W. B. YEATS : A LIFE
II : THE ARCH-POET
1915–1939

R. F. FOSTER

OXFORD
UNIVERSITY PRESS

OXFORD
UNIVERSITY PRESS

Great Clarendon Street, Oxford OX2 6DP

Oxford University Press is a department of the University of Oxford.
It furthers the University's objective of excellence in research, scholarship,
and education by publishing worldwide in

Oxford New York

Auckland Bangkok Buenos Aires Cape Town Chennai
Dar es Salaam Delhi Hong Kong Istanbul Karachi Kolkata
Kuala Lumpur Madrid Melbourne Mexico City Mumbai Nairobi
São Paulo Shanghai Taipei Tokyo Toronto

Oxford is a registered trade mark of Oxford University Press
in the UK and in certain other countries

Published in the United States
by Oxford University Press Inc., New York

British Library Cataloguing in Publication Data
Data available

Library of Congress Cataloging in Publication Data
Data available

ISBN 0-19-818465-4

1 3 5 7 9 10 8 6 4 2

Typeset in Adobe Caslon by
Jayvee, Trivandrum, India
Printed in Great Britain
on acid-free paper by
T. J. International Ltd.
Padstow, Cornwall

In memory of Francis Stewart Leland Lyons

He who attains Unity of Being is some man, who, while struggling with his fate and his destiny until every energy of his being has been roused, is content that he should so struggle with no final conquest.

A Vision (1925), p. 28

Works of lyric genius, when the circumstance of their origin is known, gain a second beauty, passing as it were out of literature and becoming life.

W. B. Yeats's Preface to *The Lemon Tree* by Margot Ruddock

After all one's art is not the chief end of life but an accident in one's search for reality or rather perhaps one's method of search.

W. B. Yeats to Ezra Pound, 15 July 1918 (Yale)

CONTENTS

CONTENTS

LIST OF ILLUSTRATIONS

Robert Gregory, drawing of Ballylee   *front endpaper*

LIST OF TEXT ILLUSTRATIONS

ACKNOWLEDGEMENTS

As WITH the first volume of this study, my first debts are to the late Leland Lyons, the late Anne Yeats, and Michael Yeats. As the Foreword to *The Apprentice Mage* pointed out, this biography is in no sense a joint production, but I owe much to the sources amassed by Leland Lyons before his death, and am immensely grateful to the generosity and friendship of his widow, Jennifer, in making them available to me. I must also renew my profound thanks to Michael and Anne Yeats for their discerning care of the Yeats material in their possession and the courtesy and generosity with which they have always met scholarly inquiries. This is a debt I share with all Yeats scholars. However, my particular task over the last fifteen years has been immeasurably lightened by the sympathetic but deliberately impartial stance they have taken in relation to a biography that is authorized but in no sense 'official'. I am deeply grateful to them both and to Gráinne Yeats for unfailing courtesy, frankness, and helpfulness.

My induction into Yeats studies was also made far less daunting than it might have been by the generosity of Yeatsian scholars at large. In particular, John Kelly's friendship, advice and information smoothed many paths; his own great edition of Yeats's letters represents a central aspect of biographical enterprise, and he has been a constant support. Once again I must record my debt to William Murphy, whose unrivalled knowledge of the Yeats family was put unstintingly at my disposal, and who, with his wife Harriet, was unfailingly helpful and hospitable from the very beginning of my labours. Warwick Gould and Deirdre Toomey have provided friendship, guidance, information, and sound advice throughout, and given up a great deal of time and scholarly effort to reading the entire text, which gained greatly from their interpositions. Colin Smythe, another key figure in the creation of the scholarly Yeats industry, has been unfailingly kind in helping me find material and guiding me out of error. And I have gained much from the friendship, hospitality, and advice of Yeats scholars such as Ron and Keith Schuchard, Jonathan Allison, Douglas Archibald, George Bornstein, Wayne Chapman, Elizabeth Butler Cullingford, George Mills Harper and Meg Harper, Elizabeth Heine, Derry Jeffares, James Pethica, and George Watson.

I must also record my debt to many custodians and librarians at institutions on both sides of the Atlantic for helping me locate material and answering inquiries to do with this volume, in particular Tom Staley and Cathy Henderson at the Harry Ransom Humanities Research Center, Austin, Texas; Anthony Bliss, Bancroft Library, University of California at

Berkeley; Steve Crook at the Berg Collection, New York Public Library; Robert O'Neill at the Burns Library, Boston College; Nancy Weyant at the Ellen Clarke Bertrand Library, Bucknell University; Paula Lee at the University of Chicago Library; Steve Enniss at the Robert R. Woodruff Library, Emory University; Jennie Rathbun at the Houghton Library, Harvard University; Alexandra Mason at the Kenneth Spencer Research Library, University of Kansas at Lawrence; Alun Ford at the University of London Library; Catherine Fahy, Gerard Lyne, and Peter Kenny at the National Library of Ireland; the staff at the Firestone Library, Princeton University; Donal Tinney at the Sligo County Library; Margaret Kimball and Polly Armstrong at the Special Collections of Stanford Library; Felicity O'Mahony at Trinity College Library; Norma Jessop at the Special Collections, University College, Dublin, Archives; and Vincent Giroud at the Beinecke Rare Book and Manuscripts Library, Yale University.

Once again I am profoundly grateful to Mary-Lou Legg for helping locate material and offering sound advice, and to Declan Kiely for suggestions and help in tracing American items. Other inquiries were answered, and material or valuable suggestions offered, by many people, to whom I am deeply grateful: Bernard Adams, Nicholas Allen, the late Frederick Ashton, Hilary Browne-Wilkinson, Isobel Carlisle, the earl of Chichester, Heather Clark, Lady Elizabeth Clyde, Jeremy Clyde, Philip Cohen, Dennis Cole, Mike Cronin, Jeananne Crowley, Ivan Crozier, Julian D'Arcy, Hugh Denard, Ann Dumas, Jack Dunn, Adrian Frazier, Lord and Lady Gibson, Victoria Glendinning, Grey Gowrie, Maurice Harmon, Joe Hassett, Michael Holroyd, Clare Hutton, Sam Hynes, Nicholas Jenkins, Justin Keating, Anne Kelly, Lady Lancaster (Anne Scott-James), Louis LeBrocquy, Hermione Lee, Ben Levitas, Gifford Lewis, Lucy McDiarmid, Bill McCormack, Andy MacGowan, Jamie McKendrick, Christina Hunt Mahony, Patrick Maume, Ed Mendelson, Giovana Musolina, Shivaun O'Casey, Pegeen O'Flaherty, Margaret Ó hÓgartaigh, Keith Parsons, Senia Paseta, Tom Paulin, Hilary Pyle, William Roth, Linda Satchwell, Gaia Servadio, Miranda Seymour, Richard Shone, Diana Souhami, Jon Stallworthy, Shane Stephens, Rob Tobin, Jay Tolson, Jeremy Treglown, Marina Warner, Jane Wellesley, the duke of Wellington, and Anna MacBride White. I am particularly grateful to James Earl Roy for sending me Lucille O'Malley McLoughlin's unpublished account of Yeats and Lady Gregory, to Patrick O'Connor for his father's memories of Norman Haire, to the late George White for unpublished reminiscences about W. B. Yeats, to Diana Wyndham for material relating to Norman Haire, to Jim Condon for sharing research about Dermott MacManus, to Kate Slattery for information about the Rafferty family of Gort, to the earl of Chichester for information about Lady Elizabeth Pelham, and to Mary, Owen and Ruth Dudley Edwards for access to the unpublished writings of their mother, Síle ní Shúilleabháin. Robert Scally, Eliza O'Grady and Eileen Reilly at Glucksman Ireland House, New York University, have been unfailingly helpful and supportive on research visits to do with this volume, as with its predecessor. Ann Saddlemyer's comprehensive biography of George Yeats was published just after the manuscript of this volume had been submitted; some references to the material therein were added at a late stage, but we were, for much of our separate journeys, working from the same mines of material.

Long as it has taken, the book would have been completed far more slowly without a generous grant from the Po Shing Woo Foundation, which enabled a year's leave of absence from Oxford, and some subsequent sabbatical leave from the University as well; I am profoundly grateful to both institutions. Yet again, I owe much to the peaceful surroundings of Sheila Sheehan's house in Kerry, where a great deal of the writing was done, and to John McBratney's hospitality in Dublin. Valerie Kemp's dedication and perfectionism made the preparation of the manuscript a far easier task than it might have been. At Oxford University Press, there have been many changes since the original commissioning by Will Sulkin, but throughout I have relied upon Ivon Asquith and Judith Luna, and I must record here a great debt to the late and bitterly lamented Kim Scott Walwyn, who kept an informed interest in the project throughout and offered acute counsel and discerning encouragement. It is a great sadness that she did not live to see the second volume completed. In seeing this volume through the press I have depended much upon Frances Whistler, who has been unfailingly perceptive, helpful, and judicious; its visual appearance also owes much to the talents of Sue Tipping, the picture research of Sandra Assersohn, and the original design of Paul Luna. Douglas Matthews laboured heroically on the index. The text was also much improved by being read by Selina Hastings and Andrew Motion, and I am enormously grateful. Gill Coleridge, nonpareil among literary agents, also not only read every word but has proved a rock of support throughout. And I have been equally fortunate in my editor Donna Poppy, whose literary flair and exacting eye are complemented by a wide knowledge of Yeats's world. Her commitment to this volume, as to its predecessor, has added decisively to its final form.

My children Phineas and Nora have spent much of their youth under the shadow of this biography, and I am more grateful to them than they know for their forbearance. My wife, Aisling, has been unfailingly supportive throughout. None of the shortcomings in this volume are the responsibility of my family, friends, or fellow scholars, but I am acutely conscious that I would never have finished the project without them.

ACKNOWLEDGEMENTS

Poetry, prose and unpublished writings by W. B. Yeats and other members of the family appear by permission of Michael Yeats. The poem 'Albâtre' by Ezra Pound is quoted with the permission of the estate of Ezra Pound, Faber and Faber Ltd, and New Directions. Quotations from the letters of Lennox Robinson are by permission of the Trustees of the Abbey Theatre, and from those of Iseult Stuart by permission of Christina Bridgwater. For other permissions I am grateful to Margaret Farrington and Elizabeth Ryan (Thomas MacGreevy's writings) and Colin Smythe Ltd on behalf of Veronica Jane O'Mara (Gogarty quotations) and the estates of Augusta Gregory and Diarmuid Russell. I am also grateful to the following holders who have granted access to previously unpublished material: Harry Ransom Humanities Research Center, University of Texas at Austin; Bancroft Library, University of California at Berkeley; John Quinn Memorial Collection and Henry W. and Albert A. Berg Collection, New York Public Library (Astor, Lenox and Tilden Foundations); Bodleian Library, Oxford; Ellen Clarke Bertrand Library, Bucknell University; Burns Library, Boston College; the Syndics of the Fitzwilliam Museum, Cambridge; the Provost and Scholars, King's College, Cambridge; University of Chicago, Special Collections Research Center; University of Delaware Library, Newark, Delaware; Robert W. Woodruff Library, Emory University, Atlanta; Houghton Library, Harvard University; Huntington Library, San Marino, California; Lilly Library, Indiana University; Kenneth Spencer Research Library, University of Kansas, Lawrence, Kansas; University of London Library; Meisei University; William M. Murphy; the Trustees of the National Library of Ireland; the Trustees of the National Library of Scotland; Charles Deering McCormick Library of Special Collections, Northwestern University Library, Evanston, Illinois; the Department of Rare Books and Special Collections, Princeton University Library; the Public Record Office; the Public Record Office of Northern Ireland; Sligo County Library; Morris Library, Southern Illinois University at Carbondale; Department of Special Collections, Stanford University Libraries, Stanford, California; the Board of Trinity College, Dublin; University College, Dublin, Archives; Beinecke Rare Book and Manuscript Library, Yale University. Every effort has been made to establish contact with the holders of original copyrights; in cases where this has not been possible, I hope this general acknowledgement will be taken as sufficient.

INTRODUCTION
Accidence and Coherence

THE STORY of W. B. Yeats's life, perhaps more than that of most writers, raises immediate and pressing questions about the relationship between everyday life and creative work. Reading J. M. Hone's biography of her husband in 1942, George Yeats realized that 'the lack of co-ordination of Yeats's poetic development with his life was almost inevitable in a book of this sort'. For one thing, the poems as they appeared in collected form were 'far from being in a chronological order'. For another, 'Unless a biographer's mind is naturally so concerned and saturated with poetry that he is compelled against his own will to write from that bias, what can he do but tell a story that will make a picture? Someone else will write another "Life" from the only point of view that I myself care for at all – poetry.'[1] Several such 'Lives' have been written in the intervening sixty years, revolving around the production of poems – most recently, and with great critical distinction, by Terence Brown. Nor are biographies of the poet 'telling a story that makes a picture' in short supply. Richard Ellmann's *The Man and the Masks* brilliantly attempted to marry both approaches, at a time when he was travelling into uncharted territory – though his approach struck horror into Edith Sitwell's heart when he interviewed her in 1946 . 'His one interest is exactly what terms Mr Y was [on] with Mrs Maud Gonne and others. He says he is going to base the book on the effect this had on his poetry!!! Oh, oh, oh! Is it not awful that every great man has got to be exhumed and nailed down at the crossroads with a stake through his heart?'[2] Ezra Pound, who read the eventual result, put it just as forcefully in his own way. 'AND I admit the twaddle by idiots who dig up biography (recent eggzamble re/WBY) is enuff to discourage most anyone.'[3] Nonetheless, one thing is clearly established in the story told in the following pages: WBY himself expected biography to happen, and thought it both inevitable and important. He constantly instructed his collaborator Augusta Gregory about the importance of the way their lives would be interpreted for the history of their times, and of their country. 'We may come at last', he remarked in 1934, 'to think that all knowledge is biography.'

This volume opens in 1915, his fiftieth year. By then he had become 'WBY' a decisive and mythologized presence in the history of modern literature; he 'had achieved Yeats', as Francis Hackett put it.[4] The achievement imposed a certain distance between immediate experience and creative output, further refined by his famous insistence on polishing up his public persona. As he muttered to Rupert Doone, pausing at his reflection on the Savile Club staircase, 'one must adjust the image'.[5] In this volume, as in its predecessor, *The Apprentice Mage*, the challenge of getting behind the adjustments is faced by a rigorous reliance on chronology and the reconstruction of the everyday – what WBY himself called 'accidence'. 'A poet writes always of his personal life,' he declared in a summation of his own creative existence; but he quickly added that this was transformed by the 'phantasmagoria' whirling around his imagination. 'He never speaks directly as to someone at the breakfast table . . . he is never the bundle of accident and incoherence that sits down to breakfast; he has been reborn as an idea, something intended, complete. A novelist might describe his accidence, his incoherence; he must not.'[6]

But a biographer might. And, for all his insistence on foretelling patterns in life, WBY knew well the importance of accident, a word which frequently recurs in his reflections about himself. Responding to a tribute from Arthur Power on his seventieth birthday, he remarked, 'I have tried to create standards, to do and say those things that accident made possible to me, the accident being I suppose in the main my father's studio'.[7] Earlier he had described his own art (to Ezra Pound) as 'an accident in one's search for reality or rather perhaps one's method of search': an admission important enough to stand as an epigraph to this book. The conditions of incoherence surrounding the accidents of life clearly deserve elucidation, though how far they illuminate the work that emerged will always be debated. But, though everybody knows that the 'I' of a poem is not necessarily the 'I' of the poet, WBY's own point about the primacy of personal life in poetic inspiration needs to be kept in mind. Poetry was, after all, born out of 'the quarrel with oneself'. The frequent and matter-of-fact references in WBY's letters and lectures to the direct connections between his experience and his poems may be unwelcome to dismissive post-modernist or new-critical authorities, but they are there in black and white. The importance he gave to the creation of his own autobiography, closely traced in this volume, supplies corroborating evidence. WBY has received many kinds of biographical treatment, and will require more. But there is certainly a case for writing about his life in terms of ascertainable facts: the kind of biography, it should be remembered, which Samuel Beckett – of all people – thought most desirable. 'What I want is the straws, flotsam, etc., names, dates, births and deaths, because that is all I can know . . . I want the oldfashioned history book of reference, not the fashionable monde romancé.'[8]

'All we can know' is problematic in the case of WBY. The form in which his life-story comes to us is intensively mediated: through his own fame and astute sense of publicity, his meticulously rearranged autobiographies, the

accretion of subsequent commentary, and the inflections lent by his combative attitude to life. He was fond of repeating his friend Charles Ricketts's
belief that people who have something to give to the world are always
troublesome; unlike AE, Gogarty once remarked, WBY's opposites were his
opponents.[9] This readiness to be contentious was even more marked in the
second half of his life, which is dealt with here. In his struggle towards reality, antagonists reared up across his path and he invariably took them on. As
in the first volume, certain poems appear as manifestos or declarations,
responses to immediate circumstances. This is sometimes indicated by the
immediacy of WBY's manuscripts: the increasingly erratic and jagged writing, the mind flying impatiently ahead of the pen, the line of script reflecting the excitement of creation and resembling, in Daniel Albright's phrase,
'a mouse's electrocardiogram'. The chronology of composition and the form
of first printing therefore has its own biographical importance, and is
reflected here in the way certain poems are embedded in the text – and in the
life. This is particularly relevant to the great sequences written at the time of
the Irish revolution and civil war, but it remains true for the poems influenced by his supernatural investigations at the time of the First World War,
as well as for the lyrics he was writing as he awaited death in the south of
France.

But there is more than one sense in which WBY is 'troublesome' for the
biographer. For one thing, his intellectual omnivorousness increases with
age. It was enough to put Sean O'Faolain off writing the life of a poet for
whom he always felt a guarded and baffled admiration. 'I[n] point of fact I
did begin some years ago to compile data for a biography of W. B.,' he
admitted privately in the late 1930s,

and still have stacks of notes. I gave it up when I gave up trying to be a scholar, and
anyway I found that W. B. had, in his time, dived down so many caverns of knowledge and as quickly returned, bringing many pearls with him, that if I were to write
about him with any authority of knowledge I should have to dive down the same
caverns, stay much too long, and bring back very little – all to be able to write about
his voyaging with an assurance about things I could not be interested in for their
own sakes . . . He has a quick receptive mind and skims the cream off with ease.
I surrendered, and the only effect was that I was left with a profound feeling that
W. B. Y. can be very insincere: and very profound (apparently) on very little basis,
and that he is a great lyric poet and nothing but a great lyric poet.[10]

Had O'Faolain dived down some of those caverns and followed the trail of
bubbles left by his subject, he might have come to the surface with a different opinion. Following WBY's intellectual track, and reading his prose as
closely as his poetry, one is driven to the conclusion that while his greatness

as a lyric poet is unassailable, he was very much more than simply that. This can be proved not only by employing a multiplicity of voices from other spheres, but by examining WBY's non-poetic writings in detail: unpublished tracts like the manuscript of 'Leo Africanus' as well as underestimated apologias like *Per Amica Silentia Lunae* and 'If I were Four-and-Twenty'. His father once remarked that poets were necessarily solitaries, and that every poem was a social act done by a solitary man; but the judgement needs to be adapted for his elder son.[11] WBY's writing in the second half of his life repeatedly struck public poses and was put to public purposes. 'Posterity', David Garnett wrote after WBY's death, 'may recognise what has escaped his contemporaries: his enormous influence upon practical affairs.'[12] This is borne out by several episodes related in this book, especially during the 1920s and 1930s. They stretch further than the notorious brief fling with an Irish right-wing party from 1933 to 1934. His ambition to play a political role in the new Irish state decisively predated his nomination to the Senate. His interest in a new order in politics dates back to the Russian Revolution of 1917 and is reflected in his reading throughout the 1920s. If the drama of his early life was played out against the background of a country developing towards national self-consciousness, the backdrop to the second half was not only the achievement of Ireland's independence but war, dislocation, and the rise of totalitarianism in Europe, all of which affected him deeply.

In other ways too the great design of his life wove the outside world closely around him: his enduring need for audiences, his construction of *cénacles* of like-minded people, his passionate friendships with women, his growing preoccupation with both sexual and religious ecstasy. Paradoxically, on one level his desire for supernatural investigation might be seen as a way of claiming a relationship with the 'real' world at large and engaging with other people. His occult interests can no longer be dismissed as merely credulous, silly, or fantastical. The intensive analysis by George Mills Harper and others of the material produced by George Yeats's automatic writing shows that these interrogations were closely integrated into his poetic imagination. The patterns didactically posited in *A Vision* infuse his drama as well as his verse. Further, this material also contains clear biographical signposts, both dictating everyday decisions and influencing WBY's own analysis of his life so far. In the second half of his life the place of occult investigation is as important as in the first, but the form it takes is introspective rather than ritualistic.

Yet that 'real' world dominates. It is worth remembering Virginia Woolf's judgement that WBY's mental world was like an immensely complex thicket of undergrowth where 'every twig was real' to him.[13] His enormous effect on his contemporaries was an established fact by the time he was fifty. Nor was it restricted to cultural nationalists: even Violet Martin of 'Somerville and Ross', whose politics were sceptically Unionist, told Augusta Gregory in 1915 that when she looked back it was as if WBY 'had flung open a great window' and let an atmosphere of true poetry into the stuffy Ireland of her youth.[14] The authority which he had so single-mindedly striven for in the years of his apprenticeship was now settled upon him. Partly because of this, the materials recording his life in the quarter-century from 1914 to 1939 are immense and have been added to by intensive biographical studies of his friends, brother, sisters, father, and, most of all, his wife – whose decisive part in the direction of his creative as well as his everyday life is fully dealt with in this volume. But if the quantity of both printed and manuscript sources is now gigantic, this does not mean that there is nothing new to say – even about the composition of as closely scrutinized a poem as 'Sailing to Byzantium'.[15] Nor will the sheer mass of personal material automatically yield up all the clues and secrets: the ear must be attuned to a chorus of voices from the edge.

This volume continues and completes themes laid out in *The Apprentice Mage*: notably the needs created by early emotional insecurity, the desire to achieve wholeness and pattern in life and work, and the complex and passionate relationship between the poet and his country's history. WBY's reconstruction between 1916 and 1922 of his relationship to Irish politics is a central theme, decisively affecting his publication strategies and the actual content of poems and plays. His increasingly embattled stance in independent Ireland, and the implicit and explicit querying by others of his claims to 'true' Irishness, suggests that many themes and motifs of the early 1900s are replayed in the 1920s and 1930s, only with new antagonists. In other ways too the wheel turns back to his youth: as ever, he is dividing his time between England and Ireland, impelled as much by romantic as professional reasons.

When Richard Ellmann remarked that for T. S. Eliot the creative process was an escape from personality, the contrast with WBY must have been in his mind.[16] 'Personality' remained a dominating preoccupation in WBY's imagination and life: 'achieving Yeats', again. This happened neither by accident nor by incoherence. But his negotiation of the unexpected accidents of everyday life, 'the delight in the unforeseen' which he thought essential to true creativity, needs to be recaptured if the process is to be fully understood. Hence the chronological and contingent nature of this narrative, like its predecessor. For the biographer, following WBY's path through life often recalls Edmund Dulac's description of walking with him in the country. 'Sometimes, in the early winter, we had to walk in pitch darkness along lanes that were soaked with rain. Yeats would invariably come back with his shoes spotless. I was spattered with mud to the knees.'[17] But the fascination of what's difficult remains. Meeting WBY in 1915, after a long and resentful interval, Edward Martyn grudgingly had to admit 'he has got much more interesting; his critical remarks are especially so, & he is dreadfully hard to please'.[18] As the following Prologue shows, at that point WBY stood at a crossroads in his life. But his critical and creative intelligence stayed unblunted through all the strange excursions and obsessions chronicled here; and he remains throughout as interesting as ever.

A Note on the Text:

Poems are generally quoted in their first published form: deviations are indicated in the footnotes.

Sums of money are given without today's equivalents, but in 1914 a multiple of around fifty provides a rough guide to present-day purchasing power. From 1915 to 1925 financial instability reduces this formula, which should be reckoned at about half by 1920, but from *c*.1930 until 1939 a multiple of fifty once again gives a general indication.

Prologue : CROSSWAYS

'MOST of the books written about W.B.Y.', Jack Yeats drily remarked twelve years after his brother's death, 'have a great many noisy gaps.'[1] This book begins at the start of 1915; the noisy gap of the previous half-century is filled by the earlier volume, *The Apprentice Mage*. In one sense the story continues *in medias res*, but it is also a new beginning – as the poet himself realized. At the end of 1914 WBY had finished writing his memoir of childhood with the 'old thought' that all life was 'a preparation for something that never happens'. The elegiac note matched his mood. He had recently published the first version of *Responsibilities*, the volume which can now be seen to establish in his poetry a bleak new edge, as well as a tone of introspection and disillusionment. He had decided to write poems that would be, as he put it much later, 'not at all a dream, like my earlier poems, but a criticism of life'.[2] He would plumb his family and personal history, his long wrangle with Irish politics, and his supernatural searches as the material for his art.

But he needed to cultivate distance, and he knew it. Summers were spent at Coole Park in County Galway with his closest friend, Augusta Gregory (and her resentful son and daughter-in-law, Robert and Margaret); his Dublin world was still dominated by the Abbey Theatre, his and Gregory's joint creation, which had survived ten years of crisis to become a great Dublin institution while constantly trembling on the edge of financial disaster. For WBY, its fortune and achievements were inescapably bound up with the work and life of John Millington Synge, influential out of all proportion to their brevity. The angry audience-reaction to Synge's masterpiece *The Playboy of the Western World* in 1907, and the playwright's premature death two years later, still haunted WBY as an enduring emblem of the antagonism he had himself encountered when waging cultural war in Ireland. So did the more recent explosion set off by the attempt made by Gregory's nephew Hugh Lane to establish a collection of modern art in Dublin. WBY's interim *Poems Written in Discouragement* in 1913, particularly the scornful polemic eventually called 'September 1913', had signalled his mood, just as the recurrent image of 'estrangement' expressed his feelings for Ireland after Synge's death. He had put a wide distance between his current political stance, as a supporter of Redmondite Home Rule (which had reached the statute-book but was suspended for the duration of the war), and his youthful Fenianism; the growth of radical nationalism in Ireland since the Ulster crisis of 1912 had apparently left him untouched. His creative life depended on the link to Coole, which released his lyric gift during the long summers of walking in the woods and reading in the library. In Dublin he was embattled.

But despite his exasperation with the life of the city, in all its pieties and asperities, it belonged to his youth and his family history, and he was intermittently part of it. His oldest collaborator and friend, George Russell ('AE'), was still immersed in Sir Horace Plunkett's agrarian cooperative movement, still exploring mystical insights in his painting and poetry, still offering what WBY thought was undiscriminating encouragement to fledgling writers at his haphazard Rathgar salon. For all their mutual irritation, AE observed and recorded his boyhood friend with unwavering fascination. So did the novelist George Moore, considered an enemy since the publication of his own masterly autobiography *Hail and Farewell*, which created an enduring caricature version of WBY. So did his friend and boon companion, the medical littérateur Oliver St John Gogarty. The Yeats sisters, Lily and Lolly, were also Dublin institutions, running their Cuala arts and crafts business at Dundrum, which printed the first versions of all their brother's books. Jack was established in Dublin too, drawing from Ireland the inspiration for his own painting, which WBY would belatedly realize had moved from illustration and commentary to 'an art of excitement'.[3] And the extraordinarily gifted family knew how much of their inspiration stemmed from their brilliant but improvident father, John Butler Yeats. 'When I look back on Papa's life,' Lily reflected much later, 'I marvel at his gay courage – talking literature & art & life – & no income, an invalid wife, four children growing up without education or prospects. If we had not had that spark or whatever it is that we have we would have gone down out of our class. Anyway he lived to see Willy famous, Jack a fine painter whose work will live [and] Lolly & I are not nonentities.'[4] This was no more than the truth. And at the end of 1914 the old painter was himself very much alive, living a charmed life on no money at all in New York, heavily dependent on the help of his son's friend and patron, the lawyer–collector John Quinn. His escape had been provided for by American energies and American generosity; these also remained an important resource for his eldest son, whose reputation there was now securely established.

But it was in London that WBY's working life was centred, as it had been for decades. While he was now a heavyweight figure in the literary establishment of clubs and organizations, prominent on Edmund Gosse's Academic Committee of English Letters, and dining with senior politicians and society hostesses, he had not abandoned the world which he had first conquered in the days of the Rhymers' Club and the *Savoy* magazine twenty years before. In his shabby but atmospheric rooms in Woburn Buildings, conveniently and symbolically situated between the British

Museum (for intellectual inspiration) and Euston Station (for the boat-train to Ireland), WBY contrived to entertain literary and artistic Bohemia. The 'friends of his youth' were changing and receding, to be fixed and memorialized in further instalments of his disingenuous autobiography. But the red-and-black painted staircase was still climbed on Monday nights by intimates like the painter Charles Ricketts, the engraver and designer Thomas Sturge Moore, and above all the young American poet Ezra Pound. Pound had already spent a working winter with WBY in the cottage which they rented at Coleman's Hatch in Ashdown Forest on the Kent–Sussex border; his place in WBY's London life, and his less certain influence on the older poet's work, was established. And WBY's dependence on much older friends continued – all of them women. The unconventional Florence Farr, one of his first lovers and a collaborator in occult learning and dramatic experiments, had left for Ceylon, but WBY regularly visited the dying Mabel Beardsley, another old flame from the nineties, in Hampstead. Above all, Olivia Shakespear remained the centre of his London life, still beautiful, still married, still ironically world-weary. Their early love-affair and long friendship gave her a unique place in his affections, and him in hers.

The same was true of the woman whose enduring image had driven the love-affair with Shakespear on to the rocks. In 1914 WBY's stormy but perdurable attachment to Maud Gonne survived, though the embers of their romantic relationship, briefly rekindled five years before, had died down. Still a zealous Irish revolutionary and Catholic convert but long separated from her Fenian husband, John MacBride, she was living in France with her children Iseult and Seán. Like WBY she was approaching fifty, but she carried a dominating role in the phantasmagoria of his emotional life, and she continued to haunt his poetry. As in all his close associations with women, the relationship was fuelled by a commitment to joint occult and psychic investigations, recently renewed when they had travelled to a French country village to inspect a 'miracle'. And he had just finished his long meditation 'Swedenborg, Mediums, and the Desolate Places', which testified to his search for confirmation from the void, through study as well as revelation. Both paths led to his alter ego Leo Africanus, encountered in a seance and pursued in encyclopedias. The need for a supernatural faith, and the inability to establish one, dominated his mood in late 1914, as the world went to war and he returned to his solitary life in London.

Some projected work, such as his play *The Player Queen*, lay obstinately unfinished (it was beginning to loom over his middle age as the similarly recalcitrant *The Shadowy Waters* had haunted his youth). But he had completed *Reveries over Childhood and Youth* and written a series of exploratory

3

poems that cast back into his own past. Memory remained the mother of the muses, and for all his occult investigations he was uncertain what the future would bring. Yet at the beginning of 1915 he knew he could rely on his own astonishing resilience and the resources of his legendary imagination. Shortly afterwards their father wrote to Jack, trying to bring encouragement at a time of personal and artistic crisis:

You do not stand still. A man of genius should be like a young boy who is never, never and never will be a grown up. He must have a new style & new methods. Not for fashion's sake, but because he has outgrown the old ways. People are offended with Willie because he won't go on writing Oisins & lyrics. They are fools for their pains & I anathematise them.[5]

That confidence to break old moulds was one of the inheritances which would sustain WBY when he reached a crossroads in his life at the end of 1914. Lying ahead were seismic transformations in his personal, artistic, political, and spiritual life, and public acclaim beyond anything he had ever known; but, throughout it all, the 'young boy who never will be a grown up' remains discernible beneath the achieved grandeur of the poetic personality.

Chapter I : ACCOMPLISHMENT AND NOH
1915–1916

> Here in Ireland there is nothing but excursions and alarums sickening recruiting measures, opposition meetings of Volunteers, threats of National Registration and conscription, counter-threats of armed, or partly armed, recalcitrants, etc., etc. – such is the air we breathe in an island where a year ago we were only thinking of – Home Rule, at the worst, and at best, 'nine bean rows' and 'a hive for the honey bee'!
>
> Joseph Campbell to Ernest Boyd, 18 August 1915[1]

I

BY THE New Year of 1915, the year in which he would turn fifty, WBY had reluctantly left Coole, coming back to wartime London and the established pattern of his English existence. 'For all his poetry,' AE wrote snappishly to John Quinn in New York, '[he] is as conventional in his life as if he was a trained butler in an aristocratic family.'[2] The atmosphere of the wartime city was oppressive, and he spent as little time as possible there before once more taking up residence with Ezra Pound in Ashdown Forest. The reflective mood induced by finishing his memoir persisted, and his family noted his tiredness; according to JBY, his son had only narrowly avoided a 'break down' after his tour of America the previous April.[3] 'How does the war affect you?' Florence Farr asked him in one of her jaunty letters from Ceylon late in 1914. Though he could no longer keep it at bay, with Zeppelin raids afflicting London from late spring, WBY's opinions had not changed. 'It is merely the most expensive outbreak of insolence and stupidity the world has ever seen,' he wrote to Quinn, 'and I give it as little of my thought as I can. I went to my club this afternoon to look at the war news, but read Keats's Lamia instead.'[4]

Quinn, who was fanatically anti-German, disapproved deeply of WBY's stance, though he held his counsel until later. As far as possible, WBY adhered to this approach: probably in early February, he wrote a short poem on a poet's duty in wartime, echoing Maeterlinck's statement that those not carrying rifles should remain silent.[5] Later he would send the lines to Edith Wharton, for publication in *The Book of the Homeless*, as 'the only poem I have not bartered to somebody or other'. This was in aid of two refugee charities in Paris; though Henry James was the intermediary, WBY may have been swayed by accounts from Maud Gonne describing the suffering of the wounded in France. As transmitted to Wharton, however, the lines conveyed a certain impatience at the whole exercise, and Quinn thought them 'quite unworthy of you and of the occasion':

> I think it better that at times like these
> We poets keep our mouths shut, for in truth
> We have no gift to set a statesman right;
> He's had enough of meddling who can please
> A young girl in the indolence of her youth
> Or an old man upon a winters night.[6]

He told James that it was the only thing he would write about the war, being determined to lie low 'till bloody frivolity is over' (though he would take part in a poets' reading for the Belgian Relief Fund a year later). H. W. Nevinson was similarly assured that 'the war made no difference to his writing; a man must follow his line'.[7]

In keeping with this, he tried to abstract himself at Stone Cottage from early January 1915; the flat at Woburn Buildings was scraped and repapered in an effort to remove insect life, though WBY still returned there for his Monday evening entertainments, and often came up to Pound's Thursday dining-club in Soho or the Friday gatherings at Charles Ricketts's. But he saw more of the irrepressible Ezra Pound than anyone else. Pound was as energetically offensive as ever, wearying the Monday night regulars; in late April he was silenced only by W. T. Horton revealing that he had seen seven black phantom dogs enter the room with the American, 'barking and circling round him'. Others, like the appalled Belfast novelist Forrest Reid, saw Pound himself as a canine. 'He is obviously very much as God made him. My quarrel with him is that he so glories in the unfortunate fact . . . Do you call it writing or barking? I imagine he is an epileptic, but possibly he is only very virile and tense, and this peculiar Pomeranian style is the style of the future.'[8] Pound was certainly part of WBY's future. With his marriage to Olivia Shakespear's daughter, Dorothy, Pound's adoption into the Yeats circle was formalized, and the two poets were no longer alone in Stone Cottage. WBY gave an avuncular version of their life together to Mabel Beardsley:

Ezra Pound & his wife are staying with me & are to read out to me when artificial light makes my eyes useless – it is a problem what I do with my eyes every winter. Ezra Pound has a charming young wife who looks as if her face was made out of Dresden china. I look at her in perpetual wonder. It is so hard to beleive she is real; & yet she spends all her daylight hours drawing the most monstrous cubist pictures. I am sure her real test would be to paint with very little brushes, & draw neat outlines with a pencil she took half the morning making sharp enough. She is merely playing up to the revolutionary energy of her husband (whom I have shocked by bringing seven volumes of Wordsworth's poetry). I feel quite sure that Ezra & his wife who are obviously devoted must have fallen in love out of shere surprize & bewilderment they are so unlike each other. I am still patching my 'Memoirs' here & there. They are finished except for the patching and I have plays to read, or rather to listen to, for the Abbey Theatre. I always long for a life of routine & seldom attain it but here I shall have it & that will make the life of my thoughts much more vehement. I think a monastery, if only it could come to terms with your sex, would be the most exciting & delightful place imaginable – but alas it will never get over that ancient misunderstanding.[9]

The weather was dry, calm, and clear; wby found that he came in from his moonlight walks 'full of thoughts'. He and Pound continued to read together (including, that winter, Norse sagas, Doughty's *Travels in Arabia Deserta*, and Bram Stoker's *Dracula*). As Pound corrected the proofs of the poems which would be published as *Lustra*, wby continued to work on his memoirs, dictating additions to Pound and arguing by post with Lily, who still objected to his inclusion of comments about Agnes Gorman, their mentally unstable aunt.[10] By now his preoccupation with family had taken deep hold; he told Lily he would like to inherit the family miniatures possessed by their Morehampton Road aunts, which had helped inspire passages of his memoir. In turn he would undertake to leave them to 'whoever might keep some family memory and tradition' – qualities he now valued more strongly than ever. The bookplate he ordered from Thomas Sturge Moore in February bore this out: it used the supposed Yeats heraldic emblem of a goat.[11] But family dignity still took second place to artistic integrity. He stood his ground about including the incident of their aunt Agnes Gorman's breakdown – though he was prepared for censorship in other areas, as he made clear to Quinn.

I write amiably for I find I do not remember slights & wrongs but still I cannot write let us say of Hughes & Shepherd my fellow-students at the Art School as freely as if they were dead. I cannot describe the virtuous Hughes wanting to fight the English modelling master because the master had suggested that a pain in Hughes thighes (I cannot spell this morning because of that Dracula) came from sexual excess & of Hughes rapid fall from virtue after he left Dublin. These things will go into chapters for my own entertainment perhaps. I stopped short before I came to the Rhymers for the same reason.[12]

Stone Cottage exerted its charm; the quiet routine of reading and work was punctuated only by visits to the ancient pub for cider, and he refused to return to London for meetings of Edmund Gosse's Academic Committee. But he was heavily dependent on the local post office, and his correspondence streamed on unabated. Much of this had to do with the Abbey Theatre, for here too the effects of the war could not be ignored. Some of the problems were chronic, such as Sara Allgood's threats to leave, though she was temporarily wooed into staying by a salary rise that had to remain secret. But the impossibility of sending tours to wartime England had precipitated a crisis, with the main theatre rented out as an emergency measure. The financial year ending in February 1915 nonetheless brought a deficit of over £1,200, and the directors had to raise an overdraft of £600. Drastic measures loomed. Pound, modern-minded as ever, suggested closing down as a theatre and converting to a cinematograph, but A. D. Wilson, the manager, offered the more traditional counsel of music-hall engagements – a tendency towards 'vulgarisation' which WBY put down to his Belfast background. This was at first resisted, and somehow a London production of *Deirdre of the Sorrows* was planned for May. (The disgruntled Wilson threatened resignation during the run, and stayed for only two months more.) But by June W. F. Bailey (a leading trustee) was sending WBY a bleak financial analysis. Staff, salaries, and the players' share of the earnings must all be cut; the trustees refused to be liable for the approaching crash and pressed for a closure. WBY spiritedly argued that an American tour would bring in $1,200 a week, but Bailey remained unconvinced. As it happened, the offer of an Australian tour staved off disaster; as the players' contracts came up for renewal in the summer, the despised music-hall engagements were reluctantly accepted as the only way out.[13]

Yet these distractions remained distant enough from Ashdown Forest to enable him to write. On 31 January Pound could tell Harriet Monroe that his companion had sent five poems to his agent for transmission to *Poetry*; three more, just written, were still concealed in his desk. ('Her Praise', 'The People', 'His Phoenix'). If these poems reflected his autobiographical immersion in late 1914, they were also influenced by the company he kept. Pound (and his girlfriends) are a definite presence in 'His Phoenix', and some of Pound's own poems of this era 'answer' WBY's.[14] But this new work also hinted at the impatience WBY's companions sometimes felt with the old obsession about Gonne, as he 'turned the talk by hook or crook/Until her praise should be the uppermost theme'. The closing lines of 'Her Praise' clearly established the world of Stone Cottage, but transposed the surrounding landscape to Ireland.

> I will talk no more of books or the long war,
> But walk by the dry thorn until I have found
> Some beggar sheltering from the wind and there
> If there be rags enough he will know her name
> And be well pleased remembering it, for in the old days,
> Though she had young men's praise and old men's blame,
> Among the poor both old and young gave her praise.[15]

'The People' dealt even more directly and specifically with Gonne. Cast in the conversational mode of 'Adam's Curse', it provides in some ways both a counterweight to that pivotal poem and a sequel. It also cast back into the past, to the time of her separation from MacBride, and recalled the many times she had spoken (and written) to him of her reverence for the crowd. More clearly than ever before, the poem outlined the alternative existence, first shown to him on his Italian tour with the Gregorys nearly eight years before, which his determination on an Irish public life (and his obsession with Gonne) so regularly disrupted.

> 'What have I earned for all that work,' I said,
> 'For all that I have done at my own charge?
> The daily spite of this unmannerly town
> Where who has served the most is most defamed,
> The reputation of his lifetime lost
> Between the night and morning. I might have lived –
> And you know well how great the longing has been –
> Where every day my footfall should have lit
> In the green shadow on Ferrara wall;
> Or climbed among the images of the past,
> The unperturbed and courtly images,
> Evening and morn, the steep street of Urbino
> To where the duchess and her people talked
> The stately midnight through until they stood
> In their great window looking at the dawn.
> I might have had no friend that could not mix
> Courtesy and passion into one, like those
> That saw the wicks grow yellow in the dawn.
> I might have used the one substantial right
> My trade allows – chosen my company,
> And chosen what scenery had pleased me best.'
>
> Thereon my phoenix answered in reproof:
> 'The drunkards, pilferers of public funds –
> All the dishonest crowd I had driven away –
> When my luck changed and they dared to meet my face,
> Crawled from obscurity, and set upon me
> Those I had served and some that I had fed;
> Yet never have I, now nor any time,
> Complained of the people.'
>
>   All I could reply
> Was: 'You that have not lived in thought but deed
> Can have the purity of a natural force;

> But I, whose virtues are the definitions
> Of the analytic mind, can neither close
> The eye of the mind nor keep my tongue from speech.'
>
> And yet, because my heart leaped at her words,
> I was abashed, and now they come to mind
> After nine years, I sink my head abashed.[16]

The penultimate stanza directly transposes a letter she had sent him eight years before, when the collapse of her marriage brought angry recriminations from advanced nationalist circles: 'the frauds who I had exposed, the publicans & drunkards I had driven out the cowards who I had made own their cowardice all join MacBride's party and whisper calumny against me – but in neither of our cases were the people generally to blame'. Thus she dominated his imaginative life as much as ever, and possibly his emotional life as well. 'The People' must be the poem he sent her in February, which she acknowledged distractedly at the end of a long letter describing her exhaustion and depression at the conditions of the war, and her impatience with Iseult, now a disconsolate twenty-year-old beauty, who spent her days chain-smoking and writing desultory fragments. 'I have never thanked you for the poem. To me you are too kind – You have often tried to defend & protect me with your art – & perhaps when we are dead I shall be known by those poems of yours – '[17]

They both knew this perfectly well by now. In his poems of early 1915 WBY returned to the sense of his life as a 'past' woven into a pattern; this is closely connected with the construction of his memoirs. The volume that would appear as *Reveries over Childhood and Youth* was as good as finished (he had wanted it to be with Lolly's press by mid January), but his recollections were already moving on to the next phase of his life. Though his account of the late 1880s and 1890s would not appear until 1922 (as *The Trembling of the Veil*), in January 1915 he was discussing his memoirs of this era with friends and correspondents; Pound knew all the Rhymer anecdotes (they would surface in his *Hugh Selwyn Mauberley*), and Gonne was offering help with his account of their early friendship. The fact that WBY was himself being written about, and pursued by Joseph Hone and Ernest Boyd for autobiographical details, reinforced the sense of his own history – and of the past as a story.[18] Little wonder that the theme of memory pervades the poems of this Stone Cottage winter. In January 1915 his memories of the time when he first met Gonne twenty-six years before, and 'the troubling' of his life began, were a constant accompaniment to the recondite readings with Pound, and the muffled reverberations of the war offstage.

Another ancient preoccupation sustained him too, as he settled to the notes he had offered to provide for Gregory's long-running *Visions and*

Beliefs in the West of Ireland. These brought him back twenty years, when she had first taken him, at a low point in his emotional life, around Galway cottages in search of folklore. (The very first sentence of her text invoked their friendship and intellectual collaboration.[19]) But the notes also incorporated material from the books on China and Japan read to him by Pound, where stories of ancestral ghosts and folk magic occurred as regularly and matter-of-factly as in his and Gregory's Irish investigations. The project preoccupied him more and more, and by late April he told Gregory that he wanted the freedom of an Appendix in order to wax obscure and irrelevant. 'I dont want to be bothered with the general reader at all.'[20]

His own writing bore this out: both drama and poetry were swayed by his determination not to talk down to a popular audience. By mid February he thought *The Player Queen* was successfully 'reduced to two manageable acts', and he was as preoccupied as ever by avant-garde staging. Ricketts had produced a dramatic theatrical set for *The Well of the Saints*, and offered to design costumes both for it and *On Baile's Strand* for £20. 'It will be a return to our first thought in principle,' WBY excitedly told Gregory: 'that old decorative scheme of the play that you and I made.' Indeed, Ricketts's plan was for *On Baile's Strand* to be played against undyed sacking, lit by coloured filters, as in the memorable production of December 1904.[21] This was also dictated by expediency, since it turned out that all the coloured jute hangings from previous productions had disappeared from the theatre, taken home by members of the company to drape their walls. Above all, at Stone Cottage and in Pound's company he could write the kind of poetry which had been announced in *Responsibilities*: at once personal, lofty, and colloquial. Some of the reactions to that latest Cuala volume had missed the point, which is why an important late review by J. M. Hone in the *New Statesman* of April 1915 pleased WBY so much. 'The very few who praise my later work', he told Hone, '(& you have been the most subtle) have praised it in words full of intellect & force. That convinces me, that & my own emotion when I write, that I am doing better & plunging deeper.'[22]

The poems sent to Monroe show this, none more decisively than 'The Fisherman'. It was probably first drafted the previous summer, arising from a 'subject for poem' entrusted to his notebook in March 1914.[23] The poem is an evocation of the ideal reader who is also an ideal Irishman: a solitary, proud 'country person' whose image is at once a reflection and an inspiration. Echoes from 'J. M. Synge and the Ireland of his Time' are impossible to miss. 'The Fisherman', like much of WBY's work at this period, reprises the themes and imagery of that essay: popularity versus solitude, a natural sense of aristocracy, and the essential artistic integrity that resides in an Irishness above hackneyed commonplaces. Synge is present, not only as 'the dead man that I loved' but as the Fisherman himself: moreover, as always, when WBY wrote about his dead friend, he wrote about life as he felt he himself should live it.

> Although I can see him still –
> The freckled man who goes
> To a gray place on a hill
> In gray Connemara clothes
> At dawn to cast his flies –
> It's long since I began
> To call up to the eyes
> This wise and simple man.
> All day I'd looked in the face
> What I had hoped it would be
> To write for my own race
> And the reality:
> The living men that I hate
> The dead man that I loved,
> The craven man in his seat,
> The insolent unreproved –
> And no knave brought to book
> Who has won a drunken cheer –
> The witty man and his joke
> Aimed at the commonest ear,
> The clever man who cries
> The catch cries of the clown,
> The beating down of the wise
> And great Art beaten down.
>
> Maybe a twelve-month since
> Suddenly I began
> In scorn of this audience,
> Imagining a man,
> And his sun-freckled face
> And gray Connemara cloth,
> Climbing up to a place
> Where stone is dark with froth,
> And the down turn of his wrist
> When the flies drop in the stream –
> A man who does not exist,
> A man who is but a dream;
> And cried, 'Before I am old
> I shall have written him one
> Poem maybe as cold
> And passionate as the dawn.'

Neither the deceptively simple structure (short lines, strictly alternate rhymes, and an insistently iambic metre with intriguing variations) nor the deliberate archaisms ('Knaves', 'clowns') compromise his new radicalism; while the last lines, throwing together a sudden conjunction of antithetical coldness and passion, supply both an enduring image and one of WBY's most magnificently assertive signatures, fixed by his characteristic metrical 'trick' of an unexpected polysyllable in the last line. Piquantly, JBY had written to him just before this, infuriated by Pound's critique of 'The Two Kings' in *Poetry*; to the old man, his son's poetic imagination conferred 'a liberating splendour, cold as sunrise'. WBY admitted that he had taken his concluding image directly from this comment. 'Cold and passionate' was also a description he had applied directly to Synge.[24] More broadly, 'The Fisherman' looked back to the quarrels, bitternesses, and inadequacies of WBY's public Irish life over the past few years. But in its celebration of authenticity, in its radical compression, in the concreteness, exactness, and economy of its imagery, even in the very idea of 'cold beauty', it reflected the aesthetics mediated by Pound, notably the influence of Japan.[25]

II

His own existence could not remain as loftily removed as the Fisherman's, nor would he really have wished it so. Writers, as he had always known, live in the marketplace, and during the summer of 1915 he devoted much time to obtaining financial security for an Irish artist just as uncompromising as Synge. WBY's commitment to James Joyce's genius had been strengthened by *Dubliners* and especially *A Portrait of the Artist*, though Gonne, who both hated and disapproved of the autobiographical novel, found it hard to believe that WBY had really read it. Indeed, when he began to sound out the inevitable arch-fixer, Edmund Gosse, regarding a Royal Literary Fund pension for Joyce in early July 1915, he gave *Chamber Music* and *Dubliners* as qualifications; the real masterpiece, he told Gosse, was 'a most lovely poem' in Katharine Tynan's anthology *The Wild Harp* (he apparently could not remember the poem's name, though it must have been 'I Hear an Army'). The formal submission to the Fund, however, cited the serialization of *A Portrait* appearing in the *Egoist*, 'which increases my conviction that he is the most remarkable new talent in Ireland today'.[26] Perhaps not coincidentally, in the extracts currently appearing, Stephen Dedalus's constant reference-point was WBY's own work: reworking WBY's favourite Thomas Nashe line, 'Brightness falls from the air' and questioning Michael Robartes's wish to take in his arms 'the loveliness which has long faded from the world'. Though Stephen disagrees ('Not at all. I desire to press in my arms the loveliness which has not yet come into the world'), his thoughts circle around WBY's canonical phrases, just as Joyce's did: the extracts in the *Egoist* that summer showed that WBY, alone of his nineties contemporaries, still magnetized the coming generation.[27]

Gosse initially worried that Joyce might harbour subversive opinions about the war effort – a scruple which WBY managed to head off without revealing his own opinions. And eventually Gosse offered strong support, even prepared to call a special Fund meeting; WBY, probably remembering their previous disagreements over Tagore and Gosse's insulting letter to Gregory regarding the poet's own pension in 1910, quoted Bridges's opinion that Gosse was 'a wicked man [who] now tries to do good'.[28] By the end of August the 'wicked man' could assure WBY 'it is all right about Joyce', who had been voted 'a substantial sum' – but, as usual with Gosse, there was a cavil, and it concerned WBY's politics, still arousing suspicion in the heart of the establishment. 'Neither his own letters nor yours expressed any frank sympathy with the cause of the Allies, and I would not have let him have one penny if I had believed that he was in sympathy with the Austrian enemy. But I felt that you had taken the responsibility in the matter.' WBY's reply was masterly:

My dear Ghosse: I thank you very much for what you have done; but it never occurred to me that it was necessary to express sympathy 'frank' or other wise with the 'cause of the allies'. I should have thought myself wasting the time of the committee. I certainly wish them victory, & as I have never known Joyce to agree with his neighbours I feel that his residence in Austria has probably made his sympathy as frank as you could wish. I never asked him about it in any of the few notes I have sent him. He had never anything to do with Irish politics, extreme or otherwise, & I think disliked politics. He always seemed to me to have only literary & philosophic sympathies. To such men the Irish atmosphere brings isolation not anti English feeling. He is probably trying at this moment to become absorbed in some piece of work till the evil hour is passed. I again thank you for what you have done for this man of genius.[29]

During that summer, the financing of genius was much on WBY's mind, focused by the need to bail out his cheerfully improvident father in New York. Not counting the Civil List pension of £150 a year, his own earnings for the years ending 1913 and 1914 had hovered around £400, but for 1915 they would plummet to £150: the war was taking its toll.[30] This entailed careful husbandry, and menacing but unsuccessful dunning letters to his drunken and near-bankrupt publisher A. H. Bullen.[31] In 1914 he had sent £40 to help with a permanently outstanding bill at the Petitpas boarding house, where JBY continued to hold court with bohemian Manhattan. By January 1915 WBY was once again receiving letters from his parent requiring 'a dollar or two', as he was 'wonderfully and fearfully hard up'; Gregory, visiting New York, was dispatched to find out just how poor he was. Ten pounds was sent, but Gregory's reports made clear that further subventions were necessary by the spring of 1915, and a guaranteed £100 per annum. WBY had continued to send odd sums, including a major payment of £100, which came out of invested capital, and wondered about selling his Sligo Steamer shares. But this could not continue. The eternally tricky question was broached about bringing him home; but, Lily warned Quinn, '[it] will have to be done with tact, of which Lady Gregory has not much. Willy thinks she has an enormous amount. I say she has none, but goes for what she wants straight over everything in her way. I call her the Juggernaut. She hurts people in a way that would surprise her if she knew it.'[32] JBY told Lily that Gregory's interrogations resembled a session on the rack, but he escaped being crushed by the juggernaut. As usual, someone else took on the responsibility.

An arrangement was now formalized with John Quinn, through Gregory: if the lawyer made a regular allowance to JBY, WBY would, in turn, pay him in manuscripts. Thus was laid the basis of Quinn's great collection, and JBY's continuance in New York was ensured, to the relief of all parties. Meanwhile WBY ruefully saw his manuscripts turned rapidly into hard currency to support his father, just as his early magazine earnings had vanished down the 'swally hole' at Blenheim Road thirty years before. He initially offered Quinn the manuscripts of *Reveries*, the Swedenborg essay, 'and say a dozen poems. I am a slow writer and this has been about an average year's work. I write a great deal more of course, but destroy what I do continually.' Quinn, according to Gregory, was prepared to pay for WBY's prose at the same rate as Conrad's.[33] Jack, 'hard hit by the war' (and a nervous breakdown), was unable to contribute to their father's upkeep, and there was no other source available. The principle was quickly agreed: WBY wondered whether Quinn could take eighty pounds' worth of manuscripts a year, hoping unrealistically that JBY might earn the balance necessary for subsistence. But the old man was courteously prepared to be as dependent as ever. The reprobate's other children breathed an audible sigh of relief. 'I am as pleased as Papa must be to hear of Willy's generosity,' Lily wrote to Quinn.

He is as fine as a man as he is as a writer, and that is saying a good deal. I know that up to his getting the Civil List pension he had a very hard struggle to keep himself going even with his modest wants. None of us have ever known the peace of a regular income. Willy has it in a small way with his pension, and now his books must be bringing in a good deal . . . Your offer about the MSS is most generous. I think I have most of Willy's old MSS, Mosada, Countess Cathleen, and odds and ends, so Willy is sure to be writing me about them, or it may be you are getting newer work. I don't for a moment consider the MSS mine, though I would have given you 'The

Countess Kathleen' if you would have taken it. I just saved them from destruction long ago and kept them safe, being something of a magpie in these matters. What I have are very anyhow scratched in and out and written on odds and ends of paper. If you would like to look through any of them let me know and I will send it at once to you by registered post. You cannot imagine what a relief this all is to me. I was always worrying about Papa, which did him no good.[34]

Clearly, Quinn lost no time in contacting the other members of the family, with a view to building up his collection – while enjoining them to secrecy. A few weeks later Lily again told him that, though she did possess manuscripts of her brother's, she considered them to be morally his: she also made clear that she knew their potential value.

He knows I have them but I do not remind him of them as in an expansive moment he might let 'Aunt Augusta' have them all, and I feel they have a better right to be in my oak chest than locked away for little Richard in the Archives at Coole, to be probably sold by little Richard when he has become big Richard and wants a wife or a motor. I said nothing to Willy about you and his MSS and he has said nothing to me.[35]

Quinn also contacted Jack, while emphasizing that WBY had asked him not to tell his siblings. In the same letter Quinn said the agreed rate was a pound per thousand words. By September 1915 he had offered £50 for the manuscript of *Reveries*, to start the fund. The details of the negotiation were kept from its beneficiary, who wrote, insouciant as ever, to his old confidante Rosa Butt:

I have had a lot of worry, very much in debt to these nice people, but W. B. Yeats sent me £50 *I had not asked for it* or even hinted at it. It was a pleasant surprise, and money can't be abundant with him, but he lives always in the most thrifty way, never wanting to spend money on himself, in this like his mother.[36]

Characteristically, JBY undervalued his son's sacrifice – much as he underestimated the extent of Quinn's exasperation. In fact, the attractions of Irish cultural entrepreneurship were wearing thin for Quinn. He had taken to sending vituperative letters to would-be Irish lecturers who 'assume that I have the time or the leisure to attend to his or her special "mission", to use a favourite phrase of those who come here from Ireland';[37] post-Impressionist painting monopolized more and more of his aesthetic energies. But Quinn's eye for quality ensured that his obsession with the work of WBY, and soon James Joyce, would endure. And so did his role in subsidizing the poet's father.

The son's generosity was all the more striking because he had a private project in mind: the purchase of his first house. He had long been struck by the stark beauty of a medieval tower-house or castle keep buried in a little river-valley near Coole, and had written of it in *The Celtic Twilight*: the 'old square castle, Ballylee, inhabited by a farmer and his wife, and a cottage where their daughter and son-in-law live, and a little mill with an old miller, and old ash-trees throwing green shadows upon a little river and great stepping stones'.[38] It was Gregory territory, and since the Land Purchase Acts and the crisis of the war, part of the estate was being sold off. The tenants wanted the land but not the tower. In January 1915 Gregory suggested that WBY should consider buying it; her old friend's answer, written just when he was learning about his father's difficulties, clearly shows his state of mind as his fiftieth birthday approached.

Now about my own affairs. Your sale to the tenants has come at a bad time for me. I am quite serious about Ballylee (though I should want to see it again now the trees are gone); but I cannot bid for it now. If I remain unmarried I would find it useless (I am too blind for the country alone & too fond of company) & it would use up the money my father or sister may need, & remain empty. Can you put it in the government's care? (under the clause we got passed) & that I suppose would leave it still to be got. If after a couple more years I find myself as I am I shall give up thoughts of the country & shift from Woburn Buildings to Greys Inn in 'The Temple' where I can have more dignified circumstances, though in a moment of folly I have just spent 17 or 18 pounds getting the walls of two of my rooms scraped and repapered to exterminate as I hope those summer insects. It will soon 'be time to be old & take in sale' as Emmerson said, & I am not too gloomy at the prospect.[39]

For the moment, nothing would happen about Ballylee, but the sense of a new phase opening up in his life is palpable. 'Friendship is all the house I have,' he had written during Gregory's life-threatening illness six years before. Now he had put his eye on a house whose association with his closest friend could not be stronger, and whose romantic solitude accorded with his increasingly hieratic sense of history.

III

On 7 May Violet Martin, walking by the sea near Castletownshend, County Cork, saw the liner *Lusitania* pass 'in beautiful weather'. Half an hour later the ship was torpedoed by a U-boat: nearly 2,000 perished. 'That afternoon the news was called to me from a cottage door – in horror,' she wrote to Gregory. 'The shadow of it has been over us ever since.'[40] That shadow fell heavily over Coole, for one of the casualties was Gregory's celebrated, controversial, and beloved nephew, Hugh Lane.

Since the 1913 débâcle over his plans for a Dublin gallery of modern art, when he had withdrawn in pique after a bruising encounter with the

Philistines,[41] Lane had pursued his way unhampered: quarrelling with Christie's, arguing with the National Gallery in London about which of his pictures they should hang, and turning ever more profitable deals. When he met his end, he was returning from a New York visit where he had sold a Holbein and a Titian of his own to Henry Clay Frick. Having gone there to face down a financial crisis which had threatened him with the loss of all his pictures, he was – by a tragic irony – returning in triumph.[42] In February 1914, however, he had become a director of the Dublin National Gallery (a part-time post), and his attentions had shifted back to Ireland. This had not been an easy passage: attempts had been made to exclude him on the grounds of his trusteeship (which he resigned in favour of the inevitable W. F. Bailey), and even after his appointment the Treasury refused to accept him as a civil servant. He was a controversial figure, dismissed by more scholarly aesthetes like Charles Ricketts as 'an uneducated flunkey'.[43] While his dealing activities were looked on with disapprobation, it was risky to alienate Lane, as he continued to offer munificent bequests. 'I gave pictures to the value of at least £10,000 at last meeting [of the Dublin Gallery],' he had told Gregory in May 1914, '& I was going to give an important Gainsborough to London & some good French pictures to fill important gaps in the collection at next meeting, but I feel rather angry at the moment. I've a good mind to write to Mr Birrell [the chief secretary] & demand a "damnation" to confound my enemies.'[44]

Despite his repeated declarations of dislike for Dublin, and his readiness to flounce off, his basic commitment had remained. 'You give me to[o] much credit for my intention toward Dublin,' he had told his aunt after the gallery fiasco in late 1913. 'I hate the place, the people, & the "Gallery". But I am simply ashamed to have my name associated with a bad collection, & would like to make it really good of its kind. I don't think that I will ever bring back these pictures, as I could best work up a fresh interest (to myself & Dublin) by making a fresh collection.'[45] He had subsequently willed his collection to the London National Gallery, which had accepted them on loan, 'to found a collection of Modern Continental Art in London'. But this was in October 1913, before his appointment to the Dublin National Gallery – and his quarrels with London over their cavalier attitude to his collection, much of which they put in store without consulting him. Recent research has shown that before Lane's death the trustees of the London Gallery were, ironically, preparing to return Lane's pictures to him 'in polite but definite terms'. In any case, his strategy, as he airily told AE the day before he sailed for America, was 'to make threats to frighten people here [in Dublin] to get them to move'.[46] Both Gregory and WBY were convinced that Lane had reverted to his intention to give thirty-nine pictures, most of them by modern French painters, as the foundation for a modern art gallery in Dublin.*

After Lane's tragic death WBY put the position succinctly in a letter to Quinn:

The only properly signed and witnessed will found, was made some years ago and at a time when he was angry with the Dublin Corporation. It made a few private bequests, amounting in all to very little. He left the pictures that had been offered to Dublin, to go towards the foundation of a modern gallery in London and left all the rest of his property to the Dublin National Gallery. From various things Lane had said to various people, Lady Gregory believed there was a later will, and a search started by her, resulted in the discovery of an unwitnessed codicil leaving back the modern pictures to the Dublin Municipal Gallery on certain conditions. They were to make a fitting building for them and put it in a fitting place, and of place and building Lady Gregory was to be the sole judge. We are now trying to get a competent successor to Lane, appointed by the Governors of the Irish National Gallery. I daresay we shall fail and have to submit to some local job, for with few exceptions, they are local nobodies . . . . It is wonderful the amount of toil and intrigue one has to go through to accomplish anything in Ireland. Intelligence has no organization whilst stupidity always has. I suppose because it is the world itself. I have often thought that all ages are the equal of one another in talent, and that we call an age great merely because it knew better how to employ talent.[47]

Lane's friends and intimates knew of his intention to make another will:[48] within three days of his death WBY was in touch with Elizabeth Radcliffe in the hope that Lane's spirit might make contact through automatic writing. Further seance investigations with established psychic divas like Etta Wriedt, Mrs Cannock, Charlotte Herbine, and Geraldine Cummins followed, and Hester Travers Smith claimed Lane's spirit had contacted her at a seance before the news was announced in Dublin. In fact, a codicil to Lane's original will, dated February 1915, was swiftly discovered by looking in his desk at the Dublin Gallery – Gregory's practical suggestion, though

---

* As listed in Lady Gregory, *Case for the Return of Sir Hugh Lane's Pictures to Dublin* (Dublin, 1926), pp. 47–8, the thirty-nine pictures left to the Dublin Municipal Gallery in Lane's codicil were: C.-O. Monet, *Vétheuil: Sunshine and Snow*; P.-A. Renoir, *Les Parapluies*; E. Manet, *Le Concert aux Tuileries* and *Portrait of Mlle Eva Gonzalès*; C. Pissarro, *Printemps, vue de Louveciennes*; E. Vuillard, *The Mantelpiece*; E. Boudin, *Le Rivage, entrée de Tourgeville*; E. Degas, *La Plage*; B. Morisot, *Un jour d'été*; J.-M.-J. Ingres, *Duc d'Orléans*; J.-L. Forain, *In the Law Courts*; A. Mancini, *Portrait of Marquis del Grillo, En Voyage, Aurelia*, and *La Douane*; J. L. Brown, *The Mountebank*; R. Madrazo, *Portrait Study of a Woman*; C.-F. Daubigny, *Portrait of Honoré Daumier*; A.-L. Barye, *Forest at Fontainebleau*; J.-B.-C. Corot, *Avignon: Ancient Palace of the Popes, Landscape: A Summer Morning*, and *An Italian Peasant Woman*; E. Fromentin, *The Slave*; J.-D.-G. Courbet, *The Snow Storm, The Pool, In the Forest*, and *The Artist*; N.-V. Diaz de la Peña, *The Offspring of Love*; J.-L. Gerome, *Portrait of a Naval Officer*; J.-H.-F. Fantin-Latour, *Still Life*; F. Bovin, *Still Life*; T. Rousseau, *Moonlight*; P.-C. Puvis de Chavannes, *The Toilet* and *La Décollation de Saint Jean-Baptiste*; A. Monticelli, *The Hayfield*; H. Daumier, *Don Quixote and Sancho Panza*; J. Maris, *Feeding the Bird*; A. Stevens, *The Present*; J. B. Jongkind, *Skating in Holland*.

WBY preferred to think it was 'revealed' to her by 'Lane's spirit'.[49] The codicil left his pictures back to Dublin on condition that the Corporation made a building suitable for the purpose within five years; Gregory was appointed executor. The codicil was, however, unwitnessed and therefore not legal. The question at once arose as to whether there was a further, complete will, and through June WBY pursued spiritualist investigations, recorded at great and apparently credulous length, including harrowing cinematic impressions of the last moments on board the doomed ship. Lennox Robinson was also instructed to seek contact through Hester Travers Smith, his future mother-in-law. In the end WBY suspected that the professional mediums were simply relaying back 'telepathy from my unconscious mind', and he retained confidence in only one Greek word produced by the reliable Miss Radcliffe. Faced with this long account, Gregory replied warily:

That evidence is very impressive – tho' I suppose it might be the reflection from your mind – I want to know if I said to you on Sunday that I thought he might have taken the new will with him, & been dissatisfied with it & torn it up? The impression came to me when I was at Cheyne Walk [Lane's house] on Sunday, & I said it either to you or Ruth [Shine, Lane's sister] – If I did not say it to you, I would feel Mr C. ['Coulter', Mrs Herbine's 'Control'] got it from him – I think myself the message was from him – but we should sift evidence as closely as possible . . . if Hugh had been rescued he could have suffered terribly from the shock of what had happened to others – it is strange if it can be so on the other side –[50]

Nonetheless, the codicil seemed to prove Lane's intentions, and a strong letter from his colleague Ellen Duncan to the *Irish Times* the following year, written in collaboration with Gregory, carries conviction. 'All the bitterness which he felt in 1913 after the defeat of the Bridge Site scheme had passed from him, and his interest in the Gallery had revived.'[51] By late 1916 the unthinkable would become clear: the London National Gallery was going to stand on the letter of the law and fight for the original bequest, and no politician was prepared to back the Act of Parliament that would be necessary to legalize Lane's unwitnessed codicil. And also by late 1916, due to utterly unforeseen political upheavals, Gregory and WBY would no longer be able to wield political influence through their highly placed friends Birrell and Asquith.

In the sad summer of 1915, however, the immediate problem seemed to concern Lane's replacement at the Dublin Gallery rather than the implementation of his will. Several names familiar in aesthetic London were suggested: Wilde's friend and defender Robbie Ross, the poet Laurence Binyon, and WBY's candidate Eric Maclagan among them. Arguing for a local candidate, WBY also introduced the name of the painter Dermod

O'Brien, but really as a stalking horse in a deep-laid strategy, to bring in Robert Gregory. When Lane had resigned as a trustee, Gregory had already tried to float her son's name as a replacement.[52] Now, she prompted WBY to advance him as the new director. WBY accordingly pressed the appointment of Robert, who would provide, he claimed, the inspiration necessary to make a great gallery. His advocacy of Robert's qualities contradicted the opinions confided to his notebooks regarding the young man's dilettantism and lack of direction, though he had come to admire his artistic talent (particularly one painting shown at the New English Gallery that summer, 'a decorative landscape suggested by Coole Lake, full of airy distinction'[53]). The candidate's mother and WBY moved on to lobby influential trustees like Sarah Purser and W. F. Bailey, receiving wary and temporizing replies. Bailey's remark that Robert was 'not well known to the Governors' received a withering response from Woburn Buildings:

It will be a scandal if the Governors appoint a man merely because he is 'well-known personally to several of them'. I often think that talent is much more nearly equal in all ages than people think, and that a great age is merely an age that knows how to employ it. Nearly all incompetents are appointed because they are 'personally known to somebody'.[54]

A copy was sent to Coole, but the campaign got nowhere; WBY and Gregory had to content themselves with trying to block the candidature of Thomas Bodkin, and attracting more glamorous figures from Lane's London circle, like Robert Clermont Witt, a founder of the National Art Collection Fund and author of several works on art appreciation. Robert Langton Douglas eventually succeeded, though WBY confided to Gregory the hope that Witt would be appointed, and then rejected because he refused to live in Dublin; this would leave the way open for the equally cosmopolitan Robert rather than Bodkin, whom he saw as unworthy and lightweight. 'I am an old politician and I believe that I am in the right though I know what I am doing could be misrepresented . . . I said to-day to Richard [*recte* Robert] Witt, "a line of Edmund Spenser's has been in my head all day, 'The fox has fouled the lair the badger swept'".'[55]

The Lane tragedy left other ripples in its wake. Though his estate was at one point estimated at £300,000, there were claims outstanding (£10,000 for a Sargent, plus money owing on pictures lost on board ship). WBY raged at the reluctance of Lane's executor, the banker J. J. Meagher, to defend the bequest to the Dublin Gallery: 'I thought him a typical Catholic as we know the better sort in Ireland,' he told Gregory, 'charitable, loyal to personalities, but without any grasp on principles. I suppose public life is a Protestant creation.'[56] Thus the Lane affair revived all the bitterness and prejudices of

'September 1913'. It also reminded wby of his old conviction that the history of their generation's influence on Ireland would be written in their life-stories, since a biographer had to be appointed for Lane. He refused to do it himself, having 'not the training to marshal a mass of facts, and besides, I have made a vow with myself now, never to do anything again that is not creative literature'.[57] Various candidates were canvassed, including Lewis Hind, D. S. MacColl, and Robert Witt once more; but both Witt and MacColl would turn out to be in the camp of the enemy, upholding the London Gallery's claims, and within a year Gregory had started making notes for a biography herself. It was just one of the burdens which Lane's death, and his troubled bequest, deposited on her strong shoulders. The major weight would prove to be the destination of his pictures, but in the summer of 1915 this had not yet become clear. Birrell was assuring them that the spirit of the codicil would be observed, though the executor of Lane's will had his doubts. wby sarcastically defined this worthy's ideal solution: 'if only the modern pictures could somehow be suspended in the air, nobody making out a clear right to them'.[58] In fact, this is more or less the situation that evolved decades later. The moral right, in the view of himself, Gregory, and all shades of Irish opinion, lay firmly with the mooted Dublin gallery of modern art: but, as things turned out, ownership of the pictures would indeed enter the realm of suspended animation.

In grappling with the problem, wby turned swiftly to psychic investigation. At just this time he wrote to Hone explaining why he had left occult affairs mostly out of *Reveries*: 'I may do so in detail when I continue but what is "occult" will be so mixed up with my present affairs, that they may have to await publication till after my death.'[59] In fact, the resort to mediums in May was by no means an isolated impulse that summer. wby's old occultist friend W. T. Horton, still beset by visions, had returned to his circle; he and his platonic love, Audrey Locke, were regulars at Woburn Buildings and put wby in touch with a medium who introduced historical personages, excitedly checked in biographical dictionaries. The demanding correspondence with Elizabeth Radcliffe continued. And Mrs Wriedt was still providing psychic contacts; Leo Africanus looked in during early June (though wby, as ever suiting his tone to his correspondent, confided to Agnes Tobin, 'I think he is masquerading and gets himself out of an encyclopaedia': perhaps referring to his own copy of *Chambers's Biographical Dictionary*, where Leo appeared two lines above Leonardo da Vinci). In late July Wriedt actually contacted George Pollexfen who – more obliging than in earthly life – solicitously inquired after all the family.[60] wby's friend Edith Lyttelton, who was deeply interested in psychic research, worried that his growing preoccupation with 'materialistic seances' meant 'that you are within the circle of influence of some rather undesirable spirits or mediums'; she herself received a communication indicating that 'Yeats is a prince with an evil counsellor.'[61] But his appetite remained unappeasable: he experimented with planchette, and in March obtained a reader's card for Trinity College Library in order to reread Adam Clarke's memoir of magical and alchemical happenings in eighteenth-century Dublin. On the same Dublin visit he was still reading *Dracula*, and was interested enough to plan a visit to the Count's Transylvanian castle with the psychic investigator Everard Feilding – never consummated. Writing 'with love' to Mabel Beardsley, from his respectable new quarters at the Stephen's Green Club, WBY tried to explain his ideas:

I have been rehersing plays & reading the 17th century platonists in the College Library, & making psychic experiments with two friends who have written out with a ouja [ouija] board (a sort of Planchet) words which I have held up before their tightly blindfolded eyes. As they cannot see the words if I hold them out of the line of sight I beleive myself to have proved that more than one life looks through our eyes & that lives more sensitive than ours can see by the light that passes through thick cloths. Are we perhaps the senses of a whole invisable world? Perhaps the angels & devils can read the books we merely glance at in passing, & hear sounds too far for our hearing though not for our ears.[62]

The need for verification of life beyond the grave still possessed him: death was all around. (Audrey Locke, whom he had come to admire, died suddenly in June, a month after Lane.) The idea of a simultaneous 'invisible world' existing in another time-dimension had long been with him, but it was fuelled by reading *An Adventure*, written pseudonymously by Charlotte Anne Moberly and Eleanor Jourdain, two Oxford dons who, on a visit to Versailles, had shared an intensely detailed vision of the time of Louis XV. Their account, published in 1911, had created a cause célèbre, and perhaps because of its popularity, WBY did not refer to it publicly as much as to old guides like Agrippa, Lévi, and Swedenborg – all of whom he was rereading. But the depth of corroborative research produced by Jourdain and Moberly (whom he later met) appealed to him. All this was put to practical use in the notes for Gregory's *Visions and Beliefs*, as well as answering the echoes struck by Pound's Japanese ghosts. The first long note WBY provided for Gregory's book was, in fact, an essay on the rebirth of the soul, and he took pleasure in citing 'Father Sinistrari', a Catholic theologian of Padua, in support of the existence of alternative worlds. Probably in reading St John Seymour's recently published *Irish Witchcraft and Demonology* for his notes, he found local references which would subsequently emerge, not only in *Visions and Beliefs* but in his later verse.[63]

For, as so often, the obsessive pursuit of arcane wisdom and the search for
'evidence' of other worlds was directly connected with a creative surge. On
13 June he turned fifty, but found his artistic energy unabated. By the end of
that month he was telling Robert Bridges of poems recently written and not
yet typed up; a letter to Quinn around the same time shows how cheered he
was by the successful revival of *On Baile's Strand* in London.

By a beneficent accident there was no press to tell me I am a fool for my pains; the
result is that I am full of new poems – dramatic and lyrical. All my mythological
people have come alive again, and I want to begin the completion of my heroic
cycle. I have also nearly finished my Notes for Lady Gregory's book, and that has
laid the ghosts for me. I am free at last from the obsession of the supernatural, having got my thoughts in order and ranged on paper.[64]

This was wishful thinking. But he was ready for the peace of Coole and
longed to write – sending ahead two dozen bottles of Marsala ('which is
what I usually drink now I find') and trying to sort out the Abbey business
which was detaining him in London. The Australian tour, organized to
keep the company afloat, capsized when Sara Allgood finally defected to
play *Peg o' My Heart* on Broadway; WBY had his wish and sacked the manager Wilson, who had been allegedly cutting out the directors by making
contracts to his own advantage, intercepting music-hall offers from
America, and informing the players that 'all was up with the Abbey
Theatre'.[65] Eventually, after much negotiation, the directors appointed the
talented Ulster playwright and littérateur, St John Ervine. It was a delicate
situation, since he had submitted his own plays to the Abbey, and his wife
was not only an actress but an inadequate one. WBY made the appointment
on his own authority, as Gregory was in America. Then, freed at last, he followed his Marsala to Coole, where he spent August and September.

Anxious though he was to write poetry, he occupied himself with *The
Player Queen*; as a result of the summer's work, he could (wrongly) consider
it finished by the end of the year. As it eventually turned out, he felt it would
be unsuitable for Mrs Pat Campbell, who had wooed him with wine so
many years before, though he felt he should read it to her for form's sake.
The early drafts, more or less abandoned since 1910, had remained unresolved – as well as becoming uncomfortably lengthy, with the tone veering
uneasily from farcical action to tragic ending. During the summer of 1915 he
had had a kind of breakthrough.[66] Blank verse was now replaced by free-
wheeling prose, and he visualized a fantastic production, 'with scenery in
the manner of Bakst'; but thought the play 'less possible for Dublin than
ever', being sexually explicit, iconoclastic, and avant-garde ('I imagine that
Dublin would outdo its Playboy enterprise').[67]

This was an exaggerated expectation. The play, as it stood in 1915, has more in common with *Where There is Nothing* than with any controversial play by Synge. Like every project which WBY had trouble finishing (*The Shadowy Waters, The Speckled Bird*), there is a highly personal subtext: the play, which he had begun at the time of his affair with Mabel Dickinson and of Mrs Pat's infatuation with him, features a powerful woman who takes lovers where she will. The version that emerged in late 1915 revolved around her partnership with an artistic free spirit, Septimus: self-described (in his cups) as 'a player, a playwright, and the most famous poet in the world'. Another of his women accuses the Player Queen of making miserable 'a great genius who can't take care of himself': yet this wild character emerges as the prophet of a dawning new world. It is set, rather uncomfortably, in a never-never land *à la* Dunsany, complete with fairy-tale palace, reclusive queen, scheming Prime Minister, strolling players, and transformative magic – symbolized, significantly, by masks.

Finally, the 'Player Queen', Decima, though 'born in a ditch between two towns and wrapped in a sheet that was stolen from a hedge', replaces the real queen, a would-be nun obsessed with sainthood. Images of copulation with animals (including, eventually, a unicorn, which became a central symbol for WBY from this time), poems composed in a lovers' bed (the poet tapping out the beat on his beloved's spine), and the celebration of a 'beautiful, bad, flighty woman' would not have unequivocally pleased Dublin audiences. Nor would an incident involving the neglect of a holy statue, which was subsequently left out. When the play eventually reached the Abbey in 1919, W. A. Henderson noted frigidly that 'marriage is made very light of',[68] while the *Evening Telegraph* decided that WBY 'glimpsed Ruritania in the Celtic Twilight and resurrected François Villon and sent him reeling drunk through the lantern lit street of its capital', in order to annoy the respectable. Three years and yet more revisions (including a gentle and reconciliatory ending) would pass before WBY felt ready to let it be performed. It would not be published, still further altered, until 1922. The play continued to mean more to him than it ever would to his audience: 'is not Septimus yourself?' he would be asked in a future, highly collusive session of psychic exploration.[69] On an abstract level, it worked out the themes of self and anti-self, mask and reality, which preoccupied him at this time; it also suggested the annunciation of a new age and the mutability of apocalyptic times. WBY's friend Edmund Dulac perhaps understood it more than most when he defined its theme as 'the idea that complex self-expression can only be accomplished when man and his image are united in the same person'.[70] More concretely, it expressed WBY's view of, and relationship with, the world of theatre itself. *The Player Queen* is, finally, a play about performance.

IV

As usual, the return to London in October restored the problems of every-day. Only now, five months after Lane's death, the real issues about his bequest became clear. WBY had thought the main problem with the thirty-nine pictures simply concerned whether they hung in the projected Municipal Gallery or the established National Gallery; either way, they would stay in Dublin. This thorny question seemed near resolution: W. M. Murphy and other old adversaries now supported a new gallery, a site was agreed by the Mansion House, Sir Horace Plunkett initiated an approach to the Carnegie Trust, and it looked as if the stipulation in Lane's codicil (a modern art gallery within five years) would be comfortably met. But a new and greater danger threatened: powerful figures in the London art world decided the London National Gallery should take a stand on the terms of Lane's 1913 will. By mid October WBY could tell Gregory that ostensible friends like Henry Tonks, Robert Witt, and probably D. S. MacColl

are furious with the National Gallery for proposing to give up the pictures. They think it merely a symptom of the general incompetence of the Governors who are going to give up the pictures because they are too stupid to know their value. They choose to believe that the codicil was written in momentary irritation of [sic] the English National Gallery; they threaten a Press campaign which will 'create such a public opinion against the Governors that they won't dare to give up the pictures'.

WBY threatened Witt in turn, telling him that 'we would make quite as good a fight, and that the moment they took that line, it will be an international question between Ireland and England, and that the next time the English Government refused something that all Ireland wanted, they would give Ireland the pictures'.[71]

Thus, in his view, politics loomed large behind the issue of the paintings; as so often, a property bequest inflamed tensions and resentments stretching back into ancient history. WBY's excitement may be gauged by the length of this letter – twelve typewritten pages, even though its composition was interrupted by a Zeppelin raid ('I have just said to Miss Jacobs [the typist] – twenty minutes is enough for the Day of Judgement so I will take up the thread of my letter'). As in 1913, Ireland's cultural maturity was at issue, and the enemy was now not the Dublin bourgeoisie but the English establishment. An interview with Sir Charles Holroyd of the London National Gallery in early November gave him some hope, but by the end of the month news of the disagreement over observing the terms of Lane's codicil had broken in the papers.[72] Gregory sailed magnificently into battle, opening fire in the threatened public campaign; it would dominate the remainder of her life, ending only in a messy compromise long afterwards. For WBY, the contest over the Lane pictures showed British official attitudes towards Ireland at their most intransigently self-interested, and it would play its part in the shift of his own political opinion, precipitated by the political upheavals of the next year.

All the same, he moved easily in the highest establishment circles. The lion-hunting Lady Cunard arranged a lunch at the Ritz for WBY to meet Lord Wimborne, the new lord-lieutenant, who was struck by the poet's 'great knowledge' of Ireland (and probably surprised at receiving an 'exposition of Irish politics a good deal clearer than it seems Irish viceroys are usually given').[73] Emerald Cunard was born Maud Burke in Chicago and rapidly jettisoned both names. She had a special line in fashionable artists – usually musicians and composers, since her liaison with Thomas Beecham had begun four years before, succeeding a long involvement with George Moore. Diminutive, racy, and slightly scandalous, she had successfully broken into Edwardian high society, and was currently renting the Asquiths' house in Cavendish Square while they occupied 10 Downing Street. From late 1915 she mercilessly cultivated WBY. He put up with it, while confiding privately that she seemed to represent 'the triumph of the Barbarian: she jumps upon all our altars – and dances the can-can there'. In mid November he complained to Alick Schepeler that the 'energetic' Lady Cunard was 'eating up much of my time.'[74] 'Eating' was the *mot juste*: after the lunch with Wimborne, she arranged a dinner with Arthur Balfour at the end of November, which WBY reported fully to Gregory:

There were 3 men including Balfour and 3 women and I regret to say I did all the talking. I am afraid I can say nothing of Balfour expect [*sic*] that he is a most charming and sympathetic listener, so charming and sympathetic that he lures one on into more and more vehemence of speech. The conversation became general at a saying of mine about Carlyle, I was talking to Lady Cunard and I said, 'Carlyle was a sheer imposter, the French Revolution is now as unreadable as McPherson's Ossian.' Lady Cunard repeated this to Balfour who agreed, very pleased with the Ossian comparison. I said, I spent an evening reading Walpole's letters to get Carlyle out of my head. Balfour then said, 'Walpole was just the kind of man Carlyle despised and called insincere, and yet Carlyle himself was the most insincere of all'. Then I told tales about George Moore and at the end of [the] scandalous tale, Lady Cunard – who enjoyed my stories immensely – pointed over the table at Balfour and cried out, 'Oh, look at Mr Balfour's face!' Sturge Moore was one of the guests, I had been engaged to dine with him and Lady Cunard told me to bring him with me as a way out of the difficulty. He was very silent but looked so extraordinarily like himself and so unlike anybody else that I am not sure he was not the success of the evening.[75]

27

The indefatigable Emerald Cunard also arranged WBY's lecture on 6 December at the duchess of Marlborough's, raising over £200 for the beleaguered Abbey. WBY did not enjoy the experience, finding the select audience hard to move and his own performance earthbound. And life lived at this level brought other dangers too. The letter describing dinner with Balfour was dictated to a typist, but carried a handwritten and highly confidential postscript:

As I came away from the Balfour dinner Lady Cunard said 'the Prime Minister means to be very gracious to you at the New Year, & Mr Balfour has just said to me that he is in full agreement,' I began 'o please not – ' but Lady Cunard interrupted me with 'well you may as well have it offered, & you can refuse.' I told Bailey about it in confidence & said in spite of the real satisfaction I would feel at the increased respect of railway porters & spirit mediums I would have to refuse. He could not understand & argued that it would help me in England. He told me that he has been promised a K.C.B. but that for certain reasons it has been put off for the moment. I told him that if I accepted my family would be shocked & last night at dinner (my two sisters Ervine & myself dined with him) Lilly said 'They will accuse you next of wanting to be knighted'.

In fact, ten days later WBY told Lily about his refusal:

Lady Cunard had already sounded the authorities & asked me about it today. Please keep it to yourself as it would be very ungracious of me to let it get talked about in Dublin. It was very kindly meant. I said 'As I grow old I become more conservative & I do not know whether that is because my thoughts are deeper or my blood more chill, but I do not wish anyone to say of me "only for a ribbon he left us."' Lady Cunard then said 'Well you can have it whenever you like'.[76]

Lily did keep it quiet ('Willy often tells me secrets which I hold tight even when he tells them to others who tell them to me'); but Lady Cunard 'told it everywhere', so he released his sister from discretion.[77] Gregory was of course informed at once, and responded briskly. 'As to the proposed "honour" it is annoying to be offered something that is of no use & that you are better without – some Oxford honour would be worth more to you – tho' I don't see you want anything at all but your own name, now the civil list has removed the danger of poverty.' WBY might have been forgiven for thinking that this robust dismissal came more easily from someone with a title of her own. But acceptance was never a possibility, though the recognition was gratifying. Radical nationalist opinion had its ears to the ground and was waiting to pounce. Within weeks Arthur Griffith decided that AE's 1907 satire on WBY as the 'Chief Poet of Ireland', promised a knighthood by Cathleen ni Houlihan, was 'so appropriate today that [we] must reprint it'.[78] WBY knew all too well what the Dublin of Griffith and D. P. Moran – not to mention Maud Gonne – would have made of Pensioner Yeats as a Knight of the Realm. But the Jamesian minuet of lunches, hints, exchanges after dinner, measures the distance travelled since WBY had chaired the Wolfe Tone Memorial Committee and denounced royalty fifteen years before, though the establishment would never be completely sure of him.

He was still able to invoke the world of 'influence' when Shaw provided yet another cause célèbre that November. After the problems with *John Bull's Other Island* and *Blanco Posnet*, his latest play, *O'Flaherty VC*, gave St John Ervine, just installed as Abbey manager, his trial by fire. The play was supposed to encourage Irish recruitment, but – Shaw being Shaw – contrived to argue the case on the grounds that Ireland was so unbearable, Irish patriotism so mindlessly ignorant, and Irish domestic life so violent that the only hope for any Irishman in search of a quiet life was enlistment for the Western Front. The *Playboy*, as Shaw admitted guiltily to Gregory, would seem 'a patriotic rhapsody by comparison'.[79] He knew perfectly well it might be banned in England, and thought it 'much safer for Ireland and America'.[80] Since it argued that 'no war is right', the military authorities in Ireland unsurprisingly objected to its being played. WBY decided the issue was not worth fighting, but Shaw, infuriatingly, told him that Gregory, absent in America, would disagree, if only from a love of mischief. 'I told him that was a misunderstanding of your character,' WBY primly assured her, but he was nettled enough to negotiate with the under-secretary and the Castle authorities ('as courteous and obliging as possible, & everybody professes to be a friend of the theatre, especially [Sir Matthew] Nathan').[81] A paragraph in the *Freeman* scared everybody, and the play was postponed; as Nathan remarked to Birrell, the chief secretary, it would 'be looked upon as too much a recruiting play by the Irish and as an anti-recruiting play by the English', which may have been exactly Shaw's intention.[82] The eruption passed and ordinary Abbey troubles resurfaced instead, such as Ervine's problematic wife, 'too inexperienced', 'exceedingly fat', and disliked by WBY 'as much or more off [the stage] than on it'.[83] Shaw's version of wartime Ireland would not be played by the Abbey until 1920, when the world had changed. Even then they risked it only in London.

The Abbey's affairs had brought WBY back to Dublin in early December, but he told Quinn that he was tied to 'this noisy London' by 'the need of a woman friend'. This was his intermittent mistress Alick Schepeler, once again a regular attendant on Monday nights this autumn, and the recipient of flirtatious letters and even presents from WBY. ('It looked too large to go in any parcel but a friend I consulted said that there is such a thing as a muff corded up in a bundle.'[84]) The year before she had stayed with him at Coole and – according to Gregory – left WBY 'quite disconsolate' when she returned to London. She also accompanied him on spiritualist inquiries, which revealed, among other things, that 'I am not the only dark man in your tortuous existence'. Nor was he. The pale and passive Schepeler continued to be admired by much of London's artistic Bohemia; her appearances at Woburn Buildings may lie behind Pound's 'Albâtre', published in the *Catholic Anthology* at the time when his poems and WBY's often conducted a surreptitious dialogue with each other.

> This lady in the white bath-robe, which she calls a peignoir,
> Is, for the time being, the mistress of my friend,
> And the delicate white feet of her little white dog
> Are not more delicate than she is,
> Nor would Gautier himself have despised their contrasts in whiteness
> As she sits in the great chair
> Between the two indolent candles.[85]

As for WBY himself, when he was involved with another woman his thoughts inevitably spiralled back to Gonne. His notebooks for October and November 1915, exactly the period when he was seeing Schepeler, are full of drafts of poems about Gonne – including 'A Deep-Sworn Vow', 'The Dawn', 'Presences', and 'Broken Dreams'.[86] This last not only celebrated Gonne's 'burdensome beauty', but announced its decay: the cancelled first line in the first draft, 'Lines are about your eyes your hair is gray', was replaced first by 'Cobwebby lines – hair that is getting gray!', and finally became, starkly, 'There is gray in your hair.' But the theme of the poem is the renewal of eternal beauty in death, and his vision that in another world he will see her 'Leaning or standing or walking, / In the first loveliness of womanhood' – except, he hopes, for her one flaw, 'small hands', which he wants left unchanged, 'for old sake's sake'. The finality of the vision is decisive; if Gonne has become grey and lined, her admirer appears as a vague old man rambling in his chair. He was just past his fiftieth birthday, and she was forty-nine.

Even more strikingly reflective is the intellectual and spiritual history attempted in the long dialogue poem he wrote in December, first called 'The Self and the Anti-Self', and later 'Ego Dominus Tuus', a title borrowed from Dante's *Vita Nuova*.[87] In Dante's poem, the words are spoken by Love, and another inspiration was William Morris's 'Hopeless Love', also a dialogue between 'Hic' and 'Ille'. But in WBY's poem, the master he acknowledges is the occult power of artistic inspiration. The first exchange raises the whole question of arcane studies, symbolism, and artistic inspiration, using the duality represented by the personae of Michael Robartes and Owen Aherne in his early fiction. Here the two voices are simply identified as 'Hic' and 'Ille' ('This one' and 'That one'), and suggest that he was determinedly anticipating a life of scholarly seclusion in the tower-house of Ballylee.

> *Hic.* On the grey sand beside the shallow stream,
> Under your old wind-beaten tower, where still
> A lamp burns on beside the open book
> That Michael Robartes left, you walk in the moon;
> And though you have passed the best of life still trace
> Enthralled by the unconquerable delusion,
> Magical shapes.

> *Ille.*   By the help of an image
> I call to my own opposite, summon all
> That I have handled least, least looked upon

> *Hic.* And I would find myself and not an image.

'Ille' replies that this 'modern hope' means the loss of creative 'nonchalance' in favour of criticism. The debate moves on to the nature of poetic creativity in the modern age, instancing Dante and Keats and arguing about the relationship of 'personality' to 'reality' in their works. For all WBY's dismissals of Carlyle, he borrowed Carlyle's celebrated description of Keats 'hungering after sweets he can't get':[88] his declared ambivalence about 'luxuriant song' may be yet another repudiation of the early work which had made his reputation, and which he had long been trying to put behind him. Yet the most heartfelt arguments are given to 'Ille', powerfully denying that immersion in the world is a route to real inspiration:

> For those that love the world serve it in action,
> Grow rich, popular and full of influence,
> And should they paint or write still it is action:
> The struggle of the fly in marmalade.
> The rhetorician would deceive his neighbours,
> The sentimentalist himself; while art
> Is but a vision of reality.
> What portion in the world can the artist have
> Who has awakened from the common dream,
> But dissipation and despair?

As with Robartes and Aherne, the authorial voice sounds both through the robust pragmatism of 'Hic' and the dedicated supernaturalism of 'Ille'. But by ending with a powerful invocation to his own guide, Leo Africanus, WBY makes clear where his commitments lie:

> I call to the mysterious one who yet
> Shall walk the wet sands by the edge of the stream

And look most like me, being indeed my double,
And prove of all imaginable things
The most unlike, being my anti-self
And standing by these characters disclose
All that I seek; and whisper it as though
He were afraid the birds, who cry aloud
Their momentary cries before it is dawn,
Would carry it away to blasphemous men.

He had not long since privately remarked that Leo may have 'got himself out of an encyclopaedia', and there are strong circumstantial reasons to bear him out. Nonetheless, this dramatized philosophical dialogue, halting in places but forceful in its characteristic blend of formality and colloquialism, delineated clearly the creative imperative behind WBY's search in arcane wisdom for something outside the self – and the 'double vision' that was its inseparable accompaniment.

WBY's 'fiftieth year had come and gone', leaving him, at the end of 1915, with the knowledge that his writing still magnetized the younger generation, while the authorities tried to load honours upon him. It was only appropriate that December would see the long-delayed publication of his early memories, *Reveries over Childhood and Youth*.

This came at a time when the theme of family was much in his mind. Earlier in the year Jack had broken down from overwork, as WBY revealed to Gregory on 20 December; his intense privacy, and his wife's protectiveness, excluded the family, to their annoyance. 'He works at his pictures as if it was counterfeit coin he was making,' Lily told Quinn. 'Willy gives you all that is in his mind, spreads it all out, work, plans, thoughts.'[89] To their father's pleasure, the brothers had spent some time together in July, but this reflected WBY's solicitude for Jack's health rather than any meeting of minds. Lily too had been ill earlier in the year, and the Cuala enterprise was still financially shaky: WBY continued to press the claims of high art, asking aesthetic friends like Sturge Moore to provide embroidery designs for the sceptical Lily, and lecturing Lolly about the costings of her press. Meanwhile, their father merrily went his improvident way – though now provided for by the deal with Quinn. Another project had emerged, as usual mediated by others on his behalf: WBY had decided during the spring that his father's letters – high-flown, generalizing, written more and more with an eye to posterity – should be published, and the unlikely figure of Pound was appointed to edit them. The old man was delighted, but WBY had an additional reason for pleasing him. The publication of *Reveries* was approaching, and he was worried about his father's reaction. The official publication date was March 1916, but copies were available from the previous December. WBY had made fewer changes than usual in proof, though he had left it to Cuala to 'put in the punctuation' as they went along.[90] Breaking it gently to his father, WBY chose to emphasize the portrait of Edward Dowden, as if this were the only thing that might offend JBY:

I am rather nervous about what you think. I am afraid you will very much dislike my chapter on Dowden, it is the only chapter which is a little harsh, not, I think, really so, but as compared to the rest, which is very amiable, and what is worse I have used, as I warned you that I would, conversations of yours. I don't think the chapter good, there have been too many things I could not say because of the living, the truth is that it is the one chapter in the biography which would have been better if I had written it for my own eye alone and delayed publication many years. I couldn't leave Dowden out, for in a subconscious way, the book is a history of the revolt, which perhaps unconsciously you taught me, against certain Victorian ideals. Dowden is the image of those ideals and has to stand for the whole structure in Dublin, Lord Chancellors and all the rest. They were ungracious unrealities and he was a gracious one and I do not think I have robbed him of the saving adjective. The chapter I should tell you, gives particular satisfaction to Lady Gregory who felt in Dowden a certain consciousness of success which makes it amusing to her that I have quoted from you a very kind analysis of the reasons of his failure. If you feel inclined to be angry with me remember the long life of a book. If it is sincere it has always a diffi-cult birth and can not help disturbing the house a little. Amiable as I have been, I wonder if Mrs Smith, Dowden's daughter, whom I like, but whom Lilly has named 'the cobra', will invite me to any more seances in her house. I am going on with the book but the rest shall be for my own eye alone, and perhaps I may redo that Dowden chapter, the first Mrs Dowden, her sister, the young family all set out in order this time, and leave it to be substituted for the other chapter some day. I think you will like [the] early part, and I would like from you any reveries or suggestions that occur to you.[91]

This was disingenuous. Though Quinn had had possession of a manuscript for months, it was deliberately kept from JBY's eyes until fixed in print, for reasons that had nothing to do with Dowden. Much of what WBY had writ-ten about family relationships and early life in London was more directly hurtful. And in the portrait of JBY was etched all his negligence, improvi-dence, and superb carelessness – as well as the alarm he aroused in his chil-dren. The unhappiness which pervades the book could be read as an indictment of the world created (or unmade) by the author's father, even if the implicit message was that insecurity acted as the nursery of genius.

All this was a far harder blow to JBY than the treatment of Dowden, for whom he in any case nurtured an enduring resentment. His friends tried to console him. 'Absurd, all those contrasts of you and W.B.Y.,' wrote Oliver Elton. 'They forget (a) how much of him is *you* (b) on the other side, how you & he are *incommensurables* – to be pedantic. I don't know what W.B.'s humanity & wisdom will be when he reaches your years. He has his share of them now, but no one could confound or compare your minds.'[92] But, according to Lily, their father told WBY 'that he had dreaded the book's coming and that it was worse than he had expected'. She added, with a thrust worthy of JBY, 'The Yeats dont like it, I know – the Pollexfens never read so have no opinion to give.' JBY's public reaction was to turn a dry quip: it was, he said, 'as bad to be a poet's father as the intimate friend of George Moore'.[93] But the cut went deeper than that.

V

By Christmas WBY and the Pounds were back at Stone Cottage, where they stayed, on and off, until March. It was at this point – midwinter 1915 – that, in D. H. Lawrence's words, London finally gave way to the war: 'perished from being the heart of the world, and became a vortex of broken passions, lusts, hopes, fears and horrors . . . the genuine debasement began'.[94] Even in Sussex, they did not entirely escape the war: in one farcical incident, the poets attracted the suspicion of the police because of their proximity to military installations. The Pounds were 'aliens in a prohibited area', as Ezra would later put it: yet again, WBY was put to writing to influential friends on behalf of a youthful (and more disreputable) fellow artist.[95] Meanwhile, they continued their shared reading programme (there was a sudden craze for Walter Savage Landor), and Pound worked at his translation of *Dialogues des Morts*. As for WBY, he continued to examine his past and his beliefs, clarifying the search for certainty beyond the grave and extending the imaginative boundaries of his work; this reflects not only the occult readings at Stone Cottage, but the psychic investigations and spiritualist inquiries precipitated by Lane's death.[96] Simultaneously, inspired by Pound's enthusiasm for Ernest Fenollosa's translations of Japanese Noh plays, WBY turned to drama again, and wrenched it in a radical new direction. He began writing *At the Hawk's Well* in January 1916; by 4 February he had hit upon the right form for it; by 16 February he was planning its production.

The contrast with the long-drawn-out *Player Queen* could not be greater, and the rapidity with which WBY headed off in this new direction proved his dissatisfaction with Mrs Campbell's albatross. He was no longer convinced that it had found its final form, as a prose farce with a few lyrics. This reflected a wider disillusionment with theatrical forms, perhaps echoed in his lack of enthusiasm for Shaw's *O'Flaherty VC*. His companion's advocacy of Noh drama came at exactly the right time. As so often with Pound, this was more a matter of aggressive marketing than original discovery. The

Japanese craze had flourished in London's artistic world since the 1880s (it was a central part of the Bedford Park aesthetic); Noh theatre was being performed in London in the mid 1870s and discussed in *The Times* by the 1890s. WBY's friends Charles Ricketts and Max Beerbohm admired the Kabuki theatrical effects brought by the Imperial Court Company to London at the turn of the century; Symons, always attuned to the current vogue, had some time ago led him to the Japanese prints in the British Museum, which strongly influenced WBY's notions of stage-settings. He knew Binyon's commentaries on Japanese art by 1909, and long before, in his *Savoy* days, had met Osman Edwards, who published on Noh drama in 1901.[97] In the spring of 1914 Yone Noguchi had lectured on Noh theatre in London; four years before, Noh dancing had been featured in a Japanese–British exhibition at Shepherd's Bush, inspiring Gilbert and Sullivan's *The Mikado*, and a *Times* special supplement carried an article about the revival of what it called the 'lyrical drama' of the Noh.

This was not an accurate definition. The origins of this dramatic form lay in religion, providing a commentary on Buddhism much as medieval miracle plays did on Christianity; they ended classically in an assertion of forgiveness and harmony, and the affirmation of 'the concepts of non-attachment and peace'.[98] This element meant less to WBY than the dramatic conventions upon which it rested. The Noh effect relied on a blend of formalism and intimacy, using strategies which WBY had already established at the centre of his ideal drama: symbolic scenery, masks, dance. Much in his article 'The Tragic Theatre', written for Edward Gordon Craig's journal the *Mask* in October 1910, was perfectly in line with the conventions of Noh. Just as strikingly, the subject matter concerned aristocratic values, archetypal personalities, duty, and the otherworld, and the dramatic presentation involved choruses, pauses, and repetitions. Put like this, proto-Noh elements are discernible in many of Yeats's earlier plays, notably *Deirdre* and the 1911 production of *The Hour-Glass* – though often coexisting, not uncomfortably, with the formulations of classical tragedy. WBY consciously followed the main lines of the classical Noh play in *At the Hawk's Well*, but only in so far as it fitted the format he had already grasped.

What happened at Stone Cottage in January 1916 was that the imagery, concision, and ellipsis which Pound found in Fennolosa's translations, and wrote about in his essay '"Noh", or Accomplishment', showed WBY how his core poetic values, so painfully evolved, could be expressed in drama. This was done by finding a theatrical form which had at its centre the presentation of occult themes, and for which an elite audience was a requirement rather than a disadvantage. A long letter to JBY in March shows vividly both how much Pound's modernist associations had influenced him in this – and how little.

You asked for examples of 'imitation' in poetry. I suggest that the corresponding things are drama & the pictorial element & that in poetry those who lack them are rhetoricians. I feel in Wyndham Lewis's Cubist pictures an element corresponding to rhetoric arising from his confusion of the abstract with the rhythmical. Rhythm implies a living body a breast to rise & fall or limbs that dance while the Abstract [is] incompatible with life. The cubist is abstract. At the same time you must not leave out rhythm & this rhythm is not imitation. Impressionism by leaving it out brought all this rhetoric of the abstract upon us. I have just been turning over a book of Japanese paintings. Everywhere there is delight in form, repeated yet varied, in curious patterns of lines but these lines are all an ordering of natural objects though they are certainly not imitation. In every case the artist one feels has had to *consciously* & deliberately arrange his subject. It was the impressionists beleif that this arrangement should be only unconscious & instinctive that brought this violent reaction. They are right in beleiving that they should be conscious but wrong in substituting abstract scientific thought for conscious feeling. If I delight in rhythm I love Nature though she is not rhythmical. I express my love in rhythm. The more I express it the less can I forget her.

I think Keats perhaps greater than Shelley and beyond words greater than Swinbourne because he makes pictures one cannot forget & sees them as full of rhythm as a Chinese painting. Swinbourne's poetry all but some early poems is as abstract as a Cubist picture. Carlyle is abstract – ideas, never things or only their common worn out images taken up from some preacher, & today he is as dead as MacPhersons Ossian. In sincere and theatrical he knew nothing, he saw nothing. His moral zeal cast before his mind perpetually 'God' 'Eternity' 'Work' & these ideas corresponding to no exact pictures have their analogy in all art which is without imitation. I doubt if I have made myself plane. I seperate the rhythmical & the abstract. They are brothers but one is Abel & one is Cain. In poetry they are not confused for we know that poetry is rhythm but in music hall verses we find an abstract cadence, which is vulgar because it is a part from imitation. The cadence is a mechanism, it never suggests a voice shaken with joy or sorrow as poetrical rhythm does. It is but the noise of a machine & not the coming & the going of the breath.

It is Midnight & I must stop.[99]

In fact, though *At the Hawk's Well* relies for its scenario on the Noh play *Yoro* (not published by Pound), it is built around familiar themes which invoke Celtic mythology as well as William Morris's *Well at the World's End*. Cuchulain as a young man comes in search of immortality to a miraculous well whose waters appear and disappear (like the lake at Coole). The well's guardian, a miraculous figure who takes the guise of a hawk, mesmerizes him by a marvellous dance; during this, the waters run and dry up again, unnoticed by the hero until it is too late. The first draft ended with a reflection (later excised) which exactly repeated the conclusion to *Reveries*: 'Accursed is the life of man – between passion and emptiness what he longs for never comes. All his days are in preparation for what never comes.'[100] Thus the drama would take its place in the series of Cuchulain plays which WBY returned to throughout his life. It establishes the pattern of the Promethean hero doomed to disappointment, and the Yeatsian moral – as expressed in the play's conclusion – that 'wisdom must live a bitter life'. The bleakness reflects the lonely conditions of his life when he began to write it. Stylistically, WBY was determined on austerity: written in a kind of free verse, the play was cut down, draft after draft, to remove descriptive passages and focus on 'a single metaphor, as deliberate as the echoing rhythm of line in Chinese and Japanese painting'.[101] But the two apparently Eastern innovations in the play's presentation were derived from nearer home. One was the use of marvellous masks worn by the players, designed by Edmund Dulac; the other was the dance performed by Michio Ito.

By 1916 the 34-year-old Dulac was one of the most eminent illustrative artists of the day, his status recently confirmed by work for the bestselling 'Gift Books' produced for the war effort. A reticent, dapper, Anglophile Frenchman, who had moved to London in 1904 and subsequently taken out British citizenship, his unassuming manner belied the sensuous, erotically charged style of his art, which owed as much to Beardsley as to Rackham (whose mantle he assumed); he was much influenced by Persian miniatures, Léon Bakst, and Japanese prints. Though celebrated for his fairy-tale illustrations, the projects which most suited his style were perhaps *The Arabian Nights* (1907) and *The Rubáiyát of Omar Khayyám* (1909). Dulac's world had intersected with WBY's for several years: he had worked for the theatre, illustrated Verlaine's *Fêtes Galantes* (1910), and frequented the Ricketts–Shannon salon from 1912, when he moved to the artists' studios built by Edmund Paris in Ladbroke Road, Holland Park. Through his wife Elsa Bignardi he became interested in seances and spiritualism. His Leicester Gallery exhibition of November 1914 had included a caricature of WBY, physically supporting the Abbey Theatre: by then they were well acquainted, and Dulac was a natural choice to design *At the Hawk's Well*.[102] He had already done costumes and sets for Maud Allan's unperformed ballet *Khamma* (with music by Debussy), and for Thomas Beecham's 1915 production of the Bach cantata *Phoebus and Pan*.

Dulac was notoriously expensive as an illustrator but in 1916 was ready to collaborate on a new venture, tempted by the stimulation of working with WBY, and hoping to revive his own flagging energies. In a recent accident he had nearly lost the sight of one eye, wartime commissions were not

37

lucrative, and his wife was suffering severe nervous trouble. His influence on the production was immense, and through it he developed a close friendship with WBY. The multi-talented Dulac created costumes, properties (including a black backcloth with a symbolic gold hawk), and the famous masks, and was also a passionate advocate of modern and exotic music: a visitor once found him sitting cross-legged on his studio floor, with a cotton-wool plug up one nostril to let a steady stream of air from the other into a Polynesian nose-flute which he had just constructed; he was also able to provide Puccini with chinoiserie musical themes for *Turandot*, and to introduce Constant Lambert to Diaghilev. (Another route to the WBY circle may have been through Pound's friend the avant-garde composer Walter Morse Rummel, who was close to Dulac as well.) Much influenced by Satie, Dulac felt that *At the Hawk's Well* needed music based on simple chords, with a flute melody underlying vocal intonations. This was in line with current thought; Pound was preaching that music and poetry were essentially connected, and this should be made dramatically effective.[103] WBY had already approached the violinist Maud Mann (brought by Horton to his Monday evenings). An aggressive devotee of Indian musical instruments, she had improvised a wordless song to her own accompaniment. Dulac found this repellent. First he forced her to perform behind a backcloth, then engineered a public row, and finally saw to it that her services were dispensed with after the first performance. Then he was free to alter the score and increase the musicians to three – one playing a series of bamboo flutes in different scales (inevitably constructed by Dulac), another a harp, while the composer himself performed on drum and gong.[104]

The effect was archaic and remote, just as WBY wanted; he had recently decided there were definite tunes behind the rhythms of his own verse (alerted to them, ironically, by the ill-fated Maud Mann). Dulac's musical contribution fascinated him, but the painter's influence did not stop there. In November 1915 Dulac had begun an oil painting of a Japanese dancer, Michio Ito, in the costume of a medieval Japanese *daimyo* jointly designed by Ricketts and Dulac. Thus he also brought to WBY the ideally authentic Noh interpreter of the Guardian's dance.

Or so it must have seemed. In fact, the dramatically handsome Ito was a habitué of the Café Royal and a disciple of Nijinsky and the *Ballet Russe*; he had come to England after several years in Germany studying Dalcroze's 'eurhythmics'. He was also patronized by Lady Cunard, who launched his performances on London drawing rooms, where WBY first saw him dance. Much as the language in *Diarmuid and Grania* had achieved 'authentic' Irishness by transmigrating through French and English, the Japanese Ito was reborn as a Noh performer under the instruction of a Frenchman, an

Irishman – and an American, since Pound was arranging for Ito to perform five dance-poems in Noh mode by October 1915. There were inevitable gaps of comprehension (when WBY read his poems aloud Ito thought he was speaking Gaelic), but the Japanese dancer took to it all the more readily as there were echoes of Mallarmé, Maeterlinck, and the aestheticism of the 1890s. He was the logical interpreter for WBY's new passion; in early March 1916 he went to the zoo in Regent's Park with Dulac and WBY to spend an absorbing Sunday studying the movements of birds of prey. (The birds remained sleepily uncooperative, despite encouraging prods from an umbrella.) But this approach owed more to Isadora Duncan than to the traditions of Noh. True to his real passions, Ito would subsequently gravitate to New York, where he partnered Martha Graham, before returning to Japan to run a dance studio and a few 'discreetly lit bars'.[105]

A year before, WBY had told Mabel Beardsley he preferred rehearsals to performances: at that stage, he felt, there was still room for creativity, 'but always when the performance comes somebody eats the apple & it is all finished. The audience is the serpent & the tempter seducing by its boredom & by its interest.'[106] The rehearsals of *At the Hawk's Well*, over three weeks of March 1916, were certainly exciting. Maud Mann angrily demanded whether Dulac was going to take charge of make-up as well as everything else (he did): for his part, WBY listened to her music with trepidation and eventually sided firmly with the dictatorial Dulac.[107] Pound told Quinn that his own 'undefined managerial function' was to watch WBY 'rushing about a studio shouting "Now . . . NOW . . . Now . . . Now you really must . . . etc . . ., etc."' But the serpent-audience was going to be kept firmly in its place: elitism ruled offstage as well as on it. The scheme was, Pound wrote, for 'a theatreless stage – very noble & exclusive – his new play and a farce of mine are to be performed before an audience composed exclusively of crowned heads and divorcées'.[108] This was an only slightly fanciful account of the main charity performance, on 4 April at Lady Islington's. Those in attendance included Queen Alexandra, Princess Victoria, the Grand Duchess George of Russia, the Princess of Monaco, the Ranee of Sarawak, the Spanish ambassador, Margot Asquith, the duchess of Marlborough ('too late to find a seat'), and Lady Randolph Churchill ('full of the burglary of her artistic treasures, which had taken place that morning'[109]). It had been well advertised in the *Morning Post* and the *Observer* on 2 April (see next page).

'None of my friends were there,' WBY told Alick Schepeler, anticipating the slight disdain with which he would describe the occasion at Lady Islington's in his published 'Note' on the 'first performance'.[110] But the real first performance had taken place two days before, when it had been tried out at Lady Cunard's – where the avant-garde mingled with high society. They did not include a rather disapproving Augusta Gregory, though she was in London: 'I don't feel much at home among the war-charity ladies.'[111] However, among the *cognoscenti* was Pound's new protégé, the 26-year-old T. S. Eliot. Having come to England in autumn 1914, he had just made up his mind not to return to academic life in America. In September 1914 he had made himself known to Pound, whose unique literary radar had already registered the 'funny stuff' his young compatriot had been writing at Harvard. Eliot, precociously ruthless in his judgements, thought Pound's verse already strangely old-fashioned, and even 'touchingly incompetent':[112] but he knew, like many others, what he had to learn from him.

MASKS ON THE STAGE.

NEW W. B. YEATS PLAY FOR A CHARITY.

Lady Cunard has organised a performance at Lady Islington's, 8, Chesterfield-gardens, W., to be given on Tuesday next, at 3.30, for the Social Institutes' Union for Women and Girls, of which the Countess of Ancaster is the President. It provides dinners for many thousand factory girls and munition workers. There will be a play of an unusual kind, given for the first time. It is called "The Hawk's Well, or The Water of Immortality," and it is written by Mr. W. B. Yeats. Mr. Henry Ainley will act the hero, and Ito, the Japanese dancer, will take the part of the hawk's spirit. Masks will be used for the first time in serious drama in the modern world. The masks and costumes have been designed and executed by Mr. Edmund Dulac. Mr. Henry Ainley will wear a mask resembling an archaic Greek sculptured face. Instead of scenery, there will be a chorus of singers and musicians, who describe the scene as well as commenting on the action.

The performance is under the patronage of Queen Alexandra, who will be present. A limited number of tickets at a guinea may be obtained from the Countess of Ancaster, 95, Lancaster-gate, W.; Lady Edmund Talbot, 1, Buckingham Palace-gardens, S.W.; Lady Cunard, 20, Cavendish-square, W.; and Mrs. Arthur James, 3, Grafton-street, W.

1. *Observer*, 2 April 1916.

Formal, watchful, and withdrawn, from early 1915 he entered Pound's London circle, attending his Thursday dining club at Belotti's restaurant in Soho; he first met WBY in January 1915.[113] In literary terms, they rubbed shoulders in issues of the *Egoist* as well as in Pound's *Catholic Anthology*, where the landmark 'Love Song of J. Alfred Prufrock' had appeared the previous November after its first outing in *Poetry*, again at the inevitable insistence of Pound. For Eliot – as avid for intellectual enterprise as Pound but in a more feline way – *At the Hawk's Well* confirmed 'Yeats rather as a more eminent contemporary than as an elder from whom we could learn'.[114] The influence would recur in his own drama, and perhaps in 'Ash Wednesday'.[115]

'No press, no photographs in the papers, no crowd,' WBY had told Quinn. 'I shall be happier than Sophocles.'[116] There was a photographer involved, but it was the experimental and artistic Alvin Langdon Coburn; at Lady Islington's a press man who offered 'a whole page somewhere or other' was disdainfully dismissed. As for the audience, the reaction of the shrewd social butterfly and literary man-about-town Eddie Marsh (who got into the select preview at Lady Cunard's) was probably fairly typical:

I had to go away in the middle, which was wretched, as I was getting quite worked up and impressed. I find I can manage quite well without *any* scenery at all, but they had been a little too careful not to disturb the room, and I couldn't help being disconcerted. Just when I had persuaded myself that I had before me a wild mountain track of semi-historic Ireland, to notice the characters skirting round a Louis XV table covered with French novels. The actors wore masks made by Dulac, awfully good, and I found it quite easy to accept the convention. But I had an odd sensation before the play began. Henry Ainley had a mask very like his own face and I didn't know it wasn't his own self till he came up to me roaring with laughter and not a muscle of his mouth moving, it was quite uncanny. The play began with atmospheric keening and a man in black solemnly pacing to the front – he got there, made an impressive bow to the audience, then started, and said, 'Oh, we've forgotten to light the lanterns!' – lighted them, retired, paced solemnly forward again and began his speech.[117]

For WBY, however, the success was not necessarily to be confined to aristocratic drawing rooms. The Noh enterprise had restored his old faith in an experimental Irish travelling theatre. He wrote excitedly to Gregory from rehearsals, suggesting that they adapt a room in the Dublin Mechanics' Institute for plays of this kind, with masks and no scenery. 'We would not invite the press and would have some form of society. The aim would be to get those who cared for poetry and nobody else.' Their old Abbey collaborator Frank Fay might even come back to teach there; they could undertake tours; perhaps they could play in Irish, working with the Gaelic League.[118] The 'accomplishment' which Pound had associated with the

Noh form had infused a decisive new energy into WBY's drama, but it also brought him back to familiar ideas, though they had long proved unfeasible on the Abbey stage. There, crises continued to erupt. Ervine's insistence on rehearsing two plays a day would lead to a mutiny and dismissal notices in May. In June things reached such a pass that the directors seriously thought of bringing in Pound as manager: there could have been no more eloquent signal of desperation.[119]

As it happened, Dublin was denied this spectacle, and Pound himself, as usual, moved on after his raid into Japanese exoticism. A year later he was telling Quinn, 'China is fundamental, Japan is not. Japan is a special interest, like Provence or 12–13 century Italy (apart from Dante). I dont mean to say there aren't interesting things in Fenollosa's Jap stuff . . . But China is solid.'[120] Equally characteristically, WBY's interest would be sustained: the mask Dulac made for Henry Ainley ended up hanging on his wall, a permanent inspiration as well as a reminder.

He had composed, in January 1916, 'Lines Written in Dejection', reflecting the feeling that his creative life had reached a crossroads:

> When have I last looked on
> The round green eyes and the long wavering bodies
> Of the dark leopards of the moon?
> All the wild witches those most noble ladies,
> For all their broom-sticks and their tears,
> Their angry tears, are gone.
> The holy centaurs of the hills are banished;
> And I have nothing but harsh sun;
> Heroic mother moon has vanished,
> And now that I have come to fifty years
> I must endure the timid sun.

Almost immediately moonstruck inspiration had flooded in, with *At the Hawk's Well*: he felt he had hit upon a new form which responded to the harsh new age, and he ended his 'Note' on the first performance with a rallying call reminiscent of the manifestos he had issued in *Samhain* when shaping the Irish National Dramatic Society.

We must recognise the change as the painters did when, finding no longer palaces and churches to decorate, they made framed pictures to hang upon a wall. Whatever we lose in mass and in power we should recover in elegance and in subtlety. Our lyrical and our narrative poetry alike have used their freedom and have approached nearer, as Pater said all the arts would if they were able, to 'the condition of music'; and if our modern poetical drama has failed, it is mainly because, always dominated by the example of Shakespeare, it would restore an irrevocable past.

By April life had been transformed. The artistic success of the new play was followed by a financial bonus when the completed transfer of all his books from Bullen to Macmillan promised a much needed payment of £250 (eventually reduced to £210).[121] The publication that spring of *Reveries*, and of Hone's perceptive short biography, had confirmed the centrality of WBY's place in modern Irish culture. But Hone laid a decisive emphasis on his place in Irish contemporary politics too, quoting his speech at the Thomas Davis centenary celebration two years before:

All who fell under [Davis's] influence took this thought from his precept or his example: we struggle for a nation, not for a party, and our political opponents who have saved Ireland in some other way may, perhaps, be the better patriots. He did not, as a weak and hectic nature would have done, attack O'Connell, or parade with a new party; no venomous newspaper supported his fame, or found there its own support. When the quarrel came it was O'Connell's own doing, and his only; and the breach was so tragical to Davis that in the midst of the only public speech he ever made he burst into tears. It is these magnanimities, I believe, that have made generations of our young men turn over the pages of an old newspaper, as though they were some classic of literature, but when they have come as some few have, to dream of another 'Nation' they do not understand their own lure, and are content to copy alone his concentration and his enthusiasm.[122]

Thus WBY had used Davis's large-mindedness to score a point against the 'venomous newspapers' of his own day, and to reiterate – as he had done since his elegiac essay on Synge in 1910 – that extreme politics were no longer the politics of intellectual freedom. After the second performance of *At the Hawk's Well* he set off to spend Easter sitting for his portrait by Rothenstein, in Gloucestershire. While there, he would receive news that showed the 'concentration and enthusiasm' of a new political generation was capable of convulsing the Irish political landscape beyond recognition, and WBY's apparently settled life with it.

Chapter 2 : SHADES AND ANGELS
1916–1917

The Irish are essentially a dramatic people as the French are, as the English and Germans are not. When Mr W. B. Yeats created the Irish Theatre it was with an almost uncanny knowledge of the needs and capacities of the Irish.

Daily Chronicle on the Easter Rising, 9 May 1916

I

ON 15 APRIL 1916 Elizabeth Asquith organized what sarcastic observers described as a 'seance' in aid of charity: poets, including WBY, read their work to a paying audience of 400 in a hall off Piccadilly. The occasion was chaired by Augustine Birrell, the literary-minded chief secretary of Ireland, who for most of the event 'sat with his head buried in his hands'.[1] Within ten days, he would bury his head from more than mere embarrassment. On Easter Monday, April 24, a group of Irish Republican Brotherhood revolutionaries led by WBY's old adversary Patrick Pearse marched into Dublin and took possession of several central locations – notably, the General Post Office in O'Connell Street. Dublin Castle had heard of plans for an impending Fenian coup with German aid but had thought the enterprise aborted or postponed – as, indeed, it was, at least in its original form. Those who led the doomed 'Rising' were opposing their own leadership, and knew they represented a minority of a minority. They were, however, possessed by a transcendant Pearsean idea: in taking arms, they would redeem Ireland's 'soul' from the compromises and collaborations of the constitutional movement, and confront the ancient oppressor on the field of battle.

This démarche failed to address the real reason why independence had not been granted, but it reflected discontent with Redmond's pro-war stance, as the conflict dragged on, and also disillusionment at the postponement of Home Rule for the war's duration. The rebels were further frustrated by Unionist Ulster's refusal to agree a modus vivendi with Home Rule triumphant – an intransigence encouraged by the apparent inability of Asquith's government to cut the Gordian knot. The war had strengthened the Unionist hand; it had also presented the IRB strategists with a traditional opportunity to strike in Britain's hour of need. But their counsels were divided, and the cataclysm burst on Dublin from an apparently clear sky.

44

There had nonetheless been rumbles offstage, relayed to WBY in London. From the summer of 1915 Gregory had heard rumours of rebel encampments in the Galway hills, drilling by night, and preparations 'to fight the English'.[2] As the fear of conscription mounted, she had learned from her housekeeper that 'reservists in Limerick are deserting to America, afraid of going mad as some have done by all the horrors of the war. The [missioners], as you know, are emphasising these, as an illustration of the torments of hell. I think Redmond's difficulty will be getting the priests to support him, and he certainly won't get many of the farming class to go.' She also attributed the fomenting of discontent to Sinn Féin, led by the Abbey's ancient enemy Arthur Griffith, and denounced their local representatives as 'corner boys'. WBY, always politically interested, had noted in November 1915 that the atmosphere in Dublin had turned antagonistic, reflected in the probable reaction of the Abbey audience to a viceregal visit: 'our Pit in which all the ancient suspicions are alive again in all probability will either desert the theatre or boo the viceroy'. A month later he told Gregory that nationalists were now interfering with the mail of well-known Unionist sympathizers, like the land commissioner and Abbey trustee W. F. Bailey.[3] But neither he nor Gregory, in common with the doomed Birrell and most of the Irish population, expected the Rising to happen as and when it did.

Misinformation was general. Griffith in fact had opposed the idea of a Rising, as had the Volunteer leader Eoin MacNeill, and been kept in ignorance; the leadership came from a dissident IRB wing, not from Sinn Féin as such. But as Dublin blazed, and troops were hastily poured in to douse the conflagration, WBY was reliant on rumour, speculation, and what letters could get through to London. He heard the news when staying at Oakridge, Will Rothenstein's idyllic farmhouse overlooking a Cotswold valley near Stroud; strangely, his sister Lolly was also marooned in Gloucestershire, spending Easter with Sir William Wedderburn a few miles away. 'How many years will Ireland take to recover?' she wrote in her host's visitor-book. 'The bitterness on both sides will be hard to bear.'[4]

For the transfigured participants, Easter Week 'seemed one long, sleepless, fantastic space of time fused into one';[5] but observers saw it differently. Bitterness at what appeared a wanton and destructive assault indeed dominated the initial reactions of the Yeats circle. 'Did you ever hear or know of such a piece of childish madness – clever children – there is not one person in the whole of Ireland that is not the worse for this last fortnight's work,' Lily wrote to Quinn.[6] Gregory too, who was friendly with both Birrell and his under-secretary, Sir Matthew Nathan, initially blamed the event on Sinn Féin. But both she and WBY were shocked by the fact that several of the leaders had been personally known to them. Pearse, after early attacks on their theatre, had come to admire their work (and WBY allowed St Enda's School to act his plays for nothing); Thomas MacDonagh, the critic and university lecturer, had dedicated a book of poems to WBY; Joseph Plunkett came from an affluent nationalist family well known in Dublin cultural circles. Constance Markievicz had been a figure in WBY's life since his Sligo youth, much though he disapproved of her later incarnation as the most strident of republican socialists. Several Abbey and Cuala employees turned out to have been involved as well. So, notably, did Maud Gonne's estranged husband, John MacBride.

By 1916 WBY's ideological and political disagreement with such people was clear-cut: he had disassociated himself from Pearse's politics on a public platform, and written scathingly of the mystical schoolteacher and his Gaelic League colleague Eoin MacNeill as 'flirting with the gallows-tree'. As for Griffith, he was 'a mischievous personality & better out of the country'.[7] As Pound put it to Quinn, WBY had 'said for years that Pearse was half-cracked and that he wouldn't be happy until he was hanged. He seemed to think Pearse had Emmet mania, same as some other lunatics think they are Napoleon or God.' Pound looked forward wolfishly to 'chaffing Yeats about the Dublin Republic. He dont like republics. He likes queens, preferably dead ones, but he has been out of town for three days and I shall assume that he was at Stephen's Green.'[8]

In fact, when WBY returned from the Cotswolds his mood was cautious. He wrote to Lolly:

I am writing for news of the Abbey & shall not go over unless it has been burned or badly damaged. There is nothing to be done but do one's work & write letters. That 'introduction' [to Pound's *Certain Noble Plays of Japan*] by the by is somewhere in the post on its way to Dundrum.

I know most of the Sinn Fein leaders & the whole thing bewilders me for Conolly is an able man & Thomas MacDonough both able & cultivated. Pearse I have long looked upon as a man made dangerous by the Vertigo of Self Sacrifice. He has moulded himself on Emmett.[9]

To St John Ervine of the Abbey he wrote about ten days later: 'I have been a good deal shaken by Dublin events – a world one has worked with or against for years suddenly overwhelmed. As yet one knows nothing of the future except that it must be very unlike the past.'[10]

When WBY visited Ricketts four days after the Rising, his host noted his 'strange Irish impartiality' on the subject, 'as it was all a sort of game'. Following this cue, the artist assured him 'that a paternal government would discover that Roger Casement was insane, imprison the leaders during the war pending the investigations over the extent of German intrigues in the matter, discover that these men were misguided dupes, and probably amnesty them after the war'.[11] But this is exactly what did not happen. All WBY could rely on was reports from Ireland, in newspapers or – more vividly and influentially – from friends; and through these the shift of opinion can be gauged, as the government declared martial law and began to execute the rebel leaders after brief trials for treason. Damning anecdotes also began to circulate about the behaviour of the security forces, notably the murder of the pacifist Francis Sheehy Skeffington, a popular Dublin figure, well known to the Yeats circle. As news seeped out, it was relayed to WBY through a series of letters from Gregory in Galway – long, urgent, and intense. These swayed many of his own reactions. If a letter from Gonne supplied the central idea that 'tragic dignity had returned to Ireland', his changing sense of what the rebellion represented followed the trajectory traced out in his correspondence with Coole.

In the immediate aftermath of the Rising, Gregory, reporting on 27 April, was still distracted by accounts of guns landed at Kinvara, armed men marching by night, barricades and encampments cutting off Gort from Galway. But she also astutely anticipated what would happen in Dublin. 'It is terrible to think of the executions or killings that are sure to come,' she wrote to WBY, 'yet it must be so – we had been at the mercy of a rabble for a long time, both here and in Dublin, with no apparent policy, but ready to take any opportunity of helping on mischief.' As the executions were carried out, however, Ascendancy prejudices were sapped by doubts and regrets. On 7 May she heard that MacBride had been executed,

the best event that cd. come to him, giving him dignity – And what a release for her! a smoothing away of confusion, which I have come to think is the worst thing that can come into any body's life – Perhaps I think it because now that the railways are mended, & the barricades on the Galway road have been thrown down, papers & letters of the last fortnight are rushing in, & we had learned to do so well without them . . . I am sorry for Pearse & MacDonnough [sic], the only ones I knew among the leaders – they were enthusiastic – [12]

A week later, with the news of more executions, her thoughts had crystallized further.

Thank you for your letter & the papers – I haven't looked at them yet, but they wouldn't make any difference – because my mind is filled with sorrow at the Dublin tragedy, the death of Pearse & McDonough, who ought to have been on our side, the side of intellectual freedom – & I keep wondering whether we could not have brought them into that intellectual movement – Perhaps those Abbey lectures we often spoke of might have helped – I have a more personal grief for Sean Connolly, [the Abbey actor] who I had not only admiration but affection for – He was shot on the roof of the City Hall – there is no one to blame – but one grieves all the same – It seems as if the leaders were what is wanted in Ireland – & will be even more wanted in the future – a fearless & imaginative opposition to the conventional & opportunist parliamentarians, who have never helped our work even by intelligent opposition – Dillon just denounces us about Playboy in his dull popular way.[13]

The 'papers' which WBY had sent her included the current *Westminster Gazette*, which carried an antagonistic analysis of the Irish political outlook. Gregory preferred to take her position on a text from the Coole library, which was calculated to appeal strongly to WBY too – Shelley's political testament.

I have read those papers you sent, but they are hardly worth considering, in questions like this one must go to one's own roots – I think Shelley right & that he goes to the roots when he says we know so little about death that we have no business to compel a person to know all that can be known by the dead . . . to punish or reward him in a manner & a degree incalculable and incomprehensible by us – And he says what is very applicable to this moment Persons of energetic character, in whom as in men who suffer for political crimes, there is a large mixture of enterprise and fortitude & disinterestedness, and the elements, though misguided & disarranged, by which the strength & happiness of a nation might have been cemented, die in such a manner as to make death appear not evil but good – the death of what is called a traitor, that is, a person who, from whatever motive would abolish the government of the day, is as often a triumphant exhibition of suffering virtue as the warning of a culprit – [14]

She went on to remark that the government would 'suffer for the stupidity' of giving over their own business to soldiers, though she inveighed against 'armed bullies' and 'village tyrants', and felt that the military authorities were taking a carefully lenient line with 'terrorizing gangs' in the country at large. As often before, her attitude towards the world that centred on Gort was notably less nationalistic than her stance in Abbey matters. And here, she regretted that St John Ervine was about to produce *The Playboy of the Western World*, which Sinn Féin had attacked nine eventful years before.

On the other hand, what I am rather upset by today, is the putting on of 'Playboy' at this moment – Our managers have shirked it for years – now it seems as if we were snatching a rather mean triumph in putting it forward just as those who might have attacked it are dead or in prison – I don't know if this is folly, & I suppose we can't remonstrate with Ervine anyhow for fear of shaking his nerves – But I don't like it – And I wish we could have won that 'enterprise & fortitude and disinterestedness' to our side – I believe we should have done so but for the rising –

'I see the whole affair through as it were two glasses,' she confessed to Wilfrid Scawen Blunt in late May. 'I don't know if [the executions] were necessary from an English point of view – probably they were – But I grieve, because these men were more akin to us than the politicians, or the Ancient Order of Hibernians – I knew MacDonagh – Pearse a little – John [Eoin] MacNeill (being tried today 23rd) I knew & liked & respected – They were all enthusiasts, brave, sincere – Beside them we seem a little insincere, we have all given in to compromise – '[15] She signed a circular letter of sympathy for James Connolly's family organized by AE, though she worried it was too sympathetic 'to what he considers Sinn Feinism':[16] her own view of the movement continued to be considerably less benign. But the individual heroes, more and more clearly seen as martyrs, were another matter. A terse letter from Edward Martyn (who had spent Easter Week trapped in his Leinster Street house, saved from starvation by food from the Kildare Street Club) said what many were feeling: 'I am as well as a man can be who has had a lot of his friends executed & deported.'[17] While the ambivalence caught in Gregory's letters persisted, Dublin's literati were shocked by the immediacy of what had happened: people they had known with familiarity, and even regarded with contempt, had joined, at a stroke, the mythic company of Emmet, Fitzgerald, Tone. Whatever was felt about Sinn Féin's political programme (let alone that of the IRB), the contempt WBY had expressed in 'September 1913' rang hollowly now. The 'romantic Ireland' of O'Leary's sacrificial nationalism had returned from the grave.

Further barometric readings might be taken from Lily's letters, the only member of the family to be in Dublin for the Rising. Before the executions had completely run their course, she was as caustic as ever:

What a pity Madame Markiewicz' madness changed its form when she inherited it. In her father [Sir Henry Gore-Booth, the Arctic explorer] it meant looking for the North Pole in an open boat, very cooling for him and safe for others. Her followers are said to have been either small boys or drunken dock workers out of work, called the citizens army. I don't think any others could have followed her. I would not have followed her across a road. I often heard the elder Pearse speak at his school prize days and such things. I though he was a dreamer and a sentimentalist. MacDonagh was clever and hard and full of self conceit. He was I think a spoilt priest.

Maud Gonne is at last a widow, made so by an English bullet. It must have been some humorist who got him the post of water bailiff to the corporation.[18]

In early May, MacBride's drunkenness, MacDonagh's egocentricity, Pearse's impracticality, Markievicz's eccentricity could all still be seen as material for a good Dublin story. But Lily's subsequent reaction to the government's draconian policy was stupefaction, followed by fury. 'This whole work here is so horrible I hate to write of it, this shooting of foolish idealists, not a vicious man among them except perhaps MacBride, Maud Gonne's husband.' By mid May she thought the situation ruled out any possible accommodation with Britain: it had been a catalogue of folly and blunder. 'We can never understand each other. I felt like that when I was a girl and an Englishman wanted me to have him. I felt we could never understand each other. He would have thought he understood me the whole time, which would have been maddening, I cannot believe they make good colonist[s], it is impossible.'[19]

Among all WBY's friends the reaction was the same. Pound, who had begun by seeing the Rising merely as something to 'give that country another set of anecdotes to keep it going another hundred years', was among the most vehement. 'Damn it all the government, i.e., the executive, must *know*. I mean they must understand *why* things happen if they are to act intelligently. In the case of the Irish outbreak they didn't know. Nobody seems to have known. Yeats certainly didn't know. He thought as Birrell thought, that it was all fireworks.'[20] By 29 May, W. K. Magee noted that 'the barbarities of the military and chivalrous conduct of the insurrectionists are the universal topic in AE's circle'. Opinions were setting towards radical nationalism, and only 'the aegis of Plunkett's respectability' kept even the saintly AE out of hot water.[21] Out of fury at the government's ineptness, a slow recognition began to stir: that what had happened might be, in Lily's words, 'the beginning of Ireland'. The shock of the executions was followed, as her sister put it, by 'a queer undercurrent of excitement everywhere – not expressed – but there nevertheless'. By the end of June, AE judged 'Ireland a political corpse with lively atoms: a disintegration before a new synthesis'.[22]

II

WBY's reactions developed against this background of echoes from Ireland. He started like Gregory, from a point of distinct antipathy to the Sinn Féin ideologues who were generally supposed to have planned the Rising. In January 1916 Arthur Griffith's latest newspaper, *Nationality*, attacked WBY as an 'imperialist' who had 'gone over to the enemy': 'a poseur in patriotism precisely as Chesterton is a poseur in Catholicism'. This was the issue that reprinted AE's sharp parody of *Cathleen ni Houlihan*, first published at the time of the *Playboy* riots:[23] the reverberations of those old battles never fell quite silent. Nor were WBY's opinions of Pearse, MacDonagh, Markievicz, and MacBride substantially different from those retailed by Lily, before her change of heart; he told Ricketts that Ireland was 'like a man diseased who can only think of his disease', obsessed by 'the folly of one idea'.[24] By 11 May, however, the news of the executions and 'many miscarriages of justice' preoccupied him. Disturbed and ill, he kept largely to Woburn Buildings, too unwell to attend the funeral of Mabel Beardsley on 10 May, and worriedly seeking consultations through Elizabeth Radcliffe with her spirit instructors.[25] He was also in more prosaic communication with Gregory. Not all of his letters survive, but on 11 May he wrote of his 'sorrow and anxiety' at seeing so many of their colleagues and acquaintances undergoing imprisonment and worse, while the political outlook – so optimistic before the war – was uncertain and gloomy.

If the English conservative party had made a declaration that they did not intend to rescind the Home Rule Bill there would have been no rebellion. I had no idea that any public event could so deeply move me – & I am very despondent about the future. At this moment I feel that all the work of years has been overturned, all the bringing together of classes, all the freeing of Irish literature & criticism from politics. Maud Gonne reminds me that she saw the ruined houses about O'Connell St & the wounded & dying lying about the streets, in the first few days of the war. I perfectly remember the vision & my making light of it & saying that if a true vision at all it could only have a symbolical meaning. This is the only letter I have had from her since she knew of the rebellion. I have sent her the papers every day. I do not yet know what she feels about her husbands death. Her letter was written before she heard of it. Her main thought seems to be 'tragic dignity has returned to Ireland.' She had been told by two members of the Irish Party that 'Home Rule was betrayed.' She thinks now that the sacrifice has made it safe.[26]

Already, however, Maud Gonne's comment that the rebels had 'raised the Irish cause again to a position of tragic dignity' was working in his mind. 'I am trying to write a poem on the men executed – "terrible beauty has been born".'

By 23 May, sending Quinn the typescript of *Reveries* in accordance with the arrangement worked out to support JBY, WBY could describe the late rebels as 'the ablest & most fine natured of our young men'. He also confessed a desire to return to Dublin to live, '& begin building again', despite the fact that he had extended his empire in Woburn Buildings to the floor below. His letters to Quinn also show that he was increasingly preoccupied by an issue close to the lawyer's heart too: the cause célèbre gathering around the figure who would become the last of the Easter martyrs – Roger Casement.[27]

Casement was a uniquely dashing figure. Born to an Irish Protestant background, he had entered the consular service and become celebrated (or execrated) for revealing the horrific exploitation of South American Indians in the rubber trade and of native workers in the Belgian Congo. His conversion to Irish nationalism rapidly followed, and he had pursued the cause with characteristic impetuosity: after the outbreak of war he had tried to recruit a revolutionary force for Fenian purposes from Irish prisoners of war in Germany. This enterprise resoundingly failed in its set purpose, but succeeded in establishing him in the eyes of British officialdom as the worst kind of traitor. Casement's general lack of success in galvanizing a decisive level of German support for Irish revolution convinced him that the Rising must be cancelled. Ironically, he had landed secretly in County Kerry to advocate caution but was arrested. His trial, and condemnation to death, took place in July. At once a strong campaign was set in motion, led by several prominent Irish people such as Bernard Shaw – no friend to Sinn Féin but convinced that Casement did not deserve the death penalty.

The condemned man had not been part of WBY's circle; only a few months before, Gregory had written to WBY wondering who Casement was. WBY was, nonetheless, brought on board for the campaign, though he preferred to pursue it his own way. When Eva Gore-Booth, Constance Markievicz's sister, wrote to him in late July asking for his support, he replied from Gonne's Normandy house that he had already written to the home secretary, with a copy to Asquith. In fact, he sent a cable to the prime minister the following day, pleading clemency for Casement. The case was, WBY felt (and told Quinn and Eva), overwhelmingly strong. But already the waters were being muddied. Members of the government were attempting to defuse the campaign for clemency by circulating portions of Casement's alleged diaries, which obsessively recounted homosexual exploits on his travels abroad. WBY would not learn of this whispering campaign until much later, but it certainly produced the desired effect in some quarters, and Casement was hanged on 3 August. The hangman remembered him as 'the bravest man it fell to my unhappy lot to execute'.[28]

WBY's reply to Eva, expressing sympathy for the trouble brought to them by Constance's arrest and imprisonment, strikes an anticipatory echo of a poem written much later: 'Your sister & yourself, two beautiful figures among the great trees of Lissadell, are among the dear memories of my youth.'[29] The tension of the politically charged summer after the Rising and the executions was translated, almost at once, into creative energy. He was not alone in this: AE swiftly wrote his 'Salutation' to the dead rebels and circulated it privately, while WBY's old acquaintance from Dublin, Dora Sigerson, married to the editor of the *Sphere*, Clement Shorter, was working on the verses which would be printed as *Poems of the Irish Rebellion, 1916* and sent to WBY later that year. (Two were about Casement; one was called 'Sixteen Dead Men'.)

As early as 1 May, H. W. Nevinson's account of a conversation with WBY at the Kardomah Café shows that the images of his poems about 1916 were building up:

Talked the whole time about the Irish Sinn Fein rising: does not know Casement personally: deeply laments part of other leaders – James Connolly (who as half-hearted working man could be easily deceived by vague hopes & promises), the Countess whom he knew with her sister as the toasts of Sligo, beautiful as gazelles, Pearse that schoolmaster who ran the model lay-Catholic school . . . & especially MacDonagh: a professor of literature & author of an excellent book on English prosody: thought MacNeill realised the folly & tried to stop it at last moment: supposed they had expected a German landing, or were otherwise deceived: had heard nothing about the Skeffingtons: said he went on with his writing & other work every day through all the stress and turmoil: was anxious to hear whether the Abbey Theatre was burnt down.[30]

On 23 May WBY told Quinn he was 'planning a group of poems on the Dublin rising but cannot write till I get into the country'. He had already accumulated enough poems before the Rising to make the Macmillan edition of *Responsibilities* far more substantial than the Cuala version of two years before: he was even keeping back poems to provide a brand-new small book for Cuala the following winter. This would become *The Wild Swans at Coole*. But the poetic energy infused by the Rising would take him in a different direction, and publishing the work which it inspired raised more difficult questions yet.

He had, moreover, still not been to Dublin since the cataclysm a month before. But he could not postpone it for ever, and in late May he was summoned firmly by Gregory to come back and put 'new life' into the stricken Abbey.[31] The players were furiously opposed to St John Ervine's dictatorial ways; 'cocksure and ill-mannered and thick-skinned', as Lily put it, he had tried to sack several actors for refusing to rehearse two plays a day and then tried to impose his wife as a leading actress. But here too post-Rising trauma had exacerbated matters. Arthur Sinclair, one of those dismissed, declared that the company also disapproved of Ervine (an Ulster Unionist) 'dabbling in politics', and the players rebelled openly on 29 May. Ervine remained for some weeks, but by early July Gregory was determined that he must go, and that WBY must sack him 'as you engaged him'.[32] Ervine was forced to resign; after Ezra Pound was briefly floated as his successor, J. Augustus Keogh was appointed, on the firm understanding that Gregory and WBY were the sole directors ('which seems to have slipped from peoples' minds') and kept entire control over all dramatic and artistic matters. Had Pound actually been appointed, there would certainly have been problems on this score, since at this very moment he was embroiled in a savage quarrel with his publisher Charles Elkin Mathews over the alleged obscenity of the poems in his forthcoming collection, *Lustra*. Though WBY manfully weighed in on his side, quoting Donne to the effect that 'a man ought to be allowed to be as indecent as he liked', this would not have augured well for the sensibilities of Dublin audiences.[33]

Moreover, Irish public opinion was now poised on a hair-trigger over issues even more explosive than sexual frankness. On his visit during the first week of June, WBY stayed in the Stephen's Green Club, and surveyed the wreckage of much of the city centre; he needed a pass from the Dublin Metropolitan Police to travel even as near as Greystones, just outside the city on the Wicklow coast, where Jack was recovering from his nervous breakdown. All in all it was a sobering visit, dominated by talk about the late Risings; but it helped fix in WBY's mind the idea of irrevocable change as a subject for his own poetic commentary. 'He is writing a series of poems on things here,' Lily told Quinn.[34] The correspondence with Gregory had taken him back, not only to his abiding love of Shelley, the eternal revolutionary, but to his own memories of the '98 centennial organizations, and the row over the *Playboy* when he had apparently watched 'the dissolution of a school of patriotism that held sway over my youth'.[35] The Irish earthquake entailed a reckoning with his past, and particularly with those elements from which he had thought himself liberated. Since the news of MacBride's execution his thoughts (as his letter of 11 May shows) had been with Gonne; he swiftly decided to spend the summer in France. Gregory was disappointed, 'for I feel the need of a talk with you, a new beginning as it were'. But, for WBY, Gonne's changed position after MacBride's death meant a new beginning too. He had discussed with Gregory in Dublin his intention to travel to France and propose marriage once more. The day after he left his old friend wrote resignedly, 'Coole seems lonely without the certainty of your summer here . . . I hope all may go well with you whatever happens.'[36]

He had already consulted another, equally inevitable oracle: a few days after MacBride's execution he was sending urgent letters to Elizabeth Radcliffe. There were sessions on 14 and 17 May. WBY wrote, as a query to Radcliffe's 'Instructors' (but hidden from the medium), 'should I marry MG. Is this the torches splendour.' The answer was vague enough: 'Not misjudged. Meeting point abridged.'[37] But it was enough to send him to France with Iseult, who had been staying in London, on 22 June.

The atmosphere at Gonne's seaside house in the aftermath of the Rising is best conveyed by a letter from WBY to his old friend Florence Farr, now terminally ill in Ceylon.

I am writing in France, where I am staying with Maude Gonne . . . She belongs now to the Third Order of St Francis & sighs for a convent. She & her family are returning to Ireland in October. When she heard the news of her husbands execution she went to Iseult, paper in hand & looking pale and said 'MacBride has been shot' & then went to her little boy who was making a boat & said 'your father has died for his country – he did not behave well to us – but now we can think of him with honour' and then said to Iseult 'Now we can return to Ireland'. Thereon a hanger on, a Miss Delaney began 'May a soul of an English man be lost for every hair upon his head' and the like till Iseult took her by the shoulders & shook her and said 'Delaney this is nonsense' & then Delaney wept & said 'You have no heart'.[38]

This account must have been relayed to WBY by Iseult. The year before, trying to encourage her translations of Tagore into French, WBY had ruefully concluded 'she is too young and beautiful to be industrious'.[39] But for about three years she had been sending WBY letters mingling self-doubt and self-dramatization, thanking him for caring whether 'I am going to waste sordidly my life in futility or to make a great task of it.'[40] She appealed for advice, railed against the ennui of life, and between the lines gave him news of Maud. But by late 1915 she was making it clear that her reliance on him extended beyond ancient family friendship. 'You are the only person who has encouraged me to work, in the real sense of the word. You are the person in whose mind I trust and believe in most.' She sent him her efforts at writing, which he closely criticized; she poured out her exasperation with her mother, whose powerful character and dramatic way of life perhaps accounted for many of Iseult's insecurities. Now twenty-one, she was lazy, neurotic, and beguiling: despite her haunting beauty, she was touchingly awkward (at six feet tall), shy, and increasingly dependent on WBY. Their relationship had been considerably strengthened by her visit to London in May, to try to arrange a passport which would enable her mother to travel to Ireland. WBY had taken her around the salons of his friends, and to the opening of Rothenstein's exhibition at the Leicester Gallery, where she had been much noticed. Her looks had attracted the attention of admirers as diverse as G. B. Shaw, W. T. Horton, and Ezra Pound: on a visit to Stone Cottage both Dorothy Pound and George Hyde Lees were struck by her originality and distinction, set off by a charming Franco-Irish accent.[41]

By 1916 her interests had moved on to the new generation of French Catholic poets – Francis Jammes, Paul Claudel, and Charles Péguy, whose *Le Mystère de la charité de Jeanne d'Arc* was Iseult's latest translation project (doomed, like much else in her life, to remain unfinished). WBY proclaimed his interest in her was avuncular at most, but his friends were interrogating him closely about it: histrionic and nonchalant by turns, Iseult was already affecting the world-weary sarcasm which WBY had found appealing in Olivia Shakespear. In London she had told WBY she would 'bring him back to Colleville with her';[42] and even though WBY accompanied her to France, in order to propose to her mother, Iseult's presence provided a powerful secondary reason. When he duly asked Maud to marry him, and was duly refused, his thoughts shifted with surprising speed to her daughter. A long letter to Gregory made this unabashedly clear.

I have little to report. I asked Maude to marry me, a few days ago. She said that it would be bad for her work & mine, & that she was too old for me. 'I have been always ten years older than you. I was when we were both twenty & I still am.' Next day she said 'were you not very much relieved that I refused you?' & then 'I dare say it would be better for the children if we married but I do not think it would work'. Perhaps she was hesitating, perhaps not. I have not returned to the subject and she has not. I think she would find it hard to give up politics & I have given her a written statement of my political creed. Probably she has finally decided. She says 'I have always thought a woman of my years should not marry.' I am very much taken up with Iseult, not in the way of love or desire, but her joyous childhood absorbs my thought, & I hardly know what I feel. It makes Madam Gonne seem older than she is. Should my feeling change towards Iseult I shall leave at once, as I think 30 years too great a difference for her happiness, but I have little fear. I am more & more convinced of her genius. I find the little boy attracts me too. He is very gentle & well bred & intelligent – rather a surprize to me. Every one is indeed peaceful & gentle. Madam Gonne helps the servant with the housework in the morning & spends her afternoon drawing flowers. She does nothing with these drawings, but packs them away in portfolios, or loses them. Today she eat her lunch with a bird in a cage on the table beside her. The little boy had his white rabbit beside him. We have three & thirty singing birds, a green Parrot, a white Japanese cock which perches on the back of our chairs at lunch, two dogs, two guinea pigs, two rabits & a black Persian cat. Our one anxiety is how we are to limit Iseults ciggarettes.[43]

The denial that 'love or desire' came into his feelings for Iseult is unconvincing. It was also disingenuous to describe someone approaching her twenty-second birthday as a 'joyous child'; writing to Maud in May, he had remarked that Iseult was 'quite a commanding person now, no longer a fanciful child'. In any case, Gregory was not taken in, quickly replying:

I am relieved on the whole – I was growing more & more doubtful of the possibility of its going well – it sometimes seemed as if it wd separate you from the Ireland you want to work for [rather] than bringing you nearer – As to the other matter I dont think the difference of age an objection, you are young in appearance & in mind & spirit – she may look on you as but a family friend – but I have always thought it possible another feeling might awake & in that case I see no reason why happiness might not come of it – [44]

WBY may have been influenced by this explicit encouragement. He stayed on into the summer, lulled and magnetized again by the world Gonne created wherever she went. But it was the lure of Iseult's company, rather than her mother's political fixation, that bound him to the large house on the bare Normandy beach. After that summer, Iseult would write to him: 'I wish we were both on the shore now, outlining pentagrams in the sand, counting on our fingers 12345 (5 was the right number I think), seeing some yellow come into the sky and our shadows lengthen and discussing with the greatest seriousness whether the sea could really be paler than the sky and what we should say when we came in late for dinner.'[45] She conjured up intimacy; they discussed their respective tendencies to depression, and he taught her mantras to induce resignation. By mid August he could write to Gregory a much fuller account of the developing relationship, though he still presented his role as that of a therapeutic presence in the life of a difficult child, in conflict with an equally difficult mother.

I think by your silence that you may blame me for staying on here – & I know that my last letter was not quite candid – there are things it is easier to say. However that is only a conventional idea. I am staying on here for the sake of that young girl, in whom we are both interested. (I will not give the name to a possible censor). To look at her dancing on the shore at the edge of the sea or coming in with her arms full of flowers you would think her the most joyous of creatures. And yet she is very unhappy – dying of self-analysis. Everything becomes food for an accusation on sin Last night we had a painful scene. 'I hear a voice always' she said 'saying "worthless, worthless, worthless"'. A moment ago she brought in a pack of cards & asked me to keep it & never let her have it again. She has been accustomed to play 'patience' after lunch in her room, & Maud Gonne has very probably made a sin of it – there has been a contest of will over it. Yet the worst is not these definite sins ('Patience is sensuality' she says in her quaint English) but metaphysical sins – she has not enough love for God & enough love for others & so on. And then there is the real trouble of ciggarettes – she is getting nicotine poisoning, & Maud Gonne by allowing the little boy to taunt her constantly about it at meals (till I stopped that) has armed the craving against her reason. She put that matter in my charge, & now after some rebellions she seems to be really trying to conquer the craving herself. I am dealir g with the metaphysical sins in a way I learned from you. 'If you do not love so & so enough, do something for them, sacrifice something & you will love them.' Maud Gonne has feared she was going into melancholia, & supports my belief that I can do more for her than others & so I stay on. My own relation with her is now perfectly candid. She is really a child & when she trusts trusts comple[te]ly. She has told me that when she was in Dublin four years ago – the time you met her – she wished to marry me ('You were the only person of my own race I had met' she means the only person of culture) & that she had this wish for two years. She has shown me in her diary such sentences as 'I have an affection for him; he has, I think, an affection for me' (I had given her books since she was a child) and a record of a conversation, in which I said I would like, if I married, to live in some out of the way place like Bayeux in an old house. She took this quite seriously & chose the house at Bayeux. This thought lasted two years, & then she made up her mind she was not in love, & that perhaps she would fall in love with someone of her own age. I need hardly say that I told her that she might marry me if she would & that there were exceptional cases where even 30 years difference would not prevent happiness. We discussed it nearly without emotion as we might any other problem – her usual analysis – 'Ah if you were only a young boy' she said & I left it there & am now established not as husband not as father (though she rejects the word 'father' which has I imagine no very pleasant associations). She has grown to be a great beauty & has had many proposals and so is all quite natural. She says however 'do not tell Lady Gregory that it is quite certain I am not going to marry you for if you do she will not be kind to me'. I think my own feelings are those of kindness & affection, natural to my years.[46]

This time, Gregory's reply took a firmer line. She now understood his 'apparent indifference to Ireland after your excitement after the rising', but he must come back and bring his great weight of cultural influence to bear on the unrest and discontent. 'There is nowhere for the imagination to rest – but there must be some spiritual building possible just as after Parnell's fall, but perhaps more intense, & you have a big name among the young men – I daresay your being away & having time for thought & your thinking of the '98 time may be all a help in the end.'[47]

At the end of August WBY wrenched himself away from the caged singing birds, the wide beach, kite-flying with Seán, and Iseult's seductive moodiness; her mother's passport had finally come through, but would permit her to travel to England only. He arrived back in London on the 31st. On 15 September he went to Dublin, where he met Gregory to attend the Abbey's first production of *John Bull's Other Island*, which Shaw had mischievously written to launch their theatre so many years before. The next day they proceeded straight to Coole.[48]

There he stayed until early October. He wrote to Iseult asking if she was 'too young to know what a test of affection letters are'; she replied 'now I am in great gloom and oppressed by that old sense of sinking and failure. You are one of the very few whose thought brings me a life giving power.'[49] She also told him how much she had missed him during the early autumn at Colleville; they were soulmates, and he was the voice of her daimon. Her long letters employed a romantic shared language, and repeated the rules of life and thought she had learned from him. 'Only the fool or the saint can stand serene amid the discordance of modern civilisation, for the first is part of it and the other stands above.'[50] If she was in part testing her own sexual powers upon her legendary mother's famous admirer, she was also expressing an intoxicating dependence on him. He was deeply affected. And, as always, romantic excitement fuelled his imaginative powers. At Coole, on 25 September, he finished the poem on the Rising which he had been meditating upon since May, and writing in Colleville. In a provisional contents page for *The Wild Swans at Coole* (where it did not appear) he placed it first – with the bare title '1916'. But it was first published, to a privately circulated audience, as 'Easter, 1916'.[51]

The roots of the poem stretch back, not just to the revelation of May that 'terrible beauty has been born again', but also to the quarrels with conventional nationalism which had convulsed the life of Dublin's avant-garde in the rows over Synge's plays, and to WBY's own experience of hardline political attitudes in the '98 centennial movement. All these conflicts and memories had been thrown into sharp relief by the transformation of his political and intellectual antagonists into the martyred heroes of Easter Week. The poem analyses the way that this has come about, but also the extent to which WBY's own ambivalence about fanaticism had really been overcome. In its intellectual complexity, subtly modulated argument, and tightly controlled changes of mood and form, 'Easter 1916' reached a new level of achievement among WBY's political poems: the ringing declamations of 'To a Wealthy Man . . .' and 'September 1913' have been replaced by something much closer to the dramatic dialogue of a meditation like 'Ego Dominus Tuus'. Here, however, the dialogue is not only with, but within, the uncertain self. Transcending politics, it is also a last, elegiac love-lyric to Gonne. The poem circulated in samizdat form the following spring begins, in diminuendo mode, by conjuring up Dublin before the revolution; the city's Georgian squares and terraces are inhabited by bureaucrats from the nationalist petite bourgeoisie, whose strict Sinn Féin platitudes seem bathetically ill attuned to the necessities of modern compromise – political and cultural – in a dwindled world.

> I have met them at close of day
> Coming with vivid faces
> From counter or desk among grey
> Eighteenth-century houses,
> I have passed with a nod of the head
> Or polite meaningless words,
> Or have lingered awhile and said
> Polite meaningless words,
> And thought before I had done
> Of a mocking take or a gibe
> To please a companion
> Around the fire at the club,
> Being certain that they and I
> But lived where motley is worn:
> All changed, changed utterly:
> A terrible beauty is born.

The tone suggests expiation for having trivialized the subjects of the poem, before they had translated themselves into heroes. The second stanza memorializes selected revolutionaries: oddly, the same four referred to in Lily's sardonic letter, but they are celebrated in a very different sense. At the same time he conveys a certain restraint, especially where Constance Markievicz is concerned:

> That woman at while would be shrill
> In aimless argument;
> Had ignorant goodwill;
> All that she got she spent,
> Her charity had no bounds:
> Sweet voiced and beautiful,
> She had ridden well to hounds.

The version eventually published in the *New Statesman* was more graceful, inverting the last description into a classical Yeatsian rhetorical question; but the effect was hardly less impatient. Pearse and MacDonagh were more kindly treated:

> This man had managed a school
> An[d] our wingèd mettlesome horse.
> This other his helper and friend
> Was coming into his force;
> He might have won fame in the end,
> So sensitive his nature seemed,
> So daring and sweet his thought.

But a real, and surprising, penance was done in the lines on MacBride, for so long seen by WBY as the betrayer of Gonne and molester of Iseult, both now 'near to his heart'.

> This other man I had dreamed
> A drunken, vain-glorious lout.
> He had done most bitter wrong
> To some who are near my heart,
> Yet I number him in the song;
> He, too, has resigned his part
> In the casual comedy;
> He, too, has been changed in his turn,
> Transformed utterly:
> A terrible beauty is born.

Following a private logic, the introduction of Maud and Iseult leads into the third stanza, where the tone of memorial invocation suddenly yields to meditation.

60

Hearts with one purpose alone
Through summer and winter, seem
Enchanted to a stone
To trouble the living stream.
The horse that comes from the road,
The rider, the birds that range
From cloud to tumbling cloud,
Minute by minute change.
A shadow of cloud on the stream
Changes minute by minute;
A horse-hoof slides on the brim;
And a horse plashes within it
Where long-legged moor-hens dive
And hens to moor-cocks call.
Minute by minute they live:
The stone's in the midst of all.

A year before, writing to Ernest Boyd, he had attacked 'Dublin talkers' who 'value anything which they call a principle more than any possible achievement. All achievements are won by compromise and these men wherever they find themselves expell from their own minds – by their mind's rigidity – the flowing & living world.'[52] The image and the thought find their way into the poem, but the 'talkers' had now opted for action. Simultaneously this stanza reprises, yet again, his enduring plea to Gonne over the years. Most vividly, it recalls the great passage in 'J. M. Synge and the Ireland of his Time' six years before, also composed at Colleville, where he had written of the sterility that comes from giving oneself to an abstract idea of the nation: 'till minds, whose patriotism is perhaps great enough to carry them to the scaffold, cry down natural impulse with the morbid persistence of minds unsettled by some fixed idea'. In that essay he had argued for 'intellectual innocence, that delight in what is unforeseen, in the mere spectacle of the world, the mere drifting hither and thither, that must come before all true thought and emotion': now symbolized in 1916 as cloud-shadows on water, a rider splashing though a stream, the flux of life. Those who renounce the world 'no longer love, for only life is loved, and at last, a generation is like a hysterical woman who will make unmeasured accusations, and believe impossible things, because of some logical deduction from a solitary thought which has turned a portion of her mind to stone'.[53]

In 1910 this had been implicitly addressed to Gonne; in 1916 she knew that the third stanza of 'Easter, 1916' was another appeal. Twenty-three years later, she recalled her guest working all night on the poem that Colleville summer.

Standing by the sea shore in Normandy in September 1916 he read me that poem, he had worked on it all the night before, and he implored me to forget the stone and its inner fire for the flashing, changing joy of life, but when he found my mind dull with the stone of the fixed idea of getting back to Ireland, kind and helpful as ever he helped me to overcome physical and passport difficulties and we travelled as far as London together.[54]

But she must have noticed that his romantic attention had been deflected, and there are also less important inaccuracies and conflations here. He left Colleville before September, and the journey back together happened a year later. He finished the poem in Gregory's house, not Gonne's; the transformation of his own opinions about the Rising had been heavily influenced by Gregory. Above all, the appeal to share his life, and thus to embrace the living world rather than intellectual abstractions, had been directed most recently towards Gonne's daughter rather than to herself. Nonetheless she stands at the centre: all the more so, as the values of uncompromising, 'advanced', Anglophobic nationalism which she had always personified had been spectacularly embodied by the 1916 martyrs. And the last stanza of the poem took up the question of martyrology. While the names are 'told' at nightfall like the beads of a rosary, the poem subtly links the rebels' sacrifice to a life of dreams and delusion, and reminds the reader (now as then) that Home Rule had after all been passed into law, and the crisis over its implementation was still awaiting resolution.

> Too long a sacrifice
> Can make a stone of the heart.
> O when may it suffice?
> That is heaven's part, our part
> To murmur name upon name,
> As a mother names her child
> When sleep at last has come
> On limbs that had run wild.
> What is it but nightfall?
> No, no, not night but death.
> Was it needless death after all?
> For England may keep faith
> For all she had done and said.
> We know their dream; enough
> To know they dreamed and are dead.
> And what if excess of love
> Bewildered them till they died?
> I write it out in a verse —
> MacDonagh and MacBride
> And Connolly and Pearse

Now and in time to be,
Wherever green is worn,
Are changed, changed utterly:
A terrible beauty is born.[55]

It was this last stanza which Gonne seized upon, in a magnificently defiant letter that November, when she had been sent the final version. 'Your poem on the Easter week has been the cause of great argument in our household as to the nature and value of sacrifice,' Iseult warned him. 'Moura who cannot admit Art for art's sake would willingly admit sacrifice for sacrifice's sake, and I have come to admit neither exactly.'[56] But her mother's certitude was uncompromising.

My dear Willie,
   No I don't like your poem, it isn't worthy of you & above all it isn't worthy of the subject – Though it reflects your present state of mind perhaps, it isn't quite sincere enough for you who have studied philosophy & know something of history know quite well that sacrifice has never yet turned a heart to stone though it has immortalised many & through it alone mankind can rise to God – You recognise this in the line which was the original inspiration of your poem 'A terrible Beauty is born' but you let your present mood mar & confuse it till even some of the verses become unintelligible to many. Even Iseult reading it didn't understand your thought till I explained your [?retribution] theory of constant change & becoming in the flux of things –
   But you could never say that MacDonagh & Pearse & Conally were sterile fixed minds, each served Ireland, which was their share of the world, the part they were in contact with, with varied faculties & vivid energy! those three were men of genius, with large comprehensive & speculative & active brains the others of whom we know less were probably less remarkable men, but still I think they must have been men with a stronger grasp on Reality a stronger spiritual life than most of those we meet. As for my husband he has entered Eternity by the great door of sacrifice which Christ opened & has therefore atoned for all so that praying for him I can also ask for his prayers & 'A terrible beauty is born'
   There are beautiful lines in your poem, as there are in all you write but it is not a great WHOLE, a living thing which our race would treasure & repeat, such as a poet like you might have given to your nation & which would have avenged our material failure by its spiritual beauty –
   You will be angry perhaps that I write so frankly what I feel, but I am always frank with my friends & though our ideals are wide apart we are still friends.[57]

She had unerringly spotted the poem's central ambivalence, missed by those who concentrate on the images of terrible beauty and rebirth through sacrifice. Throughout the mounting rhetorical questions, wby's doubts about the utility of self-immolation and the dangers of fanaticism beat an insistent rhythm. Nonetheless, in 1916 it would have read principally as a passionate endorsement of the rebels' cause, and WBY was extremely cautious about releasing it. Copies were sent to selected friends in the autumn (Gonne, Gregory, Ernest Boyd), and on 7 December he read it to a small group at Lindsey House, where Gregory was staying;[58] Gregory found it 'extraordinarily impressive', and had to read some Hilaire Belloc afterwards to lessen the tension. At some point that winter WBY drew up a contents page for his next Cuala volume, placing '1916' first, but he abandoned the idea, deciding instead on a private printing with Clement Shorter, to whom he sent a copy the following March. The delay, as he told Shorter, was at Gregory's request. She 'asked me not to send it you until we had finished our dispute with the authorities about the Lane pictures. She is afraid of it getting about & damaging us & she is not timid.'[59] This, indeed, seems the principal reason for discretion, though the conditions of the war also imposed a certain inhibition. On 10 September 1916 he wrote to Gregory that there had been a proposal to take away his pension, on the grounds that he was pro-German: 'Is it not a curious Russian state of things when one's private, or supposed private conversations, are reported to government . . . I am rather afraid I will find that the Dublin rising has brought suspicion on us all.' She replied wrathfully, telling him to go straight to Asquith.[60] It is likely that his support of Casement (hanged in August) was being held against him in some political circles; and a year later, in May 1917, WBY told Quinn that the forthcoming *Wild Swans at Coole* would be '24 or 25 lyrics or a little more if the war ending enables me to add two poems I have written about Easter week in Dublin'.[61] But above all hovered the matter of Lane's contested bequest, which dominated Gregory's and WBY's London lives in the winter of 1916/17.

'There are no politics in the matter,' WBY wrote in a letter to the *Spectator* yet again setting forth the arguments for honouring Lane's unwitnessed codicil leaving his modern collection to Dublin.[62] But in a private letter to Ellen Duncan in Dublin he directly contradicted this: since parliamentary action would be needed, 'it will certainly be a political matter': Lloyd George now had to be cultivated rather than Asquith, and the moment seized when he would take it up.[63] Since the débâcle of the Rising, Birrell (who had swiftly and inevitably resigned) lost influence. With Lloyd George's coup of December 1916, Asquith was also relegated. And, as Birrell warned Gregory, after Easter 1916 the National Gallery could count on 'the present unpopularity of Ireland & the Irish in both Houses of the country'.[64] Moreover, the matter of supporting the Easter Rising was all the more difficult, since the only government minister unequivocally in favour of Gregory's campaign happened to be the Unionist leader Edward Carson, who promised to work on his Trinity College constituents; his Ulster colleague in the Unionist cause, James Craig, was equally committed.[65] But their support was unlikely to survive their ally's publication of a poem extolling the Easter Rising.

From late November, when WBY joined Gregory in London, they were engaged in a round of intrigue. WBY wooed Strachey of the *Spectator* and Robinson of *The Times*, setting up the publication of a 'statement' by Gregory. Meanwhile she laid siege to hostesses like Margot Asquith and Leonie Leslie, pursued Redmond to his gloomy Kensington flat, and bearded Lord Northcliffe. By January Birrell's successor as chief secretary, H. E. Duke, was being cultivated relentlessly. But by then the enemy were advancing into the open. The National Gallery would only hint at a loan arrangement covering part of the collection; WBY wrote angrily to *The Times* denouncing the idea. Robert Witt had now been identified as an arch-opponent.[66] The ex-viceroy Wimborne warned Gregory that the National Gallery was determined to fight; they disingenuously claimed the pictures were worth only £6,000, but rapidly put them on display. Most damaging of all, the distinguished critic D. S. MacColl, who had been retained to write Lane's life, revealed that he was in the National Gallery camp, arguing that the matter should be decided on the basis of Lane's opinions and wishes in 1914, not 1915. MacColl's letter to the *Observer* in mid December was, WBY confided, the only salvo of importance fired against them; his own reply appeared on 21 December, and he also planted an interview in the paper, as well as writing copious letters to other journals. Though a Dublin committee was set up to agitate for the pictures' return, Gregory and WBY kept the operation in London firmly under their control. 'I am doing nothing but this dispute,' he gloomily told Duncan in January.[67]

There were faint signs of hope in February, with T. P. O'Connor mediating approaches to other MPs; but WBY's visit to the House of Commons on 9 February to try to organize a committee of Irish Parliamentary Party members was a disappointment, and a note from Lloyd George's secretary, saying that the question of the pictures would be pursued, was scant comfort.[68] Nonetheless, all this unproductive lobbying and organization had a direct effect on WBY's work. In the 1917 printing of *Responsibilities*, for instance, two paragraphs about the struggle over Lane's gallery were dropped from the notes, at Gregory's request, and he threw himself into composing a pamphlet stating the case. Though nominally under Gregory's name, it was largely written by WBY.[69] Above all, this level and intensity of political wire-pulling required tact, discretion, and an avoidance of controversy. Little wonder that 'Easter 1916' was withheld from both the Cuala and Macmillan versions of *The Wild Swans at Coole* (1917 and 1919 respectively) and stayed out of public circulation until its publication in the

New Statesman on 23 October 1920 – when the political situation in Ireland, and Anglo-Irish relations with it, had changed more utterly than anyone could have foreseen.

III

Through the summer at Colleville WBY had been writing hard: not only 'Easter 1916' and drafts of other poems, and 'patching' *The Player Queen*, but the next instalment of his memoirs. He arrived determined to get them down on paper, and by 1 August had written more than half. They were not, however, for immediate publication, as he made clear to Quinn.

It will be published 20 years after my death & I hope to find some public institution – T.C.D. library perhaps – to take charge of it till then. It is my life from the close of 'reveries' to about 1900. I am using Maud Gonnes memory as well as my own. It is perfectly frank & containing besides my own life studies of Henley, Symons, Wilde, Maud Gonne of course & of all the little group in Dublin.

The same message went to Farr: 'Do you want to go in over a nom-de-plume or not? It is a very candid book & will be quite unpublishable unless the world grows more free spoken.' He stressed his wish for complete psychological honesty. 'I will lay many ghosts, or rather I will purify my own imagination by setting the past in order.'[70] He read instalments aloud to the Colleville household as the work progressed – Iseult being 'interested & impressed', while Gonne objected to much that he said about Dublin. This was hardly surprising: 'it is so far almost as much a study of Maud Gonne as of myself'.

Thus he was writing about the first agonies of his youthful love for her, and his repeated proposals, at the very time when – both past fifty – he was proposing to her all over again. The draft ended, in fact, with his exhausted inability to pursue her further, after the traumatic revelations of December 1898. It was indeed published posthumously in 1972, as *Memoirs*, and it is frank and direct on some sexual matters: he was now acquainted with the ideas of Freud and Jung, and wrote about his first experiences of sexual arousal and masturbation 'that some young man of talent might not think as I did that my shame was mine alone.'[71] But, as with all his autobiographical writing, it is also a masterpiece of reordering and manipulation: 'getting in all the characters is rather like writing a play', he told Quinn. He was determined to choreograph his varied acquaintances of the 1880s and 1890s against the backdrop of their times, and write his own history of the literary revival along with it, to rival or dispute those of W. P. Ryan and Boyd. The sexual frankness forbade publication of the most personal passages: he would recycle much of the political and literary material from it in his later autobiographical writing. But in those personal passages lie the distinctiveness and intensity of *Memoirs*. The very first sentence plunges into a quarrel with his father (over Ruskin), when 'he broke the glass in a picture with the back of my head'. Bedford Park in the late 1880s frames his ideas: the nervous boy of *Reveries* is deliberately teaching himself to debate, and measuring his lack of self-possession against figures as theatrical as Morris, Wilde, Blavatsky, Mathers, the astonishing cast who marched through the drama of his early life. Occult studies and mystic insights are introduced early on. His shyness is extended to a self-confessed dread of the subject of sex, and a persistent inability to act as he wishes. The recollected personality is not the impetuous, charismatic figure who is reflected in his early letters, and who entranced the people who met him at that time. Yet when his fate appears, in the person of Maud Gonne, he recognizes it at once. If the passage where he describes the impact of her appearance ('I had never thought to see in a living woman so great beauty') was among those he read out at Colleville in the summer evenings, she cannot have been displeased. But her revolutionary ruthlessness, and their abiding disagreements, are sharply delineated from the start, and so is the vulnerability which bewitched him as much as her beauty. If he read her the passages describing her grief after her first son's death in 1891, she must have been unbearably moved. Unsurprisingly, she objected to the draft being located in a library in Britain or Ireland; she also declared an (unfulfilled) intention to add a corrective political appendix.[72]

Above all, *Memoirs* is written with the sharp consciousness that politics in the years after 1891 were in the crucible, and WBY claims to have recognized that 'the young, perhaps for many years to come, would seek some unpolitical form for national feeling'. Thus the circumstances of 1916 permeate the memory of the nineties. He returned yet again to the conflict between the parti pris propaganda of conventional nationalism and the intuitive imperatives of the artist's development: this may have been one of the issues disputed by Maud Gonne while *Memoirs* was being written. (Another may have been his statement that in November 1895 'she had secretly wished to take me for her husband': it is deleted in the manuscript, possibly after he read it to her.) Recalling the intrigues, miseries, and uncertainties of the 1890s, at a time when Irish politics were in flux once more, added a particular vividness. And the self-critical, regretful description of the way his obsession with Gonne ended his affair with Olivia Shakespear (disguised as 'Diana Vernon') owes something to the fact that during that summer of 1916 he was once more preoccupied by the desire for love, and the limits of passion. 'All our lives . . . [we] long . . . for our destruction, and when we meet it in the shape of a most fair woman, can we do less than leave all others for her? Do we not seek our dissolution upon her lips?'

The patina of anecdotes recalling the sexual exploits of Dowson's or Symons's would-be bohemianism is polished through retelling; though chronology is sometimes reversed or telescoped (the account of the '98 centennial movement is particularly distanced and disjointed), *Memoirs* is written as fluently and excitedly as *Reveries* had been two years before. Some images and ideas would transfer directly into the mystical reflections which were written shortly afterwards and published as *Per Amica Silentia Lunae*. The ending is particularly powerful, introduced by another bewildering chronological reverse, which this time seems to be a deliberate dramatic effect. The controversy over *The Countess Kathleen* in 1899 is recounted as a bravura set-piece, using Martyn and Moore as brilliantly and mercilessly as Moore himself had satirized Gregory and WBY five years earlier. Then, in an abrupt change of perspective, the telescope swings to the apocalyptic fervour of 1897–8, that time of shared visions and passionate hopes – which, in the narrative of *Memoirs*, seems to follow (rather than precede) the imbroglio over the Irish Literary Theatre. This brings Maud Gonne back to centre stage, at her most entrancing, and it ends, breathtakingly, with their shared visions of December 1898, her revelations, by the fireplace in the Crown Hotel, of her secret life with Millevoye, the death of her first child, and her agonies of confusion and guilt. As for himself, he recalled his own determination only 'to touch [her] as one might a sister':

If she was to come to me, it must be from no temporary passionate impulse, but with the approval of her conscience. Many a time since then, as I lay awake at night, have I accused myself of acting, not as I thought from a high scruple, but from a dread of moral responsibility, and my thoughts have gone round and round, as do miserable thoughts, coming to no solution.

A few pages before, he declares that he did not summon her image in erotic dreams: 'I think I surrounded her with too great reverence and fear.' Here speaks once again the uncertain, self-analysing, irresolute boy. Though they are vouchsafed a final double vision, the sexually implicit 'initiation of the spear', *Memoirs* ends with his own insufficiency. Gregory, as ever, urges decisiveness on him, offers him money, tells him to pursue his advantage with Gonne 'till I had her promise of marriage, but I said, "No, I am too exhausted; I can do no more."'

Though he had finished the draft, 'setting the past in order', by 19 August,[73] it is unlikely that he read this final section to Iseult and her mother that August in Colleville; but writing it against a background of a marriage proposal repeated and refused, with a certain air of ritual exhaustion on both sides, must have strongly influenced its composition. There is a hint of this in a letter from Iseult later in the year:

It is very curious indeed that prophecy of Horton 'Your sins have found you out . . .' I do not quite understand: and you say it is a version of what you have been going through. Now when I think of last summer I see what I did not realise at the moment, that you must have gone through a terrible deal. While you were writing your biography I was merely interested in those evocations of the past, but little did I think of the agony of it and of the courage it needs to settle memories into a definite order. You did it to give a lasting life to the soul, but did you not at the same time have to give the last death stroke to many old pathetic illusions? I read the other day: 'All confession is a destruction.' And it is true and nothing hurts as much as to destroy – I don't understand about your sins finding you out: but you have found out your delusions to be sins: and that is a great suffering. Do not think to[o] much of me Willie you might find me out also.[74]

Memoirs, written that summer, is a vivid and vital guide to the turmoil of WBY's life in the 1890s, but it also enshrines the ending of a phase in his relationship with his 'phoenix' which occurred in the summer of 1916.

The emotional and intellectual excitement of the summer was sustained by avid reading as well as writing: notably the modern French Catholic writers beloved of Iseult, who sent him long extracts from Péguy and Claudel. Pound told Quinn that since 'staying in bigoted circles in France . . . [WBY] has got a new mania. French *Catholic* dramatists. Gosh!' George Moore also reacted in character, furiously denouncing WBY for affecting to understand verse in a language which he could not speak.[75] Though WBY had reservations about the school of Jammes, Claudel, and Péguy, he was struck by Irish parallels and potentialities – or so he claimed – when trying to find a publisher for Iseult's projected translation of Péguy's *Le Mystère de la charité de Jeanne D'Arc*. 'For various reasons I am very anxious to introduce the French school of Catholic writers to Ireland, & look upon this book as a start.'[76] But his own writing was still dominated by the surge of autobiographical energy which brought *Memoirs* to completion by 19 August. A few days later he sent Lily a draft poem commemorating their Uncle Alfred Pollexfen, the latest of their mother's great clan to die. It is an awkward elegy, studded with fine phrases in an uncertain and slightly banal catalogue, and one quatrain, recalling George Pollexfen's funeral, would be used against him for the rest of his life:

> And Masons drove from miles away
> To scatter the Acacia spray
> Upon a melancholy man
> Who had ended where his breath began.[77]

That aspect of George's splendidly archaic funeral had appealed greatly to WBY's hieratic sense, at the time and later. But to his enemies like Moran and Griffith, Freemasonry stood for a secret Protestant conspiracy running Irish business life and leagued together in a specifically anti-Catholic alliance. The tactless boast about George's connections fuelled the campaign waged by pious nationalism to identify WBY with reactionary – even Orange – Protestantism. His current interest in the fervently nationalist, and fervently Catholic, writers introduced to him in France by Iseult, and his wish to proselytize on their behalf in Ireland, owed something to the change of national mood which he sensed after the sacrificial Easter Rising; but it may also have represented one of those public demonstrations, periodically necessary but never wholly effective, that his soul was in the right place. In any case, Catholic Ireland remained as unconvinced as ever.

His credentials for conventional piety would have carried even less weight if the depth of his current supernatural involvements had been generally known. Since May he had been bombarding Elizabeth Radcliffe with requests for insights into his personal dilemmas. After his return from Colleville on 31 August he resorted to seances with various mediums, following through the preoccupations which had sustained him since Lane's death. (Prolonged exposure had shaken even Gregory's stout-hearted scepticism: reading Oliver Lodge's *Raymond* that autumn helped her to accept 'proofs' of life after death, though she added the characteristic rider that the Catholic Church should now stop 'asking for money to get a soul out of purgatory when it is saying that it is well & happy'.[78]) As for WBY, he spent the weeks up to Christmas visiting mediums like Alfred Vont Peters, accompanied by like-minded friends. One was Dulac; another, recently encountered, was Una, Lady Troubridge, the discontented young wife of a distinguished admiral. WBY addressed excited letters to her throughout this winter, and consulted her about 'private psychic matters'. His interest clearly went beyond the spiritual, but he was fated to disappointment. Her inseparable companion in these experiments was the lesbian poet and novelist Radclyffe Hall, and the two women would sustain a scandalously open liaison for most of their lives.[79]

As so often during critical periods in WBY's life, sexual excitement, supernatural investigations, and artistic creativity reacted in a potent fusion. The atmosphere of that winter of seances is preserved in two long pieces of experimental prose, where WBY interrogated the beliefs and inferences which sustained him, mining the vein which he had explored in the reflective essay 'Swedenborg, Mediums, and the Desolate Places', written two years before (though as yet unpublished). A conversation recorded by

Nevinson at a Woburn Buildings Monday on 30 October clearly shows his preoccupations:

Yeats was in most interesting mood: talked of his entrance into Spiritism fr. the magic of old days: his attendant spirit Leo Africanus, a man of the 14th cent. who converses in Italian: also the spirit of a policeman Emerson who drowned himself fr. Putney bridge [in] 1850, as he found in Somerset House records: also Louise Kirsch, the friend of Goethe, fr. whom he had messages. All this he absolutely believes. Then talked of Freud & Jung and the subconscious self, applying them to art; said the great thing is to reduce the conscious self to humility, as by imitation of some ancient master, leaving the unconscious free to work: said all reading of con- temporaries & imitation of them was bad. The self in poetry must be a dramatist, regarded by poet as spectator, & have a universal outlook or appeal. This I have always vaguely thought. Some discussion also of Vers Libres, with sidelong shots at Ezra Pound. Much praise of Pater's Marius, which he has just re-read with intense admiration for sentence & style. He traces English prose only through Pater, Landor, & Sir T. Browne, but admitted parts of Swift. The man himself is full of interest – a fine mind in every sense.[80]

Some of these ideas about drama in art are preserved in his revealing but long unpublished dialogue 'The Poet and the Actress'. It is an imagined exchange between a Poet, who wants to reform the language of the stage, and a sceptical Actress, who, though unnamed, speaks in the unmistakable accents of Mrs Patrick Campbell; the impulse may have been wby's current dissatisfaction with the 'stage-struck types' frequenting the Abbey.[81] His established preferences for Japanese-style formalism, dance, and masks are given full rein, and so is his dislike of 'plays of the new scientific kind'. (This apparently included James Joyce's *Exiles*, which the Abbey turned down in 1917.) Dramatic art must focus on the unwinnable 'battle with reality itself'. This was not new, but the dialogue also explored ideas just beginning to take possession of him. Certain artists (Keats, Shelley, Dante) are discussed as archetypes rather than as individuals, placed in a scheme much as in 'Ego Dominus Tuus', and the Poet also introduces the concept of 'a whole phan- tasmagoria' to express the fundamental antagonisms of life. 'There must be fables, mythology, that the dream and the reality may face one another in visible array.'[82]

Those who try to create beautiful things without this battle in [the] soul, are mere imitators, because we can only become conscious of a thing, by comparing it with its opposite. The two real [or new?] things we have are our natures, and the cir- cumstance that surrounds us. We need in both a violent antithesis, nor do I believe that art has anything to do with happiness. When we say we are happy we mean that we are doing all kinds of pleasant things, that we have forgotten all painful things. The end of art is ecstasy, and that cannot exist without pain. It is [a] sudden sense of power and of peace, that comes when we have before our mind's eye a group of images, which obeys us, which leaves us free, and which satisfies the need of our soul.

The 'passion for reality' can be expressed only through the use of a mask, and the Poet tells the Actress at the outset that she must act in one, which he has brought her from Fez. At the end, she laughingly repudiates it, but he turns the tables on her once more: 'There is no mask. I have never been to Fez.'

However, Leo Africanus had, and several of the ideas in the dialogue, as well as the introduction of an exotic Moorish city, anticipate another unpublished meditation written at this time. In December 1916, inspired by a supposed command in a seance, WBY composed a 'letter' to his established familiar and alter ego Leo Africanus, and also supplied an answer, written as from Leo himself. Like *Memoirs*, but for different reasons, this was fated to remain unpublished in his lifetime. It is a strangely irresolute text, admitting at the end not only that Leo may be an impostor (even if the euphemism 'secondary personality' is used), but that WBY himself has remained unconvinced since the first clear revelation in 1912.[83]

The genesis of the 'letter' was in a session of automatic writing at Woburn Buildings on 22 July 1915, when a friend of Sturge Moore had relayed a demand from Leo. 'He asked me to write him a letter addressed to him as if to Africa [?] giving all my doubts about spiritual things and then to write a reply as from him to me.'[84] In fact, this agenda was dictated through WBY's 'conversation with the control'. Given that his habit was to ask extremely leading questions in such circumstances, and he had already 'several times' thought of constructing an 'imaginary dialogue' with Leo, the idea probably owed much to Landor's *Imaginary Conversations*, and WBY's ancient habit of creating dialogues between literary personae in order to clarify his own mind on abstract difficulties. The intensity of his psychic investigations in late 1916 concentrated his mind on this project: it seems likely that Leo (conjured up for him by the obliging Olivia Shakespear, among others) had recently manifested himself by courtesy of Peters. The 'letter', as constructed in late 1916, assembles the history of WBY's pursuit of his 'daimon', but it also places that phenomenon firmly in the context of self and anti-self, explored by 'Ego Dominus Tuus'. The 'curious doctrine' that a spiritual alter ego could be psychically established, whose opposite qualities and identifications would complete WBY's own personality, was clearly inspirational: but so was the historical Leo's *Description of Africa*, which WBY had now tracked down and read.

Yet he returned to the question of doubt, instancing the possibility that the medium had created Leo out of a biographical dictionary: the proofs that reassured him are not particularly persuasive. In discussing the arguments for the spirit-Leo's independent existence, WBY ranged back to youthful Dublin experiments at Dr Sigerson's, remembered his own early readings in folk and faery lore, and rehearsed many examples from the profuse records of mediumistic investigations. The very awkwardness and circuitousness of the language suggest feelings which were not fully resolved, for all his claims that spirit existence was now irrevocably demonstrated.

Can in fact a secondary personality draw from many sources & so build up a complex knowledge, & even of different languages. Certainly I am incredulous, but maybe that is only a dolts reason abashed by the unknown. [Have] I not after years of investigation accepted the most incredible facts. You may have built up a being as complex as my own & yet require from me an intermitted attention, & a measure of belief to keep you from dying.

Later, he posed a more general question:

Does in fact the human mind possess a power like that of the amoeba of multiplication by division? Perhaps every mind has originated at conception so, & the seance room but uses in a new way, a faculty necessary to nature, & thereby looses upon the world a new race of bodiless minds, who after they are first created grow & change according to their own will & continually seek a more solid and hard being [&] are in the end dependent not upon an individual body, but upon the body of the human race as a whole. The thought has some support from antiquity.[85]

Spirits, in fact, may be a kind of succubus needing to ransack and fasten on to the 'thoughts and images' by which the living construct biographies. Thus the Leo who speaks to WBY is partly created by the research WBY has put into 'proving' his existence – and by WBY's own hard-won belief. 'Does he even know that he deceives, when the definition has gone so far, that he has divided himself, from the thoughts & activities of the mind where he was born.'

At one level, this seems an extremely elaborate rationalization of auto-suggestion: but it presupposes, even at an attenuated level, the independent existence of the wandering spirit mind. In the much longer 'answer' which WBY drafted from Leo himself, that independent existence is unequivocally stated, while his daimon scolds him for adhering to a dogged belief in literal proofs. 'You insist on considering spirits as unknown causes, though they have interfered in your own life often enough.' Further admonitions suggest that the function of this experimental dialogue was, as so often, a therapeutic analysis of WBY's personal life at a disquieting juncture:

You are sympathetic, you meet many people, you discuss much, you must meet all their doubts as they arise, & so cannot break away into a life of your own as did

Swedenborg, Boehme, & Blake. Even the wisdom that we send you, but deepens your bewilderment, for when the wisest of your troop of shades wrote you through the ignorant hand of a friend 'Why do you think that faith excludes intellect. It is the highest achievement of the human intellect, & it is the only gift that man can offer to god. That is why we must leave all the winds of time to beat upon it'[,] you but sought the more keenly to meet not your own difficulties but the difficulties of others. Entangled in error, you are but a public man, yet once you would put vague intuition into verse, & that insufficient though it was might have led you to the path the eye of the eagle has not seen. I will speak to you & not your friends, & will therefore begin by assuming the existence, of myself & of the shades that are my fellows.[86]

The ancient reassurance came again: 'All living minds are surrounded by shades, who are the contrary will which presents before the abstracted [?] mind & the mind of the sleeper ideal imerges'. Patterns, pre-existence, assonances confirm to the mind of the adept (or artist) a fuller meaning to life rooted in the common mind. The Neoplatonist Henry More is much invoked, to help build up this notion of 'Spiritus Mundi', 'the place of images & of all things [that] have been or yet shall be'. By this point, the simulated voice of Leo has effectively become that of 'Ille' in 'Ego Dominus Tuus', reaching out to his alternative daimon. 'I have shared in your joys & sorrows & yet it is only because I am your opposite, your antithesis because I am in all things furthest from your intellect & your will, that I alone am your Interlocutor.' When he adds 'yet do not doubt that I was also Leo Africanus the traveller', it is hard to feel that the creator of the dialogue believes him. The final coda, written as from WBY, admits 'I am not convinced that in this letter there is one sentence that has come from beyond my imagination': in writing it he has tried to make his mind blank (almost as if preparing to receive messages through automatic writing) and to avoid the smooth 'railway tracks' of argument. But there has been no sense of special spiritual illumination or guidance. The imaginary conversation with Leo Africanus ends as irresolutely as it begins. Yet it remains a centrally important examination (if not clarification) of the difficulties besetting him at the end of 1916 – not least because it prepares the way, and rehearses the arguments, of a much more important testament which he wrote immediately afterwards.

The text in question is *Per Amica Silentia Lunae*, written early in 1917 and published the following year, as a short and elegant series of *pensées*. The original name, 'An Alphabet', suggests the basic building-blocks of his personal philosophy, but the chosen title, suggesting reflections in the friendly silence of moonlight, is more apposite. These thoughts, philosophical, speculative, and occasionally autobiographical, are placed between a Prologue and Epilogue addressed to Iseult. Thus his starting-point is alleged to be their joint readings in Catholic writers: but the theme of *Per Amica* is really to be found in a sentence earlier addressed to Leo. 'I do not doubt any more than you did when [among] the alchemists of Fez the existence of God, & I follow tradition stated for the last time explicitly in Swedenborg & in Blake, that his influence descends to us through hierarchies of mediational shades and angels.'[87] WBY himself described it as 'an explanation of the religious convictions & philosophical speculations that I hope govern my life'. It was carefully framed to move from considering the individual creative soul to the world's 'great memory', and to try to define the relationship between the two. The style recalls Pater's lapidary paragraphs, and the book itself is in some ways a return to the question raised in the similarly constructed *Discoveries* a decade before. 'Doing it is a kind of cleansing of one's soul.' 'I used to think', WBY told Gordon Craig when he was writing it, 'when a boy, that no man should be permitted to public life till he had written first: an account of the world to come; second: a practicable scheme for the perfection of this world and sworn to the two.'[88]

Per Amica is also a distillation of the ideas trailed in 'Swedenborg, Mediums, and the Desolate Places' and the manuscript of 'Leo Africanus', building in material from lectures given in America.[89] In its original form, it confronted the ideas of Freud and Jung more specifically than he had done before (though their names were excised for the published versions). It also forecasts the astrological pattern-making on which he would shortly begin to construct *A Vision*.[90] *Per Amica* is constructed, like *Discoveries*, in short aphoristic reflections, and divided into two sections. The first, 'Anima Hominis', is dated 25 February 1917. It begins with the old question of the origins of artistic inspiration, and its relationship with spiritual life: Dante (again, an interest stimulated by his summer readings with Iseult) is a brooding presence. The poem 'Ego Dominus Tuus' is printed as a kind of dedication at the beginning of the volume, and a famous passage on the making of poets reprises some of the queries it raises:

Nor has any poet I have read of or heard of or met with been a sentimentalist. The other self, the anti-self or the antithetical self, as one may choose to name it, comes but to those who are no longer deceived, whose passion is reality. The sentimentalists are practical men who believe in money, in position, in a marriage bell, and whose understanding of happiness is to be so busy whether at work or at play that all is forgotten but the momentary aim. They find their pleasure in a cup that is filled from Lethe's wharf, and for the awakening, for the vision, for the revelation of reality, tradition offers us a different word – ecstasy.[91]

But he also declares, more clearly than ever before, the need to override the passivity induced by Romantic doctrines of 'sincerity and self-realisation', and to cultivate an alter ego that will be masterful and heroic. This can be achieved by meditating on an opposing mask: his reflections on the seeking of opposites, the sense of destiny, and the truth that comes through dreams refine and extend ideas tried out in (and on) 'Leo Africanus'. Here too he draws upon ideas and theories encountered in the course of psychic research. While he had long been conscious of Freud's and Jung's work (initially through Ernest Jones's writings in the *Journal of the Society for Psychical Research*), the ideas he had been reviewing during his reading for 'Swedenborg, Mediums, and the Desolate Places' and 'Leo Africanus' rang some clearer bells: notably, the belief that 'the most minute particulars which enter the memory remain there and are never obliterated'.[92] WBY, however, principally related this to the Platonic theory of recollection, and its employment – or unlocking – through poetry. His long-standing preoccupation with the revelation that comes through dreams (or between waking and sleeping) raised Freudian echoes, but was also a commonplace of occultist experimentation. Section XII confronts the discovery by 'the doctors of medicine . . . that certain dreams of the night, for I do not grant them all, are the day's unfulfilled desire, and that our terror of desires condemned by the conscience has distorted and disturbed our dreams'. In the first draft, this reflection is attributed to 'Dr Freud and his pupils', and Jung's observations on group hysteria are further instanced. However, WBY adds:

I did not get my thought from Freud but from my own observation, & letters from my father that I shall quote presently. Now however that I skim through a couple of books of the Psycho Analysts I find no great difference except in what they call the censor – The dreams they have studied express [?] which the waking man thinks shameful . . . But the dreams of the poet are an illumination of the conscience, & the censor tries rather to exclude our waking life.[93]

WBY prefers to follow unfulfilled spiritual passions into the realm of vision, which brings inspiration: but, again, the path cannot be an easy one. The final section masterfully compresses his ideas of self and anti-self, his reading in Stone Cottage, and his own sense – in his fifty-second year – of incipient age and past experience.

A poet, when he is growing old, will ask himself if he cannot keep his mask and his vision without new bitterness, new disappointment. Could he if he would, knowing how frail his vigour from youth up, copy Landor who lived loving and hating, ridiculous and unconquered, into extreme old age, all lost but the favour of his Muses?

> The Mother of the Muses, we are taught,
> Is Memory; she has left me; they remain,
> And shake my shoulder, urging me to sing.

Surely, he may think, now that I have found vision and mask I need not suffer any longer. He will buy perhaps some small old house, where, like Ariosto, he can dig his garden, and think that in the return of birds and leaves, or moon and sun, and in the evening flight of the rooks he may discover rhythm and pattern like those in sleep and so never awake out of vision. Then he will remember Wordsworth withering into eighty years, honoured and empty-witted, and climb to some waste room and find, forgotten there by youth, some bitter crust.

With the second section, 'Anima Mundi', the theme moves from the personal to the collective unconscious, employing the concept of a common mind, explored through psychic investigation and Neoplatonic reading: 'great memory', as WBY put it, 'passing on from generation to generation'. This was, however, an inadequate concept to express the specificity and familiarity of the images which drifted up from that 'vast luminous sea', at whose shallow edge 'our daily thought was but the line of foam'.[94] Henry More's Platonism, adventures with mediums, spirit photographers, and the folk beliefs of Connacht are all instanced: once again, the ideas aired in 'Leo Africanus' and the essays written for Gregory's book have been polished and faceted into these reflections – brief, beautiful, and obscure. Here too he considers the ideas of 'dreaming back', recurrence and repetition on the spiritual plane, which he had learned about long before, encountered again in Japanese ghost-plays, and would utilize in his own work until the end of his life.

Spiritism, whether of folk-lore or of the séance-room, the visions of Swedenborg, and the speculation of the Platonists and Japanese plays, will have it that we may see at certain roads and in certain houses old murders acted over again, and in certain fields dead huntsmen riding with horse and hound, or ancient armies fighting above bones or ashes. We carry to *Anima Mundi* our memory, and that memory is for a time our external world; and all passionate moments recur again and again, for passion desires its own recurrence more than any event, and whatever there is of corresponding complacency or remorse is our beginning of judgment; nor do we remember only the events of life, for thoughts bred of longing and of fear, all those parasitic vegetables that have slipped through our fingers, come again like a rope's end to smite us upon the face . . . The soul can indeed, it appears, change these objects built about us by the memory, as it may change its shape; but the greater the change, the greater the effort and the sooner the return to the habitual images.[95]

The argument recapitulates the ideas in 'Leo Africanus' about the dependence of disembodied spirits upon their own memories and the energies and intuitions of the living. Pound had drawn his attention to a resonant line in *The Odyssey*, 'the departing soul hovers about as a dream', and WBY was also struck by the connection between spirit existence and memory postulated in Henry More's *The Immortality of the Soul*, which he was reading at this time.[96] One section of *Per Amica* that was written later echoes the thought of 'The Cold Heaven':

Awhile they live again those passionate moments, not knowing they are dead, and then they know and may awake or half awake to be our visitors. How is their dream changed as time drops away and their senses multiply? Does their stature alter, do their eyes grow more brilliant? Certainly the dreams stay the longer, the greater their passion when alive: Helen may still open her chamber door to Paris or watch him from the wall, and know she is dreaming but because nights and days are poignant or the stars unreckonably bright. Surely of the passionate dead we can but cry in words Ben Jonson meant for none but Shakespeare: 'So rammed' are they 'with life they can but grow in life with being.'[97]

Much of this seems sonorously plangent but deliberately vague. It eventually becomes clear that WBY is finding reasons for the unsatisfactory nature of much mediumistic communication, and the openness of seances to accusations of imposture. The state of the disembodied minds, slipping in and out of different time-systems, the volatile and malleable nature of their memories as they interpenetrate those of the living, the sense of repetition, familiarity, and déjà vu, make the spirits vulnerable rather than authoritative. 'We bewilder and overmaster them, for once they are among the perceptions of successive objects, our reason, being but an instrument created and sharpened by those objects, is stronger than their intellect, and they can but repeat, with brief glimpses from another state, our knowledge and our words.'[98] Towards the end, inevitably, he reverts to autobiography and self-analysis, circling around a particular instance of grace, which he would remember again fifteen years later in 'Vacillation'.

At certain moments, always unforeseen, I become happy, most commonly when at hazard I have opened some book of verse. Sometimes it is my own verse when, instead of discovering new technical flaws, I read with all the excitement of the first writing. Perhaps I am sitting in some crowded restaurant, the open book beside me, or closed, my excitement having over-brimmed the page. I look at the strangers near as if I had known them all my life, and it seems strange that I cannot speak to them: everything fills me with affection, I have no longer any fears or any needs; I do not even remember that this happy mood must come to an end. It seems as if the vehicle had suddenly grown pure and far extended and so luminous that the images from *Anima Mundi*, embodied there and drunk with that sweetness, would, like a country drunkard who has thrown a wisp into his own thatch, burn up time.

It may be an hour before the mood passes, but latterly I seem to understand that I enter upon it the moment I cease to hate. I think the common condition of our life is hatred – I know this is so with me – irritation with public or private events or persons.[99]

Reading *Per Amica* a year later, AE was unimpressed. 'It has a kind of distinguished remoteness from reality, but I do not think for all its distinguished style the philosophy is either fine or deep. He is best at poetry.' JBY despaired of ever understanding it, 'at least with my reason – but in time I shall get his "points of view".' Gordon Bottomley, writing to Sturge Moore, was more effusive. 'He enchants, entrances, charms me and makes me feel on every new occasion as I did twenty years ago, how grateful I am to him for showing me of what an exquisite, enriched yet mystery-stirring precision my native language is capable'.[100] This was another way of saying that WBY employed exact and didactic language to convey extremely cloudy concepts. 'Precision' might not seem the *mot juste* to everybody.

But the book, while it casts forward and back through WBY's supernatural preoccupations, is also about his life in the early spring of 1917.[101] Strikingly (and here too the influence of Colleville rather than Coole is ascendant) the language approaches more closely to religiosity than is usual for WBY, particularly in the first draft. As published, Section V of 'Anima Hominis' begins with one of his most famous aphorisms: 'We make out of the quarrel with others, rhetoric, but of the quarrel with ourselves, poetry.' In the manuscript it continues 'or if we have a moral sense, sanctity', but this is later cancelled. In an early draft too the phrase 'Anima Mundi' often appears as 'Spiritus Mundi', which was perhaps changed to tilt the tone towards Jungian psychology rather than religion. And the concluding paragraph of the Epilogue (originally a 'Prologue') dedicated to Iseult (called by her chosen pseudonym 'Maurice') addresses the question of religion and tradition. Iseult's love of Péguy and Claudel reminds him of his own early devotion to Mallarmé and Verlaine, and WBY recalls his encounters in 1890s Paris with initiates and would-be magi; and though the new Catholic poets look to 'Mother France and Mother Church' rather than to 'the soul, self-moving and self-teaching', he can understand this too. However, he originally wrote, 'I have not found my tradition in the Catholic Church, for in Ireland to a man of my descent the Catholic Church with its Guido Renyi [*sic*] and its manuals does not now seem very traditional.' This did not quite pass muster at Colleville. Iseult warned him that she found his remarks 'extremely puzzling', while 'Moura, of course, was a little shocked by what you say of Catholic tradition in Ireland.'[102] For publication WBY accordingly watered it down: 'Have not my thoughts run through a like round, though I have not found my tradition in the Catholic Church, which was not the Church of my childhood, but where the tradition is, as I believe, more universal and more ancient?' Finished April–May 1917, the Epilogue stamps this book (magical in more ways than one) as a gift to Iseult, rather as he had dedicated his poetic notebook 'The Flame of the Spirit' to her mother before she was born.[103] And, by another strange stroke of symmetry, *Per Amica Silentia Lunae* would play an important part in dictating a new body of occult revelation, which would come to him through another woman before the year was out.

The writing of *Per Amica* may be mapped through WBY's search during the early spring of 1917 for proofs of psychic certainty. On 8 February Arnold Bennett encountered him at a seance with Peters, organized by Madame Lalla Vandervelde: Roger Fry was also one of the party, and Bennett was deeply impressed by Peters's telepathic recognitions associated with selected objects.[104] Moreover, WBY had just embarked upon one of his most bizarre and credulous involvements yet. He discovered that David Wilson, a mildly deranged chemist (and part-time solicitor) in St Leonards-on-Sea had constructed a machine which received and amplified voices from the spirit world. 'It seems', wrote Wilson with modest pride, 'to constitute a kind of ear-hole into the unknown region.'[105] The Society for Psychical Research commissioned an investigative report. By early February WBY had visited Wilson and been instantly converted. 'The more I think it over the more clear is it to me that you may have made the greatest discovery of the modern world. Even the elixir of life seems possible.'[106]

The cause of this excitement was an apparatus which Wilson described as 'a kind of syntonizer between and [*sic*] incarnate and discarnate intelligences', by means of electricity and 'metallic medium'. WBY christened it 'the metallic homunculus'. It could allegedly 'listen in' to messages and overheard conversations from the Other Side, identify secretly marked playing-cards, produce coded sounds, and make pictures, but it was unfortunately prone to interference from mischievous spirits ('little beasts', Wilson briskly called them).[107] The inventor had been an assistant to the Nobel Prize-winning physicist and inveterate psychic sleuth, Sir William Crookes, which may have enhanced his credibility in WBY's eyes. However, Wilson's chief obsession was financial rather than spiritual: he was convinced the homunculus would make his fortune, and WBY readily agreed to help raise money for its development. But there were complications. An article about Wilson in *Light*, the journal of the College of Psychic Studies, recklessly revealed that he had received a message in German. The police descended and impounded the machine as an illegal wireless, forcing WBY to intercede with Gerald Balfour and highly placed contacts at the Home Office. But the chief need was to convince others. WBY told Wilson that the opinion of Dulac would carry great weight and so would that of Radclyffe Hall – 'a rich, able woman who is giving all her time to psychic research' and who was considering putting money into the invention. On 13 February he tried to get the formidable novelist, known to her intimates as 'John', to invest, but she was not an easy proposition. Her lover Una Troubridge fondly recorded, 'Yeats writhing like an unhappy Irish beetle upon the pins of John's business attitude,' and he came away empty-handed.[108] Dulac, WBY, and Sir Edward Denison Ross (a scholar of Persian, who founded and directed the School of Oriental Languages) all inspected the apparatus, and Ross addressed it in varieties of Arabic. The homunculus proved to be well connected, introducing John Dee, Paracelsus, Oscar Wilde, and the inevitable Leo. To WBY's pleasure, 'all seemed anxious for us to know that there was a universal mind and that if we spoke to them, it was as but links with this mind'.

In late March WBY worked through his notes; on 4 April he lectured to the Ghost Club in London about Wilson; but he was becoming less convinced that the invention was 'the greatest event of the modern world' after checking the credentials of various tests it had been put through. Wilson himself remained 'in a state of violent excitement and thinks that his machine is going to make an immense Fortune'.[109] His plans were, however, short-circuited by conscription, and he subsequently disappeared from history, without becoming rich. 'His instrument is now out of reach till the war is over,' WBY wrote regretfully in the summer. 'It did wonderful things but I was only just starting my investigation to prove what degree of independence it had from David Wilson's own organism. Did personal mediumship act through it, as through a moving table which moves without physical contact with the medium, or was the machine as David Wilson beleives, it self the medium? I do not know.'[110] But the strange adventure demonstrates that the questions which he had raised in 'Leo Africanus' and *Per Amica Silentia Lunae*, especially the reflections on muffled or scrambled messages from the dead, were not only for philosophical discussion. They dominated his everyday life, and he lived in the hope and prospect of revelation.[111]

IV

These frenzied enthusiasms coincided with a burst of creative energy, and possibly sustained it: at the very time WBY was telling David Wilson that his invention might change the world, he was writing to Gregory that he could send her a new poem called 'The Swans' 'in a day or two'.[112] This became 'The Wild Swans at Coole' ('Wild' being added at a comparatively late stage), the title poem of his next collection and one of his supreme achievements. By early April he would provide Pound with no less than eight new poems for the American *Little Review* – later reduced to seven, appearing in the June number, but all in Pound's view 'Excellent'.[113] Cannily, they were also placed with Clement Shorter in the *Sphere*. The suite of poems on Mabel Beardsley were offered to Harriet Monroe, but – to her annoyance – WBY decided the payment she offered was inadequate; and they appeared in the *Little Review* in August.[114] (The incident helped close Pound's stormy but influential career as 'Foreign Correspondent' for *Poetry*.) WBY now knew his worth, and others knew it too. When Macmillan published the extended version of *Responsibilities* late in 1916, JBY noted the reaction. 'I can see by these critiques that Willie is now a classic, a sort of sovereign poet & anointed King. This is new to me in criticism of his work.'[115] But 'Easter 1916' stayed unpublished, and so did the other 'Rebellion poems', such as 'The Rose Tree', which he wrote in April 1917. In May, when AE tried to get his backing for the initiative which produced a 'Convention of Irishmen' determined to negotiate the continuing political impasse, WBY stayed cautious. 'I do not want to take a political part however slight in haste so he will perhaps have to do without my name.'[116]

Still, he was possessed by the need to fix himself. 'The Wild Swans at Coole', drafted in February 1917 and published in the June *Little Review*, is a poem – written in sublimely plain language – about alienation, belonging, companionship, and love. The lyric's apparent simplicity emerged from intensive redrafting and distillation, and its intellectual descent is also more complex than might appear: the central theme and image echo a passage of *Alastor*, and reflect the attention WBY had been paying, yet again, to Shelley and, perhaps, less typically, to Wordsworth.[117] But, more personally, the lyrics commemorate the passing of time and the fact that he had been seeking solace by Gregory's lake among the seven woods for nearly twenty years.

> The trees are in their autumn beauty
> The woodland paths are dry
> Under the October twilight the water
> Mirrors a still sky
> Upon the brimming water among the stones
> Are nine and fifty swans.
>
> The nineteenth autumn has come upon me
> Since I first made my count.
> I saw, before I had well finished,
> All suddenly mount
> And scatter wheeling in great broken rings
> Upon their clamorous wings.

As written, and first published in the *Little Review*, the next stanza runs:

> But now they drift on the still water
> Mysterious, beautiful;
> Among what rushes will they build;
> By what lake's edge or pool
> Delight men's eyes when I awake some day
> To find they have flown away?

The last two verses focus on the observer, his loneliness, and – implicitly – his lack of a mate.

> I have looked upon these brilliant creatures
> And now my heart is sore.
> All's changed since I, hearing at twilight
> The first time on this shore
> The bell-beat of their wings above my head,
> Trod with a lighter tread.[118]

> Unwearied still, lover by lover,
> They paddle in the cold
> Companionable streams or climb the air;
> Their hearts have not grown old,
> Passion or conquest, wander where they will,
> Attend upon them still.

Thus the original poem ends on the note of the poet's lost youth and passion; whereas, when WBY rearranged it for subsequent publication, he shifts the attention to the mysterious swans, and the impossibility of eternalizing the present. The climax of the poem now invokes the poet's future, rather than his past. It is a decisive change, not only radically improving the poem but signalling an alteration in WBY's mood between the summer of 1917 and the autumn. This in turn reflected a change of circumstances.

He felt the need to root himself, and had done so in the most concrete way possible by at last buying a house. He had already extended his holding at Woburn Buildings. 'The drunken lady in the rooms under Yeats set the place on fire and has been kicked out,' Pound had reported in May 1916, 'so he has taken on the floor, painted the stairs sky blue, ordered a large board table like mine, and Woburn Blds. is shaken to its foundation.'[119] The aesthetic effects did not stop there: in his new study the floor and woodwork were promptly painted black, and the room hung with orange. But the lease of the whole building had only a few years to run, and the neighbouring Gwalia Hotel wanted to take it over. WBY was already reflecting on the need to return to Ireland 'and begin building again'. Edward Martyn offered him Dungory Castle for nothing, if he repaired it, but WBY had already fixed his interest on the abandoned castle keep built by the powerful de Burgo clan three miles north-east of Gort, with its attached cottage.

By the autumn of 1916 he was negotiating directly for Ballylee with the Congested Districts Board, which now owned it, the farmland having been disposed of to the tenants. The tower is probably sixteenth century, though its origins may go back to the fourteenth century and WBY certainly liked to date it earlier ('The Normans had form, Gogarty, the Normans had form').[120] Up to the turn of the twentieth century the old tower had been the home of the Spellman family; before that, the adjoining cottage had been built by a nineteenth-century master of Loughrea Workhouse for his young family, while he occupied two floors of the tower. It had been inhabited when WBY discovered it in 1898 or 1899, searching for stories about the local beauty Mary Hynes. But by 1916 it had fallen heavily into disrepair. For a derelict tower with no acreage, in the wake of a rebellion and in the midst of world war, it was hardly a seller's market. In October he had written to the ubiquitous W. F. Bailey, clearly stating his position, and Bailey forwarded the letter to Sir Henry Doran at the Land Commission.

For years I have coveted Ballylee Castle, on this property [Coole], or what was this property and which has now been bought by the C. D. B. It has got a tolerably good roof on it, good rough old Elizabethan chimney pieces, and I could restore it to some of its original stern beauty and have a place to keep my pictures and my books. At present it is worth nothing to anybody, and will soon become ruinous, and that will make the neighbourhood the poorer of romance. Now I want to know if I could get it from the Congested Districts Board. The tenant who had possession of it says he hears they are going to lock it up. He says also that a couple of acres have been kept with it, which would be useful to keep a few trees which are there now from being cut down. I might not be able to live there for some little time, but I should be sorry if I found it had been possible to get it and that it had slipped away. You would do me a great service if you would find out informally if such a purchase was possible. I need not say I could not give much for it, especially as I should have to lay out money in doing it up.[121]

Doran authorized the purchase, and by November WBY was negotiating with the Congested Districts Board about boundaries and price. He went over the castle with a local builder on 19 November, and by the end of the year knew that he would need to spend twice as much as he had intended – £200 or £300 to put on a roof and make it habitable.[122] The romantic position, down a small valley on a tiny island made by a tributary of the rushing river variously called the Ballylee, the Turra, and the Cloon, meant that floods were endemic; floor levels had to be raised and doors altered. Pound, unforgivably, referred to it as WBY's 'phallic symbol on the bogs – Ballyphallus or whatever he calls it with the river on the first floor'.[123] Though two of the floors were sound, another needed rebuilding, and it was roofless; but, to WBY's delight, the 'winding stair' (which he mentioned frequently in describing the building) was perfect, and there was a gargoyle's head fixed high on one wall. The cost of the fee simple was estimated at no more than £25, since the building was effectively a ruin, but the Board wanted £80.

Obsessed though he was, WBY bargained as hard as he knew: a romantic Yeats gesture was pursued with Pollexfen hard-headedness. He was suffering 'an attack of nerves financially', since his publishing income had declined with the war. He had already had to borrow from Gregory again, to tide over an awkward patch. His extended Woburn Building holding cost £50 a year. An inheritance of £35 from Uncle Alfred was earmarked for Ballylee, but got swallowed up by the cost of his election to the Savile Club and the plates for the illustrations to *Reveries*.[124] But he knew he could sell something, or make money by an American tour; the tower could be done up slowly 'but rather well, that I may keep the sentiment of the past'. Dulac offered to decorate the rooms for nothing. The negotiations dragged on through February and March, complicated by the Board's wish to bring a road across the island by two bridges, establishing a right of way. WBY was driven nearly demented: 'I did not sleep till seven this morning with worrying over Ballylee,' he told Gregory on 1 March. However, he accepted the new road for the aesthetic reason that it meant 'some picturesque old stepping stones' could be kept: they appear in Robert Gregory's atmospheric drawing of the castle, which WBY had reproduced as a postcard in April.[125] More pragmatically, since the bridge interfered with the property, the price came down. On 27 March he accepted it for £35, exactly the sum of Alfred's legacy. Sligo had made possible a purchase on Galway.

He delegated the final negotiations to Gregory. By the beginning of June she had taken formal possession on his behalf and sent on to him the 'seisin', or symbols of possession: a bunch of grass from the field, a handful of thatch from the cottage, a stone from the castle wall, and two florins from the sale of a fallen tree. At the Savile Club on 30 June 1917, WBY signed the deed of sale, which stipulated a public right of way through the yard. Ballylee also gave him a purchase on Coole. Gregorys had owned it, Robert had drawn it, even the Gort builder was Michael Rafferty, whom WBY decided must be related to Raftery, the great local poet whose life Gregory and WBY had commemorated in the distant early days of their relationship twenty years before. And from early April he deluged her with inquiries and suggestions. Should the cottage be saved by a buttress ('Margaret seems to have a prejudice against buttresses whereas I having seen them upon cottage walls in Ireland, all my life, think of them as an added beauty, a gift of antiquity')? Could Margaret provide a scale-drawing, which he could bring to the Society for the Preservation of Ancient Buildings to get free advice? Could a temporary tarpaulin roof be made ('they put a tarred tarpaulin upon Wagner's theatre in '75 and it is still there')? Would his books be safe?[126]

Gregory's less romantic demurrals were briskly rejected ('You certainly cannot wash your face from the Castle walls in summer. All those heavy old walls "sweat" a little'). His bank could advance £200, which would enable a floor, a roof, doors, and windows. He had chosen a Dublin architect, William Scott, an Arts and Crafts enthusiast who specialized in restorations, was approved of by Martyn (the local expert on castles), and had executed several ecclesiastical buildings around Galway. By July the roof was going on. WBY found that the bank could now give him an overdraft of £300, after he had spent £200 making the cottage habitable; and he had £90 in the bank after paying the Board their £35 in June. 'He already feels such an Irish landlord that he has begun by putting a mortgage on it,' Gregory remarked drily to Quinn.[127] So he suddenly had an overwhelming reason to make money. He gave fee-paying lectures in Dublin, and started planning an American tour, possibly speaking on Blake, Calvert, and Palmer – with illuminated slides. 'Binyon lectured with slides in America – it is quite dignified.'[128]

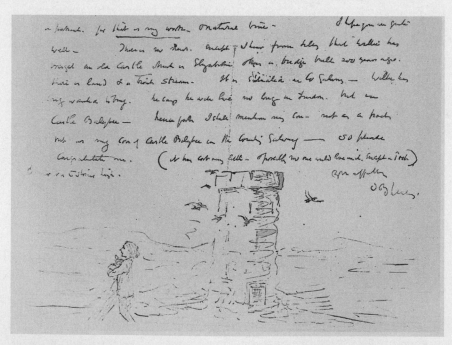

2. 'He says he will live no longer in London but in Castle Ballylee – henceforth I shall mention my son – not as a poet but as my son of Castle Ballylee in the County Galway – so please congratulate me. (It has cost very little – & possibly no-one could live in it. Except a Poet.)' JBY to Julia Ford, 21 November 1916.

His family watched with amused pleasure. 'So Willie owns landed property – & a castle,' JBY wrote delightedly to Gregory. 'Lolly sends the words, is he asking "Where are the Butlers now?"'[129] There was, indeed, a sense of historic repossession in this great step. And though he could not yet know the wealth of symbols and associations Ballylee would provide, its possession clarified a sense of insufficiency in his personal life. This was clearly expressed by WBY in a letter to Farr: 'I am fifty one myself & do not like it [at] all & keep thinking of all the follies I have committed not to have somebody to talk to after night fall & to bring me gossip of the neighbours. Especially now that I am going to own a castle and a whole acre of land.'[130] On several occasions he mentioned spending the summers in his castle with 'a friend'. In March he expanded on the subject to Gregory: 'Ballylee may be very necessary to me. The truth is my domestic arrangements here seem to be broken up. I have had a slight difference with G. W. [?] & this brought things to an end (you might if you keep this letter blot out this part).'[131] The 'G. W.' is not blotted out, but it clearly began life as other initials, and was tactfully disguised by Gregory. It does not seem to fit Iseult. Given his renewed visits to the Tuckers at this time, it could be a reference to his on-off flirtation with Nelly's daughter, Georgie Hyde Lees. But he had continued his association with Alick Schepeler: the initials have been read as 'O. S.', and could be 'A. S.'. Through spiritualist investigations he had met Lalla Vandervelde (wife of the Belgian ambassador), with whom he had a dalliance, but his thoughts came back to a more settled relationship, and he as usual confided in Coole. On 13 June Gregory wrote about his Ballylee plans: 'With the prospect of your marriage question being settled within the next few months, it seems a pity not to consult your "comrade's" inclinations before plunging into expense.' His reply reiterated his commitment to the castle above all. 'If I marry', he wrote on 20 June, 'my London arrangements will depend on my wife, if I do not I should take two rooms at £25 a year.'[132] And as the summer of 1917 approached, so did the prospect of a reunion with the Gonnes by the Normandy seaside.

And if Ballylee stood for a more settled future life, it also meant a fuller commitment to Ireland: a feeling that had grown upon him since the news of the Rising the eventful year before. He was anxious not to be drawn too far into Abbey matters, wanting to withdraw to 'a slight connection . . . getting a Dublin board of governors to take over the general management and the financial management. I would then be free to raise some money to carry out, on the Abbey boards, experiments that interest *me*, and belong to my own art.'[133] But this old dream would remain, for the moment, unfulfilled. Political tensions in Dublin necessitated careful selection of productions. The Convention continued to meet, but public opinion was tilting in

Sinn Féin's direction: the barometer was set by election of the 1916 survivor Eamon de Valera as MP for Clare in July. WBY was – as he had warned – a notable absentee from a letter to the *Irish Times* supporting AE's 'Thoughts for a Convention' – a manifesto on behalf of a pluralist solution to the national problem, 'aiming at a diversity of culture, and the greatest freedom, richness and diversity of thought'.[134] He had endorsed exactly these principles on numerous past occasions, but caution ruled in the summer of 1917. He would 'risk' putting on *The Parnellite* at the Abbey because it was agrarian in theme, rather than a Sinn Féin tract; but *Cathleen ni Houlihan* would be, under present circumstances, politically electric. His own politics were to be kept private, he told Ellen Duncan, while he was 'in negotiation' over the Lane pictures;[135] but he had by now written 'The Rose Tree', a ballad about the Easter sacrifice which endorsed Pearse and Connolly more clearly than had 'Easter 1916', and he would shortly begin his play *The Dreaming of the Bones*, which linked the rebel cause back to the twelfth-century Norman invasion – Fenian teleology in Noh form. 'The best play I have written for years,' he told Gregory: '& I am afraid only too powerful politically.'[136]

Much of it had been written at Coole, where he settled in late April, staying on through May. William Scott came down to prepare drawings for Ballylee, and the legal transfer of ownership took place in June. WBY had planned to renovate the cottage first, but Scott was impatient to get to work on the castle (fortunately, since he drank heavily and had only a year to live). There were four floors in the tower, of one room each, connected by the celebrated winding stair embedded in the seven-foot-thick wall; an additional flight of steps led to the battlemented roof level. A second cottage was planned, and furniture and ironwork commissioned locally. All this would be expensive, and WBY threw himself into work. He was revising, yet again, *The Player Queen*; Mrs Patrick Campbell complained that he had delayed it 'till her jaw sagged with age'.[137] But he was also working on the new play, rewriting the second part of 'Anima Mundi' for the book which he still thought would be called *The Alphabet*, and planning the arrangement of his new collection, to be called 'The Swans at Coole'. 'It will be published in Autumn and be among my best books.' 'The book of poems you must not send for review,' he warned Lolly, 'about the other I am not quite sure yet. I might have to take advice.'[138]

The traditional routine of 'order and labour' at Coole was enhanced by the plans for renovating Ballylee, so his return to London at the end of May was all the more debilitating. He had firm instructions from Gregory to lobby James Craig and other Irish MPs about the Lane pictures, which he dutifully did, even visiting the House of Commons in hopes of an unscheduled interview – though he dolefully warned her 'this is a technique I do not understand & I feel helpless'. Though Craig was helpful, others were not. Lloyd George remained elusive, and WBY was driven to considering an approach through 'Julia James his very pretty light comedy actress'.[139] But his mind was elsewhere: renaming his philosophical treatise, choosing illustrations for a projected book of his verse plays (Dulac's masks and costumes for *At the Hawk's Well* had been glamorously reproduced in *Harper's Bazaar* for March 1917), and longing to return to Galway. Afflicted by exhaustion, the London heat, and indigestion, at the end of June he gloomily warned Gregory that he 'might break down like my brother unless I get back to routine'.[140] He was also deeply saddened by the news of Florence Farr's death, after her long struggle with cancer. She had told him of her mastectomy in one of her inimitable letters, but assured him the tumour was benign; only to her other old friend and lover, Shaw, did she outline the seriousness of her condition. Ceylon had, in the end, given her much of what she wanted. She had, she told Shaw a year earlier, spent her time there liberating herself from 'barriers' including 'my secret horror of death, I mean of the death-bed scene – I have been through it once or twice & it's nothing after all'.[141] Her death, like Mabel Beardsley's, marked a divide between WBY's present life and his 1890s youth, soon to furnish another section of the memorial frieze of his autobiography.

In the immediate present he was under pressure to make money for Ballylee. At the end of May he was excited by an approach from the University of Edinburgh: a lectureship at £300 a year, for six lectures only, which could be given over a few weeks. It would be a guaranteed income and remove the need for American tours.[142] However, nothing came of it, and with the imminent prospect of America entering the war, the New York agent James Pond warned him that there was no point in arranging a tour. He made some money by selling some of his own first editions to Yale University, but he needed more. Another prospect was raised in late June by his old acquaintance, the journalist George Mair, who had married Synge's fiancée Molly Allgood in 1911 and was now a publicity officer at the Foreign Office. He suggested a series of four lectures in France under the auspices of the FO, to be given in September, for a fee of £40. There was the additional inducement of facilitating a wartime passport.[143] WBY offered three trusty familiars – one on 'Synge and Ireland', and two on the poets of his own generation – but proposed a fourth on 'Ireland Today': he explained it as a political, literary, and social survey of modern Ireland, which would 'clear up my own mind'.[144] This intriguing project never came off, though WBY was still planning it in the autumn. For one thing, the Foreign Office took fright at 'Ireland Today' and suggested a lecture on Blake instead, to WBY's relief. But it supplied yet another reason for caution on WBY's part when it came to publishing 'Easter 1916' (now privately printed by Shorter), 'The Rose Tree', or *The Dreaming of the Bones*.

In early July he managed to return to Ireland. In Dublin he stayed, for the first time, with Gogarty in his large town house at Ely Place, adjacent to the premises that had once housed AE's Theosophist commune, which the two young mystics had decorated with murals so many years before. AE, indeed, called in on him at Gogarty's and so did Douglas Hyde and James Stephens; and WBY sat for a bust by the young sculptor Albert Power, commissioned by his host. The subject found it 'admirable . . . I look rather humorous and intellectual than poetical'.[145] Fortified, he went on to Coole and his castle, where he spent a fortnight. He also attended a committee meeting for the founding of a new 'Society of Irish Tradition', an ecumenically inclined organization celebrating matters like folklore and Gaelic culture in a determinedly unpolitical way and, given the temper of the times, doomed to speedy extinction.[146] But he was back in London on 27 July, arranging publication of a distinguished group of poems in the *Sphere* – they included the 'Dying Lady' sequence about Mabel Beardsley, 'Ego Dominus Tuus', 'Presences', and 'A Thought from Propertius'. The Macmillan publication of *Per Amica* was planned, with a beautiful Sturge Moore cover depicting a mystic rose. But his sojourn in London was intentionally brief. On 3 August he travelled to Paris; by 7 August he was once again in Gonne's house at Colleville, drawn there – and possibly summoned – by Iseult rather than by her mother.

Her letters through the winter had continued – lengthy, introspective, expressing ardent friendship and literary homage in between earnest discussions of Rudolf Steiner. 'Whatever happens, Willie, you are wrong to say that I shall gradually forget that I am your pupil (and your teacher??).'[147] Their 'common memory' kept them near while apart; it provided 'gold' that she played with in solitude, like a miser; she thought of him 'continually'. He must have arrived in a fever of expectation. While he worked on the lectures he expected to give in September, and his head throbbed 'full with poems',[148] his reasons for being there were primarily emotional, as Gregory well knew. 'It will be a great excitement to you going to France', she wrote, '& being fetched in so romantic a way – I am sure you will be glad to be out of London for a while and see things in perspective – and I hope the expedition may be all for the good.'[149] Rumours that WBY and Iseult were to marry had been circulating in Dublin since the previous winter, but WBY told Gregory on 12 August that though they were 'on our old intimate terms', she was disinclined to accept him. All would remain undecided until they parted. Gonne, moreover, 'is no longer bitter and she and Iseult are on good terms now and life goes on smoothly'.[150]

But beneath the surface tensions were building; nor was WBY as resigned as he claimed to be. In the third summer of the war, conditions were deteriorating. The Colleville household depended for food on the vegetable garden planted at Easter, and torpedoed fish washed up on the beach, while at night the house shook with the reverberations of naval bombardment. Gonne was temporarily exhausted. 'You I believe still see beauty in war,' she wrote to Quinn. 'I did once but hospitals and broken hearts and devastation and destruction of all art and beauty have changed me and I bow to any peace advocate.'[151] She set herself to planning her return to Ireland, bringing a resentful Iseult with her: WBY's suggestion that the latter would be better off in London caused, he admitted, one of the few violent outbursts from Gonne. On 28 August the household removed to Paris: the Gonnes to their temporary flat in Passy, WBY to the Hôtel Gavarni near by.[152] From here he wrote urgently to Elizabeth Radcliffe for guidance: had her controls received messages about him? While Gonne tried to arrange her return to Ireland, against the reluctance of the authorities to release such a well-known 'agitator' into the political crucible, WBY continued to agonize about his future. After a week in Paris he wrote to Gregory:

I am really getting ready a mass of work to start on in Dublin and London if I can make some settlement in my life. I am just now too restless. Iseult has always been something like a daughter to me & so I am less upset than I might have been – I am chiefly unhappy about her general prospects. Just at the moment she is in one of her alarming moods – deep meloncholy & apathy, the result of having left the country – and is always accusing herself of sins – sins of omission not of comission – She has a horoscope that makes me dread melancholia. Only in the country is she amused & free of this mood for long. Maud Gonne on the other hand is in a joyous & self forgetting condition of political hate the like of which I have not yet encountered. As soon as I reach London I shall be in the midst of another crisis of my affairs, (about which I need not write for the possible eye of the censor,) so you must not expect to get much good of me for a while.[153]

On 14 September the Gonne–MacBride family, accompanied by WBY, set off for London.[154] Gonne, still considered a severe security risk, was detained and humiliatingly searched at Southampton, while WBY raged and complained – an incident she remembered with fury all her life. Under the Defence of the Realm Act they were forbidden to travel on to Ireland. So they stopped in London. The Gonnes occupied Woburn Buildings, while WBY stayed at the Arts Club, in Dover Street. On 20 September Pound could report to Quinn: 'Yeats is back from Paris bringing Maude Gonne, 10 canary birds, 1 parrot, 1 monkey, 1 cat, two members of MG's family, and the hope that she will lead a tranquil life.'[155]

Pound, as usual, was slightly off the mark. Maud was no longer upper-most in WBY's thoughts, and he was still uncertain where he stood with Iseult. But the 'crisis of my affairs' which he had expected to break on his return to London was located elsewhere. As soon as he returned his old acquaintance Nelly Tucker invited him to a house she had rented near Ashdown Forest – prompted by a letter he had sent her from France. They had kept in touch through Olivia Shakespear and had encountered each other at Eva Fowler's Kent cottage in the summer of 1915; while Nelly's daughter, Georgie Hyde Lees, had helped WBY's occult researches the fol-lowing winter, met him regularly through her closest friend, Dorothy Pound, and drawn close to him in the spring of 1917. After a summer of rebuffs and dislocations, and temperamentally exhausted by the proximity of the raging Maud and irresolute Iseult, it is not surprising that WBY took refuge in these supportive and admiring circles, wrapped in seances and reassurances, rather than in the histrionics of Colleville and Passy.

But Gregory alone seems to have been prepared for just how decisive that turning away would be. On 18 September, just after the traumatic journey from Paris, he wrote to her of Iseult's depression: at Le Havre she 'went off by herself & cried. Because she was so ashamed "at being so selfish" "in not wanting me to marry & so break her friendship with me." I need hardly say she had said nothing to me of "not wanting". Meanwhile she has not fal-tered in her refusal of me but as you can imagine life is a good deal at white heat.' He added that he now was uncertain about going to Mrs Tucker's, since the prohibition on Iseult's travelling to Ireland changed matters: 'I wrote to Mrs Tucker from France thinking that Iseult was going to Dublin & that I would not see her for months', but now she would need his presence in London, as 'Maud Gonne will certainly do something wild'. He asked for a letter of advice, which Gregory obligingly provided.

You are certainly in a muddle, but 'it's well to be off with the old love before you are on with the new' and I don't feel as if you could go straight off and engage yourself to another in the present state of affairs. You could not do so with a quiet mind, & that would be a bad beginning. I rather think you ought to tell Mrs Tucker simply of the political difficulty, and that you do not like to leave while you may be needed or of use.[156]

It crossed with a short and agonized note, dated 19 September, bearing the news which she alone among WBY's friends may have expected.

I wrote you a very disturbed letter yesterday. Since writing I have decided to be what some Indian calls 'true of voice'. I am going to Mrs Tuckers in the country on Saturday or Monday at latest and I will ask her daughter to marry me. Perhaps she is tired of the idea. I shall however make it clear that I will still be friend and guardian to Iseult. Last night Maud Gonne returned to that strange conviction of hers that Iseult is my child because when Iseult was born she was full of my ideas. Perhaps at that time Maud Gonne was in love with me. I have seen Iseult today and am doing as she wishes. All last night the darkness was full of writing now on stone, now on paper, now on parchment but I could not read it. Were spirits trying to communicate? I prayed a great deal & beleive I am doing right.[157]

Chapter 3 : THE SENSE OF HAPPINESS
1917–1919

'A woman who marries an artist,' he said with much animation,
'is either a goose, or mad, or a hero. If she's a goose, she drives
him to earn money. If she's mad, she drives him mad. If she's
a hero, they suffer together, and they come out all right.'

Francis Hackett's recollection of a conversation
with wby in March 1914[1]

I

wby's decision to go down to the Tuckers' rented house in Crowborough on 24 September and formally propose to Georgie Hyde Lees appears a sudden swerve of direction, and the subsequent marriage struck his friends like a thunderbolt. When the news eventually broke, Susan Mitchell was phoned at once by Lily. 'She got me to repeat it, and then said "The telephone has burst!"'[2] But from the point of view of the prospective bride (first rechristened 'George' by Ezra, which wby determinedly adopted), it was the culmination of a long and often agonizing flirtation. Nor were the agonies over yet. In subsequent intensive analysis of critical moments in their joint lives, the date of May 1913 is identified as romantically climactic for them both; it also relates to the joint supernatural investigations which marked their relationship from its origins, and would decisively influence their marriage. Long afterwards wby told a later lover that George had been more or less 'reared' to be his wife by Nelly Tucker and Olivia Shakespear, who directed her interests towards mysticism as a preparation; he apparently claimed they had been alone together only once before they became engaged. This seems to be a self-interested version. In November 1915 wby's attentions had been so marked that George's mother, Nelly, half expected a proposal.[3] A younger cousin and confidante of George, Grace Jaffe, had been told in secret at around this time of her intention to marry wby, responding, unforgivably, with 'George . . . you can't. He must be dead.'[4] The upheavals of 1916 had intervened, but he was back in touch with the family in March 1917, before the summer in France and his mounting obsession with Iseult: again, a date of special romantic significance for George. wby's choice of bride was not a sudden 'rebound'; but his treatment of her was insensitive and opportunist, and he reproached himself with this in the difficult weeks after their wedding. She, however, judiciously put up with it, and was rewarded. It would help fix the pattern of their marriage.

94

She knew, by and large, what she was taking on. Just about to turn twenty-five, she had grown up moving from place to place, the child of a separated mother (whose marriage to Olivia Shakespear's art-collecting brother did not take place until George was nineteen). Nelly Tucker came from the Woodmass family, who were noted for a strong strain of unconventionality, feuds between mothers and daughters, artistic tastes, and ample money: much of it by now diverted elsewhere. Her daughter, George, was wise beyond her years. Her assured place in the Shakespear circle meant that she must have known of Olivia's history with WBY, and, through Dorothy Pound, most of Ezra's gossip about 'the Eagle' would have been promptly relayed. She had been fascinated by him since their first meeting in 1911, though she recalled a strange foreboding when she had glimpsed him for the first time.[5] The fact that she was less than half WBY's age does not mean that she was either ingenuous or naive: though a private and even secretive person, her more unbuttoned letters show a fierce, slangy wit and a brisk impatience with pious cant or convention for its own sake. Thirty years later she speculated that her own supposedly 'sanguinary' temperament was 'attracted to the neurotic', but added that the definition 'neurotic' seemed to apply to nearly everyone she had ever met. 'Personally I just like that which is "most unlike oneself".'[6] Meeting her three years later, JBY was struck by her calmness, self-control, and tact; too intelligent not to be bored by people, she was able to conceal it.[7] Like her future husband, she had begun to train as an art student but abandoned painting. And, like him, she was an autodidact, and read omnivorously in obscure texts, particularly the Neoplatonists. Unlike him, she was both musical and a gifted linguist. The worldly-wise and slightly rackety background of her family, together with the confidence of the financially independent upper middle classes, and her own inclination to cosmopolitan and bohemian life, equipped her to take on the unconventional aspects of WBY's background; her intellectual and occultist interests accorded perfectly with his. This was unsurprising, since he had in part shaped them; but their cooperation, begun episodically four years before, would soon pay unexpected dividends.

WBY's past was one thing; his present, another. After the agonies of the summer, the nightmare journey to London with the Gonne–MacBride family, and their arrival at Woburn Buildings, WBY had determined to go to Mrs Tucker's country retreat and renew his proposal to George. But he nonetheless endured a traumatic meeting with Iseult on 19 September in a Lyons tea-shop, where she made clear her anguish at how her rejection had hurt him. Like her mother, she had quickly discovered ways to keep him captive while withholding herself from him. Again like her mother, unattainability may have been a part of her charm, but so was her haunting beauty, her distance, her sadness, her strangeness: time and again he would compare her to a mountain hare or a wild bird. His future wife, on the other hand, epitomized (in his mind) the virtues of safety and domesticity. This was made embarrassingly clear in a letter to Gregory three days after his meeting with Iseult.

My dear Lady Gregory: I have just got your letter. Since I wrote to you I have had talks with both Iseult & Maud Gonne. I have done exactly what you suggest. I have explained that I might be occupied with the political difficulty for some time. Iseult said to me yesterday 'even if I loved you wildly (and I do not love) I would not marry you because it would distress Moura so deeply'. I acted I as did when wrote to Mrs Tucker from Paris because I wished to start my new life so seemingly heart free that my wife would not be jelous of Iseult & would make no difficulty in the kind of guardianship I have taken up. Strange to say I think that guardianship possible & Maud Gonne insists upon it. The strange conviction that Iseult is my child has grown upon her. I have not I think been in love with Iseult – I have been nearly mad with pity & it is difficult to distinguish between the two emotions perhaps. I want to get rid now of all ambiguity & to make my relation-ship definite & final. I go to Mrs Tuckers on Monday, & now that Iseult knows that I will not allow anything to break our friendship (I had for a time thought it my duty to break it) she seems to me content, though a little indignant, as Maud is also, with what they think my prosaic marriage plans. Both wish me to settle things so decissively that Mrs Tucker will not think there is anything to dread from either. Both on these grounds dissaproved of my letter putting things off. I am doing little things for them both. I think I have persuaded Maud to study design at the Central London Art School, instead of taking up some wild political plans. All this will seem strangely cold & calculating. But I have only come to it – in my way – after sleepless nights & prayer. About 3 mornings ago I awoke calm & decided – had a last inter-view with Iseult & wrote the deciding letter. I need hardly say that all this has left me but little time to think or plan of my own future but I beleive all will go well. Perhaps Iseults account is true – she gave it to Maud – 'he is tired of Romance & the normal & ordinary is now to him the Romantic.' I certainly feel very tired & have a great longing for order, for routine and shall be content if I find a friendly servis-able woman. I merely know – we had our talk alone two years ago – that I think [this] girl both friendly, servisable & very able. After all I want quiet more than any other thing & with me quiet & habit create great affection.[8]

He did go down to Sussex on 24 September. After discussions with Nelly on the 25th, the formal proposal came on the morning of the 26th and was promptly accepted.[9] A week later George went to London with Dorothy Pound to issue the banns for the marriage. Despite WBY's indecisiveness, she evidently did not hesitate. Though he had agonized over the age difference regarding the 22-year-old Iseult, the fact that George was only two years older apparently did not bother him. However, it certainly worried her mother. The day before George went up to London, Nelly Tucker addressed a desperate appeal to Coole.

Georgie has sent you her photograph and Mr Yeats tells me he has written to you to say they are engaged.

I now find that this engagement is based on a series of misconceptions so incredible that only the context can prove them to be misconceptions, on my part and my daughter's. I was very much afraid that Mr Yeats meant to propose to my daughter in Nov. [19]15. I did not consider him free to do so then. But it was only a mutual interest in astrology which they shared, which is, so Mr Yeats tells me 'a very flirtatious business'! The war and its interest helped to keep us apart for some time, but unluckily, last March, having no idea that Mr Yeats's life was in any way changed, and feeling a little unkind at my long neglect of him I asked him to come & see me, never supposing that there could be any question of his marrying my daughter.

Other, and most annoying misconceptions arose, a mutual friend interested him in my daughter, the idea occurred to him that as he wanted to marry, she might do. Fortunately she has no idea of all this unpleasant background, she thinks he has wanted her since the time of the astrological experiments, and when he proposed to come & see us here, I told her he was now free. But it has dawned upon her that there is something amiss, after a long talk with Mr Yeats yesterday. I have decided that the best thing to do is to write to you, and I have told him to confide in you frankly and without any idea of consideration for me or my daughter's possible feelings. She is under the glamour of a great man 30 years older than herself & with a talent for love-making. But she has a strong and vivid character and I can honestly assure you that nothing could be worse for her than to be married in this manner, so there will be no harm done and a rather unpleasant episode can be closed. She has told no one of the affair, and only a few intimate friends of Mr Yeats (who we do not know) are aware of the matter. Mr Yeats has the kindest heart and I feel that only you can convince him of the entire undesirability of this engagement. Georgie is only 24 and is to begin work at the F.O. in October of a very interesting nature. I am not selfishly trying to keep her from marrying, but the present idea seems to me impracticable.

I had the pleasure of meeting you once at a show of your son's pictures and you took me to see Marlborough House, a never forgotten treat. Perhaps we may meet again some day when this affair is pleasantly closed.

Yours sincerely,
E. E. Tucker.[10]

P.S. I feel sure you will understand that my knowledge of the deep affection and reverence that Mr Yeats has for you is my justification in writing this to you. If Georgie had an inkling of the real state of affairs she would never consent to see him again, if she realised it after her marriage to him she would leave him at once.

My letter to you is his release if he wishes it.

Nelly obviously thought that Gregory knew more of WBY's recent entanglements than George did. Her remark that he was 'not free' to propose in November 1915 is also intriguing, and may well refer to Alick Schepeler. But it seems clear that WBY, talkative as ever, had subsequently revealed to George's mother the depth of his commitment to Iseult. He may also have told her of his intention to flee, as so often, to Coole – which he promptly did, after introducing George to Maud and Iseult at Woburn Buildings. He wrote to his new fiancée from Dublin on 3 October as 'My beloved': a short letter of practical instructions about a sugar-ration card, adding,

I am sorry to give you this trouble & yet glad too. It makes me think of the time when I shall find you, when my work is over, sitting at the gass fire or dealing firmly with Mrs Old. As the train passed through Wales I noticed a little house at the roadside & thought of Stone Cottage & myself walking home from the post to find you at the tea table.[11]

The next day he was at Coole. Gregory, already in possession of Nelly Tucker's letter, had sized up the situation with her habitual firm generalship. Despite her original approval of Iseult as marriage candidate, she probably decided that things had gone too far in Sussex to be reversed. Within an hour of arriving, WBY was able to write to George a letter of palpable relief:

Lady Gregory thinks that we should get married as soon as possible & that I should bring you here before the weather grows very cold & gloomy that we may make our Ballylee plans together while the castle looks well. She does not want us however till we are married – that one candle being I think the danger, or at least what the neighbours might say about the possible number of our candles. I was at the theatre last night, & I know that today or tomorrow Lady Gregory will show me a list of proposed plays with several of mine. I shall cross mine off the list, for this winter at least I will have no rehersals to distract us. We shall be together in the country, here I hope & in Stone Cottage & then we shall be alone in France & Italy. You found me amid crowds but you will lead me to lonely places. Let us begin at once our life of study, of common interests & hopes. Lady Gregory is very pleased at the thought of our marriage, & thinks it the best thing that could have befallen me. I grow more fond of you every time we meet, but never quite escape my dread of that old intreaguer Neptune. I shall have no ease of mind till he has been finally put to rout. Lady Gregory is writing to your mother & I think her letter will compell him to take his trident out of our flesh. You will soon see me again – what day I cannot say till I have had another talk with Lady Gregory & learn what necessary business there is, if there is any. There are generally a few plays which have to be read – and then I long to recieve from you one or two letters. Remember you have never yet written to me. I think I must go downstairs as I am to row the children across the lake. I kiss your hands.

Yours affectionly[*sic*]
W B Yeats

This makes clear not only the influence Gregory brought to bear but also his preoccupation with astrological influences – as Elizabeth Heine has shown, a powerful motivation in his desire to be married before 1917 was out.[12] Gregory's letter to George's mother was evidently effective: Nelly replied on 9 October, reassured that her original letter 'seems to have been unnecessary. As long as Georgie has no idea of what I told you I think all will be well now. I am much reassured by your opinion of Mr Yeats's feelings.'[13] That reassurance was, however, only temporary. Gregory also wrote encouragingly to George, who replied gratefully. And while at Coole wby sent her daily letters which seem designed to convince her of his affection, in an oddly formulaic and uneasy way. 'My thoughts are always with you – at first you were but a plan & a dream & then you became a real woman, & then all in a moment that real woman became very dear . . . O my dear child if you can add your eyes to mine we will do together fine & stirring things'.[14] He also assured her that since meeting them in London she was approved of by Gonne, and liked by Iseult. Gonne's relief that her old friend was not to become her son-in-law may easily be imagined, and she had sent wby a letter of slightly condescending congratulation. wby continued to write dutifully to his fiancée; the day before he left he described Ballylee, their future life together, and the astrological conjunctions which would make her 'strong magnetism' 'a foundation for lasting love'. There is a certain clumsy constraint in all this, bearing out Arland Ussher's judgement that in sexual matters 'Shaw's coyness was a sort of disguised attack, Yeats's ardour almost a camouflaged retreat'.[15]

O my dearest I kiss your hands full of gratitude & affection – do not draw them away while my lips are still hungry. Am I not Sinbad thrown upon the rocks & weary of the seas? I will live for my work & your happiness & when we are dead our names shall be remembered – perhaps we shall become a part of the strange legendary life of this country. My work shall become yours and yours mine & do not think because your body & your strong bones fill me with desire that I do not seek also the secret things of the soul. That magnetic Mars will not make me the less the student of your soul.[16]

But he was also evoking the notion of mystical marriage which had echoed in his imagination since he had tried to write *The Speckled Bird* twenty years before.

He arrived back in London on 9 October. The next day a wedding date was fixed, for 20 October. And this precipitated yet another shattering crisis of doubt and self-examination, lasting three days. On 13 October he wrote to Gregory:

I have not written for until this morning I have been in the grip of the subconscious. I came over full of thoughts of the future & only anxious for fear the marriage might not take place. Then the day was fixed & I fell into wild misery. I thought I loved Iseult & would love to my life's end and that I wrote that letter to Mrs Tucker to end by a kind of suicide an emotional strain that had become unendurable – my sheer bodily strength was worn out. Then I became a little happier remembering that I had two main thoughts when I wrote (1) that I might become unhappy through a long vain courtship (2) that Iseult might become unhappy through accepting me out mere kindness and gratitude. Then I spent most of yesterday with Iseult (Georgie would not come saying that we should be alone) & she was so noble & sweet & made me feel as well as know that neither of us could think of anything now but George's happiness that I became more content. This morning the storm has shifted & I think the marriage a great promise of happiness & tranquil work. Your letter too has given me great pleasure for you had hurt me very much by something you said about being married in the clothes I bought to court Iseult in. I knew that whether this marriage is or is not for the happiness of George & myself & Iseult at least 'not easily did we three come to this'. I know I have not been selfish or had any vulgar motive. When you write you need not speak of this letter. I send it to you that I may keep nothing back. I am longing for all to be over that a new life of work and common interest may give George & myself one mind & drive away after a time these wild gusts of feeling. I believe that in spite of all I shall make her happy and that in seeking to do so I shall make myself happy. She has great nobility of feeling. I have always believed that the chief happiness & favour of my life has been the nobility of three or four woman friends.

Gregory reassured him that his new life would be 'a re-birth', which necessarily meant a certain 'pain and travail'; she admitted that she had been 'a little shocked' by his tranquillity following the sudden swerve from Iseult to George, and had expected a bout of insecurity and worry. As to George, he should be 'full of gratitude' to her, 'and I believe that love as well as gratitude will ensure her happiness and yours'. But she still insisted that he 'send a wire when the ceremony is over'; she appears to have had her doubts that it would really take place.[17]

He continued to see George daily for the week before their marriage, entertaining her at Woburn Buildings and possibly spending the night before their marriage at her rented flat in North Kensington.[18] The impending event remained secret to all but the chosen few. Iseult learned the date from her mother and wrote 'wishing you and Georgie great happiness and mutual understanding'. 'There is much in her of the quality of the sphinx, and she has awoken greatly not only my admiration but my curiosity; you must feel the same, and wherever there is curiosity and admiration together, there is romance.'[19] Like Gregory, Iseult was assuring WBY that though he was not in love now, that emotion would follow. But the prospective bridegroom's caution persisted. He wrote to JBY a letter timed to arrive after the event, telling the old prodigal the details that would interest him most, and giving a tactful but inaccurate version of his relationship with the Shakespear–Tucker circle.

My betrothed is a Miss Hyde Lees, comely & joyous & aged but 24. She is a great student of my subjects & has enough money to put us above anxiety & not too much money. Her means are a little more than my earnings & will increase later, but our two incomes together will keep us in comfort. I have known her for some years, ['but' deleted] & ['also' deleted] a very dear friend of mine has long wanted to bring this match about. Then when I found the girls mother wished it, ['I decided' deleted] I thought I might marry so young a girl & yet not do her wrong.[20]

The 'very dear friend' must be Olivia Shakespear, whose influence may also be indicated in Nelly Tucker's irate outpouring to Gregory. But there is no record that she attended the wedding in Harrow Road Register Office, where Ezra was best man. The only other witnesses were George's mother and Dorothy Pound. Olivia does not seem to have seen much of the new couple in subsequent years; certainly she never visited them in Ireland over the twenty-odd years up to her death, though she remained the 'centre' of WBY's life in London. Nelly remained equally detached, firmly kept at a distance by her daughter. The courtship had been inauspicious enough: it was up to George to make the most of the marriage.

No photographs survive, but the couple who emerged into the Harrow Road that Saturday must have looked ill assorted. The groom was fifty-two; the beady-eyed Maurice Bowra, spotting him in the Savile Club earlier that year, has left a description of him. 'He was tall and quite heavily built. His hair was turning grey; he had a fine straight nose, and dark eyes, which had that look of peering into infinity which is the privilege of the short-sighted. He carried his glasses on a black ribbon, and manipulated them with a ceremonial care.' As for the bride, she was handsome but by no means beautiful. ('Not bad looking,' Ezra Pound grudgingly told Quinn.) Her new sister-in-law Lily (who had liked her at once) recorded an artist's first impression:

She is not good-looking, but is comely; her nose is too big for good looks; her colour ruddy and her hair reddish brown; her eyes are very good and a fine blue, with very dark, strongly marked eyebrows.

She is quiet but not slow. Her brain, I would judge, quick and trained and sensitive . . .

She also apparently had 'curious legs, ankles very thick'; she would lament the short-skirted fashions of the twenties and longed for hems to return to Edwardian lengths. Her colouring was markedly high; WBY loyally referred to her 'barbaric beauty', but Lily found her complexion too ruddy, and this heightened with age. But she had her own 'artistic' style and a shy charm, and could – Lily noted – assume 'a look she often had, as of a light shining out from her . . . It is most attractive.'[21] What everyone noticed was her palpable intelligence.

The newlyweds intended to slip away to the Ashdown Forest Hotel, while the news broke. In Dublin Susan Mitchell was not the only person to feel the telephone had burst in her hand. '*What* do you think of WB?' wrote an Abbey friend to the actress Máire Garvey.

I'm not a sentimentalist but I feel cheated – I feel the Romantic age is really, really dead – it was something in the drudgery pulling the devil by the tail to feel he was there – virgin and above – sacrificed for 'a barren passion's sake'. High-ho, we grow cold, we know, as we grow old & comfortable houses with young faces and voices are fearfully tempting – I have a feeling that he did it as a protection – He felt now *she* was a widow he'd wake up & find himself married to *her* some morning & that would compel him to revise *all* his love poems of the last four or five years.[22]

As this illustrates, Gonne's supposed feelings aroused vivid speculation, which Lily impatiently dismissed. 'Lady Gregory and Maud both I believe are pleased,' she told John Quinn, 'and why shouldn't they be, they have both, so to speak, had "their whack", the latter a very considerable whack of her own choosing, but she will live forever in Willy's verse which is a fine crown and tribute to her beauty. Lady Gregory would, I expect, have liked to choose the bride, but Willy liked in this to be his own master.'[23] JBY was assured, in a carefully phrased letter from Gregory, of his new daughter-in-law's suitability. She prophesied a happy marriage, though she wrote of George mainly as part of the furnishings acquired for Ballylee. 'He had come to have a passionate almost romantic longing for a hearth & home of his own & in gaining this he has also gained a young & charming & well-endowed wife. She is naturally the centre, the [?] in that romantic setting, as a poetess could never have been, bringing the draughtiness that surrounds Miss Meynell or Miss Harriet Moore.'[24] JBY's own reaction was no less characteristic. He wrote philosophically to Rosa Butt:

The lady is too young, but then she is very intelligent and well-educated, so that they can talk together and live together on equal terms. It is better to live with an elderly man all whose ideas you can share than with a young man, however handsome, with whom you had not an idea in common. Willie wrote that they are going to Ireland taking with them two servants, the 'two servants' is an artistic touch, and lets me see that they are in a sort of atmosphere not common hitherto in Willie's rather bare and lonely life.[25]

The 'two servants' remained for the moment in the realms of artistic imagination. George's private income from her father's estate was about the same as WBY's at the time of his marriage – which, according to a schedule of

ASHDOWN FOREST HOTEL

FOREST ROW, SUSSEX

A.A.   TEL. NO. FOREST ROW 10   R.A.C.

Adjoins the two famous Royal Ashdown Forest Golf Links

The Hotel faces south and is situated in one of the most charming positions on the Forest, well away from the main road and ten minutes walk from Station and Buses

London, Tunbridge Wells, East Grinstead and Coast, within easy reach

Good riding from reliable stables

Miles of Forest for the ardent hiker and pleasant strolls for the quiet ambler

Good English Cooking, Invalid and Children's Diet a speciality

Hot and cold running water and either gas or electric fires in all Bedrooms.   5 Bathrooms.   Private Suites available.   3 Lounges.   Pretty Garden.   Latest interior sprung mattresses to all beds.   Moderate Terms with reduction for long stay

Resident Proprietors : Mr. and Mrs. Hyde-Clarke

3. The rather forbidding prospectus of the hotel where the honeymooners arrived on 22 October 1917.

earnings drawn up in 1917, usually averaged around £600 a year over the five previous years.[26] But in 1917 £1,200 a year, while comfortable, was not a great deal to sustain a life lived between England and Ireland, with a Galway castle to renovate and a potential family to provide for. The rumour that WBY had married for money was ill founded; if he was seeking anything, it was, as he repeatedly said in his first letters to George, 'peace'.

But their first days together showed little sign that he would find it. The night before the wedding he had 'a feverish attack . . . followed by great exhaustion';[27] though he got through the ceremony he was incapable of leaving London, and the honeymooners had to wait two days before departing to the gloomy Ashdown Forest Hotel. 'Resident Proprietors keep a watchful eye to ensure every comfort,' the brochure promised, 'and we can well say that in a world of bustle and strife "Here is PEACE!"' It was badly needed.

The cause of the bridegroom's illness was, as he well knew, psychosomatic. Four days after the wedding he told Gregory:

I am troubled for I cannot banish another image. How little one knows one's self. I think I am all the more attentive to Georgie because I am troubled but I dread some accidental revelation. I imagine that I have suffered for a long time from over-strain & perhaps if I keep in the country & idle for a while I shall have less to fear. I think for the last year & a half I have suffered from a kind of suppressed excitement, which came to its climax only this autumn.[28]

His fear of mental collapse was exacerbated by a terrible sense of inadequacy and betrayal − of George, of Iseult, of himself − and a sense of doomed repetition. Twenty years before the image of Iseult's mother had come between Shakespear and himself, with destructive results. As for George, though WBY told Gregory she was 'most gentle & sympathetic & I believe that she is happy', this was far from the case. By her own account, she rapidly reached a point where she − like Olivia − might have 'gone weeping away'. It seems likely, from these conditions and scattered later references, that the marriage was not, for the moment, consummated. On 24 October, at a particularly low point, WBY drafted a poem which he later sent to Gregory but withheld from publication for seven years.[29]

> A strange thing surely that my heart when love had come unsought
> Upon the northern upland or in that poplar shade,
> Should find no burden but itself & yet should be worn out.
> It could not bear that burden and therefore it went mad.
>
> The south wind brought in longing, & the east brought in despair,
> The west wind made it pityful & the north wind afraid;
> It feared to give its love a hurt with all the tempest there;
> It feared the hurt that she could give & therefore it went mad.
>
> I can exchange opinion with any neighbouring mind,
> I have as healthy flesh & blood as any rhymer's had,
> But oh my heart could bear no more when the upland caught the wind;
> I ran, I ran from my love's side because my heart went mad.[30]

And in this troubled first week of his marriage he was still writing to Iseult. On 26 October she replied, coincidentally using Gregory's metaphor of rebirth:

I burnt your first letter: it made a very ghostly little flame in the chimney.

All our thoughts about the immediate moment were there, such rubbish after all, since memories are so much more important. I felt your trouble as if it was mine, and it is . . .

I happened this afternoon to enter into a little Protestant church, quite bare but welcoming. I spoke to God there (for it was in the spirit of the place) as if he was a simple old friend, a kind of outlaw like ourselves yet with some influence on the authorities. 'Why should Willy of all people, not be happy; why should I who have always loved him in all affections have had any share in causing his sorrow and could it all be arranged?' . . .

If only as one more kindness to me try to be happy. It is too late and it is too early just now to look into yourself. An abruptly new condition is bound to have a little of the fearfulness of a birth, though it may be for the better. Though it may feel dreary to you, would it not be better to renounce for a time the life of emotion, and live on a few maxims of the early Patricians?

But here I am speaking as if I knew when really all I know is that I share your sadness and will share your joy when you will tell me: 'All is well'.[31]

This seemed, for the moment, an extremely remote possibility.

II

Only a 'miraculous intervention' could have saved the situation, and that is exactly how WBY described the events of 27 October, a week after the wedding, to Gregory.

Two days ago I was in great gloom (of which I hope, & believe, George knew nothing). I was saying to myself 'I have betrayed three people' when I thought 'I have lived through all this before'. Then George spoke of the sensation of having lived through something before (she knew nothing of my thought). Then she said she felt that something was to be written through her. She got a piece of paper, & talking to me all the while so that her thoughts would not effect what she wrote, wrote these words (which she did not understand) 'with the bird' (Iseult) 'all is well at heart. Your action was right for both but in London you mistook its meaning'. I had begun to believe just before my marriage that I had acted, not as I thought more for Iseults sake than for my own, but because my mind was unhinged by strain. The strange thing was that within half an hour after the writing of this message my rheumatic pains & my neuralgia & my fatigue had gone and I was very happy. From being more miserable than I ever remember being since Maud Gonne's marriage I became extremely happy. That sense of happiness has lasted ever since. The misery produced two poems which I will send you presently to hide away for me – they are among the best I have done . . .

I think Georgie has your own moral genius. She says by the by that you are the only friend of mine she has never feared. Should have said that after Georgie had written that sentence I asked mentally 'when shall I have peace of mind' & her hand wrote 'you will neither regret nor repine' & I think certainly that I never shall again.[32]

This letter clearly fixes the breakthrough automatic writing as 27 October, though in later years both WBY and George would identify 24 October as the date his new wife began her experiments.[33] Either these failed to illuminate or convince until three days later, or her first occult divinations were merely astrological (WBY told Dulac on 25 October 'I am writing verses and my wife is casting horoscopes').[34] George remained reticent about her mediumship (and was irritated by her husband's talkativeness on the subject), but she did say that she began the automatic writing as a diversion, even a stratagem, and was surprised to find herself the bearer of messages from a variety of 'Controls' and 'Instructors'. Those messages at first brought WBY consolation and encouragement at a moment of hopelessness; later they would extend to suggesting, in his mind, a formidably complex 'System' of explaining and codifying fate, psychology, and history. It should be remembered that at an earlier point of despair in his love-life (Mabel Dickinson's supposed pregnancy in May 1913) the automatic writing practised by Elizabeth Radcliffe had provided a way out: and that George Yeats had been involved with him in checking messages relayed by Radcliffe. The 'method' and its potentialities were novel neither to her nor to WBY. Flournoy's *Spiritism and Psychology*, which he had read, contained much on the exploration of mediumistic power and the function of spirit communicators as teachers, and George had wide experience of consulting mediums such as Oliver Lodge's Mrs Leonard since at least 1915. She was deeply versed in the literature of psychic research, with a particular admiration for the works of William James; her biographer believes that she was familiar with automatic writing as early as 1913. She also had a formidable knowledge of astrology, and had collaborated on horoscopes with her future husband for years.[35] Even more directly, Olivia Shakespear used occasionally to enter trance-like meditations in order to pronounce answers to WBY's spiritualist inquiries, and George may well have known of this.[36] She had certainly been prepared by WBY's letters before her wedding for a relationship of joint spiritual exploration, echoing his old fantasy of the marriage of Nicolas Flamel or Raymond Lully. In July 1914, when their relationship looked like deepening, she had been initiated by him into the Order of the Golden Dawn, at the usual obscure suburban address. She chose the motto 'Nemo Sciat' ('Nobody Must Know'). From that point her studies had been guided by the obscure didacticism and rotund phraseology of the Order, probably with instruction at least in part by WBY; in July 1916 she was seeking astrological information about a wide range of Irish nationalist heroes, including Pearse and Connolly, which suggests yet another aspect of their collaboration.[37] It is not surprising that she turned to this channel, knowing her husband's susceptibilities. But it is probable that she got more than she bargained for, both in the way that the process 'took off' and in WBY's rapidly developing obsession with it.

They postponed their planned departure to Ireland, staying on at the Ashdown Forest Hotel until 7 November, when they took over WBY's old haunt, Stone Cottage. From 5 November a vast body of automatic script accrued; this has since been devotedly examined by a phalanx of scholars, a study pioneered by George Mills Harper. The sessions took place in the evening, continuing until the medium's energy gave out – a juncture usually signalled by a helpful warning from the void. The records show how decisively the process was driven by queries from WBY: even if the answers apparently came from 'unknown Instructors' speaking through George, the effect is of transactional analysis. This impression is all the stronger because of the nature of the questions. The various 'Instructors' speaking through George were required to elucidate the patterns of WBY's life, to bring reassurance about his recent passages with Iseult, and to clarify his long and extraordinary relationship with her mother. Above all, reading the profuse evidence, it is clear that through this strange process the principals were getting to know each other for the first time.

The records begin on 5 November, and were ordered and catalogued by George – as she would henceforward order, preserve, and arrange drafts of her husband's writing. Effectively, the 'automatic script' represents her own creative work; it also hints at her decisive intervention on various issues where she may have felt he needed guidance. The 'Communicators' warned him against placing his trust in Leo Africanus, told him to ask fewer questions about the Gonnes, forecast 'government difficulty' if Maud tried to get back to Ireland, advised against lecturing in France, and instructed him to take regular exercise; early on he was warned not to 'lay yourself too open to belief'.[38] The dialogues also broadened to take in aspects of their own married life. These 'instructions', which borrow the sonorous and peremptory intonation of Golden Dawn handbooks, coexist with the drawing of speculative cosmic patterns based on astrological constructions, cyclical notions of history, and archetypes of personality which would form the basis of the volume published in 1925 as *A Vision*. But in November 1917 the chief creative inspiration of the automatic-writing experiments was a play, *The Only Jealousy of Emer*, which WBY had begun by 3 November. Dealing with Cuchulain and using the Noh form, it apparently fits into the developing cycle already sketched out by *On Baile's Strand* and *At the Hawk's Well*; but the theme of jealousy, wifely sacrifice, and a man torn between three women had an immediate personal relevance, and the automatic script shows how conscious WBY was of the parallels with his own recent entanglements. 'Much that I have felt lately seems coming in to it.' Each of the Cuchulain plays, he was told, bore 'a relation to the state of my life when I wrote it'.[39]

Thus, in early November, questions to George's first 'Control' (whom she named 'Thomas of Dorlowicz') concerned the development and symbolism of his work as well as the pattern of his life. The answers were often obscure or confused, the medium needing more time to think, or blaming the inter- ference of 'Frustrators'. The names invoked suggest the authorities encoun- tered in George's esoteric studies, mingling ersatz classicism, Gothic medievalism, and the whimsical identifications chosen by mediums for their visiting 'Controls'. When questions turned to areas of his life and work unfamiliar to George, such as the symbolism and rites created for the Celtic Order twenty years before, the medium returned smartly: 'No I may not speak of these mysteries'; she often begged for time. Over subsequent years WBY would develop several interlocking theories about the way communi- cations were generated, using symbolic images and telepathic processes: the communicators supplied several versions too, telling him on 6 November that visionary images and truths 'were taken from the inner wisdom of your own consciousness by selection'.[40] But the form in which answers came could mean that his wife was using her familiarity with occultist termin- ology and the language of symbols and invocation, her wide reading, her knowledge of his own poetry, her own interest in Freudian psychology – mediated through free association, half-asleep speculation, and thinking on her feet. If this is so, her influence on his mystic thought is decisive.

From the beginning their dialogue tried to construct a psychological analysis which could explain both behaviour and fate, based on WBY's ancient notion of the divided self as well as on Freudian ideas of the uncon- scious. Many inquiries revolved around the nature of creative genius, with an initial concentration – inevitably – on Iseult's psychology. Definitions emerged which WBY was anxious to project on to others, whether friends like Horton and Mrs Patrick Campbell, or great artists of the past, like Shelley or Michelangelo. There was much stabbing around in an attempt to hit upon a theory explaining the emergence of genius. In the dialogues of November 1917, ideas floated in the shortly-to-be published *Per Amica* are refined further, and related to his own mentality, balanced between intuitive artistic genius and everyday pragmatist: 'antithetical' and 'primary' selves. (The 'Instructors' seem to have had a good working knowledge of the proofs.) Always a dedicated categorizer, ever since his boyhood interest in scientific lists and typologies had been transferred into the bureaucracy of the Golden Dawn, WBY evolved the idea of a 'System' early on, constructed around archetypal artistic personalities. But his questions circled back repeatedly to Iseult and her mother, to the gathering impatience of the medium. While some questions do not survive, the answers are indicative: 'Yes have you met a man who did actually fall in love with a woman who *was* really his ideal' and 'Admiration & sexual love had little in common'. Asked how he could help Iseult, the 'Control' advised 'go on with work she did with you years ago – lazy now – no solid work indolence stopped her obstinate as a mule'.[41] Over and over again, WBY was reassured that Iseult would survive. Once again, however, these personal questions were scaled up to universal significance in the lengthy discussions about the origins and meaning of physical beauty. This took up much of a long and exhausting session on their last night in Stone Cottage before they left for London, and several of the ideas resurface in *The Only Jealousy of Emer*. The answers recorded for a later session on 7 December, while only one side of the dialogue, clearly illustrate the trend of WBY's questioning, and George's exhaustion:

No I came for something but cant remember what it was – wait better leave this for a month – go back to something else –
 You will be better for leaving it
 Yes
 Yes better not
 too much strain on thought
 Finish before you leave – dont work any in London
 Yes dont work or read late at night
 Yes verse and reading
 Yes much better
 You should not ask her a mental question you want to ask
 She is all right – take her about while you are both in London & get her affairs fixed
 [In mirror writing] You need not have any of the old fear about her and need not doubt that you should have done otherwise – she will assert herself
 All possible identity papers and work & so on
 no but dont *write*
 not a snub but I may not answer[42]

When they went to London, George was introduced to friends such as Horton at Woburn Buildings. A weekend with Edmund Dulac in the country cemented a long friendship, though his neurotic wife Elsa was shortly to disappear from the picture, to be replaced by Helen Beauclerk. They returned to Stone Cottage on 20 December, and at once embarked on lengthy sessions, with WBY's questions becoming more and more 'leading'. But when he asked 'Are my questions guided from your side' the answer was 'Yes'. His preoccupations remained the same, but he concentrated more and more on the symbolism of his play, where dream and reality face each other, symbolized by dancers in masks. Cuchulain's body, in a death-trance, is battled over by his wife, Emer, his mistress, Eithne Inguba, and the supernatural

Fand – figures emblematic of George, Iseult, and Maud. Meanwhile his 'anti-self', Bricriu, hovers over him, in a contest over the hero's tortured soul. While the personal metaphors are clear, there were larger patterns too; WBY later noted that he filled the play 'with those little known concepts about the nature of beauty which Robartes found among the Judwalis in the "Speculum of Gyraldus"'. Thus he linked it directly to the structure of *A Vision*.[43] 'Wife-Eithne-Sidhe', WBY was told, represented respectively 'race-passion-love'. 'Race' seems to have meant, unromantically, family and domestic solidarity: much as, in later imaginative guises, George would figure as a hearthside cat but Iseult as a wild hare.

Subsequent sessions revealed another preoccupation which would recur in his work: the idea of repetitive 2,000-year cycles in history, placing Christ in a continuum rather than as a unique revelation. The intensive questioning persisted, and so did warnings from George against running his life according to supernatural promptings. 'The reliance absolute reliance on the supernatural and the consequent abandonment of personal judgement is as great a temptation as any other.' Simultaneously she helped him evolve towards the idea of a 28-phase progression, based on the lunar cycle, where human personalities could be assigned to different phases, and the whole reflect a cycle of historical development. (It could also explain, to the medium's satisfaction, why Gonne possessed an ugly mind in a once-beautiful body.[44]) George and her husband shared a close knowledge of astrological symbols and structures, repeated throughout the several thousand pages of 'script' accumulated in hundreds of sessions over the first three years of their marriage. The 'System' mapped the soul's progress through the heavenly mansions, reflected the experience of several lives, and related stages of the journey to psychological archetypes. This required a familiarity with the symbolism of Dante's poetry, Blakean dialectic, Neoplatonic philosophy, Freud-derived psychology, and Kabbalistic esoterica; it reiterated ideas floated in 'Swedenborg, Mediums, and the Desolate Places', as well as *Per Amica*. Here, unsurprisingly, the developing theory was driven by WBY's leading questions, but George's close study of the writings of Pico della Mirandola probably helped her to hold her own.[45] Still, as the 'System' developed and the questioning became more didactic, she took refuge behind 'Controls' like 'Marcus', who pleaded incapacity or exhaustion.

The proportion of conscious to unconscious suggestion relayed by George will always be debated, but for much of the time she must have known what she was doing. The hypersensitive and susceptible condition of exhaustion and nervous tension during the traumatic start to their honeymoon was clearly a predisposing factor, not always easily sustained in later circumstances. The utilitarian functions of the 'Instructors' for everyday matters such as exercise, diet, and sexual relations are clear, as is their usefulness as mechanisms to relegate Maud (and Olivia) to distant history, and to keep Iseult in her place. Hypnosis may have facilitated the stream of answers; from time to time the medium clearly had to think them through, and demanded time to get it right. What remains astonishing is the depth, ingenuity, and oracular confidence of the bizarre wisdoms she imparted. From her side, the phenomenon is convincing evidence of her powerful mind and wide reading. From his, it reveals a good deal about what he wanted to know, and what he wished to be true. This applied not only to the voices from the void and his belief in the possibility of two minds sharing access to a common thought, but to the dilemmas of his personal life.

wby's line of questioning was spurred on by a strange combination of personal self-analysis and historical generalization; but the dialogues also expose deeply laid *idées fixes* which would emerge over the next twenty years. One was his preoccupation with physical beauty in women and men – its essential meaning, its relation to creative genius, the validity of beauty as evidence of high achievement in a previous incarnation. In part, this stemmed from wby's obsession with the Gonnes. In his private iconography Maud had long filled the place of Helen of Troy; now that age and fanaticism had dulled her own beauty, Iseult carried the torch. The idea that spectacular good looks might be a kind of creative achievement in themselves was not new. Reading Castiglione and others had prepared him for it, and he had celebrated it in 'Adam's Curse' many years before. But the notion that 'ugliness' itself indicated the lower levels of a journey towards perfection on one level, and civilization on another, was ominous (James Stephens's combination of ugliness, genius, and sweetness of character created something of a stumbling-block to the 'System'). One of the enduringly obscure areas of the developing theory remained the relation between physical beauty to the creation of beauty in the work of (for instance) Keats and Shelley.

For immediate purposes the turn taken by their marriage meant that Iseult could (as bidden by the 'Instructors', and desired by wby) be incorporated into their life. An effort was made, but the project was doomed. This was partly because wby's feelings for her were still too volatile for such a comfortable resolution, and partly because Iseult lived up to her emblem of the 'wild bird' and refused to follow the path laid down by wby, though her letters continued – affectionate, confiding, fey. Through his SPR friend Edward Denison Ross he had found her a part-time job as assistant librarian at the School of Oriental Languages, near Woburn Buildings, where she was also to study Bengali and Sanskrit. The arrangement began in late November, just before wby's marriage, but it was not a success. In

March 1918, when this foundered, he would try to organize work with Pound on the *Little Review*. Iseult had already been introduced to Mrs Tucker, for no very clear purpose; she stayed at Woburn Buildings on 15 December, and WBY fondly imagined that she and George were 'becoming great friends'; she was invited to join them at Stone Cottage a week later, and spend Christmas in a larger house they rented near by. When her ménage with Wyndham Lewis's girlfriend Iris Barry turned sour the following year, she would be once again installed in the vacant Woburn Buildings. WBY would determinedly continue the connection, but others, like George and Gregory, saw the danger more clearly: according to George, Gregory was determined never to have Iseult to stay in the same house as WBY.[46] The relationship eventually resembled that of an errant stepdaughter and a mildly besotted father-figure. Iseult would turn to him for succour at critical moments in her unhappy life, just as her mother had done, and at other junctures she went her own way. One reason why her employment by Pound did not work out was that he rapidly seduced her, probably in early 1918, and very likely in Woburn Buildings: he was soon claiming that he would leave Dorothy for her. Though WBY sent Iseult reproving letters about Pound, based on reports from Gonne's scandalized maid Josephine, it is unlikely that he ever discovered how far things had gone.[47]

Meanwhile, in London with his new wife, convinced that he could manage his obsession with Iseult and inspired by the recent surge of occult divination, WBY was writing again. On 17 December he finished a poem about the Easter Rising, 'Sixteen Dead Men', which charts the growing radicalization of his opinions; like 'Easter 1916', it would remain unpublished for the moment. But he was anxious to continue work on his Cuchulain play, and its development had come to depend upon the instructions received from the automatic script. When he and George returned to Stone Cottage on 20 December, he bombarded his medium-wife with questions about Cuchulain, his own plays, the poem 'Ego Dominus Tuus', and the ideas of the 'mask' which he had been refining for so many years. Long ago, describing his idea of Cuchulain in *On Baile's Strand* to Frank Fay, the parallels with his own perceived personality had been clear; now the idea of the mythic hero as his own alter ego was specifically established.[48] The archetypal 'System' of *A Vision* would put Cuchulain, like Nietzsche, in the heroic Phase Twelve: he was also established as WBY's own mask, or solar opposite. And when George's 'Instructors' told WBY that Cuchulain's 'Evil Genius' was banished by his rejection of the Hawk Woman, Gonne's surrogate in *At the Hawk's Well*, the medium knew exactly what she was doing. Even more immediate to his concerns was the demonstration that the three women in *The Only Jealousy* not only represented Iseult, George, and Maud but also – respectively – danger, peace, and a combination of the two. Given his own self-reproaches over the past traumatic weeks, the interpretation of Bricriu as Cuchulain's dark other self, banished by a loving wife's sacrifice, must have carried equal resonance. 'Who will C. love?' he inquired on 7 January. 'I cannot tell you till you know yourself,' replied the medium, 'and you do know I think unconsciously.'[49]

The advent of the corporeal Iseult for Christmas disrupted these self-interrogations. Before her arrival, 'Thomas' enjoined WBY to 'remember your pledge of secresy/private script always as I said before', though, to judge by WBY's letters, he kept little to himself. George's 'Controls', when asked about Iseult's melancholia, tended to reply unsympathetically in terms of laziness, indolence, and obstinacy.[50] 'Thomas' also encouraged WBY to anticipate Iseult's marriage and 'be comforted in the thought of her happiness': 'it will be a marriage ring soon to be on her hand let there be no doubt in her heart or yours – we do not err when we make judgement on these matters'. This may have been overplaying her hand a little; when they returned to supernatural soundings a few days after Christmas, WBY's questions stayed with the safer, if fruitless, matter of Lane's missing will. The Yeatses returned to London for New Year, and then on 2 January 1918 moved to 'charming old rooms' at 45 Broad Street, Oxford. George's 'Instructors' had issued the welcome advice that they should avoid an early removal to Ireland.

At Broad Street the occult interrogations continued, building up through 'lists' the patterns of 'placing' great artists into different phases of the system. 'I live with a strange sense of revelation', WBY told Gregory on 4 January, 'and never know what the day will bring.' Part of the reason for choosing to locate themselves in Oxford concerned the city's intellectual and scholarly atmosphere, against which WBY expected to refine his 'System': long ago, the beauty of the streetscapes and buildings had suggested to him life lived against an opera set. The Yeatses were also swayed by a belief that spirit communication was less easy in the blacked-out capital. 'He had hated London of late,' Gregory told JBY, 'although little boys had left off shouting "Kitchener needs you" as he walked to his club, Fashionable Ladies bothered him to give readings & tho' he professed to think London darkness an artistic improvement one gets tired of peering thro' the gloom.'[51] George may also have been ready to move her husband to a distance from earlier associations: she had told him, after all, that Gregory was the only one of his established friends whom she did not fear. Nonetheless, as WBY put it to Quinn, she never knew 'which to be most surprised at, the hats or the minds of the dons' wives, and is convinced that if we live here every winter, which is possible, she will be driven to great extravagance out of the desire for contrast.'[52]

Later WBY would inquire if he and George had been brought to Oxford 'to find certain mystic associates'. 'Yes', the answer came through George, 'but only the orderly and philosophic.'[53] The SPR was certainly active in Oxford; the resources of the Bodleian Library were round the corner; he could visit the dons Anne Moberly and Eleanor Jourdain, who had written *An Adventure*, the occult time-travelling testament which had preoccupied him for years: indeed, he was told by George's 'Instructors' that Miss Moberly expected him to call.[54] He was also excited by the so-called 'Glastonbury script', apparent evidence that psychic inference through a medium had revealed the whereabouts of the lost Glastonbury Chapel. The script was published at Oxford, by Basil Blackwell, and WBY made an expedition to the site. But principally, both the Yeatses wanted peace, and it is likely that George baulked at immediate exposure to her husband's Irish life. WBY's excuses to Gregory for postponing their visit until Easter – an attack of influenza and rumoured food shortages in the west – do not ring convincingly. He also revealed that they planned '(if we like Oxford) living here when not in Ireland & making this a center for my Noh plays which have to be worked out with Dulac'.[55] Within a week they were looking at houses with a view to spending the winter there.

He also revealed to Gregory his continuing excitement with the 'very profound, very exciting mystical philosophy' being revealed to his wife and himself, and confided, 'I am writing it all out in a series of dialogues about a supposed medieval book . . . You will be astonished at the change in my work, at its intricate passion.' By 17 January he had sent the commentary on this invented text, '"the Speculum Angelorum et Hominum" by Gyraldus & a sect of Arabs called the Judwalis', to Dulac. Less exotic commitments persisted: plans for the theatre, projected books for Cuala, letters to the builder Rafferty about Ballylee, the Lane pictures campaign. He had regained all his intellectual energy and confidence. Social life remained muted, though WBY saw Robert Bridges at Boar's Hill, renewed his acquaintance with the charismatic classicist Gilbert Murray, and visited the critic Walter Raleigh. Guests came at weekends, including Iseult, Bessie Radcliffe, and Horton. But the visiting presences who meant most to him were the shadowy 'Instructors', summoned up at night by his extraordinary wife.

As the collaboration continued during evenings at Broad Street throughout January 1918, WBY questioned George's 'Controls' about patterns in his past life. He sought insights about people he had worked with, such as Pound and Gregory ('unbalanced – you created she transferred not real colaboration') and those to whom he had been linked by a 'lightning flash' – represented by the zigzag line through his life which marked critical junctures, often fusions with significant people. Unsurprisingly, she refused to prophesy the phase where the lightning might next strike; she also took the opportunity to instruct him not to take on too many outside lecturing commitments and to concentrate on his own work. On occasion the everyday advice (rest, nerves, digestion) recalls Gregory's admonitions in his early bachelor days about regular habits and warm underwear. Sometimes the motivation behind the instructions is touchingly clear: 'do not forget your youth now that you have past it – if you have not forgotten how you felt when young – that is answer to your last question.'[56] No wonder George was tired. There are ample indications that the 'Instructors' often prescribed erotic relations, perhaps to give the medium a respite from her other activities. Her warnings against Gonne, thinly disguised as the 'Woman of the Sidhe' in the Cuchulain plays, continued ('she is not emotionally objective – she is intellectually so because she is cunning – in her desire – deliberate – she desires for desire not for love'[57]). When WBY instanced his 'Archer' vision at Tillyra twenty-two years before, and asked if Gonne was one of the seers then mentioned who would 'attain a wisdom older than the serpent', George's 'Instructor' briskly countered 'she will attain to the wisdom of folly'.[58]

At times WBY himself queried the veracity of the spirit messages. There are moments of near-confrontation when he asked whether the medium knew if the messages relayed were false. 'Why [are] you trying to impress upon me some contrast between Medium and M[aud] G[onne],' he asked sharply on 2 February. But the idea of 'Frustrators', producing a kind of astral radio-interference, was supplied to get over this difficulty. (George used this to condemn Leo and warn WBY against being swayed by bogus prophecies.) However, questions about 'contact' (often meaning sexual relations), and how its refusal or denial spurred on creative effort, were guaranteed unequivocal answers. Like so much else in the automatic script, this confirmed ideas and principles which he had already built into his life and laid the foundation of his personal myth. Not only was his long-cherished idea coming true, of a mystical marriage partnered in adepthood as well as in sexual union, but the 'Controls' also – after some prompting – supported his notion of himself as a public man. '"I think it would be a fitting thing to send me on an embassy like Dante unfitting to set me to right [write] pamphlets like Dante?" "Yes."'[59] George would bring in an even more intoxicating new dimension by introducing, on 15 January, the idea that she would bear him a child who would reincarnate past ancestors, as well as play the role of 'Initiate', or spiritual guide, in their personal religion.[60] From late February

George conjured up a distant Butler 'ancestress' from the late seventeenth century – Anne Hyde, wife to the second duke of Ormonde, who died in childbirth in 1685. WBY spent much time in the Bodleian verifying her existence. In this case, the spirit was not an 'Instructor' but a visitant who confirmed WBY's expectations that he would prolong the family line and, with George, 'incarnate' a figure of importance in the historical cycle now dawning. On 4 March, just before they left Oxford, the 'Instructors' declared that the couple were to have a child, later defined as the reincarnation of Anne Hyde's stillborn son. But they should keep up precautions against this for three months longer until WBY was quite sure he wanted it. 'The child would only give her happiness in being your child she does not want a child for its own sake.'[61] They had already discussed his 'conscious creation of a personality' and, implicitly, the effect of marriage on his creative powers. There was also the possibility of George collaborating on plays with him. She firmly quashed the idea, but all that had happened since 27 October proved that she was now indispensable to his life.

In *The Only Jealousy of Emer*, WBY was fitting his creative work into a cosmic system of allegory and archetype: the long-time student of Blake felt he was writing, at last, in a pure Blakean mode. On 26 January he began thinking of a play about Christ and Judas, which became *Calvary*. The ideas for it were floated in a long series of interrogations, which were also related to his interest in the ending of cycles, the annunciation of a messiah, and the advent of a new spiritual age towards the millennium.[62]

He was full of plans for literary entrepreneurship, pressing Gregory to produce an anthology of translated Gaelic poetry for Cuala, telling Lolly of his intention to make James Stephens write an autobiography for her, and making clear his vision of the press. 'I try to keep a certain unity in the books . . . In no case must you have books if it can possibly be avoided which are an authors ordinary output only dearer & smaller . . . I dare say I shall try several people for autobiographies & succeed with somebody. We have a very small group of authors to draw from – as I dont think I can go to English writers unless I can relate their work to Ireland in some way by elaborate prefaces.'[63] As public opinion in Ireland shifted towards more radical nationalism and anti-English feeling grew, WBY's intellectual antennae picked up the signals of cultural nationalism as sharply as they had done in the 1890s. Letters and pamphlets pressing the case of the Lane pictures were dispatched from Broad Street, but he was anxious to shift the weight of the lobbying on to Ellen Duncan and the Dublin committee. Gregory was unsympathetic, complaining to Lane's sister about WBY's indignation at being 'stirred up . . . "I have married a wife & therefore I cannot come!!"'[64] But he had become tired of being 'sent from one polite man to another', and remarked to Gregory that 'strong pressure from some recognised political party is what is wanted. Perhaps a speech by de Valera might help.'[65] Thus, ten months before the general election in which the reconstituted Sinn Féin party swept the board, he had identified Eamon de Valera, 1916 survivor and apparently implacable revolutionary, as the coming man.

He was nonetheless determined to remain in Oxford, spending days in the Bodleian (where his table was 'covered with such things as the etchings & wood cuts of Palmer & Calvert'[66]), recruiting his strength after influenza and receiving guidance from his wife's 'Instructors'. *Per Amica* appeared in late January, mystifying the general public but, to WBY, vindicated by the supernatural revelations of the past weeks. And on 29 January he sent Clement Shorter seven poems, 'some I think among my best', drawing his attention particularly to 'The Wild Swans at Coole'.

III

Just as WBY's life was becoming reorganized, that of his closest friend was blown apart. On 4 February he received a tragic few lines from Gregory. 'Dear Willie – the long dreaded telegram has come – Robert has been killed in action. I came here [to Galway] to tell Margaret – I will go home in a day or two – It is very hard to bear.' She added a postscript: 'If you feel like it some time – write something down that we may keep – you understood him better than many.'[67]

For months she had been preoccupied by missing aeroplanes, ever since Robert had been sent out from the flying-scout centre at Gosport with the reputation of an 'exceptionally capable pilot'. He had met his death on 23 January returning from a mission in Italy, near where he had travelled with WBY and his mother eleven years before, and was buried at Padua. In fact, he had been shot down in error, by an Italian plane, though this was not yet known.

For Gregory, the worst imaginable had come true. Having so often imagined the horror, she found it no easier to take, and, though she bore it with heroic fortitude, she told WBY 'a spring seems to have broken'. 'The machinery of my life will not change much I think,' she told Blunt. '26 years ago I came back here alone, to keep things together & keep the house open – now I feel I have been put back there again – but a quarter of a century older & with half my income gone – last month I was planting for Robert – this month it is for [his son] Richard.'[68] WBY helped her as she had asked, first with a brief article in the *Observer*: she was grateful that it stressed Robert's abilities as artist, since his military career 'was a small part of his life in a way – tho' an intensification of much that had been in him before'. She preferred to think of his 'few lovely pictures', his courteous relations with his tenants, and the abilities he would have brought to 'the building of Ireland'. But what she really wanted was a poem from WBY, and by 25 February she knew he was working on an elegy. 'It seems as if the intensity and crystallisation of thought in verse would go best with ones memory of him.' Already an image of Robert was forming, upon which WBY would build a series of poems over the next two years. Gregory often showed him letters from JBY, and in April the old artist wrote consolingly from New York, describing Robert's 'ideal life' in terms which anticipate the image celebrated by WBY's memorial poems.

His happiness (for he says he was happy) [lay] in his strenuous forgetting of self. Pleasure lies in remembering yourself, happiness in forgetting it – & we can only forget ourselves by attaining to the maximum of strenuousness – he lived at the highest pitch of exertion . . . Sometimes people live to be old because they have never lived – these are the prudent tho' time serving – your son did otherwise & has paid the penalty . . . . as it were, he said to himself I will live even tho' it means death.[69]

For WBY, the project of commemorating his friend's son was not an easy one: a certain constraint runs through his letter to Iseult a week after the news came.

I have been deeply moved by the loss for his mother's sake & for his own. He had a strange pure genius, full of vast austere rythms [sic]. I always felt that he had a luck-less star and have expected the end . . . His wife has asked me to write something about him & I shall do some article or other now, & later on some fuller & more meaning thing.[70]

His own relationship with Robert Gregory had never been easy. He had periodically expressed impatience at the younger man's casual and dilettante approach to projects such as sets for the Abbey, and Gregory's wife, Margaret, nursed a settled antipathy towards Coole's perpetual summer resi-dent.[71] In later years WBY came to appreciate Robert's distinction as a land-scape painter and to see in him something of his mother's qualities – but they had never really got on. There was also the difficulty of the manner in which Robert met his end. By early 1918 feeling in Ireland was setting hard against the endless war; this would be sharply exacerbated by the government's move towards imposing conscription in Ireland in the autumn. Since the executions of 1916, opposition to the British war effort had spread widely even among political moderates, while the tone of nationalist propaganda was vitriolic. These feelings were not shared by Robert Gregory; his views had long been anti-Sinn Féin and he seems to have fully supported the war effort, joining the Royal Flying Corps with alacrity early in the war. In the first commemorative poem which WBY wrote, these difficulties were avoided by deliberately pitching the elegy in the form of a Spenserian eclogue. Later, in 'An Irish Airman Foresees his Death', he would posit Gregory's commitment to fighting as purely existential, and even attribute to him an alienation from empire for which there is little evidence. By 22 February he was at work on his elegy, a dialogue, eventually called 'Shepherd and Goatherd' (for its first publication he confusingly used the title of an earlier fragment, 'The Sad Shepherd'). By 19 March it was finished. Its archaism lends an additional awkwardness to a poem written, as it was, to order: Robert Gregory is pastoralized into a Virgilian landscape, his paintings becoming 'sorrowful, austere, sweet, lofty pipe tunes'. The fact that he was unprepared to take over Coole (though it was technically his possession since his twenty-first birthday) was put in a laboured way that cannot have been entirely welcome to his wife (or his mother):

> You cannot but have seen
> That he alone had gathered up no gear,
> Set carpenters to work on no wide table,
> On no long bench nor lofty milking-shed
> As others will, when first they take possession,
> But left the house as in his father's time
> As though he knew himself, as it were, a cuckoo,
> No settled man . . .

Where the elegy comes alive is in the Goatherd's song, framed within the poem. The reason is that it concerns what was closest to WBY's mind and heart that February, the supernatural theories of the soul's progress which he and George had been piecing together. The Goatherd's song visualizes Robert's death in terms of 'dreaming back', the notion of a return to prenatal innocence through reliving one's life in reverse after death:

> Jaunting, journeying
> To his own dayspring,
> He unpacks the loaded pern
> Of all 'twas pain or joy to learn,
> Of all that he had made.
> The outrageous war shall fade;
> At some old winding whitethorn root
> He'll practise on the shepherd's flute,
> Or on the close-cropped grass
> Court his shepherd lass,
> Or run where lads reform our daytime
> Till that is their long shouting playtime;
> Knowledge he shall unwind

> Through victories of the mind,
> Till, clambering at the cradle side,
> He dreams himself his mother's pride,
> All knowledge lost in trance
> Of sweeter ignorance.[72]

But the poem as a whole might be judged in the Shepherd's words, deprecating his own song:

> I worked all day,
> And when 'twas done so little had I done
> That maybe 'I am sorry' in plain prose
> Had sounded better to your mountain fancy.

Always acutely attuned to weaknesses in his own work, WBY probably recognized the unwieldy nature of 'Shepherd and Goatherd'. It was only the first of four poems written about (or to) Gregory, a more inspirational figure in death than in life. There is a marked contrast with the hard-edged and declamatory 'An Irish Airman Foresees his Death', written a few months later, which matched a ringing metre to an uncompromisingly 'pure joy': part of the reason why it would become, second only to 'Innisfree', a standard for schoolbooks. This turned out to be the 'war poem' which WBY had told Edith Wharton he would or could not write. But it also identified Gregory with Galway and Ireland, repudiating England and empire, reflecting the fact that WBY was writing it in Ireland. The same would be true of his most substantial commemorative poem to Gregory, 'In Memory of Major Robert Gregory', which would also constitute a sombre celebration of his own new state of life, and a chapter of his own autobiography.

After Robert Gregory's death, his mother would live for her three grandchildren, Catherine, Anne, and Richard, hoping to keep Coole for them as it had been.[73] But the lands had been sold out to tenants under the purchase schemes introduced by a series of government measures culminating in 1909; and the house and demesne, inherited by Robert at his majority, were left by him (in a brief and hasty will made in 1916) to his widow, who was to enjoy 'the fullest freedom in the upbringing of my children and the management of my house and estate'.[74] The wording suggests that he anticipated potential conflicts with his powerful mother, who retained rights for her lifetime. For her fatherless grandchildren, as recalled by Anne in her enchanting memoir, Augusta Gregory was the most perfect of grandmothers, the lodestar around which the beloved Galway house and its denizens revolved, but their mother found herself cast adrift. The pretty Welsh art student had become a disconsolate war widow, left in technical possession of a house and diminished lands which she did not control, in a country which she did not care for, and which was just about to descend into guerrilla war and civil strife. In a few short months WBY's relationship to Coole had changed dramatically. He would return to a house of mourning, with an undertow of uncertainty and resentment about its ownership; and he himself would be coming back to Gort as possessor of a new wife and his own property in the neighbourhood. Little wonder that a certain tone of trepidation marks the correspondence between Oxford and Coole, discussing the arrangements for the Yeatses' visit at Easter.

Moreover, since Robert's death the terms of their projected sojourn at Gort had changed. When the news came, WBY had offered at once to go to Ireland, but Gregory – slightly to his relief – refused. However, he now determined to live at Gort while Ballylee was finished. Ballinamantane House was a modest dwelling (three bedrooms, two sitting rooms, a kitchen) belonging to the Gregory estate, and situated near the entrance to Coole. It had to be furnished on a temporary basis, since the Ballylee furniture was being designed by Scott and custom-made: the Ballinamantane floorboards remained bare throughout their occupation. It had other disadvantages; Gregory had drawn it to WBY's attention when he was house-hunting, and he had summarily dismissed it. Now, since Robert's death, the very proximity and dependence which had put him off seemed desirable.[75] Plans were made to stay at Coole for Easter, and then move into Ballinamantane. Practical as ever, even in her desolation, Gregory warned him about local food shortages, and suggested that they wait till the harshness of March was over and come in Easter week when the children would be in residence and the house less cheerless: 'I should not like your wife to see it as it is now.'[76] On 8 March the Yeatses left Oxford. But they had already seen an ancient house near the Bodleian which would be vacant in September, and they planned to return.

On 9 March the Yeatses arrived in Dublin. The next evening George was introduced to Lolly and Lilly at Dundrum, who approved of her thoroughly; they also attended the Abbey to see a new play by Gogarty. But after four days in the city they settled for the time being at the Royal Hotel, Glendalough – a famous beauty spot in the Wicklow mountains, beside an ancient monastic site on the lakeside. It was near enough Dublin to make business calls there and plan a series of lectures to raise money for the Abbey,[77] but WBY was by now convinced that urban conditions inhibited the spirit voices mediated by George. He also – to judge by the evidence of the automatic script – believed that the round tower at Glendalough had an occult significance for their researches. In these isolated conditions they set once more to work. From 19 March WBY was engaged in an intense interrogation about the spiralling movement of the soul's progress through existence: 'the image', as a 'Control' put it, 'of shutter spiral and funnell', which would be sustained throughout the several drafts and versions of *A Vision*.

The conditions in Wicklow suited him. He and George acquired a white cat ('Pangur', after a similar animal commemorated in a celebrated medieval lyric by an Irish monk). They moved to another hotel in the neighbouring valley of Glenmalure on 27 March, to escape Easter holidaymakers, but he had already finished 'Shepherd and Goatherd', partly helped by occult discussions about 'dreaming back'; he also wrote 'Solomon to Sheba', a concealed tribute to his wife. In early April they returned to Dublin, where George was introduced to a widening circle of her husband's friends, whose curiosity had already been aroused. 'I gather she will write for him, read for him, type for him, communicate with the dead or living for him, and will make the ideal poet's wife,' AE told Quinn.[78] On 6 April they travelled to Coole, where they stayed a fortnight.

It was not an auspicious beginning. Though permission had been sought, and given, to bring Pangur, the cat had to be left off at the stables; he was later smuggled into their room. Ballylee was disappointingly far from completion, though WBY believed 'a month's steady work would make it ready'.[79] George took on the necessary work of chivvying the builder Rafferty (unfairly described by WBY as 'a morbid man who cries when anything goes wrong'), marking out a garden, and following up materials. Scott was a pioneer in the use of Irish vernacular detail and local stone, flags, and slate. Thus the aesthetic correctness learned by WBY in his Bedford Park apprenticeship was maintained, with roof beams cut by adze rather than machine-sawn, and ancient timbers and stone salvaged from a nearby mill.[80] But they were Gregory's guests, and social life at Coole was strained. The Yeatses were still, in a sense, getting to know each other: long afterwards George recalled her surprise when her husband, who had talked much of fishing, revealed his ignorance of the may-fly on their first expedition. (They abandoned the attempt, and sat on a bank while he told her the story of Florence Farr's love-life instead.[81]) When they were alone, WBY insisted on continuing their sessions of automatic writing, though George did all she could to dissuade him ('thick air – joyless – heavy').[82] Gregory and her daughter-in-law were still mourning Robert, but under any circumstances WBY's introduction of a new wife would not have been easy. Gregory had told him she did not want to meet George 'until you were married and nothing could be done about it', which was hardly enthusiastic. She set herself to be kind to the bride, but George knew it was a strain. For her own part, she hated the 'routinised' life at Coole and found the enforced attendance at their hostess's readings out loud after dinner excruciating: she thought Gregory was snobbish and puritanical. An added cause of resentment was George's con-sciousness that they had in fact met in London in 1914, but the older woman had determinedly forgotten the encounter. This may have been insensitive, but it was unlikely that they would ever be soulmates, differences of age and background apart: George was uneasily aware of Dorothy Pound's alle-gation that 'at one time Yeats and Lady G had planned to be married', though she never dared ask him.[83]

The strain told on their own relationship. The 'Controls' apparently accused WBY of 'boredom and coldness of heart towards the medium',[84] but he insisted on pursuing their investigations. Finally, the various tensions came into the open. WBY allowed himself to be provoked by Margaret Gregory's unremitting petty sarcasms into a violent riposte at dinner; he reduced her to silence and the Yeatses retired early to bed. That night, for the first time (and against the previous advice of the 'Instructors'), they abandoned precautions against conception.[85] On 20 April they moved tem-porarily into lodgings in Galway. The claims of his new marriage had asserted themselves over those of his ancient friendship.

As he harassed George's 'Controls' with questions, WBY was trying to track cycles of history. The notion that, in 1918, a phase of civilization was coming to an end, with the spiral movement of historical time opening out to demotic chaos, seemed borne out by the conditions around them. The political atmosphere in Ireland was increasingly ominous: they heard in Galway that all the young men were buying hatchets and crowbars with the intention of using them on railway lines and telegraph poles. The storm-cloud over government plans to impose conscription was swelling to critical proportions. On 23 April there was a one-day general strike of protest, which affected all Ireland outside Ulster. WBY longed to go quietly to ground, and felt that anything could happen. On 2 May they moved into Ballinamantane, having borrowed some basic furniture from Coole. The government imposed permits for travel between Britain and Ireland; public meetings were forbidden; mail was more and more crudely censored. In these circumstances WBY determined to cancel his projected lecture at the Abbey, especially as he had intended to deal with 'the poetry of the Irish rebellion'.[86] 'Times are too dangerous for me to encourage men to risks I am not prepared to share or approve,' he told Shorter. 'If the government go on with conscription there may be some disastrous outbreak – I doubt the priests & the leaders being able to keep the wild bloods to passive resistance. I have seen a good many people here in the west & I cannot imagine a more dangerous condition of things, the old historical passion is at its greatest in-tensity'.[87] He had just sent a letter to the *Nation*, also signed by Gregory, Stephen, AE, and Hyde, deploring the idea of introducing conscription as a death-blow to 'all hope of peace in Ireland and good will towards England in our lifetime'.[88] The very next day the government swooped on Sinn Féin leaders, including de Valera, Griffith, and Markievicz, and arrested them, simultaneously proclaiming evidence of a 'German plot' between Irish republicans and the Kaiser's secret service: 'a bee in somebody's inkpot', as WBY contemptuously put it to Pound.[89] This inept and trumped-up manoeuvre helped swing public opinion yet further behind Sinn Féin. And it affected WBY directly, through Gonne.

She was still in England, but determined to evade Defence of the Realm Act regulations: in January 1918 she and Seán had temporarily fled from London in disguise, aided by Sylvia Pankhurst and Eva Gore-Booth, and materialized in Dublin, to the horror of friends like AE.[90] Iseult's immediate reaction had been to send a distraught letter to WBY, appealing for help. Her indomitable mother remained actively involved in republican propaganda, and in the sweep of May 1918 she was arrested in London and sent to Holloway. Frenzied letters arrived at Gort from Iseult, suggesting, *inter alia*, that Maud be induced to go to live quietly in Oxford, an idea that must have filled both Yeatses with foreboding. But WBY's bond with Iseult was strengthened by their joint disdain for Maud's political opinions and associates, and by Iseult's appeals to him at times of trouble. He was still trying to arrange a job for her with Pound on the *Little Review* (secretly subsidized by himself), but he was worried about her association with such a potentially scandalous publication, not to mention its predatory editor.[91] George was pressed into service – sending money to Iseult, keeping track of Seán, and writing to Pound in a tone which suggests that WBY's sentimental idea that she and Iseult might become soulmates was far removed from the truth.

Anyhow M [Maurice, or Iseult] will have to be got work from some other source than the L.R. with its social reputation . . . As a matter of fact Shorter is in a sentimental condition over Ireland & might get Maurice a job on the Bookman or some other god forsaken bilge. Turpitude can easily be produced in WB's brain & hashed up by M . . . whether M will concent [*sic*] to any machine work I doubt . . . WB will be unpersuadable over the whole time job. He will be less so if he does not imagine you are paying from your own pocket for the workhouse fare of distressed beauty – But his view of LR is of course final . . . WB has an exaggerated view of M's suspicious nature. In other words I dont imagine she'll have the faintest idea if she gets 10/- more than normal.[92]

She ended by complaining about WBY 'trotting up to Coole', adding 'Lady G & I cant *both* be right! And she's as cautious as any priest LR no place for a young gal etc!' It is one of the few occasions during this period when George's own voice can be heard, and it comes as a bracing corrective to the version of events and relationships sustained by WBY, for his own self-preservation.

During this crisis George herself was spending a few days in Dublin, reading medieval philosophy at the National Library, attending the Abbey, ordering furniture for Ballylee, and getting to know the city which would be her home for the rest of her life. WBY's letters to her are unaffectedly tender, with none of the stiltedness of those he had sent from Coole before their hasty marriage. 'I miss you beyond words & have carefully watered your seeds on the windowsill as the only form of attention I can show you & am now going to the garden to water the rest. They do not require watering but I am doing it to satisfy my feelings so they must endure it.' 'I cannot bear the thought of being away from you again. I say to myself everyday that is one day less of parting. She will be home in so many days . . . I feel always that I am just filling up an empty space in life waiting your return.'[93] The quarrel with Margaret Gregory had brought them together in more ways than one. At Ballinamantane their life at last seemed to have settled into the regular pattern so long dreamed of: a marriage like that of Nicolas Flamel or Raymond Lully. Evenings would be spent in occult divination; for company they had the Angora cat Pangur, soon joined by another kitten and two tame hares – who multiplied to five before they left.[94] The routine was dictated by George's 'Controls', who firmly handed out a 'time table' on 12 May: work five mornings a week, idle one morning, 'potter over paper' another; expeditions in the afternoon; automatic-writing sessions two nights a week, and two evenings 'codifying' the material already accumulated (which presumably gave the medium an opportunity to revise). 'You are to go to bed earlier & get up earlier – much better for you. Now I have done for the time being.'[95] It seemed a good omen that on the day they moved in, a long-awaited talisman arrived: a gold ring cast from a design by Dulac, incorporating their twin symbols of butterfly and hawk, wisdom and intuition.[96] And, though they did not yet know it, George was pregnant.

The new regime brought results. 'WB has *stacks* of stuff eating its head off for want of print,' George told Pound at the end of May. 'In fact he is going to take two weeks holiday to recover from overwork.'[97] He had just finished his second elegy, which would become 'In Memory of Major Robert Gregory', published the following August. This time, Robert's mother and widow were determined to supervise. Working on the stanza 'that is to commend Robert's courage in the hunting-field', WBY confided to George:

It has been a little thorny but we have settled a compromise. I have got from her a list of musical place-names where he has hunted & hope for a new representation of the place. I have firmly resisted all suggested eloquence about aero planes '& the blue Italian sky'. It is pathetic for Lady Gregory constantly says 'it is his monument – all that remains'.[98]

WBY thought it 'one of my best poems' and he was anxious to publish it as soon as possible; Margaret and her mother-in-law were both involved in choosing where it would first appear (the *English Review* in August, and – via Pound – the American *Little Review* in September).[99] Their approval may have been tempered by the way that the poem centred on Ballylee and Yeats rather than on Gregory and Coole. Though it owed much to the elegiac tradition he had attempted less successfully in its predecessor, 'In Memory of Major Robert Gregory' is also WBY's first celebration of the tower and its place in his own life. It might even be seen as another instalment of his memoirs, summoning the dead friends of his youth as Robert Gregory's fit company – though the war hero alone is given the accolade of achieving unity of being. WBY's metaphor for a short life, joyously lived, is a fire of straw: an image which reprises JBY's letter of condolence to Augusta Gregory.

> Some burn damp faggots, others may consume
> All the combustible world in one small room
> As though dried straw, and if we turn about
> The bare chimney is gone black out
> Because the work had finished in that flare.
> Soldier, scholar, horseman, he,
> As 'twere all life's epitome,
> What made us dream that he could comb grey hair?[100]

Above all, the elegy is a roll-call of ghosts – a theme to which he would return, and which reflected closely the preoccupations brought by his marriage.

It was not the only poetic profit. On 6 June WBY wrote excitedly to Pound (still his conduit to American publication) about the two 'philosophic poems' he had written, 'an attempt to get subjective hardness': these were 'The Phases of the Moon' and 'The Double Vision of Michael Robartes'. He grouped them with his fantasy about the imagined sect of 'Judwalis', as part of the background to his 'System'. *The Dreaming of the Bones*, which he sold equally hard as 'the best play I have written for some years', was similarly rooted in the circumstances of his current life. 'Recent events in Ireland have made it actual, & I could say in a note that but for these events I should not have published it till after the war'. There was also *The Only Jealousy*, his memoirs in progress, and 'a bundle of stories & dialogues concerning Michael Robartes' which he had in his head. And he was 'writing more verse than I ever did before'.

The upheavals of the previous year had subsided; his marriage had settled into a happy pattern; even his old fantasy of playing father-figure to Gonne's children was indirectly coming true. She was still in Holloway (where WBY arranged for her to receive the *Theologiae* of Thomas Aquinas: she had told him 'one needs very sound doctrine to prevent imagination going wild in meditation'[101]). At AE's request the Yeatses took Seán to Ballinamantane for July, until they moved into the cottage quarters at Ballylee. The question of his schooling also preoccupied WBY, since 'he will have to make an income someday for his Mother has no longer enough for herself & him & Iseult. She will be able to give him something but not a livelihood. This is private.'[102] Seán's visit was a success: 'a gentle solitary boy', WBY told Quinn, '& whether he has talent or not it is impossible to say for he is still too much the boy, thinking of what he does & sees but not forming judgement'. Not everyone agreed; to Arthur Symons, visiting the Gonnes at Woburn Buildings that autumn, the boy seemed like a nihilist revolutionary student, forever conspiring.[103] But, as always, WBY had come to the aid of 'the oldest friend I have' in adversity. His sympathy for Gonne in her plight was all the stronger because he was less opposed to her 'advanced' brand of politics than he had been for years. He continued to keep his 'rebellion poems' from publication, and was cautious about the offence which *The Dreaming of the Bones* might cause; the *Bookman* turned it down because of the political implications.[104] But, WBY told Pound, 'I share the Irish point of view myself completely . . . and think England has no business whatever (as I think you put it) to obtrude her affairs on Ireland.'[105]

IV

Life at Gort in that first Ballylee summer was not entirely solipsistic. WBY continued to grapple with the Abbey's problems from a distance, drum up commissions for Lily's embroidery (using artist contacts in London such as Sturge Moore and Dulac), and to press the claims of Joyce on the eternal patron Quinn, prompted by Pound, the eternal advocate.[106] And on a visit to London in mid August, he was keenly reminded of his susceptibility to Iseult. Her Chelsea life with Iris Barry, 'a scandalous person [who] seems to have kept Iseult in submission with tears & temper', had foundered. Iseult, irresolute as ever, had to be 'kidnapped' by both Yeatses with 'her maid, her cat & birds & all her furniture & transferred to Woburn Buildings'. 'It was George who got the furniture van & seized the furniture glad to exercise her hatred of Chelsea.' WBY's position as avuncular guardian was slightly compromised because his ex-mistress Alick Schepeler, well established in the louche world that circled round Augustus John, had been partly responsible for Iseult's falling into fast company. 'Maud Gonne has brought Iseult up in such a strange world that she is not shocked at what other girls are shocked at,' WBY told Gregory; he added, 'Iseult is afraid of the young woman, of Ezra, of me, of everybody & thats the very devil.'[107]

Iseult refused to join them at Ballylee for the summer, but her allure remained. Her correspondence with WBY had not abated: the previous month he had sent her new poems to type out, including 'Solomon to Sheba' and 'Under the Round Tower'. And when George left London, probably to visit her mother in Devon, WBY took Iseult to dinner before he departed for Dublin. He sent her two long letters as soon as he arrived there, clearly showing that his obsession with her remained in the blood.

My dear Maurice: We must not let the old 'link' be broken. For so many years you were to me like a very dear daughter, & cannot you be that again. Nothing indeed can break this link – never up to this broken in my thoughts – but the unhappiness of another. Every year of life has shown me that there is nothing in life worth having but intensity & that there cannot be intensity without a certain harmlessness and sweetness in the common things of life.

I made a mistake in something I said to you about your 'Mask' – I said it belonged to active life & was perhaps 'a shepherdess with her flock'. I had seen the symbol wrongly. I enclose a diagram. Your Mask is at 28 (called the phase of the Fool but in its high aspect the Fool means a mind absorbed in God not the convinced absorbtion of the Saint who is at phase 27 – but a natural or enforced absorbtion). The ego is folding up into itself & scales as an escape this absorbtion in God. By this Mask & by the creative genius (from 16) which is a kind of emotional intuition (I will write more of this and less vaguely when I have besought the help of Thomas) the ego escapes from 'the enforced love of the world' the personality of Fate from 2 (where Natural life the vehement life of the race begins.) Tell me if you can understand this?

When I come to London next we will have some long talks & we will see each other at Oxford where you will come & stay with us. Later on you will come to Ballylee. Meanwhile my dear child be friends with George & with her friends too if you can. George has become happy only very lately but in a little while she will have become used to happiness & then I shall dread no more that thought that used to persecute her – the thought that she had come between old friends by an accident. Write to me more often & send me your work.

Yours affectly
WB Yeats[108]

That evening he wrote again, enclosing 'The Phases of the Moon' and further refining his analysis of her personality as defined in his 'System'. The formulation said something about himself as well.

Your evil genius is 'terror' and being from 16 is caused by the subconscious memory the souls at 16 possess of the deepening vision haunted loneliness with which the spiritual incarnation of 15 begins a kind of agony in the garden. You escape this by the creative genius. The creative genius & the mask together protect you from the personality of Fate 'enforced love of the world' and from the ego's absorbtion in itself. The ego & the personality of Fate left to themselves are slavery and all good is freedom. To be free is to be self determined but we come to the self through the mask 'a form created by passion to unite us to ourselves' and express it thro [ugh our? – page torn] creative genius. The ego is merely free will, that which makes one man different from another & the Personality of Fate, or the environment of the ego, is the creation of its past & other lives.

I think the reason why the mask is a form created not by 'emotion' but by 'passion' is that we make it not by thinking alone but while struggling with the Personality of Fate. Your PF makes you 'passionate' & in that condition you desire 'serenity' & live not in the world but in God.[109]

She replied at length, assuring him that 'the link our friendship will never be weakened'.[110] And though the subject of her letter was ostensibly religion and mysticism, this had always provided their metaphorical language of emotion. During her mother's imprisonment, she would continue to turn to him as dependently as ever.

However, the opposing magnetic pull of the domestic life he was building in Ireland exerted a stronger and stronger influence. George was now four months pregnant, and she enlisted the 'Instructors' to emphasize this in a dramatic manner calculated to absorb all of WBY's attention and direct it away from the bewitching Iseult. By 24 September the nightly dialogues had established not only that an Avatar was coming to impose a new order on the world, but that he would be born to a family associated for five generations with the sacred mountain of Ben Bulben. The 'completion of this philosophy through self & medium is part of this Being's work'. The picture was building up, and, after exhaustive questioning, it was clarified that the unborn Avatar would, in fact, be the Yeatses' coming child.[111] This astonishing prospect was calculated to put even Iseult's glamour in the shade. But her image, like her mother's, had a way of persisting. That autumn WBY wrote, and sent to Iseult, 'Two Songs of a Fool', a poem which framed his symbolic images of George and herself, tame and wild, as cat and hare. It also expressed his sense of responsibility for her – 'Fool' though he was – and his fears for her future: all too prophetic, as it would turn out.

I

A speckled cat and a tame hare
Eat at my hearthstone
And sleep there;
And both look up to me alone
For learning and defence
As I look up to Providence.

I start out of my sleep to think
Some day I may forget
Their food and drink;
Or, the house door left unshut,
The hare may run till it's found
The horn's sweet note and the tooth of the hound.

I bear a burden that might well try
Men that do all by rule,
And what can I
That am a wandering witted fool
But pray to God that He ease
My great responsibilities.

II

I slept on my three-legged stool by the fire,
The speckled cat slept on my knee;
We never thought to enquire
Where the brown hare might be,
And whether the door were shut.
Who knows how she drank the wind
Stretched up on two legs from the mat,
Before she had settled her mind
To drum with her heel and to leap:
Had I but awakened from sleep
And called her name she had heard,
It may be, and had not stirred,
That now, it may be, has found
The horn's sweet note and the tooth of the hound.

'It is beautiful,' Iseult wrote in acknowledgement,

and pathetic with the pathos I admire most – destiny. I was thinking to myself after reading it: 'All, even hysteria, becomes respectable when set spinning by the thumb of fate, and it is part of the fate of hares to run wild and to be hunted.' Then I began to think of it as applied to myself and my speculations became less dreamy, more precise. Why did you feel anxious about me, I mean anxious in that way? The hare seems to me a symbol of personality – as helpless – but more active than mine, of one that both fears yet has to encounter danger, altogether a more dramatic personality. I don't really think I belong to that order of things. Sometimes I wish I did ('enforced love of the world' I suppose), but I doubt that it is my destiny ever to meet directly with drama, unless it be the obscure drama of the mind in the hard process of sheding [*sic*] illusions.[112]

When wby returned to Gort, Ballylee was still not ready. George joined him after a week, and they visited Gogarty at Renvyle, moving on to Sligo and Rosses Point (they rowed around Lough Gill without being able to find the by now legendary Innisfree). Finally, on 12 September, they moved from Ballinamantane into the cottage adjacent to the castle. 'Little of house is yet habitable,' wby told Pound a week later,

but we have kitchen & servants room, & our bedroom, & a sitting room with a most romantic old cottage fire-place with a great hood and a great flat hearth that makes our two cats purr whenever they think of it. Then also we have a hall with open timbers, and out of it is the great castle door with its 14th or 15th century arched top. As George moves about she would shock your modern mind by composing into 14 century pictures against the little windows with their orange curtains, & the rough whitewashed walls.[113]

The fireplace hood was made of wicker, an idea encouraged by Charles Ricketts, who also helped produce 'medieval' candlesticks. Scott's massive furniture designs were being made up by local carpenters. All the window frames were made and being installed by late October. The setting was as carefully crafted as that of Woburn Buildings but with more resources, thanks to George's money. 'I do be anxious for safety of buildings,' wrote Rafferty, 'now that there is so much cost with them.'[114] Floods persisted, mice were rife, autumn was closing in, and wby began to spend more time in Dublin. There was the Lane pictures business, precipitated by the threat of the Tate Gallery claiming the hoard for their new wing. The series of lectures planned for the Abbey was coming to fruition, and he booked a performance by his old Bedford Park acquaintance Gilbert Chesterton – tempted by wby's promise that he would debate against Larkinite socialists '& might start a movement'.[115]

But he was also concerned with less Utopian politics, as the conscription crisis rumbled on. Three weeks after wby's return to Dublin, Francis Cruise O'Brien, an Arts Club acquaintance and a member of the War Aims Committee, asked wby to write to the senior Liberal politician Lord Haldane. A long and powerful letter was dispatched in early October:

I write to you because you are a man of letters, and we, therefore, may speak the same language. I have no part in politics and no liking for politics, but there are moments when one cannot keep out of them. I have met nobody in close contact with the people who believes that conscription can be imposed without the killing of men, and perhaps of women. Lady Gregory, who knows the country as few know it, and has taken down, for instance, hundreds of thousands of words in collecting folk-lore from cottage to cottage and has still many ways of learning what is thought about it – is convinced that the women and children will stand in front of their men and receive the bullets. I do not say that this will happen, but I do say that there is in this country an extravagance of emotion which few Englishmen, accustomed to more objective habits of thought, can understand. There is something oriental in the people, and it is impossible to say how great a tragedy may lie before us. The British Government, it seems to me, is rushing into this business in a strangely trivial frame of mind. I hear of all manner of opinions being taken except the opinion of those who have some knowledge of the popular psychology. I hear even of weight being given to the opinions of clergymen of the Church of Ireland, who, as a class, are more isolated from their neighbours than any class anywhere known to me. I find in people here in Dublin a sense of strain and expectancy which makes even strangers speak something of their mind. I was ordering some coal yesterday, and I said: 'I shall be in such and such a house for the next four months.' The man at the counter, a stranger to me, muttered: 'Who, in Ireland, can say where he will be in four months?' Another man, almost a stranger, used nearly those very words speaking to me some two weeks ago. There is a danger of a popular hysteria that may go to any height or any whither. There is a return to that sense of crisis which followed the Rising. Some two months after the Rising I called on a well-known Dublin doctor, and as I entered his room, an old cabinet-maker went out. The doctor said to me: 'That man has just said a very strange thing. He says there will be more trouble yet, for "the young men are mad jealous of their leaders for being shot".' That jealousy is still in the country. It is not a question as to whether it is justified or not justified, for these men believe – an incredible thought, perhaps, to Englishmen – that the Childers Committee reported truthfully as to the overtaxation of Ireland, that the population of Ireland has gone down one-half through English misgovernment, that the union of Ireland, in our time, was made impossible because England armed the minority of people with rifles and machine-guns. When they think to themselves: 'Now England expects us to die for her', is it wonderful that they say to themselves afterwards: 'We shall bring our deaths to a different market.' I read in the newspaper yesterday that over three hundred thousand Americans have landed in France in a month, and it seems to me a strangely wanton thing that England, for the sake of fifty thousand Irish soldiers, is prepared to hollow another trench between the countries and fill it with blood. If that is done England will only suffer in reputation, but Ireland will suffer in her character, and all the work of my life-time and that of my fellow-workers, all our effort to clarify and sweeten the popular mind, will be destroyed and Ireland, for another hundred years, will live in the sterility of her bitterness.[116]

When Chesterton did visit Dublin, and the king's health was proposed at a dinner for him, WBY 'was so angry – as I knew the difficulty it put all the

Sinn Féin part of our audience in – that I did not stand up'.[117] By the late autumn Sinn Féin had transformed itself into a credible political force, winning by-elections on a platform of boycotting Westminster and setting up alternative civil institutions. It had also redefined its organization and nature in the aftermath of 1916: it was now an openly republican party, with a policy which remained deliberately ambiguous about the use of violence. For WBY and his friends, it was no longer a motley collection of chauvinists centred around the malevolent Arthur Griffith but a body representing the sacrificial politics of 1916, in the tradition of the Fenians, and epitomized by Eamon de Valera. This was how the revolutionary cause figured in *The Dreaming of the Bones*, and WBY was now anxious to see the play published – the war effort notwithstanding. Haldane replied to WBY's letter, offering an interview, but it was postponed. WBY feared that in any case it was too late to do anything.

If conscription is imposed upon Ireland it will be neither imposed nor met in cold blood. I have just been speaking to a man who had said to an officer this morning 'Why do you want conscription with the War nearly at an end?' And the officer had replied 'We want the chance of teaching these people a lesson.' He went on to explain that a barber at Kingstown had refused to shave him, & the refusal of that barber may yet cause some man's death. There will be incidents that will become anecdotes & legends according to whether they are told by the educated or by the poor, & the legends of the poor never die. Each side will have its wrongs to tell of & these will keep England & Ireland apart during your lifetime & mine. England will forget the anecdotes in a few years, but the legends will never be forgotten.[118]

By mid October the danger of imposing conscription was belatedly recognized, and the arrival of American troops relieved the crisis. But WBY was not wrong in his reading of the public mood, nor in his sense – as his wife would put it in the distant future – of 'how things would look to people afterwards'.

From mid September he was based at the Stephen's Green Club, dispatching a stream of letters to Ballylee about the usual trail of missing belongings. The tone had moderated: 'My dearest' had become 'My dear George', and 'Yours with love', 'Yours affy, W. B. Yeats' – his habitual superscription in letters to his family. Practicalities were taking over. A base had to be found in Dublin for the winter, and by early October WBY had hit on a solution. Before her imprisonment under the DORA regulations, Gonne had taken a lease on a house on Stephen's Green. The Yeatses would take it over for six months. Lily helped to organize furniture and fuel. It seemed a convenient arrangement, and WBY's closeness to Gonne was further signalled by his intercession on her behalf with the chief secretary, Edward Shortt, which took place on 3 October.[119] WBY got permission for Gonne to be examined by a doctor chosen by her friends, and to return to France, but gloomily doubted whether she would agree: 'she has refused to give her parole not to engage in politics if released'. By mid October he was facing the prospect that they might have to give up the house to her, if she were released on grounds of ill health. On 14 October wby asked the Home Rule MP Stephen Gwynn to request this on the grounds that the abandonment of conscription would make her release safe.[120] But for the moment he had a Dublin base, not before time: he calculated that in the past eventful twelve months he had inhabited exactly twenty different houses.[121] George joined him at Stephen's Green. She was now nearly six months pregnant; she was also exhausted, as she had had to close down Ballylee as the waters rose. The solicitous 'Instructors' rapidly administered some supernatural nagging: her husband must recognize her needs and condition, allow her rest, and stop his garrulity about psychic affairs to all and sundry. This was indeed becoming a joke. Gogarty went round Dublin promising entertainments when wby would expound his 'secret doctrines of the Sun and Moon to an audience limited to 28 and selected by me', while Pound ironically reported the Yeats pregnancy to Quinn in terms of 'awesome expectations with portents, signs and excursions'.[122] A young Canadian who visited the Yeatses in Stephen's Green had clearly picked up the gossip. He was struck by their distinction as a couple: wby's 'short, aggressive nose, small firm mouth, quick penetrating eyes and proud, even arrogant poise and carriage', and George's long 'pre-Raphaelite' hair, warmth of manner, and lack of affectation. But, he noted, she seemed wrapped in 'some strange power of divination'. Meanwhile wby talked hypnotically and mystically about the phases of the moon until the problems of financing a repertory theatre came up, when he became at once 'completely objective and realistic'.[123]

Late October and early November were spent getting the house ready, preparing the Cuala publication of *Two Plays for Dancers* (*The Only Jealousy of Emer* was to be published first in *Poetry* and *The Dreaming of the Bones* in the *Little Review*),[124] and negotiating Sturge Moore designs for a bookplate and the cover of Macmillan's much extended *Wild Swans at Coole*. The Abbey was once again taking up his time, and there was the proposal of a revival of *On Baile's Strand*, using Ricketts's wonderful sets and costumes. Interest was expressed from the Stage Society in London in *The Player Queen*, though wby doubted its commercial viability. He was once again excited by a new thespian initiative, the 'Drama League', set up a few months before to put on modern plays and bring in international experimentation.[125] In some ways his Dublin life promised to revive the enthusiasms of twenty years before. But suddenly, crisis struck.

First, on 17 November a delayed cable from New York announced that JBY was ill. Lily at once planned to cross the Atlantic.[126] At this very point, George collapsed. WBY first put it down to exhaustion and stress, but she had fallen a victim to the virulent influenza epidemic sweeping Western Europe. Within a week she had developed serious pneumonia. The gynaecologist, Bethel Solomons, called in a specialist; a day nurse and a night nurse were installed in Stephen's Green, and WBY moved out to his club to make room. His family noted how distraught he became: JBY remarked to Quinn (on Lily's authority) 'if she should die, Willie will be a wreck within six months'.[127] She was not out of danger until 29 November, and remained very weak, 'but sweet & patient through it all, trying to think of everybodys comfort', WBY told Gregory;[128] she was not to move for at least a week. And, to provide a dramatic climax, Gonne arrived illegally in Dublin, having been released from Holloway (thanks partly to Quinn's intervention) and disguised herself to evade port security at Holyhead. She made her way straight to Stephen's Green, and WBY turned her away. With nursing staff in residence there was, for one thing, no room even for himself: more importantly, with a heavily pregnant wife seriously ill, the risk of a military raid could not be taken. But after this confrontation they could no longer stay under Gonne's roof. 'The patriot was, so to speak, banging on the door the whole day long,' Lily told Quinn, 'wanting to get into her own house, and was living in *ostentatious* discomfort in rooms.'[129] The household moved further down the Green to lodgings at No. 96 for George's convalescence, and WBY wrote ruefully to Gregory:

I cannot go to the house in Stephens Green because Madame Gonne has come out of prison with Neurasthenia & her hatred has pitched on me. She writes me the most venemous letters. It all started with my refusal to allow her to stay there while George was ill. It has finally taken the form of beleiving that I have conspired with Shortt to shut her up in an English sanatorium that I might keep possession of her house. It would be much simpler to call it possession by the devil & then one could beleive that it might be over – after a Mass or two.[130]

Gregory must have applauded him, but it had been deeply traumatic for Gonne. Weakened by prison, worried about her children, obsessed by politics, she felt betrayed by someone who had been staunch through all her troubles and who had, after all, promised to move out of her house when she was released. Iseult (who had followed her mother to Dublin) detachedly judged that 'they have both behaved as badly as they could', her mother having been 'more tactless and Willy more in the wrong . . . there should be a law by which after 50, people should be placed under the tutelage of their juniors'. She also sardonically recounted a confrontation between the two in Stephen's Green, 'among the nurses and perambulators'.

M: 'If only you would stop lying!'

W (gesture of arms): 'I have never lied, my father never told a lie, my grandfather never told a lie.'

M: 'Now, Willy, you are really lying.'

The quarrel after the Jubilee of 1897, when he had restrained her from joining the Dublin street riots, was as nothing compared to this. Iseult remained friendly, visiting George and planning a trip to Ballylee, but both the Yeatses needed peace. As for Gonne, Lily cynically reported to Quinn that she had 'gone to the country. I can't imagine her in the country, no limelight, no audience, no one but her very difficult family – But it shows that for the present she has abandoned the "arrested on her deathbed" tableau, or perhaps only postponed it.'[131]

By mid December George was well enough for them to go to Wicklow. Dublin now seemed to WBY 'a foul form of English life'; 'even you', he told Pound, 'would prefer a mountain to this town.'[132] His native city had certainly not lost its taste for guying him. Susan Mitchell had recently published a collection of anonymous parodies by divers hands, *The Secret Springs of Dublin Song*, in which WBY featured over and over again. AE had a poem entitled 'Michael Robartes to His Beloved, Telling Her How the Greatness of His Verse Shall Open to Her the Door of Heaven', and Gogarty wrote a skit of the First Musician's song from *Deirdre*, mocking WBY's social aspirations:

> Peeresses a shining ring
> Yearn about me as I walk,
> If a poet cannot sing
> He must talk, he must talk.

But the most vitriolic (and best) parody was by Seumas O'Sullivan.

> The Wild Dog Compares Himself to a Swan

> Though crowds once gathered if I raised my hand,
> I have grown now to be like that old swan
> That, lonely, swimming, frowns the summer through,
> Because he finds his voice inadequate;
> Or that he must so constantly seek out
> The base intruders that have built their nests
> In difficult places underneath his wings.[133]

O'Sullivan knew that he had been one of the 'fleas' whom WBY had 'refused to praise' when asked to do so by AE for his *New Songs* anthology ten years before, and he took a poet's revenge.

They returned to their Dublin lodgings for Christmas, but the strain of the recent upheavals told on WBY. By early January he was ill with eye trouble, 'heart bother & general nervous weakness', blaming it on 'my fathers illness, Georges illness, & the row with Maud Gonne'. He first thought of taking refuge at Coole, but Gregory put him off, and the Yeatses withdrew to the Lucan Spa Hotel just outside Dublin. Here he worked on the lectures which he was giving to the Arts Club on psychic phenomena ('I want to break through our conventions of opinion'[134]). These paved the way for two public debates on psychic phenomena (one at Belfast) and a discussion of 'Psychical Research from the Catholic Point of View' held at the Abbey. WBY was opposed by one professor from the National University and chaired by another; he vigorously rebutted arguments that psychical research was unethical and forbidden by the Church. Science, in his view, had proved that communications with the dead could and did take place (though he did not instance Wilson's metallic homunculus as his proof). 'The country should make up its mind for itself and have an Irish point of view.' Unbelief had poisoned the world; he wanted to change that and could quote words that had come to him from a spirit: 'The love of God is infinite for every human soul, for every human soul is unique. No other can satisfy the same need in God.' This seemed like a clever finesse, and WBY assumed that he had finished his opponent off. It had been, he told Pound with satisfaction, 'a wild week of lectures'.[135]

As he buoyed himself up with controversy, George recovered, and so did his father. Though WBY sent Quinn the old man's fare home to Dublin ('he can be put into the University Club where he can talk to the other atheists'[136]), JBY remained in New York, probably to his family's relief. But it was not a happy time, and WBY was once again worried about money. Ballylee had absorbed most of the Yeatses' joint resources, and in January the builders stopped work for the time being. 'My feudal ambitions have left us both impecunious', WBY ruefully told Pound.[137] Now that Iseult had left London, he was anxious to make some money from letting Woburn Buildings before giving the flat up for good at the end of June.[138] Down the Green, Gonne remained a reproachful presence. 'She looks ghastly,' WBY reported to Quinn.

I heard a young English officer speak of her the other day as a tragic sight. The trouble is that she has no fixed conviction about herself &, after being really alarmed, now thinks herself much better than she is & wont see a proper doctor. Her lung is I believe affected & there is certainly great nervous trouble, & it was this last that caused the difficulty with me. She was in an unnatural state throughout, complicated no doubt by the fact that ever since Easter 1916 her convictions have been fixed ideas, always making her judgement unsound.[139]

By the end of January he found her 'sane & amicable again & I think anxious to make up'; Gogarty claimed that WBY had brought her into line by threatening to revise his early love poems to her. Their quarrel had revived some of his own antipathy to those 'fixed ideas'.[140] 'He is out of touch with latter-day Ireland and I imagine all he likes about Ireland is its past and its scenery,' AE told Quinn at the end of the year.[141] This was not accurate, but certainly at Lucan he drafted a bitter poem which he described to Pound as 'a denunciation of Madame Marckievicz that might get me into trouble . . . When Madame Gonne quarrelled with me I felt it necessary to denounce – Madame Marckievicz.'[142]

It was not published until November 1920, with the title 'On a Political Prisoner'. Much as in 'Easter 1916', Markievicz's present politics were placed in opposition to his own memory of her youth as a county belle: but the contemptuous reference to demotic politics reflected his current disenchantment with Dublin, and hinted that his Sinn Féin sympathies had limits.

I

She that but little patience knew,
From childhood on, had now so much
A grey gull lost its fear and flew
Down to her cell and there alit,
And there endured her finger's touch
And from her fingers ate its bit.

II

Did she in touching that lone wing
Recall the years before her mind
Became a bitter, an abstract thing,
For thought some popular enmity,
Blind and leader of the blind
Drinking the foul ditch where they lie?

III

When long ago I saw her ride
Under Ben Bulben to the meet,
The beauty of her country-side
With all youth's lonely wildness stirred
She seemed to have grown clean and sweet
Like any rock-bred, sea-borne bird:

IV

Sea-borne, or balanced on the air
When first it sprang out of the nest
Upon some lofty rock to stare

Upon the cloudy canopy,
While under its storm-beaten breast
Cried out the hollows of the sea.

But Gonne, as he had admitted to Pound and to George, stands behind the poem too: not only in the denunciation of abstract bitterness and the politics of the crowd, but also in the image of a white sea-bird, associated with her as far back as their tryst at Howth in 1891, and transferred to Iseult in the audacious opening image of *The Only Jealousy of Emer*:

A woman's beauty is like a white
Frail bird, like a white sea-bird alone
At daybreak after stormy night
Between two furrows upon the ploughed land:

The transposition of woman to bird conjures up vulnerability, wildness, and single-mindedness, the characteristics WBY indelibly associated with both the Gonnes. His poem lent Markievicz some of these qualities, but it also takes its place in what would become a poetic commentary about the political sea-change now gathering pace in Ireland, his own receding past, and the price paid for the insights of experience.

This was apposite, for his life was entering another phase. He was about to become a father. On 26 February George gave birth to a healthy child, nearly three weeks early. 'George, who had not cried a tear all through her pains burst into tears when told it was a daughter,' WBY told Gregory. 'I think a daughter (family ambitions and dissapointed relations apart) pleases me better.'[143] The 'Instructors' had not, after all, been infallible: first of all they had specifically forecast the reincarnation of Anne Hyde's son ('She will not want you to reincarnate her herself only her boy because she looks on you as on her husband & on medium as on herself '[144]), and then they had raised the bidding by promising an Avatar. Still, the child was named Anne Butler, presumably after their supernatural visitant and putative ancestress, Anne Hyde. And the 'Instructors' rapidly reassured the parents that their daughter fitted into a foretold daimonic design which made her actually 'a form of the Avatar' (though, being female, a passive form).[145] All was for the best, after all. It was not yet eighteen months since WBY had decided, in a desperate plunge, to make George Hyde Lees his wife; but he knew by now that the decision had been triumphantly vindicated. He was rooting himself once more in Ireland and had (as he had written just after the Rising) begun building again. Established with wife, house, child, and writing poetry with a vigour which he had thought lost years before, he would now record and interrogate what was appearing more and more clearly a crucial turn in the historical cycle which so preoccupied him: the advent of the Irish revolution.

Chapter 4 : A Feeling for Revelation
1919–1920

> Are our personal daimons with us in
> this life only
> No permanent
>
> > automatic script, 7 April 1919[1]

I

ONE month before Anne Butler Yeats's birth, two policemen guarding gelignite at a quarry near Soloheadbeg, County Tipperary, were shot by a detachment of Sinn Féin 'Volunteers', now becoming known as the Irish Republican Army. The more aggressive Volunteers were determined to press the military initiative, rather than rely on 'politics', meaning either a negotiation of dominion home rule or a reliance on international goodwill for Sinn Féin representatives at the Versailles peace negotiations. Those who, like Gregory, had gradualist preferences – wishing for a republic but believing that dominion status would produce it eventually, and that Sinn Féin's monopoly of Irish parliamentary representation gave them the negotiating advantage – were, for the moment, outflanked. From Soloheadbeg, a percussion of 'incidents' against policemen and security forces escalated into a guerrilla war – unevenly prosecuted over the country but violently disruptive and increasingly bitter in areas of Munster and Connacht. In February 1920 Lloyd George's government decided to send in 'Auxiliary' forces to impose order on the most disturbed districts: the most notorious mercenaries became known as 'the Black and Tans'. Gregory's published journals provide one of the most vivid testaments to the drunken tyranny waged around places like Gort. As a government policy decision, it ranked in ineptitude with the post-Rising executions, and it completed the alienation of much Irish nationalist opinion from a compromise approach to independence.

But in early 1919 the Black and Tans were still in the future, and hopes remained high for a negotiated solution. 'Here, a new Rising is prophesied for Easter,' Gregory told her old friend Wilfrid Scawen Blunt in April:

but I don't think it likely, there may probably be something spectacular, like the escapes from Mountjoy prison, to keep the world interested, but Sinn Fein has so tremendously strong a hand just now they should play warily. They have USA and Labour, and especially USA Labour behind them. No American President can afford to ignore them, or rather Ireland, for we are all more or less Sinn Fein.[2]

But she also noted that local 'bad characters' were able to get away with small crimes and intimidation, 'sheltered by the name Sinn Fein, and the idealism that is connected with it'. She hoped for an end to 'the stupidities of the Military Government we live under', and the offer of a self-government scheme 'large enough to put responsibility on the people themselves, and spectacular enough to excite the imagination, or rather to turn the already excited imagination of the young to building instead of breaking'.[3]

Many felt the same way, including WBY. These were the very arguments and metaphors which he had used after Easter 1916. But hopes of American diplomatic intervention, or compromise over Ulster, waned as the hawks of the IRA waged low-intensity warfare against police barracks, state institutions, and 'informers'. For the newly fledged Yeats family, the situation was both ominous and uncertain. The question of where to live continued to preoccupy WBY, as did the weight of family responsibilities. One such responsibility was the irrepressible JBY, more and more of a burden to the long-suffering Quinn in New York; another was the new-born Anne. Conveniently ambiguous horoscopes were cast for her by her mother, by Dulac, by Cyril Fagan of the Irish Astrological Society. 'Yes the child is a great joy,' WBY wrote to Harriet Monroe, 'for she fills the future.'[4]

She also stood for the ancestral past. WBY told Elkin Mathews that the name Anne had been chosen because 'it "cannot be clipped" and has the advantage of not being too poetical; it is a family name on both sides'.[5] But there was more to it than that. The records of the automatic script demonstrate his obsession with fitting her into the history of his uncertain ancestress Anne Hyde. Since she was not a boy, he decided she could not be the reincarnation of Anne Hyde's stillborn son; the interrogations of George's 'Instructors' indicate that he canvassed the idea of his daughter as Anne's own reincarnation, and himself as the reincarnation of both husband and son. 'I want you to fully grasp the meaning of your having been Anne's lover & now her father & the husband of her child who is now her mother,' remarked 'Ontelos' later in the summer, an injunction that confused even WBY.[6] Unsurprisingly, George steered him away from this line of speculation, and his delight in the child for her own sake was patent, though the story that he celebrated her arrival by buying her a bag of sweets may be apocryphal.[7] 'I find that having a child seems to prolong ones own life,' he wrote cheerfully to Quinn in June. 'One thinks of oneself as perhaps living to 1970 or even with luck to the year 2000. (That would be Annes 91st [sic] year) It makes ones family more venerable too now that ones Grandfathers are all great grand fathers. It almost enobles ones ancestors as if it were a Chinese emperror.'[8] His arithmetic was as inaccurate as ever, but the buoyancy of tone is unmistakable.

WBY's sisters and father were equally gratified; Nelly Tucker less so, waiting nearly a year before coming to Oxford to inspect the granddaughter whose arrival she 'regretted', according to WBY. 'She has now compromised with the grandmother so far as to permit herself grey hair instead of the snow white it was a week ago,' he waspishly told Gregory.⁹ The visit, when it came, was not a success. Despite bribes, Anne 'howled' whenever her grandmother went near, and it helped fix George's 'strong feelings' against her mother, whom she considered self-dramatizing and domineering.¹⁰ As for Mrs Tucker, her resentment against the marriage seems to have moderated, though she rarely visited again. Her daughter had, after all, taken someone from 'her' circle, and she may once have had an eye to him herself. Though they visited her in England, and she helped out with – for instance – the evacuation of Woburn Buildings, she would maintain a certain distance from the Yeats household for the rest of her life, and they from her.

This was made possible by George's financial independence, though she had to sell stocks worth £100 to meet the expenses of her peripatetic confinement, and had put a good deal of money into Ballylee.¹¹ But by the spring of 1919 they had to watch money carefully. The effects of the war had left its mark on WBY's income, and regular large sums drained away to New York. In June he had to send a sudden £234 to meet JBY's further expenses, preferring to do this rather than send manuscripts to Quinn. Within two years further payments had used up nearly all his Pollexfen inheritance. By late 1920, he noted ruefully 'all my money and George's goes to mere living expenses'.¹²

With the arrival of a child came a maid and a nurse, while further strain was put upon expenditure by the Yeatses' unsettled life style. From mid March until May they were once again in a rented Dublin house, Dundrum Lodge, down the road from Lily's and Lolly's uneasy ménage at Gurteen Dhas. The sisters welcomed them with a party for fifty people, 'representing the most diverse political opinions from extreme Protestant Unionist to Sinn Fein', according to Lolly, 'and everyone who was at it seemed to enjoy themselves immensely'.¹³ Dublin society mirrored the polarization of Irish politics, but Lolly hoped that their party showed that 'we are perhaps here in Ireland drawing together more and throwing down the doors of our watertight compartments'. Within a year she and Lily would find themselves on the Library Committee of the local Sinn Féin Rural Council, with two Protestant clergymen and two priests. 'The two Priests never came at all, the two parsons did (true we looked *them* both up).'¹⁴

At Dundrum life settled into some kind of routine, and here too began a concentrated assault course of automatic writing, the very day after they moved in. First, the 'Instructors' had to cover themselves against any

complaints about Anne's sex: 'Such a son could not be *willed* – to will ster-
ilises choice – & chance – no – ours corresponds exactly because we make it
from its *image & being* . . . we gave you Anne – is not that horary remarkable
enough.' They also made clear that one more child would suffice: otherwise,
the fourfold pattern intrinsic to the revelation of a coming Avatar would be
disrupted.[15] WBY's questions beat incessantly at the door of revelation and
prophecy, particularly concerning the future birth of his son: the conditions
of conception now become related to the language of 'Iniatory' and 'Critical'
Moments and the 'Passionate Body', already established in his 'System'. He
asked about dates referring back to his own emotional history with
Shakespear, Dickinson, and Gonne. The function of personal daimons in
bringing about the turning-point of a life was anxiously probed, circling
round and round the eternal triangle of Maud, Iseult, and George. The
'Interpreter', as his wife now styled herself, became accordingly exhausted,
vague, and snappish, finally issuing a kind of contract on 29 March:

For every public speech or lecture you give after tomorrow during the next 6 months
– For every occasion you talk system in private conversation one month – Yes you
must begin writing – Yes but dont fish for questions.[16]

Nonetheless, she took the opportunity to convict him of 'delusion', built up
by himself, not only in his 1890s love-poems to Gonne but also in the poetry 'in my last book which is inspired by her'. And he was told he was too separate from 'people – Interpreter among others'. Much of this was scaled up
to cloudy generalizations, but through the sessions recorded at Dundrum
Lodge comes an overwhelming impression of WBY's insistence on asking
'personal' questions about the patterns of his past, and of George's mingled
impatience and readiness to make a point about his behaviour. Above all,
when he asked if the 'lunar symbolism' of the script was from her own spiritual memory, 'pre-existant in anima mundi', she told him firmly that the
'System' they were developing was a created philosophy rather than the
revelation of an eternal reality.

No that is what I have been waiting for – This system is *not* preexistent – it is developed & created by us [the 'Instructors'] & by you two or you three [WBY, George,
and Anne] now – from a preexisting psychology – all the bones are in the world –
we only select & our selection is subordinate to *you both* – therefore we are dependent on you & you influence our ability to develop & create by every small detail of
your joint life.[17]

Perhaps because of this answer, which he analysed closely, from this point
onwards (9 April) his questions about the developing system of astrological
fate, personal character, and historical cycles become more and more

assertive: effectively, statements to which the 'Interpreter' assents or not. WBY was searching inexorably for a consistency behind responses which often seem desultory or self-contradictory. And from now on the link between the supernatural and sexual 'contact' was emphasized. The theory emerges that the 'Instructors' used and relied upon the sexual connection between WBY and George in order to be able to provide full knowledge rather than 'fragments'. And their 'complete sympathy' was dated specifically back to the occasion when, at Coole, six months after their marriage, they had retired to bed, excited by the confrontation with Margaret Gregory, and 'omitted our usual precaution against conception'. Moreover, Ballylee was 'in both fates': as with the expected reincarnation of Anne Hyde, the pattern of their marriage had been preordained. Much of this found its way into poems such as 'Solomon to Sheba', patterned against the Yeatses' shared knowledge of, and identification with, *The Arabian Nights*.

The questions about their sexual relationship would continue to dominate automatic-writing sessions, but from mid May the Yeatses were unsettled once more. WBY travelled to London to move finally out of Woburn Buildings; its last tenants had been the novelist Douglas Goldring and his wife, followed by two theatre people, who had left it in a state of creative squalor, down to an abandoned banjo on the floor. Thus the bohemian connections of the court behind St Pancras Church were kept up until the very end of what his housekeeper Mrs Old would always remember as the 'blessed days' of WBY's tenure. But he felt tired of the city. He planned to return to England in the autumn, as throughout his adult life, but not to London. When George joined him, after checking up on Ballylee and installing Iseult there for a holiday, they spent a weekend house-hunting in Oxford, visited friends like Dulac, and oversaw the surprisingly successful Stage Society production of *The Player Queen*. Having found an Oxford base, they moved the Woburn Buildings furniture there in early June, dispatching Anne and her nurse to Lily and Lolly. By the middle of the month they were back in Dublin, en route to a summer in Ballylee. Here they stayed, with intermittent visits to the Gogartys at Renvyle, a hotel at Oughterard, and a trip to Dublin and Kilkenny in early July, when they tried to research the background of Anne Hyde.

Meanwhile the tower was inching nearer completion, and its decorative style suggested Woburn Buildings would perpetuate itself in another form. The Cuala workers made up curtains dyed 'wonderful brilliant colours, orange and deep blue' in roughly woven fabrics. The archaic effect was set off by striking 'blew' paintwork, and candles in imposingly large stands. WBY could write 'at a great trestle-table which George keeps covered with wild flowers' in 'the great ground floor room of the castle – pleasantest room I have yet seen, a great wide window opening over the river & a round arched door leading to the thatched hall'. Trout could be caught in the river outside, and otters played on the bank.[18] A room was being plastered for Anne's nurse, the cottage was becoming comfortable, George's garden was taking shape, and a local girl was engaged to help with the baby. But down the road at Gort, local disorder was building up, as much based on land hunger as on political disaffection. After a series of local shootings, guns were impounded by the police, and the mail train was robbed. Nationally, the political situation looked no clearer; the Versailles settlement was signed, with no reference to Sinn Féin's optimistic demands for Irish autonomy.

While the Yeatses reviewed their future, an intriguing invitation arrived. On 9 July wby received a letter from the University of Keio Gijuko, Tokyo, asking him to lecture there for two years, with accommodation provided. wby was at once drawn to the idea; by July it was being generally canvassed, for all his fear that Gregory would 'think I am diserting my duties'. 'I shall come back to find Ballylee finished so far as structure goes & all trees planted,' he told Pound: 'it is beautiful now but untidy here & there.'[19] The thought also occurred that he would return to a quieter Ireland. 'It would be pleasant to get away from Irish politics and some patriots for two years', Lily shrewdly remarked to Quinn, while wby himself ruminated on the delights of disappearing

until the tumult of war had died down, & perhaps Home Rule established & even the price of coal settled on. But would one ever come back – would one find some grass-grown city scarce inhabited since the tenth century where one seemed surpassing rich on a few hundred a year; and would I mind if Shinn Fein took possession of my old Tower here to store arms in or the young scholours from the school broke all the new windows. I think my chief difficulty in accepting will be my Tower, which needs another years work under our own eyes before it is a fitting monument & symbol & my garden which will need several years, if it is to be green & shady during my lifetime. Ballylee is a good home for a child to grow up in – a place full of history & romance with plenty to do everyday.[20]

At any rate, by the end of July plans had solidified. On 9 August, he firmly told Quinn (who had been deluging him with doom-laden warnings against the step), 'I have accepted subject to reasonable terms.' They would travel on to Tokyo from his American lecture-tour in the early spring, according to Lily. He had confronted Gregory with the news: she implied, disapprovingly, that the decision was due to George's 'restlessness'.[21] Enthusiasm cooled slowly. By late August he was having doubts, and at the end of September Lily reported that the project would probably be dropped because of the climate and the general disruption involved. But he was still mentioning the possibility to Bullen in mid November. Not until the end of the year did he relinquish the idea of 'some forgotten city, where the streets are full of grass, except for a little track in the centre made by pilgrims to some budhist shrine; & where there is no sound but that of some temple bell'.[22] The Tokyo of the 1920s might have disappointed him; this vision was as poetic as the Byzantium fantasy he would dream up in a few years' time. But his long interest in Japanese aesthetics and dramatic forms remained unslaked, and in fact the eventual refusal was prompted from outside. In a session of automatic writing on 17 November George's new 'Instructor', 'Ameritus', issued a firm warning. 'Tower this year – I said before no Japan next year.' He was ordered to 'write temporising & await official letter', and finally 'wire impossible come next autumn'.[23] Instead, he was to get on with writing up 'the System'. The idea of a retreat to Japan remains preserved as a flourish in the last sentence of WBY's testament 'If I Were Four-and-Twenty', written that first summer in Ballylee; its abandonment bears witness to the powers wielded by the advisory voices speaking through his wife.

'If I Were Four-and-Twenty', written for the liberal-nationalist *Irish Statesman*, testifies to other preoccupations too. As an expression of 'thoughts on the present state of the world', it airs the preoccupations which would shortly pulse through poems such as 'The Second Coming' and 'Nineteen Hundred and Nineteen'. It also shows that WBY continued to be preoccupied by his own autobiography. 'One day when I was twenty-three or twenty-four', the essay begins, 'this sentence seemed to form in my head, without my willing it, much as sentences form when we are half-asleep: "Hammer your thoughts into unity".'[24] The hint of auto-suggestion is not pursued, and the preoccupation with uniting literary, philosophical, and nationalist interests is not related to the 'System' so recently revealed by George's writing. But in the essay, self-assured to the point of stridency, WBY announces that he has become, through thirty years of intellectual effort (which he calls, rather affectedly, 'idleness'), a cultivated man. That unity of philosophy, literature, and patriotism which he had preached in the 1890s might today be demonstrated in France by Péguy, Jammes, and Claudel (Iseult's household gods); in Ireland, the ancient places of pilgrimage, and the confluence of early Christian and Neoplatonist doctrines like that of purgatory, should 'nationalise' religion and contribute towards a form of politics more characteristic of Irish genius than the Connolly-inspired socialism currently fashionable among the young. In fact, those looking for national unity should read Balzac to realize his vision of social order as the creation of two struggles, that of family with family, that of individual with individual, and that our politics depend upon which of the two struggles has most affected our imagination. If it has been most affected by the individual struggle we insist upon equality of opportunity, 'the career open to talent', and consider rank and wealth fortuitous and unjust; and if it is most affected by the struggles of families, we insist upon all that preserves what that struggle has earned, upon social privilege, upon the rights of property.[25]

This is the most original thought in the essay. WBY goes on to reflect on the economics of redistribution and cooperation, the idea of the family unit as the basis of civilization, and the inherited ideals of beauty which fuel not only culture but sexual choice. These are all themes that would affect his work over the following years, and perhaps it was his opinions on these matters that provoked Pound to pronounce the essay 'a bundle of the worst rubbish he has ever written'.[26] But WBY believed that the crisis of Western civilization (which his generation had anticipated in the 1890s) was finally upon the world, and that the form it had taken was materialism and Bolshevism. At a debate in Trinity he aired his anxiety about the Irish Labour movement seeking a revolutionary alliance with extreme nationalism, and he wrote to AE pointing out that Russian communists had killed not 400 but 13,000 people. 'What I want is that Ireland be kept from giving itself (under the influence of its lunatic faculty of going against everything which it believes England to affirm) to Marxian revolution or Marxian definitions of value in any form. I consider the Marxian criterion of values as in this age the spear-head of materialism & leading to inevitable murder. From that criterion follows the well-known phrase "can the bourgeois be innocent?"'[27] He put the same idea more rhetorically in 'If I were Four-and-Twenty':

Logic is loose again, as once in Calvin and Knox, or in the hysterical rhetoric of Savonarola, or in Christianity itself in its first raw centuries, and because it must always draw its deductions from what every dolt can understand, the wild beast cannot but destroy mysterious life. We do not the less need, because it is an economic and not a theological process, those Christian writers whose roots are in permanent human nature . . .

If we could but unite our economics and our nationalism with our religion, that, too, would become philosophic – and the religion that does not become philosophic, as religion is in the East, will die out of modern Europe – and we, our three great interests made but one, would at last be face to face with the great riddle, and might, it may be, hit the answer.

In an unpublished variant he speculated that the Irish 'belief in evil' meant that they would probably adopt 'Balzac's view of the world' and solve problems as they arose, choosing 'the old gambling table of nature' rather than relying on a political system based upon logic.[28] This seems his inclination too. But in the conclusion he hints once more at the importance of supernatural connections, and the web of influence set up between all men by an ancient Anima Mundi: suddenly connected, by a jolting insight, to the advent of totalitarian rule.

With Christianity came the realisation that a man must surrender his particular will to an implacable will, not his, though within his, and perhaps we are restless because we approach a realisation that our general will must surrender itself to another will within it, interpreted by certain men, at once economists, patriots, and inquisitors. As all realization is through opposites, men coming to believe the subjective opposite of what they do and think, we may be about to accept the most implacable authority the world has known. Do I desire or dread it, loving as I do the gaming-table of Nature where many are ruined but none is judged, and where all is fortuitous, unforeseen?[29]

These ambiguous questions would return to him, precipitated by Europe's lurches into historical crisis, over the next twenty years: the striking fact is how clearly he anticipated them in 1919.

II

'He hasn't done much work since his marriage,' Gregory had written in a slightly disapproving letter to Blunt.[30] This was almost ludicrously far from the truth. The Macmillan version of *The Wild Swans at Coole*, which appeared in February 1919, contained seventeen poems not included in the Cuala book of November 1917. They transformed the tone of the volume from introspective reflection to personal assertion.[31] The richness of the work which had been written in the interim, especially 'In Memory of Major Robert Gregory', was universally praised by reviewers. If poems like 'The Fisherman', 'Ego Dominus Tuus', and the suite of poems to Gonne's departing beauty and indomitable spirit[32] belonged to the period before the great upheavals of 1917, a series of lyrics had been inspired by that obsessive summer and autumn. 'Men Improve with the Years', 'The Collar-Bone of a Hare', 'The Living Beauty', 'A Song', 'To a Young Beauty', 'To a Young Girl' are only the most explicit of the poems declaring his feelings for Iseult. Less obviously, and through a subtle use of his own personal imagery for Iseult and George, hare and cat, 'Two Songs of a Fool' movingly declares his own sense of inadequacy and of divided responsibility, as well as his fears for poor Iseult's ultimate fate, all too well founded. To crown the volume, 'Solomon to Sheba', 'The Phases of the Moon', 'Another Song of a Fool', and most of all 'The Double Vision of Michael Robartes' reflect or even record the supernatural insights brought by George's mediumship: writing to Frank Pearce Sturm two years later, WBY told him that all his 'thesis of incarnation' was contained in 'The Phases of the Moon' and 'The Double Vision'.[33]

Seen thus, the 1919 *Wild Swans at Coole* is one of WBY's most autobiographical volumes of verse, commemorating a period of emotional turmoil as well as occult revelation. In this it stands with *The Wind Among the Reeds*, and Pound thought it his strongest book since then.[34] Some modern critics agree, but it was not an opinion generally shared at the time. WBY remained resentfully conscious of the fact that his early work continued to sell best, and that this was where his popular audience remained: the Unwin *Poems* still brought in as much as all his more recent Macmillan volumes together.[35] The influential J. C. Squire wrote an antagonistic piece on *The Wild Swans at Coole*, attacking the rough language, unevenness, and wilful obscurity. *The Times Literary Supplement* found it 'easy, lazy, masterly fiddling': old tunes played with variations. John Middleton Murry, forcefully wrong-headed, thought WBY's personal mythology had dissolved into a dreamy 'phantasmagoria', incapable of animating the poems with vigour, so the collection betrayed emptiness and impotence.[36] Other reviewers regretted the loss of 'delicacy of diction, the atmosphere of legend and myth, vital and all pervading, the penetrating insight that made the poetic fancy but an interpretation of one's struggling thought'. Few saw that the 'thought' reflected in the new poems was more idiosyncratic than ever before, rooted in a bedrock that owed little to Celtic mythology or public politics, and expressed in a language quarried for the new purpose. Within two years, as it happened, Squire's very own *London Mercury* would be printing some of WBY's most impressive poems yet.[37]

The volume also deliberately left out the whole series of political poems which had stemmed from the Easter Rising. These would have added a much more accessible 'public' dimension, but at the cost of disrupting the secret coherence of the whole. When WBY expressed disappointment at the volume's reception, Gregory told him he 'would have made a better and richer book if he had kept it back till he could put in his rebellion poems – and he agreed – but does not know when that can be'. (In her journal she added, with ill-concealed distaste, 'he is still interested in his philosophy'.[38]) Yet it is unlikely that she would have encouraged him: she herself still subordinated all public expressions of nationalist sympathies to the Lane pictures campaign, as she admitted to Blunt.

I am keeping clear of politics . . . But though I would take Dominion H.R., or even Federalism, and even under Coercion would continue to do my work as best as I could, I am more and more drawn to a Republic. It is the only thing that would excite the imagination of our young men to such an extent as would lead them to the enthusiastic building of the nation. And it would bring America in with enthusiasm and without patronage. But I cannot say this in any public way, because – so are we bound – Carson's men are in charge of the Lane picture business just now, and I must pray for Carson's health to bring it through.[39]

Moreover, while *The Wild Swans at Coole* was going through Macmillan's press, WBY was writing a poem which not only reflected his views of the anarchy seeping into Irish politics but dramatically conveyed the sense of historical apocalypse suggested by world events since 1917, clarified (in his own mind at least) by the 2,000-year cyclical tides of history discussed with George's 'Instructors'. In its title too 'The Second Coming' suggests the idea of the Avatar which dominated so many of the automatic-writing sessions. Above all (unlike the poems published in *The Wild Swans at Coole*), it achieved a language which could be intuitively, if not rationally, understood by the entranced reader: which *would*, in the words of the disappointed reviewer of that volume, 'make the poetic fancy but an interpretation of one's struggling thought'. An audaciously long sentence opens the poem, cast as the first octave of a sonnet, and a shocking question closes it. The effect anticipates the mystery and grandeur of his later verse at its most plangent. Like the best poems of his youth, but in a very different way, 'The Second Coming' would – from its first publication on 6 November 1920 in the *Nation* – crystallize the doubts and feelings of a generation at a moment of flux.

> Turning and turning in the widening gyre
> The falcon can not hear the falconer;
> Things fall apart; the centre can not hold;
> Mere anarchy is loosed upon the world,
> The blood-dimmed tide is loosed, and everywhere
> The ceremony of innocence is drowned;
> The best lack all conviction, while the worst
> Are full of passionate intensity.
>
> Surely some revelation is at hand;
> Surely the Second Coming is at hand.
> The Second Coming! Hardly are those words out
> When a vast image out of Spiritus Mundi
> Troubles my sight: a waste of desert sand;
> A shape with lion body and the head of a man,
> A gaze blank and pitiless as the sun,
> Is moving its slow thighs, while all about it
> Wind shadows of the indignant desert birds.

> The darkness drops again but now I know
> That thirty centuries of stony sleep
> Were vexed to nightmare by a rocking cradle,
> And what rough beast, its hour come round at last
> Slouches towards Bethlehem to be born?[40]

The poem may take its rise from the same reaction to the unleashing of Bolshevism which prompted 'If I were Four-and-Twenty', but its imagery trawls as wide a net of influences as any poem in WBY's canon. Echoes are stirred from Shelley, Wordsworth's *The Excursion*, illustrations by Blake and Ricketts, Flaubert's *La Tentation de Saint Antoine*, Burke's *Letters on a Regicide Peace* (with its description of a dog-headed Egyptian monster), Gustave Moreau's paintings, and WBY's early studies in Egyptology with MacGregor Mathers, Farr, and the fringe of the Golden Dawn; the last lines reflect the interest in New Testament cosmogony which had been pre-occupying him for more than two years.[41] But the surreal vividness of the apocalyptic imagery in 'The Second Coming' stands independent and entire, with no need of reference or explanation: as much as any Yeats poem, it expresses what T. R. Henn calls 'that curious clarity of vision which is not a clarity of detail, but rather of imaginative focus: a sense of the procession-al element in life and in history'.[42]

Nor was this all. During the early summer at Ballylee he completed another major piece of work: the first poem to celebrate his house at length, dedicated to the baby now sleeping there in a seventeenth-century cradle.[43] Like 'The Second Coming', 'A Prayer for my Daughter' reflects his appre-hension at a world descending into formless anarchy, though it is constructed as a formal ode, in the manner of his poem in memory of Robert Gregory.

> I have walked and prayed for this young child an hour,
> And heard the sea-wind scream upon the tower,
> And under the arches of the bridge, and scream
> In the elms above the flooded stream;
> Imagining in excited reverie
> That the future years had come
> Dancing to a frenzied drum
> Out of the murderous innocence of the sea.

In the much reworked first drafts of the poem Anne is addressed directly, and Coole, the swans, the lake, and WBY's own collaboration with Gregory take centre stage; but these references were systematically removed or played down, as the injunctions offered for his child's future became more formal and abstract. Perhaps his sense of future chaos sent him back to the past, in the deliberately archaic prescriptions for Anne's life which have

vexed or puzzled generations of readers. There is nothing here to indicate
that the women WBY himself admired were without exception independent,
strong-minded, gifted, and intellectually curious. Instead he prays for
beauty (but not 'overmuch'), courtesy, and kindness: a word he constantly
used to describe his wife. The fifth stanza, in fact, may be read as a development of the Maud-versus-George trope which preoccupied (to the
medium's annoyance) so many sessions of automatic writing.

> In courtesy I'd have her chiefly learned;
> Hearts are not had as a gift but hearts are earned
> By those that are not entirely beautiful.
> Yet many, that have played the fool
> For beauty's very self, has charm made wise;
> And many a poor man that has roved,
> Loved and thought himself beloved,
> From a glad kindness cannot take his eyes.

The seventh and eighth stanzas are directly autobiographical, dealing with
the price paid by legendary beauty *à la* Gonne, and the additional danger of
Maud's fanaticism.

> My mind, because the minds that I have loved,
> The sort of beauty that I have approved,
> Prosper but little, has dried up of late,
> Yet knows that to be choked with hate
> May well be of all evil chances chief,
> If there's no hatred in a mind
> Assault and battery of the wind
> Can never tear the linnet from the leaf.
>
> An intellectual hatred is the worst,
> So let her think opinions are accursed.
> Have I not seen the loveliest woman born
> Out of the mouth of Plenty's horn,
> Because of her opinionated mind
> Barter that horn and every good
> By quiet natures understood
> For an old bellows full of angry wind?

And we are reminded that the soul 'recovers radical innocence' in learning
how its journey is guided by 'Heaven'. If this is read as 'the Heavens', the
lessons of the unknown 'Instructors' and the developing 'System' recur yet
again. On one level, the poem is another 'self and soul' exercise in personal
analysis. But, in the end, it apparently resolves itself into a prayer for marriage couched in the most archaic and aristocratic terms:

And may her bridegroom bring her to a house
Where all's accustomed, ceremonious;
For arrogance and hatred are the wares
Peddled in the thoroughfares.
How but in custom and in ceremony
Are innocence and beauty born?
Ceremony's a name for the rich horn,
And custom for the spreading laurel tree.

On a cursory reading, the poet's possession of a 'castle' seemed to have gone to his head, and his youth spent in the company of women as unconventional as Farr, Gonne, and Shakespear to have been conveniently forgotten: 'A Prayer for my Daughter' early on became a target for feminist literary criticism.[44] But it could equally be said that the poem is a deliberate repudiation of the kind of life Gonne led, and the kind of existence she had bequeathed to her own daughter. It is also a celebration of the tranquillity which WBY thought his own marital home had brought him, after the storms of his early life. And the Renaissance-style archaism of the sentiments, as well as the formality of language and structure, should be read in terms of the belief (which currently possessed him) that his daughter represented the reincarnation of a seventeenth-century countess of the house of Ormond (who would, indeed, have been a duchess if she had lived).[45] Just after finishing the poem, he and George set off to Kilkenny to look for evidence of Anne Hyde, inevitably returning disappointed.

Not only, then, had he just published a volume which included a large body of poems directly produced from his marriage; by the spring of 1919 he was writing as vigorously as he had ever done. Gregory's strictures, however, also owed something to her suspicion that his involvement in the Abbey was cooling. George's involvement in the Dublin Drama League, which had formed itself more or less in opposition to Abbey traditions, cannot have helped.[46] From February 1919, when the Abbey's current manager Fred O'Donovan deserted them, WBY had been arguing that Lennox Robinson, despite his disastrous handling of the 1911 Abbey tour, should yet again take over: he jumped the gun by offering Robinson the post, only to be hauled back into line by Gregory, who had her own candidate. WBY (who in early March had himself tried to fill the gap by producing Brinsley MacNamara's play *The Rebellion in Ballycullen*) was impatient to press Robinson's case. '[His] appointment will be popular; then too he will never use us as a springboard for a new leap for himself & he is thoroughly educated – which last is perhaps most important of all.'[47] He told Gregory forcefully in early March that a new generation, committed to Ireland, must take over, and that his own priority must be his poetry. He was even ready to cede Robinson his own place as director. 'I do not feel, as I am so much away, that I should be asked again to work with an uneducated manager of the Wilson-Fay-O'Donovan type without a resident director.'[48] He got his way, but the argument brought out a fundamental difference between the two old comrades, summarized in the discussions about the Abbey's direction which WBY precipitated at the theatre's Sunday evening lectures. His own speech was so critical of the Abbey's recent direction that he had to try to repair the damage by arranging newspaper interviews, a published dialogue with Robinson at the end of April, and an open letter to Gregory published in the *Irish Statesman*.[49] As he put it privately to Gregory, he thought 'the quality of plays has fallen off and it is necessary to say so', whereas she took the opposite view. (This was hardly surprising, since a good deal of the Abbey's fare consisted of plays of her own like *The Dragon*, about which WBY had been noticeably chilly.) He argued powerfully against the authenticity of modern popular drama and the need to get down – as she and Synge had allegedly done – to the bedrock of tradition. But his conclusion called for 'an unpopular theatre and an audience like a secret society', unequivocally advocating his own recent departures into the world of dance plays and the Noh. This reflected, again, his private expostulation that the Abbey could not rely entirely on 'popular peices', as it would always be outbid in that game: such material should simply 'pay for the better work & for experimental work'.[50]

These were the arguments that had bedevilled the directors since the Horniman days, though WBY was now prepared to let his own feelings come much further into the open. And, just as in the Horniman days, he was anxious to keep the Abbey as a forum for his own experimental work. He was excited by the success of the Stage Society production of *The Player Queen* in London, with Máire O'Neill (Molly Allgood, Synge's original 'Pegeen') as Decima; the play struck him as far more dramatically viable, as well as far more amusing, than he had feared. Like *The Shadowy Waters*, or any project which he had been unable to finish to his satisfaction, it represented a deep level of personal identification. At an automatic-writing session the night before the play opened in London, one of George's 'Instructors' inquired, 'Is not Septimas yourself', and WBY subsequently introduced prophecies into the speeches of his poet-protagonist which chime with his own developing 'System'. His reaction, after the first London rehearsal, was to suggest 'hiring the scenery & clothes & giving it in Dublin'.[51]

But when the play was produced at the Abbey in early December, WBY stayed in Oxford. It had a mixed and noisy reception which, given its anarchic philosophy and sexual frankness, was hardly surprising: the bawdy bestiality had the desired effect. Iseult told him 'the fury of the pro and the anti-Dreyfusards of my childhood was no worse than that of the pro and the anti-Unicornians among certain people I know: Mrs Salkeld (anti-Unicornian) says she will never be the same person again!' The crotchety Joseph Holloway found it baffling but beautiful, and Gogarty loved it, but the Dublin press were uniformly unfavourable: 'as unappreciative as if the play had been in verse', WBY remarked sourly, '& may indeed have thought it was'. Gregory paid him back for *The Dragon* by staying in Coole, and telling him that she 'didn't care for it myself as for the verse plays'. But what he really wanted to know was the reaction of the popular audience, and this was unlikely to have come up to the level he expected.[52] Much as in the days of the Fays and Horniman, Dublin's readiness for WBY's kind of dramatic experiment was strictly limited, and this helped confirm his disillusionment with the Abbey. The feeling was intensified when Frank Fay suddenly turned up in his life, arriving for tea in Oxford: the 'beautiful speaking voice' immortalized in the dedication to *On Baile's Strand* now 'talked with a strong cockney accent'. The early Abbey days seemed far away. 'The Fays', WBY remarked cynically to Gregory, 'as they recede in time have ever nobler vistas conferred upon them.'[53]

III

As Gregory suspected, the kind of energy WBY had once directed into the theatre was now absorbed by another world of ritual and revelation. He was working on a play with a religious theme, which became *Calvary*: 'constantly reading the Bible', JBY heard, 'not because his mind is going weak, but for a play on the New Testament'.[54] The life and death of Christ were to be treated − rather iconoclastically − to accord with the historical and philosophical patterns provided by the insights of George's 'Instructors'. Christ, as an 'objective' personality, ushers in a new age and provides an exemplar of the soul's journey from end back to beginning, through 'dreaming back'. In his exchanges with Lazarus and Judas, the Yeatsian message is preached about personality, determinism, and fate. The play was not performed in his lifetime, but it remains one of WBY's first creative works founded closely on the 'System' which he would formalize as *A Vision*. The record of the automatic script shows how closely Jesus and Judas were located in their lunar 'phases', paired as interdependent and opposing principles. George's 'Instructors' put it with uncharacteristic clarity, perhaps helped by *Per Amica*. 'The point is that man frees himself through his opposite.'[55]

Meanwhile the 'System' itself was being codified as his own book of revelation. In July AE reported to Quinn about WBY's 'big prose book he is working at, his philosophy of mysticism'. AE had, in fact, been a partial confidant since October 1918, when he told Quinn that WBY was

obsessed by some fresh mystical doctrine about the phases of the moon. There are twenty-eight and we all pass through them, it appears, twelve times in a cycle of 336 incarnations. All I can gather is that I am in phase 25 and am next to being a saint, with which attribution my knowledge of myself is at variance. Though he talks with great solemnity about this new doctrine revealed to him, I suspect that there is a great deal of humour underlying these manifestations of mysticism.[56]

Though this may have been calculated to set the implacably anti-mystical Quinn's fears at rest, the 'humour' remained deliberately arcane. From June to September, in the atmospheric surroundings of Ballylee, as the country around went – in WBY's words – 'reeling back into the middle ages without growing more picturesque,'[57] he pursued his supernatural search for a system of historical recurrence and astrological explanation. The questions put to his 'Interpreter' wife were now written down by her, with answers in ordinary handwriting; the impression is less and less 'automatic'. Moreover, their exchanges at first avoided the large-scale philosophical diagrams which WBY was trying to trace: the 'Interpreter' was most anxious to warn him 'not to be drawn into anything – possible trouble in Ireland . . . you may be tempted to join in political schemes if there is trouble – & you must not'.[58] The 'Instructors' had risked some specific suggestions about finding Anne Hyde's tomb and family papers at Kilkenny, but the futility of that expedition seems to have directed the Yeatses' attention back to questions of personal psychology and 'sexual health': by the end of July the patience of the 'Interpreters' was straining to breaking point. In early August they returned to the more congenial task of plotting Anne Hyde's life and death. Here George's 'Instructors' suggested the kind of sources familiar to her from biographical research at an earlier stage of her relationship with WBY, and Iseult was pressed into service as a research assistant too.[59] But again a certain desperation took over, when on 19 August WBY was informed that he was the reincarnation of an eighteenth-century French revolutionary, the bastard son of the duchess of Orleans and Camille Desmoulins. Even WBY found the detail of this hard to swallow (Desmoulins would have fathered him when eleven years old): he reproachfully elicited from the 'Instructor', 'Ontelos', an admission that he had been simply 'trying your credulity', to cure him of 'hammering for facts'.[60] More warnings followed, from other 'Instructors': 'keep off personal or be precise', 'personal is dangerous', 'I cant see this leads anywhere except to platitudes'. Yet in late August he was still peppering the weary 'Interpreter' for details about his past lives (several responses were rather desperately lifted from Kenelm Digby's *Private*

Memoirs). George cannot have been particularly pleased when he repeatedly requested information about his relationship with Gonne in previous incarnations, and she provided notably sharp answers.[61]

In a commentary added some years afterwards, WBY noted the shortcomings of these exchanges, and the prevalence of 'Frustrators'. What burns through most strongly, however, is the will to believe, and what is hardest to understand is the passionate credulity which lies behind these endless sessions, and would produce the irrational exactness of *A Vision*. 'Yeats . . . queer in his head about "moon",' Pound told Quinn in December, 'whole new metaphysics about "Moon", very very very bug-house.'[62] WBY had often enough examined his own need to believe, and its coexistence with a kind of rarefied scepticism: the tension runs through his several volumes of autobiography, as well as through meditations like *Per Amica*. But the faith placed in the automatic script draws on another source as well: the need to make sense of his sudden and apparently desperate marriage, indeed to make a triumphant success of it. The messages from beyond, the preordained children, the placing of his new family into a great historical pattern at a time of apocalyptic change, foretold in the stars: all this had built up a solid reef of emotional and intellectual support, on which he rested after the storm-lashed passages of 1917. Sexual relations within his marriage were closely linked to the creative process, with male and female daimons interchanging at the moment of 'contact'. 'Pure energy' was confined to creative genius and sexual intercourse – which was, the 'Instructors' told him, 'a perpetual drama, which has for its real theme the nature of the unborn child, for whom the daimons have laid their plans'.[63]

Moreover, the strange pattern of his and George's private exchanges had also brought him, as he would later put it in a famous phrase, 'metaphors for poetry'. Whatever Gregory thought, he was writing at his best. The sceptical, or tired, or embarrassed reader has often wanted to leave the function of the automatic script exactly there. But as a factory for mysterious images assembled into great poems, its rationale should be recognized. For WBY, it was a confirmation that he had been rescued from a personal, emotional, and intellectual void.

The desirability of WBY's new life was amply demonstrated when he, George, Anne, nurse, and housemaid settled into 4 Broad Street, Oxford, on 11 October 1919 – 'such a house as I love', he told Gregory, 'all harmonious & severe, nothing looking expensive or too cheap but a dignified natural house for intellectual people'.[64] Facing Balliol, at what was then the narrow neck where Broad Street met St Giles, it was destined for eventual demolition, to allow street widening; inside, it was irregular, oak-floored, and atmospheric. The furniture from Woburn Buildings fitted into place. WBY's treasured Kelmscott Chaucer was placed on its blue-painted lectern, between two brass candlesticks four and a half feet high; George's Blake engravings of 'Job' were hung on the stairwell with those of Dante brought from Woburn Buildings; singing-birds were installed in cages, as in Gonne's Passy house. He had created another refuge, the kind of house, he told Lily, 'that ought to be in Sligo and never was'. It was even slightly but agreeably haunted: mysterious smells of incense arrived, and objects were moved around by inexplicable 'apports'.[65] Since it could easily be let to a don when they were away, they envisaged keeping it as a permanent base.

Their social circle widened, beyond the tea-tables of Boar's Hill. Undergraduate societies heard that the poet had come to town and asked him to speak. Those intrepid enough to make WBY's acquaintance included the future novelist Richard Hughes and the medical student Raymond Greene, who tried to effect a meeting between WBY and his younger brother Graham, who had literary ambitions. (It does not seem to have come off.[66]) Acolytes like Willam Force Stead (later chaplain at Worcester College) became friends, and young dons like Maurice Bowra set out to cultivate the new arrival.[67] So did the great world. WBY had slightly known Lady Ottoline Morrell since at least 1914, when he had discussed with her obtaining designs by her lover Henry Lamb for Lily's embroidery.[68] They may have collaborated more closely in the campaign to save Casement in 1916: Lady Ottoline, whose mother was Irish, had passionately thrown herself into it. She was a friend of Eva Gore-Booth, and well known (if considered slightly outré, not to say scandalous) in the London drawing-room world now regularly frequented by WBY. By 1919 her famous salon at Garsington, a few miles outside Oxford, was a magnet for writers, artists, some dons, and intrepidly aesthetic undergraduates; it was going through a palmy period before over-spending, backbiting, and personal tragedy forced her to retrench and move to London. She at first found WBY 'too rhetorical and pompous', but was quickly won over by 'his really good intellectual qualities'.[69] He was tailor-made for Garsington and rapidly became a fixture. In some ways Lady Ottoline was tailor-made for him too. Tall, soulful, still eccentrically beautiful at forty-five, she decorated both herself and her house in a high style, where gypsy-chic met mock-medieval splendour. Her love-affairs, intellectual aspirations, and personal affectations made her an easy target for mockery, as a duke's sister striking cultural attitudes while bent on lion-hunting in Bohemia. This did her much less than justice: she was generous, astute, by no means rich, and genuinely committed to those artists she believed in. Both the Yeatses took to her. They went gratefully to Garsington for weekends from December 1919, while Lady Ottoline's unmistakable pony-carriage and 'red heels' made regular appearances at

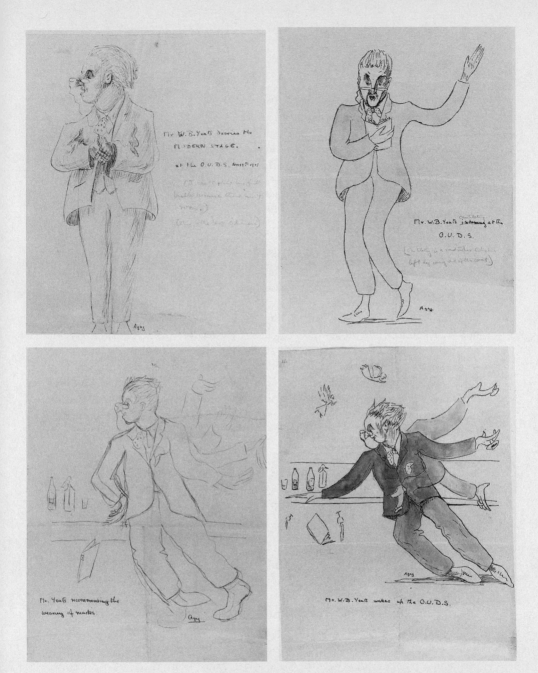

4. A series of drawings by Richard Hughes (the future novelist), made when WBY addressed the Oxford University Dramatic Society on 19 November 1919. 'Mr Yeats decries the MODERN STAGE.... (I can't show his full bulk, because there isn't room.) (This is the best likeness.)' 'Mr W. B. Yeats ~~intoning~~ cantilating at the O.U.D.S. (Cantilating is a sound rather like his left leg coming out of the coat.)' 'Mr. Yeats recommending the wearing of masks.' 'Mr. W. B. Yeats wakes up the O.U.D.S.'

Broad Street. One dazzled Irish undergraduate, James O'Reilly, recorded such a sight:

One afternoon in the autumn or early winter of 1919 when I was an undergraduate of St John's I was strolling along Broad Street by the walls of Balliol. The door in a stone Georgian house opposite opened and two remarkable figures came down the curved steps. The first was Lady Ottoline Morrell, a famous lady of those years, a Cavendish Bentinck, half sister to the then Duke of Portland, friend of conscientious objectors, rebels, poets and writers of every description, she was a tall, wraith-like creature, fantastically dressed in clothes suggesting some bygone period of aristocratic grandeur. The other was W. B. Yeats hatless in dim coloured tweeds with a huge knotted black tie.

> 'The noble head held high
> The brown unageing face . . .'

Lady Ottoline paused on the steps and took his arm and they descended to the pavement. Philip Morrell in a great fur coat and 'high low' hat was waiting in a little phaeton with two beautiful horses tandem. A groom in cockaded top hat, blue tailed coat and white britches was standing at the leader's head. Yeats, his greying hair blown by the wind, bowing low, kissed Lady Ottoline's hand and helped her up to the seat beside her husband. The leader's head was released, the whip cracked, the horses moved off smartly and the little groom swung himself up to his perch behind the rear wheels. Yeats stood on the pavement gazing after them with his open hand above his head in salute. I was not the only passer-by who stopped for a moment or two to watch that performance which I think no one enjoyed more than the poet actor himself.[70]

Though the Yeatses may have joined occasionally in the irresistible pastime of satirizing Garsington life, it was an enduring friendship and would outlast the Morrells' country salon. For the moment the house, the company there, the highflown if wayward elegance of the Morrell world, gave WBY a kind of replacement for Coole.

In the suitably ancient atmosphere of Broad Street the invisible guides were consulted once more as autumn set in, but it was the last sustained period of automatic writing before new methods of divination were devised, less stressful for the 'Interpreter'. The Yeatses' research in the Bodleian concentrated upon the seventeenth century; they traced peerages and family histories as well as astrological almanacs, and sought revelations about a possible reincarnation within their own household.[71] In mid October George led the discussion towards the interpretation of dreams, subconscious desires, the artist's acquisition of images locked into *Anima Mundi*, via the 'fantastic consciousness'. She also prescribed joint readings of Dante, and suggested that a mythical ancestor of Yeats, Thomas Hyde, might have written in his imagination a sacred book which was to be transmitted to

WBY via the 'Interpreter': a nudge towards the origin myth of *A Vision*.[72] But her own astonishing resources were becoming limited, and the directions relayed by 'Ameritus' accordingly peremptory. Sittings were forbidden during the medium's menstrual periods; WBY must stop asking for 'facts' and 'verification'; he was to take long walks in the Magdalen deer-park ('good for your nerves').[73] From late October she insisted that they concentrate upon defining the system ('wheel') rather than treading yet again over the dead ground of past personal relationships. And in one memorable intervention, the 'Instructors' were asked, 'What is the opposite of the abstraction which produces the rage to destroy?' The answer that came through George's mouth could not have been simpler: 'family love'.[74]

As George Harper has pointed out, from 24 October 'even the pretence of questions was abandoned as George began recording phasal characteristics', much in the forms in which they would appear in *A Vision*: she 'had come to the table well prepared for revisions and final decisions'.[75] The relationships between Fate, Genius, and Mask were drawn out, with descriptive details and examples. WBY's questions were at first cautious, slightly cowed, and easily satisfied; but he soon began laying down the lineaments of the emerging 'System'. Particular attention was paid (on 4 November) to cyclical developments in history, the function of 'revelation as shock', and the relationship of this to current wars and revolutions: 'the revelation of subjective avatar [will] be by shock'.[76] 'The Second Coming' can be fitted precisely into this part of the system: as Gregory remarked, 'it makes the philosophy clear'. By early November the bit was between the subject's teeth: dealing with the transference of images from Anima Mundi into the personal iconography of the creative artist, he defined the 'begetting' of images which he would tackle in a famous later poem.[77] And the transmission of artistic intensity across the ages from a writer like Keats is also linked into a pattern of recurrence and inheritance. Indeed, one effect of these months of psychic discussion about the seedbed of creativity was to send him back to the Romantic poets of his youth: Shelley, Keats, and Blake. Through the transference of symbolic thought from Anima Mundi, poets could be seen as unacknowledged legislators in a cosmic sense. 'It means', concluded WBY (not the acquiescent 'Instructor'), 'that if Homer were abolished in every library & in every living mind the tale of Troy might still emerge as a vision.'[78]

He had not given up his attempt to discover 'personal' truths, and the 'Instructors' were interrogated at length about, for instance, the reliance of psychic communication upon an active sexual relationship between the medium and himself.[79] But from early December the 'Instructors' flagged. They made excuses for their inability to respond, suggested other means of inquiry, and pleaded exhaustion: 'simply too much script'. In one revealing metaphor, George described the medium as an unwilling Persephone, repeatedly dragged down to a dark underworld by Pluto, away from the richness of natural life. By the 8th a new method was being floated, a 'kind of sleep', in which the medium and her 'daimon' would be most strongly linked. Again, the potential effect could be strengthened by sexual relations ('the moment of the supreme activity of the daimons'). The sleep-trance also required a half-hour nap for the medium, which was probably the least she felt she deserved. 'Ameritus' thoughtfully struck another deal, stipulating that she had two nights a week off, and went to bed very early on one of them. The use of 'automatic' writing, by this stage something of a misnomer, more or less came to an end as a regular activity on 22 December. By then, much of the interrogation concerned the preparations for the conception of their second child and reflected George's impatience with her husband's uncertainty on the subject. But WBY's last questions returned yet again to the crisis over Iseult at the time of his marriage, the question of responsibilities, and the formative or traumatic moment of their joint lives.[80] '*Stop now*,' ordered 'Dionertes', vainly for the moment; but on 23 December he announced, 'You must always now *refuse* any script which refers to your past present or future relations.' Instead, the 'Interpreter' continued with the schema of the 'System', defining the characteristics of the 'Creative Genius' at certain phases. These terms, yet again, would transfer straight into the formulae of *A Vision*.

On Christmas Day 1919 'Dionertes' ordered: 'do a marriage invocation over one of interpreters rings'. There were further, rather desultory sessions before departing for the United States in early January. On their lengthy American tour they would from time to time consult their oracles in the old style, but from now on revelation was generally expected to come in a trance or sleep. The marriage invocation is an interesting final ritual. It is as if George were affirming categorically what the sexually charged exchanges about their joint 'daimons' had so often implied: that her unique insights, on which WBY had come to depend so much, were an intrinsic part of her position as his wife and the mother of his children, and that there was no room in their marriage for anyone outside the four-cornered diagram of their two selves, their daughter Anne, and the child to come.

IV

The American tour had been planned since the summer, through J. B. Pond's Lyceum Bureau. With the end of the war it was the obvious way to make money for Ballylee, though WBY hoped his 'gathering years and increasing weight' would not lessen popular enthusiasm.[81] It was an ambitious undertaking: WBY planned to be away the best part of four months, and insisted upon a less hectic schedule than previously. Leaving Anne in Lily's care, the Yeatses fortified themselves with a few days in London, reading Blake in the British Museum. They sailed on 13 January, arriving in New York on the 22nd, where they stayed at the Arts Club in Gramercy Park, and then at the Algonquin Hotel. They could review JBY's situation at first hand, while he approvingly inspected his new daughter-in-law. 'She is good looking, & but for a drawn look in her mouth would be very good looking – however she looks distinguished & that is best.' Above all, she told him she could 'always conquer [Willie] by pretending not to sympathise with what he is telling her. She has merely to remain silent while he talks, she says. He will change the subject and do everything to get her to reply to him and be interested. After this has gone on for a while she ends it by bursting out laughing.'[82]

He also shrewdly noted that George was 'exceedingly companionable – she is as Quinn says calm always calm that is because she has a keen sense of the underlying facts, which the impetuous man – Quinn for instance – is always forgetting, & Willy also'.[83] Impetuous or not, WBY had an opportunity to discuss with Quinn the prospects for JBY's remaining years, and from this point applied heavy pressure to recall him to Dublin. George was in favour: she took to the old man, and preferred drinking wine with him at Petitpas to meeting rich New Yorkers like the loquacious woman who told WBY that her favourite among his poems was 'The Everlasting Mercy'. When he gently pointed out it was by Masefield, her hitherto silent husband rounded triumphantly on her with 'Stung again!'[84] Nonetheless, George spent much time in New York while WBY embarked upon a punishing tour. She joined him in Washington, Yale, and Chicago, and travelled out to California with him, but avoided many of his engagements. For all the stimulation of New York, WBY noted how she missed Ballylee and Anne. 'One night I heard her singing something in her sleep – it was hush a by baby on the tree top.'[85]

She threw herself into managing the tour, in spite of this: telephoning, booking train tickets, and dealing with the slippery Pond. It was a lengthy and demanding schedule[86] and JBY put his son's well-being down to his wife: 'at the end of his tour he found himself in better health than he had been for years. It was all because she was with him.'[87] The lectures he offered comprised 'A Theatre of the People', 'The Friends of my Youth', 'William Blake and his Friends' and 'The Younger Generation'. There were also 'Readings', mostly early poems – 'everyone assures me that the older I grow the more unintelligible I become' – though 'On a Political Prisoner' and 'An Irish Airman' also featured. The Blake address aroused little interest and was never used. The theatre lecture reprised his public discussions with Robinson and Gregory the year before, advocating his 'noble' drama for the few, played in drawing rooms. The others were stock autobiographical fare. While reactions were usually effusive and often ecstatic, one disgruntled reporter judged the 'Friends of my Youth' performance harshly. 'Distinctly of the "light-entertainment" kind; he did not go deep into any subject of literature nor did he touch upon the Irish political question, but swung along through an hour and a half of bursts of Irish wit and a steady flow of English self-conceit.'[88]

WBY claimed that the material was new, never printed or delivered before, and that he lectured extempore from notes.[89] This was slightly disingenuous, but he had certainly gained greatly in confidence and reputation since his herculean first tour of 1903/4. He struck one observer as grey-haired, portly, and 'in all respects the handsome and distinguished man of middle life'; JBY recorded rather smugly that his son now weighed fourteen stone, which he put down to the pint of milk which George had waiting for him after every lecture.[90] He could travel in style, with a factotum from the Lyceum Bureau making all arrangements. Despite paying his expenses, including luxurious hotel bills, he expected 'to bring home more money than ever before'. Pond was told to send the Gort builder £100 'for the Ballylee roof for which we have bought beautiful slates of different colours and sizes'.[91] He kept a Pollexfen eye on accounts, and was worried by the reports of Pond's financial doings which were given to him by the agency representative, Boyer ('an agreeable person very anxious to get into politics for the sake of "the graft" as he explained'[92]). But Boyer turned out a mixed blessing. By the time he arrived in California in early April, WBY was sending Quinn worried telegrams about money owed – precipitated by Boyer's allegation that Pond's business had collapsed. Pond took offence, and WBY blamed unsatisfactory accounting by Boyer, who had himself a taste for extravagance and ran up large bills unwillingly met by WBY. The apprentice politician was right in the end: the Lyceum Bureau went temporarily bankrupt within a year, though Pond later resurrected it.[93] WBY cleared about £500, but would have preferred to have spent less on travelling and brought more back to Ballylee. All his profits were reserved for the tower, except for two personal luxuries: a green parrot, and a set of pewter dinner plates and dishes for the Oxford house.[94]

But if the tour was dictated by the state of his private affairs, it was impossible to avoid public politics. WBY's American visit coincided with a new turn in the Irish crisis, as Lloyd George sent over mercenary troops and the Sinn Féin publicity machine intensified its efforts. De Valera was also touring America, and President Wilson was being pressed hard by

Irish-American activists. As on previous occasions, WBY spoke more forth-rightly to American journalists than to interviewers in Britain or Ireland; as soon as he arrived on 24 January, he announced that Ireland was now 'a country of oppression', stifled by censorship, and called for 'some form of self-government'. But he stressed the value of dominion status, and empha-sized that Ulster should not be 'coerced any more than the remainder of the country; there should be some way to permit both to work out their destiny'.[95] He also avoided giving an opinion about de Valera's American publicity campaign and disclaimed – as he was often to do – that he himself was any kind of a politician: though this did not prevent him issuing a ringing endorsement of the Jewish campaign for the establishment of 'a homeland in Palestine'.[96] Moreover, if the disclaimer was technically true, nonetheless he certainly possessed enough political sense to avoid being trapped into the position of a Sinn Féin mouthpiece, and Quinn's advice was firmly against embroilment in the Irish-American political cauldron.

In Toronto on 2 February, he continued to distance himself, stressing that he and Griffith 'have not been on speaking terms for some years', blaming British policy over the 1912 Home Rule Bill for creating Sinn Féin's success, and preferring to concentrate upon financial relations between the coun-tries. 'England is always doing the right thing at the wrong time': in other words, blundering rather than malevolent.[97] Nor did he condone the tactic of violence, though he feared that 'England may be criminal enough to grant to violence what she refused to reason'. When questioned about Sinn Féin, he emphasized that they possessed a mandate from the country at large. And time and time again, he said that politics and propaganda had been banished from the Abbey, and that their audiences bridged the polit-ical divide. On at least one occasion his 'Readings' introduced 'On a Political Prisoner' by a severe denunciation of political fanaticism as 'a bitter acid that destroyed the soul': the poem (and by implication Constance Markievicz) illustrated 'this spirit that was the curse of Ireland'. His lecture on the theatre contemptuously rejected attempts at propaganda plays: when the Abbey tried Gaelic plays they invariably 'ended up with somebody tearing off a white collar or dickey as a symbol of renunciation of English civilisa-tion and at last everybody laughed at them'.[98] (Synge was, yet again, employed as the paradigmatic artist 'incapable of a political thought'.) He did smuggle in politics through poetry – but it was the poetry of others. His lecture 'The Younger Generation', comparing new poetic modes to those of his own apprenticeship, allowed him to read some of the poems of 1916 – at least in Boston, where the effect was maximized.[99] If the ostensible reason was to illustrate poetry's need for passion and poignancy rather than for abstract ideas, the nationalist political message did not go unheard. But he addressed politics on another level too, one whose implications were less obvious. Denouncing modern materialistic culture to an audience at Oberlin, he ended his speech with a ringing assertion. 'Democratic Ireland and its symbols he would change to an intellectual aristocracy. He would go back to the Middle Ages, back to the time of Thomas Aquinas. "The values are changed," he said.'[100]

He had time for other reflections too. His tour took in new experiences such as lecturing to two Mormon universities in Utah, provoking a deadpan description for Olivia Shakespear.

I hope to ask questions about their doctrine of continuous inspiration. They claim that the miraculous has never ceased among them. They have great wealth, number about 750,000 & now alas pride themselves on never having more than one wife. They claim that their once generous plurality was a temporary measure after a great war – so at least an enthusiast for the faith has been explaining to me I told him that America & Germany had both made the same mistake, the mistake of standardizing life, the one in interest of monarchy, the other in interest of democracy but both for the ultimate gain of a sterile devil. That once both America & Germany had been infinitely abundant in variation from type & now all was type.

Tell Ezra to come to America to found a paper devoted to the turning of U.S.A. into a monarchy to ballance Germany.[101]

Mid April found him introducing the poets of the 1890s to Waco, Texas, a lecture which 'seemed to pass over the heads of most of the audience', according to the local papers.[102] He was also, piquantly, telling the strictly teetotal Baylor University about poets who were 'slaves to intoxicants: writing their best poem[s] while they were somewhat dissipated'. Baylor had set the tone for the whole United States: Prohibition had been introduced only a few months before, providing one of the few instances where WBY became embroiled in 'politics'. In Chicago, he had unguardedly remarked that Prohibition was 'hell', and put it down to the reforming zeal of enfranchised women. 'After women become more accustomed to political freedom they will seek less reform. They will become constructive. I understand they are even going to bar cigarets in this country.'[103]

This was a godsend to reporters, who besieged him for more and racier quotes: but he firmly if belatedly invoked his 'no politics' rule. However, the journalists noted that during this exchange Harriet Monroe arrived in the room with a half-pint flask, and further relief was supplied by an illegal drinking-club called the 'Alcohol Alumni' who happened to be meeting in his hotel and invited him to a session. WBY 'appeared to be startled and not so sure of what had brought him to the party' until a drink was put in his hand; he then lowered two large measures with evident appreciation. One of the group recalled what followed:

'I should like to ask you', said Mr Dillon, 'if there is any little thing you would like to tell us about the future of poetry in Ireland, or in the United States.'

'There is not,' replied Mr Yeats, in a tone which indicated that he meant it.

'Then you shall not be asked,' replied his interlocutor. 'Our chief aim in all this celebration is just to see you are happy. When your glass is empty, please indicate.'

'I find the whiskey unexpectedly good,' replied Mr Yeats, as he downed another generous slug.

However, after this promising beginning, 'a woman sailed into the room. Mr Yeats quickly downed what was left of his liquid and arose with great dignity.' George, briefly introduced, promptly steered him to the door.[104]

There were other memorable moments. The audience for his public lecture at Chicago was huge, with 200 seats placed on the stage to accommodate the spill-over, and it was once again followed by a banquet hosted by *Poetry*. A more personal tribute was paid to him at Portland, Oregon, described in a letter to Dulac on 22 March.

A rather wonderful thing happened the day before yesterday. A very distinguished looking Japanese came to see us. He had read my poetry when in Japan & had now just heard me lecture. He had something in his hand wrapped up in embroidered silk. He said it was a present for me. He untied the silk cord that bound it & brought out a sword which had been for 500 years in his family. It had been made 550 years ago & he showed me the maker's name upon the hilt. I was greatly embarrassed in the thought of such a gift & went to fetch George, thinking that we might find some way of refusing it. When she came I said 'But surely this ought always to remain in your family?' He answered 'My family have many swords.' But later he brought back my embarrassment by speaking of having given me 'his sword'. I had to accept it but I have written him a letter saying that I 'put him under a vow' to write & tell me when his first child is born – he is not yet married – that I may leave the sword back to his family in my will.

His benefactor was Junzo Sato, a young Japanese working at Portland. Already a devotee of WBY's poetry, Sato was electrified by hearing him in person and, 'after reflecting all night', had made his way to his hero's hotel, bearing the gift 'wrapped up in a piece of beautifully embroidered cloth, from some ancient lady-in-waiting's dress'.[105] The sword must have appeared to WBY as both a sign and a symbol, and he treasured it. Like the tower of Ballylee, it was built into his verse: an emblem of continuity, ancestry, and noble austerity. Sato, to whom the encounter was immensely important, saw them off to the west the next day, waving till the train was out of sight.

WBY was anxious for Pond to arrange as many final lectures in the New York area as possible before they left at the end of May. 'I am not in the least fatigued & am indeed better than I have been for years': if he could give two lectures a day in ninety-degree heat at Sherman, Texas, he felt capable of anything.[106] But he had strained his throat, and a New York specialist told him a tonsillectomy would be necessary – though he postponed this until his return. The long rest he had demanded in the middle had coincided with his stay in California, which he found idyllic; by the end of the tour he had read all Jane Austen 'with great satisfaction'.[107] They arrived back at the Algonquin on 30 April, later moving to Quinn's apartment on Central Park West. Though not many lectures had been arranged for his last weeks, the tour had been a success. WBY gave a leisurely interview in which he reflected on the rise of modernism, the fashion for 'photographing reality', the desirability of diverting attention from politics into culture, and most of all the need for a spiritual revolution which would combat materialism.

I know we are approaching some kind of philosophy which will deal with the social state. But I avoid politics merely because I feel that our opinions will not long hold. To my way of thinking, speculative interests are our true interests for the time being. The more I ponder it, the more I am confident that the only salvation for the world is to regain its feeling for revelation.[108]

He could also enjoy the varied distractions of New York, two of which he described to Gregory:

Today I go to have a record taken of myself for a new kind of moving picture – a picture that talks as well as moves. Last night I & Quinn went to see De Valera. I was rather dissapointed – A living argument rather than a living man, all propaganda, no human life, but not bitter or hysterical or unjust. I judged him persistent, being both patient and energetic but that he will fail through not having enough human life to judge the human life in others. He will ask too much of everyone & will ask it without charm. He will be pushed aside by others.[109]

The judgement was based not only on de Valera's public address on 11 May but on a meeting which he requested with WBY and Quinn at his hotel. The Sinn Féin organization evidently hoped to enlist WBY in the public advocacy which he had carefully avoided. If so, they were unsuccessful. But de Valera's presence in America to raise money for the paramilitary campaign at home was a reminder of what awaited WBY at Ballylee. He at once sent Gregory a second letter asking how dangerous things were around Gort: if it was unwise to bring Anne there, they would summer in Oxford instead.

On 29 May they left from Montreal, travelling first class on the 'Megantic'. WBY had hoped to bring JBY back with him. This was a wish devoutly shared by Quinn, who, in a fit of exasperation, told JBY that his patience was exhausted and 'the expense of your remaining here is up to W.B.Y.'.[110] But the old man – now eighty-one – clung to Manhattan like a limpet. 'My father has decided to stay in New York,' WBY told Gregory. 'He says his return would be "to sink into the cradle of his second childhood". I shall return to the point again but I think his mind is made up. He beleives he is at last going to paint a masterpeice – his portrait of Quinn – & is as full of the future as when I was a child.'[111] The 'masterpiece' was actually a self-portrait commissioned by Quinn, and would inevitably and appositely remain unfinished. JBY would carry on defining and reassessing himself, as a public performance for the entertainment of others, until he died.

George had accompanied WBY to the west, where one of the last formal sessions of automatic writing took place in the improbable surroundings of a flowery bungalow hotel in Pasadena on 29 March. Here, 'Dionertes' finally dug his heels in. 'I do not want script here – I prefer to use other methods – sleeps – I have given you three opportunities lately and you have not taken any of them.'[112] WBY was instructed to 'always wait till she murmurs' before instituting sleep-interrogation. Thus the 'Interpreter' astutely arranged to retain the initiative, as she had learned to do throughout. The very last response of the 'Instructor' to WBY's questioning was airily dismissive: 'Quite easily obvious – Goodnight.'

Mobilise the poets . . . Perhaps Yeats would use his muse for
Ireland now.

Arthur Griffith, memorandum to Dáil Éireann issued
from Gloucester Prison, 23 January 1919[1]

I

THE Yeatses returned to find their Oxford house let until mid July, Ballylee
still full of builders, and the Irish situation worsening daily. They took the
Pounds' flat off Kensington Church Street and hoped (vainly) for Ireland in
September. WBY settled down to preparing his new book of poems for
Cuala and sending anxious inquiries to Gregory about Ballylee. The prob-
lems which he was facing seemed trivial to her – worries about missing
building materials and a threat to their Ballylee servants, Delia and Mary-
Ann Molloy, for fraternizing with a local farmer disapproved of by Sinn
Féin.[2] While WBY was touring America, Gregory's nephew Frank Shawe-
Taylor had been shot and her brother boycotted. Intimidation on the one
side, and atrocities on the other, had proceeded apace. Her Ascendancy
neighbours were beginning to abandon their houses, and Margaret was
determined to follow suit. Local feeling, Gregory's nationalist beliefs, and
her readiness to consult the local Sinn Féin authorities kept Coole inviolate
for the moment, but Gort was electrified by 'shootings and burnings by the
Military always'.[3] WBY's worries about the fabric of Ballylee seemed incon-
sequential by comparison. However, from late July he was writing to her
about another crisis, which wrenched him back to Dublin, and to the traumatic scenes of his earlier life.

In America he had received a letter from Lennox Robinson giving 'the
bare news of Iseult's marriage'. 'I need not tell you how distressed I have
been at the way things fell out,' WBY told him, 'I did my best, though for an
obvious reason I did not tell you so at the time.'[4] This referred to the
attempts made by George and WBY to bring about a match between Iseult
and Robinson himself the year before. Lily, entertaining the couple to sup-
per, had thought the gangling, effusive Robinson 'willing, but I cant tell
from her anything of her thoughts. She is charming – has very little self-
confidence, is indolent and something of a charming humbug – enormously tall and rather gaunt – like Maud says little but looks much – She hates

170

politics and her mother's political friends, so can't be very happy. Her position is too uncomfortable.'[5] She did not choose to remedy it by marrying Robinson, whom Dublin in any case assumed to be homosexual. Instead she ran away to London in February 1920 with an 18-year-old ex-public-schoolboy, Francis Stuart, and married him. Her intention to do so had been confided to WBY two months before.[6] On her return to Dublin, she had to go and see the redoubtable Sarah Purser, now the grande dame of Dublin's artistic circles. 'So, you have married your poet,' Miss Purser remarked. 'Your mother had more sense.'[7]

It was certainly an unwise decision. Pound jauntily said that Stuart's chief fault was that he was a *bad* poet: but he also showed himself unstable, aggressive, immature even for his years, and – in WBY's repeated judgement – sadistically cruel to Iseult. He had come from an unsettled Ulster background, and just left Rugby. Endowed with an adequate private income and a vague literary ambition, he had drifted into Dublin's artistic Bohemia, attracted – among other things – by an admiration for WBY's poetry. (This did not stop him stealing books WBY had dedicated to Gonne and selling them to collectors.[8]) For all his awkwardness he was handsome, compelling, and inarticulately scornful in a way that appealed to Iseult. In his disguised memoir *Black List Section H* Stuart described long afterwards the strange elopement of two lost, neurotic, self-absorbed spirits. In Iseult's account to WBY she was first attracted because 'he asked a series of naive questions, and made a series of naive statements suggesting an extreme simplicity till she at last said to herself "he is a blessed angel," – plainly she was hoping for "God's Fool".'[9] Even more poignantly, in an effort to gain approval Iseult presented the marriage to WBY as a kind of proxy union with himself. Her first mention of Stuart had stressed his 'adoration which amounts to a religion for you', and, when telling WBY of their intention to marry, she added:

You have often told me that I am your spiritual child, perhaps he is even more that than I; there are times when I wonder even if you might be his real father. Many young people have imitated your manner and your style as he does from the things they knew about you and from your books, but when I see in him a reflexion of things in you which only I know, then I am amazed.[10]

Robinson 'showed great generosity' by having Stuart to live with him until the wedding, but otherwise only Gregory encouraged the match, probably because she thought Iseult should be put safely out of harm's way.[11] If so, things did not turn out as anticipated. Almost at once the marriage lurched into crisis. To WBY the recurrence of a pattern was heartbreakingly clear. Writing to Robinson from America, he had clearly cast his mind back to the Gonne–MacBride marriage of 1903:

I myself once suffered so much that I think I know all it means. All one has to trust to is the old rhyme 'good days and bad days and all days pass over.' . . . I think that the one refuge in mental pain is doing some work which keeps one surrounded by other people, at least I have found it so. Solitary work is little help and workless solitude is the worst possible.[12]

When Iseult's marriage apparently collapsed, much as her mother's had done, WBY felt a weight of irrational responsibility. This was partly because he had watched her infatuation with Stuart but 'I could not understand her mind and was trusting to him', and partly – though he could not say so – because he felt his own marriage had prevented him from protecting Iseult as she needed. And in late July the old pattern reasserted itself even more clearly: after sending a letter outlining 'horrible family trouble', Gonne dispatched a telegram begging him to come to Dublin immediately and help. He left at once.

By 31 July he had arrived at Gonne's lonely cottage in Glenmalure, County Wicklow, where the Stuarts had been staying. Iseult had already written to WBY about her wretchedness and Stuart's cruelty, fuelled by his 'half unconscious but fierce' longing for power.[13] According to Iseult, he had locked her in her room, deliberately deprived her of sleep and food, and burned her clothes; he was demented by jealousy and hatred of her friends. Moreover, she was pregnant. Gonne and WBY tried to persuade her to rest in a nursing-home while they forced Stuart to agree to conditions for a settlement, but Iseult – perverse as ever – then elected to defend him. 'On one occasion he kept Iseult without food all day because she did not like his prose. Iseult confirms all, when one insists, but never showed indignation but once & that was when she told me that he liked de la Mare's poetry which she considers second rate.' In a telling slip, WBY added, 'Whether Maude [recte Iseult] is still in love with him I dont know – she sometimes talks as if she was.'[14]

It was left to WBY to arrange medical treatment for Iseult with the Dublin gynaecologist Bethel Solomons, to collect evidence about her maltreatment, to open negotiations with the Stuart family for a separation settlement, and then to find a refuge for Iseult. As ever, he turned to Coole:

I have just come up from Glenmalure where Iseult & MG are, and am now going to Dr Solomon to get Iseult into a nursing home for a few days that we may decide what is to be done with her & about her. She has been starved, kept without sleep & several times knocked down by her husband who is mad. His father died in a lunatic asylum & his mothers father died of drink. He has never given her any money – he has an income of £365 I beleive – & Iseult from pride or from some more obscure impulse has not asked for any. By a singular machination settlements were prevented. Iseult has £75 a year & when Maud who is very poor gave gifts – about

£50 – to Iseult that she might have food enough, he got her to sign the lease for the flat & left her to pay the rent. Often Iseult has not had food enough through lack of money but on other occasions he has locked up all the food in his room & left her all day without any (once because she did not like something he has written). I have the signed statement of a young man who found her one evening weak & hungry not having eaten all day & got her food. I have spoken to an elderly woman, once a ladies maid who lives at the house next the Gonnes house at Glenmalure and she told me – a statement confirmed by Iseult and Madam Gonne – how he drove Iseult out of doors in her dressing gown & then heaped her clothes in the middle of the floor and burned them. The elderly woman came to give help, thinking the house on fire. This woman also told me how he used to lie in bed all day & compelled Iseult to fetch wood for the fire down an uneven swampy mountain path a mile & a half long & this every day – 'a strong mans job' she said.

Iseult has at last wished to assert herself because she is with child & she says 'I know now that I must not any longer be starved or kept without sleep because of the child.' He keeps her without sleep by making scenes all night – here I have independent witness – & once by banging on her door till he broke the panel. He would then sleep all day while Iseult did the housework.

When she is in the Nursing home he will be informed that she will not return till enough is settled on her & the child to insure that neither shall starve & that after her return, she has decided to leave for ever after the first scene. But it is vital to this plan that when the few days in the nursing home (which are all MG can afford) are over she can dissapear & leave no address. May we send her to you. To take her for a couple of weeks will be an act of mercy and kindness. She would go down by herself & perhaps I then might go for a couple of days (as there may be things needing explanation & she will defend her husband through all & minimise all his wrongs) & think that if I was to be there she would feel less strange. I would not however think it right to stay longer & besides I shall probably have to negotiate with the young mans family. MG is too angry Iseult thinks to make a good negociator . . .

The young man is I think a Sadist one of those who torture those they love, a recognized lunatic type.

'Alas,' he added in a second letter, '"The horn's sweet note and the tooth of the hound."'[15] 'The Second Song of the Fool' now looked like a sinister prophecy.

But Gregory failed him. She had her own troubles, as she was currently fighting a rearguard action against Margaret's efforts to sell Coole. ('Just a little suburban minx who has been to a school of art and gathered a little knowledge there,' fulminated Lily, 'and in the suburbs they like to move every three years and have no feeling or understanding of anyone not of their generation.'[16]) Gregory was desperately trying to come to an accommodation with Margaret, wishing to keep Coole at least for her lifetime, and if possible for her grandson. Meanwhile the country round about was catching fire; she felt distanced from WBY over the theatre, over her own writing, over what she saw as his diminishing commitment to Ireland. Most of all she did not trust anything to do with the Gonnes. She had met Iseult at Ballylee the year before, and probably anticipated trouble; she was disinclined to take sides in a marriage which she had encouraged. At any rate, she was not about to have Iseult at Coole with her antagonistic daughter-in-law. 'It is a terribly distressing account & I feel very deeply for poor sweet gentle Iseult. I wish indeed I could have her – nothing could please me better were I alone, or alone with the children.' Later she wrote more strongly: 'so please put away this idea from any plans you may make for her. I am sorry you told her you had asked me to have her, for it will make it awkward for me to see her should I be in Dublin again.'[17]

This was a blow. But there was no awkwardness from the quarter whence it might have been expected. George had firmly and magnanimously accepted the responsibility which Iseult somehow managed to impose. She had suggested lending Ballylee to Iseult the previous May, and she had encouraged WBY in his mission to Glenmalure. 'I felt it was right to come,' he told her, '& I thank you for letting me do so. All that happens but shows me some new side of your goodness.' 'As for my "goodness" in letting you come,' she replied, 'that was really nothing but the foreseeing that you would have found it difficult to forgive me had I dissuaded you – if you cannot do much, at least you can do "something."'[18]

But her 'goodness' was indeed heroic, considering that at this very time she suffered an early miscarriage (her second) and was imprisoned at Broad Street with Lily as an unwanted house guest. This coincided with an interminable visit from the Theosophist G. R. Mead and his wife, who talked about 'The Lamb – The Jews – Tibet – Theosophy'. While George fumed at Lily's unintellectual chatter, and despaired of the mutual silence between her and the Meads, Lily was reporting back to JBY about her fellow guests: 'they want to attend a course of lectures on subjects they hate by men they abominate'.[19] 'I am hungering for a mind that has "bite"', George wrote desperately to WBY, 'I am too dependent on you – I am lost when you are away.' 'I too feel lost without you,' he replied. 'I do not take care of myself & I tire myself out & there is no order in the day or peace in my thoughts.' And he was careful to reassure her that there was no danger of reawakening his old obsession with Iseult:

I give you my word of honour that to my own surprise I have suffered little. I have had bad hours, but they are nothing compared to the even serenity that rather shocks me. The truth is that so much has happened since that time in Normandy that though I admire Iseults subtle thought I have no contact with her mind. Lennox is in contact & is suffering horribly & I greatly wish I had told him nothing. I beleive that ever since my return from America I have had a need of action &

that this activity has been very good for me. I am even gay as if I were hunting some beast. I remember how Francis Stuart, shortly after the marriage, sold Iseult's engagement ring; & then I think of him confronted with the necessity of losing her or consenting (he is a minor) to a substantial portion of his income being paid to her direct. It is precisely because I am not deeply moved that I am useful, I can banter both Iseult & MG till they put away subjectivity and see bare fact. I am some Ezra Pound, putting his head against the wall, & laughing, as MG is the enfuriated philospher.[20]

At the same time the breach with Gonne was fully repaired – all the more easily, as he was acting towards Iseult *in loco parentis*, the role for which Gonne had always cast him. But it had been a taxing time. Even getting Iseult into a nursing-home had been fraught with crisis (pony-car accidents, missed trains); once there, even with the sympathetic Bethel Solomons fully enlisted, she began to make difficulties. George, playing Elizabeth Radcliffe's part in yet another reprise of a previous crisis, suggested to WBY that Iseult's pregnancy was 'not a reality': she had cast a horoscope which suggested 'deception & entanglement of all kinds, especially in Vth house matters'.[21] But Solomons confirmed the pregnancy and Iseult's ill-health; he interviewed the father-to-be on lines set out in a letter from WBY.[22] It was becoming clear that Iseult would not give Stuart up, so he had to be forced to allow her some financial independence, and forbidden to see her until she had recovered.

Undertakings were made and withdrawn. Gonne took offence at Iseult's reluctance to return to the discomforts of Glenmalure. ('The slight on the house was what she could not forgive,' WBY told George ironically. 'There is no easy chair no carpets, no sanitation whatever except the noble sanitation of the fields. I was very glad to get away.'[23]) And for all the stern talking from doctors, the solicitors' letters, and the consultation with 'a doctor in lunacy' (Gregory's suggestion), Iseult refused to abide by the advice of her would-be protectors. The ill-starred marriage would continue until Stuart's flight to Nazi Germany twenty years later. WBY, as a last resort, arranged an invitation for her from Ottoline Morrell, but he received a passionate response from poor Iseult:

I cannot help feeling it was right to act as I did about the money question: for the sake of the child I will have enough energy to earn my living if Francis and I live apart; and if anything brings us together again it is on my part a mixture of generosity and firmness . . . No no I will not go to Lady Ottoline. The only part of it that tempts me would be the thought of being near you and able to see you sometime; but it is at all times an effort for me to stay in the house of people I don't know and just now the effort would be too great. I was very thrilled by what you wrote of initiatory moments, do write me when you can of such things as you are allowed to say: it is a great stimulus.[24]

One of WBY's stranger suggestions was that Stuart should come to him at Oxford for a time (George must have blenched): 'he has talent & one may do something with that'.[25] But both Yeatses felt the marriage and the child were doomed. A banshee had cried at the Glenmalure cottage, and the horoscope cast by George was ominous. 'One can only put off tragedy with a child tainted with madness at the end of it.' Even more chillingly, he remarked to Gregory, 'it must be taken from her at once, & brought up by strangers'.[26] But after Iseult's daughter was born seven months later, he wrote a charming if highly loaded letter, sending a horoscope, implicitly reminding her of the time his own obsession with her had begun, and placing himself in a family relationship to her once more.

I found your horoscope & with this to help have written enclosed but I wish I had had your husband's also . . . I am out of practice with natal figures but have probably done as well as anybody you could get in Dublin. If I am alive when she gets to 17 or 18 we shall have a long consultation as to what is to be done to make her marriage lucky. Perhaps we may marry her with my family. By that time I shall be very old & stern & with my authority to support yours she will do in that matter what she is told to do. By that time you will no doubt have completed your studies & become a celebrated Bengali scholar . . . You will be still very handsome & an Indian prince will have attempted upon your visit to his country in search [of] Bengali manuscripts – according to rumour – to carry you off.[27]

George's prophecy was the correct one. Iseult's daughter was dead from meningitis within three months. 'Perhaps', wrote WBY to Gregory, in a comment that needs no gloss, 'it is well that a race of tragic women should die out.'[28]

II

By 13 August he was back in Broad Street, which (once the Meads and Lily were safely dispatched) seemed a refuge of sanity and order. There were distractions such as the Lane imbroglio, the constant uncertainty about the fate of Ballylee, and the hopeless task of persuading JBY to come home,[29] but he could return to writing. Impelled by the upheavals of the last weeks, and the recent deaths of old friends and occultist comrades like Farr, Horton, and Mathers, his theme was memory – and the dead. By 7 October he had completed another major poem, built around the idea of the dead revisiting on All Souls' Night – though this anniversary fell over three weeks after the first draft of the poem was completed.[30]

He pursued memory even further back by beginning the next instalment of his memoirs. The frank and private draft which he had read to Maud and Iseult at Colleville in 1917 remained in existence, but he now set himself to cover the same era in a form that could be published.[31] At first he intended to cover the period from the family's return to London in 1887 up to 1894; but his scope contracted to the period up to Parnell's death in 1891, now firmly fixed as a Rubicon in WBY's version of history. *Four Years* would accordingly be the title of the instalments published in the *London Mercury* in the summer of 1921 and produced as an elegant little book by Cuala in December.

His mind may have been concentrated by the discovery of a collection of his very early manuscripts, which Lily had preserved and presented to him in October 1920: early drafts of works like *The Countess Kathleen* and even *Mosada*. 'George says they ought to make Willy kind to young poets, some of it is so bad.'[32] By mid December he had written about 14,000 words, covering the Bedford Park set, the Rhymers' and Blavatsky. This comprised the section eventually published as *Four Years*: he was moving on to 'Ireland after Parnell', envisaging 20,000 to 30,000 words altogether.[33] While the scene is seductively set in 1880s Bedford Park, and architectural details employed to point up the atmosphere of youthful ambition and high art, *Four Years* is really a demonstration of the interrelationships among character, fate, and artistic achievements. From a different perspective, therefore, the book explores the governing preoccupations of *A Vision*. JBY's circle – John Todhunter, J. T. Nettleship, F. York Powell – supply one kind of lesson or warning; W. E. Henley, Wilde, Morris another. WBY's chosen scheme can impose a certain mechanical shape on his analysis of – for instance – Morris, but Wilde is brilliantly illuminated, for what he represented about Ireland as well as for his own genius. WBY's memories of the occultist circles around Blavatsky and Mathers are lit up by gleams of merciless humour, but the intention is serious and the effect powerful. Visual detail is employed with an artist's eye; people are interpreted as portraits, in a characteristic pose, or compared to an archetype by Titian or Rossetti.

Above all, in *Four Years* WBY excels at revealing inadequacies among the artistically ambitious, either because they were led astray by abstractions and theories, or because – like the Rhymers' – they refused to base their deeply felt artistic principles upon a philosophy of life. 'They were artists and writers and certain among them men of genius, and the life of a man of genius, because of his greater sincerity is often an experiment that needs analysis and record. At least my generation so valued personality that it thought so.'[34] Morris's life was exemplary – and enviable above all others – because his 'intellect, unexhausted by speculation or casuistry, was wholly at the service of hand and eye, and whatever he pleased he did with an unheard-of ease and simplicity, and if style and vocabulary were at times monotonous he could not have made them otherwise without ceasing to be himself.'[35] Many of the ideas with which WBY had dazzled or bewildered listeners on his American tour find their place here: the fragmentation of world culture from the time of the Renaissance, the disabling introspection of romanticism, the need to reverse 'abstraction' by creating and evoking symbols which linked back to a common consciousness (or subconsciousness). This led, by Yeatsian logic, to his particular kind of nationalist commitment. 'A nation or an individual with great emotional intensity might . . . give to all those separated elements, and to all that abstract love and melancholy, a symbolical, a mythological coherence.'[36] And a literary revival would provide the key. As WBY told Russell, the idea that unity of culture could be achieved by a nation that eschewed materialism in favour of spirituality would follow 'the chapters on Madame Blavatsky, Morris, Macgregor, Henley and so on and will come as a logical deduction'.[37] Though he later moved the section on the Irish Literary Society to his next autobiographical instalment, it appeared in the 1921 *Four Years* in obedience to this exact logic. (By contrast, the sections on Farr and Gonne were added after the first publication, for the extended volume called *The Trembling of the Veil* which Werner Laurie published in October 1922: while of prime autobiographical importance, they were less central to the theme drawn out in the original publication.) Some of his more stringently elitist beliefs were edited out of the published version.[38] Above all, in 1920 WBY was determined to place his own early beliefs, even the most exotic, credulous, and supernatural, in a context which would lead, indirectly but inexorably, to the Irish revolution which had exploded all around him. The connection would be made more and more explicit in the section which he wrote after the first *Mercury* publication, 'Ireland after Parnell'.

Even his familiar reflections on the Rhymers', polished up in countless renditions of his stock lecture 'The Friends of my Youth', were used to equate his own experience to that of Ireland, like the nationalist heroes of Young Ireland. This was introduced by a memory of Joyce in his ruthless apprenticeship.

A young Irish poet, who wrote excellently but had the worst manners, was to say a few years later 'You do not talk like a poet, you talk like a man of letters', and if all the Rhymers had not been polite, if most of them had not been to Oxford or Cambridge, the greater number would have said the same thing. I was full of thought, often very abstract thought, longing all the while to be full of images, because I had gone to the art schools instead of a university. Yet even if I had gone to a university, and learned all the classical foundations of English literature and English culture, all that great erudition which once accepted frees the mind from restlessness, I should have had to give up my Irish subject-matter, or attempt to found a new tradition. Lacking sufficient recognized precedent, I must needs find out some reason for all I did. I knew almost from the start that to overflow with reasons was to be not quite well-born; and when I could I hid them, as men hide a disagreeable ancestry; and that there was no help for it seeing that my country was not born at all.

Towards the end of the book WBY referred again to the evolution of his thought, in terms which he would shortly embody in *A Vision*; he ended the passage with a ringing aphorism:

I generalized a great deal and was ashamed of it. I thought it was my business in life to be an artist and a poet, and that there could be no business comparable to that. I refused to read books and even to meet people who excited me to generalization, all to no purpose. I said my prayers much as in childhood, though without the old regularity of hour and place, and I began to pray that my imagination might somehow be rescued from abstraction and become as preoccupied with life as had been the imagination of Chaucer. For ten or twelve years more I suffered continual remorse, and only became content when my abstractions had composed themselves into picture and dramatization. My very remorse helped to spoil my early poetry, giving it an element of sentimentality through my refusal to permit it any share of an intellect which I considered impure. Even in practical life I only very gradually began to use generalizations, that have since become the foundation of all I have done, or shall do, in Ireland. For all I know all men may have been so timid, for I am persuaded that our intellects at twenty contain all the truths we shall ever find, but as yet we do not know truths that belong to us from opinions caught up in casual irritation or momentary fantasy. As life goes on we discover that certain thoughts sustain us in defeat, or give us victory, whether over ourselves or others, and it is these thoughts, tested by passion, that we call convictions. Among subjective men (in all those, that is, who must spin a web out of their own bowels) the victory is an intellectual daily re-creation of all that exterior fate snatches away, and so that fate's antithesis; while what I have called 'the Mask' is an emotional antithesis to all that comes out of their internal nature. We begin to live when we have conceived life as tragedy.[39]

The notion of an integrated life, the only one proper to an artist, is expressed through the idea of 'Unity of Being', an existence which has overcome fragmentation and 'abstraction'; and this in turn is projected on to his idea of a national literature. 'Might I not, with health and good luck to aid me, create some new *Prometheus Unbound*; Patrick or Columcille, Oisin or Finn, in Prometheus' stead; and, instead of Caucasus, Cro-Patrick or Ben Bulben? Have not all races had their first unity from a mythology that marries them to rock and hill?' The closing appeal addressed 'the present state of the world' in terms of the spiritual revelation he had sought through George's 'Instructors', and intermittently referred to in his American lectures. But it circled back to Ireland in the end.

I used to tell the few friends to whom I could speak these secret thoughts that I would make the attempt in Ireland but fail, for our civilization, its elements multiplying by division like certain low forms of life, was all-powerful; but in reality I had the wildest hopes. To-day I add to that first conviction, to that first desire for unity, this other conviction, long a mere opinion vaguely or intermittently apprehended: Nations, races, and individual men are unified by an image, or bundle of related images, symbolical or evocative of the state of mind which is, of all states of mind not impossible, the most difficult to that man, race, or nation; because only the greatest obstacle that can be contemplated without despair rouses the will to full intensity.

A powerful class by terror, rhetoric, and organized sentimentality may drive their people to war, but the day draws near when they cannot keep them there; and how shall they face the pure nations of the East when the day comes to do it with but equal arms? I had seen Ireland in my own time turn from the bragging rhetoric and gregarious humour of O'Connell's generation and school, and offer herself to the solitary and proud Parnell as to her anti-self, buskin followed hard on sock, and I had begun to hope, or to half hope, that we might be the first in Europe to seek unity as deliberately as it had been sought by theologian, poet, sculptor, architect, from the eleventh to the thirteenth century. Doubtless we must seek it differently, no longer considering it convenient to epitomize all human knowledge, but find it we well might could we first find philosophy and a little passion.[40]

He had often told Gregory and Russell their lives would be seen as part of Irish history, and *Four Years* began the process of putting them there. 'I wrote all that about unity of culture with great excitement,' he told Gregory, 'feeling that at last I had got something I had long wished to say upon paper.' But he also admitted elsewhere: 'One thing I did not see, the growing murderousness of the world.'[41] Irish history since 1916 had taken a direction which threatened to marginalize and make redundant their enterprise of creating a common culture that would be pluralist, avant-garde, English-speaking yet distinctively Irish. But for WBY this simply made it all the more imperative for his generation to claim their rightful place.

In any case, as the winter of 1920/21 drew on, the present could not be forgotten. Dublin life was punctuated by gunfire: 'it is possible we may get so accustomed to sensation', AE wrote grimly, 'that we would not stop a discussion on Yeats's last poems to rush to the window to see what the firing in the street was about'.[42] Around the country the Black-and-Tan terror had a firm grip on certain areas, and the moral authority of Sinn Féin had been correspondingly strengthened – most of all by the policy of 'reprisal' killings, inflicted on the populace apparently at random after a policeman or soldier was murdered. In June 1920 Lily had written light-heartedly about her arguments with Susan Mitchell, who claimed to be a Sinn Féiner. 'I don't think she is a true S.F. because I don't think she really believes that the police are shooting each other dead to oblige the English government. A real S.F. believes this.' But in December, after six months of Black and Tan atrocities, having just seen a lorryload of them roar past her house, revolvers in hand, with 'Reprisals Galore' scrawled on the side, she wrote to her father: 'As you know I was no Sinn Feiner a year ago, just a mild nationalist – but now – '[43]

The tension mounted inexorably over the weeks leading up to the death of the imprisoned hunger striker Terence MacSwiney, the Sinn Féin lord mayor of Cork, on 25 October. WBY went to Dublin on 9 October, to have a tonsillectomy performed by Gogarty. But his very first action was to seek out Horace Plunkett and discuss a publicity offensive against the government's Irish policy. Plunkett recorded that his visitor 'has been talking to Asquith and wants AE and me to stir him up to a Midlothian campaign against the "Irish atrocities"'. But, he added, 'alas Squiff is not Gladstone.' This was all too true, and though WBY continued to lobby the Liberal leader, who visited him at Oxford, Asquith's instincts were towards brokering a peace plan rather than assailing Lloyd George.[44] Further political discussions in Ireland were curtailed by WBY's operation on 13 October, his subsequent weakness, and the fact that he had to be rushed back to England for fear of being stranded by a rail strike.[45] This was his only visit to Ireland, but he was kept in touch with terrible events around Gort through Gregory – still campaigning to keep Coole against Margaret's wishes, still lobbying local Sinn Féin representatives about the disposal of the estate's farmland, and finding refuge in reading *Du côté de chez Swann* as houses were burned and shops looted around her. She had been voting Sinn Féin since the summer and contributing anonymous articles to the *Nation* attacking government policy.[46] On 26 October the news of MacSwiney's death came to Gort. Ten days later Ellen Quinn was shot dead outside her front door in Kiltartan, from a military lorry passing by, a baby in her arms.[47]

This horror struck deeply home. The murdered woman was the young wife of Malachi Quinn, one of a well-known Gort farming family, who rented Ballinamantane from the estate; the killing was utterly random. After a huge funeral and angry demonstrations, an official 'inquiry' applied some unconvincing whitewash. Gregory followed it through closely, taking over the compensation case brought by the widower and bringing pressure to bear where she could. Meanwhile, the climax of horror was reached in Dublin: early on Sunday, 21 November, fourteen army officers or alleged intelligence agents were killed off-duty in a brutally effective operation by Michael Collins's 'squad'. That afternoon the military opened fire indiscriminately on a crowd at a Gaelic football match, killing twelve civilians. And in Gort in early December a new level was plumbed when two local boys, with no IRA connections, were murdered by the Black and Tans for 'impudence', their bodies thrown into a ditch after being dragged behind one of the dreaded lorries until they were unrecognizably mangled.

The lurid glare of these conflagrations reached as far as the reflective rooms of the Yeatses' ancient house in Oxford. For WBY the time had come to take a public stand. Despite all Gregory's delicate lobbying, the Lane pictures issue was no nearer solution (both WBY and Gregory blamed Curzon's implacable hostility in Cabinet). Temporizing seemed pointless. 'I think the cause wants a martyr,' AE would shortly write to Gregory. 'If anyone went to jail over the pictures it would add the finishing touch to the controversy. Personally I think the man to go to prison is W. B. Yeats. He has had a long & pleasant & famous life & it wants accent. I think he would shine in prison better than you or I and he would write a volume of prison poems.'[48] WBY might not have been prepared to risk imprisonment for Lane's pictures, but the issue would no longer inhibit him about taking a Sinn Féin line about events in Ireland, and declaring it publicly. He was not alone in this. Liberal opinion in Britain was becoming increasingly worried about the Irish policy of the Lloyd George government. The *New Statesman* took a leading part in the campaign in support of Terence MacSwiney, and it was there that WBY decided to publish 'Easter 1916' at last. It appeared on 23 October. MacSwiney had gripped WBY's imagination; he decided to rewrite his old hunger-strike play, *The King's Threshold*, in case 'the Mayor of Cork may make it tragically appropriate'.[49] At the time of MacSwiney's death, the Abbey were actually considering his own play *The Revolutionist*. Four days after his death, WBY wrote to Robinson about the drama.

All the womens parts are bad. Probably he has, apart from his wife who seems simple & charming, lived among harsh political types. The women in the play are not political but they have the ungraciousness of politics. Yet I think in time he could have created true & original types of women. These women are good at moments. . . . The more however the play is kept close to its political story the better & the more it remains in the mens hands. It is not a good play, but it certainly increases ones respect for the Lord Mayor. He had intellect & lived & died for it. One feels that he died not because he would not dissapoint friends (fine as that had been) but because he would not dissapoint himself. I think the last pages would greatly move the audience who will see the Mayor in the plays hero.[50]

Played the following March, it would be one of the Abbey's great successes.

Throughout his long convalescence from the tonsil operation WBY brooded on Ireland. As the horrors mounted, he worked on another poem: centred on Gort, it took its place in his series of elegies for Robert Gregory but struck a very different note. Like so much of his recent work, it was addressed directly to a phantom:

> Some nineteen German planes, they say,
> You had brought down before you died.
> We called it a good death. Today
> Can ghost or man be satisfied?
> Although your last exciting year
> Outweighed all other years, you said,
> Though battle joy may be so dear
> A memory, even to the dead,
> It chases other thought away,
> Yet rise from your Italian tomb,
> Flit to Kiltartan cross and stay
> Till certain second thoughts have come
> Upon the cause you served, that we
> Imagined such a fine affair:
> Half-drunk or whole-mad soldiery
> Are murdering your tenants there.
> Many that revere your father yet
> Are shot at on the open plain.
> Where may new-married women sit
> And suckle children now? Armed men
> May murder them in passing by
> Nor law nor parliament take heed.
> Then close your ears with dust and lie
> Among the other cheated dead.

'Reprisals' remained unpublished, not from WBY's caution, but because Gregory sent a telegram asking him to suppress it. He had sent it to the *Nation* (sympathetic to the Irish nationalist case) and simultaneously posted a copy to Gregory. She wrote in her journal:

Yeats writes enclosing lines he has written and has, without telling me, sent to *The Times* [*sic*], I dislike them – I cannot bear the dragging of R. from his grave to make what I think a not very sincere poem – For Yeats only knows by hearsay while our troubles go on – and he quoted words G. B. S., told him and did not mean him to repeat – and which will give pain – I hardly know why it gives me extraordinary pain and it seems too late to stop it . . .[51]

But stop it she did, telling WBY that the moment was unpropitious, after the Bloody Sunday killings in Dublin ten days before. Above all, though, she disliked the poem, and the exploitation of Robert's ghost. This was a message he preferred not to pick up, as his reply makes clear:

I wired at once to 'The Nation' but have not yet heard. As I had had no proof I have no doubt I was in time. I think the poem good & wrote it, after the subject had been six weeks in my head, less because it would be a good poem than because I thought it might touch some one individual mind of a man in power. At the same time I do not for one moment doubt that you have good reason for your wire. I had long hesitated before I wrote, as I have hesitated about other things in this tragic situation. In any case there were a thousand chances to one against any poem having any effect. If you think over the poem 'the nineteen planes' 'the battle joy' (so no pacificist crank) you will see that all was calculated. I hope your objection is entirely on public, or local grounds, & not on any personal dislike to it.[52]

This disagreement accentuates their distance from each other over the Irish crisis: he had, for example, no idea that she had written the articles for the *Nation*, whereas in earlier times she would certainly have consulted him. When she did tell him, he must have felt abashed.[53] For her part, she was understandably impatient with letters from Oxford worrying about damage to door locks at Ballylee, after a Black and Tan break-in, while she was trying to negotiate a pathetically small 'compensation' payment to Malachi Quinn for his murdered wife. When wby asked anxiously 'to what military authority in Gort we should write, or get Georges solicitor to write to', Gregory transcribed the query in her journal with an ironic exclamation mark.[54] Matters were not helped by his tendency towards cosmic generalizations: 'The trouble is that there is world wide reaction owing mainly to Russia & everywhere governments & military power are let do much what they like. People speak quite calmnly of a large part of Europe sinking back into barbarism & compare it to the break up of civilization at the fall of the Roman Empire. They cling to any authority.'[55] This may have been closely linked to the historical cycles dictated by George's 'Instructors', and in line with the poems he was hatching on the current state of the world, but in Gort it would have seemed rather off the point.

At the same time his memoirs were taking shape. And he presented these to Gregory, rather defensively, as in part a political testament.

I have written about 14000 words of my new memoirs but about 3000 are not for present publication. They are mainly the history of my kind of national ideal & how it formed in my head – the rags I picked off various bushes. I think it will influence young Irish men in the future, if for no other reason than that it shows how seriously one lived & thought. I know from my own memory of my youth in Dublin how important biography can be in Ireland.

I hope you will go on with your Nation essays & re-print them in some permanent form. It is even more important to England than to Ireland that the English policy of these last months should be recorded for judgement. If not judged & cast out it will become a precedent of Government & if it does – *Exit Britannia*. I wonder if I ever wrote you so political a letter.[56]

But 'Reprisals' remained the only poem he wrote directly about the Irish troubles at this time, and he was more anxious to get into print his latest

Noh play, *Calvary*, which owed much to late-night sessions with George and her 'Instructors'.[57]

He was also worried about money. This anxiety lay behind his suggestion of reorganizing his work into a newly arranged collected edition with Macmillan,[58] and was also a strong incentive to continue his memoirs. And his initial reaction to the rumour that Ballylee had been 'wrecked' was to retrench by planning a full-scale retreat to Italy, letting the Oxford house for half the year and settling in a cheap villa near Florence in time for the birth of their second child, due in August. When he told Gregory this at the end of the year, she must have felt completely deserted – especially as the curfew in Dublin had temporarily closed the Abbey, and the time had come for an appeal and a campaign to keep it going. But he was insistent on the necessity of 'getting George away': 'I think the only desire George has ever expressed to me has been this desire to go to Italy, where she was very happy as a child, & it was growing on her even before this last news.' It was a particularly difficult pregnancy, and she felt trapped in Oxford. Against Gregory's strictures about working for Ireland, WBY stressed his own need to make money: living expenses devoured all their income. He made periodic but doomed efforts to persuade his father to return to Dublin (where he could be supported on 35s. a week instead of £4). But JBY remained a master of the art of getting his own way. When his son pleaded that in order to support him, another arduous American lecture tour would be necessary, the old man's 'only reply was that I musn't on any account go to lecture without bringing George'.[59] In June WBY made yet another effort to bring him back to Dublin (though 'dreading his inability to recognise curfew'). The old man baulked and feinted, and once again, rather than paying JBY's debts direct, WBY had to send rather contrived 'manuscripts' to Quinn ('I write in lost pages & George finds the old pages').[60] Financial worry abated a little with a favourable royalty statement at the end of January – *Poems* earned more than twice its previous maximum, and the sale of his other works showed a healthy increase.[61] He still meditated increasing his earnings by issuing a new *Collected Works* with Macmillan, but they remained evasive.[62] More than anything, he still wanted peace, to develop the patterns which he now discerned in his work as a whole.

The Italian project came to nothing, and was soon replaced, rather less glamorously, by the prospect of living in Cork. 'You must not think we are deserting Ireland,' he assured Gregory on New Year's Day 1921, repeating the same message to Robinson. A later letter to Gregory elaborated on their future plans, stressing George's part in them:

She is very happy & satisfied so far as the future is concerned & of course hopes for a son. It is her idea to leave this for Cork on our return – I had suggested it half seriously – partly because she wants to be near Ballylee to look after it & partly because she hopes to get a house on the edge of Cork city, a town house, & yet with a garden & thinks we should economise enough by the move to have a motor which would carry us to Ballylee & back. I am insisting however on nothing definite being settled even in thought until we have been there & found what kind of architecture we could hope for & what sort of society. I would prefer to stay out of Ireland till my philosophy is complete & then to settle there and apply its doctrine to practical life. The fact that we can let this house for six months in the year & get back our rent & taxes has to weigh in the ballance & makes the economy doubtful. I have always wished however to live in Cork & start some kind of movement or theatre there . . . I had proposed Oxford as a place to live in because I thought it unfair to George to live wholly out of Ireland [*recte* England]. I now find she would have preferred Ireland from the start.[63]

It is unlikely that Gregory's mind was set at rest – especially as WBY suddenly precipitated one of his periodic quarrels with Lolly and resigned his position as editor at Cuala. The conflict had a familiar ring, arising from their acceptance for publication of 'a little book of patriotic verse by Russell, which I thought extraordinarily bad, as indeed I think all his recent verse'.[64] 'If you have the courage,' AE had appealed to Lolly, 'print "Michael", "Brixton Prison", "To Some I Know Who Are Dead" & "Sackville Street 1917"'; he understood 'the delicacy of the position', but 'it would go in the USA'. Lolly agreed, without consultation.[65] WBY therefore resigned, announcing he would take his memoirs elsewhere. Gregory replied firmly, calling him back, as so often before, to the line of duty. 'When so much is being torn down we like to keep any work going, & without you it will fizzle out & lose its good name . . . I think you may have been too hasty . . . I feel that this is a bad moment to abandon Cuala.'[66] She also wrote reassuringly about Ballylee, where the damage turned out to have been exaggerated. By early February the trouble with Cuala had blown over, the Italian plan was abandoned due to a crisis over Nelly Tucker's health, and Cork remained, like Tokyo, in the realms of imaginary destinations.

But his relationship with Gregory did not immediately improve. For one thing, he continued to tell her that 'the constant bad news from Ireland kills my power of poetical work . . . & I own that for my own sake also I dread going nearer to the fountain of that news.' Rather defensively, he explained, 'I came here [Oxford] to live because I knew that if I did not get out of every kind of public life I would lose my poetical power. Years ago I had so much passion it did not matter what I did, but now emotion has to be brooded over in solitude to get it to the intensity for verse.' This may not have been an entirely acceptable excuse, especially since they also fell out over his merciless criticism of her new comedy, *Aristotle's Bellows* ('I do not like the play . . . I get the impression of it being written against the grain, by sheer will. Probably the state of Ireland caused that . . . it is never rich. Of all your plays it is the only one where the dialogue is mechanical').[67] He advised against putting it on and only a gushing letter from Robinson restored her faith in herself. She was also worried – but, it appears, not surprised – when she saw WBY's name cited as a supporter of a benefit for the army in Ireland – inaccurately, as it turned out. He wrote a powerful public letter disassociating himself, but, as the year closed, she was still describing him, with some disapproval, as 'having practically left Ireland'.[68] But WBY had a further defence: he claimed his memoirs as a 'testament' which would encourage the young to begin building in Ireland, when the struggle was over. 'I think that you should prepare too,' he told Robinson, 'for you are young and can do more than I who become more and more absorbed in abstract thought and suggestion. I can help to make the keys but I will never turn them in the locks.'[69]

This was amply contradicted by his venture into the public arena in mid February. WBY had by now become something of an Oxford 'figure', sought out by undergraduates, befriended by dons, and acting as honorary president of the Oxford Irish Society. This provided a conduit to Irish undergraduates like Edward Pakenham and L. A. G. Strong, himself a future poet and novelist. WBY made a point of entertaining undergraduates at his 'Monday evenings', where he read extracts from his memoir in progress, as well as poems. As in Woburn Buldings he dispensed aphorisms and drink, though the 'tea and whiskey' had been replaced by wine in long-stemmed Venetian glasses.

His involvement with the Irish Society came about through the initiative of James O'Reilly, the undergraduate who had observed the ballet with Lady Ottoline on the steps of 4 Broad Street. O'Reilly's opinions were republican, and WBY closely quizzed him about the political complexion of the Society, pleased that it represented 'all shades of Irish opinion from extreme republican separatism to die-hard Unionism'. 'He was amused and interested', O'Reilly recalled, 'when I told him that the die-hard Protestant Unionist at Oxford became more and more Irish and indeed anti-English, if still remaining anti-nationalist, the longer he was out of Ireland no matter how vehemently he might have started by denouncing Sinn Fein and all its works: and that there was a "Castle Catholic" type whose hope was to be mistaken for an Englishman.'[70] He presided over the annual dinner, where Horace Plunkett bored them all to sleep, including the honorary president (another Irish undergraduate, Hubert Butler, noticed that WBY and Plunkett were 'each deaf in the wrong ear').[71] On 16 February he spent a convivial evening addressing the Society on 'The Irish Intellectual Movement', saying, to O'Reilly's recollection, 'pure culture is necessary for a nation in the fight against the east which has nations with culture'. But he was also astutely observing undergraduate opinion about Irish affairs, and testing the ground; he had already told both Gregory and Robinson that he was trying to use his presidency of the Oxford Irish Society to 'get at some young men, who may come to have importance'.[72] Walking home with O'Reilly after his address to the Society, he spoke about his invitation to debate at the Oxford Union the following day, declaring, 'I will tell them their King's soldiers are murderers.'

He was as good as his word. His appearance on 17 February 1921 electrified a capacity audience. As the *Oxford Magazine* put it, 'Mr W. B. Yeats, who was very well received by the House, immediately gave expression to his feelings on the Irish Question. He gave an oration rather than a debating speech, holding the attention of the House by the manner in which he passionately extolled Sinn Fein justice, denounced the Prussianism of the "Black and Tans", and appealed to the England of Gladstone and Disraeli. We have never heard so full a speech delivered in seven minutes.' The motion was carried by a majority of 90, after 'the most successful debate of the term'.[73] O'Reilly's judgement bears this out, far more vividly:

. . . the most eloquent speech I have ever heard. He made no attempt to debate or to argue. He denounced and defied the English. Pacing up and down away from the table at which the speakers stand, his fists clenched in his dinner jacket pockets, he roared and stormed with his splendid voice. 'Honourable members opposite say they approve of reprisals. They are not speaking the truth for they have no conception of what they speak . . . I see before me the bust of Gladstone . . . England has changed since his day. Ireland has not changed and it is Ireland that will survive.' He spoke for about twelve minutes only, twelve minutes of bitter and blazing attack on the English in Ireland. He ended pointing at the busts of the Union's Prime Ministers: 'Gladstone! Salisbury! Asquith! They were Victorians. I am a Victorian. They knew the meaning of the words "Truth" and "honour" and "Justice". But you do not know the meaning of them. You do not understand the language I speak so I will sit down.' He was cheered to the echo. The Union had never heard eloquence like that. Yeats must have been the greatest orator of his time, certainly the greatest I ever heard. But this was the only speech of the kind I heard Yeats make. Here then was another Yeats. There was no acting or posing that night at the Union, there was real fury; no one who heard that speech could question his sincerity as an Irish nationalist.[74]

Yet he carefully declared that he was 'not a Sinn Feiner', and praised the regular troops for keeping control.[75] Nonetheless, though Gregory might have pointed out that his impassioned account relied entirely on vicarious experience, he had nailed his colours to the mast. (He was rewarded by an attack in the *Morning Post* and a congratulatory report in the *Westminster Gazette*, which reported that Oxford had been 'very highly privileged to hear him break the political silence of thirty years with words of imagination and fire'.[76]) A week after his triumph at the Union he wrote a revealing letter to Gregory, congratulating her on her recently published memoir of Hugh Lane:

Young men will read it, when we are all dead & canonised & take out of it facts & opinions for the final history of the last thirty years in Ireland & it is possible that those thirty years may set the tune in Ireland for a hundred years . . . It gives me a great impression of intellectual energy & not only in its writer. One gets the impression of a group of people, with Lane for centre & principal, living a life of intense activity & intellectual energy. I myself often write with that object in mind – I am so writing my new memoirs – because more than anything else is it necessary to make young Irish men understand what an intellectual society is. In a way it makes me a little sad for that vehement companionable life may never be mine again. I have been given a more solitary task. It is partly longing for that lost life that makes me think of living in Cork when this war is over, but even there my strange work will keep me solitary. I am like a man looking for the philosopher's stone or like a man who has found it but doubts if any will beleive his chemical gold is anything but brass or copper.[77]

But he was not as removed from the world as this might suggest. Like Gladstone, whom he had just invoked in his Union speech, he was demonstrating, yet again, the gift of 'right-timing'. The placing of his publications over the next months would confirm this talent further still.

III

WBY published *Michael Robartes and the Dancer* in February 1921, less than two years after his previous collection. Partly, this reflected the poetic productivity which had come with his marriage: 'Solomon and the Witch', 'Under Saturn' (commemorating his visit to Sligo with George, and addressed to her), 'Towards Break of Day', 'The Second Coming', 'Demon and Beast' (inspired by their visit to Kilkenny in search of Anne Hyde), 'A Prayer for my Daughter', and his dedication-poem to Ballylee all bore witness to this. ('All Souls' Night' was held back.) But he also published – deliberately placed in sequence – 'Easter 1916', 'Sixteen Dead Men', and 'The Rose Tree'. That last poem, employing a favourite occult symbol for a new purpose, stands as his most unequivocal 'rebel ballad'. The ambiguity of 'Easter 1916', and the hard edge of 'On a Political Prisoner' (which directly followed it) make much less immediate impact, though they are far more accomplished poems.

'O words are lightly spoken,'
Said Pearse to Connolly,
'Maybe a breath of politic words
Has withered our Rose tree;

> Or maybe but a wind that blows
> Across the bitter sea.'
> 'It needs to be but watered,'
> James Connolly replied,
> 'To make the green come out again
> And spread on every side,
> And shake the blossom from the bud
> To be the garden's pride.'
> 'But where can we draw water,'
> Said Pearse to Connolly,
> 'When all the wells are parched away,
> O plain as plain can be
> There's nothing but our own red blood
> Can make a right rose tree.'

He had written 'The Rose Tree' four years before, in April 1917. Like 'Easter 1916', it had been first released at the critical moment (November 1920), and then placed in a volume which constituted the political statement he was now ready to make. For WBY himself, however, the kernel of *Michael Robartes and the Dancer* probably lay in the three difficult dialogue-poems which open the book. The title poem referred, inevitably, to himself and Iseult: his alter ego provocatively presents the arguments about the incompatibility of beauty and 'opinion' put more didactically in 'Prayer for my Daughter' and implied in his questioning about 'Phase 15'.

> *She.*   I have heard said
>   There is great danger in the body.
>
> *He.*   Did God in portioning wine and bread
>   Give man His thought or His mere body?
>
> *She.*   My wretched dragon is perplexed.
>
> *He.*   I have principles to prove me right.
>   It follows from this Latin text
>   That blest souls are not composite,
>   And that all beautiful women may
>   Live in uncomposite blessedness,
>   And lead us to the like – if they
>   Will banish every thought, unless
>   The lineaments that please their view,
>   When the long looking-glass is full,
>   Even from the foot-sole think it too.
>
> *She.*   They say such different things at school.

If 'Michael Robartes and the Dancer' is for Iseult, 'Solomon and the Witch' (which follows it immediately) is for George; a poem about mystic marriage, where 'Chance is at one with Choice at last'.

> A lover with a spider's eye
> Will find out some appropriate pain,
> Aye, though all passion's in the glance,
> For every nerve: lover tests lover
> With cruelties of Choice and Chance;
> And when at last that murder's over
> Maybe the bride-bed brings despair
> For each an imagined image brings
> And finds a real image there;
> Yet the world ends when these two things,
> Though several, are a single light,
> When oil and wick are burned in one;
> Therefore a blessed moon last night
> Gave Sheba to her Solomon.'

But 'An Image from a Past Life' is more personal and less mystic. Poet and his lover are haunted by the image of his lost love, floating by the shadows of a starlit river:

> *He.*   Why have you laid your hands upon my eyes?
> What can have suddenly alarmed you
> Whereon 'twere best
> My eyes should never rest?
> What is there but the slowly fading west,
> The river imaging the flashing skies,
> All that to this moment charmed you?

> *She.*   A sweetheart from another life floats there
> As though she had been forced to linger
> From vague distress
> Or arrogant loveliness,
> Merely to loosen out a tress
> Among the starry eddies of her hair
> Upon the paleness of a finger.

There is a curious reversion here to ninetyish language and the diction of *The Wind Among the Reeds*. It is hardly accidental that the images are those he had conjured up for Olivia Shakespear over twenty years before, when he had also been distracted by 'an image from a past life'. The doubleness of the poem reflects the doubling of a pattern in WBY's life: Gonne's image displacing Shakespear's, George's fear that Iseult's would replace hers.

She. Now she has thrown her arms above her head;
　　Whether she threw them up to flout me,
　　Or but to find,
　　Now that no fingers bind,
　　That her hair streams upon the wind,
　　I do not know, that know I am afraid
　　Of the hovering thing night brought me.

The fifteen poems of *Michael Robertes and the Dancer* span, with radical compression, the themes and preoccupations of 1917 to 1920. Those who found *The Wild Swans at Coole* incoherent and directionless had their rebuttal, though they may not have realized it yet. The new book was not a full 'trade' collection, but an interim statement. There would not be another full-scale collection for seven years, and when it appeared it would be his greatest achievement.

For the moment, in the spring of 1921, life remained uncertain. Ireland seemed less and less safe, and George was restless in Oxford: O'Reilly was struck by WBY's repeated complaints that she lacked company and did not meet the dons' wives (though, O'Reilly added, 'even if she were in the way of meeting them I can think of very little in common between Mrs Yeats & the average don's lady in North Oxford or on Boar's Hill'). In March they decided to economize by letting Broad Street and moving to a cottage in Shillingford, fifteen miles away. Life in Oxford had palled: his chief social occupation, he told Quinn, was trying in vain to get Masefield – 'imbedded in concrete blocks of marriage' – to come to lunch without his wife. (The Masefield daughter was forbidden to know George and WBY 'because we might talk astrology, or magic, or say something unclassifiably wicked'.) As for academic society, there were too many literate people 'especially among the Dons wives. Max Beerbohm says that the Dons have married such ugly wives from a habit that arose when they were first permitted marriage some 60 years ago. They thought marriage very improper at the best, but not quite so improper if the woman was ugly.'[78] The supposed activities of the dons rankled as much as the alleged plainness of their wives. Strong overheard WBY informing two college tutors: 'You seem to be busy with the propagation of second and third and fourth hand opinions about literature. Culture does not consist in acquiring opinions, but in getting rid of them.'[79]

They let 4 Broad Street 'for a pot of money' (£5. 10s. a week) and moved out on 2 April.[80] The cottage had a large garden, where Anne could play and recover from whooping cough and George could rest, though the rural surroundings made her pine for Ballylee. At any rate, WBY was able to write. *Four Years* was completed, attracting gratifying – and profitable – interest from publishers. The serial rights were taken with alacrity by the *Dial* in

America and the *London Mercury* in Britain. Werner Laurie offered WBY £500 for an extended version, to be printed in an expensive edition. This had to be cleared with Cuala, but came as a great relief – even if it showed 'how much more profitable it is to write about poetry than to write it'.[81] But he was writing poetry too. By early April he was at work on the complex sequence which would eventually bear the confusing title 'Nineteen Hundred and Nineteen', inspired by the ideas of apocalypse and recurrence which he had explored through George's 'Instructors' and amplified – as he told Olivia Shakespear – in further reading.

One finds that Greeks & Romans were very religious & that their religion was full of all those images you & I have found in vision. The things wild people, half scholars & rhapsodical persons wrote about, when you & I were young, & were scorned by whole scholars for writing, seem now proved . . . I read many books of this kind now, searching out signs of the whirling gyres of the historical cone as we see it & hoping that by their study I may see deeper into what is to come.

I am writing a series of poems ('thoughts suggested by the present state of the world' or some such name). I have written two, & there may be many more. They are not philosophical but simple & passionate, a lamentation over lost peace & lost hope. My own philosophy does not much brighten the prospect, so far as any future we shall live to see is concerned, except that it flouts all socialistic hope if that is a brightening.[82]

But 'the world' really meant Ireland. The next day he told Gregory:

I am writing a series of poems all making up one poem on the state of things in Ireland & am now in the middle of the third. I do not know what degree of merit they have or whether I have now enough emotion for personal poetry. I begin to find a difficulty in finding themes. I had this about twelve years ago & it passed over. I may have to start another Noh play & get caught up into it, if these poems turn out badly. The first poem is rather in the mood of the Anne poem but the rest are wilder. Newspapers & letters alike await now till my work is finished: 'bring out weight and measure in a time of dearth' Blake wrote.[83]

The weight and measure were undeniable; for all the doubts of this letter, the complex poem-series became one of his masterpieces. First published as 'Thoughts upon the Present State of the World', by the time it was collected into *The Tower* (1928) it had been rechristened 'Nineteen Hundred and Nineteen', obscuring the date of its creation – and the nature of its content, since that year would by then be identified as the start of the Anglo-Irish War. The eventual title might also signify his preoccupation with historical cycles lasting around 2,000 years, or slightly less, which had recently featured in exchanges with George's 'Instructors'. Thus the opening poem of the series concerns the advent of apocalyptic times and the decay of civilizations. Beneath the high polish of the surface lies a complex pattern of preoccupations: the fall of Athens, the self-deluding liberal certitudes exploded by 1914, the memory of an exchange heard while watching a regiment exercising in Hyde Park in the summer of 1914, the illusion that war was a thing of the past.[84]

> Many ingenious lovely things are gone
> That seemed sheer miracle to the multitude;
> Above the murderous treachery of the moon
> Or all that wayward ebb and flow. There stood
> Amid the ornamental bronze and stone
> An ancient image made of olive wood;
> And gone are Phidias' carven ivories
> And all his golden grasshoppers and bees.
>
> We too had many pretty toys when young;
> A law indifferent to blame or praise,
> To bribe, or threat; habits that made old wrong
> Melt down, as it were wax in the sun's rays;
> Public opinion ripening for so long
> We thought it would outlive all future days.
> O what fine thoughts we had because we thought
> That the worst rogues and rascals had died out.[85]

The 'we', whose expectations of an untroubled civilization are so bitterly confounded by the anarchy of 1919 to 1921, deserves consideration: so does the era recalled here. On one level, it is obviously the late-Victorian world of Home Rule expectations (and Pax Britannica). On another, the language, concepts, and tone of aristocratic confidence summon up a more distant elite. The classical imagery of the first stanza, the disdain for the 'multitude', the implication of 'public opinion' as the possession of a class (or caste) suggests the identification with eighteenth-century Ascendancy values which was already coming to mark WBY's work. But the fourth stanza (which would supply some of the most resonant phrases and images in WBY's canon) sharply shifts the focus to the anarchic present – and, even more specifically, to the horrors of Black and Tan rule in south Galway.

> Now days are dragon ridden, the nightmare
> Rides upon sleep: a drunken soldiery
> Can leave the mother, murdered at her door,
> To crawl in her own blood and go scot-free;
> The night can sweat with terror as before
> We pieced our thoughts into philosophy,
> And planned to bring the world under a rule
> Who are but weasels fighting in a hole.

The poem goes on to posit that the horrors of the present suggest the impermanent effect of great art, the illusion that civilization and its ornaments are ever here to stay: Keats's Grecian Urn reversed.[86] For the artist (Athenian or Irishman), 'ghostly solitude' is all that is left to him.

> And other comfort were a bitter wound:
> To be in love and love what vanishes.
> Greeks were but lovers; all that country round
> None dared admit, if such a thought were his,
> Incendiary or bigot could be found
> To burn that stump on the Acropolis,
> Or break in bits the famous ivories
> Or traffic in the grasshoppers and bees?

WBY later altered the first lines to address a more poignantly idiomatic question:

> But is there any comfort to be found?
> Man is in love and loves what vanishes,
> What more is there to say? . . .

Removing the specific reference to Greece, and the equation of artists with deluded lovers, hides the central argument, and the symmetry between first and last stanzas. But it adds a philosophical question, cast in the most immediate and personal form. The effect of the change is to make the lines at once more memorable and more obscure – a trick his later poetry would turn to perfection.

What follows in the sequence could not be more different: a memory of the 1890s, inevitably suggested by the autobiography he had just completed. The American dancer, and choreographer Loie Fuller (one of Arthur Symons's passions) conjures up – yet again – the returning cycles of history which so preoccupied him.[87] The connection with the stanzas that precede and follow this lovely *aperçu* is as deft as it is surprising. Artistic illusion creates a dragon out of whirling silk, which suggests humanity being devoured by cycles of historical recurrence. Yet the next sequence takes up both Blake and Shelley (though not by name) and raises once again the theme of the artist's lonely triumph, hinting that his inspiration can ride even the levelling winds of history, prepared to welcome the advent of chaos and destruction. In the deployment of certain images (the swan, the labyrinth, the death of the body, the rage against fate), as well as in a distinct air of intellectual swagger, this sequence announces the essential qualities which would eventually define 'late Yeats'.

Some moralist or mythological poet
Compares the solitary soul to a swan;
I am content with that,
Contented that a troubled mirror show it
Before that brief gleam of its life be gone
An image of its state;
The wings half spread for flight,
The breast thrust out in pride,
Whether to play, or to ride
Those winds that clamour of approaching night.

A man in his own secret meditation
Is lost amid the labyrinth that he has made
In art or politics;
Some platonist affirms that in the station
Where we should cast off body and trade
The ancient habit sticks,
And that if our works could
But vanish with our breath
That were a lucky death
For triumph can but mar our solitude.

The swan has leaped into the desolate heaven:
That image can bring wildness, bring a rage
To end all things, to end
What my laborious life imagined, even
The half imagined, the half written page.
O but we dreamed to mend
What ever mischief seemed
To afflict mankind, but now
That winds of winter blow
Learn that we were crack-pated when we dreamed.

Again, this complex meditation is followed by a short interjection which reprises the earliest idea of disillusionment; again, added impact is lent by compression, and colloquialism.

We, who seven years ago
Talked of honour and of truth,
Shriek with pleasure if we show
The weasel's twist, the weasel's tooth.

'Seven years ago' would mean 1912, going by the poem's eventual title and supposed date of composition; but since it was composed over the two years up to its publication in 1921, with a title which does not 'mention' 1919, the reference seems to suggest 1914 and the pre-war world. The fifth sequence calls for a mockery of 'the great', 'the wise', and 'the good', who thought they could create permanence and placed their faith in 'leaving some monument behind', ignorant of 'the levelling wind'. The poet finally turns the tables by 'mocking mockery', the critics and quidnuncs who 'traffic in mockery' instead of 'helping good, wise or great / To bar that foul storm out'. But the sequence as a whole denies that such efforts could ever be more than temporary pallia-tion. The last section piles up visionary images of destruction, using – once again – a memory of the 1890s: Arthur Symons's 'Dance of the Daughters of Herodias', harbingers of vengeance and anarchy, whom WBY himself had instanced in a note to *The Wind Among the Reeds* twenty years before.

> Violence upon the roads, violence of horses,
> Some few have handsome riders, are garlanded
> On delicate sensitive ear or tossing mane;
> But, weary running round and round in their courses,
> All break and vanish, and evil gathers head.
> Herodias' daughters have returned again:
> A sudden blast of dusty wind and after
> Thunder of feet, tumult of images,
> Their purpose in the labyrinth of the wind;
> And should some crazy hand dare touch a daughter
> All turn with amorous cries, or angry cries,
> According to the wind for all are blind.
> But now wind drops, dust settles; thereupon
> There lurches past, his great eyes without thought
> Under the shadow of stupid straw-pale locks,
> That insolent fiend Robert Artisson
> To whom the love-lorn Lady Kyteler brought
> Bronzed peacock feathers, red combs of her cocks.

A note to the poem partly explained the final mysterious image. 'My last symbol, Robert Artisson, was an evil spirit much run after in Kilkenny at the start of the fourteenth century.' In fact, the reference is to a tale of witch-craft and sexual obsession rehearsed in detail in St John Seymour's *Irish Witchcraft and Demonology* as well as in histories of Kilkenny; this inspired, if obscure, closing image is probably another by-product of WBY's researches into the shadowy background of Anne Hyde. Arcane reading and personal symbolism coincide in a jarringly vivid historical image. What is yet to come is the idea which he would advance in his next great poem-sequence, 'Meditations in Time of Civil War', the theory that those apocalyptic horses can herald a new creativity and growth, coming out of the destruction of a superficially assured civilization. But he had already established the theme of much of his poetry over the next decade, which owed a great deal to the explorations behind *A Vision*: the artist regarding himself in the mirror of history. And the poem finally called 'Nineteen Hundred and Nineteen' revealed the combination of qualities which would define his future work: an ability to synthesize arcane learning, philosophical speculation, and political judgement, in a poetic language that made the most of open rhythms and idiomatic address. The achievement came not only from renewed self-confidence but also from a new technical proficiency. The uniquely authoritative tone of 'late Yeats' would rest upon this challenging combination of intimate meditation and public voice; it owed a great deal to the reflection and analysis enforced by the upheavals in his life over the past five years.

For the moment, the Yeatses marked time in Shillingford, hoping to hear of some cessation in violence in Ireland that would allow them to spend the summer in Ballylee, rather wearily keeping track of the inevitable latest row in the Stella Matutina Order[88] to which they both still belonged, and – in WBY's case – arranging some benefit lectures for the Abbey in London. This brought him to an enforced stay in Chelsea lodgings during early May – 'lonely, bored, tired, becolded in the head, toothachy, out of temper, Saturnian, noise-distracted, excemaish, bathless, theatre-hating, woman-hating, but otherwise well & cheerful'.[89] The news from Ireland worsened. Margaret Gregory, returning from a tennis party in an army officer's car, was the only survivor of an IRA ambush: all the men, and one woman, were shot by the roadside. Gregory advised WBY not to take George to Ballylee. The Yeatses gave up hope of Galway and moved to Cuttlebrook House in the high street of the neighbouring village, Thame, for July to September. He was now convinced that his correspondence was under police surveillance. 'The government seems to have committed itself against everything Ireland might accept,' WBY wrote gloomily to Robinson, suggesting that they close the theatre till the storm passed. But, he added, once the troubles were over, 'we shall find an opportunity greater than we have ever had. There have arisen a new mass of dramatic motives and dramatic emotion. I dread our not being able to live till that day comes.'[90]

Meanwhile, Cuttlebrook House was a consolation. Belonging to three spinsters and their mother, it was full of the clutter accumulated by a country family over generations, pleasing WBY 'better even than fine taste without a history'. It also recalled the Victorian atmosphere of Sligo in his youth. 'I shall end up reading Charles Kingsley & liking him.'[91] In fact, he read Trollope, and enjoyed the favourable reception of *Four Years*, serialized in the *Mercury* from June. In the most English of settings, in a large room looking out over the sleepy high street to John Hampden's school and an ancient church, he began on 1 July the lucrative enlargement of his memoirs. The published extract had not pleased JBY, as much because of the lofty amusement with which his son discussed his father's artistic circle as because of reflections on the family. The old man wrote querulously about it to Lolly, who transmitted the complaint to her brother, adding sharply 'we were not quite nonentities'. WBY warned her caustically that it might have been far worse.

You can tell JBY that the published parts are not all, that I have written much more which cannot be published during my life time, & that this does not give an unfriendly account of any of you. I am sorry if stray passages without their context have seemed unjust. I cannot write of living people for publication except in the most cursory way. I cannot write of any one, much less of my family, if I have to think of any point of view but my own & making that just in my own eyes. Probably I should have put in words of commendation, but, such sound conventional when used of relatives. I will try if I can amend things in the new enlarged edition for Werner Laurie, (for which by the by I am after all to get that £500) but I cannot promise.

In spite of his cheerful letters I judge from a letter to Quinn that JBY would much sooner be left in New York so probably at the moment he is feeling a little ruffled. There are also many things in my book (apart altogether from what I say of him or you) which he must dislike. My point of view is that of my generation & there is always antagonism between two generations. In old days at Bedford Park he once broke a picture glass with the back of my head, & another night as Jack will tell you wanted to fight me because of that quite legitimate difference between the ideas of his generation & mine. The cause of dispute was entirely abstract & impersonal. In his last letter he insists that I would have done much better, if I had written in the way in which he & York Powell (if 'you had stayed with us' is his way of putting it) would have preferred, been what he calls entirely human or some such phrase.

My aim through out was to leave you all out from the published memoirs as far as possible. I think this was right. I had to put JBY more fully into 'Reveries' but always wrote with difficulty & hesitation.

I thought of writing of your art books – you will remember I questioned you for the purpose – but when I thought over the matter I thought it would sound like family advertisement. Lilly had to come in because of Morris.

This £500 comes in the nick of time to save me from an immediate lecture tour to pay JBY's bills & return home. The £200 I sent is already spent I think.[92]

Thus he not only defended his right to recall the family history as he saw it, but reminded her that the weight of supporting their irrepressible father fell on him.

IV

On 9 July a truce was declared between the IRA and the security forces, and the preliminaries to a tortuous negotiation began. Gregory told WBY that in their locality people were 'anxious for a settlement, but there may be bitterness in other parts it will be hard to overcome; here the feeling is "it is time to stop. There is plenty done on both sides." '[93] As the participants moved uneasily towards each other, WBY was immersed in the Irish struggles of thirty years before – writing the section of his autobiographies which would become 'Ireland after Parnell'. After the passionate plea for unity of culture with which he closed *Four Years*, written 'with great excitement', the quarrels and intrigues over the foundation of the National Literary Society traced a different line. '[I am] arranging all so as to show the ungraciousness & crudeness of the Dublin of that time,' he told Gregory. 'All the while too I am making a social & literary philosophy for our young men as I dream.'[94] He and AE were corresponding again. The thoughts of both were driven back to the 1890s, that time of signs and portents, when apocalypse seemed just around the corner. AE reminded him that Blavatsky had forecast an 'iron age' for Britain and France, which was now dawning, whereas 'Ireland will lift itself out of its long obscuration by virtue of an idealism which is in its people . . . I agree with you that Europe is in for a period of reaction and repression and I do not think that there is enough idealism in the French or English to throw it off.'[95]

In reviewing the literary battles of the early 1890s against the background of Ireland in 1921, WBY repositioned his own youthful politics. In 'Ireland after Parnell' he appears as the defender of artistic standards against nationalist platitudes: this conceals the fact that contemporaries had seen him as heading a faction determined to tilt the National Literary Society in a Fenian direction. O'Leary is presented as guardian of nationalism and moral conscience, whose high standards were to be abandoned by his successors: but in the end he too was 'a victim, I think, of a movement where opinions stick men together, or keep them apart, like a kind of bird-lime, and without any relation to their natural likes and tastes, and where men of rich nature must give themselves up to an invitation which they no longer recognise because it is always present'.[96] Later he returned to the ideas advanced in 'Synge and the Ireland of his Time' and repeated in 'Easter 1916'. 'Nationalist abstractions were like the fixed ideas of some hysterical woman, a part of the mind turned into stone'. Unionist prejudices, their mirror image, took the form of cynical indifference. WBY's IRB activities are recounted with weary amusement: by mounting a series of vignettes, several out of sequence, he contrived to distance himself from the political passions of the past as of the present. Already he is anticipating the coming of Synge and the exposure of chauvinist practices.

'Ireland after Parnell' concludes with a leisurely, affectionate, only slightly barbed survey of Russell and his circle of mystics in the Ely Place days: another route to enlightenment which runs into the sands. And the metaphor of losing one's way on the road of spiritual exploration supplies

PLATE I

Michio Ito photographed in Japanese martial costume by Alvin Langdon Coburn in 1916, the year of *At the Hawk's Well*.

PLATE 2

Above left: Henry
Ainley as Cuchulain
in *At the Hawk's Well*,
1916, wearing Dulac's
Noh-style mask,
which—according to
Eddie Marsh—was
unnervingly like the
actor's own features.

Above right: Allan
Wade (the future
editor of WBY's letters)
behind the mask of
the Old Man in *At
the Hawk's Well*.

Right: Ito dances as
the Guardian of the
Well.

PLATE 3

Left: Iseult Gonne, *c.*1917.

Below: George photographed by her sisters-in-law in their Dundrum garden, 1918. Her thin and drawn appearance was probably the result of several months' intensive mediumship.

PLATE 4

The Yeatses in the USA, 1920.

Maud Gonne MacBride (on the right) with her friend Charlotte Despard at the Dublin Horse Show, August 1922; Dublin wits referred to them as Maud Gone Mad and Mrs Desperate.

PLATE 5

WBY photographed in his study at 82 Merrion Square
after winning the Nobel Prize (New York Times,
9 December 1923).

PLATE 6

Above: The Tower and cottages (with garage and vegetable-garden in the foreground) in 1926.

Left: The legendary winding stair.

PLATE 7

Interiors of the Tower
photographed by
Thomas Hynes
in 1926, showing
the solidly-made
local furniture, great
fireplace hood, and
painted ceilings.

PLATE 8

Above: A garden party given by the Gogartys during Aonach Tailteann, 1924. *Front row, left to right*: WBY, Compton Mackenzie, Augustus John, Edwin Lutyens. *Back row, left to right*: G. K. Chesterton, James Stephens, Lennox Robinson.

Below: The dinner on the Abbey stage, 8 August 1925, to celebrate the government's subsidy. Lennox Robinson, standing, addresses Ernest Blythe, third from right. Sean O'Casey and Barry Fitzgerald are third and fourth from the left. Maureen Delany is to the right of Blythe and WBY has Mrs Blythe on his right. May Craig is turned around in profile in the right-hand foreground, looking at Robinson; Shelah Richards is beside him.

PLATE 9

Ezra Pound staring out to sea from his Rapallo roof-
garden, photographed by James Jesus Angleton in the
later 1930s.

PLATE 10

Rapallo, *c*.1930.

82 Merrion Square, sold in 1928 when the
Yeatses temporarily abandoned Dublin winters
for Rapallo.

12/8 via Americhe, Rapallo. WBY's apartment
gives onto the top corner balcony.

PLATE II

Above left: A bearded WBY convalesces at the Caffè Aurum in the spring of 1930.

Left: WBY, Gogarty, and Augustus John (in painter's smock) at Renvyle, where John was painting WBY's portrait, July 1930.

Above right: WBY as John saw him, paunch tactfully concealed by the hat.

PLATE 12

Above: Augusta Gregory after Robert Gregory's death.

Right: AE painted by Hilda Roberts in 1929, against one of his own canvases.

PLATE 13

Augusta Gregory sitting underneath her catalpa tree
at Coole, August 1927.

PLATE 14

Above: WBY with a group from the Abbey at a dance in the Metropole Hotel, September 1931.
Back row, left to right: Shelah Richards, Lennox Robinson, Mick Dolan, F. J. McCormick, Denis O'Dea, Arthur Shields, Fred Johnson, P. J. Carolan.
Front row, left to right: Maureen Delany, WBY, May Craig, Eileen Crowe, unidentified, unidentified, Barry Fitzgerald.

Right: May Craig as the medium in *The Words upon the Window Pane*, 1930.

PLATE 15

Above: WBY holding forth in the New York Arts Club, January 1933, with (*from left to right*) Count John McCormack, Hamilton Harty, and Gogarty.

Left: WBY and T. S. Eliot at Harvard, December 1932.

PLATE 16

Clockwise from top:
Riversdale; Michael Butler Yeats
(against a background of JBY's family
portraits); Anne Butler Yeats.

the theme of the next section of *The Trembling of the Veil*, 'Hodos Chameliontos'. WBY's own search for unity through the Celtic Mystical Order appears as a path embarked upon after disillusionment by political divisions, an interpretation which conceals the connections between the high political fever of 1898 and the visionary expectations of the Yeats circle at the same time. And the experiments and passions of the 1890s were seen as frantic and inchoate precisely because WBY was then ignorant of the synthesizing supernatural philosophy which he had been developing since 1917. Maud Gonne's influence, fully recognized in *Memoirs* (then unpublished), is not given its due, and his own withdrawal to London from 1894 to 1897 is unmentioned. Instead, the way of the chameleon is straightened out by a spiritual insight: the idea of guidance through discovery of one's anti-self. The concluding meditation abandons autobiography for philosophy. 'Revelation is from the self, but from that age-long memoried self, that shapes the elaborate shell of the mother and the child in the womb, that teaches the birds to make their nest; and that genius is a crisis that joins that buried self for certain moments to our trivial daily mind.' As with all his autobiographical writing, *The Trembling of the Veil* reflects more accurately the poet's priorities while he was writing it, than the events which it purports to describe.

Above all, in the later section of the autobiography, particularly the chapter called 'The Tragic Generation', WBY's treatment of the lives (and deaths) of his friends was closely influenced by the schemes of character and fate which he was developing for *A Vision*, and had hinted at in 'All Souls' Night'. The anecdotes sparkle, and he employs the gift for impressionist scene-painting discovered in *Reveries over Childhood and Youth*; but his companions, acquaintances, and mentors, stranded within their various 'phases', never quite link up with their fates. Their search for reality, in artistic achievement or occult wisdom, leads to disintegration instead of fulfilment. In the process, Todhunter, Henley, Farr, Wilde, Johnson, Mathers are discussed as exemplars rather than as personalities. This approach would raise difficulties if they happened to be still alive, like Ernest Rhys (who disputed the treatment of the Rhymers') or Mrs Mathers (who sent a furious remonstrance when WBY's 'fantastic and grotesque' portrait of her husband was printed). As with his now-perfected version of the Abbey Theatre's history, the friends of his youth were placed in apposition to the revealed pattern of his own life, and his own evolving consciousness. 'I am certain that there was something in myself compelling me to attempt creation of an art as separate from everything heterogeneous and casual, from all character and circumstances, as some Herodiade of our theatre, dancing seemingly alone in her narrow moving luminous circle.'97 For all the apparent randomness of the recollections in 'The Tragic Generation', it is no accident that the anecdotes climax in WBY's first encounter with Synge at the Hôtel Corneille.

After a kaleidoscopic whirl of remembered incidents and images, the patterns are finally woven through to a conclusion in the last section, 'The Stirring of the Bones'. In his most blatant chronological reversal, he begins with the '98 centennial activities: presented as his last, misguided attempt to create a unity of culture where none could exist, when he suffered 'the worst months of my life'. The Jubilee riot of 1897 is then introduced, and the passions which thus found temporary release are connected directly to the 1916 Rising nearly twenty years in the future. And then the searchlight is thrown further back, without mentioning the year, to WBY's pivotal journey west in 1896: the visit to Tillyra the lunar invocations which preceded his 'Archer' vision, and finally the summons to Coole, with its woods by water. This final refuge appears as the fulfilment of his invocation, the end of his experimental wanderings on the chameleon's way. At Coole he could find his revelation, through withdrawal, concentration, and – in time – the development of his own philosophy. 'It was at Coole that the first few simple thoughts that now, grown complex through their contact with other thoughts, explain the world, came to me from beyond my own mind.'

Thus he hints that 1897 marked the end of an era – though a good deal of the material assembled in *The Trembling of the Veil* actually post-dated that year. He would not return to his autobiography for thirteen years. When he did, the next and final section ('Dramatis Personae') would revolve around Gregory and the world she helped him build. The last words of *The Trembling of the Veil*, completed in Oxford, celebrate her. Though she seems (in a phrase deliberately borrowed from 'Nineteen Hundred and Nineteen') 'indifferent to praise or blame', the coming generation 'to whom recent events are often more obscure than those long past, [should] learn what debts they owe and to what creditor'. The 'recent events' suggest the Irish revolution, now all but accomplished: *The Trembling of the Veil*, whose title is itself a reference to the advent of revelation, deliberately ends by placing the triumvirate of Synge, Gregory, and himself in the position of cultural founding fathers of the new Ireland.

As WBY put his past life into order, the future was taking tangible shape. Finally, after an anxious wait, the new baby arrived on 22 August, a boy, named at first William Michael, then Michael Butler. 'William' was dropped, WBY told Lolly, 'at my suggestion, being a soft, wishy washy, moist day sort of name'; however, if a girl, she was to have been 'Stuarta'. He was sickly, and there was a critical bowel haemorrhage shortly after his birth, necessitating a transfusion of George's blood and serum. A doctor was summoned from Oxford, 'disguised as a chemists assistant sent with a medicine' to allay WBY's fears.[98] In late September the family visited Dublin, where Solomons operated on an infantile hernia (which later ruptured again). Perhaps because of these complications, the Avatar idea was aired much less obsessively than at the time of Anne's birth. The 'Instructors' apparently decided that this was too 'personal' a subject and discouraged numerous inquiries. George may well have decided it was unwise to burden her children with such demanding expectations. In a less ambitious mode, Quinn and Robinson were asked to stand godfather, and the child's horoscopes turned out to be gratifyingly compatible with a diplomatic career, which Lily had earlier forecast in a vision.[99]

Back in Broad Street, working on his memoirs, WBY's mind ran on history, families, and continuance. 'I think no Irish movement will have had a more complete record than ours,' he wrote to Gregory. 'I hope another record will not be the stark walls of Coole & a stark roofless Ballylee ("May these characters remain/When all is ruin once again") for Americans to photograph: but that both may some day house our descendants.'[100] On a lecturing trip to Glasgow in November, he was excited to find a Middleton relation, a portrait painter who at sixty 'has just married a wife younger than George',[101] and another artist relative, Miss Raeburn, whom he remembered coming to Sligo in his childhood. In October *Four Plays for Dancers* appeared, at a time when devotees like Allan Wade and Nugent Monck were reviving WBY's early plays, and *The King's Threshold* (with a new ending) was put on at the Abbey: WBY's additions stressed the parallel with MacSwiney's death by hunger strike.[102] And when Cuala published *Four Years* in December, it set the seal on the part of his life irrevocably gone by. The rest of his memoirs, he told Olivia Shakespear, 'will grow less personal, or at least less adequate as personal representation for the most vehement part of youth must be left out, the only part that one half remembers & lives over again in memory when one is old age, the passionate past'.[103]

The book was Cuala's fastest seller ever, and all the copies printed were devoured at once.[104] But even while celebrating the past, present politics could not be forgotten. His lectures attracted some anti-Irish reaction in Scotland and he had to abandon a trip to Aberdeen.[105] On his return he was taken ill yet again; from his sickbed in early December he followed the political situation anxiously. For weeks, a delegation from Dublin, led by the guerrilla supremo Michael Collins and the architect of Sinn Féin, Arthur Griffith, had been negotiating in London with Lloyd George's coalition government, while Eamon de Valera stayed in Dublin. Once Collins proved to be both decisive and amenable to compromise, intransigent republicanism was under-represented by the delegation; nor did such intransigence reflect opinion in Ireland at large, which was overwhelmingly in favour of the settlement eventually mooted. Twenty-six counties were to have a wide sphere of autonomy, with dominion status within the commonwealth. Comprehensive powers were ceded regarding police, revenue, coinage, and other matters withheld under the old Home Rule blueprints. The new six-county political entity of 'Northern Ireland', set up the year before, would continue in existence pending review of its territory by a Boundary Commission. An oath of fealty would be imposed on members of the new Irish parliament – to the monarch of Great Britain as head of the commonwealth.

This was the point on which de Valera and other republican purists chose to break. The delegates who signed the Treaty on 6 December returned to tense debates in the Sinn Féin assembly, Dáil Éireann. The arrangements battered out in London were ratified by a small majority on 7 January 1922. A split was inevitable. Just before Christmas WBY had written to Olivia Shakespear in terms which reflect his ancient sense of divided identity, exacerbated now by the responsibility of having children.

I am in deep gloom about Ireland for though I expect ratification of the treaty from a plebecite I see no hope of escape from bitterness, & the extreme party may carry the country. When men are very bitter, death & ruin draw them on as a rabbit is supposed to be drawn on by the dancing of the fox. In the last week I have been planning to live in Dublin – George very urgent for this – but I feel now that all may be blood & misery. If that comes we may abandon Ballylee to the owls & the rats, & England too (where passion will rise & I shall find myself with no answer), & live in some far land. Should England & Ireland be divided beyond all hope of remedy, what else could one do for the childrens sake, or ones own work. I could not bring them to Ireland where they would inherit bitterness, nor leave them in an England where being Irish by tradition, & my family & fame they would be in an unnatural condition of mind & grow as so many Irish men who live here do, sour & argumentative.[106]

But Gregory, reading the conclusion to *Four Years*, had got the point at once. 'It will make a fine prologue for your Irish work, tho' I'm afraid you will be doing a sword and egg dance in writing that. Some how all the work you & I & Hugh & Hyde & others have done seems to be worth so much more now that independence is in sight – it is a sort of deposit account to the credit of the country.'[107] For all WBY's doubts and reservations, by historicizing the work of his literary generation he had prepared his place in the new dispensation, and he was going to occupy it. In the end, he knew the time had finally come to return to Ireland.

Chapter 6 : LIVING IN THE EXPLOSION
1922–1924

> 'If, by touching a button on that lamp-post, you could kill a
> person in China and get all his goods without fear of detection
> or punishment either here or in hell, would you touch the
> button?'
> Mr Griffith laughed, but focused the problem.
> 'I would not touch the button,' he averred.
> 'Would O'Connolly [*sic*]?' I urged. 'Would Russell? Or
> Montgomery, or Gogarty?'
> 'Yeats would,' said Mr Griffith . . .

> Arthur Griffith in conversation with James
> Stephens, March 1922[1]

> Yeats as observer SAW that problem after ANY revolution is:
> what to do with yr / gunmen.

> Ezra Pound to Gladys Hyne, n.d. [1954][2]

I

THE ratification of the Anglo-Irish Treaty in early January 1922 marked a
decisive stage in the Irish revolution, but for the moment no one quite discerned the fault-line that was opening beneath them. On one side, large
concessions had been made by the British state, but if twenty-six counties of
Ireland had gained potentially effective independence under democratic
institutions, the extent of this concession had to be concealed by Lloyd
George in order to retain his conservative allies. On the other hand, in an
exactly symmetrical process, the ultra-republican formal demands of Sinn
Féin had been eroded, so Griffith, Collins, and the other signatories had to
claim that the traditional desideratum was still potentially within their
grasp. Ironically, the British government's strenuous underestimation of
what had been conceded added apparent credibility to the arguments of disgruntled republicanism. Around these uncertainties of definition, a sterile
but obsessive argument about the very nature of the state developed: had the
Treaty a legal existence? Was republican government still vested in the
'Second Dáil', reliant on the *status quo ante* the Treaty, despite its narrow
ratification? Was the creation of the Free State an 'Irish Thermidor',[3] a
bourgeois reaction which sold both republicanism and egalitarianism down
the river? It is clear that a substantial section of republican militants felt that
the claims of 'democracy' in early 1922 were simply a cloak thrown over a

pusillanimous sell-out. It is equally clear that these feelings were not recip-rocated by any substantial proportion of the Irish population, and that this was recognized by 'gunmen' rapidly turning into politicians.

Writing to Russell, WBY grasped the situation more clearly than many.

I am by constitution a pessimist & never thought they would get as much out of Lloydd George & so am pleased, nor am I distressed to see Madam Markiewicz and other emotional ladies among the Non-jourors. I expect to see Griffith, now that he is the universal target, grow almost mellow, and become the fanatic of broad mindedness and accuracy of statement. Hitherto he has fired at the cocanuts but now that he is a cocoa nut himself he may become milky.[4]

He was right. A new political class would do their best to anchor the new ship of state as the ice-floes of the stranded revolution ominously cracked around them. One of those ex-guerrillas used a different metaphor in a cele-brated description of the atmosphere of 1922. The provisional government, he remarked, were

simply eight young men in the City Hall standing amidst the ruins of one adminis-tration, with the foundations of another not yet laid, and with wild men screaming through the keyhole. No police force was functioning through the country, no sys-tem of justice was operating, the wheels of administration hung idle, battered out of recognition by the clash of rival jurisdictions.[5]

This eloquent image comes from Kevin O'Higgins, subsequently minister for Economic Affairs in the new government, and the post-revolutionary politician whom WBY would come to admire most. By mid January Dublin Castle had been handed over to Michael Collins, and British troops had evacuated the Curragh military camp. By this point too WBY was experi-encing at first-hand the tensions of the rapidly polarizing political situation, through his visit to the Irish Race Congress in Paris.

This cultural jamboree had been planned before the Treaty as a demon-stration of international solidarity among the Irish worldwide; WBY was one of the delegates from Dublin. Unfortunately, the participants assembled in Paris in mid January 1922 just as battle-lines were being drawn up over the question of Treaty ratification. 'Politics' were supposed to be excluded, but cultural demonstrations were a traditional Irish method of conducting politics by other means, and the Irish Race Congress conformed to pattern. The Paris gathering quickly replicated the divided Dáil at home in Dublin, instead of serving – as its South African-Irish progenitor had hoped – as 'a family reunion on a worldwide scale'.[6] Proceedings were riven by boycotts, splits, and near-confrontations, as one side or the other tried to score polit-ical points to assert precedence, rather than celebrate the unity of the sea-divided Gael. The turn-out of Gaels was also disappointing, though for the

Yeatses the presence of the resolutely unGaelic Ezra Pound offered some compensation. The Irish of Canada and the United States stayed away, carpetbagging 'spokesmen' turned up from the exiguous Irish communities of Bolivia and Java, and recently returned missionaries were wheeled on to represent the Irish of China. WBY was nominated by his old adversary Arthur Griffith, as President of the Dáil government, along with Eoin MacNeill, Douglas Hyde, and a few other safe moderates. Griffith's new opponent de Valera was allowed to send a parallel delegation, and riposted by choosing Constance Markievicz, Mary MacSwiney, and Harry Boland – the most intransigent of republicans. The nervous permanent officials devoutly hoped that delegates would confine themselves to promoting a 'cultural' agenda for a projected world organization of the Irish abroad: hence the first session was addressed by MacNeill, Hyde, and WBY.[7] Pound thought 'W. B. Y. arrived for Irish conference not quite knowing why and left leaving others in I think same state of uncertainty', but this judgement was as skewed as usual. Gregory accurately perceived that it 'identifies you with the new state of things'.[8]

Though partisanship rapidly took over, and the short-lived new organization became – as so much else – a battlefield for contesting interpretations of the Treaty, WBY had been clear from the beginning that 'politics' could not be avoided. For all the muddied waters stirred up by the uncertain circumstances of January 1922, he was at last officiating at an occasion which presented Ireland's newly won independence on an international stage, if a circumscribed one. His intentions, as declared to Gregory, show a firm grasp of the political necessities: 'I have chosen for subject "The Plays & lyrics of Modern Ireland" – I shall insist on the national value of the Abbey & ballance Synge by the poets of 1916. I have accepted partly to identify the Abbey with government propoganda.'[9]

He was as good as his word, and his performance in Paris showed his determination to support the provisional government from the outset – even to the extent of quoting Pearse's poetry in his speech.[10] It was no surprise that this commitment would lead to conflict with Gonne, but it precipitated other estrangements too, as civil war loomed and the government embarked on an inevitably ruthless struggle against those who denied its legitimacy and turned their weapons against it. Several of WBY's circle, while far from being 'gunmen', felt ambivalent about the new dispensation. Jack Yeats was firmly anti-Treaty in his sympathies; Gregory also inclined towards de Valera ('I feel tilted towards the republican side by those clauses that must be swallowed – the oath that will be taken insincerely by all but the two Trinity T.D.'s, and that preposterous Governor General who will be but a fly-paper for the vulgar'[11]). Nonetheless, she believed that the exceptional freedom conferred by the Treaty under the cloak of dominion status would enable Free State diplomats to negotiate their way to independence. In this, her habitual canniness was vindicated.

WBY's feelings were far less ambiguous. As soon as the Treaty split became evident, he told Gregory that he was pleased to see 'the non-jurors will include all those whose political influence in Irish government I dreaded . . . Griffith isolated from the "impossibilist" people may be better for our purposes than the old Griffith'. The fears of some English friends, that he would take the intransigent side, were unfounded, and his commitment to the new government went so far as to contemplate a swerve in his career. Shortly after the Paris conference, he heard that he might be offered the ministry of Fine Arts in Griffith's administration: 'It would certainly tempt me for I could do a great deal – I see several precise things to do.'[12] A letter of 23 February makes it clear that he was considering it very carefully. His Civil List pension, so long an object of nationalist taunts, would have to be given up; but 'my having had it in the past should not count against me considering that I promised nothing in return, much less swore any of those 14 oaths of allegiance which Collins says have been taken by members of the Dail'. Moreover,

If I was asked to be Minister I should have to get certain conditions of an obvious kind. There are however questions that should be taken up by the Irish Government such as the application of art to industry – this has been greatly studied in Germany & but little in England, & I hope that whoever is Minister of Fine Arts will get some enquiry made into this.[13]

By playing a public part in Paris and taking a governmental appointment, he might claim an influential place in the new Ireland apparently emerging from six years of chaos. In fact, no such ministry was set up by the new government. But WBY's ambition is of a piece with his decision to memorialize those *fin de siècle* years when Ireland had been like wax, and he and his friends had been able (in his view) to mould it.

Not all of those friends saw it like that, and at this very point his old sparring-partner Magee published a commentary on the published extracts of *Four Years* that was calculated to throw cold water on WBY's determined appropriation of the revolution. The recent upheavals, 'John Eglinton' contended in the *Dial* of February 1922, had relegated the 'Literary Renascence' and its 'hero' into distant history.

Mr W. B. Yeats is already – the frequent fate of Irish political and literary heroes – something of a 'back number' in Ireland. But yesterday the Abbey row, the *odium theologicum* investing the Countess Cathleen, seemed charged with all the moving forces of Ireland's spiritual destiny, and already these things have receded into the dim past, almost as much as the Belfast Address of Professor Tyndall. For the last year or two, as far as literature is concerned, A. E. has perhaps been the dominating figure, but if he reads this page he will, I feel sure, smile in approving acceptance of my *memento mori*! Ireland may be a land of just and old renown but it is certainly not a land in which freedom slowly broadens down from precedent to precedent. Each new phase of its political and spiritual history seems to require new personalities to express it; and just as Griffith and Collins have blotted out Redmond and Devlin, so the literary influence of P. H. Pearse and his band has seemed, at all events for the moment, to cast into the shade the movement in which Mr Yeats was so recently the protagonist.

Therefore, wby had been galvanized into a mode of reminiscence by the sense of a period ending. 'Eglinton' was right that wby sensed the passing of a baton, but utterly mistaken in assuming that the 'hero' was ready to retire to his tent. 'We have to be "that old man eloquent" to the new governing generation,' he grimly told Gregory; 'if we write our best the spiritual part of free Ireland will be in the books & "the Free State's" struggle with the "impossibilists" may even make some of our unpopular struggle shine with patriotic fire.'[14] He was already planning to return to the fray. Seven years after he had started the process of buying Ballylee, it was finally to be ready in April, but he meditated a move back to the centre. When they returned from Paris, George was dispatched to Dublin to find them a house. wby chose to explain his reasons satirically. 'Oxford society is intolerable,' he told Gogarty: 'a woman today & in a quite respectable house recommended me to read Alfred Noyes and Stephen Phillips. I want to go & live somewhere where public opinion permits me to be rude: & have selected Dublin.' May Morris was given a different but equally appropriate reason: his decision to move was precipitated by hearing 'that our new Government had appointed as curator of the Municipal Gallery a man who had been very useful to them in identifying exhumed revolutionary corpses'.[15] But these deadpan jokes concealed a real commitment to the new Free State, and a desire to play a public role in it.

He knew exactly the style of life he wanted, and where he wished to live. 'Nothing modern, no random modern improvements, if possible . . . Ancient names cut on the glass of the windowpanes, if possible.' This was a reference to the Swift-haunted Glasnevin house owned by the Gogartys, where he had stayed in 1909 and 1910.[16] But the locations he now required were significantly different. 'Mountjoy Square, Rutland Square, Stephens Green, Ely Place, that street where Dillon lives [North Great George's Street].' These were the great Georgian *quartiers* where the politicians of the last independent Irish parliament had lived, and subsequently the haunts of Dublin's upper professional classes; even where the decline into tenements had encroached, these addresses declared an assertive, if fading, grandeur. An almost identical letter went to Lennox Robinson; here too WBY made the practical point that Castle officials must be starting to slip away 'and leave their holes empty – a Castle rathole should be a comfortable place'.[17]

What he got was very far from a rathole. Merrion Square was now the grandest of the Georgian squares: south of the Liffey, safely removed from the social decline of the city's north side, hard by Trinity College, and flanked on one side by the National Gallery. In JBY's Dublin days the denizens had included legendary figures like Lord Justice Fitzgibbon and Sir William Wilde; earlier residents had included Sheridan Le Fanu and Daniel O'Connell, and WBY liked to recall that the duke of Wellington had been born there. Though occasional eminences like Sir John Arnott still maintained houses in the square, most local plutocrats had moved further out. Many of the vast 1740s dwellings had now become offices, accommodating institutions as varied as the Criminal Investigation Department and Sir Horace Plunkett's cooperative Irish Agricultural Organization. The house George found, and promptly leased, was only two doors down from 'Plunkett House'. The Yeatses had not expected to afford anything so grand, but the political turmoil had brought rents down, and she immediately let the top floor and the mews. WBY earmarked the £500 from Werner Laurie for his memoirs, planned another lecture tour, and took out a bank mortgage, but they had made a good bargain, and rents began to rise as political life stabilized. WBY was delighted by the great rooms full of north light, with their carved marble chimneypieces, but his pleasure was more than aesthetic: 'it puts back my family into some kind of dignity & gives my children a stately home, & myself a background for old age'. He had dreaded returning to a house 'like that Rathgar villa where we all lived when I went to school, a time of crowding & indignity . . . I think constantly that our children will have that spacious home I lacked after I left Sligo.' And he took an especial pleasure in hearing that 'my uncle Issac & my old Aunts all went altogether & looked at the outside of 82 Merrion Square & approved'.[18] After the long trials of his *déclassé* youth and peripatetic adulthood, he had settled, at least in residential terms, into the traditions of his caste – at just the point when those traditions were dispersing and disappearing.

The one family member who might have had reservations was the old bohemian living on West 29th Street, far from Manhattan's equivalent of Merrion Square. JBY had long before written that he always gave up hopes of people who went to live in that very square because they became 'as others there': 'in those magnificent abodes I am as a tainted person'.[19] He would nonetheless have appreciated his son's restoration of the Yeats family position in a newly independent Ireland. But at that very moment, with his customary flair for doing the unexpected, he went to sleep on the night of 1 February and did not wake up. There had been ominous signs of deterioration in his health, which he had determinedly hidden from everyone except the eagle-eyed Quinn, and he completed his campaign to stay in New York with resolution and success. He even had $14 in the bank. His last words, the evening before, had been to John Quinn's companion, the beautiful Jeanne Robert Foster, who was deeply attached to the old man. 'Remember you have promised me a sitting in the morning.' Jeanne Foster put it crisply and reassuringly to WBY: 'Yes, I think he died as he would have wished to die. "He set the scene and played all the parts", J.Q. has aptly said. No one asked him for *messages*; no one gave him a solemn face. We laughed and talked and then he went to sleep.'[20] His eldest son's feelings were mixed. No one could have described JBY as a rock of support, but he had certainly been a cardinal compass-point to steer by: sometimes pointing out a challenging intellectual course, sometimes conveying an awful warning, often exasperating, always stimulating. Their relationship had been eased and strengthened by WBY's spectacular achievements, which JBY felt vindicated his own equally spectacular failures. Ingeniously, the old man had come to claim credit for nurturing greatness, by selflessly demonstrating the dangers of artistic improvidence. In his own view, he had sacrificed himself as a great painter in order to create a great poet.

It was a self-centred as well as self-serving analysis, but, as WBY put it to Olivia Shakespear, JBY had long ago become a friend and intellectual sounding-board as much as a father. Even after his demise, he still seemed to be 'thinking and writing'. The amputation of death left the sense of a continuing limb. By now WBY could see how much those early years of aesthetic effort and material struggle had been shaped by JBY's charisma, imagination, and selfishness; by now, too, his parent's determined abjuration of respectability exerted a certain wistful charm. But the way ahead could only have been a steady decline, for all the old man's masterful self-deception, as WBY pointed out to the heartbroken Lily. His letter shows how much the event turned his own mind back to their distant youth:

It is possible that things have happened in the best way, for he has had no growing infirmities, no long illness. He wrote to me but a little while ago, saying that he felt in such good health, and his mind had lost nothing of its vigour. I had a letter 2 or 3 weeks ago that was among the best he ever wrote. If he had come home he would have lived longer but he might have grown infirm, grown to feel himself a useless old man. He has died as the Antarctic explorers died, in the midst of his work & the middle of his thought, convinced that he was about to paint as never before. And in all probability he has died in sleep after an illness that was almost all sleep, and so without any consciousness of death. Several times lately (the last, two or 3 months ago) he wrote of dreaming of our mother and of seeing her in his illness of 1919 and also last summer. I was turning over an old note-book the other day and I find that she came to me at a London séance & told me that from then on she would be much with me. I think in spite of his misfortunes that his life has been happy, especially of recent years; for more than any man I have ever known he could live in the happiness of the passing moment. I think we did all for him that could be done and that there is nothing to regret.[21]

In death as in life, JBY reaped the dividend of charm by being cared for by others. Jeanne Foster arranged the burial in Chestertown, New York, while she and Quinn packed up the sketchbooks, drawings, papers, and unfinished masterpieces which had piled up around him to the end. A month after his father's death, WBY and George visited a 'direct voice' medium in London – a 'dark room & voice in the dark. A voice spoke & gave the name "John" & then as an initial "B" & then "John B" sent a message to my sister' – proving his credentials with the intelligence, later corroborated, that Lily's neighbour's dog had been recently run over. 'The voice spoke of being happy & said this with emotion.'[22] JBY's death had at last eased his restlessness, and marked a point of passage in his son's life. And, as 'John Eglinton' pointed out, it also represented the passing of a whole type of existence.

It is hard to see how an Ireland in which Sinn Fein ideals have triumphed will continue to produce men of the type of Mr Yeats' remarkable father, moving easily between one country and the other, bringing to England the charm of irresponsibility and unworldliness, and back to Ireland the liberal atmosphere of a larger world. In this type the union has been to some extent justified, at all events intellectually. These men, amphibious in their nationality, 'specialised' in ideas almost as the Jews in finance. Some of them cultivated a certain idealistic hatred of England, but this sentiment, far from developing as it has done in Ireland, into a disturbing political fanaticism, was consistent with being good citizens, and certainly with being excellent company.[23]

WBY's move back to Dublin, catching this very moment, reinforced the symbolic significance of his father's death. The Yeatses returned ready to take possession of a new Ireland, for which they could work and which would in turn celebrate the traditions which made them the independent Protestant nationalists that they were. At least, so it may have seemed to WBY in February 1922. But he was also returning to a country about to descend into the abyss of civil war, and the outcome would make him question how far the traditions he most valued were really safeguarded by the new state.

II

By mid March he had left Oxford, and was preparing to follow George to Galway, intending to stay at Coole until Ballylee could accommodate them both. The Oxford house was sub-let until September, when the final move to Dublin would take place. At least two rooms in Ballylee were to be completed by the end of April. As it was, the bedroom was more or less ready, and WBY's third-floor study slowly followed. The summer could be spent there, as planned. In the dining hall downstairs, a large deal trestle-table, painted dark red, was established on an uncovered stone floor. Other furniture was unvarnished oak or elm, locally made to Scott's designs. Upstairs, walls were painted blue, with ceilings picked out in red, green, blue, black, and gold – perhaps dictated by the magical colour codes of the Golden Dawn, or the colour symbolism of the Tattwa cards used for clairvoyance and astral travel, though George invariably told people she was just using up whatever paint-pots were to hand.[24] Straw rugs were strewn around, and dyed 'bainín' curtains hung from brass poles. These had to be removed in winter, because of frequent floods, which left behind a deposit of mud and worms. The permanent damp seeping through the limestone walls also forbade pictures, prints, or photographs of any kind. The adjacent cottages continued to provide bedrooms for children and servants; light was provided by oil-lamps and storm-lanterns; river-water was heated in a large copper. It was all extremely simple, not to say uncomfortably austere: 'a fourteenth-century picture', in WBY's view.[25] Medievalism supplied the motif. They rechristened it 'Thoor Ballylee', to avoid the modernized ring (and Anglo-Irish associations) of 'Castle', though 'Thoor' was in itself a rather idiosyncratic Anglicization of the Irish túr. From this appropriate stronghold the Yeatses watched as the country around them threatened to regress into the very anarchy which the tower's ancient walls had been built to withstand.

By the spring it was clear that the legalistic quibbling about the Treaty would – like Swift's war between Big-endians and Little-endians – be translated into fratricidal strife. WBY had already determined which side to support. Besides his own inclination to conservatism and order, those who accepted the Treaty tended – in the formulation of a later authority – to opt for 'civic nationalism' rather than 'ethnic nationalism', and for someone of WBY's family and religious tradition this was the obvious course to take.[26] The oath of fidelity was no obstacle to him, nor was the loss of the six counties now making up Northern Ireland ('I have always been of the opinion that if surly disagreeable neighbours shut the door, it is better to turn the key in it before they change their mind'[27]). Nevertheless, coming through

Dublin in late March, he had determined – despite Gregory's urgings – not to take a public stance in the rapidly polarizing situation. 'I could do no good in this whirlpool of hatred.'[28] The Dáil elections of June 1922 did not lower the temperature; by the summer 'Irregular' army dissidents were taking on detachments of the new Free State Army, which had been formed from IRA elements that had supported the Treaty. The issues which galvanized a minority of the political elite, and de Valera's denunciations of 'cowardly reason and its thousand misgivings', meant little to the populace at large. Around Gort, as in the Anglo-Irish War, unrest usually took the form of threatened land seizures, and confused visitations by disguised bands of young men late at night. From time to time WBY stayed at Coole, more at risk than Ballylee, and he and Gregory worriedly tried to forecast the future ('he thinks there will be a Republican rising again after some years').[29]

Around Ballylee the houses of the gentry stood empty, except for Coole and Tillyra, where Edward Martyn sat immobilized by the stroke which would kill him the next year. Some houses were occupied by wandering soldiers, others protected by government forces, others burned to the ground. In the uncertain atmosphere mail could be held up for weeks, or robbed, blockades were imposed and lifted without warning, cross-country travel was fraught and unpredictable (motoring to Dublin meant removing drystone walls and taking to the fields whenever a road was mined or blocked). The atmosphere appealed to WBY's sense of the dramatic: it was a good time to be living in a castle.

A few days ago a man driving a cart stopped his cart & looked up at the castle & said 'You could put up a good fight.' 'No' I said 'a bad door.' 'What you want' he said, 'are steel shutters' and drove on. No trains, no post, no telegraphs, & roads blocked with stones & trees.[30]

Rumours came and went; occasionally a car passed with a coffin end-up on the back seat. The controversial bridge at Ballylee, which had figured so prominently in the purchase negotiations five years before, was targeted by local rebels for demolition early on. It had been a condition of sale that a right of way across the bridge and through the castle yard be preserved for travellers. This was its death-warrant, as de Valera's forces in the area were determined to disrupt communications. George asked the Irregulars to blow up the small bridge further downstream rather than the main one beside the tower, but it was duly detonated on 19 August. She described the incident coolly to Ottoline Morrell on 1 September:

Our bridge which you [know] is built right up to & touches the tower was blown up a week ago the men gave us 1½ hours warning. I consulted them as to where the safest place would be to bring the children & maids & they said half way up the tower.

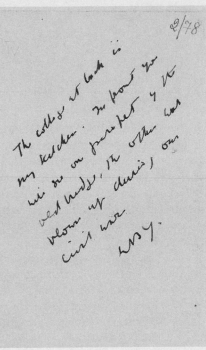

5. A photograph of the renovated Tower sent by WBY to Thomas Sturge Moore on 2 June 1927, to help with the cover design for *The Tower*. 'The cottage at back is my kitchen. In front you will see one parapet of the old bridge, the other was blown up during our Civil War.'

They behaved very well & when the fuses were lit & all the men ran off as hard as they could pelt, one man stayed behind to say 'in a few minutes now, there will be two explosions. Good night, thank you'(!)

As though he was thanking us for the bridge! After two minutes, two roars came & then a hail of falling masonry & gravel & then the same man shouted up 'All right now' & cleared off. We had gone round opening all windows to save the glass & nothing was damaged. Not a hole in any roof, though some stones went right over the tower (130 feet & more up) or fell on the cottages on the other side.

It was all over about 1.15 am. then we went out to put up barricades & lamps burning in the great window on the ground floor. At the time, *after* a feeling of panic when we heard the irregulars knocking at the door & had to go out to speak to them, one felt nothing but a curiosity to see how it was done & to try & save windows etc. But since then we have both felt rather ill & our hearts both hopping & stopping. I think that although the noise did not seem as tremendous as the explosions – when one was close – of the German bombs during the war, the vibration was tremendous. The explosions were heard at Loughrea 16 miles off. And our windows are 6 feet from the bridge & 14 feet up! the bridge is a lamentable sight. One can walk over but one side is completely gone.[31]

215

Both Coole and Ballylee determined to sit out the storm in circumstances of reflection and writing. By chance, the atmosphere in the house, on a day when WBY, George, and Anne were visiting, has been recorded. Charles O'Malley, an American journalist, was in Gort with his family in early July and visited Gregory. Seventy-five years later, his daughter still recalled it with absolute clarity:

I remember Lady Gregory very vividly, and Yeats too, though not his wife. Lady Gregory was most gracious. I wasn't very big. I was the same now as I was then, and it seems to me she and I were about the same size. And she was most gracious, just lovely, and she invited my parents most hospitably to come in and chat with her. And who should be visiting but William Butler Yeats, his wife and daughter. And everyone just sat down and started chatting. Lady Gregory said to us children, just go into my library and you can look at anything you want in there. Can you imagine the treasures? We looked around, we looked at all the books, we were not, I must say, particularly impressed because we were not old enough to be impressed. One thing I remember about the library which intrigued me was an elephant's foot about two feet high, a real elephant's foot with nails in the heel and everything; and it was full of canes. It seems to me, as I remember it, that she walked with a cane.

Then we were all told to sit down, that Mr Yeats was going to give a reading to us. Well, that was fine. I mean, I wasn't impressed. Maybe my brothers were, being older and smarter, but I was so young. And so he started in, 'A Prayer to My Daughter.'

I don't know why he picked that one out, it had been written a year or two before. Except for the fact, perhaps, that his little one was playing around at his feet – she appeared to be about four or five. I don't know why, really. But he stood up with a great flourish and began. It was all very dramatic. He was 'flourishing' as they say, waving his arms, declaiming on the poem. I was watching the child, who just wouldn't leave him alone. Her nose, well, her nose was running enormously, and she kept coming up to him and yanking his coat. And the mother – you know, I have no recollection of her at all – she was there, but she wasn't there if you know what I mean.

So the daughter kept yanking at his coat. Why the mother didn't grab her I don't know, but the girl was annoying Yeats . . . not seriously, you know, but she was sort of a beloved nuisance, if you see what I mean. He may have been annoyed with his wife, why doesn't she take her away, I don't know. He didn't repulse her or chase her off, he just stopped everything and took care of it. He put the book DOWN, reached into his pocket, took out a large handerchief which he had been flourishing earlier, went down – BLOW! – a loud blow. Put it back in his pocket and continued reading.[32]

Lucille O'Malley noticed that the chatelaine of Coole and the Yeatses seemed 'as if they were all part of a family'; and Gregory relied heavily on the comfort her new neighbour brought. Since the previous November she had been occupying Coole as a leaseholder from her unsympathetic daughter-in-law, with full responsibility for its upkeep. Desperate to make money, she was at work on the memoir that would become *Seventy Years*. She read it to wby, who offered criticism which she began 'interjecting into the text, like a Greek chorus'. The objective retailing of old letters and diary extracts struck him as the opposite of his own method, as she helped type out the full version of his *The Trembling of the Veil*, dispatched to A. P. Watt by the end of May. The past was made all the more vivid when Cuala sent the proofs of jby's posthumously published memoirs: scrappy though they were, they reinforced wby's conviction that 'Hyde, Russell, Lady Gregory, myself, my father, will all be vivid to young Irish students a generation hence because of the memoirs we are writing now'.[33]

For recreation, he sent lengthy letters of advice to young poets, and alternated between reading Trollope and Joyce's newly published *Ulysses*. But the writing which would immortalize this summer, for a far wider and more lasting audience than 'young Irish students a generation hence', was the long poem he began working on in June, first while spending a few days at Coole, then in his study up the stone staircase – its silence surprised and delighted him. By 27 July he had written three of the envisaged four parts: eventually it comprised seven sections, linked together as 'Meditations in Time of Civil War'. Gregory's journals record its progress through the long, strange summer of off-stage alarms and excursions. If there is a tension in all wby's work between the real and the symbolic, often refracted through self-interrogation, it is resolved most successfully in this great poem. In many ways a companion-piece to 'Nineteen Hundred and Nineteen', it balances vision and concreteness with an equal audacity, and similarly manipulates a sequence to confer variety of form and freedom for exploration.

Though the first section, 'Ancestral Houses', is inspired by Garsington rather than by Coole,[34] the questions it raises are rooted deep in Irish history, and in the distant past of settler families like Gregory's and his own, as the great houses of Galway tottered around them. The poem opens with an overture imagining country-house life at its most Arcadian:

> Surely among a rich man's flowering lawns,
> Amid the rustle of his planted hills,
> Life overflows without ambitious pains
> And rains down life until the basin spills,
> And mounts more dizzy high the more it rains,
> As though to choose whatever shape it wills,
> And never stoop to a mechanical,
> Or servile shape, at others' beck and call.

The rhetorical question is, however, quickly subverted. In fact, the poem tells us, the appropriate symbol for the aesthetic achievements of apparently secure, inherited wealth is not an effortless fountain but a washed-up seashell, deposited by a random flood. This effectively smothers the echoes of Jonson and Penshurst evoked by the first stanza. And the artful ease of a country estate rests, originally, upon expropriation: the word 'planted' does duty for invasion and displacement as well as for arboriculture.

> Some violent bitter man, some powerful man
> Called architect and artist in that they,
> Bitter and violent men, might rear in stone
> The sweetness that all longed for night and day,
> The gentleness none there had ever known;
> But when the master's buried mice can play
> And maybe the great-grandson of that house
> For all its bronze and marble, 's but a mouse.

The old Ascendancy fear of degeneration and unworthy inheritors, closely linked to a fundamental sense of insecurity, surfaces here – as it would, more and more clearly, in his later work. But the challenging last stanzas, piling up images of privilege, revolve around one uncomfortable question: are violence, bitterness, and grandeur inseparable? Is the decline and destruction of inherited greatness not only inevitable but somehow encoded within the qualities which created a house like Garsington (or even Coole) in the first place? And, if so, can it really be regretted? (Gregory, sharp for her purposes, told him that he might make a living by writing poems for landlords, showing that they were leaving their estates for the best possible reasons.[35])

> Oh, what if gardens where the peacock strays
> With delicate feet upon old terraces,
> Or else all Juno from an urn displays
> Before the indifferent garden deities;
> Oh, what if levelled lawns and gravelled ways
> Where slippered Contemplation finds his ease
> And Childhood a delight for every sense,
> But take our greatness with our violence.

> What if the glory of escutcheoned doors,
> And buildings that a haughtier age designed,
> The pacing to and fro on polished floors
> Amid great chambers and long galleries, lined
> With famous portraits of our ancestors;
> What if those things the greatest of mankind,
> Consider most to magnify, or to bless,
> But take our greatness with our bitterness.

The theme of inheritance and continuity is wound through the entire sequence of 'Meditations', superficially different though the individual instalments are. That difference is deliberately stressed in the next section, as a kind of balance. 'My House' was written just after 'Ancestral Houses': Gregory records him adapting it on 2 July. Where the latter is flowing, classical, and polished, like the houses it describes, 'My House' is deliberately irregular, summoning up a different kind of building, and an alternative inheritance – which may preserve its own contrasting vitality. It must be quoted in full, not only because of its exact evocation of Ballylee in the summer of 1922 but because of the close-meshed argument. A scholar–poet, committed to his midnight toil, can be a 'founder', as much as the original Norman baron. The struggle with implacable philosophical forms, as much as the conquistador's efforts to subdue a locality and create an estate, can fuse 'greatness' and 'violence'; austere medieval (or Renaissance) virtues outweigh the inheritance of Georgian manners.[36]

> An ancient bridge, and a more ancient tower,
> A farm-house that is sheltered by its wall,
> An acre of stony ground,
> Where the symbolic rose can break in flower,
> Old ragged elms, old thorns innumerable,
> The sound of the rain or sound
> Of every wind that blows,
> The stilted water-hen
> That plunged in stream again
> Scared by the splashing of a hundred cows.
>
> A winding stair, a chamber arched with stone,
> A grey stone fire-place with an open hearth,
> A candle, and written page.
> *Il Penseroso's* Platonist toiled on
> In some like chamber, shadowing forth
> How the demonic rage
> Imagined everything.
> Benighted travellers
> From markets and from fairs
> Had seen his midnight candle glimmering.
>
> The river rises, and it sinks again;
> One hears the rumble of it far below
> Under its rocky hole.
> What Median, Persian, Babylonian,
> In reverie, or in vision, saw
> Symbols of the soul,

> Mind from mind has caught:
> The subterranean streams,
> Tower where a candle gleams,
> A suffering passion and a labouring thought?
>
> Two men have founded here. A man-at-arms
> Gathered a score of horse and spent his days
> In this tumultuous spot,
> Where through long wars and sudden night alarums
> His dwindling score and he seemed castaways
> Forgetting and forgot;
> And I, that after me
> My bodily heirs may find,
> To exalt a lonely mind,
> Befitting emblems of adversity.

In the later 'Meditations' the Japanese sword presented to WBY in Oregon becomes yet another symbol of continuance and commitment to artistic tradition. Perhaps still thinking of his father's death, WBY has the idea of inherited accomplishment here take a different turn, one more laborious in its expression. The stanzas on 'My Descendants' follow as a natural progression, looking back to the 'old fathers' present in his mind since he began constructing autobiographies, and forward to what he himself will leave behind. A momentary inclination to condemn the hard-won tower back to ruination, 'if my descendants lose the flower', is followed by a more philosophical reflection. In the end, 'natural declension of the soul' and the sinuous line of Nature explored in Anima Mundi may account for the kind of necessary decay hinted at in 'Ancestral Houses': even the qualities proudly asserted in 'My House' will not guarantee continuance.

> The Primum Mobile that fashioned us
> Has made the very owls in circles move,
> And I, that count myself most prosperous
> Seeing that love and friendship are enough,
> For an old neighbour's friendship chose the house
> And decked and altered it for a girl's love,
> And know whatever flourish and decline
> These stones remain their monument and mine.

The conclusion is slightly pat, and not altogether convincing. But in any case the next two sections explode the illusion of philosophical consolation. They laconically depict the events and atmosphere of life in the tower during that summer of civil war and, in doing so, continue to raise unanswerable questions. 'The Road at my Door' records dealings with soldiers from both sides, as they exercise that controversial right of way through the castle yard, and cast further doubt upon the scholar's success in achieving the abstract consolations of withdrawal. The tight construction, regular rhyming pattern, and biting clarity of diction make it one of the least showy but most assured of WBY's short poems, and one of the most successful of the sequence.

> An affable Irregular,
> A heavily built Falstaffian man,
> Comes cracking jokes of Civil War
> As though to die by gunshot were
> The finest play under the sun.
>
> A brown Lieutenant and his men,
> Half dressed in National uniform,
> Stand at my door, and I complain
> Of the foul weather, hail and rain,
> A pear tree broken by the storm.
>
> I count those feathered balls of soot,
> The moor-hen guides upon the stream,
> To silence the envy in my thought;
> And turn towards my chamber, caught
> In the cold snows of a dream.

If 'Meditations' ended with its penultimate section, 'The Stare's Nest by my Window', the coherence and beauty of the whole would be unassailable. It is an invocation against 'the whirlpool of hatred', calling up by contrast the observed ecology of the ancient tower wall: bees swarming, birds feeding their young, as below them the events of civil war are exactly recorded. (He had begun working on the poem on 2 July; on 15 July a Free State soldier was shot at Gort railway bridge, 'a boy from Connemara', and WBY then added the third stanza.) It is no accident that 'Meditations' shares an obvious kinship with 'Easter 1916': the image of stream and moor-hen, the challenges of 'what if', the tension between an ambivalent observer and the ruthless clarity of action. But in 'The Stare's Nest' the political and historical implications become unambiguous, and cut clean to the bone. With the wall loosening, and the starlings abandoning their nest, the injunction to overcome fanaticism and 'start building again' (as he had wanted to do since Easter 1916) has a despairing ring.

> The bees build in the crevices
> Of loosening masonry, and there
> The mother birds bring grubs and flies.
> My wall is loosening, honey-bees
> Come build in the empty house of the stare.

> We are closed in, and the key turned
> On our uncertainty; somewhere
> A man is killed, or a house burned,
> Yet no clear fact to be discerned;
> Come build in the empty house of the stare.
>
> A barricade of stone or of wood;
> Some fourteen days of Civil War;
> Last night they trundled down the road
> That dead young soldier in his blood:
> Come build in the empty house of the stare.
>
> We have fed the heart on fantasies,
> The heart grows brutal from the fare,
> More substance in our enmities
> Than in our loves; oh, honey-bees
> Come build in the empty house of the stare.

As published, however, the sequence did not close on this ostensibly simple chord. The finale, under the ninetyish title 'I see Phantoms of Hatred and of the Heart's Fullness and of the Coming Emptiness', displayed WBY at his most apocalyptic, obscure, and plangent. It recalls a vision of anarchic and fratricidal violence conjured up by the story of the Knights Templar and the judicial murder of their last grand master, Jacques Molay, in the early fourteenth century. This allows for reference to occult philosophy, secret tradition, Freemasonry, gorgeous imagery, mass delusion, the dissolution of civilization, the irrational satisfactions of destruction. Much of the material may have arisen from an argument he had been having with a paranoid member of the Stella Matutina Order about Freemasonry, and from George Sand's novels about the 'Illuminati' tradition which Gregory was reading to him at the time.[37] The vision is conjured up by the transfigured view from the top of the tower, but in tone, extravagance, and obscurity it jars with the subtle symmetry that has gone before. Only the last stanza restores the note of autobiographical interrogation which unites 'Meditations' with a commentary on Irish history in flux, and with the ambivalence expressed more economically in 'The Road by my Door'.

> I turn away and shut the door, and on the stair
> Wonder how many times I could have proved my worth
> In something that all others understand or share;
> But oh, ambitious heart had such a proof drawn forth
> A company of friends, a conscience set at ease,
> It had but made us pine the more. The abstract joy,
> The half-read wisdom of demonic images,
> Suffice the aging man as once the growing boy.

The Wordsworthian diminuendo should not conceal the fact that this stanza reprises all the hypotheses and possibilities raised in the sequence so far: the decay and renewal of historical traditions, the powers conferred by scholarly withdrawal, the dynastic expectations inherent in founding a family, the possible transmission of artistic genius through the generations, the self-deceptions practised by those hypnotized by violence and extremism. Finally, the nightmare of history is inferred through vision and race memory. If solitude, self-knowledge, and resilience constitute the bitter lesson learned at the end, it was, for him, hardly a novel message: his own life up to then repeatedly confirmed it. But he had never expressed it with a comparable virtuosity, clarity, and force. The 'Phantoms of Hatred' are kin to the 'Daughters of Herodias'. 'Meditations in Time of Civil War' would eventually be published alongside 'Nineteen Hundred and Nineteen' in *The Tower*, with the equally misleading date of '1923' appended, but its contents are as intimately linked to the dislocations of 1922, and the collision of personal and national histories, as those of 'Nineteen Hundred and Nineteen' are to the events of 1920.

III

The Yeatses left Ballylee on 21 September, depositing the children at Coole for several days until the Merrion Square house was ready. Their departure from the tower was precipitated by a sudden flood in the ground floors, since the demolished bridge had dammed the river. The month of August had seen equally decisive changes in the political situation. With extraordinary rapidity the two strong men of the Free State government had disappeared: Griffith collapsed and died on 12 August, and Michael Collins was killed in a County Cork ambush ten days later. At a stroke the government lost its chief voice for moderation (Griffith was now considered by many the only 'real' Free Stater) and its only popular leader. To WBY's fury, the *Independent* reprinted his youthful poem on Parnell's death, 'Mourn – and Then Onward!', a piece of juvenilia that regularly returned to haunt him. (Gregory asked him if he saw no grain of merit in it, and he bleakly answered 'None': but consoled himself with the thought that he would get some credit for supposed sympathy with his old enemy.[38]) The new men, William Cosgrave, Kevin O'Higgins, Richard Mulcahy, were less glamorous and evoked less affection; they were also prepared to be tougher. De Valera's followers were driven yet further into the wilderness. Shortly before the Yeatses left Ballylee, WBY inquired about distant gunfire and was told that it was an Irregular 'firing at something eatable at last'. 'One hopes the taste will grow,' he added.[39]

Random firing was by no means unknown in Dublin, but the Irregular forces had no real presence there. WBY and George set themselves to creating yet another house, which had a claim to be their first family home. Not that 82 Merrion Square was built to be homely. Their Oxford furniture looked lost in the great bare rooms, and aesthetic arbiters like Dulac and Shannon tried to persuade them to invest in Harrods' 'literal copies' of Persian carpets rather than the squares of pure colour favoured by George. But the proportions and grandeur appealed to them both. The first-floor drawing room had three tall windows overlooking the square gardens: 'my wife will receive at tea her half a dozen guests,' WBY told William Force Stead, 'where the first owner entertained a score to dinner, or several score for a dance'.[40] The house soon followed their established principles of style. Ricketts watercolours of stage-sets hung in the hall. George introduced some Omega Workshop precepts into the Georgian rooms: there was painted furniture, blue and orange hangings, tall candles everywhere. A cage of canaries took up residence in the study window, woodcuts were grouped on the walls, carved tables were piled with books. A bedroom ceiling was painted blue with gold stars; Anne noticed the decorator subsequently brought friends past the house, pointed in the windows, and laughed. Vestiges of bohemianism remained: V. S. Pritchett was entranced when WBY, producing a fresh pot of tea in his fine drawing room, threw the previous contents out of the window into the square. Later, seeing his guest out, WBY noticed he was wearing only one sock; the poet unaffectedly took the other out of his pocket and, leaning on his young visitor's shoulder, pulled it on.[41] But it is clear that WBY considered the house appropriate for his re-entry to Dublin life, as a public and established figure. The kaleidoscope of Irish life had rotated dramatically, establishing – among other novelties – the old anti-Parnellite T. M. Healy in the governor-general's mansion in Phoenix Park. WBY tried to buttonhole him about the Lane pictures and received a legendary reply: 'My dear Bard, Come to this un-Bee-loud glade as often as the spirit moves you.'[42] Even his old adversaries at Trinity had mellowed towards him, offering him an honorary degree. This was eventually conferred in December: 'effect of Merrion Square, I conclude', he remarked drily to Gregory. On 2 October 1922, barely a week after they moved in, he reinstituted his Monday evenings, taking their place in the rota of Dublin conversaziones (AE on Sundays, Sarah Purser on Tuesdays, Gogarty on Fridays, Jack Yeats's studio on Saturday afternoons).[43] Old friends and adversaries watched and waited with interest, as AE reported to Quinn.

Dublin will be more interesting with him there. He has lived too much out of Ireland. He has become a very distinguished kind of person, so distinguished that it is really difficult to be intimate with him as I was when I was a boy. I see he is writing very inaccurate memoirs of my dead youth & my friends of the Hermetic [Society]. There is hardly a single fact accurate. He came to me to ask questions, I said 'if you will show me the MSS I will correct the facts'. 'Oh' he said 'I do not want accuracy I only want a picturesque sentence' and I said 'you can do that without my assistance' . . . If Willie would write about his own imaginations, moods & feelings it would be really valuable. But I wonder could he be accurate about anything or sincere except in making his work as beautiful as possible. I hear his wife is humanising him & I hope when he comes to live in Dublin I will be able to renew my ancient intimacy. For years he talks when he meets me as if he was lecturing a public meeting about art or literature and I am bored.[44]

Like most people, Russell failed to grasp WBY's intention in writing his memoirs; and for intimacy WBY would turn to the younger generation whom he was trying to influence. This was not always successful. The young poet Monk Gibbon agonized for decades about WBY's supposed condescension towards him after he spoke out of turn on a Monday night, and Francis Stuart remained resolutely outside the charmed circle. But both were prickly and self-obsessed to the point of neurosis, writing books to prove it.[45] For his part, WBY reflected privately on the decline of manners among young artists.[46] Still, he made sure the young Free State minister Desmond FitzGerald (also a poet and disciple of Pound) was invited to his first Monday to discuss a possible subvention to the Abbey. He rapidly re-established contact with Horace Plunkett. And while avidly listening to gossip he avoided talking politics, mischievously telling Maud Gonne he belonged to a society whose members were not allowed to do so without a fortnight's notice to the secretary. His endorsement of the Free State yet again opened a deep political divide between them, though she allowed him to use his influence to try to get compensation for a car which had been stolen from her by the Black and Tans, and it may have been because of her that he pursued Kevin O'Higgins on the question of prison conditions. Their ancient connection, and his readiness to come to her aid, somehow survived.[47]

But his own views were privately setting in a direction very far from hers. As the organized Irregular campaign faltered in the countryside, and the Free State Army recaptured important strongholds in Munster, the guerrillas nominally (and inexpertly) commanded by de Valera fell back on assassinations, random bombings, and house-burnings. Even in Merrion Square, WBY's Monday evening on 30 October was disrupted by a bomb attack on Oriel House (where the Free State Army interrogated Irregular suspects), cracking the glass in his windows. The sentry on the corner 'answered our questions in a gentle, depressed & rather educated voice &

then said "I think this is a dangerous place for you as they may start shoot-ing at me any moment."[48] An Arts Club entertainment a few days later was punctuated by bombs in the street. Writing to Quinn in mid October, WBY had affected insouciance: 'When one thinks of all the destruction one won-ders at one's own cheerfulness. Probably general destruction is less depress-ing to the elderly intellectual than to others. One has one's mind on the re-building and one finds some compensation in ample space for it'.[49] But after nearby explosions in early November he remarked to Gregory that *The Unicorn from the Stars* seemed a strange prophecy of the communism and anarchy now apparently rife in Munster under the sway of socialist republicans such as Liam Mellows. 'All talk here is conservative & eyes are turned full of enquiry towards Italy,' where Mussolini had just been invited to form a government after the threatened March on Rome. Order, WBY told Ricketts, was now 'a conspiracy of the few', a belief he repeated to Shakespear: 'everywhere one notices a drift towards conservatism perhaps towards Autocracy'. He now specifically traced Ireland's descent into an-archy back to Easter 1916. 'Perhaps there is nothing so dangerous to a modern state, where politics take the place of theology, as a bunch of martyrs. A bunch of martyrs (1916) were the bomb & we are living in the explosion.'[50] And, as he continued to work on his 'System', he discerned a growing sense of recognition in the patterns of history, and in his own work as commentaries upon them. If *The Unicorn from the Stars* had been a prophecy, so – to an Ireland now indelibly marked by sacrificial revolution and hunger striking – were *Cathleen ni Houlihan* and *The King's Threshold*.[51]

By the time he had arrived at these reflections, the Free State government had taken a further decisive step towards authoritarianism. On 27 September a Public Safety bill was introduced into the Dáil, setting up mili-tary courts, with powers of life and death, to try offences such as the har-bouring of arms. After a brief amnesty period the court came into operation on 15 October, inaugurating a period of brutal reprisals and counter-reprisals. Though the army's loyalty was strained to breaking-point, the policy was sustained – with the ostentatious support of the Catholic hier-archy. De Valera and his followers clung to the theoretical tatters of the Second Dáil's sole legitimacy, but what WBY called the 'impossibilist' pos-ition was clearly more and more untenable. The government could rely on the general support of even unlikely sections of the Irish population, as Lolly had pointed out to Quinn when things were lurching into anarchy the previous July:

Everything seems crumpling up. *Yet* if we can hold on, I am sure all will yet be well. And one thing this fight has done. It has made one huge party on the Free State side, all ready to work together. People have *drawn together* in the most unexpected way. The old Unionist has become a good Irishman and proud of the young Irish army. And they all swear by the Great Michael [Collins].[52]

The Great Michael was now gone, but, relying on this unity, his colleagues moved ruthlessly ahead. The first executions of men caught with arms took place on 17 November, just as WBY left to give some lectures in England. Attention was now concentrated upon the fate of the most high-profile prisoner awaiting a similar trial: Erskine Childers.

Childers had come (rather unfairly) to stand for the archetype of embittered republican zealot and wrecker. He was marked out by his English background, Haileybury education, imperial service, and presence at the negotiation of the Treaty, which he had obsessively and influentially opposed. At an earlier stage of his life he had won fame as a thriller-writer and journalist. In Ireland liberal as well as republican opinion was firmly against his execution. George's letters to WBY, who was staying at Garsington when Childers was tried and condemned, hinted that he would be asked (possibly by Gogarty and the journalist Francis Cruise O'Brien) to join in a petition for clemency: they also show that she had developed an acute sense of the politics of her adopted country, independently of her husband.

I hope you weren't angry with me for wiring you about Childers? It is not so much a question of Childers, as of the other men. If they don't shoot Childers there is a better chance for the others, and any way it is a good thing for the ministry to see that people do care. The four men they shot last week were shot without the knowledge of the Teachtai [members of the Dáil], and the wives and relatives were not informed until the men had been dead eleven hours . . . They will probably have to shoot men, but if they do it in this way and before the constitution is passed in England the country will turn as it did after the Maxwell executions [in 1916]. No one cares a damn about the MacSwineys [Mary MacSwiney had recently been on hunger strike], but there is great feeling about these unauthorised shootings.[53]

But even as she completed the letter, a stop press announced Childers's execution. From a later reference of George's, it is clear that WBY had in fact written a remonstrating letter to Cosgrave's colleague Ernest Blythe, and equally clear that his old adversaries were not going to let him get the credit for it.

Maud Gonne is publishing wide and broadcast your statement that you wouldnt do anything for Miss MacSwiney Also that you want the English government back – that you are not even a free stater. I was told this twice, both times by republican women who wanted to know was it true. I think the way they make hay, or try to make hay, of your reputation for the sake of propaganda is too disgusting. I have set in motion amongst the de Valera feminine branch a contradiction of the second statement, although I find on roundabout investigation that it is not believed outside the [Charlotte] Despard group. I am not at all sure from the evidence that the record statement has its origin in M.G. It sounds to me more like Helena Malone [Moloney]. It is a very poisonous thing to start just at the moment. Number one woman who came to me on the matter gave herself away most beautifully. She was saying that only three letters of protest about Childers were received by the Gov. So I said I knew of four for a fact that were sent to Blythe. And she said 'O but they wouldn't come under the heading of government letters if they were personally addressed to him.' So I said 'You mean he would have opened them himself instead of their being opened by the officials who open government letters?' And she said 'yes'. So I said 'And therefore the republicans wouldnt get told about it.' She got very red and said nothing more.[54]

Blythe, a ruthless Ulsterman, would not have paid much attention. He remarked, about this time, that the Irish had to realize they were not 'a race of superidealists whose misfortunes are due entirely to the crimes and blunders of outside enemies', but an untrained and undisciplined people trying to build a stable national polity. 'We are marching into freedom ankle-deep in blood, and by all signs are likely to go still deeper.'[55]

During the week of executions Dublin rocked with sniper fire and explosions: George, on her way from the cinema with the young poet Thomas MacGreevy, found herself dodging bullets in Grafton Street. Meanwhile WBY moved between Garsington and the Savile Club, crossing swords with Edmund Gosse (an enemy once more) about Joyce and *Ulysses* and lecturing profitably in Leeds, London, Liverpool, and Leicester.[56] His worries about what George was enduring in Dublin took the – for him – practical form of buying her a pair of black and gold evening shoes (chosen with the approval of Olivia Shakespear). During his absence, which lasted till mid December, his letters signed off with deeply affectionate declarations. 'I miss you constantly & am always wondering if I am as much missed.'[57]

A fortnight after his departure she could tell him that his public role was to be recognized formally – not by an appointment to a ministry but by his nomination to the Senate of the Dáil. On the early evening of 1 December Gogarty called by with the confidential news, inscribing 'Senator Yeats' in the fog on the doorplate. Later that night two young government emissaries arrived and asked a hastily dressed George if her husband would accept nomination as one of a 'panel' of three members who would offer advice on education, literature, and the arts. She telegraphed to the Savile, but there was no doubt about his answer. As long ago as 1912 he had expected to be in the upper house of a Home Rule parliament; he now occupied the kind of platform that suited him best, political but detached from parties. He

hurried back to Dublin in time for the Senate's first meeting on
11 December. Strangely, it took place in the eighteenth-century chamber of
Leinster House, which had once been part of the National Library, and
where he had read Goethe and the Elizabethan poets forty years before.[58]

'We are a fairly distinguished body,' he told Dulac, 'much more so than
the lower house, & should get much government into our hands.'[59] This was
sanguine. The 1922 constitution had set up an upper house of sixty, thirty
senators elected for three years and thirty appointed for six. Its function was
to review legislation from the Dáil, though it could not veto any proposal
already passed, and it could initiate non-financial legislation on its own
account. An unstated intention behind the nomination of members was the
desire to attract into the legislature representatives of the Unionist community (which was one reason why de Valera reformed it so drastically after he
took power ten years later). All the same, the Senate's constitutional powers
amounted to less than many Unionists expected from Griffith. Though
Gogarty credited himself with arguing WBY's name to the Nominating
Committee, Ernest Blythe recorded that it was Desmond FitzGerald who
proposed him, and that there was no opposition.[60] And WBY's chief mentor
in the Senate would be his father's old friend Andrew Jameson, a distilling
magnate, director of the Bank of Ireland and quintessential *ancien régime*
Unionist making terms with the new order. It was a telling choice, considering that other empanelled members included the nationalist historian
Alice Stopford Green, and the influential lawyer and constitution-
draughtsman, James Douglas. When Horace Plunkett retired from the
Senate in late 1923, both Gregory and Quinn lobbied WBY on Hyde's behalf,
but he firmly held that Plunkett had been considered 'the representative of
the group of men who acted together with Andrew Jameson in the Irish
Conference', so the successor figure – in the event, a conservative lawyer –
was up to them.[61] This association with a family friend, like Merrion Square
and the Trinity degree, represented a certain return to tribal tradition, fixed
in stone when Jameson proposed him for the Kildare Street Club. When he
declared his hope in the Senate that 'this country will not always be an
uncomfortable place for a country gentleman to live in' and described himself as 'a crusted Tory' in his support of 'a leisured class',[62] there was an air
of deliberate identification: he was by now a 'country gentleman' himself.
But it did not endear him to many of the friends of his youth.

WBY entered the Senate at a critical time. On 30 November, in response to
the Public Safety Acts, the Irregular forces had turned the ratchet of violence
another notch, by declaring a 'shoot on sight' policy against listed categories
of government supporters, which extended to politicians, judges, and
senators. The government, for its part, authorized reprisal executions of

prisoners, without even invoking the Public Safety Act. The subsequent character of the war has been described as 'vendetta on a national scale'.[63] Colleagues of WBY, like Horace Plunkett and Richard Bagwell, saw their houses burned and themselves threatened with abduction and murder. Gogarty, theatrical as ever, went one better when he foiled a kidnap attempt by diving into the Liffey on 12 January. He temporarily returned to London and a Grosvenor Square practice, and – always a rabid anti-Semite – from this point took to referring to de Valera as 'the Jewish rat'. WBY set himself about analysing the situation in an equally characteristic manner by trying to get hold of de Valera's horoscope.[64] By the end of February 1923 thirty-seven senators' houses had gone up in flames. The government held to its draconian policy: thirty-four prisoners were executed in January. Defensible or not, it seems certain that this broke republican morale. But the threat to public figures associated with the Cosgrave regime continued: Ballylee was entered by Irregulars and 'knocked about', and armed guards were posted to 82 Merrion Square. Just before Christmas the house was fired upon. One bullet came into the nursery and knocked plaster out of the wall, hitting (though not injuring) George, who was soothing Anne on her knee. Another bullet entered the drawing-room window, passed through the folding doors into the bedroom beyond, and embedded itself in the wall. 'Mary Ann [the housemaid from Gort] is ill & scared & will go home for a time,' WBY told Gregory, 'but George & I we are quite cheerful & I dont think the children mind.'[65]

This was not the full truth. But for the moment WBY's mind ran on the possibility of defusing the situation by modifying the Treaty. In early January he was in London once more, suggesting 'a slight modification that might have a great effect and bring peace much nearer' to the Irish peer Lord Granard. It evidently concerned adapting the oath in a way that might bring round the republican opposition. He thought he had won over Lord Southborough, whom Granard proposed as intermediary, and hoped to be put in touch with someone who could negotiate between both governments and the republican side (perhaps Lionel Curtis, the Colonial Office adviser on Irish affairs). On his return to Dublin he referred mysteriously to 'my plan for peace'. Four years later the republican TD Patrick McCartan claimed that WBY had travelled as Cosgrave's envoy 'to confer with the British Government regarding the abolition of the oath of allegiance'. According to McCartan, WBY came back with the message that they would not object to abolition if it ended the civil war, but the Irish government in the end preferred to keep the oath (and the war) rather than admit republicans into the political process. WBY denied that he visited London at Cosgrave's behest, 'nor did I see any member of the British Government on the subject, nor did I make any such report to the Irish government'.[66]

McCartan accused him of quibbling, and certainly his denial would not cover seeing Curtis, or giving a verbal account to Cosgrave. McCartan's authority was WBY's fellow senator Douglas, to whom WBY had allegedly given the full story. According to McCartan, O'Higgins and another minister, Patrick Hogan, had dissuaded Cosgrave from proceeding with the abolition of the oath. (De Valera did this in 1933.) In fact, abolition can hardly have been in question; it does not fit with 'a slight modification', and it would have been political suicide for Bonar Law's recently elected Conservative government. But it seems clear that some alteration in the oath's wording was accepted in London and rejected in Dublin: probably because it was not enough to appease republicans and would simply deflate the Cosgrave government's hard-won reputation for toughness.

WBY returned to Dublin to attend the Senate debates, as 'my absence would look bad in light of threats etc.', coming back to London a week later to use his new-found senatorial authority in the cause of the Lane pictures. He was probably still pursuing his private peace mission too. However, he was becoming unsettled. He learned from Eddie Marsh that a commission was to be formed to consider the Lane pictures, and briefly revelled in 'the world I knew ten years ago [which] for the moment is amusing – beautiful ladies who are so gifted that they seem to know everything yet know nothing'.[67] But he also saw several politicians, and – as suggested – the influential Lionel Curtis, who recorded WBY's opinions on the 'General Position' in a memorandum registered on 27 January (they had met on the 20th). Given the inadequacies of the new Civic Guard, WBY warned him, if Ireland were unable to carry out the provisions of the Treaty, the British government might have to reoccupy the country by force: they should threaten this in public, so republicans would see that destabilizing the new state would not result in anarchy.[68] (This was a dubious argument: many republicans thought, rightly or wrongly, that the return of a British presence would unite the country in patriotism and bring public opinion around to their side.) From the perspective of London, he was irritated at unthinking support among *bien pensant* Liberals for all Irish revolutionaries.

[Lord Buckmaster] was full of admiration for Ireland, train wreckers, murderers & all. 'Ah if only the Germans were like that, they would soon get rid of the French but they have been too much drilled.' I said 'Yes; & I hear that the Egyptian nationalists have asked an Irish politician to hire them a few gunmen as they say there [*sic*] own people lack moral force' – he became a little grave. It struck me that the liberal party mind was shifting about to find out if it could not take up the republicans.[69]

But he was past idealizing what he had come to see as anarchy. His home was protected by an armed guard, and, though he went about Dublin unaccompanied, he could have been an assassination target. At this time, in a letter that no longer survives, he evidently wrote to George suggesting that the family leave Dublin; the attack on Gogarty seems to have swayed him. Her reply, dated 1 February, is remarkable:

I *do* feel that things now are at the climax – and therefore that one should if it is in any way possible, stick it out. If it is, in any way, any use being here at all – that is if it is to be of any use in the future – this is the decisive moment

Mrs Humphreys – in her house Ernie O'Malley was taken – came to Mrs Buck Mulligan [Mrs Gogarty] & said she wished her to know that De Valera & *his* H.Q. had *not* given the order for the kidnapping & that they were extremely sorry about it. It is *just* possible that Dev. may at last have the courage to disassociate himself from the extreme element. Do not think that I for one moment do not realise the upset to you that all this is, or that I neglect the possibilities of danger to you.

I am not suggesting that you should come back – except for the senate – but I do think that a general removal might be a bitter mistake. Anne has slept through *everything*. That she is a little deaf may be a godsend to her. She is sleeping as she has never ever slept before & curiously enough seems to have lost all sense of fear at strange noises. It seems strange to me that I have no feeling of fear over the future, but this very lack of anxiety increases my belief that there is no need for fear, for if I do not fear for you when you are my whole world surely my instinct is right?

In a letter to Gregory of this time he mentions moving the children from Dublin, using Anne's 'nerves' as the reason,[70] but it seems clear from George's letter that a 'general removal' was planned. As it happened, George's political instinct was right. Late January was probably the critical point, though O'Higgins, who had emerged as the voice of coercion in the Cabinet, advocated executions in every county, summary shootings for anyone in possession of arms, a policy of transportation, and 'the ruthless application of the Iron Hand'.[71] The Irregulars had effectively lost the war already. By late April peace negotiations were under way, brokered by WBY's senatorial colleagues Andrew Jameson and James Douglas; they astutely reported back that de Valera appeared to be 'trying to get his followers to hold together as a constitutional party'.[72] This accurately forecast his future path. Meanwhile, internment continued. Iseult, her husband, Francis Stuart, and Seán MacBride were all in prison in April, along with Maud Gonne, who promptly went on hunger strike. WBY brought influence to bear on Iseult's behalf, and she was released after ten days.[73] For the present, the war petered out when the Irregulars announced a grudging ceasefire on 24 May. For zealots the issues, such as they were, remained unresolved, with the idea of an inalienable 'republic', owing allegiance only to the long-dead 'Second Dáil', floating somewhere in the ether. The traumatic psychological wounds had cut deep, and time did little to cauterize them. The govern-

ment introduced a new Public Order bill in June, which sustained internment powers and established flogging as a punishment for arson and robbery. 'When you come face to face with stark anarchy,' O'Higgins declared,
'worse still if it masquerades as political idealism, you have got to be reactionary.'[74] Irreconcilables like Maud Gonne devoted themselves to the cause
of Republican prisoners, 12,000 of whom remained in Free State gaols
after the ceasefire. But the revolution was over, having – true to classical
form – devoured many of its own children.

IV

From early February 1923 WBY was in full senatorial harness. His official
protection continued late into the year.[75] He was at last a politician, even if
not all his policies could be put into practice. ('If the Pope, as a neutral
Authority, would agree to store all republican arms in the Vatican,' he suggested to Gregory at Christmas 1922, 'to keep or deliver up again at his discretion, all would be settled. It does not seem to have occurred to him &
aparently nobody else likes to suggest it.'[76]) The appointment to the Senate
brought a small income (£30 a month), as well as public kudos ('relations of
whom I have seen nothing call on me & are kind, & old acquaintances press
my hand'[77]). His first intervention, supporting the nomination of the controversial ex-Unionist Lord Glenavy as chairman of the assembly, was characteristic. 'I think we should put aside once and for all all diplomacy in
dealing with the people of the country. We have been diplomatised for a
generation. Let us stop it.' The past, he went on to say, was dead and they no
longer met as 'nationalists' and 'Unionists'. 'I shall speak very little', he told
Shakespear a week after he entered the Senate, 'but probably intrigue a good
deal to get some old projects into action.'[78]

First among these, predictably, was the matter of getting government support for the Abbey. This was a long and deep-laid plan. Even before the Treaty
negotiations had been concluded, over a year before, he had been urgently
corresponding with Gregory. Proposals for a national theatre were already in
existence, and the Abbey directors feared Griffith's traditional enmity and
Markievicz's established theatrical ambitions: could they move fast by offering a new Irish state the existing Abbey in its entirety, and, if so, could they
expect to retain any control? Rather surprisingly, WBY was inclined to ask for
an annual subsidy, rather than handing the enterprise over. As early as
December 1921 he was thinking in concrete terms of at least £1,000 a year.

Robinson would have to find out the constitution of, say, the Comédie Française or
of some representative German State Theatre and submit a scheme. Our case is

this: owing first to the World War and then to the Irish war we have used up most of our small stock of capital and that in any case we always intended (you will remember our public declaration on that subject) to hand the Theatre over to the Nation. The Government, on its side, would feel that the National Theatre must be so far as building stage decoration and payment of actors, worthy of the Nation.

I cannot think that we could be refused if we act quickly. Should the Government lay down some condition we could not accept – and the only condition we could not accept would be some interference with our artistic freedom – we could refuse and would then face a rival Theatre with the advantage of standing for intellectual independence. A situation would have been created which, even though we were finally beaten – and we might not be beaten – would be a fine definition of our position and our work.

Perhaps, he added, an interim subsidy might be offered, with the right to consider a more comprehensive takeover at the end of a certain period.[79] But for all his eternal desire to be freed of 'theatre business', when it came to the point he could not bear to relinquish control of the unique institution which he had done so much to bring into being, and whose development he tried so hard to dictate.

Gregory was readier to let go, partly because she doubted if such a flexible arrangement would be offered. She suggested letting the Dáil leaders know, informally, that it had always been the directors' intention to bequeath the Abbey to an Irish government: could it be taken on as a national theatre, or should it continue independently?[80] WBY suggested approaching Desmond FitzGerald with this outline, via Lennox Robinson, and this strategy was pursued in early January, as the terms of the Treaty were fought over. (Gregory thought 'when one reads the Dail debates one feels that to mention such a thing as a theatre wd be as Mr Dooley says like "reading a chapter from the Lives of the Saints in a meeting of the Clan na Gael"!'[81]) From the outset, WBY was determined to establish the traditional right to experiment, and to protect the theatre against interference from 'a Government Jack-in-office': hence his close interest in the mooted ministry of Fine Arts, a post which must be saved from a ludicrous figurehead like Count Plunkett (arts minister under the previous Dáil government) and directed towards someone like Desmond FitzGerald – or himself. Finally, 'an intelligent Minister of Fine Arts and the Abbey Theatre nationalised would give us considerable influence with Government which would help us, perhaps, to press the problem of the Lane pictures'.[82]

As it turned out, the infant Free State would be preoccupied by the more visceral matter of sheer survival and did not create a ministry of Arts at all. But as soon as the secession of extreme republicans became inevitable, it was clear that Griffith would be isolated, and no longer a dangerous enemy.

WBY's goal therefore became the establishment of a state theatre with the Abbey directors as part of its governing authority. They might still have to hand over their creation, but must try to prevent it 'from sinking either into politics or commerce.'[83] In January FitzGerald assured them that the provisional government looked kindly on the Abbey, and that there was no immediate plan to create an alternative national theatre. Matters were then muddied by rumours that Sara Allgood was to be asked to organize the Abbey as a national theatre by the irrepressible Plunkett. Gregory swiftly countered by planting out newspaper interviews asserting the Abbey's historic position, and pursuing the embarrassed Allgood for a private retraction.[84] Through all the tension of the civil war, her eagle eye remained fixed on the question of the Abbey's future; with WBY's return to Dublin in September 1922, the campaign began again. In late October Robinson presented a long memorandum to Desmond FitzGerald, minister for External Affairs, asking for a subsidy (Gregory, characteristically, was annoyed that the original draft stressed WBY's activity in fundraising rather than her own). The memorandum was accompanied by a deeply disingenuous letter from Robinson, whose arguments were clearly dictated by WBY. He advocated a brand-new state theatre, to seat 2,000, with 'all the latest contrivances – Fortuny lighting, a revolving stage, etc., all the things that are revolutionising the art of the theatre. I am sure you have been in, or have seen photographs of the new Continental and American theatres and you know the kind of theatre I have in mind.' Then the Abbey could continue as an adjunct 'Gaelic Theatre'.[85]

If one thing was clear in the straitened circumstances of October 1922, it was that the Free State government would not conjure up the funds for an extravagantly ultra-modern and cosmopolitan state-of-the-art theatre. Robinson's accompanying memorandum made the more practical points that the Abbey was a valuable property, that it existed principally for the production of Irish plays, that it had a noble record of paying its way but now needed money. The directors had always wanted to hand it over to an independent Irish government, which should have an institution to rival the Comédie-Française or the Moscow Art Theatre. The Abbey alone could fulfil this function at a low cost. It also intended to develop an Irish-speaking subsidiary. Effectively, and with a delicate hint of moral blackmail, the government was offered an intellectual treasure which already amounted to a national aesthetic possession, and which was also a good bargain.

The Directors would regret being forced to let the theatre to a cinema company (they have already refused an offer) even in order to gain money with which to open later on: & to sell the whole property which is now a valuable one, in which case they would apply the money to other intellectual purposes in Dublin. They wish to avoid the breaking up of a business that is, both on artistic and intellectual grounds, an advantage to Dublin. For eighteen years they have carried on its work. They carried it on in spite of the European war (which killed every repertory theatre in England save one), and in spite of the English war in Ireland. Ungrudgingly and without pay they have given their services to the creation of the Irish drama, they have created the Irish Theatre – a mass of plays, dramatists that have brought honour to Ireland all over the world, a type of activity that has largely become the model of all modern acting, players of genius. They think that the time has come when the responsibility of the Theatre should be borne by the State.[86]

This memorandum bears a distinctly Yeatsian stamp, and the accompanying suggestion is in effect exactly what WBY had proposed several months before. The government should make the theatre a grant for the next twelve months (£500 for repairs, £1,500 for running costs) and recognize the Abbey as the national theatre. At the end of twelve months the position should be reviewed, and a permanent form of association (and subsidy) decided upon. No immediate reply was forthcoming, but the pressure continued. FitzGerald was invited to Merrion Square for dinner the day WBY joined the Senate, and George was detailed to discuss the matter when WBY was in England.[87] Gregory continued to oppose what she saw as exchanging the theatre's independence for an inadequate grant. She wanted to hand over the entire thing (a prospect which Eoin MacNeill, the minister for Education, greeted with horror).[88] Financial troubles mounted: by June 1923 the directors were mortgaging the buildings, to clear an overdraft which had now reached £2,000. In August an emergency council at Coole drew up a memorandum for financial reorganization, and then went cap-in-hand to the Carnegie Trust, who turned them down.[89] The government dug in its heels for another eighteen months, and by November 1924 Gregory herself was petitioning the minister for Finance, Ernest Blythe, for a subsidy. Eventually (early in 1925) FitzGerald and Blythe offered £1,000 as an annual subvention towards performances. This established the principle of the state providing support without taking over artistic control, much as WBY had wished. When it came through later that year, it had been reduced to £850, but WBY could still describe the Abbey as 'the first state-endowed theatre in any English-speaking country'.[90]

As a senator his chief concerns continued to be cultural, but he was determined to speak on other matters as well. AE ironically noted that WBY was reading volumes on economics, taxation, and other matters 'so that he may do his duty in that rank of life to which it has pleased God to call him'.[91] He intervened forcefully on procedural issues such as the inadvisability of forming strictly defined standing committees, and paid generous tribute to his old enemy Arthur Griffith when supporting a bill to provide a pension for his widow. He offered comments on bills about property damage and personal injuries, and supported Jameson's attempt to defer Ireland's admission to the League of Nations. In matters such as the location of the parliament, he argued unsuccessfully for the old Houses of Parliament on College Green, which remained the stronghold of the Bank of Ireland. He warned against altering such a 'priceless masterpiece' as the late-seventeenth-century Royal Hospital at Kilmainham – which to many of his hearers would have been tainted by its military connections. (It was, in fact, allowed to decay for decades before its restoration as the Museum of Modern Art sixty years later.) He pursued a long campaign about fire risk in the National Museum, harassing reluctant civil servants at the Board of Works.[92] His interventions, often prefaced by elaborate disclaimers of any special knowledge, could arouse a testy response from the chairman, but on basic matters, such as the constitutional relationship to the Dáil, his comments were to the point. His political speeches outside the chamber were few, but could be both concrete and weighty – as when he supported the candidature of Bryan Cooper (a Sligo grandee with a liberal Unionist background) as an Independent in April 1923, blinding the Rathmines electorate with economic statistics and financial credit issues.[93] The long apprenticeship in political and literary pressure-groups of thirty years before now paid its dividend. Walking from his house in Merrion Square, past the government buildings in Merrion Street and into the Senate debating chamber, he not only felt part of a new nation but consciously followed the footsteps of eighteenth-century Irish parliamentarians. And it was this tradition that he invoked with gathering frequency and force.

AE felt that the new senator was neglecting his writing, but this had as much to do with the effort still being lavished on WBY's recalcitrant philosophical 'System'. The other main project which absorbed his energies was, inevitably, the Lane pictures. Official interest had to be kept up; just before the Anglo-Irish War the chief secretary had got so far as bringing a bill to Cabinet. On his London visit in late January 1923 WBY lobbied Beaverbrook, Curtis, Lord Peel, and the duke of Devonshire (whose secretary, Eddie Marsh, also provided access to Winston Churchill). Another new contact was drawn into the web: a mysterious and slightly shady Irish adventurer in English political journalism, Brendan Bracken. WBY met him at an Irish Literary Society soirée held at the home of the editor J. L. Garvin in the summer of 1922. Bracken cemented their friendship by borrowing the rich novelist Frederick Britten-Austin's country house for the weekend, inviting WBY and passing the place off as his own. He even presented the poet with a book from the library as a memento. 'What does he do for a living?' wby nervously asked another guest: it was a good question.[94]

Officially, Bracken was editing *English Life*, which would publish wby's coded narrative of George's automatic writing, 'The Gift of Harun Al-Rashid', in January 1924. But Bracken's real passions were high finance and political intrigue. He promised to press the case for the Lane pictures with his highly placed friends, sent portentous telegrams about the imminent return of the collection, and stayed at Merrion Square during October 1923. In the end it is doubtful if he did very much (and later in life, as a trustee of the English National Gallery, he opposed even the 'loan' arrangement by which the pictures were eventually shared). Gregory, indomitably pursuing the cause from Coole, betrayed to her journal a certain scepticism about wby's efforts ('still in London "dining out" R[obinson] says and "sending for more dress shirts"'). They clashed over strategy. She wanted a Dáil and Senate resolution asking directly for the pictures back, and wby preferred the idea of the Dáil's declaring the codicil legal. But he followed her instructions and introduced the Senate resolution in May – in a carefully researched speech, supported by Jameson and Lord Glenavy.[95] The Lane Bequest had become a settled grievance, regularly raised in Irish parliamentary debate, and as regularly met by a smokescreen of indifference from British officialdom. As the paintings soared in value and popular appeal, the National Gallery in London sheltered behind its legalistic defence. Only Gregory's great spirit remained undaunted.

The Lane pictures and the Abbey's finances were long-standing battles; other cultural issues would emerge in the new Free State and in turn become lifetime campaigns. Nine months before wby's appointment AE had approached him about the government's mooted 'National Academy' for Ireland. wby had been proposed as someone who might be asked to become a foundation member. As reported in the press, the list of other 'literary' names was suspiciously patchy. Gregory, Moore, Shaw, Standish O'Grady, 'John Eglinton', Katharine Tynan, Stephen Gwynn were excluded: apparatchiks and academics unknown to Russell (or, presumably, to wby) were suggested instead.[96] wby agreed in finding the suggested body 'preposterous', 'absurd', and 'childish', and refused to countenance the project. AE withheld his support on the grounds that it would duplicate the work of the Royal Irish Academy, the Hibernian Academy, and the Royal Irish Academy for Music. He did not, presumably, pass on Susan Mitchell's description of the proposed body as 'a kind of Catholic Young Men's Association' or his own belief that one of the obscure nominees 'owed his immortality to his genius in illuminating addresses to parish priests'. But both AE and wby felt that those excluded were left out either because they were Protestant or, like Tynan, not nationalist enough.[97] The abortive suggestion helped inspire wby's own ideas about such a body. But the fact that he at once decided any decent Irish Academy must include James Joyce indicates just how far his ideas diverged from the scheme floated by the government.

From an early stage too he used the Senate as a platform for arguing against what he conceived of as a narrow or solipsistic approach to national culture. In June a backwoods senator made an unsupported proposal to exclude children under sixteen from cinemas, except in school parties. wby took the opportunity to call for 'leaving the arts, superior or inferior, to the general conscience of mankind', a foretaste of battles to come. More combatively, in November he opposed a resolution to read the Prayer in Irish and English every day:

I wish to make a very emphatic protest against the histrionics which have crept into the whole Gaelic movement. People pretend to know a thing that they do not know and which they have not the smallest intention of ever learning. It seems to me discreditable and undesirable. I hope this will not be taken as being unsympathetic to the Gaelic movement. In the Abbey Theatre, on Monday night, a play in Irish was produced, and the theatre was packed with an enthusiastic audience. They knew Irish, and they were able to understand the language of the play, but I think this method of histrionics and going through a childish performance of something we do not know, and which we do not intend to learn, will ultimately lead to a reaction against the language. I wish to say that I wish to see the country Irish speaking.[98]

Nothing here was inconsistent with the opinions he had long held. But in the Free State of 1923, which officially stressed a commitment to cultural Gaelicization if only in order to combat accusations of political pro-Britishness, this smacked of dangerous heterodoxy. Even worse, to some suspicious minds it also suggested aboriginal Unionism.

By the middle of 1923 the institutions of the state – military, peacekeeping, legal – had evolved, borrowing from the old and incorporating the new. In creating stability, and a viable independent polity, even de Valera would later privately concede (when he had become a conservative too) that the Cosgrave government did 'a magnificent job'.[99] He owed his opponents this accolade, since the ruthlessness with which they established the new system freed de Valera's own hands to enter constitutional politics. It also enabled an uneven but surprisingly fast return to 'normal life', even in those rural areas where order had broken down during the last terrible year. For wby, the summer was spent between Ballylee and Merrion Square, scattering a constant trail of forgotten personal belongings to be recalled by telegram. Gregory was back at Coole, having spent early June convalescing at Merrion Square after an operation to remove a breast tumour. The balance of their old relationship was in some ways reversed: he now provided sustenance, 'quiet and fine linen', and an established refuge on her visit to Dublin, while at Coole her resources were further and further strained. 'I think I went through my wealthy days with simplicity', she told her diary; 'now I must go through these straitened days with dignity.'[100]

She was helped in this resolve by her combative friendship with WBY, still central to both their lives. Gregory's journals record amicable disagreements with her guest over the republican issue. She retained her admiration for de Valera, and, entertaining Jack Yeats that August, found her opinions closer to his than to his brother's. In November she would clash with WBY again, about 400 republican prisoners on hunger strike: she wanted to write a public letter suggesting that their cases be examined, and a compromise reached. He was 'violently against any protest, says it is necessary to the stability of Government to hold out; says they cannot publish the accusations, because many are on suspicion, or as they think certainty, but they have not evidence that can be given.'[101] They continued to argue, but he presented an implacable government line. As usual, she followed her conscience and did write a letter to the papers, with Lennox Robinson and James Stephens; then she told WBY what she had done and offered to leave his house, since he would disapprove. 'He would not allow that, and after talking for a while thought perhaps we had done right.' Again, the reversal of positions is striking: twenty-five years before, he had burst into Coole full of Gonne's ideas about seizing landlords' property, and Gregory had pulled him firmly into line.[102] But their shared history enabled them to weather such changes. And similar accommodations were, on several levels, happening all around them.

The summer of 1923 had also seen a certain amount of family upheaval, centred on the Cuala Press. The Yeats sisters now produced highly defined artefacts for an established clientele – including many dedicated collectors on both sides of the Atlantic. The printing oeuvre enshrined a particular version of the Irish Revival as well as the commodification of the Yeats family aesthetic (poems by WBY with decorated initial letters, cards and engravings designed by Jack). The booklist had remained beautiful, distinguished, and expensive, and was similarly dominated by the first appearances of WBY's volumes, with occasional additions from his friends. But, like any small Irish business, Cuala had been buffeted by the storms of war and revolution. Though sales were buoyant, a 'huge overdraft' was established by 1917, and by 1923 it had reached £2,000.[103] The dislocations of these years made things worse. Some of their staff were arrested during the civil war, and in July 1922 the sisters were given notice by their landlord. By January 1923 Lolly was considering converting the business from a cooperative to a limited company, in order to survive; the printing was paying well, but the embroidery doing badly.[104] Matters were therefore difficult enough when, in early July 1923, Lily fell seriously ill with a disease first thought to be tuberculosis. WBY's reaction to the practical implications was immediate: 'I imagine what ever happens George & I will now become responsible for Cuala.'[105]

They certainly became responsible for part of it. They had been planning to buy 'a large old Dublin house' and let it to the sisters, but the cost of Lily's illness ruled this out. So the business was installed in the capacious ground-floor rooms of 82 Merrion Square, taking over their dining room. George, whose name now joined the firm's notepaper, was to commandeer the embroidery side of the business and 'try and pull it round', with projects such as blouses for evening wear (which did not catch on). The move was accomplished on 23 August; appositely for this family business, the book that had just been bound was JBY's *Early Memories,* and it was the first volume issued from Merrion Square. It was to be followed by a collection of Gogarty's poetry: 'a little of it beautiful & all with some charm', according to WBY, who was nonetheless slightly shocked at his facile friend's ability to churn out verse at short notice in order to fill up blank pages.[106] By the following Christmas, when they sold 1,600 hand-coloured cards, Lolly could judge that the business had done 'immensely better' since the move.[107]

The same could not be said of poor Lily. Her illness was at first mysterious, and Lolly persisted in describing it as 'neurasthenic', but a substantial correspondence between WBY and her doctors confirms both the seriousness of the malady, and his commitment to looking after her. On 19 July he went to London to book her into a specialist nursing-home for an indefinite period, anticipating a cost of £400; from surviving bills, it was in fact considerably more.[108] The treatment for tuberculosis revealed retrosternal goitre, creating a congenital bronchial obstruction which impeded her breathing, and she settled in for a long recuperation, remaining in the clinic until the following April. The doctors wrote angrily that part of the problem was Lolly, who plagued them with letters asserting her own diagnosis, and whose visits to the nursing-home produced havoc, infuriating the staff as well as Lily. (Lolly's quintessentially Yeatsian reaction was to get an angry letter from the matron 'psychometrysed' by the family seer, Lucy Middleton, who warned that it gave off a sinister aura.) WBY was inexorably drawn into this, explaining to one bemused doctor 'the whole family are exceedingly nervous and suggestible. I remember once being crippled with rheumatism and my instant cure by an unexpected half hour's animated conversation. We are not a normal family.'[109] For all his determination to keep out of his sisters' disastrous relationship, from the summer of 1923 the long crisis of Lily's illness and Cuala's fortunes imposed a burden on his domestic life as well as on his finances.

He was, nonetheless, building a Dublin life with the energy he had always devoted to constructing societies, projects, *cénacles*. To have an art printing press downstairs carried a certain flavour of Bedford Park days. High hopes about the Lane pictures were artificially boosted by Bracken's descent upon Merrion Square, 'an engaging visitor but of insatiable energy'.[110] WBY brought him to see Cosgrave, whom he misled as thoroughly as he did everyone else. It suddenly seemed that the Royal Hospital at Kilmainham might house both the paintings and the Senate. WBY plotted about appointments to the National Gallery and tried to persuade the government to set up an artistic committee to advise it on aesthetic matters, covering 'stamps, medals, seals, etc.'; he hoped to enlist Orpen, Lavery, and Shannon.[111] The Drama League continued to try to sustain an avant-garde existence. Best of all, Plunkett was to revive his journal the *Irish Statesman*, perhaps with the young Belfast essayist Robert Lynd as editor: 'Lynd should be an addition to our group here.'[112] Tedious and monomaniacal though he could be, Plunkett's real integrity and self-lessness shows in his determination to create something of value to Irish cultural life, only weeks after Kilteragh, his beloved house at Foxrock, had been burned to the ground by Irregulars. He saw the new paper, he told Gregory, as a forum where he could again gather the kind of people who had once congregated at Kilteragh. 'Yeats too must show that the paper is going to uphold the very best traditions of the best days of our literature and art. Thus alone can we bear what we see around us in the Bedlam British tinkering has made.'[113]

In the event, AE took on the *Irish Statesman* and made it one of the brief glories of the liberal Irish intellectual tradition. 'I intend to make it as good-natured as I can,' he told Gregory, 'and to do my best to interest the Irish people in ideas & literature. I think it likely Yeats & Robinson will be on committee.'[114] It would become the house magazine for what WBY was already calling 'our group here', and this would bring its own backlash. But for the moment, he was organizing his life. The Senate sat in the after-noons. In the mornings he wrote, still working on the interminable 'System' behind his book of philosophy. By the end of October he was drafting the 'last most difficult chapter' and had a contract from Werner Laurie for a private printing of 500 copies. Half would be taken by WBY himself, clearly indicating the kind of semi-private production he expected it to be. George had been induced to provide more material through a sleep-trance: this would be incorporated in the 'Gates of Pluto' sections of the book – which he now knew would be called *A Vision*.[115]

This did not leave much room for verse, and in June Gogarty had told Boyd that WBY was neglecting his writing. However, according to his ancient pattern, a retreat to the west brought the concentration and inspiration that he needed. On 1 August he had written to Herbert Grierson from Ballylee:

I have all the thought I ever had, but it is a fire of straw. Alas I have to return to Dublin in a couple of days. There one gets angry & writes prose but here beside a little stream I write poetry & think of nothing else. I suffer nothing worse than occasional horse-flies which on very hot days drive me on to the castle-roof & into the shadow of the big chimney. I am writing nothing but curses upon old age which distress my wife who says I am not old enough to justify them. I am resisting Wordsworthian calm.[116]

But the most noteworthy product of that late summer and autumn was a short and forceful poem, which would achieve a unique notoriety among his work: 'Leda and the Swan'. From Gregory's journal, it is clear that he was working on it in September, thinking he had finished it in the middle of the month but constantly impelled to further revision. It is also clear that politics were preoccupying him as much as angry memories of youthful passion. Staying at Merrion Square on 17 September, Gregory recorded:

Yeats talked of his long belief that the reign of democracy is over for the present, and in reaction there will be violent government from above, as now in Russia, and is beginning here. It is the thought of this force coming into the world that he is expressing in his Leda poem, not yet quite complete. He sat up till 3 o'c this morning working over it, and read it to me as complete at midday, and then half an hour later I heard him at it again.[117]

WBY put the same idea in the note to the poem as it appeared in *The Cat and the Moon* in 1924, adding that although he had been asked to write a poem for 'a political review', the sensual theme overwhelmed its original political inspiration, and 'bird and lady took possession of the scene'. Certainly Russell felt it was too scandalous for the *Irish Statesman*. It was much altered for its first printing in 1924 (and would be changed further before the final form revealed in *A Vision*). But the sonnet detonates a powerful sexual charge, even in the first published version.

> A rush, a sudden wheel, and hovering still
> The bird descends, and her frail thighs are pressed
> By the webbed toes, and that all-powerful bill,
> Has laid her helpless face upon his breast.
> How can those terrified vague fingers push
> The feathered glory from her loosening thighs!

> All the stretched body's laid on the white rush
> And feels the strange heart beating where it lies;
> A shudder in the loins engenders there
> The broken wall, the burning roof and tower
> And Agamemnon dead.
>   Being so caught up,
> So mastered by the brute blood of the air,
> Did she put on his knowledge with his power
> Before the indifferent beak could let her drop?

The technical virtuosity of the poem owes much to its compression and concreteness, grounded on a specific image of the much-illustrated rape of Leda, which WBY showed to Gregory during her visit. It was this immediacy, together with the disturbing implication of the girl's acquiescence, which would turn the poem into 'the foul swan song' of the *Catholic Bulletin*'s fevered imagination.[118] The theme of mythical copulation with animals was not new in his work, running through *The Player Queen*, but there the general obscurity of the play had muffled the shock-effect. Swans had long been a favourite Yeatsian image: the idea may have been recently focused by Gogarty's collection *An Offering of Swans*, printed at Merrion Square and using Leda as a reference point. 'Leda and the Swan' also strikes echoes back to Blake, Spenser, Irish legend, and many of WBY's earliest inspirations. Above all for WBY, the weight of the poem falls in the sestet, where he returns to his old theme of the gestation of violence, the wheel of fate, and inherited guilt. Helen, born of this fabulous congress, caused the destruction of Troy: Leda's other progeny, Castor and Pollux, were the harbingers of war. At the point of conception, did the mother recognize and see the terrible future, and even – momentarily god-like – glory in it? He would paraphrase the thought in the section of *A Vision* called 'Dove or Swan', also written at this time. 'I imagine the annunciation that founded Greece as made to Leda, remembering that they showed in a Spartan Temple, strung up to the roof as a holy relic, an unhatched egg of hers; and that from one of her eggs, came Love and from the other War.'[119] From this angle, 'Leda and the Swan' is linked to 'Meditations in Time of Civil War', and Gregory's version of its political and historical roots seems more comprehensible.

The drafts show how the focus persistently shifts from the god to Leda, a balance which he was not satisfied with until the poem's third printing, in *A Vision*. But the idea of a violent political annunciation from above was powerfully present in 1923. The *Dial* carried 'Leda and the Swan' in June 1924, but for Irish readers two months later WBY would choose 'a political journal' of a very different stamp to the *Irish Statesman*.

V

For the moment, the impact of 'Leda' was deferred. Given the attention about to be focused on its author, this was just as well. WBY's astrologist friend Cyril Fagan had recently forecast money and travel for him: perhaps, like WBY himself, Fagan had noted speculations in the papers about the Nobel Prize for Literature, which bracketed WBY with Thomas Mann as leading contenders. The announcement came on the evening of 14 November, telephoned through to Merrion Square by his fellow Sligoman Bertie Smyllie, the editor of the *Irish Times*. It had appeared through the office wire at 11 p.m. Allegedly, the new Laureate's reaction was pure Pollexfen. 'How much Smyllie, how much is it?'[120] Then – according to Lily – the Yeatses 'sat up till 1 a.m. answering the telephone and being interviewed, then at 1 o'clock went down to the kitchen and fried sausages, next morning marched out and bought new stair carpets'. More expansively, they also had a celebratory dinner with MacGreevy in the Shelbourne the following night.[121] Normal life went on: within two days WBY was lecturing the Trinity College Elizabethan Society on 'The Irish Dramatic Movement' in the mundane surroundings of the Ritz Café, Grafton Street. But the deliberate historicizing of the literary movement, which such lectures were designed to promote, was strengthened by the international recognition of the Nobel Prize. He would use the opportunity of his acceptance speech, on the very same subject, to drive the message home.

WBY was well aware of the larger implications. An Irish winner of the prize, a year after Ireland gained its independence, had a symbolic value in the world's eyes, and he was careful to point this out. His reply to the many letters of congratulation was consistent: 'I consider that this honour has come to me less as an individual than as a representative of Irish literature, it is part of Europe's welcome to the Free State.'[122] This dignified reaction enabled him to duck sniping from English literary quidnuncs like Edmund Gosse, furious that Thomas Hardy had been passed over. Nearer home, WBY could utilize this international recognition in his battle against the Irish puritanism and philistinism that was slowly gathering force. He was also determined to make the most of the presentation. The medal and cheque could be sent to Dublin, but he chose to make the expensive journey a fortnight later to Sweden. His old chinchilla coat, purchased so long ago in America and famously mocked by George Moore, was disinterred and relined; on 6 December he and George set sail for Stockholm via London.[123] All his preparatory homework about Sweden came out of the *Life of Swedenborg*, and he referred enthusiastically to the sage in interviews given in Stockholm, going so far as to imply that he was a fully committed believer in the New Swedenborgian Church and had wished to be married according to its rites.[124] He had time to inspect some Swedish architecture, give a lecture, and repel Robert McAlmon, one of Pound's restless band of avant-garde literary commandos, who stormed his hotel armed with an introduction.[125] He would later describe the Nobel visit, in suitably portentous terms, within the covers of a small Cuala volume. The version retailed by Lily, whom he visited in her nursing-home on his way back through London, is more vivid.

I want to tell you about Willy. He came on Xmas Eve and was delightful, told me about the splendours of Stockholm. He said it was like the Prisoner of Zenda, a fine spectacle. There was the giving of prizes. He had to walk backwards up five steps coming from the King. There was a banquet. He sat by a Princess, George by a Prince, who talked with her in French the whole time and told W. B. that she spoke without accent. The royal family are very cultivated people and have people of intellect about them. One prince is a good artist, another an authority on Chinese painting, one a poet. The princesses all wore white and sat and stood grouped together. The uniforms were very magnificent. Sweden does not ennoble any one, but bestows orders on literature, art, science. These orders were worn and looked fine. There was a big evening reception, and the theatre gave a performance of Kathleen ni Houlihan in Swedish and a play by Goldsmith.

Willy gave an address on the 'Irish Theatre.' This, he was told, was immensely admired. The Swedes are not speakers and were surprised at his powers.

He and George dined at the English Ambassador's and were interviewed and photographed all day long. He got a gold medal as well as the cheque.

The English man of science, Hill [Archibald Vivian Hill, the physiologist], who shared the prize with a German, was an amazing specimen, Willy says, wishing he supposes to show how democratic he was and no admirer of the pomp of Courts. He spoke his thoughts aloud and said, seeing the orders worn, 'Medals, where did they get those, not fighting, I'll be bound.' Again, at the military breastplates, 'Tin,' and when the queen passed with pages carrying her train he said, 'Look at that. Man hasn't to put up with indignity of that sort, thank goodness.' I forget if it was the English Ambassador or one of the ministers who conveyed Willy to and fro in his motor and the Mr Hill, but after his last remark he collected Willy and went off with him, leaving Mr Hill to find his own way. Willy is going to write a full account of his experiences and publish it, as a slight acknowledgment of all the hospitality and kindness. He was also sending autographed copies of his books to some of the princes and ministers.[126]

'The prize has made a boom in his books,' she added, 'and he is seeing Macmillan and his agent so as to get the most out of it.' Letters poured in: two months later he was still answering '17 or 18 in an afternoon'. The recognition marked a milestone in his long ascent of Olympus. It also meant that at last he possessed capital. Only a fortnight before the news, he had had to apologize to Quinn for being as yet unable to pay off all the debts inherited from his father, adding, 'I see I have a chance of the Nobel Prize. If I get there I shall be well off once more & can pay my debts but at the worst I should have my affairs right in a few months.' When it came through, he frankly told Stead, 'I am glad of the prize and glad of the money.'[127]

The answer to the question he had asked Smyllie was gratifying: about £6,800. Part would go to pay off the Cuala overdraft, which used up more than expected. Before this calculation, he outlined his plans to Gregory:

I have invested £6,000 of the money, & kept £500 to go to pay off the debt on this house [Merrion Square], or pay Lilly's expenses as the case may be. There was almost £400 which we have largely spent on our trip to Sweden & on completing the furnishing both of this house – my book cases, stair carpets, a carpet for the study, plates dishes, knives & forks & something I have always longed for a sufficient reference library – *Encycopaedia Britannica* Cambridge Medieval, Ancient & Modern History & a good edition of Gibbon & some art books. As I look at the long rows of substantial backs I am conscious of growing learned minuite by minuite.[128]

Quinn feared that he would now pour money into Ballylee, but WBY assured him that none of it would disappear into the tower by the Cloon. He still had the proceeds from his January lectures set aside for a concrete roof, and expected to spend less and less time there, with the demands of the Senate and Cuala. For investment advice he went to a stockbroker recommended by Andrew Jameson, and by mid January had put £3,500 into various railway stocks. This was far less than he had expected to invest, but much of the residue was swallowed up by Cuala's £2,000 overdraft.[129] He expected an average 5 per cent return on what seemed, in 1924, a safe stock, but within a few years the convulsions of the financial market would alter these prospects for the worse. Between the demands of Cuala and the effect of the depression, the financial security brought by the Nobel represented a brief interlude, not a settled future.

At the same time as placing half the money where he thought it would be safe, he began writing what he called privately 'a sort of "bread & butter letter" to Sweden, & at last a part of my autobiography'.[130] This was completed early in 1924 and would be published by Cuala as *The Bounty of Sweden* later in the year. It is an account of his impressions of the visit to Stockholm, bound with a printed version of the lecture on the Irish Dramatic Movement which he subsequently gave to the Swedish Academy. The opening paragraph of *The Bounty of Sweden* is pure Yeats, disconcertingly different from anything the reader may be disposed to expect.

Thirty years ago I visited Paris for the first time. The Cabbalist MacGregor Mathers said, 'Write your impressions at once, for you will never see Paris clearly again.' I can remember that I had pleased him by certain deductions from the way a woman at the other end of the café moved her hands over the dominoes. I might have seen that woman in London or in Dublin, but it would not have occurred to me to discover in her every kind of rapacity, the substance of the legendary harpy. 'Is not style', as Synge once said to me, 'born out of the shock of new material?'

The ostensible rationale for the dramatic paragraph is to establish the validity of writing down immediate impressions of the strange and the new. But it also establishes WBY in his chosen role (so recently demonstrated in *The Trembling of the Veil*) as chronicler of his times, a prophet from the now near-mythological era of the nineties, and a seer of the avant-garde. Further, he identified himself as 'but a writer of plays', mentioning his 'gift of lyric writing' almost as an afterthought. This is hardly convincing, but creates the persona which he wishes to inhabit for this consummately self-conscious performance. The journey on the Harwich boat with commercial travellers is described with lofty amusement, and he is careful to retail what he says about Ireland to Danish journalists in Copenhagen en route: 'If the British Empire becomes a voluntary Federation of Free Nations, all will be well, but if it remains as in the past, a domination of one, the Irish question is not settled. That done with, I can talk of the work of my generation in Ireland, the creation of a literature to express national character and feeling but with no deliberate political aim.'

Politics, however, are hardly absent. His reaction to a possible socialist government in Denmark is 'to wonder what Denmark will make of that mechanical eighteenth-century dream; we know what half-medieval Russia has made of it'. Sweden, by contrast, is presented as the land of the philosopher-king, or at least of the artist-prince, a country where members of the royal family help to decorate the recently completed Stockholm town hall, and the populace turn out to admire the visiting Nobel Prize winner. Again, his own status as a revenant from the nineties is established by his memories of Strindberg in Paris, and messages from survivors of that circle are delivered to his hotel. The royal presentation is described in laboured detail, at a court 'where life herself is praised' and intellectual orders are recognized in the rituals and hierarchies. Against this dreamy idealization, a long and complex passage of reverie shows how WBY's particular blend of historical fantasy and personal identification intensified the moment.

I had thought how we Irish had served famous men and famous families, and had been, so long as our nation had intellect enough to shape anything of itself, good lovers of women, but had never served any abstract cause, except the one, and that we personified by a woman, and I wondered if the service of woman could be so different from that of a Court. I had thought how, before the emigration of our poor began, our gentlemen had gone all over Europe, offering their swords at every

Court, and that many had stood, just as I, but with an anxiety I could but imagine, for their future hung upon a frown or a smile. I had run through old family fables and histories, to find if any man of my blood had so stood, and had thought that there were men living, meant by nature for that vicissitude, who had served a woman through all folly, because they had found no Court to serve. Then my memory had gone back twenty years to that summer when a friend read out to me at the end of each day's work Castiglione's commendations and descriptions of that Court of Urbino where youth for certain brief years imposed upon drowsy learning the discipline of its joy, and I remembered a cry of Bembo's made years after, 'Would that I were a shepherd that I might look down daily upon Urbino'.

Even more suggestively, his mind turns to the question of ancient privilege and inherited talent, explored in 'Meditations in Time of Civil War', but given here a more concrete form:

Nature, always extravagant, scattering much to find a little, has found no means but hereditary honour to sustain the courage of those who stand waiting for the signal, cowed by the honour and authority of those who lie wearily at the goal. Perhaps, indeed, she created the family with no other object, and may even now mock in her secret way our new ideals – the equality of man, equality of rights, – meditating some wholly different end. Certainly her old arrangements, in all pursuits that gain from youth's recurring sway, or from its training in earliest childhood, surpassed what begins to be a world of old men. The politic Tudor kings and the masterful descendants of Gustavus Vasa were as able as the American presidents, and better educated, and the artistic genius of old Japan continually renewed itself through dynasties of painters . . . How serene their art, no exasperation, no academic tyranny, its tradition as naturally observed as the laws of a game or dance. Nor has our individualistic age wholly triumphed in Japan even yet, for it is a few years since a famous player published in his programme his genealogy, running back through famous players to some player of the Middle Ages; and one day in the British Museum Print- Room, I saw a Japanese at a great table judging Chinese and Japanese pictures. 'He is one of the greatest living authorities,' I was told, 'the Mikado's hereditary connoisseur, the fourteenth of his family to hold the post.' May it not have been possible that the use of the mask in acting, and the omission from painting of the cast shadow, by making observation and experience of life less important, and imagination and tradition more, made the arts transmittable and teachable?

The scientist, Hill, is anonymously employed to represent the 'Jacobin' spirit of insecure, levelling ignorance. The Sweden of wby's imagination is a united intellectual polity, bound together by a sense of place – the characteristic he sees as distinguishing Swedish Impressionist art. The contrast with Ireland is nearly always implicit, but sometimes strikingly breaks through:

I am constantly reminded of my brother, who continually paints from memory the people and houses of the village where he lived as a child; but the people of Rosses will never care about his pictures, and these painters paint for all educated

Stockholm. They have found an emotion held in common, and are no longer, like the rest of us, solitary spectators.

Finally, he turns to his Swedish Academy lecture, 'The Irish Dramatic Movement'. The reason for choosing this subject, he claimed, was, first, to enable him to 'commend all those workers, obscure or well-known, to whom I owe much of whatever fame in the world I possess'. He went on to say, with superb disingenuousness, that if he had not 'become through this Theatre the representative of a public movement', he would not have been nominated for the prize in the first place, which was certainly news to the Nobel jury. The Academy had been expecting him to speak about himself and read his poems.[131] The idea that WBY's plays rather than his poetry had created his international reputation is laughable, but meshes tightly into the historical construction underpinning these apparently rambling auto-biographical impressions. There was also a practical consideration: he had given so many lectures on the Irish Dramatic Movement, on both sides of the Atlantic – most recently three weeks before – that it provided a ready-made subject for his public address. He then permitted himself a reflection which, though it incensed Gregory, would remain more or less unchanged in its many printings.

I am speaking without notes and the image of old fellow-workers comes upon me as if they were present, above all of the embittered life and death of one, and of another's laborious, solitary age, and I say, 'When your King gave me medal and diploma, two forms should have stood, one at either side of me, an old woman sinking into the infirmity of age and a young man's ghost. I think when Lady Gregory's name and John Synge's name are spoken by future generations, my name, if remembered, will come up in the talk, and that if my name is spoken first their names will come in their turn because of the years we worked together. I think that both had been well pleased to have stood beside me at the great reception at your Palace, for their work and mine has delighted in history and tradition.' I think as I speak these words of how deep down we have gone, below all that is individual, modern and restless, seeking foundations for an Ireland that can only come into existence in a Europe that is still but a dream.

The excessive modesty rings hollow, but the peroration is important. It leads on to a consideration of the architecture of the art nouveau Stockholm Town Hall, applauded as a sort of Morrisite master-work, where 'myth-makers and mask-makers worked as if they belong to one family', under 'the authority of a Prince and the wisdom of a socialist Minister of Culture'. 'No work comparable in method or achievement has been accomplished since the Italian cities felt the excitement of the Renaissance, for in the midst of our individualistic anarchy, growing always, as it seemed, more violent, have arisen once more subordination, design, a sense of human need.'

The autobiographical section of the essay closes with some impressions of the Swedish Royal Theatre's performance of *Cathleen ni Houlihan*, and a final comment on the warmth and comforts of the city: structure and tone remain ostensibly random. But the text of his Royal Academy lecture, which follows, would become canonical. It fixed in print WBY's particular analysis of the Irish Literary 'Renascence' (as it was now being called) as well as of the dramatic movement, and the part played in it by himself, Gregory and Synge, who had set themselves – he wrote in a deleted passage – 'against all Jacobin envy'.[132] And it also related that historic era firmly to the politics of the present. 'The modern literature of Ireland, and indeed all that stir of thought which prepared for the Anglo-Irish war, began when Parnell fell from power in 1891. A disillusioned and embittered Ireland turned from parliamentary politics; an event was conceived; and the race began, as I think, to be troubled by that event's long gestation.' Thus Easter 1916 was born a quarter-century before the event: a Leda's egg hanging in the temple of the Abbey Theatre. He went on to link the early theatre movement to Hyde's enterprise of Gaelic revival and the work of the Gaelic League, ignoring at once the avant-garde ambitions of its avatars, their Irish establishment backing, and the existing Dublin theatrical experiments which it had subsumed. The Fays especially were treated with the kind of dismissal to which they must by now have become resentfully accustomed. Most of the troupe, according to WBY, might as well have been chosen by names put into a hat; but 'our two best men actors were not indeed chosen by chance, for one was a stage-struck solicitors' clerk and the other a working man who had toured Ireland in a theatrical company managed by a Negro'.[133] Inghinidhe na hÉireann were at last noticed, but not by name. 'We got our women, however, from a little political society which described its object as educating the children of the poor, or, according to its enemies, teaching them a catechism that began with this question, "What is the origin of evil?" and the answer, "England".'

Past politics, however, are kept in their place in this version of history. The controversy surrounding the theatre is interpreted as the conflict between ancient country values and 'town thoughts': the effort of the literary movement to teach 'reality and justice' incurred the hatred of the crowd. Here and elsewhere, WBY's personal history and achievement are treated interchangeably with that of the theatre, an interpretation which infuriated several of his old associates.[134] The arguments with Griffith over Synge's plays, and with Dublin Castle over *The Rising of the Moon*, are explained by an argument taken, almost word for word, from 'J. M. Synge and the Ireland of his Time'. 'Every political party had the same desire to substitute for life, which never does the same thing twice, a bundle of reliable principles and assertions.' The political agendas of the post-Parnell era are notably absent. More accurately and more concretely, he emphasized that the theatre eventually triumphed through the advent of Miss Horniman's money, and Synge's genius.

WBY's lecture enabled him to annex Synge yet again, to tell the established story of how he found him in a Paris garret and sent him to Aran, to stress Synge's inability to harbour 'a political thought or a humanitarian purpose'. He treated *The Playboy* (alone among the plays mentioned) in great detail, explaining why it first 'roused the populace to fury', and then became acceptable. In a carefully constructed argument, Synge, Gregory, and WBY himself are subtly placed in the history of developing revolutionary consciousness in Ireland over the past decade.

Our victory was won by those who had learned from him courage and sincerity but belonged to a different school. Synge's work, the work of Lady Gregory, my own *Cathleen ni Houlihan* and my *Hour-Glass* in its prose form, are characteristic of our first ambition. They bring the imagination and speech of the country, all that poetical tradition descended from the Middle Ages, to the people of the town. Those who learned from Synge had often little knowledge of the country and always little interest in its dialect. Their plays are frequently attacks upon obvious abuses, the bribery at the appointment of a dispensary Doctor, the attempts of some local politician to remain friends with all parties. Indeed the young Ministers and party politicians of the Free State have had, I think, some of their education from our play ... It is too soon yet to say what will come to us from the melodrama and tragedy of the last four years, but if we can pay our players and keep our theatre open something will come. We are burdened with debt, for we have come through war and civil war and audiences grow thin when there is firing in the streets. We have, however, survived so much that I believe our luck, and think that I have a right to say my lecture ends in the middle or even, perhaps, at the beginning of the story.

WBY's final remarks, which he had proudly adverted to in the autobiographical 'Bounty of Sweden', claim a share in the Nobel Prize for Synge's ghost and the decrepit Gregory, now described as 'a living woman sinking into the infirmity of age' (not much of a rejuvenation, from her point of view). His fellow workers, he believed, would have been inspired by the vision he had seen in Stockholm, where rank and intellect were recognized in the hierarchy of the state. 'No like spectacle will in Ireland show its work of discipline and of taste, though it might satisfy a need of the race no institution created under the influence of English or American democracy can satisfy.' This ominous last sentence should not be ignored. 'The Bounty of Sweden', taken as a whole, shows both WBY's brilliant ability to reconstruct history in terms of its meaning for himself and to place his work, and his circle, at the centre. It also shows how the aesthetic lessons of the nineties, the fear of a potential anarchy terrifyingly demonstrated in the events of the last four years, and an appreciation of grandeur not easily discernible from unashamed snobbery, reacted with each other to reinforce his natural elitism. In the circumstances of the early 1920s, the political implications of this would become inescapable.

Chapter 7 : BAD WRITERS AND BISHOPS
1924–1925

> 23rd [March 1924]. Mr and Mrs Yeats staying. I wish I could
> remember Yeats' conversation accurately – not that it is lost as
> I believe he puts it all in lectures and essays, but because it is
> such a delight. The clearness and beauty of his phrases, and
> never without an interesting idea. He was developing the
> theory that shock is necessary to achievement – he cited
> Wordsworth, whose young revolutionary ideals had such a
> shock when he saw the French Revolution in practice that it
> made a great poet of him for 10 years, and then drove him out
> of active life altogether after which he inevitably deteriorated.
> Perhaps unconsciously he was explaining his own new
> absorption in politics as necessary to his literary life.
>
> Lady Dunsany's diary

I

BY EARLY 1924, the new Nobel Laureate could define his Dublin life to
Quinn.

Politics are amusing and don't take much of my time. I am pressing upon the
Government the appointment of an Advisory Committee of Artists, and have got
Orpen, Shannon and Lavery to promise to act upon that Committee, I think I shall
succeed. I am also trying to get designs for Irish lace improved, but do not yet know
what success I shall have. In the Senate I speak as little upon politics as is possible,
reserving myself for the things I understand. Dublin's social life is becoming interesting, various classes wanting to meet each other, and not knowing how.[1]

While he admitted this could produce horribly contrived occasions, where
'carrying on conversation was like shaking a sack of wet sand', it is clear that
he was settling into the life he had made. The routine between Merrion
Square, the Senate, Dublin clubland, and Ballylee had replaced the old axis
once fixed between Woburn Buildings and Coole. Weekends with the
Jamesons at Sutton House, or at Dunsany Castle, alternated with his efforts
to cultivate a circle among younger intellectuals, a constituency which
included a growing number of disillusioned republicans. The time was ripe,
WBY told Dulac, for performances of the sort of elite theatre they both
believed in. 'The psychological moment has come, for Dublin is reviving
after the Civil War, and self government is creating a little stir of excitement.
People are trying to found a new society. Politicians want to be artistic, and
artistic people to meet politicians, and so on.' He ironically urged Dulac to

find a hostess with genius, wealth, and an Irish ancestor; she could come to Dublin and do great things.[2]

Such letters pass over something already evident in early 1924: an organized reaction against the kind of latitudinarianism and heterodoxy which WBY had always been held to represent. This would soon produce yet another public row focused upon the theatre. But resentment against the unique and prominent position he held in public life was, for the moment, concentrated upon his political pronouncements. The *Leader*, still an enemy, opposed his appointment as a senator, and he was an object of suspicion to others as well. From the end of 1923 the editor of the *Catholic Bulletin*, Timothy Corcoran, set himself to expose the pretensions and ambitions of WBY as explosively as D. P. Moran had ever done, borrowing his predecessor's terms of abuse but without Moran's occasional quirky sympathy for the overall enterprise in which the embattled poet was engaged. In December 1923 WBY's public statement about education and libraries allowed the *Bulletin*'s first leader free range over WBY's entire oeuvre:

Mr William Butler Yeats, having recently added to his English Civil List pension for poetical writings a much larger annual sum from the pockets of Irish ratepayers, and given no special value in exchange for it, has now joined the new Ascendancy movement, a criticism of Gaelic Ireland. Hence many persons were astonished, and a good deal more than astonished, to find him lecturing, on literature in general and on himself in particular, on behalf of the Central Catholic Library Committee . . . The pensioner poet has long made it quite clear that he has no use for Christianity, and that he prefers, both on aesthetic and on ethical grounds, if you please, the pagan past.

The *Bulletin* was incensed not only by WBY's importation of 'neo-pagan, materialist, agnostic, freemason' influences into the 'school hall of a Catholic Convent' but by the presence there of 'a large number of Catholic nuns', conveyed 'by motors and otherwise', to hear the thought of someone whose 'objections to the influence of Catholic truth on Catholic life in Ireland are frank and specific'. This theological point was ingeniously illustrated by reference to lines from *The Land of Heart's Desire*, but the *Bulletin*'s essential point was political. WBY's pronouncements before the upheavals of 1916 were triumphantly brought to witness, deliberately discounting all his efforts to reposition himself since then.

Not a few of Mr Yeats' audience in the Catholic Convent Hall, in the middle of November, 1923, must have come from those Catholic Irish families whom he treated to derisive scorn in his 'September, 1913', as composed of persons who –

> 'fumble in the greasy till,
> And add the halfpence to the pence,
> And prayer to shivering prayer',

and whom he told, in that month and year, that 'Romantic Ireland's dead and gone,' and that 'the delirium of the brave' had vanished with it. It may be a lesson to them – it has been no lesson to W. B. Yeats – that less than three years later Padraic Pearse was writing to his mother his final lines, opening with a very different note from the cultured paganism of the lecturer of 1923:

> 'Dear Mary, thou who saw thy first-born Son
> Go forth to die amidst the scorn of men.'

And Michael Mallin [executed in 1916] wrote on such a morning: 'Una, my little one, be a nun. Joseph, my little man, be a priest if you can.' Very different indeed, is such a note from the writings of one who told the Irish people that they 'have dried the marrow from the bone' by their concept that 'men were born to pray and save.' This is the philosophy that in its own pitiable audacity of irreverence wants the restoration of a paganism that will look on serenely while 'God stands winding his lonely horn.'[3]

From this point, nearly every issue of the *Bulletin* pursued its vendetta against the 'New Ascendancy', which it saw epitomized by people like WBY, Gogarty, Plunkett, and Russell, and entrenched in institutions such as the Royal Irish Academy, Trinity College, and the Senate. The Nobel Prize, and Gogarty's florid congratulations to WBY on behalf of the Senate, provided further good copy in January:

Senator Gogarty directs attention to the fact that on this issue there was recently a tussle between the English colony in Ireland, and the English of England, for the substantial sum provided by a deceased anti-Christian manufacturer of dynamite. It is common knowledge that the line of recipients of the Nobel prize shows that a reputation for Paganism in thought and word is a very considerable advantage in the sordid annual race for money, engineered, as it always is, by clubs, coteries, salons and cliques. Paganism in prose or in poetry has, it seems, its solid cash value; and if a poet does not write tawdry verse to make his purse heavier, he can be brought by his admirers to where money is, whether in the form of an English pension, or in extracts from the Irish taxpayer's pocket, or in the Stockholm dole.[4]

But the really sinister development, in the *Bulletin*'s view, was the imposition of WBY's work as an accepted model of literary Irishness.

The New Ascendancy has very skilfully secured itself various underground approaches towards official power, and is busy in constructing new political lines through them. Already Senator William Butler Yeats has been imposed on Irish schools as the model literary man. This has been done since 1922, and quite recently he has declared himself as deeply influenced by what we must call the perverse lunacies of Emmanuel Swedenborg. It needs little perspicacity to see that through the tunnel so obligingly constructed to admit Senator Pollexfen Yeats, other literary personages, true to type as above, will soon be found advancing. Has it not been said, by the literary agency of their tribe, that the re-discovery of the Gaelic culture created them, the exponents of Anglo-Irish literature? Davis, Mangan and Mitchel are abolished, and the new Pagan school ascends instead into national influence, as the real and positive outcome of the Gaelic Revival.[5]

Thus, for all wby's hopes of 'a new genuine society being born', where 'all we wanted to do begins to seem possible',[6] the ancient battalions of the turn-of-the-century *Kulturkampf* were wheeled into place once more.

And his own ancient genius for impartially irritating all quarters was equally unabated. He was unable to trim the sails of his magnificent conversational abilities, even for people like the deeply devout minister for Defence, General Mulcahy. wby ill-advisedly told the general of Cardinal Vaughan's reply when reproached for living in a luxury which contrasted with the life of Christ: 'It would be presumptuous of me to put myself on a level with my maker.' 'A shadow passed over Mulcahy's face,' wby told Gregory sadly. 'I think I shock those people, they don't respond.'[7] To respectable nationalist Ireland, wby's idiosyncratic style of slightly bohemian grandeur seemed archaic, affected, and un-Irish. Yet Unionists of a less accommodating (and less intelligent) stamp than Andrew Jameson still could not abide his politics. 'It is often pathetic to see great minds finding the most ingenious excuses for murder,' wrote Lady Dunsany in her journal, after wby and George visited them in March. 'It makes for tolerance no doubt but also for insincerity.'[8] Even with the civil war over, Dublin life had its pressures and tensions: it took its toll on George (whom Lady Dunsany found 'practical, appreciative and not a shadow'), and she became ill in April, probably the result of accumulated strain. 'You have been working too hard & taking no care of yourself,' wby told her. He removed himself to Coole, which could indicate thoughtfulness, or the opposite; she spent several weeks recuperating in England.[9]

Finally, early March 1924 saw the excitement of what appeared to be a threatened army mutiny, though the would-be mutineers were disaffected old Collins men rather than irredentist republicans. An ultimatum was presented to the government, demanding army representation in Cabinet. wby had been involved in alerting the government to military disaffection, through his eccentric friend Dermott MacManus, fairy folklorist, occultist, and Free State army officer, and in the early stages of the crisis used his good offices with the reputed 'strong man' of the government, Kevin O'Higgins. A confidential letter from Colonel Jephson O'Connell, director of Inspection in the army, shows that both wby and Jameson were involved as early as the previous September. O'Connell had been brought by MacManus to see wby and tell him of ominous developments in the army;

according to a memorandum drawn up by O'Connell, which did not name WBY, 'it was decided that he and another senator [Jameson] should approach the Minister for Home Affairs [O'Higgins] to discuss the whole affair'. WBY's papers show that both he and George took a close interest in the crisis. The IRB had been much involved, and possibly WBY's ancient Fenian associations may have drawn him in.[10] For all his avowed determination to stay out of political controversy, he anxiously canvassed information: dining at the Glenavys on 11 March, the Yeatses met O'Higgins, and talked of nothing else. It apparently pleased WBY to be seen as a channel for communication and part of the web of political intrigue spun between the Dáil, the government, the 'Independent' senators, and – perhaps – some discontented ex-gunmen. A week later, at the point when resignations were being demanded, WBY cast a horoscope to find out 'what will the eventual outcome of the current crisis be?' The stars foretold that General Mulcahy, minister for Defence, would resign, and so it turned out. There was to be no post-revolutionary *coup d'état* and the would-be mutiny was defused. Tension remained high, especially after dissident republicans (dressed in Free State uniform) opened fire on an unarmed British naval party arriving at Cobh, County Cork, killing one person and injuring several; WBY gave notice of a motion of protest in the Senate, but did not turn up to sponsor it. In the end the mutiny scare was used by WBY's friend O'Higgins 'to undermine the militarist-republican wing within the regime',[11] a project with which WBY was deeply sympathetic. It was a time for taking stock of what the recent revolution had really meant: and whether it was really over.

This was as true in the theatre as anywhere else. WBY's remarks about the Abbey at Stockholm had been purposefully vague concerning recent developments, but, for all the financial travails and hopes for a state-aided rescue, it was going through something of a renaissance. This was in part due to a new generation of actors, such as F. J. McCormick, Barry Fitzgerald, Arthur Shields, and Eileen Crowe, described by the *Dublin Magazine* in April 1926 as 'the best company by far the Abbey has had'.[12] And their talents were met by the brilliance of a new playwright, seen by many as Synge's successor.

Sean O'Casey had been first noticed by the Abbey in November 1921. Though his early efforts were rejected, Gregory in particular encouraged his gift for characterization and his ear for dialogue. O'Casey, a communist in the process of rejecting extremist nationalism, had grown up a poor Protestant in the Dublin tenements (if not in quite as deprived circumstances as he later implied); in April 1923 his first Abbey success, *The Shadow of a Gunman*, owed something to Synge in its flights of lyrical language undercut by salty idiom, and also in the protagonist's fantasy-identification with violence.[13] It provided the Abbey with its most successful first night since *Blanco Posnet*, a hint that controversy was expected. The *Shadow* did not, as it happened, offend the guardians of either political or religious probity, and brought in a considerable profit. But this was eclipsed by O'Casey's next triumph, *Juno and the Paycock*, a huge success in the first week of March 1924. Gregory thought it 'a wonderful and terrible play of futility, of irony, humour, tragedy'. At once utilizing and subverting the convention of melodrama, it gave Sara Allgood one of her greatest parts as 'Juno' and conveyed a distinct scepticism about the efficacy of the Irish revolution, as well as the tragedy of the civil war. One astonishing aspect of the play was the author's readiness to expose what he saw as the self-serving posturing of both sides in that embarrassingly recent conflict; equally striking was the readiness of the Dublin public to hear this message. O'Casey's success brought money to the box office and attracted London reviewers to the Abbey once more. The playwright himself began to turn up at Monday evenings in Merrion Square (where on 10 March the talk was of the army mutiny, the delay of the Fishery bill in the Senate, and the uses of hashish). He did not fit in.[14]

Nor is it likely that O'Casey enjoyed the Drama League's performance of *At the Hawk's Well* reverently put on in the Merrion Square drawing room on 30 and 31 March (with Frank Fay, of all people, as the Old Man). wby had decisively argued against accepting O'Casey's first play, and did not record an opinion about *The Shadow of a Gunman*, which probably seemed to him another instalment of 'realism'. His own contrasting ideas about dramatic production were epitomized in the Introduction to *Plays and Controversies*, published at this time. *Juno* took him by surprise, 'reminding him', Gregory recorded, 'of Tolstoi: he said when he talked of that imperfect first play "Casey was bad in writing of the vices of the rich which he knows nothing about, but he thoroughly understands the vices of the poor."'[15] This was not a good sign. For one thing, neither of the playwright's names was 'Casey' (he was born 'Cassidy', and adopted 'O'Casey'); for another, the play is certainly not about the vices of the poor. O'Casey and wby were fated to mutual misunderstanding. Both masked shyness and insecurity with assertiveness (and a certain amount of personal fantasy), both nursed preoccupations about social standing and easily imagined slights, both were uncompromising about their artistic creations. The particular kind of grandeur now wrapped around wby like a cloak might have been calculated to drive O'Casey into silent resentment. Any chance of a deeper relationship was probably also inhibited by Gregory's adoption of O'Casey, whose characteristics were adapted to please her just as certainly as they were guaranteed to annoy wby. In 1924 the younger writer seemed to be taken on and taken up by her, just as wby had been a quarter-century before: soon he was staying at Coole, determinedly adhering to his cloth cap and collarless shirt, talking happily at length about deprivation. Her grandchildren and her servants saw this as an irritating affectation, but Gregory could not have enough of it.

In one way, however, O'Casey was on the side of the angels as far as WBY was concerned, because his work seemed likely to annoy the guardians of morality. When *Juno* was taken to Cork, local pressures forced the players to remove 'everything that made any reference to religion' and to rewrite the part of the plot that depended upon the seduction of an unmarried girl.[16] The public morality of the Free State was, by 1924, specifically and unsurprisingly Catholic, with Cosgrave's government deliberately expressing fidelity to the Pope. Confessionalism was implicit in the legislation for censoring films introduced in 1923, after aggressive lobbying from the Catholic Truth Society and the Irish Vigilance Association. (WBY subsequently served on the Appeal Committee.) Ominously, a campaign against 'evil literature' followed, pursued in the hierarchy's Lenten pastorals as well as in the Catholic press (which extended far beyond the *Bulletin*[17]). Since, to these authorities, 'evil literature' included information about contraception, the debate would rapidly centre upon civil rights for the half-million Protestants within the Free State: thus from an early point the censorship debate took on a sectarian complexion. This would become marked around the time of the Censorship bill at the end of the decade, but the writing appeared on the wall in 1924. And as regards 'evil' literature in the sense of what was generally called 'smut', the issue had been focused on the publication of an Irish masterpiece in Paris two years before: *Ulysses*.

The publication of Joyce's great book had genuinely excited WBY: the intense, handsome, scornful wunderkind he had helped twenty years before was now a figure of acknowledged European significance. Joyce had never let himself become a protégé, and WBY had turned down his play *Exiles* for the Abbey five years before, but his literary fortunes had remained close to WBY's heart. He had lobbied for Joyce's pension, and the fact that Pound and Eliot were fellow admirers gave Joyce a special position. The scandal over the prosecution of the *Little Review* in New York during February 1921 for publishing extracts, and John Quinn's key role in the defence of the published book, was cause for even closer involvement. Reading *Ulysses* at Ballylee in the summer of 1922, WBY had shared his enthusiasm with several correspondents. He told Pound that he could see the 'immense importance' of Joyce's book, and read it 'a few pages . . . at a time as if he [*sic*] were a poem. Some passages have great beauty, lyric beauty, even in the fashion of my generation, and the whole book incites to philosophy.'[18] On his visit to London in the subsequent December, he talked excitedly about Joyce and his work throughout a three-hour lunch with Eliot, who at last 'charmed' him.[19] Once settled in Merrion Square, WBY had sent a graceful letter to Joyce, inviting him to come and stay, and meet his new generation of admirers in Dublin. Joyce refused, but allowed himself to be pleased.[20] WBY's belief in the genius of the great leviathan published in Paris was genuine, and if he subsequently wrote about it authoritatively without having read every word, he was not the only one. On 8 November 1923, responding to a quintessentially pompous undergraduate address on 'The Modern Novel' at the Philosophical Society in Trinity, WBY contradicted the speaker's assertion that *Ulysses* in 'reaching the ultimate limit of realism ... was open to the charge of dullness'. His countering argument was both forceful and carefully historicized:

James Joyce was certainly as voluminous as Johnson's dictionary and as foul as Rabelais; but he was the only Irishman who had the intensity of the great novelist. The novel was not his [Mr Yeats's] forte. All he could say was there was the intensity of the great writer in Joyce. The miracle was possibly there; that was all he felt he had the right to say; and, perhaps, the intensity was there for the same reason as the intensity of Tolstoi and Balzac.

When James Joyce began to write in Ireland they had not come to their recent peril – or the robbery and the murder and the things that came with it – but he thought that the shadow of peril was over everyone when men were driven to intensity. The book *Ulysses* was a description of a single day in Dublin twenty years ago. He thought it was possible that Ireland had had that intensity out of which great literature might arise and it was possible James Joyce was merely the first drop of a shower.[21]

He was probably neither surprised nor displeased that the seconder of the address, Professor Magennis of the National University, nonetheless referred to *Ulysses* as 'moral filth'. Moreover, endorsing Joyce carried the added gratification of aligning him against the kind of English middlebrow opinion he despised (Alfred Noyes, Edmund Gosse). And the opposition the book aroused in Ireland, given the gathering storm over censorship in the early 1920s, was an augury of further conflicts.

Without a censorship Act in operation, the book could not actually be banned, though Irish booksellers generally refused to handle it. The issue was brought to the fore by the British authorities, not the Irish: in May 1924 499 copies were seized at Folkestone by the Customs as obscene and apparently destroyed, and Pound – spoiling for a fight, and for publicity – pressed WBY to take the matter up. WBY saw the sensitivity of his own position at once, pointing out to Olivia Shakespear that he and Russell were already 'accused of being in a conspiracy to destroy the Catholic faith through Irish education'.[22] As long as the 'ecclesiastical terrier' was objecting to authors like Tennyson, it was 'hunting in its dreams', but to invoke *Ulysses* would awake it in earnest. To Pound, he sent a temporizing letter pointing out that 'all our liberties are surreptitious', and that though he would talk to 'the intelligent head of a department', he could probably do nothing. 'You could probably get copies sent in here if nobody knows anything about it but it would be ruinous to let the fact be whispered in Government offices. Here we have a few intelligent men who have to keep always on the watch not to give clerical ignorance any opportunity of attack.' He inquired politely if the seizures had been made under the League of Nations Charter. Pound replied in terms that do not lend themselves to paraphrase:

???? I know that England her ministers, her academic committees are a mass of moribund filth and that the League of Nations was invented by one of the worst fahrts nature ever let loose from her copious and inexhaustable arse-hole.

WOT I wanted to know from you was whether free and assassinous Ireland was still under Henglands bhloody thumb: or whether she acted for her evergreen and bhlossoming self in these little matters;

Does a manifestation of bigoted idiocy on the part of Gawd's own boss of the traffic in Southampton, imply an identical or DIFFERENT idiocy on that of Mikky Grogann boss of the port of Cork?? Or wd, the noted conthrariety of yr. esteemed comphatriots incline them to insist of having something because England thought it unsuitable to their consumption.

In reply WBY straight-facedly promised to 'call on somebody, probably [Desmond] FitzGerald . . . armed with your very lucid and persuasive letter'.[23] It is unlikely that he did so. As he told Pound, though a prosecution could technically be brought against *Ulysses* in Ireland under British law, this had not yet taken place. It was obtainable in the Irish Bookshop, and indeed on display in the window, and sleeping terriers should be let lie.[24] But the questions explosively raised by Pound were important. And they propelled WBY to issue Pound a pressing invitation to come to Dublin – as an official 'Guest of the Nation' at the forthcoming 'Tailteann Games' in August. He particularly wanted his erratic and irascible ex-acolyte on hand

when I crown in the name of the Irish Academy certain books – the best Irish products in that line of manufacture for the last three years, produced by citizens of the Free State living in Ireland. I shall have a small Committee acting with me, selected by myself and you will hear Joyce sufficiently commended I hope, though certainly not crowned, for he is excluded by the terms of reference. You will also probably be invited to certain country houses, and will be generally made much of, and meet everybody who is to be met, and have admirable opportunities for your usual violence and brutality.[25]

It must be a matter of lasting regret that Pound eventually refused the invitation – though he continued to fulminate against Irish censorship, demanding of Desmond FitzGerald 'ARE you a nation or a dung hill?' and advising him to 'keep condoms and classics in sepharte parts of your law-book ?!!!!'.[26] But the fact of the invitation, and a similar (though equally unsuccessful) solicitation sent to Joyce, shows that WBY was already prepar-ing to occupy high public ground in the battle against censorship, and to nail his colours to the mast of avant-garde outspokenness.

II

The Tailteann Games, or 'Aonach Tailteann', were not the most obvious forum for such a demonstration. This festival was originally planned – under the chairmanship of the postmaster-general, J. J. Walsh – as a kind of national Olympic games, crossed with a cultural congress. The rising min-ister Desmond FitzGerald, whose sensibilities were more exquisite than those of his colleagues, thought it promised to be a 'nightmare.'[27] But the draft invitation to 'Guests of the Nation' produced by WBY as chairman of the invitations committee, suggests that visions of Stockholm still swam in his mind.

Now that Ireland is once more free, she has decided to resume such old traditions and ancient customs as are compatible with the circumstance of modern life. From time out of mind a Tri-annual athletic festival was held at Tailteann, which gave the youth of Ireland its poets and craftsmen an opportunity to show their skill and it is intended to revive this festival next August. As it is the desire of the People of Ireland that this, their greatest traditional celebration, be attended by representa-tive men in Science, Literature, and Arts from different countries, the committee has the honour to invite you, as its guest, for 'The Festival of Tailteann', and asks you to choose any date which may be convenient to you for coming to Ireland between 1st. and 18th. August.[28]

Lennox Robinson gleefully told Thomas MacGreevy that 'W.B., full of fresh intrigues', had settled the guest list, claiming that it included Picasso, Benavente, Rossignol, and Pound ('Who will come? Only Ezra, I bet').[29] Gogarty, as usual involved in the wings, further fantasized about inviting D'Annunzio and Sigmund Freud, and subsequently turning Freud loose on both D'Annunzio and Yeats. As it was, the guest list was distinctly more staid (Chesterton, Belloc, Lutyens, Compton Mackenzie, Sir Thomas Lipton, the Laverys, John Devoy, the foreign minister of Sweden, the Persian prince Mirza Riza Khan, the ambassador to the League of Nations, and the legendary cricketer Maharaja of Nawanagar, K. S. Ranjitsinghji, inevitably accompanied by C. B. Fry).[30] The Games were timed to overlap with the Horse Show, to maximize their social cachet, but WBY's determination to import high culture was less successful. Pound's main interest in coming had been to force on the Abbey his new opera based on the works of François Villon, but this was a non-starter. More prosaically, he also wanted to acquire an Irish passport.[31] Neither project bore fruit.

For WBY, the chief point was to honour great Irish artists, however controversial. He called a special meeting of the committee to press for an official invitation to Joyce but – as expected – it was turned down with horror, though WBY enjoyed the pleasure of outraging his fellow committee member, the Marquis MacSwiney, chamberlain to the Pope, a figure who himself might have come out of a Joycean fantasy. WBY invited Joyce in any case as a private guest to Merrion Square for the festivities. 'You will find a great many admirers of your genius in Dublin and altogether a very different city from the city you remember.'[32] Even if Joyce had not been undergoing a series of eye operations, he would hardly have come. If he had done so, the opportunities for official Dublin to snub him would have been limitless, but WBY wanted to run the gauntlet.

All in all, the response from distinguished exiles was not positive: Shaw was equally uncooperative.[33] The Games opened on 31 August, threatened by a strike of municipal workers and a 'barefoot march' of the unemployed through central Dublin, but in the event these recalcitrants were relegated to the background. (De Valera was prudently kept locked up until the celebrations ended.) Crowds of up to 60,000 assembled, and a profit of £3,000 was made.[34] The entertainments included an industrial exhibition, a John McCormack concert, plays (including *Cathleen ni Houlihan*), receptions and garden-parties; the athletics took in tennis, golf, clay-bird shooting, cycling, gymnastics, and archery, as well as hurling. There were aerial displays, and music by the Garda Síochána band. Gogarty's 'Tailteann Ode' addressed to the athletes, a grisly exercise in pseudo-classicism, was much reproduced and sung by a massed choir at the Theatre Royal. The organizer in chief, J. J. Walsh, defined the *raison d'être* of the Games as 'racial pride, national outlook, love of the Homeland': though the original Games had lapsed some time in the ninth century, hopes of reviving them 'never died in the Irish people' and this was their apotheosis.[35]

WBY's opportunities for using such an occasion as a celebration of literary experimentalism, or a platform for his own political pronouncements, were clearly limited, but he manipulated events as best he could. The first chance he seized was in his speech at the Tailteann Banquet on 2 August, proposing the health of 'Our Guests'. The opening remarks were apposite but, for the occasion, surprisingly sombre:

In our long struggle for National Independence our people have been scattered through the world, in the seventeenth century our nobility, and in the nineteenth our poor; and I see round me many representatives from those countries of the Old World into which our nobility carried their swords, and many representatives of that New World into which after our Great Famine and in the years of poverty that follow[ed] our poor have carried their labour. It was natural and fitting that we should call you together now that at last we are an independent nation, a victor at last in the struggle of centuries. The nation is as it were a young man just entering upon his property, and of whom it is impossible to say whether he is a wise man or a fool, whether he will enlarge his estate, or a mere spendthrift. He is celebrating his coming of age and asks the good will of his neighbour. Certainly he finds himself in a very difficult and troubled world.[36]

If Ireland had attained Home Rule under Gladstone, that world would have been pleasanter: in 1886, WBY recalled, Churton Collins at Oxford had prophesied to him that the twentieth century would hold no more war and no more poverty. This was a general belief held by educated opinion, based on 'physical science and democratic politics'. 'There will never be another war, that was our opium dream.' This implicit paraphrase of 'Nineteen Hundred and Nineteen' was followed by a yet more ominous passage, which would be quoted against him in the future.

That is all gone, and Ireland celebrates its coming of age in such a different world. We do not believe that war is passing away and we are not certain that the world is growing better. We even tell ourselves that the idea of progress is quite modern, that it has been in the world but two hundred years, nor are we quite as stalwart as we used to be in our democratic politics. Psychologists and statisticians in Europe and America are attacking the foundations, and as a great popular leader has said to an applauding multitude, 'We will trample upon the decomposing body of the Goddess of Liberty.'

This invocation of Mussolini may seem jarring, but it recalls his comments to Shakespear about 'all eyes turning to Italy' and carries through some of the implications of the conclusion to 'The Bounty of Sweden'. How far the repudiation of democracy applied to Ireland was as yet not quite clear, but it was hinted at in a passage partly deleted from his draft of the speech and not given to the banquet audience. This began by referring to the industrial unrest which had nearly sabotaged the opening of the Games.

It may be that some in our own town have had some similar thoughts this week on discovering that public life was at least normal as the word normal is understood in Europe today. We have exchanged revolver shots for strikes, illegal violence for the legal violence of a small minority that has claimed the right to deprive of the necessities of life and health many thousands.

This attack on labour militancy contrasted strongly with his attitude during the employers' lock-out of 1913, when he had taken the workers' side against William Martin Murphy.[37] But it was only the preliminary to looking into the dark future:

It is impossible not to ask oneself to what great task of the nations we have been summoned in this transformed world where there is so much that is obscure and terrible. I see about me the representatives of nations which have suffered incomparably more than we have, more than we may ever suffer. Our few months of war and civil war must seem in their eyes but a light burden. To them, as to us perhaps, it seems that the world can never be the same. Is it not possible perhaps that the stream has turned backward, and that a dozen generations to come will have for their task, not the widening of liberty, but recovery from its errors: that they will set their hearts upon the building of authority, the restriction of discipline, the discovery of a life sufficiently heroic to live without opium dreams.[38]

Even without this addition, his speech was marvellously at odds with the general tone of the evening. It made a strange preliminary to welcoming 'two of the most famous cricketers who ever lived', the Brazilian minister to the Vatican, a Persian poet, the Swedish ambassador to the Court of St James, and a veteran Fenian.[39] The Maharaja (who owned the great Galway salmon fishery of Ballinahinch Castle) replied with graceful self-deprecation, as a 'tongue-tied son of the Orient', and other speeches of varying degrees of adroitness followed from Devoy, Chesterton, Lord Glenavy, General Mulcahy, and the governor-general. WBY's political gauntlet was left lying on the table.

However, before the Games closed he mounted another challenge. Under the patronage of the Aonach Tailteann, the Royal Irish Academy presented a number of literary awards, and here WBY could not be stymied by the Marquis MacSwiney: the judges numbered himself, Russell and Robinson. In fact, the idea originated with the Nobel Laureate himself.[40] Unsurprisingly, the three gold medals went to Stephen MacKenna for his Plotinus translation (he refused it on republican grounds), James Stephens for his *Deirdre*, and Gogarty for his Cuala volume *An Offering of Swans*. On WBY's initiative a fourth prize was raised by subscription: a financial award to 'a poet under thirty, a writer of promise rather than achievement'. This appropriately went to Iseult's wayward husband, Francis Stuart, for *We Have Kept the Faith*, in which WBY found 'no perfect poem, [but] constant beauty of metaphor and strangeness of thought and so no lucky accident, but a personality'.[41] Stuart, a good learner in begrudgery if little else, remembered the ceremony as 'having the mixture of the serious and the ludicrous, the innocence and the falsity, that he came to associate with Yeats'.[42]

Joyce was excluded by reason of non-residence, but WBY took the opportunity to single out *Ulysses* for praise, in a judgement reprinted by the *Irish Statesman*: 'We feel, however, that it is our duty to say that Mr James Joyce's book, though as obscene as Rabelais, and therefore forbidden by law in England and the United States, is more indubitably a work of genius than any prose written by an Irishman since the death of Synge.' This was amplified by a subsequent piece in the *Irish Statesman*, regretting that non-resident Irish writers were ineligible, so that Joyce could not be honoured as he deserved. 'I would like him to know', WBY told Pound, 'that we all recognised his claim would have been paramount but for the [terms of] reference.'[43]

The ecclesiastical terrier was to be woken up after all, and the speech certainly acted as a bugle to the hounds of the *Catholic Bulletin*. The Academy was already firmly placed on the *Bulletin*'s personal Index as an organ of Ascendancy elitism: the election of 'the only and inevitable Senator Pollexfen Yeats' to that body had been denounced in a leading editorial.[44] The 'recent literary manoeuvre' at the Tailteann celebration was duly denounced. While Gogarty's plot to import 'Maeterlinck, d'Annunzio and others of their kind' had come to nothing, he and WBY had commandeered the Academy for their mutual admiration enterprise, and as a forum for trumpeting the merits of 'obscene' works. The literature advocated by the Yeats circle was

confined to the petty little field of the Anglo-Irish; and there is no use now in attempting to impose that on the mass of the Irish people as being at all a genuine article worth preserving in Irish culture. It is an upstart of yesterday, alien in source, in models, and in such little inspiration as it can boast; and many of its avowed leaders are simply exhibits of literary putrescence.[45]

WBY's poems were again hauled into the dock, notably 'The Gift', and – a favourite theme of the *Bulletin*'s – the verses on George Pollexfen which celebrated his Masonic funeral. ('What a touch was lost in the delicate distinctiveness of the Dawson Street awards, when officers of the Ascendancy Academy failed to remember that Molesworth Street [the Masonic offices], hard by, could furnish Acacia spray!')

Freemasons were rather tired game by now, but Joyce was a comparatively new quarry, and the *Bulletin* truculently stood by its 'criticism of the activities of Senator Yeats' and his 'frank contempt of the Irish people'. Most of all, its fury was directed at the 'obtrusive laudation' bestowed at the Aonach 'on what was avowedly obscene and repulsive'.[46] The *Bulletin* was supported by the *Irish Monthly*, which considered even *Deirdre* 'sheer filth to all who hold an ideal of chaste manhood and womanhood', and believed Joyce to be 'afflicted with a shameful mania; but his works are but little read by sane folk'.[47] To the *Bulletin*'s delight, a more unexpected ally joined in – Professor W. F. Trench, who had succeeded to Dowden's Trinity College chair of English instead of WBY in 1910. This ancient rival wrote to the *Statesman* to protest at WBY's praise of *Ulysses*:

J. Joyce rakes hell and the sewers for dirt to throw at the fair face of life, and for poison to make beauty shrivel and die. Now, the Dublin aesthete discovers Joyce, and Dr Yeats undertakes that no citizen of Dublin shall fail to know his name. In season and out of season he has proclaimed him a genius . . .

Joyce's genius was 'bestial', and Trench pleaded with WBY 'to cry halt to the aesthete's publicity campaign on behalf of that which is so foul'.[48] But the 'campaign' was now well under way. It would soon become evident that even while making his controversial pronouncements at the Tailteann Games, WBY had been meditating another salvo in the battle against puritanism. This exploded just after the distinguished visitors left Dublin.

III

In June he had heard from Iseult and her husband that they wanted to start a radical new review, with the poet F. R. Higgins and the novelist Liam O'Flaherty. Francis Stuart, WBY would later say, was 'the moving spirit'. As WBY retailed it to Shakespear, he had originally suggested that they trump the forces of Catholic reaction by declaring that they stood for the doctrine of the immortality of the soul, whereas 'most bishops and all bad writers' were essentially atheists. On 20 June the Stuarts had visited him with the news that they had adopted his suggestion '& been suppressed by the priests for blasphemy': in fact, much as with Joyce's *Dubliners*, the printer had refused to handle the sheets ('no mention must be made of the Blessed Virgin'). The Nobel Laureate and the Young Turks had sworn alliance together. 'My dream is a wild paper by the young which will make enemies everywhere & suffer suppression, I hope a number of times, for the logical assertion with all fitting deductions of the immortality of the soul.'[49] He told much the same story a week later to Gregory, adding, 'now they are to print in England & I am advising generally . . . If they have the courage to fight on I will write for them regularly – I have sent them a contribution as it is – & I think it may be the start of a great deal. It is about the only cause for which I am prepared to turn journalist.'[50]

This may be slightly disingenuous. It is clear that WBY wrote the manifesto which formed the editorial of the first issue of the short-lived review *To-Morrow*, which appeared in August: it repeated exactly the argument he expounded to Shakespear and was written on 22 June, two days after the 'deputation' visited him. The content of the pages first rejected by the printer is unknown, but they probably did not contain 'The Madonna of Slieve Dun', a story by Lennox Robinson about a country girl who is raped and subsequently believes she is chosen to re-enact the Incarnation. This, like WBY's contribution, was acquired after the June meeting.[51] (It had been written thirteen years before and already published in the US in 1920.) But the editorial contributed anonymously from Merrion Square deserves full quotation, from the draft which WBY retained.

To all artists and writers

We are Catholics, but of the school of Julius the second and the Medichean Popes who ordered Michael Angelo and Raphael to paint upon the walls of the Vatican and upon the ceilings the doctrine of the Platonic Academy of Florence, the reconciliation of Gallilee and Parnassus. We proclaim Michael Angelo the most orthodox of men because he set upon the tombs of the Meccidi Dawn and Night, vast forms shadowing the shape of antediluvian portraits and the lust of the goat, the whole handiwork of God, the horn of his abundance.

We proclaim, that we can forgive the sinner but abhor the atheist, and that we count among the atheists bad writers and the Bishops of all denominations. 'The Holy Spirit is an intellectual fountain' and if the Bishops believed the holy spirit would have descended upon them and soon shewn itself in decoration and architecture of their churches, in their daily manners and their written style. What devout man can read the pastorals of our hierarchy without horror at a denial of God that shows in a style rancid, coarse and vulgar like that of the daily papers? We condemn modern art and [letters] because no man can create, as did Homer, Sophocles, Shakespeare, who does not believe, but with all his blood and nerve, that man's soul is immortal; because the evidence is plain to all men, that where that belief has declined men have turned from creation to photography. We condemn, though not without sympathy, those who seek escape from banal mechanism, through technical investigation and experiment. We proclaim that these can bring no escape, for new form comes from new subject matter and new subject matter must flow from the human soul restored to all its courage, all its audacity. We dismiss all demagogues & call back the soul to its kingly throne, & declare that it can do whatever it pleases, being made, as antiquity affirmed, from the imperishable substance of the stars.[52]

To experienced readers of WBY, the piece needed no signature. Neoplatonic secret tradition, ancient wisdoms, the outflanking of religiosity by invoking the faith of the soul, all are here in his unmistakable polemical style. It also might be read as a self-plagiarism of Martin Hearne's paean to destruction at the close of *The Unicorn from the Stars* ('We will destroy all that can perish! It is only the soul that can suffer no injury. The soul of man is of the imperishable substance of the stars!'). There are also more recent echoes of the sections of *A Vision* currently under construction. But the deliberately offensive note in the attack on the episcopacy is new, and was signalled by the battles into which he had been drawn over the past months. No one would be taken in by the profession that bishops 'of all denominations' were being targeted, and the 'rancid, coarse and vulgar' style can only have meant the *Catholic Bulletin* and its stablemates. If that journal had known of this manifesto, written by 'Senator Pollexfen Yeats' weeks before the Tailteann awards, the endorsement of Joyce would have appeared a venial sin by comparison. As it was, he was preparing to give them even greater cause for outrage when the first issue of *To-Morrow*, printed in Manchester, finally appeared in August.

In the meantime, he pressed the case of the review's editors on a wide range of correspondents, sending circulars, accompanied by explanatory letters, to Ottoline Morrell, Dulac, Shakespear, Pound, Frank Pearce Sturm, L. A. G. Strong, Harriet Monroe, and – mischievously – G. K. Chesterton. The issue of freedom of speech in sexual matters loomed larger and larger, perhaps further galvanized by his experiences on the Film Censorship Appeal Board. 'Yesterday . . . my fellow censors refused a film because a pair of lovers who had lived together without wedlock go through great suffering & are finally married,' he gloomily told Ottoline Morrell. 'The board would only allow the film if the marriage was taken out as that was to admit that sin could end happily. The lovers must be punished. This makes me wish that circular which I sent had contained more of its leading article especially that sentence charging Bishops with atheism.'[53] His own further contribution to *To-Morrow* would bring the question of sexual propriety firmly into the open. 'I do not know what their paper will be like', he told Sturm just before it appeared. 'I have seen nothing but the leading article.'[54] This was untrue. He had also handed them another bombshell, and this time a signed one: 'Leda and the Swan', which had been published by Cuala in *The Cat and the Moon* a month before.

The swan motif added fuel to the fire. Gogarty's prize-winning volume had been called *An Offering of Swans*, invoking his gift of a pair of swans to the River Liffey, as a thanksgiving for his rescue from his kidnappers in January 1923. This rather stagey gesture had been much noted in the newspapers: when it took place on 26 April 1924, attended by President Cosgrave as well as WBY and Lennox Robinson, the *Bulletin* described it crisply as 'the swan stunt'.[55] Already incensed by the recent history of swans, poets, and the mutual backslapping of the 'New Ascendancy', the editor was moved to new heights of invective, when a copy of *To-Morrow* fell into his hands:

If Dr Wilbraham Fitzjohn Trench has seen the new issue, 'hell and the sewers' will probably have appeared to him an inadequate phrase: but, above all, he will have seen how Senator W. B. Pollexfen Yeats has chosen to reply to the remonstrance from Dowden's successor as Professor of English Literature. The new literary cesspool of the clique of aesthetes, prize-winners or laurel-bearers at the recent games, blazons under its titles: 'Contributors include W. B. Yeats, Lennox Robinson'. The former contributes a 'poem', which exhibits Senator Pollexfen Yeats in open rivalry with the 'bestial genius' which Senator Yeats has so recently championed. For bestial is the precise and fitting word for this outburst of 'poetry'. The 'swan-motive' has been prominent in the aesthetes' circles for a year or more: it has now found characteristic utterance in the title and texture of these fourteen lines signed 'W. B. Yeats'. To such foul fruition have come the swan-sequence of Coole, of the Liffey; the mutual prefaces, the mutual awards; the posed photographs on the river-side, including Mr Lennox Robinson, Senator Yeats and the Senator who made the offering of Swans to the river, and received from Senator Pollexfen Yeats therefor a wreath of laurel spray. Professor W. F. Trench is answered. We may even say that J. Joyce will be envious when he reads the effort of Yeats, and will call for a more effective rake. 'Hell and the sewers' are not in it. It is when resort is had to the pagan world for inspiration in the 'poetry' of the obscene, that the mere moderns can be outclassed in bestiality.

To Senator Yeats therefore must be accorded the distinction of bringing the Swan Stunt to its quite appropriate climax. The Swan Song which he has uttered will not be forgotten to him.[56]

'Leda' was not the only sexual shock contained in *To-Morrow*'s two broadsheet pages. 'Colour', a short story by Margaret Barrington (the wife of a Trinity professor, Edmund Curtis), dealt with a love-affair between a black man and a white woman. And as far as the *Bulletin* was concerned, the crowning horror was reserved for 'the repulsiveness and villainy' of Robinson's story, 'a sustained and systematic outrage on all that is holiest in our religion'. As AE resignedly put it, the magazine had given a free hand to 'industrious ghouls . . . trying to make it appear that the whole of Anglo-Irish literature is based on the raping of some-body'.[57]

To-Morrow did not achieve wide circulation, but the fall-out from the detonation was considerable. Robinson had already drawn attention to himself by writing to the *Irish Statesman* complaining about the printers' refusal to set the pages of *To-Morrow* and announcing that it would be printed in England.[58] He probably underestimated the volume of condemnation about to be loosed on his head, though he had had fair warning, since the Talbot Press had already refused to print it in a book of short stories, and the *Nation* had turned it down as indecent. (He had temporarily loosened his ties with the Abbey and – courtesy of Bracken – was now a contributor to the *Observer*.[59]) Gregory, always slightly suspicious about Robinson, took the matter up with George Yeats:

She [George], though she didnt support me when I told him so – is sorry Willie is writing for them, says everyone will recognise the manifesto as his though he doesn't believe they will, and that he has given them his Leda poem and a fine thing among his other poems in the Cuala book, but [it] is, now it is known it goes into *Tomorrow*, being spoken of as something horribly indecent. However she says he was feeling dull in Dublin and it has given him a great deal of amusement.[60]

Her own instinct was more cautious. As soon as she had heard of the *To-Morrow* project she worried about the effect on the Abbey and – implicitly – on the fight for the Lane pictures, though 'they seemed to have faded from his mind'.[61] And all for no purpose 'but to fill the Stuarts' idleness': both she and George may also have thought that Iseult's influence, intentionally or not, usually meant trouble.

They were not wrong. Ernest Blythe told WBY that Cosgrave had contemplated suppressing *To-Morrow* by government order; he was stopped only by O'Higgins (as minister of Justice) remarking that 'the prosecution would merely represent the moral attitude of a certain people and place and time'.[62] Meanwhile the public reverberations from 'The Madonna of Slieve Dun' spread far beyond the *Catholic Bulletin* and the *Irish Rosary*, rocking the Carnegie Library Committee, which employed Robinson as secretary. A committee member, Father Finlay, resigned in protest.[63] The chairman, Provost Bernard of Trinity, decided to force Robinson to go. On the committee support was not forthcoming from AE, who 'hated the story', though he was subjected to an angry visitation from WBY. Gregory reluctantly supported Robinson, as did F. H. O'Donnell, a Catholic member who thought the story both 'beautiful' and true to life. But the provost was determined to press the issue to resignation. He was equally outraged by 'that horrible story about the blacks': Gregory told him it came from Trinity, and, after some incredulity, he decided to haul up the offending Mrs Curtis. But she had, it transpired, just run away with Liam O'Flaherty, and the provost 'got the wrong Professor, and the wrong Professor's wife, "on the carpet".'[64] Driven beyond endurance, on 22 October Bernard threatened his own resignation, hoping to force the beleaguered secretary out. WBY sent Robinson a letter more or less forbidding him to go.

Your desire would be to escape from so much annoyance by that easy act but when you consider public opinion in this country I think you will stay where you are. You have done nothing needing explanation or apology. You have but claimed the same freedom every important writer of Europe has claimed. Neither Flaubert nor Tolstoy, nor Dostoieffsky nor Balzac, nor Anatole France would have thought your theme or your treatment of it illegitimate. Ireland must not be allowed any special privilege of ignorance or cowardice. Even if your resignation helped the Libraries for the moment it would injure them in the end perhaps irreperably because it would injure the position of literature. We must not surrender our freedom to any ecclesiastic.[65]

'Not very wise linking himself with three heretics,' Gregory tartly remarked, 'and they were not paid secretaries of an educational Board.'[66] But WBY saw this letter as yet another manifesto in the threatening public storm, telling Robinson he could put it to any use he liked. This was not the unwilling heretic's intention; he in fact expressed his regret to the committee and dissociated himself from WBY's manifesto ('he was not aware before the issue of the first number of the nature of the paper to which he had contributed it').[67] Nonetheless, the row simmered on. The provost resigned, and Robinson temporarily stayed, but by the end of the year the whole committee had been suspended and the Library movement slowly atrophied. Robinson was saddled with an undeservedly heterodox reputation which would – for instance – raise potential problems over the government's support for the Abbey, exactly as Gregory had feared.[68] WBY, the bit between his teeth, told Gregory that he suggested to the editors that they apply to the Pope for an opinion about the blasphemous nature of 'The Madonna of Slieve Dun'. She may have thought it a joke, but the Stuarts actually drafted a letter to the Holy Office.[69] As for *To-Morrow*, it limped through to a second number, but – according to Gregory – by late November it was 'practically extinct, as it is going to become a Republican paper, and thus cuts off Yeats and L. R. and other "intellectuals" from it, and it from theology'.[70]

This nicely pinpoints WBY's circumscribed position in his efforts to mark out a battleground where he could fight about politics, religion, and free speech. He was seen as inadequately Irish and even pro-imperial by hardline republicans, as a heretic with a cess-pool mind by Catholic zealots, and an intellectual trouble-maker by like-minded ex-Unionists who simply wanted a quiet life. In some ways, his situation in the Dublin of 1924 now curiously echoed that of his youth, when enmeshed in different quarrels in the very different city of thirty years before. But he was now deliberately taking the offensive, and the struggles of the early 1920s showed up a fundamental contradiction in his evolving thought. On the one hand, he wanted intellectual freedom, the artist's traditional right to experiment: on the other, he repudiated what he saw as outworn forms of democracy and dreamed nervously of an authoritarian, coherent rule of life as mediated through politics, invoking an inherited aura of tradition. At about this time, casting his mind back to the intellectual searches and struggles of his youth, he wrote, 'I wished for a system of thought that would leave my imagination free to create as it chose and yet make all that it created, or could create, part of the one history, and that the soul's.'[71] If the subsequent years brought any message, it would be that the fortunes of intellectual freedom were safer with the necessary muddles and compromises of political democracy than with an idealized authoritarianism. But this was not an easy or welcome insight for an astrologer and mystic, surveying the wreckage of war and civil war, and trying to develop a system of philosophical analysis that would make sense of total history. And this was what he was completing in the book of montages that became *A Vision*.

IV

Now, as in his youth, he disappeared to London for a different kind of sustenance, and a different level of admiration. He had been there in July, 'living in museums' and reacting to *Saint Joan* with all the angry ambivalence only Shaw would arouse in him: 'I thought her clearly thought of but obscurely felt & so not beleivable. A woman who has spoken wth God & has no dignity & no simplicity – but is half cockney slut, half nonconformist street preacher. Even the wind does not change for such as she.'[72] English life revolved around Shakespear, Dulac, and weekends at Garsington. Since the Nobel award, his own great reputation could be a barrier to easy enjoyment: both he and Dulac winced when an American newspaperman insisted on an introduction.

Before dinner was served he crossed his hands in front of him & said 'This is the most important evening of my life. I went to Harvard in such & such a year' & then proceeded with his biography. Having finished with it he said 'now I make only one request to you, that you speak to me out of your deepest thought & your deepest emotion.' As you can imagine conversation languished.[73]

There was a more entertaining echo of the world's acclamation when he read John Buchan's *The Three Hostages*, and suspected that he had inspired the character of the villain Dominic Medina ('an Irish poet, who[se] verse is highly finished & very melancholy. He is a hypnotist, a murderer, and an anti-English politician, and has a mother who looks like Maud Gonne as she is today, but I am glad to say he has excellent manners').[74]

After the distraction of the Tailteann Games in August he returned to London for a month, to represent the Dublin Corporation at the lengthy and inconclusive commission on the Lane pictures. He also worked on his philosophy book at the British Museum, convincing himself yet again that he was reaching an end. He had now decided to encase the 'System', to be published as *A Vision*, in a fictionalized framework inspired by *The Arabian*

Nights. Dulac was asked to produce imaginary portraits, and local colour checked out with knowledgeable friends. (When 'The Gift of Harun Al-Rashid' had appeared earlier that year, tainted by an inescapable air of stately hokum, Sturm had sent a sharp letter pointing out the incompatible age-spans of the protagonists: a flaw left uncorrected by WBY.[75]) But finishing the book, 'getting all that abstraction put in concrete form', made him feel better. He interpreted his sense of well-being in a characteristic way to George: 'perhaps I now am a medium & my force is used'. For her part, she felt it should be completed 'on October 24th – then it will be exactly 7 years since we started it. I feel that if you dont finish then you will go on for another 7 years at the one book.'[76]

Their marriage, once so dependent on the investigations which made up that 'one book', had settled into a predictable pattern. He utterly relied on her in everyday things, but their intellectual companionship persisted too – even if he did not take her advice on matters like *To-Morrow*. He wrote and thought about his children more than some later authorities have allowed, but was as *distrait* as any father who is also a writer, working at home; his benevolently removed attitude is not to be wondered at, in a man at the end of his fifties, with a Victorian background and a long life as a bachelor behind him. His children were kept, by and large, at a distance. But even if George had to prompt him to buy a mechanical toy in Hamleys for Michael, he still went to considerable trouble to do so, and Anne's sayings were devotedly reported and repeated by her father. His letters to George from London this summer and autumn mention her tiredness and need of rest, and are particularly solicitous: 'if I were a rich man my dear I would go to Dublin just for that one day when you will be there but as it [is] I can only tell you that you are always in my thoughts'. After contemplating an Italian visit in early September he decided, 'No I think I would sooner be alone somewhere with you at least for a time than even with Ezra & Dorothy.'[77] He was slightly disorientated by changes around him, and looked back to the preoccupations of his youth; much time was spent writing a Preface to a translation of *Axël*, by H. P. R. Finberg (another acquaintance from his Oxford days). WBY's contribution was composed 'entirely of my memories of the first performance', a milestone in his never-completed journey towards the perfect symbolist drama.[78] And in early August another historic chapter was closed when he heard, with shocking suddenness, of another death in New York. On 29 July, less than three years after JBY slipped away, his impatient but solicitous benefactor John Quinn was carried off by liver cancer.

The fussy, obsessive, generous lawyer with the miraculous eye for avant-garde art had toiled endlessly for all the Yeats family, and for WBY in particular, as Quinn himself well knew. 'I am damn sick and tired of Yeats seniors and Yeats sisters and Yeats sisters-in-law and Yeats cousins and Yeats nieces and Yeats sister-in-law sister's brats and Yeats slim and Yeats fat', he had exploded a few years before.[79] But his commitment to the poet himself was staunch, and WBY recognized it. He wrote to Jeanne Foster:

Quinn was the only man friend – except George Russell of whom I had seen much less in my most active years – who had remained to me. How much he was bound up with us all . . . I have known no other man so full to overflowing with energy & benevolence & these always arising out of his nature like a fountain & having the quality of his nature. I mean his benevolence expressed him as a work of art expresses the artist. I, as you know, have great cause for gratitude to him on my own & on my fathers account. The lecture tour he arranged for me many years ago brought me the first substantial sum I ever earned. To that tour he must have given daily thought for weeks or rather months. All this week [of the Tailteann Games] I have been wishing that he had seen Dublin with all its flags, & the joyous crowds (war & civil war put away at last) as it has been for the last few days. He did his share to bring it all about.[80]

He was haunted by a remark of Goethe's: 'I have never for many years heard of a friend's death without envying him.' 'Geothe [sic] was one of the most successful men who ever lived & one of the least morbid & yet he had that thought. Is there not that instinct in us all.'[81]

If there is such an instinct, it is usually manifested in the tiredness of late middle age. WBY's next birthday would be his sixtieth. Intimations of mortality had reached his own generation: Lily's illness, Quinn's death, the news from Iseult that Gonne's nerves had given way, 'worse than an ordinary breakdown', and she had been sent away for complete rest.[82] He was writing when he had the time, but his recent publications had mostly been compilations and new editions. Cuala published *The Cat and the Moon and Certain Poems* in July 1924, but most of his creative energy was still being poured into *A Vision*. Composition had its particular difficulties. 'He has separate statements but is trying to get them into a synthesis,' Gregory noted that summer; 'it is all right if he accepts what comes, but if he begins to think it all goes wrong. I said Moses must have had "the Devil of a job" getting the ten commandments fixed in stone. He says Yes, that is just it.'[83]

After his return to Dublin in September, there were the demands of the reconvened Senate. He had spent much of the previous session drawing up a report on Irish manuscripts, presented to the Senate on 4 June 1924; his 'passion' had been noted in a heartfelt speech objecting to printing all railway tickets, signs, and notices in Irish ('if the Gaelic League or any other Irish national interest is injured it will be injured by an attempt to force Irish on those who do not want it. Endow creation by scholarship, and press that on to Government, but do not set up a pretense of people knowing a language that they do not know by perpetually printing, and in other ways exhibiting something in the Irish language').[84] In August the *Irish Statesman* had printed his 'Compulsory Gaelic: A Dialogue': it approached the subject as a Platonic philosophical exchange, airing the arguments on each side while coming to a deliberately indeterminate conclusion.[85] But he was prepared to march into even more sensitive territory. On 17 October there was a heated debate on relations between the Free State and Northern Ireland, when a motion was put suggesting 'an agreed solution' to the vexed question of the Border before the Boundary Commission appointed under the terms of the Treaty met. Senator Farren, a reliably myopic bigot, called for 'asserting our manhood and setting aside all this humbug and nonsense about goodwill and toleration for people who will not have toleration, and who will not meet us in a spirit of goodwill'. WBY said that Farren did not understand the issue. Though WBY told a correspondent that he had spoken 'in a panic' and 'knew nothing' about the Border, his words were both prescient and powerful:

Results of a very evil kind may happen from the report of the Commission no matter what way it reports, and it is exceedingly important that no responsibility for those results should lie with the Government of the Free State. I have no hope of seeing Ireland united in my time, or of seeing Ulster won in my time; but I believe it will be won in the end, and not because we fight it, but because we govern this country well. We can do that, if I may be permitted as an artist and writer to say so, by creating a system of culture which will represent the whole of this country and which will draw the imagination of the young towards it.[86]

His opposition to compulsory Gaelic, the war against censorship, and the determination to expose Ireland to chosen aspects of the avant-garde were all of a piece with this belief: he told Gregory that he thought the enforcement of the Irish language in the educational system would alienate Ulster beyond repair. The issue of legislation to prevent divorce in Ireland was already looming, with positions being marked out in the press,[87] and the battle over Robinson's position after the *To-Morrow* scandal was under way. At this very point, he received his own intimation of mortality: immediately after concluding his speech on 17 October, he was gripped by severe breathlessness and pain. On 20 October his doctor T. G. Moorhead[88] diagnosed dangerously high blood pressure and ordered complete rest. 'My life has been too exciting it seems and I must now pay for it,' he told Sturge Moore. 'A book with me has been like a drinking bout, or at any rate the doctor seems to think so, having questioned me in vain for more normal excess.'[89] The excitements of Dublin (not only the Senate but quarrels with bishops and dinners with the Stuarts at the Moira Hotel) were to be put behind him, and he was dispatched to rest at Coole on 29 October.

In a calm autumn, the woods and water exerted their old spell. He wrote to George: 'My only distress is absence from you & I miss you always, & when I see a lovely sight – evening light on the beeches & light – long for you that I may talk of it. Is not love being idle together & happy in it. Working together & being happy in it is friendship.'[90] This considered reflection may have been prompted by the fact that nearly thirty years on, he and Gregory were 'working together' once more. He amended early poems 'as if for a competition in eternity', Gregory remarked, worked on *A Vision*, and discussed prospective Abbey plays with his hostess. There had recently been a coolness over his tactless opposition to reviving her play *The Image* ('says it has an act too much and is slow in action'), which she had taken to heart, and she also resented George's Drama League poaching the Abbey's players and props.[91] The disagreement rumbled on at Coole, where he ill-advisedly referred to her play as 'rubbish', but they came to an agreement, read *Phineas Finn* together at night, and talked about literature. She recorded in her journals his *obiter dicta* on Hardy, Shelley, Keats, Browning, his dislike of formal education, and his interest in Trollope's engaging Irish hero. ('When we read about Mr Kennedy keeping Lady Laura in such order, not allowing her to see anyone or to read a novel on Sundays, I said "What ought she to have done?" and he said "What Jack said Masefield ought to do come home drunk and dance a sailors' hornpipe on the table".'[92]) This echo of lost times was matched by his new-found interest in his early poetry. He was pleased by rereading *The Wanderings of Oisin*; and, though he described 'The Sorrow of Love' as 'an absurd old poem of mine', he put considerable effort into redrafting it: 'says you can't write well without self-control, and he had not that when it was first written'.[93] He stayed a fortnight and, according to Gregory, left 'a picture of health and high spirits', having arrived looking like the hollow-cheeked spectre of his father's early portraits.

His blood pressure, however, was reduced by only ten points, and he was banished to the Tuckers at Sidmouth for further rest – without the intellectual stimulation of Coole. 'My wife & the doctor have decided that I am to finish my philosophy & keep out of Dublin for a while.'[94] George was still anxious to remove him from local excitements. Devon meant attempts at golf (in which he had been improbably tutored by Bertie Smyllie, editor of the *Irish Times*), detective stories, and respectable boredom, but he managed to fit in lunch with Bracken and dinner with Beaverbrook in London en route, as well as meeting Dulac (now with his 'new love' Helen Beauclerk).[95] He wrote to George from her mother's cottage:

Always when I [am] first away I get more or less desperate & I think I cannot get any order or peace into my life without your help but after a time – though I always want you – I get into some sort of pleasant existence which serves for a season. Harry & your mother take great care of me & life is pleasant, but I shall want you before long for all that.[96]

They planned to meet in London before returning to Dublin in early December, and to go south in January: WBY was already thinking of Sicily. *A Vision* continued its difficult gestation, and he continually convinced himself that it was finished. This was a false hope, but the rest cure did its work. By late December his blood pressure was down to 170, having been 220 at the crisis of October, and it was safe to get away. On 5 January he and George left for southern Italy, planning to stay away for six weeks.

They travelled first to Sicily, where they joined the Pounds, and then to Naples, Capri, and Rome. Ezra later remembered WBY trying out the acoustics at the amphitheatre near Syracuse, and viewing the Byzantine mosaics at Monreale, which created a lasting impression, supplying images that recur in his writing.[97] But he took the injunctions to rest very seriously, more or less abandoning everything to George.[98] By the time he arrived in Rome in February, he had recruited his strength: Joseph Hone saw him 'refuse a lift in the Borghese Palace and dash up two flights of stairs'.[99] Sight-seeing was addressed seriously, with repeated visits to the Vatican Galleries and the Sistine Chapel (another abiding image). George was dispatched to buy books 'dealing with the spiritual antecedents of the Fascist revolution'. He had already read Croce, and was now anxious to follow up Gentile's ideas about education. He also discussed with Hone the possible formation of a new anti-democratic Irish political party, influenced by what was going on around him.[100] He would not, however, give up his work on *A Vision*: two of its Books are dated 'Finished at Syracuse, January, 1925', and the Introduction ends with some vivid local colour from Capri. It also conveys not only the euphoria of his own regained health but an implicit excitement at Italy's apparent renewal:

I would forget the wisdom of the East and remember its grossness and its romance. Yet when I wander upon the cliffs where Augustus and Tiberius wandered, I know that the new intensity that seems to have come into all visible and tangible things is not a reaction from that wisdom but its very self. Yesterday when I saw the dry and leafless vineyards at the very edge of the motionless sea, or lifting their brown stems from almost inaccessible patches of earth high up on the cliff-side, or met at the turn of the path the orange and lemon trees in full fruit, or the crimson cactus flower, or felt the warm sunlight falling between blue and blue, I murmured, as I have countless times, 'I have been part of it always and there is maybe no escape, forgetting and returning life after life like an insect in the roots of the grass.' But murmured it without terror, in exultation almost.[101]

V

In a notebook on 23 April 1925, at Merrion Square, he wrote: 'Yesterday I finished "A Vision".'[102] He sent the same message to Dulac, saying that at long last it had left his hands and gone to George's whose task was to make the endless corrections legible. Dulac was to send his 'diagram' (of the Great Wheel on which the book's astrological pattern depended) and all could then go to Watt and subsequently Werner Laurie.

It has really been the book I think that made me ill – for it has not been out of my mind for years. I have grown well as I got it out of my head. I have now a free mind for the first time in years . . . I do not know what my book will be to others – nothing perhaps. To me it means a last act of defence against the chaos of the world; & I hope for ten years to write out of my renewed security.[103]

This defines the importance of *A Vision* to its author, but what it meant to others would always be problematic. Sturge Moore believed that by the time WBY finished it, he had forgotten the central idea,[104] and bemusement or embarrassment would greet its appearance in January 1926. Shakespear found the 'System' 'rather terrible – all so unending & no rest or peace till one attains an unattainable goal', but consoled herself that at least there was nothing in it about Love ('I believe that men are so made that they naturally hate each other &. all their talk about Love is Bunkum'[105]). Gogarty presciently called it 'a geometrical rendering of the emotions; a mixture of Einstein and myth'; probably to him, as to Gregory, WBY had claimed affinities between Einstein's demonstration of relativity theory and his own attempt to destabilize the positivist universe.[106] As finally submitted to the printer, the book gathers up two preoccupations: the attempt to arrive at a diagrammatic representation modelling the process of historical change and recurrence, and an (equally schematic) 'System' of personal and historical archetypes, concentrating upon creative or artistic personalities and related to the phases of the moon. This is astrology at its grandest. It also represented a flight from 'objectivity' into the symbolic via what the chief authority on the book has called 'psychic geometry'.[107] The same scholar has described the book, more helpfully, as a 'spiritual autobiography', and this is where its biographical importance lies. George's 'Instructors' during the transfigured first years of their marriage hover behind much of it: but so do psychic investigations stretching back to before the war. (As early as the summer of 1914 he had been trying to assemble random suggestions from Edith Lyttelton's automatic writings into coherent images which would dictate a pattern of life.) A preoccupation with the occult significance of numbers and colours goes back further still, to his earliest studies in the Order of the

Golden Dawn, and his attempts to construct a Celtic Mystical Order.[108] And he had always, one way or another, tried to classify types of human personality. But as outlined in *A Vision*, his ambition was nothing less than summing up 'all thought, all history and the difference between man and man'.

It is also a meditation on artistic inspiration, and this links it (as WBY wished) to *Per Amica Silentia Lunae*. The sun and the moon had for long been his favourite antithetical images, standing for sexual union as well as for complementary supernatural influences. Sometimes rather inconsistently interpreted, they nonetheless dominate the pattern of *A Vision*. Joyce, characteristically, admired the 'colossal conception', only regretting that 'Yeats did not put all this into a creative work'.[109] WBY worked from the huge accumulation of automatic-writing transcripts, and the card file in which the Yeatses had attempted to codify the random 'knowledge' that they had hit upon: the fruit of his ancient habit of docketing and arranging information, and George's determination to bring order to his study. Later he would claim he wrote it 'for a devoted Catholic and revolutionary who has engaged me in argument since my twenty-third year' – inevitably, Gonne – 'and for a Scotch doctor in the north of England': his fellow occultist Frank Pearce Sturm.[110] But, unsurprisingly, the directly personal issues which had brought about the crisis of 1917, and which dominated so many of his questions to George, were not used as illustrations to the system in *A Vision*: Iseult and George, hare and cat, sit outside the borders of the sacred book, and Maud's presence remains veiled. Like Farr, Shakespear, Gregory, and Mrs Patrick Campbell, she appears as a nameless 'type'. He was also – at this stage – determined to keep George's contribution undefined. Freudian or Jungian ideas, specifically employed at the time of the interrogations, were also kept out of *A Vision*, as apparently ill fitted to its deliberately archaic and occult pattern. His method of writing involved a concentrated effort to bring together the great mass of material under intelligible headings, as a way of illustrating the diagrams of recurrence symbolized by the spiralling movements of 'gyres' – contracting to a point at which they begin unfolding again in reverse motion, two cones continually interpenetrating. This was the final outcome of his many years' reading about historical cycles and astrological geometry.[111]

Early drafts suggest that he thought of writing *A Vision* in dialogue form, like so many of his philosophical poems. He had resurrected his invented alter egos Michael Robartes and Owen Aherne for the purpose, as representatives of alternative paths on the search for spiritual wisdom. More lasting was the idea of setting off the book by medieval Arabic window-dressing, which was in WBY's mind as early as 1917. He had been collecting ideas about personal archetypes and affinities from a similarly early stage: it became a kind of private parlour-game between himself and George, extended to privileged correspondents like Iseult. (George, through her 'Controls', periodically tried to make him hold his tongue on the subject.) A draft of the first section, and possibly much more, had been in existence since late 1922; George Harper has closely analysed the stages of writing and rewriting over the next two and a half years.[112] Ideas of a dialogue-book, or two aphoristic volumes (after the model of *Discoveries* or *Per Amica*), early on gave way to an Introduction and four sections of exegesis. In the process of writing, especially for the section on 'History' (eventually titled 'Dove or Swan'), he incorporated ideas from non-occult sources (such as *The Education of Henry Adams*, read at Oxford in early 1921). But he abandoned the attempt to divide up actual historical chronology into sequential partitions corresponding to the twenty-eight 'Phases', for which the reader can only feel gratitude.

A Vision represents a little of the best of WBY, and most of the worst. Leaps of imagination, audacious strokes, unforgettably sonorous phrases, and brilliant imagery come in flashes; he retains his ability to make the esoteric and irrational at once universal and uniquely strange. But far more of the material is ponderous, self-regarding, wildly didactic, inconsistent, and unconvincing. The generalizations on which the archetypes are erected, the arbitrary and self-referencing symbolism, the incomprehensibility of it all to anyone not already versed in his own thought and life, rob it of any general intellectual interest. He came to see this himself with embarrassing rapidity, with the unfortunate result that the great autodidact set himself to producing an alternative version, published twelve years later.

The value inherent in the volume dated 1925 (though published in 1926) is as an autobiographical lode. Much of it is cloaked by an abstruse and self-referential game, starting inside the front cover with Dulac's frontispiece, a woodcut of the medieval 'Giraldus' on whose writings the volume is supposedly based, bearing, as Iseult playfully remarked, 'a quaint resemblance' to the real author.[113] The dedication, signed 'Capri, February 1925', has an equally private provenance, reflecting a quarrel of the year before: the book is offered to 'Vestigia', the Golden Dawn motto of Moina Mathers. When *The Trembling of the Veil* was published, she had written him a violent remonstrance about what she saw as his travesty-portrait of her late husband. WBY had mollified her and vaguely promised changes (never carried out). Instead, the dedication appears as an implicit apology, and a roll-call of the occultist 'friends of his youth': it is a kind of prose version of his 1920 poem 'All Souls' Night', which he would place at the end of the book as the Epilogue. 'We all, so far as I can remember, differed from ordinary students of philosophy or religion through our belief that truth cannot be discovered but may be revealed, and that if a man do not lose faith, and if he go through certain preparations, revelation will find him at the fitting moment.'[114] *A Vision* was to demonstrate, therefore, that this hope was not in vain: 'A system of thought that would leave my imagination free to create as it chose, and yet make all that it created, or could create, part of the one history, and that the soul's.' In a curiously apologetic passage, he warned lovers of his poetry to avoid the mathematical exegesis, and to stick to the historic philosophy and the poetry, and he admitted that he had written 'nothing of the Beatific Vision, little of sexual love' (the very elements most central to the inspiration that had come via the 'Instructors'). In fact, he implied, the whole point of the elaborate exercise had been to liberate his poetic creativity.

I am longing to put it out of reach that I may write the poetry it seems to have made possible. I can now, if I have the energy, find the simplicity I have sought in vain. I need no longer write poems like 'The Phases of the Moon' nor 'Ego Dominus Tuus' nor spend barren years, as I have done some three or four times, striving with abstractions that substituted themselves for the play that I had planned.

Many readers must have devoutly wished that this were the case. As sent to Werner Laurie in 1925, *A Vision* opened with an Introduction in which WBY revisited (as at Coole the previous autumn) his own work of the 1890s. The volume was presented, with heavy playfulness and elaborate reference to WBY's early occult fiction, as an invented manuscript – mediated by the magus figure of Michael Robartes and the spiritual searcher Owen Aherne (who 'wrote' the Introduction). The text had allegedly been discovered as a sixteenth-century treatise, and its mystic diagrams gathered among the magicians of an Arab tribe. All this was given to WBY to 'expound'. The Introduction is in itself an occult short story, mingling esoteric references, local colour, and sexual swagger. It features Woburn Buildings, Watkins Bookshop in Cecil Court, Thoor Ballylee, and WBY himself – strangely described by Robartes as 'a man who has thought more of the love of woman than of the love of God'. Aherne's description of WBY suggests that the 'spiritual autobiography' aspect of *A Vision* had been affected by his recent battles with the guardians of religious piety: '"Mr Yeats has intellectual belief but he is entirely without moral faith, without that sense, which should come to a man with terror and joy, of a Divine Presence, and though he may seek, and may have always sought it, I am certain that he will not find it in this life."' The Introduction, in fact, revives the old Aherne–Robartes antithesis: a reliance on faith and inherited authority (Aherne) is posited against Robartes's ruthless search for magical experience. Robartes *redivivus* owes even more to MacGregor Mathers here than in his previous incarnation. But the poem that follows, 'The Wheels and the Phases of the Moon', unites Aherne and Robartes in an exposition of the 'phases of the moon' theory of astrological-historical development: delivered as they stand outside Ballylee, observing WBY at his midnight toil.

These internalized references and invented histories continue throughout the first 'Book' of *A Vision*, dressing up the theory of lunar phase. The twenty-eight divisions of a full circuit are arbitrarily related to objective (or 'primary') qualities giving way to subjective (or 'antithetical' qualities): the enduring tension between external and internal life, balanced out through various combinations or aspects of the chief human faculties. These are reduced, in WBY's ideally tetradic system, to four rather ill-defined concepts derived from Blake's *Prophetic Books*: Will, Creative Mind, Body of Fate, and Mask.[115] Already the reader is being lured into a secret language, founded on the occult geometry and cyclical theory which had coloured WBY's reading since the 1890s.[116] A series of didactic generalizations about personalities and a ludicrously specific 'Table of the Four Faculties' recall the voices of George's 'Instructors', inexorably interrogated, coming up with a series of statements where airy certainty is mingled with driven desperation. This is adulterated, when it comes to defining embodiments, or examples, of people caught in the various phases, by a good deal of table-talk; WBY's impression of Dostoyevsky's novels, or his memories of John Morley's remarks about Parnell, or his hatred of Carlyle are thrown, as it were, into the conversation. 'Phase Twenty-one' is an excuse for a violent character sketch of George Moore, and 'Phase Twenty-four' is a profile of Gregory as WBY wanted her to be. It is hard not to think of George's caustic remark, made much later in life, that her husband had no real interest in people for themselves, but was endlessly absorbed by the way they behaved.[117]

This uneasily formulaic approach sets the tone. *A Vision* is the work of a mind that tries to see people as constructs. There is little evidence of the side of WBY that revelled in the self-deceptions and venial idiocies of his fellow men; no sign of his ability to etch with an acid lightness the outlines of the 'friends of his youth' in *The Trembling of the Veil*, or to spellbind listeners in Merrion Square on a Monday night, or to entertain Gregory in the library at Coole. The idea of defining personality, especially by adopting or creating a 'Mask' in a 'free' rather than an 'enforced' manner, carries some autobiographical resonance, and so do many other generalizations.

Discords, Oppositions and Contrasts

The being becomes conscious of itself as a separate being, because of certain facts of *opposition* and *discord*, the emotional *opposition* of *Will* and *Mask*, the intellectual *opposition* of *Creative Mind* and *Body of Fate*, discords between *Will* and *Creative Mind*, *Creative Mind* and *Mask*, *Mask* and *Body of Fate*, *Body of Fate* and *Will*. A *discord* is always the enforced understanding of the unlikeness of *Will* and *Mask* or of *Creative Mind* and *Body of Fate*. There is an enforced attraction between *opposites*, for the *Will* has a natural desire for the *Mask* and the *Creative Mind* a natural perception of the *Body of Fate*; in one the dog bays the Moon, in the other the eagle stares on the Sun by natural right. When, however, the *Creative Mind* deceives the *Will*, by offering it some *primary* image of the *Mask*, or when the *Will* offers to the *Creative Mind* an emotion that should be turned towards the *Mask* alone, the opposition emerges again in its simplicity because of the jarring of the emotion, the grinding out of the *Image*. On the other hand it may be the *Mask* that slips on to the *Body of Fate* till we confuse what we would be with what we must be.[118]

But potential insights are obscured by the schematic grid imposed on these psychological reflections. The distinction between 'personality' and 'character' is just one of many that seems clear to WBY but not to his reader. Some economies of the imagination are made: the definition of certain 'phases' seems to rely almost entirely on choosing a specimen personality and analysing it (Dowson, as described in *The Trembling of the Veil*, apparently dictates the formulation of Phase Thirteen). Since George's first messages, seven years' thought had imposed layer upon layer of interpretation and generalization, and the arrival at 'rules' for discovering true and false masks, creative minds and body of fate. What is new, as Richard Ellmann pointed out, is the binding of traditional elements in WBY's cosmogony into a pattern of 'furious movement'.[119] But in the end, following the 'System' requires the suspension not only of scepticism but of the faculty of rational analysis. As Ellmann, again, points out, *A Vision* is – fortunately – not a guidebook to WBY's poems. Nonetheless, it provides necessary illumination for a key section of his oeuvre – even if that includes poems which meant more to him than to his readers. And the book's real value is to students of Yeats's mind, and of his aspirations. Some passages carry a deeply personal intensity:

He who attains Unity of Being is some man, who, while struggling with his fate and his destiny until every energy of his being has been roused, is content that he should so struggle with no final conquest. For him fate and freedom are not to be distinguished; he is no longer bitter, he may even love tragedy like those 'who love the gods and withstand them'; such men are able to bring all that happens, as well as all that they desire, into an emotional or intellectual synthesis and so to possess not the Vision of Good only but that of Evil. They are described as coming after death into dark and into light, whereas *primary* men, who do not receive revelation by conflict, are in dark or in light. In the *Convito* Dante speaks of his exile, and the gregariousness it thrust upon him, as a great misfortune for such as he; and yet as poet he must have accepted, not only that exile, but his grief for the death of Beatrice as that which made him *Daimonic*, not a writer of poetry alone like Guido Cavalcanti. Intellectual creation accompanies or follows in *antithetical* man, the struggle of the being to overthrow its fate and this is symbolised by placing the *Creative Mind* in the phase opposite to that of the *Body of Fate*. Unity of Being becomes possible at Phase 12, and ceases to be possible at Phase 18, but is rare before Phase 13 and after Phase 17, and is most common at Phase 17.[120]

And Phase Seventeen is where WBY located both Dante and himself, destined by astrology to be superpoets. For *A Vision* demonstrates WBY's tenaciously-held belief in life as the journey of the soul, and death as the soul's journey back to the beginning of life – parallelled by successive civilizations (in his favourite formula from Heraclitus) 'living each other's death, dying each other's life'. There are coded references to George's 'Instructors' throughout, and the whole founding myth of the 'System' is given again in 'Desert Geometry, or The Gift of Harun Al-Raschid', reprinted as an Introduction to Book II: George and WBY, as Arab philosopher and his girl-bride, exploring occult and sensual mysteries while through her 'a Djinn spoke'. The poem also suggests, however, that he was more aware than has sometimes been suggested of the psychological dependence that had arisen between them as a result of their occult traffickings, and more conscious of the emotional covenant that they had sealed.

> Even to-day, after some seven years
> When maybe thrice in every moon her mouth
> Has murmured wisdom of the desert Djinns,
> She keeps that ignorance, nor has she now
> That first unnatural interest in my books.
> It seems enough that I am there; and yet,
> Old fellow student, whose most patient ear
> Heard all the anxiety of my passionate youth,
> It seems I must buy knowledge with my peace.
> What if she lose her ignorance and so
> Dream that I love her only for the voice,
> That every gift and every word of praise
> Is but a payment for that midnight voice
> That is to age what milk is to a child!
> Were she to lose her love, because she had lost
> Her confidence in mine, or even lose
> Its first simplicity, love, voice, and all,
> All my fine feathers would be plucked away
> And I left shivering. The voice has drawn
> A quality of wisdom from her love's
> Particular quality. The signs and shapes;
> All those abstractions that you fancied were
> From the great Treatise of Parmenides;
> All, all those gyres and cubes and midnight things

Are but a new expression of her body
Drunk with the bitter-sweetness of her youth.
And now my utmost mystery is out:
A woman's beauty is a storm-tossed banner;
Under it wisdom stands, and I alone –
Of all Arabia's lovers I alone –
Nor dazzled by the embroidery, nor lost
In the confusion of its night-dark folds,
Can hear the armed man speak.[121]

The alternative title, 'Desert Geometry', hints that against the phases of astrologically determined personality a diagrammatic version of historical process is to be sketched out. This replicates a spiral movement, for which WBY found authority in philosophers back to Heraclitus, and which also expresses the form of each person's journey into consciousness, in constant tension with his 'daimon'.

As man's intellect, say, expands, the emotional nature contracts in equal degree and vice versa; when, however, a narrowing and a widening gyre reach their limit, the one the utmost contraction the other the utmost expansion, they change places, point to circle, circle to point, for this system conceives the world as catastrophic, and continue as before, one always narrowing, one always expanding, and yet bound for ever to one another.[122]

Planetary transits are also attached to this pattern of motion, and – in a section of 'The Great Year' – calculations of apocalyptic periods are presented along with an essentially Neoplatonic framework of the soul's journey. Christ is to be found grouped as one of the 'great victims of Antiquity', with Caesar and Socrates, representing Love, Justice and Truth.[123]

In the third section, 'Dove or Swan', Yeatsian theory meets the Yeatsian idea of fact, as the history of civilization is mapped against the pattern of the historical cones.

A civilisation is a struggle to keep self-control, and in this it is like some great tragic person, some Niobe who must display an almost superhuman will or the cry will not touch our sympathy. The loss of control over thought comes towards the end; first a sinking in upon the moral being, then the last surrender, the irrational cry, revelation – the scream of Juno's peacock.[124]

'Meditations in Time of Civil War' as well as 'Nineteen Hundred and Nineteen' might hint that he placed contemporary Ireland's experience at this point in the pattern, with himself as witness. 'Dove or Swan' is introduced by the latest version of 'Leda and the Swan', with its theme of the death of a civilization encoded in its birth. But the entertaining exegesis that follows is a ramble through classical history, speculative and subjective, with

WBY alighting at certain points because he happens to find them all alluring, as much as because they conform to his pattern. It also traces some of WBY's constant preoccupations – notably the creation by Greek sculptors of styles of beauty, and the way great civilizations borrow and feed from each other:

Each age unwinds the thread another age had wound, and it amuses one to remember that before Phidias, and his westward moving art, Persia fell, and that when full moon came round again, amid eastward moving thought, and brought Byzantine glory, Rome fell; and that at the outset of our westward moving Renaissance Byzantium fell; all things dying each other's life, living each other's death.[125]

He engagingly admits that according to the 'System', the rise of the Byzantine state should occur at a different historical stage from that in which it actually happened, but, nonetheless, in one of the few passages often quoted from *A Vision*, he asserts his own identification with it:

I think if I could be given a month of Antiquity and leave to spend it where I chose, I would spend it in Byzantium a little before Justinian opened St Sophia [AD 537] and closed the Academy of Plato [AD 529]. I think I could find in some little wine shop some philosophical worker in mosaic who could answer all my questions, the supernatural descending nearer to him than to Plotinus even, for the pride of his delicate skill would make what was an instrument of power to Princes and Clerics and a murderous madness in the mob, show us a lovely flexible presence like that of a perfect human body.

I think that in early Byzantium, and maybe never before or since in recorded history, religious, aesthetic and practical life were one, and that architect and artificers – though not, it may be, poets, for language had been the instrument of controversy and must have grown abstract – spoke to the multitude and the few alike.[126]

It is never exactly clear why this should be so, but WBY's vision of Byzantium remained a gleaming personal emblem, later to shine through two of his most luminous poems. A formalist aesthetic, the blend of the antique and the early Christian, the irrecapturable exoticism of it all, conferred 'a supernatural splendour' – expressed to WBY's eyes by the mosaics he had just seen in Sicily.[127] But the great synthesis crumbled, the images were destroyed, 'Europe grew animal and literal'. Towards the end of the first millennium AD, WBY discerns an unspoken but evident parallel with the rise of zealotry and anarchy in his own day. Though he dropped some anti-Christian passages from the manuscript draft, his Gibbonian view of the Western Church would not have surprised the *Catholic Bulletin*.

Three Roman Courtesans who have one after another got their favourite lovers chosen Pope have, it pleases one's mockery to think, confessed their sins, with full belief in the supernatural efficacy of the act, to ears that have heard their cries of love, or received the Body of God from hands that have played with their own bodies . . . In monasteries and in hermit cells men freed from the intellect at last can seek their God upon all fours like beasts or children.[128]

The millennium up to the present is treated in a series of sweeping aesthetic judgements, closely tied to WBY's canonical figures: Dante, the Italian painters before Raphael, Chaucer, Villon (related ingeniously to Aubrey Beardsley). The Neoplatonic Academy of Florence represents a brief revival of synthesis, doomed because out of phase.[129] With the age of 'Michaelangelo, Rabelais, Aretino, Shakespear, Titian', secular intellect bursts loose, and then 'the gyre ebbs out in order and reason'. The disruptions of the seventeenth century, in art, intellect and politics, are bewilderingly telescoped forward to the nineteenth, seen through William Morris's vision:

Personality is everywhere spreading out its fingers in vain, or grasping with an always more convulsive grasp a world where the predominance of physical science, of finance and economics in all their forms, of democratic politics, of vast populations, of architecture where styles jostle one another, of newspapers where all is heterogenous, show that mechanical force will in a moment become supreme.[130]

The current era, ending in 1927, is 'like that from 1250 to 1300 . . . a period of abstraction'. 'Our generation has stood at the climax, at what I call in "The Trembling of the Veil" *Hodos Chameliontos*, or has witnessed a first weariness, and when the climax passes will recognise that there common secular thought began to break and disperse.'[131] Though he briefly refers to 'recent mathematical research', it is in cubist art and abstract sculpture (seen by WBY as an end, not a beginning) that the first phase of the last quarter (Phase Twenty-three) has been announced. And this leads to a literary reflection on what was not yet called 'modernism'.

I find at this 23rd Phase which is it is said the first where there is hatred of the abstract, where the intellect turns upon itself, Mr Ezra Pound, Mr Eliot, Mr Joyce, Signor Pirandello, who either eliminate from metaphor the poet's phantasy and substitute a strangeness discovered by historical or contemporary research or who break up the logical processes of thought by flooding them with associated ideas or words that seem to drift into the mind by chance; or who set side by side as in "Henry IV," "The Waste Land," "Ulysses," the *physical primary* – a lunatic among his keepers, a man fishing behind a gas works, the vulgarity of a single Dublin day prolonged through 700 pages – and the *spiritual primary*, delirium, the Fisher King, Ulysses' wandering. It is as though myth and fact, united until the exhaustion of the Renaissance, have now fallen so far apart that man understands for the first time the rigidity of fact, and calls up, by that very recognition, myth – the *Mask* – which now but gropes its way out of the mind's dark but will shortly pursue and terrify.[132]

The last phrase betrays the political dimension behind all this. The climax of 'Dove or Swan', completed at Capri in February 1925, is deeply affected by contemporary European upheavals, and categorically questions the utility of democratic forms of government. Perhaps this is one of the reasons why it was excised from the 1937 version.

In practical life one expects the same technical inspiration, the doing of this or that not because one would, or should, but because one can, consequent licence, and with those 'out of phase' anarchic violence with no sanction in general principles. If there is violent revolution, and it is the last phase where violent revolution is possible, the dish will be made from what is found in the pantry and the cook will not open her book.

How Phase Twenty-four will avoid revolution is a moot point: the suggested alternatives are either the invocation by Péguy and Claudel of a traditional hierarchy, or the loss of 'egotism' (and greatness of intellect) in ceaseless activity of the masses submerged in 'duties' conceived of as the general will. This is a Roman-style decadence, coming to terms with the revelation of a new era, which can be discerned, in a phrase resurrected from 'The Wanderings of Oisin', like 'bubbles in a frozen pond'.[133]

When the new era comes bringing its stream of irrational force it will, as did Christianity, find its philosophy already impressed upon the minority who have, true to phase, turned away at the last gyre from the *Physical Primary*. And it must awake into life, not Dürer's, nor Blake's, nor Milton's human form divine – nor yet Nietzsche's superman, nor Patmore's Catholic, boasting 'a tongue that's dead' – the brood of the Sistine Chapel – but organic groups, *covens* of physical or intellectual kin melted out of the frozen mass. I imagine new races, as it were, seeking domination, a world resembling but for its immensity that of the Greek tribes – each with its own Daimon or ancestral hero – the brood of Leda, War and Love; history grown symbolic, the biography changed into a myth. Above all I imagine everywhere the opposites, no mere alternation between nothing and something like the Christian brute and ascetic, but two opposites, each living the other's death, dying the other's life.[134]

From 1927, with the increasing separation of 'the cultivated classes' from the community, a new philosophy will take hold – concrete, fixed, relying for sanction on the ideas of man's immortality and the 'soul's re-embodiment' rather than on 'God or any exterior unity'. The conclusion is resoundingly elitist:

Unlike Christianity, which had for its first Roman teachers cobblers and weavers, this thought must find expression among those that are most subtle, most rich in memory . . . among the learned – every sort of learning – among the rich – every sort of riches – among men of rank – every sort of rank – and the best of those that express it will be given power, less because of that they promise than because of that they seem and are. This much can be thought because it is the reversal of what we know, but those kindreds once formed must obey irrational force and so create hitherto unknown experience, or that which is incredible.

Though it cannot interrupt the intellectual stream – being born from it and moving within it – it may grow a fanaticism and a terror, and at its first outsetting oppress the ignorant – even the innocent – as Christianity oppressed the wise, seeing that the day is far off when the two halves of man can define each its own unity in the other as in a mirror, Sun in Moon, Moon in Sun, and so escape out of the Wheel.[135]

This was the last section of *A Vision* to be finished (though not the last in the book) and may stand as some kind of testament to WBY's political expectations in the mid 1920s. He had now experienced war, civil war, and the birth of a new Irish polity, as well as playing a political role himself. The fact that he was writing in the Italy of Mussolini, whose sinister rallying-cry about trampling on the decomposing body of the Goddess of Liberty WBY had himself quoted a year before, cannot be ignored: nor can his simultaneous plunge into reading seminal works of the Fascist movement. He was also discussing with Joseph Hone the formation of a distinctly undemocratic political party in Ireland. The message of *A Vision* may be aristocratic as much as determinist, but it certainly expects 'irrational violence' and totalitarian government to replace a decadent democracy. This may mark a stage towards 'unity of being', but that desideratum seems far away. Democratic art had been rejected long ago by WBY; democratic politics were now condemned by association.[136] Selectively quoted, and read in retrospect, 'Dove or Swan' is an ominous text. That its readership was both limited and bewildered may have been to the advantage of the author's reputation, and so was his decision to drop its conclusion from the later version.

The final section, 'The Gates of Pluto', deals with death, life, and the shifting boundaries between the two – including dreams and reincarnation. Before his illness he had written to Force Stead: 'I am well & contented as a man can be who is growing old & knows that there is little worth having but youth & vigour . . . I think the dead are our emotions & by their senses I pray that when I am dead I may look out upon the world through young mans eyes.'[137] However, there is little that is new to those well versed in 'Swedenborg, Mediums, and the Desolate Places' or *Per Amica Silentia Lunae*, and the title of the opening section, 'Stray Thoughts', is all too apposite. By WBY's own admission it is the 'least finished' of the sections in this collage of a book, 'a series of unrelated statements & inaccurate deductions from the symbols & were little but hurried notes recorded for my own future guidance'.[138] Certainly it reads as garrulous, confused, and obscure – perhaps because whole sections are direct rephrasings of insights dictated by George's 'Instructors'.[139] He had written an 'Epilogue', addressed once again to Vestigia, to end the book. But it was rejected, and he employed instead 'All Souls' Night', written five years before and already published in the *New Republic* and *London Mercury* for March 1921.

The poem fits neatly enough, since it summons ghosts, constructs an imagery of winding spirals, celebrates the occultist mentors of his youth, and asserts that those who map the soul's journey have themselves a peculiar and special relation to death – which, so far from ending this existence, completes it. But 'All Souls' Night' may also have been chosen because its ending anticipated the reaction of many readers when they closed one of the 500 numbered copies of *A Vision*. Further, it declares that their incomprehension was irrelevant.

> I have mummy truths to tell
> Whereat the living mock;
> Though not for sober ear
> For maybe all that hear
> Should weep and laugh an hour upon the clock.
>
> Such thought – such thought have I that hold it tight
> Till meditation master all its parts,
> Nothing can stay my glance
> Until that glance run in the world's despite
> To where the damned have howled away their hearts,
> And where the blessed dance;
> Such thought, that in it bound
> I need no other thing,
> Wound in mind's wandering,
> As mummies in the mummy-cloth are wound.

Chapter 8 : VANITY AND PRIDE
1925–1927

Some quotations from Chekhov's letters. 'Somehow everything has suddenly become less interesting. I must sit on some
gunpowder'; and 'It is as if everybody had been in love, had
now fallen out of love, and were now seeking for other infatuations' seem to match our mood in Ireland. And we can't be
infatuated with Cosgrave and the Treason Bill . . .

Lady Gregory's journal, 26 February 1925

I

BY THE spring of 1925 WBY was back in Merrion Square. *A Vision* was
dispatched in late April, his blood pressure sank to normal, and his good
health returned. Like Chekhov, however, he felt the need to sit on gunpowder, and a suitably explosive issue presented itself. A debate was due in
the Senate on the question of divorce – one of the areas of civil law where the
new Irish administration was moving towards legislation which would
reflect a distinctively Catholic ethos rather than following the English
norm. WBY had plenty of time to prepare his position. Nearly a year before
his Senate colleague James Douglas produced a report on the question, violently attacked by the *Catholic Bulletin* as a plot inspired by the Masonic
Order and Trinity College (or 'Queen Elizabeth's Academy in Dublin').[1]
The Catholic Bishop Cohalan of Cork weighed in, declaring that divorce
should not be allowed in Ireland: 'It would be said that Protestants would be
denied what they enjoyed under British rule . . . but why should any party in
the State get facility for doing what the Catholic Church regards as a viol-
ation of a Divine Law?' In response, the *Irish Times* attacked the potential
infringement of Protestants' civil liberties and pointed out that a measure
outlawing divorce would 'crystallize' the partition of Northern Ireland.
This alerted the *Catholic Bulletin*, which kept up the pressure, demanding
that the Catholic Truth Society devote their Conference to the question,
and warning the faithful of an impending assault by the ungodly.[2] Thus the
battle lines were drawn well before WBY's first public intervention.

This came – inevitably, the *Bulletin* must have thought – in the pages of
AE's *Irish Statesman*, which carried on 14 March 1925 the text of 'an undelivered speech' by the Nobel Laureate. It had been prepared for a debate on
4 March, which was to discuss a resolution from the Dáil proscribing the
introduction of divorce bills, but the initiative had simply been ruled out of

order. WBY's delayed salvo attacked the 'quixotically impressive' ambitions of Cosgrave's government in legislating for the morals of non-Catholics, comparing it to that of medieval Spain. He moved rapidly to the probable effect on Ulster.

This country has declared through every vehicle of expression known to it that it desires union with the North of Ireland, even that it will never be properly a nation till that union has been achieved, and it knows that it cannot bring this union about by force. It must convince the Ulster Protestants that if they join themselves to us they will not suffer injustice. They can be won, not now, but in a generation, but they cannot be won if you insist that the Catholic conscience alone must dominate the public life of Ireland.[3]

He went on to instance the hypocrisy inseparable from countries which have regarded marriage as indissoluble and quoted, with relish, the mother of a Balzac heroine who tells her, on the eve of her marriage, that if she does not love her husband she may take a lover, so long as she 'does nothing against the family'. The argument against divorce, according to WBY, was based simply on the utilitarian protection of the family rather than on divine ordination, for all the claims of Catholic apologists. As for himself, he finally felt unmuzzled.

For a long time there has been a religious truce in Ireland, men like myself have kept silent about all those matters that divide one religion from another, but President Cosgrave has broken that truce, and I will avail myself of the freedom he has given me. Marriage is not to us a Sacrament, but, upon the other hand, the love of man and woman, and the inseparable physical desire, are sacred. This conviction has come to us through ancient philosophy and modern literature, and it seems to us a most sacrilegious thing to persuade two people who hate each other because of some unforgettable wrong, to live together, and it is to us no remedy to permit them to part if neither can re-marry.[4]

The Gonne–MacBride separation may have been in his mind here, and the 'undelivered speech' enshrines the convictions of a man formed in the bohemian 1890s and familiar with the worldly circles of Olivia Shakespear and her friends, as well as the self-consciously unshockable reader of the classics and connoisseur of Gogarty's bawdy verse. These identifications would not have rung many answering echoes from his companions in the Senate, but the peroration of his speech went straight to the political core of the issue:

I do not think that my words will influence a single vote here, nor am I thinking of this House, I am thinking only of a quarrel which I perceive is about to commence. Fanaticism having won this victory, and I see nothing that can prevent it unless it be proved to have overstepped the law, will make other attempts upon the liberty of minorities. I want those minorities to resist, and their resistance may do an over-whelming service to this country, they may become the centre of its creative intel-lect and the pivot of its unity. For the last hundred years Irish nationalism has had to fight against England, and that fight has helped emotional energy, and had little use for intelligence so far as the mass of the people were concerned, for we had to hurl them against an alien power. The basis of Irish nationalism has now shifted, and much that once helped us is now injurious, for we can no longer do anything by fighting, we must persuade, and to persuade we must become a modern, tolerant, liberal nation. I want everything discussed, I want to get rid of the old exaggerated tact and caution. As a people we are superficial, our Press provincial and trivial, because as yet we have not considered any of those great political and religious ques-tions which raise some fundamental issue and have disturbed Europe for gener-ations. It must depend upon a small minority which is content to remain a minority for a generation, to insist on those questions being discussed. Let us use the weapons that have been put into our hands.[5]

What he did not do was specifically advance the claims of the Protestant Ascendancy to their place in the faltering new Irish sun, but that was to come.

Meanwhile he kept his hand in by writing an article, 'On the Need for Audacity of Thought', sparked off by the condemnation by some Christian Brothers of a medieval carol dealing with Mary's pregnancy: the editor of *Our Boys* publicly burned the magazine which printed it. WBY quoted the carol in full, noted that Hyde had reproduced an Irish version twenty years before, and urbanely suggested that the Christian Brothers could find the verses offensive only because 'they do not believe in the Incarnation. They think they believe in it, but they do not, and its sudden presentation fills them with horror, and to hide that horror they turn upon the poem.' The bit between his teeth, he moved swiftly on to Lennox Robinson's controversial story, which had created such a furore the year before. 'Mr Lennox Robinson and I want to understand the Incarnation, and we think that we cannot understand any historical event till we have set it amidst new cir-cumstance. We grew up with the Bible; the Mother of God is no Catholic possession; she is a part of our imagination.'[6] This was a distinctly Protestant 'we', and he compounded the offence by arguing that 'the intel-lect of Ireland is irreligious', apart from Johannes Scotus Erigena and Bishop Berkeley, both forgotten. But, above all, he attacked the 'ignorance' of men like the Christian Brothers and, in Gregory's words, 'the general intolerance that is afoot'.[7] Russell refused to print the piece; WBY thought he had been 'terrified' by the undelivered speech, and unable to deal with the controversy.[8] Their disagreement, when revealed, drove the *Catholic Bulletin* into delighted paroxysms of multiple exclamation marks, and 'The Need for Audacity of Thought' lay fallow until its appearance in the *Dial* the following February. But it forecast the deliberately confrontational terms embraced by WBY when he finally came to speak on divorce in the Senate on 11 June.

The debate, enshrined as one of WBY's supreme public moments, was precipitated by the report of the Committee on Standing Orders regarding 'matrimonial orders'. The outcome (never in much doubt) was that a private bill of Divorce, the only option possible for Irish citizens, had to receive a first reading in each House in order to proceed. This amounted to ruling such bills out completely. WBY's position was already well advertised, and he entered the lists at once. He read from a carefully prepared text, which survives.[9] It was a hot day, and observers noted that, as his words grew more inflamed, his colour rose and he began to sweat profusely. He began gently enough, regretting that it was apparently impossible for Catholic senators simply to absent themselves while a Divorce bill 'that concerned Protestants and non-Catholics only' might be passed. But he accepted that this would not happen, and moved quickly to the question of the North, and the inevitable effect of 'passing more and more Catholic laws' in the Free State. From early on he resorted to the language of religious confrontation, rather than the more tactful rhetoric of pluralism which had characterized his *Irish Statesman* essay: naming senatorial colleagues (to their discomfiture), specifying the influence of the Catholic archbishop (whom he misnamed), and declaring 'once you attempt legislation on religious grounds you open the way for every kind of intolerance and for every kind of religious persecution'.[10] In terms of personal attack, Archbishop Byrne was lightly treated compared to the Jesuit Father Peter Finlay, who had declared that suttee was a more defensible practice than divorce. Finlay was described as a man of 'monstrous discourtesy', who was likely to exert undue influence over the legislators of the country simply because he was a priest: whereas the Protestant bishop of Meath, who had also (in WBY's view pusillanimously) supported the criminalization of sexual laxity, would not sway a single vote. 'It is one of the glories of the Church in which I was born that we have put our Bishops in their places in discussions requiring legislation.'[11]

WBY's speech ranged widely, taking in the unhistorical nature of the Gospels, the backwardness of countries that did not countenance divorce, and the inevitability of 'irregular sexual relations' in a society which forbade remarriage. And over and over again, he aggressively set himself against his colleagues in the Senate, as well as the presumed opinion of the wider Irish world.

I know something of the opinions of those who will make the next generation in this country. I know it, perhaps, better than most of the members of this house, and

I am going to give those young people, speaking here, a piece of advice, though they are, perhaps, of a far less excitable temperament than I am. I urge them not to be unduly excited. There is no use quarrelling with icebergs in warm water. These questions will solve themselves. Father Peter Finlay and the Bishop of Meath will have their brief victory, but we can leave them to it.[12]

Had the speech ended there, it would have been possibly more graceful, and certainly more emollient. But this was not the effect that WBY was bent upon making. He had made some excisions: the original version accused the pro-divorce lobby of vindictively pursuing 'with particular sternness' members of their own faith who acquiesced in divorce laws elsewhere, and he also deleted a reference to John O'Leary refusing to have ex-papal soldiers in the IRB.[13] What remained was sufficiently offensive. Anticipating that 'when the iceberg melts [Ireland] will become an exceedingly tolerant country', he went on to instance the monuments in Dublin's streets to Parnell, Nelson, and O'Connell – all, by WBY's definition, adulterers.[14] The 'Protestant Bishop of Meath', he suggested, 'should advocate the removal of Nelson on strictly moral grounds'; there was a concealed double irony here, since as a Unionist the bishop would have revered Nelson's column in central Dublin, considered an affront to nationalists (and in fact detonated by an IRA bomb forty years later). According to WBY, Daniel O'Connell (whose statue stood further down Sackville Street) had the reputation of swelling the workhouses with his countless illegitimate children, 'but he believed in the indissolubility of marriage and when he died his heart was very proper-ly preserved in Rome'. And Parnell, whose monument marked the other end of the same thoroughfare, not only was convicted of adultery but mar-ried Mrs O'Shea after her divorce.

At that point, Glenavy as Speaker could bear no more, interjecting, 'Do you not think we might leave the dead alone?' WBY's reply was in every way characteristic: 'I would hate to leave the dead alone.' But the most famous passage in this long and astonishingly outspoken speech came at the end. It would be endlessly quoted, fuel the perception of WBY as an unregenerate Ascendancy elitist, and forecast many of the preoccupations explored in his writing over the next years.

I think it is tragic that within three years of this country gaining its independence we should be discussing a measure which a minority of this nation considers to be grossly oppressive. I am proud to consider myself a typical man of that minority. We against whom you have done this thing are no petty people. We are one of the great stocks of Europe. We are the people of Burke; we are the people of Grattan; we are the people of Swift, the people of Emmet, the people of Parnell. We have created most of the modern literature of this country. We have created the best of its political intelligence. Yet I do not altogether regret what has happened. I shall be able to find out, if not I, my children will be able to find out whether we have lost our stamina or not. You have defined our position and given us a popular following. If we have not lost our stamina then your victory will be brief, and your defeat final, and when it comes this nation may be transformed.[15]

In a country where a sense of religious difference, while pervasive, was always treated with polite evasiveness, where Protestant assertiveness was distinctly bad form, and where Catholic authority was now firmly in the ascendant, this attack was breathtakingly direct. It was also very carefully crafted. The Protestants whom WBY listed were all 'patriots', claimed by the nationalist tradition; he deliberately identified his caste as 'one of the great stocks of Europe' rather than in terms of English descent; the claim that most of Ireland's modern literature had been produced by Protestants strategically ignored many of the writers whose claims he had advanced in the past (Mangan, Carleton, Joyce), but may be taken as yet another assertion of the primacy of himself, Gregory, and Synge in the re-creation of national culture. Finally his declaration of the need to assess the 'stamina' of Protestant Ireland echoed the question raised by 'Meditations in Time of Civil War', which would continue to preoccupy him – in poems like 'The Statues' and plays like *Purgatory* – until the end of his life.

To his listeners, like the appalled Colonel Moore, WBY had taken 'an absolute sectarian view of the matter': one of the silent rules of Irish life had been loudly broken. Defending himself, WBY claimed that 'I had to give my speech what members thought was a religious turn, because it seemed to me that the only argument that I had to meet was a purely religious argument; I have seen no discussion in the Press and heard no discussion in this country which was not a purely religious argument, and it would be pure hypocrisy to deal with it on other grounds.' This conveniently ignored the fact that one of his adversaries was the Protestant bishop of Meath. He also attempted to clarify his remarks about Nelson, Parnell, and O'Connell, arguing that 'genius has its virtue, and it is only a small blot on its escutcheon if it is sexually irregular'. But to his audience, in the Senate and the wider Irish world, he had deliberately identified himself not only with Protestant tradition but with sexual licence and unashamed social snobbery.

To anyone following the current of his thought over the previous period, this cannot have been entirely unexpected. The political 'Protestant' chained up within him had burst out before, notably at the time of the 1912 Home Rule crisis, and WBY's quarrel with the blanket imposition of Catholic principles on Irish social and cultural life went back further still, to the quarrels with Cardinal Logue over *The Countess Kathleen*. But in those days he had occupied the same political quarter as John O'Leary, and been identified as an 'advanced nationalist' as well as an avant-garde artist. Nowadays he spoke from Merrion Square and the Kildare Street Club, and had taken his place in the group of senators who included Andrew Jameson, James Douglas, and other representatives of land, money, and the remnants of Ascendancy – willingly claimed by WBY himself as his 'party'.[16] It was all the *Catholic Bulletin* had ever expected of him, and more: phrases from his divorce speech would join its ritual canon of invective along with references to *To-Morrow*, 'Leda', and WBY's Civil List pension. Catholics who had defended WBY 'were "asking for it", and they have got it. They can now sample the satanic arrogance of what we have always termed the New Ascendancy.'[17] Less predictably, the *Irish Times* carried a rather pained editorial, and the bishop of Meath was only one of several prominent Protestants who would have preferred not to be identified with this particular crusade. Glenavy criticized WBY's speech to Gregory afterwards, though more for its oratorical flourishes than for its content. But Lily stoutly approved, telling her niece: 'It was very fine and a great effort, someone had to do it.' According to her, people like 'Canon Somerville & most of the young [Protestant] clergy' thoroughly agreed; the bishop of Meath was not typical. What is more, liberal Catholics such as Lord Fingall said it was 'common sense from beginning to end.'[18] But this was probably as unrepresentative a reaction on one side as the bishop of Meath's was on the other (Lord Fingall happened to be a notably complaisant husband). WBY himself claimed that the typist who had to copy it out did so in floods of tears.[19] All the same, he told Gregory, 'I get constant congratulations on my speech . . . the situation seems to be that educated catholics despise ecclesiastics of the sort I have attacked but are helpless and silent because of the control those ecclesiastics have over the masses'.[20] Though a devout Church of Ireland communicant, as WBY was not, Gregory seems to have held a view that was more restrained than that of her friend's; it is another instance where the balance of their positions had subtly tipped. Her record of their conversation about a fortnight later is illuminating:

Willie talking this morning of the notes and articles he is writing on Ireland, and of Burke and Berkeley influences. I said 'we Protestants did not like to boast, while we were "the oppressors", of our intellectual superiority and moral courage, but now we are under a Catholic majority we can do so.' And when he talked of English Protestantism I said 'Ours has and will have more force; theirs is vague and merging into Rome. We will never do that, we being a minority will stand solid and keep our strength. The smaller our congregations are I think the greater should be our pride that we can do and create so much.'[21]

Thus she ceded his right, against all traditional etiquette, to 'boast of intellectual superiority and moral courage'. But her conception of Irish Protestantism was primarily doctrinal and confessional, while WBY's was above all social and historical.

He would continue on the path marked out. By November he was further outraging pious opinion, and probably embarrassing fellow Protestants, by pointing out that 'immoral' France had a lower illegitimacy rate than 'Catholic Austria' – in a speech at what the *Catholic Bulletin* called 'Queen Elizabeth's Irish Academy'.[22] The divorce issue had reaffirmed his sense of historic commitment to 'all those who have held power in Ireland', and it also focused his mind on the necessity to fight for freedom of expression, in the battle over censorship that was already gathering force.

II

Since WBY was simultaneously working to arrange a government grant for the Abbey Theatre, the arena of so many battles with Irish public opinion, his sudden notoriety threatened to impede negotiations. Robinson's position also raised difficulties: at one point FitzGerald had, after all, suggested that, in view of the *To-Morrow* débâcle, the author of 'The Madonna of Slieve Dun' might have to temporarily resign his directorship, a suggestion WBY refused to countenance.[23] Instead a new director was appointed to 'balance' him, the economist and littérateur George O'Brien. By July an annual grant of £850 had been arranged, along just the lines WBY had planned before,[24] but he was warned not to thank Desmond FitzGerald and Ernest Blythe in the Senate debate on Appropriations, for fear of 'irritating' others and reawakening animosity over the divorce issue. Instead, the Abbey directors decided to express their appreciation by entertaining Blythe to a dinner on the Abbey stage, which duly took place on 8 August.[25] WBY came up from Ballylee, having concocted a speech with Gregory. His sense of pride and relief was palpable: 'we have become the first state-endowed theatre in any English-speaking country'. But his address was also notable for presenting the view of Georgian Ireland which was beginning to take hold of his imagination:

In the eighteenth century there were two or three decades during which Ireland produced an intellectual expression for herself that did rise with the first rank, and became famous through the whole world, and that was because during those decades she created an assembly, the old Irish parliament where a section of the Irish people could discuss their own life and their own problems . . . The day of oratory has passed but in this theatre we have created an assembly where we can discuss our own problems and our own life, an assembly more representative of the people as a whole than that of the 18th century, and I think we have the right to claim that we have founded an art of drama and an art of acting which are in the first rank . . . I think at this moment I may be permitted to boast of our own work for without doing so I cannot praise the Government awright [*sic*] for this new manifestation of their courage and intelligence.[26]

He was well aware of the elite nature of the eighteenth-century Irish parliament, as changes in the draft of the speech show, but this would not, in his eyes, have been a disadvantage.[27] Nor since its very early days had the Abbey ever been anything like a democracy. For WBY, central to the new arrangements was the continued control of the original directors. And his own dislike of demotic realist drama continued unabated. He was enraged by the success of plays like Brinsley MacNamara's *Look at the Heffernans*, played the following April, and railed against it to Shakespear. He argued about contracts, read potential scripts, and intrigued to keep the best actors – notably the young Shelah Richards, whose work he admired.[28] Another young actress, Mary Manning, noticed WBY's penchant for Richards; she also observed George Yeats's efforts to fit in at Drama League rehearsals and subsequent dinners, drinking a good deal while keeping a slightly nervous eye on her husband. (Manning also dreaded the Green Room teas and the institutionalized barm brack, a vast cartwheel of fruit bread baked at Gort: she was unable to keep a straight face when Barry Fitzgerald asked her 'Would ye like a bit of bog?'[29])

WBY's possessiveness about his and Gregory's joint creation was not lessened by the government subsidy. Towards the end of the year the Abbey's twenty-first birthday was celebrated with an evening of speeches and a special programme of plays by the original triumvirate of directors: *The Hour-Glass, In the Shadow of the Glen*, and *Hyacinth Halvey*. The sense of *temps retrouvé* was heightened by the inclusion of Frank Fay in the cast. Gregory, whose heroic energies were beginning to flag, was brought by WBY in a taxi, and gave a memorable address. Officialdom was represented by O'Higgins and Blythe, both of whom also spoke. But for all WBY's compliments to the government's 'courage and intelligence', Gregory had in fact been chosen to represent the directors because both Robinson and WBY were currently too controversial to share a platform with Cosgrave's colleagues.[30] Lily Yeats sent the inevitable report to her niece:

Everyone we knew was there, all the grey heads that had been there as brown and red and blond, 21 years ago. Willy sat in the middle of the stalls locked in a deep dream, with moments of intense observation. He did not speak. Lady Gregory made a charming speech, clever. She had difficulty in controlling her tears at first, the applause was so great. Her Galway voice added to the charm. She, poor woman, has suffered much in the 21 years . . .[31]

So, in his way, had WBY; and so had the newly independent country whose national theatre had begun in such an unlikely manner at the turn of the century, developed and preserved by the energy, talent, guile, and ruthlessness of the two surviving original directors. They were now 'history'. The Abbey, in its new incarnation, was integral to the way the 'Irish Renascence' was being historicized into the great myth enshrining the birth of the nation. This process was symbolized by JBY's portraits of O'Leary, WBY, Standish O'Grady, Hyde, Moore, and AE, which had just come back to Ireland, bought for the National Gallery from the Quinn collection by philanthropic Irish-Americans.[32] WBY's consciousness of a generation of cultural founding fathers, centred on the Abbey, developed through his autobiographies and canonically defined in his Stockholm speech, was now built into the edifice of Irish history.

For Gregory, however, one crowning task remained, in order that Ireland might enter its independent existence with a full cultural inheritance: the restitution of the Lane pictures. In the late summer of 1925 a British government commission reported unsatisfactorily. While accepting that Lane believed his codicil leaving the paintings to Dublin was a legal document, the Report found that it had no legal force, and so legislation would have to be passed in the British parliament to change the will – which the commission stopped well short of recommending. Legal complications, apparently, outweighed moral claims.[33] Gregory at once enlisted WBY to continue battle. The issue was now complicated by the existence of Duveen's Tate Gallery extension, which enabled the British side to assert they were fulfilling Lane's wishes for an appropriate home dedicated to the paintings. 'Their claim seems to me', WBY told Glenavy, 'exactly as if the Forty Thieves were to say they had a right to their treasure because they had been to the trouble of digging a cavern to contain it.'[34] From now on, much of his annoyance would be directed at this ploy: he particularly resented the king's opening of the Tate extension the following March, since he had hoped to appeal to the monarch, as head of the commonwealth, to favour the case of his new Irish dominion.[35] In the meantime the endless round of lobbying got under way once more. Gregory now had an Irish government to make representations on their behalf, and was also cultivating the opposition. By 1928 she had de Valera firmly committed to founding a gallery which he characteristically hoped would 'express both in its architecture and in its content, that love for the arts which has ever been a characteristic of the Gael'.[36] But she also relentlessly placed pressure on WBY to use his influence in the political drawing rooms of London.

None of this was welcome during a summer which he wanted to devote to writing. In May he was working on a short visionary play,

The Resurrection, developing his preoccupation with Christianity as the annunciation of a historical cycle now moving to its close; by the autumn he was engaged upon the long poem which would become *The Tower*. But in between came a series of distractions: not only Abbey business and the revival of the Lane pictures campaign but the publication of *The Bounty of Sweden*. It was Cuala's first production from its new premises in Baggot Street; they had finally vacated WBY's dining room. The oracular tone and apparent self-regard of the meditations attracted adverse attention from, among others, Gosse, requiring a magisterial letter of self-defence from WBY.[37] Then there was the world of politics, and the demands of fame. 'Never tell folk I can get them to see W.B.', Lily cautioned her niece that autumn, 'because I can't. He was never very approachable, now he is very unapproachable. The Senate gives him much work, committees and other work. Then he has his writing and letters and the Abbey. He has to rest in the afternoon, and so must protect himself from callers. He would get no peace.'[38]

Nonetheless he was determined to retain his active involvement in enterprises such as Cuala. 'W. B. is editor of the Cuala Press,' Lolly told Symons, 'in the sense that *I can not* print any book he does not *agree to my doing . . .* my brother is most helpful & I could not run the Press at all without him. He doesn't in any way supervise the work here – merely gets in the books – but *that is a very important part of it.*' As to disagreements, 'brothers & sisters often have these storms – I too am hot – & they bear no malice ever.' Not so sisters and sisters, or even sisters and sisters-in-law: Lily, back from her London nursing-home, continued to chafe under Lolly's 'hysterical egoism' and 'insane jealousy', while Lolly herself privately resented George's control of her brother's everyday life and felt that she was entertained in Merrion Square 'as a distasteful duty'. But Lolly had to live her life, as George resignedly put it, 'as a series of short dramatic one-act plays'.[39] As for George herself, she had begun to chafe under the restrictions of Dublin life, and her letters to friends like Robinson and MacGreevy hint at an ominous current of discontent and frustrated creativity. She also longed for travel. In August 1925 there was another visit to Italy, via Switzerland, where WBY gave a lucrative lecture for the Lunn travel company (and had to recite 'Innisfree' 'with an air of suppressed loathing'). They went on to Milan to meet MacGreevy, who was struck by WBY's attachment to the country; he talked of the permanent effect his 1907 visit had left, and the beauty of the mosaics in Sicily and Ravenna. Milan offered less; he dismissed the cathedral as 'Nottingham lace architecture' and identified a painting of Christ and Simon the Pharisee as 'Our Lord dining with the Lady Cunard of the day'.[40]

Returning to Dublin did not improve his temper. From the autumn of 1925 confrontations resurfaced in another traditional sphere, as the Abbey began to get to grips with O'Casey's latest play, the third in his great trilogy about the Irish revolution. *The Plough and the Stars* was set in Easter Week 1916 and completed the examination of patriotic heroics begun by *Shadow of a Gunman* and *Juno and the Paycock*. If the first two plays had laid bare the world of the city tenements to the Abbey audience, the third used that tenement world to evaluate the revolution itself. In doing so, O'Casey projected an even more sceptical light upon the lives of 'ordinary' people caught up in national tragedy, using the device of an aggressively nationalistic panorama rather than a developed plot. The sympathetic portrayal of a prostitute, 'Rosie Redmond', on stage created one problem; another arose during a pub scene, when the words of a distinctly Pearsean speech come floating through the window and into the cross-talk of the bar-room habitués, striking a note nearer bathos than heroism. ('The dramatic effect is a terrible one,' a disapproving reviewer would write, 'more terrible when one remembers that one is Irish.'[41]) In his previous two plays O'Casey had introduced a certain scepticism about the Anglo-Irish War and the civil war that followed it: this had been acceptable. But in *The Plough* he would represent, with irony and distance, the Easter Rising – an event which did not allow an ambiguous or irreverent interpretation. That 'paratheatrical' event occupies the same relation to O'Casey's play, Nicholas Grene has remarked, as *Hamlet* does to Stoppard's *Rosencrantz and Guildenstern are Dead*.[42] This time those offended were likely to be not only the guardians of conventional morality but the inheritors of nationalist piety. Little wonder that when the play was sent to Gregory at Coole in August, she felt a tremor. It was the spectre of the *Playboy*.

Ireland in 1925 was a different country from the Ireland of 1907, and the Abbey's position too had changed: it had just become, in WBY's proud boast, 'the first state-endowed theatre in any English-speaking country', and the new director George O'Brien was effectively a government nominee. By September, encouraged by disquiet among some of the actors, O'Brien was involved in a lengthy correspondence with WBY and Robinson. Cuts were demanded, both in language and structure. O'Brien wanted Rosie Redmond banished completely, a point forcefully rebutted by WBY:

... she is certainly necessary to the general action and idea as are the drunkards and wastrels. O'Casey is contrasting the ideal dream with the normal grossness of life and of that she is an essential part. It is no use putting her in if she does not express herself vividly and in character, if her 'professional' side is not emphasised. Almost certainly a phrase here or there must be altered in rehearsal but the scene as a whole is admirable, one of the finest O'Casey has written. To eliminate any part of it on grounds that have nothing to do with dramatic literature would be to deny all our traditions.[43]

WBY, Robinson, and Gregory were prepared for some changes. But when O'Brien crudely warned them against provoking 'a movement of hostility that would make it difficult or impossible for the Government to continue or to increase its subsidy', they united against him, prepared – in Gregory's words – to risk the subsidy to retain artistic freedom. O'Brien was brought unhappily on board, but by the time of rehearsals in January 1926 two key actors, Eileen Crowe and F. J. McCormick (playing Mrs Gogan and Jack Clitheroe), were refusing to speak certain lines. Gregory favoured temporizing, but WBY was furious. By the time the play opened on 8 February, public expectation was running high, and the one-week run was booked solid ten days before the play opened.

At first the directors seemed to have got away with it. The controversial second act, featuring Rosie Redmond and off-duty republicans roistering in a pub, drew no fire; there was an ovation for the author, and reviews were lengthy and favourable.[44] The first-night audience included the novelist Liam O'Flaherty, the politicians Blythe and O'Higgins, and Lord Chief Justice Hugh Kennedy; neither O'Higgins nor Kennedy liked it, but kept their disapprobation private. This discretion was encouraged by the fact that the ministerial party dined with WBY beforehand, and were shepherded by him to meet the players at the interval. The only discordant note so far was provided by Joseph Holloway, who referred loudly to the governmental representatives as 'bloody murderers' when they passed his seat.[45]

This sign that the civil war furies were not yet appeased was prophetic of the political upheavals to come. The following evenings were less dominated by Dublin's *bon ton*, and objections began to be heard, particularly to the national flag being brought into a pub. By the third night Rosie Redmond's appearance was hissed. On the fourth night, 11 February, the second act was greeted with uproar; in the third, stink-bombs were thrown, the stage was rushed, and actors attacked: a man who struck the actress playing Bessie Burgess was allegedly felled by a punch from Barry Fitzgerald. The police were called in, and – as recounted by the *Manchester Guardian* correspondent – WBY himself took the stage.

Senator W. B. Yeats, the well-known poet and dramatist, who is a director of the theatre, came forward to the accompaniment of a torrent of boos and hisses. What he said was quite inaudible to a large section of the audience who knew he was speaking only by the movement of his lips and the waving of his hands in dramatic gesture. This was his speech: 'I thought you had got tired of this. It commenced fifteen years ago. You have disgraced yourselves again. Is this to be an ever-recurring celebration of the arrival of Irish genius? Once more you have rocked the cradle of genius. The news of this will go from country to country. You have once more rocked the cradle of a reputation. The fame of O'Casey is born tonight. This is his apotheosis.[46]

This makes clear that some text of WBY's remarks was made available to reporters. He had, in fact, taken the precaution of delivering it to the *Irish Times* office, slipping out from the theatre during the riots. He admitted later that he knew he need say only one sentence and the rest would be drowned in uproar. 'I went on pretending to speak and then went back to the newspaper office and wrote the speech the audience thought I had given.'[47] The paper's version of his remarks included the phrase 'Synge first, and then O'Casey'; certainly the riots of 1907 had prepared him for 1926. And this time the police summoned to the Abbey were the civic guards of the new state, not the Dublin Metropolitan Police from the Castle. One journalist described his appearance on stage as 'a Sydney Carton attitude', another observer thought him 'stiff, pompous and furious'; all agreed he was inaudible. But Gabriel Fallon, who was present backstage, noted his energy, and the delight with which he said, 'I am sending for the police, and *this time* it will be *their own* police.' 'The old war-horse', Fallon added, 'was hearing once again trumpets sounding the vindication of Synge.'[48]

Smyllie's paper obligingly carried the fullest coverage. The most prominent opponents of the play were, by now, a group of women described by one of their number, Hanna Sheehy-Skeffington, as 'the widows of Easter Week'. Objecting to what they saw as the trivialization of heroic sacrifice, they included the historian Dorothy MacArdle, the widow of Tom Clarke, Patrick Pearse's mother, and the sister of Kevin Barry. 'From start to finish the whole thing was a woman's row, made and carried on by women,' according to the *Irish Times*. This ignored the man who had been punched off the stage, but suggested that O'Casey's aim to portray women as victims of history did not always find its mark. After the theatre closed that night, WBY congratulated the actors in the Green Room. 'That such a small minority could be found in Dublin to try and stop the showing of Mr O'Casey's play was a proof to him that Mr O'Casey had in "The Plough and the Stars" cut very close to the bone.' This supposedly private meeting was, once again, reported verbatim in the *Irish Times*. 'Yeats', Holloway sourly reported, 'was in his element at last.'[49]

The symbiotic relationship between WBY and the *Irish Times* is further evidenced by the paper's Saturday leader. This directly connected the reaction to O'Casey's play with the campaign to institutionalize literary censorship, already taking hold in certain quarters of the government. WBY wanted to prolong the discussion into a public debate, as with the *Playboy*, but Gregory squashed the notion, astutely noting that the widows of 1916 could prove more formidable and embarrassing opponents than those who had naively defended Irish peasant virtues against Synge's supposed traducement. Her instinct was proved right by Hanna Sheehy-Skeffington's letter to the *Irish Independent* the following week, which emphasized the 'supposedly national' status of the Abbey.

Your editorial misses what was apparent in your report regarding the Abbey Theatre protest. The demonstration was not directed against the individual actor, nor was it directed to the moral aspect of the play. It was on national grounds solely, voicing a passionate indignation against the outrage of a drama staged in a supposedly national theatre, which held up to derision and obloquy the men and women of Easter week.

The protest was made, not by Republicans alone, and had the sympathy of large numbers in the house. There is a point beyond which toleration becomes mere servility, and realism not art, but morbid perversity. The play, as a play, may be left to the judgement of posterity, which will rank it as artistically far below some of Mr O'Casey's work. It is the realism that would paint not only the wart on Cromwell's nose, but that would add carbuncles and running sores in a reaction against idealisation. In no country save in Ireland could a State-subsidised theatre presume on popular patience to the extent of making a mockery and a byword of a revolutionary movement on which the present structure claims to stand.[50]

This last observation dealt an effective blow against WBY's claims as published in *The Bounty of Sweden*, and Sheehy-Skeffington went on to describe the Abbey 'in its subsidised sleek old age jeering at its former enthusiasms'. Anticipating the ground that WBY would take up, she added, 'the only censorship that is justified is the free censorship of public opinion'. These were far weightier issues than Joseph Holloway's celebrated assertion that 'there are no streetwalkers in Dublin' (or at least not 'till the Tommies brought them over'[51]) or the lengthy accusations and counter-accusations about O'Casey's own chequered relations with James Connolly and the Citizen Army, given full rein in the *Voice of Labour*. Other, less powerfully argued letters followed Sheehy-Skeffington's in accusing WBY himself of suppressing public opinion, 'dictating Mussolini-like to a Dublin audience'.[52] O'Casey's ripostes did nothing to lower the temperature: 'The heavy-hearted expression by Mrs Sheehy-Skeffington about "the Ireland that remembers with tear-dimmed eyes all that Easter Week stands for", makes me sick. Some of the men cannot even get a job.'[53] The argument revolved around the propriety of using recent Irish history as O'Casey had used it, and the question – as it often is in such cases – was one of tone as much as of content.

Interestingly, one of the strongest attacks (if not an entirely coherent one) came from the novelist Liam O'Flaherty, himself an avant-garde socialist-realist whose work was considered offensive to conventional opinion. In O'Flaherty's view, WBY's 'protest against the protest of the audience was an insult to the people of this country . . . it is not a good thing that pompous fools should boast that we have been "cut to the bone".'[54] Yet again, an issue of national opinion and political rectitude was complicated by the impact of WBY's public personality. A barely suppressed resentment against him is apparent in other contributions, notably from the young poet Austin Clarke, railing against 'Anglo-Irish coterie criticism'.[55] Even F. R. Higgins, a future acolyte of WBY, raised the Nobel Laureate's own celebrations of 1916 against him, pointing out that 'some have forgotten the cold logic of *Sixteen Dead Men* and their influence on those "That converse bone to bone", and of a time when "A terrible beauty is born".'[56] Sheehy-Skeffington's unremitting campaign constantly returned to WBY's calling in the police to discipline the *Playboy* audience nineteen years before. One issue of the *Catholic Bulletin* spread itself over eight pages on the subject of 'subsidised New Ascendancy linked up with the Associated Aesthetes and the Mutual Boosters', personified by the 'Subsidised Director in Chief and Orator at Large, W. B. Pollexfen Yeats, Declaimer on Divorce and Elocutionist on Education' (an interest of WBY's which it found particularly galling). Above all, the *Bulletin* took up the *Irish Statesman* reviewer Walter Starkie's approving endorsement of O'Casey's line 'There's no such thing as an Irishman or an Englishman, or a German or a Turk: we're all only human bein's.' Thus interpreted, the play decried not only nationalism but the very fact of nationality itself – for which, after all, the sacrifices of the last decade had been made.

The controversy continued until (and after) the play was revived in May, but WBY avoided further public statements. (Maud Gonne, on the other hand, entered the lists, though without the benefit of having actually seen the play.) Over the next fifty-odd years, the Abbey performed *The Plough and the Stars* nearly a thousand times. Like the *Playboy*, it graduated quickly from controversy to acceptability. Even the *Catholic Bulletin* soon turned its energies to campaigning against the plans of the 'Persse-Pollexfen Theatre' to import the work of Eugene O'Neill.[57] The author of *The Plough*, however, was destined to go on causing controversy. He was already meditating a move to London (where *Juno and the Paycock* had been playing simultaneously, with tremendous success). The theme of the Great War raging in Europe had filtered into *The Plough and the Stars*, and O'Casey was planning a new play on internationalist themes which could only promise trouble.

For WBY, the struggle clarified his opinions about the new Ireland and its sensitivity to criticism. Ten days after the disturbances at the Abbey, he had an opportunity to speak his mind again, this time to a more receptive audience. Giving the lecture 'My Own Poetry', he invoked a name which would have surprised even the *Catholic Bulletin*:

He had been told the previous night that he was a Cromwellian, and there was a valuable part of Ireland – the Cromwellian part – which had its own patriotism. It was chosen, and it had great qualities. To illustrate this patriotism he read his recent poem: 'The Airman Forsees His End'. [*sic*].

After the lecture a member of the audience asked would Mr Yeats express his opinion on the patriotism that resented the faults of a country being exposed. Were the people of other countries as sensitive as the Irish, if a play showing their faults was put on the stage, and was such a play likely to be hounded down in other countries, or to be considered beneficial, as having the effect of curing their faults?

Mr Yeats said that he thought that a nation was likely to go through that phase, and it was a very natural phase; but he was quite sure that when it reached intellectual maturity it got over that feeling; but every country that had had in any way the opinion of other nations thrust upon it felt that way for a time. The moment a nation reached intellectual maturity, it became exceedingly proud and ceased to be vain and when it became exceedingly proud it did not disguise its faults, because it was satisfied to know what were its qualities and powers; but when it was immature it was exceedingly vain, and did not believe in itself, and so long as it did not believe in itself it wanted other people to think well of it, in order that it might get a little reflected confidence. With success came pride, and with pride came indifference as to whether people were shown in a good or bad light on the stage. As a nation came to intellectual maturity it realised that the only thing that did it any credit was its intellect.[58]

The distinction between vanity and pride, and the assured place of the intellect in national life, were crystal clear to him; but it was increasingly apparent that his definition did not command unanimous assent in circles outside the Monday evening gatherings at 82 Merrion Square.

III

By the time the storm broke over *The Plough and the Stars*, WBY's intellectual isolation had been demonstrated in a different way. In February, the first version of *A Vision* had been published. In keeping with its private and hieratic status, it was released to the reading world largely by subscription, and guaranteed further exclusivity by a three-guinea price tag. Even those closest to WBY were slightly guarded. 'I was thrilled to get your book,' Iseult wrote in late January:

I have not yet been able to read it very far because unfortunately for me Francis is equally interested and as we neither care to read aloud to each other, since the book has come we are living on terms of a dangerous chilly politeness! Who made the picture of Geraldus? It has a quaint resemblance to you. It is almost a miracle to have embodied the exposition of a difficult system in such a clear beautiful poem as that dialogue between Aherne and Robartes.[59]

But she rapidly changed the subject to social arrangements and the recent revelations of Krishnamurti. Lennox Robinson could not pretend to understand it all but found 'some great stuff in it', and was relieved that its shock-value was limited ('it's non-Christian of course but no-one for years has suspected W. B. of Christianity').[60] AE's reaction took the form of a long review in the *Irish Statesman*, which was more or less the only formal response the book elicited (WBY gloomily suspected that the publisher had sold the other three copies designated for review: it would make only a faint and far-off splash, he told Shakespear, like the stones he used to drop into a well as a child[61]). Even AE wrote: 'Here I fall away from a mind I have followed, I think with understanding, since I was a boy'. The determinism of WBY's system disconcerted him, though he felt the concentrated and

6. Dulac's frontispiece woodcut for the first edition of *A Vision*, allegedly 'by an unknown artist of the early sixteenth century', though Dulac chose an earlier style still, 'better suited to a book of that kind than the "Durer" manner'. Iseult thought it bore 'a quaint resemblance' to WBY, which was of course the point.

aphoristic style might make it seem more reductionist than its author intended. Faced with the 'hard geometrical core', supported by the 'long and brilliant meditation' on the cycles and changes of history, AE took refuge in the idea that the divine origin of the soul meant that all human speculation had to follow some approximation to eternal truth preserved in the 'Oversoul'. But, in the end, like many readers of *A Vision*, he was reduced to accepting it as a sort of arcane parlour-game. Contemplating in bewilderment the archetypal personalities in their phases, he admitted defeat in the face of WBY's relentless subjectivity:

It is not a book which will affect many in our time. It is possible it may be discussed feverishly by commentators a century hence, as Blake's prophetic books, so ignored, so unintelligible a hundred years ago, are discussed by many editors in our time, and he is found to be the profoundest voice of his own age. It is possible *A Vision* may come to be regarded as the greatest of Mr Yeats' works. It is conceivable also that it may be regarded as his greatest erring from the way of his natural genius, and the lover of his poetry may lament that the most intense concentration of his intellect was given to this book rather than to drama or lyric. Personally, I am glad that it was written. I do not doubt that though the seeds of his thought do not instantly take root and fructify in my mind that they will have their own growth, and later I may find myself comprehending much that is unintelligible.

The intimate and slightly self-regarding tone shared by AE and WBY, along with the easy assumption of a kind of esoteric brotherhood, might have been calculated to enrage outsiders, such as the inevitable *Catholic Bulletin*. It had already taken to referring to Russell as 'the Mahatma' or the 'Great Ego', and to Yeats as the 'Grand Visionary'; now it was faced with the 'loony slovenliness' of *A Vision*.

What are *we* to do meanwhile, uncivilised and uneducated as we are? If even the Great Ego finds the Great Visionary 'now unintelligible', what is to be done? But the Reviewer of the Vision has already given us cause for hope: for he writes also in this strain: 'I may have missed some implication, and there may be some way out.' Let us wait for a new Oration from the Orator at Large; a Phase, an Apotheosis, a Vision; any of these may be vouchsafed us in 1926, epoch of the New Nationalism and the New Education.[62]

Even those more sympathetic were somewhat flummoxed. The young painter Norah McGuinness, visiting Merrion Square for the first time, found herself dining alone with WBY while George and the children were sequestered with measles upstairs. *A Vision* had just been published, and he made it the sole subject of conversation, oblivious to the fact that she had not read it – a pose kept up when the Monday night visitors assembled afterwards and WBY appealed to her on several disputed points of his interpretation. 'I was to learn it was Yeats's way of thinking aloud & elucidating for himself.'[63]

Another kind of critical reaction came from his old occultist acquaintance Frank Pearce Sturm, a fellow habitué of Watkins Bookshop in Cecil Court, now marooned for life in a Lancashire medical practice. Sturm read the text with a very different kind of attention from Russell's, and forwarded slightly grumpy remonstrations. 'The Moon doesn't move from West to East; she is never retrograde; but moves along the Zodiac in the same direction as the sun, not in the opposite direction. You base so much on the opposite movements of the Lunar & Solar circles, where no opposite movement exists, that some kind of explanation is needed to smooth out the wrinkles here.' 'Unless some dull dog with an eye for detail & accuracy goes over Book II, it will remain incomprehensible simply because of inaccuracies . . . the text simply does not explain the figures.'[64] WBY's reply gamely disputed Sturm's interpretation of his astrological symbolism, but admitted some carelessness, and ended with a plaintive appeal:

I was afraid that Book II would be almost unintelligible but I could do no better. I have no gift for explanation & am the least mathematical of men. I made myself ill over it. It took me months to understand the simplest things. I understood nothing till the whole mass was before me, & little then for months . . . Think of my symbolism as a thing in itself & only when you have mastered it compare it with any astronomical system.[65]

Though Sturm wrote a mollifying answer about lunar and solar movement, he continued to pinpoint errors, such as Cicero writing *Scipio's Dream* in Greek rather than in Latin, and – even more embarrassing – a grammatical mistake in the frontispiece caption,[66] also denounced by G. R. S. Mead in the *Quest* as 'a "howler" for which Smith Minor at a preparatory school would receive condign punishment'. Sturm tried to make up for his relentless amendments of *A Vision* by finding encouraging parallel references to gyres in a wide range of authorities from Thomas Aquinas to John Dee, but the corrections rankled. Thus, any apparent evidence that made *A Vision* less idiosyncratic was eagerly welcomed. In May 1925 WBY had written excitedly to his collaborator Dulac:

A German called Oswald Spengler has lit on a number of the same ideas as those in my book. The American *Dial* has just published a long essay by him – the introduction to his book now being translated – which might have been a chapter of 'A Vision'. He applies the fundamental thought to things outside my knowledge, but his thought & mine differ in nothing. It seems that the thought came to him suddenly & with great excitement.[67]

WBY continued to proselytize about Spengler, the first volume of whose

Decline of the West he obtained in the summer of 1926 and read avidly. Spengler's cyclical view of history, and belief that the era marked by the dominance of Christian civilization was drawing to a close, seemed to WBY exact parallel revelations to his own: that Spengler's book was 'passing through the press in Germany' in 1918, just when the Yeatses were interrogating the 'Instructors' about the 'System', seemed a confirmation. 'Coincidence is impossible – his mind [and] mine were in contact – through intermediaries, & not embodied into mediaters.'[68] His belief in Spengler's 'vast learning' and profundity was firmly established, though other authorities such as Vico and Berkeley would partially displace him. WBY gradually shifted his emphasis to Spengler's imagination and away from his scholarship, which was just as well; three years later, when WBY was immersed in Spengler's second volume, his philosophically minded correspondent Sturge Moore crisply dismissed the German schoolmaster-sage as 'worthless . . . no one takes him seriously I find'. WBY still defended him, though less committedly than on his first acquaintance.[69] But, above all, the assonances with Spengler's book seemed to add credence to WBY's old idea of Anima Mundi, adhered to since his early apprenticeship to Swedenborg, the Neoplatonists, and Blake; universal ideas could be absorbed by the individual mind, if subjected to the necessary disciplines.

Nonetheless, responses to *A Vision* left him slightly chastened. 'Don't get it', he advised an importunate correspondent.

It is horribly expensive, £3.3.0 when published & some booksellers have already put up the price – it was privately published – It is only a first draft of a book & intended for students of Plotinus, the Hermetic fragments & unpopular literature of that kind. The chances are a hundred to one against your liking it & in three years time I will bring it out expanded & corrected at 10/-. So please wait. It may be worth risking 10/- on.[70]

This Pollexfen approach to the book's value should not conceal its real importance to WBY, but reactions like Sturm's had convinced him that much of it should be rewritten. He would do so, though over a far longer period than three years. The apparent existence of parallel theories, whether among Church fathers, Elizabethan astrologers, or contemporary German philosophers, provided both consolation and encouragement. And for this he now had to look elsewhere than George. Just when *A Vision* was being published, she confided to her friend Tom MacGreevy, 'there's nothing in his verse worth preserving but the personal. All the pseudo-mystico-intellecto-nationalistico stuff of the last fifteen years isnt worth a trouser-button.'[71] Her opinions may have had some effect. Gregory noted that in January 1926 the publication of *A Vision* had turned him to love poetry and 'freed him from philosophical preoccupations'.[72] But this last was wishful thinking. He could not leave them alone.

During the summer of 1926 he returned to reading Plotinus; his philosophical correspondence with Sturge Moore remained intense; and his preoccupations, as ever, were translated into the verse which he had fled to Ballylee to write. Over 1926 and 1927, he himself thought, his poetry was 'at its best'.[73] 'Yeats is extremely well,' Gregory reported to Gogarty from Galway in May 1926, 'has begun a new poem and has another in his head jostling it. And another part of his mind is occupied with threat of drainage of a bog, which he is afraid will convert Ballylee into an an [*sic*] island, or possibly into part of the country-under-wave. He is prepared to resist this with all the land forces of the neighbouring farmers, who will bring their pitchforks out to resist the threatened flood.'[74]

Ballylee had, indeed, given him both the title and the organizing symbolism of the sequence he had completed late in 1925 under the title 'The Tower'. It also stands behind 'A Dialogue of Self and Soul', which took shape afterwards,[75] and a series of later poems which reprise the images of Sato's sword, winding staircases, and Ascendancy inheritances. In part, 'The Tower' reflects the bleakness with which he surveyed life from the vantage of sixty years – and his growing readiness to broadcast unpopular opinions and air thoughts long kept silent. (The following spring, Cuala planned a new book called 'Bitterness, being fifty thoughts from a Diary kept by William Butler Yeats in nineteen hundred and eleven', but for publication 'Bitterness' became 'Estrangement'.[76]) Yet as he told Lady Londonderry, 'The Tower' represented affirmation. 'I am making this gaunt tower the centre of many poems. It is a deliberately chosen symbol of some difficult truths. I feel that those who are fortunate enough to live at the foundation of a nation (& this nation is in the main knew [*recte* new] despite its gaelic dream) can affect the future as men of greater genius elsewhere cannot.'[77]

Yet if national history is one theme of 'The Tower', it takes second place to personal history: the encroachment of age, the failure of love, and (more painful still) the memory of failure through insufficient commitment – or desire.[78] The poem begins on a note of desperate derision, mocking the old age that has been 'tied to me/As to a dog's tail' – and declaring that creative writing must be abandoned in favour of philosophical cogitation. The rest of the poem triumphantly refutes such an idea – first implicitly, in the brilliance with which he summons up the passionate, devious, bewitching ghosts of the Ballylee locality, and at the end openly, when the poet affirms his faith in the power conferred by inheritance, and his belief in a humanist unity of being, founded on inspiration as much as on learning. It is noticeable – given the political struggles enmeshing WBY – that his heroes and inspirational figures are country lovers, Gaelic poets, and Georgian gentlefolk, all embodying the blend of ruthlessness, anti-puritanism, and *sprezzatura* by which he identified one kind of Irish ideal. (The heroic delusions wrought through passion and drink are part of it too.)

It is time that I wrote my will;
I choose upstanding men,
That climb the streams until
The fountain leap and at dawn
Drop their cast at the side
Of dripping stone; I declare
They shall inherit my pride,
The pride of people that were
Bound neither to cause nor to State,
Neither to slaves that were spat on,
Nor to the tyrants that spat,
The people of Burke and of Grattan
That gave, though free to refuse –
Pride, like that of the morn,
When the headlong light is loose,
Or that of the fabulous horn
Or that of the sudden shower,
When all streams are dry
Or that of the hour
When the swan must fix his eye
Upon a fading gleam,
Float out upon a long
Last reach of glittering stream
And there sing his last song.
And I declare my faith;
I mock Plotinus' thought
And cry in Plato's teeth,
Death and life were not
Till man made up the whole,
Made lock, stock and barrel
Out of his bitter soul,
Aye, sun and moon and star, all,
And further add to that
That, being dead, we rise,
Dream and so create
The final Paradise.
I have prepared my peace
With learned Italian things
And the proud stones of Greece
Poet's imaginings
And memories of love,

315

Memories of the words of women,
All those things whereof
Man makes a superman,
Mirror resembling dreams

And at the loophole there,
The daws chatter and scream,
And drop twig, layer upon layer;
When they have mounted up,
The mother bird will rest
On their hollow top,
And so warm her wild nest.

The final stanzas apparently hand on the torch of physical, passionate affirmation to the next generation, while the poet removes himself into abstraction:
but, given the visceral energy of what has gone before, and the controlled
power of the poem as a whole, this abdication is hardly convincing:

I leave both faith and pride
To young upstanding men,
That climb the mountain side,
That under bursting dawn
They may drop a fly;
Being of that metal made
Till it was broken by
The sedentary trade.

Now shall I make my soul
Compelling it to study
In a learned school
Till the wreck of body
Slow decay of blood
Testy delirium
Or dull decrepitude,
Or what worse evil come –

The death of friends, or death
Of every brilliant eye
That made a catch in the breath –
Seem but the clouds of the sky
When the horizon fades;
Or a bird's sleepy cry
Among the deepening shades.

Personal icons are positioned throughout the poem like household deities.
The local beauty, Mary Hynes, doubles – as ever – for Helen of Troy. WBY's

youthful invention Red Hanrahan ('old lecher with a love on every wind'), composite poet-lover, identifies the sacrifices and delusions of obsessive love. The Norman *condottieri* who haunt Ballylee take their places in the inherited history of Irish power relations. The deliberate evocation of 'The Fisherman' recalls Synge and what WBY was coming to define as his Anglo-Irish solitude. And at the centre, yet again, lies the question which all George's 'Instructors' had never answered: why, how, could he never quite reconcile himself to his failure with Gonne, and whose fault had it really been?

> Does the imagination dwell the most
> Upon a woman won or woman lost?
> If on the lost, admit you turned aside
> From a great labyrinth out of pride,
> Cowardice, over some silly subtle thought
> Or anything called conscience once
> And that if memory recur, the sun's
> Under eclipse and the day blotted out.

Through the spring and summer of 1926 he was being driven back to the memories of his youth, summed up in the series 'A Man Young and Old' and recorded in regretful, half-flirtatious observations dotted through his letters to Olivia Shakespear, who told him briskly he was 'a little morbid' about the inescapable fact of age.[79] Approaching his sixty-first birthday, he was grimly determined to hold on to the vanities of youth, but in March he had over-exerted himself with Swedish exercises, which caused a rupture. Henceforth he had to wear a surgical belt. 'So he will probably get fat, which is sad,' Lily summed up to Ruth Lane-Poole. 'He is still a handsome man.'[80] He did not get particularly fat (though Gogarty told him he 'waxed and waned like the moon'), and he remained impressively handsome. After nearly ten years his marriage had subsided into quotidian domesticity, a state less welcome to George than WBY assumed. Taking a settled home life for granted, he was more intent on restlessly reviewing the great changes in his life over the past decade.

He was also reviewing his apprenticeship in philosophy. His play *The Resurrection*, now drafted but not to be performed for some years, returned to the idea of the Christian era as a cycle developing antithetically out of the pre-ordained mythologies of antiquity. The publication of *A Vision*, and his combative public stances, had reignited the need to define his heterodox philosophy, and to spread his eclectic and idiosyncratic sources before his reading public. This was often done with what one exasperated future critic would call 'the assertion/denial, give-with-one-hand/take-away-with-the-other and always-have-it-both-ways strategy that Yeats practises whenever anything of the occult is in question'.[81] But the strategy is also a form of antithetical debate. WBY was always drawn to the dialogue form, and from this time the pattern of his philosophical poetry constantly pits soul against self, saints against swordsmen, Dionysius against Christ.[82] And in all that he wrote during this period of reassessment and reaffirmation he responded to the 'need for audacity of thought'. His growing preoccupation with the dangers of censorship, together with the recollections and regrets associated with his late sexual maturing, infused his poetry with a new erotic frankness. Thus the poetic developments of the later 1920s forecast the direction (if not the notoriety) of his work in the next decade.

For the moment, in 1926, the sexual references were lightly handled, often answering an earlier voice. The series 'A Woman Young and Old' was probably begun this summer.[83] Here the antitheses are man–woman, sun–earth, dark–light: parts of the poem were originally intended to figure in a series called 'Two Voices'. His adoption of a woman's voice (and often a face-painting, coquettish, frankly sexual woman at that) must be related to his growing impatience with the repressive Irish attitude towards sexual love. The brief and lovely poem 'Consolation', sent to Shakespear in a near final form a year later, is, like 'Chosen', an earthy comment on a reference from John Donne.[84]

> O but there is wisdom
> In what the sages said;
> But stretch that body for a while
> And lay down that head
> Till I have told the sages
> Where man is comforted.
>
> How could passion run so deep
> Had I never thought
> That the crime of being born
> Blackens all our lot?
> But where the crime's committed
> The crime can be forgot.

In 'A Last Confession', more plain-spoken still, the female speaker aggressively divorces sexual need from romantic love. The daringly titled poem echoes both Blake and Milton, if in a way neither would have expected, by turning the ultimate earthly religious ritual into a paean to eternalized sexual congress beyond the grave.

> What lively lad most pleasured me
> Of all that with me lay?
> I answer that I gave my soul

And loved in misery,
But had great pleasure with a lad
That I loved bodily.

Flinging from his arms I laughed
To think his passion such
He fancied that I gave a soul
Did but our bodies touch,
And laughed upon his breast to think
Beast gave beast as much.

I gave what other women gave
That stepped out of their clothes,
But when this soul, its body off
Naked to naked goes,
He it has found shall find therein
What none other knows,

And give his own and take his own
And rule in his own right;
And though it loved in misery
Close and cling so tight
There's not a bird of day that dare
Extinguish that delight.

'Would it be less shocking if I put a capital to "he" in the last stanza?' WBY asked Shakespear.[85] She must have ironically compared these laconic, sexually charged lyrics to the indirect and yearning verses he had written for her during their love-affair thirty-odd years before. Central to the development of this elliptical and mysterious series (unpublished until *The Winding Stair* in 1929) is the subtle patterning whereby the interpenetrating gyres and cones of occult astrology are equated to the physical act of love: a fusion of the spiritual and the erotic which for WBY connects not only to Swedenborgian cosmology but also to his early (and future) interest in Indian philosophy. But this intellectualized rationale is not the only way WBY approaches sex in the poems which poured out through 1926. Erotic congress also represents insufficiency, lack of fulfilment, impossible longings, and gnawing regret.[86]

He was also transmuting more everyday preoccupations and incidents into poetry which contrived to be at once complex, suggestive, and resonant. He had been appointed to a government committee investigating Irish schools, and from the end of 1925, in *Irish Statesman* articles and Senate speeches, had been adverting to the subject of national education – again, much to the *Catholic Bulletin*'s fury.

If one wants to realise how putrid and pestilential, how deadly to all moral life the 'training' of the young could be among the rich, the Protestant Ascendancy of Ireland, could be and actually was, one has only to read the squalid story which tells of boyhood and its experiences in the 'Reveries' of William Butler Pollexfen Yeats. They are the proper prelude to the Sordid Swan Song of 1924, to the Divorce Diatribes of 1925, and to the Educational Effort of 1926.[87]

Lily put it more modestly: 'It is a surprise to many finding him writing as a strongly religious man,' she remarked to her niece. 'He has been inspecting all the National Schools lately.'[88] His speeches on education were practical, stressing the need for renovation of school buildings, larger classrooms, organized school meals, and hygienic conditions. His work on the committee appointed to research national education conditions, much resented by George, had influenced him deeply, and so had his reading of Italian educational theory. (He was not alone: by 1926 Gentile had become something of an in-house philosopher for the *Irish Statesman*.[89]) He advocated a child-centred approach and – despite the religious difficulties – the appointment of local committees responsible for school buildings in their districts. He also called for greatly increased government expenditure, brandishing sheaves of comparative statistics from other European countries.[90] And on 26 May he 'suddenly' began a poem ostensibly about the education of schoolchildren.

Here WBY's thoughts on education, art, and life, strangely but potently mixed with memories of the loves of his youth, are put through the prism of Neoplatonic philosophy. The educational visit which impressed him most, and which he mentioned more than once in his Senate speeches, had been to St Otteran's School in Phillip Street, Waterford, an institution which followed Maria Montessori's ideas in educating children up to seven, and those of the Parents' National Education Union for older children. Both stressed self-development and creative freedom. WBY described the school approvingly to Gregory:

Our work is being embodied in the programme & I was amused in one class when a child on being asked to give the 'narration' last learned (my visit was unexpected) repeated my biography out of 'Who's Who' – poor intellectual diet – & another child Sigerson's – disgusting diet. The children had no idea who I was. This however was not typical. The literary work prose & verse was very remarkable – one little girl had written a poem to a giant cat in 'Gulliver' containing these lines

> 'Its purr is like the noise of guns
> Its eyes like great green fields.'

Another on being asked to tell Swifts life turned it into pure folklore thus 'He was the servant [of] an English Statesman. He liked him. He came to Ireland but he thought the people did not like his sermons so he went to the sea-shore & preached to the birds and the fishes.' The childen were all clean & neat, & sometimes had embroidered little patterns of their own design on their dresses.[91]

The claim that he was incognito is not altogether true. Though his first visit to the schoolroom may have indeed been unheralded, his return the next morning was intensely anticipated, with the art room decorated by Jack Yeats reproductions and in pride of place a portrait of WBY himself. The initial entertainment at the school was equally celebratory, as recorded by George in a violently funny letter to MacGreevy. (The ellipses are her own.)

Willy has been in the thick of – I *wont* use an epithet – Education Bills. We were at Waterford last weekend to see the Sisters of Mercy's School . . . We lunched with Mother De Sales on Sunday . . . terrible O terrible . . . pale green washed walls and sacred pictures of the late eighteenth century, a dreadful plaster – very whitened plaster – Christ in the centre of the mantelpiece draped in red push [*sic*] with tassels flanked on either side by two oriental and purely mundane figures, one of each sex, very markedly so and these in turn flanked by two of the worst vases I have ever seen . . . Then we were conducted into another room for lunch . . . The Reverend Mother did not eat with us. Perhaps one does not eat in the presence of a man? But O Tom – the lunch . . . soup, half sherry . . . chicken with brandy sauce . . . already my head reeled, but though I refused port the brazen William drank two large glasses after refusing whiskey and brandy that were urged upon him . . . spent near two hours over curriculums, Montessori apparatus, P.N.E.U. (otherwise known and [*recte* as] Parents National Education Union . . . it invaded Ireland about the time we chucked you over!) Willy asking blushing nuns how often the floors were washed . . . asides to me from Sister Mary Ellen 'O DEAR! I wouldn't mind saying ANY-THING to you . . . but a man . . . O DEAR . . .' 'Do the children come clean? Or do you have to wash them?' More blushes. Then at last back to the Convent where Reverend Mother awaited us with hot milk. I started off boldly and joyfully being half frozen . . . stopped . . . realised . . . twas hot brandy with a dash of milk. But I had to drink more than half for the Reverend Mother with a most baffling and unequalled courtesy kept handing me the glass. I was in dread I wouldnt be able to walk straight down the drive, remembering the black and white framed faces that watched our arrival from all the windows. On Monday I refused to go again. I couldnt face it twice. They make one feel ashamed, ashamed of life and drinking and smoking. And caring for nothing not even husband and children or relations (*who* really does?) or anything but a line written in a book and a particular person that is but part of one's own supreme egotism.[92]

The reaction of one of the schoolchildren has been preserved. The author of the poem about the cat was twelve at the time. She remembered, sixty years later, being called up to receive the great poet's approbation, but nothing of what he said. 'He was seeing a school-age Maud Gonne, and I was seeing a strange man who briefly interrupted my day.'[93] For WBY, however, the (comparative) freedom of intellectual development, the emphasis on creativity and art, the development of the individual spirit, resonated strongly with the ideas he had been propounding in speeches and articles – originally inspired by what he knew of Gentile's educational reforms in Italy. They also chimed with the belief in 'radical innocence' which he had reiterated in 'The Need for Audacity of Thought'. Most of all – as Donald Torchiana has shown – the thoughts built into his lecture 'The Child and the State', which he had given to the Irish Literary Society in London on 30 November 1925, seemed echoed and vindicated by the sight of those twelve-year-old girls reading their poems and stories in the Waterford classroom.

The proper remedy is to teach religion, civic duty and history as all but inseparable. Indeed, the whole curriculum of a school should be as it were one lesson and not a mass of unrelated topics. I recommend Irish teachers to study the attempt now being made in Italy, under the influence of their Minister of Education, the philosopher Gentile, the most profound disciple of our [our] Berkeley, to so correlate all subjects of study. I would have each religion, Catholic or Protestant, so taught that it permeates the whole school life . . . that it may not be abstract, and that it may be part of history and of life itself, a part, as it were, of the foliage of Burke's tree . . . every child in growing from infancy to maturity should pass in imagination through the history of its own race and through something of the history of the world, and the most powerful part in that history is played by religion. Let the child go its own way when maturity comes, but it is our business that it has something of that whole inheritance, and not as a mere thought, an abstract thing like those Graeco-Roman casts upon the shelves in the art schools, but as part of its emotional life.[94]

The principle of indivisibility in culture, and of the permeation of life with a sense of religion leading to the liberation of the individual spirit, lay in his mind as he was led through the classrooms at St Otteran's. Torchiana has pointed out how the Montessori literature stressed the physical results of a full and balanced education, leading to 'a special grace of action' and an expression of 'serene brilliance' reflecting the 'flame of spiritual life'.[95] Gentile's *The Reformation of Education* was read by WBY as yet another formulation of the unity of being. Gentile described culture as an indivisible part of spiritual life, 'in no manner comparable to a moving body in which the body itself could be distinguished from motion'. This very image was echoed unforgettably in 'Among School Children', the poem WBY wrote a few weeks after his Waterford visit, projected – as so often – through memories of personal experience and past love. Yet he is aware, as ever, that 'experience' could be a deceitful teacher. In the first prose draft of the poem's idea, he went back to the last words of *Reveries over Childhood and Youth*, reminding himself to 'bring in the old thought that life prepares for what never happens'.[96]

The poem bears this out. The first draft begins with the image of a young mother nursing a child, replaced in the final version by the elderly poet walking through the Waterford classroom. From viewing himself as 'a sixty-year-old smiling public man', to remembering Maud Gonne's unhappy childhood and visualizing her as a girl like those before him, the poet invokes Platonic theories of soul and body, sharply delineating what has become of Gonne, and of himself:

> Her present image floats into the mind –
> Did Quattrocento finger fashion it
> Hollow of cheek as though it drank the wind
> And took a mess of shadows for its meat?
> And I though never of Ledaean kind
> Had pretty plumage once – enough of that,
> Better to smile on all that smile, and show
> There is a comfortable kind of old scarecrow.

But in one of WBY's most consummately executed swerves of direction, the conclusion moves to considering how the hopes held out by mothers are inevitably disappointed, and the inadequate approaches to a philosophic understanding of the world epitomized by classical theories of education.

> Both nuns and mothers worship images,
> But those the candles light are not as those
> That animate a mother's reveries,
> But keep a marble or a bronze repose.
> And yet they too break hearts – O Presences
> That passion, piety or affection knows,
> And that all heavenly glory symbolise –
> O self-born mockers of man's enterprise;
>
> Labour is blossoming or dancing where
> The body is not bruised to pleasure soul,
> Nor beauty born out of its own despair,
> Nor blear-eyed wisdom out of midnight oil.
> O chestnut-tree, great-rooted blossomer,
> Are you the leaf, the blossom or the bole?
> O body swayed to music, O brightening glance,
> How can we know the dancer from the dance?

The last two stanzas instance once more the world of disillusion prepared by conventional education and religion. The closure is provided by Gentile's idea of culture as an instinctual unity of being, echoing WBY's own remark in *Per Amica Silentia Lunae* that at certain high points of creative activity he did not know when he was 'the finger, when the clay'. There are also echoes of Symons, his occultist correspondence with Sturm, and – as so often Shelley's 'Defence of Poetry'.[97] But above all the poem is a synthesis of the highest order, written at a time when what he called 'ascetic Platonism' was beginning to infuse the social legislation of the infant Irish state. Taken with the deliberate invocations of Leda, 'Among School Children' carried a public, political charge as well as posing the most personal of questions in language as memorable as any he ever wrote.

IV

Throughout the summer and autumn of 1926 WBY continued to write, driven on by old memories as well as new philosophical inspiration. He was meditating a new instalment of autobiography (never written) and still rehearsing the lost passions of the 1890s. Rediscovering a beautiful photograph of Shakespear in the *Literary Yearbook* of 1897, her profile 'like a Sicilian coin', he told her, 'One looks back to one's youth as to [a] cup that a madman dying of thirst left half tasted. I wonder if you feel like that'.[98] The image, and the preoccupation, entered the series eventually called 'A Man Young and Old', which began life as 'Songs' from 'An Old Country-man' and 'A Young Countryman'. This introspective series (in ballad metre suited to the peasant personae) moves from memories of Gonne, stony as a statue of Diana, and Iseult, a vulnerable hare, to regrets at the lost opportunities for fulfilment in his youth. The first stanzas have been read as political metaphors, partly based on the reworking of imagery from 'Easter 1916';[99] but that poem had also been addressed to Gonne, and, since the Countryman (Young and Old) uses the language of stone, of classical beauty, and Helen of Troy, her presence in 'A Man Young and Old' cannot be denied. One particular memory apparently conveys, with odd and rather sinister directness, the brief consummation of their affair eighteen years before:

> The women take so little stock
> In what I do or say
> They'd sooner leave their cosseting
> To hear a jackass bray;
> My arms are like the twisted thorn
> And yet there beauty lay;
>
> The first of all the tribe lay there
> And did such pleasure take –
> She who had brought great Hector down
> And put all Troy to wreck –
> That she cried into this ear,
> Strike me if I shriek.

The last stanzas predict old age, conjuring up personae whose brutal humour and distracted wits would characterize much of his verse to come. Madge and Peter anticipate Crazy Jane and Tom the Lunatic, who would similarly subvert conventional restraint in sexually explicit ballads. Perhaps the most astonishing thing about WBY's great creative burst in the spring and summer of 1926 was the coexistence of these demotic voices and poetic forms with the allusive, philosophical plangent tone achieved in 'The Tower' and 'Among School Children'. These two voices were more and more fully realized sides of his multiple poetic personality, and would sustain themselves for the rest of his writing life.

As if to celebrate the breakthrough, in the late summer of 1926 he vanished to a Kerry country house specifically to write a poem which represents his work at its most complex, hieratic, and eerily suggestive. He knew from early on that it would revolve around his preoccupation with the magnificence of medieval Byzantium, sustained by his reading of W. G. Holmes's *The Age of Justinian and Theodora*. In *A Vision* he had already established to his own satisfaction that the climactic Phase Fifteen coincided 'with Justinian's reign, that great age of building in which one may conclude Byzantine art was perfected'. (The dates, unsurprisingly, do not always fit.[100]) In mid August WBY had left Ballylee to stay with the Jamesons at Howth, but 'fled [to Muckross] to write verses'.[101] His Kerry retreat was magnificent in its own way. Muckross House was a great Victorian 'Tudorbethan' pile built by the Herbert family in a ravishing location on the lakes of Killarney, with a lushly planted park that reminded WBY of Santa Barbara. (He probably did not know that his father, at the outset of his artistic career, had stayed there sixty-odd years before and painted several of the Herberts.) The owner was now an Irishman, Bourne Vincent, who had married an American heiress: they seem to have been acquaintances rather than friends of WBY, but he needed a refuge. The Kerry weather was brilliantly hot, the company distractingly smart (Shane Leslie and his wife, and *mondaine* young women 'got up as sheer Mont-Martre to shock the county').[102] The Vincents' young son remembered WBY's visit all his life, and not only because he let his nursery bath overflow to deluge the poet in the Queen's Bedroom below. He was astonished to find his parents' visitor walking wildly among the Kerry oaks in the park, and reported, 'That fellow's mad: he's talking to the trees.'

An abandoned draft of the first verse is all about a sleepy Ireland, where the old poet dozes amid the young 'at their gallantries', against the ravishing summer backdrop of 'the changing colours of the hills and seas'; all of this owes something to his immediate surroundings. A letter to Lady Londonderry indicates, however, that the direction of WBY's thought was heading far away from lipsticked flappers or plutocratic mansions:

The only thing for which I have ever envied wealth is that it permits a family to put down deep roots into some soil. You are right to find the *Sidhe* no phantasy. I often feel when I talk to some old woman in Connaught that I am not far from Plotinus. At the break up of the Roman Empire refugees – flying from a horror like that of Russia today – refugees, both Pagan & Christian, came to Ireland. When I hear the *Sidhe* called 'The Ever-living' & such names I think of such phrases as 'Authentic Existants' – Mackennas translation – 'True Being' or so on applied to souls in eternity by Plotinus. Connaught even still sometimes seems to me half Greek. I think – without evidence doubtless – that St Patrick & his Christians were not the only missionaries. I came here to write a poem about a medieval Irishman longing for Byzantium – Dublin was too full of distractions – so am rather full of the thing. I want to bring not only Modern but Ancient Ireland into the great world.[103]

Though antiquity was much in his mind since the pattern-making of *A Vision* and the visual stimulation of research for the Coinage Commission (planned in 1925), 'Sailing to Byzantium' is anchored in Ireland as much as in WBY's imagined city on the Bosporus. After all, as T. R. Henn pointed out, Byzantium's break from Rome was to echo Ireland's from imperial England.[104] In a much later comment on the poem WBY remarked, 'When Irishmen were illuminating the Book of Kells and making the jewelled crozier in the National Museum, Byzantium was the centre of European civilisation and the source of its spiritual philosophy, so I symbolise the search for the spiritual life by a journey to that city.'[105] This tends to place his idealized 'Byzantium' as rather later than the mid sixth century. But his chief concern was to parallel it with Ireland. 'There was great Byzantine influence upon Ireland,' he told his publisher Frederick Macmillan excitedly a few months later; 'in two Irish private collections there are wooden crucifixes entirely Byzantine in type and of great beauty, and these crucifixes continued to be made in North Connaught and perhaps elsewhere till about 80 years ago.'[106]

This reflected a concurrent project that brought Ireland and Byzantium together: a new edition of *The Stories of Red Hanrahan*, bound with *The Secret Rose*, to be illustrated by the young painter Norah McGuinness 'in the style of Byzantine wall-pictures'. Just twenty-two, she had recently designed a Drama League production of *The Only Jealousy of Emer*, and danced in it as well. WBY was usually reluctant to see his work illustrated, but he decided to 'launch' McGuinness in an experimental artistic project, in which his early stories were framed by illustrations consciously modelled on Byzantine motifs. The collaboration recalled early Bedford Park days but also anticipated later enthusiasms for working with much younger women.

And the reprinted stories with their stylized pictures were to be prefaced by his new poem, 'Sailing to Byzantium', in its second printing. As with its first appearance in *October Blast* and its canonical placing in *The Tower*, it came first. It was always to signal a point of departure.

> That is no country for old men. The young
> In one another's arms, birds in the trees,
> – Those dying generations – at their song,
> The salmon-falls, the mackerel-crowded seas,
> Fish, flesh, or fowl, commend all summer long
> Whatever is begotten, born, and dies.
> Caught in that sensual music all neglect
> Monuments of unageing intellect.
>
> An aged man is but a paltry thing,
> A tattered coat upon a stick, unless
> Soul clap its hands and sing, and louder sing
> For every tatter in its mortal dress,
> Nor is there singing school but studying
> Monuments of its own magnificence;
> And therefore I have sailed the seas and come
> To the holy city of Byzantium.
>
> O sages standing in God's holy fire
> As in the gold mosaic of a wall,
> Come from the holy fire, perne in a gyre,
> And be the singing-masters of my soul.
> Consume my heart away; sick with desire
> And fastened to a dying animal
> It knows not what it is; and gather me
> Into the artifice of eternity.
>
> Once out of nature I shall never take
> My bodily form from any natural thing,
> But such a form as Grecian goldsmiths make
> Of hammered gold and gold enamelling
> To keep a drowsy Emperor awake;
> Or set upon a golden bough to sing
> To lords and ladies of Byzantium
> Of what is past, or passing, or to come.

WBY's peculiar idea of Byzantium was already emblematized in *A Vision*, where he fantasized about spending 'a month of Antiquity' there, circa AD 550, under Justinian's rule. It may owe a sizeable debt to William Morris's reiterated belief that the organic unities of Gothic art were Byzantine in origin.[107] Thus, for WBY the ancient Byzantines, like the Connacht peasantry, were directly connected to unworldly realities. Elsewhere in *A Vision* he had written that early Byzantium brought 'religious, aesthetic and practical life' together, specifically instancing mosaic-workers and goldsmiths as expressing 'the vision of a whole people' and 'a unity of creative being'. This thought pervades the poem he wrote at Muckross. More immediately, the final version rehearsed the themes of 'The Tower'; by the third stanza the heart has become something 'sick with desire', 'fastened to a dying animal'.

There are echoes of Blake and of Shelley in the 'flight from nature' (a cancelled line from an early version) to perfection.[108] However, the poem's preoccupation is not so much with a heavenly city on earth as with the question that ended 'Among School Children': is artistic absorption in the act of creation the reflection of true reality? The poet's creative soul will, in fact, at the end be located in the eternal artifice of a mechanical bird.[109] As in 'The Tower', sensual and passionate realities are to be abandoned in favour of the search for philosophical truth; but, as in 'The Tower', an energetic irony undermines the premise. This comes through clearly in the final, canonical version.

The unashamed exoticism became inseparably intertwined with his poetic persona. Frank O'Connor and Padraic Colum would later see WBY himself as a Byzantine. But though the wrought perfection and dazzling finish of the poem resemble the golden bird itself, Jon Stallworthy has shown in a classic study of the manuscript drafts that it was not an easy journey from the beginning in a Killarney heatwave to the typescripts which emerged a month later. The first outlines were almost totally different; only the last two lines came easily and stayed the same. Nor did WBY remain totally satisfied. Rehearsing a radio broadcast nine years later, he swiftly changed the first line to 'Old men should quit a country where the young', saying that the original was 'the worst bit of syntax I ever wrote'.[110]

When WBY drafted his first outline of the poem, he returned yet again to his own lost loves, remembered in impotent old age, though the thought is progressively generalized throughout the drafts. Reflections about the peasantry's direct line to ancient deities also make an early appearance, in line with his letter to Lady Londonderry. They too fade into the background, as Byzantium takes on its own sharply realized shape and colour – though the descriptive physical details are reduced to the single image of saints against a gold-ground mosaic, derived from his visits to Ravenna with the Gregorys nearly twenty years before as well as his journey to Sicily in 1925.[111] WBY's audacious gift for allusive compression does double duty in suggesting – beside glittering local colour – purification and the transcendence of physical reality. As for the first two stanzas, they emerged in a great rush of images during a radical rewrite a month after he left Muckross. And, characteristically, several of the images they displaced were not abandoned altogether, but remained in the Procrustean bed of WBY's iconographic treasury, to surface again in a second Byzantium poem four years later.

V

The summer of 1926 was spent in a round of country-house visits. With a detachment from his older haunts came new confidantes like Lady Londonderry, while Gregory's journal for this time indicates that her friendship with WBY was slightly diminished. Reading the proofs for the extracts from his 1909 diary published as *Estrangement*, she was struck by how she missed 'those years of close companionship' – even though she was staying in Merrion Square at the time.[112] Still, the toing and froing between Coole and Ballylee continued, and there was – yet again – a flurry of activity over the Lane pictures. In June 1926 it was clear that the British government would agree to a loan arrangement at most, taking their stance from the Commission report which, while admitting Lane's intention to leave the pictures to Dublin, claimed that it could not be legally recognized. WBY and Gregory frenziedly lobbied Cosgrave and his colleagues, and parliamentary questions were raised in London and Dublin, to as little avail as ever. That same month the king opened the Duveen Galleries at the Tate. This seemed to reveal the motive behind the determination to retain the pictures in London, since Joseph Duveen had been promised that Lane's Impressionists would hang there. WBY was resolved to denounce this unworthy acquisitiveness in public.

On 14 July he delivered what Gregory called 'a good and well reasoned and documented' speech in the Senate, attacking what he saw as the royal sanction given to the government's immoral denial of a testator's wishes. He cleverly scaled up the issue to raise the most far-reaching of political questions:

It is the policy of most of us in this country, seeing that very lately we preferred a king to a president and that we fought a civil war that we might be governed by a king rather than a president, to remain upon the friendliest terms with the King of England, who is also the King of Ireland. We have been told I do not know whether truthfully or not, that the King is personally friendly to us, that a certain speech which influenced our affairs for good was made on his own initiative. Statements of that kind are frequently untrue; they are put out for policy, but, whether true or not, we have no desire to disturb the impression that they have left. Our relations with Ulster make this more essential. But it would be impossible to preserve this attitude towards Royalty if certain obvious conditions are ignored. When the King was urged to perform an action which seriously compromised the claim made by this nation, when he was urged to intervene in this international dispute, was it pointed out to him that he should be advised not only by his English Ministers alone, but also by the Governor-General, or otherwise by his Irish Ministers? We have no means of questioning Ministers in this House, and I would be glad, therefore, if someone in the Dáil would ask President Cosgrave if his Government was consulted before the King recently opened the new modern gallery in London. Important as our claim for the Lane pictures is, this question seems to me to raise an issue of far greater importance, one vitally affecting the constitutional position not only of this country but of every Dominion. I can imagine the British Government replying in the evasive spirit of its Commission that as our claim was moral and not legal the King was not bound to take cognizance of it, but in disputes between nations – and the British Government itself has, within its terms of reference to the Commission, called this dispute international – it is not legal but moral and material issues that cause trouble. A day may come when the action of the King may prejudice some claim involving the most fundamental rights. I see by the daily papers that Canada and the Irish Free State are to seek at the next Imperial Conference for some clarification or modification of the relations between the Crown and the Dominions. I think that this recent experience of ours shows that one or the other is necessary.[113]

wby's criticisms, and his questioning of the use of royal authority to favour the claims of one of the dominions over another, raised echoes of long-ago rows when he had denounced British sovereigns – but only among members of the Irish *ancien régime* like the Arnotts, and some of his English friends. Probably with an eye to this, he warned Lady Londonderry in advance, outlining his feelings forcibly:

Our little group of intellectuals is at the moment wholly taken up with the Lane picture question. It is to us as vital a matter as (say) the coal question to your London politicians and rouses quite as bitter passions. Had Lane lived he might have endowed both Dublin and London, & sometimes talked of doing so, but he made the codicil because he knew that if he died upon the voyage he could endow only one city and preferred that it should be Dublin. If this dispute had been between England and Canada it is inconceivable that England would have refused the claim. The matter has been complicated by the fact that the English Government persuaded the King – it was certainly not his own thought – to open the new wing of the Tate while the matter was *sub judice*. I know from what I hear said, or from what is written to me that the most vocal people in Ireland think this raises the constitutional question whether the King has the right to act on the advice of his English ministers alone in a matter which concerns the vital interests of a Dominion. I have just had a letter from a London Irish journalist begging me to take the matter up. Whether I shall do so or not heaven knows. The only thing that makes me hesitate is the thought of the use the Republicans will make of it, but the chances are, whether I do or not, that we shall all be in full cry in a week.

You ask if our Players want to go to Belfast. Certainly they want to, but heaven knows whether you will want us if this pot boils.[114]

In October he was in London, pushing the latest pamphlet on the Lane affair (written by Gregory but revised by WBY), working hard on Lady Londonderry, dining with Beaverbrook to meet Churchill, persuading Cecil Harmsworth 'to stir up Rothermere', and even cultivating columnists like Lord Castlerosse on the *Express*. Lord D'Abernon, the National Gallery's most steely champion, 'told Lady Lavery that I was a charming person but as obstinate as a mule'.[115] The time and energy devoted to the cause is as striking as ever. The same was true of his campaign to have commissioned new legal robes for the Irish judiciary, designed by his friends the great aesthetic arbiters Ricketts and Shannon. Lengthy correspondence was undertaken, examples summoned up, and a campaign mounted in the Senate, lost by one vote: 'much better than carrying it by one, and having the robes worn by restive judges', Gregory reflected.[116]

WBY also tried to steal a march, and provoke a public controversy, by having the proposed designs publicly exhibited, but he was smartly smacked down by Lord Chief Justice Kennedy.[117] His Senate speech took a high line on the importance of the question. 'This country has passed through one of those crises which all countries have made the occasion of a new act of energy for the creation of tradition. No country that I know, after a revolution such as we have gone through, has been content to take without examination the traditions of the past, and I cannot imagine any place where innovation is more necessary than in the outward image of the law' – most of all because it had been seen for so many generations as an alien imposition.[118] His wife thought these senatorial campaigns were making him 'damnably national', to the detriment of his poetry.

As long as there was any gesture in it, as long as there was a war on and so on and so on, it was worth it, but really now to spend hours listening to rubbish in and out of the Senate and going to committees and being visited by fishermen's associations, and Freddie Ryans' and nincompoops and miaows and bow-wows of all sorts mostly mongrels is a bit too much.[119]

But for WBY the visual symbols of the nation were more than details, and he was determined to have a hand in shaping them. This was why the question of a Dublin gallery housing Lane's pictures was even more relevant than it had been before independence. To his ancient belief in the vital importance of models of artistic greatness in public places was added his recent preoccupation with the education of the new country by exposing it to European standards of excellence. 'If we do not give Ireland intellectual pride in this generation', he warned Beaverbrook, 'it will grow into some sort of papistical potato-digging republic, in fact if not in name, a mischief to itself and its neighbours.'[120]

He had put this more tactfully in a long letter to Ernest Blythe the previous summer, suggesting that the government 'get the best available expert on the applications of art to industry and give him such post in connection with the Technical Board as will give him complete control over the Art Schools of Ireland. I think that the best man would possibly be a Swede, as Sweden has within the last ten or twelve years re-created its applied arts.' The object was to equip 'Irish hands' to furnish and decorate Dublin's great buildings, such as the Four Courts and Customs House, and eventually to design a worthy House of Parliament. Already Irish achievements in stained glass and the generation of painters represented by Tuohy and Keating showed what enlightened example might do. But WBY was anxious to see new aesthetic principles brought to 'not merely furniture, but electric light fittings, mosaic pavements, plaster work, Textile[s], wall decoration in all its kinds, and glass-making as distinct from stained glass'. Ireland, like Sweden, could excel through inspired art education and – again like Sweden – reignite the applied arts in which it had been supreme in the eighteenth century.[121] William Morris was his master still.

It is doubtful if this allegiance was shared by Blythe, a dour and penny-pinching Northerner. But it suggests that, in WBY's protean imagination, Dublin could reach Byzantium by way of Stockholm – decorated by buildings which reflected a unity of artistic genius, embellished with a gallery containing the greatest contemporary European art, even presided over by judges attired in robes designed by a master of modern stage-craft (Shannon's 'Irish descent' was craftily invoked as an additional qualification). None of these enterprises bore fruit, but they relate closely to the project which WBY did manage to commandeer in 1926: the committee to create a new Irish coinage.

This was planned from 1925, but the first meeting did not take place until 19 June 1926.[122] WBY presided, and reported afterwards to Lady Londonderry with unconcealed satisfaction. The nominees included the art curator Thomas Bodkin, the painter and president of the Royal Hibernian Academy, Dermod O'Brien, Leo McCauley, Lucius O'Callaghan, director of the National Gallery, and Barry Egan TD, a silversmith by profession. None was a match for WBY. He had steered things so that they were free 'to find our designs anywhere in Europe so it will be our fault if we do not get a good coinage. If we succeed I shall try to get something done about the stamps.'[123] A letter swiftly went to Dulac, crisply spelling out WBY's own agenda and confirming his domination of the committee.

I hear you have done a very fine medal. Can I have a photograph of that & of any similar thing you may have done. I am Chairman of the committee of coinage design. The Free State is bringing out a silver & copper coinage of its own. There will be a limited competition, each competing artist getting a fee, whether his work is accepted or not, & we are not limited to Irishmen. We shall probably arrange for a competition of 5–2 Irish to satisfy patriotic feeling. Of course I cannot judge what five of the world's artists shall be chosen. Where my friends are concerned I shall probably think it decent to merely present their work & let the others decide. We are only collecting photographs at present. Milles the Swede has however sent a very fine medal.

Every coin will have a harp on one side but we can put what we like on the other. I am pressing on the committee certain simple symbols which all can understand as expressions of national products – say a horse, a bull, a barley sheaf, a salmon, a fox or hare & a grey hound. Somebody else urges symbols of industries, but we have so few industries & doubt the decorative value of a porter bottle. The government will have to pass our symbols, or prefer others. We will probably only insist on their being simple – emblems or symbols & not pictures.[124]

Before a single entry had come in, WBY had already laid down more or less exactly the symbolism to be used – elegant, racy of the soil, and utterly unpolitical. 'We have asked the government to let us put on the reverse of the coins a series of national products, a horse (hunter), a salmon, a hare, a hen & chickens, a pig & a woodcock.'[125] (The pig would create particular problems, for both symbolic and representational reasons, and the minister pressed for a ram instead.) WBY determined to spend August studying medals and coins – probably adding to his personal poetic store of images from antiquity. Through the autumn and winter, entries were pored over. WBY introduced designs by Ricketts and Shannon, while declaring he could not vote on them, as they were his friends; he also admired the medal struck by the Swede, Milles, though his ambition to have an entry from the Croat sculptor Mestrovic was blocked. Three Irish artists were listed: Albert Power, Oliver Sheppard, and Jerome Connor. By February the finalists' designs were anonymously presented: a fortunate precaution insisted upon by WBY, since the unanimous choice turned out to be an Englishman, Percy Metcalfe (a medallist rather than a monumental sculptor). His slightly stylized designs did not have an easy passage. The Ministry of Finance raised difficulties, calling in a chief livestock inspector from the Ministry of Agriculture who denounced the bull as 'all wrong' and insisted on referring the dog to the president of the Irish Wolfhound Club. At one point, in October 1927, the committee had to threaten resignation *en masse*.[126] But all this was mere bagatelle to someone who had steered the Abbey Theatre through nearly three decades of squalls, and the committee brought its coinage to fruition almost unscathed. When Metcalfe's designs were revealed there were grumbles, notably from Maud Gonne, who denounced

7. Percy Metcalfe's designs for 'the beast coinage' as finally issued. WBY regretted that due to the intervention of the Minister of Agriculture and his experts the hunter had 'lost muscular tension', the bull was adapted to suit 'the eugenics of the farmyard', and 'the state of the market for pigs' cheeks' made the initial design of sow and piglets impossible. 'We have instead querulous and harassed animals, better merchandise but less living.' Nonetheless he was delighted.

a coinage 'designed by an Englishman, minted in England, representative of English values, paid for by the Irish people'. The Cathedral Chapter of Tuam levelled accusations of 'paganism' at the imagery, and an anonymous priest sent a letter to the *Irish Independent* pointing out that the coinage represented 'the thin edge of the wedge of Freemasonry sunk into the very life of our Catholicity', in an attempt 'to beget a land of devil-worshippers'. (WBY must have suspected the resurrection of his old traducer Frank Hugh O'Donnell.) But, despite some snide newspaper paragraphs, the new coinage was generally approved of.[127]

WBY's own delight in it comes clearly through in his characteristic introduction to the committee's report, 'What We Did, and Tried to Do', a sprightly account which gives no hint of the clashes and brinkmanship behind the scenes. It had provided exactly the kind of involvement he had yearned for since the foundation of the Free State, when he had dreamt of being appointed minister of Fine Arts. And his committee was vindicated. Metcalfe's designs stood the test of time, and became recognized modern classics. But the *Catholic Bulletin*, sharp as ever for its purposes, made a different connection.

The Pollexfen strain has come to have its revenge on the Paudeens and the Biddys, to use the Senator's own choice phrases. When, in the near future, they (again in the select Senatorial sentences) 'fumble in the greasy till, and add the halfpence to the pence', they will have to use small coins of various ignoble values. These coins, it would appear, have had their designs fixed for them by the Coinage Design Committee, to which Senator W.B. Yeats was elected as a Chairman by

Governmental decision, 1925–1927 (Compare *Responsibilities*, 1914, page 230: 'No Government appointed him'.) The beast coinage from Yorkshire is the result. It is just what is suitable, in the Pollexfen type of mind, for 'onionsellers' and the like, who 'fumble in a greasy till'. It suits Paudeens and Biddies. It is appropriate to what the Stateley Weekly has termed our 'petty peasant nationality'. The Pollexfen Pride has had in 1927 a suitable revenge for the defeat it encountered in 1912. We are to see that we are not at all 'beyond the fling of the Wild Ass's hoof'.[128]

VI

These public involvements threatened to overwhelm him, and George was not alone in expressing dissatisfaction. 'I see Uncle William occasionally,' Desmond FitzGerald wrote to Pound at the end of 1926. 'I hope he is writing poetry. His conversation at social functions is very unquintessential.'[129] Dublin life imposed other demands. He was famously seen at Punchestown races, in a top hat (the first time he had been to such an occasion for fifteen years, according to Lily), and he and George gave large dinner-parties in Merrion Square for ministers and their wives. Late November saw a particularly grand occasion for the Swedish architect Östberg, catered by a chef and attended by the Gogartys, the O'Higginses, Lennox Robinson, the Jamesons, and the Cosgraves; a Yeats cousin, Claud Armstrong, had too much claret-cup and insisted on trying on Dulac's Noh masks, which were hanging on the wall.[130] This kind of life ensured the continuing estrangement from Gonne, who now hated the Free State establishment as cordially as she had ever loathed England.

Less predictably, wby's older, bohemian friends were conspicuously absent from these occasions: though AE – hard hit by the death of his great love Susan Mitchell in March 1926 – remained grateful that wby 'always turned up' at his Friday tea-parties.[131] To this period, however, belongs Isa MacNie's celebrated caricature of wby and AE on Merrion Square unconsciously passing as they set off to visit each other. 'It really happened,' Lily told her niece. 'W.B. left 82 to call on AE at 84 [Plunkett House, the offices of the cooperative movement]. At 83 they passed each other, one looking up and one looking down.' As for Gregory, she relied on wby and George during her treatment for cancer, spending sojourns at Merrion Square; she was once again grappling with the equally terrible possibility of leaving Coole, pleased when the Yeatses told her 'Ballylee means Coole' and they would leave if she did.[132] By April 1927 the house and demesne had been sold by Margaret to the Forestry Commission, while her mother-in-law retained the right to live there until her death. wby was facing into his sixties with his social landscape eroding and resettling all around him.

8. 'Chin-Angles, or How the Poets Passed': Isa MacNie's cartoon of WBY and AE setting out to visit each other in Merrion Square.

One refuge was the grand world of such Irish country houses as remained, and society hostesses like Edith Londonderry – invited to visit Ballylee, a rare honour, in the summer of 1926. The impulse leading WBY to rediscover the Ascendancy world was not entirely intellectual: country houses and London clubs were a necessary part of his life. The Nobel money was still cushioning his finances, though Cuala's debts swallowed £2,010 in the end, and continued to be a drain on Merrion Square.[133] There were still the sales from *Autobiographies* which brought in a good income in 1926/7; even a new edition of *The Land of Heart's Desire* the previous year earned him £100, a good deal for a 'sentimental trifle', as WBY remarked to Gregory.[134] However, his Macmillan royalties to June 1927 were only £171. 1s. 10d. after tax and Robinson heard that summer, probably from George, that they were 'very hard up'.[135] George's income was strengthened by a further family legacy, adding £250 to her annual income. She was the family financial manager, and she kept her own money separate but from time to time had to bail him out, though they were both acutely conscious that her capital had to be conserved as a 'rampart round the children'.[136] By and large, WBY was living a gentlemanly life on resources which, as Lily regretfully noted, left him no margin.

He had, however, acquired lifelong habits which he would not renounce. One was the deep-rooted determination to accumulate around himself a group of younger writers, meeting regularly at his house and forming a centre of resistance to the pieties of conventional culture. It was not entirely easy. Francis and Iseult Stuart were originally groomed to play such a part, but proved unreliable. Other tyros, such as Seumas O'Sullivan, had long been marked down as enemies. Lennox Robinson remained faithful, but was more and more regularly drunk. The young poet F. R. Higgins came nearer to filling the bill, though he had gone wrong over *The Plough and the Stars*. Thomas MacGreevy was appreciated for his gossip and grew particularly close to George, but departed to seek his literary fortune in London and Paris. The Cork writer Frank O'Connor's translations also appealed to wby, and O'Connor, like Higgins, would become a supporter at the Abbey – though wby continued to make enemies effortlessly through his uncompromising attitude to 'realist' dramatists like Brinsley MacNamara.[137]

By early 1926 George was anxious for him to leave the Senate and devote his time to poetry rather than to 'insular and provincial politics',[138] but wby refused. The effect of the divorce debate, the *Plough and the Stars* controversy, and the threat of literary censorship further concentrated his mind, and in late July 1926 he fired the opening shot in a long campaign to found a literary academy on the French model. This would not only recognize distinction but – implicitly – would also defend the interests of writers as a profession. The initial suggestions sent to the president of the Royal Irish Academy were signed by Russell, Robinson, and wby, but addressed from 82 Merrion Square. Names floated included Shaw, Stephens, MacKenna, O'Casey, Hyde, St John Ervine, and Forrest Reid – a notably non-Catholic *galère*. 'Once such a body were established it would have no difficulty in finding out duties for itself, our feeling is that at the beginning of a new State, where conditions are unsettled, it is important to have an authoritative body, not merely in matters of learning but in creative literature.'[139] The Royal Irish Academy took the idea no further at this point, but wby was not going to leave it alone. His public pronouncements continued to outrage the *Catholic Bulletin*: opening an exhibition by the Radical Painters group that summer, he remarked with magnificent nonchalance that they should break a bottle of champagne on a bust of Archbishop Mannix, an icon of nationalist as well as of religious piety.[140] Moreover, his own thoughts had turned back to the theatre, and to subjects which took on conventional opinion.

During this year of intellectual and artistic fireworks, he had been simultaneously following a more ancient preoccupation – a version of Sophocles' *Oedipus* plays. A draft of his rediscovered version of *Oedipus Rex* had gone to Robinson from Ballylee in June,[141] and by December it was in production. Twenty years before, WBY had commissioned a translation from Gilbert Murray, and in 1912 he had himself adapted and simplified the R. C. Jebb version – all with an eye to flouting conventional opinion, since the play had been censored in England.[142] Nothing had come of the project, but now he was ready again. He thought of extending his scope to *Oedipus at Colonus* and pared down still further his already truncated version of *Oedipus Rex* (a cause of abiding affront to Sophocles scholars). 'I want to be less literal & more dramatic & modern . . . bare hard & natural like a saga'. The tension and horror of the ancient story were to stand out unrelieved, and he was once more anxious to challenge censorship, this time Irish rather than English. 'How will these Catholics take it?'[143]

When *King Oedipus* opened at the Abbey on 7 December, strangely paired with Shaw's *The Shewing-Up of Blanco Posnet*, the audience (Catholics or not) took it very well. F. J. McCormick turned in a magnetic performance, backed by an austere chorus; the restraint of the whole treatment was a deliberate contrast to Max Reinhardt's celebrated extravaganza production fourteen years before. There was a tremendous ovation and rave reviews as far afield as New York. At home, the *Irish Times* called it 'the most notable event of many theatrical years . . . the most powerful thing the Abbey Theatre has ever staged'. WBY was congratulated for staying close to the original, a judgement far from the truth.[144] Thus encouraged, he at once set to work on *Oedipus at Colonus*, which would be played the following September, and was even looser in its relation to Jebb's translation than its predecessor.

Always energized by dramatic success, WBY planned to travel to Cambridge in late January to see a version of *On Baile's Strand* very much after his own heart – 'the poor & blind man masked, & elaborate dancing of the witches & strange lighting'.[145] But in January illness struck again. Influenza was followed by inflammatory rheumatism, and he was confined to bed well into February, driving George – who also had Gregory in the house for a month on end – to the end of her tether. 'There IS a mass of verse bad and goodish,' she told Pound, 'but it has to be sorted . . . and until there is solitude in the house it seems impossible to get this done.'[146] If 1926 had been a poetic *annus mirabilis* for WBY, the energy expended had taken its toll. But he had triumphantly vindicated the claims made at the opening to 'The Tower' –

> Never had I more
> Excited, passionate, fantastical
> Imagination, nor an ear and eye
> That more expected the impossible –

The harvest of that frantic year's writing would stand very near the summit of his artistic achievement.

In December AE had reviewed WBY's *Autobiographies*, taking the opportunity to consider his astonishing friend's views of his contemporaries (including the reviewer) and his way of placing them in their times. AE grumbled gently at WBY's omission of 'internal life' and preference for weaving external patterns and 'mirroring notable personalities'; he pointed out the 'chasm' between the inner life of mutual friends and WBY's version of their outward personae. In AE's view, the 'fourth dimension' so magically apparent in WBY's best poetry was rigorously excluded from this story of his early life. But AE's conclusion showed that he fully understood the function which WBY intended *Autobiographies* to fulfil:

That is the virtue of Yeats' story telling about his friends, that what he says about them is rarely trivial, but the incident or words quoted have some symbolic value, and it is probable that he only remembers what fits into the pattern of his own vision. We have had many books about modern Ireland, but they have been for the most part political and historical, dealing with externalities and but little with the cultural current out of which modern Anglo-Irish literature, as important as anything else in that period, was born. To some extent these memories where they touch on the poet's life in Ireland, fill up the spiritual emptiness in our records of the years which preceded our revolution, and in which that independence, which came afterwards in the political sphere had already been achieved on the cultural or spiritual lane of our national being. Any real history of our time must draw not only upon the records of the fighters and the political chieftains, but upon the thoughts and emotions of those who were working in another sphere, but who were letting loose those imponderable elements which give infinity and profundity to national consciousness and without which no great man of action would bestir himself to the upsetting of society. Books like the life of Michael Collins need a spiritual background to be true histories of their time, for assuredly Ireland from 1890 to 1916 was abundantly and richly alive and in many ways, all of which added to each other's vitality. Some time a real historian will unite both the body and the soul of Ireland in a history of our times, and it will be seen that few nations, contemporary with ours, had a richer life.[147]

The spiritual element in national consciousness was still at the centre of WBY's thought, and much of his recent poetry reflected it. But for the moment he was exhausted. He recovered slowly during the spring of 1927, and the promised brief visit to London and Cambridge, to see his plays performed, was all he could manage. (In Cambridge, however, he was excited by the ballet arranged by Ninette de Valois, a young Irishwoman 'who has, I think, inventive genius . . . we might want her in Dublin if we continue to prosper'.[148]) The early summer was spent between Dublin and Ballylee, where Gregory recorded long and leisurely conversations.[149] Life in Merrion Square during June and July was also recorded – by Horace Reynolds, a young American observer determined to plumb literary Dublin to its depths. Reynolds indefatigably attached himself to Gogarty's accommodating coat-tails and as indefatigably transcribed his impressions into a diary: again, his observations suggest life taken at ease, under George's watchful eye.[150] It was the comfortable existence of the leisured bohemian bourgeoisie, where doors were hospitably left open, lunches at Jammet's or the Dolphin Hotel lasted all afternoon, and the nearby sea and mountains beckoned for drives out of town on the endless summer evenings. But WBY could afford to rest on his laurels. That summer Cuala published a short volume called *October Blast*, containing – among other glories – 'Sailing to Byzantium' and 'The Tower'. Gregory, though already familiar with the poems, was astonished by their power ('a trumpet call'):[151] the echo would sound long and clear when they reappeared in the extended volume published by Macmillan the next year. But Dublin's tranquil life was suddenly convulsed by a thunderbolt, revealing that what AE would have called 'external' realities and antipathies still seethed below the surface of the Free State. On 10 July Kevin O'Higgins, now vice-president and minister for External Affairs and the strong man of the government, was assassinated on a Dublin suburban road on his way to Mass.

Though dissident republicanism led by de Valera had recently given up the gun and turned to political organization through their new party, 'Fianna Fáil', the O'Higgins murder threatened a return to the brutal vendetta of the civil war. O'Higgins was inescapably associated with the merciless execution policy carried out by the Free State government in its early days against 'Irregulars'; like Desmond FitzGerald and other political friends of WBY, O'Higgins had admired Mussolini's restoration of order to Italian public life and seemed to believe that post-revolutionary stability might require some curtailment of civic liberty. Still, his views, if right-wing, were committed to parliamentary democracy. He had certainly set his face hard against what WBY called the 'impossibilists' – with whom Maud Gonne, for one, had long thrown in her lot. The O'Higgins murder (though condemned by de Valera, now becoming a belated constitutionalist) brought such antipathies into sharp relief, and WBY felt them bitterly. Of all the government ministers, O'Higgins had been the nearest to a friend: apart from colluding in various political matters, they dined in each other's houses, and by 1927 O'Higgins's political stance mirrored WBY's own conservatism most closely. From 1922 he had been obsessed by threats to the Irish social fabric and had turned against what he called 'rabid Republicanism'. In November 1926, when WBY had been in London on

Lane business, O'Higgins was there too, cultivating the same politicians but pursuing the bizarre agenda of suggesting to the Imperial Conference that the Free State declare itself a monarchy under George V. It came to nothing, but indicates how far O'Higgins had travelled from traditionalist republicanism. A product of the Irish middle class, closely related to the old Home Ruler elites, expensively educated, French-speaking, and intellectually assured, he was seen by more rough-hewn colleagues as suspiciously cosmopolitan and sophisticated.[152] But the executions of 1923 and the army mutiny of 1924 had proved him to be a tough politician, and Cosgrave's almost certain successor. His brutal murder was probably occasioned by his past actions rather than his present identification or his probable future, but it transformed Irish politics, and fell on WBY as a great personal blow. O'Higgins would join Parnell in his personal pantheon of lost Irish leaders who had not been afraid to be unpopular.

A long letter to Olivia Shakespear showed that the shock had driven him back on speculation about occult foreknowledge, and also that he had no qualms about carrying through the kind of political measures O'Higgins himself would have felt necessary.

You were right about our peace not lasting. The murder of O'Higgins was no mere public event to us. He was our personal friend, as well as the one strong intellect in Irish public life & then too his pretty young wife was our friend. We got the news just when we reached the Gresham Hotel where we were to dine & we left without dining & walked about the streets till bedtime. The night before George had suddenly called the dog out of the way of what she thought was a motor car – there was no car – & a moment after when inside our own door we both heard two bursts of music, voices singing together. At the funeral at the Mass for the dead I recognized the music as that of the choir which – just before the elevation of the Host – sang in just such short bursts of song. You will remember the part the motor car had in the murder. Had we seen more he might have been saved for recent evidence seems to show that those things are fate unless foreseen by clairvoyance & so brought within the range of free will. A French man of science thinks that we all – including murderers & victims – will, & so create the future. I would bring in the dead. Are we, that fore-know, the active or potential traitors of the race-process. Do we as it were forbid the banns when the event is struggling to be born. Is this why – even if what we foresee is not some trivial thing – we foresee too little to understand.

I have finished those love poems – 14 in all – and am now at a new Tower series partially driven to it by this murder. Next week I must go to Dublin to help write the more stringent police laws the government think necessary. I hear with anxiety that they will increase the number of crimes punishable by death & with satisfaction that they will take certain crimes out of the hands of jurors. But I know nothing except what I find in the papers.[153]

The event reverberated all around him, reaching into intimacies past and present: for Dublin rumour quickly pointed an accusing finger at Maud Gonne's son, Seán MacBride, heavily implicated in the most intransigent circles of the IRA. The poem which subsequently formed in WBY's mind, 'Blood and the Moon', confronted the idea of inherited hate, and the closed circles of Irish history. All his work on senatorial committees, his belief in creating a new and independent Irish aesthetic, his own evolution into a smiling public man, weighed little when balanced against the gunshots in Booterstown that Sunday morning. But the government, aided by special powers, survived the crisis, and, for all his quarrels with conventional opinion, WBY's own position in the new state was now unique. Horace Reynolds, characteristically, had positioned himself in the front row at O'Higgins's great public funeral procession and noticed WBY pacing behind the coffin, wrapped in a penumbra all his own. 'The first poet of Ireland walks before the fire brigade.'[154]

Chapter 9 : Striking a Match
1927–1930

> Poets, as much as politicians or publicists, may be permitted
> to observe the emotions which move through the multitude as
> greater minds. That Mr Yeats should still find picturesque or
> heraldic expression for moods of public hate, enthusiasm or
> violence, is a particular gain.
>
> Austin Clarke reviewing The Tower in
the TLS, 1 March 1928

I

THE MURDER of Kevin O'Higgins resonated in WBY's life like the fall of
Parnell: indeed, his later political poetry would put the two events in fateful
conjunction. And he probably knew more about aspects of O'Higgins's life
which, at the time of the assassination, were a closely kept secret from the
Irish public: his recent attempts to bring Unionists and nationalists together in a 'Kingdom of Ireland' under the British Crown for one thing, his
bedazzled and obsessive love-affair with WBY's friend Hazel Lavery for
another.[1] To the Irish public, O'Higgins still appeared – rather unfairly –
the implacable Robespierre who had ordered seventy-seven executions of
his ex-comrades during the civil war. At thirty-five he had moved rapidly
from revolutionary republican to reactionary hardliner; had thirty-five more
years been spared to him, his trajectory would certainly have carried him, at
least initially, further to the right, and his party with him. In the general
election of June 1927 de Valera's Fianna Fáil, only recently brought into the
constitutional arena and strongly tinged with irredentist republicanism,
won a very nearly equal share of both popular vote and parliamentary seats.
O'Higgins, wishing to 'see Ireland consciously and deliberately relegate
separatism and Anglophobia (as distinct from Independence) to the waste
paper basket',[2] had defined the alternative Irish future to that cherished by
de Valera, and was thus a figure with a particular appeal for WBY.

De Valera and Fianna Fáil rapidly demonstrated their new-found consti-
tutionalism by deploring the assassination, but the government cracked
down hard nonetheless. A sweeping Public Safety Act gave the military
free-ranging powers of arrest and detention, and simultaneously an electoral Amendment Act was introduced, forcing Fianna Fáil deputies to take
the hated oath of fidelity before entering the Dáil. The new-minted parliamentarians reluctantly complied; to their Irregular comrades who had

stayed in the purist faith of the IRA, they had now sold out and joined the turncoats who had accepted the Treaty. This was the line taken, inevitably, by Maud Gonne and her indomitable entourage, centred on Roebuck House in Clonskeagh, where she was attempting to organize her own republican variant of Cuala industries, advertising 'Funeral wreaths made from Irish shells'. And one of the first suspects arrested under the Public Safety Act, and interrogated about O'Higgins's murder, was her son Seán MacBride. For all the political distance now separating them, she called, as always, on WBY for help. And, as always, he responded: visiting Cosgrave to ask for Seán to be allowed out of prison to visit his old nurse's deathbed and offering to be personally responsible for him. The request was refused, but, yet again, Gonne's appeal in a time of trouble salvaged their relationship.[3] The terms of her claim, however, did not compromise her political principles.

Of course both Seagan [Seán] & I are Republicans & I still believe what I believe[d] ever since I was [a] girl that Ireland has a right to be independent. You believed that too once long ago – but what is the use of writing this long letter to you who by your vote made yourself responsible for the Public Safety Act & put the Police above the magistrates & made law a mockery & derision.

Her own derision took the form of a mocking reference to *Cathleen ni Houlihan*, the play she had made her own. 'In the Public Safety Act the Free State legislators have given their measure. They will [be] remembered by it for all time.'[4]

Thus she simultaneously reproached WBY for abandoning his Fenian past and enlisted his help in agitating – unsuccessfully – for Seán's release. WBY's reply directly confronted her accusation of coat-turning and took up the theme which now preoccupied him above all in Irish public affairs: the politics of hate.

You are right – I think – in saying I was once a republican, though like you yourself I would have been satisfied with Gladstone's [1886 Home Rule] bill. I wonder if I ever told you what changed all my political ideas. It was the reading through in 1903–4 of the entire works of Balzac. Today I have one settled conviction 'Create, draw a firm strong line & hate nothing whatever not even, if he be your most cherished belief – Satan himself'. I hate many things but I do my best, & once some fifteen years ago, for I think one whole hour, I was free from hate. Like Faust I said 'stay moment' but in vain. I think it was the only happiness I have ever known.[5]

Her reply, though it preached her own belief in divine love, had all the fierceness and passion he had once loved in her, savagely attacking what she saw as the inhumanity of the Free State government. WBY remained uncompromising. 'The great political service that Balzac did me', he told her, was that he made authoritative government (government which can, at need, be remorseless, as in his *Cathedral Des Médicis*) interesting in my eyes – that is what I mean by the 'strong line', a line drawn upon the fluctuating chaos of human nature – before I had read him only movements for liberty – movements led by lyrical idealists – seemed to me interesting. In some ways you & I have changed places. When I knew you first you were anti-Drefusard all for authoritative government, – Boulanger – & so on; and I was Drefusard & more or less vaguely communist under the influence of William Morris. Today if I lived in France I would probably join your old party – though with some reservations – & call myself a French national-ist. You I imagine would join the communists.[6]

Those 'reservations' probably meant the anti-Semitic company he would be keeping. In reply Gonne crisply dismissed Dreyfus as 'an uninteresting jew . . . too much money was spent on his cause for it to be an honest cause' and declared her sympathy, as a nationalist, for 'French nationalists who ob-jected to the Jews & international finance interfering in their country'.[7] While WBY's politics set further and further to the right, he avoided the anti-Semitic identification which disfigured the correspondence of so many of his contemporaries (notably Gogarty and Sturm).

In early October he drew up for Gonne a statement 'of what I believe to be the ancient doctrine – which must soon be modern doctrine also – of the effects of hate & love. The whole of mystical philosophy seems to me a deduction from this thought.' Following the theory of Plotinus (and Berkeley) that 'things only exist in being perceived', the eternal realities are thoughts and emotions which remain in existence through the Anima Mundi; and the passion of hatred can be exorcized only when people 'who are in the mystic sense of the word Victims . . . dissolve that passion into the totality of mind' by an act of sanctification. Long before, in the 1890s, he had agonized about the way Gonne's 'life of hatred' condemned her to live in a kind of hell, and he returned to it now, thirty years later. 'Those who hate [receive] the influx of hate, subjecting themselves as old writers believe to streams of disaster, those who love [receive] the influx of love, human and divine.'[8] On these themes, their correspondence continued: she probably agreed with him that 'we will never change each other's politics; they are too deeply rooted in our characters' – but she had returned to signing herself 'Always your old friend'.

Their eternal argument, the memories it evoked, and the political tension after O'Higgins's death are reflected in two poems WBY wrote at this time. 'Blood and the Moon' was written at Ballylee, and deliberately declared the part the tower played in WBY's personal iconography – epitomizing both the 'bloody arrogant power' of the building's (and Ireland's) history and the intellectual associations of towers in classical antiquity, Babylonian

345

astronomy, and Shelley's poetry. The poem is an uneven performance, obscure and declamatory by turns, replete with wonderful phrases and open questions. It begins by consecrating the tower, but moves on to suggest that the violence and hatred carried in Irish blood present the constant threat of defilement. While O'Higgins's death inspired WBY to reflect upon Ireland's savage history ('odour of blood on the ancestral stair'), the poem was WBY's most decisive declaration yet that his own identification lay with the Ascendancy tradition, into whose company the murdered politician was posthumously co-opted. The tower, rising from its cottages, suggests the arrogant power that 'rose out of the race': a deliberate indication that the Irish elite was intrinsically Irish, not composed of foreign settlers. (Anglo-Normans are, for these purposes, elided into Anglo-Irish.) WBY ringingly claimed as his intellectual ancestors an Irish-Georgian quartet very far from the 'old fathers' of mercantile Sligo or bohemian Bedford Park:

> I declare this tower's my symbol; I declare
> This winding, gyring, spyring treadmill of a stair is my ancestral stair,
> That Goldsmith and the Dean, Berkeley and Burke have traveled there;
>
> Swift beating on his breast in sibylline frenzy blind
> Because the heart in his blood-sodden breast had dragged him down
>   into mankind;
> Goldsmith deliberately sipping at the honey pot of his mind;
>
> And haughtier headed Burke that proved the State a tree
> That this unconquerable labyrinth of the birds, century after century
> Casts but dead leaves to mathematical equality;
>
> And God-appointed Berkeley that proved all things a dream,
> That this pragmatical preposterous pig of a world, its farrow
>   that so solid seem
> Must vanish on the instant if the mind but change its theme,
>
> *Saeva Indignatio* and the labourer's hire
> The strength that gives our blood and state magnanimity of its own desire
> Everything that is not God consumed with intellectual fire.

Thus Anglo-Ireland was associated with uncompromising intellectual achievement (Swift and Goldsmith), conservative and anti-egalitarian politics (Burke), and Neoplatonic philosophy (Berkeley, with some special pleading) – all core values held by WBY himself. Possession of the tower, and the work that it inspired when he climbed the 'treadmill' stair up to his study, symbolized his claim to this strain of Irish history; it also fortified Burke's emphasis on the necessity for perpetuating property within the family, as a way of perpetuating society itself.[9] In the end, for all these proud declarations, WBY staked his faith on the purity of insight gained through concentrated mystic reflection – much as in *Per Amica Silentia Lunae*, and using the same image:

> Is every nation like the tower
> Half dead at the top? no matter what I said
> For wisdom is the property of the dead,
> A something incompatible with life; and power,
> Like everything that has the stain of blood,
> A property of the living, but no stain
> Can come upon the visage of the moon
> When it has looked in glory from a cloud.

'Half dead at the top' is a radically compressed reference to the unfinished state of Ballylee's topmost storey, Swift's consciousness of mental decline ('I shall be like that tree, I shall die at top'), and the failure of authority in democratic states: in the next publication WBY added the adjective 'modern' to 'nation'.[10] But it should be noted that the poet's chosen ancestors are far removed from the well-ordered Augustans of the English eighteenth-century tradition: their extremeness, posturing, eccentricity, and originality complement the 'bloody arrogance' of their caste. And all qualities may be needed for the 'modern nation' standing on seven centuries of 'blood-saturated ground'.

This may seem to sit oddly with WBY's injunctions to Gonne about casting out ancestral hatreds through an act of sanctification. But in the autumn of 1927, while they argued about politics and mysticism, he was working on another poem about hatred and history, inspired by another death. On 15 July his old friend and enemy Constance Markievicz had died in the public ward of a poor Dublin hospital, worn out by years of frantic campaigning in republican and labour politics. The huge funeral demonstration proved that she was remembered for her creation of the republican youth movement, her military activity in the 1916 Rising and subsequent imprisonment (after which she had returned to Dublin like a queen), her brief ministry in the First Dáil, her violent stand against the Treaty, and her socialism. All this, set off by her dashing and theatrical style, her imperiousness, and the remains of an aquiline beauty, made her an iconic figure for the Dublin public. Gregory, while admiring the Countess's nationalist commitment, also remembered her 'in her Castle days when she was rather a jealous meddler in the Abbey and Hugh's Gallery'.[11] WBY's memories, also mixed, were far more intense. Constance's sister, Eva, like her a committed radical, had died a year before after a career of socialist and feminist activity in England. Both women's lives ended in middle age, impoverished and worn out, having embraced careers and principles which

carried them far from the great neoclassical house wreathed in the mists of
Raghly Bay in Sligo, where WBY had first encountered them thirty-five years
before. The Gore-Booth family were all, as he had noted at the time, 'inflam-
able' and 'ever ready to take up new ideas and new things'.[12]

For all his progressive irritation with her radical style and his deep dislike
of her shambolic Polish husband, WBY had continued to find the Countess
an object of fascination. A few years before, his poem 'On a Political
Prisoner' had shown how the memory of her beauty, and the unpredictable
trajectory of her astonishing life, could both ignite the long fuse of a potent
memory and illuminate his own reaction to the disasters of the present. He
once said that he had written about Con in order to avoid writing about
Maud; now, embroiled in his never-ending argument with Gonne, he
began to write in memory of Eva and Constance Gore-Booth. The elegy
was finished in early October; WBY kept it unpublished for two years.
Eventually he would place it as the first poem in *The Winding Stair* in 1929,
striking the keynote for that collection as ringingly as 'Sailing to Byzantium'
did for *The Tower*. This is appropriate, for it is far more than a poignant
memory of youth and beauty; it confronts the very question of inherited
abstract hatreds which he had examined (less deftly) in 'Blood and the
Moon', and argued about so eloquently with Gonne.

The poem opens with a double portrait from the 1890s, suggesting a
canvas by Lavery or Osborne, but moves swiftly to the ravages of time.

> The light of evening, Lissadell,
> Great windows open to the south,
> Two girls in silk kimonos, both
> Beautiful, one a gazelle.
> But a raving autumn shears
> Blossoms from the summer's wreath;
> The older is condemned to death,
> Pardoned, drags out lonely years
> Conspiring among the ignorant.
> I know not what the younger dreams –
> Some vague Utopia – and she seems,
> When withered old and skeleton-gaunt,
> An image of such politics.
> Many a time I think to seek
> One or the other out and speak
> Of that old Georgian mansion, mix
> Pictures of the mind, recall
> That table and the talk of youth,
> Two girls in silk kimonos, both
> Beautiful, one a gazelle.

The beauty of the sisters is clearly sacrificed to their opinions as much as worn by the passing of years. The second and final section projects this thought further, opening with a compassionate but despairing invocation to the ghosts of the lost girls and ending with an image that is at once plangent and mysterious in WBY's high style.

> Dear shadows, now you know it all,
> All the folly of a fight
> With a common wrong or right.
> The innocent and the beautiful
> Have no enemy but time;
> Arise and bid me strike a match
> And strike another till time catch;
> Should the conflagration climb
> Run till all the sages know.
> We the great gazebo built,
> They convicted us of guilt;
> Bid me strike a match and blow.

If the poem simply expressed his wish to burn away the years and restore Constance and Eva to the innocence and beauty they possessed in their (and his) youth, it would be an achievement of poignant clarity. The couplet towards the end, however, returns to his preoccupation with the hatreds and the confrontations of Irish history. It is possible to read the 'we' as uniting WBY with the two sisters in their dreams of youth, building a 'great gazebo' of hopes; and the 'they' as faceless critics, modern Irish philistines, soi-disant sages. Considering the direction of his own thought in 1927, and his condemnation of Eva's and Constance's politics, it might be interpreted very differently. A first draft read 'I the great gazebo built/They brought home to me the guilt.'[13] The Georgian image of a 'great gazebo' suggests the fragile structure of Ascendancy achievement which WBY used as a gauntlet flung down in Senate speeches and poems such as 'Blood and the Moon'; 'we' embraces WBY and his chosen Ascendancy ancestors; and the people who convicted 'us' of guilt are not the 'sages' but the Gore-Booth girls themselves, who denounced the Anglo-Irish world from whence they came. In her histrionic speech against the Treaty, Constance Markievicz had declared: 'By that bad black drop of English blood in me I know the English': the abstract bitterness which WBY had already identified in 'To a Political Prisoner' was rooted, he now hinted, in a personal repudiation of a world to which he had decided to pledge his allegiance. 'In England you have never met the hatred that is a commonplace here,' he told Olivia Shakespear. 'It lays hold upon our class, I think, more easily than upon the mass of the people – it finds a more complicated & determined conscience to prey upon.'[14] Thus he may have been placing Markievicz among the phantoms of hatred, the innumerable harpies with their clanging wings, who haunt the last stanzas of 'Meditations in Time of Civil War' – and at the same time claiming his own place in the same 'class' of Anglo-Irishry.

At such a time of demoralization and introspection, it is not surprising to find him at Ballylee and Coole during August and September, rereading his early work, rewriting sections of *A Vision* (already), and visiting Gregory. She was enduring her own time of trouble, overseeing the disposal of the estate which Margaret had sold to the Land Commission and Forestry Department. They formally took possession on 29 October, though the tenancy of the house remained hers for life. Indomitable as ever, she set herself to memorialize the house and estate in a book, which would allow her a kind of continued possession. Cuala agreed to print it. They had already produced a small volume of WBY's recent verse, *October Blast*: WBY read from it to some visitors at Coole on 23 August. 'And then he talked of clairvoyants, and of religion, the need of an intellectual belief,' Gregory recorded, adding waspishly, 'poor Mary [Studd] fidgetted, having taken the R.C. sleeping draught'.[15]

But if WBY's reputation for dangerous heterodoxy was well established in Ireland, so was his fame in the wider world. Yeats tourism had spread from Sligo to Gort, with regular visitors arriving at Coole in search of places named in his poetry. And in mid September he was offered a flatteringly lucrative deal by the American publisher Crosby Gaige – £300 for sixteen pages of verse, with all rights reverting to WBY after six months. Much of it could, he thought, be accounted for by *Oedipus at Colonus*, so, as he told Gregory, 'I am well off for the moment.'[16] It would eventually provide the first version of *The Winding Stair*, beautifully published by the Fountain Press of New York in 1929. But the commitment came at a time when, as he told L. A. G. Strong, he had already been writing lyrics for 'some months',[17] and it developed into an incubus. The published volume would include several poems already written or in the process of gestation (including 'In Memory of Eva Gore-Booth and Con Markiewicz' and 'Blood and the Moon'), but much effort was devoted to 'a new Tower poem' (eventually 'A Dialogue of Self and Soul') and the arrangement of the short, questioning sexually explicit lyrics grouped together as 'A Woman Young and Old', several of which he had already sent Shakespear. They provide a curious, complicit subterranean current in the stream of gossipy, worldly, reflective letters that flowed between Shakespear and himself, as well as bearing witness to the restless preoccupation with sex increasingly evident in WBY's writing since he turned sixty. In part, this reflected his determination to confront the threat of literary censorship, but it also represents a mounting tension in his own personal life.

II

In November 1927 George told Lennox Robinson that she had 'felt for years that life was quite unnecessary & if only a landslide would remove me they [her husband and family] could have jointly a nurse a governess a secretary & a housekeeper & all get on so much better'.[18] This is not an unusual reaction for an overworked and underappreciated mother of small children, with a much older husband who had just been seriously ill; but her frustration had now lasted 'for years'. With the disappearance of her role as spirit-medium, the erotic dimension of their marriage had clearly faded. It is also significant that she confided in Robinson, whom she relied upon as a 'perfect oyster'. He was closely integrated into the household at Merrion Square: as Michael's godfather, as a reliable sounding-board for WBY (who, in George's words, needed Robinson to 'hold his hand in the long evenings'), and as the recipient of George's exasperation.[19]

With Robinson, she went to the cinema, entertained the Drama League, and drank rather too many cocktails. Now forty, Robinson was lanky, fruity-voiced, and still unmarried, so even Dublin tongues were unlikely to wag. Though still professing a hopeless love for Iseult Stuart, he was pursued instead by what George called 'rumours and gossip of the Oscar Wildish sort'.[20] WBY was, in more than one sense, behind the obsession with Iseult: not only because he had encouraged it before her marriage to Stuart, but possibly because, since Robinson had cast WBY as a father-figure, to pursue the daughter of Maud Gonne completed the necessary symmetry. And Robinson brought into the Yeats circle his friend Thomas MacGreevy, together with his own future wife, Dolly Travers Smith.

MacGreevy was an introspective and saturnine Kerryman, hell-bent on aestheticism, who would, after a long apprenticeship in Paris, become an interesting modernist poet and an influential art critic and director of the National Gallery of Ireland. George affectionately called him 'a missed-priest . . . living in a magnificent vortex of vicarious enjoyments'.[21] From the early 1920s he was a regular visitor to Merrion Square, and visited the Yeatses in Italy in 1925. In May 1927 WBY even tried to advance MacGreevy (aged twenty-four and more or less untried) for director of the National Gallery, against Thomas Bodkin – far better qualified but an old adversary of Gregory and WBY. This was a spectacularly premature manoeuvre, though MacGreevy would succeed to the directorship twenty-three years later.[22] In the mid 1920s he was still a fringe figure in Dublin's cultural life. He had shared lodgings with Robinson, and, like him, had lived at Plunkett's home in Foxrock; constantly thrown together, they had, as their correspondence shows, a close friendship founded on mutual irritation as well as on shared interests (Robinson was annoyed by MacGreevy's self-obsession, MacGreevy was impatient with Robinson's thespian gush). For WBY, they were disciples and surrogate sons. For George they provided a necessary alliance, a point of contact outside her demanding domestic role, and a safety-valve for her inevitable explosions. And from 1926 the duo that played this part in the Yeats household was extended to a trio by the introduction of Dolly Travers Smith.

Strangely, she was the granddaughter of WBY's old patron and sometime adversary Edward Dowden. Her mother, Hester, was Dowden's daughter, and well known to WBY as a spirit medium and author on psychic matters; but after his marriage it is unlikely that they often met. This may have been because Hester lived in London but also because she was a particular *bête noire* of George's. 'The unbending hard essence of everything I loathe mentally emotionally and temperamentally, she makes me think of lumpy beds, russian fleas and ipechuana wine.'[23] Hester (three years younger than WBY) certainly appears as something of a monster: vain, demanding, cruelly critical of her daughter, she liked to appropriate Dolly's young men and – according to Robinson – was slowly poisoning both their lives. Nonetheless, MacGreevy lodged with her in Chelsea in the mid 1920s, and she exerted a considerable power over Robinson, forcing him to escort her on Continental holidays and hectoring him about Dolly's prospects and short-comings. Robinson was caught between mother and daughter. He had sustained a friendly, quasi-avuncular relationship with Dolly since her childhood, building up her confidence and encouraging her ambitions to be a painter. She was fifteen years younger, evidently adored him, and probably saw him as an escape route. MacGreevy and George both realized she was in love with Robinson; MacGreevy thought a marriage would be disastrous, George disagreed. By the time the inevitable union happened, in 1931, she may have had her own reasons for supporting it.

Robinson did not introduce Dolly to Merrion Square until October 1926: she was twenty-five years old, artistic, funny, appealingly plump, and an instant success. A month later George told MacGreevy: 'I love Dolly. Dont generally much like females but she adds one to the small collection I do like.'[24] By early 1927 Dolly was painting sets for *The Emperor Jones* at the Abbey and living at Merrion Square; she was greatly liked there, and given the pet-name 'Chinatown'. Both Yeatses joined the Robinson–MacGreevy conspiracy to find Dolly regular Dublin work, which would enable her to escape from Hester. In May there was even a plan to set up a cinema associated with the Abbey, with a managerial role for Dolly built in, but nothing came of it and she returned sadly to the dragon of Cheyne Row. 'I miss Dolly terribly', George told MacGreevy, '& wish she *did* live here.'[25] And by October 1927 she returned to Dublin, producing notably successful sets for *Caesar and Cleopatra* at the Abbey, staying on to do *Spreading the News*, and working in Harry Clarke's stained-glass studio. But things were no longer sunny. 'Tom McGreevy arrived yesterday,' WBY told Olivia Shakespear on 2 October, '& some obscure quarrel between him, Dolly Dowden – otherwise Chinatown & Lennox Robinson is disturbing life. I think the trouble is that Tom came here when he should have gone to Lennox and as Dolly's cap is set at Lennox she too feels angered.'[26] But there may have been other tensions too. In the same letter he remarked to Shakespear, 'I am still of opinion that only two topics can be of the least interest to a serious & studious mind – sex & the dead.' Dolly would later claim that WBY himself became increasingly attracted to her, and paid her attention to a degree that upset George and provoked at least one public scene.

Yet George retained her affection for Dolly, and even encouraged her to try automatic writing for WBY.[27] This was playing with fire; but, looked at another way, it may have reflected George's desire to provide distraction for her husband at – almost – any cost. At any rate, Dolly's presence at Merrion Square certainly raised the temperature. Unsurprisingly, George became anxious to see her married to Lennox and scolded MacGreevy for his opposition to the idea. As for Robinson, he continued to raise Dolly's expectations with solicitous and half-romantic letters, while telling MacGreevy as late as 1930 that, though he had not seen Iseult for a year and a half, 'whenever I see her my heart stops and when we meet I can say nothing but banalities'.[28] Nonetheless, a few months after that letter, he finally married Dolly, despite Hester's fury and MacGreevy's misgivings. The marriage would be close, companionate, and childless, featuring small dogs and heavy drinking. Robinson's alcoholism continued apace, and his dramatic writing never matched up to the early promise of *The Big House* or *The White-headed Boy*. All this lay in the future in the autumn of 1927, when emotions were running high in Merrion Square. And at this point illness struck again.

In mid October George guardedly admitted to Gregory that WBY had flu and 'a slight congestion of the left lung; he is *not at all* seriously ill and has to be kept very quiet'. On 23 October Lily found him still bedridden, and composed the scene with an artist's eye: 'he looks still handsome and a poet in bed, which is more than many could do. He has a fur rug on the bed, and on himself a yellow coat . . . and his rich colouring and thick hair makes a really fine picture.'[29] But he was much more ill than he seemed: the congestion had taken hold, and was followed by a haemorrhage. An Irish winter boded ill. Even before his collapse, George had been planning a trip south to Rapallo to see the Pounds; now she advanced the plan, switching to Spain (which she had never visited, though – resourceful as ever – she spoke and read the language).[30]

At the beginning of November they departed by ship to Gibraltar, and thence to Algeciras and Seville. WBY was still extremely weak, and George at the end of her tether. 'WB of course is making his last will & testament at all hours of day & night,' she told Robinson, 'hurrying to finish a poem but has not been able to begin yet. "Of course I shall never be able to go on with the autobio now ..." etc etc. All poppycock. However in the same breath he talks of writing a poem on the herons at Algeciras "in a few years time". ... What a pillaloo!'[31] The herons at Algeciras, flying in from Africa, remained a pre-occupation, and they eventually came to roost in a poem. But his recuperation did not develop as hoped: the lung was not healing, and when they moved north to Seville he was still coughing blood. Worse still, mental confusion had overtaken him, and, to George's alarm, he thought he was in Siena. The weather was cold, and the hotel barely heated. Once again they set off, and by 25 November were at last comfortably settled at Cannes, in the Château St Georges – a quiet hotel on the Route Fréjus ten minutes from the town, with a beach across the road, warm rooms, and a south-facing veranda where WBY could sit 'purring all day', according to George, and comparing the outlook to Rosses Point.[32] Reluctantly she agreed to stay six weeks, and to bring the children out for Christmas; telegrams were dispatched to Robinson asking him to convey Michael and Anne to Cannes (a proposal that terrified him). And WBY at last began to recover. George, irritated by rumours relayed from Dublin, wrote to Gogarty to counteract them:

I hear that in spite of all our efforts it has got round Dublin that Willy has some 'disease of the lung' & so I hasten to write to you as the best centre of contradiction – the hamorrage [sic] in the lung was due to very high blood pressure (it was 260) & since the B.P. has come down to 230 the haemorrage has practically ceased. There is a small spot on the lung – since the congestion last October I imagine – & the man here thinks it quite unimportant – the blood pressure is what he concentrates on – W. is allowed no reading (but detective stories) no work & no exercise at present. No food after 4.30 pm at all. No wine nothing but toast for tea & breakfast. The diet suits him admirably.[33]

As for WBY, he was sharply conscious that he had suffered 'my first serious illness ... I hardly expected to recover.'[34] But apparently he did. The detective stories were supplemented by Wyndham Lewis's *Time and Western Man*. Visitors from Dublin began to call (the MacNeills, Lucy Phillimore). To Shakespear he wrote of his determination to finish *The Winding Stair* for the American publisher (whose £300 was paying for WBY's convalescence) and extolled 'the subsconcious gaity [sic] that leaps up before danger or difficulty; I have not had a moment's depression – that gaity is outside one's control, a something given by nature – yet I did hate leaving the last word to George Moore.'[35] When Robinson arrived to stay in December, he was shocked to find wby weak, exhausted, and bedridden.[36] He was not yet sure of recovery, and in mid January he caught flu and relapsed. To his shock, the local doctor told him – in George's words – 'he need never expect to regain his original health and vigour'.[37] This was a staggering blow. wby obsessively recurred to it as to a sentence of death, and the depression which he had boasted of avoiding now descended in earnest. George hurriedly instructed MacGreevy and Robinson to send him encouraging letters:

That ass-doctor came earlier than expected and filled W. with despair by telling him he need not expect ever to get back his original health . . . etc, etc. So W. proceeded to have a complete breakdown, and 'of course he had never realised before how completely his interest in life had been in his work and if he isnt going to be able to work and etc and etc.' and 'You must tell Lennox. I know he has always thought I did not take my fair share of the burden of the Abbey . . . etc etc' So I made him dictate the beginning of a scenario for ballet, many letters, and walked him into town today and he ate an enormous meal at the Majestic grill room and then wandered about looking at a seaplane which was taking people for short flights and landing near the Majestic on the sea, and only at 2-30 did he remember that he must be getting tired![38]

This shows that he was no longer as ill as he feared; but it also conveys the shock that the doctor's pronouncement had given him and the realization of how little in his life mattered besides his work. This, in turn, was hardly a reassuring revelation for George, now coping with an ill son as well as an ailing husband, since Michael had been struck down by a severe glandular infection which threatened tuberculosis. 'Had I known that all this might happen,' she confessed to MacGreevy, 'I should certainly never have had a family'.[39]

wby continued to regain his strength, to send entertaining letters to Shakespear, to cogitate about Wyndham Lewis and their 'fundamental agreement' about philosophical matters. He had met Lewis through Sturge Moore nearly twenty years before, and kept desultorily in touch, but it took the philosophic readings of the later 1920s to convince him that Lewis's cosmopolitan modernism had elements in common with his own 'System'.[40] Shakespear, who commissioned paintings from Lewis, put them in touch with each other, and a cautious intellectual relationship developed – wby even allowed Lewis to use a quotation from him to publicize *The Childermass* in America. They shared the notion that reality was shaped by perception, which chimed with wby's readings in Berkeley and Gentile;

there was also a mutual debt to Nietzsche and a distrust of the democratic age in politics. On return visits to London, WBY met Lewis at Dulac's house in Ladbroke Grove and visited his studio; for his part, Lewis's subsequent painting incorporates preoccupations shared by WBY.[41] They were, however, separated by as much as united them, including basic differences on issues such as historical cycles, psychic research, nineties aestheticism, and Celticism: Lewis's satirical picture of the young Yeats in his magnum opus, *The Apes of God*, though conceived in the early 1920s, determinedly survived to appear in 1930. Nonetheless, the relationship showed that WBY could still attract the younger generation of avant-garde artists. This was true also of those in the theatre.

He had already noted the work of the young ballerina and choreographer Ninette de Valois, and his mind now ran on dance-plays; the fact that de Valois was both beautiful and Anglo-Irish could only add fuel to the fire. Robinson was quizzed as to the relative musical merits of Constant Lambert and Walter Rummel (already a friend, who had visited Dublin) for ballet music; at Cannes 'he re-wrote & simplified [*The Only Jealousy of*] *Emer* into a ballet,' Robinson reported to Gregory, 'and I left it with Miss de Valois in London.'[42] With music by George Antheil, it was produced by de Valois at the Abbey the following June, to ravishing effect. By mid February WBY was well enough to leave Cannes for Rapallo, and the heady restorative of Ezra Pound's company. But the doctor's pronouncement on 14 January had struck an echo which reverberated. From now on he knew that time could not be wasted; he was more and more fiercely impatient with any impediments, obstructions, evasions which might come between his work and what he wanted it to say; and he would pursue that lost vigour with a single-minded commitment, determined to demonstrate that he could recapture the force of youth in his life as well as in his work. The aftershock of 'first serious illness' reverberated not only in his subsequent writing, but in the experiments with politics, philosophy, and love which would mark the next phase of his life.

III

Nonetheless the tranquillity of Rapallo seemed, for the moment, the answer. Beautifully placed on the Ligurian coast near Portofino (less grand than the French Riviera or the Italian Lakes), the little town looked due south and was sheltered by mountains behind it. A curving beach was fringed with oleanders and palms, and bathing-platforms with private huts jutted out into the water. Its accessibility, cheapness, and famously mild climate meant it was modestly fashionable all year round, and attracted a colony of foreign residents on literary incomes. These had in the past included Nietzsche; current inhabitants numbered Pound, Max Beerbohm, and the German playwright Gerhard Hauptmann, while long-term visitors included Richard Aldington, Emil Ludwig, Franz Werfel, Basil Bunting, and young American acolytes like Robert Fitzgerald and James Laughlin. Pound had even begun editing a little magazine called, appropriately, the *Exile*. On 20 January he sent George a surprisingly practical letter, full of information about the relative warmth of different hotels (offering to test them out himself), the use of oil-stoves, and the flavour of life at the Albergo Rapallo, where the Yeatses eventually decided to stay.

The 'terasse' of the [Albergo] Rapallo is where we normally sit from 11.30 till after lunch. Hauptmann sits on the other side of the shrub box, ten feet off at the Aurum (i.e. the jazz hell in our basement). Probably the slight va et vient will provide Wm with mild object of observation. The 'gardens', are against hill side, with dampish rocks at strategic points.

At any rate the foci of solar heat are at 'Albergo Rapallo', on our elevated terazza, and on a tin bench the other side of a bathing pavillion to the north of the Chris. Colombo monyment. Does Wm know, like, dislike or what Hauptmann. My present relations with same are limited to ceremonious bow.[43]

The Yeatses arrived at the Albergo Rapallo on 17 February; they were reunited with the Pounds that same evening. For George, the relief of being among old friends of her own generation was immense, though the limitations of life in a watering-place quickly dawned on her. WBY took to the atmosphere of the Italian resort immediately. Sitting in the sheltered sunshine, he could turn from contemplating the sea to looking at a little white monastery on the top of a mountain behind the town, inhabited by three or four old monks – a prospect that particularly appealed to him.[44] Down below, all was serene, though all was not perfect. Ezra's testiness and choosiness about people created obstacles. When visitors like Siegfried Sassoon passed through and were liked by both Yeatses, they were usually condemned by Pound (however nice Sassoon was, he 'wanted a good brain as well'[45]). WBY's American acolyte was no longer the charming hothead of fifteen years before, and his attitude to 'old Unc. Wm.' sometimes jarred.[46] Besides, the Pound marriage had entered choppy waters. Ezra's lifelong association with the violinist Olga Rudge was well advanced, and her daughter by him was nearly three years old; while Dorothy's baby son, Omar, was not part of the Rapallo scene, being brought up by Olivia Shakespear in London. The marriage endured but under high tension; upon arrival, WBY expected George and Dorothy 'to renew all their old friendship', but the world and their lives had moved on. The Pounds' complicated ménage made Rapallo less idyllic than expected.

Then there were Ezra's politics. In *Time and Western Man*, Lewis had typified him as 'the revolutionary simpleton', and WBY concurred. But Pound's ideas of revolution had by now tipped towards endorsement of the peculiar revolution instituted by Mussolini. From 1925 he was declaring his admiration for Il Duce; soon he began dating his letters Fascist-style, from the March on Rome in October 1922, and emblazoned his letterhead with the Fascist motto 'Liberty is a duty not a right'. And he had become obsessed by the economics of money circulation, a subject to which he devoted much of his manic intellectual energy, and which tended towards denunciations of 'usury', international capitalism, and Jews. The *Exile* (which lasted four issues) printed some poems by WBY and others among Pound's star-studded literary network, but it was sabotaged by the editor's diatribes against politics and commerce, calling for a *'rappel à l'ordre'* and renouncing modern government. Full-blown Fascism and virulent anti-Semitism developed along with mood-swings into dictatorial incoherence: all characteristics which gradually infected his montage-series of *Cantos* constructed on increasingly bewildering principles. By the mid 1930s several of his friends and acquaintances, including James Joyce, thought Pound's manic energy had edged over into madness.

Since 1926 WBY had been reading modern Italian philosophy (notably Gentile and Croce), revising *A Vision* in the light of Italian thought, and excitedly relating the ideas he encountered to those of Plato, Plotinus, and Berkeley. Much of this was cast as a critique of materialism and Marxism, as well as an affirmation of the unity of opposites, and the Vico-derived notions of cycles which move from civilization to barbarism.[47] He was not, however, impressed or convinced by Pound's ranting: he and his old acolyte 'disagreed about everything', he told Gregory. 'He has most of Maud Gonne's opinions (political & economic) about the world in general ... The chief difference is that he hates Palgraves "Golden Treasury" as she does the Free State Government, & thinks even worse of its editor than she does of President Cosgrave. He has even her passion for cats & large numbers wait him every night at a certain street corner knowing that his pocket is full of meat bones or chicken bones. They belong to the oppressed races.'[48] The 'oppressed races' (with the rather large exception of Jews) were far closer to Gonne's heart than to Pound's, but for the moment WBY saw the 'revolutionary simpleton' in Pound rather than the committed Fascist.

The Rapallo routine was limited enough, given WBY's weakness, but a future life in the little seaside town was now part of the Yeatses' plan for transforming their existence. The previous November an exhausted George had told Robinson 'William is re-planning his future − Resigning from everything he can resign from − no Ballylee − that anyway will be a relief − a house near sea – perhaps Killiney – winter months here [Cannes] – I have given up the future so apart from getting rid of 82 [Merrion Square] can't be bothered.'⁴⁹ After the shock of his Cannes doctor's diagnosis in mid January, WBY had dictated a long letter to Gregory outlining a new pattern of life: winters abroad, summers in Ireland (though not at Ballylee), abandonment of the Senate and other work, except for his Abbey directorship. The Merrion Square house had already been put with an agent, and Robinson instructed to look for a smaller Dublin establishment, 'which must be, both for Michael's sake and mine, on high ground and near the sea'.⁵⁰ This was written when things were at their gloomiest, but the plans stuck. A week after arriving in Rapallo, George set off to Switzerland with Michael. She installed him in a school at Villars, where his glandular illness would respond to the climate; a mild tubercular infection was suspected, and he was still unwell. Now in much sunnier mood, WBY wrote to Shakespear about their envisaged future:

We have made great changes of plan & intend now to take a flat here & move over some of our furniture, & let all but one floor of 82 Merrion Square. We can then spend say from August to April here & the rest of the year in Dublin, with passing visits to London. Doctors tell us the Dublin climate will no more suit Michael than his father so we think to keep both children at a Swiss school & fetch them here for summer & winter holidays (hence August is included in our time here). George is longing for the freedom of flats & daily help & all heavy meals out. We have the refusal – George decides on her return from Switzerland – of a large flat – 9 or 10 rooms – with balconies & the most lovely view imaginable. Better not tell Nelly of all this as George may want to do so at her own time. We shall live much more cheaply & this change of place & climate at my time of life is a great adventure one longed for many a time. Once out of the Senate – my time is up in September – & in obedience to the doctors out of all public work there is no reason for more than 3 months of Dublin – where the Abbey is the one work I cannot wholly abandon. Once out of Irish bitterness I can find some measure of sweetness, and of light, as befits old age – already new poems are floating in my head, bird songs, of an old man. Joy in the passing moment, emotion without the bitterness of memory. At last I am really convalescent – all the exhaustion gone. I think I could do a day's work again, but under doctor's orders shall idle out this month, walking in the mornings by this brimming sea, in bed in the afternoon and from 7 to 9 or 10 with Dorothy or Ezra, or alone with George. Then from 10 to 11 or 11.30 base fictions in bed, any sort of swift adventure that can break the stream of thoughts. Part of my cure, by the by, is to walk slowly, even turn my head slowly, that my thoughts from sympathy with my movements may slacken. If it does not I may become my own funeral pyre.⁵¹

Crucially, he felt he had found a refuge where he could write. 'Here I shall put off the bitterness of Irish quarrels, & write my most aimable verses.

They are already – though I dare not write – crowding my head.'[52] By mid March George could tell MacGreevy that they had 'revolutionised existence'. They had committed themselves to the promised Rapallo flat, situated in a leafy suburb on the road to Santa Margherita and Portofino, and looking back to the town (where Pound held court in his apartment at the centre of the seafront). wby could walk towards the sea, cross a footbridge by the Columbus monument, and sit in the sun by the Lido; an alternative route took him by a grass-grown Roman arch, the Ponte Detto D'Hannibale, to find Pound feeding his cats in the seafront garden. The flat itself was unlike anywhere the Yeatses had ever lived. On the fourth floor of a new block on via Americhe (now corso Cristoforo Colombo), it was not yet finished. The decoration looked back to florid *fin de siècle* rather than twenties modernism, but George was able to dictate where electricity switches went, choose plain tiles throughout, and veto Italianate ornamentation and glass doors. wby would have an interconnecting study and bedroom with French windows on to the balconies, which ran around the corners of the building, giving morning sun and views of mountain and sea. The expansive lay-out allowed George to plan for a schoolroom, several bedrooms, and even her own small study, all for £98 a year. Most important of all, it had steam-driven central heating, besides auxiliary electric radiators and gas. Both in its aesthetics and its comforts, Via Americhe 12-8 presented the greatest possible contrast to Ballylee. Living in a symbol had proved to be a mixed blessing, and they would not return to the tower by the Cloon.

This pleased George, but she worried privately about the longeurs of spending too much of the year in the restricted environs of Rapallo; and she knew how painfully they would both miss the Merrion Square house and all it had stood for. Robinson's idea that they sublet it and keep the top floor as a flat was reluctantly abandoned. He, and others who had congregated there on Monday nights, found the prospect of its loss 'hellish', and Dolly Travers Smith 'wrote piteously' to MacGreevy.[53] By mid April wby was strong enough to return to Dublin. His doctors, Moorhead and Abrahamson, pronounced him well on the way to recovery; Lily found him slimmer and better, but still plagued by bronchial trouble. He went on receiving vaccinations for his chest problems for nearly a year. Social life was once more possible ('I am a fire of straw,' he told Hone, 'but bright enough while it lasts').[54] George began to reorganize their lives. By the end of May No. 82 was sold, to be vacated by 1 August. In the frenzy of packing and moving furniture there was no time to find a suitable flat; George and the children took rooms in Howth for the summer, and wby prepared to remove to Coole, determined to avoid being roped into the second Tailteann Games. In Galway too all was changing: with Edward Martyn dead, wby visited Tillyra, 'getting in through an old disused avenue . . . the only visible life was an incredible old slattern'. At Lough Cutra, Margaret Gregory's new fiancé Guy Gough had deserted his castle and moved into a converted stableyard house, where WBY found him 'looking in humble but puzzled misunderstanding at a picture of Jack's somebody had presented to him'.[55] And at Coole, though Gregory remained the central, controlling figure that he required her to be, her house was no longer her own.

Back in Dublin, the Yeatses were scaling down their lives. At the last minute they found a flat near by at 42 Fitzwilliam Square, above the consulting rooms occupied by an acquaintance – Bethel Solomons, the eminent gynaecologist who treated George and had advised Iseult during the crisis of her marriage eight years before. WBY had a large study overlooking the square, which George decorated in blue and gold. The flat cost £100 a year – cheaper than the norm, but Solomons did not want strangers. (There were hidden costs too: at fund-raising events for Solomons's hospital, George took a stall selling ices and ordered her husband to 'walk about and be seen'.[56]) By keeping an Irish residence, they forfeited the right to waive income tax, and their rental costs were now about £200 a year, but they both felt it was worth it. By the end of August they had left their great town house. 'I feel very sad about it,' Lily told her niece.

I loved the house and I hate change. George says it has served its purpose and I suppose I ought to feel that way also.

I feel it is the end of the Yeatses as Irish. Anne and Michael will be cosmopolitan and have no abiding place. I understand Willy's wish to get to the peace of Italy away from Irish politics now that he is older and not very well . . . But perhaps this is only my low-spirited view. They will still be here five or six months in the year and always have Ballylee. Anyway I keep my fears to myself. George makes and unmakes plans with such rapidity no need to worry over any one plan.[57]

But this plan was definite, and the shape of their life was fixed. Nor, for WBY in his current mood, was the 'cosmopolitanism' of his children's future a disadvantage. 'They will know Ireland from Ballylee & Coole (& they very naturally much prefer Coole to Ballylee),' he told Gregory.

& then they will come here [Rapallo] for Xmas & as they grow older will see Rome & Florence, & the few people they meet will be intellectual persons. I would not have liked London for them, or anywhere that would bring them into contact with people much richer than themselves, & I dreaded Dublin because people much poorer are even worse. Then too they will grow up with perfect French & Italian.[58]

This was a rather chilly prospect for two lively Irish children, and one in which George did not entirely concur, but WBY repeated the prescription in more than one letter. It sits oddly with his youthful view of national culture

and identity, 'rooted to rock and hill', and with his achieved image as an ornament of a newly independent Irish state. But it reflects his growing impatience with what that state was making of itself, the anxious desire to simplify
his life after a traumatic illness, and the liberation apparently offered by life
in Italy – even if his long-held vision of Ariosto, a tower in the Apennines,
and the ducal patronage of Urbino had been replaced by a steam-heated flat
in a Rapallo apartment-block. He was also sensing, as he recovered, the
revival of a desire to shape his life into a new adventure. And the very year
that he abandoned the actual tower for good, he published the book which
immortalized the name and the image. With his great architectural and historical symbol realized in a great book, the real building became redundant.
Symbolically, the first poem in his new collection was 'Sailing to Byzantium':
like the 'medieval Irishman' whose vision is enshrined in the poem, WBY was
setting his face towards new shores, driven by the onset of old age and the
overwhelming impulse to create an art that would defy mortality.

The Tower, published by Macmillan in February 1928, proved he could do
precisely that. It was rapidly seen as a supreme achievement, and has been
recognized as one of the key books of the twentieth century. Popular taste
still favoured his early work, to WBY's annoyance; Gregory told him that a
particular expression always crossed his face 'when you find the play or poem
some charming lady is gushing about is either Land of Heart's Desire or
Innisfree'.[59] But the short volume published by Cuala in 1927, *October Blast*,
had suggested just how powerful an effect WBY's new poems of the 1920s
could make when grouped together; *The Tower* carried through the promise,
for a much wider readership. Between 'Sailing to Byzantium' and 'All Souls'
Night' were gathered nineteen poems, many of consummate subtlety and
force. They included 'The Tower', 'Meditations in Time of Civil War',
'Nineteen Hundred and Nineteen', 'Leda and the Swan', and 'Among School
Children'. Beginning with the great sequences about history and violence, the
rhythm is modulated by lapidary lyrics like 'Youth and Age', and – at long last
– 'The New Faces', a premature anticipation of Gregory's old age written in
1912. Another long-repressed theme from his previous life surfaced in a series
of poems about his obsession with Iseult, withheld from *The Wild Swans at
Coole* and *Michael Robartes and the Dancer*. They included 'The Hero, the
Girl, and the Fool', 'Owen Aherne and his Dancers' and 'A Man Young and
Old'; while 'The Gift of Harun Al-Rashid' was a coded account of his rescue
into marriage. He also included the savagely interrogative 'Two Songs' from
The Resurrection – a very idiosyncratic perspective on the Christian message.
None of this harmed sales, and by April it was getting fast through a second
printing. 'This is very unusual for poetry,' Lily told her niece. 'It is very diffi-
cult, I find, but feel its stateliness and intellectuality and strength.'[60] These are

THE
TOWER
W B
YEATS
THE TOWER
BY W. B. YEATS
MACMILLAN·AND·CO
TSM
DEL

9. Thomas Sturge Moore's cover design for *The Tower*, stamped in gold on olive-green cloth: 'a most rich, grave and beautiful design', WBY told him, 'admirably like the place'. He also approved of Sturge Moore's 'completing Tower symbolism by surrounding it with water'.

well-chosen words, conveying the uncompromising nature of the poetry as well as its grandeur – qualities perfectly expressed in Sturge Moore's lovely design, an image of Ballylee and its reflection blocked in gilt on the cover. WBY's correspondence with Macmillan from the time he sent in the manuscript the previous September shows how carefully he monitored the production of what many would consider his greatest book.

In *The Tower* WBY's sense of drama was allied to a passionately personal testimony and an acceptance of his divided self: a modern critic has judged it 'a quintessentially modernist achievement, [giving] the same kind of satisfaction as *The Waste Land*, with its surface of unrelated voices and its submarine element of personal conviction'.[61] But it is also the supreme record of the upheavals and obsessions which had plagued and inspired him since 1917: Iseult, the civil war, the insights and study that had produced *A Vision*, and finally his determination to challenge the pieties of the new Irish dispensation as aggressively as he had ever challenged the old. Reading the new volume, however, he found himself 'astonished by its bitterness'. 'Yet that bitterness gave the book its power and it is the best book I have written.'[62]

More surprising yet – to WBY himself at least – was the warmth of its reception. 'Perhaps the reviewers know that I am ill, & think that I am so ill that I can be commended without future inconvenience. I gather that I am the last Victorian (with George Moore as a kind of last but one). Even the Catholic press is enthusiastic.'[63] This is a tongue-in-cheek misrepresentation. The consensus of critical judgement emphasized how WBY had transcended his poetic origins to arrive at an original and authoritative synthesis that was both distinctive and modern. His 'greatness' was now assured. In a huge *TLS* review the young Irish poet Austin Clarke traced another interesting distinction: the acerbity of *Responsibilities* had been translated into 'intellectual anxiety and indignation', strangely conveyed through 'an imaginative and prosodic beauty that brings out the pure and impersonal joy of art'.[64] Though highly individual, the results were more sympathetic and accessible than 'the work of Mr Yeats's middle age'. Clarke was equally perceptive about the philosophical underpinnings of the volume, noting a 'sharp division of physical from mental fact', reminiscent of 'popular medieval dialogues between body and soul' but signifying 'an individual doubt for the commonplaces or mysteries of creed'. Overall, the book seemed an exploration of spiritual restlessness and loneliness: a cry from a kind of internal exile.

Regarding WBY's philosophical bent, the less engaged and analytical reviewers tended to be preoccupied by the question of whether his poetry had – so to speak – survived *A Vision*. This curiosity was well put by the American critic Theodore Spencer: 'Would the philosophy be sufficiently absorbed not to override the emotion? Would the escapist element, now that a philosophic symbolism had been substituted for a nationalist one, still be too predominant? Would the personal feeling be so related to the external order that they would be fused into a single whole?'[65] The answer was yes: 'the poems in this book are among the finest Mr Yeats has written'. WBY's idiosyncratic philosophy now provided a symbolic language rather than an analytical structure (much as WBY would shortly write that George's automatic-writing voices had once brought him 'metaphors for poetry'). However mysterious (or inconclusive) the resolutions of the poems, many triumphantly achieved not only an echoing richness of tone, but a hard-won emotional reality. If this was 'Victorian', it was 'Victorian' in a very particular (and little-used) sense.

Three years later, Edmund Wilson's ground-breaking study *Axel's Castle* would stress above all WBY's apprehensions of reality: 'his greatness is partly due precisely to the vividness of that sense'. Wilson also noted that with *The Tower* WBY 'has passed into a sort of third phase, in which he is closer to the common world than at any previous period' – losing (in Wilson's view) a certain Dantean intensity along with his Dantean haughtiness. 'He has become more plain-spoken, more humorous – his mind seems to run more frankly on his ordinary human satisfactions and chagrins: he is sometimes harsh, sometimes sensual, sometimes careless, sometimes coarse.' But above all he had maintained 'a profound and subtle criticism of life'. *The Tower* had established this beyond all doubt. In the same year even Ezra Pound's splenetic *How to Read* had to except WBY from his indiscriminate thunderbolts ('the language is now in the keeping of the Irish (Yeats and Joyce); apart from Yeats, since the death of Hardy, poetry is being written by Americans'[66]). The young F. R. Leavis, congenitally suspicious of WBY's trajectory since the Celticism of the 1890s, paid tribute to the 'intellectual passion', 'difficult and delicate sincerity', and 'extraordinarily subtle poise' of *The Tower*. When it was awarded laurels at the Tailteann Games, even the *Catholic Bulletin* stayed quiet. At a moment of crisis and flux in his personal life, WBY had had his greatest critical success yet. But his triumph coincided with a literary row on another front, which rocked the Abbey, seismically altered the career of its new star playwright, and showed WBY at his most implacable, domineering, and thoughtless.

IV

As the laudatory reviews of *The Tower* were appearing, just after the Yeatses returned to Dublin and began to reorganize their life, WBY was reading the manuscript of Sean O'Casey's new play, which had been waiting for him at Merrion Square. His reaction was hasty in every sense. They had arrived, after an endless sea journey from Cherbourg to Cork, on 16 April 1928; on 20 April WBY wrote long letters to O'Casey and to Gregory which amounted to a swingeing condemnation, and an unequivocal decision that the Abbey directors should reject the latest work by the dramatist whose trilogy of plays about the Irish revolution had restored their audiences, their profits, and their dramatic edge.

The row was waiting to happen. The directors were already annoyed with O'Casey for negotiating a separate London deal for *Juno and the Paycock* in October 1925. Robinson had argued that the Abbey should put on the first London production, but O'Casey preferred James Fagan, and the Abbey received only a small percentage of the profits from an immense success.[67] Robinson nurtured a particular resentment of O'Casey, perhaps fuelled by jealousy: he was the nearest thing to a rival O'Casey had, especially after his success with *The Big House* two years before, but O'Casey effortlessly garnered all the publicity. Producing *The Plough and the Stars* in late 1925, Robinson had complained incessantly about the play's structure and O'Casey's unhelpfulness.[68] The fact that the Abbey turned down a play of Robinson's own in November 1927 because Gregory feared it might endanger the subsidy cannot have made him feel any better.[69] It was Robinson who read *The Silver Tassie* first, in March, while WBY was still in Rapallo; and Robinson who produced the first, negative response, particularly to the fourth act, though he kept it from O'Casey – who in blissful ignorance continued to assume that all was well and to suggest possible cast-lists for the first production.[70] Gregory's diary for 28 March records her 'absolute agreement' – to Robinson's relief. 'If you had disagreed with me,' he told her on 30 March,

I'd have suspected myself of all sorts of horrid sub-conscious feelings. I shall send the play at once to W.B.Y. and avoid writing to Sean until W.B. has read it. We can't do it before the end of this season and if W.B. agrees with you and me Sean will have time to think over his last act before July or August.[71]

Until WBY saw the play, then, the difficulty was with the fourth act, which even Robinson thought could be overcome with 'a simplified 3rd Act'. Finding the play awaiting him in Dublin, WBY read it at once – without, he claimed, looking at the opinions of his fellow directors. His reaction on 20 April critically exacerbated the problem, though it is unlikely that Robinson dissuaded him. It could not but be a terrible shock for O'Casey: as recently as 2 March Gregory had written to him in enthusiastic expectation ('I am sure the wine you have filled it [the 'Tassie', or cup] with is of the best vintage'[72]). He thought it was his best play.

Most authors in a state of post-natal euphoria think no differently, but there are wonderful things in *The Silver Tassie*. Beginning in Dublin's dockland as men set off to fight in the trenches, it follows its footballing hero, his sweetheart, his best friend, and his family through the horrors of war, disablement and then the almost equal horror of a return to 'normal' life after the trauma of the trenches. The second act, set on the war front, is a tour de force of expressionist theatre, constructed as a sort of secular cantata. The bitterness of the maimed hero, his rage and self-pity, and the survivalist instincts of his girlfriend and family are mercilessly shown. If Robinson had had his way and docked the fourth act, which returns to the Avondale Football Club and brutally shows how people adapt to survive, much would have been lost. (Remarkably, the women are no longer the saintly standbys of O'Casey's previous plays: they get by through cunning, self-love, and self-deception, much as the men do.) It is not an easy play, but it is a powerful one – and, in 1928, well ahead of its time. *The Silver Tassie* achieved great success seventy-odd years later when adapted as an opera, perhaps its natural destination.

O'Casey had already moved to London when he wrote it, and was in thrall to avant-garde ideas, as well as determined to write a play where the Irishness of the characters was incidental to their fates; in the stage directions, Dublin is merely a city 'in the Empire'. In 1920s Ireland, where the commitment of a large section of the populace to Britain's imperial war had been hastily brushed under the carpet, this was a sensitive political issue in itself. But this was not the reason WBY disliked it. Fundamentally, he believed the playwright had cut himself off from his creative roots and his play had therefore withered on the vine. This uncompromising message was indirectly expressed in a long letter, addressed to O'Casey ('Dear Casey') but sent first to Gregory. WBY levelled the charge of didacticism at the playwright, in a celebrated letter whose own didacticism needs to be quoted in full.

I had looked forward with great hope and excitement to reading your play and not merely because of my admiration for your work for I bore in mind that the Abbey owed its recent prosperity to you. If you had not brought us your plays just at that moment I doubt if it would now exist. I read the first act with admiration, I thought it was the best first act you had written and told a friend that you had surpassed yourself. The next night I read the second and third acts, and tonight I have read the fourth. I am sad and discouraged, you have no subject, you were interested in the Irish civil war and at every moment of those plays wrote out of your own amusement with life or your sense of its tragedy; you were excited and we all caught your excitement; you were exasperated almost beyond endurance by what you had seen or heard as a man is by what happens under his window, and you moved us as Swift moved his contemporaries. But you are not interested in the great war, you never stood on its battlefields or walked its hospitals and so write out of your opinions. You illustrate those opinions by a series of almost unrelated scenes as you might in a leading article, there is no dominating character, no dominating action, neither psychological unity nor unity of action, and your great power of the past has been the creation of some unique character who dominated all about him and was himself a main impulse in some action that filled the play from beginning to end. The mere greatness of the world war has thwarted you, it has refused to become mere background and obtrudes itself upon the stage as so much dead wood that will not burn with the dramatic fire. Dramatic action is the fire that must burn up everything but itself, there should be no room in a play for anything that does not belong to it, the whole history of the world must be reduced to wallpaper in front of which the characters must pose and speak. Among the things that dramatic action must burn up are the author's opinions; while he is writing he has no business to know anything that is not a portion of that action. Do you suppose for one moment that Shakespear educated Hamlet and King Lear by telling them what he thought and believed? As I see it Hamlet and Lear educated Shakespear, and I have no doubt that in the process of that education he found out that he was an altogether different man to what he thought himself, and had altogether different beliefs. A dramatist can help his characters to educate him by thinking and studying everything that gives them the language they are groping for through his hands and eyes, but the control must be theirs, and that is why the ancient philosophers thought a poet or dramatist Daimon-possessed.

This is a hateful letter to write, or rather to dictate – I am dictating to my wife – and all the more so, because I cannot advise you to amend the play. It is all too abstract, after the first act; the second act is an interesting technical experiment but it is too long for the material; and after that there is nothing. I can imagine how you have toiled over this play. A good scenario writes itself, it puts words into the mouths of all the characters while we sleep, but a bad scenario exacts the most miserable toil. I see nothing for it but a new theme, something you have found and no newspaper writer has ever found. What business have we with anything but the unique.

Put the dogmatism of this letter down to splenetic age and forgive it.[73]

This torpedo was sent to Coole, along with a covering letter to Gregory – pointing out that, with Robinson away and O'Casey announcing to journalists that the play was now with the Abbey, there was no time to be lost. He suggested that she send on his criticism 'if you agree with it', enclosing a covering letter to soften the blow. He added:

I did not think it tactful to say in my letter that he has left his material here in Dublin and will in all likelihood, never find it anywhere else because he cannot become a child again and grow up there. I did not say that to him because I thought he might suspect me of exaggerating some of his faults to lure him back. By all I hear James Stephens knows now that he has lost his material, but is fixed where he is by some heavy anchor, probably his wife.[74]

The last sentence, and indeed the preceding remarks, left no doubt that WBY's covering letter was for Gregory's eyes alone. So was a subsequent letter from Merrion Square, written on 25 April and suggesting that O'Casey be allowed to save his face by voluntarily withdrawing the play 'for revision' – 'he should say that he himself had become dissatisfied and had written to ask for it back . . . I want to get out of the difficulty of the paragraphs saying that the play has been offered to us.' WBY wanted Gregory to write 'making this suggestion'. Instead, with the staggering tactlessness of which she was occasionally capable, she sent to O'Casey not only WBY's devastating letter but his covering letters to herself, suggesting strategy.[75] This made matters even worse than they needed to be. 'The letters [from WBY to Gregory] came into his hands by Lady Gregory, who of course had no right to show them,' Lily reported. '"She, obstinate old woman, will never even say she is sorry", says George.' As for WBY, he frostily began his next missive to Coole 'Please regard this letter as private.'[76]

But it was not entirely foolishness or unintentional tactlessness. Gregory, who was far closer to O'Casey than WBY, also wanted to divert most of the playwright's anger towards her fellow director and away from herself.[77] In this she succeeded, as a letter from O'Casey to Robinson swiftly made clear.

If W. B. Yeats had known me as faintly as he thinks he knows me well, he wouldn't have wasted his time and mine making such a suggestion [as voluntary withdrawal]. I am too big for this sort of mean and petty shuffling, this lowsey [*sic*] perversion of the truth. There is going to be no damn secrecy with me surrounding the Abbey's rejection of the play. Does he think that I would practice in my life the prevarication and wretchedness that I laugh at in my plays.[78]

He proved as good as his word, writing an even more scorching letter to WBY, and then enlisting the help of St John Ervine to get all the correspondence published in the *Observer*, which obligingly carried it on 3 June. WBY had already been warned by AE that O'Casey was trying to publish their letters; all the publicity which he had feared broke on their heads like a deluge.[79]

The language of O'Casey's letters was a godsend to journalists and a joy to Dublin opinion, which relished O'Casey's annotations of Yeats's letters ('Could anything equal the assumption of Zeusian infallibility?') as much as the exchange itself. A further letter from Merrion Square, attempting to mollify the playwright by retailing the ecstatic reception given to a current revival of *The Plough and the Stars*, evoked a splenetic sneer from St John's Wood on 11 May.

You seem Mr Yeats, to be getting beautifully worse; you astonish me more and more. There seem to be shallows in you of which no one ever dreamed.
What have packed houses, enthusiastic (cheering, says Mr Robinson) audiences for *The Plough* got to do with your contention that *The Silver Tassie* is a bad play?[80]

In fact, quite a lot. As a recently discovered prompt-book for the first production of *The Plough and the Stars* shows, the Abbey directors had made O'Casey radically alter the conception of its central characters; and he had done so because the original representation of Jack and Nora Clitheroe as a middle-class couple, rather than tenement-dwellers *pur-sang*, was inept and unconvincing. Once already, therefore, the directors had persuaded O'Casey that his invasion of unfamiliar social territory was a mistake.[81] On that occasion, he had listened to their advice and followed it to the letter – rewriting his central characters 'down a social class'. Arrogant and hurtful though it was, WBY's reaction to *The Silver Tassie* echoed this critique. O'Casey should write about people he 'knew'. 'Ideas go to the head of the uneducated man,' WBY wrote loftily to Olivia Shakespear; 'while they are content to observe & feel all is well.'[82] But O'Casey's position was no longer that of 'the uneducated man', and in 1928 he stood on very different ground from two years before: major international success, the plaudits of London society, and a recent marriage to a beautiful musical-comedy actress had boosted his self-confidence (and his own arrogance). Refusing to alter a word, he opted instead for maximum publicity.

WBY was, of course, a veteran in this game and moved fast on several fronts simultaneously: threatening a legal action against the *Observer* through the Society of Authors, and attempting to hijack the *Irish Statesman*'s coverage of the row by inserting a belated statement from the fourth Abbey director, Walter Starkie, hastily written to order in the Merrion Square study. 'It is of course of the utmost importance that O'Casey should not know that the writing out of Starkie's opinion has been so long delayed.'[83] Starkie's judgement, however, was not what WBY wanted: though the characters were shadowy and the play itself an unachieved dramatic synthesis, he 'felt that the author is experimenting in a new world of drama; for this reason I feel strongly that the Abbey Theatre should produce the play.'[84]

Posterity may agree and so did Gregory, when she saw the eventual London production a year later.[85] But by the time the dust had settled, Dublin opinion had had a field day. The delight of the *Catholic Bulletin* at this falling-out among the ungodly was predictable; but even Russell's *Irish Statesman* milked the affair for all it was worth, caricaturing WBY booting O'Casey down the Abbey steps ('Of course, Mr O'Casey, you must on no account take this as being in the nature of a rejection. I would suggest that you simply tell the Press that my foot slipped').[86] WBY hoped for vindication from the ambivalent reactions to the play when it was published, and the difficulty O'Casey experienced in finding a producer in London as well as in Dublin. He told Gregory: 'the tragedy is that O'Casey is now out of our saga'. As usual, his eye was on history. Gregory did her best to keep O'Casey in her own saga – sending him affectionate and regretful notes, to which he replied in terms that veered between friendly gratitude, stand-offishness, and obsessive breast-beating. The storm passed, newspapers began to reject O'Casey's frenetic letters about the Abbey's decision; only Shaw offered comfort and support, cheerfully dismissing WBY with the delicate ridicule which had served him well since their conflicts over Florence Farr thirty years before:

With all his extraordinary cleverness and subtlety which comes out just when you give him up as a hopeless fool and (in this case) deserts him when you expect him to be equal to the occasion, [he] is not a man of this world; and when you hurl an enormous smashing chunk of it at him he dodges it, small blame to him . . . Give him a job with which you feel sure he will play Bunthorne and he will astonish you with his unique cleverness and subtlety. Give him one that any secondrater could manage with credit and as likely as not he will make an appalling mess of it.[87]

In fact, as O'Casey's biographer has shrewdly noted, Shaw liked *The Silver Tassie* for nihilistic reasons which would have shocked O'Casey if he had understood them; WBY's rejection, for all its high-handedness, was based on a more reasoned perception of the play's weaknesses. But O'Casey heard

10. 'I would suggest that you simply tell the Press that my foot slipped': the *Irish Statesman*'s view of WBY rejecting *The Silver Tassie*, 9 June 1928.

only what he wanted to hear. His understandable resentment calcified into malevolent paranoia about 'the many Artistic & Literary shams squatting in their high places in Dublin',[88] even after C. B. Cochran's expensive and star-studded (though short-lived) production got under way in October 1929. There was no rapprochement with wbY until 1933; two years later the Abbey finally produced *The Silver Tassie*. But there would be no success in O'Casey's life to equal that of the first three plays about the Irish revolution which made his name, and no collaborators produced, presented, and edited his work with the sensitivity of the Abbey in the early 1920s.

V

As the row over *The Silver Tassie* simmered during the summer of 1928, another confrontation was brewing. Pressed hard by voluntary societies and 'vigilance' associations, the Free State government was moving towards introducing legislation against the dissemination of 'evil literature'. This had been a cloud on the horizon ever since the film censorship Act of 1923; the scandal of *To-Morrow* had raised the issue already, and the *Catholic Bulletin* had been spearheading a campaign since the mid twenties. Book-burnings and the forcible removal of English newspapers from mail trains were periodically organized by voluntary associations. In February 1926 O'Higgins, pressed hard by the Catholic Truth Society and the Catholic Social Guild, had formed an Evil Literature Committee to consider the necessity of new legislation; it was carefully constituted (two Protestants, three Catholics, no zealots), but those who presented 'evidence' were unanimous in calling for legislation. By March 1926 the *Irish Times* was sounding a warning about the implications of 'O'Higgins's committee', and the increasing stridency of the 'smug voice of cant' – a tocsin which the *Catholic Bulletin* immediately connected to the campaign of Yeats, 'Orator at Large', foisting O'Casey's anti-national plays on the Irish people. 'Thus is the stage set for the Houses of Pollexfen, Persse and Plunkett, with all the Associated Aesthetes, with the watchword of the New Nationalism as their clarion call: "There's no such thing as an Irishman".'[89]

A series of recommendations appeared in December 1926. The *Irish Statesman* warned that they could lead to 'a censorship obnoxious to many cultured people', since at least one writer called for banning Rabelais, Balzac, and the unexpurgated Shakespeare. 'The danger is that a group of mediocre minds acting together as censors might easily, because they have no real wisdom or profundity, paralyse the expression of national genius as a clot on the brain, the tiniest clot, may make of a strong man a paralytic.'[90] Through 1927 a paper war raged between the *Irish Times* and *Irish Statesman* on one side, the *Catholic Bulletin* and *Irish Monthly* on the other – violently determined to expose 'the Ascendancy keynote', the sneering at 'the poor vulgar Irish' under the guise of criticizing the proposed Censorship Boards.[91] wby's name featured incessantly, as perpetrator of *To-Morrow* and defender of Joyce. The *Bulletin* made the necessary connection. '*Evil Literature* is neatly linked up with Essential Irish. The claim that one must purvey a Divorce Act in the name of "Religious Freedom" now becomes an equally audacious demand that Unlimited Literary Filth is to be given a free field to spread itself over, and that the National Language must be displaced from its due normal status in education, in the sacred name of "Spiritual and Intellectual Freedom".' The subtext had as much to do with national identity as with literature, and the contested territory of Irishness. And the New Ascendancy were on the losing side.

A bill based upon the Evil Literature Committee's recommendations was introduced in July 1928, horrifying liberal opinion by allowing for the input of 'recognised groups of associations of persons' – granting carte blanche to the shadowy vigilance organizations. Excluding pornographic magazines was an issue most public opinion agreed upon, but the proposed legislation was clearly intended to extend to books. And though Ireland was by no means alone in introducing such legislation at this time, Irish conditions lent a particular sensitivity to the definitions of 'evil' literature. According to the eventual Act, these comprised works which were 'in general tendency indecent or obscene', which devoted too much space to 'the publication of matter relating to crime', and which advocated, or gave information about, contraception ('Race Suicide', according to the Vigilance Association – though the grounds for opposing it were based on Catholic doctrine rather than on population decline). The interpretation would be employed against 'England's filth' ('the insidious Legions of the Great Mental Invader'); it could also be seen to oppose the civil rights of Ireland's Protestant minority. Liberal Catholics such as Padraic Colum were equally appalled at the prospect of 'giving outsiders the impression that the mental age of Catholic people is about seven and a half',[92] but the weight of opposition came from a few beleaguered Protestant intellectuals, speaking through the *Irish Statesman*. The 'real Ireland' was now to be defined specifically as totally Catholic.

But by the time this issue entered public debate, wby was no longer active in the Senate; his last brief speech, 'followed by a minute of great pain', was on 18 July, and he was fixedly determined to retire from public life.[93] During the late summer of 1928 he worked at a projected essay on Pound and his poetry– never completed in that form. From mid August he was at Coole, Ballylee being considered too rough-and-ready for his delicate health. 'I am longing for Rapallo to get away from damp and political agitation,' he told Pound.

The Government has just introduced an Evil Literature Bill which will enable the pietists, if they have the nerve, to make it illegal to import into the country any book on the Roman Index. The Government hate the Bill as much as I do, but for the moment the zealots are all powerful, in the struggle between Free State and Republic each party promises them whatever they want. I have been interviewed and may probably write but I can speak no more, it makes me too ill and in any case I shall be in Rapallo before the fight comes.[94]

The 'interview', on 22 August, had been with the *Manchester Guardian*. As the *Catholic Bulletin* sharply pointed out, it was synchronized with a powerful *Irish Statesman* editorial on 24 August, making many of the same points.[95] In the interview WBY attacked the idea of censorship as 'moral cowardice' trumpeted by religious zealots, and condemned the persistently low standard of Irish education: 'we are one of the most uncultivated of races, if the quality of our culture can be judged by the number or kind of books read in the Free State'. As for literature explaining birth control:

There is the taint of hypocrisy about the whole proceedings. Everyone knows that the practice of the well-to-do class will not be affected by this legislation. It is the poor who are to be condemned to continue in virtuous ignorance and to suffer accordingly. The zealots are alarmed by what people call 'the post-war demoralization', and they would therefore drive our young people in blinkers. The young people of Ireland do not deserve to be treated as if they were fools or dolts, and I do not think they will stand it. They need no more protection than the young people of England or France. Let our zealots do what they will, they cannot retain the old order unchanged in Ireland. The new world keeps breaking in.

He was now in full campaigning flood, setting himself to writing letters to the papers and articles for the English and Irish press. 'The Censorship and St Thomas Aquinas' appeared in the *Irish Statesman* on 22 September; WBY sent it on to Pound, with a draft of another piece, 'The Irish Censorship', which was printed in the *Spectator* a week later.[96]

As the letter to Pound shows, WBY thought the initiative came from the 'zealots' in organizations like the Vigilance Association and the Catholic Truth Society rather than from the government; indeed, earlier in the summer he had arranged to bring together the influential minister Ernest Blythe and Arland Ussher, who had just translated Brian Merriman's bawdy Irish masterpiece *The Midnight Court* (subsequently banned under the new Act).[97] But he may have been too sanguine. Attitudes were hardening, and WBY's other highly placed friend, Desmond FitzGerald, irritably defended the bill to Pound, dismissing WBY's objections.

An enlightened committee – and Uncle William and the Irish Times notwithstanding the committee will be enlightened – will not only not prevent any single person from reading anything that you or I think it desirable should be read but also that committee will have an enightening effect . . . I happen to know something about the history, teaching, philosophy etc of the Catholic Church, and I also know that Yeats and the editor of the Irish Times, etc, are more than average ignorant . . . Knowing something about the Catholic Church I am annoyed when people who know nothing (such as Uncle William) make ignorant assertions and expect me to accept them as proved.[98]

Pound's reply brilliantly exploded FitzGerald's argument that a Catholic revival would cure all Europe's ills, and WBY continued to plan an Irish Academy of Letters, as a rallying-point for dissident intellectuals. A cancelled passage from his *Spectator* article read: 'An educated press and a tacit understanding among creative writers could give something of positive direction as they have in other half-born nationalities.'[99] This was, of course, exactly the lofty tone which annoyed people like FitzGerald, and incensed the *Catholic Bulletin.* The article for the *Spectator* sustained the argument that the threatened legislation would bring together intellectuals across the political divide in Ireland; he was encouraged by the fact that Maud Gonne (unnamed in the article) had recently greeted him with the words 'We are of the same mind at last.'[100] He also rehearsed another of his favourite themes – the ignorance of Catholic ecclesiastics about the traditions of their own Church. But the brunt of the article spelt out, with brutal clarity, not only the provisions of the bill but their inevitable intellectual effects:

The Bill is called 'Censorship of Publications Bill, 1928,' and empowers the Minister of Justice to appoint five persons, removable at his pleasure, who may, if that be his pleasure, remain for three years apiece, and to these persons he may on the complaint of certain 'recognized associations' (The Catholic Truth Society and its like) submit for judgement book or periodical. These five persons must then say whether the book or periodical is 'indecent,' which word 'shall be construed as including calculated to excite sexual passions or to suggest or incite to sexual immorality or in any other way to corrupt or deprave,' or whether, if it be not 'indecent' it inculcates 'principles contrary to public morality', or 'tends to be injurious or detrimental to or subversive of public morality.' If they decide it is any of these things the Minister may forbid the post to carry it, individual or shop or library to sell or lend it. The police are empowered by another section to go before a magistrate who will be bound by the Bill's definition of the word 'indecent' and obtain, without any reference to the committee or the Minister, a right to seize in a picture-dealer's shop, or at a public exhibition where the pictures are for sale, an Etty, or a Leighton – the police have already objected to 'The Bath of Psyche' – and fine or imprison the exhibitor. Another section forbids the sale or distribution of any 'appliance to be used for,' or any book or periodical which advocates or contains an advertisement of any book or periodical which advocates 'birth control.' The *Spectator,* the *Nation*, the *New Statesman*, and *Nature*, are, I understand, liable to seizure.

375

This Bill, if it becomes law, will give one man, the Minister of Justice, control over the substance of our thought, for its definition of 'indecency' and such vague phrases as 'subversive of public morality,' permit him to exclude *The Origin of Species*, Karl Marx's *Capital*, the novels of Flaubert, Balzac, Proust, all of which have been objected to somewhere on moral grounds, half the Greek and Roman Classics, Anatole France and everybody else on the Roman index, and all great love poetry. The Government does not intend these things to happen, the Commission on whose report the Bill was founded did not intend these things to happen, the holy gunmen and 'The Society of Angelic Welfare' do not intend all these things to happen; but in legislation intention is nothing, and the letter of the law everything, and no Government has the right, whether to flatter fanatics or in mere vagueness of mind to forge an instrument of tyranny and say that it will never be used. Above all, they have no right to say it here in Ireland, where until the other day the majority of children left school at twelve years old, and where even now, according to its own inspectors, no primary schoolmaster opens a book after school hours.[101]

Equally threatening were the implications for a free theatre: under legislation like this, his 'theatre, now the State Theatre, would never have survived its first years'.[102] As for birth control, he sounded a clarion call: 'those who belong to the Church of Ireland or to neither church should compel the fullest discussion', since the Treaty enjoined the government to treat all religions equally. Equally resonant was his invocation of the principles which had inspired the Literary Revival thirty years before independence – and an implicit, regretful reference to the disagreement that had driven O'Casey away from the Abbey.

Our imaginative movement has its energy from just that combination of new and old, of old stories, old poetry, old belief in God and the soul, and a modern technique. A certain implacable and able Irish revolutionary soldier put me to read Berkeley with the phrase: 'There is all the philosophy a man needs'; and I have long held that intellectual Ireland was born when Berkeley wrote in that famous notebook of his after an analysis of contemporary mechanistic thought: 'We Irish do not think so,' or some such words. The power to create great character or possess it cannot long survive the certainty that the world is less solid than it looks and the soul much solider – 'a spiritual substance' in some sense or other – and our dramatists, when they leave Ireland, or get away from the back door in some other fashion, prefer cause or general idea to characters that are an end to themselves and to each other.[103]

WBY's manifesto for the *Irish Statesman*, 'The Censorship and St Thomas Aquinas', was shorter, more pointed, and more mischievous – claiming (in the way that so infuriated Desmond FitzGerald) that he possessed a superior knowledge of Thomist philosophy to the Church that professed it. Further, he asserted that the history of religious art, as well as Catholic apologetics, showed up the censorship bill's notions of 'indecency' as a hilarious blunder – the soul being, in Thomist doctrine, 'wholly present in the whole body and in all its parts', as witnessed by religious paintings from Giotto to Titian – an 'art of the body'. Though he excised from the published version a reference to his old adversary Professor Trench as 'a goose',[104] wby had by now abandoned all efforts at tact, revelling in his and Lennox Robinson's reputation for immorality among the Catholic establishment. The battle to defeat the bill by simple weight of votes could never have been won; its opponents set themselves instead to modifying it by amendment.[105] The role of 'recognised associations' disappeared, suggested penal clauses were dropped, and the definition of indecent literature was altered, eliminating the notion of 'inciting to sexual passion'. The *Irish Statesman* tried to look on the bright side. 'We have managed things much better than at one time seemed possible, and the fact that this was accomplished by the good sense of a body of representative Irishmen who set themselves to discover a middle way, encourages the hope that something will be done to keep in check for the future the zealots whose antics have made us a laughing-stock to the outside world.'[106] wby was less optimistic. In his view, the legislature of the Free State had faced a great test and failed it, to the detriment of its intellectual vitality. His sense of alienation was strengthened – and so was his determination not to censor his own work, however wild and elemental the voices that spoke through it.

Defeat over the censorship bill in the summer of 1928 came at a time when the sense of an ending was all around him. Ballylee and its discomforts were now out of the question. He retired to Coole in mid August, though the woods and lake did not provide an infallible refuge; Gregory recorded his fury with a visiting German journalist who admired Charlie Chaplin's films, Ernsı Toller's expressionist drama, and Upton Sinclair's novels. wby further shocked the Gort rector's wife by 'apparently belittling the Christian active virtues and preaching contemplation'.[107] It was not an easy time. With Margaret Gregory's marriage to Guy Gough in September, the Coole ménage came a step nearer to breaking up. Though the Yeatses thought that getting rid of Margaret took fifteen years off her mother-in-law's age, in fact Gregory's health was slowly collapsing, with the return of her cancer (there would be a further operation in February 1929).[108] Nor was wby's need for a country refuge met by an invitation that September to Kilmacurragh in Wicklow, rented by the rich but famously argumentative novelist Lucy Phillimore; he managed to have a 'blazing row' with his hostess and tried to give her a wide berth in future.[109] In October George went to Gort to close down Ballylee for the last time. The tower would slowly decay until its restoration as a Yeats monument over thirty years later. 'I was sad at leaving Coole & the woods today,' George wrote in a rare letter to Gregory. 'Your long-suffering kindness to me these eleven years had made many things easy that might – otherwise – have been most difficult.' In her journal Gregory added, 'But the kindness has been from her rather than me.'[110]

When the Yeatses set off for Rapallo later that month, an era of hopes, public and private, seemed to have dwindled to a close. In a final pugnacious interview WBY delivered over his shoulder a blow at censorship and clerical interference. The new cultural regime, he said, might put paid to Dublin's vigorous intellectual life, drive writers into exile once more, and drag down all that he, Gregory, Synge, and AE had tried to achieve – 'something at once daring and beautiful and gracious' – into 'a mire of clericalism and anticlericalism'. He had done all he could, and was now glad to be out of politics. 'I'd like to spend my old age as a bee and not as a wasp.'[111]

VI

Before their departure, WBY had informed an American acquaintance that, though ordered to a milder climate, 'he intended to return to fight the beasts at Ephesus'; but he told Olivia Shakespear that he would not accept a proffered invitation to return to the Senate after a year's recuperation. 'I am tired, I want nothing but the sea-shore & the palms & Ezra to quarrel with, & the Rapallo cats to feed after night fall.'[112] The plan was to stay in their new Italian flat until April. They left on 31 October, visiting the children at school in Switzerland en route. Their belongings followed them out at an even more leisurely pace. By 28 November they had moved into the large, bright flat on via Americhe, with its 'electrical gadgets', warmth at the touch of a button, modern furniture ordered in Genoa, 'without curves and complications', 'amazing views from all the windows', and 'great balconies to sleep on in the sun'.[113] They could sit inside the plate-glass windows and contemplate the shape of their new existence.

Social life would not be sparkling. George, a good linguist, was annoyed at WBY's refusal to learn Italian ('She little knows us,' Lily ruefully remarked.[114]) The local emigré community watched each other closely from balconies and café tables. WBY's arrival was expected, and an acquaintance reported on the first sighting of the poet, uncertainly walking by the shore in a black coat and hat, suddenly surprised to be joined by George. ('"Who is this stranger? Can it be . . . ? It is! It's my wife." Relieved, he allows her to lead him to the Savoia for the café-Belge he loves.'[115]) Intellectual discussion was not necessarily brillant; when the expatriate American composer George Antheil arrived, he was surprised to find that the Rapallo writers merely talked obsessively about the latest murder mysteries. (Inspired, he

wrote one, which was published by Faber; he claimed the original manuscript was annotated with suggestions by Yeats, Pound, Hauptmann,
Werfel, and Ludwig.[116]) There was little or no contact with Beerbohm. The
playwright Gerhard Hauptmann soon became a dining companion but not
an entirely satisfactory one for WBY (too little English, and too much champagne); Hauptmann also returned obsessively to the fact that the Irish poet,
despite their contrasting appearances, was only two and a half years younger
than himself.[117] Pound called daily. 'We disagree about everything,' WBY
told Gregory, 'but if we have not met for 24 hours he calls full of worry &
almost dumb aggression.'[118] The Yeats circle was also joined by Ezra's 'savage disciple', Basil Bunting: 'he got into jail as a pacifist & then for assault-
ing the police & carrying concealed weapons & he is now writing up
Antheil's music; George & I keep him at a distance & yet I have no doubt
that just such as he surrounded Shakespeare's theatre, when it was
denounced by the first Puritans'. This impression was confirmed by
Bunting's chance remark that 'there was no good in Shelley whatever except
perhaps that he had recommended incest, which might be the best foundation for domestic tranquillity'. WBY appreciated the idea, but remarked that
if the general public could overhear the conversation of poets 'they would
hhhhang the lot of us'.[119] George tried to give more respectable local
English residents a wide berth, though some of them took to calling on
Sundays; intimate friends were issued with instructions for a coded doorbell
ring.[120] Desperation drove them to visit Lucy Phillimore in Monte Carlo,
but this was no more attractive – 'a wondrous land of the rich with no side-
walks upon the roads which are intended only for murderous motor-cars'.[121]

Overall, the Yeatses' Rapallo life relied upon birds of passage like themselves. WBY's reputation in Italy was growing; translations of his poems by
Carlos Linati had been published there since 1914, and Giuseppe Tomasi di
Lampedusa (later famous as the author of *The Leopard*) had published a long
and sympathetic critique of his work in 1926. WBY had corresponded since
1919 about occult matters with Lampedusa's cousin Lucio Piccolo, poet and
Rosicrucian; Piccolo described himself as a disciple of 'il vecchio Butler',
but they do not seem to have met when the Yeatses were in Sicily. Eugenio
Montale came to Rapallo to see Pound and was intrigued by the legendary
Irish poet, but found the language barrier impassable.[122] For all WBY's
enthusiasm for Italy, the people he met were not Italians. Some friends were
imported from Ireland, including MacGreevy, who came for Christmas,
and proved useful in arranging a papal audience for Michael's nurse. The
governor-general of Ireland, James MacNeill, and his wife were also in
Rapallo; they would be followed in February by Lennox Robinson, and two
survivors from Pound's literary life in London, the novelist Richard

Aldington and his new lover, Brigit Patmore. Patmore once overheard WBY reminding George to send a second invitation to yet another guest from Ireland: 'We have invited a gunman to come here and are anxious he should make no mistake, or think we do not want him. They're so sensitive, these gunmen.'[123]

Patmore visited the Yeatses in their flat, where she found the modern decor strangely mixed with the Yeatses' books and engravings; George relieved her boredom and imposed a further Yeatsian touch by painting the furniture Chinese red. WBY generally put on an elaborate performance. On their first visit he read Patmore and Aldington 'Three Things', just completed, in a rhythmic chant – a disconcerting experience, at which Aldington shook with nervous laughter. Perhaps because of this, Patmore was – by WBY's request – invited on her own the next time; he discoursed to her about 'energetic, eager young American girls who come over to study with Freud', remarking that one of them 'talked about the phallus as if it were no more than a carrot'. Later the Yeatses dined with Patmore and Aldington in their apartment, on a night of freakish snow: WBY wore thick woollen socks over his gloved hands, giving the alarming impression of arms ending in stumps. At dinner he suddenly asked: 'How do you account for Ezra?'

'Here we have in him one of the finest poets of our time, some erudition, and a high intelligence and yet he is sometimes so . . . amazingly clumsy. So tactless and does what one might call outrageous things.'

We made no attempt to account for Ezra, and Yeats murmured: 'And those little books of poetry by new writers he shows me.' He slanted his head back and said firmly: 'They are just shell-shocked Walt Whitmans.' Then down sank the noble head. 'But we are all just pebbles on the beach in the backwash of eternity.'

George had acquired the habit of bending her head over her plate and, with her eyes fixed on some ice-pudding, she said in a low voice: 'Willie talking poppycock.'[124]

But the 'poppycock' reflected his attempts to grapple with Pound's work, currently running into the sands: his current project was, in fact, all about 'accounting for Ezra'. Pound had pressed upon WBY some translations of Cavalcanti, which mercilessly exposed how far apart their interests had drifted since the quasi-collaboration in Stone Cottage before the war. As Pound's style, opinions, and poetics headed further and further into his own Ezraic realm of obscure and laconic didacticism, interspersed with shafts of brilliant light, WBY found it harder and harder to simulate appreciation. The last approbation he managed to summon up was for *Hugh Selwyn Mauberley* in 1920, and then he restricted himself to the first fourteen pages. Here, WBY told his former acolyte, 'you have discovered yourself – a melancholy full of wisdom & self knowledge that is full of beauty – style which is always neighbour to nobility when it is neighbour to beauty, a proud humility, that quality that makes ones hair stand up as though one saw a spirit.'[125] This analysis oddly predicts the impact of the *Pisan Cantos* written during Pound's desolation after the war, but in the 1920s 'proud humility' was a Yeatsian characteristic, not a Poundian one.

Given this apparent enthusiasm on WBY's part, Pound was determined to have the master's accolade in print, and WBY intermittently tried to provide one; but it foundered when Pound sent him his idiosyncratic Cavalcanti translation in the summer of 1928. 'I read it and it was almost clear to me,' WBY told him with fatal if courteous frankness, 'but the meaning I found had no relation to that time. I dare not risk it without a whole apparatus of learning, for they would either accuse you of bad translation, or me of bad scholarship.'[126] Pound directed his fury through violent letters to George. 'If he is too ill to be responsible for his actions . . . one will say no more about it. No one cd possibly accuse Wm. of scholarship in ANY FORM, anyhow.' WBY tried to mend the fence: 'I wish you could make yourself do another & fairly conjectural version which was clear. I would delight to comment upon it in this strain "Whether this is Cavalcanti or not I neither know nor care – it is Ezra & that is enough for me." I would then go on, all out of my own head & without compromising you in any way, & say that it was your religion, your philosophy, your creed, your collect, your nightly & morning prayers . . .' But it was too late. Pound retaliated by brutally dismissive reactions to WBY's own new work, which hurt the older man more than he allowed.[127] Besides his ancient fondness for the colourful if erratic Ezra, he was afraid that his incomprehension was a sign of old age. There is a revealing passage in the book which began as a critical study and ended as *A Packet for Ezra Pound*:

It is almost impossible to understand the art of a generation younger than one's own. I was wrong about *Ulysses* when I had read but some first fragments, and I do not want to be wrong again – above all in judging verse. Perhaps when the sudden Italian spring has come I may have discovered what will seem all the more, because the opposite of all I have attempted, unique and unforgettable.[128]

But by the time of this reflection, he had decided to abandon the attempt to account fully for Ezra. *A Packet* turned, instead, into an attempt to account for himself.

The short book that Cuala would publish the following June is, in fact, an assemblage. The first section, 'Rapallo', dated March and October 1928, was the final residue of his attempt to analyse Pound, and it deliberately ducks the issue: the first drafts are full of excisions and abandoned passages, including a reflection on how warped Ezra's judgement had been by his 'persecution in America & neglect in England'.[129] But WBY, recalling discussions of the *Cantos* in the Pounds' roof-garden above the sea, cleverly locates the poem in the artistic context of what was not yet called modernism:

I have often found [in the *Cantos*] some scene of distinguished beauty but have never discovered why all the suits could not be dealt out in some quite different order. Now at last he explains that it will, when the hundredth Canto is finished, display a structure like that of a Bach Fugue. There will be no plot, no chronicle of events, no logic of discourse, but two themes, the descent into Hades from Homer, a metamorphosis from Ovid, and mixed with these medieval or more modern historical characters. He has tried to produce that picture Porteous commended to Nicholas Poussin in 'Le Chef d'Oeuvre Inconnu' where everything rounds or thrusts itself without edges, without contours – conventions of the intellect – from a splash of tints and shades, to achieve a work as characteristic of the art of our time as the paintings of Cézanne, avowedly suggested by Porteous, and 'Ulysses' and its dream association of words and images, a poem in which there is nothing that can be taken out and reasoned over, nothing that is not part of the poem itself.[130]

WBY finds this approach frankly unintelligible – crafted only for what he later calls 'this hard, shining, fastidious modern man, who has no existence, who can never have existence, except to the readers of [Pound's] poetry'.[131] Perhaps, he soliloquizes, Pound feeds the cats of Rapallo because they are 'oppressed'; perhaps his instincts, like Maud Gonne's, are to battle with the powerful on behalf of the outcast.

I examine his criticism in this new light, his praise of writers pursued by ill-luck, left maimed or bed-ridden by the war; and thereupon recall a person as unlike him as possible, the only friend who remains to me from late boyhood, grown gaunt in the injustice of what seems her blind nobility of pity: 'I will fight until I die' she wrote to me once 'against the cruelty of small ambitions.' Was this pity a characteristic of his generation that he survived the Romantic Movement, and of mine and hers that saw it die – I too a revolutionist – some drop of hysteria still at the bottom of the cup?[132]

Thus Pound, for all his idiosyncrasy, is co-opted into the Yeats generation, at least as far as his inspiration goes: the last paragraph of 'Rapallo' looks briefly at Pound's collection *Personae*, giving the younger poet credit for 'passion, self-possession . . . self-abandonment that recovers itself in mockery . . . masterful curiosity'. But these qualities exist in spite of 'faults and flaws', and Pound's desire to create 'a new man' along with 'a new style' is implicitly judged hopeless – a judgement aided and influenced by the strictures Wyndham Lewis had delivered (to WBY's relief) on Pound's work in *Time and Western Man*.[133]

By far the greater part of *A Packet for Ezra Pound* is taken up by a commentary on the writing of *A Vision*, completed on 23 November, which would eventually serve as the Introduction to the second version published nine years later. By a deliberately ironic juxtaposition, WBY's sceptical account of Pound's alphabetical and geometrical patterning behind the *Cantos* – a code 'scribbled on the back of an envelope', defining 'emotions or archetypal events . . . all whirling together' – is followed by a description of his own secret 'System', announced by George's 'Instructors' in the first years of his marriage. The reader is implicitly required to dismiss one, and accept the other.

The 'Introduction to the Great Wheel' is an ostensibly straightforward account of the genesis, progress, and pattern of the automatic-writing experiments begun in Ashdown Forest 'on the afternoon of October 24' 1917: the initial signals, the circumstances of trance, the exposition of phases, incarnations, faculties, cones, gyres, published nearly three years before. He thought carefully about how to present George's contribution, writing and then deleting that she 'suggested', 'proposed', 'intended to amuse me by some invented message'.[134] Supernatural signs and insights are exhaustively rehearsed: the tone is all the more deliberately matter-of-fact as the subject-matter becomes more bizarre. WBY's own early spiritual influences – Blake, Swedenborg, the Kabbalah, the revolt against Victorian positivism – are instanced, but the 'Instructors' arrived, it is emphasized, as a new revelation: voices from the void. Yet, at the outset, it is made clear that the work behind *A Vision* was not to be an end in itself, nor a project to take over WBY's writing life. 'We have come to give you metaphors for poetry.' This was one defence against incomprehension and ridicule. At the close of these reflections, the defensive tone recurs:

Some, perhaps all, of those readers I most value, those who have read me many years, will be repelled by what must seem an arbitrary, harsh, difficult symbolism. Yet such has almost always accompanied expression that unites the sleeping and waking mind . . . We can (those hard symbolic bones under the skin) substitute for a treatise on logic the Divine Comedy, or some little song about a rose, or be content to live our thought . . .

Some will ask if I believe all that this book contains, and I will not know how to answer. Does the word belief, used as they will use it, belong to our age, can I think of the world as there and I here judging it? I will never think any thoughts but these, or some modification or extension of these; when I write prose or verse they must be somewhere present though not it may be in the words; they must affect my judgement of friends and of events; but then there are many symbolisms and none exactly resembles mine. What Leopardi in Ezra Pound's translation calls that 'concord' wherein 'the arcane spirit of the whole mankind turns hardy pilot' – how much better it would be without that word 'hardy' which slackens speed and adds nothing – persuades me that he has best imagined reality who has best imagined justice.[135]

Thus he came back at the end to Pound – and his insufficiency as a translator. The modernist 'System' had been patterned against the revelations of the unknown 'Instructors' and found wanting. As an *envoi* WBY added a letter to Ezra advising him, on the strength of WBY's own experience, to keep out of politics, and telling him the cyclical revelations of *A Vision* echo one of the rare Pound poems unequivocally praised by WBY – 'The Return'.

But taken all in all, *A Packet for Ezra Pound* is unlikely to have pleased its dedicatee. It certainly displeased George, who had tried to dissuade her husband from publishing the details of their psychic experiments. Later she said grimly that the publication of *A Packet* caused the one serious quarrel of their marriage. Her powerful sense of privacy and fear of ridicule recoiled from this exposure; it also threatened to dilute the powers which she had exerted to create a secret bond between her husband and herself.[136] Gregory and AE were equally doubtful about WBY's frankness. But for him, self-centred as ever, the public declaration cleared the decks, concluding his dogged attempt to make sense of Ezra and fixing his decision to rewrite *A Vision* into a form that would encompass his philosophical reading since 1925. The little book also included, as markers between its two prose sections, two poems finished in early February 1929: 'Meditations upon Death', inspired by the great birds he watched flying into Algeciras in November 1927, and two stanzas recalling Mohini Chatterjee's advice to him in Dublin forty years before. This poem reworked an unsatisfactory early lyric, 'Kanva on Himself', into a simple yet subtle philosophical reflection which is, in its way, a 'meditation upon death' as well.

> I asked if I should pray
> But the Brahmin said
> 'Pray for nothing, say
> Every night in bed,
> "I have been a king,
> I have been a slave,
> Nor is there anything,
> Fool, rascal, knave,
> That I have not been,
> And yet upon my breast,
> A myriad heads have lain."'
>
> Thinking to set at rest
> A boy's turbulent days,
> Mohini Chattergee
> Spoke these, or words like these.
> I add in commentary
> Old lovers yet shall have

All that Time denied –
Grave is heaped on grave
That they be satisfied –
Over the blackened earth
The old troops parade –
Birth is heaped on birth
That such cannonade
May thunder Time away,
Birth-hour and death-hour meet
Or, as great sages say,
Men dance on deathless feet.

Intentionally or not, these poems, with their elliptical, questioning, author-itative air, demonstrated that WBY was capable of much denied to Pound. They also showed that, at least, he was writing verse freely once more: 'I never wrote with greater ease.'[137] The 'Rapallo Notebooks' which contain the drafts of so many of his new ideas are sacred objects in the great Yeatsian mine of manuscipts. The entries and outlines, jammed together in close proximity, show how freely and excitedly he was writing in his sunny eyrie above the road to Portofino.[138]

The previous November, he told Walter de la Mare that he had been suddenly struck by the fact that he had written hardly any poetry over the past year of illness, except for finishing up his commitment to Crosby Gaige: his returning energies had gone into reworking *A Vision*, writing his Introduction, and reading Swift.[139] But this was about to change. When AE sent a gloomy letter looking for help in bailing out the troubled *Irish Statesman* in late January, he added: 'I hope that you are writing poetry; now that you are a good many hundreds of miles away, Ireland may appear worth a song as it did when you were in London and wrote the Lake Island [*sic*] of Innisfree.'[140] The 'songs' were, in fact, already coming, as George told MacGreevy in early February:

William is exceedingly well, has been writing verse hard and says he is full of themes – yesterday came dashing along from his cot to announce that he was going to write twelve songs and I had got to purchase 'a musical instrument' at once and set them to music . . . All said songs being of a most frivolous nature![141]

The desire for music was fuelled by a new friendship with Antheil, who was working on the dance-plays and whose 'revolutionary' energy excited WBY greatly: 'there will be masks & all singing within the range of the speaking voice – for my old theories are dogmas it seems of the new school'.[142] Above all, he was writing. A list of poems prepared by George shows that between early February and the end of March twelve poems were indeed written: 'Meditations upon Death', 'Mohini Chatterjee', 'Mad as the Mist and

Snow', 'Three Things', 'Cracked Mary's Vision', 'The Nineteenth Century and After', 'Cracked Mary and the Dancers' ['Crazy Jane Grown Old looks at the Dancers'], 'Those Dancing Days are Gone', 'Lullaby', 'I care not what the Sailors Say' ['Crazy Jane Reproved'], 'Cracked Mary and the Bishop' ['Crazy Jane and the Bishop'], and 'Girl's Song'.[143] Later he would recall that at this time

Life returned to me as an impression of the uncontrollable energy and daring of the great creators; it seemed to me that but for journalism and criticism, all that evasion and explanation, the world would be torn in pieces. I wrote 'Mad as the Mist and Snow', a mechanical little song, and after that all that group of songs called in memory of those exultant weeks Words for Music Perhaps.[144]

This renewal also brought WBY another alter ego: 'Cracked Mary', later renamed 'Crazy Jane', through whose mouth the unsayable would be said and respectable opinion outraged. The original 'Cracked Mary' was a deranged woman who wandered the roads around Gort, known for 'the wild imaginings of her mind'; 'the local satirist and a really terrible one', WBY told Shakespear.[145] She also apparently possessed second sight, and had long been a subject for conversation at Coole. ('One of her great performances is a description of how the meanness of a Gort shopkeeper's wife over the price of a glass of porter made her so despair of the human race that she got drunk. The incidents of the drunkenness are of an epic magnificence.') One of the poems written at this time would be swiftly censored, since it was a scurrilous attack on the monarchy called 'Crazy Jane on the King', whose refrain ran 'May the Devil take King George'. WBY wanted to publish it the following June, to coincide with a current controversy about the National Anthem and Trinity College, but AE thought it too offensive; it was preserved only through a copy later made by Gregory, and Gogarty's capacious memory. (Not only had the king opened the Tate Gallery wing containing Lane's pictures, though Gregory and WBY had been privately assured that he would refuse to do so because he believed the paintings should go to Dublin, he had also recently ennobled Hamar Greenwood, last chief secretary of Ireland, whose defence of the Black and Tans during the war of independence still rankled with WBY.[146]) The other poems, at once more substantial and challenging, were very far from George's judgement of 'frivolous'. WBY, who thought of the series as 'all emotion and all impersonal', would publish several of them the following November and collect the full series in a book published by Cuala two years after that.

The first Crazy Jane poems may have been written in Rapallo during the spring of 1929, but the inspiration is powerfully linked to WBY's deliberately offensive statements about Irish censorship and Catholic puritanism the previous year. Jane's adversary 'the Bishop' is mockingly compared to her lover Jack the Journeyman, as a coxcomb to a solid man; the imagery is earthy, the voice strident, the poetics those of an audacious ballad. Parallels have been noted with some of Swift's verses, which chimes with WBY's reading that Rapallo spring: Swift too gave him the idea that the Irish Ascendancy were naturally anti-Hanoverian ('May the Devil take King George').

> The bishop has a skin, God knows,
> Wrinkled like the foot of a goose,
> All find safety in the tomb,
> Nor can he hide in holy black
> The heron's hunch upon his back,
> But a birch tree stood my Jack:
> *The solid man and the coxcomb.*

Over the next year WBY would use Jane's voice to deliver judgements at once sharp-edged, jolting, and philosophically interrogative. The most famous, and most shocking, was 'Crazy Jane talks with the Bishop', which did not appear until the 1933 edition of *The Winding Stair* and was written two years after her first materialization, as Cracked Mary, in Rapallo. The poems written that spring were often more delicate, alternating mystery with simplicity, but already showing the intellectual bite of their successors. And the pre-occupations which he had described to Shakespear – sex and death – resound through the first of his new verses to be published, which he thought the best of the series. It was also the poem he read to Patmore and Aldington in the via Americhe – 'Three Things'.

> 'O cruel death give three things back,'
> Sang a bone upon the shore;
> 'A child found all a child can lack
> Whether of pleasure or of rest
> Upon the abundance of my breast';
> A bone wave-whitened and dried in the wind.
>
> 'Three dear things that women know'
> Sang a bone upon the shore
> 'A man if I but held him so
> When my body was alive
> Found all the pleasure that life gave';
> A bone wave-whitened and dried in the wind.
>
> 'The third thing that I think of yet'
> Sang a bone upon the shore;
> 'Is that morning when I met

Face to face my rightful man
And did after stretch and yawn';
A bone wave-whitened and dried in the wind.

VII

Rapallo had restored his health, reawakened his creative energy, and given him the opportunity to read and think – in particular, to follow through the interest in Swift and Berkeley, encouraged by Joseph Hone and his Italian collaborator, Mario Rossi. While WBY's poetry referred more and more frequently to Berkeley's idealist philosophy in general terms, it was the *Commonplace Book* that particularly influenced him, with its laconic, explosive, jolting reflections. These came to represent for WBY the best of the Anglo-Irish mind, and their inspiration is reflected in the elliptical fragments of verse which are interspersed throughout his long sequential poems in collections like *The Winding Stair*.[147] Ireland called, and by April the Yeatses were more than ready to return to Dublin.

They were spurred by the plan to present Ninette de Valois in three of WBY's dance-plays at the Abbey at the end of the month, set to music by Antheil: *At the Hawk's Well*, *On Baile's Strand*, and *The Only Jealousy of Emer*, renamed *Fighting the Waves*. The plays, written at different times under very differing circumstances, were now being drawn together as a Cuchulain trilogy. In the event, the production was postponed until August, and WBY and George made their way back more slowly via London. Here WBY visited Olivia Shakespear, Ninette de Valois, Ottoline Morrell, Dulac, Sturge Moore, Ricketts, and – disappointingly – Wyndham Lewis ('both of us too cautious, with too much sympathy for one another not to fear we might discover some fundamental difference'[148]). He also called on 'a couple of mediums' and lectured to the Ghost Club for an alleged three hours on the 'System': discretion about the 'Unknown Instructors' was now, apparently, thrown to the wind. He made a pilgrimage to the Round Pond in Kensington Gardens, watching the model boats as in his childhood, though they were now powered by miniature steam-engines. But, he told Gogarty, 'I find there are fewer & fewer people here I want to see especially now that I have given up all public life & have not even "Lane Pictures" to consider'.[149]

By mid May he was back in Dublin. Based in the Fitzwilliam Square flat, the Yeatses' social life resumed: lunches for visiting friends, meeting a new generation of actors (including Mícheál Mac Liammóir), viewing Jack's latest paintings ('very strange and beautiful in a wild way: Joyce says that he and Jack have the same method'[150]). His lodgings seemed cramped after

Rapallo, and he was plagued by 'Americans with introductions . . . I suppose I am one of the sights just now.' They escaped to Glendalough in late June, visiting Iseult and her increasingly taciturn husband on their chicken farm – Stuart remaining silent 'unless one brings the conversation round to St John of the Cross or a kindred name'.[151] In mid July WBY removed himself to Coole, though even there he was not guaranteed peace ('A Dutch student who is writing a thesis on his work has gone off in pursuit of him, and a German priest called at Cuala yesterday for information. He is also writing a book on him and says he is very much read in Germany'[152]). George stayed in Dublin on the excuse that she had to put an electric stove into the flat – 'immensely happy all by herself', according to Robinson. Her husband was not unconscious of this, telling Gregory that she needed 'a clear fortnight's rest from attendance on me'.[153] He remained at Coole until early August, working on *A Vision* in the mornings, reading Trollope in the evenings, and writing hard. Lolly, lunching with him on one of his trips to Dublin in early July, was told he had written nineteen new poems; she 'was glad to feel that his old vigorous attitude to life was returning – & his old enjoyment of controversy'.[154] Coole remained his base until late September, punctuated by visits to Dublin to dine with the governor-general at the old viceregal lodge, and, much more excitingly, to see the de Valois dance-version of *Fighting the Waves*.

The rehearsals, in strange masks made by the Dutch artist Hildo van Krop, filled WBY with enthusiasm: the old days of artistic experiment seemed to have returned to the Abbey stage. However, the combination of de Valois, Antheil, Cuchulain, and WBY was a shock to Abbey audiences. As far as Joseph Holloway was concerned, 'when I heard that Yeats liked the music, that was enough for me – as he has no ear for sound'. The composer, Antheil, famous for his *Ballet mécanique*, boasted that his style could break the strings of any piano except a Steinway, and the discords drove people from the theatre as soon as the ballet started. While the dancing was 'decorative and beautiful to the eye', the music was compared to 'the falling of a tin tray on the flags'.[155] WBY privately admitted that 'if I knew one tune from another I should probably hate it', since Pound had told him Antheil's 'affinities are all with the youngest of the young. Not knowing anything about music, however, I am delighted to find a man whose theories about the relations between words and music seem to be exactly my own.'[156] As to the wider world, he was proud that his play was mentioned in an *Irish Times* leader ('an interesting experiment') and told Shakespear it had been his greatest success since *Cathleen ni Houlihan*: 'everyone here is as convinced as I am that I have discovered a new form by this combination of dance, speech & music as the theatre was packed night after night so the play will be revived'.[157] His optimism remained unconquerable, and he was content to feel he had brought the avant-garde and the esoteric back to the theatre where it belonged.

There was also a more unexpected entertainment, gleefully described by Lennox Robinson to Dolly in mid July:

We all went to motor races on Fri. Between you and me, dullish. Imagine, 4 hours for one race! Give me the 30 second bow-wows. We thought poet who was dragged there would be bored to death. Not at all. You see there were ITALIAN cars running and shades of Mussolini and Rapallo hovered, he was as excited as a boy that Italy should win, but alas Italian-driven car crashed and driver of winner was a Russian. It spoiled it a little but not entirely.[158]

Though George and the children came and went, a life between Coole and Dublin seemed like a return to the settled patterns of earlier times; he even went back to Sligo at the end of the summer, staying *en famille* in a hotel at Rosses Point (Lily reported that WBY wanted to show his children 'our old paradise'[159]). The Yeatses then visited Bryan Cooper (who had been a colleague in the Senate, as well as an occasional Abbey playwright) at the massive and gloomy Markree Castle, outside Collooney. Bryan Cooper's son Peter remembered the poet's visit as 'a great nuisance . . . he was deposited by his long-suffering wife, with instructions not to let him go out in the wet grass in his slippers, and she then disappeared off to Galway with the children'. Ursula Cooper was equally unimpressed when WBY wrote a poem and read it to her. However, he told Mrs Cooper that he had 'realised the ambition of my life . . . as we have always looked on the Coopers and Markree Castle as greater than the Royal Family and Buckingham Palace'.[160]

The visit to Sligo may have been an attempt to lay claim to the past; but in Galway changes gathered momentum below the surface, moving as inexorably as the underground river that emptied Coole Lake. Gregory's relatives at Castle Taylor were threatened by shootings. There were further confrontations and workmen's strikes at Lough Cutra, prompting Margaret Gregory and her new husband to move near Dublin. Coole itself would be taken over by the Forestry Commission at Augusta Gregory's death, and she now knew that – for all her hopes – no Gregory would possess it after her. As for herself, with the return of her cancer and approaching infirmity, she set herself to leaving a memorial of the house and her love for it. She continued to work on the volume called *Coole*, which Cuala would publish in 1931. This edition contained chapters on 'The Library', 'The Woods', and 'The Gardens'; but the full manuscript shows that the book memorialized not only the rooms of the house but the ghosts of friends and family who had inhabited them. A chapter on 'The Drawing-room', not published by

Cuala, fixes WBY in the house through the presence of his books in a bookcase:

The front of that shelf brings happier meditations, filled as it is with Yeats bounty from end to end. The earlier volumes shine and glitter through the glass; golden designs, by a genius, of leaves and birds and the mystic rose. The later volumes have become quieter in tone: Macmillan and [*recte* 'in'] pale green, and mauve: grey *Vision* and *Trembling of the Veil*. Some of his books are dedicated to me; many of the poems and plays were dictated to me in this room, I, never a very expert typist, sitting in a window recess, blackening my fingers as I changed the ribbon of my Remington, or forgetting to reverse the carriage so that the ribbon was in holes through standing still; he suggesting changes to the cast as he walked up and down the room. For all but a score of summers he spent here brought a good harvest in the quiet of the lake and shadows of the woods . . .

The tone is proudly elegiac, and WBY was ready to match it. In November 1928 he had promised her 'an introductory poem' for the book; on 2 July 1929 he told her 'I have a longish poem in my head about Coole'; now in September, he began to work on it. The poem, 'Coole Park, 1929', completed over the next month after many drafts,[161] not only summoned up the history of the house and the distinction of its inhabitants but took its place as a chapter of his own autobiography. And, at the end, with true poetic prescience, it anticipated both the death of the great chatelaine, and the destruction of the house itself by its new institutional owners.

I

I meditate upon a swallow's flight,
Upon an aged woman and her house,
A sycamore and lime tree lost in night
Although that western cloud is luminous,
Great works constructed there in nature's spite
For scholars and for poets after us,
Thoughts long knitted into a single thought,
A dance-like glory that those walls begot.

II

There Hyde before he had beaten into prose
That noble blade the Muses buckled on,
There one that ruffled in a manly pose
For all his timid heart, there that slow man
That meditative man John Synge and those
Impetuous men Shawe-Taylor and Hugh Lane,
Found pride established in humility,
A scene well set and excellent company.

III

They came like swallows and like swallows went,
And yet a woman's powerful character
Could keep a swallow to its first intent;
And half a dozen in formation there,
That seemed to whirl upon a compass point,
Found certainty upon the dreaming air,
The intellectual sweetness of those lines,
That can cross time and cut it withershins.

IV

Here traveller, scholar, poet, take your stand
When all those rooms and passages are gone,
When nettles wave upon a shapeless mound
And saplings root among the broken stone,
And dedicate – eyes bent upon the ground,
Back turned upon the brightness of the sun
And all the sensuality of the shade –
A moment's memory to that laurelled head.

'One lives to see so much fine life broken,' he wrote to Gregory after he left Coole; while he longed for continuity there, he felt it was coming to a close. 'Meditation' pervades the poem, and the sense of an ending was powerfully present; at the same time, he was brought back to his own beginnings, 'ruffling in a manly pose', with companions now dead. He continually rewrote the description of his youthful self; an early draft ran 'Here I beaten by every wind that blows/The character of my own mind unknown/But hiding under young embittered pose/That ignorance.'[162] But autobiography is finally subdued and the poem climaxes – like *The Trembling of the Veil* – with what modern Ireland owes to Gregory and, by extension, himself and Synge. Coole is at once a house and an ethos, standing for a culture fixed at the centre, revolving around established foundations of decorum, commitment, steadiness, and 'pride established in humility'. But a swallow's flight, after all, presages winter and the poem is unequivocally a farewell, confronting the death of both Gregory and her house. Perhaps because of this, though 'Coole Park, 1929' is one of WBY's finest tributes to his friend and collaborator, her own reaction to it – like Pound's to his *Packet* – remains unrecorded.

Back in Dublin, WBY's energies seemed intact, especially where the theatre was concerned; violently attacking a play submitted by the romantic republican Dorothy MacArdle, and terrifying Robinson by his readiness for experiment. (When Robinson, in a moment of drunken frivolity, suggested doing the Broadway hit *Green Pastures*, WBY 'fastened on the idea and loved it' – leaving his colleague wondering desperately how to manage twelve scene changes and find sixty black actors.) WBY was, however, distracted by commitments outside his own work, and felt the summer in Ireland had been 'half-poisoned' by having to work on a Preface to Gogarty's *Wild Apples* for Cuala.[163] The offer, yet again, of a one-year university post in Japan briefly tempted him, though he knew George would veto it. In June he had 'bowled her over' by saying casually that he could easily winter in Dublin: according to Robinson, she was 'afraid to hope', and she was right.[164] As autumn came on, they planned to return to Rapallo; but, yet again, there was a crisis over WBY's health.

At the end of October he set off via London, where he was on the track of some absorbing documents to do with the much disputed origins of the Golden Dawn; he was also anxious to make contact with a Stella Matutina group in Bristol. He settled into the Savile Club, dined with Dulac and Beaverbrook, and arranged tickets for the Cochran production of *The Silver Tassie* and Eisenstein's revolutionary film, *The Battleship Potemkin*.[165] But his plans were cut short by a sudden illness. A severe cold turned into congestion, just as a year before; it was followed by a haemorrhage from his left lung. WBY blamed over-strenuous Swedish exercises, but Carnegie Dickson, chest specialist as well as Golden Dawn initiate, suspected a recurrence of infantile tuberculosis.[166] Other consultants advised rest; after what seemed a safe interval, punctuated by a cautious social life, the Yeatses proceeded to Rapallo, arriving in late November. From there, WBY wrote gaily to Lennox Robinson, who had just had a success with a new play and was receiving American offers: 'meditate on the day when you will be the last Edwardian and fabulously rich. You can then give interviews and say you knew the last Victorian and his unlucrative art. (I intend to outlive Shaw, Moore, and Bridges.)' But Robinson was not convinced, and wrote sadly to MacGreevy:

The London affair was frightening but all the X rays etc say no lung trouble, lots of other minor bugs. If everything goes pianissimo all will be well. It may sound awful to say but now I wish he would die quickly. I can't bear this petering out. He was in splendid form in Dublin before he left and I saw him for half an hour at his Club in London, he looked like the Sargent drawing and was full of fun and life – then three days later – this. But anything better than this crawling round in heavy overcoat to a cafe in the middle of the day, a slow walk, then bed.[167]

This sounds melodramatic but was well founded. The warmth and comforts of Rapallo were not enough to sustain WBY's recovery: in early December he rapidly succumbed to an alarming and debilitating illness initially diagnosed as typhoid. By Christmas Eve his temperature, which rose ominously every evening, was hovering above 104°; on 21 December he made a brief emergency will, witnessed by Pound and Bunting, leaving everything to George, 'to be employed by her according to my known wishes, for the benefit of my children'.[168] He was more ill than he had ever been. George resourcefully wired to London for the name of the best local specialist, who diagnosed brucellosis (Malta fever) and began to treat it with injections even before the tests confirmed his report.[169] By mid January he was out of danger. But the knell of mortality had sounded for the third time in as many winters, more insistently than ever, and he could not ignore it. He had, as it happened, exactly nine years of crowded life left to him, but in January 1930 this seemed far from guaranteed. With recovery came a sense of urgency. 'Nobody running at full speed has either a head or a heart,' he had written almost twenty years before.[170] But he would now attack what was left of his life with all the reserves of ruthlessness, *sprezzatura*, and self-centredness which he held to be necessary for the artist's survival.

Chapter 10 : One Last Burial
1930–1932

Freedom from obsession brought me a transformation akin to religious conversion. I had thought much of my fellow-workers – Synge, Lady Gregory, Lane – but had seen nothing in Protestant Ireland as a whole but its faults, had carried through my projects in face of its opposition or its indifference, had fed my imagination upon the legends of the Catholic villages or upon Irish medieval poetry; but now my affection turned to my own people, to my own ancestors, to the books they had read.

'Ireland 1921–1931', *Spectator*, 30 January 1932

. . . now I am like that woman in Balzac who, after a rich marriage and association with the rich, made in her old age the jokes of the concierge's lodge where she was born.

Pages from a Diary Written in 1930

I

THROUGH January 1930 WBY lay seriously ill in the Rapallo flat. The Malta fever (also guessed by Gogarty at a distance) was confirmed by blood tests, and treated by serum injections and arsenic; it may have been contracted from contaminated milk before he left Ireland. An English day nurse was hired from Florence, at considerable expense, and stayed from late December until the end of February. George did day duty. The treatment acted slowly, his lungs remained congested, and he was unable to write letters until early February, when his temperature finally abated. George reported to Gregory that he was 'delighted' to be wheeled in a chair from his bedroom to the study next door. He was unable, as yet, to walk or stand alone.

Gregory, though her own health was failing, considered going out to Italy 'to read Trollope to him and be a help to George',[1] whose reaction can be imagined. George wrote desperately to Robinson, outlining WBY's weakness and querulousness, her own exhaustion, and the 'two or three days of panic that William might die *here*. Some day of course he will have to die but I do hope it will be in Dublin or at least London. Here one is absolutely helpless. More than ever I believe that no one should be dependent on anyone.' She longed for the moment when the nurse could take over the day shift 'and the first day that happens I shall go down to the Aurum and drink three Luigi's one on top of the other! (A Luigi is orange juice, gin, 5 drops of curocoa . . .)'[2] An American doctor in Nice prescribed an equally racy convalescent treatment of 'sunshine, wine, women and song', and was non-plussed by the patient's objection: 'He had found it such a popular prescription and was said to have made a fortune out of it.'[3]

Though WBY relented so far as to drink champagne on his own doctor's orders (supplied by Hauptmann), along with port and brandy egg flips, his progress was slow through February. Unable to shave, he grew a grey beard, which became the subject of regular bulletins to friends (and was even reported in the *Irish Times*). Snapshots, he warned Gregory in mid March, did not do it justice: 'my beard, though for domestic reasons it will probably disappear, is a unique and beautiful beard.' 'Quite dreadful! Banish it!' she replied: 'A little longer & you will be like old Sigerson.'[4] Pound, now cautiously overcoming his hypochondria to visit once more, thought it qualified his friend to become first minister of Austria. The beard stayed until May, when the children voted on it: Michael in favour, Anne (the aesthete) against.

Forty years before, Madame Blavatsky had warned him about dispersing the mesmeric energy that collected in a beard by shaving it off, but by the spring he was drawing strength from his own recovering health. The weather in March was surprisingly bitter, but he could totter as far as the Aurum Café, which at first afflicted him with agoraphobia after his long incarceration. Gogarty sent the usual breezy advice:

The account you give of your health is excellent. The blood pressure appears to me to be normal for you, because there is a harmless type of pressure which is indispensable for creative work and has not been considered until the poet or artist becomes a patient, when it is attributed to the illness and not the $\delta\iota\acute{a}\theta\epsilon\sigma\iota\varsigma$ [diathesis] or 'nature of the beast'. But that beard will only prevent you forgetting illness. So shave it off at once . . . as you have a visible mouth and chin, it can only be a visible mark of years, a deceptive calendar. You will be much better when you are restored to your pristine looks and form. Leave such things to Joyce and Rasputin.[5]

For the moment the beard remained, and he spent much of the day in bed, in the company of a white Persian cat abandoned by the discarded mistress of a local playwright. WBY's concentration was still patchy and his energy low. At the end of February he had told Robinson that he was unable to read or study, had 'exhausted the detective stories of the world', and was now reading biography – 'but am keeping off Swift and Burke as everything about Ireland is too exciting.' Nonetheless, his choice of biographical subjects was prophetic – Walpole, and Edith Sitwell on Alexander Pope. A preoccupation with eighteenth-century life, literature, and philosophy was taking hold, which would dominate his thought as he recovered his strength.[6]

This interest is reflected in the aphoristic diary he began to keep in April, when he and George moved to a hotel in wooded grounds above the sea at Portofino Vetta, a few miles up the coast.[7] A fortnight there set WBY on the road to real recovery; he felt his energy return, and was further inspired by the knowledge that Nietzsche had spent a productive month in the same location. Pope, Bolingbroke, and – increasingly – Swift continued to 'fascinate' him, placed into a characteristically Yeatsian pattern of literary history: 'in Bolingbroke the last pose and in Swift the last passion of the Renaissance, in Pope whom I dislike an imitation both of pose and passion'.[8] By the time they returned to Rapallo in mid April, his routine was set.

I work for an hour in my bed after breakfast for two or three days, then stop work for two or three. Almost all mornings I read Swift till twelve when I get up. In the afternoon I go out for an hour & lie down for an hour or so & read nothing above the level of a detective story. At night my wife reads out one of William Morris's long prose stories.[9]

The *Diary*, written as a series of *pensées* and clearly intended for publication, records how his mind was turning to philosophy and politics, stimulated by his regular immersion in Balzac and recent reading of eighteenth-century biography and some modern history (notably F. S. Oliver's *The Endless Adventure*). His reflections may also have been affected by the political atmosphere around him, and Pound's increasingly noisy admiration of Mussolini's authoritarian rule:

Struck by this in Swift's *Discourse of the Contests and Dissensions between the Nobles and the Commons in Athens and Rome*. 'I think that the saying "Vox populi vox Dei" ought to be understood of the universal bent and current of a people, not of the bare majority of a few representatives, which is often procured by little art, and great industry and application; wherein those who engage in the pursuits of malice and revenge, are much more sedulous than such as would prevent them.' (Vol. II, page 408 of Sheridan's *Swift*.)

The whole essay leads up to Burke so clearly that one may claim that Anglo-Ireland re-created conservative thought as much in one as in the other. Indeed the *Discourse* with its law of history might be for us what Vico is to the Italians, had we a thinking nation.[10]

'Laws of history', of course, held a traditional fascination for him, as long as they were not derived from Marxian materialism. In a few months he would recur to the 2,000-year cycles laid down in *A Vision*, and decide that the Western civilization 'which began in AD 1000' was approaching its 'meridian' and would shortly see a 'counter-birth': 'I can only conceive of it as a society founded upon unequal rights and unequal duties which if fully achieved would include all nations in the European stream in one harmony.' But this, he reflected, was as incapable of full realization as the idealized egalitarianism of early Christianity or Rousseauist philosophy. Here, as elsewhere, WBY framed the Europe of his day against the insights suggested by his new passion for the conservative thought of Swift and Burke:

Spengler is right when he says all who preserve tradition will find their opportunity. Tradition is kindred. The abrogation of equality of rights and duties is because duties should depend on rights, rights on duties. If I till and dig my land I should have rights because of that duty done, and if I have much land, that, according to all ancient races, should bring me still more rights. But if I have much or little land and neglect it I should have few rights. This is the theory of Fascism and so far as land is concerned it has the history of the earth to guide it and that is permanent history.[11]

Yet, he added, the 'plasticity' of modern society complicated matters, and enjoined more complex decisions about rights and duties: 'we are no longer archaic, we control our material'. By August he would reflect further that abstract egalitarianism created 'a government only possible among those that need no government': and, returning as so often to Swift, came to the conclusion 'that the liberty he served was that of intellect, not liberty for the masses but for those who could make it visible'.[12]

If this is nearer Burke than Mussolini, that seems a fair reflection of his thought in 1930. The reading pursued by WBY in his convalescence through that spring and early summer lies behind all that he would write in the coming months; but his attention centred upon Ireland's uneasy democracy, rather than Mussolini's experimental Italy. And freedom of the intellect would remain the standard by which he judged the operations of government, especially in so far as it affected the minority consciousness which he felt was represented by himself and his friends.

This might be illustrated by the way that his worries about the Abbey's fortunes kept pace with his recovering health. The theatre's 'national' status was no guarantee of solvency; as early as 19 March he was fretting at his fellow directors Gregory, Robinson, and Starkie, trying to arrange future programmes, and worrying that no play of his own except *Cathleen ni Houlihan* showed any hope of bringing in money. The question regularly arose of bringing in the young playwright Denis Johnston as a director, to inject new energy − a possibility complicated by the fact that WBY had rejected Johnston's work, though Gregory had taken most of the blame.[13] The author of *The Old Lady Says 'No!'* was also connected with the new Gate Theatre, where Hilton Edwards and Mícheál Mac Liammóir were embarking on the sort of enthusiastic experimentalism which WBY had once craved at the Abbey. But even from a day-bed in Rapallo, WBY was alive to the political advantages of poaching Johnston. 'I think I have overwhelming arguments for him as a Director – or rather one such argument. If she [Gregory] and I were to die criticism in the Dail and the Press would compel the Government to insist on Con Curran as not only the Right Religion but an Obvious Expert.'[14] Johnston's appointment would short circuit such an outcome. Gregory disagreed, yet the campaign continued. So did WBY's determination to assert himself. By mid April he was demanding to 'read every play which you think possible for production . . . nothing must be accepted till I have seen it.'[15] The theatre continued to stagger into debt, threatened by its new rival. By June the last quarter's losses approached £1,000; the only profits had been made by George Shiels's *The New Gossoon* and, inevitably, *The Plough and the Stars*. Even *Cathleen ni Houlihan* had lost them £80. The alienation of O'Casey continued to rankle with Gregory, and, to make matters even more sensitive, the contract for his early plays was due for renewal in September; WBY's reiterated comments about the impossibility of *The Silver Tassie* by now had a distinctly defensive ring.[16] A progressively disgruntled Lennox Robinson decided WBY was losing his grip. 'He has been the biggest thing in my real life,' he tactlessly told Dolly,

and with that prop gone (and it seems to be) I feel helpless. And the whole theatre is going in a direction I can't follow with much pleasure or sympathy. That's why I want to get Denis Johnston in as a fellow-Director. (Did you know that? Don't say it aloud because the Old Lady has to be squared.) It's awful to feel old-fashioned but I do. I know I was born a generation too late. I should have died in 1912.[17]

As usual, the introspective and self-pitying Robinson was more perceptive about himself than about WBY. The barrage of instructions from Rapallo presaged not only a recovery of physical strength but of dramatic power; within six months WBY would write a play set in modern Dublin which – unique in his oeuvre – was at once accessible, haunting, and dramatically effective.

For the moment, he fretted in Rapallo at further depressing news from Dublin. The *Irish Statesman* for 29 March announced that it would cease publication on 12 April; the Wall Street crash had put paid to the American subsidies which were all that kept it going, and it had been brought nearer collapse by a bizarre libel case over a particularly recondite book review.[18] WBY wrote to AE that he 'regretted it on all public grounds – it leaves us "sheep without a shepherd when the snow shuts out the day" – but not on private for now you can write books'.[19] But this was charitable dissimulation. AE had lost his *raison d'être*, and Dublin's already beleaguered liberal intellectual clique had lost its house magazine. Everything conspired to draw WBY back to Dublin. In early May Michael and Anne arrived in

Rapallo from their Swiss school, fetched by Bunting, and wby outlined the family's projected future to Masefield:

They dominate our plans, & for their sake we shall try & settle in Ireland again. I shall hope, like the tramp [W. H.] Davi[e]s in one of his poems, for a small house and a huge garden. I have always wanted to live always in one place and have never managed it yet. If that one place should be Ireland (now that I am free of the Senate) I shall see something of you for I shall be at liberty to cross the water to my friends. You, Dulac, Sturge Moore, Lady Ottoline & perhaps one other exaust the list. My mystical system, all those cones & gyres that have taken most of my time for years, is now on paper & I am at peace. There is now no reason why my shade should walk after I am buried. Being at peace I shall have the more time for friends.[20]

Rapallo, indelibly associated with illness and debility, had lost its attraction; even the climate had failed in its promise, and George felt imprisoned. As early as March wby was considering spending the next 'experimental winter' in Fitzwilliam Square, moving the children (now eleven and nine) from their Swiss school. Reunited with them during May and early June in Rapallo, and with the leisure to study them, he noted their characteristics and behaviour with amusement – Anne quick, uninhibited, decisive, Michael careful, considerate, abstracted. 'She works to please others,' wby told Gregory, 'Michael to please himself.' One characteristic incident was reported with pleasure by their father, but hints that the children already sensed the penalties of fame. 'Michael stepped on to the road incautiously upon which Anne struck him rather hard on the face & said "Michael dont you understand that if you are killed there will be nobody to continue the family".'[21] wby decided that Dorothy Pound missed much by leaving her son, Omar, under Olivia Shakespear's care in London. He read Anne and Michael narrative poems at bedtime (*The Lay of the Last Minstrel*, *Lays of Ancient Rome*, *The Ancient Mariner* – his own childhood diet). During the day they all sunbathed on one of the jetties projecting into the bay, anointed with olive oil (wby's idea, acquired through reading about Greek athletes). He Boswellized the children's conversation for Gregory:

Cafe waiter.   'Yes that is the oldest palm tree in Rapallo – it is 60 years old.'
Michael.   'When my father was born that tree was not even planted.'
Anne.   'My father can swim under water.'
The last remark, which so obviously scored off the palm tree was the result of my diving for a lost bathing slipper.

The evidence of his recovered health seemed irrefutable. His worry was now for George, completely exhausted after months of nursing, tired to death of watering-place life, and inclined to be snappish. His diary ruefully recorded an exchange in mid June, when he remarked, '"Now that my vitality grows less I should set up as sage." She said: "What do you mean by that?" and I said "Adapt my conversation to the company instead of the company to my conversation." She said: "It is too late to change."[22]

A further incentive for returning home came in a letter from Gogarty, suggesting that Augustus John paint 'a serious portrait' of WBY at Renvyle, as he had done at Coole so many years before. WBY was attracted by the idea, but it brought home to him the ravages of illness and – worse – time.

. . . to-day I have been standing in front of the hotel mirror noticing certain lines about my mouth and chin marked strongly by shadows cast from a window on my right, and have wondered if John would not select those very lines and lay great emphasis upon them, and, if some friend complain that he has obliterated what good looks I have, insist that those lines show character, and perhaps that there are no good looks but character. In those lines I see the marks of recent illness, marks of time, growing irresolution, perhaps some faults that I have long dreaded; but then my character is so little myself that all my life it has thwarted me. It has affected my poems, my true self, no more than the character of a dancer affects the movement of the dance. When I was painted by John years ago, and saw for the first time the portrait (or rather the etching taken from it) now in a Birmingham gallery, I shuddered.

Always particular about my clothes, never dissipated, never unshaven except during illness, I saw myself there an unshaven, drunken bar-tender, and then I began to feel John had found something that he liked in me, something closer than character, and by that very transformation made it visible. He had found Anglo-Irish solitude, a solitude I have made for myself, an outlawed solitude.[23]

But for all this sense of 'outlawed solitude', he was ready once more to confront Irish life. On 3 July the Yeatses left Genoa by sea; by 9 July he was installed at the Savile Club in London, while his family proceeded to Dublin. He spent a week there, dining with Dulac and Ottoline Morell, gossiping with the poet W. J. Turner, and finding his way back into metropolitan social life.

After yet another serious illness he had been, in a sense, reborn: and the great poem he was working on during his convalescence, which 'warmed him back into life',[24] dealt with rebirth after death. A letter from Sturge Moore in mid April had taxed him with the image of eternal creative life constructed in 'Sailing to Byzantium':

[Santayana] thinks the Indian philosophers the most spiritual, but his arguments leave me sceptical as to whether mere liberation from existence has any value or probability as a consummation. I prefer with Wittgenstein, whom I don't understand, to think that nothing at all can be said about ultimates, or reality in an ultimate sense. Anyway, I can say nothing that approaches giving me satisfaction nor am I satisfied by what others say. Your *Sailing to Byzantium*, magnificent as the first three stanzas are, lets me down in the fourth, as such a goldsmith's bird is as much nature as a man's body, especially if it only sings like Homer and Shakespeare of what is past or passing or to come to Lords and Ladies.[25]

WBY could not have disagreed more profoundly with the idea that nothing could be said about ultimates; within a fortnight he was making notes for a poem about 'Byzantium as it is in the system towards the end of the first Christian millennium' – but also envisioned as a Heavenly City, or at least a sort of supernatural staging-post on the way to paradise, where transfigured beings walk the inlaid streets, and dolphins in the harbour transport the souls of the dead to Elysium. (The diary note is carefully worked and rewritten, showing he returned to the idea more than once.[26]) While Sturge Moore's querulous remark about the golden bird may have been the point of departure, 'Byzantium' is also deeply rooted in Platonic imagery (notably, the gong beaten as the soul descends to Hades), and even (in the opening lines) in Coleridge, whom he had just been reading to his children. By mid June a complete version existed.[27] From the first drafts, he sustained his vision of a city at night, where the brawling tumult of life is subsumed into fabulous starlit images of the supernatural. Initially, the poet is summoned and led by a Dantesque guide from the other world, wound (in an echo from 'All Souls' Night') in 'mummy cloth'. The gold bird reappears, defined (in deference to Sturge Moore) in clear contradiction to 'natural' life, but it rapidly gives way to the spellbinding supernatural image of a soul dancing in a purifying fire.

> The unpurged images of day recede;
> The Emperor's drunken soldiery are a-bed
> Night's resonance recedes, night-walkers song
> After great cathedral gong;
> A starlit or a moonlit dome disdains
> All that man is;
> All mere complexities,
> The fury and the mire of human veins.
>
> Before me floats an image, man or shade,
> Shade more than man, more image than a shade;
> For Hades' bobbin bound in mummy cloth
> May unwind the winding path;
> A mouth that has no moisture and no breath
> Breathless mouths may summon;
> I hail the Superhuman;
> I call it Death-in-life and Life-in-death.
>
> Miracle, bird or golden handy-work,
> More miracle than bird or handy-work,
> Planted on the star-lit golden bough,

Can like the cocks of Hades crow;
Or, by the moon embittered, scorn aloud,
In glory of changeless metal,
Common bird or petal
And all complexities of mire or blood.

At midnight on the Emperor's pavement flit
Flames that no faggot feeds, nor steel has lit,
Nor storm disturbs, flames begotten of flame,
Where blood begotten spirits come
And all complexities of fury leave,
Dying into a dance,
An agony of trance,
An agony of flame that cannot singe a sleeve.

A straddle on the dolphin's mire and blood,
Spirit after spirit! the smithies break the flood,
The golden smithies of the Emperor,
Marbles of the dancing floor
Break bitter furies of complexity,
Those images that yet
Fresh images beget,
That dolphin-torn, that gong-tormented sea.

The physical actuality of Byzantium is rapidly elided into a supernatural site, inhabited by the spirits of the newly dead – carried by dolphins from the world of men through the sea of immortality to paradise. This precisely echoes the movement of the poem as a whole, from concrete details (echoing, as in 'Sailing to Byzantium', the histories of Gibbon and Holmes) to supernatural symbols. The unifying image is supplied by mosaic: the immobile flames of the 'Emperor's pavement', can stand as a literal description of a symbolic inlaid floor, as well as a purgatorial vision in Byzantium at midnight. The 'golden smithies' in the last stanza sustain the occult imagery produced by the imperial mosaic-workers, creating the legendary marble city washed by the tide of dolphin-borne souls, who leave behind the incoherence and bloodiness of earthly life for the summons to paradise. Yet it is the roughness and violence of their passage which dominate the poem's astonishing closure, rather than the starlit calm of their Byzantine destination.

On 11 June he wrote out this stanza in a near-final form; though the poem would be tightened and tuned up by many minor changes, it was essentially created by the time he left Italy in early July. Two remaining points should be made. One has to do with music. Obscure as the content of 'Byzantium' may seem, its effect (and popularity) partly depends on play of sounds.

Echoes and repetition are notably manipulated in the climactic lines, but they occur throughout the poem, strengthened by the assonance and alliteration in lines like 'Flames that no faggot feeds, nor steel has lit', and a carefully stressed rhyming system (already used for complex long poems like 'A Prayer for my Daughter'). The other key to this consummate poem is its deliberate reference to so many canonical influences in WBY's past life, and to so many preceding poems. 'Sailing to Byzantium' lies behind it, but so do 'All Souls' Night' and 'Among School Children', while the intellectual inspirations include *The Golden Bough*, Plato, Plotinus, Leo Africanus, Blake, Coleridge, and Japanese drama. The images invoked are equally central: winding stairs, golden boughs, religious mosaics, and transfiguring dances. Into this poem about the trauma of death and the hope of rebirth, written as he recovered from his own close brush with extinction and rediscovered the sense of life, WBY incorporated a succession of personal references and signatures. It works as both an introit into the next world and a celebratory return to everyday life and work. This in itself says much about the artistic uses of WBY's particular kind of supernaturalism.

II

WBY's appearance in Dublin in mid July was welcomed with relief by his friends. The city had seemed 'very *dry* without you,' Gregory told him, 'and now the *Statesman* is gone it seems even more arid.'[28] For the moment they were based in the Solomons' flat in Fitzwilliam Square, where Jack and Cottie Yeats were now installed up the street. But with the prospect of staying on into the autumn and winter, George soon began to look for a house and garden to rent, away from the city centre, where WBY could write. In Dublin his reputation and public status would always mean that controversy was just around the corner; nor was he reluctant to meet it. In fact, he had narrowly avoided it that summer by not being elected Poet Laureate. Robert Bridges (who had sagely remarked in 1923 'Poor Yeats! He's finished'[29]) had died in April 1930, leaving the post vacant, and WBY's name was widely canvassed from the start. Much more surprisingly, he seems to have considered accepting it.

His eminence was unquestioned. Literary journalists generally concurred that the field of potential laureates was made up of Kipling, Watson, Masefield, and Yeats – whose dominion citizenship made him eligible. The *Observer, New Statesman, Daily News*, and *Weekend Review* all called for him, as did the *Manchester Guardian*, but with the proviso that his nationalist opinions would prevent his accepting the post. This might readily be assumed, and certainly his family thought so. Gregory, however, floated the idea at the end of April, and wby's reaction was ambivalent. He kept the newspaper cuttings which had advanced his case, and when Masefield was appointed, wby wrote to Gregory in terms that suggest he would not have ruled the post out.

'The Observer' pressed my claims very eloquently & I am grateful but Masefield has wide sympathies I can make no claims to & a popularity only surpassed by Kipling. He is an ideal Laureate from the point of view of a labour government & I am more relieved than anything else, for I have no quality that could have moved the great mass of English readers & I would have had to postpone the new edition of 'A Vision', (the great wheel as I shall probably call it) not to hurt their feelings.[30]

This suggests strongly that he would have accepted. If so, the reaction of the *Catholic Bulletin*, and even Fianna Fáil, can easily be imagined. But his response shows a recognition that – as he would later put it – he owed his creative soul to the great tradition of English literature, even if he was realistic enough to know that he could not appeal to a mass audience. In any case, the contest kept wby's name in the newspapers. His fame was further evidenced by the reaction when Gogarty (in desperate need of money after the stockmarket crash), attempted to arrange the sale of a version of the 1907 Augustus John portrait to the Cork Municipal Art Gallery. The trustees turned down the purchase 'because Yeats insulted Daniel O'Connell', reviving the storms over his speech on divorce (and the subsequent poem, 'The Three Rascals'). (They bought instead a Barry portrait of a much more notorious adulterer than 'the Liberator', the Prince Regent.) Gogarty's idea of a second John portrait was inspired by this imbroglio. Hearing of it through a news cutting in late May had brought home to wby the slings and arrows of everyday Irish life.

I am feeling at my worst & yet can honestly say that I mind neither my rejection for the Laureateship nor by Cork. What I do mind is an article by Sean O'Faolain, sometime Cork Republican only praising to give point to blame & that blame the common carping of Dublin, my association with Madam Blavatsky – she expelled me however – & so on, my general lack – tracable thereto – of solid qualities . . . It is nothing to these people that one sought like ones predecessors not solidity but ecstasy. Sean O'Faolain has printed in his article two poems of mine which I had entirely forgot, one with some faint fanciful merit and not because he likes them or dislikes them but out of pedantry provincial respectability collects, like a fly paper. Think of old Sigerson's house.[31]

Back in Dublin, he had to navigate once more these familiar but treacherous waters, which made him all the more anxious to leave the small flat and travel west towards Coole. On 22 July he set off in high good humour to Gogarty's hotel at Renvyle, to meet John for sittings, leaving

George 'having a holiday' on her own in the flat.[32] There was a rail strike, so Gogarty arranged a lift with Edward Pakenham, now Lord Longford, whom WBY had known as an Oxford undergraduate. Longford and his wife, Christine, a novelist and dramatist, were now dividing their time between the Gate Theatre and the ancestral Westmeath mansion, a vast Gothic barracks brightened up – to WBY's approval – by Lady Longford's penchant for scarlet paint. They spent a night there en route and WBY recorded his feelings after arriving at Renvyle: 'I have talked most of a long motor journey, talked even when I was hoarse. Why? Surely because I was timid, because I felt the other man was judging me, because I endowed his silence with all kinds of formidable qualities. Being on trial I must cajole my judge.'[33] When Christine Longford read the published diary years later, she was astonished: her memory was that her husband was worried by the responsibility of his famous passenger, missed several turnings, and arrived late.

How could Yeats possibly have been timid? How could he have found Edward formidable? A young man worried about the car and the road, that was why he was silent. He was quite sure that Yeats was a major poet, the greatest now writing in English, very likely the best in the world. But wait, we must remember that Yeats was a magician, nothing escaped him. Strange as it seems, he may have sensed a resistance. Edward was not his disciple in some things, not in religion or politics, he didn't believe in the ghosts or in Toryism or Anglo-Irish Ascendency. He wouldn't and couldn't have argued, but was he daring to judge?[34]

It is a vivid illustration of the barriers often imposed by WBY's public reputation and personal style, and his habit of hiding behind them because of his enduring sensitivity to disapproval. Those who refused to be cowed (notably Gogarty) tended to fare best, and in turn to draw out the best in him. This meant that the company he chose to keep was, at times, unexpected.

Nobody was at their best at Renvyle, where the atmosphere was tense. The hotel had been opened only three months before on the site of the family house burned down by republicans in the civil war. WBY's bust by Albert Power had turned up in the excavations, 'much improved by its burying, a fine green glaze'.[35] The rooms were luxurious, decorated tastefully in local Connemara materials, and the heating reached American standards; but WBY and Augustus John found each other changed. John was struck by WBY's silver hair, increased girth, and over-rehearsed storytelling.

The conversation at dinner consisted of a succession of humorous anecdotes by Yeats, chiefly on the subject and at the expense of George Moore, punctuated by the stentorian laughter of his lordship and the more discreet whinny of his accomplished wife. I was familiar with most of these stories before, or variants of them: for

406

the Irish literary movement nourished itself largely on gossip . . . My difficulties while painting Yeats were not lightened by the obligation of producing an appreciative guffaw at the right moment, and I fear my timing was not always correct.[36]

WBY thought (correctly) that John had declined: dependent on alcohol and women, surrounded by an entourage of frivolous admirers, and all too ready to disappear off in mid brush-stroke for three-day drinking sessions at Galway Races. Sittings were continually postponed, and to make things worse the dreaded 'Lion' Phillimore turned up at the hotel on 31 July. However, WBY reported to George, 'once established that we are enemies we were in great amity. "Why do you hate me?" she said. "Because you crush my chickens before they are hatched."'[37]

Amid all the distractions WBY worked on rewriting *A Vision* (on 30 June he was convinced, yet again, that it was finished), and the portrait took shape. '[It] promises to be a masterpiece,' he told George, 'amusing – a self I do not know but am delighted to know, a self that I could never have found out for myself, a gay, whimsical person which I could never find in the solemnity of the looking-glass. Is it myself? – it is certainly what I would like to be.'[38] But John kept repainting, declaring he wanted to make his subject more 'monumental'. The final result did not carry his ambition out. Though the subject's tousled hair is silver-grey, it is John's youthful Yeats portrait reinterpreted – high colour, gypsy cheekbones, red mouth ironically puckered, but decked with the appurtenances of old age. WBY is viewed full face, a large hat held tactfully over his paunch, a tumbling Connemara landscape of clouds and mountains crowding behind. Though there is a rug on his knees, his face is freakishly thin and unrealistically youthful. Long before, WBY had identified John as 'a painter who has a profound instinct for detecting the decaying elements to represent' and, intentionally or not, the 'dilution' which John perceived in WBY's personality was reflected in the portrait: it lacks all the intensity of the earlier masterpiece. He looks like a self-satisfied mountebank. If it reflects anything, it is the way his affected public persona gave rise to misapprehension.[39]

On 7 August he arrived at last at Coole, anxious to get to work. But his reunion with Gregory was shadowed by her own illness. Before his arrival she had sensed the return of her breast cancer, and, instead of resuming his ancient summer routine, he found himself accompanying her to Dublin for another operation. George was privately dismayed, and made no bones about it in a letter to Dorothy Pound.

Had a [dental] operation when I got back here and imagined W. safely disposed of for three weeks! But no, Lady G had to have an op: and the two of them buzzed up to Dublin the day after I had my stitches out, and since then – that's 11 days ago – life has been a perpetual fro and to and to and fro, but thank God I've had such a bad cold these last four days I couldn't risk giving it to her!! Christ how she repeats herself now . . . she'll tell you the same saga quite literally three times in less than an hour, and repeat it again the next day, and the day after that too. Burn when read . . . She has recovered in her usual miraculous manner, may be going home tomorrow or Monday. She wants W. to go down to Coole for most of September, and I hope he will – he doesn't seem to mind the re-iterations. Personally they send me nearer lunacy than anything I ever met.[40]

By late August, WBY and Gregory were finally together at Coole; indomitable as ever, Gregory was completing her essays on the house to be published by Cuala, with WBY's 'Coole Park, 1929' as dedication. Poem and book took their place in the historicizing process which enshrined both house and literary revival together. For WBY, installed once more in his traditional bedroom, walking in the woods as the weather turned to autumn, and embarking on a concentrated programme of reading and writing, the thirty-odd years since his first visit had apparently evaporated (not to mention his marriage; George stayed in Dublin, and the children remained at school abroad). But things were not the same. Coole, after all, had been sold to the Forestry Commission, and Margaret Gregory wanted to remove furniture and books to her new house – as WBY complained to Lily on a visit to Dublin in early September. ('Suburban and greedy,' Lily summed her up, with the insouciant Yeats snobbery. 'Little girls' like her, married gaily when young, 'have a way of growing up into hard greedy women without imagination'.[41]) WBY stayed on at Coole until mid October, George came west for a brief visit, looked at Ballylee, and left. Her husband made sorties to Dublin – on one occasion to see a revival of *The Hour-Glass*, which delighted him. Craig's screens had been repainted, and the technology of lighting effects could at last approximate to his intention – 'gold & shimmering'. Sidney and Beatrice Webb, guests of the governor-general, attended, and WBY reported a brief exchange between them: 'What does it mean?' 'It means nothing.' This, like Webb's inquiry about the 'economic increment' represented by the paintings in the Municipal Gallery, confirmed all WBY's prejudices about scientific socialism.[42]

Through it all Gregory's health declined inexorably (there was another scare in September). Nonetheless, WBY's presence sustained and consoled her – all the more so as he was working with an energy released by the months of enforced inactivity ('full of life and fire sprung from the ashes of his illness', she noted approvingly[43]). Macmillan was planning a new volume: the title *The Winding Stair* echoed his 1929 American volume, but the new collection included many more poems. It would be a sister volume to *The Tower*, with another Sturge Moore cover (WBY was already dreaming up images). In a moment of rapid inspiration, he wrote a poem for Gregory's pretty and vivacious granddaughter Anne, celebrating her 'yellow hair', which temporarily conquered the young Gregorys' scepticism about Coole's semi-permanent guest – though their grandmother made him read it aloud six times. Her forgetfulness was becoming chronic, and she clung to WBY's presence: not just for his company and his conversation, but because his residence reaffirmed the *raison d'être* of their friendship, the house, and their shared creative past. Above all, he was writing at concentrated speed, drawing on the house's eighteenth-century library and receptive atmosphere to inspire a one-act play about Jonathan Swift.

Since the early summer in Rapallo, he had pursued his notions of the Irish eighteenth century – further enthused by a request from Joseph Hone and the Italian scholar Mario Rossi to write an Introduction to their book on Berkeley's philosophy. This was an important connection. Philosophically, Berkeley was supposed to be akin to modern Italians such as Gentile and Croce. For WBY, and probably Hone, the Bishop also represented an Irish era when a patriotically inclined elite ruled, defining themselves *contra demos*; they were equally contemptuous of Britain, and distinguished by intellectual adventurousness and scepticism about levelling Whiggery. (Hone had, only a few years before, discussed with WBY the formation of a political group based on notions of a 'new Ascendancy' – ideas inspired by exposure to the new Italian politics.[44]) WBY made a direct connection between Berkeley's experimentalism and modern Ireland. 'He is of the utmost importance to the Ireland that is coming into existence . . . I want Protestant Ireland to base some vital part of its custom upon Burke, Swift and Berkeley.'[45] Anglo-Irish conservatism in the eighteenth century, when seen as the precursor to the brief and idealized 'Grattan's Parliament' of 1782, held lessons for the Free State as de Valera's 'slightly constitutional' Fianna Fáil party grew in strength and prepared to take power through the ballot box.

Berkeley's essay on *Passive Obedience* asks a question that Berkeley, through the lack of a historical sense, cannot answer. Dreading, as Swift dreaded, a return of public disorder he forbids opposition to the State under all circumstances, though when such opposition has arisen, and the headship of the State is vacant or in doubt, a [man] may choose his party. No modern man can accept a conclusion that confounds red and white armies alike. Burke answered the question, and Swift, had he taken up again the thought of his essay on the Dissensions of the Greeks and Romans, could have answered it. Berkeley spoke his speech in the great drama of Anglo-Irish thought. The answer came when the curtain rose upon the second act. A State is organic and has its childhood and maturity and, as Swift said and Burke did not, its decline. We owe allegiance to the government of our day in so far as it embodies that historical being.[46]

The day after this diary entry, he was haunted by a dream of Sandymount Castle, the Gothicized Dublin house lived in by his uncle Robert Corbet, now preserved only in a family album of Victorian photographs. Sandymount and Coole merged in his dream into decline and ruin. His own identification with Ascendancy Ireland could not be clearer; and it is no coincidence that, in the Swift play he was writing, the young scholar who explains the context of Swift's appearance at a seance in modern Dublin is called 'Corbet'.

The 'Swift play', begun in late August and in a near-finished state by the end of September, contains other autobiographical resonances too. The very title, *The Words upon the Window Pane*, recalls Fairfield at Glasnevin, where he had taken rooms in 1909 and been shown some lines allegedly engraved on glass by Swift himself; while the relationship between Swift and Stella – at once romantic and tutelary – echoes that between wby and Iseult. In the play, the lines on the window become Stella's poem to Swift about her education (found by wby in the Coole library); the play revolves around the ancient conundrum of the nature of Swift's relationship to Stella and Vanessa, expressed through a medium at a seance in a Swift-haunted house. The presence of the scholarly Corbet allows a certain amount of didacticism, and the transmission of essential information. The dialogue is rapid, economical, and idiomatic; the stagecraft is adroit and effective (George suggested certain details, such as Mrs Henderson declaring she will not accept money but surreptitiously checking what each sitter gives her). The essential dramatic idea of voices coming through an ignorant medium, culminating in Swift's despairing cry 'Perish the day I was born', is genuinely chilling. It provided a wonderful part for an authoritative actress, exploited fully by May Craig in the first production. On many levels, it was the best play wby had written (or would write), and emerged with astonishing speed: the first handwritten draft of the scenario is surprisingly full. Swift's harangue against Vanessa remained much as first written – it spills on to the page almost as if wby himself were possessed. And Swift's last terrible cry as the kettle boils stays unchanged from the first draft.[47] Its apparent dramatic simplicity works all the more strongly because of the philosophical and historical inflections which shadow it.

It could be enjoyed by an audience as no other play he wrote, but was underpinned by wby's ideas about history and supernaturalism – as he later told MacGreevy.

You haven't fully understood my 'Words upon the Window-Pane'. . . . One is always dramatising. One of the characters gives what he supposes to have been Swift's point of view, that is all. Swift the arrogant, the exclusive, appears or speaks to common people at a common séance. To me, mediumship is the antithesis of the highly developed, conscious individuality you may even call it democracy in its final form. I always dramatise, even in my essays; every truth has a counter-truth. One expresses oneself strongly or clearly only when one remembers that.[48]

The philosophical and historical theories behind the play would be distilled into the long Introduction which WBY wrote at Coole the following summer (and published in the *Dublin Magazine* at the end of 1931):[49] he told Shakespear it would make up part of a 'scheme of intellectual nationalism'. Here, he returned to the question of what Irish 'national life' should consist of – and looked once again to the eighteenth century. By then, he would write, 'Swift haunts me; he is always just around the next corner.' He defended the judgement of the Irish eighteenth century he had put into Corbet's mouth in his play: 'everything great in Ireland and in our character, in what remains of our architecture, comes from that day . . . we have kept its seal longer than England'. This reversed his own youthful dismissal of Goldsmith, Swift, and Burke, whom he had once judged insufficiently Irish by background and intellectual inclination. It was still sensitive political territory, but WBY was prepared to claim a kind of exclusive patriotism for the Ascendancy world that had been erected on the ruins of Jacobite Ireland.

The battle of the Boyne overwhelmed a civilisation full of religion and myth, and brought in its place intelligible laws planned out upon a great blackboard, a capacity for horizontal lines, for rigid shapes, for buildings, for attitudes of mind that could be multiplied like an expanding bookcase: the modern world, and something that appeared and perished in its dawn, an instinct for Roman rhetoric, Roman elegance. It established a Protestant aristocracy, some of whom neither called themselves English nor looked with contempt or dread upon conquered Ireland. Indeed the battle was scarcely over when Molyneux, speaking in their name, affirmed the sovereignty of the Irish parliament. No one had the right to make our laws but the King, Lords and Commons of Ireland; the battle had been fought to change not an English but an Irish Crown; and our parliament was almost as ancient as that of England. It was this doctrine that Swift offered in the fourth *Drapier Letter* with such astringent eloquence that it passed from the talk of study and parlour to that of road and market, and created the political nationality of Ireland.[50]

No one who had noted WBY's Senate speeches could be surprised that he held this view of Irish history, or that he claimed pre-eminence among Irish writers for those from the Anglo-Irish tradition. But the reaction against these views was building up, from sophisticated critics like Daniel Corkery as well as blunt instruments like the *Catholic Bulletin*. When WBY returned to the theme of Anglo-Ireland the following summer, his immersion in Berkeley and Swift had equipped him for another engagement in the long war about defining Irish identity, which had so often impelled his interventions into public life for over forty years.

For the moment, with *The Words upon the Window Pane* finished and sent off to the Abbey, he could return to Dublin, where he spent late October dictating the revised *A Vision* to a typist. 'If I dictate to George it would almost certainly put her nerves all wrong,' he told Shakespear. 'I don't want any more mediumship.'[51] This reflects a pattern of distance in their marriage. Since the return from Rapallo three months before, they had spent barely a week under the same roof. But this was partly because the Fitzwilliam Square flat was so confined. They had firmly decided not to go back to Rapallo ('I can stand the Irish winter now'[52]), and let the flat on via Americhe to Ezra Pound's parents. George was already looking for a house in the suburban coastal village of Dalkey, where WBY would be safe from pursuit by eccentric admirers. (Gregory's journals for this time record regular materialization at Coole of literary pilgrims wanting to walk in the woods or count the swans.) In the meantime, after less than a fortnight in Dublin, WBY was off to England: partly to attend a strange occasion arranged by Masefield at his Oxford house on 5 November. This was a formal homage to WBY, celebrating the thirtieth anniversary of their meeting; his work was recited by five girls, and Masefield read his own tribute, later printed as a flowery private pamphlet.

Mr Yeats is the choicest poet and the greatest poetical influence of our time. Sometimes I have thought of him as of a Greek poet from Byzantium who, having attain'd immortality in Arabia, came, seeking wisdom, to Renaissance Italy, and then having watch'd from some high tower, the decline of life during three centuries, descended in the late Victorian time, to say that Unearthly Beauty lives, and that her Shadow, cast on the mind of some turbulent wanderer, whom the world slays, is lovelier than those great possessions that numb the mind, and redden the land with suburbs and blacken the towns with death.[53]

The emphasis on WBY as a dramatic poet with full fin de siècle trimmings is archaic enough; the accompanying performance of little plays by Gilbert Highet ('a young poet of lively promise') and the Anglo-Irish Oxford don Nevill Coghill must have made for a fairly grotesque afternoon. WBY found it 'very embarrassing' but 'strangely overwhelming'.[54] Masefield probably intended it as a clumsy gesture of compensation for WBY's missing the laureateship. It carried an echo of the peacock dinner for Blunt, nearly twenty years before, with WBY now cast as the great survivor, before whom the younger generation offered homage.

A further reminder of the passage of time came with a visit to May Morris at Kelmscott the next day: memories of Bedford Park in the nineties came flooding back. But another encounter brought him firmly into the present. On 7 November Ottoline Morrell entertained him with Walter de la Mare and Virginia Woolf.

De la Mare thought no one understood a word WBY said, and Woolf's letters gave a fantastical and mocking account, but her diary showed that she was deeply impressed. The force of WBY's personality and the power of his conversation at full flood seem to have called out her extrasensory powers of sympathetic perception, rather than the dazzling malice which often marked her observations of other people. (Morrell, for her part, was not sorry to see Woolf have 'the wind taken out of her sails' by WBY's brilliance.) They had met, glancingly, twenty-five years before, but this was the first direct encounter, and WBY struck Woolf as almost unnervingly large and solid, 'a solid wedge of oak'. His talk, similarly, was direct, idiomatic, humorous ('with men perhaps he might be coarse'). Full of his recently completed play, he talked of dreams and the soul 'as others talk of Beaverbrook & free trade – as if matters of complete knowledge'. He seemed to have worked out 'a complete psychology' – and (though she did not put it this way) a theory of history, where he and de la Mare 'wrote "thumbnail" poems only because we are at the end of an era'. Her own approach, she felt, seemed 'crude and jaunty' compared to the intricacy of his art –

its seriousness, its importance, which wholly engrosses this large active minded immensely vitalised man. Wherever one cut him, with a little question, he poured, spurted fountains of ideas. And I was impressed by his directness, his terseness. No fluff & dreaminess. Letters he said must be answered. He seemed to live in the centre of an immensely intricate briar bush; from wh. he could issue at any moment; & then withdraw again. And every twig was real to him.[55]

One of the themes of their conversation was, in fact, conversation. Woolf remarked that talk did not come easily or equally to English people, and that 'we hide in little sets'. WBY asserted that things were different in Ireland, where he had valuable exchanges with strangers met in trains, and a kind of equality of dignity was encountered 'if you visit in the cottages'. Nor was the contrived American notion of 'democracy' relevant in his country. Here, he was himself recurring to his idealizations of thirty years before; at home in Ireland, his argument might have been different. But it was a stimulating encounter. Woolf believed WBY had never heard of her, but he subsequently read *The Waves*, and compared its approach to that of *Ulysses* and Pound's *Draft of XXX Cantos*: 'mental and physical objects alike material, a deluge of experience breaking over us and within us, melting limits whether of line or tint; man no hard bright mirror dawdling by the dry sticks of a hedge but a swimmer, or rather the waves themselves'.[56] As for Woolf, her recognition of WBY's creative force and power was accurate. Even if he claimed, inaccurately, that he was reduced to 'thumbnail poems', the quatrain that he wrote the next day to enshrine the idea shows his mastery of the form.

> We that had such thought,
> That such deeds have done,
> Must ramble on – thinned out
> Like milk on a flat stone.[57]

III

WBY was back in Dublin for the opening of *The Words upon the Window Pane* at the Abbey on 17 November. At last, he had a great dramatic success. Lily wrote ecstatically to Ruth of the play's 'beauty and strangeness', and the excitement of the reception; Mícheál Mac Liammóir, star of the rival Gate Theatre, told Gregory he was 'shaken by its power . . . I had never imagined anything like it'. WBY was, reasonably enough, gratified. 'It is a fine thing to be old,' he told Ottoline Morrell. 'Four morning papers have praised my stagecraft, & one, that for years had reminded me that I was poet & not a dramatist, has something about my hand having lost nothing of its cunning – or some such phrase. Was it Watson who wrote "O blessed age beyond the fret & favour"?'[58]

Energized by this success, WBY plunged back into theatre business: rewriting *The Resurrection* (which he now thought 'rather bad' in its earlier incarnation), working on a series of Introductions to his one-act plays, evaluating new offerings, objecting to George Shiels's attempt to write plays without plots, and trying to stem the Abbey's mounting tide of debt. The accounts for 1929/30 were grim, with long lists of unprofitable productions, and drastic measures were required.[59] By the summer of 1931 WBY was arguing that the theatre should be rented out to recoup their losses. Despite the success of *The Words upon the Window Pane*, the Abbey was in decline. The passing of its glory days was symbolized by the death, in January 1931, of Frank Fay: by a terrible irony he had contracted throat cancer, his golden voice reduced to 'a hoarse croak'. An appeal was raised to provide for his children, and WBY worried that the Abbey's association with this might imply they were 'responsible' for his poverty; despite Robinson's reassurances, a feeling persisted that the Fays had not been well done by.[60] With the new decade, change and decay crept in all around. Another subscription had to be raised to provide for AE, bereft of the *Irish Statesman* and deeply depressed since Susan Mitchell's death.[61] In mid April 1931 WBY's first 'literary' comrade, Katharine Tynan, died. He had long outgrown their friendship, but her death snapped the link back to the days of his early apprenticeship, when he had discovered John O'Leary and the world of nationalist culture.

All the boundaries were shifting, a feeling exacerbated by financial insecurity. With the stock-market crash of 1929 and a contracting Irish economy, the investments made with WBY's Nobel Prize money had drastically declined, and to the expenses of his illness were added the increasing drain of the Cuala enterprise. By 1930 WBY was paying rent and taxes for his sisters – though, Lily admitted, 'I know he has no margin.'[62] The following year he added an allowance of £7 a month for Lily, as her embroidery business had declined to nothing; never in complete health since her long illness of 1923/4, she was by now selling books to meet chemists' bills, and early in 1931 the bank refused her a further overdraft and she was unable to pay salaries. Though the embroidery business was formally wound up in January 1932, he would continue to suggest projects and commissions. 'George is extraordinarily good, so comforting & you can trust her,' Lily told her niece. 'She is so big in her ways & mind & Willy the same. They fill me with hope & comfort.'[63] Lolly indomitably continued the printing business, while the rest of the family treated her with a certain nervousness. 'She is in so many ways just Grandfather Pollexfen over again & everyone avoided him like poison but he was silent & he'd not her quick mind & tongue & also was kept in check by a very wholesome fear of the Wrath of God, which is entirely absent in her.'[64]

There were further outgoings associated with the return to Dublin: school fees for the children[65] and – not least – finding a place to live. In November 1930 they agreed to return to the Hones' house at Killiney, though the move was delayed until the following February. WBY's bank accounts from the early 1930s show fluctuating small balances and few lodgements apart from stock dividends and other reduced investments; his railway shares now brought in about £160 a year, the only residue of the great Nobel windfall. His current account balance between 1930 and 1933 hovered at around £40 or £50, and he had to sell out stock in 1932. The need to make money became insistent, and it was specifically instanced as a motivation behind the project preoccupying WBY from December 1930: a new collected edition of his work, to be produced by Macmillan.

As described by WBY to several correspondents, this was to be 'an expensive limited edition' – or 'edition de luxe', as he told Shakespear. Macmillan was 'insisting on new work which has not been serialised making a part of it', as well as canonical versions of work already published. 'Months of rewriting – what happiness . . . I have a great sense of abundance – more than I have had for years. George's ghosts have educated me.'[66] He envisaged his oeuvre since 1917 as the core of the work, with the still developing *A Vision* occupying a central place: it was to be ready 'next autumn at latest'. The Yeatses were counting on the income that would be produced. In May, telling Gregory about the demands put on him by Cuala, WBY summed up: 'What however is quite certain is that George and I will be very hard up for the next twelve months, or until the edition de luxe brings in some money, as I have published nothing for a long time.'[67] George was equally conscious of the new edition's financial potential. 'I don't want to get an "advance" from Macmillan this year,' she wrote later, 'because I want to have the cash from the collected edition kept beautifully isolated.'[68]

But this was a vain hope. The negotiations with Macmillan were long and tortuous, and the new edition's fate in America (where large profits were to be hoped for) remained an open question. WBY declared a profound aversion to the New York branch of the firm, for their 'atrocious' covers and lavish misprints.[69] A much amended draft letter to his agent, probably written in the summer of 1931, outlines his financial strategy and shows how his income had declined.

When Macmillan wrote to me a few months ago about the Edition de Luxe he said that he proposed to publish next spring, or if I let him have the material by June, this autumn, I gave him the material for six of the seven volumes when I was in London [May 1931] and promised the remaining volume at three weeks notice. He then said that he could not publish before autumn of next year (1932) and when I explained that this would give me two ['several' deleted] very lean financial years he very generously said he would advance the money for the edition de luxe at any time.

I have been going into my accounts, and I find that my average income from Macmillan (London) calculated over some five years is £211. I haven't the papers to calculate with equal accuracy what I receive from the American firm but the average is certainly somewhat higher. The present year, that ending June 30 1931, will certainly fall very much below the average in both countries. It will probably fall to the level of 1929, £131 (from London) and a proportionate amount from America – a year when there was no new book or recent new book There is nothing in my agreement with them to prevent my publishing my new work in America, provided I do not do so in a signed limited edition. There are several new books incorporated in the edition de Luxe which could be published in America at once. I do not want however to do anything which is not in the spirit of my agreement with Macmillan.

My own feeling is that American publications, if not limited signed editions, would not interfere with the sale of the edition de luxe. Macmillan is however the best judge on that matter.

I calculate that for the year ending June 1931 and for the year ending June 1932 my income will fall, counting England and America together, by £150 in each year. Now if Macmillan advance me that amount on the edition de luxe I should be financially solvent, but I confess that I have been counting on some substantial gain from the edition de luxe when it came out. For that reason I would very much prefer a much smaller advance from Macmillan and ['permission' deleted] an understanding that I may publish what I like in America so long as I do not publish in a signed limited edition.

He added but deleted, 'Another reason is that it is unadvisable to leave one's public too long without new work, especially in America where my reputation will not be stimulated by the edition de luxe.'[70] These priorities would remain, but as the publishing recession continued Macmillan procrastinated and the edition de luxe was never published. Its ghostly existence nonetheless helped to dictate the arrangement in which future collections of wby's work would appear, and set the terms for editorial battles long after his death.[71]

He began the new year of 1931 'entirely occupied with what I hope is the final revision of my work for Macmillan . . . It is pleasant work as it means seeing my work as a whole & finding that it is whole.' This comment in a letter to Gregory was immediately followed by a new verse he had just drafted 'at the end of my re-written "Resurrection"':

> Everything that man esteems
> Endures a moment or a day:
> Love's pleasure drives his love away,
> The painter's brush consumes his dreams,
> The Herald's cry, the soldier's tread
> Exhaust his glory & his might
> For man has nothing but the light
> That his resinous heart has fed.[72]

The idea of art as a fusion of process and product was not new, but he was powerfully conscious of it as he prepared for an intensive bout of work. Amid domestic upheavals (Anne's measles, and the long-awaited move to temporary quarters in the Hones' Killiney house) he finished amending *A Vision* and removed himself to Coole: 'I have done more work since I came back than during any previous period of my life.'[73]

The rewritten book, he admitted to Shakespear, was a 'myth' rather than a philosophy, 'but then one can believe in a myth – one only assents to a philosophy. Heaven is an improvement of sense – one listens to music, one does not read Hegel's logic . . . When I was young – but ah my dear old men must be content with philosophies.'[74] By mid February he was installed at South Hill, 'a beautifully situated house, in the near distance the sea through eucalyptus boughs', fulminating against censorship. 'The pietists are in a state of wild excitement,' he told Masefield, 'the last shock being an article in the *Daily Mail* suggesting that Christ was a hunchback. Thousands of young men all over the country are doing penance for having seen some copy of the Daily Mail at some time or other.'[75] A disputed custody case in a 'mixed marriage' provoked him to send a violent squib to Gregory:

Here is a quatrain written 'upon a recent incident'. (You probably saw it in the paper, a protestant mother, whos[e] yelling children were taken from her in open court to be taken to catholic institutions)

> When Rousseau dropped his babies in
> The Foundling-basket it was sin;
> But who dare call it that, if Rome
> Prefer the basket to the home.

I shall put it [in] my nex[t] book and an appendix with the Judges name & suchlike detail.

In the event, the mother won her appeal and the quatrain remained unpublished.[76] But he was ready to take up the cudgels and, spurred by these incidents, decided at this point to revive his project of an Academy of Letters.

It is important if it is to be done at all that it should be done while Shaw is still living, he has promised his name and will be an immense gain to national propaganda. Moore will I suppose refuse the moment he finds Shaw is there, but then his letter of denunciation will be of great value to propaganda.[77]

A year after his close brush with death in Rapallo, all his old combative energy seemed restored; that summer, Jack Yeats thought he had never seen his brother in such good health. By the time he went to England in May, he was able to deliver six of the projected seven volumes of the edition de luxe. He made a triumphant return to Oxford, where he received an honorary degree (wearing a brown suit to the ceremony, since – he told the vice-chancellor – 'prolonged inactivity and gluttony had made my dark clothes impossible'[78]). There was a dinner in his honour at Wadham, arranged by Maurice Bowra (who had proposed him for the degree); the guests included Elizabeth Bowen, Kenneth Clark, John Sparrow, and Nancy Mitford. WBY read afterwards from *The Tower* and *The Winding Stair* (notably 'In Memory of Eva Gore-Booth and Con Markiewicz' and 'A Dialogue of Self and Soul'), and was asked 'what had of recent years so deepened' his poetry. (He might have answered that a brush with death had much to do with it, and his decision to channel his combativeness into art.) He then read some earlier work ('The Cap and Bells' and 'The Happy Townland'), but refused to read 'The Man who Dreamed of Faeryland' ('It is a bad poem') and remarked after reading 'The Lake Isle of Innisfree' that it was 'full of faults'. Afterwards, he told Bowra that he appreciated his host's understanding of 'poems that I like and that have not been much noticed . . . I have not written verse for some months, and it may be owing to you and your friends that I am eager to write it.'[79]

But if he had not been writing new poems, it was because he had been immersed in editing his old ones. After Bowra's dinner he stayed with Masefield before returning to London to give his six volumes to Macmillan on 2 June. The seventh, 'entirely philosophical, with a small amount of fantastic romance', was evidently the still not quite finished *A Vision*, with rewritten Michael Robartes stories.[80] While in London that early June, he gave an interview to a perceptive journalist, Louise Morgan. Though it was squeezed in at a Piccadilly tea-shop en route to lunch with Sturge Moore in Hampstead, WBY was at his most eloquent, energetic, and persuasive. (Since he was given the opportunity to correct her transcript before it was published, some of his statements are polished to particularly high gloss; but it also means that he was prepared to stand by them.[81]) Morgan was struck by his vigour and youthfulness. 'There is not the remotest suggestion of age about him, and inspite of his grey hair; he looks fifteen or twenty years younger than his sixty-five years.' (WBY would have been pleased at this, as he had become worried about his thinning hair, and tried abandoning a hat in order to encourage its growth.[82]) His voice, with 'almost a separate life of its own', cast a spell: 'intimate, quiet, with a touch of brogue and more than a touch of humour'. His views on modern poetry were trenchant and challenging. 'We are moving away from the Victorians and on towards the modern equivalent of Pope. We are developing a poetry of statement as against the old metaphor. The poetry of tomorrow will be finely articulated fact. T. S. Eliot fascinates us all because he is further on towards their consummation than any other writer' – but he ducked the question of whether he approved of the process. (The fact that he loathed Pope is a clue.[83]) The romantic cult of 'personality' had passed; a literature of 'spirited conviction' was on the way. She asked him about his own work habits, and he described his mornings of labour, sitting down 'like the galley-slave to his oars', and the difficulty of starting. 'The thing that gets you over the horrible business of beginning is the momentum of the subconscious. The subconscious is always there lying behind the mind, ready to leap out. The weight of its momentum grows with experience. The whole aim of consciousness is to make the subconscious its obedient servant. That is why as one grows older one gets happier.'

He also talked – unusually – about novelists. 'I love Jane Austen and her perilous pursuit of good breeding. With Pickwick the democratic movement began, because he offers qualities which everybody can possess. I love Henry James also. With him the perilous pursuit of good breeding begins once more!' If Jung and Freud lie behind his remarks on the subconscious, Joyce's *Ulysses* had evidently affected his ideas for future projects:

I hate international literature. The core of a thing must be national or local. But at the same time it ought to be a fundamental piece of human life, which is the same everywhere. I used to turn bad plays into good plays when I was working at the Abbey Theatre by saying to the author, 'Put that play into Japan.' If the plot survived that treatment I would say, 'Now put it back into Ireland.' I'd like to make Agamemnon a publican who comes home from America to Patrick Street, Dublin, and finds his wife has been carrying on with the bartender, and I'd like to turn Cassandra into an old char prophesying in a tea-cup. Any great play can be put into any other nation or age, but at the same time it is essentially local. A great piece of literature is entirely of its own locality and yet infinitely translatable.

Above all, he stressed the need to complete his work. 'One thing I never want to happen again. When I was ill a while ago, I was haunted by the thought of an unfinished work which I felt I might never be able to complete. It's horrifying to think of leaving unfinished work of any importance. I shall write short things, nothing that might agonize me when I am ill.'

IV

Back in Dublin, and feverishly anxious to write, he found the Killiney house less removed from distractions than he had hoped. Lennox Robinson finally drifted into agreeing to marry Dolly Travers Smith – to the fury of her mother, Hester, and the scepticism of Gregory ('I would have thought a permanent engagement might have been better'[84]). Both Yeatses encouraged the union, though Robinson himself was markedly unenthusiastic (when asked if he were very much in love, he replied querulously, 'How could I love a plum-pudding?'[85]) He was surprised at George's vehement advice against the horrors of a register office wedding, and her own expressed desire to be remarried in church; the obscure and unsettling course of her own courtship and marriage was evidently a less than happy memory. Her life with WBY had become more and more that of helpmeet, secretary, and domestic organizer; her role as muse or mediator had long lapsed. The appearance of *A Packet for Ezra Pound* had, in any case, publicized all that George's 'Instructors' had continually admonished him to keep quiet; in so doing, he may have half deliberately been breaking the spell. By 1931 George's frustration with her life is clearly expressed in her letters to friends. She was about to be forty; her own artistic and literary ambitions had been subsumed into her role as poet's wife; her activity in the Drama League had lapsed. In August Robinson reported to Dolly that George was driven demented by the domestic trivia (and Lolly's tantrums); he also noted the heavy aroma that hung around the Killiney house, and put it down to psychic causes.[86] Less friendly observers hinted at a taste for drink.

WBY had, however, abstracted himself to Coole. Gregory's decline was increasingly apparent, though both she and WBY kept up the pretence that her constant pain came from rheumatism rather than cancer. 'Her judgement is vigorous,' WBY told George, 'but her memory comes and goes.'[87] Margaret Gough asked him to spend as much time as possible at Coole, despite the traditional antipathy between them ('our courteous, indirect war has lasted for so many years', he remarked drily to Shakespear[88]). They would continue to struggle silently over issues like the old lady's medication, and WBY bitterly denounced Margaret's ambition to install Coole's library as an interior-decoration feature in her Celbridge house. But he spent most of his time at Coole from the late summer of 1931 until the end came the following May. The devotion to his old friend, marked by this nine-month residence, is often noted; the implication for his own marriage also deserves consideration. George continued to organize his life by post: 'I have three pyjama jackets & one pair of pyjama trousers,' he complained in August. 'Of course I only use the trousers as a dressing gown but the maids may not know that & be shocked.'[89] They exchanged affectionate, chatty letters. 'Yours are the best I have ever received,' he told her. 'They are so gay and vivid'; and he declared that he hated not seeing her.[90] But a certain detachment had entered their relationship, and when she could send him off to Gort or London, she did so with evident relief. From the beginning their marriage, triumphantly successful in many ways, had been an unconventional arrangement; it was now entering a different phase. This is also reflected in the tone of his letters to Olivia Shakespear – regretful, nostalgic, half apologizing for the way their love-affair had run into the sands. It is a feeling given poetic expression in the brief lyric 'After Long Silence'.

> Speech after long silence; it is right
> All other lovers being estranged or dead,
> Unfriendly lamplight hid under its shade,
> The curtains drawn upon unfriendly night,
> That we descant and yet again descant
> Upon the supreme theme of Art and Song:
> Bodily decrepitude is wisdom; young
> We loved each other and were ignorant.

But George remained essential to him. The tone of her letters to Coole, at once gossipy and laconic, blends affection, advice, and exasperation; they now deal with more practical matters than occultism and art. ('The lamp of course consumes lamp oil, paraffin. What in heaven's name else *could* it consume?! Its very form shouts paraffin oil; you could surely not have imagined that it demanded sanctuary oil, or olive oil?') He knew that her dedication had created a family life otherwise denied to him. When she told him, late that year, of some trouble Anne experienced at school, WBY replied with a heartfelt reflection:

I am greatly stirred by your letter. Most by what you quote from Anne. She could not have written like that if she was afraid of you, or if she did not want to please. There was nobody I could have written to like that. I would have been afraid to tell of my short comings, & I would not have thought of them as Anne does without moral fuss. I cannot tell you how much it has pleased me.[91]

The insecurity of his own childhood still lay poignantly near the surface.

During what was to be the last summer and autumn at Coole, visitors still came and went, but with a sense of saying goodbye. They included Jack Yeats and – in an echo of the very early days – AE, much changed and aged. 'But he came in from the lake with descriptions of the spirits as in the old days', WBY told George. 'As in the old days too he resented any suggestions that they were not just what they seemed to be.'[92] Newer friends included Joseph Hone, and his Berkeleyan collaborator from Italy Mario Rossi, a distinctly unacademic professor whom Gregory found entrancing. But her real pleasure, as always, was to see her most famous guest working. WBY's encounters with Rossi, in Dublin as well as at Coole, helped focus his mind on Berkeley in July, when he wrote his 'Introduction' to the Hone–Rossi study – a distillation of his ideas about the eighteenth-century Anglo-Irish mind and character, and the connections he saw to Gentile's *Mind as Pure Art* and Croce's *Aesthetics*. But it was also, as he admitted to Sturge Moore, 'in part Irish polemic aimed at fools & bigots at home'.[93] He was working on another Landoresque 'imaginary conversation', never published, between himself and Owen Aherne, on the theme of 'Anglo-Ireland'. They discussed the symbolism of houses (including Ballylee and Tillyra) and related the Ascendancy's decline to *Morte d'Arthur*.[94] Simultaneously he was reading – yet again – MacKenna's Plotinus translation, and writing a poem ('queer & I think good'[95]) which may have been 'Tom the Lunatic'. At the end of September George could report to Pound that her husband was 'exceedingly well, producing a large amount of activity, some of it I think rather good value'.[96] She was right. And he had returned to the theme of the Anglo-Irish eighteenth century, working on the long introduction for the published version of *The Words upon the Window Pane*, which ranged far further than the play. It was, in fact, an important instalment in the 'scheme of intellectual nationalism' which preoccupied him on and off all his life.

This was not WBY's preoccupation alone. In that same summer of 1931 the novelist and critic Daniel Corkery published his book *Synge and Anglo-Irish Literature*. Though he invoked an epigraph from Croce ('The true and complete criticism is the serene historical narration of that which has happened'), Corkery's message was the exact converse of Yeats's. So far from Anglo-Ireland representing a proudly original note, 'the Ascendancy mind' could never be part of Irish genius. In his unpublished dialogue with Owen Aherne, WBY had noted that the emblem of Protestant Ireland was a house with a high demesne wall; this was probably in response to a key passage of

Corkery's commentary, which had condemned 'Ascendancy' writing by borrowing WBY's own favourite metaphor of sculpting clay.

The ingrained prejudices of the Ascendancy mind are so hard, so self-centred, so alien to the genius of Ireland, that no Ascendancy writer has ever succeeded in handling in literature the raw material of Irish life as, say, a sculptor handles his clay. From old intimacy the sculptor's thumb assumes a quickened sensibility as the clay heats upon it; the clay seems to master him; it leads him on; this he is to do, and not that. But what if he despise the clay? If, taught of the centuries, he fear its contact, instinctively withdraw from it as one does from a stuff that is not only slimy but treacherous? No Ascendancy writer has ever succeeded in creating a living picture of Irish life: *Castle Rackrent* – which, to repeat, is the best thing they have done – is of course a picture of the English in Ireland. The life of Ireland, which is the life that counts, the national life, is not for them; it is as deeply hidden from them as the life of India is from the English Ascendancy there. An Ascendancy is an Ascendancy, and has to pay the price. We recall to vision an estate round which one of those Ascendancy families had erected a wall ten or twelve feet high and fully seven miles in length. As I read Ascendancy literature, such walls – and they are everywhere in the Irish landscape – throw their shadows across the pages. Many an Ascendancy writer must have wished to present, under the form of art, the teeming life he saw about him, many must have believed they had done so. But where now are their novels or plays? No one casts the failure in their face; it was not from any want of heart or goodness or intelligence or scholarship or craft they individually failed; it was that the system into which they were born made it impossible for them to succeed. Their hands were gloved with so thickly protective covering that the clay would not adhere to their thumbs; clay and thumb were disparate. An alien Ascendancy the artist cannot choose but loathe, it has, whether Asiatic or Roman or Spanish or British, always been so streaked with the vulgarity of insensibility.[97]

Corkery's argument was a subtler, better-read and ostensibly more flexible version of the ancient contention raised by Moran and Griffith three decades before and brought to a crude *reductio ad absurdum* by the *Catholic Bulletin* in more recent times. What was wrongly called Anglo-Irish literature was an abnormality, 'for normal and national are synonymous in literary criticism'.[98] Irish writers, writing in English for 'expatriate' audiences, were as illegitimate as 'Anglo-Irish' writers of colonial stock.

Corkery's polemic was formally a response to Synge (whose relationship to Irish culture he examined with insight and sympathy), but WBY was firmly in his sights. Synge, through empathy, might gain a *patria*, but WBY could not. He is sniped at in a footnote as a semi-expatriate (though 'it is not his habit to spend the whole of any year abroad'), and his determination to inherit Synge's 'note of intensity' is mocked ('whether there is in the themes he chooses a seriousness fundamental enough to demand its use is another question'[99]). He would not 'belong' in the crowd at a great Irish hurling match (and nor – unsurprisingly – would AE, Stephens, Dunsany, Moore, or Robinson). Even WBY's youthful rallying-cry that 'a time comes to every Irish writer when he has to make up his mind either to express Ireland or to exploit it' did not meet with Corkery's approval: 'it only needs to be pointed out that such a time never arrives for . . . the writers of any normal country'.[100] The literature produced by WBY and other 'Ascendancy minds' was, to Corkery, symptomatic of Ireland's colonial status, contributing to the alienation and disassociation of the modern Irish mind, bereft of a literature which was 'at one with national consciousness'. And it was WBY who put 'the craziest interpretation on Synge's literary pilgrimage' – the idea that he was in search of '"that old Ireland which took its mould from the duellists and scholars of the eighteenth century and from generations older still"'. 'The interpretation is so characteristically wrong that one shrinks from adding a word.'[101]

So, as WBY worked on his Introduction to *The Words upon the Window Pane* during September and October, the old claims of Anglo-Ireland on Irish identity were much in his mind, and he was determined to assert them. He was also trying to respond to the agenda which he had sketched at the end of his Introduction to the Hone–Rossi book a few weeks before:

Forty years ago intellectual young men, dissatisfied with the political poetry of Young Ireland, once the foundation of Irish politics, substituted an interest in old stories and modern peasants, and now the young men are dissatisfied again. The hereditary political aim has been accomplished; their country does not need their help; the question I have heard put again and again, 'What would he sacrifice?' is put no more, everything is upside-down; it is their aims that are unaccomplished, they need help. They have begun to ask if their country has anything to give. Joseph Hone draws their attention to that eighteenth century when its mind became so clear that it changed the world.[102]

Ostensibly addressed to the clubs that met in 'cellars and garrets' all over Dublin, drawing up schemes for 'our general improvement', he confronted – just as Corkery had – the dangers of provincialism, and the need to 'decide upon an idea of national life'. A pattern of implicit reference to Corkery's book runs through the Introduction.[103] WBY also reviewed his own early rejection of Swift, Burke, Berkeley, and Goldsmith as unIrish (again, repeating Corkery's formulation).

But now I read Swift for months together, Burke and Berkeley less often but always with excitement, and Goldsmith lures and waits. I collect materials for my thought and work, for some identification of my beliefs with the nation itself, I seek an image of the modern mind's discovery of itself, of its own permanent form, in that one Irish century that escaped from darkness and confusion.[104]

PLATE 17

Right: Dermott MacManus, soldier, Blueshirt, and fairy folklorist.

Below: The Yeats family holidaying with MacManus at Killeaden, Co. Mayo, in 1933: *left to right*, WBY, Anne, George, Michael, MacManus.

PLATE 18

Olivia Shakespear in old age, with her grandson Omar.

WBY in Walter de la Mare's garden at Taplow, 14 September 1935.

PLATE 19

Left: Margot Ruddock.

Below: Norman Haire at Ethel Mannin's Wimbledon house.

PLATE 20

Ethel Mannin photographed by Paul Tanqueray in
1930, against a backdrop painted by Ida Davis called
'Jazz'.

PLATE 21

Above: WBY and the Swami in Majorca.

Left: WBY and the Swami, perhaps with Mrs Foden.

PLATE 22

PLATE 23

Above: WBY photographed by
F. J. McCormick at Sorrento Cottage
(Lennox and Dolly Robinson's house)
in the later 1930s.

Right: Lolly Yeats in 1938.

Facing, above: Penns in the Rocks, a
conversation piece painted by Rex
Whistler, 1932–4: Valerian and Elizabeth
Wellesley are in the foreground with
Dorothy Wellesley's Great Dane Brutus,
while she appears distantly at an upper
window.

Facing, below left: WBY and Dorothy
Wellesley at the front door of Penns,
c.1936. 'He is her Prophet,' thought
Rachel Cecil.

Facing, below right: Elizabeth Pelham
in the early 1930s.

PLATE 24

Above left: Ninette de Valois in 1933.

Above right: Frederick Ashton in 1930.

Right: Rupert Doone painted by Nina Hamnett *c.*1925.

PLATE 25

Left: Warty Lads: F. R. Higgins and Lennox Robinson.

Below: WBY at the BBC microphone, 3 July 1937, broadcasting 'My Own Poetry' (amidst violent disagreements with Dulac about the accompanying musical effects).

PLATE 26

WBY, Edith Shackleton Heald, and Dulac at Steyning,
probably at the time of WBY's 72nd birthday in mid
June 1937.

PLATE 27

WBY and Dulac in Edith's garden.

WBY, Dulac, Edith (seated on the ground), and Helen Beauclerk.

PLATE 28

Above: WBY and Edith at
Menton, January 1938.

Right: The temporary grave at
Roquebrune, beside that of
Alfred Hollis.

PLATE 29

The entrance to the modest Hôtel Idéal Séjour, where
WBY died: photographed in 1987, before renovation. The
sign advertises it as a 'Maison de Repos', offering
'Arrangement pour famille'.

PLATE 30

PLATE 31

17 September 1948:
Seán MacBride
(*right*) at the
Drumcliff interment.
His companion is
Plunkett Flanagan.

Michael, Anne, and
Jack Yeats leaving
the churchyard at
Drumcliff.

Facing, above: 6 September 1948: the remains transferred to the new coffin, covered by the Irish flag, are given absolution by the parish priest of Roquebrune before starting on the journey to Ireland. A French guard of honour stands by, and the figure in the foreground is Marius Otto, a local poet who had just read a poem in homage. 'No-one present has heard of Maitre Otto's work,' reported the *Picture Post* (9 October 1948), 'but as a poet he has his say.' Sean Murphy, the Irish Ambassador to France, stands in the background.

Facing, below: Eleven days later, WBY's funeral procession enters Sligo.

PLATE 32

Looking out to Ben Bulben from WBY's grave,
Drumcliff.

The argument for an Irish Ascendancy is presented unapologetically, with Swift and Berkeley as its avatars, and wby himself as a residuary legatee: colonial decadence, far from being inherent in Anglo-Irishness, was actually a product of the Union. Above all, Swift in an early political pamphlet (*Discourse of the Contests and Dissensions between the Nobles and the Commons in Athens and Rome*) forecast the decay of democracy into confusion; wby related this to Vico's cyclical philosophy, and moved swiftly to an implicitly approving comment on Mussolini's Italy.

Outside Anglo-Saxon nations where progress, impelled by moral enthusiasm and the Patent Office, seems a perpetual straight line, this 'circular movement', as Swift's master, Polybius, called it, has long been the friend and enemy of public order. Both Sorel and Marx, their eyes more Swift's than Vico's, have preached a return to a primeval state, a beating of all down into a single class that a new civilisation may arise with its Few, its Many, and its One. Students of contemporary Italy, where Vico's thought is current through its influence upon Croce and Gentile, think it created, or in part created, the present government of one man surrounded by just such able assistants as Vico foresaw.[105]

Swift's idea of liberty was – in wby's view – inimical to 'what seems to the modern man liberty itself' (anarchic individualism). He argued that the 'national spirit' should be 'expressed as it would through such men as had won or inherited general consent': it was far more important to ensure national liberty than individual liberty. wby believed that thus a 'unity of being' might have been briefly given to Ireland, envisioned by the nationally minded eighteenth-century Ascendancy. But it was followed by Rousseau's cult of the savage, the Industrial Revolution, and the mechanical abstractions of the modern age.

The Introduction then moves, less contentiously, to a discussion of more obvious themes in the play – Swift's celibacy, the structure of seances, the idea of a 'timeless individuality' containing 'archetypes of all possible existences', accessible at moments of supernatural transcendence. 'All about us', he concludes, 'there seems to start up a precise inexplicable teeming life, and the earth becomes once more, not in rhetorical metaphor, but in reality, sacred.' This, and much else in the Introduction, reiterated familiar themes from long before. But the argument for the Irishness of the Ascendancy Protestant tradition had never emerged so clearly; nor had it been linked so directly to the reflections on successive historical cycles, and the rise and decline of sentimental and optimistic liberal democracy (coded as 'Whiggery') which he had first floated in 'If I were Four-and-Twenty' twelve years before. In an unpublished reflection, wby himself noted the change from the opinions of his youth.

When I was a young man trying to revive Irish self-confidence by talk about the concrete beauty of the old poems and stories, I boasted that in the Gaelic language 'it was almost impossible to speak an artificial thought' and now I say that the Protestant memory which seemed to me so unIrish expressed in the intellectual forms of the modern world a like vision; that they were indeed the chief modern voice of empirical speculative genius . . . [106]

By now, Georgian Dublin had become established in his mind as an analogue of Renaissance Urbino: the Irish–Italian parallel once more. Both societies, in WBY's imagination, valued style, intellect, and aristocratic authority, an attitude reflected in literature, philosophy, and architecture. He also celebrated – influenced by Jonah Barrington's memoirs and his own version of Swift's personality – the laconic, visceral, uncompromising edge to the Anglo-Irish mind. Though WBY cunningly attributed Swiftian qualities to O'Leary and J. F. Taylor, this was not an attitude shared by many conventional Irish nationalists; nor did they welcome WBY's implication that Irish culture was 'formless' before the eighteenth-century dispensation. To polemicists like Aodh de Blácam, this was horse-Protestant arrogance, pure and simple. Even Gogarty complained that WBY had become 'a poet trying it on in the pulpit'. 'The parson's blood is as persistent as a Jew's or Negro's . . . Why cant he stand over himself without, of all Churches, the pettiest and meanest "Ascendancy" that ever failed to rise?'[107] But the development might also be seen as another layer of WBY's protective and compensatory carapace which had grown over the years of insecurity and embattlement. It was now declared with a new aggression, as he sat writing in an eighteenth-century Anglo-Irish library, the doomed ornament of a house which had provided so much of his own inspiration and which was waiting to follow its great chatelaine into extinction.

V

This did not prevent him from being conscious of the coming generation's dissatisfaction, and interested in charting it. On a visit to Dublin he was charmed by the young novelist Peadar O'Donnell, Communist and republican though he was. WBY unwittingly acquiesced in O'Donnell's using the Abbey for a meeting of his revolutionary movement, 'Saor Éire', which was the object of frenzied denunciation from Church and state, and shortly to be proscribed. This incensed the government, and he had to hastily withdraw permission.[108] (A few months later O'Donnell would nonchalantly turn up at Fitzwilliam Square to read WBY a play, while on the run from the police.) WBY continued to be entranced by the ballet of the beautiful Ninette de Valois, and came back to Dublin in December for her production of

The Dreaming of the Bones. A further sign of his readiness to traffic with modernity was the beginning in August of his relationship with the BBC. WBY's version of *Oedipus* was to be broadcast from Belfast on 15 September, and the producer suggested a preliminary talk by the author on 8 September, with readings from his poetry. George negotiated a fee of thirty-five guineas, and stipulated a dummy run before the actual broadcast ('as you haven't broadcasted before I think a try out might be an advantage – you wont be able to tiger up and down the room as you usually do when you speak!').[109]

WBY's reaction was enthusiastic. His work (both plays and poems) had been performed on the radio since 1924; the radio version of *The Words upon the Window Pane* was to have an especially long and successful life. His ancient preoccupation with the importance of spoken verse was promised a new lease of life, a new medium, and a new audience. He went to some trouble with his talk, which surveyed the history of *Oedipus*, his original intention to fling down a gauntlet against censorship, and his abandonment of the idea. He credited George with persuading him to revive it and – in a novel touch – confided that his conversion to the dramatic value of the chorus had come from observing how the Salvation Army used hymns during a revivalist meeting at the Abbey. 'I found that, rested by the change of attention made possible by the hymn, the change to a different kind of attention, I listened to the exposition of one idea taken up by speaker after speaker without any sense of monotony.'[110] Talking of the play itself, he imaginatively linked *Oedipus* to both Swift and Raftery. The tone shifts easily from the personal and reminiscent to the declamatory; it recalls the introductory addresses he had liked to give before Abbey productions of his own work years before. Standing at the microphone was like standing behind the footlights.[111]

And, with the Berkeley Introduction out of the way and the Introduction to his Swift play almost finished, he was in search – as he told Sturge Moore – of a new theme.[112] It was Sturge Moore himself who provided it. In mid October he told WBY about a new Indian inspiration, a monk who had written a spiritual autobiography which was to be revised for an English version. By the end of the year he was sending chapters to Coole; by February 1932 WBY would pronounce it 'a masterpiece; a book the like of which does not exist, written with the greatest possible simplicity – marketplace, cows, children, miracles, a sort of cinema film to the glory of God'.[113] To later readers it might seem an artless piece of self-important rambling, but WBY's excitement over Shri Purohit Swami echoed earlier infatuations with Tagore and Mohini Chatterjee. In strange ways, his life at Coole during the winter of 1931/2 was a reprise of themes and patterns from his past. Once again he was reading through Balzac, who – he told George – 'has fascinated me as he did thirty years ago. In some ways I see more in him than I did, he is the voice of the last subjective phases, of individualism in its exaltation. When I read of Lucean's return to his native town & his brief triumph there I see Wilde, in his manner of speech & remember that Wilde was a Balzac scholour, perhaps a Balzac disciple – so perhaps were we all.'[114]

Gregory, weak as she was, still read Trollope aloud at night (*The Way We Live Now*, though she disliked the sections about 'English middle-class people'). But at the end of September she had noticed another lump in her breast. At first she decided not to tell her guest, but when she did he escorted her to Dublin for an examination. Her consultant produced a soothing diagnosis, but she was now in constant pain. WBY's description of 'senile rheumatism' could no longer disguise their joint recognition of her decline towards death.

But she derived comfort from the fact that 'Yeats [is] working well – that is splendid.'[115] He was also once more in the public eye. The publication of his introduction to *The Words upon the Window Pane* in the *Dublin Magazine* aroused a strong reaction, and he decided to follow it up with a lucrative piece for the *Spectator* on Ireland's eventful last decade. It started from the provocative premise that the publication of *Ulysses* inaugurated a new period of Irish history. By mid January his polemic 'Ireland 1921–1931' had been dispatched to the *Spectator*. 'I hope it is not more than you bargained for,' WBY told the editor. 'I am accustomed to speak my politics, not write them, and I have fallen into the impassioned manner of debate.'[116] The article examines Irish national myths and symbols, as they appeared at the beginning of 1932, after a decade of independence and with de Valera's Fianna Fáil party on the threshold of power. WBY started mischievously by asking himself why the colour green and the national symbol of the harp no longer offended his senses as tired clichés. The answer lay in the reality of political independence (demonstrated by the Free State's ability to execute its opponents in the civil war), which had brought 'freedom of obsession' – for WBY, at least. But it had also conferred the freedom for him to evaluate Ireland's Protestant tradition and – yet again – 'our eighteenth century', which 'now that Ireland is substituting traditions of government for the rhetoric of agitation, has regained its importance'. Nonetheless, he denounced the craven decision of present-day Irish Protestant bishops to appeal to the Colonial Conference in an attempt to keep the Irish courts subordinate to the Judicial Committee of the Privy Council in Britain.[117] WBY saw this as 'blind old men turning their backs upon Swift and Grattan', and ended with a characteristic peroration, invoking a new national hero:

If I were a young man, I would start an agitation to show them their task in life. As a beginning I might gather together the descendants of those who had voted with

Grattan against the Union that we might ask the British Government to return his body; it lies in Westminster Abbey under a flat plain stone since it was laid there, despite the protests of his followers, less to commemorate his fame than to prevent a shrine and a pilgrimage. Then I would ask the Irish Government to line the streets with soldiers that we might with all befitting pomp open the pavement of St Patrick's for one last burial.[118]

This ringing invocation of the Protestant patriot tradition was published on 30 January. Three days later the *Irish Press*, Fianna Fáil's energetic populist newspaper, carried an attack by Aodh de Blácam on 'Anglo-Irish leaders' trying to reinstate their authority through a cult of the eighteenth century; he allowed them an 'intensity of temperament' which linked them to the O's and Mac's, but still convicted the Anglo-Irish of 'rejecting the national allegiance'.[119] In fact, de Blácam had written in response to WBY's *Dublin Magazine* article and Robinson's recent biography of Bryan Cooper rather than to the *Spectator*, but it was all grist to the mill. WBY corresponded with de Blácam, hoping 'to detach him from O'Rahilly and Corkery's troop: he is an impressionable uncertain man, & probably sincere'.[120] This was to hope for too much; de Blácam, who had been born in London as Hugh Blackham, of Ulster Protestant stock, and sometimes wrote under the soubriquet 'Rody the Rover', exhibited all the zeal of the convert and would – after WBY's death – condemn him in tones of scandalized revulsion.[121] In any case, 'Corkery's troop' were in the ascendant. In the general election of mid February de Valera's Fianna Fáil won a narrow majority of seats; by early March, assured of the support of independents, they would form an administration, with the notably reactionary Thomas Derrig as minister for Education. This, together with the banning of Liam O'Flaherty's novel *The Puritan*, seemed to WBY an alarming portent. He gave an outspoken interview to the *Manchester Guardian* ('I must make a fight for this book') and reported to Gregory on the atmosphere in Dublin as Fianna Fáil prepared to take power:

One hears such comments on political events as 'when those Church of Ireland gunmen, the Gilmours, get out of jail everything will start popping' or will 'de Velera have the nerve to suppress Shawn Gonne [MacBride] before he shoots the town up', and I remember Shawn Gonne so like the Christ child that O'Delany (Maud Gonnes old retainer) said her prayers to a rosary made out of his shed buttons.[122]

Gogarty gloomily declared that it would be preferable to be English or German rather than a member of the 'stupefied' Irish race under a 'Jew-directed government'. But he also recorded that WBY's spirits were extremely high:

Yeats was in here last night and he, being the best talker I ever heard, was most entertaining. He spoke about the Whig movement in England that brought

William into Ireland and gave rise to the French Revolution, Rousseau and Locke. He is deep in the Swift and Bishop Berkeley period, having just made an ass of himself by writing an introduction to Berkeley's philosophy by Hone and Rossi. Where philosophy is concerned Yeats is as bad as a lady Theosophist or Christian Scientist, and like them he expects 'something to happen'. When he finds nothing occurred, he will be quite disappointed. He was never 'educated' and this has some disadvantages. For one, it is apt to mislead those who take all this for granted and do not realise that he is finding out in his old age what we never cared for in our youth.[123]

Gogarty missed the real importance of WBY's current obsessions: the intellectual energy and combativeness which had possessed him for months were being translated directly into one of his most intensive periods of poetic composition. The direct connection between exposure to Swiftian *saeva indigatio* and his own creativity was signalled in a short poem completed in August 1931, laconically resonant:

Remorse for Intemperate Speech

I ranted to the knave and fool
But outgrew that school,
Would transform the part,
Fit audience found, but cannot rule
My fanatic heart.

I sought my betters: though in each
Fine manners, liberal speech,
Turn hatred into sport,
Nothing said or done can reach
My fanatic heart.

Out of Ireland have we come.
Great hatred, little room,
Maimed us at the start.
I carry from my mother's womb
A fanatic heart.

His letters to Shakespear show that he returned to Crazy Jane as an inspiration in the autumn and winter, in accordance with his taste for audacious satire. But January 1932 was taken up with a different kind of introspection – a long dialogue poem initially conceived as 'Heart and Soul' but which became 'Vacillation', incorporating some poems written over the previous year into a sequence. He was returning to the theme of the conflict of opposing ambitions, and inspirations: the achievement of spiritual calm and the heroic challenge of 'living tragically'.

> Between extremities
> Man runs his course;
> A brand, or flaming breath
> Comes to destroy
> All those antinomies
> Of day and night;
> The body calls it death,
> The heart remorse.
> But if these be right
> What is joy?

The drafts of the poem show how sharply both the argument and the conclusion were fixed from the beginning – though the compressed phrasing and intense rhythm were achieved only by exhaustive reworking. He believed (inaccurately) that Gerard Manley Hopkins 'never understood the variety of pace that constitutes natural utterance',[124] and 'Vacillation' demonstrates that WBY had fought his way through to exactly such an understanding. But the content is no less demanding for that. Yet another projected title for the sequence was 'Wisdom', and it is, over all, an exercise in spiritual autobiography, taking in ancient inspirations like Charlotte Guest's *The Mabinogion* (the tree half in flame and half in leaf) and Frazer's *Golden Bough*, as well as more recent discoveries like Chinese poetry and von Hügel's *Mystical Element of Religion as Studied in St Catherine of Genoa and Her Friends*. These are interspersed with recollected moments of intense awareness and Coleridgean personal transcendence.[125]

> My fiftieth year had come and gone,
> I sat, a solitary man,
> In a crowded London shop,
> An open book and empty cup
> On the marble table-top.
>
> While on the shop and street I gazed
> My body of a sudden blazed;
> And twenty minutes more or less
> It seemed, so great my happiness,
> That I was blessèd and could bless.

He also returns (as often in his reflections at this time) to the power of remorse: '. . . not a day/But something is recalled,/My conscience or my vanity appalled.' However, in his letter to Shakespear describing what became the last stanza of the poem, there is a strong hint that Swift's tortured celibacy was not for him – 'I shall be a sinful man to the end, and think upon my death-bed of all the nights I wasted in my youth' – and the conclusion of the poem sets the poet with pagan Homer, not sanctified St Teresa or Friedrich Von Hügel's theology.[126]

> Must we part, Von Hügel, though much alike, for we
> Accept the miracles of the saints and honour sanctity?
> The body of Saint Teresa lies undecayed in tomb
> Bathed in miraculous oil, sweet odours from it come,
> Healing from its lettered slab. Those self-same hands perchance
> Eternalised the body of a modern saint that once
> Had scooped out Pharaoh's mummy. I – though heart might find relief
> Did I become a Christian man and choose for my belief
> What seems most welcome in the tomb – play a predestined part,
> Homer is my example and his unchristened heart.
> The lion and the honey-comb, what has scripture said?
> So get you gone, Von Hügel, though with blessings on your head.

Both inspiration and form probably owe something to the chapters of Shri Purohit Swami's autobiography, fed to WBY by Sturge Moore at this time. By early February he had more or less decided to contribute an Introduction and was impatient 'to question him on matters of religious practice, chiefly to get from him definitions or descriptions of meditation, contemplation, etc. In European mysticism contemplation, as distinct from meditation, is beyond the discursive mind . . . I would like to know what happens in the most concrete detail as the life of contemplation or meditation grows richer. I have perhaps just enough experience to ask such questions.'[127] 'Vacillation' addresses this issue. But it also affirms the poet's commitment – for all his belief in miraculous intercessions from the other world – to seeking an elemental reality in the strivings of the human heart.

The other thematic pulse that beats through the marvellously intricate and varying rhythm of the sequence is the philosopher's need to work towards death, not by quiescence or defeatism but 'proud, open-eyed and laughing'. This too reflected his recent experience; he had faced death and seen it retreat, while his own creative inspiration had flooded back with returning health. So had memories that took him back over the course of his extraordinary life. All these themes stayed with him, and much of the thought behind 'Vacillation' is compressed into a much shorter, and ostensibly simpler, poem written the following June.

> Stream and Sun at Glendalough
>
> Through intricate motions ran
> Stream and gliding sun
> And all my heart seemed gay:

Some stupid thing that I had done
Made my attention stray.

Repentance keeps my heart impure;
But what am I that dare
Fancy that I can
Better conduct myself or have more
Sense than a common man.

What motion of the sun or stream
Or eyelid shot the gleam
That pierced my body through?
What bids me live like these that seem
Self-born, born anew?

VI

Meanwhile Irish politics were apparently moving into a new phase with de Valera's advent to power. As it happened the fears of Cumann na nGaedhael and their supporters that this meant the ascendancy of full-blooded republicanism were misplaced. Although Fianna Fáil took up a confrontational stance on certain issues of Anglo-Irish relations, notably the repayment of land-purchase loans to the British government, they confined their hostility to constitutional matters. But the ostentatious piety of many members of the new government (not least its president) also gave liberal intellectuals cause for worry. The apprehensions of the Yeats circle are shown by a long and uncharacteristically frantic letter from George to wby on 29 February, warning him about the dangers to the Abbey under the new government, and pleading with him either to return from Coole to discuss the crisis, or to agree to 'an assignation in Galway'. A week later AE wrote shrewdly to his old friend:

I imagine the subsidence of Ireland from the heroic mood of O'Grady & his contemporaries to the mood of abject piety before the coming of the Eucharist[ic] Congress has crystalized your moods into intellectual sharpness and where before you had a dream mood you now exercise yourself with an intellectual dagger. Ireland today forces us to a heretical revolt, and if your mood and mine and [Frank] O'Connor's and others are symbolical we may be forerunners of an Irish Voltaire. What merely deflects us whose characters are already formed must inevitably I think seek out someone where it may have a complete embodiment. I cannot imagine so much musty piety to exist without some ribald iconoclast being constrained to cry out its opposite.[128]

For his part, wby was not prepared to leave the role of 'ribald iconoclast' to the next generation. This was publicly demonstrated by the 'Crazy Jane'

433

poems, placed deliberately at the opening of the new book which Lolly was setting up at this very time. (It would appear, as *Words for Music Perhaps*, in November.) WBY felt confident about it: 'I think this collection & "The Winding Stair", when combined, will make the best of my books of verse.'[129] Confidence honed his critical acumen to a sharp edge, and at this time he sent a marvellous letter of advice to his self-regarding and prickly young cousin, Monk Gibbon, an apprentice versifier. WBY's counsel also acts as an illumination and a critique of his own poetry:

You have gained greatly in intensity of diction from Gerard Hopkins but lost in naturalism. Gerard Hopkins, whom I knew, was an excitable man – unfitted for active life and his speech is always sedentary, the reverse of that of his friend Bridges when Bridges was at his best . . . Hopkins is the way out of life Bridges is the way into life . . . In my experience literature is a life-long war against the sedentary element in speech. You are too difficult and this is a sedentary element.[130]

He wrote this letter from Coole, which remained his base through the spring, but he was preparing a visit to London, where a great deal of business awaited him. There was to be a dinner celebrating the foundation of the Irish Literary Society, another BBC broadcast, and – more exciting to WBY than either – a first meeting with the Swami. He was also trying to find a publisher for Gregory's diaries, letters, and autobiographical writings; a sensitive question, since Gregory feared that after her death Margaret would excise all remarks critical of the British government and the Black and Tans.[131] As far as his own publication plans went, Macmillan was printing the copy for the edition de luxe, but had become evasive about a publication date, as the economic recession continued.

The visit was also occasioned by a political mission. The new government had revived the old republican objection to the oath of fidelity, and indeed to the entire role of the governor-general in the Free State. In private, de Valera was prepared for compromise, and discreet approaches were opened up through – among others – Edward Longford's brother Frank and J. W. Dulanty, the Irish high commissioner in London. They were not readily entertained by the dominions secretary, J. H. Thomas – erratic, viewy, and floundering out of his depth.[132] At this point, WBY was pulled in. He wrote to George from London on 7 April that he had seen Dulanty, who 'has been completely ostracised by the English government since the first note about the oath'; Lady Lavery was arranging a meeting with Malcolm MacDonald, who not only represented the Dominions Office but, as the prime minister's son, would provide access to Downing Street. 'I am amused and flattered – amused that I of all people should be selected to temper the wind to the shorn Republican lamb – or to some lamb for it is not quite clear who is to be shorn.'[133] He met MacDonald and Sir Edward Harding (permanent under-secretary at the Dominions Office) on 8 April '& put my case against the oath & described what was I believed the Irish situation'; he was pleased to find himself 'much more self-possessed & potent than I used to be: I spoke well'.[134] However, Thomas was not going to listen to reason, and a fortnight later de Valera proceeded to introduce legislation which amounted to a unilateral repeal of the oath of fidelity – without renouncing the Treaty or leaving the commonwealth. It was the first example of the balance he would strike between appeasing his irreconcilables and recognizing the reality of the Free State.

On WBY's crowded visit in early April, he also met Shaw and carried the plan for an Irish Academy of Letters forward a stage; he saw old friends, and extended his London circle into the world of Edith Sitwell and her ramshackle Bayswater *galère*. One of the attractions was high-class gossip about his old friend Lady Cunard's daughter Nancy and her black lover; but WBY's genuine admiration for much of Sitwell's poetry was a sign that his infatuation with the work of Wyndham Lewis, her enemy and traducer, was over. More exciting still, he at last met the Swami (first through Sturge Moore, and then at tea with Olivia Shakespear) and was entranced by him. So were others. As a guru the Swami was vital, funny, provocative, and very good company. A group of his influential supporters, including the explorer Sir Francis Younghusband and the mystically inclined Lady Elizabeth Pelham, would shortly form the Institute of Mysticism, to provide a London base for his mission. Olivia Shakespear liked the Swami and saw a good deal of him, but kept her distance from the 'pack of silly women' who attended his lectures and she amusedly charted the descent of the Institute into rabid power struggles among the faithful. She also noted, with her habitual percipience, that 'he must be in financial difficulties'.[135] Already, early in their acquaintance, WBY had to make the peace between the Swami and Sturge Moore, who had fallen out over money; the Swami, realizing that WBY could help him more than Sturge Moore, tried to pay off the latter with £10 and associate his autobiography with the man who had made Tagore's name in the West. Sturge Moore warned WBY of the Swami's vanity, ambition, 'silly boasting', and cupidity; he was furious when his old friend and collaborator took the Indian's side.[136] The row was fomented, intentionally or not, by a dubious follower of the Swami's called Gwyneth Foden. None of this boded well for the future.

However, the BBC broadcast on 10 April was a great success. WBY adopted an intimate tone, to an audience he envisaged 'listening singly, or in twos and threes', while he sat alone, addressing 'something that looks like a visiting-card on a pole'. He wisely took Gregory's advice to 'read them poems about women', going back as far as 'Down by the Salley Gardens', and forward to the unpublished 'I am of Ireland'. After the inevitable 'Cloths of Heaven' and 'Folly of Being Comforted', he defended the necessity of 'the now obsolete romantic movement' to which he had belonged. 'It is sometimes right to say "the spring vegetables are over", but never right to say "they have been refuted".' More poems about women followed: the 'Dying Lady' sequence and 'On a Political Prisoner', with a long description of Con Markievicz. This included a telling qualification: 'In the lines of the poem which condemn her politics I was not thinking of her part in two rebellions but of other matters of quarrel. We had never been on the same side at the same time.'[137] It was a highly effective performance, with WBY at his confiding best, delivering a commentary tailored around some of his most striking yet accessible poems, and it brought in a deluge of letters. 'One woman wrote about her ill treatment by men & enclosed a ticket from a railway station weighing machine recording her weight. Probably to show how much weight she had lost from ill treatment.'[138]

He returned to Dublin in late April, fired by plans for the Academy. Letters were sent in all directions, detailing ideas about membership, criteria, strategies. Frank O'Connor and Francis Stuart were desirable as representatives of a younger generation who had tangled with censorship. Austin Clarke's play *The Bright Temptation*, 'a charming, humorous defiance of the censorship & its ideals', similarly qualified him.[139] Seumas O'Sullivan could be useful because of his magazine. Walter Starkie deserved election only if he would be worked hard as secretary. AE was still reluctant and defeatist: 'nothing can be done in a country governed by louts . . . it is no use fighting for anything where the press is dominated by fear of priests'.[140] But WBY was on his mettle. He was also facing the future: George was house-hunting again, for 'an old detached house with a garden'. In early May he returned to Coole, where he had spent most of the winter and spring ('George said they would have to have an assignation on the streets of Galway to see each other,' Lily told Ruth). In the house among the seven woods, the last chapter of the most important friendship of his life was reaching its close.

Gregory was now very infirm, accepting medication at last and confined to one room; but she faced out her troubles to the end. In one Balzacian scene, Margaret decided to take the drawing-room curtains for her new house at Celbridge, thinking her mother-in-law would never come downstairs again. 'But she got a great wish to go over the house again and did, saw the curtains had gone, said nothing.'[141] On 9 May she told WBY that the lump in her breast had grown much bigger, and asked him to arrange a visit to her Dublin surgeon – who had privately told him there was no question of further operations. 'It is characteristic of her that all these months she has never spoken of the lump in her breast (I knew from Margaret that it was still there) & that last night after speaking of it for two or three minutes & the journey to Dublin she said "we will now dismiss the subject" and began to read out Charlotte Bronte.'[142] There was to be no journey to Dublin for her, but WBY had to return for Abbey business: a meeting with Robinson and Starkie about the players' next American visit, to be linked to a lecture tour undertaken by WBY himself. He also had to see a house that George, with her customary resourcefulness, had found in Rathfarnham, just outside Dublin, and that WBY described in a letter to Gregory on 15 May.

It is old, & has the most beautiful gardens I have seen round a small house – flower garden, fruit garden, vegetable garden, tennis & crockey lawns. A Mrs Nugent lived there till her death a short time ago, & created & tended the gardens for which she had a genius. The house is nothing except that it is old enough for dignity, but as to the gardens, we shall outdo Celbridge [Margaret's new house], for years to come.

It was the last letter in their great correspondence. WBY stayed on in Dublin, to see Gregory's doctor on 22 May (a Sunday) and to visit Michael at his boarding-school; that night he dined with the Hones at Delgany and arrived home late to a telephone call from Gregory's solicitor saying she was sinking fast. He took the first train to Gort the next morning, and was met by Catherine Gregory, who told him her grandmother had died just after midnight. To her astonishment and discomfiture, he suddenly and uncontrollably began to weep.

The tears were probably caused not so much by the inevitable event as by his absence at the last. It was a bitter blow, after his long and faithful attendance. The previous February, thinking the end was near, she had pencilled him a note, never delivered:

I don't feel very well this morning, rather faint once or twice – It may be the time has come for me to slip away – & that may be as well – for my strength has been ebbing of late – & I don't want to become a burden or give trouble. I have had a full life & except for grief of parting with those who have gone, a happy one.

I do think I have been of use to the country – & for that in great part I thank you. I thank you also for these last months you have spent with me – your presence has made them pass quickly and happily in spite of bodily pain, as your friendship has made my last years – from first to last fruitful in work, in service.

All blessings to you in the years to come[143]

It was kept among her papers, in an unstamped envelope, and he never saw it: but it said all she felt. As for him, he could only reproach himself for not being there at the end. He cannot have expected it to come so quickly, or he would not have stayed away more than a week. The account of her death, which he wrote out in obsessive and moving detail very soon afterwards, passes over this fact, but testifies that when he left Coole he thought her 'somewhat better', and – improbably – that the doctor, who thought the lump 'was not cancer or a deadly form of it', was treating her for rheumatism.[144] Back in Coole, the old conflict with Margaret crackled into life. She wanted the body taken from the house to the church at Gort before its removal for burial in Galway. WBY disagreed, and got his way. He stayed in Coole for the night, with his old friend's body in the stipulated plain oak coffin lying below, though he had initially taken a room at the local hotel.

[Margaret] was surprised that I did not mind sleeping in the house with a coffin. I said 'I am not affected by the circumstance of death, but by the parting.' Several times we returned to [the] subject & I said [to her] 'I said it is not the coffin that [w]rings my heart but all this' pointing to the books and the paintings. She said 'Yes it is your home too that is broken up.'[145]

This represents a deliberate (and rather snide) misunderstanding on Margaret's part. WBY wanted to evoke the feeling expressed by an old sculptor, come to pay his respects, when he looked at the family portraits and said sadly 'all the nobility of the earth'. 'I felt', WBY told Shakespear, 'he did not mean it for that room alone but for lost tradition. How much of my own verse has not been but the repetition of those words.'[146] Margaret, WBY pointed out in his memoir, was incapable of seeing this:

[She] thought that she had been sacrificed to Coole & seemed bitterly jealous. However I testify from my own observation & from Lady Gregory's words that there was never an ill-tempered word. It was impossible to be excitable & unrestrained in Lady Gregory's presence, & Mrs Gregory herself had been remoulded by her & by the house. These last days she was very kind to me, though we had not always been friends, unlocking without being asked the big room upstairs where I have slept & written when a young man, that I might look my last at the woods through its windows.

The sense of an ending was partly historic: the eighteenth-century Ascendancy ideal of service and patriotism, recently reinvented by WBY, had been epitomized by Gregory from the time he first knew her. AE felt it too, writing to WBY the day after her death: 'The Anglo-Irish were the best Irish but I can see very little future for them as the present belongs to that half-crazy Gaeldom which is growing dominant about us.'[147] But for WBY the severance was deeply personal too. A raw pain comes through his handwritten account, never published in his lifetime, and through his letters. 'I have lost the friend who was my sole adviser for the greater part of my life,' he told the Swami, 'the one person who knew all that I thought and did.'[148] He found himself unable to write an appreciation for the papers: 'if I ever do it it will not be soon nor I hope journalese'.[149]

Three months later, Lily wrote to Ruth:

Willy said the other day of himself that he is so hopeful that when things are difficult he has only to talk new plans for a few minutes to be filled with hope and be as
cheerful as if nothing was wrong. But of Lady Gregory he cannot speak, and the
auction and the breaking up of Coole. It depresses him too much. Again, like Papa
and the Aunts, they never speak of things that depress them.[150]

But the expression came, inevitably, through poetry. In this case, he had
already prepared himself for the loss of Gregory, and the shifting of his life's
centre of gravity. 'Coole Park, 1929', which prefaced Gregory's memoir of
the house, was already written as a kind of anticipatory elegy; and, when
keeping her company in February 1932 (just when Gregory wrote, but did
not send, her own anticipatory farewell to him), he began to develop the
thought into a longer, more complex, and more sombre poem. 'I have at last
found a rich theme for verse,' he had told George; 'I am turning the introductory verses to Lady Gregory's "Coole" (Cuala) into a poem of some
length – various sections with more or less symbolic subject matter.
Yesterday I wrote an account of the sudden ascent of a swan – a symbol of
inspiration I think.'[151] He called the poem in its first printing 'Coole Park
and Ballylee 1932', identifying it as an ode on Gregory's death; later he substituted '1931', but the implication remained. The title also connects his
house and hers, by the metaphor of the underground river that ran between
them. It surfaces in the lake at Coole, where the poet hears, on a wintry day,
the 'sudden thunder of the mounting swan' – that image which he had
made into an indelible part of the mystique of the lake, the house, and their
part in developing his own artistic genius. Here, the mysterious swan also
leads directly to the journey of the soul, and then to the dying Gregory
herself.

> Another emblem there! That stormy white
> But seems a concentration of the sky;
> And, like the soul, it sails into the sight
> And in the morning's gone, no man knows why;
> And is so lovely that it sets to right
> What knowledge or its lack has set awry,
> So arrogantly pure a child might think
> It can be murdered with a spot of ink.
>
> Sound of a stick upon the floor, a sound
> From somebody that toils from chair to chair;
> Beloved books that famous hands have bound,
> Old marble heads, old pictures everywhere;
> Great rooms where travelled men and children found

439

Content or joy; a last inheritor
Where none has reigned that lacked a name and fame
Or out of folly into folly came.

A spot whereon the founders lived and died
Seemed once more dear than life; ancestral trees,
Or gardens rich in memory glorified
Marriages, alliances and families,
And every bride's ambition satisfied.
Where fashion or mere fantasy decrees
We shift about – all that great glory spent –
Like some poor Arab tribesman and his tent.

The intellect of man is forced to choose
Perfection of the life or of the work,
And if it take the second must refuse
A heavenly mansion, raging in the dark,
And when the story's finished, what's the news?
In luck or out the toil has left its mark:
That old perplexity an empty purse,
Or the day's vanity, the night's remorse.[152]

We were the last romantics, chose for theme
Traditional sanctity and loveliness,
All that is written in what poets name
The book of the people, whatever most can bless
The mind of man or elevate a rhyme;
But fashion's changed, that high-horse riderless,
Though mounted in that saddle Homer rode
Where the swan drifts upon a darkening flood.

He already knew, therefore, how cut adrift he himself would feel when his fellow romantic, her work done, vanished like the swan into darkness. A year before Gregory's death, WBY had told his mesmerized interviewer in London, 'if you don't express yourself you walk after you're dead. The great thing is to go empty to your grave.' Gregory, indomitable to the end, had done just this; her death could only confirm WBY's commitment to go on searching 'perfection of the work', even if it meant raging in the dark and transgressing boundaries and limitations, whether imposed by his own old age or the new Ireland.

Chapter 11 : Struggles Towards Reality
1932–1933

> . . . Victorian romanticism was not the only possible answer to those modern conditions that Mr Yeats deplores. If it were, poetry would cease to matter. Adult minds could no longer take it seriously. Losing all touch with the finer consciousness of the age it would be, not only irresponsible, but anaemic, as indeed, Victorian poetry so commonly is. Mr Yeats's career, then, magnificent as the triumph was that he compelled out of defeat, is a warning. It illustrates the special disability of the poet in the last century, and impressively bears out my argument about the poetic tradition. And it cannot be repeated. No Englishman in any case could have profited by the sources of strength open to Mr Yeats as an Irishman, and no such source is open to anyone now. No serious poet could propose to begin again where Mr Yeats began.
>
> F. R. Leavis, *New Beginnings in English Poetry* (1932)

I

THE death of Augusta Gregory and the loss of her house marked a caesura across WBY's life, the cleft driven so deep that he feared the bereavement might even mean the failure of creativity. 'Did the subconscious drama that was my imaginative life end with [Coole's] owner?'[1] Luckily, it came just at the point when he and George were constructing a new home at Riversdale; and there were also the inevitable distractions, complications, and responsibilities that followed Gregory's death. But, at a crowded time of life, the creative void remained.

WBY was effectively treated as chief mourner; the governor-general's telegram of condolence was addressed to him at Coole. But his involvements did not end with the auction of the house's contents three months after Gregory's death – an event sarcastically recorded by Gogarty in a letter to an American friend. '[Augustus] John drawings and Jack Yeats pictures went for a few pounds, shillings for some . . . What a farce that legend of Coole as an Irish Bayreuth was.'[2] WBY inherited a painting by Robert Gregory, which had hung in the room where he wrote, and half of his co-director's National Theatre shares – the other half going to Robinson. But Gregory's will also bequeathed WBY 'the final decision as to arrangement and publication' of any unpublished autobiographical material in her papers. By a piquant irony, this was stated in an incorrectly witnessed codicil. Given the way that Lane's will had dominated the last seventeen years of

441

Gregory's life, it is hard to believe that this could have been an oversight: she may have intended it to have moral rather than legal force.

In any case, Margaret set herself firmly against what she saw as the ancient interloper's last invasion of family territory. As trustee and executor of her mother-in-law's estate (together with the civil servant T. J. Kiernan), she persuaded herself that Gregory had not wanted WBY to have full control of the unpublished autobiographical writings and, even more so, her unpublished diaries – whose status was left unclear in the codicil. WBY himself argued that the only reason Gregory had not given him full control was because of his ill-health at the time ('I was supposed to have "gone fut"'); after his recovery, 'some twelve or fifteen months before her death she said that she would make me the final authority'.[3] The issues at stake concerned more than literary reputation. WBY believed that Margaret's violent anti-republicanism had been crystallized by her own traumatic experiences during the Anglo-Irish War and her subsequent marriage into a diehard Unionist family. Battle-lines were swiftly drawn up for a long conflict.

Shortly before her death, Gregory had signed an agreement with Putnam, giving the company the rights to her unpublished writings (including the right of abridgement). WBY quickly took the initiative by approaching Constant Huntington, the managing director of the firm, who was doubtful about the potential of the autobiography left by Gregory; on the other hand, Sturge Moore, who was sounded out by WBY as a possible editor, thought it was publishable. WBY advanced a plan for an edited version of the diaries, with a biographical Introduction: several editors were mooted, while the Introduction would be written under his advice. Unsurprisingly, Margaret objected, standing on her authority as trustee. Equally unsurprising was Putnam's growing excitement about a far more saleable proposition: a biography by WBY himself. The idea was being floated by mid 1933, when Margaret took legal advice to see if it came within the terms of the agreements signed by Gregory before her death; in her view, the only biography necessary was the autobiographical typescript (anodyne and repetitive, by comparison with the diaries) left by Gregory and provisionally titled 'Seventy Years'. This text had the great advantage (in Margaret's eyes) of effectively stopping in 1918, before the Anglo-Irish War, in which her mother-in-law's sympathies had been firmly with Sinn Féin. Margaret feared that WBY would impose himself on his hostess after death, as he had done in life. His monopoly of *Cathleen ni Houlihan* was a continuing cause of resentment, as Gregory had become more and more outspoken in private about her claims to joint authorship – especially after the 1916 Rising conferred prophetic status upon the play. Margaret too complained about this, probably with a view to potential income rather than nationalist kudos. For WBY's part, he pointedly emphasized that his old friend had 'said she was anxious the [treatment of the] Black and Tan period might be mutilated by pro-British prejudice'.[4] He was also infuriated by Margaret's scepticism about the 1931 codicil, though Huntington repeatedly told her that Gregory had 'continually impressed upon him' her desire that WBY should have unfettered control over her literary remains. Margaret's co-trustee supported this (and clearly saw the commercial advantages of WBY writing the biography). A year after Gregory's death, Kiernan outlined WBY's position to the family solicitor, for forward transmission to the Goughs.

He will not write a life, for Putnams, based on the MSS of Lady Gregory. He does not want to press his offer against the wishes of the executors. He is considering putting into book form from memory an account of Lady Gregory as he knew her with Martyn, Moore and the Theatre folk etc as an independent piece of writing. He would I think like to use the diaries but he does not want to press his wish. He asked me to convey a request for the letters he wrote to Lady Gregory the manuscripts of which belong to the estate and the copy right to Mr Yeats. He would of course return them.[5]

By then, he had decided to make his book about Gregory into the last instalment of his own autobiography; he had written most of it, as *Dramatis Personae*, by the end of the following year. A heavily abridged edition of the *Diaries* would appear in 1946, edited by Lennox Robinson (the last person their author would have wanted); the project was fiercely contested by Margaret all the way. By 1935 WBY had decided that Gregory's own autobiographical TS was of 'doubtful' literary merit.[6] He may have been influenced by the fact that he had by then completed his own memoir, which would appear at the end of that year. But only a year after her death, he could also reflect frankly upon their professional relationship, in terms that revealed much about himself as well as her.

When two people work for a long time at any work they see it differently. Each exaggerates his or her point of view because the other point of view is there to correct it. Lady Gregory & I so differed about the Abbey. It was part of Lady Gregory's courage that she liked to take full responsibility for all that was done. She liked to say do this or do that & for that reason tolerated uneducated managers. I hate responsibility & therefore do everything by discussion. I can for this reason only work with educated managers. When I came to live in Dublin, with Lady Gregory's consent I deposed Dolan, selected by Lady Gregory, & put Lennox Robinson in his place. (He had been manager some years before.) Lady Gregory criticised him but not more than I had criticised Dolan & Fay etc. Another reason for Lady Gregory's criticism was that he represented a group of ideals & necessities that were transforming the Abbey. She loved the Abbey more than I could to the very last, &

always went there straight from the train, but never loved the later Abbey as she had the Abbey in its first years when it was a 'Folk Theatre'. Her love of 'folk' was the reason why she liked uneducated managers best.[7]

'Seventy Years' disappeared from view until the early 1970s, when it was rediscovered and published by Colin Smythe. A full edition of the diaries had to wait until 1978–87. Margaret, essentially, got her way, and though relations stayed distant, there was never an open break with WBY. But the battle over Gregory's literary estate helped to revive his own creative energies. He would still find himself unable to write poetry for many months. But the need to memorialize her propelled him into his last autobiographical essay, and her loss and the need to take stock also stand behind the thoughts he gathered into the lecture 'Modern Ireland', which he wrote shortly after her death.

As the shades descended upon Coole, de Valera and Fianna Fáil were assuming power. WBY now wanted 'to explore, for the sake of my own peace of mind, the origin of what seems to me most unique and strange in our Irish excitement'.[8] This fanaticism and intensity had coincided with contemporaneous upheavals in Italy, Germany, and Russia; but WBY located Ireland's particular force-field in the conflict between the Ascendancy self-assertiveness of Swift and Berkeley, and the rise of Catholic demos in the early nineteenth century. Parnell had fused these two energies; at his death, their courses diverged once more. At Parnell's funeral (that 'stormy autumn morning' which also, though he did not say so, marked a key moment in his courtship of Gonne) the bells tolled one of the great chords of Irish history, a seismic change signalled by portents in the night sky. Later he would refine the distinction between the preceding age and what was to follow as that between the Great Comedian (O'Connell) and the Tragedian (Parnell) – a Meredithian echo which would have pleased his father.

Gregory, a dominating presence in the lecture, represented that Ascendancy dignity, commitment, and self-sufficiency (as, less expectedly, did O'Leary); modern Irish republicanism was descended from the other strain, calling for the individual to sacrifice himself to abstract doctrine, the creation of a 'mystic victim', and a kind of anger very different from Swift's. Joyce was chosen as the exemplar here: WBY remembered him ('and he will forgive me for saying [so], knowing how much I admire his work') as 'possessed with an extreme irritation mounting to almost ungovernable rage against all that [he] saw and heard, even against the mere bodies and faces that passed him in the street'. The Christmas dinner scene in *Portrait of the Artist* epitomizes the bitterness Ireland inherited from Parnell's destruction. Yet it was Synge, not Joyce, whose influence was currently discernible in the work of O'Casey and O'Flaherty. And what succeeded the movement Joyce might have begun was the sacrificial mood inaugurated by Patrick Pearse (whose poetry WBY quoted) and Thomas MacDonagh, and now apparent in the novels of Francis Stuart.

Parnell had been the victim, the nation the priest, but now men were both priest and victim – they offered the nation a terrible way out [of] humiliation and self-detraction. Since then the substitution of the hunger strike for [the] silence of the imprisoned Fenians has helped to make deliberate suffering a chief instrument in our public life. A few weeks ago I asked an important government official about an obscure revolutionary leader, and he replied as if he was saying the most natural thing in the world, 'He has a passion for suffering; he is always compelling people to persecute him.' I do not say that this instinct is wholesome or that it is unwholesome; I may say that it is not wholesome for a people to think much of exceptional acts of faith or sacrifice, least of all to make them the sole test of a man's worth.[9]

Thus WBY believes Irish culture has lost the Aristotelian 'magnificence' attributed to O'Leary and Gregory, which should have been its dominant mode. Yet he claims that Synge and Gregory are an essential part of 'Modern Ireland', since their literary personalities were formed after the post-Parnell fall-out – in a manner that WBY's and George Bernard Shaw's were not. There is also a strong implication that the Irish are coming to a critical point in this conflict running 'in our blood'. These themes would be refracted through the only substantial poem he wrote in the year after Gregory's death, eventually called 'Parnell's Funeral' and published with notes that continue his dialogue with contemporary Irish history. By then, however, he would himself have participated briefly in a political movement to shape modern Ireland, an encounter which served only to amplify his disillusionment.

WBY wrote the notes for 'Modern Ireland' in his old haunt of Glendalough, County Wicklow. He had been dispatched there on 7 July, while George organized the move into the new Rathfarnham house. Setting off, he felt 'normal and cheerful' for the first time since Gregory's death. Before leaving Dublin, he had grappled with Abbey business, and successfully obtained a profitable ecclesiastical embroidery commission for Lily (thus providing 'that rarest of things a success in my own family'). In Wicklow he read Virginia Woolf's *Orlando* ('which I shall probably find faint of pulse & dislike') and Frank O'Connor's *The Saint and Mary Kate*, 'a beautiful strange book'. For company, he visited Francis and Iseult Stuart, and entertained them in turn at his hotel. But, he reflected sadly, 'we have not enough in common to give back a splash when I drop a stone'.[10] It was twelve years since he had come to Wicklow on a mission to rescue Iseult from her moody and violent husband. The marriage had lasted so far, but Iseult had lost her spirit, and – by a strange irony – WBY's interest was now focused more on her husband and his work, which he recommended to Shakespear:

Read 'The Coloured Dome' by Francis Stuart. It is strange & exciting in theme & perhaps more passionately & beautifully written than any book of our generation & it makes you understand the strange Ireland that is rising up here. What an inexplicable thing sexual selection is. Iseult picked this young man, by what seemed half a chance, half a mere desire to escape from an impossible life & when he seemed almost imbicile to his own relations. Now he is her very self made active & visible, her nobility walking & singing. If luck comes to his aid he will be our great writer.[11]

Against his usual practice he contributed a glowing paragraph to the dust jacket, and a year later he wrote telling Stuart that his new book *Glory* was 'a masterpiece . . . majestic, beautiful, all intellectual passion, perfect in structure, far beyond anything you have done hitherto – but sometimes vile in its grammar'.[12] Stuart and *The Coloured Dome* would find their place in 'Modern Ireland', as he worked on it down the valley. He also wrote the short poem 'Stream and Sun at Glendalough': introspective, questioning, searching for the assurance of inspiration. Epiphanic moments might be temporarily bestowed upon him, but artistic renewal remained elusive. By the end of July he was happy to leave the hotel, made noisy by holidaying families, and move into Riversdale.

Picturesque but without pretension, it was a small, double-fronted eighteenth-century farmhouse, covered in Virginia creeper. The rooms were small, but the largest – characteristically marked at once for WBY's study – had French windows which opened out into the garden. The house was far from luxurious, and the accommodation was limited (Michael slept in a room above the stables, as the Yeats children had done in Merville so many years before). Riversdale was too far from the road to bring in mains electricity without unwarranted expense, and there were only a limited number of gas-lights and none at all in WBY's study, which was lit by Aladdin oil-lamps. The house had been haphazardly decorated by the previous owner, who had simply painted around furniture and pictures without moving them. All her efforts had been concentrated upon the gardens, and on making the most of the house's remarkable location. Dublin's housing estates were already encroaching on Rathfarnham village, but Riversdale remained an oasis. Set well back from the Ballyboden Road which wound up into the Dublin mountains, it was approached by a mossy bridge over a stream. There was a little gate-lodge, occupied by unsatisfactory tenants who fortunately soon left; it was then renovated and occupied by the gardener, who was a key figure in keeping up the miniature estate. There were thirteen acres around the house, let for grazing, and a wonderful garden: ancient trees, roses on pergolas, an orchard of apples and cherries, box hedges enclosing fragrant beds of verbena and myrtle around WBY's study door, a conservatory, a croquet lawn, tennis court and bowling green, a walled vegetable and fruit garden. George installed electric bells, painted the walls and ceiling of WBY's study lemon yellow, with green and black woodwork, fenced off a hen-run, and became immersed in the garden; she and the children loved the house passionately.

Michael's future school, St Columba's, was conveniently perched further up the mountain. Both Yeatses made regular appearances there, with WBY being 'shown off' by the headmaster as a prize acquisition. Anne would leave school the following Christmas, and go to the Hibernian Academy three days a week for drawing classes. Her artistic talent was now decisively clear, and WBY was taking a more direct interest in his children's development than is often credited.[13] But his reactions to Riversdale were more detached than those of the rest of the family. The distance from central Dublin was a jolt: it was a long ride out on the number 47 bus. He tried walking as far as his sisters' house at Churchtown once, but then decided to depend upon taxis. The sense of being cut off was exacerbated by the lack of a telephone, though they had requested one; WBY took the matter up in an inimitable letter to the relevant civil servant, who fortunately was his old acquaintance P. S. O'Hegarty.

I have moved out to Rathfarnham and am finding it the devil of a nuisance not being able to communicate with the Abbey by telephone from my house. A fortnight ago the Abbey secretary was had up for stealing a motor car and I had to walk into Rathfarnham to telephone from a public-house bar, trying to disguise the nature of my communication from the assembled topers. Twice since I have had to go in to the Abbey because I could not face that bar, and when I do face it it is a quarter of an hour's walk away.[14]

A phone was duly installed within ten days. Pictures were hung, the garden began to exert a spell, and he resumed playing croquet, which had been a regular pastime at his aunts' house on Morehampton Road. WBY began cautiously to put down roots. 'At first I was unhappy for everything made me remember the great rooms & the great trees of Coole,' he told Olivia; adding, significantly, that the Gregory house had been 'my home for nearly forty years'. He was also sharply conscious that the remainder of his life would in all likelihood be spent at Riversdale. 'We have a lease for but thirteen years but that will see me out of life.'[15]

II

Nonetheless, he planned – as he had always done – for the future. Once settled in Rathfarnham, he began the serious organization of a long-cherished project: the Irish Academy of Letters. First mooted as an anti-censorship ramp in 1926, the enterprise had hung fire during the years of WBY's absence and illness; now it began to dominate his correspondence.[16] Approaches had already been made to Irish writers: Joyce, though told he was 'the first name' who came to mind, was one of the few to decline. The Academy was registered on 12 September 1932; WBY wanted to have the membership announced before a public lecture on 18 September, 'that I may have a few enemies to answer'.[17] Within a year it boasted an impressive roll-call: GBS as president, WBY as vice-president, and George MacDonnell as honorary secretary headed a membership that included AE, Lennox Robinson, F. R. Higgins, Forrest Reid, James Stephens, St John Ervine, Edith Somerville, Gogarty, Frank O'Connor, Seumas O'Sullivan, Austin Clarke, Sean O'Faolain, Padraic Colum, Liam O'Flaherty, T. C. Murray, Alice Milligan, and Shan Bullock. Associate members included Eugene O'Neill, Walter Starkie, Shane Leslie, Helen Waddell, L. A. G. Strong, 'John Eglinton', J. M. Hone, T. E. Lawrence, Ernest Boyd, Stephen Gwynn, and Elizabeth Bowen. 'Associates' were people whose work fell outside the strict criteria; they were excluded from voting rights and council membership. 'Otherwise', WBY told Joyce, 'we should have been overrun with people from England or Scotland with a little Irish blood and a great desire to acquire a national character.'[18]

To judge by the list, most of those restricted to this category either produced work which was not strictly 'creative' or lived outside Ireland – a disqualification not, of course, imposed on Joyce himself. The invitation did not overcome his disapproval of academies in principle, though he retained appreciative memories of WBY's kindness to him in his youth.[19] Sceptical observers might have noted that at least six of the full members had had difficulties with the Censorship Board, and the associates were almost entirely liberal Protestants; Gaelicism was at something of a discount, and WBY had assured Joyce that 'all the writers here who are likely to form our Council are students of your work'. He also told Joyce the Academy would vigorously try to 'prevent the worst forms of censorship'. A few months before, he had violently denounced the Censorship Board's banning of Liam O'Flaherty's *The Puritan*, a work which WBY considered as important in the history of Irish fiction as Maria Edgeworth's *The Absentee*, though the comparison would have surprised many, including the author: banning it turned 'a lamp into a bomb'.[20] AE noted that his old friend had become fired by the idea that 'with all the abilities in [the Academy] it might through its utterances affect Irish culture and government activities'. (By this he meant not only censorship policies but possible tax breaks for writers – a vain hope.)[21]

According to Gogarty, the first members had in fact been finessed into joining: in signing WBY's first circular, they found themselves automatically elected.

Genesis: for the last year Yeats has been nursing Shaw very astutely with a view to this 'Academy' of his. Shaw, filled with the considerations that it was to be a bulwark to preserve that Protestant Minority which is threatened with extinction in Ireland – responded so far as he has done: i.e. to sign the paper inviting signatories and in not blowing the whole thing sky-high. So far very astute of Yeats. But the power of gratudinous accolade with which Yeats has invested himself is beginning to show the smaller force behind the large pretentions. Making associates is a new way of getting one in on old rivals. Witness Dunsany, who will be Dunsany Furens or Furiosa, to quote from a Renaissance creation which was crystallised, that is the Renaissance, and embalmed by Academies and abolished. The minister forbear, – the inevitable origin of educated poor Protestants – is coming out in the Poet. He should stick to Parnassus and not live our 'Protestant to be.' The Irish Press having promised to publish my words if I gave them an interview broke faith and left out the gist of what I said. It is this: I did not realise when signing the petition for a Friendly Society Academy that I would be ipso facto a Member. Now if I leave it will look as if I sought notoriety at the expence of my friends and to escape or forestall criticism from the ragged Catholic weeklies who hate intelligence while crying out for 'culture' or asseverating that there is none like 'true' Catholic culture! So I got in by admiring Yeats and not by marriage, as Stewart the husband of Iseult Gone. But I can sell the Academy instead of my country to America on my lecture tour. F. R. Higgins was shocked when he found himself famous: he too having innocently signed the petition. Little did we think that we were becoming Immortals: 'ut puto Deus [. . .?]' or whatever the Emperor exclaimed. But we thought no such magnificence. What a wonderful example of Yeats's apparently foolish and fatuous ways of arriving at the significant. The letter from Yeats and Shaw only came days after the press publications of Members' names. If by not answering, one falls out, there will be a vacancy in Eternity and someone else can move up into Immortality. But when cocktails appear on the Wine List, it is time to leave the hotel. And such cocktails: who is O'Foalon and Pedar O'Donnell? . . . I am rather an ass to stay in. It is more important to select one's readers than books; and yet 'he took me in'.

> There was a kind poet called Yeats
> Who put me with those whom he rates –
>   Don't think it bad of me –
>   In his Academy;
> Off which of our heads are the slates?[22]

AE drew up the rules, as he had done so long ago for the Irish National Theatre Society. 'Its special object is the promotion of creative literature in Ireland'; the full membership (co-opted by votes of the whole body) was not to exceed twenty-five; members' work must be 'both important and Irish in character or subject'. Perhaps learning a lesson from battles in the theatre long ago, AE incorporated a scheme of arbitration for 'any dispute which cannot be settled by a majority vote of the Academicians'. More optimistically, structures were also put in place whereby trustees could deal with investments, though the only income at the outset was a £50 donation from Shaw, and the hope of money from public lectures, usually given by WBY himself, adept at prevailing upon influential society hostesses like Hazel Lavery to assemble audiences in their drawing rooms.[23] But, above all, the point was to rally forces against censorship. 'You wanted a fighting Academy,' AE wrote ruefully to WBY in America a few weeks after its foundation, 'and I have done my best to supply pugnacity in your absence.'[24]

The new body also gave endless opportunity for the advancement of protégés and the blocking of undesirables. Austin Clarke complained to F. R. Higgins 'Yeats is trying to set up a Hitler dictatorship: a Plato's Republic from which all poets but himself will be excluded.'[25] Invitations to WBY's weekly salon at Riversdale (now transferred to Wednesday nights) carried extra injunctions forbidding the discussion of Academy business in front of those outside the charmed circle, like Monk Gibbon (destined to be firmly kept there, despite his relationship to the Yeats family).[26] AE continued, as ever, to bring 'new young genius' to WBY's attention, only to see it summarily rejected; though on at least one occasion his judgement was not at fault, when he discovered 'a small farmer in Monaghan, whose verses have a wild and original fire in them', called Patrick Kavanagh.[27] WBY preferred to co-opt slightly scandalous figures, such as Francis Stuart and the literary 'gunman', Ernie O'Malley; he also enjoyed telling newspaper reporters that Dunsany had declined 'because he could not endure the thought of being only an associate member'. Gogarty characteristically claimed that Seumas O'Sullivan had initially tried to buy his way in with £3,000 from his wife, the painter Estella Solomons, which had been refused: 'thus was the newly formed Irish Academy of Letters saved from the Jews'. Alice Milligan produced a rather jarring reaction: 'I am much in favour of censorship & wd perhaps rather be on a board of censors than in an Academy.' Hyde courteously refused as it was clearly not going to concern itself with language revival. Sean O'Casey turned them down, which at least gave WBY the chance of publicly regretting their estrangement: 'I half expected it. Mr O'Casey has never forgiven us for our rejection at the Abbey Theatre of his play *The Silver Tassie*. I am afraid I played a leading part in the rejection of that play.' A few months later he took an equally leading part in protest-ing against the refusal of (English) printers to handle O'Casey's short story 'I Wanna Woman', adding 'I am glad that Mr Sean O'Casey has broken his long silence; he has moral earnestness and great dramatic genius.'[28]

wby was at the centre of the kind of activity which had always galvanized his energies, whether in the Young Ireland Societies, the Irish National Theatre Society, or the Order of the Golden Dawn: drawing up rules, admitting initiates, issuing decrees, and skirmishing on committees. He also felt that the Academy brought him into touch with the energies of the coming generation. By late September the new organization was drawing newspaper headlines: wby noted with satisfaction a letter to the *Irish Press* denouncing its members as '"the new paganism" & advocates of "race suicide" & suggesting the foundation of a real Papistical academy; that kind of thing ensures the loyalty of our friends'.[29] So did the attacks from the *Universe*, a guardian of Catholic morality. He put the case arrestingly to an American reporter: Ireland particularly needed an Academy because of the 'total lack of any critical press there, and the fact that whereas in the U.S.A. and England young intellectuals feel fanaticisms are in their favour, in Ireland they feel fanaticisms are heaped against them'.[30]

Sustaining this ambitious project required money, which raised immedi-ate political difficulties. The *Daily Mail* offered to subsidize a literary prize under the Academy's auspices, arousing the anger of those who saw the newspaper's editorial policies as implacably Hibernophobic. wby took refuge behind the Harmsworth family's Irish credentials, and also employed the kind of arguments he had used in battles over the Abbey's repertoire three decades before.

We have among our Academicians people of all sorts of politics, two or three Ulstermen for instance, and if we had refused such a prize it would have been looked upon as a political act . . . My own view is that if we were offered a prize in com-memoration of Carson we should accept it, provided he were dead and therefore a part of history. The Academy stands for all Ireland and should be a bond between contrary opinions.[31]

wby also had to combat criticism of the prize from GBS, who felt his pres-idential role licensed him to act as a loose cannon. Adjudication was, in his opinion, a job for schoolmasters or boxing referees accustomed to declaring winners 'on points'. Yet Shaw did suggest awarding a prize for 'the worst English novel. That would at least amuse the public. Donkey races are always popular.'[32]

The reaction of popular Irish opinion to the Academy was more pre-dictable. The *Irish Press* discovered that members were apparently elected 'more as a result of their success in Britain and America than because of any reflection in their published works of the real Ireland',[33] and the *Catholic Bulletin* saw it as yet another bulwark of Freemasonry and atheism. But the ultimate *raison d'être* of the Academy was neatly demonstrated only a few months after its foundation, when the president himself got into trouble with the Censorship Board over his new book, *The Black Girl in Search of God*. This Voltairean fable created, among other special effects, a living Jesus who was an odd amalgam of Shaw and Swift, and advocated racial intermarriage on a global scale, causing a gratifying uproar in South Africa, where GBS had written it. Published in December 1932, it was a runaway bestseller in Britain. The Irish censors, however, were in no doubt that its 'general tendency' was 'indecent and obscene'; they were partly influenced in this by John Farleigh's spare but sensuous woodcut illustrations. Once again history repeated itself: as with *John Bull's Other Island*, *Blanco Posnet*, and *O'Flaherty VC*, GBS handed WBY an unexploded grenade, and then bombarded him with tongue-in-cheek instructions about how to handle it. On this occasion WBY was exhorted to tell the Board that the book's intention was to justify the Church's 'objection to throwing the Bible into the hands of ignorant persons to be interpreted by their private judgement'. A somewhat safer line of argument was that the main difficulty seemed to be Farleigh's illustration of a naked girl on the cover, and this did not come within the literary terms of the Censorship Act. Famously, WBY rather spiked the legalistic side of this argument by showing Ruttledge, the minister of Justice, reproductions of the Sistine Chapel ceiling as evidence of the virtue of nudity, but the book remained banned.[34] As for GBS, he would remain a thorn in the side of Irish pieties. WBY treasured a report from the Galway County Libraries Committee a few years later announcing that they had decided to ban all Shaw's books and had therefore burnt them. 'There was no other way of getting rid of them.'[35]

By the time WBY left Ireland for the USA via London on 5 October the Academy was firmly launched. His lecture tour was planned to publicize the new body before Irish America, and also to raise money for it. After a lecture in Manchester he spent a fortnight in the Savile, seeing old friends and following up his preoccupation with the Shri Purohit Swami. They had corresponded closely since their first meeting in June 1931 and met in London through either Olivia Shakespear or Gwyneth Foden.[36] Mrs Foden, a devotee of Indian temple dancing among much else, had cast herself as the Master's disciple, fixer, and general aide; as with many of the Swami's relationships, it was not destined to end happily, but for the moment their adjacent ménages in Bayswater provided a new and exciting focus for WBY's London world. But the breach with Sturge Moore had not been mended effectively. Moore still felt the Swami had exploited him unfairly, and then deserted him for the infatuated WBY. 'We shall never get a penny out of the Swami's book,' he wrote gloomily to his wife, 'however it succeeds . . . He has gone out of our lives, and only regarded us as means to his ends and had no kind of consideration for us in any other respect. Yeats has been foolish enough or it may be wise enough to replace us – that remains to be seen.'[37] George remained detached from this latest craze; though she followed her husband to London, she stayed separately, at the Orchard Hotel, and soon returned to Dublin with two new Persian kittens. As for WBY, he sailed on 21 October for New York, and his last American lecture tour.

It was nearly thirty years since his first transatlantic venture, and the schedule was less punishing than on previous occasions.[38] There were carefully planned breaks between speaking engagements, and he took a secretary with him, Alan Duncan, the son of old acquaintances from the Dublin Arts Club.[39] Gogarty had tried to make him hand over the organization of the trip to Pond's agency, but WBY wisely resisted, engaging the rival firm of Alber & Wickes; Pond's business finally collapsed the next year, leaving Gogarty and several other lecturers in severe straits. The tour remained based on New York, where he generally returned. Quinn and his luxurious Central Park apartment were no more, and WBY stayed at the Waldorf Astoria instead. His celebrity status ensured priority treatment from his arrival at Customs, and he was besieged with telephone calls and dinner invitations. AE put him in touch with Judge Richard Campbell, doyen of cultured Irish Americans, who – with the influential republican activist Patrick McCartan – provided the kind of support and advice for which he had previously relied upon Quinn. Thanks to Brendan Bracken, he started by spending a sybaritic weekend with the socialite Mrs Harrison Williams, and he was delighted to encounter James Stephens in Toronto. Travel was eased by the Ford Motor Company, who laid on a chauffeured Lincoln in any large city he visited.

The financial arrangements had been put in place with equal care. Twenty lectures were guaranteed, at $100 per lecture; any extra would be paid at $125. WBY gave twenty-five in all. His original aim was to clear £500 or £600 profit for himself, and a few hundred for the Academy. By 15 December he had earned £500, and hoped to add £200 or more; Duncan negotiated an extra fortnight in New York on condition that he received $700 for five lectures. In the end, he brought home £500 for his new institution. Publicity was organized with similar attention. A detailed advance circular advertised his credentials as Abbey founder and Nobel Prize winner, besides being 'closely identified with the politics of Ireland during the past few decades'. This authority also promised that WBY would talk not only about the literary renaissance but about 'the new Ireland that has come into being . . . He is more than a first class lecturer. He is a genuine world celebrity, gifted with genius of a high order.'[40] Reporters accordingly often quizzed him about contemporary Irish politics, and he was careful to contrast the 'new Ireland' with the old, subtly implying that Irish-America was out of touch with the current dispensation: he also spoke supportively of de Valera's policies. While he often adverted to the iniquity of censorship, he emphasized the new tone of Irish writing, even declaring that literature had the power to unite the Free State and Northern Ireland.[41] In Boston he told a reporter that a real Irish literature would develop as 'Irishmen begin to hate and to love Ireland', rather than simply nurture illusions. And he referred, as so often in his reflections, to the significance of Joyce.

The real creator knows he must not theorise about creation. To the real creator his own creative act is continually a surprise. Men of talent live their theories. But the propagandists do otherwise. It was the propagandists who created the Ireland of illusions, just as the Communists are doing elsewhere.

Well the Irish propagandists drove James Joyce from Ireland. I think he came to hate the illusory Ireland and so he went into exile. That was thirty years ago. Since then he has spent his time studying a few days or weeks at the end of the nineteenth century in Ireland and writing about them from his own inner consciousness. And no man can say now whether it is from hate or love that he writes.[42]

The repertoire of lectures included 'The Irish National Theatre' and 'The New Ireland' – a developed version of that searching and troubled analysis he had worked on at Glendalough after Gregory's death and before the move to Riversdale. But other avenues were explored too. The Abbey was playing *Words upon the Window Pane* and *The Playboy* in New York, and WBY spoke from the stage to a capacity audience just after his arrival: the reaction was ecstatic.[43] On 14 December an 'inspired' article by Ernest Boyd about WBY and the Academy appeared in the *Nation*, perhaps in response to Francis Talbot, SJ, who had denounced the institution and its backers as not 'true Irish' but opponents of 'sane and healthful censorship' who wanted to 'open the gates to immoral foreign literature and give facilities to two or three Irishmen to disseminate filth'.[44] Boyd emphasized that the organization had 'come into being for the least academic of purposes, to wit, the protection of the intellectual freedom and integrity of Irish literature', and he criticized Joyce for not putting his shoulder to the wheel. 'In Ireland . . . political and religious obsessions, coupled with poverty and the general low level of culture resulting from a preposterous and inadequate system of national education, have reduced those Irishmen of letters whose names are universally acclaimed to a position somewhat analogous to that of the radical intelligentsia in Czarist Russia.' Boyd fulminated against the way 'Irish literature has been driven out of Ireland', condemned the 'crude provincialism' of Irish journalism, indignantly listed the works that had been barred by the Censorship Board, and scathingly quoted 'the usual gibes' levelled at the new Academicians, dismissed as unIrish because they wrote in English.

Since his arrival in this country Mr Yeats has been trying to explain to those who care to listen that the Irish Academy is a weapon of intellectual self-defense, the only weapon available to Irishmen in Ireland today. The country which appealed to the intellectuals of the world for help and sympathy, and which received both, now seems bent upon stifling all manifestations of freedom of thought . . . Paradoxical, like so many Irish phenomena when viewed by the outsider, the Irish Academy is, therefore, an academic body which seeks to enlist and deserves the support of all men of letters who value independence. The Irish Academy of Letters is unacademic. What could be more Irish?[45]

But the audience reached by the *Nation* was small, and WBY relied on spreading his message by the traditional whistle-stop tour. The pace was less frantic and the organization more comfortable than on previous occasions: and his image was now refined to a calculatedly dramatic effect. An undergraduate at Bowdoin College remembered nearly thirty years later how he seemed

a hierophant of poetry as he appeared on the platform, his aloof head tossed back in what I later learned was a characteristic gesture. The dark hair of his youth, now turned snow-white, was like the lion's mane from some Syrian bas-relief. The modeling of his high nose and chin and somewhat sensuous mouth was stylized, too, but in the manner of the later Greeks. His eyes behind tortoise-shell spectacles – then out of fashion in America, but oddly suited to him – were an oblique, almost oriental oval. On the little finger of his left hand he wore a ring with a stone so large that it extended from joint to joint. He was the most impressive man I had ever seen.[46]

Yet his listener found that WBY's 'golden voice' was more spellbinding when he spoke than when he read poetry, where the ritualized chanting was 'somewhat embarrassing'. WBY was not altogether at his ease either, and often bored: he wrote to George from Cincinnati that he 'longed for her perpetually' and already looked forward to meeting her at Southampton and having a short holiday somewhere. Ennui was briefly kept at bay by discovering D. H. Lawrence's novels (*Women in Love* struck him as 'a beautiful enigmatic book') and, when he crossed the border into Canada, being able to drink whisky again: Prohibition, while on its last legs, was still operating. On 11 December, in Boston, he attended an exciting seance at Dr Crandon's, described in detail to George: credulous as ever, he thought it remarkable that Mrs Crandon advised him, just as George's 'Instructors' had done, to 'drink water every sixty minutes'.[47] And echoes of his past life were occasionally sounded. Alleged Yeats connections approached him in Washington; 'four professional dancers', he bemusedly told George, 'who have cherished for years a conviction that they are related to us. They have adopted as their professional name their mother's name, Yates (their grand-father adopted the "American spelling"). The eldest, aged 24, (married with a son aged six,) sends me a newspaper picture of her three sisters, aged 17, 18 and 19: they are dressed alike, all in the same pose, and all exactly alike, and all smiling.' Still, he reflected, it was not impossible: 'one of my grand-father's brothers altered the spelling of the name "because he could not fight the whole world"'.[48]

In Toronto he encountered genuine relations (including 'an old woman I played with when she was a child'), and in Montreal a friend of his youth. Georgina Sime, whom he had known when he was a boy in Bedford Park, had last observed him on his visit to Canada in 1914. This time, she saw more of him. After his lecture (from a church pulpit) he 'made no pretence: the expression on his face was "I have to do it and I will" and he did'. His eyesight was noticeably failing, and as she walked him to the party after-wards he had to be guided down the steps. She had decided he was deficient in human feeling, but he won her heart completely when he suddenly spoke warmly about her artist father; at the reception he talked to her at length about Bedford Park, the ideals of their youth, and his admiration for the Morris-inspired embroidery Lily was now doing.

As he sat there he looked – 'magnificent' is the only word I find fitted to the occa-sion. Whatever he had been in youth or in mid-life, he was now a handsome, a magnificent old man. His hair, plentiful as it had ever been, was snow-white. He was dressed as carefully as he had been when I listened to his lecture in the Art Gallery almost a score of years ago, but now how differently! Then he had looked a man of the world, 'well turned out'. What he now wore was not only of a different material but it was worn in a different spirit. It had then been broadcloth; now it was home-spun of the finest kind, silver-grey in shade, spun by hand, worked out on the hand-loom, presumably at his sister's place in Ireland. His socks and tie were blue of a pale, indigo shade and they, too, I think had been made by the work of human hands. His shoes were strong and looked ready to start their wearer up a mountain. He was leaning back in his ample arm-chair and looking thoughtfully in front of him, seeing perhaps with those eyes which are not the eyes that we use to view the outside, ordinary world, some of those things he had just been recording.

As people converged upon him, she noticed how he mentally abstracted himself: 'now in the great arm-chair, which had lately held so magnificent a figure, there was not a man but a snow-capped mountain, leagues, continents away'. But 'when I bent down and said good-bye to him, taking his hand as I did so, [he] kept mine for a second in both of his, and I felt my father's ghost pass between us'. All the same, she noted that though she changed her mind about his having become 'inhuman', he was 'off the human': 'what he was really in love with and married to was art, and towards any manifestation of it he would not only be keenly sympathetic but would put himself to endless trouble in order to further it in any way he could'. This infused the admiration he retained for her father over the intervening half-century ('a fascinating man . . . I have never met anyone like him since'), and his feeling for Lily, whom he seemed to value as an artist rather than as sister.[49]

Others, less closely analytical, found him a difficult guest. His hosts at Colby College thought him impossible to talk to, and considered his lecture was seriously disordered and unsatisfactory.[50] At Bowdoin College it was believed that 'he had sent word ahead that at the dinner before his lecture no-one was to talk to him unless he spoke first' – though in the event he proved 'quite affable and talkative'. His failure to recognize people was by now legendary. At a dinner in Wellesley College on 8 December he encountered T. S. Eliot, then Charles Eliot Norton Professor of Poetry at Harvard. As Ellmann tells it,

Yeats, seated next to Eliot but oblivious of him, conversed with the guest on the other side until late in the meal. He then turned and said, 'My friend here and I have been discussing the defects of T. S. Eliot's poetry. What do you think of that poetry?' Eliot held up his place card to excuse himself from the jury.

It is a good story but, for one thing, WBY's public comments on Eliot's work were usually favourable; for another, they encountered each other fairly frequently in London and were on lunching terms (MacGreevy carried affectionate greetings from Eliot to WBY when he returned from London in 1926).[51] The story's significance lies in the fact that this was the kind of anecdote now inseparable from the Yeats mystique.

A more reliable snapshot of the Wellesley visit was preserved by Horace Reynolds, who had been taken up by literary Dublin five years before. Now teaching at Harvard, he attended the lecture and took careful notes. WBY seems to have conflated several of his usual themes, declaring 'the moment Parnell died I had an intuition which turned out to be of historical importance', and presenting the condescending line about the Fays which so annoyed their dwindling band of defenders: 'two actors of genius, one a stage-struck solicitor's clerk, the other an electric light fitter. I was to write tragedies for the stage-struck solicitor's clerk, and Lady Gregory was to write comedy for the electric-light fitter.' WBY also projected his current opinions back thirty years by claiming he had wanted 'a theatre very hard to get into, like a secret society'. The efforts of Synge, Gregory, and himself to 'create an essentially poetic literature' were defeated by the bitter realism of Catholic writers 'wishing to drag every skeleton out of the closet'. Writers must avoid propaganda, and write out of love and hate. He praised Gregory and Synge extravagantly, but his list of six favourite books is striking: 'Homer, Shakespeare, William Morris, all of him, Balzac, all of him, an anthology of the best English poetry compiled by myself, and the sixth book I have never discovered.' It is a spectacularly unIrish list, and the lecture seems to have taken an aggressive line towards the pieties of his youth.[52]

It was, therefore, rather disconcerting for the speaker when Reynolds approached him after the lecture with photographic copies of the pieces written by WBY for the *Providence Sunday Journal* and *Pilot* forty-odd years before, which Reynolds had been carefully collating. Reynolds suggested republishing them with Harvard University Press. WBY overcame his habitual distaste for his juvenilia, and agreed, though he stipulated that no suppressed early poems be included. But his mixed feelings about the enterprise persisted, and, when he eventually reread these dispatches from the passionate Irish engagements of his youth, they served to fix him even more firmly in the adversarial attitudes adopted since the late 1920s.

By Christmas he was back in Manhattan, staying at the Waldorf, visiting the swimming baths for exercise, giving occasional 'drawing-room' lectures, and recruiting his strength; he sailed on the *Bremen* for Southampton on 22 January. But another echo from the engagements of his youth was sounded by news that came through the wires just before he left. His old adversary George Moore had died in London. WBY was jolted; unsettling memories crowded in, as he recalled that unreliable but original figure who had started out his passionate admirer and ardent collaborator and ended by leading the chorus of ridicule. A journalist came to interview him only two hours after he received the news, and found WBY talked of little else. Though he admitted that 'our views diverged', he refused to talk of their estrangement, preferring to praise Moore's love of 'startling people', his vehement style of conversation, and his 'French sense of construction and logic: there is no denying his force and courage and mastery in making logical plots'.[53] But he avoided dealing with the logical plot of Moore's own life, and the fantastic embroideries of malicious detail which the novelist applied to the lives of others – above all, to WBY himself. This great subject would be left for the book which was already taking shape in WBY's mind as his memorial to Gregory, but could now also serve the purpose of his revenge on Moore.

His last weeks in New York presented him with another opportunity to reflect on the drama of his early life. He had the time to read through Horace Reynolds's collation of the articles he had poured out, often as 'The Celt in London', for American readers between 1888 and 1891. The experience discomfited him. 'It must be awful', Gogarty later remarked to Reynolds, 'to have become so good a writer, that all ones youth is ipso facto repudiated.'[54] As usual, Gogarty's reading was too crude. WBY's feelings were intensely ambivalent. He was relieved to 'make the joyous discovery' that he had no copyright, so could not prevent Reynolds's enterprise even if he had wanted to. He simply requested that the early poems remain suppressed ('some anthologist or ghastly musician will appropriate them') and corrected a couple of points in Reynolds's Introduction ('the people of Ceylon are not blacks. I remember Lord Salisbury getting into no end of a mess through calling some Indian a black man'). But, as he read through his early declamations about 'Irish Writers Who are Winning Fame', his encomia on forgotten favourites like Todhunter, Allingham, Rose Kavanagh, and Lady Wilde, his exhortation in 1890 that 'Irish Writers Ought to Take Irish Subjects', he began to think about his earlier self, bent over a proof in the National Library or his shabby room in Blenheim Road, hungry for discoveries, urgently denouncing 'oratory', passionate, edgy, insecure. Eight months later he would put these thoughts into a Preface for Reynolds's book. For the moment, he contented himself by writing a reflective letter to the editor on Christmas Eve, sitting in his room in the Waldorf:

I am glad to have read those essays of mine after so many years. I find that I am still in agreement with all the generalisations, but not with the examples chosen. I praise Todhunter and others out of measure because they were symbols of generalisations and good friends to my father and myself. The articles are much better than my memory of them, but I knew better than I wrote. I was a propagandist and hated being one. It seems to me that I remember almost the day and hour when revising for some reprint my essay upon the Celtic movement (in 'Ideas of Good and Evil') I saw clearly the unrealities and half-truths propaganda had involved me in, and the way out. All one's life one struggles towards reality, finding always but new veils. One knows everything in one's mind. It is the words, children of the occasion, that betray.[55]

III

The *Bremen* docked on 27 January at Southampton; after a short time in London (inevitably seeking out the Swami) WBY was back in his suburban fastness beneath the Dublin mountains. He seemed in good health; during the last weeks in New York, Duncan thought his employer 'as well and fit as I have ever known him'.[56] But, for all his confidence, WBY's sixty-seven years and recent succession of illnesses were telling. On the return to Ireland he collapsed with influenza and stayed bedridden till late February. His first emergence into public activity was not encouraging. He gave a lecture to the RDS on 'Modern Irish Literature', in which he referred to the Fays with his habitual condescension and drew a savage rebuke from a furious Mrs W. G. Fay: 'Both my husband and his brother, while possessing ability equal to your own, in their particular arts, have only lacked the baser qualities that make for that commercial success which I feel sure would have altered the tone of your remarks and I shall not ask your pardon for saying that, where there was so much to praise, no man of magnanimity would have been guilty of the bad taste and feeling of your reported utterances.'[57]

He could console himself with his own commercial success. His last American tour had made money: in December and January profits of £855. 0s. 11d. ($2,820.84) had been transferred from New York to his Dublin bank.[58] It was badly needed. His railway investments continued to plunge doggedly down, and the economic depression had drastically affected the book-buying market. In 1931/2, his royalties from Macmillan (outside the USA) were a modest £86. 8s. 2d.; the following year was slightly worse, at £84. 4s. 0d. Things would improve dramatically in 1933/4, with the publication of *The Winding Stair* and *Collected Poems* in 1933. The latter alone brought in £391. 18s. 11d., and his Macmillan income *in toto* was £455. 19s. 7d.[59] The figures bleakly demonstrate not only how reliant he was upon outside fees for lectures, play performances, and broadcasts but also the difference that a new publication made: and this recognition in turn lies behind his anxiety about Macmillan's dilatory approach to the edition de luxe.

As he recovered in the spring of 1933, WBY took stock of this long-running project. The agreement of a year before had revised the publishing plan into seven volumes: *Poems, Mythologies* (including *The Irish Dramatic Movement*), *Plays I, Plays II, Essays, Autobiographies* and *Discoveries* (including *A Vision*). Illustrations and portraits were already being chosen.[60] But the continuing economic slump applied a brake to progress; in August 1932, Harold Macmillan agreed to Cuala publishing a new volume of lyrics (*The Winding Stair*, with additional recent poems) on the grounds that the edition de luxe was moving so slowly. WBY was promising the final contents of all volumes before he departed for America. But at the end of March 1933 publication was still halted, 'pending better times'. The edition had always been conceived as a luxury enterprise (375 copies, with a sheet signed by WBY bound in at the beginning). Faced with a declining income, WBY needed a book to make money. This was the genesis of the one-volume *Collected Poems* mooted as a stop-gap: a consecutive arrangement of WBY's lyrics, with the longer 'narrative and dramatic' poems rearranged to go at the end.[61] By the end of June 1933 proofs were ready, and Macmillan was also prepared to publish its edition of *The Winding Stair* rather than holding it over for the edition de luxe. That opulent venture was further slowed down by the decision to go ahead with a volume of WBY's recent short plays: *Wheels and Butterflies*, comprising *The Words upon the Window Pane*, *The Cat and the Moon*, *Fighting the Waves*, and *Resurrection*, embellished with provocative Introductions. By the end of the year Macmillan had produced both *The Winding Stair* and *Collected Poems*; by February 1934 they had sold 2,280 and 1,600 copies respectively. This success galvanized WBY's publishers to suggest a *Collected Plays* in similar format, and it too would go ahead. But this provided yet another reason to postpone the edition de luxe, and WBY's literary income continued to rely on producing a series of new books.

Meanwhile, the drought of poetic inspiration that had lasted since Gregory's death showed little sign of relief. WBY's creative efforts continued to be largely directed towards arranging his oeuvre so far, writing Introductions, and devoting himself to new enthusiasms such as the Swami, whose apparently saintly qualities and undoubted storytelling abilities continued to enrapture him. On a visit to London in June, he spent much time in the makeshift ashram at Lancaster Gate, where Mrs Foden was now confiding that she had been a close friend of Constance Markievicz, and was writing a life of Casimir – neither claim likely to win WBY's approbation but both probably pure invention.[62] (Her statements that she was suffering from a serious cancer seemed more worthy of sympathy, but are equally doubtful in view of the fact that she would live until 1965.) For his part, the Swami placed great hopes on the publication of the British and American editions of his autobiography, *An Indian Monk: His Life and Adventures*, with WBY's ecstatic Introduction. But the public's appetite for tales of childhood revelations, mysterious apparitions, and the appearance of sacred marks on his body turned out to be limited. The small sales were a shock to the Swami, and he required much reassurance from his experienced new friend ('it was three years before I had sold more than about 50 copies of my first book – I sold 37 in the first year & yet I had an enthusiastic welcome from reviewers'[63]). The Introduction to *An Indian Monk*, completed in September 1932 just before WBY had left for America, catches the poet at the high point of his infatuation for a book which 'seems to me something I have waited for since I was seventeen years old'; it also suggests he was drawn to the Swami because the monk's life-experience recalled the discovery of the magical in the everyday, which WBY himself had found through his ancient collaboration with Gregory. Her absence continued to suffuse his thought throughout the year after her death.

The preoccupations of Shri Purohit Swami also echoed WBY's youthful inclination towards the exotic in Spenser, Coleridge, Shelley: 'wisdom, magic, sensation seem Asiatic. We have borrowed directly from the east and selected for admiration or repetition everything in our own past that is least European, as though groping backward towards our common mother.' And he was reminded of the lessons of cosmic unity and eternal recurrence which had attracted him in Mohini Chatterjee's teaching nearly fifty years before, as well as the philosophical acceptance that seemed, to Western eyes, moral relativism.

Our moral indignation, our uniform law, perhaps even our public spirit, may come from the Christian conviction that the soul has but one life to find or lose salvation in: the Asiatic courtesy from the conviction that there are many lives. There are Indian courtesans that meditate many hours a day waiting without sense of sin their moment, perhaps many lives hence, to leave man for God. For the present they are efficient courtesans. Ascetics, as this book tells, have lived in their houses and received pilgrims there. Kings, princes, beggars, soldiers, courtesans, and the fool by the wayside are equal to the eye of sanctity, for everybody's road is different, everybody awaits his moment.[64]

By now the Swami had also introduced WBY to a spiritual autobiography by his 'master', Bhagwan Shri Hamsa, *The Holy Mountain* – a story of travelling ascetism, transcendence, and an ascent to the icy caves of Mount Kailas, there to find wisdom in the loss of self. For this too WBY wrote a long Introduction, finished by late October 1933, which resonantly echoes his own early spiritual explorations. Through WBY's influence with Eliot, Faber and Faber agreed to publish it; but there were difficulties. Success went quickly to the Swami's head, and he became importunate. He did not appreciate WBY's advice that only a small part of the book would be worth presenting to a British market, or his firm veto on the title chosen by the Swami and Mrs Foden – 'Love's Pilgrimage'. 'There is nothing against the title as you and she understand it,' WBY pronounced in early 1934, 'but it has been spoilt by wrong usage.' Still, he remained entranced. To the same brisk letter, dictated to George, he added a handwritten message: 'Convey to Mrs Foden my good wishes; as long as I live I shall connect you both in the one friendly memory.'[65] George was less enthusiastic; WBY thought it 'remarkable' that whenever he read *An Indian Monk* to her, she fell into a deep sleep.[66] She was sceptical about the time and effort lavished on rewriting these soporific texts, but WBY found what he wanted there. And the image of one journey, both in the Swami's autobiography and that of his 'master', stayed with him: the pilgrimage to the holy mountain, advancing above the snow-line, menaced by wild beasts, sleeping in caves, and hoping to arrive at the state of *sanyasa*, or complete renunciation, and thus achieve wisdom. The Holy Mountain stands behind poems such as 'What Magic Drum' and supplies the images central to one of the very few lyrics which WBY wrote at this time. 'Meru' also suggests, however, that the wisdom gained by ascetic pilgrimage is not necessarily consoling.

> Civilization is hooped together, brought
> Under a rule, under the semblance of peace
> By manifold illusion; but man's life is thought
> And he, despite his terror, cannot cease
> Ravening through century after century,
> Ravening, raging and uprooting that he may come
> Into the desolation of reality:
> Egypt and Greece, good-bye, and good-bye, Rome!
>
> Hermits upon Mount Meru or Everest
> Caverned in night under the drifted snow,
> Or where that snow and winter's dreadful blast
> Beat down upon their naked bodies, know
> That day brings round the night, that before dawn
> His glory and his monuments are gone.

There is an echo here of the Puranic Hindu myth of the Boar who comes to spoil the world and lay foundations for a new age, and of the 'ravening and uprooting' Black Pig of Celtic apocalyptic legend as well. Yet again Indian explorations seemed to be bringing WBY back to the inspirations of his youth.

And during the same summer of 1933, when WBY was exploring Indian philosophy with the Swami, he was also writing his Introduction to Horace Reynolds's collection of his early journalism. Compressed, ironic, sharply detailed, in two short pages it both analysed the aesthetic preoccupations of his Bedford Park apprenticeship and etched a portrait of his youthful self with a painful edge: it suggests that his state of mind that July was in some ways as restless, dissatisfied, and frustrated as the lost self he so vividly and angrily remembers.

Reacquaintance with his early journalism brought home the fact that some pressures remained eternal. The same held true of politics. With Fianna Fáil's advent to power in 1932, Irish liberal and Treatyite opinion had nurtured grim forebodings about aggressively nationalist initiatives in public life. In fact, de Valera chose to tread carefully and irreconcilable 'Irregulars' were absorbed easily enough into constitutional politics. But WBY and his circle were alert to signs that the censorship mentality might extend beyond the written word, and early in 1933 their fears seemed justified. The office of the minister for Finance, prompted by de Valera himself, sent a sharp letter to Lennox Robinson about the plays brought by the

Abbey to the USA. Irish-American societies and 'influential individuals' had allegedly complained that the theatre's repertoire was 'open to serious objections on various grounds' – 'filthy language, drunkenness, murder and prostitution, and holding up the Irish character generally to be scoffed at'. The government subsidy might therefore have to be made conditional on an acceptable programme for future US tours, and would in any case be reduced from £1,000 to £750. Almost incidentally, the information was offered that the minister gave 'consent' for the appointment to the Abbey Board of Professor William Magennis: a firm advocate of right-wing Catholic values, who had frequently condemned Joyce and denounced WBY's enterprises in the *Catholic Bulletin*.[67]

This was all that WBY had feared ever since the Abbey had become dependent on a government grant eight years before. A reply was swiftly drafted for the Department of Finance and a copy sent directly to de Valera, making clear that the correspondence would be made public within a certain space of time.[68] WBY calculated that the government had played such a crude hand that they would be denounced by public opinion: his letter pointed out contemptuously that *The Playboy* was now a subject for 'lectures in American universities and schools', there had been no difficulties with audiences since 1911, *Juno* packed out the Abbey again and again, and his own recent lecture tour had caused no controversy. It is clear that he felt able to take a markedly aggressive line about wounding the susceptibilities of Irish-American societies, let alone the imposition of Magennis.

If we are to retain our grant we must leave out of our American repertory all plays that offend such persons or societies, that is to say the chief work of Synge and of O'Casey. We refuse such a demand; your minister may have it in his power to bring our Theatre to an end, but as long as it exists it will retain its freedom. Your letter adds that 'the Minister has consented to the appointment of Professor W. Magennis of the National University of Ireland as a government representative on the board of directors'. Who asked for his 'consent'; we never heard of Professor Magennis's candidature until we received your letter. I find that word 'consent' interesting. We refuse to admit Professor Magennis to our Board as we consider him entirely unfitted to be a Director of the Abbey Theatre. It is not necessary to state our reasons for this opinion as my Directors empower me to say in their name and in my own that we refuse further financial assistance from your government.

Old politician that he was, he included a loophole to allow the government to save face. The ministry had also complained about the words 'By special arrangement with the Free State Government' appearing on the American tour programmes. WBY admitted that they were 'at once accurate and misleading': accurate because they had signed the contract only after explaining to Blythe, the previous minister for Finance, the reasons why the tour was imperative, and misleading because they had not made any such arrangement with the government now in power. He therefore agreed that the words should be omitted in future.

And the government was open to negotiation. The proposal of Magennis was dropped, and Richard Hayes substituted: a more intellectual figure, who had recently written an article bravely attempting to claim WBY as a Catholic poet.[69] (His eyes were quickly opened and he subsequently opposed *The Herne's Egg* as blasphemous; he later became film censor as well as director of the National Library.) The theatre continued to receive its subsidy. However, the complaints persisted; a year later an Irish-American lobby complained about the Abbey's touring repertoire yet again, and managed to get questions asked in the Dáil. De Valera responded that he had 'informed the directors of the theatre that it is my opinion if they produce certain plays that are on the list for production in America . . . then it is clear that they will damage the good name of Ireland and they will cause shame and resentment to the Irish exiles'. This was true so far as it went, but the letter sent to Robinson, while making this point, went on to say that 'the selection of plays for production by the Abbey Company is, of course, a matter for the Directors of the National Theatre Society'; the important thing was to make clear that the government had no responsibility for the company's repertoire. The letter from de Valera also complained, in a muted way, about statements made by WBY in newspaper interviews regarding the directors' recent meeting with the new head of government, apparently because the impression had been given that he was trying to dictate which plays were to be included. If de Valera had wanted to exercise such power, the attempt misfired: WBY, not for the first time, had used a publicity offensive to finesse his opponent. Compared to the projectile of February 1933, de Valera's subsequent letter of 17 April 1934 was a gentle rebuke, and seems to have been intended to protect himself from the Irish-American complaints inseparable from the Abbey's tours, and to retract any impression that he was to censor the repertoire. He had given up hope of banishing Synge and O'Casey. By October 1934, when stories to this effect resurfaced, WBY could write to the newspapers urbanely explaining that relationships with the government were friendly, and all that had been at issue was the note on the programme about responsibility for choosing the plays.[70] By then, however, he had himself been through a brief period of political involvement which reflected the frustration and disorientation he had felt since the loss of Gregory. Transient as this flirtation was, the waves created would rock his own political reputation for many years after his own death.

Chapter 12 : A New Fanaticism
1933–1934

> Think what the people have made of the political thought of
> the eighteenth century, and now we must offer them a new
> fanaticism.
>
> WBY, *Autobiographies*, p. 542

I

IN AUGUST 1932, shortly after moving into Riversdale, the Yeatses gave a
garden party. De Valera's government was only a few months old and ex-
ministers arrived in Rathfarnham accompanied by armed guards. Lily
noticed WBY and Desmond FitzGerald 'walking up and down under the
rose pergola for an hour; I did want to know what was said and what they
think is going to happen'.[1] Such conversations were happening all over
Ireland after the ex-gunmen had come to power. De Valera himself, who
had never been comfortable as a guerrilla leader, rapidly came to terms with
the politics of compromise, and elevated to a fine art the technique of com-
bining abstract 'irreconcilable' rhetoric on issues like partition and the language question with a cautious pragmatism in the management of everyday
politics. But to supporters of Cosgrave's conservative regime, who by now
included imperially minded ex-Unionists as well as supporters of the
Treaty, the new president of the Executive Council seemed like a Kerensky
figure who would shortly be eclipsed by the shadowy forces behind him.[2]
And, to such imaginations at least, these sinister elements included
Bolsheviks as well as republicans. Saor Éire, a Communist organization
linked to the IRA, provoked a panic out of all proportion to its membership;
when the Irish 'establishment' met at venues like the Riversdale garden in
the aftermath of the 1932 election, the talk was of drastic alternatives, especially when they looked to events in contemporary Europe. Gogarty, for
one, expected a military dictatorship. The election of de Valera proved, in
his opinion, that the Irish were unfit for self-government and needed a
leader like Mussolini.[3]

There was, moreover, a subterranean current of discontent within both
the army and the police which had briefly surfaced in the threatened 1924
'mutiny' and had never gone away. This consisted of ex-revolutionaries who
felt the political classes had monopolized the spoils system, shown a cavalier appreciation of the contribution of the 'old IRA' to independence, and
made a mess of running the country. These malcontents saw de Valera's

advent to power as proof of this corruption and mismanagement, and they looked to a military leader to restore the proper balance. From early 1932 the economic policies of the Fianna Fáil government marshalled another platoon of the discontented. The previous government had agreed to pay land annuities to the British Exchequer, maintaining arrangements made under the Land Purchase schemes of the *ancien régime*; de Valera refused to continue them. Britain retaliated by imposing tariffs on Irish imports, and the ensuing 'economic war' hit Irish farmers hard. Cattle prices slumped to disastrous levels, and the discontent of the 'strong' farming classes (already supporters of Cosgrave rather than de Valera) was added to the disaffection of some army officers and the fears of the Irish elite. It could have been a potent combination, especially as a leader was apparently waiting in the wings: General Eoin O'Duffy.

O'Duffy had been appointed commissioner of the new police force in 1922, and was strongly identified with Cumann na nGaedheal. He had been a prominent campaigner against Fianna Fáil's return in 1932, working with an organization called the Army Comrades Association that essentially represented those elements which felt they had done badly out of the war and wanted to halt what they saw as a slide into anarchy under Fianna Fáil. O'Duffy himself had been exhorting the government to wake up to the dangers of an IRA takeover since the late 1920s and to impose permanent coercive legislation; his name was frequently associated with rumours of a *coup d'état* by the army to short-circuit the 1932 election.[4] He was also a vociferous participant in the growing chorus warning about how easily Ireland could 'go Communist' – in which WBY's friend Desmond FitzGerald was well to the fore.

The objective conditions for Fascism were apparently in place in 1932–3, and a movement shortly emerged which would ride these ominous currents: malcontents in the army, making their feelings felt through the Army Comrades Association and the National Defence Association, formed the background to the political organization known as the 'Blueshirts'. Superficially, WBY's affiliations seem clear. He had himself written apocalyptically of the coming of Communism since the Russian revolutions. He was a firm supporter of the Cosgrave government, and a friend of Desmond FitzGerald. WBY's ally Ernest Blythe was influentially involved in the new organization. Another friend, Dermott MacManus, WBY's link to army circles during the 1924 'mutiny', had been closely associated with O'Duffy in earlier times and would become general organizer of the new Blueshirt party. MacManus had been a friend of WBY since the civil war period. An eccentric figure, from an old Catholic gentry family in the west of Ireland, he had gone to Sandhurst and served as an officer in the British

Army before joining the IRA in 1920, and subsequently the Free State forces; he shared WBY's interests in psychical research, Indian philosophy, and, as it happened, sexual rejuvenation techniques.[5] WBY admired the way MacManus struck extreme attitudes and talked matter-of-factly about fantastic experiences – a figure from Jonah Barrington, though to others he might have seemed closer to Baron Munchhausen. But their friendship certainly provided the link between WBY and the discussions which produced the fully fledged 'National Guard' in the spring of 1933. MacManus, who was also friendly with George, visited Riversdale frequently, and the Yeats family stayed, as paying guests, at Killeaden, the MacManus family home in County Mayo, that summer.

WBY had anticipated political reconstruction through totalitarian rule in Europe since 1919; indeed, he was increasingly sceptical about the efficacy (and benefits) of democratic government. He admired, like many, the apparent achievements of modern Italy in the 1920s, but in terms which might not be immediately recognizable nowadays. He had told MacGreevy ten years before that Mussolini 'represented the rise of the individual man as against what he considered the anti-human party machine', which seems, in retrospect, to have interpreted the movement exactly the wrong way round.[6] His views on National Socialism in the early 1930s are less easy to trace. Though he had a devoted following in Germany, he did not visit the country. He was vague about the provenance of the Goethe-Plakette medal awarded him by Frankfurt in 1934, which was in any case specifically for *The Countess Kathleen*, just played in Germany for the first time; attempts to identify this episode as a recognition by the Nazi state of a distinguished fellow traveller have been comprehensively rebutted. (The regime, in fact, later put WBY on a list of forbidden writers, condemning his work as 'depressive art'.[7]) Though he refused to sign a petition got up by English writers against the Reichstag Fire tribunal proceedings in March 1933, it is likely that this is because it seemed a Communist ploy. Unlike Iseult and her mother, he was neither anti-Semitic nor pro-Nazi. Gonne, years after the post-war revelations of genocide, was still saying that if she had been German, the only thing that would have stopped her becoming a Nazi was their exclusion of women from positions of power; she also boasted of telling Richard Ellmann ('a young American Jew') that, compared to Hiroshima and Nagasaki, Hitler's death-camps were 'quite small affairs'. By contrast, as Jack later remarked, no one ever heard his brother 'say anything against Jews or ever show any kind of dislike for them'; to Rothenstein, WBY once remarked approvingly that 'the Irish and the Jews were alike in that they are at their best and most fruitful as a ferment among men of other races'.[8]

Nor was he a natural Blueshirt in Irish terms. In many important ways, WBY was at odds with the emerging opposition to de Valera – whether he recognized it or not. He certainly feared the effects of Fianna Fáil zealotry on those aspects of Irish cultural life which meant most to him; by early 1933 he was linking together de Valera's government, clerical denunciations of the Academy, and the Minister of Finance's attack on the Abbey's pro- gramme, and telling Pound 'the liberty of thought is very seriously threat- ened here'.[9] Shortly afterwards he would employ automatic writing to try to infer the future of Irish politics, receiving messages about 'reconciliation' through 'government from below'.[10] But his fears differed from those of friends like FitzGerald, or anti-de Valera intellectuals like James Hogan. FitzGerald's anxieties were grounded in fervent neo-Thomist apologetics, and poured out in letters to Jacques Maritain. While WBY equally approved of rejecting the rationalism and positivism derived from the Enlighten- ment, he was very far from sharing FitzGerald's attachment to the papalist political thought pioneered by Pius XI at this time. As the struggle against censorship had already shown, WBY and FitzGerald opposed each other regarding freedom of expression, particularly where sexual morality was concerned. For FitzGerald, the struggle against Communism was bound up with the struggle against sexual licence in literature. His opinions about the banning of Liam O'Flaherty's works could not have been more diametrically opposed to WBY's:

Nowadays it seems to me that there is a short cut to being recognised as a great writer by favouring Communism and stressing filth. One would almost weep at the waste of fame of the man who wrote only on urinal walls instead of in printed books. I think if you eliminate Bolshevism and muck-raking from Liam O'Flaherty you have a very unimportant writer left.[11]

WBY had sustained philosophical discussions with FitzGerald from the late 1920s, though the areas of disagreement yawned widely. FitzGerald had sent Berdyaev's works to Coole during the winter of 1931, and they corres- ponded about cyclical theories of philosophy; when Cumann na nGaedheal lost power, FitzGerald had more time for such distractions, and both men began to think in terms of a political philosophy to meet Irish needs. Towards the end of his American lecture tour in December 1932, WBY wrote to FitzGerald

to remind you of a conversation we had two or three months ago. You were to get together a few persons who would join us in considering the Marxian revolutionary theory in relation to St Thomas and modern philosophy. We thought we might be able to think out something among us which could give a foundation for advanced thought in Ireland. I wonder if you have done anything in the matter? You spoke of

Professor Tierney as a possible person. I have a feeling that Ireland is so passionate it might think out some philosophy of action, if we gave the first push, that might be important to the world as well as to itself.[12]

Tierney would become one of the theorists of the Blueshirt movement, and the author of an influential tract called *Could Ireland Go Communist?* Both he and FitzGerald subscribed to an austere Thomist doctrine which dictated views of intellectual freedom, as well as of political organization, that were very far from WBY's.

Nor did WBY agree with the right-wing Cumann na nGaedheal elite that de Valera was either a demonic wrecker or the harbinger of Communist chaos. During his American tour, his expressed views on de Valera's approach to Anglo-Irish affairs were extremely favourable and, indeed, contradicted the Cumann na nGaedheal party line.

'I am a Cosgrave man', he said when I mentioned politics, 'but I believe that de Valera is dead right in his dispute with Great Britain. Cosgrave and de Valera do not disagree in objectives: the difference between them is on the methods which they employ. De Valera has a right aim, but whether Ireland can stand the racket or not is a ticklish question. Ireland can only meet the English embargo on her cattle by becoming more or less self-supporting. De Valera's aim is to make Ireland economically independent of the rest of the world. Before the winter is over the question must be settled, and it would not surprise me if during that time all imports were rationed.'[13]

His sympathy for de Valera remained; he even compared him to Swift, as representing a nation's 'turbulent self-assertion.'[14] He also retained his liking for Peadar O'Donnell, a republican Communist prominent in Saor Éire. He had elevated himself above the atavistic fears, reactions, and obsessions which fuelled Irish party politics. After de Valera was returned to power in January 1933 with a hugely increased popular vote, and the policy of so-called 'economic war' with Britain bit more sharply into the Irish rural economy, WBY's reactions remained very different from those of the disgruntled farming classes, who supported increasingly radical opposition tactics. When he went to see de Valera about the Abbey's programme, he came away intrigued: 'I was impressed by his simplicity and honesty though we differed throughout. It was a curious experience, each recognised the other's point of view so completely. I had gone there full of suspicion but my suspicion vanished at once.'[15] His favourable view was vividly recorded by Edith Somerville in early March, when she met WBY for the first time at a Dublin luncheon party.

Yeats is a huge man, more like a country-gent than the typical poet (wh. I had believed him to be). A brown, healthy, good looking face, & charming wavy grey hair (*not* long hair). Very interesting talker, though at moments he fell into abstraction. A nice voice, decided Dublin tone, (rather reminding me of G.B.S.'s) & *no* assumption of high brow or stuffed-shirt-ness ... [James Stephens] & Yeats began, at lunch, to discuss de Valera, & I grieve to say, they both seem to have been subjugated by his abominable charm. Olive backed me up in describing the ruin he was bringing on farmers, but both these poets were only concerned with the brute's personality, & kept re-iterating that he was sincere, & a gentleman, & a patriot, & neither of them cared tuppence for the people to whom he has brought starvation. I must admit they were very interesting, & quite temperate & well-mannered, & obviously, they knew *nothing* about why wheat couldn't be grown on the Killarney mountains, or cattle sold at a profit for pence apiece.[16]

Ottoline Morrell also noted, late in 1933, his 'great admiration' for de Valera, whom he thought 'a very able man'.[17] The ex-revolutionary was coming out in his true colours as a cautious conservative, prepared to move swiftly against the forces of anarchy while publicly adhering to the old Sinn Féin orthodoxies from simpler times. This view of Fianna Fáil, very different from that of Cumann na nGaedheal, is reinforced by a note in WBY's journal of 1933: 'What I have seen of the present government I get a sense of vigour and sincerity, very unlike the old government party in the Senate, who left upon the mind an impression of something warm, damp & soiled, middle class democracy at its worst. They are success become logical.'[18] His attitude here was certainly elitist and oligarchic, but this does not make it Fascist.

Irritatingly Olympian as he may have seemed to some, WBY stayed detached from the immediate political crisis which produced the Blueshirt movement. De Valera now headed the first majority government in the history of the state. The stage was set for his domination of Irish politics for decades, controlling a dynamic, populist, political organization, that married traditional clientelistic Irish political techniques with up-to-date manipulation of public opinion. The opposition was demoralized and bewildered; Cosgrave's Cumann na nGaedheal seemed to have lost control, and ex-ministerial friends of WBY like FitzGerald and Blythe had to face up to a long period of retrenchment. Blythe threw himself into organizing the Army Comrades Association, whose members, during the election, had made a practice of intervening aggressively at public meetings and forming a guard of honour for opposition speakers. At the end of February 1933 de Valera challenged the opposition directly – by dismissing O'Duffy from his post as Garda commissioner. From March the ACA formed a kernel around which an extra-parliamentary opposition coalesced. Disbanded soldiers were joined by economically hard-pressed farmers and disgruntled ex-politicians (notably T. F. O'Higgins, the brother of WBY's murdered friend). Paramilitarism, anti-Communism, and populist Catholicism characterized the Blueshirt movement, which may have numbered nearly 30,000 by early 1933. When O'Duffy became leader in July, he tried to introduce the trappings of contemporary European Fascism; a uniform, a salute, a dynamic youth movement, the fetish of physical fitness, aggressive rallies and marches (he also tried, unsuccessfully, to persuade his colleagues to spell 'comrades' with a 'k', for added effect). The ACA was rechristened the 'National Guard', but the name 'Blueshirt' stuck. The movement used a network of leisure pursuits to bind its youthful supporters throughout the country. Blythe's articles in the *United Irishman* in the summer of 1933 called for 'a great national, patriotic association' overriding the electoral system and asserting 'the national will' against 'gabblers'. The new organization also advocated vocational organization within a corporatist state, and announced that membership would be reserved to 'citizens of Irish birth or parentage who profess the Christian faith'. Xenophobia and anti-Semitic opinions were freely expressed, particularly by O'Duffy himself.

Whether all this defined the movement as Fascist is debatable; the label of 'para-fascism' seems most appropriate, indicating that, while not objectively Fascist, the Blueshirts could easily have become so.[19] In later years, the word was strenuously avoided by those who had been connected with the movement. Before Mussolini's alliance with Hitler and the rise of the Third Reich, it carried fewer sinister connotations, and WBY for one felt little compunction about using it. Through Dermott MacManus, he was involved in the discussions about a new extra-parliamentary opposition in the spring of 1933, but his contribution was purely intellectual. 'At the moment', he wrote to Olivia in April, 'I am trying in association with [an] ex-Cabinet Minister [Blythe or FitzGerald], an eminent lawyer [Samuel Lombard Brown[20]] a philosopher [MacManus], to work out a social theory which can be used against Communism in Ireland – what looks like emerging is Fascism modified by religion.'[21] An unpublished letter to Desmond FitzGerald shows that their philosophical discussions had indeed continued, and that WBY was anxious both to introduce the ideas he had examined in Italy ten years before and to move the project to a more abstract plane. WBY sent FitzGerald a list of 'four philosophical positions', positing the descent of Communism from Hegelian dialectic on one side, and the opposing progression of ideas from Vico through Croce and Gentile whereby 'the individual is preserved as a process of the whole without which the whole could not exist. The past is honoured, hatred is condemned.' The 'practical result' means that 'the Fascist philosophy is accepted but there is something in man, which lying deeper than intellect, is not affected by the flux of history'. In fact, the 'new philosophy' is not – any more than the Hegelian dialectic – 'a solution of the antinomies which are insoluble by the human intellect, though they are solved in the heroic life, in the saintly life, in the work of art'. In the accompanying letter WBY added, 'What I think most important is to preserve the dynamic element of Fascism, the clear picture of something to be worked for. We have to take everything we legitimately can from our opponents.' He then wrote but deleted: 'Perhaps even more from communism than Fascism has taken. Fascism is perhaps as much entangled with right-hand Hegelianism as communism is.' But he added: 'To ask ourselves, for instance, how much even of the materialistic theory of history we can reinstate and absorb.'[22]

FitzGerald was interested in this kind of abstraction, but not many of his fellow politicians followed him. If any of WBY's interlocutors were interested in Continental theories rather than immediate Irish circumstances, their interest probably stopped at corporatist and vocational ideas of political organization, much in the air both in Ireland and Italy. As the summer of 1933 wore on, the sense of crisis gathered, and the movement became more distinctively Irish and less like an Italian variant. On 20 July O'Duffy proclaimed a new constitution centred on reunification of the island, opposition to Communism, and fervent Catholicism – as well as the creation of a national association for farmers, upon whom the movement increasingly depended for popular support. He also planned a 'March on Dublin', ostensibly to commemorate the fallen Cumann na nGaedheal heroes Griffith, Collins, and O'Higgins. Gogarty's invocation of an Irish Mussolini seemed about to be answered.

WBY's own political excitement took the characteristic form of wondering whether the Abbey should stage *Coriolanus* in Blueshirt uniform. More reflec:ively, he wrote to Shakespear a week before O'Duffy unveiled his new constitution:

Politics are growing heroic. De Valera has forced political thought to face the most fundamental issues. A Fascist opposition is forming behind the scenes to be ready should some tragic situation develop. I find myself constantly urging the despotic rule of the educated classes as the only end to our troubles. (Let all this sleep in your ear.) I know half a dozen men any one of whom may be Caesar – or Cataline. It is amusing to live in a country where men will always act. Where nobody is satisfied with thought. There is so little in our stocking that we are ready at any moment to turn it inside out & how can we not feel emulous when we see Hitler juggling with his sausage of a stocking. Our chosen colour is blue, & blue shirts are marching about all over the country, and their organiser tells me that it was my suggestion – a suggestion I have entirely forgotten – that made them select for their flag a red St Patrick's cross on a blue ground – all I can remember is that I have always denounced green &

commended blue (the colour of my early book covers). The chance of being shot is raising everybody's spirits enormously. There is some politics for you of which your newspapers know nothing (I can write it because my letters are not being opened).

History is very simple – the rule of the many, then the rule of the few, day & night, night & day for ever, while in small disturbed nations day & night race.[23]

As this hints, he was at work once more on *A Vision*, and trying to relate the current upheavals to the historical cycles which preoccupied him (Hegel versus Vico again). The distanced, sceptical tone about politics is notable, as well as the studied vagueness about his own part in discussions. Shortly after this letter was written, still determined to convert his famous friend into the Blueshirt D'Annunzio, MacManus brought O'Duffy to Riversdale on 24 July, 'that I might talk my anti-democratic philosophy', as WBY put it. The meeting was not a success: George, who thought O'Duffy was a buffoon, 'noticed they spoke on different levels and neither listened to the other'.[24] The general was far from being an intellectual: his political strengths, such as they were, resided in myopic stubbornness, physical stamina, a hard head for drink, and obdurate bigotry. WBY recorded the interview in his note-book, in a form which suggests he thought of publishing it some day in one of his collections of discursive *pensées*.

McManus [*sic*] brought him [O'Duffy] that I might talk about the situation. If the I.R.A. attempt to seize power (& MacManus believes they will but I do not) or if the economic war brings chaos, then democratic politics will be discredited in this country & a substitute will have to be found. Talk was on the usual lines: the organised party directed from [a]bove, each district dominated by its ablest men, my own principle 'That every government is a tyranny but by the government of the educated classes & that the state must be hierarchical throughout. 'De Valera has described himself to somebody as the autocrat expressing the feeling of the masses. If we must have an autocrat let him express what Swift called 'the bent & current of a people', not a momentary majority. I urged the getting of a recent 3 volume description of the Italian system (FitzGerald talks of it) & putting some Italian sc[h]olars to make a condensation of it. I urged also that unless a revolutionary crisis rose they must make no intervention. They should prepare themselves by study to act without hesitation should the crisis arise. Then, & then only, their full programme. I talked the 'historical dialectic', spoke of it as moving itself by events as the curvature of space was proved (after mathematics had it worked out) by observation during an eclipse. O'Duffy probably brought here that I might talk of it.

What O'Duffy made of this may be imagined. He was probably no further enlightened by the 'Genealogical Tree of Revolution' sketched by WBY in the same notebook. One branch descended (on the left-hand side) from Nicholas de Cusa through Marx and dialectical materialism, eventually 'crushing the past, justifying hatred', and putting the party above the state –

'the Proleteriat justified, because having nothing it can reject all'. On the right-hand branch, a different kind of evolution descended through, once again, Neoplatonism and Italian philosophy, to arrive at a political system in which 'the past is honoured, hatred is condemned, the state is above the party, and Fascism is "the final aim"'.[25]

This was wby's preferred route, but his idea of 'Fascism' was not everybody's. For one thing, 'the family and the individual' were judged 'wiser than governments'. wby carefully lists principles upon which 'creative individuals' and their families deserve privilege in order to achieve 'complete culture': they should be allowed to 'prolong the education of [their] children for as many years as their nature & gifts demand'; 'structure and tradition' must be preserved. This is little different from the oligarchic and aristocratic ideas he had been drawn to all his life. The Italian ideas which he had inspirationally reinvented since his 1907 visit to Urbino and Ferrara with the Gregorys and his subsequent discovery of *Il Cortegiano* were at least as influential as Mussolini's march on Rome. The notion of 'new kinds of aristocracy' was in line with Mussolini's early rhetoric but had little to do with what Fascism meant by 1933. As MacManus later put it, 'Yeats was not a fascist, but he was an authoritarian.'[26] O'Duffy's idea of Irish *fascisti* was dramatically different from wby's. MacManus's visionary streak was more appealing, but again his prophecies were retailed by wby with an ironic distance.

'We shall be assassinated', he said, 'but others have been chosen to take our place' – his dream perhaps but possibly not. Italy, Poland, Germany then perhaps Ireland. Doubtless I shall hate it (though not so much as I hate Irish democracy) but it is September and we must not behave like the gay young sparks of May or June.[27]

Thus wby not only anticipated a historical cycle bringing in a revolutionary ascendancy, but expected that he himself would be at odds with it – probably because of O'Duffy's aggressive Catholicism. As Grattan Freyer has put it, instead of eighteenth-century elitism the Blueshirts seemed to offer – yet again – clerical autocracy. And this, for wby, was the most ancient enemy of all.

As it happened, MacManus's 'heroic' expectations were punctured a fortnight later, when de Valera banned the March on Dublin. The National Guard (though constitutional and, so far, law abiding) were banned on 21 August. They remained an ominous presence, but instead of directly threatening the powers of the state they regrouped as the League of Youth and began to merge into a general anti-Fianna Fáil coalition. This would produce the new parliamentary party Fine Gael, launched in early September. O'Duffy remained for the moment the dominant figure, but the trend of opposition politics shifted to straightforward anti-government rhetoric rather than imported Fascistic trimmings. Nonetheless, the autumn of 1933 saw the disruption of political meetings, a certain amount of street fighting, and tough government measures against prominent members of the Young Ireland Association. O'Duffy became noticeably erratic, and was increasingly perceived as an embarrassment. His colleagues fell back on the traditional cries of popular nationalism and an end to the economic war: xenophobic echoes and corporatist organization would remain the only political inheritances of the para-fascist movement. Banned or not, the Blueshirt presence remained active in 1934, organizing rallies and maintaining its following of about 30,000 supporters. But by then de Valera's government was taking a firm line with the IRA through military tribunals; the Communist threat was no more apparent than it had ever been; and the ominous linkage between the Blueshirts and disaffected elements in the army and police forces had perished. O'Duffy, fuelled by alcohol and instability, adopted more and more stridently Fascist views. In December 1933 Ottoline Morrell remarked to WBY that she had heard Hitler described as 'a "medium" only to express the desires of a Nation'; WBY responded 'that was the case with O'Duffey [*sic*]'.[28] But by the summer of 1936 the general was marching determinedly towards the political waste land.

Well before then, WBY had carefully diluted his support. His correspondents in England were now treated to Irish politics as a comic spectacle, with O'Duffy as Punchinello. In August he told Dulac, 'Here we are in the excitement of "the blue shirts". Fashist ideas started up in the country some two or three months ago & now they cannot make the shirts fast enough. The government is like a disturbed ant-hill.'[29] Even the misspellings suggest detachment. Yet his imagination had certainly been stirred by the crisis, and his extravagant and dramatic descriptions of events suggest a hope that excitement was returning to Irish politics, and perhaps even the chance of a transfiguring moment. And he was prepared to write 'songs' for the movement: or, perhaps, to hope that the stirring of political excitement might stimulate him to write poetry again.

References to the Blueshirts are rare in his correspondence after the summer of 1933. From that autumn until the following spring, the movement increased its popular membership, becoming more aggressive in its tactics and less like 'Fascism modified by religion'. By the spring of 1934 political activity was concentrating on the rural issue of cattle prices, and O'Duffy's increasingly hysterical leadership was driving 'respectables' away from the movement, though his invocation of Fascist principles continued to raise echoes in Ireland. WBY's Abbey Theatre colleague Walter Starkie, who was married to an Italian and lived part of the year in Liguria, emerged as the leading Irish advocate for 'the import of Italian Fascism';[30] however, he was also a passionate devotee of Central European gypsy culture, which would not fare well under National Socialism. Ernest Blythe was another enthusiast, producing the most closely detailed outline of an Irish Fascist political system. Otherwise, Irish intellectuals who advocated Fascism tended to be fervently Catholic university professors and politicians – never a constituency immediately sympathetic to WBY.

And yet he wrote 'Three Marching Songs' for the movement between the unrest of the autumn of 1933 and February 1934 – when the *Spectator* published versions, with WBY's elaborate disclaimers of his own political commitment. 'A friend' had suggested that WBY write something for the movement; this may have been MacManus, but drafts of the 'Marching Songs' exist in Ernest Blythe's papers, amended by WBY and apparently sent by him in late November.[31] Blythe, moreover, in his 'Onlooker' column for the Blueshirt paper, was publishing songs for the movement from October 1933, echoing current Dáil debates about the alleged need for a new 'National Song'. WBY's efforts were sent to him a week after this public discussion. The Blueshirts had adopted the Gaelic air 'O Donnell Abu' as its theme-tune, and WBY wrote three 'songs' to fit its lilting rhythm, which was difficult enough, since each stanza ended with four stressed beats. (It was composed in the early nineteenth century by a talented Irish regimental bandmaster in the British Army, who also invented the Kent bugle.) Unsurprisingly, the Blueshirts adopted a simpler doggerel, under the title 'Blueshirts Abu'.[32] But there were other reasons for rejecting WBY's productions: the 'three songs', even in the versions he eventually published, are at once strident, obscure, and bathetic.

The first 'song', as originally written, presents the imperatives of sacrificial Irish history: 'Justify all those renowned generations,/Justify all that have sunk in their blood'. The attached chorus makes an elephantine attempt at the demotic:

> *Those fanatics all that we do would undo;*
> *Down the fanatic, down the clown;*
> *Down, down, hammer them down,*
> *Down to the tune of O'Donnell Abu.*

However, an incident of February 1934 suggested a different refrain to WBY, which he substituted on its next publication at the end of that year. George, 'who hates Blueshirts', had complained to their Blueshirt-supporting neighbours, the Weldons, that their dog had killed one of her beloved hens, and been told that the dog was promptly destroyed – with three others. ('Note the Hitler touch,' WBY pointedly remarked.) To her added horror, the missing hen subsequently turned up, and WBY advised that it be hastily consigned to the pot. This domestic incident, like a black version of a tale from *Cranford*, was to be clumsily introduced into a 'song' celebrating the 'renowned generations' who 'defended Ireland's soul':

> 'Drown all the dogs,' said the fierce young woman,
> 'They killed my goose and a cat.
> Drown, drown in the water-butt,
> Drown all the dogs,' said the fierce young woman.

The point about this ludicrous change is that almost as soon as the 'songs' were published, WBY disclaimed the apparent political intention behind them; he was determined to introduce private, obscure references in order to destabilize or subvert the public 'message'. The second 'song', as it appeared in the *Spectator*, invoked 'Grandfather', an emblem of you-be-damned insouciance, preaching from the gallows in 'the great Rebellion' that 'good strong blows are delights to the mind'. On the next printing of the 'songs', it was promoted to first place. The third 'song', as originally published, began

> Soldiers take pride in saluting their Captain,
> The devotee proffers a knee to his Lord,
> Some take delight in adorning a woman.
> What's equality – Muck in the yard:
> *Historic Nations grow*
> *From above to below.*

On its next outing, the strident fourth line turned into the Yeatsian reflection 'Troy looked on Helen, it died and adored', and the last couplet, 'Great nations, blossom above;/A slave bows down to a slave'. WBY's doubts had been there at the beginning. The rationalization which he offered to the *Spectator*'s readers when the poems were published on 23 February 1934 deserves quotation in full:

In politics I have but one passion and one thought, rancour against all who, except under the most dire necessity, disturb public order, a conviction that public order cannot long persist without the rule of educated and able men. That order was everywhere their work, is still as much a part of their tradition as the *Iliad* or the Republic of Plato; their rule once gone, it lies an empty shell for the passing fool to kick in pieces. Some months ago that passion laid hold upon me with the violence which unfits the poet for all politics but his own. While the mood lasted, it seemed that our growing disorder, the fanaticism that inflamed it like some old bullet imbedded in the flesh, was about to turn our noble history into an ignoble farce. For the first time in my life I wanted to write what some crowd in the street might understand and sing; I asked my friends for a tune; they recommended that old march, 'O'Donnell Abu.' I first got my chorus, 'Down the fanatic, down the clown,' then the rest of the first song. But I soon tired of its rhetorical vehemence, thought that others would tire of it unless I found some gay playing upon its theme, some half-serious exaggeration and defence of its rancorous chorus, and therefore I made the second version. Then I put into a simple song a commendation of the rule of the able and the educated, man's old delight in submission; I wrote round the line 'The soldier takes pride in saluting his captain,' thinking the while of a Gaelic poet's lament for his lost masters: 'My fathers served their fathers before Christ was crucified.' I read my songs to friends, they talked to others, those others talked, and now companies march to the words 'Blueshirt Abu,' and a song that is all about shamrocks and harps or seems all about them, because its words have the particular variation upon the cadence of 'Yankee Doodle' Young Ireland reserved for that theme. I did not write that song; I could not if I tried. Here are my songs. Anybody may sing them, choosing 'clown' and 'fanatic' for himself, if they are singable – musicians say they are, but may flatter – and worth singing.

His letter to the *Spectator*'s editor on 18 February also betrays a certain nervousness.

If you care for the enclosed poems and preliminary note I would be greatly obliged if The Spectator could publish them as soon as possible. A great deal has happened about them here. They were to have been sung from the Abbey Theatre stage tomorrow night but at the last moment I have been compelled to withdraw them. The situation both between the Government and the I.R.A. and between the Blueshirts and the I.R.A. has become too acute. For certain reasons I am very anxious to have them published immediately and in some paper that has no connection with Irish parties.[33]

George typed this letter, and her influence may have been brought to bear. She hated the Blueshirts and, though she thought the Songs 'terrible', may have encouraged WBY to defuse them by getting into print with a disclaimer as soon as he could.[34] As for the Blueshirts themselves, they had more or less given up hope of enlisting the National Poet. Their official journal carried an item on 3 March 1934:

Songs by Yeats

In the issue of the London 'Spectator' of February 23rd there are three interesting songs by WB Yeats, who is the greatest living poet writing in English. The three songs are all to be sung to the tune of 'O'Donnell Abu'. One of them seems to be a poetical restatement of the central doctrine of Fascism. Another is a light whimsical song which might make a barrack room ballad. The remaining song is one which would not be unsuitable for occasional singing at League of Youth functions, though possibly that is to some extent ruled out by the fact that the official rallying song is to the same tune.

The 'official rallying song', 'March of Youth', was much nearer the mark than WBY could aim.

Ireland we serve! To the death we shall serve thee,
Mother of Collins, the upright and gay.
Mother of Griffith, O'Higgins, O'Reilly,
Glory shall crown thee at the eve of our day.
Tyrants would have us quail,
Onward we'll never fail –
Leal as Hugh Reilly who died for the Blue.
Plighted to God and Right
Naught can resist our might
On, youth of Erin; the Blueshirts Abu![35]

For the next printing of his own 'Songs' in *Poetry*, WBY extended the accompanying note. He also changed the title of the ironic accompanying squib from 'A Vain Hope' to 'Church and State'.

Here is fresh matter, poet,
Matter for old age meet;
Might of the Church and State,
Their mobs put under their feet.
O but heart's wine shall run pure,
Mind's bread grow sweet.

That were a cowardly song,
Wander in dreams no more;
What if the Church and the State
Are the mob that howls at the door!
Wine shall run thick to the end,
Bread taste sour.

By the time the 'Three Songs to the Same Tune' had been sanitized and reprinted, WBY's creative power had returned. That same month, December 1934, would see the publication of the wonderful 'Supernatural Songs', which anticipated the great achievements of his last five years. He had already proved he could write a great political poem in a very different mode: 'A Parnellite at Parnell's Funeral'. Here, a fusion is achieved between the comet that appeared the dark night of Parnell's funeral, the Archer vision which had obsessed WBY since his haunted visit to Tillyra with Arthur Symons nearly forty years before, the myth of the Platonic Year, and his own disillusionment with Irish politics.

Under the Great Comedian's tomb the crowd;
A bundle of tempestuous cloud is blown
About the sky, where that is clear of cloud
Brightness remains; a brighter star shoots down;
What shudders run through all that animal blood?

What is this sacrifice? Can someone there
Recall the Cretan barb that pierced a star?

Rich foliage that the starlight glittered through,
A frenzied crowd, and where the branches sprang
A beautiful seated boy; a sacred bow;
A woman, and an arrow on a string;
A pierced boy, image of a star laid low.
That woman, the Great Mother imaging,
Cut out his heart. Some master of design
Stamped boy and tree upon Sicilian coin.

An age is the reversal of an age;
When strangers murdered Emmet, Fitzgerald, Tone;
We lived like men that watch a painted stage.
What matter for the scene, the scene once gone:
It had not touched our lives; but popular rage
Hysterica Passio, dragged this quarry down.
None shared our guilt; nor did we play a part
Upon a painted stage when we devoured his heart.

Come, fix upon me that accusing eye,
I thirst for accusation. All that was sung,
All that was said in Ireland is a lie
Bred out of the contagion of the throng,
Saving the rhyme rats hear before they die.
Leave nothing but the nothings that belong
To this bare soul, let all men judge that can
Whether it be an animal or a man.

First published in 1932, it was reprinted in the *Spectator*, on 19 October 1934, with a coda headed 'Forty Years Later'.

I pass the rest – one sentence I unsay –
Had de Valera eaten Parnell's heart
No loose lipped demagogue had won the day,
No civil rancour torn the land apart.

Had Cosgrave eaten Parnell's heart, the land's
Imagination had been satisfied,
Or lacking that, government in such hands
O'Higgins its sole statesman had not died.

Had even O'Duffy – but I name no more –
Their school the crowd, his master solitude,
Through Jonathan Swift's dark grove he passed and there
Plucked bitter wisdom that enriched his blood.

This announced a return to Olympianism. By the light of Parnell's aristocratic star, de Valera was a demagogue, Cosgrave earthbound and uninspir-
ing, O'Duffy not even worth considering. The images appropriate to the
lost leader come from Frazer's *Golden Bough* and Dante's *Inferno*, proper
companions for a dead king and a great poet. And Swift, as ever, represents
the brilliance of intellect by which a nation should be rightly ruled, but
never would. As for the Blueshirts, WBY's disillusionment arose not from
the fact that they became Fascist, but that their commitment to Fascism, as
he understood it, did not go far enough.

WBY's excitement about an Irish Fascist movement in 1933 should be
seen in the light of his own creative stasis, and his fear that the loss of Coole
a year before had meant the loss of his inspiration. As always, he was
prepared ruthlessly to search out themes in unlikely places, and work up
his own poetic energies through a willing suspension of incredulity. He had
infused himself with creative power through bizarre transactions often
enough before this, from Golden Dawn rituals to the invention of Leo
Africanus. But his interest in the Blueshirts is also a logical development
from his reactions to 'the present state of the world' in 1919, through his
anticipation of totalitarian developments in European politics in 'If I
were Four-and-Twenty', to his interest in the Fascist dispensation created
by Mussolini. His withdrawal from O'Duffy's movement is principally
explained by the fact that, rather than becoming an interpretation of
Italian Fascism, it seemed by early 1934 to be drawing on elements in
Irish politics that were all too familiar – Catholic zealotry, nationalist
exclusiveness, and rural agitation. WBY's interest in Fascism, which he had
come to through cloudy philosophy and distaste for lumpen-democracy,
remained; but he avoided publicly endorsing the Blueshirts (or, interestingly, Fine Gael, though he apparently voted for them). In so far as Irish
politics went, he would look more and more kindly on de Valera. The
Fascist tag stuck, and his very late political writings would revive it. But this
was partly a question of cultivating a furious style *pour épater* the Irish
bourgeoisie. The distinguished soldier and diplomat Ian Hamilton, asked
in 1940 by WBY's first biographer to put down on paper his reminiscences of
the poet, ended with a mischievous comparison which Hone had some
reservations about printing:

During my two hours talk last year with Adolph [*sic*] Hitler, as I listened to his
eager, nervy voice running up and down the gamut of the emotional scales – laughter, sorrow, pity – the thought kept on rising at the back of my head like a question
mark – 'where ever have I heard some one speak like this – who would it have been?'
– then suddenly, as he spoke of his nightingales, the mirror of memory flashed and
there I was listening again to Yeats.[36]

To an extent perhaps unrecognized, WBY's affinity with Fascism (not National Socialism) was a matter of rhetorical style; and the achievement of style, as he himself had decreed long before, was closely connected to shock tactics.

II

The 'Three Songs to the Same Tune' remained one of the few poetic products of the months since Gregory's death. 'I have written little poetry during the last two years,' he told Sturm. 'I have been writing philosophical essays for the most part, finishing what would otherwise be unfinished. I pack my old age with thought to balance the excessive emotionalism of my youth.'[37] He continued to work on the Introduction to Bhagwan Shri Hamsa's *The Holy Mountain*, spurred on by gushing letters from the Swami, who seems to have learned the patois of his female followers ('the way you have interpreted the thing seems to me so romantic & exalted'[38]). These were interwoven with more disgruntled reflections on the incomprehensible fact that Macmillan was selling hardly any copies of the sage's own autobiography; by April 1934 WBY, like many others, was chipping in with financial contributions to pay the Swami's Bayswater rent ('it was very sweet of you to send it'[39]). But for the moment his thoughts were turning away from Indian asceticism, and back to the lost demesne of Coole.

In early 1934 WBY immersed himself in the planned memoir of Gregory, conscious as ever of the way biography would fix both their images in Irish history. (At this time too, Oliver Edwards began interviewing him for a full biography, and Sean O'Faolain was already at work on a similar project; neither would approach completion.[40]) A letter to Shakespear conveys something of the excitement with which he relived the days when he first discovered sanctuary among the Seven Woods – the period of his life when he had loved and (foolishly, he now thought) lost Olivia herself.

I come out of my reveries to write to you. I do nothing all day long but think of the drama I am building up in my *Lady Gregory*. I have drawn Martyn and his house, Lady Gregory and hers, have brought George Moore on the scene, finished a long analysis of him, which pictures for the first time that preposterous person. These first chapters are sensational and exciting and will bring George much household money when she sends them out to English and American magazines. I am just beginning on Woburn Buildings, building up the scene there – alas the most significant image of those years must be left out . . . It is curious how one's life falls into definite sections – in 1897 a new scene was set, new actors appeared.[41]

Ten days later he told Harold Macmillan that he had written fifty pages: 'it will be a considerable book and contain a great deal that is new'.[42] He had been 'collecting material, letters, etc.' (mainly his own letters to Gregory, returned since her death), and it would be his principal work for the next year. He was, in a sense, cauterizing the wound left by the loss of Coole, and bidding a last farewell to his old friend. As he began to write in January, he recorded that an apparition which had appeared ten times in recent months had finally materialized as 'an arm waving goodby at the edge of a screen beside my door; it has not appeared since'.[43] He no longer described the project as a biography of Lady Gregory but as 'a book about the Irish literary movement' and its personalities. The eventual title almost suggested itself: *Dramatis Personae.*

The notebook in which he began writing that early spring of 1934 has a fair number of excisions, but the first draft (though still titled 'Coole Park') is strikingly close to the book published by Cuala in 1935.[44] The opening paragraph is almost word for word. A long time ago, in another age, the young hero, like Childe Roland or the protagonist of a Maturin novel, approaches a mysterious castle.

When I was thirty years old the three great demesnes of three Galway houses, Coole House, Tulira Castle, Roxborough House, lay within a half-hour or two hours' walk of each other. They were so old they seemed unchanging; now all have been divided among small farmers, their great ancient trees cut down. Roxborough House was burnt down during the Civil War; Coole House has passed to the Forestry Department; but Tulira Castle is inhabited by blood relatives of those who built it. I went there with Arthur Symons, the editor of the *Savoy* magazine [in 1897]. I was taking him here and there through Ireland. We had just been sightseeing in Sligo [& Aran]. Edward Martyn, met in London, perhaps with George Moore, had seemed so heavy, uncouth, countrified that I said as we turned in at the gate: 'We shall be waited on by a barefooted servant.' I was recalling [perhaps] a house seen at Sligo when a child. Then I saw the great trees, then the grey wall of the Castle.

It is a wonderful prelude, establishing atmosphere and characters with magical deftness. But WBY moves swiftly to destabilize and subvert all these impressions. The Castle is of course not 'so old it seems unchanging' but (in a passage much redrafted) 'among the worst inventions of the [modern] Gothic Revival'. Martyn's taste is anything but 'uncouth' – 'an abstract mind that would see nothing in life but its vulgarity and temptations' and – in a deleted passage – 'had learned from some priest that almost all lost souls were lost through sex'. WBY's delineation of Martyn's imprisonment in lifedenying aestheticism is brilliant in its subtle suggestion of a 'secret torture'; he deleted a phrase about how his host 'always resisted homosexuality', perhaps because it is hardly necessary. His conclusion that Martyn 'would never learn to write; his mind was a fleshless skeleton' may be unfair, but connects neatly to WBY's other explanation for this host's 'sterility'. 'Two traditions met and destroyed each other in his blood', when his father, from the old Catholic Galway gentry, married a woman 'but one generation from the peasant'. This not only restates the central apposition of 'Modern Ireland' and 'Parnell's Funeral' but anticipates a theme that would pre-occupy WBY for the final years of life and dominate his last play, *Purgatory*. The portrait of Martyn's frustrated and inverted life also serves as a contrasting prelude to the great theme of the book: the culture of Coole as an Ireland that might have been.

In the first draft WBY's portrait of Gregory follows hard upon that of Martyn, succeeded by a description of Coole. He then reversed the two, moving from his speculation about Martyn straight to a description of the house which he 'came to love more than all other houses', and which taught him the value of the eighteenth-century inheritance and the meaning of an accumulated culture, symbolized by lovingly itemized objects, paintings, and traditions. It is no accident that the catalogue highlights, among the marble statues, Mughal paintings, and great silver bowls, a framed letter from Edmund Burke. The house's chatelaine is drawn with equal care: WBY excised his original remark that 'old Mrs Martyn had said that [Lady Gregory] was clever and that women were afraid of her', as well as a more flowery reflection that her face had 'all the charm a vivid character can give by expression & with every charm of character'. The final version paints her with restraint and a certain eighteenth-century directness.

Lady Gregory, as I first knew her, was a plainly dressed woman of forty-five, with-out obvious good looks, except the charm that comes from strength, intelligence and kindness. One who knew her at an earlier date speaks of her dark skin, of an extreme vitality, and a portrait by Mrs Jopling that may have flattered shows con-siderable beauty.

In fact, when they met first that vitality had been very much in evidence; the record of the time suggests that WBY's first reconnoitre of Coole was marked by a mutual excitement as well as a charged atmosphere of storytelling and hilarity. He also diluted a reference to her tolerance of sexual misconduct.[45] Nor does his description suggest Gregory's mischievous humour, or her facility for ruthless manoeuvring. She represents the 'feudal, almost medieval' culture of the Persse family, Protestant seventeenth-century planters: marked by strong passions and distinctive enthusiasms. But 'all had lacked intellectual curiosity until the downfall of their class had all but come.' And then they produced John Shawe-Taylor the land reformer, Hugh Lane the art connoisseur, and their aunt Augusta Gregory.

Thus *Dramatis Personae* is infused with reflections which owe their perspective on the distant 1890s to the conditions of de Valera's Ireland (WBY carefully notes that 'Free State Ministers were fond of recounting the adventures of Lady Gregory's "Seven Brothers"', which sounds like rather special pleading). Moore's accusations of Protestant proselytizing by the Persses is dismissed. So is anything else in Gregory's background and character incompatible with WBY's intention to immortalize her in the fresco of an Irish tradition which – in his idealized view – amounted to a natural aristocracy, directly related to the faith of the people.

She knew Ireland always in its permanent relationships, associations – violence but a brief interruption –, never lost her sense of feudal responsibility, not of duty as the word is generally understood, but of burdens laid upon her by her station and her character, a choice continually renewed in solitude. 'She has been', said an old man to me, 'like a serving-maid among us. She is plain and simple, like the Mother of God, and that was the greatest lady that ever lived'.

Yet *Dramatis Personae* is also intended to establish WBY himself at the centre of Irish experience. Adrift though he had felt when he came to the harbour of Coole, he had already founded (by implication, single-handedly) the Irish Literary Societies of London and Dublin – adding, with superb inaccuracy, 'no political purpose informed our meetings'. Now he wanted to reach another Irish audience; he outlined his hopes that, even if he had to live outside Ireland, his books would return there like the crows who congregated nightly in the vast rookeries of Tillyra.

There follows what became the canonical account of the founding of the Irish Literary Theatre, when Gregory takes him to de Basterot's lonely house on the Clare–Galway coast: a scene straight from *The Speckled Bird*. The ensuing organization, fundraising, and agitation are ascribed entirely to Gregory and himself; in the original draft he mentions Martyn's contribution and his offer to guarantee expenses, but this was ungraciously deleted. The other drama of his personal life – his 'miserable love affair' – is mentioned, but only as the background to the revelations that come through his folklore-collecting expeditions with Gregory, recording 'actual experience of the supernatural'. The story of the theatre drives the narrative on, and climaxes in a masterly and malicious dissection of George Moore: described proudly by WBY himself to Macmillan as 'a very vivid and surprising account'.

This is no more than the truth. The generosity of WBY's reaction in his American interview on hearing of Moore's death was not to be sustained. As long ago as 1927 Horace Reynolds had heard that 'Yeats is writing up himself and Moore to be published after Moore's death'.[46] He had long meditated his revenge for *Hail and Farewell*, and here it was. Moore is set off against Martyn, 'the peasant sinner, the peasant saint' ('Lady Gregory once told me what marriage coarsened the Moore blood, but I have forgotten': the theme of *Purgatory* again). Moore's artistic and dramatic understanding is limited: 'He knew nothing but facts' and only felt 'sincere remorse when he thought he had injured somebody's financial interests'.[47] Above all, in personal relations he 'sacrificed all that seemed to other men good breeding, honour, friendship in pursuit of what he considered the root facts of life'. In a much redrafted series of vignettes, WBY conveyed Moore's vulgarity, posturing, and pathos. He is glimpsed gushing over the proofs of WBY's Blake book, denouncing a cab-driver, showing off about his alleged sexual liaisons. Some stories are too good not to allow his subject a 'brutal wit', and WBY tells them with a flair that suggests the kind of conversationalist he must have been. They also betray the pleasure to be found in keeping company with Moore.

He and I went to the town of Galway for a Gaelic festival that coincided with some assembly of priests. When we lunched at the Railway Hotel the room was full of priests. A Father Moloney, supposed to know all about Greek Art, caught sight of Moore and introduced himself. He probably knew nothing about Moore, except that he was some kind of critic, for he set out upon his favourite topic with: 'I have always considered it a proof of Greek purity that though they left the male form uncovered, they invariably draped the female'. 'Do you consider, Father Moloney,' said Moore in a voice that rang through the whole room, 'that the female form is inherently more indecent than the male?' Every priest turned a stern and horrified eye upon Father Moloney, who sat hunched up and quivering.

At the centre of this economical but complete character assassination was the assertion that in matters of art (Moore's guiding, indeed only, principle) he was as maladroit as he could be in everyday social life. His great realist novels lacked style, depth, variety. WBY deleted from his first draft an interesting comment on his own reaction to *Esther Waters*: he took six weeks to read it 'to [Moore's] great disgust for I am a slow reader but I read it with admiration'. Moore's fundamental ignorance betrayed him in every aspect of life (even down to his not knowing how to attach braces to the waistband of his trousers).

He had gone to Paris straight from his father's racing stables, from a house where there was no culture, as Symons and I understood the word, acquired copious inaccurate French, sat among art students, young writers about to become famous, in some café; a man carved out of a turnip, looking out of astonished eyes.

This inspired image was suggested by Manet's wonderful portrait, but WBY was offhand even about Moore's indisputable acuity as critic of the great post-Impressionists. Every old score was paid off. Moore had laughed at

WBY's inability to speak French, so WBY dismissed Moore's own command of the language; Moore had hilariously recounted WBY's allegedly chaste pursuit of Maud Gonne, so WBY satirized the motives behind Moore's supposed conquests, as well as his literary affectations. The last sentence of this pen-portrait, which achieves its murderous effect through an amused tone of casual condescension, says it all: 'In later life he wrote a long preface to prove that he had a mistress in Mayfair.'

With the characters established, WBY turns back to his life in the closing years of the previous century: Florence Farr's chanting to the psaltery, his own impoverished life in Woburn Buildings, the visits to saturnine George Pollexfen, the world of the Golden Dawn (unnamed), and the '98 centennial movement. The trigger of all these memories was the great cache of his letters to Coole. Gregory's indomitable spirit, her impeccable standards, her unobtrusive generosity are implicitly counterpointed against the ridiculous Moore. In a telling passage WBY described ('after a struggle with myself') how she subsidized him over the years until he made enough on an American tour to pay her back. He added but deleted, 'Since then I have never had a debt to any one & it hurts my pride to record the debt but it is right that I should witness to her generosity & to her wisdom.' It is a moving passage, frank and surprising: but what Margaret Gough made of it can well be imagined.

The central sections of the memoir deal with the venture of the Irish Literary Theatre: high comedy, with Martyn and Moore acting their allotted *opera buffa* parts. The marvellous theological row over *The Countess Kathleen* is played for all it is worth; the perspective of WBY's account is decisively influenced by his renewed struggles with Irish censorship over the past decade and his invention of Crazy Jane. 'The Countess sells her soul, but she is not transformed. If I were to think out that scene today, she would, the moment her hand has signed, burst into loud laughter, mock at all she has held holy, horrify the peasants in the midst of their temptations.' The account of *fin de siècle* politics, in one of the few structural infelicities, intervenes before the narrative returns to the Theatre's next season. WBY's preoccupations of the 1930s seep into his analysis of nationalism at the turn of the century. 'Protestant Ireland . . . lacked hereditary passion. Parnell, its last great figure, finding that this lack had made the party of my father's old friend Isaac Butt powerless, called in the peasants' tenacity and violence, but for months now the peasants had stood aside and waited, hoping that their old masters might take the leadership again.' This is a very idiosyncratic reading indeed. But in great set-pieces like the public dinner given by T. P. Gill at the Shelbourne in May 1899, WBY presented a beautifully worked refutation of the version immortalized by Moore in *Ave*. J. F. Taylor's oratory, and Standish O'Grady's prophecy of a military movement that would follow literary revival, intone a Wagnerian overture to the still-distant revolution. Where Moore ridiculed, WBY conjured up a sense of the transforming history to come.

Against this, the drama behind the scenes of the Literary Theatre is played out at Coole: the agonized Martyn–Moore collaboration over *The Bending of the Bough*, Moore's increasingly exaggerated and coarse behaviour ('He was like a mob – as I have told him – always an enthusiastic supporter or a noisy interrupter' [deleted]). The first seasons of the Irish Literary Theatre are treated quite perfunctorily: again and again, the focus fixes on Moore, his manic demands for attention, his fabulism, his plagiarizing of stories from Huysmans or Maupassant to claim as part of his own life. Even his complaints about the food in the Shelbourne are vitiated by both culinary ignorance and linguistic insufficiency. '"He has written to the proprietress", said the manager, "that the steak is like brown paper. How can you believe a word such a man would say, a steak cannot be like brown paper."' As Robinson had remarked to Reynolds, 'Moore can say cruel things only after he has spent some time thinking them up. Yeats has the advantage in that he can put them off the end of his tongue.'[48]

Finally, the account of WBY's collaboration with Moore on *Diarmuid and Grania* allows him to puncture Moore's literary ineptness with the skewer-point of WBY's own commitment to style, and to enjoy a long-postponed compensation for Moore's victory at the time. The question of achieved style, in fact, sparks off one of WBY's most intense (and revealing) passages of self-scrutiny. He compares his father's inability to finish his pictures, which 'sank through innumerable sittings into final confusion', to Goethe's failure to represent Faust. This is in turn related to the 'religious and philosophical confusion' that awaited twentieth-century man[49] and his own abandonment of his 'first manner . . . the sentimental *Land of Heart's Desire*, the tapestry-like *Countess Cathleen*'. It is not a complete repudiation. The connection between his early style and 'popular songs and stories' was powerful enough, he reflects, for it to have, perhaps, some unfulfilled potential: here, the poet of the mid 1930s can be discerned, moving to a new style after a period of stasis, and rediscovering a form which echoes ballad and rann. But, as far as Moore was concerned, 'his nature, bitter, violent, discordant, did not fit him to write the sentences men murmur again and again for years'. The echo of 'Easter 1916' is intentional: WBY by now had spectacularly demonstrated that his own work had achieved this immortalizing effect beyond question. As for Hyde, he had had the potential to do the same, but had given it up – though the purity and concreteness of his beautiful translations from Irish showed the path Gregory would take and illuminate in her own way.

Thus the characters of the story are interwoven with their *raison d'être*, the revival of Irish literature; the behavioural comedy of life is constructed with appropriately Balzacian flexibility, capaciousness, and mastery of the malicious aside. The story moves through the magnificent episode of the Benson production of *Diarmuid and Grania*, and wby's ensuing depression, uncertainty, and unpopularity in Dublin, to the discovery of William and Frank Fay and the first – already legendary – production of *Cathleen ni Houlihan* in April 1902. Here, in contrast to the condescending character-izations of his Stockholm speech and American lectures, wby is careful to identify the Fays only as leaders of a respected 'amateur company': the fury of Brigit Fay had, perhaps, made its mark.[50] *Cathleen ni Houlihan* was, he carefully notes, 'written with Lady Gregory's help', as was *The Pot of Broth*; slowly, repertoire and interpretive style evolved. But Moore cannot be kept out. The last great set-piece, much rewritten, retails their quarrel over the plot of *Where there is Nothing*, and wby's stealing a march to victory by pub-lishing his version in *United Ireland*.

I look back with some remorse. 'Yeats,' Moore had said, 'a man can have only one conscience, mine is artistic.' Had I abandoned my plot and made him write the novel, he might have put beside *Muslin* and *The Lake* a third masterpiece, but I was young, vain, self-righteous, and bent on proving myself a man of action.

Now, he could afford to be generous. But to make this incident the basis of his estrangement from Moore deflected attention from *Hail and Farewell*, the text which lies beneath *Dramatis Personae*. wby deleted some specific references to it in his first draft, and he never mentions Moore's wounding portrait of Gregory and their subsequent enmity. Reviewing the book a year later, Padraic Colum offered a pertinent critique:

'Hail and Farewell' exists in its own right: its historic justice or reality is something that readers of the future will trouble themselves very little about. Yeats's counter-attack in 'Dramatis Personae' does not show good generalship. He does not attempt to outflank the gigantic line of 'Hail and Farewell' – instead he attacks a little salient and the attack is not very well organised.

Moore, as Colum points out, was more original, talented, and (as it happened) aristocratic in his attitudes than wby allows: 'Yeats makes too much of George Moore's ignorance and he is not really the man to establish it.' Moore might have written a novel about the thirteenth century in which the hero attends Parisian salons, but in *Dramatis Personae* itself wby asserts that the *Bhagavadgita* was composed before the Gospels. 'Imaginative writers who want to manipulate the facts of cultural history had better leave each other alone.'[51]

Colum also criticized the odd detachment in wby's portraits of Synge and Gregory: they are presented as embodied attitudes, not as people who inspired the author's affection. This is true, but it misses the point of WBY's presentation. The conclusion of his memoir moves back to Gregory, analysing the motives which impelled her to write and the literary figure who emerged: an achieved personality whose tradition, background, and style are integrated in a manner impossible for Moore. And it is with Moore that WBY's final reflection begins:

A writer must die every day he lives, be reborn, as it is said in the Burial Service, an incorruptible self, that self opposite of all that he has named 'himself'. George Moore, dreading the annihilation of an impersonal bleak realism, used life like a mediaeval ghost making a body for itself out of drifting dust and vapour; and have I not sung in describing guests at Coole – 'There one that ruffled in a manly pose, For all his timid heart' – that one myself? Synge was a sick man picturing energy, a doomed man picturing gaiety; Lady Gregory, in her life much artifice, in her nature much pride, was born to see the glory of the world in a peasant mirror.

Thus Gregory, prepared to 'die every day she lived', comes to epitomize one of WBY's most famous creative imperatives. The book ends with Gregory's version of Grania's song over the sleeping Diarmuid, offered as an elegy to the author herself. *Dramatis Personae* was in some ways, as intended, a wonderful evocation of Coole, a portrait of Gregory, and a celebration of her work. But, as the changes of title show (from 'Lady Gregory' to 'Coole Park' to *Dramatis Personae*), it turned into the story of WBY and Moore. WBY's old adversary was not after all (as he had feared during his recent illness) to have 'the last word'. He 'filled the scene as he did in life,' WBY told Margaret Gough rather disingenuously, 'though I had not intended that he should.' Gregory might not have been altogether pleased at her own relegation, but she would have approved of the unsparing malice with which the enemy was dispatched. Many years before, when WBY began to publish his autobiographies, John Quinn had remarked that 'the texture of Yeats's memoir is Beauvais or Burgundian tapestry: Lady Gregory's will be like a Manet painting.' This did not turn out to be true. Her single memoir is (especially compared to her journals) faintly coloured and mannered, whereas WBY's final volume of autobiography is as capacious, startling, energetic, and varied as any of the great Impressionist ensemble paintings which Moore himself loved so much.[52]

III

In that spring of 1934 WBY was compelled to review his early life and the evolution of his style: not only through writing what would be his last volume of autobiography but through the reviews of his *Collected Poems*, which had appeared in late 1933. The same themes dominated his reaction to

Horace Reynolds's collection of his youthful journalism, published in 1934 within a beautiful Sturge Moore cover suggesting the lost swan-children of Lir. As this hints, wby had taken a close interest in the production. He annotated the draft Introduction which Reynolds sent him[53] and the volume carried the Preface that he had written in July 1933 – in itself another instalment of autobiography. Reading the salvos he had fired from his study in Blenheim Road all those years ago, he 'noticed that I had in later life worked out with the excitement of discovery things known in my youth as though one forgot and rediscovered oneself'. The Clubhouse in Bedford Park had been the setting for his first theatrical epiphany, when Florence Farr acted in Todhunter's *Sicilian Idyll*; from those early experiments in Arts and Crafts suburbia came all the artistic endeavour that he had made his own. He could note his own capacity for passion, his fanatical attachment to Blake and Swedenborg, his 'isolation from ordinary men and women', his 'asceticism destructive of mind and body, combined with an adoration of physical beauty that made it meaningless'. The Preface to *Letters to the New Island* does not reflect – as it well might have – on the extraordinary achievements of the man who began his career with these excited flourishes of literary criticism; instead, the author looks coolly back on his youthful self.

The article that interests me most is that written in the Dublin National Library, where everybody was working for some examination, nobody, as I thought, for his own mind's sake or to discover happiness . . . I can remember myself sitting there at the age of twenty-six or twenty-seven looking with scorn at those bowed heads and busy eyes, or in futile revery listening to my own mind as if to the sounds in a sea shell. I remember some old man, a stranger to me, saying, 'I have watched you for the past half hour and you have neither made a note nor read a word.' He had mistaken the proof sheets of *The Works of William Blake, edited and interpreted by Edwin Ellis and William Butler Yeats*, for some school or university text book, me for some ne'er-do-well student. I am certain that everybody outside my own little circle who knew anything about me thought as did that cross old man, for I was arrogant, indolent, excitable. To-day, knowing how great were the odds, I watch over my son, a boy at the preparatory school, fearing that he may grow up in my likeness.

'Sometimes', he added, 'the barrier between myself and other people filled me with terror' – a terror which provided the theme for the final version of *The Shadowy Waters*. Unable to communicate normally, he poured his 'hatred and adoration' into 'verse that expressed emotions common to every sentimental boy and girl', thus ensuring that his early poems would remain his most popular.

This harsh judgement perhaps reflects the fact that he was supervising Macmillan's publication of his *Collected Poems*, and that he was uneasily conscious of having written next to no poetry for over a year. The reviews of

11. Thomas Sturge Moore's highly-charged design for the 1934 Harvard University Press edition of *Letters to the New Island*, in dark green on light green cloth. It combines the exile-motif of the Children of Lir, transformed into wandering swans, with images of letters sealed by the masks of comedy and tragedy.

the *Collected Poems* six months later should have brought solace. Desmond MacCarthy noticed the continuity of the oeuvre, and challenged the idea of a complete shift of tone around *Responsibilities*: 'There are not two poets, Yeats I and Yeats II; one whose poetry the most modern poet can afford to ignore, the other one whom they recognise as a master. From the first he wrote out of the basis of his nature, which cannot change. The poems of the Celtic period are not to be regarded as poems of a youthful novitiate, but as an integral part of his genius.'[54] The tricks of 'compression and sudden finality in suggestion' striven for by modern 'Imagists' and 'Vorticists' were central to WBY's armoury long before: so was 'the spoken word, the homely, the perhaps harsh image, the detail fetched from life'. MacCarthy analysed WBY's continuing (if idiosyncratic) use of symbolism and incantation, his mastery of love-poetry, and – finally – the voyages of intellectual exploration which provide the freight of experience behind his most recent poetry. The change from early to late expression is not so much a change of style, in MacCarthy's view, as a change of preoccupation: from the *fin de siècle* idea of 'the artist as a being apart, shut in the world of his reveries' (just as WBY recalled in his Preface for Reynolds), to 'the predicament of the poet in the modern world', best expressed in 'Ego Dominus Tuus'.

Other critics (notably Herbert Read), reviewing WBY's work as a whole in 1934, quibbled at the effect of some of his rewriting;[55] but Edith Sitwell noted that the early and late lyrics are united by the unearthly ability to fuse sound and sense, and perceptively analysed WBY's vowel schemes, their relationship to the rhythmic plan of his poetry, and how they created a passionate and moving effect.[56] Critics in their thirties, evaluating WBY at sixty-nine, placed him at the cutting-edge of modernity. In *The Times Literary Supplement* of 5 October 1933, George Buchanan noted that WBY was now 'stirring the marrow of the younger English writers', just as he had mesmerized his own Irish generation forty years before. Ten pages of the April–June issue of the *Dublin Magazine* were devoted to reviews of *The Winding Stair, Collected Poems*, and *Letters to the New Island*. Padraic Fallon, another poet–critic in his early thirties, hailed the most recent poems as proofs of WBY's 'shape-changing energy . . . casting skin after skin till now, at the age of sixty-eight, he emerges as nearly naked as a poet may'. In Fallon's view, 'this period of *The Tower, The Winding Stair* . . . is more important than any of the earlier periods': intellectual realization had replaced romantic sensation. WBY had 'put himself under X-ray: any commonness will show clearly as a broken bone'. The iridescence of poems like 'In Memory of Eva Gore-Booth and Con Markiewicz' was infused with harmony as well as light; throughout, 'plain words in a seemingly usual combination set the mind in a whirl'. When Fallon in the end accuses WBY of chiselling his art out of an Anglo-Irish civilization 'half dead at the top', representing the last light of a sinking epoch, this judgement is implicitly contradicted by all he has already said about the energy, mystery, and verve of the latest lyrics.

The same conclusion is repeated over and over again by reviewers of the *Collected Poems*: astonishing changes of style are underpinned by an integrated unity of themes. Such evaluations, taken with the construction of *Dramatis Personae* and the appearance of *Letters to the New Island*, made early 1934 a time of introspection. It is no coincidence that WBY's latest broadcast, from Belfast on St Patrick's Day, was called 'The Growth of a Poet'.[57] Reviewing his own development, WBY came back to his search for simplicity, 'the natural words . . . in the natural order'. Though the latest of his poems included was 'The Fisherman' (now twenty years old), the text of the broadcast stressed his lifelong struggle to advance his intellectual enterprises against the opposition of others. 'I had to make my thoughts modern; modern thought is not simple; I became argumentative, passionate, bitter.' WBY's various representations of himself in March 1934 echoed the reception of his *Collected Poems*: the Last Romantic had liberated himself into the modern age, through austere discipline, mystic explorations, and passionate engagement with the world. But privately he was sharply conscious that, for all his great achievements, the creative impulse had remained recalcitrant since Gregory's death. The attempt to throw himself into a public role as the Blueshirts' D'Annunzio had failed to inspire anything beyond the inadequate 'marching songs'; he would be seventy the following year. But he was about to try another route. 'What has endured in him', wrote one of his admiring young critics the year before, 'is the unabated desire for life. He has not finished with life before life has finished: hence his great interest as a poet.'[58] In one of the governing myths of his creative imagination, Leda's rape by Zeus had engendered the twin representatives of love and war. As WBY distanced himself from the warriors led by O'Duffy and organized by MacManus, he turned to the other source of energy epitomized by the miraculous egg hung in the Spartan temple: a search for inspiration through sexual rejuvenation.

Chapter 13 : PASSIONATE METAPHYSICS
1934–1935

> Art bids us touch and taste and hear and see the world, and
> shrinks from what Blake calls mathematic form, from every
> abstract thing, from all that is of the brain only, from all that
> is not a fountain jetting from the entire hopes, memories and
> sensations of the body.
>
> *Essays and Introductions*, pp. 292–3

I

WBY's engagement diary for Thursday, 5 April 1934, records one Harley
Street appointment: 'Norman Haire 12'.[1] This laconic entry is the record of
an encounter that convulsed his life and changed his work beyond all expectation. On that day or the next, WBY received the so-called 'Steinach operation' at Beaumont House Hospital – actually a simple vasectomy, intended
to increase and contain the production of male hormone, thus arresting the
ageing process and restoring sexual vitality. This procedure (rather than the
much mythologized idea of injections with animal extracts) had been pioneered by Eugen Steinach's experiments, which apparently demonstrated
the invigoration of endocrine cells by increasing blood flow to the testes.[2] (It
also had the incidental benefit of reducing blood pressure and the less welcome effect of weight gain.) Steinach had been performing such 'rejuvena-
tions' since 1918; in 1922 he released a film showing the results; in 1923 Freud
himself submitted to the operation. By 1930 the fashion amounted to a
'craze', surviving even the case of Albert Wilson, a Steinach patient who
dropped dead the day before he was due to lecture at the Albert Hall on
'How I was Made Twenty Years Younger'. By then too Norman Haire was
recognized as the foremost British practitioner of the procedure, which he
was performing from 1922 – often on patients referred by WBY's old acquaintance, the sexual psychologist Havelock Ellis.

In 1924 Haire had also published *Rejuvenation: The Work of Steinach,
Voronoff and Others*. He had begun his colourful career as a gynaecologist in
Australia, where he was born as Norman Zions in 1892. He left Sydney
under a slight shadow in 1919, and rapidly established himself as a fashionable sexologist – writing a series of popular books about sex, cultivating pion-
eers in the field like Ellis and Magnus Hirschfeld, organizing the World
League for Sexual Reform (On a Scientific Basis). This organization, which
had close links to Hirschfeld's celebrated Institute, was also connected to

the Eugenics Society: it had been initially convened by A. M. Ludovici, Rodin's secretary, who was an enthusiastic pro-Fascist, though the usual tendency of the League was strongly to the left. While Haire continued to practise as a gynaecologist (Marie Stopes referred women to him for abortions), he was determined to dominate the developing movement for the organization of sexual knowledge.[3] He made a good deal of money through pandering to the anxieties of the well-off, though he also continued to provide contraception and sterilization services to a more impoverished clientele at the Cromer Street Welfare Clinic. In the 1920s he was a prominent figure in the Walworth Birth Control Clinic, but had to leave after he 'got too intimate with a policeman'. In 1929 he took a leading part (with Dora Russell and others) in the London conference of the World League for Sexual Reform, a large-scale jamboree held at the University of London's School of Hygiene, where papers were read on eugenics, venereal disease, abortion, sexual tolerance – and (by Peter Schmidt) on 'Six Hundred Rejuvenation Operations'. He also travelled around Britain giving shock-effect lectures (a role he reprised, with relish, in Australia during the last phase of his eventful life).[4] Haire's approach was to utilize medicine rather than radical sociology in the cause of sexual liberation: 'he tapped into the medical world in order to talk about sex in a respectable way, while also managing the other pseudo-medical and lay discourses'.[5]

Haire was a complex character. Immensely tall and fat, attired in 'Rational Dress' uniform, he reminded one acquaintance of a great neutered cat: when cultivating people like Ellis and Hirschfeld he could be both sycophantic and devious. Others found him more rebarbative, and he made influential enemies in the British Society for the Study of Sex Psychology, where he was frequently accused of aggressive self-aggrandizement. To the popular novelist and journalist Ethel Mannin, who also read a paper at the 1929 Congress, he initially seemed as inspirational a figure as the radical educationalist A. S. Neill. In the early 1930s she celebrated Haire as a guiding light in the reform of outdated attitudes, a wildly amusing companion, a generous friend. To the nineteen-year-old Anthony O'Connor, fortuitously appointed first secretary of the Glasgow branch of the World League for Sexual Reform and then of the central body, Haire represented 'a great gust of fresh air blowing through the stuffy atmosphere', at once outrageous, flamboyant, and kindly. O'Connor relished the parties at Haire's extravagantly decorated Harley Street house, where he encountered figures like J. B. S. Haldane, his sister Naomi Mitchison, Magnus Hirschfeld, and – once – W. B. Yeats.

With his extravagance, shadiness, and readiness to shock, Haire recalls many of the charlatan figures in WBY's past. His chinoiserie-festooned consulting rooms were the obvious destination for anyone interested in a Steinach operation in the early 1930s, though the book in which WBY first researched the topic was probably not Haire's *Rejuvenation*, but *The Conquest of Old Age*, published by Peter Schmidt in 1931.[6] WBY's interest in the movement for sexual tolerance is consistent with his record in anti-censorship activities (another area of interest to the World League); it also echoes his support of Wilde, his attraction to the demi-monde of the nineties, and his participation in the worlds of Theosophy, psychical research, and occult study – whose memberships often overlapped. But there were far more pressing reasons too. The creative dearth which he constantly linked to the disappearance of Coole also coincided with other losses. The succession of serious illnesses since 1930 had altered the nature of his dependence on George, whose role as nurse, protector, and organizer had taken over from that as psychic and sexual collaborator. This occurred at a time when WBY's letters to Olivia Shakespear became more and more insistently – if nostalgically – erotic in their content. And both developments were closely connected with the decline of his own sexual potency.

The subject of impotence, often in the form of deferred, or surrogate sexual relationships, is a constant theme in WBY's work throughout his creative life, but in the early 1930s it achieves a new urgency. It was at this time that the young Montgomery Hyde, bravely asking WBY about his experience of visiting a brothel, received the discomfitingly vivid answer, 'It was terrible. Like putting an oyster into a slot machine!'[7] The recurring vision which he recorded after his 1930 illness, where a coat on a coat-hanger turns into a body and then materializes more specifically into a young woman who approaches his bed, was famously recounted to Virginia Woolf in terms of a sexual annunciation: 'Then – I finally recovered my potency.'[8] Over six months earlier, 'a friend' (almost certainly Dermott MacManus, who also suffered from impotence) told WBY about the possibility of rejuvenation operations; he read Schmidt's book in Trinity College Library, and found his way to Haire. Haire, interviewed by Richard Ellmann in 1946, said that WBY 'told me for about three years before I saw him he had lost all inspiration', a process triumphantly reversed after the operation; Haire also told Ellmann that WBY was technically impotent, but it is intriguingly unclear whether this means before or after April 1934. WBY continued to receive regular courses of injections from the Harley Street magus.[9] It is also indubitable that he believed the Steinach procedure had restored his vitality, and that this extended to a renewed ability to feel desire and to have sexual relations.

The benefits of the Steinach procedure have been generally supposed illusory, so it is usually accepted that WBY's presumptions were the result of psychological rather than physiological stimulation. However, experiments carried out in 1995 suggested that a vasectomy operation can increase libido, and WBY was certainly convinced. Just over a month after his visit to Haire's clinic, he wrote to Macmillan:

That operation has almost made me a young man. I do not yet know how it has affected my blood-pressure but it has given me back my energy. I no longer feel myself at the end of life putting things in order or putting them away. They say that I shall lose this first stream of vitality in a few weeks and then recover it in greater measure.[10]

A letter to Shakespear a fortnight later suggests more intimate disclosures: he was 'still marvellously strong in some ways better than I was at Woburn Buildings, at least towards the end'.[11] Since Woburn Buildings had been the scene of their lovers' trysts nearly forty years before, and the affair had collapsed because of his diminished ardour, this suggests that he was indeed feeling renewed desire. (How far it was the result of a ligature to the *vas deferens* is another matter.) WBY showed a remarkable lack of reticence on the matter: Macmillan was hardly an intimate friend. Dublin was soon revelling in the story; Gogarty, who had not been consulted beforehand, was particularly scathing.

The poor old fool has undergone Stienach's [*sic*] operation and is now trapped and enmeshed in sex. When I parodied his poem into

> I heard the old, old men say
> everything's phallic

little did I think that he would become so obsessed before the end. He cannot explode it by pronogrhphy [*sic*] (as Joyce) or jocularity as I try to do.[12]

This was written in October, only six months after the operation. Gogarty's implication that sexual interest for those past middle age was something to be baffled, obscured, and evaded was directly contrary to WBY's belief. He made no secret of the experiment, advocated it for contemporaries like Sturge Moore (who took his advice) and AE (who did not), and – to the discomfiture of many – liked to pose as the 'wild old wicked man' of his own poetry by encouraging ribald talk. 'When you get to be as old as I am,' he told Frank O'Connor, 'the thing you will find you need most is a young man [F. R. Higgins] to come and tell you dirty stories.'[13] But he did not mean that storytelling did duty for everything else. Nor did he consider the love-lives of the young a thing apart. A month after the operation he wrote quizzically to Olivia about Denis Johnston and Shelah Richards:

Here is a problem. An Irish dramatist & an Abbey actor, both very handsome people, married three or four years ago & moved into a little flat with a single bed Now each has a lover & without the least disguise but they still inhabit that little flat. Does each say to his or her admirer 'I sleep on the sofa'? Does the admirer believe it? Are they often unfaithful with one another. Do they discuss their admirers in the small hours? How does modern realism consider this situation? Is it so realistic that it sees no situation at all? Perhaps, it thinks that our generation through Ibsen, made a whole system of morals out of a mole-hill.[14]

Subsequent letters descanted upon the affairs of acquaintances like Norah McGuinness, whose 'artistic aim changes with each lover', and Austin Clarke, whose advances were indignantly repulsed by a Donegal girl who had founded all her expectations of sex on the activities of domestic animals.[15] By the autumn of 1934 WBY was powerfully preoccupied by sex and apparently anxious for an adventure. By the act of undergoing a rejuvenation operation, he was convinced that he had induced both potency and creativity to return.[16]

And he was writing again. For some time he had been working on a short one-act play, *The King of the Great Clock Tower*. Begun as an exercise to start him writing lyrics, it would have a brief run at the Abbey at the end of June. It was nearly finished when George and WBY went to Rapallo at the beginning of that month to take their final leave of the flat on via Americhe, and to arrange for their furniture to be shipped back to Dublin. WBY brought the play with him. At this stage it was a short parable, borrowing his customary Japanese stage-settings (masks, drum, gong, abstract hangings) to frame a faux-medieval parable, involving a King, his mysterious and mute Queen, and a strolling troubadour obsessed by her beauty, who is beheaded for his impertinence and whose severed head sings a love-duet with the bewitched Queen. The impotence theme is implicit, yet again. But even more striking is how deliberately WBY has plundered his early work: there is specific reference to the dominant motifs of *The Wanderings of Oisin*, incidents from *On Baile's Strand* and *The Countess Kathleen*, and the story of 'The Binding of the Hair' (dropped after the 1897 edition of *The Secret Rose*). Forgael's search for beauty in *The Shadowy Waters* is also suggestively echoed, and the whole thing is – as the *Times Literary Supplement* remarked – 'a rather Ninety-ish fable'.[17] The deliberate evocation of Salome's dance and the deathly Queen inviting 'desecration and the lover's night' are anchored firmly in the world of Gustave Moreau, Aubrey Beardsley, and WBY's youthful adventures with the *Savoy*.

This being the case, WBY should not have expected too much when, on that brief return to Rapallo, he gave *The King of the Great Clock Tower* to Ezra Pound and asked for his opinion on the lyrics it contained. Pound had already departed far from the paths of his one-time mentor. 'When the Hell did I ever Berkeley-ize?' he had recently demanded of FitzGerald. 'When did I say it was round *an'* flat? *Who* has the record fer having coonthradicted

Unc. Wm. more times per week, hour, moment, year and decade, than yer ole fren' Ez?'[18] This was no more than the truth, and he was about to do it again. As wby later recalled it,

He said apropos of nothing 'Arthur Balfour was a scoundrel', and from that on would talk of nothing but politics. All the modern statesmen were more or less scoundrels except 'Mussolini and that hysterical imitator of his Hitler'. When I objected to his violence he declared that Dante considered all sins intellectual, even sins of the flesh, he himself refused to make the modern distinction between error and sin. He urged me to read the works of Captain [Frederick] Douglas [the monetarist-reform crank] who alone knew what caused our suffering. He took my manuscript and went away denouncing Dublin as 'a reactionary hole' because I had said that I was re-reading Shakespeare, would go on to Chaucer, and found all that I wanted of modern life in 'detection and the wild west'. Next day his judgement came and that in a single word 'Putrid'.[19]

This encounter marked the effective end of a long literary association and to a certain extent a personal friendship too. Pound, who predictably told wby the play was written in 'nobody language', was even crueller to others in private. The Eagle had decayed into 'the buzzard', and become unreadable; Pound himself hoped to be chloroformed 'before I get to THAT state'. But the exchange also shows that wby was now far more anxious to talk about poetry than Fascist politics, which had cast a much shorter shadow than his preoccupation with being, once more, able to create.

For Pound's splenetic strictures did not stop his old mentor writing, though his direction changed slightly. The Yeatses returned from Rapallo and spent the summer in Dublin. wby corrected the proofs of *Collected Plays*, oversaw the first production of the new play and a successful version of *The Resurrection* at the Abbey in August, and – as he told T. S. Eliot – 'wrote against time to keep my sister's press going'.[20] The resulting product was a surprising mélange. Under the title *The King of the Great Clock Tower, Commentaries and Poems*, it would gather the new play, the only substantial poem written in the bleak period after Gregory's death ('A Parnellite at Parnell's Funeral'), the notorious 'Three Songs to the Same Tune' (with changes), copious 'commentaries' on the contents – and a new series of 'Supernatural Songs', still being worked on as the copy went through the press that autumn. The book is genuinely 'occasional', indirectly reflecting wby's developing sequence of thought, through the commentaries linking play and poems as well as the new-minted quality of the lyrics. wby's appended 'notes' to *The King of the Great Clock Tower* are actually a consideration of the dramatic effects achieved by music and singing: the memory of Florence Farr and the far-off days of Dolmetsch's psaltery came vividly alive.[21] But he also argued in favour of abstract dramatic content. 'I say to the musician "lose my words in patterns of sound as the name of God is lost in Arabian arabesques. They are a secret between the singers, myself, yourself."' No clue was given about the symbolic meaning of the play, beyond the link between the severed-head dance and 'the old ritual of the year: the mother goddess and the slain god.' But this cunningly leads to a specific treatment of the slain god theme: 'A Parnellite at Parnell's Funeral'.

By now, he had added the coda which directly related the lost possibility of an Irish political annunciation to the failed promise of O'Duffy. But it is placed after the 'Commentary' on the four original stanzas. This is a boiled-down version of WBY's personal view of Irish history, which answers the 'Four Bells' signalling world-changing events: the Flight of the Earls in 1607, the Battle of the Boyne in 1691, 'the coming of French influence among our peasants' after 1789, and the 'beginning of our own age' in the post-Parnell fallout. WBY's ancient taste for defining eras had not deserted him, and nor had his more recent penchant for idealizing the Irish Ascendancy, even if their natural authority had declined, after the Union, into the 'Garrison mentality'. Here, again, a grappling hook is cast deftly forward to the next item in the book: the 'Songs' written for the Blueshirts, reprinted with tactful changes. The attached 'Commentary' (dated April 1934) is just as carefully calculated: it deals largely with the Abbey, before expressing an idealistic wish that the 'sacred drama' of the entire Irish nation might be emblematized by the kind of government or party apparently impossible today. A further postscript, dated August 1934, finally disclaimed all support for O'Duffy's party. What had gone before showed that WBY's political commitments were anchored to a more archaic, less sinister kind of authoritarianism. What followed – the 'Supernatural Songs', 'written while this book was passing through the press' – showed that his creative inspiration was now blazing a new trail. Michael Roberts, writing in the *Spectator* a year after their publication, hailed them as 'among the best that Mr Yeats has written'; they proved he could make poetry out of abstractions because of a miraculous gift of striking an echo from 'habits of thought and emotion which are so deeply ingrained in us that they appear to be part of the structure of our mind'.[22] These alone showed that WBY was not confined to 'nobody language': the languid embellishments of the play's lyrics are answered by the directness of Crazy Jane, and a Blakean sense of mystery and transcendence. WBY's revived interest in Indian philosophy, his ancient neo-Platonic schema, and motifs from an idiosyncratically earthy version of Celtic Christianity are fused in the persona of the hermit Ribh. Through his eyes, at the tomb of the legendary lovers Baile and Aillinn angelic intercourse is presented as a kind of transcendental Tantric sex; while the slyly iconoclastic 'Ribh Considers Christian Love Insufficient' raises a characteristically awkward question.

> Why should I seek for love or study it?
> It is of God and passes human wit;
> I study hatred with great diligence
> For that's a passion in my own control,
> A sort of besom that can clear the soul
> Of everything that is not mind or sense.
>
> Why do I hate man, woman or event?
> That is a light my jealous soul has sent.
> From terror or deception freed it can
> Discover impurities, can show at last
> How soul may walk when all such things are past,
> How soul could walk before such things began.

In his study or sitting in the garden at Riversdale that July and August, enigmatic epigrams (two of them based on his children's horoscopes) and brief poetic queries suddenly came with the accustomed felicity; as so often before, a running commentary was preserved in his letters to Shakespear. The published 'Supernatural Songs' would climax in the beautifully crafted 'Meru', inspired by reading *The Holy Mountain* over a year before; the poem suggests the insubstantiality of human ambition (intellectual as well as material). But the force of the 'Supernatural Songs' resided in their sexual charge. Tantric images, lovers coiled and circled together, orgasmic metaphors (shivering, sweetness, crying) express the confluence of divine inspiration and carnal erotics: the soul penetrated by the Godhead.

> At stroke of midnight soul cannot endure
> A bodily or mental furniture.
> What can she take until her Master give!
> Where can she look until He make the show!
> What can she know until He bid her know!
> How can she live till in her blood He live!

Taken together, *The King of the Great Clock Tower* and the 'Supernatural Songs', both products of the post-Steinach summer of 1934, forecast much of WBY's late work, where a rather forced archaism alternates with swift, elemental, earthy confrontations. Sex is an urgent, imperious presence, ultimately unsatisfying unless linked to some kind of revelation. 'The point', WBY told Olivia that summer, 'is that we beget and bear because of the incompleteness of our love.'[23] 'Passionate metaphysics', WBY's own phrase,[24] partly sums it up. But the passion would inevitably attract more attention than the metaphysics.

II

As so often in his earlier life, a creative surge was associated with erotic excitement. Schemes succeeded each other with bewildering rapidity. He made connections to the world of avant-garde drama in London (notably Rupert Doone and the Group Theatre), with a view to reviving misunderstood work like *The Player Queen*, and he planned a revival of pamphlet 'Broadsides' to boost Cuala's flagging fortunes (the first series, from 1908 to 1915, had become collectors' items). At the beginning of 1935 the plan would be unveiled: a hundred sets, bound and signed, using music, ballads, and pictures. The material was to be 'old and new' (including Gogarty's bawdy medical-student extravaganza, 'The Hay Hotel'); later the project would incorporate new friends and collaborators like Dorothy Wellesley. The appearance of the 'Broadsides' was conformed to Cuala house-style design, now an accepted modern Irish classic. They often featured Jack's inimitable illustrative line, learned in his caricaturist mode long before and retained even when his idiosyncratic oil-painting style became wilder and wilder. If nothing else, the 'Broadsides' enabled the first collaboration between the brothers, after a long period of political estrangement.

They were also inspired by WBY's desire to experiment with ballads, bawdiness, and scatological jokes – encouraged by new boon companions like F. R. Higgins as well as old ones like Gogarty. This discomfited listeners like Iseult ('it was not pretty', she told Richard Ellmann) and the permanently pursed-lipped Monk Gibbon. For WBY, it was all part of the twisted rope of sexual and supernatural experience, which winds through his letters to Shakespear. 'Strange that I should write these things in my old age,' he remarked, 'when if I were to offer myself for new love I could only expect to be accepted by the very young wearied by the passive embraces of the bolster.'[25] It is a curious reflection: the 'very young' do not generally seek out the very old for a first sexual experience. At the end of the summer, however, the longed-for erotic adventure presented itself, via importunate letters from a beautiful amateur poet and actress called Margot Ruddock. All that WBY had anticipated seemed to be coming to pass: he always referred to her as a 'girl', though when they met she was in fact a 27-year-old wife and mother.[26]

She took the initiative, writing to him about her poetry at the end of August; his first reply, in early September, was cautious ('even in London I have sometimes a vacant hour for a fellow-artist'). But by 24 September, when he was planning a visit to Rome by way of England, the tone of their correspondence was surprisingly intimate for two people who had not yet met.

I shall go to London on October 3 and ring you up before 11 on the morning of October 4. With the exception of a doctor I must see (nothing serious) I shall not tell anybody of my arrival until we have arranged our meeting – indeed perhaps not then. As a poet I am a solitary man, though I live in a crowd – one word of yours pierced that solitude. You spoke of the 'trueness' of my work, if you had said its 'veracity' or used any other word, such as reviewers use, it would have meant nothing. The fact that you found this word, our own word, made me see you, it was as though I saw your face. I do not want compliments but I want to know what people are like. I wanted to be sure, I wanted you to say just what you have said in your latest letter, that is why I asked whether you preferred my early or my latest work. I wanted to find your 'trueness' in your discovery of mine. Do not think that I await our meeting with indifference. Shall I disappoint you or shall I add to the number of my friends? . . .

We shall ask each other questions, perhaps; perhaps I shall put a book into your hand and ask your [*recte* you] to read out some poems, that too is one of the ways to knowledge. When I was young I think I wanted to be deceived, but now I want wisdom always or as much as my blind heart permits.[27]

This heated language reflects WBY's determination to revive the erotic dimension in his life and his correspondent's ready flirtatiousness. But the intensity was heightened by the fact that Margot Ruddock was mentally unstable, and her temperament continually trembled on the edge of full-blown mania.

Even in the early stages of their relationship, this is indicated in her letters. But her obvious attractions disguised the danger. The febrile energy and ecstatic creative surges often associated with a manic-depressive personality intensified the magnetism of her dark, sensual good looks. When she approached WBY, she was living with her second husband, a rising actor called Raymond Lovell, and their six-month-old baby in London; a previous husband and child had already been abandoned. As Margot Collis (the surname came from her first brief marriage), she had played in provincial theatre companies, and now nurtured ambitions to create a poets' theatre – a sure way to awaken WBY's interest. Their meeting in early October was a success: he was delighted by her 'distinguished beauty of face and limb' and her thrilling contralto voice: the conjunction between the Poet and the Actress, played at in the past with Stella Campbell and Florence Farr, suddenly seemed an intoxicating possibility. At their first meeting on 4 October he seems to have declared a wish to find a base in London where he could entertain more discreetly than at the Savile Club; she promptly suggested self-contained service flats in Seymour Street, near Marble Arch, and he as promptly took one. 'You are bound to nothing, not even to come and look at me.'[28]

He then went on to Rome, where the Reale Accademia d'Italia had invited him to the annual Alessandro Volta Foundation Congress on the theatre: but her image pursued him. In Rome he was surrounded by theatrical people, including Ashley Dukes of the Mercury Theatre in London, and WBY's old friend and collaborator Gordon Craig; Ruddock received vivid letters describing encounters with them, and promising her much more. 'I am rewriting *The King of the Great Clock Tower* giving the Queen a speaking part, that you may act in it.' (Since the play revolves around the Queen's mysterious muteness, this was a considerable and rather troublesome accolade.) 'O my dear my mind is so busy with your future and perhaps you will reject all my plans – my calculation is that, as you are a trained actress, a lovely sense of rhythm will make you a noble speaker of verse – a singer and sayer. You will read certain poems to me, I have no doubt of the result, and October 19 I begin the practical work.'[29]

Erratic as she was, Ruddock could not but see the advantages of this connection with an infatuated great man. Even amid the distractions of Rome, he was preoccupied by her (as soon as he returned, he began investigating her horoscope, though unfortunately it does not seem to have warned him of any of the upheavals that were to come). In Rome WBY presided over a general session of the conference. Since he was unable to speak Italian, he used a sharp rap of his gavel to cut speakers off after ten minutes, a tactic not appreciated by the voluble Futurist Marinetti.[30] He also gave his by now well-worn lecture on the Irish Theatre, and the origins of cultural revival amid the disillusionment of Parnell's fall: the Abbey Theatre was presented as 'the parting gift' of a declining Ascendancy to 'the new Catholic Ireland that was about to take its place'.[31] But his mind was elsewhere. The conference ended on 14 October; he and George travelled back separately, she to Dublin, he to Seymour Street.

The idea of a 'poet's theatre', working with the new generation represented by Dukes, Doone, and Frederick Ashton, glowed in his mind, lent further phosphorescence by the allure of Margot Ruddock. At a meeting in Dulac's house on 26 October Doone's Group Theatre agreed to act and produce a series of Yeats plays, but at first insisted on their being in a public theatre. This was a coup, but the apparent contrast between WBY's style and the plays by Auden and Eliot which Doone had pioneered, presented a problem. Doone, Robert Medley, and the Auden–Isherwood clique were also in search of a stylized approach, surreal effects, and the collaboration of avantgarde musicians – all principles familiar to WBY. The leftist political identification of the Group Theatre was not an obstacle; one of their first productions was by WBY's friend Walter Turner, who certainly did not share their politics, and he may have provided the initial link between Doone and

WBY. Another attraction was the adherence of T. S. Eliot, now experimenting with verse plays. *Sweeney Agonistes* would provide a great success for Doone the next month, and *Murder in the Cathedral* brought even more *réclame* to Ashley Dukes a year later. By the end of October everything seemed arranged. A 'poetical theatre', run by Dukes at his Mercury Theatre in Notting Hill, would open with *Fighting the Waves, The Player Queen*, and the new version of *The King of the Great Clock Tower* (retitled *A Full Moon in March*). Constant Lambert would provide music; and, at WBY's insistence, the repertoire would mix his own work with that of 'the poetical left' – Auden and Isherwood as interpreted by the Group Theatre. Doone and his friends wanted to take a Yeats play to Germany and – WBY excitedly reported to George – had asked for an article by him for their journal explaining their theatrical approach. 'This means that they allow me to direct their policy to some extent.'[32] In fact it meant no such thing, and on that rock the enterprise would founder.

But for the moment WBY seemed to have found, at long last, a dramatic venture which he could dominate. The Young Turks of the Group Theatre movement seemed to appreciate him; John Allen later remembered that they excepted 'Craig, Stanislavsky, Yeats and Eliot' from the general rule that anyone over thirty was old hat. Both Auden and Eliot had noted WBY's dance-plays a few years before, and their influence is discernible in *Sweeney*. That the ethos of the Group was, in Cyril Connolly's phrase, 'homo-communist' did not unduly bother WBY. 'There is great tecnical skill in the little theatres & this is the moment to use it . . . I am doing great work here – seeing all kind[s] of people, dancers, musicians actors & think there will be no difficulty in launching here just such a theatre for "No Plays" as I have described & always wanted.'[33] He also told George that he was avoiding friends and immersed in the new project. But the fact that *The Player Queen* and *A Full Moon in March* were designed to showcase the scanty talents of Ruddock is not mentioned, nor are the injections which he was still receiving from Haire.

He was back in Dublin in early November. *Wheels and Butterflies* was published on the 17th, containing WBY's recent plays and their provocative Introductions; Lolly was also bringing out *The King of the Great Clock Tower*, while he worked on its poetic successor.[34] All the same, he was soon taking the mailboat and train back to London on 6 December 1934, his mind fixed on the more concrete issues of his new theatrical enterprise, and his reunion with Margot Ruddock. During his time in Dublin he had been writing to her as 'My dearest'; though their correspondence was conducted through the Kildare Street Club, she was instructed to 'write an occasional letter' to Riversdale, as 'my wife knows that we work on the theatre enterprise'; he did not mind a postponement of Dukes's production of his plays, 'for it will leave December to us'; he held out the promise of launching her on the BBC as 'a "sayer" of my verse'; he promised her poems, including the opening song of *A Full Moon in March*, 'partly addressed to you'.

> Should old Pythagoras fall in love
> Little may he boast thereof
> (*What cares love for this and that?*)
> Days go by in foolishness
> But O how great the sweetness is
> *Crown of gold or dung of swine.*

'How did you and I choose each other?' he added. 'I think even before we had seen each others' faces.'[35]

Her first letters to him do not survive, but it seems clear that, if days went by 'in foolishness', this was a *folie à deux*. Ruddock assured WBY that her husband no longer slept with her; she took WBY to see him on the stage, as some kind of reassurance, with the result that Lovell became jealous and started to pay attention to her again.[36] She apparently worried that people might suspect an 'intrigue': he reassured her 'I think our work will throw us much together, that is if you do not weary of me, fame will link our names for the work's sake, and doubtless, to use a phrase of George Moore, people "will hope for the best".'

What George Yeats hoped for is another matter. As subsequent correspondence made clear, she knew all about the Margot fixation and viewed it more as a health hazard than as anything else. In spite of WBY's efforts to conceal letters arising from this and later entanglements, he was as transparent as ever in affairs of the heart. George's own independence of mind, and her weariness at the demanding role into which she had slipped, meant that she cast a philosophical eye on her husband's obsessions, and may even have responded to them with a certain relief. Drink was playing a large part in her life – a common pattern with mediums whose powers have failed – and when he had been dispatched to London on one of his adventures, she often took to her bed for a day, telling the maid to say she was out.[37] She remained utterly certain of her own role as helpmeet and – to a certain extent – editorial collaborator. By now, she had brought some organization to her husband's vast and expanding archive; lists were kept of the manuscripts in a large steel filing-cabinet and the key deposited with the family solicitor when the Yeatses were abroad. Revisions were collated, and dates of composition recorded. Her typing skills were as essential as ever. But her contribution was far greater than that. Both her editorial insights and literary opinion were valued commodities; neither the *Collected Poems* of 1933 nor the projected edition de luxe would have been conceivable without her help. The same would be true of the *Oxford Book of Modern Verse*, which WBY was first approached about editing in October 1934. Her role as the Caliph's gift was well past; never a beauty, she no longer tried to counteract her ruddy colouring and increasing stoutness by dressing fashionably, and the hens at Riversdale occupied the time once spent on Drama League productions and expeditions to the cinema with Lennox Robinson. However, she privately retained at least some of her own artistic ambitions; her attempts at play-writing did not survive, but in 1935 she was writing a novel (and raged at WBY for his indiscretion on the subject: 'leave me to stew in my solitary juice'[38]). Everyone noted that she was an unaffectedly loving, efficient, and appreci-ated mother, from Joyce Barcroft, who worked for the family, to George White, Michael's housemaster at St Columba's. She was essential to WBY in countless ways, he missed her when away for too long, but the romance of their relationship had faded. Nonetheless she was a tough-minded and unsentimental realist, and in some ways the direction the marriage had taken was not unwelcome to her.

She also knew better than anyone the fragility of her husband's health, and his worries about the loss of potency. She had accompanied him to London for the Steinach operation; his subsequent activities were hardly a surprise to her. How far they were a surprise to Margot Ruddock is another matter. From their letters it seems that some kind of physical intimacy was achieved during his November visit to London, but also that what he called 'this nervous inhibition' had made it less than complete. He wrote to her of his efforts to console himself by lining up Gogarty and Higgins to tell him 'Rabelaisian stories of the Dublin slums', and by unburdening himself to Dermott MacManus, who claimed to have cured his own impotence by 'Oriental meditations'. This letter included a brief love-poem, actually called 'Margot' and wisely left unpublished: it rehearsed his 'famine struck' state, 'gazing on a past/That appeared constructed of/Lost opportunities to love', before her 'generous eyes' were cast on his: his plea 'let me be loved as though still young' strikes an unfortunately maudlin note. Always con-scious of repetitive patterns in his life, he must have thought of his first efforts with Olivia Shakespear, and his failures with Maud and Iseult Gonne; his marriage is not invoked in this version of his history. Had he been rational rather than infatuated, it might have struck him that the two most successful erotic relationships of his life so far had been with notably generous, balanced, and thoughtful personalities, Olivia and George; an unstable, discontented, and self-obsessed actress, already twice unhappily married and with a small baby to take care of, was hardly likely to offer him the understanding he needed. But a good part of WBY's own capacity for self-preservation and self-renewal lay in his self-centredness, and in a surprisingly short time he learned to look elsewhere.

For the moment, he was back in London, receiving injections from Haire, reading the latest version of *A Full Moon in March* to Rupert Doone, lunching with Eliot, attending *Sweeney Agonistes* (on the same night as Bertold Brecht), and dining with Frederick Ashton. Ashton, who was fascinated by WBY and liked him personally, was nonetheless unconvinced that work like *A Full Moon in March* could be paired with plays by 'the poetic left': sixty years later, asked about WBY's avant-garde credentials, he retorted, 'Avant-garde? He was *pure nineties.*' WBY confirmed this judgement by his wish to revive in dance-play form *Diarmuid and Grania*, the strange fruit of his long-ago collaboration with George Moore, but his new friend rejected the idea at once.[39] Ashton also became impatient with the constant attendance of Margot, whom he remembered as 'that dreadful mad girl', utterly obsessed with the great poet. She remained very much on the scene – promised the leading role in the production of *The Player Queen* projected for the spring, brought to visit Ottoline Morrell in Gower Street, and to dine with Dulac in Holland Park. (WBY's old collaborator caused difficulties by objecting to the increasingly 'bloody' symbolism of the new version of *The King of The Great Clock Tower*: like Ninette de Valois, he preferred the first version, which WBY now thought 'dramatically coherent, spiritually incoherent'.[40]) WBY had sent Ruddock long letters from Ireland about the best way to recite his verse, and continued to try to school her – but admitted to Ottoline Morrell that 'some of my rehersals have been stormy'.[41] He remained closely in touch with Dublin through George and Lennox Robinson, and complained that his co-directors Richard Hayes and Walter Starkie stayed away from many of the theatre's current productions. But all his energies were concentrated once more on life in London, where he stayed through Christmas. By then, however, his affairs had taken another bewildering swerve. A two-line letter to Olivia Shakespear, written on 27 December, said it all. 'Are you back? Wonderful things have happened. This is Bagdad. This is not London.'

Most surprising of all, the Arabian Nights adventure which had overtaken him had nothing to do with Margot Ruddock. In mid December Norman Haire invited him to meet Ethel Mannin, the successful novelist and journalist involved in the World League for Sexual Reform. As she recalled it, Haire encouraged her to dress seductively, joking that the efficacy of WBY's operation had to be tested.[42] The dinner in Haire's Chinese dining room was not an unqualified success from his point of view, but his two guests were mesmerized by each other. They left the teetotal Haire's table, where the food was luxurious and plentiful but wine non-existent, and went back to Mannin's house to drink burgundy, and there forged a lasting friendship. This may be a censored version. Almost at once WBY was sending her fevered letters invoking private references, arranging rendezvous, fervently discussing (as always with his lovers) her work, and thanking her for the 'blessing' she had brought him. By 23 December he wrote to her as 'My dear O My dear'; on 27 December, the same day as his ecstatic note to Olivia, he drafted a 'theme for a poem' which, extending the verses already sent to Margot Ruddock, evokes an 'Artemis' figure who first appears 'implacably lipped', a statue to be worshipped, but ends by offering sexual comfort to an old man:

> Port[r]ayed before his Eyes,
> Implacably lipped,
> It seemed that she moved;
> It seemed that he clasped her knees
> What man so worshipped
> When Artemis roved?
>
> He sat worn out & she
> Kneeling seemed to him
> Pitiably frail;
> Loves anxiety
> Made his eyes dim
> Made his breath fail
>
> Then suffered he heart ache;
> Driven by Love's dread
> Alternate will
> A winding pathway took,
> In Love's levelling bed
> All gyres lie still.[43]

The date at the end of one of the drafts suggests that it was Mannin (whose looks indeed resembled an art deco Artemis), rather than Ruddock, who 'blessed' WBY by convincing him that erotic love was still a possibility, even if it had to take a 'winding pathway'. But it is unlikely that she was infatuated in the same way. At this stage of her life Ethel Mannin, despite her Marxist politics, was a free spirit determined on sexual radicalism. Affairs with people like Bertrand Russell had left her with something of a reputation as an apostle of 'free love', which later came back to haunt her. When WBY met her she was thirty-four, had – like Margot Ruddock – a young daughter from an early marriage, and was a determined collector of 'interesting people'. She had recently published *Confessions and Impressions*, part precocious autobiography, part series of profiles of her avant-garde contemporaries, including Haire, Russell, and A. S. Neill. It also included a large element of strident personal and political credo, reprised in several self-centred volumes (she stuck to a schedule of producing two books a year, one novel and one non-fiction, and had turned out over a hundred by the time she died). An inveterate traveller, she visited, admired, and wrote about Soviet Russia; and she produced a series of bestselling novels, including *Crescendo*, described as 'a saga of sex'.[44] A few years later her *Women and the Revolution* argued straightforwardly for free love, equal sexual rights and opportunities for men and women, instant divorce, and abortion on demand. Her racy reputation, good looks, and decisive style made her a sought-after lecturer. Hearing her speak on 'The Gospel of D. H. Lawrence' had led the young Anthony O'Connor to *Confessions and Impressions*, and subsequently the World League for Sexual Reform; later he was told 'that Ethel got Lawrence all wrong, but I didn't know or care. It was *new*.'[45] She was a member of the Independent Labour Party, and her ideology in the 1930s tended to anarcho-syndicalism rather than hardline Communism, but she was emphatically and vociferously left-wing. The many publicity photographs of the era show classically clean-cut good looks; her literary style was intelligent, assertive, and slightly brash. Her relationship with WBY inaugurated a high point of sexual excitement for him, but she seemed determined to keep the emotional side of it under control, soon absenting herself for long periods of foreign travel and pointedly writing to him about her love-affairs. Whatever kind of 'beatitude' she promised him on his visits to her at Oak Cottage, Burghley Road, Wimbledon, meant a good deal less to her than to him.

Their relationship is obscured by Mannin's later swerve into Anglo-Catholicism, her second marriage to a high-minded Quaker, and her recantation of faith in Norman Haire and his works. The great sexologist is evoked with admiration and affection in *Confessions and Impressions*, and was still a close friend in 1935; but a decade later she denounced him to Ellmann as 'that horrible doctor . . . a liar, and [WBY's] operation was a failure'.[46] In *Young in the Twenties* (1971) she described Haire roundly as a 'monster'. Late in life she burnt letters from WBY about his 'rejuvenation', telling her daughter she found the operation 'quite disgusting and revolting'.[47] This was very far from her attitude at the time. She also told Ellmann that WBY had talked of his 'lack of sexual potency in his early years . . . he told me he was "impotent" – *the word he used* – until [the] age of 26 . . . He was always, in any case, obviously much more romantic than actively sexual.'[48] According to Gogarty, 'Ethel Mannin told me that she "did my best for him" after the operation; but, of course, without effect!' and to Ellman she described WBY's 'hunger for a swan-song of passionate love . . . and his inability to secure it'. But the tone of his letters to her suggests that their relationship enabled him to believe that he was once again capable of satisfied desire. On 30 December he told her: 'You are right, the knowledge that I am not unfit for love has brought me sanity and peace. Yet that is not altogether why I came from you with the feeling that I have been blessed.'[49]

She at once supplanted Ruddock's place as his companion for dinner at the Ivy with the Dulacs (on one occasion sabotaged by WBY falling asleep at the table) and visits to the Swami, whom she disliked. He postponed his return to Dublin, preoccupied by the plans for producing his plays at Easter, an interview with his hopeful biographer Oliver Edwards, the continuing negotiation with publishers and solicitors over Gregory's literary estate – and, above all, Ethel Mannin. But the excitement took its toll. On his return to Dublin in late January, he once again fell seriously ill with congestion of the lungs. He seemed to recover, and then on 27 January he had a visit from the solicitor representing Margaret Gough, who was still trying to prevent the publication of her mother-in-law's diaries. 'I was holding my own,' he told Olivia, 'until I collapsed spitting blood, panting, shivering, too exhausted to stay still a moment.'[50] George, who had kept him supplied with gossipy letters during his month's absence, was once again precipitated into the role of nurse: an emergency X-ray machine was brought to the house, and in the absence of mains electricity had to be powered by a hundred-yard cable from the gate lodge. On 29 January she scribbled a note to Gogarty which reveals a good deal about their marriage, and her remarkable temperament.

I cannot telephone to you because every word I say can be heard by W. B. in his bedroom.

He had a 'relapse' on Sunday night – yesterday, Monday, Dr Shaw (51 Rathfarnham Road) brought out Dr Stewart with his portable X Ray apparatus. Today, at 2.45 p.m. Shaw told me the print showed not much of a serious nature in the left lung but showed a considerable enlargement of the heart.

What I want you to do, if you will consent, *is to allow me to ask Shaw to consult with you* as 'you are Willy's oldest friend in Ireland & know him physically & *temperamentally* better than any one else'.

I do not want Willy to be made an invalid or a fool. I think too that *if* any of these things are serious, I would rather he died in happiness than in invalidism. He may not have told you of all his past 18 months' activities. One of them is that he has been very much in love with a woman in London. I tell you this that you may understand why I am most anxious that he should not be tied to an unnecessary invalidism.[51]

Gogarty believed that the frankness of this reference 'goes to show that she knew his love-making was altogether mental';[52] but this does not necessarily follow. She had already written humorously to Dulac asking him to tell Ruddock ('as from yourself!') that WBY was anxiously watching the post for letters from her ('From which you can gather that he has discoursed largely on the subject – !')[53] The fact that George knew all about Margot Ruddock (if not yet about Ethel Mannin) was part of her recognition of his complexity, his insecurity, his romanticism, his wilfulness; only a few weeks before, reading through the records of his life in search of information for Oliver Edwards, she told him 'all these investigations have quickened my memory of the strange, chaotic, varied and completely unified personality that you are'.[54] She also recognized his need for dignity and privacy, and was determined to observe it. The doctor's diagnosis of heart disease carried a certain inevitability, after the constant trouble with his lungs and kidneys. Lily, while relying on her brother's 'wonderful powers of recovery', was uneasy. 'Willy is a very great man but he is also my very dear brother. I always pray I go before he and Jack do.'[55]

He recovered, but slowly. Bedridden until the end of February, he was unable to stay up for protracted periods until early March. Gogarty visited and played Boswell. 'Strange that all his attention revolves on sex. "Women are educated by their lovers." And, "As we grow old our mistresses grow younger," . . . "Ethyl Manin [sic] learned much from Bertrand Russell whose mistress she was."' Asked by Gogarty what he had been taught by women, WBY's reported response shows that Mannin's feminist opinions had had some influence – up to a point.

'Only this: never to regard them as half-creatures to be triumphed over, nor madonnas to be worshipped. But just equals who have to sustain the destiny of our daughters or our mothers: a lot so disproportioned to ours, that it becomes incumbent on us to conceal our pity for them lest they take offence. Because their courage outsoars their destiny, they are more touchy than we imagine. Our "chivalry" insults them: at least in these ways.'[56]

It was a time of enforced reflection. Reading Balzac yet again, interposed with *The Arabian Nights*, he had to come to terms with the news about his weakened heart. As at Rapallo five years before, the medical sentence precipitated a state of self-doubt. 'A week ago', he wrote to Mannin,

I was given some information that came as a shock, & kept my thoughts for some days on the one theme: I went over & over my life for the last twenty years, & the lives of those dear & near to me & saw what suffering, even demoralization had been caused by an instinct like that which made the followers of Dionysius gash themselves with knives. The vertigo of self-sacrifice is one of the means whereby we escape from thought. It is more dangerous to our subtle finished civilised souls than egotism . . . I find my peace by pitting my sole nature against something & the greater the tension the greater my self knowledge.[57]

'The vertigo of self-sacrifice' was the phrase he had used for Patrick Pearse and his companions in the sacrificial Rising nearly twenty years before; but now WBY was thinking of his own wilfulness and determination to take on experience at whatever costs. 'Vertigo' was the right metaphor for the dizzying welter of emotional intensity he had embraced since the operation in Beaumont Street the previous April. But however reflective his mood was during his convalescence, he still recognized his own hunger for 'self-knowledge'. A pattern of behaviour had been set long before, and it would endure.

III

Ill as he had been, as soon as his strength returned he was anxious to get back to London. Notwithstanding the proofs of *Dramatis Personae*, and the projected work on what he persisted in calling the *Cambridge Book of Modern Verse*, he was preoccupied with the hoped-for Dukes production of his plays, and desperately wanted to be there. His correspondence with Ruddock had cooled in tone, and his expressed wish was now to 'look at her', rather than anything else. Other distractions apart, her behaviour was giving cause for concern; the Swami wrote plaintively about the difficulty of getting her to 'control herself' on the committee of his tottering Institute in Kensington. WBY's letters to Mannin had also become calmer and more analytical: though she was still 'My dear', he wrote searchingly about their intellectual differences. For Mannin, her socialism was 'something deeply, fundamentally, felt, colouring all one thinks and feels, all one's reaction to people and things'.[58] She was involved in a controversy with Sean O'Casey about the use of political propaganda in drama, where she argued a strong Communist line; WBY, who had been touched and pleased by a letter from O'Casey commiserating on his illness, sent her some heartfelt advice: 'do not let it [propaganda] come too much into your life. I have lived in the midst of it, I have always been a propagandist though I have kept it out of my poems & it will embitter your soul with hatred as it has mine.' He continued this advice with a new reflection, on the necessarily feminine side of the artist's psyche – which suggests, again, that the theories of Mannin and the Sexual Reform set had had influence on him as well.

You are doubly a woman, first because of yourself & secondly because of the muses, whereas I am but once a woman. Bitterness is more fatal to us than it is to lawyers or journalists who had nothing to do with the feminine muses. Our traditions only permit us to bless, for the arts are an extension of the beatitudes. Blessed be heroic death (Shakespear's [*sic*] tragedies) blessed be heroic life (Cervantes) blessed be the wise (Balzac). Then there is a still more convincing reason why we should not admit propaganda into our lives. I shall write it out in the style of *The Arabian Nights* (which I am reading daily). There are three very important persons: (1) a man playing the flute; (2) a man carrying a statue; (3) a man in a woman's arms. Goethe said we must renounce, & I think propaganda – I wish I had thought of this when I was young – is among the things these three renounce.[59]

The thought remained and would resurface in one of his very last poems. But though he added a postscript endorsing Scheherazade's statement that 'it is not shameful to talk of the things that lie beneath our belts', his private metaphor of 'beatitude' is here deliberately offered to Mannin without its habitual erotic implication. When he returned to London on 25 March, she was in the South of France. In any case, he was preoccupied by theatre matters: his one letter to her is mostly about his conversion to the plays of her friend Ernst Toller, which he now wanted to bring to Dublin.[60]

And he urgently wanted to clarify matters about the plan to produce his plays with Ashley Dukes and Rupert Doone, which was lurching to a halt. His initial belief that in the Group Theatre he had found his longed-for interpreters was mistaken. Dukes (who was determined not to cede control to Doone) had muddied the waters by warning WBY of the Group's Communist 'label' and their anti-romantic agenda.[61] Worse still, Doone and his friends were unaccountably reluctant to take dictation from the master, whom they privately regarded with some irreverence (Doone ecstatically reported how WBY had paused on his way down the Savile staircase after lunch, peered at his reflection in a glass, and murmured, 'One must adjust the image'[62]). WBY now worried that his work would be unsuited to their method and tried to insist on retaining the right to approve cast and production: he was also privately determined to get Margot Ruddock the lead in *The Player Queen*, a play which he now thought should be produced by the new wunderkind Tyrone Guthrie, rather than by Doone. His plans were further impeded by a violent cold which struck as soon as he arrived and more or less confined him to his Seymour Street lodgings until mid April. He was still determined to attach himself to the avant-garde, and not yet ready to recognize that both the Group Theatre's repertoire and Ashley Dukes's opposing ambitions would be monopolized by Eliot and the new generation already focused on the dazzling Wystan Auden. The play Auden had written with Isherwood, *The Dog beneath the Skin*, was now Doone's priority.

Ill as he was, WBY summoned Auden from Birmingham for an Ivy lunch 'to settle a point about his play'.[63] This may have been the only occasion they met, but Auden retained lifelong ambivalence about the towering figure who would inspire one of his own greatest elegies. Nonetheless they had several friends in common (notably Gerald Heard and Edith Sitwell), and

WBY was more attuned to the Auden generation than is often allowed; the fragmentary, parodic effects and harsh juxtapositions of some of his own poetry in this period may represent an echo of the Auden–Isherwood dramatic tone, and Auden's interest in experiments with dance, music and speech were – in principle, if not in effect – closely compatible with WBY's enduring but unrealized ambition for a poet's theatre. Auden's biographer has described him as 'seeking to make some kind of intellectual order out of the chaos of human history, knowledge and belief',[64] which suggests a definite affinity with the author of *A Vision*. But their intellectual bases were sharply opposed, and Auden – like Mannin – was at this stage of his career a determined materialist in philosophy and a fellow travelling left-winger in politics.

Prospects for the theatre season darkened. Dukes was distracted, not only by the prospect of Auden's play but by the idea of doing Eliot's *Murder in the Cathedral*. Both Doone and Guthrie had privately decided to back out of the projected Yeats season, though Doone did not yet admit it to WBY.[65] Dulac, who had been lined up to do costumes and scenery, also wearied of the contentious atmosphere that infected anything to do with the edgy, insecure, and dictatorial Doone: 'the happy atmosphere of the Hawks' Well production' seemed far away.[66] On 19 April, believing himself fully recovered, WBY borrowed Gwyneth Foden's flat in a Bayswater boarding-house ('a great room with Chinese tapestries, a golden gasolier, a bad painting of the Scott School – mountain and mist'). He lived frugally on 'bread, olives and burgundy' and felt well enough to admit to George how ill he had been. In response to an anxious telegram he had replied, 'Nearly well again. Yeats.' 'The "Yeats" made [George] shout for joy,' Lily remarked. 'There she had her man. No other man would so end a telegram to his anxious wife. And then all the 8 paid for words wasted.'[67] But he was still driving himself too hard, trying to rescue the Mercury Theatre project (now altered to a summer fortnight of WBY's plays in celebration of his seventieth birthday), negotiating with Constant Huntington over Gregory's literary estate, and seeing friends. After a few days in Lancaster Gate Terrace the congestion in his lungs returned, so severely that Dulac summoned George by telegram; she arrived promptly and nursed him until he was well enough to return to Dublin in early June.

When partially recovered, he invited Sean O'Casey to visit him – an occasion O'Casey recorded in his memoirs. He found WBY surrounded by books of poems, from which he was selecting for the Oxford anthology, mixed in with the whodunnits and Wild West adventures prescribed for relaxation. O'Casey refused to pass judgement on the poetry, but they talked of their mutual love of Elizabethan and Jacobean tragedy, with its glamorous chiaroscuro of emotion. Suddenly WBY's enthusiasm brought on an alarming attack.

> The teeming thoughts of Yeats turned suddenly into himself as a tremulous stoppage of breath started an outburst of coughing that shook his big, protesting body, stretching his wide chest on a rack of straining effort to rid itself of congestion, or end the effort by ending life. His hands gripped the sides of his chair, his fine eyes began to stare and bulge, showing the storm within, as he leant back and bent forward to sway with the waves of stuffy contortion that were forcing resistant life from his fighting body. The whole stately dignity and courage of the poet was crinkling into a cough. He has caught an everlasting cold, thought Sean. His own black oxen are treading him down.[68]

O'Casey's memories of the conversation are heavily laden with baroque imagery and internal rhapsody, but subsequent letters confirm several of the subjects which he records discussing, and at least one point strikes true: WBY's close questioning of his guest about Communism and its contemporary appeal. 'What is this Communism: what is its divinity – if it has any; what is its philosophy? Whatever the State, there must be a governing class placed by wealth above fear and toil.' Unsurprisingly, he was unconvinced by O'Casey, who argued the economic-determinist case and claimed that Communism meant a process of levelling up, not down. 'It isn't enough. What I've heard of it, O'Casey, doesn't satisfy me. It fails to answer the question of What is life. What is man? What is reality? It tells us nothing of invisible things, of vision, or spiritual powers: or preternatural activities and energy beyond and above man's ordinary knowledge and contemplation.' They moved to safer territory – the need to bring modern European plays to the Abbey – but WBY's testy queries probably echo questions raised by his attempted collaboration with the Group Theatre and his arguments with Ethel Mannin. And she had returned to his life, sending flowers and visiting Lancaster Gate several times; his letters to her regain a little of their fervour (and he discreetly advised her, like Ruddock, to write to him in Dublin via the Kildare Street Club). But she had by now met her future husband, Reginald Reynolds, and the 'beatitudes' she offered WBY played a decreasing role in their relationship.

With his recovery he cautiously entered social life again. Rothenstein, lunching at his club with Ramsay MacDonald and G. M. Trevelyan, noticed that the convalescent WBY at first could hardly speak, but gained in strength and ended by dominating the table. As he talked of Swift and Berkeley, Trevelyan tried to interrupt with mundane historical corrections but was masterfully kept in check by WBY's raised hand.[69] It may have been at this time too that Mannin and Ernst Toller tried to persuade WBY to sign a petition by Nobel Prize winners, arguing for the prize to go to Carl von Ossietzky, currently imprisoned by the Nazis. Collecting WBY at the Savile, they went to the bar at Claridge's, and – having been fortified by vodka at the Soviet Embassy – begged him to lend his name. 'I knew before Toller had finished', she wrote later,

that Yeats would refuse. He never meddled in political affairs, he said; he never had. At the urging of Maud Gonne he had signed the petition on behalf of Roger Casement, but that was all, and the Casement case was after all an Irish affair. He was a poet, and Irish, and had no interest in European political squabbles. His interest was Ireland, and Ireland had nothing to do with Europe politically: it was outside, apart. He was sorry, but this had always been his attitude.[70]

Though this was a rather contorted view of his political past, it was probably true regarding his attitude to the European arena. A year later Dermott MacManus tried to enlist his support, probably regarding Mussolini's flouting of the League over Abyssinia, and received exactly the same reply: he 'had always refused to have any part, however slight, in international politics'.[71] Though exceptions were made for literary causes (he had signed a letter of protest against the Spanish government's treatment of Unamuno y Jugo in 1924[72]), the word 'international' was carefully placed; the focus of his political attention continued, however resentfully, to be Dublin.

But his artistic and social interests were still centred on London, visiting Margot Ruddock, Eliot, and Ottoline Morrell. And through his London circle he was introduced to Dorothy Wellesley, one of the new poets whose work he had dutifully been reading for the Oxford anthology. She had written to him on 28 May, after Ottoline and Rothenstein had told her WBY liked her poems. On 3 June he and Ottoline travelled to Penns in the Rocks, Wellesley's romantic house near Withyham on the Sussex–Kent border, to dine and stay the night. The meeting was, for them both, an epiphany. 'Within two minutes of our first meeting,' Wellesley later remembered, 'standing in the hall at Penns, he said "You must sacrifice everything and everyone to your poetry."'[73] Though she told him this was impossible, a note had been struck which would be sustained throughout their friendship, and an intense correspondence began as soon as he returned to Dublin on 9 June.

IV

Four days later he celebrated his seventieth birthday. This had been long anticipated: during his illness six months before, a well-wisher involved in the planned celebrations had implored George, 'O Mrs Yeats dont let him slip away before June.'[74] The Irish branch of PEN announced a celebration banquet, to which WBY reacted with some alarm: he did his best to dissuade friends like Masefield from travelling to attend it. ('It is great audacity on their part. I hope you will not think of going upon that boring journey. They are a small unimportant Dublin Society. I had refused to join them, but when they offered this banquet was grateful to them.'[75]) The Laureate came anyway, and even brought his dreaded wife. Masefield was also a moving spirit in arranging a presentation from fellow artists: the committee included Lawrence Binyon, de la Mare, Dulac, Eliot, Augustus John, Gilbert Murray, Rothenstein, Sturge Moore, and Ralph Vaughan Williams.[76] 'When he was 40,' Gogarty wrote sarcastically to Horace Reynolds, 'Lady Gregory gave him a Kelmscott Chaucer (at our expense). Who will be as off-handed now that she has gone?'[77] In the event, the joint present took the form of a drawing by Rossetti: the subject was Lucrezia Borgia, a figure who, WBY courteously responded, had always 'charmed' him – 'her infamous reputation, Bayard's declaration that she was his ideal woman, the hair-shirt found on her dead body'.[78]

This faintly bizarre presentation inaugurated a general chorus of celebration, confirming WBY's status as – in Gogarty's phrase – 'The Arch-Poet'. The *Irish Times*, as Lily put it, 'came out strong and was nearly all W.B.Y.'[79] A leading editorial was followed by contributions from Francis Hackett, Sean O'Faolain, Denis Johnston, A. E. Malone, and Aodh de Blácam. Less predictably, the Fianna Fáil *Irish Press* also printed a laudatory piece, attributing the 1916 Rising to the influence of WBY's theatre.[80] This gave him a certain pleasure, but the *Irish Times* leader placed him more precisely where he would like to be seen:

From the national viewpoint W. B. Yeats occupies an almost unique position in Irish life; for he is virtually the first man since Swift who has been able to bring the Anglo-Irish tradition into line with a positive nationalism. He took his inspiration from the ancient Celtic legends of the west; but he has always been proud of the fact that he comes of Anglo-Irish stock . . . Thus he has reconciled in his life and work a tradition that is purely Gaelic, with the younger, but no less vital, tradition of his Anglo-Saxon forebears . . . He is Anglo-Irish and he is a Protestant. Yet there is no other Irishman of his day and generation who has done one tithe of his work for his native land.[81]

This put WBY squarely in the Thomas Davis tradition, and implicitly rallied the *Irish Times*'s traditional Protestant readership as full citizens of de Valera's Ireland. In an interview for Radio Éireann WBY delivered the same message: 'Anglo-Ireland is already Ireland . . . there may be pure Gaels in the Blasket Islands but there are none in the Four Courts, in the College of Surgeons, at the Universities, in the Executive Council, at Mr Cosgrave's headquarters . . . I hate all hyphenated words. Anglo-Ireland is your word not mine.'[82] Other essays simultaneously published by the paper took up this theme, with Francis Hackett hailing him as the epitome of his country. For Hackett, WBY was a self-created artistic phenomenon, developing from the 'necromantic cadence' of his early plays and lyrics through to the subtlety and tension of the later work.

. . . like Beethoven's later sonatas, a mobile medium, in which the warmth and impress of mood are communicable . . . He is still Yeatsian, but the sensitiveness has become virile and inclusive. Had Yeats been educated in a grand tradition, had Coole been a Weimar, he could have been our Goethe. As it is, the world knows him as our national poet, the one Irishman who has given form to our lyric and lyric to our theatre. He has spread his dreams under Ireland's feet. May she tread softly.

It was a distinguished evaluation by a perceptive admirer, and WBY kept a copy in his papers.[83] O'Faolain covered some of the same ground, but emphasized the intellectual conflicts running beneath the brilliant surface of language. 'That has been his task and his torment, to find a philosophy in which man is at once free and creative, absolute possessor of himself in this life, and possessor at the same time of everything that is outside the individual substance of his body and his span. The arrogance of it is immense.' Higgins similarly discussed WBY's position in Ireland, as creator of a literary 'movement' rather than of a 'school' – in his view, a valuable and liberating influence. Both the celebratory tone and the high standard of criticism were abruptly deflated in Aodh de Blácam's sour-faced contribution, which took a directly contrary line by stressing the selfish 'subjectivity' and unnational nature of the Anglo-Irish tradition. It was the Gaelic League that truly expressed 'the old racial tendency' in literature; WBY's controversies with 'patriots' were regrettable; the only 'Anglo-Irishman' to truly express the voice of the nation was John Mitchel, 'most majestic of all Irish prose authors'. By comparison, WBY epitomized the Spenglerian decline of the Ascendancy.

Yeats's late essays are studded with phrases quoted for their verbal atmosphere, with an unclassical, un-Gaelic disregard for their logical setting. Sensation rises over reason, art over conscience, style over matter in this autumnal writing. Yeats came at last to compose those strange 'Plays for Dancers' which reject all common appeal, and he declared in 1916 that 'public art' belonged to 'an irrevocable past'. Harmony of mind was ended.

In de Blácam's view WBY perversely challenged 'sacred things', preferring to praise Brian Merriman's *The Midnight Court*, 'a morbid freak, totally untypical of Gaelic letters with their stern chastity'. In commissioning de Blácam, the *Irish Times* may have felt constrained to demonstrate just what WBY had devoted his later life to opposing.

The *Irish Times* essays were printed in a celebratory booklet, circulated by the Irish branch of PEN. On the day itself, WBY received forty-two cables and telegrams from well-wishers as diverse as James Joyce, Margaret Gough, Micheál Mac Liammóir and Hilton Edwards, Edith Sitwell, Ethel Mannin, Margot Ruddock, the Dulacs, the Morrells, and Gwyneth Foden. The Rossetti drawing arrived accompanied by a white vellum book with a high-flown Masefieldian inscription and a list of subscribers.

We, friends of the Arts, wish to offer to you on your seventieth birthday a token of our admiration.

Some of us who have had the privilege of knowing you have felt the encouragement of your sympathy. All of us have known the beauty and strength of your inspiration.

We hope that this power, which has grown steadily and is still growing, may continue for many years to delight mankind.

The names attached numbered 108. They included ancient friends and collaborators (Gordon Craig, Dulac, Herbert Grierson, Augustus John, H. W. Nevinson, Ernest Rhys, Shaw), new associates (Dukes, Eliot, Robert Lynd, Sassoon), society figures (Sibyl Colefax, Lord Crewe, Eddie Marsh), prominent literati (A. E. Housman, Compton Mackenzie, Vita Sackville-West, R. H. Tawney, G. M. Trevelyan, Maurice Baring), theatre people (Granville-Barker, John Martin Harvey, Lillah McCarthy) and large-minded adversaries (Dunsany, St John Ervine, D. S. MacColl). The list profiled WBY's London world, past and present.

This was joined by an eclectic range of presents, including some pre-1815 brandy 'from an English admirer' and (a fortnight later) a Chinese carving in lapis lazuli from Gogarty's friend, the wealthy but erratic young poet Harry Clifton, which at once joined Sato's sword as a sacred and inspirational object.[84] On 13 June there was a small family dinner at Riversdale: 'duck and green peas, meringue and cream, coffee and champagne to drink Willy's health', Lily recorded.[85] But a fortnight later the PEN banquet provided more to write about. Two hundred and fifty people came to eat six courses and toast WBY at the Royal Hibernian Hotel on Dawson Street. 'Everyone who was anybody' was there, though the Yeatses had to fish for an invitation for poor Mrs Masefield, whose ubiquitous husband proposed the toast to WBY. 'You like him and what he says immensely as he says it,' reported Lily, '& then somehow cannot recall it.' Other speeches were made by Francis Hackett, Desmond MacCarthy, Sean O'Faolain; 'It was a very un-noisy evening,' Lily told her niece.

Lots of talk but no fooling. Willy, I suppose, really set the note . . . [He] looked very fine and about 65. The speaking was good . . . It was a proud evening for the

Yeats[es]. Aunt Fanny was quite overcome, and I thought that stoic George was also. But it was also sad. Willy is now an old man, and we are old.

Willy said little, but said it well, so true and finished. He ended with 'I probably am standing at the door saying goodbye'.[86]

The sense of parting was sharpened by the imminent loss of his earliest friend. For all their intermittent coolnesses and resentments, AE and wby had been allies since their art-school friendship and occultist experiments in the distant Dublin of a half-century before, when they had wandered home to Terenure arguing about supernatural experiences. By 1935, never really recovered from Susan Mitchell's death and the collapse of the *Irish Statesman*, disappointed by his family and disillusioned by Ireland, AE had sold his house, books, and pictures, and embarked on a life of American lectures, Bloomsbury boarding-houses, and sojourns in Bournemouth to recruit his failing health.[87] The day after wby's birthday, he wrote apologizing that he was incapacitated by his medical regime and could not travel to Dublin for the birthday celebrations. The formality with which he addressed his boyhood friend suggests a considered valediction.

I read with great pleasure the articles in Irish Times on your seventieth birthday. You have such an endowment of intellectual & physical energy that you may well after eighty be to Ireland what Goethe was in Weimar, and may go on creating new masterpieces of lyrical & dramatic beauty, and studies in more profound philosophy when those who were your contemporaries are long silent. I hope it may be so for the sake of Ireland which indeed has to be overawed by a great reputation world wide like yours, out of the mood of the bosthoon & easy cynicism which is a cloak for ignorance. I think you will be the pivot round which Ireland will turn from its surfaces to more central depths. There are deeps in the Irish character to be sounded. I could not sound them. I could only find intermittently access to some spiritual nature which is not more Irish than Hindu. But to find access to that however intermittently was the only thing I really care about in life & it is the reason why so often I could not or would not be with you in your work or policies for I dreaded that a nature more formidable and powerful than my own would lead me away from my own will & centre. It is of no importance now, for I have written all I had to write, and there will be no more poetry from me good or bad. This letter is only to assure you of my profound respect for your genius & to join with your other contemporaries in paying my tribute to it.[88]

This was the last letter he would write to w b y, but his half-suspicious fascination with his extraordinary friend remained as intense as ever. Just before he died, he was prompted by Sean O'Faolain's article to send him a long letter reviewing his ancient arguments with wby over mysticism and magic:

The poet was naturally idealist. His father was sceptical and because of this early influence there are layers of faith & scepticism in Yeats mind. It was I think to get rid of the sceptical element in himself so that he might have a whole faith that he adventured into magic and spiritualism hoping for the clear fact or experience, or sign, which would enable him to have an untroubled faith.[89]

AE's own adventurous journey was almost over; he died of stomach cancer in Bournemouth a month after WBY's birthday. There was an enormous funeral in Dublin, which would stay in WBY's mind as exactly the kind of *envoi* he wanted to avoid when his own time came. It commenced with a reception committee of notables, and a fly-past of assorted aeroplanes organized by the scandalous aviatrix Lady Heath, and went on relentlessly for hours. 'Willy had a long day and felt it very much,' Lily told Ruth. 'He and others of the Irish Academy of Letters met the mail boat at 6.30 [a.m.] and then the coffin was taken to Plunkett House. From there the funeral was at 9.30 a.m., a mile-long procession following.'[90] Some surprise was expressed when he declined to give a funeral oration, but he was harder hit than many people recognized, and did not want to contribute any further rodomontade. He was also exhausted by having 'to use all my powers of intreague & self assertion to prevent a fanatical woman from making it a political demonstration by draping the coffin with a tri-colour.'[91] But he was nagged by regret at not having gone with Gogarty and Con Curran to visit the invalid at Bournemouth, and felt unable to appear even at his sisters' annual summer party a week after the funeral: 'he felt AE would be talked of, and he cannot yet talk of him'.[92] He wrote a kind of private elegy in a letter to Dorothy Wellesley:

All is well with AE. His ghost will not walk. He had no passionate human relationships to draw him back. My wife said the other night 'AE was the nearest to a saint you or I will ever meet. You are a better poet but no saint. I suppose one has to choose'.[93]

George's astringent summing-up may have provided some comfort. However, the death of his oldest friend, following hard upon his seventieth birthday, forced him to take stock. He resumed his plans to reform the Abbey, currently foundering in a rut of well-worn comedies and losing its key players to Hollywood contracts. In London he and O'Casey had agreed that the only hope for a real revival lay in putting on Continental and American plays; WBY was already nurturing a plan to start up a 'Second Company' again, devoted to just such work.[94] In February, while convalescing, he had given an interview to the *Irish Times* on forthcoming changes to the Abbey, following the resignation of the latest manager, Bladon Peake (an Englishman awarded the traditional hostile reception by the players). WBY's plan was to set up an advisory committee to inject new energy into the theatre, and bring in modern Continental drama. He also wanted to incorporate people like F. R. Higgins, who could outflank recalcitrant directors. His comments on the slackening standard of new Irish plays had brought an angry rejoinder from Sean O'Faolain and Frank O'Connor, who blamed the dilatory and discouraging approach taken by the Abbey management towards any new work submitted.[95] Illness and WBY's long London visit intervened, but during his convalescence in London in early May he dictated a long letter for the consideration of the Abbey Board, suggesting a public competition, with cash prizes, to elicit new plays: 'a jury of, say, 60 regular Abbey patrons should be formed to make the final selection'. This envisaged an astonishing surrender of the powers he had guarded so jealously for so long.[96] On his return to Dublin, he corresponded with O'Casey about possible new set-designers, and a modern repertoire: the ancient hunger for 'foreign masterpieces' had possessed him once more. The 'advisory committee' never came off, but two new directors (F. R. Higgins and Ernest Blythe) joined the quadrumvirate of WBY, Robinson, Walter Starkie, and Richard Hayes: so, briefly, did Brinsley MacNamara. As it happened, the great Abbey event of the summer of 1935 would be neither a reorganized management nor a new second Company, but – finally – a production of *The Silver Tassie* in August. WBY's rapprochement with O'Casey made it possible, but his ready admission of the mistake made in 1928 testifies to the effect of the new theatre of the Auden generation, and WBY's reappraisal of political playwrights like Toller. And the response would be all that he had hoped for: violent attacks in the press, a resignation from the board. The great days of Abbey controversy promised to be returning, and with them his own energies.[97] But he had realized that he was too old to play a public role.

Just before the June celebrations, he had been invited (for the second time) to become Charles Eliot Norton Professor of Poetry at Harvard for the spring semester in 1936: a lucrative and distinguished post, but ruled out by WBY's ill-health and the Massachusetts climate.[98] Still, he hesitated over it, and the offer – as he wrote to Mannin – 'brought to a head' the need to look forward into the rest of his life.

I have had to make an important decision. Have I written all the good poetry I can expect to write? Should I turn my measure of fame into money for the sake of my family? . . . I am about to cut myself adrift, as far as I can, from all external circumstances (the Abbey Theatre will soon be able to go its own road), I want to plunge myself into impersonal poetry, to get rid of the bitterness, irritation & hatred my work in Ireland has brought into my soul. I want to make the last song, sweet & exultant, a sort of European *Geeta*, or rather my *Geeta*, not doctrine but song.[99]

The birthday accolades, and AE's funeral, drove him to consider yet again his relationship to Irish life, and the need for liberation. Shortly before, Austin Clarke (whose review of *The Tower* seven years before had testified to WBY's status among the younger Irish poets) published a searching and rather tendentious article on 'Irish Poetry Today',[100] arguing that WBY had now turned away from Ireland and back to the 'rich imaginative associations' of the English tradition. Hailed by Eliot, Wyndham Lewis, and their 'English' generation, he was looking back to the sources of his 'nineties' youth. Clarke posed an insinuating question: did this mean the Irish Revival had been 'a flash in the pan', and a distinct Irish literature 'no more than a clearing house or a training-depot'? But, he went on, WBY's own trajectory proved this was not the case.

When we match the jigsaw puzzles of his various phases, we can see that his flightiness belongs to the adventurous, restless Anglo-Irish type of the past, those writers who lacking lares of their own, were extraordinarily responsive and adaptable to any environment in which they happened to find themselves, Wilde, Shaw and so forth ... Mr Yeats, coming too soon before the new forces of racial recovery, was unable to find that complete identification of interests which others found, and with rare artistic integrity continued his search, turning to the metaphysical Anglicans and modern intellectual encyclopaedism. In expressing so completely his own type, Mr Yeats presents us with the case for integrity.

This constructed an urbane version of Corkery's and de Blácam's 'outsider' thesis, directly contrary to the *Irish Times*'s celebration of WBY as Irish in his Anglo-Irishness. Clarke (whom WBY dismissed as 'an unbalanced person') was never impartial on the subject; years later he would tell Richard Ellmann 'I hated Yeats and he hated me.'[101] But he was right to sense a swerve in WBY's artistic affections and a readiness for adventure just when his weakened physical resources might have suggested limiting his horizons. Dr Shaw was in regular attendance during June, ordering the patient to avoid strain, rest for three months, and – WBY told Mannin with a certain faux insouciance – to observe 'celebacy'. But these strictures, like his birthday apotheosis, came at a moment when – as he also told Mannin – he wanted to cut loose from both domestic and Irish associations and antipathies. The destinations where this impulse would carry him had already been signposted.

V

One of them was the refuge promised by Dorothy Wellesley at Penns in the Rocks. The meeting in early June had created a sense of excited anticipation. In his first substantial letter WBY wrote effusively about Wellesley's poetry: 'Your work resembles & contrasts with that of Edith Sitwell. She too loves minute exquisite detail but her world is literary, artificial, almost that of Russian Ballet, whereas you play with the real world as a child, as a young girl, as a young man plays, you are full of poet's learning but it is the learning the unlearned desire & understand.'[102] She sent him Vita Sackville-West's poems, which, WBY assured her, were eloquent and technically skilled, but her friend was not a poet and lacked Wellesley's 'masculine rhythm'. When Dorothy Wellesley published WBY's correspondence five years later (to the horror of more reticent members of WBY's circle like Dulac), she called the volume 'Letters on Poetry', and this is the ostensible theme. But even in the early exchanges there is an extra dimension. To remark that Wellesley played with the real world 'as a young man plays' in poems of a 'masculine rhythm' carried its own message. So did her gift to

12. William Rothenstein's drawing of Dorothy Wellesley in 1925.

527

him of Sackville-West's poetry: several of Sackville-West's poems, including a long passage in *The Land*, were addressed to Wellesley. For WBY's fascination with Dorothy Wellesley was partly to do with her exoticism, both as an aristocrat and as a well-known lesbian.

Born in 1889 as Dorothy Ashton, she was rich and well connected. The early deaths of her father and brother had left her an heiress, and after her mother's marriage to the tenth earl of Scarbrough she grew up between Lumley Castle and other great country houses. In 1914 she had married the architect Lord Gerald Wellesley – later, rather unexpectedly, to become seventh duke of Wellington. The couple had two children but separated in 1922. (Since he had already been engaged to Violet Keppel, Sackville-West's first lover and a spectacularly histrionic personality, he was something of a glutton for punishment.) Married or not, Dorothy Wellesley's life was closely woven into the tangled web of upper-class lesbian intrigue spun around the glamorous Vita Sackville-West. Their own love-affair was over when WBY met her, and her long relationship with the influential BBC producer Hilda Matheson had begun, which would last until Matheson's early death. Tiny, slight, auburn-haired, 'with blazing blue eyes' and an equally blazing temper, Wellesley was always at odds with her surroundings. Sackville-West wrote much later that Dorothy was 'a natural rebel, rejecting all conventions and accepted ideas, loving to proclaim herself an agnostic, a fiery spirit with a passionate love for beauty in all forms': early on she was marked by 'temper, pride and combativeness'.[103] Harold Nicolson, less diplomatically, reflected that 'Dottie makes a mistake in trying to be at one and the same time the little bit of thistledown *and* the thistle';[104] her bad temper could deteriorate into malevolence and neurosis. As with Sackville-West herself, Wellesley possessed bohemian instincts that were at war with the dynastic grandeur and *noblesse oblige* of her public role. She was already, since her rejection by Sackville-West, trying to escape the tension through alcohol. Later, after she lost Matheson, she would give in to it completely.

Sackville-West was well known to be a lover of women (Edith Sitwell's tongue-in-cheek proposal of her as Poet Laureate in 1929 had stated 'Miss Sackville-West, had it not been for a flaw in fate, would have been one of Nature's gentlemen'[105]), and her liaison with Wellesley was no secret to Ottoline Morrell and her circle; WBY must have been forewarned. Nonetheless, he became infatuated with Wellesley and her world, curiously reminiscent of Woolf's *Orlando*: an androgynous, *difficile*, creative spirit, immobilized in the heraldic tapestry of historic English aristocracy. Early on she confided that she had been entranced when he told her his regret, after first reading her work, at learning about her social position. 'I know that you realised instantly how difficult and exhausting it all is. Hardly shall a rich man enter into the temple of the muses. I have tried to keep faith since a child, and now I am happier and shall probably make my peace with the Pharisees of all sorts. Is this right or wrong?'[106] To many, this agonizing about privilege, assuaged by frequent flights to southern Europe or the Near East, seemed a tedious affectation: her daughter would later describe her as 'a phony Bohemian'. Nor was WBY really regretful about his new friend's quasi-ducal status. Later, Ottoline Morrell would remark acidly that he had left her for Dorothy Wellesley's chef. There was also a Mayfair flat, and a Rolls-Royce, and the wonderful Sussex house. But the attraction was more profound than that.

From Wellesley's side, WBY's fascination was immense. She was struck by his style, his own type of grandeur, his looks. And he genuinely admired the 'passionate precision' of her poetry, to the stupefaction of many. Sackville-West was probably envious of the endorsement offered to her friend by WBY, and certainly annoyed when Wellesley later published letters declaring his low opinion of Vita's own work. She got her own back by delivering a stinging judgement on Wellesley's poetry after her death, declaring that her imaginative gifts were never equalled by intellectual power: she 'dashed off poems as fast as she could write them down', too lazy and headstrong to revise them.

Grammar and syntax bored her; impatiently she rejected the counsel of her friends . . . Fancying herself as something of a philosopher, with a sense of history and a smattering of archaeology, all somewhat amateurish, she often imposed upon her verse a weight it should never have been asked to carry. She felt; she saw; she interpreted. Her undoing, as a poet, sometimes, was that she thought she could think.[107]

Even the vaunted 'preciseness of observation' of Nature could, in Sackville-West's opinion, approach myopia. Privately, Woolf and Sackville-West referred to 'Dotty' with some impatience. But WBY thought he had found a poet who represented the aristocratic *sprezzatura* of an Urbino courtier or an androgynous Hilliard miniature. After he had known her a few months, he analysed Wellesley's horoscope:

It has greatly surprized me, your profile gives a false impression, it suggests cumulative energy, masculinity. You are not sensual, but emotional, greatly wishing to please and to be pleased; fundamental common sense but too impatient for good judgement until deliberation call up this common sense; deeply imaginative but the star that gives this makes drugs attractive . . .[108]

By then, he knew that she was erratic and affected as well as intelligent; he may also have observed the two bottles of white wine which were conveyed to her bedroom every night. But the limits of their relationship had been conveniently demarcated. A 70-year-old man with a strained heart and potency problems was not likely to inflict amorous demands which a 46-year-old lesbian would find unwelcome. Their friendship would settle into an *amitié amoureuse*: Ottoline Morrell could safely assure George (apparently recalling Margot Ruddock, whom she had met) that Dorothy was not a 'minx'.[109] Wellesley, chronically unsure about her talent and partly trapped in a conventional and self-assured world which ignored her literary ambitions, had found both an admirer and a mentor whose greatness was unassailable. He read her work closely, made suggestions, encouraged her, and told her to sacrifice everything to her writing. She clung to this advice for the rest of her life, without ever being able to follow it.

He could offer practical help by drawing attention to her poetry – not only in the Oxford anthology, but by suggesting to Macmillan (already her publishers) that he edit a selection of her work and contribute an Introduction.[110] This aspect of their relationship would arouse some derision, but Wellesley was (at least compared to Margot Ruddock) a moderately accomplished if minor poet, and the quality of some of her work has been vindicated by time. For WBY, the echoes from his past were irresistible. By the end of the year he was telling his hostess and correspondent that she could, for all her ambition, 'write like the common people'.[111] As a writer, a great lady, and the possessor of a house which would give him a creative refuge, Dorothy Wellesley appeared, in the summer of 1935, to offer a glamorous replacement for Gregory and Coole. 'How anxious she was to take Lady Gregory's place as a Platonic Muse and flame behind the Bardic throne,' reflected Shane Leslie, who knew them both, 'and Yeats sighed for a last rose of autumn with a pink suffusion of passion, but all in vain.'[112]

As with Gregory, the relationship was cemented and symbolized by a house. Penns was as emblematic of Englishness as Coole of the Irish Ascendancy. Its discreet white gate, sunk below the road between Crowborough and Groombridge, led into a long, winding drive through bluebell woods and great trees; as at Coole, the world fell away behind the traveller. The house, at first glimpse, was a small, dignified early-Georgian manor in rose-coloured brick; careful early-Victorian additions had filled it out into a more expansive shape, and a larger dwelling lay concealed beneath the regular doll's-house frontage. The drama lay in the setting. Penns looked across huge sloping lawns to the surprising natural feature which gave it its name: a great outcrop of sandstone rocks, like something out of a brooding Italian romantic landscape. Trees grew out of them and on top of them, and walks wound around them: Ashdown Forest stretched for miles beyond. Strangely, only a few miles to the east lay Coleman's Hatch and Stone Cottage, where WBY had spent his honeymoon, and wintered with Pound in the early years of the war. Like Coole with its seven woods and disappearing lake, the house was hidden in a secret and surreal landscape, haunted by memory. There were walled gardens, restored by Wellesley when she bought the house in 1929, *allées*, high yew hedges; a lily pond and a romantic swimming pool were added in 1935. On the south side of the house, where a large downstairs chamber was designated WBY's bedroom, wide windows commanded a view of a huge cedar and another great lawn stretching down to a river. Vanessa Bell and Duncan Grant came over from Charleston to decorate the dining room with large *fauvist* nudes; Wellesley's appalled son and daughter surreptitiously flicked mashed potato to cover up the 'rude bits' on the paintings, but WBY much admired them.[113] The house and its slightly brooding atmosphere were legendary. Both are preserved in a celebrated painting by Rex Whistler, a close family friend. In the dramatic foreground the two beautiful Wellesley children (who resented WBY's presence much as the young Gregorys had done) lounge gloomily among the Rocks, with a gun and a Great Dane; the house floats four-square in the distance, their mother's distant face framed in a window. Intentionally or not, she seems to be glaring.[114]

The echo of Coole and Gregory is suggested in another long letter sent by WBY, immediately after his first – asking if he could stay with her in August 'long enough to see your woods. By that time I shall be well enough to walk there. I shall not be a burden to you, for the trees will entertain me.'[115] The postscript shows that they already had few secrets from one another. 'I find my present weakness made worse by the strange second puberty the operation has given me, the ferment that has come upon my imagination. If I write more poetry it will be unlike anything I have done.' And her reply responded to his implicit request. 'This house is yours to work in, at peace, at any time all yours.'[116]

In August he travelled to Penns, bringing Anne, whom Wellesley had invited to meet her own sixteen-year-old daughter. He had resumed, after a four months' silence, his correspondence with Margot Ruddock, in a notably cautious tone. She had offered to meet him at the boat, but he declined. A response to one of her poems carried a clear message:

I understand what you mean about the word 'love'. I too hate that word and have I think avoided it. It is a name for the ephemeral charm of desire – desire for its own sake. I do not think that it is because I have grown old that I value something more like friendship because founded on common interests and think sexual pleasure an accessory, a needful one where it is possible.[117]

The Wellesley house-party included Iris Mountbatten, and WBY derived a certain satisfaction from Anne's beating of 'Victoria's great-grand-daughter' at croquet (and from retailing Lady Iris's belief that 'the Mona Lisa is a song, though she had heard a lecture upon the subject').[118] George had been invited but declined. WBY was by now well advanced on compiling the Oxford anthology, declaring that Wellesley, Elinor Wylie, and Richard Hughes had been the most exciting discoveries; they would be followed by equally sudden passions for George Barker and W. J. Turner. 'I did [not] forsee that the work would bring me your friendship,' he told Wellesley, '& for that you have my gratitude.'[119] At Penns they worked together, on both his selection from Kipling for the anthology and her own compositions. 'I have made a selection from her poems which I want her to offer to Faber & Faber,' he told George; 'I finished it yesterday. I cut long passages out of certain poems & got her to re-write others. Such a volume, about 50 pages, should establish her fame.'[120] He was as good as his word, arranging a meeting with Eliot in London on 24 April. 'I told him there was no question of your paying for the book, Faber & Faber must take it at their own risk.' (As it happened, to Eliot's slight embarrassment, they did not. WBY blamed the 'ultra-radical influence' of Robert Graves and Laura Riding.) If Penns were to play the role of Coole, he would press the claims of Wellesley's poetry as strongly as he had boosted *Cuchulain of Muirthemne*.

In London he worked through forty-five books of modern poetry in the British Museum, had a satisfactory check-up with Norman Haire, dined with Dulac, and returned to Dublin before the end of the month. He arrived back to the full-blown row over *The Silver Tassie*, which had opened just before his departure. Brinsley MacNamara, appointed a director only a few months earlier, had come out against the play, but WBY managed things, as he boasted to Wellesley,

so that he must publicly apologise or be expelled, not for attacking us, or the play (he would like that) but for breach of trust. (He had published in his excitement what took place at board meetings.) When he saw what was happening he was almost pathetic in his helplessness & I spent a gloomy evening wondering whether I am as my wife says 'ruthless'. But I must have a governing body in complete agreement or the mob wins.[121]

In the theatre too an ancient pattern seemed to be reasserting itself. As always, WBY was energized by the conflict; after his enforced summer of rest, September and October saw a welter of activity. The Mercury Theatre season of his plays had evaporated, and Ashley Dukes now seemed, he told Margot, 'a swamp we got mixed in'. But she knew Nancy Price of the People's National Theatre Company, and sent on the plays to her. Price responded favourably and wrote to WBY in September, suggesting a brief matinée season in the Little Theatre. By early October she was casting *The Player Queen*, to be produced along with *The Hour-Glass* and *The Pot of*

Broth. WBY, determined as ever to interfere, pressed the case of Margot Ruddock as Decima, emphasizing the need for a tragic undertone: 'Through all the play Decima in the midst of her farce is keeping down with all the force of her will the hysteria of her tragedy. I write not only as dramatist but as producer.' He added that actresses in Dublin could play comedy but not tragedy. 'I said to the women members of my company once "Why aren't you tragedians? Exactly similar women are tragedians in France. I will tell you why. You sprinkle yourselves with Holy Water. In France they sprinkle each other with vitriol."'[122]

He did not get his way. Price demoted Margot to the secondary role, and Decima went to Joan Maude, who happened to be Price's daughter. But WBY continued to bombard the impresario with suggestions, instructions, and rewritten songs, determined to get away from the 'sentimental atmosphere, that I came to hate'. And the rewritten song from *The Pot of Broth* which he sent to Price on 11 October, to the tune of 'Paistin Finn', recurred yet again to an old man's impotent passion:

> That blonde girl there is my heart's desire
> But I am shrunken to skin and bone
> For all that my toil has had for its hire
> Is drinking her health when love, alone –
> *Aro Aro,*
> *Tomorrow night I will break in the door.*[123]

He had promised Price not to turn up at rehearsals, but he planned to be in London from 18 October, nine days before the plays were performed to a favourable reception but an infinitesimal audience. WBY predictably found Joan Maude's Decima 'commonplace', while Margot was 'accomplished, distinguished, flawless.'[124]

This was partly a strategic reaction. Ruddock herself was racked by doubts and distracted by loss of confidence about her acting. By November her letters were increasingly disjointed and erratic. WBY had to ply her with soothing reassurances. But by the time the plays opened, he had had his own worries. His plans to travel to London had to be postponed when a lump was found on his tongue which had to be removed immediately. The operation was on 16 October; two days later it was diagnosed as benign. He managed to get over in time for the Little Theatre matinées and recuperated for a few days at Penns with Wellesley and Matheson, where his hostess proudly summoned Vita Sackville-West to meet him. WBY read some of his Introduction to the Oxford anthology aloud, and performed as best he could, but Sackville-West was resolutely unimpressed.

He is the sort of person who has no small-talk at all, but who either remains silent or else plunges straight into the things that matter to him. So little small-talk has he that he doesn't even say 'How do you do?' when shaking hands on arrival. He just sits down on the sofa, looks at his nails for two minutes' silence, and then tells one stories about Manley Hopkins or Lady Gregory or Gogarty; or else expounds his views on T. S. Eliot and *les jeunes* . . . A handsome man, with a fine head but also unfortunately a fine tummy.[125]

There was clearly a clash of styles. But it is symptomatic that T. S. Eliot was on WBY's mind, because on his return to London he saw *Murder in the Cathedral*, produced by the unreliable Ashley Dukes, and found 'it is to my great surprise a powerful religious play'.[126] Then he returned to Dublin, but not for long. Yet another scheme of escape was about to come to fruition.

During his convalescence the previous summer, he had decided that the constant setbacks to his health, and the new threat to his heart, meant that he must resume his habit of wintering abroad. Moreover, with the Oxford anthology as good as compiled, he wanted to work on translating the Hindu *Upanishads* with the Swami. A plan had evolved of a journey to the sun together in October, accompanied by Gwyneth Foden, who took upon herself all the arrangements and made a considerable fuss about them. The chosen destination was Majorca, perhaps suggested by Ethel Mannin, who had wintered there in 1932. The departure was constantly postponed, first because of the Little Theatre season, and then WBY's operation. Finally a date was fixed for late November, with a stay envisaged of three months. There was a welter of organization to be got through, much of it involving the copy for the *Oxford Book of Modern Verse*, largely handled by George. At this very time, yet another large publishing venture was mooted, in the shape of an American collected edition, published by Charles Scribner & Sons, to be sold by subscription. This – it was hoped – would bring in a lot of money for not much effort: in early November excited letters flew between Scribner, Macmillan in New York, and WBY's agent A. P. Watt. WBY hoped the project would make him 'a minimum of something over 2500 dollars or a maximum of a little over 4800 dollars'.[127] Scribner wanted the edition to be 'definitive' and to carry a new General Introduction by WBY. The large question of competition from the edition de luxe, still in train with Macmillan in London, was, rather disingenuously, not mentioned.[128] This would complicate life for editors of WBY's work in the future; but at the time it was first floated, his priority was to maximize his writing income, as he was faced with the disappearance of his investments and the prospect of resuming a life of winters abroad. His letters outlining arrangements for the Majorcan sojourn show how narrow his margins were ('I cannot pay more than £3 a week'[129]).

Since the summer he had gazed in his study at Riversdale at Harry Clifton's lapis lazuli carving, which carried an odd suggestion of the monastery perched above Rapallo: 'a mountain with a little temple among trees half way up, and a path leading to it and on the path an ascetic with his pupil. The ascetic, pupil and little temple prophesying perhaps the Swami and myself at Mallorca.'[130] After the excitements of London and Penns in the Rocks, he was fretful. Iseult, who visited Riversdale just before he left for Majorca, found him depressed. 'He said everything was terrible, he and his wife had gradually been alienated – he said that she was a mother rather than a wife – she had humiliated him in public.' To Iseult's surprise, he said to her, 'Ah, if only we had married.' 'Why', she replied, 'we wouldn't have stayed together a year.'[131] On 28 November he and George travelled to Liverpool: she handed him over to the care of his strangely assorted travelling companions, due to take ship on a Henderson Line steamer to Palma, and headed back to Dublin. 'I'm sure Mrs Foden thought it most odd of me not to wait to see the boat steam out of the docks,' she later wrote to him. 'I felt too like the dog who sees his masters going for a walk and leaving him at home.'[132] As matters turned out, she would shortly wish that she had followed him on board; and, for all his desire for liberation, so would he.

Chapter 14 : FIRE AND EATING
1936–1937

> Yeats & Aldous agreed, the other day, that their great aim in
> writing is to avoid the 'literary'. Aldous said how extraord-
> inary the 'literary' fetish had been among the Victorians.
> Yeats said that he wanted only to use the words that real people
> say. That his change had come through writing plays. And
> I said, rashly, that all the same his meaning was very difficult.
>
> *The Diary of Virginia Woolf*, 1 January 1935[1]

I

WBY's collaboration with Shri Purohit Swami on translating mystical
Hindu writings was not a sudden passion. His Introduction to the Swami's
autobiography, and still more to *The Holy Mountain* (which echoes through
poems like 'What Magic Drum?' as well as 'Meru'), show that his long-held
fascination with India had survived the many vicissitudes of his philosophical journeyings.[2] Poems like 'Vacillation' and 'A Dialogue of Self and Soul'
strike a strong chord with the best known of the *Upanishads*, the 'Katha',
and some themes in *A Vision* (notably the Four Faculties) similarly echo
Indian mystic writings.[3] WBY's long-held belief in parallels between ancient
Indian and Celtic consciousness had been preserved since his youth; so had
his idea that Indian and Irish *mores* were both pitted against British materialism and philistinism. This could apply to current politics as well as to
philosophical traditions. 'I have been watching with delighted amusement
the controversies with Gandhi,' he had written to Lily four years before.
'Gandhi writes to the Viceroy as one well-bred man writes to another he has
met in friendly intercourse, the Viceroy adopting the time-honoured
method of politics replies like a journalist, then Gandhi the well-bred man
answers him, & the Viceroy has probably a sleepless night then correspondents write to the Times saying that something must be done to restore
British prestige, without understanding that it is a question of style.'[4]

Now the question of style preoccupied him in a different way. As he prepared to winter abroad in the autumn of 1935, WBY was impelled to try to
rediscover Mohini Chatterjee, who had inspired him in Dublin a half-
century before. Finding out Chatterjee's address, WBY wrote recalling 'the
wealth of talk when you were in Dublin' as 'a very beautiful young man'; it
'did much for my intellect, gave me indeed my first philosophical exposition
of life'.[5] There was no reply. Chatterjee (who had long since abandoned

536

asceticism for a successful law practice in Bombay) himself died a year later. The Swami, however, was very much alive, and still on the spiritual trail. WBY continued to put his faith in him, despite strenuous warnings from Sturge Moore. 'He wants to be the Vivekananda of this century, but he is neither so gifted nor so outstanding in character. This desire of his is his weakness and makes him to some degree resemble the many poets who want to be Tagore.'[6] The Swami did indeed nurture literary ambitions: starting out as a poet, he had tried to get to England in Tagore's wake in 1913 and was inordinately proud of his recent translation of the *Gita*. But his appeal for WBY was as a spiritual guide.[7] The Swami apparently epitomized an integrated and distinctly unpuritan life, where spirituality was fused with a bantering humour, physical enjoyment, good looks, a spontaneous, extravagant manner, and a cultivated attractiveness to women. He also represented the 'suspension of thought' that WBY extolled in his Introduction to *The Mandukya Upanishad*, and had been exploring in his Yogic studies since meeting the Swami in 1931. Much of what he had read awoke ringing personal echoes: the swan as symbol of the soul, the importance of mastering the technique of the non-sleeping dream-trance, the round of miracles, pilgrimages, revelation. Through the Swami, WBY had approached Patanjali's meditative techniques, though his teacher believed (conveniently enough) that the highest state of concentration was neither possible nor desirable for more than a chosen few. The Yogic idea that you could be 'fire or an eater', ascetic or sensual, struck WBY powerfully. Immersed once more in Balzac, he had decided 'that great eater' would draw him back into the world of human relations. But Indian philosophy seemed to allow, more than most intellectual systems, for the pull between rival ideals of heroism and abstraction.

This was particularly true of the Tantric system of affirmative and dynamic divinity; and WBY had possessed and read the Tantric texts translated by Sir John Woodroffe (as 'Arthur Avalon') since their first appearance in 1914.[8] (Their geometric images may, in fact, have suggested the revolving and interpenetrating gyres of *A Vision*.) And this connects directly to another of WBY's preoccupations in the 1930s: for the Tantric system emphasized the mystical and symbolic use of sex, through the transfiguring power of desire and the possibility of externally realizing ecstasy. These ideas had found their way into WBY's recent changes to *A Vision* (where both the Swami and Bhagwan Shri Hamsa were also belatedly inserted into the Great Wheel). Tantric philosophy advocated the integration of a physical dimension with spiritual insight – which was, at this stage of his life, more exciting to WBY than the Vedantic philosophy of transcendent calm suggested long ago by Chatterjee. Much of what he studied with the Swami taught the allowance for human passions included in Puranic Hinduism, and expressed by Patanjali's Yogic discipline.[9] The Swami, who supposedly had attained the penultimate stage of spiritual concentration, would be his guide in this – as in interpreting the *Upanishads*, though the translations they produced together have been judged manifestly inadequate, due to the Swami's carelessness and ignorance of the texts.[10] But at the end of 1935, fired by what he had called his 'strange second puberty', WBY was alive to the insights and possibilities offered by collaboration with the Swami during a mild Balearic winter.

What kind of possibilities were offered by the third member of the party remain doubtful. Mrs Foden, who sometimes appeared before her fellow Institute members as Lady Gwyneth Foden, had bombarded WBY with letters since the summer, as the escape to Majorca took shape. He wrote back at length, and defended her pretensions to sceptics like Olivia Shakespear. 'Probably Mrs Foden felt there were so many titles in or near the family that she was entitled to one. Her grandmother, Swami says, was an Italian countess and so on. She is good hearted & her vanity is on the surface so one forgives her.'[11] In fact, as John Harwood has established, she was not even 'Mrs Foden'; her maiden name was Gertrude Woolcott, her legal name (acquired through a shadowy marriage at eighteen) Gertrude Riddell. If her past were chequered, her activities in the present became more and more irritating. She had quarrelled with many of the members of the Swami's Institute, allegedly throwing Lady Elizabeth Pelham down the stairs (possibly incensed by jealousy of a genuine title). Mrs Foden was taking a vehemently proprietorial role in the guru's life – which extended not only to the preparations made for Majorca but to WBY as well. Her sweeping offer to pay all his expenses was quickly rejected, and may have been as unreliable as several of her other claims. He had to assert himself in matters like insisting on a cabin of his own, and moving to an affordable pension rather than a hotel. The eventual arrangement was that WBY and Foden would share the expenses, thus providing for the Swami.[12] For all his courteous letters, the claim that WBY had been briefly 'infatuated' with her seems unlikely.[13] If it had ever been the case, her imperious and erratic behaviour on board ship must have dispelled it.

More sinister traits would subsequently reveal themselves, but for the moment Mrs Foden appeared (in WBY's letters to George) as a figure of fun. She embarked on a 'war' with the purser about the status of their cabins; she threatened to disembark, with her distinguished charges, at Gibraltar; she complained violently when a bouquet which George had presented her with ended up on the captain's table; she danced 'badly, but with contagious good humour' in sacred temple clothes at the ship's concert, astonishing the

Hindu seamen. At the same event WBY read three poems 'introduced with the usual patter, & Swami sang a passage from the Upanishad announcing that India had sung it exactly as he did for 5000 years'.

All these diversions were played out against a horrifically rough crossing, which delayed them two days. But at last they reached Palma on 13 December and collapsed into a hotel, intending to find more self-contained lodgings. Contact was established (fortunately, as it turned out) with the British vice-consul, Captain Alan Hillgarth, a part-time novelist and fellow member of the Savile Club.[14] As it happened, they stayed on in the centrally heated Hotel Terramar purely so they might not be 'at the mercy' of Mrs Foden, who was now irritating George with letters about 'your beloved poet'. Before long, WBY had decided she was 'devoted, benevolent, practical & beyond belief tyrannical, self-seeking & silly'. A week later he had realized she was both 'very tiresome' and seriously deluded: 'she wept at intervals for a week & without intervals was in a black temper because she discovered that I did not admire her writing. I think she came out hoping to be in the [Oxford] anthology.'[15] He settled into work, sitting up in bed until lunch-time (possibly another evasion technique); he had been planning a verse play to express the Swami's 'philosophy in a fable', and now a prose scenario began to take shape, 'the strangest, wildest thing I have written'. On 21 December he began the verse version of what would become *The Herne's Egg*.[16] In the afternoons, they worked together on the translations of the *Upanishads*. At home, George was overseeing the arrangement of the Oxford anthology and the typing of the Introduction which WBY had left behind him. *A Full Moon in March* was about to be published, and long extracts from *Dramatis Personae*, copiously illustrated, had just appeared in R. A. Scott-James's *London Mercury*. In Majorca the collaborators stayed away from local distractions. Ethel Mannin, who had spent some weeks in Palma four years before, described it as 'infested by every kind of foreign undesirable, drug addicts, dipsomaniacs, crooks, idle rich, and every kind of parasite'.[17] Across the island at Deya, Robert Graves maintained an already notorious ménage with Laura Riding, but there was no fraternizing in that direction either. Graves had issued a grandiloquent diktat that WBY was 'not to call' on him. This antipathy went back to a disagreement about inclusion in the Oxford anthology, though a few months later WBY would change his mind about Riding's poetry and conduct an amiable correspondence about incorporating her work in the collection.[18] The sun poured in on the white walls of his bedroom, the Swami arrived every afternoon in his pink robes, and for nearly a month the regime seemed to be working perfectly.

On 14 January George Yeats suddenly woke up in her bedroom at Riversdale and seemed to hear her husband 'saying "O, O, O, O" continuously like a groan'; she ran into his room, and only then remembered that he was in Majorca.[19] She wondered if his lung congestion had returned but decided not to wire – 'the British Consul would know all about doctors and nurses'. Her prescience was eerily accurate. Around this time WBY had indeed collapsed with acute breathing difficulties. A Spanish doctor came, diagnosed irregular heart rhythm, and put him on a drastic diet. He wrote to George around the 16th, putting it down to food poisoning, and to Wellesley a few days later, believing that he was mending; but he collapsed again, and on 26 January his breathlessness was so severe that the Swami wired for George to come from Dublin.[20] By the time she landed at Palma, the trouble was clearly much more serious than WBY had pretended: kidney disease (nephritis) and heart trouble had reduced him to delirium. The Swami sent a note to Margot Ruddock on 29 January, saying that 'the doctor does not promise great hopes for him' and she should prepare for the worst. The London papers of 31 January carried reports that he was 'gravely ill' after a heart attack. The crisis was aggravated by Mrs Foden, who – in the manner of tyrants – had now become distinctly paranoid, spying upon the Swami and WBY, opening their letters, and sending telegrams in WBY's name.[21] There had finally been an open scene. 'In that cloudy beginning of my illness,' WBY later recalled, 'when I don't clearly know what happened I turned Mrs Foden out she has avenged herself not by attacking me but by attacking the Swami. She said "Leave him, he is dying, he is dead", & Swami said "then I will follow his bones to Ireland".' George arrived on 2 February and, after some awkward passages, saw her off. WBY gratefully remarked that Mrs Foden had 'never had to deal with a rock before'.[22] During one of his bouts of delirium he was heard shouting, 'George, George, call the sheriff' – perhaps he was dreaming of pursuit from Mrs Foden, who had now assumed demonic proportions.

The final confrontation took place on 21 February. She returned to London, but they had not heard the last of her. The Swami's disciple seems to have made at least part of her income by blackmail, and now commenced a campaign by letters to the Sturge Moores, Lady Elizabeth Pelham, and others of the Swami's circle, past and present. At least one ready listener was Ethel Mannin, who had always been suspicious of the Swami, and added her own voice to the rumours that ran around London. The Swami was accused of peculation, dishonesty, and seduction. Mrs Foden claimed she had had a child by him in 1932, though this seems about as likely as her fantasies of cancer. WBY was accused in a more shadowy way, of guilt by association; but for several years she threatened to reveal her records of all she had witnessed between him and the Swami, which would reflect badly on them both. Mysterious bundles of manuscripts recording 'unreserved' conversations with WBY were offered to her appalled correspondents and quickly withdrawn. Revelations were promised to an 'American author' who was writing his life. It was, as George wearily wrote to the Sturge Moores, 'an untidy mess'. As it turned out, Mrs Foden's only eventual production was a fanciful account of nursing the ill poet in Palma, masquerading as a review of WBY's *Last Poems*, which she sent to his biographer after his death.[23]

As soon as she arrived, George had sent as reassuring a report as possible to Lolly and Lily in Dublin. She had found WBY weak and slow in speech but not looking as bad as expected; he was propped up in bed receiving visits and presents from the Hillgarths. On 10 February she sent Dorothy Wellesley a friendly but businesslike letter, trying to defuse the rumours of serious illness already widely reported after Mrs Foden had granted an interview to the Reuters correspondent. Ominously, Margot Ruddock had offered to fly out, and been hastily dissuaded by WBY. By late March WBY was well enough for Anne to join them; George moved the family into a local villa (steam-heated, and with a terrace) on the 23rd, and Michael joined them a fortnight later. The plan was to stay until June, when WBY should have recruited his strength. She told him firmly 'You must never go away without Anne or me'; and, WBY remarked dolefully to Olivia, 'that will not suit me at all . . . O my dear, as age increases my chains, my need for freedom grows.'[24]

It was a slow, resentful convalescence. The Dulacs arranged for a wheelchair to be sent out from London, but WBY had to live a very restricted life. George told Lily she felt like 'a child of five in charge of a Tiger in a wire cage & she is tired of being sent for when the Tiger escapes from the cage'.[25] By early April he was working on the *Upanishads* again, drily observed by George. The collaborative murmurings of WBY and the Swami were punctuated by the flatulence of the holy man, who ate great quantities of rice. 'So you would hear them saying something like "the ineffable wisdom of the blessed sushupti" and the next moment you'd hear . . . a loud rrrppff from the Swami. Or W. B. would be saying "the deep and dazzling darkness of the Eternal Mind", followed by rrreeeppp! again from the Swami.'[26] When released from this activity, WBY spent much time idly reading. Wellesley was asked to recommend modern novels 'that are philosophies', like Aldous Huxley's (he hated Vita Sackville-West's *The Edwardians*). She recommended *The Waves* (which he had read) and *Orlando*. Respectability had intervened once more, in the shape of visits from the Hillgarths, and Provost Gwynn of Trinity and his wife. The Villa Pastor was a stockbroker's summer place – marble pillars, white walls with stucco panels, and purple curtains, 'a setting for a film'. From this 'charming but melodramatic house' he wrote an important letter to Ethel Mannin on 6 April – the day after he had got dressed for the first time. In a return to the sexual frankness of their early relationship, he told her that the night before he had felt, for only the second time 'in months', a spasm of desire. But he was really writing to refuse a favour. Once more she was trying to enlist his support for von Ossietzky, still imprisoned though now a Nobel laureate, and this time WBY produced a powerful statement of his beliefs.

Do not try to make a politician of me, even in Ireland I shall never I think be that again – as my sense of reality deepens, & I think it does with age, my horror at the cruelty of governments grows greater, & if I did what you want I would seem to hold one form of government more responsible than any other & that would betray my convictions. Communist, fascist, nationalist, clerical, anti-clerical are all responsible according to the number of their victims. I have not been silent; I have used the only vehicle I possess – verse. If you have my poems by you look up a poem called 'The Second Coming'. It was written some sixteen or seventeen years ago & foretold what is happening. I have written of the same thing again & again since. This will seem little to you with your strong practical sense for it takes fifty years for a poet's weapons to influence the issue.

If the Nobel Society did what you want it would seem to the majority of the German people that the Society hated their government for its politics not because it was inhuman – that is the way their newspapers would explain it. What victim of the Russian government had been given the peace prize & so on? If Germans are like my own country-men the antagonism so roused would doom the prisoner you want to help, either to death or to long imprisonment.

Forgive me my dear, & do not cast me out of your affection. I am not callous, every nerve trembles with horror at what is happening in Europe. 'The ceremony of innocence is drowned.'[27]

On the same day, writing to Wellesley about his dislike for her friend Vita's novel, he remarked:

It is not true that it is easier to live a profound life in an artic hut than at Knowle, unless the artic hut means the ascetic's contemplation. Do you remember that phrase in one of Dante's letters 'Cannot I anywhere look upon the stars & think the sweet thoughts of philosophy'? Some few of us, you, Turner, I have in the very core of our being the certainty that man's soul is active. I find this dialogue in the *Upanishad*: 'I want to think.' 'You cannot think without faith.' 'How can I get faith?' 'You cannot get faith without action.' 'How learn to act?' 'Be happy'.[28]

As he lay on the sunny balcony of his film-set villa, his thoughts ran on self-reflection as a road to revelation. But the stormy sea of irrational emotions, into which he had plunged in the fevered aftermath of his Steinach operation exactly two years before, was about to break on him again. He wrote yet another lengthy letter that first week of April, to Margot

Ruddock. She had bombarded him with her writing, and he told her what he thought of it. A play she had sent, while 'well constructed and well written', would not be accepted by any producer; nonetheless, it 'has greatly increased my admiration for [your] intellect and made me confident of your future'. But the last paragraph of his letter was merciless, especially in the light of the extravagant praise which he had previously awarded her poetry.

I do not like your recent poems. You do not work at your tecnic (I cannot spell the most familiar words because of my illness – this is my first real letter) you take the easiest course – leave out the rhymes or choose the most hackneyed rhymes, because – damn you – you are lazy. Leave off verse for a time. When your technic is sloppy your matter grows second-hand – there is no difficulty to force you down under the surface – difficulty is our plough.   Yours affectionately,

W. B. Yeats.[29]

Her letters to him since his arrival in Majorca had been cast in a very different mould: wild, excited, recounting nights spent in manic bouts of writing '*because* of you'. Furious impatience with her life, her husband, her child, alternated with ecstatic insouciance ('we are sued on all sides, but it doesn't worry me in the very least. Lovely not to care what happens') and surges of depression, combated with drink. A manic behaviour-pattern is ominously clear between the lines ('extraordinary things are happening in my head! Sometimes with regard to people'). By 5 April she was hearing voices, and being told she was a religious maniac. 'People say I am mad, it doesn't matter. They've always said it from my first husband onwards.'[30]

Unfortunately, they were right. By late April she was writing to Palma every few days, and obviously in the grip of mounting dementia. Finally, early in May, she acted out the often-rehearsed fantasy of joining him in Majorca. wby's bemused account to Wellesley on 22 May did not appear in Wellesley's published edition of their correspondence:

It has been a wild week. Some eight or nine days ago Margot Collis – you compared some of her verse to Emily Bronte's – walked in at 6.30 a.m. her luggage in her hand. She had run away from home. After I had dressed & she had washed & breakfasted she put before me a great mass of her poems & asked were they good enough for a book. I went through them in astonishment. Some I thought magnificent tragic fragments. Others I could not judge & said I would show them to you. She seemed satisfied & after various episodes slipped out unnoticed. She had the idea, I know now, that if she drowned herself her verse would live instead of her. She went to the shore, thought of something else, & danced in the rain. She went to the loging house where Porhuit Swami was & put up for the night. He lent her some of his clothes, she was wet through, lent her some money. Next came an appeal from the British Consul in Barcelona. An English poet had climbed out of a window, fallen through a roof, broken her knee-cap, hid in the hold of a ship &

most of this time had sung her own poems to her own music. She was in some kind of ecstasy. My wife & I went to Barcelona & tried in vain to get adequate money out of her family. In the end I despatched her home with a nurse partly at my own expense (shall not be able to buy a new coat for a year). I had to get her away because the consul said that the Spanish authorities are anti-English & if they heard of her would put her in a lunatic asylum & make it almost impossible to get her out. She is now perfectly sane & was when I saw her. Both her brother, her husband & the British Consul asked my help but heaven knows what the British press have been saying. Something certainly to judge from an excited letter from my mother-in-law, who has forgotten her own & her ancestors' scandalous careers. I shall probably go to you as soon as you will have me & my doctor has finished his examinations (if my wife still insists on these) to escape the journalists this girl's husband will probably send (he thinks of little but the publicity of it all), general questions & the neighbourhood of a tragedy where I can give no more help . . . That mad girl may be a portent.[31]

This tallies quite closely with the recollection Ruddock herself wrote in a lucid interval, and published some time later – though he did not mention that, when she hid in the boat at Barcelona, it was with the intention of returning to Palma and wby. The scandal which he feared was barely averted (the fact that Mrs Foden was not on hand was a blessing). Raymond Lovell was not the only adversary to take pleasure in retailing the incident; Reuters supplied suggestive newspaper paragraphs, while Robert Graves picked up the local gossip and gleefully spread it round the island. Ruddock's manic materialization at Palma had a lasting effect. wby kept his distance personally, but continued to write sympathetically to her, and would later involve her in a broadcast performance of his work. He was already committed to writing a commentary on her poems for Scott-James's *London Mercury*; this was extended into a volume called *The Lemon Tree*, which included Margot's own account of her manic episode, which he had helped her draw up. The book was prefaced by a poem he had written about her manic episode called 'At Barcelona' (later, 'A Crazed Girl'). Much of this may be seen as a damage-limitation exercise. The tone is avuncular; George's presence is repeatedly mentioned; Margot appears as a mystic, even a Yogi, who experienced ecstasy (or madness) as a necessary step towards enlightenment.[32] She was determinedly presented as a poetic disciple and protégée rather than as an obsessed lover.

This censored version was not altogether effective. 'Old man Yeats has gone one further in the London Mercury,' Gogarty reported to Reynolds in July,

in in [*sic*] overpraising the girl who played in his Player Queen and later leaped out of a window in Barcelona after an interview with him in his retreat in Mallorca.

Frustration applied by Mrs Yeats may have been at the bottom of this affair. But as I wrote already, it's not every man of 70 who can make a woman die of love or try the Sapphic leap.[33]

And the interlude left an emotional aftershock. The image of Margot dancing by the sea carried a spectral echo of Iseult on the Normandy shore twenty years before, and WBY could not rule out a sense of responsibility – not only for the sharp critique of her poetry that had helped tip her over the edge, but for the fervent exchanges with her a year and a half before, and for so rapidly replacing her with Mannin.

In the aftermath of Margot's appearance, the Swami left for India, and the Yeatses prepared to return – as already arranged – on 26 May. Unpleasantness lingered in Mrs Foden's haranguing letters arriving by registered post to George at Riversdale ('Your illustrious husband cannot claim that his visit to Palma was a flaming success, can he?') as well as in the fall-out from the Swami's troubled financial history. A year later WBY discovered that Margot Ruddock had provided the Swami with £120 for his Majorcan expenses. Given Margot's own financial problems, the fact that WBY and Foden had met the Palma accommodation bills, and that WBY had already given the 'monk' £50 for his ticket back to India, this was distasteful. WBY devoted much effort to trying to clarify the situation, and pressed the Swami to sign an undertaking to repay Margot's debt. For the moment he would facilitate this by waiving his own claims for income from the *Upanishads* book, but the money must be returned to her from India: 'nobody must be in a position to say that I paid Margot'. The matter was eventually resolved, and the Swami returned – WBY told Wellesley – to 'his old place in my affections'.[34] But the whole Majorcan episode had become, as he ruefully described it to Olivia, 'a witch's cauldron'. By early June he had arrived back in England. George went on to Dublin, where the proofs of the *Oxford Book of Modern Verse* lay waiting, but WBY set off for Penns in the Rocks. From there, he wrote to Mannin that the recent weeks seemed 'some horrible phantastic melodrama . . . [but] life has at last taken me back into itself'.[35]

II

During his absence and illness in Majorca, the relationship with Wellesley had intensified. 'You have said to me more than once that you felt you must rebuild things around our friendship,' she wrote to him. 'I was too moved to answer. You are the Master of us all. You understand that I could not answer? Perhaps you are too modest and too great a man to realise what our friendship (8 months old I think) has meant to an obscure poet.'[36] While the

tone was that of disciple to guru, there were also echoes of his recent entanglements with Ruddock and Mannin. 'I've taken two rooms in Chelsea,' she
told him, 'where we can all meet and talk. Tiny but quiet.'[37] Even if 'all'
included Hilda Matheson, there was a sense of romance between the lines.
While WBY was in Majorca, their letters progressed to first-name terms,
though he remained 'W. B.' because of his 'detestable' Christian names; he
confided details of the various crises with Foden and Ruddock, and she
offered advice. And on April 23 she sent him, for the first time, 'some ribald
verses' she had written on classical models, dealing with – among other
things – sexual connection between women and animals. Predictably, WBY
was delighted, sending back amendments, and still referring to them a
month later, when planning their reunion on his return to England.

No I do not want other people unless you do. I want to see you & I am tired & we
have much to talk over & to plan. You seem to under rate those 'street-corner'
rhymes – I wrote today to Laura Riding, with whom I carry on a slight correspondence, that her school was too thoughtful, reasonable & truthful, that poets were
good liars who never forgot that the Muses were women who liked the embrace of
gay warty lads. I wonder if she knows that warts are considered by the Irish peasantry a sign of sexual power? Those little poems of yours are nonchalant, & nonchalance is declared by Castigleone essential to all true courtiers – so it is to warty
lads & poets. After this wild week – not without its fineness – I long for your intellect & sanity. Hitherto I have never found these anywhere but at Coole.[38]

By the time he returned from Majorca and hastened down to Sussex, the
terms of their relationship were set. Penns would give him a Coole-like
sanctuary, and its chatelaine would provide the pleasures of literary collaboration and the resources to widen the circle. But there was an additional
ingredient: many of the verses they exchanged would deal with sex, which
was emphatically not a taboo subject. Wellesley's sexual orientation (and
Matheson's presence) might rule out the kind of 'beatitude' once provided
by Mannin, but their collaboration on mildly salacious ballads acted as a
kind of sexual displacement-activity. Given the complications that his
entanglements with Ruddock and Foden had entailed, these limitations
were not unwelcome. As their friendship deepened, this shared currency
became more explicit: he wrote for her a bawdy lyric about flagellation,
never published,[39] and through the summer of 1936 they engaged upon
a game of joint composition which produced a rather laborious mock-
medieval ballad called 'The Three Bushes', dealing with substitution
and surrogate sex. Much about their relationship concerned passions
declared but safely kept in check. Jointly inspired creative works were – as he
had once said to Gonne, and Gregory had said to him – their 'children'. 'Ah
my dear,' he wrote to Wellesley later that summer, 'how it added to my

excitement when I remade that poem of yours to know it was your poem. I remade you and myself into a single being. We triumphed over each other and I thought of *The Turtle and the Phoenix*.' If their relationship was technically platonic, its creative dimension represented the kind of erotic fusion which WBY had explored in the 'Supernatural Songs'.

His sojourn at Penns in June 1936 marked a decisive advance in the relationship. As with Gregory, it was played out with a Jamesian complexity of self-presentation on both sides; as with Gregory, he would construct Wellesley into the symbol of a longed-for tradition. The fact that, unlike Gregory, she was self-indulgent, erratic, and affected scarcely mattered, but it may be one of the reasons why a poem he wrote about her later that summer lacks both the depth and the clarity of his Coole elegies. Wellesley, with her aristocratic landscape, her Great Dane, her temperament, is invoked as a cross between Orlando and a vestal virgin.

To D. W.

Reach towards the moonless midnight of the trees
As though that hand could reach to where they stand,
As though they were but famous upholsteries
Velvet to the touch; tighten that hand
As though to draw them closer yet; rammed full
Of that most sensuous silence of the night,
For since you bought the horizon strange dogs are still,
Climb to your chamber full of books and wait,
No books upon the knees and no one there
But some old dog that long had bayed the moon
But now lies sunk in sleep.
                                           What climbs the stair?
Nothing a common woman could ponder on
If you are worth my hope; neither content
Nor satisfied conscience, but that great family
Some ancient famous authors misrepresent,
The proud Furies each with her torch on high.[40]

She is a woman in control of her surroundings but bidden by creative demons. Both characteristics qualified her to join the succession of similarly endowed women in his life, from Shakespear through Gonne and Gregory to Ruddock.

On 28 June he arrived back in Dublin, met at the mailboat pier by a delegation of Abbey directors and members of the Irish Academy of Letters – probably a reflection of widely held fears that he had had a very close brush with death. (Gogarty had been forecasting 'a popular funeral – "popular" for well-attended' – only a couple of weeks before.[41]) The summer in Ireland would be spent repairing the damage caused by the Majorcan adventure, financial as well as physical. He was still weak, spending much time in bed, using a wheelchair when necessary. In August he had a relapse, but treated himself (like an Indian monk) with a diet of milk and fruit, and recovered. 'I am told that Mussolini is nourished on milk alone,' Rothenstein wrote to him, 'so you are, as artists are so often, in doubtful company.'[42]

But he made up for it by strong mental fare. In mid July he was excited by a visit from the elderly Henry Harrison, who had been one of Parnell's last followers and had devoted himself to setting the record straight about the Chief's relationship with Mrs O'Shea. Harrison's book *Parnell Vindicated* had been published, but not much noticed in Ireland, in 1931. It proved that O'Shea, far from a deceived husband, had been thoroughly complaisant, that Parnell and Mrs O'Shea had lived together uxoriously for nearly ten years before the scandal, and that a great deal of hypocrisy had been displayed on all sides; also – more controversially – that a murky part had been played by O'Shea's one-time patron, Joseph Chamberlain. In 1936 the appearance of a Broadway play loosely based on Katharine O'Shea's reminiscences, and threatened legal action by O'Shea's son, revived interest in the story, and Harrison wanted to start a campaign. 'The appreciations of Parnell, his work, his love story are yet to be formulated in the light of the amended record, where the Muses of Poetry and History hold their courts,' he urged WBY.[43] Their meeting may have – as Harrison feared – exhausted the poet's resources; his relapse into illness followed, but a few weeks later he produced the powerful ballad 'Come Gather Round me Parnellites', published in the 'Broadsides' series with a marvellous ink drawing by Jack.

Like much else that summer, it was quickly relayed to Wellesley. Letters flew back and forth between Riversdale and Penns, full of passionate protestations and interminable redrafts of 'The Three Bushes'. A letter written by WBY on 9 July shows that beneath the surface of poetic collaboration ran – as far as he was concerned – a turbulent undercurrent, with Wellesley cast in a distinctly romantic role.

I dictated to my wife a business letter which she wanted about *The Broadsides*. This must have reached you some days ago. Here however is the emotional diary of my week. Saturday night sleepless; thought I fell asleep for only a few minuites. Dreamed I was in a great country house. Dorothy came to my room in the middle of the night. She was in some trouble about Dante, thought of turning Catholic; I was furious; Maud Gonne had turned & given me up. Had D. in my arms. Carried her to my bed. Woke up – alas. Rest of night tried vainly to sleep, less for the sake of sleep than to find D. Next morning finish my play. Triumphant; believe I have written a masterpiece. That night, sleeping draught 'person' artificially quieted, good sleep. Next morning begin ballad about the poet the lady & the servant. Bad night. Next morning I finish ballad in the rough. Triumphant, believe I have written a masterpiece. Twelve verses six lines each. Will take a whole *Broadside*. That afternoon – despair. Reject my wife's suggestions for next *Cuala* Book. Beg her to take over press. She explains that my name is necessary. I say I am incapable of facing practical life. Ill. Doctor told to hurry his visit. Good night. Then on Wednesday I finish ballad in the smooth & decide to do no serious work for some days. Good night & this morning perfectly well, capable of facing anything. What the devil is that doctor coming for?

There is an account which you will recognise from your own experience as a normal four or five days of the poetical life. To me you turn only the convex side of the Mask & there is content & peace when I think about you.[44]

A different kind of excitement was provided by affairs at the Abbey, where Anne was now working with Tanya Moiseiwitch as a set-designer. The celebrated Jean Forbes-Robertson came to play wby's *Deirdre* amid considerable publicity. Not to be outdone, the author arrived at the Abbey for the opening, his first time there in three months. 'Willy wandered slowly in,' Lily recorded, 'deep in thought as if into an empty room. He was spotted, and the house clapped and cheered, people leaning out over the balcony and clapping. George says he thought the curtain had gone up.' The staginess of Forbes-Robertson's performance infuriated him: ignoring Yeatsian rhythms, she played the part like 'an Upper Tooting hen, a Camberwell canary, a Blackpool sparrow'. Frank O'Connor, who had wanted her for *The Player Queen*, thought that casting her in *Deirdre* was like making a perfect Zerlina play Isolde. Forbes-Robertson told him that she found the part hard to grasp, so 'had made up a little story' of her own and proceeded to act it.[45] Unfortunately, the audiences loved it, and the house was packed. Undismayed, wby persevered in his attack and insisted that the performance be terminated after a week 'though there is not standing room in the theatre'. The idea of cutting off his nose to spite his face seems not to have struck him, though it must have occurred to Forbes-Robertson. But he gave a garden-party for her at Riversdale on 16 August, nonetheless, and approved of at least one of her performances off-stage, which provided perfect material for a letter to Wellesley:

Miss Forbes Robertson, though commonplace & badly taught as an actress ('All the mechanics' said our stage carpenter 'but O my, what mechanics') is an audacious unexpected handsome person. Our stage manager a soft Catholic type, something between the Virgin Mary & a slug, made formal complaint to a Director. 'I could not find Dierdre's crown, so I went to Miss Forbes Robertson's dressing-room. I knocked. 'Whos there' says she. 'Stage-manager' says I. 'Come in' says she. I went in & there she was & not a stitch on her. I turned my face away & there she

549

was facing me in the mirror. I went out. 'What do you want?' says she. 'Dierdres crown' says I. She gave it me, stretching out her long bare arm. I dont mind seeing Maureen Delaney' (fat comedean) 'in her knickers but never was there anything like this in the Abbey Theatre before. At first I did not want to tell you, I did not want to insult your mind with such a story.' I need hardly say that he was told that the board did not see its way to intervene.[46]

Their correspondence also revolved around the revived 'Broadsides' project, into which he had drawn Wellesley as part of his plan to establish her poetic reputation (not helped by a derisive *Irish Times* review of the *Selections* from her poetry which he had edited). If his physical strength was erratic, his mental energy was remarkable. 'I have escaped bores business & exercise & am writing more & better than I have for years,' he told Mannin. 'It is a curious experience to have an infirm body & an intellect more alive than it has ever been. One poem leads to another as if I were smoking ciggarettes & lit them from each other.'[47]

Those summer mornings of literary chain-smoking produced not only the ballads he sent Wellesley but (by the end of July) a poem which he told her was 'almost the best I have made of recent years'. 'Lapis Lazuli' begins with reflections on the theatre provoked by the revival of *Deirdre* and takes as its final, focused image the Chinese carving Harry Clifton had given him the year before. However, the poem as a whole throws a gleaming net over the rise and fall of civilizations. The instability of international affairs in the modern world is reflected in the impatience felt by the avant-garde with the traditional formalities of art: the 'hysterical women' (in one draft, 'some queer women') who are 'sick of the palette and fiddle-bow' suggest not Gonne and Markievicz as of old but Laura Riding, Margot Ruddock, and – with her obstinately political priorities – Ethel Mannin. For his part, the poet chooses a characteristic metaphor – the way great Shakespearean actors are possessed by the essence of their art, which affirms 'gaiety'. This means stoic courage, and aristocratic insouciance, even when confronting tragedy (which, Gregory had told him long before, 'must be a joy to the man who dies').[48]

> I have heard that hysterical women say
> They are sick of the palette and fiddle-bow,
> Of poets that are always gay,
> For everybody knows or else should know
> That if nothing drastic is done
> Aeroplane and Zeppelin will come out,
> Pitch like King Billy bomb-balls in
> Until the town lie beaten flat.

All perform their tragic play,
There struts Hamlet, there is Lear,
That's Ophelia, that Cordelia;
Yet they, should that last scene be there
The great stage curtain about to drop,
If worthy their prominent part in the play,
Do not break up their lines to weep.
They know that Hamlet and Lear are gay;
Gaeity transfiguring all that dread:
All men have aimed at, found and lost;
Black out; Heaven blazing into the head:
Tragedy wrought to its uttermost.
Though Hamlet rambles and Lear rages,
And all the drop-scenes drop at once
Upon a hundred thousand stages,
It cannot grow by an inch or an ounce.

On their own feet they came, or on shipboard,
Camel-back, horse-back, ass-back, mule-back,
Old civilisations put to the sword;
Then they and their wisdom went to rack:
No handiwork of Callimachus,
Who handled marble as if it were bronze,
Made draperies that seemed to rise
When sea-wind swept the comer, stands;
His long lamp chimney shaped like the stem
Of a slender palm, stood but a day;
All things fall and are built again
And those that build them again are gay.

Two Chinamen, behind them a third,
Are carved in Lapis Lazuli,
Over them flies a long-legged bird
A symbol of longevity;
The third, doubtless a serving-man,
Carries a musical instrument.

Every discoloration of the stone,
Every accidental crack or dent
Seems a water-course or an avalanche,
Or lofty slope where it still snows
Though doubtless plum or cherry-branch
Sweetens the little half-way house
Those Chinamen climb towards, and I
Delight to imagine them seated there;
There, on the mountain and the sky,

On all the tragic scene they stare;
One asks for mournful melodies;
Accomplished fingers begin to play;
Their eyes mid many wrinkles, their eyes,
Their ancient, glittering eyes, are gay.

The poem's dramatically effective transit through varying subsections surveys the world news of the day (upheavals in Abyssinia, the Rhineland, Spain) and then imposes, in the last stanza, a signature change of perspective. Describing his own Chinese carving to Wellesley a year before, he had written: 'Ascetic, pupil, hard stone, eternal theme of the sensual east. The heroic cry in the midst of despair. But no, I am wrong, the east has its solutions always and therefore knows nothing of tragedy. It is we, not the east, that must raise the heroic cry.' By now, he had decided the subject of the carving epitomized the philosophic 'gaiety' that united artists across civilizations, offering consolation in the midst of chaos.[49] Edward Engelberg has pointed out that the poem also serves as a commentary on the 'three aspects of matter' which WBY had noted in *The Holy Mountain*: moving from frustration through activity to wisdom.[50] And it celebrates the individual's tragic impulse against synthetic mass emotion, passionate reverie against hysteria. In this it reflects his Indian reading and the upheavals in his personal life, as well as his disagreements with Ethel Mannin and her friends. For all the recent distractions and illnesses, he retained his alchemical power to transmute the tangle of experience and argument into pure poetic metal.

During the summer of 1936 another creative project reached fruition: he and George were immersed in the galley proofs of the *Oxford Book of Modern Verse*. The commission accepted lightly two years before had turned into a heavier burden than anticipated. Twenty years earlier, he had denounced the very existence of such books to Harriet Monroe.

I detest anthologies. It means being paraded before the public with a lot of people to whom one hasn't been introduced. Browning said of his wife, 'She likes being with the others', and added that he didn't. It seems to me that there are only two possible justifications for an anthology of contemporary work: first that it represents a school of young men who wish to define their position, second, that lacking this, it adds to a poet's income . . . An editor of an anthology has a pleasant idle time and if there is any money at all it should go to the authors who have had to work very hard, and if there is no money it ought not to be undertaken at all, except by some representative chosen by them.[51]

But he had, after all, begun his own literary career by compiling anthologies fifty years before, and he shifted his ground by the time he was invited to edit an Oxford volume in October 1934. 'It might bring in a great deal of money. It would not take me much trouble, the publisher will send me a mass of material.'[52] But it pitchforked him into the cauldron of contemporary evaluations, and this was always going to be problematic. In July 1935, after his crash course in reading the current crop of poets, he had written to Wellesley of his admiration for Elinor Wylie, and quoted – as so often – Dowson's description of his poetic generation as 'bitter and gay'.

'Bitter & gay' that is the heroic mood. When there is despair, public or private, when settled order seems lost, people look for strengths within or without. Auden, Spender, all that seem the new movement *look* for strength in Marxian socialism, or in Major Douglas, they want marching feet. The lasting expression of our time is not this obvious choice but in a sense of something steel-like & cold within the will, something passionate & cold.[53]

This was the theme he had returned to in 'Lapis Lazuli', written as the proofs of his anthology came in. 'I am astonished at the greatness of much of the poetry', he told Wellesley, 'and at its sadness. Most of the "moderns" – Auden, Spender etc. – seems thin beside the more sensuous work of the "romantics".' But this was a defensive reaction, and a judgement based on the bizarrely narrow range of poems chosen from the Auden generation. At the outset he had framed his 'problem', as he put it to Olivia Shakespear; '"How far do I like the Ezra, Elliot, Audin(en?) school & if I do not why not?" Then this further problem, "Why do the younger generation like it so much? What do they see or hope?"'[54] He had rushed his selection in order to get it completed before leaving for Majorca; his sudden passion for poets like W. J. Turner ('profound and lovely') deafened him to Wellesley's suggestions that he might consider Wilfred Owen, or Edward Thomas, or Stella Gibbons.[55] By October 1935 he had determined on his approach: he would ignore the starting-date of 1900 in the contract, begin in the 1890s with Blunt, Hardy, and Hopkins, chronicle the death of Victorianism, and so devote a large amount of space to his own early contemporaries. The publishers had also decided on their own strategy. 'The best chance of getting a good book and the only chance of getting it at a reasonable rate is to leave him to himself till the copy comes in.'[56]

'The publisher's circular is stressing Hopkins,' he warned Gogarty, 'because they have a bad poet in the office with a topical mind.' This was the unfortunate Charles Williams, to whom WBY sent a no-nonsense letter the same day, outlining his approach.

You speak of my omissions of certain Americans; H. D., Robert Frost, and Benét (your typist has written 'Stephen Rose Benet' there are two Benéts, one Stephen Vincent, the other William Rose.) I am acting on the advice of T. S. Eliot who said 'don't attempt to make your selection of American poets representative, you cant have the necessary knowledge and will be unjust; put in the three or four that you know and like' – or some such words. I am taking his advice and am explaining so in my introduction. As a matter of fact this will be far better for the popularity of the book as I shall not have to condemn certain popular figures. I am putting in all the people well-known on this side of the water through residence or accident, with perhaps one exception, that exception is H. D. I have known her for many years, known her and admired her, and it was a real distress to me in looking at her work after ten or fifteen years to find it empty, mere style. Aldington [H. D.'s estranged husband] also is a friend of mine, but I have always known that if I did an Anthology I would have to reject his work, just as I have had to reject everything except one poem by Squire, a friend to whom I owe certain obligations. When you get my introduction you will find why I reject Wilfred Owen and certain other war poets. I had John Davidson in but withdrew him on finding I had too much matter; I may have to restore him. I was his contemporary and we never put him on a level with Dowson and Johnson. Hulme I have left out precisely because he was the mere leader of a movement.[57]

He was determined to combat accusations of partiality, but they were inevitable. With his selection made, he had told Sturge Moore, 'Instead of giving a fairly equal amount from a lot of writers I am giving but one or two poems from most people and a great deal from a few. You will find my anthology very interesting history and not, as so many anthologies are, a glorification of the second-rate.'[58]

But that was exactly the danger he courted. His opinion (as declared to Mannin) was that 'nothing is poetry that does not run in one's head because of the sweetness or majesty of the sound. Owing to the struggle for new subject matter the younger poets today lack that sound.'[59] This would be the fulcrum of his argument for excluding – to name but one – Wilfred Owen, and awarding Eliot and Auden a representation of their work that was both limited and bizarrely chosen. Another omission that seemed glaring at the time was Robert Graves: but that was supposedly because Graves refused to be included unless accompanied by the work of his partner, Laura Riding. WBY did belatedly ask Riding if he could include three of her poems, after reading them in Michael Roberts's rival Faber anthology, which appeared early in 1936. Riding apparently demurred on the grounds that she did not want the same poems in both anthologies; since WBY was in Majorca, he promised to wait until he returned to Dublin '& make my own selection from your work'. (Neither poet seemed to think of sending a volume across the island from Deya to Palma.) In any case, since Riding and Graves had published *A Pamphlet against Anthologies* in 1928, they were hardly standing on firm ground.

Nor, perhaps, does the work of either poet present as pressing a claim now as it did in 1936. Anthologies both represent a reflection of their times and attempt to predict what contemporary work will last. Judged by this last criterion, WBY's Oxford book falls down badly. Laurence Binyon, Edith Sitwell, Sturge Moore, W. J. Turner, Dorothy Wellesley, and Margot Ruddock received respectively sixteen, eighteen, ten, sixteen, fifteen, and four pages each, which does not reflect their staying-power. (WBY himself confided famously to Edith Sitwell that Sturge Moore was 'a sheep in sheep's clothing'.[60]) The Irish representation (which was enormous) allowed Gogarty twelve pages, Higgins six, O'Connor ten, Synge seven, AE six, Gregory three, and WBY himself twelve – while completely ignoring Austin Clarke, whose *Collected Poems* had already appeared and who had won a reputation in Britain as well as Ireland. Gogarty, on the other hand, had more poems than anyone in the book, a height of appreciation he has never scaled since. No one could miss the fact that all of those most generously represented were friends and associates of WBY: Turner (now a frequent lunch companion of WBY at the Savile) was involved in the 'Broadsides' project, along with Wellesley, and WBY revised both Wellesley's 'Matrix' and nearly half of Turner's poems for their appearance in the anthology, often lending them a deliberately Yeatsian cadence. Partiality, and the assertion of his own influence against that of Pound and Eliot, could also be inferred in his choice of three poems by L. A. G. Strong, two from MacGreevy, three from the Swami, and one from Frank Pearce Sturm – whose one book of poetry WBY had helped bring to birth fifteen years before.[61] By contrast, Auden's four pages and Spender's one and a half not only drastically underrepresented the new generation but chose a strangely quixotic sample. (One of the more interesting selections, Auden's 'It's no use raising a Shout', was soon dropped from his own canon by the poet himself.) Thirteen pages were devoted to Eliot, but none of them featured 'The Love Song of J. Alfred Prufrock' or *The Waste Land* (though it is fair to note that WBY's preliminary list had included four further 'extracts'[62]). Julian Grenfell's 'Into Battle' made it, but not Wilfred Owen or Isaac Rosenberg; Sassoon was allowed two pages, but only one of his shortest war poems.

At the same time, Georgians were marked down (one poem only for Rupert Brooke) and not all the moderns were short-changed. Though WBY had an awkward relationship with Louis MacNeice and hated his version of *Agamemnon* ('we are assisting at the death of tragedy'[63]), he was allowed eight pages, Cecil Day Lewis seven, Pound and Lawrence six each, though Pound might have had more if he had been less grasping about payments.[64] Herbert Read's 'The End of a War' took up seventeen pages. Nor were all

WBY's instincts at fault. The inclusion of the unknown MacGreevy, the exotic Tagore, and the recasting of Pater's 'Mona Lisa' into free verse all look prescient now: so do four poems from Hugh MacDiarmid, and the inclusion of an imaginative range of translations (forty-one in all). There was, for the era, a notably high number of female contributors. In some ways the Michael Roberts volume assembled for Faber reflects a far narrower scope. But breadth alone was no guarantee of quality, nor of fairly representing the *Zeitgeist*.

Rumours that it would be controversial were circulating from an early stage. WBY had to write to Eliot to assure him that Auden's and MacNeice's work was not being preferred to his own. And from the beginning WBY imposed an idiosyncratic form upon the book. The limited space for moderns was not only a result of the editor's distaste for much of their work; it also stemmed from his decision to start the anthology with Victorians like Blunt (an echo of that peacock-dinner homage so long ago), Bridges, and Hopkins (recently rediscovered thanks to I. A. Richards, though WBY retained elaborately expressed doubts). This approach enabled the editor to pay old dues to long-dead mentors (Henley, four pages), collaborators (Edwin Ellis, two and a half), and above all his fellow Rhymers' (Rhys, Symons, Dowson, and Johnson all received generous space). This built the anthology into the record of WBY's own life, as created in his *Autobiographies*: to start with Pater – indeed, to rearrange him as a poet – struck a chord with the central theme of 'The Tragic Generation'. But compiling the anthology through 1935 had also forced him to reckon with the unfamiliar. George had been dispatched to trawl libraries (and exercised her own influence on the catch); WBY's London bookseller was sent lengthy orders. In the process of reading, the approach to the anthology changed. In June 1935, still entranced by Elinor Wylie, he was demanding anthologies of recent American work: but he eventually decided to sacrifice her rather than open his pages to a transatlantic influx (Eliot and Pound were treated as expatriate special cases).[65] His book orders show that he dutifully read new poets subsequently omitted, such as Charlotte Mew, Isaac Rosenberg, and the comrades in Hogarth's *New Signatures* (though possibly not Dylan Thomas).[66] In the end, however, he plumped – as he told Laura Riding – for his own tastes and instincts:

I am a despotic man, trying to impose my will upon the times (an anthology one instrument) not co-operative. My anthology has however a first domestic object, to get under one cover poems I want to read to myself, to a friend, or to my children. I do not care whether a poem has been in a hundred anthologies. I do not think that a reason for including or excluding it. If I give my anthology to a man, or as is more likely to a woman, I must be able to say this is my table of values.[67]

WBY's Introduction, completed before he left for Majorca, underlines the point. The first poets chosen are linked to his own early life and his developing taste – Hopkins, met in JBY's Dublin studio but unremembered, Bridges's books glimpsed 'behind glass doors in the houses of wealthy friends', Blunt, known 'through the report of friends', Henley, and Wilde, whose *Ballad of Reading Gaol* was partly rewritten by WBY for the anthology's purposes. 'My work gave me that privilege' – but so, it is inferred, did WBY's own connection with Wilde and his era.[68] It is literary history written as dispatches from the front. With sardonic panache, WBY recalled the literary revolt against Victorianism, the search for models like Catullus, the Jacobeans, Baudelaire, and the Rhymers' embrace of life:

the sons of men who had admired Garibaldi or applauded the speeches of John Bright, picked Ophelias out of the gutter, who knew exactly what they wanted and had no intention of committing suicide . . . Then in 1900 everybody got down off his stilts; henceforth nobody drank absinthe with his black coffee; nobody went mad; nobody committed suicide; nobody joined the Catholic church; or if they did I have forgotten.

But if 'Victorianism had been defeated', much of WBY's subsequent argument subtly suggests that certain 'Victorian' qualities, such as eloquence, retain their power and transcend the 'rhetoric' rightly rejected by WBY's generation. This is one way he implicitly sets himself against the 1930s equivalent of the Rhymers' coterie. Another is by being Irish.

For the Introduction swiftly moves into a consideration of Irish folk themes, Synge's 'masculinity', and 'passionate masterful personality' (implicitly contrasted to Housman and Hardy). Gogarty is singled out for his 'heroic song': 'one of the great lyric poets of the age'. The defence of Binyon, Sturge Moore, de la Mare as 'good poets', or Sacheverell Sitwell's sprung verse, seems rather lacklustre by comparison, though WBY's tribute to Edith Sitwell's high style of 'perpetual metamorphosis', with 'a nightmare vision like that of Webster' coiled beneath, is a compelling and intelligent defence of a writer already dividing critical opinion down the middle. In a private letter to Ottoline Morrell, he remarked that 'by intensity of vision' Sitwell 'surmounts an abominable technique', a judgement that may stand.[69] The other individuals picked out for commentary suggest that WBY was anticipating his own critics. So does his expressed reason for ignoring the poets of the First World War, which would become notorious: 'passive suffering is not a theme for poetry'. The inclusion of his own 'An Irish Airman Foresees his Death' was, in this context, no accident. The self-absorption – as WBY sees it – of the Owen generation lacks the 'tragic joy' of Greek drama or the visceral verve of soldiers' ballads and the medieval

Dance of Death (or, indeed, Gogarty jumping into the Liffey pursued by gunmen and promising the river a gift of swans – an episode rehearsed, yet again, in the Introduction). It is fair to note that WBY was not alone in reacting against the war poets (first popularized, ironically, by his friend Sturge Moore's anthology in 1918). A Harold Monro anthology in 1920 had declared that much of this work now looked 'definitely and unmistakably bad' and should be repudiated by its authors as 'the spontaneous overflow of powerful feelings'.[70] WBY's condemnation was more ringingly phrased. 'When man has withdrawn into the quicksilver at the back of the mirror no great event becomes luminous in his mind; it is no longer possible to write *The Persians*, *Agincourt*, *Chevy Chase*: some blunderer has driven his car on to the wrong side of the road – that is all.'

The deliberately modern metaphor makes WBY's dismissal all the more brutal. But by this point in the Introduction he was taking no hostages. Eliot is surprisingly compared to Pope for his 'rhythmical flatness' and an art that 'seems grey, cold, dry', until the animation of 'The Hollow Men' and 'Ash Wednesday' (apparently WBY's excuse for excluding 'Prufrock'). Though the religious power of *Murder in the Cathedral* receives approval, *The Waste Land* astonishingly goes unmentioned, and WBY's telling touchstone for his reaction to first reading Eliot is his introduction to Manet's painting, which had reduced him to misery in his art-school days a half-century before.[71] Given their friendly relations, this must have delivered a bruising blow. Eliot would get his own back later, in a feline commentary on WBY's work after his death. The dissection of Pound, on the other hand, represents WBY's own quiet vengeance for his ex-disciple's dismissal of *The King of the Great Clock Tower*. Most of it is a delicately appalled description of Pound's continuing *Cantos*: despite the grand design, 'like other readers I discover at present merely exquisite or grotesque fragments'. That damning second adjective is deliberately re-employed in the pay-off, which condemns what Pound had become as a person no less than as a poet.

When I consider his work as a whole I find more style than form; at moments more style, more deliberate nobility and the means to convey it than in any contemporary poet known to me, but it is constantly interrupted, broken, twisted into nothing by its direct opposite, nervous obsession, nightmare, stammering confusion; he is an economist, poet, politician, raging at malignants with inexplicable characters and motives, grotesque figures out of a child's book of beasts. This loss of self-control, common among uneducated revolutionists, is rare – Shelley had it in some degree – among men of Ezra Pound's culture and erudition.

Pound's influence is further blamed for 'that lack of form and consequent obscurity which is the main defect of Auden, Day Lewis and their school, a school which, as will presently be seen, I greatly admire'. This is disingenuous: when, after pages on Turner and Wellesley, he turns his attention to 'Day Lewis, Madge, MacNeice', his judgement could not be more ambiguous. If they have intellectual passion, 'words and rhythms remain gummed to one another instead of separating and falling into order'. The claim that when he likes a lyric produced by these poets, he prefers it to Eliot and even to himself, is utterly unconvincing. Auden goes conspicuously unmentioned.

WBY makes the sharp point that, even if these moderns think they are bound together by the poetry of belief ('communism as their Santa Claus'), 'this belief is not political', or at least not in the way they intend. They are working through intensity towards 'something unchanging, inviolate, that country where no ghost haunts, no beloved lures because it has neither past nor future'. This judgement could strike a chord with the young Auden; but it also carries WBY's condemnatory sense of 'abstraction'. The choice of his own poetry demonstrates the editorial approach still more clearly. The secretary to the delegates at Oxford University Press had sent breezy advice about handling WBY to the publisher of the series, Humphrey Milford, in November 1934. 'Better tell him at the outset that a popular book which ordinary people can enjoy is intended: that, even if "The Fiddler of Dooney" is inferior to his latest bits of hard and high thinking, you (at least in your capacity of publisher) expect him to fiddle.'[72] If Milford dared say as much, he was ignored. In any case, WBY's self-selection was coloured by the way his early lyrics continued to have far more popular appeal than the later work which he himself favoured. The great majority of the fourteen Yeats poems in the Oxford book are post-1920 – seven from *The Winding Stair*, two from *The Tower*, two from *Michael Robartes and the Dancer*; the earliest dates from 1913, thus excising all the early canon which still defined WBY's market popularity. This may be partly because (he claimed) George had been largely responsible: the only poem he added to her selection was 'Three Things'. But, taken together, the selection demonstrates WBY's effortless poetic control of sophisticated simplicity ('Three Things', 'Lullaby', 'The Rose Tree'), personal testament ('After Long Silence', 'In Memory of Eva Gore-Booth and Con Markiewicz', 'Coole Park, 1929') and philosophic subtlety ('Coole and Ballylee, 1931', 'Sailing to Byzantium', 'Vacillation'). And the inclusion of 'To a Friend whose Work has come to Nothing', 'An Irish Airman Foresees his Death', and 'From "Oedipus at Colonus"' drove home the message of Nietzschean tragic gaiety, which the moderns – in WBY's view – so conspicuously lacked. The message of 'Lapis Lazuli' resounds between the lines. This eclectic, scintillating, self-interested survey ends as it begins, by considering his own place in the history of poetry through his adult life:

I have said nothing of my own work, not from modesty, but because writing through fifty years I have been now of the same school with John Synge and James Stephens, now in that of Sturge Moore and the younger 'Michael Field': and though the concentration of philosophy and social passion of the school of Day Lewis and in MacNeice lay beyond my desire, I would, but for a failure of talent have been in that of Turner and Dorothy Wellesley.

This last defiant flourish would cause many reviewers' jaws to drop a year later, but it is of a piece with the bravura assertiveness of the Introduction as a whole. George thought it 'the best bit of prose he had written for years',[73] and she was right. It bears a strong affinity to the 'General Introduction to my Work', written the following year for the American project; a peculiarly Yeatsian testament of intellectual autobiography, at once affirmative and allusive, and a declaration of the sustaining power of tradition.

III

With the proofs dispatched and the tedious summer's convalescence over, he fretted for London, where another BBC broadcast awaited him. By the end of September he was on his way, followed by a brisk letter from George, with strict instructions to notify her at once if he caught a cold: 'I have a suit-case ready packed and English money'.[74] If she phoned Dulac he must not mind, but make the excuse that she was 'very fussy'. This signals his impatience at being treated like an invalid, though at the party for Forbes-Robertson only a month earlier he had been restricted to a wheel-chair. George also wrote privately to Dorothy Wellesley, in preparation for her husband's October visit to Penns. While his breathing and heart were allegedly 'excellent', he stayed in bed till mid afternoon and needed to rest after seeing people: a routine he would probably abandon when away, so he had to have a long afternoon rest. 'However as Edmund Dulac said to me "He is the most obstinate man I have ever come across". I find the only way to make him rest is to plant him in a room by himself with a detect-ive story & leave him sternly alone. I am glad he can go to England now because I doubt very much if he will be able to go over again, at any rate unaccompanied'.[75]

The strain of her role was telling, reflected in increasing dependency on drink. In June WBY wrote guardedly to Wellesley: 'you were right about my wife . . . There have been none of the old symptoms & the household is happy. My anxiety [which] was acute for many months was I think needless.

We have all something within ourselves to batter down & get our power from the fighting.'[76] While he mentions 'overwork' in the same letter, George's reliance on alcohol is indicated too – though it did not impair her efficiency with the Oxford proofs, or running Riversdale, or anxiously watching Anne begin what would prove a long and distinguished career as an artist. But as George turned her back on 'smart' Dublin life (and 'smartness' altogether), WBY's personal vanity and need for company, particularly female company, raged unchecked. Nor did the women he wanted to impress have to be poets, like Wellesley and Ruddock. Francis Stuart was amused to notice WBY's frank interest in the German swimming champion Mercedes Gleitz, when they met in a Dublin café. On another occasion Gogarty, bringing the attractive American tennis star Helen Wills Moody to visit him at Riversdale, was shocked to see signs that his host had been bleeding from the nose; but discreet inquiries revealed that WBY, 'having observed her from his bedroom window', had speedily decided to shave, and cut himself.[77] His appearance, his clothes, his poetic style made manifest, were as high a priority as when Symons had taught him to dress in black with a French tie nearly fifty years before.

And in London in early October WBY entered social life just as energetically as George had feared – dining with Margot Ruddock, and bringing Ethel Mannin to dinner at the Ivy with the Dulacs (a disaster, capsized by a political storm between his guests).[78] In return, she took him to the People's Theatre to see Nancy Price's production of Čapek's *The Insect Play* but anxiously warned Price that his health was shaky and 'he is here very incognito . . . he has been ill again, and is very much old and tired and rather a sick man these days'.[79] Though WBY's letters to Mannin retained their tone of romantic secrecy ('I want to see you and you only: I find I think of you with a growing affection'), their sexual involvement had served its purpose and was over.[80] In any case, WBY soon left the Savile for Penns in the Rocks, his base for the rest of his stay. Wellesley's Rolls-Royce brought him back to London for the radio broadcast, delivered on 11 October: a lecture on 'Modern Poetry', using the material from his Oxford Introduction and preparing the way for the publication of the anthology. He was handling the new medium with increasing confidence; subsequently Hilda Matheson, soon to become director of talks programmes at the BBC, arranged a lunch with the talks producer George Barnes and WBY, to discuss further programmes on poetry. 'He offered to sponsor two programmes of modern poetry of twenty minutes each,' Barnes recalled four years later. 'He would make the selection, introduce each programme with two or three minutes' discussion of its object and the B.B.C. would choose readers with his approval. He wanted to experiment with the use of a drum or other musical instrument

561

between stanzas or between poems, but never behind the voice, in order to heighten the intensity of the rhythm and he also wished to try out unaccompanied singing of a refrain.'[81] These ideas, which bore fruit the following year, show that the abortive experiments with the Group Theatre had revived his old interest in the technique of spoken verse. The echoes of Florence Farr's voice and Dolmetsch's psaltery still sounded seductively down the years.

He then travelled to Penns for 'a quiet I find nowhere else.'[82] He wrote affectionate letters to Mannin, struck by her recent book about travelling in the east (*South to Samarkand*): they could at last agree, he felt, in condemning 'Russian imposition of mechanical society on Asia'. There was not much company at Penns, but David Cecil, whom WBY had met as an Oxford undergraduate, and his wife, Rachel (daughter of the critic Desmond MacCarthy, an admirer of WBY), stayed en route to the local great house, Petworth. She sent a bemused report to her mother-in-law:

Dottie Wellesley and the poet Yeats are alone here. I don't know if you know her? I expect David has described her to you. It is a little difficult to do so now – she is a very odd woman, morbid and unhappy and silly; but there is something disarming and nice about her, and I am enjoying the experience of staying here, and meeting Yeats. We arrived in time for dinner last night. The evening was extraordinary. I now know what it feels like to be in a complete mental fog for several hours on end. I literally didn't quite know what the talk was about from the beginning to the end! Not that it was particularly intellectual, nor above one's head – but it was *impossible* to follow consecutively. Yeats talks slowly and clearly, in a beautiful low Irish voice, and describes people and things and books in rolling sentences which *seem* perfectly clear, and brilliantly put – and yet to me it was like standing in a tube station, with one train coming in evenly and slowly, while another one glided out simultaneously (which was Dotty Wellesley) she *adores* Yeats – in quite a touching way, she is so awed and grateful to him – but she is one of those people who can't listen, so that even though he is her Prophet, her train of thought never linked up with his once, so the conversation always had a double theme. David was also in a fog, but he managed the feat of somehow answering Dotty, and throwing Mr. Yeats a question at intervals which would set him rolling on (rather fascinatingly I must say) for another 10 minutes on end. I had often heard him described before, and some people do find him a bore and don't think him really impressive – but I did think he was like a great poet. Perhaps you have seen him? He has a wonderful face – half ugly and strange, and half beautiful – with a very sensitively drawn mouth and chin. He was dressed in a scarlet shirt and square bow-tie of pale grey silk – but he has a dignified appearance, although perhaps his personality is not exactly so.

He is of course a thundering egoist – but I found his descriptions and stories strangely fascinating, although as I said, I couldn't follow the meaning! I have never anyhow heard anyone quite like him – and after dinner he read aloud some of the poems which he had just written. One was a long sort of ballad – and although again I couldn't quite follow it – yet the sound was too lovely. He reads in singing, chanting voice, which lulls one almost to sleep – but he does it beautifully. I enjoyed that part the most, and he is so unselfconscious and spontaneous about his poetry – and it is so imaginative, that it is very moving to hear him read it. We also read out a long poem by Dottie Wellesley – but of that not *one* word could I understand, and I must say I had a awful struggle to keep my eyes open, the lulling effect was so strong! He doesn't appear until luncheon but I am quite looking forward to another hour or two of his strange company, and to being wrapped up in a fog again![83]

Penns might now have been WBY's Coole, but Wellesley herself was a very different figure from Gregory. Nor was their relationship comparable. That October in Penns, it moved on to another stage. It seems probable that after WBY's heated letters of the summer, he expected some physical passages, of the kind enjoyed with Ruddock and Mannin; but to judge from a strange letter he sent his hostess after he left, she had made it clear that her own sexual orientation ruled this out. Undaunted, WBY robustly converted it into an occasion of celebration. 'O my dear I thank you for that spectacle of personified sunlight. I can never while I live forget your movement across the room just before I left, the movement made to draw attention to the boy in yourself. Alas that so long must pass before we meet – at last an intimate understanding is possible.'[84] 'Our last' talk, he repeated in a later letter, 'has created a greater intimacy': he was 'a friend, who feels so much more than a friend'.[85] The poems he sent her in November included a first draft of poems eventually published as 'The Chambermaid's First Song' and 'The Chambermaid's Second Song', astonishingly and rather chillingly frank about post-coital *tristesse*.

I

Whence came this ranger
Now sunk into rest,
Stranger with stranger,
On my cold breast?
What's left to sigh for
Now all are the same?
What would he die for
Before night came?
May God's love hide him
Out of all harm,
Now pleasure has made him
Weak as a worm.

II

Joy left him upon my bed
Weak as a worm,
His rod, & its butting head,
Limp as a worm.
A shadow has gone to the dead
Thin as a worm,
Where can his spirit have fled
Bare as a worm.

Even Wellesley demurred at this uncompromising image; when it was eventually published, those who still cherished the WBY of 'The Fiddler of Dooney' would be correspondingly appalled. Sending a near-final version a fortnight later, WBY again rehearsed that 'intimate conversation' at Penns: 'My dear, my dear – when you crossed the room with that boyish movement, it was no man who looked at you, it was the woman in me. It seems that I can make a woman express herself as never before. I have looked out of her eyes. I have shared her desire.'[86] A month later he told her that her work relied upon its 'masculine element allied to much feminine charm – your lines have the magnificent swing of your boyish body. I wish I could be a girl of nineteen for certain hours that I might feel it even more acutely.'[87] These were love-letters passed through a bewildering prism of transference and identification – which perfectly suited the circumstances of both partners. Erotic stimulation through an exploration of androgyny, odd as it seems, was another unexpected outcome of WBY's venture into the world of Norman Haire.

But the excitements of that autumn were cut short, yet again, by illness. On a jaunt to London to see Louis MacNeice and the Group Theatre's contemporary version of *The Agamemnon* (with the chorus in dinner-jackets), which transfixed him with horror, he was felled by a violent cold.[88] His last days at Penns were spent recuperating. He arrived back in Dublin in early November, just in time for more rows at the Abbey (O'Connor was threatening resignation) and the proofs of his *Upanishads*. And there was, above all, a first-rate controversy: the reception of the *Oxford Book of Modern Verse*, published in November.

Gogarty's private quip to Reynolds – 'only titled ladies and a few friends admitted'[89] – was echoed, in varying tones of outrage, by most of the reviewers. The anthology was perceived as all the more eccentric because it carried the Oxford imprint: the blue and gold binding was supposed to convey authority, definitiveness, and permanence. But these were qualities which no reviewer was prepared to accord WBY's anthology. Even those who cautiously praised it did so because of its idiosyncrasy. Basil de Selincourt in the *Manchester Guardian* thought that another anthology could easily be assembled which would leave out all WBY's choices and yet be more representative.[90] John Hayward in the *Spectator* found the Introduction 'curious, tantalising and unintegrated . . . too perfunctory and shapeless to satisfy the reader who expects a critical survey of modern verse and not sufficiently conclusive to explain or justify Mr Yeats's predilections'.[91] The predilections themselves were analysed exhaustively and found sadly wanting; so was the incomprehensible pleasure WBY took in Wellesley's offerings, which was explicable only by 'the fact that at their best they echo his own'. *The Times* was determined to be favourable, but had to admit that the selection might appear 'wilful'; John Sparrow in the *TLS*, even more cautious, admitted that someone else might have chosen 'a more objectively "representative" selection', but the authority 'reflected its maker' – who was, after all, 'the greatest poet and the greatest critic of his age'.[92] Sparrow also pointed out that, for close readers of WBY, fair advance warning had been given of what might be expected. He also felt (perhaps reflecting his own prejudices) that the Auden generation were represented 'in full force', and that this revealed their limitations. But Sparrow's own roll-call of those who stand beside WBY himself as 'the finest poets' in the book reads, by and large, as oddly obtuse today. WBY was lucky in his reviewers.

Inevitably, opinion outside the establishment press was almost universally damning. *Scrutiny* found it perverse, eccentric, the result of 'a counsel of despair' – the exclusions indefensible, the preferences 'frankly inexplicable'.[93] There was a chorus of condemnation from the leftist camp – Stephen Spender, writing in the *Daily Worker*, violently attacked WBY's preference for Dorothy Wellesley, citing 'Horses': 'Tum-ti-tum-ti-tum rhetorical questions about donkeys for donkeys by donkeys, which nobody answers.' WBY consoled the appalled Wellesley, who must have begun to wonder what she had got into. 'One reason why these propagandists hate us is that we have ease and power. Your tum-ta-ti-tum is merely the dance music of the ages. They crawl and roll and wallow.'[94] But the 'propagandists' were in full cry, and the anthologist's own supposed politics were brought into it: a subsequent *Daily Worker* piece by R. B. Marriott linked WBY's Blueshirt poems to the opinions and preferences which lay behind his selection, and accused him of hypocrisy in preaching that poets should be above politics.[95] Day Lewis, despite his own comparatively generous treatment, condemned the selection in *Left Review*, asserting poetry's 'social function', and lamented the exclusion of Owen, who was 'the real ancestor of our new revolutionary verse'.[96] WBY's choice was 'capricious to the verge of eccentricity, scandalously unrepresentative, as arrogant in its vulnerability as any aristocrat riding in a tumbril' (a significant simile). WBY, unabashed, remarked to Wellesley, 'I did not know I was excluding a revered sandwich-board man of the revolution' and dismissed Owen's oeuvre as 'all blood, dirt & sucked sugar stick . . . There is every excuse for him, but none for those who like him.'[97]

The attacks in England were to be expected, if only because of the Irish bias of the book, and WBY responded combatively in private. But he refused to answer criticism in print, except for a restrained correction on the question of payment for permissions.[98] However, he was nonplussed by the storm of criticism unleashed in Ireland as well: he felt, he told Wellesley, 'that I have no nation, that somebody has bitten my apple all round'.[99] He should not have been so surprised. Clarke's omission strikes posterity most oddly, but that of Seumas O'Sullivan shocked Irish contemporaries even more; Dunsany's exclusion was probably generally approved of, though Gogarty made much of it. Gogarty's own spectacular elevation to Olympus was something of an incubus: Dublin gossip, inventive as ever, decided it was a *quid pro quo* for his gift to the Yeatses of a motor-car, oblivious to the fact that they never possessed such a luxury.[100] He himself chose to explain it to Reynolds in terms of tribal Irish snobberies, and WBY's own isolation.

I will find the criticisms of Yeats's selection of Irish poetry rather embarrassing. What right have I to figure so bulkily? None from a poetical point of view. But what about the Bard's society obsession? And I alone of the 'movement' stood out, refusing to 'go native' and to exalt the lowest classes in the island at the expence of all the rest. I am Kildare Streetish and the only *non-folk* friend that Yeats has in Ireland. That's why. 'Tall *UNPOPULAR* men.' Then he gets his back on all his enemies by omission . . . I set my face always against the revival of 'folk' poetry and Padraic Columism; and insisted there were better things to hear and still finer things to see in Ireland than turf smoke and cottage songs. Now, like Joyce, Yeats has put me with the Bucks![101]

Surprisingly few reviewers noted the high-octane force of WBY's Introduction, though Laurence Binyon (himself well represented) astutely pointed out that it 'is really a chapter of autobiography'.[102] Most suggestively of all, Stuart Hampshire in the *Oxford Magazine* found 'it is the prose, not the verse, which makes this book magnificent and exciting. The Introduction is a contribution to any future anthology of English prose, the rest does not even afford the raw material for an adequate anthology of modern verse.' The review acutely spotted that the Introduction embodied the unique power of WBY's later poetry, language 'at once simple, splendid and restrained, suddenly interrupted by direct, personal utterance'. Yet, Hampshire pointed out, the poetry chosen as a background to this brilliant meditation was largely anaemic and ephemeral. And, by a supreme irony, it reflected a taste for the very characteristics WBY himself had grown out of – 'richness of sound and imagery, a facility for easy, insistent rhythms, exotic epithets and smooth cadences'. Were 'the deafness and the grandeur' inseparable?[103]

The private reactions of those excluded, or inadequately included, were as pungent as the reviews. Nor were they always kept private. The mono-maniacal Lord Alfred Douglas publicized far and wide his abusive telegram to WBY. 'Why drag in Oxford? Would not shoneen Irish be a more correct description?'[104] The relentlessly middlebrow Sir Arthur Quiller-Couch, who had compiled the hugely profitable preceding volume of prose in the series, consoled Douglas: 'You should take it as a high compliment that you are not in Mr Yeats's gallery. He was a poet once; but adulation has turned his head, and Lord! *What* an anthology and *what* a preface.' (He may have been surprised to find this communication ended up in the papers too.) Auden, more dignified, kept his counsel in public but later attacked the anthology as 'the most deplorable book ever issued under the imprint' of Oxford. He would not have been much mollified by WBY's private admission, embellished by a typical mandarin flourish: 'I admire Auden more than I said in the anthology (his best work has not been published).'[105]

WBY was prepared for hostility from fellow poets, but not for the rift created in his friendship with Ottoline Morrell, arising from what she took to be his praise of W. J. Turner's *The Aesthetes*. Turner was one of many who had taken the Morrells' hospitality and later ridiculed his hostess more viciously than any of them. This book had wounded her to the quick, and after its publication in 1927 she thought he should be 'crucified with ice'.[106] This was not unreasonable: the portrait of 'Lady Caraway' is sadistically cruel and crudely recognizable. Four months after the publication of the Oxford anthology she still felt unable to meet WBY, and wrote a letter bitterly reproaching him for unnecessarily reviving a hurtful episode – especially as the book highlighted was a work of prose, not poetry. True to form, WBY sent her a mollifying letter which made things infinitely worse. She had been hoping that he had simply not read *The Aesthetes* properly – or, indeed, not read it at all – but he admitted he knew that it contained 'a disgraceful attack' on her. He claimed, however, that he had intended the opposite of praising it.[107] The fatal passage had run:

Turner himself seems the symbol of an incomplete discovery. After clearing up some metaphysical obscurity he leaves obscure what a moment's thought would have cleared: author of a suave, sophisticated comedy he can talk about 'snivelling majorities'; a rich-natured friendly man he has in his satirical platonic dialogue *The Aesthetes* shot upon forbidden ground.

As far as WBY was concerned, this was tantamount to saying *The Aesthetes* was misconceived, small-minded, and disloyal; thus, he told Ottoline, he had repudiated Turner's attack on her. He may well have thought so, but to the unfortunate victim it hardly looked like much of a defence. His obtuseness is all the more astonishing, considering that he had written in a private notebook years before that her 'grace and distinction' had been betrayed and slandered in print by her false friends, so that 'this gracious, generous and gentle person may descend to posterity as a sort of Lady Caroline Lamb'.[108] It was a spectacular instance of his ability to divorce personal sentiments from his literary arguments. As with the reactions of Moina Mathers and Bridget Fay to his portraits of their husbands, he seems to have been genuinely oblivious of the emotional reaction to his subtly calibrated constructions. For Ottoline Morrell, it was one more betrayal. 'Yeats finis', she wrote across his last letter, and their long friendship was effectively over. Typically, he never quite realized it.[109]

Even those favoured by an unexpected inclusion did not necessarily approve of their company. Sturm thought 'so many fine poets are left out entirely, and so many tootlers of tin horns and penny whistles are included that Yeats can not be altogether responsible; it is a sad production'.[110] And if feelings ran high among the excluded, there were sound utilitarian reasons beyond bruised self-regard. 'Those of us who were not between its covers', remembered the permanently down-in-the-mouth Monk Gibbon, 'could dwell on the melancholy reflection that we had lost not sixty thousand but three or four or five or six times that number of readers by our exclusion.'[111] Quiller-Couch's anthology had been a famous bestseller, and WBY's did extremely well, not hindered by controversy. In the first three months, according to WBY, it sold 15,000 copies; in the year ending March 1938, it added a further 7,000. WBY's income was considerably boosted, and he was back, emphatically, in the news.[112] As 1936 drew to a close, he could reflect that he had surmounted the Majorcan crisis, returned to an active social life, and written – in 'Lapis Lazuli' – one of his best poems.

He had also nurtured a new controversy, and a new obsession which replaced his interest in Henry Harrison's vindication of Parnell. W. P. Maloney, a Scots doctor turned honorary Irish-American, had published *The Forged Casement Diaries* raising the old issue of the way Roger Casement's alleged homosexuality had been used to swing opinion against clemency at his trial for treason twenty years before. In 1933 Maloney had approached WBY about a Casement Prize for the Irish Academy, and shown him 'proof' that the diaries were forged. WBY remained privately unconvinced. He was shocked by the use of the diaries, not the imputation of homosexuality, which – given his fin de siècle tolerance and current interest in the vagaries of sexual behaviour – was hardly likely to bother him.[113] WBY had been initially cautious when a powerful Irish-American lobby began to 'boom' the book, but he now entered battle at full tilt. 'Casement was not a very able man,' he wrote to Mannin,

but he was gallant & unselfish, & had surely his right to leave what he would have called an unsullied name. I long to break my rule against politics & call these men criminals but I must not. Perhaps a verse may come to me, soon or a year hence. I have lately written a song in defence of Parnell (about [whose] love & marriage less foul lies were circulated) a drinking song to a popular tune & will have it sung from Abbey stage at Xmas. All my life it has been hard to keep from action, as I wrote when a boy, – 'to be not of the things I dream'.[114]

As it happened, the verses came at once: two rousing ballads on Casement, denouncing those who had spread the charges, were fired off to Penns in the Rocks. Particularly singled out were the English poet and man of letters Alfred Noyes, who had indeed publicized the case against Casement, and – more surprisingly – the Oxford don Gilbert Murray. Uninhibited by an old acquaintance with Murray, who had helped with the *Oedipus* plays, WBY visualized stirring up Irish undergraduates at Oxford to sing the ballad under Murray's windows. Wellesley, whose unconventionality co-existed with the political prejudices of her class and background, nervously counselled him against it. The Casement issue continued to burn up energy, and he repeatedly denounced Gilbert Murray to Wellesley, who begged him not to make a personal attack in public. WBY remained scornful. Even if the diaries were genuine, what would she think of a 'Professor' who used the homosexual private lives of – say – Charles Ricketts or Lawrence of Arabia to ensure their execution on a capital charge?[115] Rereading the evidence, however, he suddenly realized that he had completely misconstrued Gilbert Murray's involvement, due to a hasty reading: he had, apparently, confused him with Gilbert Parker, head of the Foreign Office Press Bureau in New York.[116] 'I got in a blind rage & only half read the passage that excited it.' Wellesley's reaction prompted a famous quatrain, sent to her in apology:

> You think it horrible that Lust and Rage
> Should dance attendance upon my old age.
> They were not such a plague when I was young.
> What else have I to spur me into song?[117]

The context makes it clear that rage, rather than lust, supplied the occasion of the poem: the subject of sex was, after all, central to his relationship with Wellesley. But posterity would reverse the priority, interpreting the poem as an apologia for sexual obsession – a characteristic upon which he seems to have prided himself rather than otherwise. Still, his contrived bout of satyriasis had produced more notable mental than physical effects. Gogarty, going to visit him in mid November, summed it up:

He is not dying immediately but his Spanish doctor sent me a quaintly translated report on his case . . . *videl.*
    'We have here an antique cardio-renal sclerotic of advanced years.'
    Why! It sounds like a lord of Upper Egypt. But any touch of bronchitis this Winter is likely to carry him off. His heart is enlarged and his kidneys throw pressure back on it. He has had some bouts of dropsy. But what does one expect as the result of Steinach's operation at 70 years of age? 'A pity beyond all telling is hid in the heart of love.'[118]

Chapter 15 : Folly and Elegance
1937–1938

> Something happened to me in the darkness some weeks
> ago . . . part of my sense of solitude was that I felt I would
> never know that supreme experience of life – that I think
> possible to the young – to share profound thought & then to
> touch. I have come out of that darkness a man you have never
> known – more man of genius, more gay, more miserable.
>
> WBY, to Dorothy Wellesley, postmarked
28 January 1937

> That it is not the duty of the artist to paint beautiful women
> and beautiful places is nonsense. That the exclusion of sex
> appeal from poetry, painting and sculpture is nonsense (are
> the films alone to impose their ideal upon the sexual
> instinct?). That, on the contrary, all arts are an expression of
> desire – exciting desirable life, exulting desirable death. That
> all the arts must be united again, painting and literature,
> poetry and music. Bless synthesis; damn Whistler and his
> five o'clock.
>
> WBY's stated thesis for a radio debate with
Dulac, June 1937[1]

I

As 1936 gave way to 1937, WBY lay ill in Riversdale, afflicted by mild influenza and deep depression. He stayed in his bedroom, wrote disconsolately to Wellesley and Mannin, and distracted himself by an obsessive interest in the abdication of Edward VIII, which had been finalized on 11 December. There was an important Irish dimension, since the constitutional hiatus enabled de Valera to bring in special legislation removing references to the Crown and the governor-general from the Irish constitution, and moving Ireland's status closer to the 'external association' with the commonwealth which he had always desired. WBY, however, concentrated upon the position of the ex-king in Britain, whom he chose to see as a victim of hypocritical public morality. His fulminations are not entirely convincing, but it enabled him to take a high line with English friends like Wellesley, and gave him a subject for rhetoric which would, eventually, turn into poetry.

Thus a new series of 'Broadsides' was planned for Cuala, as 'part of a scheme to get poetry sung here', he told Edith Sitwell. 'The folk song is still a living thing in Ireland. Much of the National feeling in Ireland has been sustained by ballads.'[2] This reflects his preoccupation with getting his ballad about Roger Casement in the public prints, and sung in public as a political gesture. In December it was being considered by the *Irish Times*, who demurred; by the end of January WBY had offered it to the *Irish Press*, whose politics were dictated by de Valera and Fianna Fáil. Since the poem was to be sung from the Abbey stage on 1 February, and broadcast on the national radio network by Radio Éireann, WBY wanted it in the paper the next day. He preferred, as he graciously but disingenuously told the *Press*'s literary editor, 'that the paper should be yours'.[3] (The *Press* had printed an extract from Maloney's book about Casement that very day.) However, he desired 'the utmost publicity on national grounds' (and also wanted to know what payment would be offered). The *Press* jumped at the chance, showcasing 'Roger Casement' under the headline 'Irish Poet's Striking Challenge' and flanking the text with portraits and biographies of Yeats ('regarded by reputable critics as the greatest living poet') and Alfred Noyes, named by WBY as one of those responsible for circulating the inauthentic diaries to sway opinion against Casement. (Gilbert Murray's reprieve had arrived in the nick of time.) The poem, headed 'after reading "The Forged Casement Diaries" by Dr Maloney', had been toned down since the version sent privately to Mannin and others two months before. Murray's name had been excised, and the language tightened up and simplified into effective, if rather galumphing, polemic. The typography of the *Irish Press* was hardly elegant, and the general presentation rough and ready, but it made its point.

Finally, the effort put into the cause by the Scottish doctor Maloney, his Irish-American supporter Patrick McCartan, and local Dublin littérateurs (P. S. O'Hegarty and Bulmer Hobson) had borne fruit. This team had first tried to interest WBY in the campaign three years before, and found him evasive; but he finally lent their case his endorsement. The thesis advanced by Maloney was that the British authorities had deliberately misused a transcription Casement had made of the diary kept by depraved Peruvians – part of the Irishman's campaign to collect evidence about colonial exploitation. The legend at the top of the poem obscured the fact that Patrick McCartan had been pressing Maloney's work-in-progress on WBY for some time, and sought his help in extracting a Preface from GBS. WBY's attitude towards the whole question of Casement's sexual orientation was considerably more relaxed than that of Maloney and his Irish-American friends. 'If Casement were homo-sexual,' he wrote to Wellesley, 'what matter!'[4] The point was that the government used false evidence to present the issue to 'the middle classes', as evidence of an irredeemably tainted character. While this is tailored towards a correspondent who is herself an aristocratic homosexual, it seems to reflect his own opinions. The ballad, by contrast, implies more conventionally that Casement's 'good name' was 'blackened' by a wrongful

Irish Poet's Striking Challenge

ROGER CASEMENT

(After reading " The Forged Casement Diaries," by Dr. Maloney).

I say that Roger Casement
Did what he had to do,
He died upon the gallows,
But that is nothing new.

Afraid they might be beaten
Before the bench of Time,
They turned a trick by forgery
And blackened his good name;

A perjurer stood ready
To prove their forgery true;
They gave it out to all the world—
And that is something new.

For Spring-Rice had to whisper it,
Being their Ambassador,
And then the speakers got it,
And writers by the score.

Come Alfred Noyes and all the troup
That cried it far and wide,
Come from the forger and his desk,
Desert the perjurer's side;

Come speak your bit in public
That some amends be made
To this most gallant gentleman
That is in the quick-lime laid.

W. B. YEATS.

(Tune: The Glen of Aherlow).

WILLIAM BUTLER YEATS

Born in Dublin, 1865, son of an Irish artist. Educated at the High School, Dublin, and then studied art for three years. His first book of verse, " Mosada," appeared in 1886. Lived for many years in London, where he was the friend of William Morris, Lionel Johnson, Arthur Symons, and other poets and artists of the 'nineties. Came back to Ireland and in co-operation with Lady Gregory, George Russell and Edward Martyn, established the Irish Literary Theatre, which later became the Abbey Theatre. Since 1904 has been a director of the Abbey, where his plays, including " Cathleen ni Houlihan," " The Countess Cathleen," " The Pot of Broth," etc., have been first produced and frequently revived. Was a Free State Senator from 1922 to 1928, and was awarded the Nobel Prize for Literature in 1923. Published an autobiography last year entitled " Dramatis Personæ" and has recently edited The Oxford Book of Modern Verse. Is regarded by reputable critics as the greatest living poet.

LAND AND WATER.

ALFRED NOYES

An Englishman and a convert to the Catholic Church. Born in Staffordshire in 1880. Educated at Oxford and immediately made poetry his profession. His first book of verse, " The Loom of Years," was published in 1902. Visited the United States to deliver the Lowell lectures in 1913. Was Professor of English Literature at Princeton University, U.S.A., 1914-'23. During the war years was attached to the British Foreign Office and was prominent in circulating the Casement slanders. Wrote of Casement in the Philadelphia Public Ledger (August 31, 1916):

" . . . the chief leader of these rebels—I cannot print his own written confessions about himself, for they are filthy beyond all description. But I have seen and read them and they touch the lowest depth of human degradation ever reached. Page after page of his diary would be an insult to a pig's trough to let the foul record touch it."

Was made Commander of the Order of the British Empire in 1918. Is, in addition to being a poet, a novelist, a dramatist and a biographer. His recent Life of Voltaire has been the subject of much controversy.

THIS HAPPENED TO-DAY.

THE "MACARONI PARSON"

THERE was no preacher in London who could attract so fashionable an audience as the Rev. William Dodd. When he delivered his charity sermon at his chapel in Pimlico, the edifice was filled to overflowing, and princes and fine ladies came to listen. " The lost sheep," says Horace Walpole, " wept."

But there were many who stayed away. They did not like the pastor's flashy style of dress, nor his gilded coach, and they thought it unbecoming in a clergyman to publish a volume of verse containing epistles to dainty ladies. They nicknamed him the " macaroni parson."

Nevertheless, when the news was

HERONS

13. WBY's polemical poem, sandwiched between highly partial potted biographies, leads the Features page of the *Irish Press*, 2 February 1937.

accusation of homosexuality, and by a conspiracy to commit 'perjury' – which was never actually in question.

As such, the argument struck a chord in nationalist Ireland. WBY gleefully recorded the sudden deference shown to George in Dublin shops; when the *Irish Press* carried a page of congratulations extended to Maloney from senior figures in Fianna Fáil circles, WBY grandly interpreted them as offered to himself. Correspondents to the *Irish Press* included Shaw at his most mischievous, and Francis Stuart at his most condescending; there was a further editorial on 11 February; and – most surprisingly of all – a contrite letter from Alfred Noyes, regretting his ignorance at the time and claiming that he believed the diaries were to be subjected to a tribunal of inquiry.[5] Gogarty had been happily anticipating a libel suit from Noyes, but this rather took the wind out of WBY's sails. Noyes's name followed Murray's into tactful oblivion, though the next version retained the reference to Spring-Rice (British ambassador in the USA in 1916, ironically from a distinguished Anglo-Irish family with nationalist leanings). This was publicized in a letter to the *Press*, but WBY withdrew from taking part in any formal investigation; he had made his stand. The payment for the poem was sent to Ethel Mannin, for disbursement to a 'labour poor-box', not a political cause: a telling salvo in their continuing argument over the direction of WBY's political commitment. (She obediently gave the money to her gardener.) In a stream of eloquent letters he repeated the same message. He was still O'Leary's pupil, could be no other kind of revolutionary, saw no difference between 'communism, fashism, liberalism, radicalism . . . when all, though some bow first & some stern first, but all at the same pace, are going down stream with the artificial writing that ends every civilisation'. WBY, on the other hand, claimed to be 'a forerunner of that horde that will some day come down from the mountains'.[6] He defended his retention of the Civil List pension, and asserted his affection for the English people and his debt to English culture, but announced his dislike of 'a financial policy the people so little understand or like that they have to be tricked into supporting it', and 'the hand of English finance in the far east of which I hear occasionally'. He also stated that his attitude towards foreign crises like Abyssinia was affected by his wish not to be manipulated by Britain's priorities. Similarly, it was his old Fenian sympathies which would 'rejoice if a Fachist nation or government controlled Spain because that would weaken the British Empire [and] force England to be civil to the Indians'. But he thought that Germany and Britain were equally kept 'on one side' 'by rhetoric and manipulated news', and the artist's only consolation was withdrawal, or a Dantean exile.

This was a regular conclusion after bruising political experiences in his past, but it never provided a complete answer. The Spanish Civil War had released a wave of populist pro-Franco feeling in Ireland, where the General was seen as a defender of the Catholic faith against the assault of paganism; O'Duffy and the remnants of his Blueshirt movement organized a Volunteer movement to go to Spain and fight against the Republicans, while de Valera's government desperately tried to stay neutral. Fine Gael, whom WBY had traditionally supported, were loudly pro-Franco, partly – but not entirely – to embarrass Fianna Fáil. WBY sensed the advent of the kind of confessional politics, which always threatened his personal enterprises. 'I have noticed an ever increasing bigotry in the little pious or semi-literary reviews,' he told Mannin. 'I am convinced that if the Spanish War goes on, or if [it] ceases & O'Duffy's volunteers return heroes my "pagan" institutions, the theatre, the academy will be fighting for their lives against combined Catholic & Gaelic bigotry.' Later that year he would lend his name to a letter of support for the Second International Writers' Congress being held in Madrid, as a gesture of solidarity with the Republic.[7] Nearly half a century before, he had chosen for his masthead a quotation from Allingham: 'There are but two great parties in the end.' If this was so, his would always be the party of artistic freedom, and it was clear that this would now align him against his ex-comrades on the right of Irish politics.

At the same time, the public position he had taken up over the Casement 'forgery' issue had the intended galvanic effect. A second ballad followed, first drafted in December 1936, called 'The Ghost of Roger Casement'.[8] This poem revolves around an image from *Don Giovanni*, of an avenging ghost beating upon the door. The British Empire is contemptuously mocked, its record in India condemned, Britannia's rule of the waves threatened – perhaps, as in Casement's day, by the challenge of Germany.

> O what has made that sudden noise?
> What on the threshold stands?
> It never crossed the sea because
> John Bull and the sea are friends;
> But this is not the old sea
> Nor this the old seashore.
> What gave that roar of mockery,
> That roar in the sea's roar?
>
> *The ghost of Roger Casement*
> *Is beating on the door.*

The inspiration kick-started into life in January 1937 by the Casement controversy produced further ballads which took him back to the era of 1916, like 'The O'Rahilly'. But he also wrote some sarcastic Nietzschean epiphanies that declared a plague on all political flags ('The Great Day', 'Parnell', 'What Was Lost'). And of all the poems that emerged from this self-induced frenzy, the one that meant most to him was deliberately located in the great tradition of Gaelic bardic lamentation, rather than in current politics: based, indeed, on a Frank O'Connor translation. 'The Curse of Cromwell' was published as the eighth 'Broadside' in August 1937.

You ask what I have found, and far and wide I go,
Nothing but Cromwell's house and Cromwell's murderous crew,
The lovers and the dancers are beaten into the clay,
And the tall men and the swordsmen and the horsemen where are they?
And there is an old beggar wandering in his pride,
His fathers served their fathers before Christ was crucified.

O what of that, O what of that
What is there left to say?

All neighbourly content and easy talk are gone
But there's no good complaining, for money's rant is on.
He that's mounting up must on his neighbour mount
And we and all the Muses are things of no account,
They have schooling of their own but I pass their schooling by,
What can they know that we know that know the time to die?

O what of that, O what of that
What is there left to say?

But there's another knowledge that my heart destroys
As the fox in the fable destroyed the Spartan boy's,
Because it proves that things both can and cannot be,
That the swordsmen and the ladies can still keep company,
Can pay the poet for a verse and hear the fiddle sound,
That I am still their servant though all are underground.

O what of that, O what of that
What is there left to say?

I came on a great house in the middle of the night
Its open lighted doorway and its windows all alight,
And all my friends were there and made me welcome too;
But I woke in an old ruin that the winds howled through;
And when I pay attention I must out and walk
Among the dogs and horses that understand my talk,

O what of that, O what of that
What is there left to say?

WBY presented this brilliantly colloquial poem to Wellesley as an expression of 'rage against the intelligentsia', Cromwell being 'the Lennin of his day', but this was probably to console her for the way she had suffered at the hands of Spender and other left-wing intellectuals. More to the point, he later remarked that the poem's poignance lay in its reflection of his own state, 'watching romance & nobility dissapear'. This puts it firmly in the tradition of his poems of personal testament, developing since the early 1920s,

though the dancing rhythm links it to the ballad form he had recently rediscovered. Wellesley, increasingly irritated by what she saw as WBY's politically inspired Anglophobia, was not convinced, and replied with ballad-
doggerel of her own:

> God save us o god save us
> In all our love & hate.
> When the Irish find ancient wisdom
> They will have found it too late.[9]

In Ireland the name of Cromwell was synonymous with British oppression,
religious as well as military. Taken with the poems in honour of Casement
and O'Rahilly, Irish readers could read WBY's new poems only in terms of
immediate politics, especially as the Abdication was currently providing de
Valera's nationalist opportunity. Gogarty, as usual, probably spoke for many
in his Dublin milieu. 'The wheel swings full circle; he is reverting to his
IRB days and he can hardly be checked in his amazingly energetic invective
now that England has been found out as unworthy of a King, and its King
unworthy of his job.'[10]

This development was not unwelcome, since Gogarty was simultaneously working with Maloney's principal backer, the Irish-American Fenian
Patrick McCartan, to raise a subscription for WBY among well-off Irish-
Americans. The secretary for this endeavour was a cousin of the author of
The Forged Casement Diaries, and the committee numbered several people
involved in that earlier campaign. WBY was aware of this, and in the circumstances it was politic to draw attention to his Fenian and anti-British
credentials and to withdraw slightly from puffing Maloney's book, which
could look suspiciously like a *quid pro quo*. But above all he wanted to connect once more with the sources of poetic energy, and he had managed it. By
the end of January he felt his depression was easing and could assure
Wellesley that he was emerging into the light. Once more he sensed the
possibilities of intellectual collaboration and erotic excitement.[11] And for all
his Anglophobic balladeering, and his explanation of it in his correspondence, his thoughts turned to London, where he was already planning a new
broadcasting project with the BBC producer George Barnes. 'I like working here (Dublin) because I am not afraid of anybody and most people are
afraid of me,' WBY coyly told him in January. 'You generalize too easily
about London and Dublin,' Barnes equably replied, 'since I for one am very
frightened of you.'[12]

The plan for a broadcast of poems, chosen and introduced by WBY, was
closely linked to his current obsession with showing how poetry could be
sung and chanted in an accessible form. The BBC's fifteen-guinea fee

financed an escape from Dublin just when he was growing impatient after his long confinement. At the beginning of March George escorted her husband as far as Holyhead and put him on the train for London. He was destined, to his great satisfaction, for new quarters there. For some time he had been finding the Savile unbearably noisy, and coveted the peace of the Athenaeum, as well as access to its celebrated library. Years before he had asked Rothenstein about becoming a country member, but found the cost prohibitive. Finally, in February 1937, he was elected under a special honorary category.[13] This new refuge and resource provided consolation for the disappearance of Wellesley, who, stricken by nervous prostration, had gone to recuperate in France. Penns was, for the moment, out of reach. He settled into the comfortable mausoleum in Pall Mall, and began his negotiations with the BBC. As he had told Mannin and Wellesley, there were aspects of Englishness which had always held a place in his affections.

Not everything fell as smoothly into place. He had announced his advent to Ottoline Morrell, but received a brusque reply; WBY pleaded his case in several letters but unavailingly.[14] Mannin, like Wellesley, was away, but due to return; he wrote urgently of his desire to see her 'alone . . . I have passed a violent emotional disturbance partly health & want your advice.'[15] She came back to London in early April and they had several rendezvous, but she had by now settled down with Reginald Reynolds, and for WBY her role was purely that of confidante. In the meantime WBY occupied himself with Dulac, James Stephens, and others, and with events like the Group Theatre's production of *The Ascent of F6* by Auden and Isherwood. Collaboration with the avant-garde still in his mind, WBY sent Rupert Doone a letter of extravagant praise afterwards, suggesting a changed ending. Doone, misinterpreting the overture, promptly offered *The Dog Beneath the Skin* to the Abbey, but WBY withdrew in alarm ('the Gate [Theatre] audience is, I think, your audience'). After his Dublin winter, it was a crowded time. By 26 March he could tell Higgins, 'I have seen so many people that years seem to have past.'[16]

By then too he had to turn his attention to the official reason for his visit. The Radio Éireann broadcast of the Abbey's poetry evening on 1 February had been a technical disaster, to WBY's great discomfiture. Higgins's sound-effects had spectacularly failed to translate to the radio. But the BBC remained interested in a broadcast done under studio conditions but simulating an informal atmosphere: 'rollicking' verse performed as it might be in a pub by 'the sort of people who sing when they are drunk or in love', as WBY insouciantly put it to Barnes, revealing the malign influence of Higgins's ersatz laddishness. A preliminary rehearsal had taken place as far back as December 1936, but further developments were postponed until WBY was in

London. The final rehearsal was on 1 April, with the broadcast the next day. The poems were deliberately middlebrow – Henry Newbolt, Belloc, Chesterton, de la Mare, York Powell, Sylvia Townsend Warner – chosen for rhythm and a demotic flavour. 'All I can do', WBY said, 'is choose the poems and make certain general suggestions', but he was as interventionist as ever.[17] Barnes was astonished to find that whereas 'he could not hum a tune as his notion of pitch was wildly inaccurate . . . his ear for the sound of speech was so accurate that it outran comprehension.' This sensitivity made rehearsals harrowing, especially as WBY's own voice was not up to demonstrating what he meant. But, encouraged by Higgins, he had developed a strict theory about the proper function of music in poetry, uninhibited by his own tone-deafness. '"Music the natural words in the natural order",' he recited to Wellesley. 'Through that formula we go back to the people. Music will keep out temporary ideas, for music is the nations clothing of what is ancient & deathless. I do not mean of course what musicians call the music of words – that is all corpse factory, humanity melted down & poured out of a bottle.'[18]

The irony is that his own gift was to possess and control 'the music of words' to an almost extrasensory pitch. Yet he discounted it in order to pursue an abstract idea of rhythm and intonation, which incensed knowledgeable musicians like Dulac, much as the long-ago experiments with Florence Farr and Dolmetsch's psaltery had infuriated Shaw. These problems would emerge as the series of programmes developed. In the first broadcast on 2 April WBY announced that only experienced singers knew how to overcome the inevitable monotony of listening to spoken verse, by actually singing some of the poems. However, 'there must be no speaking through music, nothing like Mendelssohn's accompaniment to the Midsummer Night's Dream'; he had begged the BBC, 'with all the vehemence of which I am capable', to ban musical accompaniment and not to use trained concert singers. There was some music, set by Walter Turner, and the actor Victor Clinton-Baddeley was chosen to speak the poems. It seemed to work. George, a discriminating judge, wrote from Riversdale at once:

The Broadcast was entirely delightful: I don't like most of the pomes, as you know, but the result of the performance seemed to me most exciting. You spoke in your natural un-restrained voice, a voice very unlike the artificial one of 'Modern Poetry', and whatever listeners thought of any other portion of the twenty minutes a whole lot of people will have been glad to hear the real Yeats evidently enjoying himself. The whole production during its twenty minutes sounded as if you and the speaker and the drums were really enjoying yourselves and that you had locked the door on the solemn portentouous B.B.C. and had no intention of unlocking the door until you had your final laugh – which we heard *very* distinctly! . . . . Michael said 'I prefer poetry done that way' which is the nearest he ever got to any statement about 'poetry'. (He knew all the poems so I think he must secretly have been reading your anthology.)[19]

'Why not stay over for the next production?' she added. WBY did not need to be asked twice. The second programme, 'In the Poet's Parlour', was already planned for late April. He cancelled his planned return and arrived at Penns the day after the broadcast, where he was joined at the weekend by H. A. L. Fisher, Turner, and Sibyl Colefax (grandly dismissed by WBY as 'an egotistical parvenue'[20]). His hostess was still nervous and distracted, and WBY returned to London after a week to work on the projected edition de luxe for Macmillan and prepare for his second broadcast. On 16 April he met a young American admirer, the aspiring poet John Berryman, who had written a fan letter from Cambridge the year before. Facing him across the tea-table, Berryman found his hero

an utterly strange man. Taller than I thought and large; odd eyes in a great head; very weak now with heart asthma from which, he told me, he nearly died a year ago. He gives or gave me an impression of tremendous but querulous force, a wandering intensely personal mind which resists natural bent (formal metaphysics by intuitive responsible vision), to its own exhaustion.[21]

They talked of Swift, Indian philosophy, Spengler, *A Vision*, dance-plays, Parnell – all WBY's current preoccupations. Berryman carried away with him a vivid quotation: 'I never revise now except in the interests of a more passionate syntax, a more natural.' This reflects the work WBY was engaged upon upstairs in the Athenaeum library, preparing his 'de luxe' collected edition. It also echoes his thoughts on spoken poetry, and the current rehearsals for his second programme, which was broadcast six days later, on 22 April.

For 'In the Poet's Parlour' WBY was stubbornly determined to involve Margot Ruddock – the 'lynch pin', he told Barnes. It was constructed around the kind of conceit he used to plan before the curtain rose on Abbey performances: his own arguments about poetry were interrupted by other voices, dismissing him as too melancholy, and the readings then took over. The programme was less successful than its predecessor, and its effect was not helped by Ruddock's prominence. Wellesley complained about her 'tiresome lisp', and Barnes, while admiring her contralto voice, found her insufferably erratic and unable to reproduce an effect once she had got it right. Nonetheless, plans went ahead for another programme in the summer, this time featuring WBY's own poetry. For the moment he prepared to return to Dublin. But the projected BBC programme was not the only reason why he knew he would come back to London at the first opportunity. He had told

Barnes that the theme of the first two programmes, as originally conceived, was 'Love'.[22] And he was, yet again, preparing himself for an amorous involvement.

II

There are signs that, from the winter of 1936/7, WBY had been determined to find a responsive subject for his romantic energies, Mannin, Ruddock and Wellesley having proved unsuitable or uninterested. From late 1936 he had cultivated a correspondence with Moya Llewellyn Davies, a lawyer's wife with literary interests, who had involved herself with Irish nationalism during the war of independence. Now living north of Dublin, she was writing a novel and hovering around the fringes of the Abbey, working with Higgins and WBY on their plans for sung poetry. WBY advised her about her writing and repeatedly suggested rendezvous, in flirtatious letters ('you do not know enough of me to understand me yet'[23]); returning from London after the April broadcast, he wrote untruthfully, 'a month exhausts my interests here . . . I have been longing for the cat and the dog, the local gossip of my friends – for you.'[24] But he was also casting his lines elsewhere. There may have been a brief dalliance with the 31-year-old painter and occultist, Ithell Colquhoun. And, as his strength returned in the New Year of 1937, he had been considering making his long-postponed visit to India. Given his state of health, a companion was essential, but George does not seem to have been considered a candidate. On 12 March he told the Swami's 'Master', Shri Hamsa, 'I have thought of going to India with my own book of spiritual philosophy in my hand and hiding myself there for some time. But there is a practical difficulty of a personal kind which seems under present circumstances to make that impossible.'[25]

He had been negotiating with Elizabeth Pelham to accompany him. In 1937 'Betty' Pelham was thirty-eight years old. A daughter of the sixth earl of Chichester, she possessed interests in mysticism and extreme left-wing opinions that were rather at odds with her background, and she lived, on very little money, in a state of cheerful disorganization in Chelsea. When still very young she had to be extracted from an Indian ashram by her brother, and she visited Bhagwan Shri Hamsa at Lawasha in 1935. Younger relations loved her for her warm-heartedness, forthrightness, and originality; she wore eccentric clothes, said outrageous things, and was unaffectedly at ease in any company.[26] Photographs show a tall, handsome woman with a direct gaze and a quizzical smile. When WBY met her she was single; ten years later, when she was nearly fifty, she made a happy marriage to a retired army officer and talented amateur painter who shared her Indian interests. In the

early thirties WBY was evidently smitten by her: an unconventional aristocrat, obsessed with Eastern mysticism, appealed to him on every level.
What remains of their correspondence is patchy, but an agonized letter
she wrote to him on 11 March shows that his interest in her was not merely
spiritual. Though she 'feared for a second time to give you pain', they must
not 'again' be led away by 'imagination' from the right path. Her searching
for enlightenment from Shri Hamsa ruled out other attachments.

When I wrote to you a month or two ago and said that if you felt a need to see me I
would immediately come holds good – I had in mind the moment of death for some
reason, but I also mean if there is urgent need of any kind. I have found it necessary
for some years now because of the life I am attempting to lead, to quite reject personal friendships, especially those of a more serious or of a more emotional variety
– anything in fact that is likely to touch the imagination in any way . . . During the
last few days you have taken an immensely important step. I do not wish that any
mental image you have formed of me should obscure the issue for you. What am 'I'
any way – an abstraction, a dream, a symbol if you like.[27]

She repeated that his decision to go to India – the 'immensely important
step' – must be made independently of his feelings for her, though if Shri
Hamsa told her to go with him, she would. This rebuff may be the 'violent
emotional disturbance' WBY mentioned to Mannin on 24 March; it may
also explain a gnomic note from Wellesley a month later ('Am sorry about
the lady having turned into a cloud – what is to be done?'). But Pelham's
stipulations should also be read in conjunction with WBY's letter to the
Swami on 21 March:

Lady Betty of whom I have seen a good deal has suggested my going to India next
October – if your master could have me, & has offered to come too. She wrote to
your master on the subject; & this made it necessary to write. I told him that though
I longed for India there was a practical difficulty of a very personal kind that
made it impossible. You are with him I think. Please tell him of the operation
I went through in London & say that though it revived my creative power it revived
also sexual desire; & that in all likelihood will last me until I die. I believe that if
I repressed this for any long period I would break down under the strain as did
the great Ruskin. I am sorry to be kept from what might have brought me
wisdom. Once this winter after a period of gloom I thought I felt your masters
presence.[28]

This magnificent excuse should be read carefully: sexual desire, for one
thing, is not the same as sexual potency. Writing to the Swami again in mid
May, WBY offers reasons that are much less arresting. 'I must give up India
for the present. I was ready to risk going so far from my doctor but I now
find that if I did so it would cause my wife great anxiety. She has not tried to

prevent me in any way: but I have found out in various ways how great her anxiety would be.'[29] He was still, however, holding out the possibility (which the Swami eagerly seized upon) of a visit the following year. What is clear is his preoccupation with erotic love, and his determination to find someone responsive to it. To judge by his letter to the Swami, WBY was not shy about the subject with his less conventional friends. These included Dulac; and before he left London in April 1937, Dulac had introduced him to a new candidate. By late May WBY could write to him 'My correspondence with the lady is all that I could wish – & I am grateful to you.'[30]

Edith Shackleton Heald seems, on the face of it, an unlikely successor to Ruddock and Mannin. When WBY met her, she was fifty-three years old, unmarried, and neither stylish nor obviously attractive. There is an echo of Mannin, however, in the slightly racy middlebrow-feminist journalism she contributed to the *Evening Standard* in the 1920s, as special correspondent and drama critic. She also wrote a weekly column in the *Sunday Express* and, more demurely, contributed to the books page of the *Lady*, which was edited by her elder sister, Nora. They were from Lancashire. The name 'Heald' came from an absent and ne'er-do-well father, and Edith used her mother's name, Shackleton, for professional purposes: there was a distant connection to the distinguished Irish Quaker family, and the Antarctic explorer. Edith also wrote pieces for the *London Mercury*, whose editor, R. A. Scott-James, was a friend. To Scott-James's young daughters, she seemed a 'wizened, mischief-making spinster', and her sister a pathetically plain frump; more than one acquaintance remembers Edith as looking like 'a lady's companion'. But she enjoyed a certain prestige in her profession, as a member of the Critics' Circle. And Scott-James, whose views were strictly Victorian, was shocked when Edith had a blatant affair with a rich Jewish doctor, disappearing on motoring holidays to France in his large car. She had also been close to WBY's old acquaintance G. H. Mair (once married to Synge's Molly Allgood). Edith probably met him through the *Manchester Guardian*, and it may have been Mair who introduced her briefly to WBY after a lecture in Manchester in 1910.[31] Much later in life she would create even more scandal by setting up a ménage with the aggressively lesbian painter 'Gluck', and effectively evicting her sister from the house they had shared. Beneath the ordinary façade, there were hidden depths; and she was well read, talkative, and whimsical company. In 1934 she reduced her journalistic commitments and with Nora moved from Bayswater to a beautiful Queen Anne house in Steyning, Sussex, which they lovingly restored and filled with antiques; there was land, attached cottages, and servants. For two women who lived entirely by their pens, it was quite an expansive arrangement.

WBY would later claim that Edith had been the highest-paid woman journalist of her time, which – in the heyday of Rebecca West – seems unlikely. It is possible that her doctor friend provided more than the use of a motor-car.

It was with a certain match-making intent that Dulac and Helen Beauclerk introduced Edith to WBY just before he returned to Ireland at the end of April 1937. On 4 May, from Riversdale, he sent her a copy of his lectures: 'it is a tribute – that is all'. Copies of his 'Broadside' books followed, with further teasing letters: 'I am in pleasant correspondence with that lady,' he told Dulac. On 18 May he announced to her that he would be back in London in a month's time.

I am sorry to wait so long before I again ask you for a friendship from which I hope so much. You seem to me to have that kind of understanding or sympathy which is peace . . . The public does not matter only one's friends matter. Friends die, are astranged, or turn out but a dream in the mind, we are poisoned by the ungiven friendship that we hide in our bones.

Thus the theme of repression recurs; he was envisaging a markedly passionate 'friendship'. She apparently demurred about romance in middle age, but he swiftly cut off that line of retreat:

Were you younger a true intimacy would be impossible – this would be a stormy substitute full of complexes or not even that. I think the finest bond is most possible when we have outlived our first rough silver – & that it may be very sweet to the old & the half old. You see I want to increase your years to draw you nearer.

He was by now impatient to return. Turner and Dulac were detailed to find him a service flat. 'If all is as I would have it,' he told Dulac, 'I may consult [Edith] about my domestic arrangements.'[32]

WBY spent the month of May in Dublin, in a mounting state of anticipation, planning his return to London. He distracted himself by sending an angry letter to the *Irish Times* when the IRA blew up the fine equestrian statue of George II in Stephen's Green, which WBY defended hotly (as he had already defended Nelson's Pillar) on aesthetic grounds.[33] What his pro-Casement Irish-American comrades thought is not recorded. He also went to a particularly drunken dinner of the Irish Academy of Letters, where Higgins and O'Connor sang 'The Three Bushes' and 'The Curse of Cromwell', while WBY barred the door against the unfortunate waiters.[34] But, as far as he was concerned, he had now renounced Irish public life, and above all he anticipated his London visit. Dulac was asked to stage a debate with him about the arts, to accompany his broadcast; WBY's idea was to 'elaborate it into a violent row', pretending to believe they were off the air. This rather grisly contrivance was abandoned, but ironically the violent row would develop of its own accord. By the end of May all was in place for a London adventure. A service flat had been rented, at 52 Holland Park, for two guineas a week ('Do not tell anybody my address,' he told Wellesley, 'officially I am at the Club').

Impatience frayed WBY's nerves and soured his temper. He was not an easy presence at Riversdale (where he was already wont to rise from the table with the words 'I will now remove the chill my presence is causing'[35]). As he waited to return to England, even his Indian involvements were pushed aside, with a discouraging letter to the still importunate Swami. An Indian visitor, Abinash Chandra Bose, who called on him with Wilbraham Trench from Trinity on 3 June, left a telling and faintly horrified description.[36] Bose thought WBY physically frail, sitting by a hot fire on a warm June day, but when the conversation turned to mysticism and spiritual experiences, his host turned vehement. 'I am for the intellect. Tagore is vague but in my poetry I have arrived at clear, logical expression.' His mood continued impatient and bad-tempered; over tea, Trench was talking to Anne when WBY interrupted with 'NOT quite enough make-up, my dear!' 'The girl blushed and silently ate her cucumber sandwich.' Various avenues of conversation were opened up and abruptly shut off: Mohini Chatterjee, WBY scoffed, became 'just a successful barrister and nothing more', and when asked about the mystical experience he had described in 'Vacillation' he dismissed the discussion by declaring coldly, 'I felt like that.' Nor would he discuss why he had included Tagore in the *Oxford Book of Modern Verse* but not Sarojini Naidu, though he went on to complain about the difficulty of getting Tagore to express himself properly. Finally, when Bose began to talk about contrasting Indian currents of thought, WBY broke in roughly.

While I was explaining the Brāhmana ideal of peace and asceticism in some detail the poet suddenly said, 'Wait a minute', and got up and stepped into the next room and came back with a small sheathed sword. 'This sword was presented to me by a Japanese', he said. 'I invited him to dinner. At the dining table he began to praise Western civilisation. Somehow I quite disliked it in him at the moment and told him so. And having said it rather rudely I was feeling unhappy. But somebody seemed to tell me, "that was quite right". My wife was in the next room writing a letter, and at that time she found she had written the words "That was quite right" on the paper. The words had no connection with what she was writing.'

It seemed to me that my exposition of the ideal of peace was not taken by the poet to represent only one side of the case; I appeared to be preaching pacifism. This displeased him, but instead of expressing his displeasure direct, he described the parallel incident.[37]

WBY went on to criticize Bose for wasting his time on perfecting his English. Indians should write in their own languages and take a more confrontational attitude towards Britain. '"Why should India", he said, "be always thinking of peace – Shanti? Life is a conflict."' Bose reasonably asked whether India, torn as it was between opposing creeds, could afford such a philosophy, but this incensed his alarming host still further. 'Let it be. I'll tell you what to do. Take a hundred thousand men from each side and let them fight it out. Let streams of blood flow. It is found that the victor does not entirely destroy the vanquished.' He went on to claim that the 'philosophy of conflict' was already embodied in aspects of Indian thought, and the West awaited its version – though Nietzsche had anticipated it. In another account WBY is described as waving Sato's sword above his head to emphasize his point. As the Indian guest escaped down the avenue with his signed copy of the *Oxford Book of Modern Verse*, he felt discomfited. 'Sad, very sad,' he remarked to Trench. 'That a lifetime's devotion to poetry should end in so little joy.'[38]

WBY's disapproval of English literary influence in India was not new, but the violence of his expressed opinions was.[39] He despised Trench ('a goose') since their clashes over *Ulysses*, and was impatient with Bose's gentle moderation; moreover, for all his strictures to Mannin against taking part in 'international politics', he would allegedly sign the writers' manifesto in favour of the Spanish Republicans a month later.[40] But his outburst at Riversdale, stagey though it must have seemed, is of a piece with the essays he would soon begin meditating for a splenetic manifesto to be titled *On the Boiler*. It is possible that his medical condition had precipitated a few tiny infarcts, causing some disinhibition and belligerence; he was certainly in a mood for dramatic gestures and public poses. Before the Academy dinner on 26 May there had been a reception where he had 'spoken my farewell to practical life', as he put it to Edith Shackleton Heald.

Henceforth I said I would live like a butterfly & write poetry. As a matter of fact I have come to the conclusion that my two institutions here – the Theatre & the Academy – both now prosperous will go on better without me. A new generation must feel that it is in complete control. I have set myself free to go where I please.[41]

These were promises he had often made himself before; but he added his intention to return to England as soon, and often, as he could. However, his own belief in his capacities was not shared by others. After his speech at that Academy reception in the Peacock Theatre, Douglas Hyde turned to Lily and said bluntly, 'I am sorry to see Willy so shook.' The colloquial Irish expression suggests somebody badly weakened, and not long for this world. Lily recalled later that she felt a shiver when she heard it.[42]

III

Nonetheless he travelled back to London on 8 June, where his first action was to meet Edith Shackleton Heald for lunch. George stayed in Dublin, correcting the proofs of the *Collected Plays* for the Scribner edition, but Anne went to London as well, staying in a small hotel. 'She and Willy are to go about together,' Lily recorded, but he had other ideas. His rendezvous with Edith was followed almost at once by a stay at Steyning, carefully presented to George as a visit paid with the Dulacs to 'two elderly women' who could look after him. She was not so gullible, and wrote on 13 June that she hoped he was enjoying his birthday 'with the Dulacs and Miss Shackleton'. (For other correspondents, the Heald sisters were presented in yet another guise: 'my hosts are two charming Irish women', he inaccurately told McCartan.[43]) The attractions of a sleepy Sussex village in midsummer were enhanced by the fact that a house at the end of the street had once been the local register office where Parnell had married Mrs O'Shea in 1891. WBY was entranced to hear that the aged gardener at Chantry House had watched the happy but ill-starred couple emerge and drive away on another June day, forty-five years before. Long after her own romance with WBY, when Edith was an apparently demure octogenarian, she recalled his visits to Steyning as a time of afternoon drives to picture-postcard villages like Arundel and visits to Shelley's birthplace at Field Place. They also made trips to Brighton, where WBY gazed fondly at the Pier, remembering the *Liebestod* scene in Mrs O'Shea's memoir when her lover held her over the raging waves in a great storm and suggested they jump in together.[44] But for WBY, the atmosphere of his Sussex retreat was highly charged, and the memory of those earlier middle-aged lovers struck a particular chord. While no longer capable of full intercourse, his relationship with Edith was intensely sexual: surviving blurry snapshots show her sunbathing bare-breasted in the Steyning garden under his rapturous gaze. His need for romantic intimacy was being met once more, and with it his sense that he could write. On 15 June Edith drove him to Penns: he would live between the two houses and his Holland Park flat for the next six weeks. His editors at Scribner, left to deal with George, were understandably puzzled by the Yeats domestic arrangements: 'she apparently deals with him largely by correspondence', while he refused to answer her inquiries.[45] In London he dined at the Coronet in Notting Hill Gate, or with Turner at L'Escargot, and found himself – he told Edith – 'happy and at peace; my only dread that I might not please you'. The letter was signed 'with all my love'.[46]

Whether he pleased her or not, he was about to displease their mutual friend Dulac in a spectacular manner. WBY's next broadcast, 'My Own

Poetry', was scheduled for 3 July. He had chosen a selection of poems to contrast 'the tragic real Ireland' with 'the dream' – 'The Rose Tree', 'An Irish Airman Foresees his Death', 'The Curse of Cromwell', were to be set against 'Running to Paradise' and 'Sailing to Byzantium'. (These would, he hoped, defuse the political implications of the others.[47]) WBY had originally intended to employ music, set by Dulac, but he was equally determined to involve Margot Ruddock; and he had formed the opinion, unshakeably based on his powerful sense of rhythm and his complete ignorance of pitch, that poetry should be sung unaccompanied.[48] Dulac argued that music was essential to fix the modal structure, and he had produced harp settings for WBY's poems to prove it.[49] WBY had decided that a keyed instrument 'nails the musician to the mathematician's desk': the diatonic scale had joined his personal demonology of Newtonian inventions. George Barnes had assembled the actor Victor Clinton-Baddeley, of whom WBY approved, the harpist Marie Goossens, and – at WBY's insistence – the inevitable but more and more shaky Margot Ruddock. Dulac instead pressed the claims of Olive Groves, a trained singer. Rehearsals in late June exploded into animosity. Margot's incapacity was embarrassingly evident, and she was restricted to 'The Curse of Cromwell'. She wrote venomously to Dulac on 25 June, 'I can't think why WBY makes such a mess of absolutely everything . . . he is changeable as the weather not to be depended upon to do anything *unless* his reputation is at stake . . . I thought WBY liked my doing his work, evidently that too is an illusion. Why ask me in at all I wrote him why lead one to believe things not so.' By the final rehearsal she was back in the picture, and WBY was overruling Dulac's preferences: George was horrified to hear that at one point he shouted 'take that man away'.[50] The day after the broadcast Dulac angrily blamed WBY for allowing Ruddock's 'incredibly bad' performance through his 'extremely unfair behaviour' and 'queer emotional bias'. WBY's attempts to mollify him by sending George's praise of the broadcast misfired. She had praised the settings, but judged Margot (whom she had last seen out of her wits in Majorca) 'of course impossible'. 'I also now know', Dulac retorted, 'that, on certain grounds, one can never be sure of where one stands with you. Some muddled prejudice may turn up to spoil an apparently happy collaboration.' As for George's generous reaction, he scathingly added, 'her "of course" about the singer is a bit of a give away'. In the circumstances, Dulac refused to participate in the staged debate which WBY had been planning – which was probably just as well.[51]

After a welter of correspondence the hatchet was buried by mid July, as Edith Shackleton Heald confirmed to Dulac. 'The Poet . . . is in perfect agreement with your thesis and rather wondering what he has been fighting about.'[52] This is unlikely: Dulac's 'thesis' on the relations between poetry and music, sent to Steyning, condemned 'misguided' stratagems such as 'intoning of the neo-parsonic variety, improvised chanting by gifted amateurs "with no musical training but a natural melodic instinct" [and] Irish and other "folk" tune adaptations'. These were all palpable hits at WBY, who wrote firmly back to his ex-collaborator:

All my life I have tried to get rid of modern subjectivity by insisting on construction & contemporary words & syntax. It was to force myself to this that I used to insist that all poems should be spoken (hence my plays) or sung. Unfortunately it was only about a year ago that I discovered that for sung poetry (though not for poetry chanted as Florence Farr chanted) a certain type of 'stress' was essential . . . It was by mastering this 'stress' that I have written my most recent poems which have I think, for me, a new poignancy.

I want to get back to simplicity & can best do it – I believe – by working for our Irish unaccompanied singing. Every change I make to help the singer seems to improve the poem. A man of my ignorance learns from action.[53]

But Dulac was now completely sceptical about WBY's ability to judge musical settings for his poetry, and ruthlessly said so. The idea of a 'tradition' of Irish bardic chanting was an invention which merely provided an excuse for 'amateurish improvisation'. As for WBY, he adopted as his new adviser Walter Turner, who, as music critic for the *New Statesman*, had published widely and influentially, bringing (among other things) Italian opera into the domain of serious musical criticism. WBY considered Turner had the right ideas about accompaniment: though even he admitted WBY was completely tone deaf, and could not approach music 'as professional musicians understand it' (he also thought Margot's performance 'horrible – a mere whining'[54]). Dulac summed up the whole unhappy episode when writing to Pound a few months later, in Poundspeak:

Also had AI row with WBY over poatry broadcast with him asking me to do the musik for some poams the noises inbetween ah but in Doblin it aint real moosik they like, what you keep time with & real notes & all, crooning 'at's what they want and he had the harp muted so you couldn't hear it and it's Dolmetsch's old mop he would have stuffed down the singer's gullet only they woulnt let him.

All's well now, however, quite the old friends again.[55]

WBY had exerted his licence to be exasperating and didactic to the full, and now settled contentedly between Steyning and Penns. But this incident, like his treatment of his Indian visitor, showed that the rage infusing so much of his late work could break out in personal relations too.

Still, rage could bring illumination as well as bitterness. Through the early summer he was writing a General Introduction, never published in his lifetime, for the projected American edition; begun in April, he was still revising it in June, and the final version is dated six months later. It shares some of the *saeva indignatio* of *On the Boiler*, but is also a subtle and impassioned argument for a plural Irish personality, much as he had proclaimed in the interviews given at the time of his seventieth birthday celebrations, as well as a trumpet-call to ancient tradition. Most importantly, the 'General Introduction for my Work', aphoristic and scintillatingly assertive, presents at the outset one of WBY's key statements about artistic personae. Called 'The First Principle', it is in its own way a 'Defence of Poetry' as eloquent as Shelley's.[56]

A poet writes always of his personal life: in his first work out of its tragedy, whatever it be, remorse, lost love, or mere loneliness: he never speaks directly as to someone at the breakfast table. There is always a phantasmagoria. Dante and Milton had mythologies, Shakespeare the characters of English history or of traditional romance. Even when the poet seems most himself, when he is Raleigh and gives potentates the lie, or Shelley 'a nerve o'er which do creep the else unfelt oppressions of this earth', or Byron 'and the soul wears out the breast' as 'the sword outwears its sheath', he is never the bundle of accident and incoherence that sits down to breakfast; he has been reborn as an idea, something intended, complete. A novelist might describe his accidence, his incoherence; he must not.

His ancient concept of 'phantasmagoria' brings in the created, figurative world of emblems and invented personae which dominated his imagination – an imagination which was, so far as he was concerned, linked into the universal memory of tradition. Though he moves, as so often when explaining the development of his work, to personal autobiography (O'Leary, Young Ireland, Standish O'Grady, Augusta Gregory, the gathering of folklore), we have been warned. As he discusses the correspondence between Irish and other mythologies, the echoes of ancient wisdoms and folk belief, the 'great tapestry' of religion, he is placing the evolution of his extraordinary body of work in a context far transcending that of his own life and declaring its place in a 'folk art that goes back to Olympus'. Inevitably, parallel connections are made back to the world of Swedenborg, mediums, and desolate places. Christianity itself links back to Druidism, 'not shut off in dead history, but flowing, concrete, phenomenal'. (He added in a first draft, but deleted, 'for my own *A Vision* has but re-interpreted St Patrick's Creed'.) In perhaps the most striking passage of all, WBY confronts the history of Irish persecution and inherited hatreds: 'No people hate as we do in whom that past is always alive. There are moments when hatred poisons my life and I accuse myself of effeminacy because I have not given it adequate expression.' This frames the only quotation from his own poetry which he allows into the Introduction – 'The Curse of Cromwell', a further proof that he considered it one of his best poems.[57] But, he continues (writing in his Sussex village where Parnell had been married),

Then I remind myself that though mine is the first English marriage I know of in the direct line, all my family names are English; that I owe my soul to Shakespeare, to Spenser and to Blake, perhaps to William Morris, and to the English language in which I think, speak and write; that everything I love has come to me through English. My hatred tortures me with love, my love with hate. I am like the Tibetan monk who dreams at his initiation that he is eaten by a wild beast and learns on waking that he is himself eater and eaten. This is Irish hatred and solitude, the hatred of human life that made Swift write Gulliver and the epitaph upon his tomb, that can still make us wag between extremes and doubt our sanity.

The denunciation of English cultural influence in India which follows rings rather hollow, but it fits the rhetorical scheme. It also leads naturally to a third section, 'Style and Attitude', explaining why he strove for 'a powerful and passionate syntax', expressed in 'those traditional metres that developed with the language'. 'Talk to me of originality and I will turn on you with rage. I am a crowd, I am a lonely voice, I am nothing. Ancient salt is best packing.' Thus Pound (and others) receive yet again their come-uppance, and the phantasmagoria is asserted once more. The last section, 'Whither?', similarly challenges the Auden generation. They reject 'dream and personal emotion' for politics and 'action in character', attempting to achieve modernity by choosing 'the man in the Tube'. (This was exactly what the projected brotherhood of Penns in the Rocks was going to oppose.) 'They attempt to kill the whale, push the Renaissance higher yet, outthink Leonardo; their verse kills the folk ghost and yet would remain verse. I am joined to the "Irishry" and I expect a counter-Renaissance.' Thus the cycles of *A Vision* are implicitly evoked along with the principles of Dorothy Wellesley and Walter Turner. But in the last chilling paragraph it all comes back to Ireland.

When I stand upon O'Connell Bridge in the half-light and notice that discordant architecture, all those electric signs, where modern heterogeneity has taken physical form, a vague hatred comes up out of my own dark and I am certain that wherever in Europe there are minds strong enough to lead others the same vague hatred rises. In four or five or in less generations this hatred will have issued in violence and imposed some kind of rule of kindred. I cannot know the nature of that rule, for its opposite fills the light; all I can do to bring it nearer is to intensify my hatred. I am no nationalist, except in Ireland for passing reasons. State and Nation are the work of the intellect, and when you consider what comes before and after them they are, as Victor Hugo said of something or other, not worth the blade of grass God gives for the nest of the linnet.

The General Introduction, much influenced by his current stance in defiance of 'modernity', is also – phantasmagoria notwithstanding – an intensely personal statement. It reflects the life he was living in the summer of 1937, caught – as in his early years – between England and Ireland. And he continued to postpone his return to Rathfarnham and to plan to spend his remaining life, like his youth, between Dublin and London.

But he was now old and ill, and had to winter abroad as well; his mind was turning towards the money needed to sustain this pattern. The hoped for collected editions planned respectively by Macmillan in Britain and Scribner in the USA loomed large in his financial calculations, but the publishers continued to impose delay.[58] His royalty income continued to vary: in 1937 his British and Irish income was £242 without the Oxford anthology, which added a much needed £307.[59] A new book, such as *Dramatis Personae*, could be guaranteed to boost his earnings in the year of its publication, but would then lapse; his back catalogue was dominated by the *Collected Poems* of 1933 (it sold 694 copies in 1937/8, accounting for a third of his royalty income).[60] Of his plays, only the ancient *Land of Heart's Desire* made a regular appearance in the accounts columns. His American income was increasing, but still yielded not more than about $500 a year after tax. In the late 1930s his current bank account continued to fluctuate; from the end of 1934 he had been running a small but increasing overdraft.[61] The railway shares and war loan stock purchased from his Nobel money yielded a couple of hundred a year at most.[62] Unsurprisingly, he had started to augment his earnings by selling manuscripts: *Per Amica Silentia Lunae* fetched £52. 10s. 0d. in 1936. (He was not the only one: Gogarty was already adding to his own reduced income by busily procuring Yeats manuscripts from Dublin dealers and selling them on to American collectors.[63]) Lily reported in January 1937 that wby was selling off the crumpled drafts of poems she had 'picked up off the floors in Blenheim Road' fifty years before 'by degrees, and for big prices I think, to USA and other places'. Though George had some of her own money left, out of this modest and uncertain income wby had to subsidize his sisters and Cuala with 'loans' as well as an allowance; the Pollexfen shares had crashed by the end of the decade. He not only had to sustain Riversdale and 52 Holland Park; he and George paid the bills of Gurteen Dhas for telephone, taxis, and other sundries. 'He has a bad overdraft,' Lily had told Ruth in 1932, 'and his illness two years ago must have lost a great deal. And for all his fame he does not make much money.'[64]

It is little wonder, then, that his correspondence in that summer of 1937 is preoccupied by the advent of Dr Patrick McCartan to Dublin. McCartan, champion of Maloney's *Forged Casement Diaries*, was a well-off Irish-American doctor with an exciting IRB past (he had been intimately involved in the obscure dealings between de Valera's followers and Soviet Russia during the Troubles). Though he had criticized wby's mission for the Free State government in 1923, he had mellowed into devout admiration and spoken at a public banquet the year before about Ireland's lack of appreciation for the national poet.[65] Shortly afterwards he began organizing a testimonial collection for WBY – as had been done for Parnell and other national heroes in the past. McCartan's efforts on behalf of Maloney's Casement book had brought them into an even closer connection; by February 1937 WBY knew that a collection was being taken up, and stipulated that it must be made public.[66] By the summer a testimonial banquet was being organized, to be held when the Americans were in town; hence much of WBY's time in Sussex and London was spent calculating how he could maximize his time with Wellesley and Shackleton Heald, and still return in time to attend this event. (He even considered travelling by aeroplane, to George's alarm.) By late July he was installed at Riversdale, where Lily found him 'full of life and talk and enthusiasm. He looks now what he is, an old man, 72, his hair thick as ever, face very brown. The other day when I looked round at the family, the four of us all old, I got a shock. It seems only yesterday we were young.'[67]

Anyway, she added bravely, 'we are not decrepit'. Jack, indeed, defied age by removing his birth-date from *Who's Who*. But Lolly, who also noted WBY's aged appearance, felt that ever since his seventieth birthday he had 'dwelled upon' his age: it had become an obsession.[68] Nonetheless, as he prepared for the Americans' presentation on 17 August, he continued to be energetic, declamatory, and mischievous: sending Wellesley 'A Marriage Ode' on the Windsors' wedding, pressing Macmillan to produce a book of poems and music edited by himself and Higgins, correcting the proofs of *The Herne's Egg* (considered too earthy for the Abbey to produce), and writing long letters to Edith Shackleton Heald. 'When do you and I (or you and I and your sister) go abroad? I long for that.'[69]

Before then, he had to receive the American tribute. The committee set up the previous January[70] had not found their task easy. The objective was to create an annual income of $5,000 for the rest of WBY's life, by yearly donations of $100 from fifty people. The original appeal stressed that WBY was 'the only Irishman' ever invited to compile 'an Oxford anthology' and that 'his cultural writings and poetry have done much to remove the impression that Ireland is a peasant country and devoid of intellectuals'.[71] However, these esoteric achievements failed to impress many Irish-Americans. By May 1937, $3,100 had been subscribed, but there the fund languished. James Healy, one of the moving spirits, found it 'the most difficult task to raise $5000 I ever participated in'.[72] Spurred on by accounts of WBY's debility furnished by Gogarty (breaking the Hippocratic Oath for his patient's financial advantage), the appeal was relaunched the same month. The new circular pulled no punches. WBY was 'ill in body and mind as a result of the infirmities of age and acute financial worries. Those of us who have seen him recently are of the opinion that his time on this earth is somewhat limited and that he soon will be forced to greatly curtail his literary labour.'[73] This new urgency of tone was allied to a concentrated assault on networks like Yale Law School graduates and Irish actors in Hollywood, but it was an uphill battle. Faced with the collapse of business confidence (for which the businessmen on the committee unequivocally blamed Roosevelt's New Deal), the fundraisers encountered 'a trail of non-receptive Irishmen and Irish-Americans'.[74] Gogarty's interventions proved counter-productive: his scatological language offended Irish-American decencies, and he ran up debts to the organizers on his own account.[75] Meanwhile, back in the Yeats circle, rumours accumulated. Gogarty assured them that $5,000 was guaranteed. Lily heard it was £500, which at current exchange rates was half that sum. George tried to quash things by emphasizing that all estimates were exaggerated, and the continuance uncertain. In fact, by August the committee was still able to authorize only about $3,000, in the form of a cheque for £600; another instalment would arrive the following June, for £400, bringing the subvention for 1937/8 to £1,000. It was hoped to follow this up by £500 a year, but this seemed unlikely. In the end the total sum raised, with a concerted effort, was $6,000. Seventeen people had given $200 each, and there were twenty-six donations of $100. It is improbable that more would have been forthcoming.

Nonetheless, the sum subscribed in 1937 came at exactly the right time, and WBY received it with gratitude. The gift, he had told McCartan in May, would enable him to provide more poetry in the Casement ballad vein: 'more Irish, and more myself'. This was just what an old Fenian wanted to hear. As WBY had insisted, the tribute was to be made public, but a certain amount of discretion was still observed. The banquet at the Dolphin Hotel on 17 August was given, under the auspices of the Irish Academy, ostensibly to honour Patrick McCartan, Marquis Macdonald, and others for subsidizing the Academy's Gregory Medal, the O'Growney Award, and the Casement Award. (There was also an unsuccessful attempt to elect Maloney as a Fellow.) The much larger subvention to WBY came up only in his own carefully crafted speech. A few days before, he had complained to Wellesley of the necessity to be 'senatorial', and gave an ironic précis of his projected address, revolving around the importance of literature binding together the sundered Gaels worldwide. But what he said on the night was very different. He had, he admitted, his own reasons for gratitude to their guests. Though he and his wife had enough for the necessities of life and for educating their children, he had been endowed with a generous gift to enable 'dignity and ease'. This lofty tone was not sustained in all the toasts and speeches, and the Irish-American input introduced some elements not entirely compatible with the libertarian spirit of the Academy. Another old

Fenian, Denis McCullough, launched a violent assault on cinema and radio for 'completing the task that years of foreign rule failed to accomplish', and called for censorship of the airwaves and the immediate revival of the Irish language, while the satirist Niall Montgomery ('Lynn Doyle') daringly interposed that 'a lot of "bosh" was talked about the glory of the blood spilt for Ireland'.[76] The combination of the Academy's dissenting littérateurs and Irish-American nationalists was likely to produce a certain amount of combustion.

If wby had hoped the occasion would pass quietly, he was to be disappointed. Curious journalists besieged Riversdale with calls, deflected by George pretending to be a secretary. The dinner and speech were widely reported, and there was much interested gossip about his good fortune. But wby also trailed further cause for speculation by announcing in his speech that he intended to write a poem to send his benefactors: 'a poem about the Ireland we have all served, and the movement of which I have been a part'. As later printed, his speech elaborated on the theme:

For a long time I had not visited the Municipal Gallery. I went there a week ago, and was restored to many friends. I sat down, after a few minutes, overwhelmed with emotion. There were pictures painted by men, now dead, who were once my

IRISH ACADEMY OF LETTERS DINNER

At last night's Irish Academy of Letters dinner at the Dolphin Hotel. From left: Mr. W. B. Yeats, Mrs. O. St. John Gogarty, Dr. Patrick MacCartan, Mr. F. R. Higgins and Mr. Lennox Robinson.

14. The Irish Academy dinner at the Dolphin Hotel, 17 August 1937, where wby announced his American subvention, as recorded in the *Irish Times* the following day: (l. to r.), wby, Martha Gogarty, Patrick McCartan, F. R. Higgins, Lennox Robinson.

intimate friends. There were portraits of my fellow-workers; there was that portrait of Lady Gregory, by Mancini, which John Synge thought the greatest portrait since Rembrandt; there was John Synge himself; there, too, were portraits of our Statesmen, the events of the last twenty years in fine pictures: a peasant ambush, the trial of Roger Casement, a pilgrimage to Lough Derg, event after event: Ireland, not as she is displayed in guide book or history, but Ireland seen because of the magnificent vitality of her painters, in the glory of her passions.

For the moment I could think of nothing but that Ireland: that great pictured song. The next time I go, I shall stand once more in veneration before the work of the great Frenchmen. It is said that an Indian ascetic, when he has taken a certain initiation on a mountain in Tibet, is visited by all the Gods. In those rooms of the Municipal Gallery I saw Ireland in spiritual freedom, and the Corots, the Rodins, the Rousseaus were the visiting gods.[77]

The speech was printed in a pamphlet for distribution to the American subscribers, accompanied by two poems. One was an excruciatingly banal 'Dedication' addressing McCartan (who 'Travelled to and fro across the Atlantic,/He, though but a landsman, went to the mast-head'), James Farrell ('Among his children, grandchildren, and great-grandchildren'), and Dudley Digges ('Now a notable man on stage and on screen'). The other poem was the promised meditation on revisiting the Municipal Gallery.[78]

The poem, like the speech, adroitly integrated the inevitable Ascendancy triumvirate of WBY, Gregory, and Synge into the iconography of the Irish revolution and the 'people of Ireland'. That these reflections should be inspired by an institution so closely associated with Hugh Lane, and now (since 1933) located in a great Georgian town house, adds to the poignancy – and to the deliberateness of his assertion that the Ascendancy is an essential part of the new Ireland. There is also a certain challenge (especially given his old-Fenian audience) in WBY's repeated invocation (explicit and implicit) of Edmund Spenser – seen by Irish nationalists not as the master of Elizabethan allegorical poetry but as the advocate of genocidal colonial policies. 'The Municipal Gallery Revisited', written in stately ottava rima, gestures towards an old English tradition of courtly praise-poems; Casement may appear in the first verse but the style is far from balladeering, and Higgins, mercifully, would never have been able to sing it. Though the opening stanzas employ a swift impressionism, conjuring up images from paintings by Keating, Lavery, and Orpen, this is only by means of introduction. The first draft of the poem[79] declares an intention to focus on the great Abbey generation (including Frank Fay), probably as a gesture towards Dudley Digges, who had worked hard for the testimonial. But it turned out (for all its daring internal repetitions) closer to 'All Souls' Night', a reunion between the poet and the noble dead.

Heart smitten with emotion, I sink down,
My heart recovering with covered eyes;
Wherever I had looked I had looked upon
My permanent or impermanent images:
Augusta Gregory's son; her sister's son,
Hugh Lane – 'onlie begetter' of all these –
Hazel Lavery living and dying, that tale
As though some ballad singer had sung it all.

Mancini's portrait of Augusta Gregory,
'Greatest since Rembrandt' according to John Synge,
An ebullient great portrait certainly;
But where is the brush that could show anything
Of all that pride and that humility?
And I am in despair that time may bring
Approved patterns of women or of men,
But not that self-same excellence again.

My mediaeval knees lack health until they bend,
But in that woman, in that household, where
Honour had lived so long, their health I found.
Childless, I thought, 'my children may learn here
What deep roots are,' and never foresaw the end,
Of all that scholarly generations had held dear;
But now that end has come I have not wept;
No fox can foul the lair the badger swept:

(An image out of Spenser and the common tongue)
John Synge, I and Augusta Gregory thought
All that we did, all that we said or sang
Must come from contact with the soil, from that
Contact all things Antaeus-like grew strong;
We three alone in modern times had brought
All things down to that common test again,
Dream of the noble and the beggarman.

And here's John Synge, a meditative man,
'Forgetting human words', a grave deep face.
You that would judge me do not judge alone
This book or that; come to this hallowed place
Where my friends' portraits hang, and look thereon;
Ireland's history in their lineaments trace:
Think where man's glory most begins and ends
And say my glory was I had such friends.

For all the identification with soil and people, Coole was apparently better off tumbled to the ground than inhabited by inferiors. Although the poem opens with a general view of patriots and heroes, it narrows down to wby at his most exclusive. The 'friends' invoked in the last stanza are certainly not Casement, whom he had never met, nor Griffith 'staring in hysterical pride', nor even O'Higgins, but the fellowship of Coole. Yet the ending rings hollow; wby was aware that his glory would reside in his books, not in the roll-call of his acquaintance. The poem as a whole reverts to the formality of his elegies for Robert Gregory, and renounces exactly the qualities of immediacy and music which he had preached to Dulac a few weeks before. But it closes with an implicit epitaph for himself, and his own assumption into the heroic frieze of portraits. The recognition that Lily had felt a month before, when she suddenly saw him as an old man, had stabbed him too.

But it would not stop him writing, and not all of his poems were in the same sonorous vein. He told Wellesley that the Municipal Gallery poem was 'perhaps the best poem I have written for some years, unless the "Curse of Cromwell" is';[80] shortly before, he awarded a similar accolade to one of his more enigmatic ballads, 'Colonel Martin', written according to strict 'Broadside' principles. In the same letter he sent her the first draft of a short poem whose mysterious simplicity achieves a kind of Blakean transcendence; it also called a truce to their disagreements about politics, and should be read as a gentle injunction from one troubled poet to another.

> Though I have bid you turn
> From the cavern of the mind;
> (There is more to bite upon
> In the sunlight and wind).
>
> I did not say attend
> To Moscow or to Rome,
> Turn from drudgery
> Call the Muses home;
>
> Seek majestic powers
> That constitute the Wild,
> The Lion and the Harlot,
> The Virgin and the Child:
>
> Find in middle air
> An eagle on the wing;
> Recognise the fire
> That makes the Muses sing.

Following hard upon the forced polemic of 'A Marriage Ode', and accompanied by a sarcastic parody of the kind of speech expected by his American admirers, 'Those Images' shows the inventive range and power which he could summon up at will. The images invoked are inspired by Theosophy and Indian philosophy, as well as by Christian iconography. Like the Virgin and Star in the song from *The Resurrection*, Christological and apostolic emblems are worked into the tapestry of a wider antiquity. Though sent to Wellesley from Dublin, and implicitly addressed to her, Edith Shackleton Heald remembered that he first shaped it after a day spent with Elizabeth Pelham that summer at her family's house, Stanmer Park, where they had discussed the symbols of lion and virgin.[81] The poem testifies to the personal above the political, and vindicates – as a good deal of his current writing did not – his searching back into the lost simplicities and esoteric mythologies of his youth.

He kept faith too with ancient commitments like the campaign for the Lane pictures (telling de Valera that a resolution of the issue should be part of Anglo-Irish diplomatic negotiations), and the campaign to extend the Abbey's premises.[82] But he thought incessantly of liberation. On 11 September George escorted him yet again on the mailboat as far as Holyhead. As soon as he reached the Athenaeum he wrote to Edith:

I am longing for you in body & soul . . . O my dear, I want to say all those foolish things which are sometimes read out in breach of promise cases. I know what it is to think what transcends speech or what speech transcends – that is perhaps what savage tom-toms are for. I also want to say those things that belong to speech & intellect – but we shall have time.[83]

Three days later he was at Steyning, and he was based there or Penns, with visits to London, for the next six weeks. The extent to which his new passion had displaced older attachments is proved by his neglect of Olivia Shakespear. On 12 October he wrote from Steyning regretting that he had not managed to see her: 'I keep out of London as much as possible'. Nonetheless, George drily reported that he had been spotted being driven down Pall Mall 'in a racing car without a hat', and assumed that his chauffeur was Edith. WBY assured his new love that their association had his wife's blessing, and any sense of possessiveness which George might have retained seems to have been counterbalanced by relief that he was being cared for while in England.[84] Cosseted in Chantry House, he found he could write but fretted for a theme. The poem that broke through this block in mid October was 'The Old Stone Cross', drafted on Chantry House notepaper and headed 'My New Poem'.[85] Like much that he wrote at this time, a derisive balladeering tone is linked to a mysterious refrain; and the easy dismissal of politics and condemnation of an unimaginative daily life is set against an ominous hint about the decay of civilization:

> A statesman is an easy man,
> He tells his lies by rote;
> A journalist makes up his lies
> And takes you by the throat,
> So stay at home and drink your beer
> And let the neighbors vote,
> > *Said the man in the golden breastplate*
> > *Under the old stone Cross.*
>
> Because this age and the next age
> Engender in the ditch,
> No man can know a happy man
> From any passing wretch,
> If Folly link with Elegance
> No man knows which is which.
> > *Said the man in the golden breastplate*
> > *Under the old stone Cross*
>
> But actors lacking music
> Do most excite my spleen,
> They say it is more human
> To shuffle, grunt, and groan,
> Not knowing what unearthly stuff
> Rounds a mighty scene.
> > *Said the old man in the golden breastplate*
> > *Under the old stone Cross.*

As in much of his late verse, there is an echo of his Sligo youth, and an anticipation of last things: Drumcliff Churchyard, where the Sligo Yeatses were buried, was supposedly guarded by an ancient Irish warrior lying in his armour, and an ancient cross stands sentinel near by. The kernel of the poem lies in the idea that, at the end of an era, decadence triumphs and vital aesthetic distinctions become blurred: the images of folly and elegance become indistinguishable. As WBY pursued his carefully staged romantic passion for Edith Shackleton Heald, or encouraged the increasingly erratic Dorothy Wellesley (in Vita Sackville-West's cruel phrase) to 'think she could think', his own ancient ability to draw the borderline between self-indulgence and strict judgement might seem deeply compromised. But whatever effort it took him, and however contrived the necessary intellectual and erotic stimulation might be, his sense of creativity had to be preserved. He had constructed — in old age as in youth — the conditions to nurture it. 'I think', he wrote to George when he sent her 'The Old Stone Cross', 'of writing a long Noh play on the Death of Cuchulain.'

Dramatic performance, the closing image of that poem, was much in his mind in late October, when he worked with George Barnes on what would be the last of his BBC broadcasts: 'My Own Poetry Again'. It was also the most conventional. Bruised by the altercation with Dulac, WBY insisted upon no staged debate, and the musical experimentation was strictly limited. For all her tantrums, Margot was back on board (there were probably few other claims on her professional time). The poems WBY chose were, surprisingly but deliberately, all from his early career. He began with the by now canonical story of how a London shop-window display awakened his longing for Sligo, and inspired 'Innisfree'. Moving on to 'The Fiddler of Dooney' and 'The Happy Townland', he emphasized, with mock severity, that he had to read in a chanting way 'because every poet who reads his own poetry gives as much importance to the rhythm as to the sense'. He then introduced Margot to sing 'Into the Twilight' and 'The Countess Kathleen in Paradise'. 'If you listen, as a trained musician listens, for the notes only you will miss the pleasure you are accustomed to and find no other. Her notes cannot be separated from the words. Because her singing gives me great pleasure I am sure it will give pleasure to others.'[86] This may have been hoping for too much, but he had at least aimed a dart at Dulac and the 'professionals'. A nostalgic reference to Coole, 'associated with all my public activities until a few years ago', introduced the final poem: 'Coole Park and Ballylee, 1931'. 'It is typical of most of my recent poems, intricate in metaphor, the swan and water both emblems of the soul, not at all a dream, like my earlier poems, but a criticism of life.'

The broadcast went out on 29 October. Barnes found it a more moving and effective performance than its predecessors, but was alarmed by WBY's low reserves of strength. As soon as the recording was over, WBY sank back exhausted. Nonetheless, they set out, with Margot, for a celebratory dinner, but found the Ivy shut. 'Without hesitation Yeats ordered the cabby to drive on to a well-known Italian restaurant, telling us on the way of succulent meals he had had there in the past. Alas for the memory, the management had changed and a stern Scottish waitress denied us drink and eventually brought Margot a coffee and Yeats a hard boiled egg.'[87]

When they all parted outside the restaurant, it was for the last time. Plans for more broadcasts were in the air (including an overture about making a television appearance from Alexandra Palace), but nothing came of it. It was also the last of WBY's many efforts to launch Margot Ruddock in the footsteps of Florence Farr. Before the end of the year her mental instability had returned in full force, and she was committed to an institution, where she stayed until her death in 1951, aged only forty-four.

IV

On 1 November George met her husband at Holyhead, for the return journey to Dublin. By then the new edition of *A Vision* had been published, after a process of rewriting which had preoccupied him from the moment the first version had left his hands twelve years earlier, to the dismay of many of his friends.[88] WBY was unmoved. 'One goes on year after year gradually getting the disorder of one's mind in order,' he had written to JBY long before, 'and this is the real impulse to create.'[89] The 1937 version embodied some sweeping changes (as well as corrections from acid critics like F. P. Sturm), and for the moment WBY was pleased with it. 'As I turn the pages,' he told Shakespear, 'I find here & there the best prose I have written & much passion.' Finishing the proofs a few months before, he had described to Wellesley the current evolution of his philosophy:

I begin to see things double – doubled in history, world history, personal history. At this moment all the specialists are about to run together in our new Alexandria, thought is about to be unified as its own free act, and the shadow in Germany and elsewhere is an attempted unity by force. In my own life I never felt so acutely the presence of a spiritual virtue and that is accompanied by intensified desire. Perhaps there is a theme for poetry in this 'double swan and shadow'.[90]

The vision of modern thought trembling on the edge of unity is influenced by Gentile, and the link to Hitler's threatening project is arresting – as is the ominous view WBY takes of 'attempted unity by force'. The reflections on spiritual and erotic ecstasy intertwined suggest his Indian reading, and found constant reflection in his poetry. The notion of repetitions, reflections, and symmetry, mirrored both in personal lives and astrological pilgrimages, inspires the second *Vision* as the first. And WBY decisively introduces references to his own personal odyssey, particularly the influences of the 1890s. Not only does the 1937 *Vision* incorporate the revelations of *A Packet for Ezra Pound*, giving the full implications of George's involvement, but it also employs rewritten 'Stories of Michael Robartes' to construct a new origin-myth for the discovery of the sacred book. This introductory 'Phantasmagoria' of narratives uses his old Owen Aherne–Michael Robartes antithesis to bring in 1890s memories, references to *Axël*, and a deliberate sexual frankness. (The story as presented here recycles an account that had fascinated him since he heard it among Oxford students nearly twenty years before. As so often, it concerns impotence and surrogate sex: two friends share a woman, one of them being unable to perform sexually until his friend has preceded him.) Like *The Arabian Nights*, the

Michael Robartes stories deal with narratives within narratives: one, deliberately set at Coole, deals with inheritance. Embedded within the 'Stories' is the tale of the discovery of Giraldus's tome, now with the title correctly spelled. And though 'The Phases of the Moon' was retained as the Prologue, other introductory material was dropped, and the explanatory first section changed and simplified, though that is hardly the word. WBY's reading in Gentile, Croce, and Berkeley was employed more obviously, and some new political inferences had crept in.[91] So had an interest in time–space relations derived from what he knew of Einstein; the statements of George's 'Instructors' were less evident, reflecting the fact that she – twenty years older and correspondingly less starry-eyed – was now thoroughly bored by the 'System'. To a certain extent, though, WBY's reduced references to (for instance) the connection between the 'phases' of the 'System' and the transit of the moon may merely indicate an assumption that his readers were by now familiar with his governing structure. He also felt able to admit some uncertainties in the invention of a pedigree for the 1925 version. In some ways his interest in Indian philosophy has replaced the Freudian intonations of George's well-read 'Instructors', and the analysis at certain points owes more to philosophy than to psychology.[92] Recent preoccupations like Blake's 'Mental Traveller' can be discerned, along with Berkeley, and the laborious philosophy-student disagreements of WBY's correspondence with Sturge Moore. Some of the more directly autobiographical resonances were also excised.[93] On the other hand, in keeping with the development of his political ideas, a new section was added on the antithesis between aristocracy and democracy.

In many ways WBY remains faithful to the underlying structure. The archetypes of the twenty-eight incarnations remain much the same,[94] though the division of the Calendar year as related to the twenty-eight lunar phases, which had got him into trouble in the first version, is frankly pronounced 'as insoluble to the symbolist as was that between the solar and lunar year to the ancient astronomer'. The 2,000-year cycle of the Great Wheel is also very freely interpreted. There is, however, a new section on 'The Completed Symbol' (Book II), devoted to geometric symbolism and incorporating much of 'The Geometrical Foundation of the Wheel'. Book V, 'Dove or Swan', has some alterations, with the assertions of 1925 turned, more gingerly, into questions in 1937. 'The Gates of Pluto' has disappeared; and so has the Burton-meets-Browning fancy-dress of 'The Gift of Harun Al-Raschid'. It is not entirely an advantage to have more geometric diagrams instead, with would-be helpful visualizations supplied by WBY ('I can see them like jelly-fish in clear water'[95]). But the 1937 volume retains its interest (as did its predecessor) for the way the 'historical' arguments continue to mirror the author's developing preoccupations – such as a new passage on race, purity, and class:

When I look in history for the conflict or union of *antithetical* and *primary* I seem to discover that conflict or union of races stated by Petrie and Schneider as universal law. A people who have lived apart and so acquired unity of custom and purity of breed unite with some other people through migration, immigration or conquest. A race (the new *antithetical*) emerges that is neither the one nor the other, after somewhere about 500 years it produces, or so it seems, its particular culture or civilisation. This culture lives only in certain victorious classes; then comes a period of revolution (Phase 22) terminated by a civilisation of policemen, schoolmasters, manufacturers, philanthropists, a second soon exhausted blossoming of the race.[96]

But more familiar themes resurface as well. He may have deleted 'The Gates of Pluto', having decided years earlier that it 'filled him with shame . . . a series of unrelated statements & inaccurate deductions',[97] but it was simply replaced by 'The Soul in Judgment' – yet again an assemblage of anecdote and tradition seeking to prove (to WBY's satisfaction at least) the continued existence of the soul after death. Much is repeated from 'Swedenborg, Mediums, and the Desolate Places' and *Per Amica Silentia Lunae*, though the well-worn language is spiced up by reference to D. H. Lawrence's novels. 'The Great Year of the Ancients', another addition, is a meditation on cycles, history, and Neoplatonic calculations, delivered in WBY's most oracular and obscure style. ('Do not read anything after page 64,' he wrote in Dorothy Wellesley's copy.[98]) Commenting approvingly on Proclus's explication of Plato's Golden Number, defining the duration of the Great Year, WBY adds:

It is as though innumerable dials, some that recorded minutes alone, some seconds alone, some hours alone, some months alone, some years alone, were all to complete their circles when Big Ben struck twelve upon the last night of the century. My instructors offer for a symbol the lesser unities that combine into a work of art and leave no remainder, but we may substitute if we will the lesser movements which combine into the circle that in Hegel's *Logic* unites not summer solstice to summer solstice but absolute to absolute.[99]

'The Great Year of the Ancients', studded with lofty allusions, operates on a level of subjective abstraction which wraps around the most attentive reader like a dense fog: it is heavily dependent on the writers WBY had discovered since the publication of the first version (Spengler, Petrie, Heard, Vico), and it is no clearer for that. Nor is it a good sign when this section becomes an astrological commentary full of rhetorical questions and off-hand but pointless references to esoteric authorities ('I have not read [Ptolemy's] *Almagest*, nor am I likely to . . . '). Once again, an intense personal identification may be discerned in a passage trying to isolate key astrological moments which concentrate a point of 'greatest possible intellectual power'. But he admits:

An historical symbolism which covers too great a period of time for imagination to grasp or experience to explain may seem too theoretical, too arbitrary, to serve any practical purpose; it is, however, necessary to the myth if we are not to suggest, as Vico did, civilisation perpetually returning to the same point.[100]

This is a large concession. WBY's wish for history to advance towards revelation (or even annunciation) necessitated a framework which he himself knew was theoretical, arbitrary, and impractical. It is one of the junctures when the observation he had made of himself in his autobiographies, that he possessed a religious temperament unattached to a religion, rings more convincingly and illuminatingly than all his tedious efforts to debate the reality of Ruskin's cat with Sturge Moore, or drop the names of philosophical tracts he was never going to read.

He clings, moreover, to his diagrams of superimposed cones, marked out with historical eras, 'showing the gyre of religion expanding as that of secular life contracts'.[101] And, though his current political preoccupations sometimes show through, he suppresses his previous commentary on the modern symptoms of Phase Twenty-three, where he had related the writings of Eliot, Pound, Joyce, and Pirandello to the advent of revolution. In fact, the implicit prophecy of a coming 'fanaticism' and 'irrational force', 'oppressing the ignorant – even the innocent' which connects the 1925 *Vision* so clearly to WBY's experience of Mussolini's Italy, is gone. Instead there is a new reflection of 'The End of the Cycle', abjuring political prophecy. It also conjures up an oddly poignant flash of autobiography.

Day after day I have sat in my chair turning a symbol over in my mind . . . I have felt the convictions of a lifetime melt though at an age when the mind should be rigid, and others take their place, and these in turn give way to others. How far can I accept socialistic or communistic prophecies? I remember the decadence Balzac foretold to the Duchesse de Castries. I remember debates in the little coach-house at Hammersmith or at Morris' supper-table afterwards. I remember the Apocalyptic dreams of the Japanese saint and labour leader Kagawa, whose books were lent me by a Galway clergyman. I remember a Communist described by Captain White in his memoirs ploughing on the Cotswold Hills, nothing on his great hairy body but sandals and a pair of drawers, nothing in his head but Hegel's *Logic*. Then I draw myself up into the symbol and it seems as if I should know all if I could but banish such memories and find everything in the symbol.

But nothing comes – though this moment was to reward me for all my toil. Perhaps I am too old. Surely something would have come when I meditated under the direction of the Cabalists. What discords will drive Europe to that artificial unity – only dry or drying sticks can be tied into a bundle – which is the decadence of every civilization? How work out upon the phases the gradual coming and increase of the counter-movement, the *antithetical* multiform influx:

> Should Jupiter and Saturn meet,
> What a crop of mummy wheat!

Then I understand. I have already said all that can be said. The particulars are the work of the *Thirteenth Cone* or cycle which is in every man and called by every man his freedom. Doubtless, for it can do all things and knows all things, it knows what it will do with its own freedom but it has kept the secret.

Seen against the background of his own intellectual odyssey, the annunciation is to be personal and associated with creative expression. Thus in the new version, the definitions of the Four Faculties (Will, Mask, Creative Mind, Body of Fate) have become more complex and symbolic than in 1925, and man's Daimon (artistic inspiration) occupies a more central place, no longer presented simply as Muse.[102] This reflects the diminished presence of both George and Maud Gonne in the 1937 version. It may be true that the second *Vision* is more metaphysical and less autobiographical than its predecessor; Thomas Parkinson has described them as 'two separate books, the first subjective and personal, the second at least an attempt at objectivity and impersonality . . . [moving] toward creating a view of the world that is not dependent on personal or even contemporary material'.[103] But its roots in personal psychology remain, and, for all its myth-making ambition, it is still far from a philosophy of history.

Nor does *A Vision* establish a philosophical system, despite WBY's claims in his Introduction. It has found few followers since Frank Pearce Sturm, and it is hard to believe that it deserves them. Helen Vendler has brilliantly demonstrated its usefulness in explicating some late plays and illuminating difficult poems, and others have followed her. But her claim that the book is really a 'bizarre literary history', 'primarily about poetry',[104] seems perilously near wishful-thinking; the completely internalized arguments and intentional obscurity limit its usefulness in this sphere too.[105] It remains true that, as Vendler's own work shows, it can be read – on one level – as a commentary on the process and achievement of artistic inspiration: the 'System', it should be remembered, is applied principally to artists, not to all mankind. And the achievement of creativity was what had obsessed WBY in the years from 1934 to 1936, when he was revising it.

This may be why one of the most unexpectedly sympathetic reactions to the 1937 *Vision* was from Sean O'Faolain, though his attitude to WBY generally veered between guardedness and exasperation. While he felt that 'this sybilline book' would fall 'into this cynical, fragmentary, analytical age like a lark into a lime-kiln', he read it as a writer's testament – and as an idiosyncratic meditation defining an extraordinary personality, like the *Anatomy of Melancholy*.

There is no ethic, no morality. The actor and the play are One. The drama is inclusive and illuminating – as absolute as a poem – however prosy with tables and numbers – whose subject is the oldest subject in the world – the nature of man in relation to his human destiny. With such a subject and such a poet, I cannot (once the pseudo-romantic trappings have been flicked away) imagine anybody from an assayer to a tea-taster, a Communist to a pious Roman Catholic, who will not find it an exasperating, provoking, stimulating delight.

It is the Yeats who loved Blake and Shelley, who detested Sargent and admired Whistler, who wished he could prefer Chaucer to Shakespeare, who disliked the Flemish satirists, who has always been seeking a unifying image and bewails the falling asunder of life before the fraying of the intellect; it is the Yeats of the personal, fiery poems, the dramatic, hammering and hammered poems of the middle and later period; and nobody who would read these poems in mood with the poet, extract from them the ultimate pleasure of their implication and overtones, can afford not to wind his way with this book into their cavern-sources in one of the most complex and solitary minds among lyric poets since the death of Keats.[106]

Reactions elsewhere were more muted, though WBY was pleased and surprised that Charles Williams, the publisher–poet who had dealt with the Oxford anthology and been shocked at WBY's controversial omissions, reacted favourably to *A Vision*: 'he is the only reviewer who has seen what he calls "the greatness and terror" of the diagram'.[107] For WBY, at any rate, a tryst had been kept. He had reaffirmed faith with the 'System' and taken his stand as a philosopher, and was now free to turn fully to poetry. A month after the publication of *A Vision* he could tell Wellesley, 'I have finished my book of lyric poems, and a new poem which is the start of a new book.' He was also, he confided, meditating 'a *Fors Clavigera* of sorts – my advice to the youthful mind on all manner of things'. More specifically, these injunctions should 'sketch out the fundamental principles, as I see them, on which politics and literature should be based.' The reference to Ruskin's manifesto against the modern age was not accidental: he was preparing himself for battle, cranking up the unpopular opinions which would be published as *On the Boiler* and stand as one of the most unsettling testaments to the energies of his old age. In this mood he had, he told Edith, 'shaken off depression as a dog shakes off water'.[108]

As always with WBY, there was a certain Pollexfen calculation at work too. At this time he was grappling, yet again, with Cuala's slide into debt. 'The great problem of my life,' he had told Wellesley in September, 'put off from year to year, and now to be put off no more . . . [is] to put the Cuala

607

Press into such a shape that it can go on after my death, or incapacity through old age, without being a charge on my wife.'[109] WBY's productions were all that brought in money to the Press. By January 1938 Lolly had his recently completed volume in proof as *New Poems*, and it would appear three months later; but WBY also shrewdly anticipated that a series of controversial manifestos, issued (as he planned) twice a year, would add considerably to the Press's income. 'The other day', he told Mannin, 'I discovered that I must increase the income of the Cuala Press by about £150 a year & decided to issue a kind of *Fors Clavigera*. I must in the first number discuss social politics in so far as they affect Ireland. I must lay aside this pleasant path I have built up for years & seek the brutality, the ill breeding, the barbarism of truth. Pray for me my dear, I want an atheist's prayers, no Christian can do me any good.'[110]

Through a bitter December he stayed inside, longing for escape to the Riviera, but preoccupied by reorganizing Cuala. He was also at the mercy of visitors. Lily recorded his incomprehension at the descent of a 'gas bag' relative on Riversdale. She 'called him "cousin Willy", he hasn't the ghost of an idea who she is . . . and you can imagine George, who thinks all relations are just infernal nuisances'. George's unIrish briskness about family connections remained a cause for gentle regret on Lily's part ('she never sees her mother or brother: I suppose she writes now and then and will go to her mother's funeral').[111] But it may have been a rational defence strategy, given the way the whole family dreaded Lolly's incursions into their lives: WBY made a practice of hiding behind a pillar at the Abbey as she stalked by. Lily, who perpetuated their father's habit of analysing character in terms of family inheritance, thought that her elder brother was 'very much Pollexfen with the Yeats intellect', and therefore doomed to clash with Lolly, who embodied a similar combination. ('We know', WBY once asked Lily despairingly, 'that her bad temper comes from Grandfather Pollexfen, but where does her silliness come from?')[112] As for his relations with Lily, they were still, as in their youth, a 'pair'. She was touched by the way that he continued to seek out embroidery projects for her: 'he always talks to me of my work as if I was young and had a future'.[113] The designs he brought back from London were now modernistic, 'as ugly as jazz and swing music' in Lily's opinion, but his enthusiasm was unabated. In an odd re-creation of Bedford Park days, through the summer of 1937 she had been working on a panel which interpreted Oisin's Land of Youth in neo-Cubist fashion; it was followed by an equally avant-garde 'Innisfree'. 'What a pity it is we have to grow old and feeble,' she wrote in November, after a visit to Riversdale. 'But mentally we are alive, no doubt about that.' Later that month he arrived in a hired car to take her for a drive in the Dublin mountains, and in the winter sunlight she noticed how fragile he had looked ever since the illness in Majorca, though his mind was as vigorous as ever. A month later, taking Sunday tea at Riversdale, she was struck by his handsomeness in 'a camel coloured gown, with wide trousers of the same, and a dark red silk shirt, he and I now old folk, talking with vigour of our youth of embroidery, of cabbages and kings.'[114]

Such easy commerce was not possible with Lolly, but the nettle of Cuala's finances had to be grasped. In October Lolly had contacted wby in London about trouble with the bank, and he had riposted sharply, 'I like you am out of humour with the present arrangement. You owe me more than £2000.'[115] Mr Scroope at the National Bank on College Green was also out of humour. By November the Press's overdraft reached a critical level, and the bank froze the account. On 16 November wby drew up a statement, laying down his wish to leave the Press in a solvent state when he and Lolly were no longer there, and pointing out that initiatives like the 'Broadsides' could help to keep it solvent, and that it must 'remain as it always has been closely associated with the Irish intellectual movement'. He promised 'another publication to fill up the gap' between the two or three books a year which the Press produced, meaning *On the Boiler*. But he also stressed that a root-and-branch reorganization was essential when he returned from France in the spring. This was sent to Lolly with an ambitious schedule of future publications: *New Poems, On the Boiler*, a volume from Higgins, and a two-volume edition of wby's letters to Gregory.

But the bank could not wait that long, and in mid December Lolly received a chilling letter detailing the Press's position. Though wby had cleared one overdraft of £330 in January 1935 (accumulated from the embroidery side, now closed down), another account had remained outstanding and now stood at £716; while the one which wby had cleared was about to lurch into debt again.[116] wby took over negotiations, sending an explanatory and soothing letter promising that his publication plans would double output over the next two years; without consultation Lolly simultaneously sent an airy promise to reduce the debt, and wby's patience snapped. 'I suppose as your elder brother public opinion if not law considers me responsible for your debts but damn your eyes what can I do if you write one thing and I another?'[117] Henceforth wby took over negotiations, guaranteeing the debt until the following April and suggesting that Cuala's debits and credits be restricted to one account only, with the overdrawn account to be left untouched: 'I want to get into the heads of the various workers at Cuala that henceforth they can make their business a success without borrowing from anybody.' He was, he instructed Lolly, to get a weekly statement from the Press, listing bank lodgements and withdrawals.

He also demanded details of various other aspects of the business, determined to exercise close control even when abroad.[118]

But it would not detain him in Ireland. Ever since the American testimonial money arrived, he had determined to spend some of it on wintering in the sun. Sending Lolly an outline of the new arrangements on 4 January 1938, he added, 'I shall be on my way to the S. of France when you get this.' He was about to realize the dream that had kept him warm through the winter, which he had rehearsed to Edith Shackleton Heald when she suggested she travel out to the Riviera separately, for appearances' sake.

We are going out togeather. We are getting into the train at Victoria & getting out at Monte Carlo. That is clear, certain and definite. As I look out on the snow covered fields (snow has just turned to rain & all will soon be slush) I think with joy of our getting out of the train into warm bright air, or almost bright & warm air, certainly into the encouraging presence of palm-trees . . . O my dear, you are good to come so far away to take care of me but I wish there were some warm bright place nearer home so that we might be enough togeather.[119]

On 5 January the Yeatses left for London, where George handed him over to Edith. On the 8th, the train slid out from Victoria, as he had decreed, carrying Edith and himself. For public purposes, he was going out 'with friends' or 'the Shackletons'; George was to follow in a month's time. 'The only trouble', Gogarty had written to James Healy when the American testimonial fund was at last collected, 'is that it will tempt the old man to travel beyond his strength.' Nonetheless, he enjoyed the piquant spectacle of seeing the Irish-American money used in this way. 'Yeats has gone on the strength of Dr McCartan's presentation collected for him in New York for being a credit to the N.Y. Irish – to Mentone! As a poet, yes; as a gigolo – too preoccupied!'[120]

Chapter 16 : Dying Like an Empire
1938–1939

> The knowledge of reality is always in some measure a secret
> knowledge. It is a kind of death.
>
> *Autobiographies*, p. 482

I

In late January 1938 wby's old occultist friend Frank Pearce Sturm wrote regretting that he could not visit him on the Riviera. 'I got such a belly-full of War 20 years ago that I am afraid of Europe, where Mars seems to be grumbling in his sleep.'[1] His instinct was not wrong, as Germany's expansionist ambitions towards Austria and Czechoslavakia threatened a confrontation with France and Britain. But the tremors only sounded distantly at the Hôtel Terminus at Monte Carlo, where wby and Edith Shackleton Heald took up residence on 11 January. They had travelled through a snowy France and arrived to find flowers in bloom above a blue Mediterranean. wby was firmly fixed in his intentions to spend the summer and autumn in Dublin, and then return to 'this bright dream', and the American money had apparently made it possible.[2] They stayed at Monte Carlo for about ten days, and then moved to the cheaper Carlton Hotel at Menton. His companion was central to the dream, but she was to leave in a few weeks (on 5 February), when George would arrive after visiting Anne, who was studying set-painting in Paris. There was a certain amount of discussion as to whether the two women's visits should overlap; in the end they met at the station. A deliberate veil of obscurity was drawn over wby's arrangements: his sisters were told he was with his friends 'Mr and Mrs Shackleton'. By the time George came, Edith may have been ready to hand over responsibility. wby had been plagued by a stomach upset at the beginning, and went around by wheelchair in Menton. 'I am an invalid now,' he told Sturm: and, while boasting about the number of people he had outlived, he was ruefully convinced that he would 'discrase my family by dying before I am eighty'. In fact, he had exactly a year of life left before him.[3]

But – as he had himself remarked – his imagination had never been more alive, and his publication schedule kept up with it. He was working on the proofs of *New Poems*, due for publication by Cuala in April: 'more emotional than anything I have written', he told Olivia, 'second childhood is lively, even startling'. A fortnight after arriving on the Riviera, *On the Boiler* was 'all but finished' – his subversive sermons to the young, named to commemorate the drunken ship's carpenter, M'Coy, who used to harangue passersby from his perch on the Sligo quays. 'It is so tory that there is not a tory in the world will agree with it,' he told Shakespear. 'It is violent, amusing & convincing & will be put down to the declining faculties of old age.' His excitement about political and social issues suggests that those faculties were far from declining. Moreover, the impetus to write about his personal life still drove him; he was searching for a picture of the bust of Maud Gonne in the Municipal Gallery, and George was instructed to bring out his letters to Gregory and other inspirational material. His surroundings, however, encouraged other kinds of speculation, which also affected his last work. It was from Monte Carlo, appropriately, that he wrote to the Eugenics Society, inquiring about the evidence for 'intelligence quotients among the leisured classes living on unearned incomes', a subject he doggedly returned to. How was intelligence defined? 'Is it power of attention & co-ordination? Or is it a sense of the significance & affinities of objects?'[4]

His determination to address awkward ideas, and his fascination with the subjects of breeding, violence, and sex, was not new, as he was reminded when the play he had written in Majorca, *The Herne's Egg*, was finally printed. It had remained unperformed. 'It disturbed the Abbey board until I withdrew it,' he told Mannin from Menton. 'An admiring member had decided that [the] seven ravishers of the heroine are the "seven sacraments".'[5] The allegorical meaning of the mythic farce, where a priestess in charge of a magical bird's shrine is raped by a group of knights on a quest, remains obscure. Though it echoes the world of Irish sagas (as mediated through Ferguson's *Congal*), it also reflects readings in Indian mysticism and Tantric wisdom, as well as WBY's eternal belief in the expression of oracular wisdom through unlikely mediums. The contrived grotesquerie, and the tonal shifts from tragedy to farce, recall *The Player Queen*, but the stagecraft is more problematic. WBY preferred to think that his colleagues' lack of enthusiasm was caused by the themes of bestiality and inhibited puritanism, through which he explored the conflict of self and soul. Incoherent as the play is, it is certainly, as he told Shakespear, 'typical of my old age, outrageous & violent'.[6] So were the savage harangues preserved in *On the Boiler* which, he told Edith, would 'cut me off from some of my best friends'.[7] The deliberately inflammatory tone was in part dictated by his wish to produce a controversial bestseller for the Cuala balance sheet; but, taken with his other productions in the last year of his life, the ruminations on democracy, authoritarianism, and degeneration are consistent enough. This does not make *On the Boiler* pro-Fascist. In fact, he presents a critique of both Fascist and Communist governments for inhibiting the development of an able, educated elite, by 'thinking the social problem economic and not eugenic and ethnic': or, as his notes put it, 'Communism, Fascism inadequate because society is the struggle of two forces not transparent to reason, the family & the individual'.[8] Balzac, rather than Marx or Sorel, was his master still.

In mid March, at the end of this miraculously productive winter, he was still – he told Edith – wrapped in 'a dream-like absorption in my work':[9] and he was staying up late at night writing poems. The latest accommodation helped. For reasons of independence as well as economy, WBY had wanted to leave hotel life and take a flat when George joined him; their costs were running at £11 a week, more than he had expected. She found instead the perfect *pension* on the Cap Martin promontory below the rocky outcrop of Roquebrune. The Hôtel Idéal Séjour was a modest, quiet villa, in a large garden set back from the sea, which could nonetheless be seen through the trees; there were also views across to the mountains, reminiscent of Rapallo a decade before. The owner was a gifted cook, and the Yeatses' living costs were reduced to £3. 10s. a week, including taxis and tips. There were large bedrooms, the use of a sitting room, and complete peace; WBY determined to return there the following winter, and he kept his promise. The sign by the gateway described it, appropriately, as a 'Maison de Repos'.

But spring had arrived and Mars was still grumbling. On 12 March Hitler annexed Austria. A week later George and WBY set off north, finding themselves 'in a great crowd of people rushing home in fear of war'. By 23 March they had reached the Grosvenor Hotel in London. George headed for Dublin, while her husband went to Dorothy Wellesley at Penns, where he read *On the Boiler* to his hostess, Hilda Matheson, and Walter Turner – who 'accepted it all & says it is coming out at the right moment'.[10] But his real destination was Steyning, and on 28 March he was reunited with Edith at Chantry House. 'I wonder if you know how much you have given me,' he had written to her from Cap Martin. 'I ask no more of life except to see more of you . . . My dear I want your arms to make me sleep.' He would remain in Sussex for the next five weeks. 'He needs so much intellectual stimulus that you & others can give,' George wrote resignedly to Edith from Dublin, checking up on her husband's medication regime. 'And nobody can feel more passionately than I feel for him that he has to return to this desolate place!'[11]

Settled in a sleepy English village as summer came in, he completed a poem started some months earlier and accurately described to George as 'a fine lyric'.[12]

That civilisation may not sink
Its great battle lost,
Quiet the dog, tether the pony
To a distant post.
Our master Caesar is in the tent
Where the maps are spread,
His eyes fixed upon nothing,
A hand under his head.

Like a long-legged fly upon the stream
His mind moves upon silence.

That the topless towers be burnt
And men recall that face,
Move most gently if move you must
In this lonely place.
She thinks, part woman, three parts a child,
That nobody looks; her feet
Practice a tinker shuffle
Picked up on the street.

Like a long-legged fly upon the stream
Her mind moves upon silence.

That girls at puberty may find
The first Adam in their thought,
Shut the door of the Pope's Chapel,
Keep those children out.
There on that scaffolding reclines
Michael Angelo.
With no more sound than the mice make
His hand moves to and fro.

Like a long-legged fly upon the stream
His mind moves upon silence.

The final version of 'Long-legged Fly' probably owes something to conversations with Turner at Penns about European history and art, but it also crystallizes the preoccupations about individual genius and historical archetype which had dominated WBY's speculative thought since *A Vision*; he began working on the poem shortly after the second version was published. Michelangelo, as Platonist master of Blake, and prophetic representative of the climax of the Renaissance, had come to stand for the supreme delineator of religious essence reflected in 'profane perfection' – poised just after Phase Fifteen, the highest phase of human achievement. 'The painter can paint what he desires in the flesh alone.'[13] In this poem he appears as the archetypal creator, providing images capable of awakening and focusing sexual desire (and therefore susceptible to censorship: WBY may have been remembering his abortive visit to the government minister Ruttledge, armed with reproductions of the Sistine Chapel ceiling, a few years before). The preceding stanzas survey the instinctual power of two other world-historical archetypes: Julius Caesar, the conqueror, and Helen of Troy. Her fatal (and perfect) beauty is conveyed by a lovely image, which suggests the sensual child-woman Iseult as much as the Vestal destroyer Maud. In each, Creative Mind is portrayed as meeting Body of Fate: at three historical moments, Unity of Culture and Unity of Being coincide. Edith Shackleton Heald described the genesis of the poem in a radio interview long afterwards. WBY had read her a first rough draft after they had spent an afternoon at Penns, observing the pond-life in the garden pool recently made by Wellesley, and he had asked her to place a tortoise in the water to see if it could swim. Its laborious motion was not quite right for the image he wanted ('it won't do'). But there was also, as so often with WBY, a literary echo – this time from Coleridge's image of a water-insect in *Biographia Literaria*, as an 'emblem of the mind's self-experience in the act of thinking . . . by alternate pulses of active and passive motion'.[14] Heald thought the poem was 'about the necessity of silence and peace to people of creative energy', and the idea of concentration is wonderfully evoked by the water-boatman tiptoeing across the surface. But it also reflects the mysterious connections between individuals and world history – in war, love, and art – which he continued to interrogate and which even the rewritten *A Vision* could never quite explain.

'Long-legged Fly' – much worked to produce the perfect internal off-rhyme of lines like 'move most gently if move you must' – was a dramatic enough achievement, but as he finished it WBY was working on an even more ambitious poem. It would bring together his interest in philosophy, the Platonic notions of Form and Beauty, his ancient preoccupation with class, race, and Irishness, and his more recent explorations in eugenics. This does not make for a comfortable combination. In its published version 'The Statues' is identified as 9 April 1938, but he was still rewriting it in June, and the final typescript is dated September.[15]

> Pythagoras planned it. Why did the people stare?
> His numbers, though they moved or seemed to move
> In marble or in bronze, lacked character.
> But boys and girls pale from the imagined love
> Of solitary beds, knew what they were,
> That passion could bring character enough,
> And pressed at midnight in some public place
> Live lips upon a plummet-measured face.

No! Greater than Pythagoras, for the men
That with a mallet or a chisel modelled these
Calculations that look but casual flesh, put down
All Asiatic vague immensities,
And not the banks of oars that swam upon
The many-headed foam at Salamis.
Europe put off that foam when Phidias
Gave women dreams and dreams their looking-glass.

One image crossed the many-headed, sat
Under the tropic shade, grew round and slow,
No Hamlet thin from eating flies, a fat
Dreamer of the Middle Ages. Empty eyeballs knew
That knowledge increases unreality, that
Mirror on mirror mirrored is all the show.
When gong and conch declare the hour to bless
Grimalkin crawls to Buddha's emptiness.

When Pearse summoned Cuchullain to his side,
What stalked through the Post Office? What intellect,
What calculation, number, measurement, replied?
We Irish, born into that ancient sect
But thrown upon this filthy modern tide
And by its formless, spawning, fury wrecked,
Climb to our proper dark, that we may trace
The lineaments of a plummet-measured face.

The poem expresses and develops a reflection in *On the Boiler*: that our ideas of beauty are predicated upon a Greek ideal based on Pythagorean mathematical calculations of proportion – which is, he implies, superior (in every sense) to the spawning formlessness of lesser (including 'Asiatic') types of beauty. The poem went through many drafts, usually starting with a question ('What were those images?'), before he hit on the drama of the first line, giving fair warning of what to expect. The sculptors who expressed this perfection, capable of liberating and focusing the masturbatory fantasies of lovesick adolescents, were even 'greater than Pythagoras', and should take the credit for the triumph of classical civilization over 'Asiatic vague immensities'. The third stanza credits the influence of Greek statuary brought by Alexander into India with shaping certain aspects of Buddhist aesthetics.[16] But degeneration is leaching in from the mounting tide of misshapen modernity. The last stanza, with a consummate swerve of direction, suggests that the Irish revolution was an attempt to invoke classical heroic ideals of beauty as well as of sacrifice – Cuchulain, in a prose draft, is a reincarnation of Apollo. Finally, the poem instructs the new Irish nation to turn its back on formless modernity and proclaim its superiority. Thus WBY places its citizens in the position of those adolescents who project their sexual desire on the pure forms of the statues, in an antithetical reconciliation.

The conclusion credits Irish artists (and writers) with preparing the revolutionaries for the national defining moment, just as the art of Phidias lay behind the victory of Salamis. However, they were now threatened once more. The 'tide' suggests the 'multiform, vague, expressive Asiatic sea' which WBY – following Pater – believed Greek art had overcome in the ancient world, but which was now encroaching again.[17] For such an admirer of Indian philosophy and Japanese art, the identification of 'Asia' as a threatening 'horde' is surprising, but he had long decided that modern India's soul was lost in democracy. The excessive compression and allusiveness of 'The Statues', and the underlying image of Alexander bringing Greek art to India, restricts the East to the role of reconquering barbarism. The result is a poem where not only eugenicism but xenophobia and antidemocratic contempt lurk only just below the surface of oracular Platonic injunctions – some of the original prose draft of the poem resurfaces in *On the Boiler*. The poem also echoes the unpublished 'General Introduction for my Work', which he had written for the Scribner edition in 1937. In the climax of that essay WBY had attacked the heterogeneous, degenerate nature of modern Dublin and concluded:

I am certain that wherever in Europe there are minds strong enough to lead others the same vague hatred rises. In four or five or less generations this hatred will have issued in violence and imposed some kind of rule of kindred. I cannot know the nature of that rule, for its opposite fills the light; all I can do to bring it nearer is to intensify my hatred.

A year later that hatred showed no sign of diminishing. Nor did his preoccupation with the decline of intelligence among the proletariat, and the need to discover a revitalized principle of aristocracy.[18]

The thought expressed poetically in 'The Statues' and polemically in *On the Boiler* found yet another outlet during these weeks at Steyning, and one that was dramatic in every sense. In mid March he had written to Edith from Cap Martin that his work had plunged him into an obsessive dream:

I have a one-act play in my head, a scene of tragic intensity, but I doubt if I will begin it until I get to Steyning, or perhaps not till I get to Ireland. I am so afraid of that dream. My recent work has greater strangeness and I think greater intensity than anything I have done. I never remember the dream so deep.[19]

By 6 April he was 'in the middle of it', and was already considering the play-in-progress as 'something for Anne to do a setting for' at the Abbey (he had been delighted to hear she was designing *On Baile's Strand*). But the inspiration behind *Purgatory* stretched back long before her birth. The idea that damned souls revisit the scenes of their life and commit their sins over and over again was a spiritualist commonplace; and WBY's disciple Evans Wentz had written decades before of the connections between the doctrine of purgatory and the Celtic idea of rebirth, as well as ancient Irish theories that sins could be expiated which had been committed in former lives.[20] WBY himself had used it in *The Dreaming of the Bones* twenty years before. But the theological implications of the purgatory doctrine (which, Dorothy Wellesley warned him, would 'hurry us back to the great arms of the Roman Catholic Church'[21]) are turned aside: it is not a stage on the journey to expiation and transcendence. In the play he wrote at high speed during the quiet mornings at Chantry House, WBY linked these themes with his old preoccupation of Ascendancy decline in Ireland and his new obsession with the coarsening of physical beauty and moral energy through miscegenation in an exhausted civilization. Over a decade before, he and Gregory had talked 'of madness, how it destroys a family, brings them down, as the Parnell family'. She had remarked that this 'shattering' could liberate something imaginative and courageous, and he had agreed. As he wrote *Purgatory*, Coole and its environs were in his mind: the park and its trees, with the owner returning to see the May blossom, are famously evoked.[22] But the core of the story comes from a neighbouring Galway estate, Tyrone House, on a lonely peninsula beyond Ardrahan, owned by the St George family. Violet Martin had visited it as a semi-ruin in 1912, 'a great square cut-stone house of three stories, with an area – perfectly empty – and such ceilings, architraves, teak doors and chimney-pieces as one sees in old houses in Dublin'. But the family, she noted with distaste, had 'rioted' there for several generations, 'living with country-women, occasionally marrying them, all illegitimate four times over . . . about 150 years ago a very grand Lady Harriet St Lawrence married a St George, and lived there, and was so corroded with pride that she would not allow her daughters to associate with the Galway people. She lived to see them marry two men in the yard.'[23] This house and its story, a short drive from Coole and Ballylee, was common gossip in local society: long before, WBY had called a character in *The Speckled Bird* 'Harriet St George'. The version he built into *Purgatory* is violent, economical, and haunting in every sense. The play opens with an old man and his son, travelling the roads, who come to a ruined house and a stark tree. These quintessential Yeatsian emblems represent the scene of the Old Man's own conception, when his Ascendancy mother took a 'man in the yard' for her husband. (In a first draft WBY specifically suggested that this paramour was a Catholic, highlighting the Ascendancy fear of decay through 'mixed marriage'). The result was the fall of an aristocratic civilization, expressed (and unconvincingly idealized) by the son of this degenerative union. While there has been some ingenious critical discussion about the extent to which the Old Man is an unreliable narrator, his evocation of Coole expresses the playwright's own emotions.

> Great people lived and died in this house;
> Magistrates, colonels, members of Parliament,
> Captains and governors, and long ago
> Men that had fought at Aughrim and the Boyne.
> Some that had gone on government work
> To London or to India came home to die,
> Or came from London every spring
> To look at the may-blossom in the park.
> They had loved the trees that he cut down
> To pay what he lost at cards
> Or spent on horses, drink and women;
> Had loved the house, had loved all
> The intricate passages of the house,
> But he killed the house; to kill a house
> Where great men grew up, married, died,
> I here declare a capital offence.[24]

This offence had been punished by execution. Tiresias-like, the Old Man tells the history of misalliance, decline, and eventually murder – events played out at an eerily lit window in the silhouetted ruin as he speaks. (This too was an image WBY had played with before, in a song from *The King of the Great Clock Tower* as well as in 'The Curse of Cromwell'.) As the crime is re-enacted, the Old Man tries at once to expiate it and stop the transmission of bad blood by sacrificing his son (a coarse-minded thief) 'on the same jack-knife' with which he killed his worthless father. By this act, he also hopes to elevate his mother's spirit 'into the light' from the endless repetition of her sin. But the final scene, with its terrifying hoof-beats, shows that these damned souls are bound to a circle of purgatorial re-enactment nonetheless.

Purgatory shares its force, economy, and stark dramatic effect with *The Words upon the Window Pane*, but it is bleaker, more profound, and infinitely more disturbing. The echoes it arouses resonate far further than fears of Ascendancy decline.[25] It is, on one level, WBY's own *Oedipus at Colonus*. If read as a theological treatise, or – more subtly – as a parable of the relation between the artistic imagination and reality, the play is not satisfying: it is the eugenic, historical, and social preoccupations which provide its motive power and dramatic resonance, however unpleasant their implications.

There is an added irony too: the arguments for a composite Irish inheritance, and the foundation of 'greatness' in violence which he had advanced in
'Meditations in Time of Civil War', had been replaced by the implication
that a marriage between the Ascendancy and a man of the people meant
degeneracy. The politics of 'kindred' outweighed those of pluralism, as
partly forecast in 'If I were Four-and-Twenty'. Unlike *The Herne's Egg*,
Purgatory would be produced at the Abbey later that year, providing WBY
with his last theatrical controversy. And the play's language – poetic but
dramatic – finally achieved the mysterious simplicity of his finest poems.
He had also, as in his most recent plays, abandoned blank-verse metre for
the 'strong driving force' of a tetrameter beat, with subtle variations. T. S.
Eliot, a hard judge, thought that WBY had at last 'solved his problem of
speech in verse, and laid all his successors under obligation to him'.[26] This
achievement took forty years' effort, and was partly inspired by the example,
a few years before, of Eliot himself.

For all WBY's invalid status, the writing of *Purgatory*, 'The Statues', and
'Long-legged Fly' did not inhibit his social life. Visitors came and went to
Steyning, local village society was observed, and trips made to London. In
mid April WBY met George Barnes at the BBC to discuss another broadcast, but when he listened to the recording of 'The Poet's Pub' he felt only
'amused disgust'; 'my broadcasting is finished', he wrote sadly to Barnes a
few weeks later.[27] He dined with Dulac and Helen Beauclerk to read them
his new poems, and lunched with Elizabeth Pelham and her sister Prudence
(a talented artist, who studied with Eric Gill). On 23 April Walter Turner
arrived to drive him back to Penns, where Wellesley was stricken by nervous
collapse. Indomitably, WBY still hoped that there might be a chance of
assembling a company reminiscent of Coole; he wrote to George that he
was gathering people together in a conspiracy against 'Modernity' in literature, and that 'the conversation has been better [than] on any previous occasion; there are the right guests & the house is becoming a centre of activity
at last . . . the centre of intellect I have longed for'.[28] But Penns would never
be Coole, and Wellesley was a broken reed. He returned to Steyning in early
May, knowing he must go back to Dublin before long but determined to fulfil some final obligations. One was to meet Arnold Toynbee, whose *Study of
History* had excited him, with its neo-Spenglerian patterns of development
and decline. Another was his final visit to Oxford.

He was still conscience-stricken at misinterpreting a luncheon invitation
from Maurice Bowra some time before, which he had curtly refused under
the impression it came from another, unwelcome quarter, and determined
to make amends. 'I am laying a ghost, & this requires an exact ritual.'[29] The
date of 7 May was fixed for the ceremony; Edith drove him to Oxford and

they stayed at the Mitre Hotel on the High Street. WBY gave a lunch party for Bowra at Wadham, 'candidly pleased it cost so little'. His guest found him much aged, but 'as eloquent and as courteous as ever. He talked about the diatribes which he was writing in *On the Boiler*, deplored with irony his ignorance of Erse, explained how he wished to write poems which would catch the spontaneity of traditional ballads, and claimed that he could read nothing but boys' books about the Wild West.' But his mood was not entirely frivolous. That evening WBY and Edith dined at All Souls with John Sparrow, who had also invited the young philosopher Stuart Hampshire and the economist Roy Harrod. Hampshire had long admired him from afar; Harrod was invited, improbably, because WBY had told Sparrow he wanted to meet an expert on eugenics. In fact, the distinguished economist's only qualification in the field was his membership of a commission on population, and his views did not favour eugenic planning: Harrod kept presenting reassuring facts and statistics about population growth to WBY, who swept them impatiently aside, in a flood of assertions about the excessive fertility of the proletariat.[30] Hampshire, a left-winger in his early twenties, was shocked by WBY's reactionary opinions about the working class swamping the population and bringing down the general level of intelligence. He was also bewildered by the Irish poet's snobbish assertions about the long-distant middle-class origins of Bertrand Russell's family explaining the philosopher's 'vulgarity'. (Russell's affair with Ethel Mannin may still have rankled.) He escorted WBY back down the High to the Mitre, along with Edith, who had remained reticent throughout, 'rather like a lady's companion'. He never felt the same about WBY or his poetry again. As for WBY, he felt he was returning to Ireland 'well in body and in mind'. 'It is a curious [thing],' he told Wellesley the day before that All Souls dinner. 'In the last fortnight I have come to understand why people think certain things, with the result that I have new poems that I long to write. I have grown abundant and determined in my old [age] as I never was in my youth.' Yet there were moments of doubt. At Oxford, before they left the next day, he dictated a quatrain to Edith, which remained unpublished: it suggests a very different philosophic world-view from that of the pattern-maker of *A Vision*.

> What is the explanation of it all?
> What does it look like to a learned man?
> Nothings in nothings whirled, or when he will.
> From nowhere into nowhere nothing's run.[31]

II

Dublin during the summer of 1938 was as preoccupied as everywhere else by the possibility of war. From late May, German troop movements against Czechoslovakia sparked an international panic, and it seemed yet again inevitable that Britain and France should come to the Czechs' defence. WBY's own opinions were apparently detached, and a certain ambiguity comes through his report of a conversation with one of Gregory's nephews serving in the British Navy.

He had spent six months in Germany lately. He gave me a most convincing account of the state of things in Germany. I said how unbiased you are? [*sic*] He said 'Some of us have no nation now.' I said 'Remember that our class in Ireland has always chosen its nation.'[32]

The implication is that he was chiding his interlocutor for pro-British attitudes. This does not mean that WBY was pro-German: nor that he was ready to involve himself in current controversies such as the reception of Jewish refugees into Ireland, violently opposed by, for instance, Francis and Iseult Stuart.[33] Nothing in WBY's correspondence suggests any preoccupation with Hitler, and his real feelings were probably preserved in a poem he wrote shortly after returning to Dublin that May. He sent a first version to Wellesley at once.

Politics

'In our time the destiny of man presents its meaning in political terms.'

Thomas Mann

> Beside that window stands a girl;
> I cannot fix my mind
> On their analysis of things
> That benumb mankind.
> Yet one has travelled and may know
> What he talks about;
> And one's a politician
> That has read and thought.
> Maybe what they say is true
> Of war and war's alarms;
> But O that I were young again
> And held her in my arms.

By the epigraph placed at the top of the poem WBY clearly intended an ironic subversion.[34] He had in fact found the quotation in an essay by Archibald

MacLeish praising the 'public' language of his own poetry, and pointing out that 'owing to my age and my relation to Ireland, I was unable to use this "public" language on what is evidently considered the right public material, politics'.[35] The poem was, he said, his reply. The politics later itemized are those of the mid thirties, not 1938: Germany does not impinge. Nor does Ireland, even though the poem allegedly referred to a beautiful red-headed republican who used to sell newspapers at Republican Congress meetings on O'Connell Street, regularly noted by WBY as he left the Gresham Hotel.[36] But WBY could never lose his interest in current international affairs, and much in Europe's approaching *Götterdämmerung* struck resonant echoes with the apocalyptic poetry he had written since the end of the last war. His son, Michael, now nearly seventeen and fascinated by politics, found that at last they had a topic of mutual interest; in the last year of his father's life they discussed the international situation intensively.[37] But the air of detachment immortalized in 'Politics' and expressed in his letters to Ethel Mannin remained dominant. Where he did decide to air political views was in *On the Boiler*: and this, as he had told Mannin, was galvanized by the need to increase Cuala's income by a controversial publication.[38]

Money was much in his mind that summer. The receipts from Macmillan were down, and he worried that Lolly was printing too many copies of *New Poems* and that it would lose its value to collectors (George firmly disagreed). With this and *The Herne's Egg* his only new publications, much rested on his forthcoming call to arms: 'All my immediate plans for Cuala depend upon "On the Boiler".'[39] Mr Scroope from the National Bank was once more harrying Lolly, and WBY summoned her to a meeting at the Shelbourne Hotel (the one place where she could not shout at him) on 1 June. He was now embarked on a plan to convert the Press into a limited company and to reconstitute the Cuala Board to include George, himself, Lolly, and F. R. Higgins. For many years Lolly had felt the co-operative status AE had 'rushed them into' was no longer relevant, but WBY wanted a more sweeping reconstruction still.[40] His clear intention was to leave the succession tied up, hoping that Higgins would inherit his own function, there as at the Abbey. In this, as in several other ways, his estimate of his friend was ludicrously wide of the mark. 'He has joy & a man without joy cannot control our [theatre] people as they are today.'[41] Higgins's real idea of joy came in bottled form, and he was neurotically inefficient, incapable of answering letters or signing cheques. In Lolly's eyes he had no redeeming features whatsoever, and she could not bring herself to talk to him. As for Lolly, Lily tartly remarked, 'an angel from heaven' could not work with her, 'perhaps a very strong person from the other place might do it & live'.[42] The problem would fester on after his death. But by October 1938 Cuala was registered as a limited company and it would – as he wished – continue as such after his death, until dissolution in 1955.[43]

Without the income from the American testimonial, WBY's circumstances would have been very straitened indeed. In June a second instalment of £400 arrived, with a letter promising that a 'minimum of Five Hundred Pounds annually' could be expected, despite the 'total collapse of our government's political economy better known as the "New Deal"'. This was not the only reason: a disgruntled Dudley Digges wrote to Healy at the same time about Irish-American film stars' meagre response to his 'going around with the hat in Hollywood for William Butler Yeats'.[44]

WBY wrote gratefully to Eugene Kinkead, the treasurer of the testimonial committee, that he was reserving this stipend for another winter in the South of France – where he had written 'a great deal of poetry & prose which my friends tell me is at the level of my best work'.[45] Confined to Riversdale in a damp, dark Irish summer, he promptly started planning his return with Edith to the Land of Youth. Lily, visiting Riversdale in early June, found him frail but determined as ever upon dramatic self-presentation.

Willy [is] mentally very vigorous, but I feel his health is precarious, heart probably. He doesn't look ill or feeble, but is very easily tired. He was in good spirits and had got some blue pomade for his hair & got George to rub some in. He said he wanted his hair to be as blue as his shoes, which are a good deep blue. George says it is only oil & makes no difference except to give a gloss to his hair. They were very amusing over it.

I feel rather depressed about his health, but I must remember we are now old people. I don't think we feel we are. He doesn't look his age, & is handsome & distinguished & keen. Well, he is a famous man, & has known success and been honoured, & his children have been very satisfactory so far, & not likely I think to go off the rails.[46]

Another snapshot of WBY at Riversdale that summer was preserved by one of Michael's teachers, the ironic and perceptive George White. In July 1938 he was summoned to decide Michael's curriculum: WBY, according to George, was unwilling to go to St Columba's to discuss the matter 'because Willie doesn't like the Warden'. White duly turned up on a Saturday afternoon at Riversdale.

I was nervous, being filled with awe at the prospect of meeting face to face a man whom I revered, also alarmed by accounts which I had heard of the great man's capacity for rudeness: I was only thirty years old and relatively modest. My hope was that in our interview I would be protected by Mrs Yeats. My heart sank and beat furiously when I found myself ushered by a maid into a room that contained nobody but Yeats himself, seated in a low armchair. To my immense relief he was immediately friendly and polite, apologising for not getting up because 'I am supposed to have a bad heart.' He listened to what I had to tell him about his son and talked a little about the question at issue – the choice between History and Mathematics. Out of our conversation I can now remember nothing except the following exchange:

Yeats.   It seems to me a terrible thing that the boy should have to make up his mind so young which way he is going to go. I didn't know which way I was going to go till I was seventeen.

White.   Well, Michael will be seventeen next month.

Yeats.   Oh, will he?

It must have been soon after that utterance that Mrs Yeats joined us and we had tea. There was a little more discussion of the subject to which my visit was supposed to be devoted, but almost immediately we were joined by a visitor, who I am pretty sure was Mrs [Josephine] MacNeill, whose husband [James] had been Governor General of the Free State. The advent of her receptive ear stimulated Yeats to discourse at large on education: – 'If I had my way boys in Ireland would learn nothing except Mathematics, Greek and Gaelic: and they would learn the Greek and the Gaelic by translating Greek into Gaelic and Gaelic into Greek.' Naturally I did not argue this point but looked respectful, though inwardly amused by the reflection that he knew nothing of either language. Mrs MacNeill, however, with the flattering air of one privileged to hear an oracle, said 'How very interesting, Dr Yeats!' I do not know what she thought when he replied, 'Of course I'm not entirely serious.'[47]

White felt that wby, even at his most pontifical, was inwardly laughing at his hearers, and possibly at himself, but also that he would not like to be the object of the laughter of others. He also guessed that George, 'while she would never deflate him before strangers, while indeed she admired and loved him', took his theorizing even less seriously and 'only half listened to the familiar sound of his prophesying'. What lies behind the account is also the distance between father and son.

wby was assured of a more receptive ear at Steyning, and in late June he sent importunate letters to Edith Shackleton Heald. 'I do not want henceforth to be away from you for any great length of time – I am always afraid you will forget me.'[48] On 8 July George escorted him as far as Liverpool; by 12 July he was at Chantry House (where he heard of Ottoline Morrell's death, unreconciled to the end). After a week he proceeded to Penns. Wellesley had recovered from her latest breakdown, and was building a folly to commemorate the poets who visited Penns: at once a more grandiose and less impressive riposte to the tree carved with signatures at Coole.[49] wby read the new Agatha Christie, visited Elizabeth Pelham at Stanmer Park, and – with Edith – made an expedition to Shelley's house, Field Place. But, principally, he rested and wrote poetry. On this visit Hilda Matheson copied out the first version of a poem which, as much as any during this last *annus mirabilis*, summed up his questioning state of mind, and his urge to revisit the questions that had haunted him from his youth. Thus the opening query to an oracle is placed in the landscape of childhood: a mountain fissure on Knocknarea, near Sligo town. But his more recent passages with Gonne, the sad history of Margot Ruddock, and the abandonment and loss of Coole are at the front of his mind.

MAN

In a cleft that's christened Alt
Under broken stone I halt
At the bottom of a pit
That broad noon has never lit,
And shout a secret to the stone.
All that I have said and done,
Now that I am old and ill,
Turns into a question till
I lie awake night after night
And never get the answers right.
Did that play of mine send out
Certain men the English shot?
Did words of mine put too great strain
On that woman's reeling brain?
Could my spoken words have checked
That whereby a house was wrecked?
And all seems evil until I
Sleepless would lie down and die.

ECHO

Lie down and die.

'Man' forcefully rallies, calling courage into himself by remembering 'the spiritual intellect's great work': the discovery of wisdom and the journey of the soul, freed of bodily distractions and 'stupidity'. At the end of the poem, nonetheless, the philosophical invocation 'in that great night rejoice' is subverted by the distraction – yet again – of the real world, where 'some hawk or owl' has struck and killed a screaming rabbit: a jarring closure beautifully counterpointed by the use of sharp consonants and off-rhymes. The bleakness of the conclusion is arresting; WBY continued to work on the poem through August, and his changes made it no more reassuring. If, as Jon Stallworthy suggests, he intended it to be published in a sequence which continued with 'The Circus Animals' Desertion' and ended with 'Politics',[50] the personal message is poignant, resigned, and regretful. And the title of the Agatha Christie murder mystery which he read that summer oddly chimed with his own mood: it was *Appointment with Death*.

By the beginning of August he was back at Steyning. 'This village takes me very seriously,' he wrote contentedly to George. 'The woman opposite told her next door neighbour that she could not understand why a man of my importance visited at so small a house & the Head Master of the Grammar School (a Tudor building a hundred yards up the street) asked the English Master if "Mr Yeats has a police-guard" as he had "noticed some unusual movements among the police" & the English Master came over to enquire.' Any 'unusual movements' may have been to do with national security: the threat of war mounted over the summer and autumn, until Chamberlain flew to Munich at the end of September. But WBY's energies remained concentrated upon work. On 8 August George met him at Chester to convey him back to Dublin, with – he told Higgins – 'a lot of new poems'.[51] Over the next two months he sent at least fifteen poems for possible publication to Heald's friend Scott-James at the *Mercury*, and began to draft potential contents pages for a new book. He would still be planning it on his deathbed.

III

He had been drawn back by the prospect of his last great scene at the Abbey. Throughout the summer a double bill of *On Baile's Strand* and *Purgatory* had been planned, with sets by Anne. Her father was as fiercely interventionist as ever, fighting the director Hugh Hunt's desire for a moon on the backdrop, and accompanying music. WBY was determined that the play should rely on skilful lighting-effects, monochrome colouring, and a silver tree: in George's words, 'a bald production, no noise off, the whole to be concentrated on the two characters OLD MAN and BOY, and the appearance of the woman at the lit window of the burnt out house'.[52] The play's stark message was to be driven home by the production – which was to follow the theories developed by WBY forty years before.

When it opened on 9 August, the effect was all he could have wished. The acting was widely acclaimed, particularly the young Liam Redmond, and the design eerily effective. For Lily, there was an additional *frisson*, from a tragic memory of their youth at Merville. As she heard the storm of hoof-beats which announced the arrival of the ghostly bridegroom, 'all round me melted away & I felt myself back nearly seventy years in my cot on that March morning hearing the galloping of the horse flying too late for the doctor for my baby brother'.[53] The capacity audience was captivated: WBY appeared on stage at the end amid 'storms of applause' and an atmosphere of 'tense excitement'. Facing the Abbey audience for the last time, after a success nearly as controversial as Synge's or O'Casey's, he made the most of it. 'I wish to say that I have put into this play not many thoughts that are picturesque,' he told them, 'but my own beliefs about this world and the next.' Robinson had warned Blythe that the play was 'powerful', but would 'shock', and he was right.[54] WBY's theology was rapidly criticized by a Boston College Jesuit, Father Terence Connolly, who intervened at a lecture on WBY given by Higgins the next day as part of the Theatre Festival; a public discussion followed. On 13 August the *Irish Times* carried an interview with WBY, in which he chose to ignore the theological aspects of the play altogether. 'There is no allegory in "Purgatory", nor, so far as I can remember, in anything I have written,' he claimed. 'My plot is my meaning.' (He told Edith Shackleton Heald that 'the tribal dance & the drums' were arrayed against him, but he would not engage with them: 'as always I have to remain silent & see my work travestied because I will not use up my frugal energies on impermanent writing'.[55]) What followed strikes an ominous note in retrospect. WBY complained that the destruction of 'honoured houses' was taking place all over Ireland, because 'a new individualistic generation has lost interest in sanctities'.

In some few cases a house has been destroyed by a mésalliance. I have founded my play on that exceptional cause, partly because of my interest in certain problems of eugenics, partly because it enables me to depict more vividly than would otherwise be possible the tragedy of the house.

In Germany there is special legislation to enable old families to go on living where their fathers lived. The problem is not Irish but European, though it is perhaps more acute here than elsewhere.[56]

That 'special legislation' in Germany was the Hereditary Farm Law (September 1933), reaffirming primogeniture in order to keep rural Aryan families on the land. By 1938 it had been joined by a series of infamous measures, involving the expropriation and persecution of Jews and others. In this context, the statement seems – at best – unforgivably myopic. Ethel Mannin, for one, could have put him right about the motivation behind Nazi legislation. He told her more than once that he was determined to turn a blind eye to international politics, but he kept abreast of what – selectively – interested him.

It is worth remembering that Coole haunts the play, as it did WBY. When he told the *Irish Times* reporter 'I know of old houses, old pictures, old furniture that have been sold without apparent regret', Margaret's auction six years before must still have been in his mind. Earlier that summer, just at the time when he used to set off to the west for a season of writing, he had written to Edith about finding someone who might adapt his pastel of Coole, painted over forty years before, into a design for needle-point. 'I want a design for my sister to work & also for American travellers who want a memento of an Irish sacred place.'[57] That sacred place, and its desecration, stayed woven through his imagination and his regrets ('Could my spoken words have checked/That whereby a house was wrecked?'). So did his belief that the Anglo-Irish were – as AE had said to him not long before his death – 'the best Irish'; yet they had opted for decline instead of responsibility by not 'choosing their nation' aright. These Irish obsessions drive *Purgatory*, rather than any ill-digested notions about Nazi legislation.

Nonetheless, his interest in eugenics is also an undeniably powerful influence. He was not alone in this preoccupation during the late 1930s, nor was it a preserve of right-wing fanatics. The Eugenics Society, which WBY had joined in 1937, contained many representatives of the left, especially drawn by issues of 'public health'.[58] Ethel Mannin herself had just complet-ed a non-fiction book, *Women and the Revolution*, which advocated, among much else, 'legalisation of abortion, compulsory sterilisation of the unfit [including those subject to epilepsy, insanity and hereditary disease], and the destruction at birth of defective babies'.[59] Naomi Mitchison also proceeded from the League for Sexual Reform to the Eugenics Society (though Haire himself resigned from it after a disagreement). WBY's old acquaintance (and one-time landlord), the sexologist Havelock Ellis, was equally committed to the extirpation of 'the feeble-minded classes' and infanticide where 'necessary'.[60] When WBY, sending Mannin extracts from *On the Boiler*, assured her that their political ideas were converging, he may have meant eugenic matters. The interest awoken by Raymond Cattell's article on national intelligence in 1936 was not a temporary craze. Cattell's speculative interest had been aroused by the idea that 'the income-tax paying section of the community' had greater intelligence than the rest, and C. P. Blacker had added thoughts on 'The Future of Our Population'.[61] Blacker, while believing in pre-natal selection, had denounced Nazi steril-ization programmes since 1933, and his responses to WBY's barrage of ques-tions on the subject of breeding and intelligence were extremely cautious. Nor was WBY himself particularly gullible about the efficacy of tests for 'intelligence'. Though the comforting notion that eugenicists in pre-war Britain were preoccupied by issues of class rather than race has been vigorously questioned, the eugenicist beliefs of WBY's old age were driven by fears about educational and cultural decline rather than by racial prejudice.

Certainly his interest, as with so many eugenicists, derived from a passion for Nietzsche. Unlike several 1930s eugenicists, however, he never related his ideas about degeneration and racial stock to the international presence of Jews. So far as the politics of the day were concerned, WBY's views were closer to those of the (Jewish) eugenicist and Nietzschean, Oscar Levy, who saw Nazism as a symptom of the decline of the West rather than as a potential saviour. WBY would also have approved of George Adath, writing in the *Eugenics Review* in 1922, who related eugenicism to a belief in the principle of aristocracy.[62] Adath's belief that 'the social conditions of the present day are such as to favour the preponderance of what are from every point of view the lower classes, the survival of the unfit and the inevitable deterioration of the race' was repeated by WBY in *On the Boiler*. Citing Robert Burton's arguments for selective breeding and infanticide in *The Anatomy of Melancholy* and flourishing the intelligence-testing data of L. M. Terman and Cattell, WBY argued for limitation of family size among the poor, 'the stupider and less healthy'. The educated classes, he suggested, might have to wage war upon the 'uneducatable masses' in order to withhold from them the undeserved affluence which would enable them to breed uncontrollably.

The danger is that there will be no war, that the skilled will attempt nothing, that the European civilisation, like those older civilisations that saw the triumph of their gangrel stocks, will accept decay. When I was writing *A Vision* I had constantly the word 'terror' impressed upon me, and once the old stoic prophecy of earthquake, fire and flood, but this I did not take literally. It was because of that indefinable impression that I made Michael Robartes say in *A Vision*: 'Dear predatory birds, prepare for war, prepare your children and all that you can reach ... Test art, morality, custom, thought by Thermopylae, make rich and poor act so to one another that they can stand together there. Love war because of its horror, that belief may be changed, civilisation renewed. We desire belief and lack it. Belief comes from shock and is not desired.'[63]

Later he added: 'Eugenical and psychical research are the revolutionary movements with that element of novelty and sensation which sooner or later stir men to action. It may be, or it must be, that the best bred from the best shall claim again their ancient omens.' This was the kind of opinion that had shocked Stuart Hampshire – and that, as WBY himself pointed out, provided some areas of 'convergence' with Ethel Mannin's ideas about eugenics as an instrument of liberation. But they echo (even in the phrase 'the best bred of the best') work as far back as 'Upon a House Shaken by the Land Agitation' and 'To a Wealthy Man'. The 'war' he anticipated was not the war being prepared by Hitler, and the degeneration he denounced in *On the Boiler* was – as for so long – the coarsening and decadence of Irish culture through the infection of English materialism and the philistinism of a native *petit bourgeoisie*. Nietzschean 'transvaluation', anti-democratic rage, uncompromising eugenicism, and a kind of frantic class feeling are all there; anti-Semitism and pro-Nazism (even pro-Fascism) are not. He specifically denounced German and Italian policies of rewarding fecundity as 'accelerating degeneration' and deleted specific (and rather ambiguous) references to Fascism from his first draft. But his views are still stridently reactionary, and he is unashamedly prepared to forecast conflict between the many and the few. In a deleted passage he wrote 'centuries of bloodshed may ⟨follow⟩ [be] the only means of ⟨setting in all places⟩ setting in all places of authority of *power* "the best born of the best." '[64]

Eugenicist preoccupations continued to penetrate every aspect of his thought and activity – including the Abbey. 'By a curious coincidence,' he told Edith on 4 September,

a crisis germain to my thought is forming. The new players, who join us through our school, have such misshapen bodies that one of the old players, a man who incarnates our traditions, threatens to go to America because he cant stand rehersing them. Ireland is getting a prolotariot which in Dublin is pushing aside the old peasant basis of the nation. We talk of getting players from the country but dont know how to do it.[65]

In the same letter he told her he had written 'a long poem'. This was 'Under Ben Bulben', designed partly to express his views on degeneration and partly as his own epitaph. Its first draft was headed 'Creed', and began with the words '*I believe*'.

On 22 August he had written to Mannin about his wish to be buried in Sligo, at Drumcliff: 'Just my name & dates & these lines

> Cast a cold eye
> On life, on death:
> ⟨Huntsman⟩ Horseman pass by.'

George confirmed that he hit upon this legend in early August, with prose drafts of the poem following 'a week or two later'; contradicting (no doubt with some satisfaction) Dorothy Wellesley's claim that WBY had first written the lines in the margin of a book containing William Rose's essay on Rilke and death. However, Rilke's views on death are integral to the full poem – at least as WBY interpreted these to Ethel Mannin.

According to Rilke a man's death is born with him & if his life is successful & he escapes mere "mass death" his nature is completed by his final union with it . . . In my own philosophy the sensuous image is changed from time to time at predestined moments called *Initiationary Moments* . . . At *The Critical Moment* they are

631

dissolved by analysis & we enter by free will pure unified experience. When all the sensuous images are dissolved we meet true death . . . This idea of death suggests to me Blakes design (among those he did for Blairs grave I think) of the soul & body embracing. All men with subjective natures move towards a possible ecstasy all with objective natures towards a possible wisdom.[66]

The opening lines of the poem, while casting back to the ancient mysteries central to his occult thought, set a Rilkean idea of death firmly in the land-scape of Irish history. (In an early draft, Cuchulain is invoked as well for good measure.)

I

Swear by what the sages spoke
Round the Maroetic lake
That the witch of atlas knew,
Spoke and set the cocks a-crow.

Swear by those horsemen, by those women,
Complexion and form prove superhuman,
That pale, long visaged company
That airs in immortality
Completeness of their passions won;
Now they ride the wintry dawn
Where Ben Bulben sets the scene.

Here's the gist of what they mean.

II

Many times man lives and dies
Between his two eternities,
That of race and that of soul,
And ancient Ireland knew it all.
Whether man die in his bed
Or the rifle knocks him dead,
A brief parting from those dear
Is the worst man has to fear.
Though grave-diggers' toil is long,
Sharp their spades, their muscle strong,
They but thrust their buried men
Back in the human mind again.

III

You that Mitchel's prayer have heard
'Send war in our time, O Lord!'
Know that when all words are said
And a man is fighting mad,

Something drops from eyes long blind
He completes his partial mind,
For an instant stands at ease,
Laughs aloud, his heart at peace,
Even the wisest man grows tense
With some sort of violence.
Before he can accomplish fate,
Know his work or choose his mate.

IV

Poet and sculptor do the work
Nor let the modish painter shirk
What his great forefathers did,
Bring the soul of man to God,
Make him fill the cradles right.

Measurement began our might:
Forms a stark Egyptian thought,
Forms that gentler Phidias wrought.

Michaelangelo left a proof
On the Sistine Chapel roof,
Where but half-awakened Adam
Can disturb globe-trotting Madam
Till her bowels are in heat,
Proof that there's a purpose set
Before the secret working mind:
Profane perfection of mankind.

Quattrocento put in paint
On backgrounds for a God or Saint,
Gardens where a soul's at ease;[67]
Where everything that meets the eye,
Flowers and grass and cloudless sky

Resemble forms that are, or seem
When sleepers wake and yet still dream,
And when it's vanished still declare,
With only bed and bedstead there,
That heavens had opened.
                                    Gyres run on;

When that greater dream had gone
And Wilson, Blake and Calvert, Claude,
Prepared a rest for the people of God,
Palmer's phrase, but after that
Confusion fell upon our thought.

V

Irish poets, learn your trade,
Sing whatever is well made,
Scorn the sort now growing up
All out of shape from toe to top,
Their unremembering hearts and heads
Base-born products of base beds.
Sing the peasantry, and then
Hard-riding country gentlemen,
The holiness of monks, and after
Porter-drinkers' randy laughter;
Sing the lords and ladies gay
That were beaten into the clay
Through seven heroic centuries;
Cast your mind on other days
That we in coming days may be
Still the indomitable Irishry.

VI

Under bare Ben Bulben's head
In Drumcliffe churchyard Yeats is laid.
An ancestor was rector there
Long years ago, a church stands near,
By the road an ancient cross.
No marble, no conventional phrase.
On limestone quarried near the spot
By his command these words are cut:

> *Cast a cold eye*
> *On life, on death.*
> *Horseman, pass by!*

Rilke's idea of completion in death is married here to WBY's old preoccupation with the power of hatred in Ireland and the idea of going gaily to the grave – all in a driving, staccato rhythm which recalls, appositely, that early invocation of patriotism and occultism, 'To Ireland in the Coming Times'. The succeeding stanzas, however, constitute an exhortation to artists rather than to revolutionaries, defining archetypes of beauty, much as in 'The Statues', and 'Long-legged Fly', and the development of images through pictorial representation. 'It gets into narrow space what I think about the break between ancient and modern art,' WBY told Wellesley with satisfaction.[68] The penultimate stanza raises a different kind of confusion, ominously hinted at in the earlier injunction to 'fill the cradles right': the eugenic obsession again. In the same letter to Wellesley, WBY recurred to 'the misshapen lot – "earwigs" – who are growing up now', as reflected in the younger Abbey players. 'This is the origin of a passage in poem.'[69]

In the fifth section, the echo of the original title of 'To Ireland in the Coming Times' is surely intentional; so are the assonances with Frank O'Connor's translations from the Gaelic published by Cuala. The poem concluded with the epitaph he had quoted to Mannin, introduced – he told Wellesley – by 'a description of my own grave & monument in a remote Irish village. It will bind my heirs thank God. I write my poems for the Irish people but I am damned if I will have them at my funeral. A Dublin funeral is something between a public demonstration & a private picnic.'[70]

He had tried opening the epitaph 'Draw rein, draw breath', but this was dropped, deliberately arresting the rhythm, enforcing a pause, and seizing the reader's attention.[71] 'Under Ben Bulben', in all its hectoring didacticism, was planned by WBY to open his next volume of poems: all that followed would, therefore, be spoken from the grave. 'Politics' was to close it. And, like that short poem, the idea of impending war hangs behind it. Early drafts included references to bombs falling upon 'hateful cities', and to apocalyptic visions of horsemen riding out of mountainsides – along with the idea that an eternal moment of peace was contained at the heart of conflict, and as of sexual love.

He was obviously pleased with the poem and the instructions it contained, though Lily warned him the Yeatses had eschewed tombstones since the eighteenth century, since 'it had always been a gay family'.[72] Visiting her brother on 20 September, she found him 'in high spirits . . . very brown, firm, slimmer & wearing a royal blue shirt', for which he had bought a 'bog-coloured' new suit. 'I always come away from Willy feeling as if I had drunk a glass of very good wine. He is so exhilarating.'[73] Gogarty called the next day, and described the scene to Reynolds.

[I found] him sitting in his curricle chair with his silver locks blue-washed like Carmel Snow's of Harper's Bazaar! 'Yeats, you have put blue-wash in your hair!' He nodded assent as if it were an act of God or of Apollo himself at the request of all the Muses. But the allure of more mundane ladies may have accounted for it, because he changed the subject but not as much as he thought he was changing it. 'Gogarty, I have come to the conclusion that the best life consists of six weeks in England and six weeks in Ireland alternately. The best conversation is to be found in English country houses.' This is true but Yeats has first to be there to make it. He recited his epitaph which I could not memorise because it was rather inept. It addressed no[t] the passer by as antique epitaphs usually do but the 'horsemen'[sic]. And you know that the one thing I could not get him to mount was a horse![74]

But his cheerful mood, and his anticipation of escaping to country-house life in England with Heald and Wellesley, was shadowed by renewed rumours of war. Though it was now apparent in diplomatic circles that Britain and France would not, in the event, fight Germany over Czechoslavakia, Hitler kept inflating his demands, and public brinkmanship continued. On 26 September the Führer announced his decision to occupy Sudeten German territory by 1 October; France and Britain had already partially mobilized and formally threatened war if Czechoslovakia were attacked. That day WBY wrote to Wellesley:

To days news seems to make war certain. I am in complete agreement with what De Valera said at Geneva yesterday [supporting appeasement of Germany] except that I can see no hope in his remedy. The armed mobs of Europe will now tare each other into peices & the innocent will perish in the scuffle. I do not know whether I can work for I am exausted with bitterness.[75]

Nonetheless, his elegiac inspiration continued. That same month he returned to a poem about his life and the sources of his poetic inspiration that is far less strident, more poignant, and more convincing than 'Under Ben Bulben'. Gogarty would later note, astutely, how 'the symbols of the circus properties which Yeats employed in his old age [were] a revelation of his sadness and disillusionment',[76] and in 'The Circus Animals' Desertion' these images set in motion a kaleidoscope of images from *The Wanderings of Oisin* to the irresolute, retrospective present. In the back of his mind was his deliberate descent to the lowest rung of the Platonic ladder, as life ran out. In November 1937 he had completed the first version of the poem, originally called 'Despair' or 'On the Lack of Theme', reflecting his current preoccupation with the effort to find inspiration by an act of will. Paradoxically, the poem as it evolved began to turn on the record of his own achievement.[77] He had been dissatisfied by the final section, and left the ending unresolved; now, in mid-September 1938, he returned to it, jettisoned the unsatisfactory last stanza, and replaced it with one of his starkest and most memorable poetic signatures, rejecting high-flown imaginative contrivance for the 'fury and mire' of human experience.

I

I sought a theme and sought for it in vain,
I sought it daily for six weeks or so.
Maybe at last being but a broken man
I must be satisfied with my heart, although
Winter and summer till old age began
My circus animals were all on show,
Those stilted boys, that burnished chariot,
Lion and woman and the Lord knows what.

II

What can I but enumerate old themes,
First that sea-rider Usheen led by the nose
Through three enchanted islands, allegorical dreams,
Vain gaiety, vain battle, vain repose,
Themes of the embittered heart, or so it seems,
That might adorn old songs or courtly shows;
But what cared I that set him on to ride,
I, starved for the bosom of his faery bride.

And then a counter-truth filled out its play,
'The Countess Cathleen' was the name I gave it;
She, pity-crazed, had given her soul away
But masterful Heaven had intervened to save it.
I thought my dear must her own soul destroy,
So did fanaticism and hate enslave it,
And this brought forth a dream and soon enough
This dream itself had all my thought and love.

And when the Fool and Blind Man stole the bread
Cuchullain fought the ungovernable sea;
Heart mysteries there, and yet when all is said
It was the dream itself enchanted me:
Character isolated by a deed
To engross the present and dominate memory.
Players and painted stage took all my love
And not those things that they were emblems of.

III

Those masterful images because complete
Grew in pure mind but out of what began?
A mound of refuse or the sweepings of a street,
Old kettles, old bottles, and a broken can,
Old iron, old bones, old rags, that raving slut
Who keeps the till. Now that my ladder's gone
I must lie down where all the ladders start
In the foul rag and bone shop of the heart.

In *A Vision* he had similarly described the Muses frequenting 'low haunts' like 'women who creep out at night and give themselves to unknown sailors'. But 'The Circus Animals' Desertion' was also a return to the kingdom of Crazy Jane: a 'raving slut' who possessed the freedom of knowledge. The draft left aside in November 1937 had a last stanza.

> O host of triumph come and make me gay!
> If burnished chariots are put to flight
> Why brood upon old triumph, prepare to die;
> Even at the approach of the un-imagined night
> Man has the refuge of his gai[e]ty;
> A dab of black enhances every white,
> Tension is but the vigour of the mind,
> Cannon the god and father of mankind.

The poem is immeasurably enhanced by leaving this verse out, and ending with the poignant and profound refuse-dump of the heart. A draft of that last stanza was on wby's desk when he died. His preoccupation with it illustrates yet again how close the thought of his own death was, and how predominant the idea of conflict and violence.[78]

In a rejected version of *Under Ben Bulben*, wby had written:

> So what's the odds if war must come
> From Moscow, from Berlin or Rome?

But his private feelings in the autumn of 1938 reveal more trepidation. By early October, in common with many others, he was lulled by the false relief of the Munich agreement. To Wellesley (who was strongly anti-appeasement) he presented a determinedly solipsistic view:

War would have ment to me spending what remains of life here, where the winter climate makes me ill, or among unhappy & probably impoverished friends. You would have outlived even a long war (& it would have been very long) but I would never have got out of the dark tunnel. The thing has been settled as such things should be by free & able minds – I thought that day had gone.[79]

If in hindsight this seems myopic and self-centred, it was not an unusual reaction to the reprieve (Olivia strongly agreed). Freed to plan once more an escape to the sun, wby occupied himself by trying to finalize the Cuala arrangements, and by preparing his journey to England. He tried and failed to re-establish contact with Margot Ruddock; 'if she has simply cut us both out of her life we have nothing to complain of ', he told the Swami: 'she may even be quite right'.[80] But another Indian friend, Hari Prasad Shastri, subsequently told him that Ruddock was now hopelessly insane. wby immediately sent an agitated letter about the 'tragic beautiful creature', offering any financial help that might be needed. 'She was a very great help to me in taking me out in my old age.'[81] And at just this time he received a much greater shock: on 7 October he heard that Olivia Shakespear had died, suddenly, a few days before. 'For more than forty years she has been the centre of my life in London,' he told Wellesley,

And during all that time we have never had a quarrel, sadness sometimes but never a difference. When I first met her she was in her late twenties but in looks a lovely young girl. When she died she was a lovely old woman . . . She was not more lovely than distinguished – no matter what happened she never lost her solitude. She was Lionel Johnson's cousin and felt and thought as he did. For the moment I cannot bear the thought of London. I will find her memory everywhere.[82]

There may have been a certain feeling of guilt as well: he had drifted away from Olivia's London drawing room towards Steyning and Penns, and the great flow of letters had dramatically decreased. With her death, a pathway back to the days of his youth crumbled behind him, and his own mortality edged inexorably closer.

As the time drew near for him to leave Ireland, other accounts of friendship were settled. Ethel Mannin was summoned to dinner at the Shelbourne Hotel, with Reginald Reynolds. By chance, the party was spotted by the young Isaiah Berlin, writing a letter at an adjoining table. Entranced, he described WBY 'chanting verse' to his listeners ('it is perfectly audible . . . & is to me quite unknown'), while around them oblivious tourists discussed salmon-fishing and American politics.[83] In the same week WBY also summoned his oldest love for a final meeting. Maud Gonne had been a rare visitor to Riversdale in recent years, though they occasionally met in Dublin. She had remained violently alienated from the new Irish regime, and Roebuck House continued to provide a haven for irreconcilable republicans. Her letters to him often carried a waspish tone, even the one in which she acknowledged 'Among School Children'; but he always offered practical help when needed, in matters like adding inscriptions to books of his which she needed to sell. Gonne was now seventy-three, and her money had vanished along with her beauty; she had written an erratic autobiography to try to redeem her fortunes. In June 1938 she had asked WBY's permission to use material about their early relationship, and he had replied from Steyning: 'Yes of course you may say what you like about me. I do not however think that I would have said "hopeless struggle". I never felt the Irish struggle "hopeless". Let it be "exausting struggle" or "tragic struggle" or some such phrase. I wanted the struggle to go on but in a different way.'[84]

In late August he invited her to tea at Riversdale for what would be their last meeting. Their final exchange haunted her, and she often referred to it afterwards:

The last time I saw Willie at Riversdale just before he left Ireland for the last time, as we said goodbye, he sitting in his armchair from which he could only rise with great effort, said, 'Maud, we should have gone on with our Castle of the Heroes, we might still do it.' I was so surprised that he remembered, I could not reply. The whirlpool of life had sent the current of our activities wide apart. We had quarrelled seriously when he became a senator of the Free State which voted Flogging Acts against young republican soldiers still seeking to free Ireland from the contamination of the British Empire, and for several years we had ceased to meet. I stood speechless beside him with the song of Red Hanrahan echoing through my mind. 'Angers that are like noisy clouds have set our hearts abeat' – 'like heavy flooded waters our bodies and our blood' and I realised that Willie and I still 'bent low and low and kissed the quiet feet' and worshipped Her, who is 'purer than a tall candle before the Holy Rood'.[85]

Seeing her for the last time had yet again projected WBY's memory back to the 1890s, the visionary decade when so many patterns of his future life had been set. But if their ancient bond had been sustained, so had their ancient disagreement. When he left Ireland, he took her new book, *A Servant of the Queen*, with him; he wrote to her from England, regretting that they had not met again before his departure, 'but perhaps it was all for the best; I want you to read *On the Boiler* before we meet'. WBY took Gonne to task about her wish for a united Ireland: 'They are a horrid lot. Let them keep their border. Were they inside the nation they would sour all our tempers.'[86] And he wrote to George that reading Maud's version of her life had 'sufficiently upset [me] to have a not very good night. Very much herself always – remarkable intellect at the service of the will, no will at the service of the intellect.'[87] Yet, as he had written over twenty years before,

> . . . always when I look death in the face,
> When I clamber to the heights of sleep,
> Or when I grow excited with wine,
> Suddenly I meet your face.

At Menton the previous February, remembering the shock of seeing Lawrence Campbell's plaster bust of her in the Municipal Gallery, he had written a last poem about her. Yet again he pictured the child-like sadness beneath the magnificence, and celebrated her as a Helen whose legendary beauty now not only recalled the destruction of Troy, but showed up the physical decline of humankind through debased breeding. And the philosophy of the Hegelian scholar J. M. E. McTaggart formed a solid cornerstone of the poem, believing as he did that time was an illusion and that all selves existed simultaneously. Thus Maud Gonne's luminous youthful persona (symbolized for the young WBY by boughs of apple-blossom) is eternally present in the withered and obsessive old woman she has become.

Here at right of the entrance this bronze head,
Human, superhuman, a bird's round eye,
Everything else withered and mummy-dead.
What great tomb-haunter sweeps the distant sky;
(Something may linger there though all else die;)
And finds there nothing to make its terror less
Hysterico-passio of its own emptiness?

No dark tomb-haunter once; her form all full
As though with magnanimity of light
Yet a most gentle woman; who can tell
Which of her forms has shown her substance right,
Or maybe substance can be composite,
Profound McTaggart thought so, and in a breath
A mouthful hold the extreme of life and death.

But even at the starting-post, all sleek and new,
I saw the wildness in her and I thought
A vision of terror that it must live through
Had shattered her soul. Propinquity had brought
Imagination to that pitch where it casts out
All that is not itself. I had grown wild
And wandered murmuring everywhere 'my child, my child!'

Or else I thought her supernatural;
As though a sterner eye looked through her eye
On this foul world in its decline and fall;
On gangling stocks growing great, great stocks run dry,
Ancestral pearls all pitched into a stye,
Heroic revery mocked by clown and knave,
And wondered what was left for massacre to save.[88]

As in the reflective 'Hound Voice' written around this time, WBY summons up the essence of Gonne's persona through the transformation of her life, and finds it wild, vulnerable, and haunted by fear. If she herself has become a 'tomb haunter', forever mourning the republican dead and denouncing the government, perhaps this is only consistent for someone born out of her time and betrayed by the degeneration of the modern world. The eugenicist hectoring of the last stanza should not obscure the fact that WBY's last poem about Gonne shows her as a figure whose epic beauty brings tragedy in its wake: a role she had filled for him since their meeting in Bedford Park nearly half a century before.

IV

At the end of October 1938 WBY left Ireland for the last time. George took him part of the way. The journey had to be broken at Crewe because of swelling in his legs; his doctor had forbidden car journeys of more than an hour's duration. After a night in London he went to the Healds at Chantry House and subsequently (on 11 November) to Penns. The offstage rumbles of the international crisis had disturbed even these sleepy corners of Sussex; in Steyning there was unrest about the billeting of refugees, while at Penns Wellesley was arguing about Matheson's insistence that trenches be dug as air-raid shelters ('under no circumstances will I sit in a dug-out with my employees listening [to] the gramophone').[89] As before, WBY stayed in bed in the mornings, wrote, and made odd forays to London. On 15 November he gave a dinner at the Athenaeum for Ezra Pound, Edith and Nora Heald, and Walter Turner, who reported back to Wellesley. 'Truth to tell it was rather dull. Shackleton girls (!) are at least talkative tho' not inspiring. Ezra Pound was a complete wet blanket. He hardly opened his mouth but sat huddled up in a chair smiling derisively with thin lips, uninteresting eyes, but a certain light vivacity of appearance.[90] But for WBY, what mattered was that Pound, whom he would not see again, told him his recent poems were '"rather good" which for him is rapturous applause'.[91] Probably on this visit, another member of the Athenaeum noticed WBY 'wandering haltingly' around the club, wearing dark glasses, a tawny suit and a flannel shirt; or sitting in the library, 'solitary in a chair, with his head up, still with those black glasses on, meditating'.[92] He was conserving his energy for the journey south.

At Penns, plans for a movement to counter 'modernity' in poetry still went on (though it did not rule out WBY and Wellesley considering Auden and Day Lewis for the next series of 'Broadsides'[93]). A pencilled note which WBY added to *On the Boiler* may reflect these discussions:

Paul Valéry, Stephen George [*sic*], Rilke, Turner, Dorothy & myself – represent the same movement. We base ourselves on the traditional conclusions of philosophy & its modern development. We seek in words & in art what the Greeks sought. Man knows perfection for perfection's sake or for the sake of the Gods. Our thought because it needs leisure is rural like all ancient art. Modern civilization, created by industrialism, has been a violent interruption. We are not romantics but classicists.[94]

By contrast, 'Auden etc' were 'romantics gone sour – Shelleyan frenzy rioting in labour disputes'. Though a later generation would claim WBY for Modernism, the brotherhood of Penns was firmly set against it.

WBY was also still capable of a surge of energy or anger, as when he drafted a 'corker' of a letter to the young poet Sheila Wingfield, who had had the temerity to use private praise from him to puff her new book.[95] He was still revising his recent work, notably 'Man and the Echo'; and he had, just before leaving Ireland, begun a play which – as he told Mannin – brought him back again to the *alter ego* he had adopted nearly forty years before.

Goethe said the poet needs all philosophy but must keep it out of his work. I am writing a play on the death of Cuchulain, an episode or two from the old epic. My 'private philosophy' is there but there must [be] no sign of it: all must be like an old faery tale. It guides me to certain conclusions & gives me precission but I do not write it. To me all things are made of the conflict of two states of consciousness, beings or persons which die each others life, live each others death. That is true of life & death themselves.[96]

On 26 November George met him in London for their journey to France. He came up from Penns, while she stayed in a hotel near Victoria, avoiding WBY's attempts to bring her and his hostess together. However, Wellesley was to follow them out to the Riviera; she had originally offered the Yeatses her villa, La Bastide, but she now declared she needed to go there herself in order to recover from yet another bout of nervous prostration. After trying an unsatisfactory hotel in Beaulieu near by, George and WBY settled again into the Hôtel Idéal Séjour on Cap Martin. They were the only guests. The weather was turning cooler than expected, and WBY took sedation at night, but his creative energy was, as always, revived by the sunshine, the peace, the view of the sea and mountains from the windows. He considered writing a small book, perhaps with Clinton-Baddeley and Higgins, on the relation between speech and song; he coped with furious tirades from Lolly about the new Cuala arrangements; he sent unavailing bulletins to Higgins about the proofs of *On the Boiler* and 'Broadsides' and a masterly rebuke to George Barnes of the BBC, who had blithely requested a quotation for a Christmas broadcast. 'Surely a man as intelligent as you understands that if I were to write whatever I would "most like to say to the country as a whole" or to my own family as a whole, it would be altogether unprintable'.[97] But the process of building him into the history of his times was still proceeding inexorably. When Mannin, like Gonne, asked for permission to write about him in yet another book of reminiscence, he playfully took issue with the way she described him: 'Am I a mystic – no I am a practical – I have seen the raising of Lazarus & the loaves & fishes & have made the usual measurements plummet, line, spirit-level & have taken the temperature, pure mathematics.'[98]

On 22 December Michael arrived for Christmas. A year before, WBY had remarked that his son was '100% schoolboy' and he did not understand him yet,[99] but the boy could now contradict him about the Czech situation – though WBY, oblivious as ever to his son's age and independence, still recited the mythic stories of saints and heroes which he supposed suitable for children. Wellesley and Matheson were at La Bastide, and Edith (who had met Dorothy with WBY, and not liked what she saw[100]) was expected to arrive at the end of January to take over from George. The Wellesley motor went back and forth to Cap Martin, ferrying the Yeatses for dinners at La Bastide with guests like the Turners and the pianist Artur Schnabel. Fortified by admiring company, WBY insisted in early January that he felt better than he had for years; he was staying awake during the day and sleeping at night. In this energetic mood, he fired Higgins from the 'Broadsides' venture on 8 January: 'warty lads' might be all very well for the Muses, but bibulous inefficiency and productive publishing did not go together. Weakening though he was, the old entrepreneurial ruthlessness could still be drawn upon. So could the ancient reserves of his phenomenal imagination.

His mind continued to run back to the themes of his youth, and on 29 December he wrote to Rothenstein about his wish to preserve 'heroic images' from his early poems in embroidered pictures, after the Morris style.

In England the romantic movement is of course over and the average artist guys the dream. With us it is the opposite. Some of the best known of the young men who got themselves shot in 1916 had the Irish legendary hero, Cuchulain, so much in their minds that the government has celebrated the event with a bad statue. For us a legendary man or woman must still be able to fight or to dance.[101]

Each of his Cuchulain plays, George's 'Instructors' had told him long before, 'bore a relation to the state of his life when he wrote it'. Now the self-declared Last Romantic turned back to the Cuchulain legend, the subject for which he had praised Gregory so elaborately long before, as he worked on his play. Its theme, Cuchulain's death, was one he had considered addressing ten years before; but (he claimed) abandoned when 'the mood of Ireland changed'.[102] Whether or not the national mood had shifted once more, he declared his own mind had altered; 'it is more sensitive, more emotional'.[103] He decided that his old hero (who shared with Nietzsche the heroic Phase Twelve of *A Vision*[104]) would accompany him out of life, and he chose for his last play the title he had given to a narrative poem in 1892, 'The Death of Cuchulain'. With the end of the year, it was finished. He wrote to Edith on New Year's Day 1939 that he was exhausted by the excitement of bringing the drama to a close: 'strange and the most moving I have written for some years'.

This is not a generally held opinion – George, for one, recognized it as 'a bad play'. However, a certain pathos is conferred by WBY's clear intention to cast back over his adopted doppelgänger's life and bring all the relevant elements together at the end: faithful wife (Emer), misleading mistress (Eithne Inguba), avenging love-object (Aoife). The hero is warned of his death, goes out to meet it, returns dying, and is lashed to a pillar by Aoife, who prepares to kill him. But he is eventually dispatched by another revenant, the Blind Man from *On Baile's Strand*, who does it for 'twelve pennies'. The play begins with a ranting address by an old man, denouncing popular audiences, ignorant people, 'opinionated bitches', and advocating plays featuring severed heads, dancing, 'the music of the beggar man'. 'I am old, I belong to mythology.' It recalls the theatre of the *fin de siècle*, but is also an invocation of *The King of the Great Clock Tower* and a regretful tribute to Ninette de Valois.[105] This is followed by a denunciation of the debased bodies of Degas's dancers: the whole jarring harangue can be read as an echo of *On the Boiler*. These themes are reflected in the song that ends the play, which puts Cuchulain's symbolic death at the beginning of modern Ireland's sacrificial foundation myth: the Easter Rising.[106]

> Are those things that men adore and loathe
> Their sole reality?
> What stood in the Post Office
> With Pearse and Connolly?
> What comes out of the mountain
> Where men first shed their blood?
> Who thought Cuchulain till it seemed
> He stood where they had stood?
>
> No body like his body
> Has modern woman borne,
> But an old man looking back on life
> Imagines it in scorn.
> A statue's there to mark the place,
> By Oliver Sheppard done,
> So ends the tale that the harlot
> Sang to the beggar-man.

However, the play's historical and mythological resonances are tinny at best. Its interest lies in WBY's final effort to match the circumstances of his death, like his life, to the invented legend of his chosen hero. The assonances between Maeve, Aoife, and Maud Gonne[107] also echo in 'A Bronze Head': the continued relation between Emer and Eithne Inguba recalls that in *The Only Jealousy of Emer*, written in the midst of the emotional tangle set up by marriage to George while still obsessed by Iseult. Now, like Cuchulain, WBY was drifting out of life surrounded by the spirits of competing women, past and present; the final dance of the play takes place before the hero's severed head, but it is performed by his mourning wife, 'in adoration or in triumph' – the triumph being, perhaps, over her rivals. As for himself, like the dramatic chorus provided by the Old Man, he denounced misshapen modernity and invoked old mythologies. And the hero's death would come as a diminuendo, not a climax: the murderous Blind Man, like the symbolic Hunchback of *A Vision*, represents deformity as well as avarice. At the end of Emer's dance she stands 'motionless', listening to the faint notes of birdsong that suggest Cuchulain has started on his journey to the shades.

This birdsong motif would be picked up, like a fugue, in the poem which WBY wrote as a coda to the play, 'Cuchulain Comforted'. In that same New Year's Day letter to Edith which announced that his play was finished, he added, 'I am making the prose sketch for a poem – a kind of sequel – strange too, something new.' The prose sketch, dictated to George when he awoke from a vivid dream, survives. The hero is launched into the Dantean twilight of the other world, where he meets and joins his antithetical company.

A shade recently arrived went through a valley in the Country of the Dead; he had six mortal wounds but had been a tall, strong, handsome man. Other shades looked at him from among the trees. Sometimes they went near to him and then went away quickly. At last he sat down, he seemed very tired. Gradually the shades gathered round him, and one of them, who seemed to have some authority among the others laid a parcel of linen at his feet. One of the others said: 'I am not so afraid of him now that he is sitting still. It was the way his arms rattled.' Then another shade said: 'You would be much more comfortable if you would make a shroud and wear it instead of the arms. We have brought you some linen. If you make it yourself you will be much happier, but of course we will thread the needles. We do everything together, so everyone of us will thread a needle, so when we have laid them at your feet you will take whichever you like best.' The man with the six wounds saw that nobody had ever threaded needles so swiftly and so smoothly. He took the threaded needles and began to sow [*sic*], and one of the shades said: 'We will sing to you while you sew, but you will like to know who we are. We are the people who run away from the battles. Some of us have been put to death as cowards, but others have hidden, and some even died without people knowing they were cowards.' Then they began to sing and they did not sing like men and women but like linnets that had been stood on a perch and taught by a good singing master.[108]

This outline was transposed almost directly into the poem, 'Cuchulain Dead', subsequently retitled 'Cuchulain Comforted', which he dated 13 January 1939. It was written out with – for WBY – exceptionally few cancellations and changes.

A man that had six mortal wounds, a man
Violent and famous, strode among the dead;
Eyes stared out of the branches and were gone.

Then certain shrouds that muttered head to head
Came and were gone. He leant upon a tree
As though to meditate on wounds and blood.

A shroud that seemed to have authority
Among those bird-like things came and let fall
A bundle of linen. Shrouds by two and three

Came creeping up because the man was still;
And thereupon that linen-carrier said:
'Your life can grow much sweeter if you will

'Obey our ancient rule and make a shroud.
Mainly because of what we only know
The rattle of those arms makes us afraid.

'We thread the needles' eyes and all we do
All must together do.' That done, the man
Took up the nearest and began to sew.

'Now must we sing and sing the best we can
But first you must be told our character:
Convicted cowards all, by kindred slain

Or driven from home and left to die in fear.'
They sang, but had not human tunes nor words,
Though all was done in common as before

They had changed their throats and had the throats of birds.

The form he chose was a new venture into terza rima, and the sewing shades are borrowed directly from Dante's *Purgatorio*. But the atmosphere of this purgatory is, as Helen Vendler has pointed out, that of the 'Shiftings', in which – according to the first version of *A Vision* – the soul is brought to quiescence.

At the end of the *Return* . . . the *Spirit* is freed from pleasure and pain, and is ready to enter the *Shiftings* where it is freed from Good and Evil, and in this state which is a state of intellect, it lives through a life which is said to be in all things opposite to that lived through in the world, and dreamed through in the Return . . . This is brought about by no external Law but by a craving in the *Principles* to know what life has hidden, that the *Daimon* who knows intellect but not good or evil, may be satisfied . . . All now is intellect and he [the man] is all *Daimon*, and tragic and happy circumstance alike offer an intellectual ecstasy at the revelation of truth, and the most horrible tragedy in the end can but seem a figure in a dance.[109]

647

The hero, absorbed into a purgatorial otherworld, has to await resurrection and reincarnation. WBY's last poetic vision of the afterlife is not a refuge 'where the blessed dance', nor the transforming dolphin-journey to Byzantium, nor even the reunion rehearsed in numerous seance rooms, but a banishment to the company of outcasts.

There was to be one last poem. And, like 'Cuchulain Comforted', it carried him back to the world of Irish epic and the stories of Standish O'Grady, where so much had begun, so long before. 'The Black Tower' is, as George later remarked, about political propaganda, and thus far it may also reflect the immediate atmosphere of Europe in January 1939. In December he had redrafted his 'Three Songs to the Same Tune' into 'Three Marching Songs'; these too deal with impatient zealots anticipating a visionary deliverer. But the situation in 'The Black Tower' – a group of warrior-survivors, awaiting the return of a political messiah at a preordained time – comes straight from O'Grady's *The Masque of Finn*, a play he had seen at Patrick Pearse's school thirty years before. In that play, derived from O'Grady's earlier *Finn and His Companions*, the remnants of the Fianna brotherhood are hiding out in poverty, clinging to the resolution that their king will return. The warriors buried upright in their graves (according to ancient Irish practice) may be shaken awake at the day of revelation; meanwhile, the survivors live by setting traps for small game and birds, instead of the legendary deer hunts of their prime, and watch the sky for omens.[110] (Cancelled drafts of 'The Black Tower' invoke the Valley of the Black Pig, which had been WBY's image of apocalyptic Celtic war in the millennial optimism of the late 1890s – and also the Black Pig's Dyke, the rampart between Ulster and the rest of Ireland). After seeing the schoolboys of St Enda's perform the play on a dark spring day in 1909, WBY had written to Gregory: 'the waiting old men of the defeated clan seemed so like ourselves', and the identification came back to haunt him days before his death.[111] The draft of this last poem is written in a wild scrawl, and an abandoned fragment makes the approach of his own death manifest:

> Think all a vision of the air
> But they will soon be merely this
> Not yet my son not yet
> For this is no regret
> When ghost & dreams walk by
>
> What is out there, those [?]
> [cancelled: what men are these that pass in the skies]
> A dream [cancelled: by God] of the day to go
> That work all done & well
> Do I dream this sound in the sky

Do you hear [?] Father
No no not yet not yet
But [?]
Soon soon my son.[112]

These final, intense compositions were executed in the last fortnight of his life. Like Cuchulain in his play, he prepared to face into the other world, attended by the women he most cared for. He awaited Edith's arrival with impatience: she had decided to drive herself out, and was expected at the end of the month. Wellesley and Matheson visited from Beaulieu, and George was in constant attendance. Afterwards, Wellesley would describe his conversation in these last weeks,

eagerly discussing with Austrian and German acquaintances the philosophy of the poets Stefan George and Rilke. He was following with sympathetic interest and shrewd practical advice the plans of a group of English friends for giving concrete expression to ideas of a constructive democracy in Britain. After reading aloud, with undiminished fire, a new heroic play, completed within three weeks of his death, he exclaimed, throwing up his hand with a characteristic gesture: 'I have not been so excited about things for years, I want to find out the truth about the new ideas. That is why I want to live!'[113]

His mind also revolved around more ancient preoccupations, hinted at in three propositions he dictated to George on 23 December – probably to form the basis for another essay in *On the Boiler*.

I. Discoveries in eugenics will compel reversal of old politics. What must disappear? What changes in literature. Must strengthen conviction that nothing matters except poetry. What are its elements?
II. Discoveries in psychic research must revolutionize all thought even more completely.
III. Recent movement[s] in philosophy must apply everywhere to religious life the implication implied in the sentence: 'we can express truth but we cannot know it'. Get some summary. (German philosopher in Oxford or Cambridge.) Compare Vico compare Zen.[114]

The same reflection inspired a letter he wrote to Elizabeth Pelham on 4 January: in keeping with all their exchanges, it concerned the achievement of spiritual wisdom, but as with his last creative writing, he placed the sources of inspiration in personal history and the instinctual self.

I know for certain my time will not be long. I have put away everything that can be put away that I may speak what I have to speak, & I find my expression is a part of 'study'. In two or three weeks – I am now idle that I may rest after writing much verse – I will begin to write my most fundamental thoughts & the arrangement of thought which I am convinced will complete my studies. I am happy and I think full of energy, of an energy I had despaired of. It seems to me that I have found what I wanted. When I try to put all into a phrase I say, 'Man can embody truth but he cannot know it.' I must embody it in the completion of my life. The abstract is not life and everywhere draws out its contradictions. You can refute Hegel but not the Saint or the song of sixpence.[115]

This echoed a phrase of Boehme's, highlighted in Arthur Symons's *The Symbolist Movement in Literature*, dedicated to WBY over forty years before: 'man does not perceive the truth, but God perceives the truth in man'.[116] In this, as in so many ways, the great wheel of his imagination was turning at the last to the inspirations of his youth. Faith and instinct outweighed rational philosophic argument. By the same token, psychic promises, occult manifestations, and the prospect of reunion with the dead seem to have held little interest. As the icy month of January came to a close, a belt of freezing weather covered the Continent. It was snowing in Ireland, and the Riviera shivered unseasonably. WBY waited to commence that journey of the soul which he had long ago traced out in the first version of *A Vision*: rerunning the events and patterns of a life through the Dreaming Back, the Return and finally the 'Shiftings', where self-knowledge might be achieved through the soul's recognizing its opposite. In each stage, the life as lived in the world was rehearsed and examined, as a preliminary to letting it go. In a way, all the poetry and prose of his last weeks tended to this end. He had once described the thought which he fixed in his mind as he settled down to write poetry: 'I often think of a man in a little inn in the West of Ireland. There's a stormy sea and a ship. I think he's going into exile, but I'm not certain of it.'[117] Now he sat in his own room at the Idéal Séjour, looking at the sea and waiting for the ship.

'All the Pollexfens', JBY had remarked to Lily years before, 'die slowly, like an empire.'[118] The painter's mysterious eldest son elected, as so often, to follow his mother's family. On Saturday, 21 January, Wellesley, Matheson, and Turner came over to Idéal Séjour. Wellesley told Rothenstein she

had never seen [WBY] in better health, wits, charm or vitality. He was wearing his light brown suit, blue shirt and handkerchief. Under the lamp his hair seemed a pale sapphire blue. I thought during the talk 'What a beautiful man'. He read aloud his last poem. A fine affair as I remember it. He asked Hilda to make a tune for it. She went out of the hotel, and she and I walked up & down in the darkness & rain trying the tune. When we came back she sang the air; he seemed pleased. His last projective thought seems to me to be this wish for 'words for melody'.[119]

The next day the painter Dermod O'Brien and his wife, Mabel, also wintering near by, visited and found WBY in his dressing-gown but still lively, congratulating himself on getting out of his Abbey responsibilities in order to devote himself solely to poetry.[120] He had been delighted to hear that Anne was now sole designer of costume and scenery at the theatre. But the exceptional coldness was aggravating his angina, and on Monday, 23 January, he began to weaken. A planned visit to La Bastide the next day for a farewell dinner with the Turners was cancelled. On the morning of Thursday, the 26th, Matheson and Wellesley arrived again and were shocked to find him so ill: he was breathing with difficulty and receiving morphine. As Wellesley recalled it, 'I sat on the floor by his bed holding his hand; he struggled to speak: "Are you writ . . . are you writing?" "Yes, yes." "Good, good". He kissed my hand, I his. Soon after he wandered a little in his speech.'[121] He knew he was dying: one of his last decisions, taken that day, was to alter the title of his epitaph poem from 'His Convictions' to 'Under Ben Bulben'. But he yet again revised a contents list for an imagined last volume of poems: his final act of self-canonization.[122] On the next day, Friday, he sank further. Edith arrived from Paris that evening and sat by his bedside, but it is doubtful if he recognized her. He was in pain and after a bout of breathlessness early on the morning of Saturday, the 28th, the doctor was summoned and administered more morphia. At about two o'clock that afternoon he died peacefully, without pain.[123]

George was determined to follow his wishes and keep his funeral as discreet and private as possible. No announcement was to be made until the children could be telegraphed, and the interment was planned immediately. She rang the O'Briens at once, and asked them to find a clergyman; they arrived later that afternoon from Monte Carlo with the local Anglican padre, Canon Tupper-Carey, who said prayers in the bedroom at the Idéal Séjour. Looking at the dead body, O'Brien thought he detected on WBY's face 'the suspicion of a smile as if he had just had some humorous thought'.[124] That night George and Edith alternately kept a vigil by the body. The rain had moved away, and the night was intensely cold and clear, with marvellous stars. The removal took place to the hilltop church of St Pancras at Roquebrune on the Sunday evening. George spent the night at Wellesley's villa; Edith stayed alone at Idéal Séjour. Before they parted, she was presented with WBY's pen and pocket dictionary; Dorothy Wellesley was later given the manuscript of *The Death of Cuchulain*.[125] George played the part of Emer, the understanding wife, to the end.

It had long been established between George and WBY that he wanted to be buried quickly and temporarily in France, with the minimum fuss. 'His actual words', George told MacGreevy, 'were "If I die here bury me up there [at Roquebrune] and then in a year's time *when the newspapers have forgotten me*, dig me up and plant me in Sligo." He did not want the sort of funeral AE had.'[126] There was a brief Anglican service in the little church at three o'clock on the afternoon of Monday, 30 January, attended by George, the O'Briens, Dorothy Wellesley, Hilda Matheson, and Edith – with a small handful of lookers-on, huddled against the icy wind. But none of the Yeats family was at the graveside at Roquebrune that Monday. Lily believed that under French law the burying had to take place within twenty-four hours, but this was probably an explanation given by the resourceful George, to steal a march on publicity.[127] It must also have been difficult enough to manage her position as the chief of three 'widows', without the prospect of Lolly and Lily arriving. The news, still kept secret from journalists, had been telephoned through to the Yeatses in Dublin the day before – bizarrely, by Vita Sackville-West, instructed by Wellesley. Jack, who had warned Lily and Lolly that their brother was gravely ill, suddenly appeared at the door of the Dundrum house on Sunday evening. 'He was stooped & did not speak, just flung his arms out in a gesture as if saying "Gone!"'[128]

Epilogue: Genius and History

About two years [ago] – it was in the Club – he was talking
about someone, I forget who, and he said 'What will history
say about him'. And then, it came to my lips without a conscious thought, I said 'men of genius are not in history' and I
immediately knew I meant himself.

Jack Yeats to Joseph Hone, 2 February 1939[1]

IN AN abandoned line from 'Under Ben Bulben', WBY had scornfully repudiated the kind of funeral inscription that 'braggs of Irelands loss'.[2] His forebodings about the reactions to his death, and George's decisive action, were
vindicated at once. Amid the flood of obituaries and evaluations came
incessant demands for a state funeral, and a tomb in St Patrick's Cathedral.
When the news of his death came to Dublin, Lennox Robinson, 'in a state
of shock and possibly something else as well', even set off on an ill-starred
air journey to France, with Michael in tow, to plead for the return of the
body with full honours.[3] Fortunately for him, George had already set off
for Dublin the day after the funeral. She deliberately pre-empted the gathering campaign for a public burial in Dublin by placing 'Under Ben Bulben'
in the three daily newspapers on 3 February. Then, 'no-one in Ireland could
decently press what was against his own written wishes'.[4] Dublin made do
with a service in St Patrick's on 7 February; Lolly was annoyed that her
brother's Catholic friends could not enter the church ('they should work
now to get that obsolete law of the Church done away with. Now that they
are "on top" & also in the majority it seems to me so foolish'[5]). On 16 March,
the centenary of John Butler Yeats's birth, there was a London memorial
service for his son at St Martin-in-the-Fields, arranged by Masefield, interventionist as ever. The place and the occasion brought their shared London
youth vividly back to Lily. 'How often we all went by St Martin's and
waited for buses in heat and in east winds and nothing beyond the bus fare
in our pockets. Fame has come but the pockets are as lean as always.'[6]

This was true for her brother's family too. George, settling into the role as
executor and manager of the great literary estate which she would fill for just
under thirty years, found that, though her husband's estate was eventually
valued for probate at £8,329. 9s. 11d. (including copyright fees and royalties),
there was a sizeable overdraft, and the railway shares bought long ago with
Nobel money had drastically declined.[7] Financially, there was no question
of keeping up Riversdale. Lily, visiting with Jack a few weeks after George's
return, found it eerie. 'So empty & yet so full of Willy's presence: [his] vital

653

rich presence seems right through the place.'[8] As for the literary estate, though American royalties were left to Anne and European to Michael, there was no sign that this would be a profitable inheritance. The Macmillan edition de luxe, announced in April 1939, was scheduled to appear in September. 'Yeats always said you would only bring it out after his death,' George drily remarked to Harold Macmillan.[9] But it came as a shock to Scribner, who had been kept in the dark. Alarmed that their collected edition would clash with the edition de luxe, they angrily complained to Watt and tried to copy Macmillan's edition after they saw the prospectus. In any case, the Macmillan venture was delayed by the necessity of incorporating WBY's extraordinary late surge of work; and when it was ready, September 1939 brought other worries which effectively put paid to both enterprises. The very last of the copy arrived at Scribner a fortnight after Britain and Germany declared hostilities, and the war WBY had dreaded burst on Europe at last. By 1945 all of WBY's books were unavailable; even in 1949 Macmillan had only the *Collected Poems* (1933) in print.

But that same decade had cemented his reputation as arguably the century's greatest poet writing in English. And it was a reputation that, ten years after his death, was far more generally agreed in Ireland than at any time during his life. Shortly after his death his old antagonist and admirer W. K. Magee remarked to an American friend, 'There have of course been many [notices] on this side, all full of praise of the man, but most of them raising rather than fixing the question of his final standing.'[10] This was true, though praise of 'the man' had not been unadulterated: old resentments had been aired from those who felt slighted, like St John Ervine and Thomas Bodkin, and there had been predictably violent attacks by the *Catholic Bulletin* and – from an incensed Aodh de Blácam – in the *Irish Monthly*, describing him as satanic, atheistical, and above all unIrish. This last issue was aired as often in death as it had been in life: many obituaries published in Britain claimed him as an 'English' poet, and several enemies in Ireland were ready to convert this into a taunt.[11]

But by the early 1940s the tide was turning. W. H. Auden and Louis MacNeice had written their own critiques, which, while in some ways antagonistic, engaged with WBY's greatness as well as with what Auden famously called his 'silliness' and MacNeice his 'constitutional inhumanity'. The range, grandeur, severity, and tragic scale of his best work was now a critically accepted fact.[12] Moreover, Padraic Colum had pointed out how consciously WBY had celebrated and incarnated a certain kind of Irishness;[13] friends and critics like Stephen Gwynn, Frank O'Connor, and Sean O'Faolain made the point powerfully; so did the combined effect of journals which devoted special issues to WBY's achievements. Only weeks after his death the March 1939 number of the *London Mercury* had taken the form of a memorable 'Farewell to Yeats', printing for the first time 'The Statues', 'News for the Delphic Oracle', 'Long-legged Fly', and 'A Bronze Head'. This powerful volley from beyond the grave was accompanied by penetrating essays from Nevinson and Hone, and a late photograph taken at Menton, tactfully attributed to Nora rather than to Edith Shackleton Heald. The issue constituted an impressive demonstration of the way WBY's literary presence would endure. It took longer for a general realization of the originality and distinction of his late poems to dawn – partly because their arrangement in book form lacked the tightness of sequence and development so marked in *The Tower* and *The Winding Stair*.[14] Nor did celebration of violence and authoritarian rule arouse much sympathy among readers in the early 1940s. But the excitement, metrical ingenuity, variety, edginess, and jarring juxtapositions of the work published as *Last Poems and Two Plays* was recognized at once in some quarters. So was its modernity. Frederic Prokosch prophetically suggested that *Last Poems* stood in relation to WBY's earlier work as *Guernica* did to Picasso's youthful clowns and absinthe-drinkers.[15] The comparison might have surprised the poet, who in old age conceived of himself as a classicist; but his work, once seen as so distinctively Irish, was now entering the canon of modern world culture.

The life was also becoming framed in history. Joseph Hone was appointed biographer almost at once. 'It will take him two years,' remarked Lennox Robinson bitchily, 'be a fine book, & quite unreadable'.[16] Published in 1943, it was highly readable but necessarily tactful, and not always accurate. Lily thought it 'good, written with grace & dignity – no thin or hurried spots & Papa gets his due. His strong influence growing in strength is shown – he & Sligo made us.'[17] Three years later (now incapacitated by a stroke), she was giving interviews to Richard Ellmann, researching for his first book in which both life and work were read together, raising questions still provocative today, and inaugurating one of the great literary–critical industries of the age. WBY and his family were, despite Jack's disclaimer, firmly established 'in history'.

In October 1946 the invalid Lily Yeats was amused to overhear two men driving cattle past her gate in Dundrum. 'The first man shouted to the man behind him, "Do you see that woman in the garden? Well, the woman who lives in that house has two famous brothers, one writes books and the other paints pictures. They are famous all over the world."'[18] Lolly had died six years before; Lily herself would live on for three more years, dying on 5 January 1949, while Jack, the last of the artist's children, survived till 1957. And in 1948 the most famous of them was at last brought back for the long-postponed funeral in Sligo.

This was the culmination of an awkward saga, complicated by the intervention of survivors from WBY's other life in England. George had steadfastly maintained her – and WBY's – wish that his remains should lie in Roquebrune for up to a year before being shipped back to Sligo; much family discussion was devoted to the logistics of the situation. This being so, she had taken a temporary ten-year lease on the grave-site in Roquebrune, helped in the negotiations by Dermod O'Brien. The plan had been to bring the body back in September 1939, but (as with the edition de luxe) Armageddon intervened. Allan Wade reported in 1941 that the grave was well cared for.[19] But in June 1947 Edith Shackleton Heald came back to Roquebrune for the first time since she had stood by the graveside in the freezing cold on 30 January 1939 – and could not find it. To her horror, the Curé told her that the temporary 'concession' had run out after five years, and the remains had been removed to the ossuary. Edith was now living with the neurotic and overbearing painter Hannah Gluckstein, known as 'Gluck'; together they alerted Edmund Dulac. Without investigating all aspects of the situation or contacting George, Dulac, Edith, and Gluck began dealing with the confused and highly defensive local authorities at Roquebrune. Dulac felt that a story should be circulated about wartime disturbances necessitating that WBY's remains stay there permanently; he even designed a memorial stone, showing a unicorn ascending to the stars. But in January 1948 the matter of WBY's return to Sligo was raised by the Municipal Corporation, and George began to make arrangements. Dulac finally contacted her with the disastrous news. She – and Dermod O'Brien – were convinced that the graveyard concession had been for ten years, and she had retained receipts, though neither the undertakers nor the church records could provide any enlightenment. Matters became fraught, as always where Gluck was concerned. Unsubstantiated accusations of carelessness were privately levelled: George took the matter up with the French government, and the transference of her late husband's remains became an official affair. However, given the lack of documentation at Roquebrune and the increasingly inconsistent accounts from the local clergy, it was hard to find out precisely what had happened.[20]

The likelihood is that George correctly took a ten-year concession, but that the church authorities had mistakenly situated the grave in the part of the cemetery owned by the municipality rather than by private families, where leases usually ran out after five years. Certainly the body had been exhumed, without anyone informing the family. Exactly the same thing had happened to the adjacent grave, where an Englishman called Alfred Hollis had been buried a few days after WBY, also with a ten-year 'concession' which was not honoured. In any case, it proved necessary in March 1948 for

French officials to identify the remains, which was done to the satisfaction of both local authorities and representatives from Paris. The identified remains were placed in a new coffin, with the old plate affixed. Though great care had been taken to preserve discretion, rumours of confusion reached the newspapers, and some murmurs would haunt the re-interment; later, perhaps inevitably, messages on the subject even came through at a seance attended by Robinson.[21] The legend of a mystery burial, or even an empty coffin, sustains a kind of mythic life, as with King Arthur, or – more appositely – Charles Stewart Parnell.

But nothing could question the potent symbolism of WBY's spiritual return to Sligo in September 1948. The coffin was removed in state from Roquebrune on the 6th and driven with a military guard of honour to Nice, covered by the national flag. At Villefranche it was placed on the Irish navy corvette *Macha* for shipment to Galway, to be met early in the morning on the 17th by George, Michael, Anne, and Jack. The arrival at Sligo was greeted by a military guard of honour, though the family held out against a state funeral. Appropriately, there was a certain edge of controversy: George, Michael, and Anne had asked Frank O'Connor to make a graveside oration, but, to their embarrassment, this was vetoed by Jack, who disapproved of O'Connor's politics. The Church of Ireland service was conducted by the local rector, James Wilson, and Bishop Hughes of Kilmore, Elphin, and Ardagh, who privately 'felt a little doubtful as to Yeats's claim to Christian burial'.[22] The crowds were enormous. Unremarked among them was the poet Louis MacNeice, many members of WBY's Academy, and some survivors of the less charted areas of WBY's life. Edith Shackleton Heald was there, with Gluck, but she did not approach the family. Maud Gonne, afflicted with arthritis, remained in Dublin; she would die five years later, already immortalized in the Yeats legend.[23] But, with a curious symmetry, the government minister for External Affairs, closely involved throughout, was her son Seán MacBride, who, in another age, had flown kites with WBY at Colleville and been given sanctuary by the newly married Yeatses at Ballinamantane thirty years before. While the family were determined to keep control of the occasion away from the government, George gave MacBride three of WBY's manuscript books as a memento after the event. With her habitual generosity of mind, she recognized and appreciated the link to her husband's already mythologized past.[24]

In any case, the ceremony at Drumcliff on 17 September 1948 announced that WBY's reputation belonged neither to government nor family, but to the country whose consciousness he had done so much to shape, and which would declare itself a republic at the end of that year. 'Outside of Ireland his place on Parnassus is safe,' one of his obituarists had written, 'but inside of it he would perhaps prefer a place in the memory of his people's soul.'[25] In 1948 he was at last celebrated as a national poet. The arguments about 'placing' him, so marked at the time of his seventieth birthday and during the aftermath of his death nine years before, had been resolved. Long before, in 1917, T. S. Eliot had been riveted by JBY's remark that the substance of poetry was 'truth seen in passion'; and, further, that 'the poet does not seek to be original, *but the truth*, and to his dismay or consternation, it may be, he finds the original, thereby to incur hostility and misunderstanding'. In Eliot's view, this judgement 'strikes through the tangle of literature direct to the subsoil of the greatest – to Shakespeare and Dante and Aeschylus'.[26] The old painter had, inevitably, been thinking of his son; thirty years later, WBY was in the company of the greatest, and the hostility and misunderstanding had faded.

Thomas MacGreevy, closely involved in the arrangements that day in Sligo, kept impressionist notes of the journey to Drumcliff.

Ireland showed . . . in a most astonishing way. A little child just had time to bless herself. Some children wave. The nuns at Kiltimagh were lined up on the terrace of the convent with the girls, the school teacher running with her children at the Technical School at Collooney I think everywhere we went there was this extraordinary coming towards the poet and his legend for the people . . . the people knew that he had been with them in a way that was thought remote and at the back of it all there he was all the time. The spirit of Ireland.[27]

The poet who had spent his life – in Stephen Gwynn's phrase – 'smashing idols in the market place' was received with honour in his own country.[28] Nearly fifty years earlier WBY had reflected excitedly on people who set themselves to redefine or even overthrow modern civilization – that dedicated 'Remnant' who had learned all that modern life had to teach and found it insufficient, and now worked among the multitude as if 'upon some secret errand'.[29] The revolution in mass consciousness which he had expected in his youth never arrived in the way he had anticipated, but he had worked with that same singleness of mind towards a redefinition of culture for his country and himself, never quite abandoning the hope of revelation. By now, what MacGreevy called 'the poet and his legend' were becoming inseparable. 'A great poet is the antithetical self of his people,' WBY had remarked on one of his American tours, 'saying truths they have forgotten, bringing up from the depth what they would deny. He is the subconscious self.'[30] As so often, he was talking ostensibly about Synge, but really about himself. What was known of his tempestuous private existence also came to be read through his poems of introspection, of self-assertion, and of love. It was nonetheless clear that this did not exclude elements of affectation and contrivance. 'Who am I', he once asked Dulac, 'that I should not make a fool of myself?' – a remark which his friend interpreted as simultaneously the expression of justifiable pride and 'a very real and sincere modesty'.[31] For WBY himself, his life had been measured out as a series of steps towards enlightenment. 'Wisdom', as the Old Man in *At the Hawk's Well* tells Cuchulain, 'must live a bitter life', and even WBY's ruthless talent for choreography could not eliminate the contingencies and inconsistencies of fate. Even these, however, could be turned into pattern. Long before his death he had anticipated how wisdom might come through passion or even foolishness, and claimed for himself a kind of exemption. No one would withhold it now.

I shall find the dark grow luminous, the void fruitful when I understand I have nothing, that the ringers in the tower have appointed for the hymen of the soul a passing bell.

The last knowledge has often come most quickly to turbulent men, and for a season brought new turbulence. When life puts away her conjuring tricks one by one, those that deceive us longest may well be the wine-cup and the sensual kiss, for our Chambers of Commerce and of Commons have not the divine architecture of the body, nor has their frenzy been ripened by the sun. The poet, because he may not stand within the sacred house but lives amid the whirlwinds that beset its threshold, may find his pardon.[32]

APPENDIX 1

Letter and Memorandum from the Abbey Directors to the Free State Government, Opening Negotiations for a Subsidy

Abbey Theatre
Dublin

Oct. 21st, 1922

Dear Desmond FitzGerald,

I enclose the Memorandum about the Abbey. I send you two copies as you may want to hand it about and it will be convenient for you to have it in duplicate. If you will give me a day's notice I can arrange for Mr Yeats to meet Professor MacNeill and you and myself at any hour. If Professor MacNeill preferred it Mr Yeats would be very glad to meet him at 82 Merrion Square.

The Memorandum comes from the Directors and I am in entire agreement with it but I should like to add my personal view on the subject of an Irish National Theatre and I do not speak now as an official of the Abbey or as one particularly concerned in its affairs.

If the Government intends to found a National Theatre three courses are open to it: –

(1) It can make the Abbey the National Theatre.
(2) It can take over some large Dublin Theatre, the Royal, or Scala, or Queen's.
(3) It can build a Theatre for itself.

The objection to the first course is that the Abbey is too small, both as regards stage and auditorium, to be a worthy National Theatre; but a point in its favour is that it could be run with very little expenditure – it might even pay its way; another point in its favour, of course, is its tradition.

With regard to the second course the cost of buying out the proprietors would be considerable (though this might not be so as regards the Queen's). The Royal is too large, is ugly, is old-fashioned, and has no modern stage appliances; the Scala is also too large and the stage is, I believe, inadequate; the Queen's is a more suitable size but is old-fashionedly constructed without modern stage appliances and is not well situated in the city.

Undoubtedly the ideal course for the Government to take is to build their own Theatre. It need not be expensively constructed nor very large – it need not seat more than 2,000 people. It should not be elaborately constructed outside or inside except as regards the stage which should be large and equipped with all the latest contrivances – Fortuny lighting, a revolving stage, etc. all the things that are revolutionising the art of the theatre. I am sure you have been in, or have seen photographs of the new Continental and American theatres and you know the sort of theatre I have in my mind. The Abbey Theatre should be continued as the Gaelic

Theatre and possibly as a rehearsal theatre for the State Theatre. The Gaelic Theatre will have to be built up gradually as regards play wrights, players and audience just as the Anglo-Irish Theatre was. It cannot be created in a year by a Governmental act. There certainly should be special occasions when the Gaelic Company would play in the State Theatre and eventually when the Gaelic Theatre had created its repertory and its audience it, in its turn, would migrate from the Abbey to the State Theatre or to some other building worthy of it.

I am strongly of opinion that our National Theatre should be, to some extent, an International Theatre. I mean that the State Theatre should invite from time to time companies from foreign countries to show us examples of their art. The company from the Comedie Francaise, the Russian Ballet, the Moscow Art Theatre – these occur to me as companies whose work would be worthy of our State Theatre. Ireland does desperately need to be educated and made aware of the art of other countries and there is no art that is more capable of development – no art that has been so developed in our generation – than has the Art of the Theatre. But the Irish dramatist knows little or nothing of it, his only ideal is the 'well-made' play of the French and English stage and he is almost entirely ignorant of what his fellow dramatists in Europe and America are doing. While these foreign companies are playing in the State Theatre the State Company itself might be visiting other towns in Ireland or, or who knows?, playing in the Comedie Francaise or in Moscow.

This letter is only my personal view on the subject, you can show it or not as you think best.

Yours sincerely,
[Signed] Lennox Robinson

THE ABBEY THEATRE

A Statement made by its Directors
To the
Irish Provisional Government

1. The following statement is made with the object of bringing before the notice of the Government the present precarious position of the Abbey Theatre and the reasons why it should receive help from the Government.

Past
History

2. It is unnecessary to relate at any length the history of the Abbey Theatre. It began as the Irish Literary Theatre in 1899, became the Irish National Theatre Society Ltd in 1903 and, in December 1904, opened in the Abbey Theatre which was rebuilt and subsidised by Miss Horniman. In 1911, the subsidy having ceased, the Theatre was

purchased from Miss Horniman for £1,000. This money had been saved by the Theatre during the subsidised years and a further sum of money had been given through Lady Gregory by friends of the Theatre in Dublin and London. Of this sum £1,300 was used later in the purchase of that part of the building facing Lower Abbey Street. The whole building is now a valuable property worth, say, £10,000. The Theatre is entirely controlled by the Directors, Lady Gregory and Mr W. B. Yeats, who are unpaid. The Patent of the Theatre is granted to Lady Gregory and the work of the Theatre is restricted by the Patent to the production of Irish plays, plays by Irish authors and translations of foreign master-pieces. Since its inception it has inspired the writing of several hundreds of plays by Irish authors, and has always carried on its work as a repertory theatre, that is to say it changes its programme each week and does not put on plays for a 'run'. It has never earned enough money by its performances in Dublin to enable it to pay its way but before the European War it was able, by visits to England and America, to keep solvent and to give its players a fair remuneration for their work. The War put an end to touring abroad but in 1915 £206 was earned through a lecture in England by Mr Yeats and in the spring of 1921, after a disastrous winter when curfew had nearly ruined every Dublin theatre, a sum of £1,200 was raised in England by lectures given by Lady Gregory, W. B. Yeats, Bernard Shaw etc. and by subscriptions. This money paid off all debts and the Theatre's position was then clear.

The
Present

3. Since the Truce to August 31st 1922 the Theatre has incurred a loss of £683. As there is no accumulation of Cash Capital and the only assets are the premises and contents the Directors feel that they can-not indefinitely continue playing at a loss. The position during the last year has been so uncertain that they have been afraid to engage a permanent company of players and have had to depend on men and women who have other employments and who have only been able to work at the Theatre after their other work was over or during their lunch hour. Under such conditions it has been very difficult to keep up the high standard of acting and production which have been associ-ated with the Theatre; the Directors believe that, by a great effort, the standard *was* kept up but it is not possible indefinitely to continue to work under these circumstances. It has also been impossible during the last few years to spend money to keep up the fabric of the Theatre both on the stage and in the house, and at the present moment money is urgently needed for carpeting, repairing of seats, painting [repairing of seats, painting,] re-papering and repairing of scenery, lighting etc. The Directors feel that they can no longer appeal to England for help; their appeal must now be made to their own Government.

663

A National
Theatre

4. It was always the Directors' intention to hand the Abbey Theatre over to the Irish Government as soon as that Government was established. The Directors believe that they are correct in stating that every Government except that of England and its Colonies, the United States of America, and Venezuela possesses its subsidized State Theatres. The Comedie Francaise is one of the glories of France, the famous Moscow Art Theatre is subsidised by the Soviet Government, Germany possesses scores of national municipal theatres. These countries believe that a theatre which is not dependent for its existence on the caprice of the public can play a great part in the education of a nation. The Abbey Theatre may be considered by the Irish Government to be too small and too humble to be the Theatre of the Irish Nation. It may contemplate building a State Theatre or taking over one of the large Dublin theatres, but the cost of such an undertaking would be very considerable. Apart from the initial expense the State Theatre would probably be run at a heavy loss, for Irish playgoers have become to a large extent denationalised and the support given by the public would be likely to be small.

A
Gaelic
Theatre

5. The Directors know that the Government desires to build up Gaelic civilisation. They therefore intend, if the Government will assist them, to engage a Gaelic-speaking producer of plays and to form a company of Gaelic players. The number of plays in Gaelic is not considerable but if it were known that a Theatre and a company of Gaelic players were in existence the best possible impetus would be given to Gaelic writers to write for the stage. The Gaelic plays would not be mixed with the English ones but every five or six weeks the Theatre would be given over for a week to Gaelic drama. It is not possible to go into exact details in advance, much would depend on the number and the quality of the Gaelic plays submitted for production but the Directors would undertake to give every facility to the creation of a Gaelic Theatre. If the Government intend to make a great National Theatre the Abbey Theatre might eventually be turned into the Gaelic Theatre.

6. In the meantime the existence of the Abbey Theatre is in danger. The Directors would regret being forced to let the Theatre to a cinema company (they have already refused an offer) – even in order to gain money with which to re-open later on; or to sell the whole property which is now a valuable one, in which case they would apply the money to other intellectual purposes in Dublin. They wish to avoid

the breaking up of a business that is, both on artistic and intellectual grounds, an advantage to Dublin. For eighteen years they have carried on its work. They carried it on in spite of the European War (which killed every repertory theatre in England save one), and in spite of the English war in Ireland. Ungrudgingly and without pay they have given their services to the creation of the Irish drama, they have created the Irish Theatre – a mass of plays, dramatists that have brought honour to Ireland all over the world, a type of acting that has largely become the model of all modern acting, players of genius. They think that the time has come when the responsibility of the Theatre should be borne by the State.

What is
Asked for

7. For the present, and as a temporary measure to save the Abbey from closing, they suggest:–

(a) That the Government should make the Theatre a grant of £2,000, £500 of which might be spent on necessary repairs and renewals and £1,500 on carrying on the Theatre or a period of twelve months.

(b) That the Theatre should be publicly recognised by the Government as being the National Theatre of Ireland.

In return, the Directors would undertake to do everything in their power to foster the growth of a Gaelic Theatre; would give special performances on such occasions as the Government might require; would engage a permanent company of players for a year and would accept any reasonable method of supervision by the Government that the Government might desire.

A year
hence

8. At the end of the twelve months the position could be re-considered. The Government will then be in a better position to judge whether the time has come to form a National Theatre on an ambitious scale or whether the Abbey Theatre should continue to be the National Theatre. Some opinion, too, can be formed then as to the importance the Gaelic theatre is likely to assume.

9. On the next page is given an estimate of the probable expenditure and receipts. The door receipts are calculated on the season 1919–20, allowance being made for the fact that the Gaelic plays would be likely at first to draw small audiences. It should be noted that the *net* door receipts are given, the Government tax first being deducted. This tax is about 25% of the receipts so that if, as is calculated, £6,000 *net* was

taken the Government would have received £1,500, therefore the subsidy would in reality be only £500.

ESTIMATED EXPENDITURE

Actors

A Company of 12 permanent players under contract for a season of 40 weeks and 12 weeks at half-salaries, the players salaries to vary from £3 a week to £7. Also an average of 6 extra players each week, not under contract, at £2 per week.

2 players @ £7 ... £644		
4 players @ £5 ... £920		
6 players @ £3 ... £828		
6 extra @ £2 ... £480	£2,872. 0. 0.

Manager & Producer, £5 per week, 40 weeks, 12 weeks ½ salary	230. 0. 0.
Gaelic Producer & Teacher £4 per week " " "	184. 0. 0.
Secretary, £3 per week, 52 weeks full salary	156. 0. 0.

Permanent Staff, all 40 weeks, 12 weeks ½ salary

Carpenter	£184.	
Property Man	£138.	
Chars	£164. 9. 0.	
Wardrobe	£ 69.	
Box Office	£ 86. 5. 0.	
Messenger	£ 26.	£667. 14. 0.

Night Staff, all for 40 weeks only

Front of House	£520. 6. 8.	
Stage	£351. 6. 8.	
Orchestra	£700. 0. 0.	£1,571. 13. 4.

Advertising	665.
Author's Fees	340.
Lighting & Heating	330.
Wardrobe	100.
Piano	18.
Bill Posting	25.
Sundries	53.
Rents	19. 5. 4.
Insurance	100. 4. 3.
Loss on Programmes	20.
Rates & Taxes	190. 6. 8.
Audit	76. 16. 0.
	£7,681. 19. 7.

House receipts	£6,000. 0. 0.
Profit on 4 weeks lets	68.
25 Sunday lets	100.
15 afternoon lets	90.
Rents receivable	110. 17. 4.
Advertisements in Programmes	98.
Profit on Café	40. 0. 0.
	£6,506. 17. 4.

(FitzGerald Papers, UCD Archives)

APPENDIX 2

Lionel Curtis's Account of His Meeting with WBY on 20 January 1923

MR W. B. YEATS came to see me with regard to the Lane Pictures. He started talking, however, on the general situation. He was alarmed, he said, by the frequency with which he was told here that under no circumstances would Great Britain intervene in Ireland. If this meant that in the event of the collapse of the Free State Government the Republicans were to be left free to run Ireland as a Republic and if the Liberal papers ventilated that view, the greatest possible encouragement would be given to the Republican cause in Ireland. I asked him what he thought should be done in the event of a breakdown. His reply was that the government here should firmly declare that if Ireland was unable to carry out the Treaty then Ireland would be reoccupied by all the Imperial forces necessary for the purpose and would be governed as a Crown Colony, with only so much local government as it was found possible and expedient to grant. He hastened to add, however, that he was not seriously afraid of any break down in the Free State Government. The members of the Government themselves whom he saw frequently were cheerful and fully confident of their own ability to suppress the rebellion and he himself shared their confidence. The army were, of course, the weak point. When the Provisional Government finally decided in June to attack the four Courts and called upon their forces to act, they did not know which way the men would shoot. They were the old IRA, and republican in sentiment. That crisis successfully passed, they set to work to reorganise IRA into the National army, but the men refused to serve except under the old leaders who had led them in the struggle against Great Britain. The employment in responsible posts of men who had not been active members of the IRA in pre-truce days was at that time simply out of the question. Since then, however, the men themselves have begun to discover that officers who had succeeded as guerrilla leaders were unable to handle operations on a larger scale, and were now demanding the employment of experience[d] officers. The Government was therefore beginning to be in a position to employ such men. They were felt to have been too backward in accepting the service of civilian volunteers for the protection of their own localities. He thought they were coming to it now. The other day when he called on members of the Government with regard to the Lane Pictures they thought that he was coming about the protection of his house (he being a Senator) and they suggested to him that if he could get a number of younger friends to act as a voluntary guard for his house, the Government would supply them with arms. He had refused the offer as he did not like to call on his friends for such services. I suggested to him that if he and other Senators accepted the suggestion, these voluntary guards of individual houses could easily be developed into armed civilian forces, doing duty for the protection of the streets.

668

I am dealing with the subject of the Lane Pictures in a separate memorandum.

(Public Record Office CO 739/19: stamped 27 January 1923)

ABBREVIATIONS

THE following abbreviations have been adopted for frequently recurring names of publications, places, and people. Otherwise, for printed sources the usual convention has been adopted of a full citation in the first instance, followed by a recognizable shortened form. Manuscripts are cited by location, and for the National Library of Ireland, the British Library, and the Bodleian Library call-numbers are given.

AG	Augusta, Lady Gregory
AM	R. F. Foster, *W. B. Yeats, A Life. Volume 1: The Apprentice Mage 1865–1914* (Oxford, 1997)
ASD	Roger McHugh (ed.), *Ah, Sweet Dancer. W. B. Yeats and Margot Ruddock: A Correspondence* (London, 1970)
Au	W. B. Yeats, *Autobiographies* (London, 1955)
Au, CW, iii	W. B. Yeats, *Autobiographies*, edited by William H. O'Donnell and Douglas N. Archibald (New York, 1999; volume 3 of the *Collected Works of W. B. Yeats*)
AV (*1925*)	George Mills Harper and Walter Kelly Hood (eds.), *A Critical Edition of Yeats's 'A Vision' (1925)* (London, 1978)
AV (1937)	W. B. Yeats, *A Vision* (London, 1937)
Berg	The Henry W. and Albert A. Berg Collection, New York Public Library
Berkeley	Bancroft Library, University of California at Berkeley
BG	Ann Saddlemyer, *Becoming George: The Life of Mrs W. B. Yeats* (Oxford, 2002)
BL	British Library
Bodleian	Bodleian Library, Oxford
Boston College	John J. Burns Library, Boston College
Boston University	Mugar Memorial Library, Boston University
Bucknell	Ellen Clarke Bertrand Library, Bucknell University
Buffalo	Lockwood Memorial Library, State University of New York at Buffalo
CB	*Catholic Bulletin*
CH	A. Norman Jeffares (ed.), *W. B. Yeats: The Critical Heritage* (London, 1977)
CL, i	John Kelly and Eric Domville (eds.), *The Collected Letters of W. B. Yeats. Volume 1: 1865–1895* (Oxford, 1986)
CL, ii	Warwick Gould, John Kelly and Deirdre Toomey (eds.), *The Collected Letters of W. B. Yeats. Volume 2: 1896–1900* (Oxford, 1996)
CL, iii	John Kelly and Ronald Schuchard (eds.), *The Collected Letters of W. B. Yeats. Volume 3: 1901–1904* (Oxford, 1994)
CT	W. B. Yeats, *The Celtic Twilight* (London, 1893)
Delaware	Special Collections, The Library, University of Delaware
DW	Dorothy Wellesley
E & I	W. B. Yeats, *Essays and Introductions* (London, 1961)
ECY	Elizabeth Corbet ('Lolly') Yeats
Ellmann, *IY*	Richard Ellmann, *The Identity of Yeats* (2nd edition, London, 1964)
Emory	Robert W. Woodruff Library, Emory University, Atlanta
ESH	Edith Shackleton Heald
Ex	W. B. Yeats, *Explorations* (London, 1962)
FJ	*Freeman's Journal*

FS	William M. Murphy, *Family Secrets: William Butler Yeats and His Relatives* (Dublin, 1995)
GY	George Yeats
G–YL	Anna MacBride White and A. Norman Jeffares (eds.), *The Gonne–Yeats Letters 1893–1938: Always Your Friend* (London, 1992)
Harvard	Houghton Library, Harvard University
Healy	Healy Collection, Stanford University, California
Hone	J. M. Hone, *W. B. Yeats 1865–1939* (London, 1942)
Hone (1916)	J. M. Hone, *William Butler Yeats: The Poet in Contemporary Ireland* (Dublin and London, n.d. [1916])
HRHRC	Harry Ransom Humanities Research Center, University of Texas at Austin
Huntington	Henry E. Huntington Library, San Marino, California
I & R, i and ii	E. H. Mikhail (ed.), *W. B. Yeats, Interviews and Recollections* (2 vols., London, 1977)
IG	Iseult Gonne
Illinois	University Library, University of Illinois at Urbana–Champaign
Indiana	Lilly Library, University of Indiana
IT	*Irish Times*
JBY	John Butler Yeats
Jeffares, White and Bridgwater	A. Norman Jeffares, Anna MacBride White and Christina Bridgwater (eds.), *Letters to W. B. Yeats and Ezra Pound from Iseult Gonne* (forthcoming, 2003)
Journals, i and ii	Daniel J. Murphy (ed.), *Lady Gregory's Journals. Volume 1: Books 1–29, 10 October 1916–24 February 1925*, and *Volume 2: Books 30–44, 21 February 1925–9 May 1932* (Gerrards Cross, 1978, 1987)
JY	Jack Butler Yeats
Kansas	Kenneth Spencer Research Library, University of Kansas
Kenyon	Kenyon College Library, Gambier, Ohio
L	Allan Wade (ed.), *The Letters of W. B. Yeats* (London, 1954)
LDW	*Letters on Poetry from W. B. Yeats to Dorothy Wellesley* (Oxford, 1940)
Leeds	Brotherton Library, University of Leeds
LTWBY, i and ii	Richard R. Finneran, George Mills Harper and William M. Murphy (eds.), *Letters to W. B. Yeats* (2 vols., London, 1977)
MBY	Collection of Michael Butler Yeats (*all family papers not otherwise attributed in the notes were in this collection at the time of writing*)
Meisei	Meisei University, Japan
Mem	W. B. Yeats, *Memoirs. Autobiography – First Draft, Journal*, edited and transcribed by Denis Donoghue (London, 1972)
MG	Maud Gonne MacBride
Myth	W. B. Yeats, *Mythologies* (London, 1959)
MYV, i and ii	George Mills Harper, *The Making of Yeats's 'A Vision': A Study of the Automatic Script* (Carbondale, Ill., 1987)
NA	National Archives, Dublin
NLI	National Library of Ireland
NLS	National Library of Scotland
Northwestern	Charles Deering McCormick Library of Special Collections, Northwestern University, Chicago
NYPL	New York Public Library
NYU	Fales Library, New York University
OS	Olivia Shakespear
Pearce	Donald R. Pearce (ed.), *The Senate Speeches of W. B. Yeats* (London, 1961)

PF	William M. Murphy, *Prodigal Father: The Life of John Butler Yeats 1839–1922* (London, 1978)
PRONI	Public Record Office of Northern Ireland
Princeton	Special Collections, Firestone Library, Princeton University
R L-P	Ruth [Pollexfen] Lane-Poole
Reading	University of Reading Library
SIUC	Morris Library, Southern Illinois University at Carbondale
Sligo	Sligo Municipal Library
SMY	Susan Mary ('Lily') Yeats
Stanford	Special Collections, Stanford University Libraries
TCD	Trinity College, Dublin
Tulsa	Archives, Tulsa University, Oklahoma
UCDA	Special Collections in the Archives of University College, Dublin
UP, i and ii	John P. Frayne (ed.), *Uncollected Prose by W. B. Yeats. Volume 1* (London, 1970), and John P. Frayne and Colton Johnson (eds.), *Uncollected Prose by W. B. Yeats. Volume 2* (London, 1975)
VP	Peter Allt and Russell K. Alspach (eds.), *The Variorum Edition of the Poems of W. B. Yeats* (2nd edition, New York, 1966)
Wake Forest	Wake Forest University, North Carolina
YA	*Yeats Annual* (London, 1982–), followed by number and date. Nos. 1 and 2 edited by Richard Finneran; from no. 3 (1985) edited by Warwick Gould
YAACTS	*Yeats: An Annual of Critical and Textual Studies* (1983–). Various publishers, followed by number and date
Yale	Beinecke Rare Book and Manuscript Library, Yale University
YVP, i, ii, iii	George Mills Harper (ed.), assisted by Mary Jane Harper, *Yeats's 'Vision' Papers* (London, 1992). *Volume 1: The Automatic Script 5 November 1917–18 June 1918* and *Volume 2: The Automatic Script 25 June 1918–29 March 1920*, edited by Steve L. Adams, Barbara J. Frieling and Sandra L. Sprayberry; *Volume 3: Sleep and Dream Notebooks, Vision Notebooks 1 and 2, Card File*, edited by Robert Anthony Martinich and Margaret Mills Harper

NOTES

Introduction : ACCIDENCE AND COHERENCE

1. GY to Herman Peschmann, 15 June 1943, private collection. My thanks to Warwick Gould.
2. To John Lehmann, quoted in Michael Holroyd, *Works on Paper: The Craft of Biography and Autobiography* (London, 2002), 74. Ellmann's own view is worth recording. He later reflected that when he began to write about Yeats he was inclined to dismiss the material circumstances of his life; but, when he came to work on Joyce, he realized the importance of dealing with existential matters. See an interview in *Miami Herald*, 21 June 1982.
3. Quoted by Mary Fitzgerald in 'Ezra Pound and Irish Politics: An Unpublished Correspondence', *Paideuma*, 12, 2 (1983), 393.
4. *IT*, 13 June 1935.
5. See below, p. 516.
6. *E & I*, 409.
7. 20 June 1935, private collection.
8. James Knowlson, *Damned to Fame: The Life of Samuel Beckett* (London, 1996), 288, quoting Beckett in 1937.
9. For the Ricketts quote, see Thomas MacGreevy's 'Uileacháin Dubh Ó', *Capuchin Annual* (1952); for comparison with AE, Gogarty to Richard Campbell, 28 July 1935, Healy.
10. To Gwyneth Foden, 21 Oct. [probably 1936], Autograph File, Harvard.
11. *Irish Statesman*, 1920 (1st series), 2, 41 (3 Apr. 1920), 323.
12. *New Statesman*, 4 Feb. 1939.
13. See below, p. 413.
14. 6 Feb. 1915, Berg.
15. See below, p. 325–9.
16. See Ellmann's entry on Eliot in E. T. Williams and C. S. Nicholls (eds.), *The Dictionary of National Biography 1966–1970* (Oxford, 1981), 328.
17. 'Yeats as I Knew Him', a talk to the Irish Literary Society, Nov. 1948, TS in HRHRC.
18. To Ernest Boyd, 5 Oct. 1915, Healy.

Prologue : CROSSWAYS

1. To Anna Russell, 17 Nov. 1951, Healy.
2. 'My Own Poetry', BBC broadcast, 29 Oct. 1937.
3. An undated reflection in NLI MS 13,581, probably from 1929.
4. To R L-P, 15 Apr. 1935. This and later references to this correspondence come by courtesy of William M. Murphy, to whom I am deeply indebted.
5. 3 June 1916, TCD.

Chapter 1 : ACCOMPLISHMENT AND NOH
1915–1916

1. Healy.
2. 16 Apr. 1915, NYPL.

3. JBY to JY, 3 June 1916, TCD.

4. Farr to WBY, 3 Oct. 1914, *YA* 9 (1992), 242; WBY to Quinn, 24 June 1915, NYPL.

5. In the *Daily Mail*, 14 Sept. 1914, Maeterlinck published an article 'After the Victory', which began 'At these moments of tragedy none should be allowed to speak who cannot shoulder a rifle', arguing – as WBY would not have – that 'the written word seems monstrously useless, overwhelmingly trivial'. Pound took this up; see James Longenbach, *Stone Cottage: Pound, Yeats and Modernism* (Oxford, 1988), 114. On 22 Oct. 1918 Quinn told WBY: 'I never said to you before what I have frequently said to your father, and that was how much I regretted that you had not taken some part on the side of what I have always felt to be justice and right in this war.' (NYPL).

6. An earlier version is signed by WBY and dated 'Feb. 6 1915' in NLI MS 30,415, reproduced in W. B. Yeats, *'The Wild Swans at Coole': Manuscript Materials*, edited by Stephen Parrish (London, 1994), 219, where it is titled 'To a friend who has asked me to sign on his manifesto to the neutral nations'. The charities in question were the American Hostels for Refugees and the Children of Flanders Rescue Committee; the letters about the commission, dated 20 Aug. 1915, are at Yale. Quinn's comment is in the letter of 22 Oct., quoted above. Wharton's book was supposed to reach the Christmas 1915 market, but was delayed into early 1916. The general tone was stridently anti-German, making WBY's contribution stand out all the more. My thanks to Hermione Lee.

7. WBY to Ernest Rhys, 31 May 1916, Kansas; Ronald Schuchard, '"An Attendant Lord": H. W. Nevinson's Friendship with W. B. Yeats', *YA* 7 (1990), 117.

8. T. S. Moore to his wife, postcard, 27 Apr. 1915, University of London; Reid to Ernest Boyd, 21 Sept. 1918, Healy.

9. WBY to Mabel Beardsley [probably 7 Jan. 1915], Beardsley Collection, Princeton.

10. See *AM*, 528.

11. See WBY to SMY, 15 June 1915, Boston College.

12. WBY to Quinn, 21 Mar. [1915], NYPL. The remark about *Dracula* refers to his having stayed up late reading it the night before.

13. See correspondence of June 1915 in Berg, especially Bailey to WBY, 24 June 1915. For Allgood's salary, WBY to AG, 14 Jan. 1915, Berg; for Pound and the cinematograph, same to same, n.d., Berg; for the vulgar Wilson, WBY to Mabel Beardsley [May 1915], Beardsley Collection, Princeton, and a letter in Berg of 17 May 1915, from AG and WBY, telling Wilson he had to resign, because of stirring up the actors against the directors and refusing to rehearse *Deirdre*.

14. See Humphrey Carpenter, *A Serious Character: A Life of Ezra Pound* (London, 1988), 334–7, for possible use of Pound's girlfriends. The MS of 'Her Praise' is dated 27 Jan. 1915 (NLI MS 13,587), 'The People' 10 Jan. 1915 (NLI MS 30,424), and 'His Phoenix' Jan. 1915 (NLI MS 30,300); MS 30,358 in NLI dates 'The Dawn' and 'Memory' as Sept./Oct. 1915, though Longenbach thinks they were included in the poems sent to Monroe the previous January.

15. NLI MS 13,589 is an early version dated 27 Jan. 1915. The version quoted here is as first printed in *Poetry*, Feb. 1916.

16. The MS in NLI MS 30,424 is reproduced in W. B. Yeats, *'The Wild Swans at Coole': Manuscript Materials*, edited by Stephen Parrish.

17. *G–Y L*, 356–7: dated 20 Mar. [1915], but the poem had evidently been sent some time before. The letter from MG (7 May 1907) which originally inspired the poem is in *G–Y L*, 239–40.

18. See a brisk note to Ernest Boyd, 9 Feb. 1915 (private collection; sold at Christie's, 9 Dec. 1987). 'My interest in mystic symbolism does not come from Arthur Symons or any other contemporary writer. I have been a student of the medieval mystics since 1887 & found in such writers as Valentin Andrea authority for my use of the Rose . . . I do not

remember my development with that precision. I have never consciously abandoned the wish to write out of the scenery of my own country.'

19. '"The Celtic Twilight" was the first book of Mr Yeats's that I read, and even before I met him, a little time later, I had begun looking for news of the invisible world: for his stories were of Sligo and I felt jealous for Galway.' The first sentence of his notes picks this up. But in draft the passage 'Some fifteen years ago I was in bad health and could not work and Lady Gregory brought me from cottage to cottage . . .' reads 'Some twelve years . . .' (NLI MS 13,575) – suggesting 1902 rather than 1899.

20. 27 Apr. 1915, Berg. In the same letter he criticized her Introduction for its chatty references to Chevy Chase and scolded her for referring in *Our Irish Theatre* to their meeting at Lord Morris's: 'I knew that some fool would say we brought in Lord Morris because it sounded grand.' NLI MS 13,575 is an absorbing notebook and three files of notes accumulated for this project; in this first version there is far more autobiographical reference to mediums and seances than in the published form.

21. See *AM*, 328. For progress on *Player Queen*, WBY to AG, 12 Feb. 1915; for Ricketts's plans, same to same, 1 May 1915, Berg.

22. 13 Apr. 1915, HRHRC. For the reactions to *Responsibilities*, see *AM*, 520–2.

23. See MG MS Book, 18–25 Mar. 1914. A final draft of 'The Fisherman' is dated 4 June [1914] in NLI MS 30,258, and he may have sent a version to MG in Nov.: see MG to WBY, 7 Nov. 1914, *G–YL*, 352.

24. Pound's review of *Responsibilities*, which annoyed JBY, was in *Poetry*, 4, 2 (May 1914). JBY's letter invoking the cold sunrise is in *LTWBY*, i, 289. Also *E & I*, 253, for WBY's later memory of 'copying the phrase from a letter of my father's' and *Au*, *CW*, iii, 174.

25. The 'eye of the mind' would be reprised in the opening line of *At the Hawk's Well*; and for the ideal of 'cold beauty', see Hiro Ishibashi, 'Yeats and the Noh' in Liam Miller (ed.), *The Dolmen Press Yeats Centenary Papers 1965* (Dublin, 1968), 136, where this description recurs.

26. WBY to Gosse, 29 July 1915, Leeds; he first wrote to Gosse on 6 July, and two days later asked Pound to get 'the facts' from Joyce; the letter to Gosse citing the poem was 8 July 1915, Leeds.

27. See *The Egoist*, 2, 8 (2 Aug. 1915) and 2, 9 (1 Sept. 1915). Though published just after WBY's correspondence with Gosse, he would have seen the proofs with Pound.

28. To Pound, 29 July 1915, from Coole, perhaps significantly, Yale. See *AM*, 425–8, for previous difficulty with Gosse.

29. 28 Aug. 1915, Leeds; also see *L*, 600–1.

30. According to notes for taxation liability in MBY, the exact figures for 1913/14 were £413. 11s. 2d. and £423. 6s. 9d. However, in another computation done by calendar year, in NLI MS 30,398, WBY's earnings (not counting the pension) were £392. 12s. 11d. for 1913, and £432 for 1914: leaving out '£500 from America used to pay old debts of lean years before I was pensioned' (i.e., to AG; see *AM*, 503, 517). This account shows £452 for 1915, but only £173 for 1916. The discrepancy cannot be wholly explained by computing by calendar year rather than financial year: it is probable that the computation in NLI MS 30,398 was drawn up at the time of his marriage, to satisfy the Hyde Lees trustees, and errs on the side of exaggeration. On 30 June [1917] he wrote to AG recalling 'the disaster of the first year of the war, when I only made £150 above my pension & had to draw on the bank' (Berg).

31. 7 Apr. 1915, Kansas.

32. 5 Apr. 1915, NYPL. For WBY's instructions about AG's fact-finding mission, see his letter of 29 Jan. 1915, Berg. On 15 Mar. 1915 she sent a long letter estimating JBY's needs and describing Miss Petitpas as 'hard as nails' (Berg).

33. See AG to WBY, 9 Apr. 1915, Berg. 'About your M.S. – Quinn said he did not know how much to offer for it (the autobiography) till he sees it – he wd compare it with

Conrad's prices – I think he puts you on a par with Conrad – & perhaps this is right, for prose – your poems ought to have a special price being hors concours.'

34. 4 May 1915, NYPL.

35. 15 June 1915, NYPL.

36. 5 Nov. 1915, Bodleian, MSS Eng. Lett. c. 194–5, e. 87–8, letter 139. For Quinn's approach to JY, see letter of 15 Sept. 1918, NYPL; for his offer for the *Reveries* MS, WBY to Quinn, 12 Sept. 1915, NYPL.

37. Quinn to Seumas O'Brien, 24 Feb. 1915, NYPL. Two entertainingly infuriated letters from Quinn to Ernest Boyd, 31 Mar. and 3 Apr. 1915, in similar vein, have been printed by Declan Kiely in the *Recorder*, 15, 1 (Spring, 2002), 62–72.

38. '"Dust Hath Closed Helen's Eye"', *CT* (1902 ed.), 32. Also mentioned in 'The Literary Movement in Ireland', *UP*, ii, 189.

39. 29 Jan. [1915], Berg.

40. 20 May 1915, Berg.

41. See *AM*, 493–8.

42. See Lane to AG, 30 Dec. 1914 and 28 Apr. 1915, Berg. Doubts were expressed about the authenticity of some of Lane's great 'finds'. See Langton Douglas to Sarah Purser, 15 Aug. 1917, on his famous Titian (though Ricketts pronounced it a 'pearl', Robert Ross to Alec Martin, 26 July 1917). (Both in NLI MS 10,201).

43. Lane to AG, 23 May 1914, Berg; AG to WBY, 22 Feb. 1914, Berg. My thanks to Deirdre Toomey for the unpublished Ricketts quote from his diary (22 Apr. 1904).

44. 25 May 1914, Berg. The pictures given included El Greco's *St Francis in Ecstasy* and Goya's *Portrait of a Spanish Girl*. See Thomas Bodkin, *Hugh Lane and His Pictures* (Dublin, 1934), 32–3, for the rest of this astonishing list.

45. 12 Nov. 1913, Berg.

46. AG, *Case for the Return of Sir Hugh Lane's Pictures to Dublin* (Dublin, 1926), 42. For a valuable commentary establishing the London Gallery's attitude to Lane's bequest *before* his death, and indicating AG's and WBY's suspicion of Curzon, see Anne Kelly's Ph.D. thesis 'Perfect Ambition: Thomas Bodkin, a Life, with Particular Reference to His Influence on the Early Development of Irish Cultural Policy', TCD, 2001. In 1957, after a detailed investigation for the London Gallery, Dennis Mahon concluded 'the will by which the pictures are legally ours would not have come into existence at all had our predecessors made clear to Lane, when accepting his offer of a loan, all the conditions which attached to that acceptance' (Kelly, 213).

47. 24 June 1915, NYPL.

48. See the affidavits in AG, *Hugh Lane*, 37–48.

49. 'Clairvoyant Search for Will', TS in Berg and printed in AG, *Hugh Lane: His Life and Legacy* (Gerrards Cross, 1973). On 14 June 1915 WBY recorded a particularly specific set of instructions received via Mrs Cannock about Lane's desk, the position of the Trustees, and the valuation of the pictures. On 18 June yet more specific details came through 'Dr Coulter', Charlotte Herbine's control. Both are preserved in Berg. There is plenty more in NLI MS 30,081, a black notebook transcribing events of a seance, followed by a report dated 2 July 1915. WBY attended a seance with Etta Wriedt on 15 July, and on 20 July set up an automatic-writing session with Felicia Scatcherd, which helped inspire his 'Leo Africanus' manuscript (see Adams and Harper's edition, *YA* 1, 1982, 12–13) – though it probably began as a search for the will. For Hester Travers Smith, see her *Voices from the Void* (London, 1919), 34, 38.

50. [June 1915], Berg.

51. To *IT*, dated 15 Dec. 1916. Bailey said the same thing in a letter to WBY, dated 17 Jan. 1917, Berg.

52. See Lane to AG, 13 Feb. 1914, Berg; Lane pointedly told her 'it is important to have people on the spot who can attend meetings'.

53. To Quinn, 24 June 1915. It is reproduced as the back endpaper of *AM* (hardback edition).

54. To Bailey, 25 June 1915, Berg: a carbon, sent to AG by WBY. This was in reply to Bailey's restrained initial reaction: 'Your suggestion of Robert Gregory is very interesting. I am sure that he would make an excellent & accomplished Director with knowledge & taste. The difficulty I see is that he is not well known to the Governors.'

55. 15 July 1915, Berg. Witt elegantly distanced himself by telling AG that since Ross was also a candidate he could not stand in his way (8 Aug. 1915, Berg); later he came out as an implacable opponent of returning the pictures to Dublin. For AG's approach to getting Robert in, see her letter of 'Wednesday 23' [probably June 1915], Berg:

    I asked Robert yesterday if he thought Binyon would be a good man for the N. G. He said probably not very enterprising but on the whole he thought good. I don't know if Robert would take it if offered, and sometimes I think he would be better without, yet I think it right to suggest him, in view of the 'Irishman' cry that will be worked by Bodkin. Do you remember when Robert had his first exhibition Hugh said 'One sees a distinguished mind behind the pictures'. That is just what R. has, besides knowledge. However, as to that matter, our chief business is not to let Bodkin get in by default.

56. 17 July 1915, Berg. The executor, J. J. Meagher, wanted Lane's fortune to go to his family instead, though they were in accord with his declared wishes (unlike the painter Sarah Cecilia Harrison, who tried to make a claim on some of the estate on the unlikely grounds that she and Lane had been engaged to be married). WBY's description clearly identifies Meagher rather than co-executor Grant Richards.

57. To AG, 17 July 1915, Berg.

58. ibid.

59. 22 June 1915, Kenyon.

60. WBY to ECY, 24 and 31 July 1915, Boston College; for Leo Africanus and the encyclopedia, WBY to Agnes Tobin, 4 June 1915, private collection. *Chambers's Biographical Dictionary* occurs frequently in the unpublished 'letter' that WBY wrote to Leo two years later, eventually published in *YA* 1 (1982), 23, 27.

61. Messages recorded 24 May 1914, 29 July 1915, MBY. Edith Lyttelton's account is in the Chandos Papers, Churchill College, Cambridge.

62. 28 Mar. [1915], Princeton. For his long-standing interest in Adam Clarke, see *CL*, i, 373–4.

63. Notably on Dame Alice Kyteler and her incubus, who would provide the conclusion to 'Nineteen Hundred and Nineteen'. The story of Lord Orrery's butler, used in *Visions and Beliefs*, occurs in St John Seymour too. Father Ludovico Sinistrari of Ameno wrote *Demoniality, or Incubi and Succubi: a Treatise where in it is shown that there are in existence on earth rational creatures besides man, endowed like him with a body and a soul . . .*, supposedly discovered in 1872, and printed in English in 1879.

64. 24 June 1915, NYPL.

65. Offences detailed in a memo, 'Reasons for dismissal of manager, July 17th 1915', Berg. Telegrams from AG to WBY on 23 June and 16 July gave him full authority to fire Wilson, and suggested further ruthless dismissals and cuts. A letter of 'Wednesday 23' [probably June 1915] (Berg) showed how critical things had become: only music-hall profits could keep their heads above water, and she was considering begging Shaw to give a benefit lecture 'on the war or anything he liked'. Kathleen McConaghy to AG, 18 June 1915 (Berg) revealed that £800–£1,000 was necessary just to carry on for a year, having made losses of £1,200 the previous year, despite good plays and several lettings; they had lost £580 already that quarter; closure was looming. Letters from Harris and Bailey to AG tell the same story. For the Marsala, see WBY to AG, postmark 13 July 1915, Berg.

66. See W. B. Yeats, *The Writing of 'The Player Queen'. Manuscripts of W. B. Yeats*, transcribed, edited and with a commentary by Curtis Bradford (DeKalb, Ill., 1977), Chapter 12. Bradford relates this development to the writing of 'Ego Dominus Tuus'. For Mrs Campbell and the commissioning of the play, see *AM*, 385–6.

67. To AG, n.d. [but 7 Jan. 1916], Berg.

68. Bradford, *'Player Queen'*, 417.

69. *MYV*, ii, 276 (automatic-writing session, 24 May 1919); see below, p. 154.

70. 'Lecture on Symbolism', TS, Dulac Collection, HRHRC.

71. To AG, 13 Oct. 1915, Berg.

72. WBY to Horace Plunkett, 5 Nov. 1915, Plunkett Foundation, Oxford.

73. WBY to AG, 19 Nov. 1915, Berg.

74. 15 Nov. 1915, Huntington. For the can-can, see Ian Hamilton's TS of reminiscences written for Joseph Hone, Hone Papers, HRHRC.

75. 1 Dec. 1915, Berg.

76. 10 Dec. 1915, Boston College.

77. SMY to JBY, 20 Nov. 1916, transcription courtesy of William M. Murphy.

78. *Nationality*, 19 Jan. 1916.

79. Michael Holroyd, *Bernard Shaw. Volume 2: The Pursuit of Power 1898–1918* (London, 1989), 379.

80. GBS to WBY, 17 Oct. 1915, HRHRC.

81. WBY to AG, 19 Nov. 1915, Berg.

82. See Nathan to Birrell, 14 Nov. 1915, Letter-book 'Ireland', vol. 4, Nathan MS 465, Bodleian. On 16 Nov. Nathan wrote politely to GBS, after 'consulting confidentially', saying that to put it on 'would result in demonstrations which could do no good either to the Abbey theatre or to the cause that, at any rate, a large section of Irishmen have made their own'. He went on to express agreement with what (he said) GBS had argued in a letter to him: 'that this war does give to the most thinking of all peasantries the chance of contact with the wider world which enables them to rise above the hopelessness derived from their old recollections and surroundings'. My thanks to Ben Novick for these references.

83. Same to same, 1 Dec. 1915, Berg.

84. 15 Nov. 1915, Huntington. The previous month he told her, 'I want you to understand that I want you to come any Monday evening that you please. I wonder when I am to come to see you.' (n.d. [but Oct. 1915], Huntington). The reference to needing a woman friend is in WBY to Quinn, 19 Dec. 1915, NYPL.

85. The chair and the candles strongly suggest Woburn Buildings. The *Catholic Anthology* had a Futurist cover designed by Dorothy Pound, and also included WBY's 'The Scholars', Eliot's 'Prufrock', and 'Portrait of a Lady'. For WBY's remark about Schepeler's 'tortuous existence', see his letter to her of 25 Oct. 1915, Huntington; Schepeler leaving WBY, 'disconsolate', AG to Schepeler, 4 Sept. 1914, Huntington.

86. This is to accept the composition dates given in NLI MS 30,258. 'A Deep-Sworn Vow' is dated 17 Oct. 1915; the first version of the first stanza of 'Broken Dreams', 24 Oct. 1915; nearly final versions of 'Presences' in Nov. 1915 and 'The Dawn', Sept. 1915. James Longenbach has 'The Dawn' as one of the poems sent by Pound to Monroe on 31 Jan. 1915, but this seems incorrect: *Stone Cottage*, 146.

87. See George Bornstein, 'Yeats's Romantic Dante', *Colby Library Quarterly*, 15, 25 (June 1979), 103 ff., for the Dantean theme – and the way that WBY absorbed Dante via Rossetti.

88. See Brian John, 'Yeats and Carlyle', *Notes and Queries*, 215 (Dec. 1970), 455.

89. 5 Apr. 1915, NYPL.

90. This revealing comment is in ECY to Quinn, 3 Aug. 1915, NYPL. 'We have a time of it putting in punctuation for W. B. He has a lovely way of disregarding it altogether. So we

put it in as we go along and then let him have it in proof. His proof always delays us a good deal as he rewrites whole passages in proof, but with this book he hasn't rewritten so much.'

91. n.d. [but 19 Dec. 1915], Boston College, and *L*, 602–3; 'Mrs Smith' is Hester Travers Smith, the well-known medium; see below, pp. 352–3.

92. 14 July 1917, NLI MS 31,114.

93. *PF*, 448. SMY's remarks are in a letter to Quinn, 23 Aug. 1916, NYPL.

94. *Kangaroo* (1923, reprinted New York, 1970), 220.

95. Longenbach, *Stone Cottage*, 260–1.

96. See below for a consideration of his 'Letter to Leo Africanus' and dialogue 'The Poet and the Actress', which also belong to this mood. Eventually printed in *YA* 1 (1982) and *YA* 8 (1991) respectively.

97. See Sylvia C. Ellis, *The Plays of W. B. Yeats. Yeats and the Dancer* (London, 1995), 7–8, 94. For Osman Edwards see *CL*, ii, 165, 596–7.

98. Akhtar Qambar, *Yeats and the Noh, with Two Plays for Dancers, by W. B. Yeats and Two Noh Plays* (New York, 1974), 49ff. Also see Yoko Chiba, review of Masaru Sekine and Christopher Murray, *Yeats and the Noh: A Comparative Study*, *YA* 10 (1993), 298–301; and Masaru D. Sekine, 'Four Plays for Dancers: Japanese Aesthetics and a European Mind' in A. Norman Jeffares (ed.), *Yeats the European* (Gerrards Cross, 1989), 233.

99. WBY to JBY, 14 Mar. [1916], Boston College and *L*, 608–9.

100. Ellmann, *IY*, 216. The text is full of echoes, not only from WBY himself: for instance, he may have remembered the phrase 'a mouthful of air' from Seumas O'Sullivan's 'Nelson Street' in the Cuala 'Broadside', no. 1, Fourth Year (June 1911).

101. *Certain Noble Plays of Japan*. Influences in the play are fully dealt with in F. A. C. Wilson, *Yeats's Iconography* (London, 1960), Chapter 1.

102. Dulac to Hone, 16 Apr. 1940, NLI MS 5919, puts their first meeting 'in 1912 or 1913', adding that they often met at Pound's or with Ricketts and Shannon, but their close association began with *At the Hawk's Well*.

103. See his 'Vers Libre and Arnold Dolmetsch', *The Egoist*, July 1917, 90.

104. These arrangements are preserved in the correspondence, sketches, and musical scores in the Dulac collection at HRHRC.

105. See Anthony Thwaite, 'A Talk with Ito', *Truth*, 3 Aug. 1956.

106. 25 Mar. 1915, Beardsley Collection, Princeton.

107. See Mann to WBY, 29 Mar. 1916, HRHRC.

108. Pound to Quinn, 26 Feb. 1916, NYPL. Interestingly, the 'farce' was pseudo-Irish: 'The Consolations of Matrimony' by 'Oge Terrence O'Cullough'. WBY's opinion of it has not survived.

109. *Observer*, 9 Apr. 1916.

110. See *Plays and Controversies* (London, 1923), 415–19; and WBY to Schepeler, postmarked 27 Apr. 1916, Huntington. 'Hawk's Well went well & will soon be ready that my friends may see it. None were at the charity show.'

111. To W. S. Blunt, 4 Apr. [1916], Berg.

112. Lyndall Gordon, *T. S. Eliot: An Imperfect Life* (London, 1998), 100.

113. Stella Bowen, in *Drawn from Life* (London, 1941), mentions Eliot and WBY attending the Soho evenings in 1914/15. Eliot wrote on 30 Sept. 1914 that he hoped to meet WBY with the Pounds; but on 4 Apr. 1915 he told Mrs Jack Gardner 'the last time I was [in London] I had the pleasure of meeting Yeats', implying that this encounter (in Jan.) had been the first. See Valerie Eliot (ed.), *The Letters of T. S. Eliot. Volume 1: 1898–1922* (London, 1988), 58, 95. In 1920 WBY allegedly told Quinn he disliked Eliot's work: Quinn to Pound, 6 Mar. 1920 [copy], NYPL.

114. Longenbach, *Stone Cottage*, 211.

115. See Wilson, *Yeats's Iconography*, 69–72.

116. *L*, 610.

117. Letter to Cathleen Nesbitt, quoted in D. Fielding, *Emerald and Nancy: Lady Cunard and Her Daughter* (London, 1968), 70–1. Sturge Moore reported on the same performance to his wife (n.d., Sturge Moore Papers, University of London, MS 978/35/401 A): he was impressed but disliked Maud Mann's singing. 'After the play there was a sort of council of war & Lady Cunard shone. It was very interesting – she has good sense, great ability, not much taste, but courage and energy.'

118. 5 Mar. 1916, Berg.

119. Pound to Quinn, 19 July 1916, NYPL. Also *FJ*, 30 May 1916, for troubles at the Abbey: theatre-goers who turned up for a performance in Limerick the day before had been greeted by the players with hand-outs denouncing Ervine. Though Bailey, for one, thought him wasteful, extravagant, and headstrong (letter to WBY, 9 June 1916, Berg), Pound would certainly have trumped his record.

120. 10 Jan. 1917, NYPL.

121. In fact, WBY received £210 from Macmillan only in June 1916, when his agent, A. P. Watt, returned the contract for a new six-volume *Collected Edition*. The sum was reduced because Bullen handed over fewer books than expected. See Warwick Gould, 'W. B. Yeats on the Road to St Martin's Street 1900–1917' in Elizabeth James (ed.), *Macmillan: A Publishing Tradition* (London, 2002), 205.

122. Hone (1916), 40–1. There are a few small changes from the version printed by Cork University Press as *Tribute to Thomas Davis by W. B. Yeats* (1947, 1965).

Chapter 2 : SHADES AND ANGELS
1916–1917

1. *New Statesman*, 15 Apr. 1916. The favoured charity was the Star and Garter Fund.

2. AG to WBY, 11 July [1915], Berg, and 'Thursday 22' [also 1915], Stony Brook, I.2.D, Box 61.

3. See AG to WBY, n.d. [but 1915–16], Stony Brook, I.2.D, Box 61; WBY to AG, 19 Nov. and 20 Dec. 1915, Berg.

4. Wedderburn visitor-book, HRHRC.

5. Desmond Ryan, quoted in Monk Gibbon, 'Murder in Portobello Barracks', *Dublin Magazine*, 5, 1 (Spring, 1966), 14.

6. 22 May 1916, NYPL.

7. To Lennox Robinson, 7 Jan. 1915, SIUC; to AG, 2 May 1915, Berg.

8. See James Longenbach, *Stone Cottage: Pound, Yeats and Modernism* (Oxford, 1988), 256, and Pound to Quinn, 1 May 1916, NYPL.

9. n.d., [but annotated by ECY 'I got this some days ago on May 1'], Yeats Collection, Princeton.

10. 8 May [1916], HRHRC.

11. Charles Ricketts, *Self-Portrait* (London, 1939), compiled by T. S. Moore and edited by C. S. Lewis, 256. Ricketts later annotated this diary entry: 'P.S. I was an idiot.' The 'strange Irish impartiality' comment is in the unpublished version, BL Add. MSS 58107: my thanks to Deirdre Toomey. Compare SMY to JBY, quoted in JBY to Eulalee Dix Becker [copy], 30 May 1916, Yeats Collection, Princeton: 'Lincoln would have kept them in prison under a suspended sentence & then let them go – to wear out the rest of their days in penitential reflection on the misery they caused –'

12. Both these letters are in Berg, with excisions by the wartime censor.

13. 13 May [1916], Berg.

14. 14 May [1916], Berg. For the Shelley reference, see 'On the Punishment of Death', reprinted in D. L. Clark (ed.), *Shelley's Prose: or, The Trumpet of a Prophecy* (1954; new ed., London, 1988), 156.

15. 23 May 1916, Berg.

16. To WBY, 27 May [1916], Berg.

17. Martyn to AG, 19 May 1916, Berg.

18. To JBY, 7 May 1916, transcription by William M. Murphy.

19. To R L-P, n.d., and 16 May 1916, transcription by William M. Murphy.

20. Pound to Alice Corbin Henderson, 3 May 1916, in Ira B. Nadel (ed.), *The Letters of Ezra Pound to Alice Corbin Henderson* (Austin, Texas, 1993), 133; Pound to Quinn, received 13 June 1916, NYPL.

21. To Ernest Boyd, 29 May 1916, Healy.

22. SMY to R L-P, 16 May 1916, transcription by William M. Murphy; ECY to James F. Drake, 13 June 1916, HRHRC; AE to Quinn, 30 Nov. 1916, NYPL.

23. *Nationality*, 29 Jan. 1916; see above, p. 28.

24. BL Add. MSS 58107: my thanks to Deirdre Toomey.

25. WBY to Mrs Beardsley, 10 May 1916, Beardsley Collection, Princeton.

26. 11 May 1916, Berg, and *L*, 612–14.

27. See esp. WBY to Quinn, 23 May 1916, NYPL.

28. See AG to WBY, 'Tuesday 6th' [1915–16], Stony Brook, I.2.D, Box 61; WBY to Eva Gore-Booth, 23 July 1916, *Review of English Literature*, 4 (July, 1963), 24–5; Brian Inglis, *Roger Casement* (London, 1973), 386. JBY 'spent a day [in 1915] with Sir Roger Casement – Quinn tried to convince poor Sir Roger that his ideas were madness.' To Eulalee Dix Becker, 30 May 1916 (copy), Princeton. A copy of WBY's letter to Asquith is in NLI MS 10,564, dated 14 July 1916 ('the evil has been done, it cannot be undone, but it need not be aggravated weeks afterwards with every circumstance of deliberation'). According to Michael Laffan, *The Resurrection of Ireland: The Sinn Féin Party 1916–1923* (Cambridge, 1995), it is not to be found in the Asquith papers. Ethel Mannin later claimed WBY told her 'he only gave his signature to the appeal for the reprieve of Casement to please Maud Gonne, who nagged him into it': lecture notes for speech at Sligo, Mannin Papers, Boston University.

29. 23 July 1916, *Review of English Literature*, 4 (July 1963), 24–5.

30. Ronald Schuchard, '"An Attendant Lord": H. W. Nevinson's Friendship with W. B. Yeats', *YA* 7 (1990), 117.

31. AG to WBY, 25 May 1916, Berg. The letter to Quinn about getting into the country, partly in *L*, 614, is in NYPL.

32. *FJ*, 30 May 1916; Bailey to WBY, 9 June 1916, Berg; AG to WBY, 8 July 1916, Berg, telling him 'we can't let the Abbey die on the verge of Home Rule or let it die at all after all the work we have put into it'. There is an account of the players' revolt in Dawson Byrne, *The Story of Ireland's National Theatre* (Dublin, 1929), 106 ff., which sounds first-hand. Also see AG to Quinn, 8 July and 26 Aug. 1916, Berg. The cocksure description is in SMY to R L-P, 29 May 1939.

33. Pound's explosive letters, which also show the part played by WBY, are in Berkeley. Also see Longenbach, *Stone Cottage*, 252–3.

34. 11 June 1916, NYPL. The visit lasted 2–8 June.

35. See *AM*, 359–67.

36. AG to WBY, 'Thursday 25' [May 1916], and 9 June [1916], Berg.

37. White vellum notebook, kept from 1908, MBY.

38. 19 Aug. [1916], private collection.

39. To Tagore, 31 July 1915, Visra-Bharati University, Santiniketan, West Bengal.

40. IG to WBY, 25 Aug. 1915, Jeffares, White and Bridgwater.

41. See *YA* 7 (1990), 118; George Mills Harper, *W. B. Yeats and W. T. Horton: The Record of an Occult Friendship* (London, 1980), 88 ff.; Nancy Cardozo, *Lucky Eyes and a High Heart: The Life of Maud Gonne* (New York, 1978), 310.

42. *G–YL*, 378.

43. 3 July 1916, Berg.

44. WBY to MG, *G–YL*, 378; AG to WBY, 8 July [1916], Berg.

45. 2 Oct. 1916, Jeffares, White and Bridgwater.

46. 14 Aug. 1916, Berg.

47. 20 Aug. 1916, Berg.

48. Pound to Quinn, 31 Aug. 1916, NYPL, reports a wire from WBY to expect him in London that evening. WBY wrote to SMY on 15 Sept., announcing his arrival that morning, and his imminent departure: on the 17th Gogarty reported to Starkie that he had seen WBY and AG on Grafton Street two days before.

49. 2 Oct. 1916, Jeffares, White and Bridgwater.

50. 15 Oct. 1916, Jeffares, White and Bridgwater.

51. The comma was later dropped, but I am quoting the poem in the version printed by Clement Shorter and preserved (in carbon) in NLI MS 30,216. A TS copy at Huntington with WBY's corrections has the Markievicz passage as given here.

52. 20 Jan. 1915, private collection. The notion of dedication to an ideal, pitched against the claims of life, had come up in his conversation with Ricketts, and also in the autobiographical reflection eventually published as *Memoirs*, where the image of stoniness is repeatedly associated with MG.

53. See *AM*, 417–21, for a full discussion.

54. Maud Gonne, 'An Account of Yeats', 1939, HRHRC: reprinted in Stephen Gwynn (ed.), *Scattering Branches: Tributes to the Memory of W. B. Yeats* (London, 1940).

55. As in NLI MS 30,216. The substitution of Connolly for Markievicz at the end is interesting. There is an obvious reason in that he was executed and she was not, but his later poems on her verge on the denunciatory, and he was probably unwilling to apostrophize her here. The line 'wherever green is worn' is an indirect invocation of the famous rebel ballad 'The Wearing of the Green': compare his use of 'The Green above the Red' in 'September 1913' (*AM*, 496).

56. 15 Oct. 1916, Jeffares, White and Bridgwater.

57. 8 Nov. 1916, *G Y–L*, 384–5.

58. *Journals*, i, 20.

59. 28 Mar. [1917], Berg.

60. See Elizabeth Butler Cullingford, *Yeats, Ireland and Fascism* (London, 1981), 98 (quoting from a transcript of Richard Ellmann's), and AG to WBY, 12 Sept. [1916], Berg.

61. 16 May 1917, NYPL.

62. 27 Dec. 1916.

63. See WBY to Ellen Duncan, 19 Jan. 1917, and to AG, 20 Jan. 1917, Berg.

64. 18 Nov. 1916, Berg.

65. See W. F. Bailey to AG, 6 Nov. 1916, Berg, for their readiness to back a bill in the Lords; also numerous references to AG's journals and letters.

66. See a letter from AE to *The Times*, 14 Dec. 1916, denouncing him: AE was deeply committed to the Lane Gallery as a necessary decentralization of artistic resources.

67. WBY to Ellen Duncan, 17 Dec. 1916 and 19 Jan. 1917, Gilvarry Collection (sold at Christie's, New York, 7 Feb. 1986). The *Observer* interview is reprinted in *UP*, ii, 418–19. There were also letters to *The Times* dated 11 Dec. 1916, and to the *Morning Post*, 18 Dec. 1916.

68. See WBY to AG, 10 and 24 Feb. 1917, Berg.

69. See WBY to AG, 29 Jan. 1917, Berg, and 12 Mar. 1917, ibid., accompanying proofs, which clearly show his authorship. The pamphlet, called *Sir Hugh Lane's French Pictures*, was printed at the Chiswick Press in 1917.

70. WBY to Quinn, 1 Aug. [1916], NYPL, and to Farr, 19 Aug. 1916, private collection: true to form, she did not mind at all.

71. W. B. Yeats, *Memoirs. Autobiography – First Draft, Journal*, edited by Denis Donoghue (London, 1972): in these notes, *Mem*. Also see James Olney, *The Rhizome and the Flower. The Perennial Philosophy – Yeats and Jung* (London, 1980), especially 6. Olney, however, did not know the MS passage quoted below, which specifically mentions Jung. WBY's library contained a 1916 edition of Jung's *Collected Papers on Analytical Psychology*.

72. WBY to Quinn, 16 Aug. 1916, NYPL.

73. According to a letter to Farr of that date, private collection.

74. 9 Nov. 1916, Jeffares, White and Bridgwater.

75. Pound to Quinn, 3 Sept. 1916, NYPL; Moore to Eglinton, 28 Aug. 1919, John Eglinton (ed.), *Letters of George Moore* (Bournemouth, n.d.).

76. To Macmillan, 14 Sept. 1916, BL Add. MSS 55003.

77. For letter to SMY, see NLI MS 3255. The poem is simply called 'In Memory', and is postmarked from France, 24 Aug. 1916. It was printed in the *Little Review*, June 1917.

78. AG to WBY, 5 Nov. 1917, Berg.

79. See WBY to Troubridge, 3 and 13 Dec. 1916, 2 and 31 Jan. 1917, Lovat Dickson Papers, National Archives of Canada, Toronto.

80. Schuchard, '"An Attendant Lord"', 119–20.

81. As reported by SMY. 'They want women badly in the company. They are so plain, the present lot, plain and poor in type, rather the stage-struck type Willy was so anxious to keep out of the Abbey – little chorus girl types. The Allgoods have character. Sally has a kind of richness of character, Molly has character, not very deep.' (To R L-P, 7 Jan. 1917).

82. This passage continues:

That is why we poets pass on age after age an artificial language, inherited from the first poets, and always full of reminiscent symbols, which grow, richer in association every time, they are used, for new emotions. In primitive communities, where men are not yet crowded together, and so are able to find time when they speak to express emotion as well as describe facts in real language fit for the use of a great artist. Yet even Synge concentrated, and enriches the language he found in Arran, or in the Blaskets, and in the one play where he expresses his vision, without its antagonist the grotesque, he throws the events backward in time that he might obtain a more powerful phantasmagoria.

I am following the transcription of David R. Clark, who has printed 'The Poet and the Actress' in *YA* 8 (1991), 123–45.

83. See Steve L. Adams and George Mills Harper (eds.), 'The Manuscript of Leo Africanus', *YA* 1 (1982), 3–47. The date of composition, left conjectural by Adams and Harper, is fixed as Dec. 1916 by WBY's correspondence with Alick Schepeler (Huntington). For the background to WBY's association with Leo Africanus, see *AM*, 464–6. WBY believed that his 'guide' had possibly first made contact in 1898–9, but the major connection was established in 1912.

84. *YA* 1, 13.

85. ibid., 26–7.

86. ibid., 28. Some of this passage is reused in *Per Amica Silentia Lunae* (*Myth*, 332). Adams and Harper believe it originated from a script of Elizabeth Radcliffe's.

87. ibid., 22.

88. See WBY to Harriet Monroe, 21 July 1917, *Poetry* Archive, University of Chicago; WBY

to AG, 11 Feb. 1917, Berg; and WBY to Craig, 4 Sept. 1917, Arsenal, Paris (where it is misattributed to 1914). The following discussion is based not only on the published version (first as a slim book in 1918, then in a slight variation in *Myth*, from which quotations are taken), but also on MS versions in HRHRC and NLI MS 30,368 – an earlier draft. The HRHRC version was partly created for Quinn's collection. The NLI draft is probably the rejected first version mentioned in a letter to Pound, 2 May 1917, Yale. See also William H. O'Donnell and Elizabeth Loizeaux (eds.), *W. B. Yeats: Later Essays* (London, 1994), 461.

89. See *Myth*, 326, for a passage lifted from his 1914 'Theatre of Beauty' lecture, as in *AM*, 511–12.

90. See *Myth*, 328: 'When I think of any great poetical writer of the past (a realist is a historian and obscures the cleavage of the record of his eyes), I comprehend, if I know the lineaments of his life, that the work is the man's flight from his entire horoscope, his blind struggle in the network of the stars.' He goes on to 'typify' writers like Morris, Landor, and Keats.

91. *Myth*, 331.

92. *Ex*, 35. In Oct. 1916, Nevinson recorded a conversation with him about 'Freud and Jung and the Subconscious self, applying the doctrine to art' (*Last Changes, Last Chances*, London, 1928, 123).

93. NLI MS 30,368.

94. *Myth*, 346.

95. *Myth*, 354–5.

96. See Longenbach, *Stone Cottage*, 245.

97. *Myth*, 360. It is not in the HRHRC MS, and was probably inserted in proof.

98. *Myth*, 363.

99. *Myth*, 364–6.

100. AE to Quinn, 11 Feb. 1918, NYPL; JBY to AG, 1 Apr. 1918, Berg; Bottomley to Moore, 17 Feb. 1918, Sturge Moore Papers, University of London, MS 978/17/115. Bottomley was, however, deeply shocked at WBY's remarks about Keats's breeding.

101. Compare Longenbach, *Stone Cottage*, 245. He postulates close assonances between *Per Amica* and Pound's simultaneous enterprise in *Three Cantos*, both based on the poets' reading at Stone Cottage. This is suggestive, but leaves out the effect on WBY of his Colleville summer, and the connections to 'Leo Africanus'. *Per Amica* also bears interesting parallels to his friend F. P. Sturm's *Umbrae Silentes*, which was written in 1917 and published in 1918. It too deals with occult spiritual experience and aesthetic theory, displaying wide reading in arcane texts. Sturm frequented Watkin's famous bookshop in Cecil Court at this time, along with WBY, but it seems likely that his text was composed slightly later. See Richard Taylor (ed.), *Frank Pearce Sturm: His Life, Letters and Collected Work* (Urbana, Ill., 1969), 26ff.

102. 6 June 1917, Jeffares, White and Bridgwater, apparently responding to an early draft. She said that she had never discerned in his thought 'a sense of collectivity as in Péguy'; his soul followed the solitary path of the few, like Villiers de l'Isle-Adam or Pater.

103. See *AM*, 505. The published version of *Per Amica* has 'May 9, 1917' at the end; the HRHRC MS has '6' changed to '9' and 'April' crossed out, possibly a result of the page being copied later to fill in a blank for the Quinn copy (see below, p. 185). In this MS appears the original wording quoted above, and the 'Epilogue' is a 'Prologue'.

104. Arnold Bennett, *The Journals*, selected and edited by Frank Swinnerton (Harmondsworth, 1917), 404–5. He described Peters as 'a man of forty-five or so. Short, good forehead. Bald on top, dark hair at sides. Quick and nervous. Son of a bargeowner.' A barrister called Jowitt was also present, with a beautiful wife.

105. Wilson to 'Gow', n.d. [but Feb. or Mar. 1916], HRHRC.

106. WBY to Wilson, 3 Feb. 1917, Wake Forest. WBY visited Wilson on 30 Jan., a visit lasting from 2 p.m. until midnight, and returned with Dulac and Ross on 22 Mar. Estelle Stead wrote an account of Wilson's machine in *Light*, 20 Jan. 1917. The principle of the machine owed much to von Reichenbach's theory of 'Odic force', with which WBY was familiar (see *AM*, 49). WBY's lengthy report is in MBY; Dulac's more tongue-in-cheek account (with sketches) in HRHRC. The TS 'Clairvoyant Search for Will' (Berg) shows that WBY knew of Wilson as early as June 1915, when he enlisted his help to get a message from Lane. For Wilson and his machine see Christopher Blake, 'Ghosts in the Machine: W. B. Yeats and the Metallic Homunculus', *YA* 15 (2002), 69–101.

107. See Wilson to 'Gow', 25 and 29 Feb. 1916, HRHRC.

108. WBY to Wilson, 4 Feb. [1917], Wake Forest, and to Gilbert Murray, 22 Feb. 1917, Bodleian MS G.M.54; Una Troubridge's diary, 13 Feb. 1917, Lovat Dickson Papers, National Archives of Canada, Toronto.

109. WBY to Wilson, 4 Feb. [1917], Wake Forest, and to Dulac, 4 Apr. 1917, HRHRC.

110. To Gertrude Kingston, 1 July 1917, King's College, Cambridge.

111. Compare Dulac in his address on WBY to the Irish Literary Society, Nov. 1948, HRHRC: 'in our subsequent conversations, Yeats remarked that very likely Mr Wilson had some peculiar gifts but could not produce any phenomena without the help of his machine. He did not believe in the machine as such, but as an indispensable focusing point for Mr Wilson's subconscious activities.' WBY's correspondence at the time, however, shows that he gave it more credence than that.

112. WBY to AG, 24 Feb. [1917], Berg. In the *Little Review* of June 1917, it is dated Oct. 1916. There is a holograph in the Berg dated '13 July 1917', but it was composed much earlier.

113. Pound to Quinn, 3 Apr. 1917, NYPL; also see letters of 11 Apr. and 3 May (Pound was anxious to convince Quinn of the merits of his new publication, to attract backing).

114. See E. Paget's correspondence with Monroe, *Poetry* Archive, University of Chicago, letters of 11 Apr., 6 June and 8 June 1917, and WBY to Monroe, 25 June 1917. By his reckoning, 'last time' he received £16 for eight poems, now he was being offered £7 for seven poems. 'You counted pages & I counted poems.' Also see Nadel, *Letters of Ezra Pound to Alice Corbin Henderson*, 214, n. 3.

115. To AG, 20 Nov. 1916, Berg.

116. To AG, 31 May [1917], Berg. She had written on 26 May asking him to sign a letter to appear in the *IT* on 31 May. The initiative for the Convention had begun with James Douglas and Maurice Moore in Mar.; on 21 May the government announced the summoning of a representative convention; on 26 May AE began to publish his 'Thoughts for a Convention', which became a pamphlet. It was 'a last attempt to bring three parties together', he told AG (26 May 1917, Berg), but he failed to attract the extremes – though moderate Sinn Féiners and Unionists held a watching brief. WBY stayed clear: see below, p. 88.

117. *Alastor*, lines 275–90: see George Bornstein, *Yeats and Shelley* (Chicago, 1970), 104–5. For echoes of Wordsworth, see Mareck H. Darawala, 'Yeats and the Ghost of Wordsworth', *YA* 13 (1998), 215–17.

118. Speaking at Wellesley College in 1932, WBY said that 'all's changed' referred to the circumstances of the war: see Horace Reynolds's notes taken at the lecture, Harvard, b Ms Am 1787[662].

119. To Alice Corbin Henderson, 3 May 1916, in Nadel, *Letters of Ezra Pound to Alice Corbin Henderson*, 133; also WBY to Farr, 19 Aug. [1916], private collection. The 'drunken lady' was one Mary Dormer.

120. A comment recorded in Horace Reynolds's diary, 8 July 1927, Harvard, b Ms Am 1787[5803]. The Bord Fáilte announcement of the tower's renovation in 1963 described it as sixteenth century (NLI MS 30,731). Mary Hanley and Liam Miller, *Thoor Ballylee:*

Home of William Butler Yeats (Dublin, 1965, 1977), 9, describe it as thirteenth or four-teenth century. It is recorded in the *Booke of Connaught*, 1585.

121. Extract from WBY to W. F. Bailey, 2 Oct. 1916, sent on to Sir Henry Doran; Land Commission Records, Dublin. For negotiations, see further letters of 10 Nov. 1916 and 4 Jan. 1917.

122. WBY to Farr, 5 Mar. 1917, private collection.

123. To Quinn, 1 June 1920, NYPL.

124. WBY to AG, 27 Jan. [1916], Berg. These plates were, presumably, for the Cuala edition. For the loan, see an undated letter from AG, 'Tuesday 18', Berg. The context fixes it as during the war. She sends WBY £20, warning him not to pay it into his account, as it would not clear his overdraft; but also says she will have to charge him for his keep at Coole. 'I have less than half what I had a couple of years ago.'

125. See WBY to Congested Districts Board, 9 and 27 Mar. 1917, Land Commission Records. Also see letters to AG, 28 Feb., 1 Mar., 3 Mar., for the bridge issue, and 1 Apr. for the drawing. J. R. O'Brien to W. F. Bailey, 23 Feb. 1917 (NLI 30,763, copy), makes it clear that WBY's agreement to the right of way was a condition of sale (and brought the price down).

126. AG to Quinn, 3 June [1917], and WBY to AG, 4 Apr., 16 June 1917, Berg.

127. 3 June 1917, Berg.

128. Letters to AG, 30 June, 11 May 1917, Berg.

129. 22 Nov. 1916, Berg.

130. 5 Mar. 1917, private collection.

131. This letter of 9 Mar. 1917 is intriguing; if the initials were 'OS' they could not have referred to any possibility of marriage between WBY and OS (Hope Shakespear lived until 1923), but could indicate that OS had been pressing GY hard upon WBY as a candidate, and he had decided to dig his heels in.

132. Berg.

133. To AG, 23 Dec. 1916, Berg.

134. Published in *IT*, 26, 28, 29 May 1917. The letter appeared on 31 May, signed by a broad range of opinion, including AG, Alice Stopford Green, Archbishop Walsh, Gogarty, Lord Monteagle, Hyde, and some moderate Sinn Féiners. However, WBY did briefly associate himself with the 'Society of Irish Tradition', a well-meaning group arguing for cultural compromise, dominated by liberal Protestants; he attended an executive committee meeting on 26 July. See also n. 146 below.

135. 7 Apr. 1917, Gilvarry Collection; on Abbey policy, WBY to AG, 15 Mar. 1917, Berg.

136. 11 June 1917, *L*, 629. It was largely written in May and June, with a final draft in existence by Aug.

137. WBY to Farr, 5 Mar. [1917], private collection; also WBY to JBY, 12 May 1917, *L*, 624–5.

138. WBY to ECY, 13 May 1917, Boston College, making clear that he has finished *The Alphabet* 'and will dictate it to a typist in London in June'; but he would continue revis-ing it throughout the summer. The poetry book is described as 'either very small – 22 or 23 lyrics alone or with a small play Hawks Well'. The judgement 'among my best books' is in a letter to Quinn, 16 May 1917, NYPL.

139. WBY to AG, 7 and 19 June 1917, Berg.

140. WBY to AG, 28 June 1917, Berg.

141. Quoted in *YA* 9 (1992), 249.

142. To AG, 31 May 1917, Berg.

143. WBY's passport, NLI 30,219, is stamped 'Bearer is proceeding on mission for the Foreign Office', 2 Aug. 1917: inaccurately, as it turned out.

144. To AG, 28 June and 15 Aug. 1917, Berg. On 3 Aug. MG wrote to Quinn about the

planned lectures in Paris: Janis and Richard Londraville, *Too Long a Sacrifice: The Letters of Maud Gonne and John Quinn* (Selinsgrove, NJ, 1999), 208.

145. To OS, 10 July 1917, *L*, 627.

146. He did not attend again. Other leading members were Hyde, Alice Stopford Green, Con Curran, and WBY's future enemy Professor Magennis. The *Evening Telegraph* of 15 Feb. 1918 records the Society's first and last council meeting. My thanks to Shane Stephens for sharing his unpublished research with me.

147. 9 Nov. 1916, Jeffares, White and Bridgwater.

148. To Squire, 15 Aug. 1917, HRHRC.

149. Apparently dated 20 Aug. [1917] in Berg, but more probably 2 Aug.

150. *L*, 628–9. For the Dublin rumours, SMY to R L-P, 12 Nov. 1916: Lolly had met Sarah Purser, who opened the conversation with 'So Willy is to marry Isolde Gonne & Louis is seriously ill with influenza.'

151. Cardozo, *Lucky Eyes and a High Heart*, 318. WBY retained a more idyllic memory. 'Nothing of the war reached us except an occasional large green glass globe washed up on the shore, a buoy from some net for catching torpedo boats. Nobody seemed to know or care what was happening.' To SMY, 10 June 1924, Boston College.

152. Harper, *Yeats and Horton*, 57, assumes that WBY was back in London on 5 Sept. trying to get the government to agree to MG's returning to Ireland. But it seems unlikely, as he was still in the Gavarni on 8 Sept., expecting to return on the 14th.

153. 8 Sept. [1917], Berg, and *L*, 631. AG replied on 15 Sep.: 'I think that tendency to melancholy would have been against the marriage, more than almost anything – so I shall put away any regrets.' (Berg).

154. This is the date of WBY's passport stamp: NLI MS 30,219.

155. NYPL.

156. 'Thursday 20' [Sept. 1917], Berg.

157. Berg. The version in *L* leaves out the middle paragraph, by agreement between GY and Wade. The phrase 'true of voice' was borrowed from a letter of Farr's, who attributed it to 'the old Egyptian': see Farr to WBY, 17 May 1914, quoted in *YA* 9 (1992), 238.

Chapter 3 : THE SENSE OF HAPPINESS
1917–1919

1. *The Invisible Censor* (New York, 1918), 117; there is another version, from the *New Republic*, reprinted in *I & R*, i, 133.

2. SMY to John Quinn, 28 Oct. 1917, NYPL. But, according to ECY, they had been expecting a marriage that year. 'We felt sure he meant to.' She does not say to whom. ECY to Paul Lemperley, 25 Jan. 1918, Healy.

3. Nelly Tucker to AG, 30 Sept. 1917, Berg; quoted in full in John Harwood, *Olivia Shakespeare and W. B. Yeats: After Long Silence* (Basingstoke, 1989), 157–8, and below, p. 97. WBY's version was retailed to Ellmann by ESH; Iseult had also been told that WBY and GY had been alone together only once before their engagement.

4. Grace M. Jaffe, 'Vignettes', *YA* 5 (1987), 144.

5. 'Emotion like night mare', *MYV*, ii, 247.

6. Letter to Richard Ellmann, n.d. [but Dec. 1947], Ellmann Papers, Y.8, Tulsa.

7. JBY to Rosa Butt, 20 and 23 Mar. 1920, Bodleian, letters 200–1.

8. WBY to AG, 22 Sept. 1917, Berg. For the letter from AG referred to in his first sentence, see above, p. 92. She had actually advised him to tell GY and her mother that he had to remain attached to the Gonnes because of their political difficulties; WBY, significantly, interpreted it as a message to be given to IG rather than to GY.

9. *BG*, 92, gives many details.

10. See n. 3, above.

11. MBY.

12. My thanks to Elizabeth Heine for showing me a forthcoming article on this subject.

13. Berg.

14. 5 Oct. 1917, MBY.

15. *Three Great Irishmen: Shaw, Yeats, Joyce* (London, 1952), 63.

16. 7 Oct. 1917, MBY. Ann Saddlemyer (*BG*, 101) puts this a week later and thinks it arrived during their honeymoon.

17. WBY to AG, 13 Oct. 1917, and AG to WBY, 'Monday' and 'Thursday' [15 and 18 Oct. 1917], Berg.

18. See *BG*, 99.

19. 'Tuesday evening' [probably 16 Oct. 1917], Jeffares, White and Bridgwater.

20. 'Monday' [probably 15 Oct. 1917], Foster–Murphy Collection, NYPL.

21. *I & R*, ii, 395; Pound to Quinn, 3 Nov. 1917, NYPL; SMY to Quinn, 11 Mar. 1918, NYPL; SMY to R L-P, 18 Aug. 1929. For her legs, same to same, 21 July 1928.

22. Unidentified correspondent, 24 Oct. 1917, NLI MS 13,274.

23. 10 Dec. 1917, NYPL.

24. 17 Nov. 1917, NLI MS 18,674.

25. 5 Jan. 1918, Bodleian, letter 187.

26. See NLI MS 30,398:

    1913 £392. 12s. 11d. + £150 = £522. 12s. 11d.
    1914 £432 + £150 = £582
    1915 £452 + £150 = £602
    1916 £173 + £150 = £323
    1917 £440 + £150 = £590

    The recurring £150 evidently represents WBY's pension, and the remainder are literary earnings. The schedule may have been drawn up for the Tuckers. He adds that 1913/14 brought in £500 from America used 'to pay old debts of lean years before I was pensioned' (see *AM*, 517) and should be added in over the five years 'in calculating earning power', giving an average income of '£623 & some shillings'. For discrepancies from another account, see above, Chapter 1, n. 30. While GY had a trust income from her father's estate (administered on 18 Jan. 1910, following his death on 18 Nov. 1909), it is impossible to decode the contents of the trust from the will. My thanks to Mary-Lou Legg for researching this. Pound, who would have known something through the Shakespear connection, told Wyndham Lewis that GY's financial resources were 'solid but not extensive' (Timothy Materer, ed., *Letters of Ezra Pound and Wyndham Lewis*, New York, 1985, 94).

27. WBY to AG, 24 Oct. 1917, Berg.

28. ibid.

29. It first appeared as 'The Lover Speaks' in the *Dial* for June 1924 (a title significantly reminiscent of his 1890s poems to OS) and was printed as 'Owen Aherne and his Dancers' in *The Tower*.

30. NLI MS 30,358.

31. 26 Oct. 1917, Jeffares, White and Bridgwater.

32. 29 Oct. [1917], Berg.

33. See *MYV*, i, 3–5, GY to WBY, n.d. [but 1924]: 'You ought to finish the Book [*A Vision*] on October 24th – then it will be exactly 7 years since we started it'. (MBY).

34. HRHRC; see *BG*, 101–3.

35. See GY to Ottoline Morrell, 1 Sept. 1922, HRHRC, for advice on mediums; also *BG*, 43 ff., 49 ff., 52, 63–5.
36. See, e.g., 'A Biographical Fragment', *Criterion*, 1, 4 (July, 1923), 318.
37. See *BG*, 65–74, 84–5.
38. *MYV*, i, 12.
39. *YVP*, i, 91; WBY to AG, 3 Nov. 1917, Emory.
40. *MYV*, i, 14. A session on 14 Jan. 1918 (*YVP*, i, 251) produced an interesting key to WBY's symbols:

    Birds – different forms of intellect, when connected with water; emotion, when connected to the air.
    Fish – spiritual, not erotic, desire.
    Wild beasts – passion.
    Tame beasts – race.
    Butterfly – wisdom of love.
    Flying things without a sting, not birds – forms of wisdom.
    Leopards – love.
    Sea-lion – desire.
    Serpent – wisdom (of ages, not acquired, but enforced).
    Eagle – isolation or contemplation.

41. *MYV*, i, 37.
42. *YVP*, i, 159.
43. See NLI MS 30,079, an added note; there is much about the lunar symbolism which he intended to expound in 'my edition of the Robartes papers', i.e., *AV*. The connections between the play and *AV* are surveyed in Gregory N. Eaves, 'The Anti-Theatre and Its Double', *YA* 13 (1988), 34–61.
44. *MYV*, i, 103; for GY's warnings about reliance on the supernatural, *MYV*, i, 46.
45. WBY wrote proudly of this to Quinn: see *MYV*, i, 57.
46. Interview with GY, 8 Oct. 1947, Interview Book, Ellmann Papers, Y.9, Tulsa.
47. See IG to WBY, 28 Mar. 1918, for her denials, and 24 Mar. 1918 for her work on the *Little Review*: Jeffares, White and Bridgwater. Also A. Norman Jeffares, 'Iseult' in David Coakley and Mary O'Doherty (eds.), *Borderlands: Essays on Literature and Medicine in Honour of J. B. Lyons* (Dublin, 2002), 4–17.
48. See *AM*, 315–16, and *MYV*, i, 81 ff.
49. *YVP*, i, 219.
50. See, e.g., *YVP*, i, 83.
51. AG to JBY, 17 Nov. 1917, NLI MS 18,674.
52. 8 Feb. 1918, NYPL, partly in *L*, 645–6.
53. *MYV*, i, 178.
54. ibid., 178–9. The visit was something of a disappointment.
55. WBY to AG, 4 Jan. [1918], Berg, and *L*, 643–4.
56. *MYV*, i, 141, 163.
57. ibid., 124.
58. ibid., 132; for the 'Archer' vision, see *AM*, 165.
59. *YVP*, i, 307 (30 Jan. 1918).
60. *MYV*, i, 154.
61. ibid., 218.
62. ibid., 167 ff.
63. WBY to ECY, 21 Jan. 1918, Boston College.
64. To Ruth Shine, 24 Jan. 1918; NLI, uncat. My thanks to James Pethica.

65. WBY to AG, 25 Jan. 1918, Berg; also see his other letters to her at this time, and to the *Observer*, 30 Jan. 1918, reprinted in *UP*, ii, 428–9.

66. WBY to AG, 22 Feb. 1918, Berg, and partly in *L*, 646–7.

67. 2 Feb. [1918], NLI MS 18,672 (copy).

68. AG to WBY, 'Monday 18th' [Feb. 1918], NLI MS 18,672 (copy); AG to W. S. Blunt, 11 Feb. 1918, Berg.

69. 19 Apr. 1918, Berg. Compare not only 'An Irish Airman Foresees his Death' but also Stanza XI of 'In Memory of Major Robert Gregory'.

70. 9 Feb. [1918], Kansas.

71. See *AM*, 398.

72. *MYV*, i, 183 ff., comments on these ideas, which were being explored in the period just before Robert's death.

73. She had long shaped her life to this end; her American earnings were diverted into a trust fund for Richard, set up with the aid of Quinn (Gregory Family Papers, Box 2, Folder 5, Emory). Robert was apparently not expected to be much of a provider.

74. Robert's will is in Box 2 of the Gregory Family Papers at Emory, dated 14 Sept. 1916 and witnessed by two second lieutenants in his squadron. It reads, in its entirety, 'I wish to leave everything I have to my wife Margaret Gregory. I wish her to have the fullest freedom in the upbringing of my children and the management of my house and estate.' It is hard to disagree with SMY's judgement two years later (when Margaret was trying to force the sale of Coole): 'Robert Gregory made his will in the train on his way to war and just left all to his wife. No man should make his will at an emotional moment, but with careful and much thought. Lady Gregory must have had a hard task to keep silent.' (SMY to Quinn, 20 June 1920, NYPL).

75. 'Wednesday 28th' [Nov. 1917], Berg.

76. 4 Mar. 1918, Berg.

77. Later cancelled due to the influenza epidemic.

78. 11 Feb. 1918, NYPL.

79. To Dulac, 19 Apr. 1918, HRHRC.

80. WBY to Dulac, 1 July 1918, HRHRC, and to Quinn, 23 July 1918, NYPL (partly in *L*, 651–2).

81. W. R. Rodgers transcripts, HRHRC. Ann Saddlemyer (*BG*, 225) thinks this fishing expedition was in July 1919, on a trip to Oughterard. Given that he bought GY her fishing rod in 1918, when they visited Sligo and Connemara, I think it belongs to that summer.

82. *MYV*, ii, 2.

83. Interview Book, Ellmann Papers, Y.9, Tulsa.

84. *MYV*, ii, 16.

85. See *YVP*, iii, 81–2 and *BG*, 173–4.

86. WBY to Ellen Duncan, 16 May 1918, Columbia University.

87. 17 May [1918], BL MS Ashley A 2283, *L*, 649.

88. Published on 25 May 1918.

89. 15 July 1918, Yale.

90. AE to Quinn, 22 Jan 1918, NYPL; IG to WBY, n.d. [but Jan. 1918], Jeffares, White and Bridgwater.

91. A long letter of 6 June 1918 from WBY to Pound and an earlier letter of 10 Mar. from Pound (Indiana) show how much attention WBY paid to this project. IG was to receive £5 a month for three days' work a week, as well as further fees, subsidized by WBY. Though most of the work would be typing, she was not to be called a 'secretary', as this would link her too closely with Pound, but a 'foreign correspondent'.

92. 28 May 1918, Yale. Also see GY to Pound, 24 May [1918], Indiana, reprinted by Ann Saddlemyer in *YA* 7 (1990), 7–8, trying to arrange IG's summer and sending money for her. Pound's side of things is given in a letter of 10 Mar. 1918 to WBY, Indiana.

93. 28 May and n.d., 1918, MBY.

94. The menagerie is proudly described by WBY in a letter to Gogarty, 7 Sept. 1918, Yeats Collection, Princeton.

95. *MYV*, ii, 18–19.

96. WBY to Dulac, n.d. [but mid May 1918], HRHRC.

97. 20 May 1918, Yale.

98. [30 May 1918], MBY. The stanza in question is VIII, added at Margaret's request, according to WBY in a note on the MS. A Berg holograph is dated 24 May 1918.

99. See WBY to Pound, 6 June, Indiana, and 1 July 1918, Yale.

100. This is the first printing in the *English Review*. 'Fire of straw' recurs in 'The Tragic Generation'. The poem is interestingly analysed in Daniel Harris, *Yeats: Coole Park and Ballylee* (London, 1974), 126–37.

101. WBY to Francis Meynell, 13 July 1918, NYU.

102. WBY to AE, 28 June [1918], Indiana.

103. See Karl Beckson, 'Arthur Symons's "Iseult Gonne": A Previously Unpublished Memoir', *YA* 7 (1990), 204. For WBY's reaction, his letter to Quinn of 23 July 1918, NYPL. Also see a letter of 4 Sept., where he tells Quinn that both IG and Seán are 'most able courteous people & do Madame Gonne's ideas of education, that seemed wild, great credit. The boy like the girl has great sense of justice & both have strong gentle minds.' By 14 Dec. writing to AG, his tone was less favourable. 'Seugan [Seán] has no fixed habits or discipline. Iseult has done her best.' (Berg).

104. See Quinn to WBY, 25 Nov. 1918, NYPL.

105. 15 July 1918, Yale.

106. WBY's praise of the *Little Review* extract from *Ulysses* in his 23 July letter to Quinn (*L*, 651–2) should be placed alongside his letter to Pound, 6 June 1918 (Indiana): 'You want me to write to Quinn about Joyce. I think the best thing is for me to write him a letter on things in general, say something of Irish writers & then commend Joyce, & your spirit in publishing him.'

107. WBY to AG, 14 Aug. 1918, Berg, gives details of this episode; also see IG to WBY, 26 Aug. 1918, Jeffares, White and Bridgwater.

108. 18 Aug. 1918, Northwestern.

109. 'Sunday' [18 Aug. 1918], Kansas. He went on to Gort that day or the next.

110. IG to WBY, 26 Aug. 1918, Jeffares, White and Bridgwater.

111. *YVP*, ii, 70, 83, 338.

112. Probably *c.* 1 Nov. 1918 (from other remarks, it is soon after MG's release from prison and well before Christmas), Jeffares, White and Bridgwater.

113. 19 Sept. [1918], Yale.

114. 1 Dec. 1918. NLI MS 30,663 records the long correspondence between GY and Rafferty.

115. WBY to Chesterton, 1 Oct. 1918, BL Add. MSS 73210 B.

116. 7 Oct. 1918 in Dudley Sommer, *Haldane of Cloan: His Life and Times 1856–1928* (London, 1960), pp. 356–7. For circumstances of the letter's composition, see WBY to Quinn, 7 Oct. 1918, NYPL, and to AG, 15 Oct., Berg. Also see WBY to AG, 4 Oct. [1918], Berg, attacking Fisher: 'a typical officer – an empty smiling man, smooth as a billiard ball & as efficient, [who] has, on the authority of the Protestant archbishop, advised the cabinet that conscription will not be opposed'.

117. To GY, n.d. [but early Oct. 1918], MBY.

118. 12 Oct. 1918, NLS.

119. WBY reported on this to AG, 4 Oct. 1918, Berg; the chief business was the Lane pictures.
120. WBY to AG, 15 Oct. 1918, Berg.
121. To Louis Esson, 23 Oct. 1918, private collection; my thanks to John Kelly.
122. Gogarty to Leonie Leslie, 16 Nov. 1918, Bucknell; Pound to Quinn, 18 Dec. 1918, NYPL.
123. John Coulter in the *Toronto Star*, 18 Mar. 1939.
124. With some poems, this strategy brought in £20 for each: WBY to ECY, n.d., MBY.
125. A circular of 30 Sept. 1918, in the Hyde Papers, calls people to a meeting on 10 Oct. to discuss it: it was signed by Ernest Boyd, James Stephens, WBY, and Lennox Robinson. GY would later take a close interest.
126. In fact she stayed in Dublin and Quinn as usual bore the brunt. WBY wrote to thank him on 14 Dec., offering money to repatriate the old man and asking Quinn to make the arrangements. 'He has certainly given you infinite trouble – I imagine that two weeks without conversation roused all the natural wickedness of old age. However Lily says that during his one serious illness – bad indigestion twenty years ago – when we thought him near his end he refused to go to bed & sat all day his head on the table conversing with all comers. Then, too, he was quite unmanageable.' (NYPL).
127. TS by Quinn describing JBY's last days and death in 1922, NYPL, Box 53, Section 4, TS F.6. SMY also described her brother's anxiety in letters of 29 Nov. 1918 and 7 Jan. 1919.: 'Willy now says that he had given up and just thought she was dying. I felt he thought of it the night he came and called me out of the committee meeting I was at.'
128. 26 Nov. 1918, Berg.
129. 15 Dec. 1918, NYPL. ECY to Quinn, 12 Sept. 1918, NYPL, indicates that they moved on the 11th or 12th.
130. 14 Dec. 1918, Berg.
131. 29 Nov. 1918, NYPL. For IG's trenchant views, Jeffares, 'Iseult', in Coakley and O'Doherty, *Borderlands*, 13.
132. See WBY to Pound, 14 Dec. 1918, Yale, and to Quinn, same date, NYPL.
133. Published by Maunsel, Dublin, 1918. The copy in the Pierpoint Morgan Library is accompanied by a TS list identifying the contributors.
134. To Ellen Duncan, 10 Jan. 1918, Columbia University. This letter discusses how he would combine his presentation with that of a Belfast medium called William J. Crawford, and the use of slides to demonstrate materializations. Crawford was later exposed as a fraud and committed suicide in Aug. 1920.
135. For the Abbey debate on 2 Feb., see *IT*, 3 Feb. 1919. The opponent was Professor John Howley of University College, Galway, and WBY told Pound: 'He was very quaint when I got on Sinistrari [see above, Chapter 1, n. 63] he quivered with agitation & cried out "O this should never be spoken of".' (3 Feb. [1919], Yale). The chair was Professor William Magennis of UCD, who became one of WBY's *bêtes noires*. The line about 'the love of god' is recycled from *CT*: see *Myth*, 68.
136. 21 Jan. 1919, NYPL.
137. WBY to Pound, 16 Jan. 1919, Yale. Rafferty sent a graceful letter in late Jan. 'I assure you I have taken as much interest in your business as I ever did of my own.' (MBY).
138. See WBY to Pound, 16 Jan. 1919, Yale. Pound's one-time fiancée, the poet 'H.D.', wanted to rent it with a friend; businesslike as ever, WBY told Pound that he paid 20s. a week and if he sublet would have to rent the basement for storage at 5s. 'Now the neighbourhood is bad, "offices" poor, but the rooms are large & the literary associations distinguished; & however shabby the rooms may look by daylight, they put on glory by the light of candles.'
139. 21 Jan. 1919, NYPL.
140. Gogarty as quoted in Horace Reynold's diary, 4 July 1927, Harvard, b Ms Am 1787[5803]. Also see WBY to AG, 29 Jan. 1919, Berg. According to SMY, the rapprochement

had already happened. She told Quinn on 7 Jan.: 'The patriot has graciously forgiven Willy and the boy has consented to go to school on condition that he can leave at the end of the month if he doesn't like it. Isolde says he feels as if a statesman was asked to go to school.' (NYPL).

141. 28 Dec. 1918, NYPL.
142. 16 Jan. 1919, Yale. He wrote the same thing to AG, 29 Jan. 1919, Berg.
143. 26 Feb. [1919], Berg. SMY to Quinn, 4 Feb. 1919, NYPL, gives 16 Mar. as the expected date of the baby's arrival.
144. *MYV*, i, 226.
145. *YVP*, ii, 255.

Chapter 4 : A FEELING FOR REVELATION
1919–1920

1. *MYV*, ii, 249.
2. Fitzwilliam Museum, Cambridge. In the same letter she describes a visit to the House of Commons, where she saw 'such a mob of the most common and vulgar men and women evidently relations of the new MPs who came out to greet them and looked of the same class.'
3. Same to same, 27 Apr. 1919, Berg.
4. 26 May [1919], *Poetry* Archive, University of Chicago.
5. 6 Apr. 1919, Reading.
6. *MYV*, ii, 275.
7. Anne herself told it to the *New Yorker* in 1963: see Lilian Post (ed.), *The Fun of It: Stories from the 'Talk of the Town'*, *The New Yorker* (New York, 2001), 213.
8. 14 June 1919, NYPL.
9. 7 Nov. 1919, Berg.
10. See WBY to AG, 6 Dec. 1919, Berg. 'Anne is well and growing in mirth. She does not get on well with her grandmother & howled whenever she came near. She never behaved to anybody else in this way. It is curious because in the month before her birth George had a strong feeling against her mother, who on her side regretted Anne's arrival. It is rather tragic now & when Mrs Tucker went away she said "some grandmothers would cry". She had been very nice & bought toys.' GY's view of her mother is also indicated in the automatic script – see *MYV*, ii, 319–20, 322–3. The latter reference implies a possible romantic connection between WBY and Nelly Tucker in the past.
11. See WBY to JBY, 1 Sept. 1919, Boston College, for her payments.
12. See WBY to Quinn, 13 June 1919, and 9 Nov. 1920, NYPL, and to SMY, 21 June 1921, Boston College.
13. ECY to Quinn, 15 Apr. 1919, NYPL. The party was on 8 Apr.; the Yeatses moved into Dundrum Lodge on 19 Mar.
14. Same to same, 27 July 1920, NYPL.
15. *MYV*, ii, 224–5.
16. ibid., 239.
17. ibid., 249.
18. WBY to JBY, 16 July 1919, Boston College, and ECY to Quinn, 12 Sept. 1918, NYPL.
19. Undated fragment, probably late June 1919, Yale.
20. To Quinn, postmarked 11 July 1919, NYPL; also SMY to Quinn, 30 July 1919, NYPL. For Quinn's views, see especially a letter of 26 Aug. 1919, NLI MS 31,114.
21. WBY to Quinn, 9 Aug. 1919, NYPL; AG to W. S. Blunt, 3 Aug. 1919, Fitzwilliam.

22. To Quinn, 31 Dec. 1919, NYPL; also see references in SMY to Quinn, 24 Aug., 9 Sept., 29 Sept., and WBY to Bullen, 15 Nov. 1919, Kansas.

23. *MYV*, ii, 359.

24. *Ex*, 263. To judge from a TS draft in NLI MS 30,277, it originally began more prosaically, describing the objectives of the *Irish Statesman* and his own ambitions for a journal 'able and willing to submit our life to a constant, precise, unexaggerated, passionate criticism'.

25. ibid., 270.

26. To Quinn, 9 Oct. 1920, NYPL.

27. *L*, 655–6 (original in NLI MS 31,043). For the Trinity debate, see Donald T. Torchiana, *W. B. Yeats and Georgian Ireland* (Washington, 2nd ed., 1992), 216–17; the debate was on 30 Jan. Torchiana, 214–17, gives close attention to WBY's reactions to the Russian Revolution.

28. *Ex*, 277, 278. 'It may be, indeed, that we shall not only reject any plan, that would establish some committee of despotic men, at once economists, patriots and inquisitors, but declare our liking enthusiastically, seeing that "spoil-five" has been played under our hedgerows, for the old gambling table of nature.' (NLI MS 30,794). For a discussion of the essay in the context of WBY's passion for Balzac, see Paul Scott Stanfield, *Yeats and Politics in the 1930s* (New York, 1988), 118–20. Michael Baron has also discussed it in *YA* 5 (1987), 62–83, relating the essay to Wordsworth's thought.

29. ibid., 279–80.

30. 3 Aug. 1919, Fitzwilliam Museum, Cambridge.

31. As Ronald Schuchard brilliantly demonstrates in 'The Double Vision of *The Wild Swans at Coole* (1917, 1919)', *YA* 10 (1993), 111–34.

32. 'Her Praise', 'The People', 'His Phoenix', 'A Thought from Propertius', 'Broken Dreams', 'A Deep-Sworn Vow', 'Presences'.

33. 17 June 1921, in Richard Taylor (ed.), *Frank Pearce Sturm: His Life, Letters and Collected Work* (Urbana, Ill., 1969), 80–1. 'You can write anything you like provided that you deduce it from these poems, and all can be so deduced. The first part of "The Double Vision" describes spirits at phase 1 and the last part is spirits at phase 15. There are also in the same book my poems on "The Hunchback" and "The Fool", the 26th and 28th phases.'

34. See his critique in the *Little Review*, 5 (July 1918), 54.

35. So he told Macmillan on 23 Dec. 1920, BL Add. MSS 55003.

36. For the *TLS* and Murry, *CH*, 213–220; for the loss of 'delicacy', *Oxford Magazine*, 38, 3 (31 Oct. 1919): my thanks to Declan Kiely. Squire's review was in *Land and Water*, 27 Mar. 1919.

37. Including 'Nineteen Hundred and Nineteen' (Nov. 1921), 'Meditations in Time of Civil War' (Jan. 1923) and 'Among School Children' (Aug. 1927). Murry's *Adelphi*, founded in 1923, would also become a showcase for WBY's work, notably *The Resurrection*.

38. *Journals*, i, 66.

39. 3 Aug. 1919, Fitzwilliam Museum, Cambridge.

40. *Dial*, Nov. 1920. 'Thirty centuries' became 'twenty' immediately after the first printing; it seems to have been a slip.

41. See Wordsworth's 'The Excursion', IV, 11, 305–9, where the 'bad', through 'superior energies', 'Have fairly earned a victory o'er the weak, / The vacillating, inconsistent good'. T. R. Henn, *The Lonely Tower* (London, 1950), 143–4, discusses Shelleyan and Shakespearean references. For the Flaubert connection, see Malcolm Bull, 'Yeats's "Rough Beast": Sphinx or Manticore?' in *Notes and Queries*, 240 (June 1995), 209–10. Ricketts's illustrations for Wilde's *Salomé* featured a brazen-winged beast, and Moreau's painting of Orpheus and the Sphinx was a key *fin de siècle* image. Burke and the fate of Marie Antoinette are specifically mentioned in an early draft of the poem: see

696

W. B. Yeats, *'Michael Robartes and the Dancer': Manuscript Materials*, edited by Thomas Parkinson with Anne Brannen (London, 1994), 147–51. For other aspects of the imagery and its possible origins, see Jon Stallworthy, 'The Second Coming' in *Agenda*, 9, 4 and 10, 1 (Autumn–Winter, 1971/2), 24–33.

42. *The Lonely Tower*, 15.

43. He wrote to AG that he was 'at work' on it on 1 Apr.; it was completed in June.

44. Famously from Joyce Carol Oates: see '"At Least I Have Made a Woman of Her": Images of Women in Twentieth-Century Literature', *Georgia Review*, 37 (Spring, 1983), 17, answered by George Bornstein, 'Constructing Literature', Annals of New York Academy of Science, 775 (1996) in *The Flight from Science and Reason*, edited by Paul Gross, Norman Levitt and Martin W. Lewis. The most nuanced treatment is in Elizabeth Butler Cullingford, *Gender and History in Yeats's Love Poems* (Cambridge, 1993).

45. The Daphne–Apollo allusion in Stanza VI has aroused the attention of some critics to an inappropriately incestuous inference (see, e.g., Daniel Harris, *Yeats: Coole Park and Ballylee* (London, 1974), 142, n. 38). However, the Anne Hyde theme helps explain it; WBY was already in some confusion about the implications of reincarnation for family relationships (see above, p. 141).

46. Gabriel Fallon records that AG 'hated' the League, which took over the Abbey on Mondays ('Profiles of a Poet', *Modern Drama*, 7, 3 (Dec. 1964), 336–7). *IT*, 30 Jan. 1922, reports the League putting on plays by Chekhov, Schnitzler, and Wilde; players then included Shelah Richards, Geoffrey Phibbs, and Alan Duncan, with music by John Larchet.

47. WBY to AG, 2 Mar. 1919; also see WBY to Robinson, 28 Feb. 1919, with thanks to John Kelly.

48. 12 Mar. 1919, Berg. For his reflections later about AG, himself, and uneducated directors, see below, pp. 443–4.

49. *FJ*, 26 Apr. 1919. The draft of the 'Open Letter', published in the *Irish Statesman*, is NLI MS 30,195; it is reprinted in *Ex*, 244–59, as 'A People's Theatre'. Also see WBY's 'Instead of a Theatre' in *Theatre Arts Magazine* (Jan. 1919). Many of these ideas and pronouncements resurfaced in the speeches on his US tour.

50. To AG, 3 Apr. 1919, Berg. For the 'secret society' reflection, see *Ex*, 254.

51. Same to same, 18 May 1919, Berg; also see *MYV*, ii, 276. The play was produced on 25 and 27 May at the King's Hall, Covent Garden.

52. IG's comment is in an undated letter of Dec. 1919, Jeffares, White and Bridgwater; she refers to WBY reading the play out loud at Colleville, and closely criticizes the performance. WBY reported this and Gogarty's opinion to AG, 13 and 19 Dec. 1919, Berg; Holloway's reaction is in Robert Hogan and Michael J. O'Neill (eds.), *Joseph Holloway's Abbey Theatre: A Selection from His Unpublished Journal 'Impressions of a Dublin Playgoer'* (London, 1967), 206. For WBY's curiosity about the audience, see letters to Robinson, 19 and 24 Dec. [1919], SIUC; for AG's reaction, n.d. [but c. 20 Dec. 1919], NLI MS 18,676.

53. 13 Dec. 1919, Berg, referring to an anonymous article which WBY thought was written by Ernest Boyd (currently enraged with the Abbey for turning down a skit he had written about an arms raid).

54. JBY to Rosa Butt, 1 May 1919, Bodleian, letter 196.

55. *YVP*, ii, 19. Also see Janis Haswell, 'Resurrecting *Calvary*: A Reconstructive Interpretation of the Play and Its Making', *YA* 15 (2002).

56. AE to Quinn, 18 Oct. 1918, 10 July 1919, NYPL. AE was, however, still not given the full picture; he told Quinn on 10 July 1919, 'I think he gets a lot of it through his own [or] somebody else's automatic writing.' The 1918 revelation may stem from WBY's address on the subject at Gogarty's; see above, p. 134.

57. To Quinn, postmarked 11 July 1919, NYPL.
58. *MV*, ii, 292–3: the warnings are specifically against MG's influence.
59. See IG to WBY, 3 Aug, '17 [*recte* 1919], Jeffares, White and Bridgwater.
60. *MV*, ii, 307. GY was perhaps inspired by the story of Lord Edward Fitzgerald's wife, Pamela, alleged daughter of 'Philippe-Égalité', Duc d'Orléans.
61. '"Why did her having to come to me cause our relations in this life to have their special character?" "The fact that she was of a different class & status & had to come in secret to you unacknowledged with no recognised position weighed on her – She hated your wife & tried to destroy her."' (*MYV*, ii, 313). GY possessed *The Closet of Sir Kenelm Digby, Knight, Opened*, edited by Anne Mcdonnell (London, 1910): see *YA* 4 (1986), 282.
62. 13 Dec. 1919, NYPL.
63. *YVP*, ii, 115; also see *YVP*, ii, 291–2, 349. Frequency of intercourse, and technique, were often discussed in indirect ways.
64. 'Saturday' [27 Dec. 1919], Berg.
65. GY to WBY, 8 Aug. 1920, for the hauntings; other details from SMY to JBY, 15 Aug. 1920, Boston College, and WBY to AG, 27 Dec. 1919, 2 Jan. 1921, Berg.
66. My thanks to Philip Cohen for showing me the correspondence between Raymond Greene and WBY.
67. On Force Stead, see George Mills Harper, 'William Force Stead's Friendship with Yeats and Eliot', *Massachusetts Review*, 21, 1 (Spring, 1980), 9–38.
68. WBY to R L-P, 2 Sept. 1914, Boston College.
69. Ottoline Morrell's diary for 17 Dec. 1919; my thanks to Miranda Seymour.
70. James P. O'Reilly, 'W. B. Yeats and Undergraduate Oxford 1919–1922', TS, dated Aug. 1953, HRHRC; also quoted by Oliver J. Gogarty in 'My Father's Friend' in Jim McGarry (ed.), *The Dream I Knew: Memories of Thirty Years of the Yeats International Summer School, Sligo* (Collooney, Sligo, 1990), 76.
71. My thanks to John Kelly for tracing their book-requests.
72. *MYV*, ii, 324.
73. *MYV*, ii, 333–5; 'Martha' is a code for menstruation.
74. *MYV*, ii, 362.
75. *MYV*, ii, 338–9.
76. *MYV*, i, 342–3.
77. *MYV*, ii, 347–8. Gregory's remark is in a letter to WBY, 10 Mar. 1921, referring to the note attached to the poem in *Michael Robartes and the Dancer*.
78. ibid., 352.
79. ibid., 360. He pointed out that they had not had sex for three months before Anne's arrival, and yet messages had come via automatic writing; but she smoothly pointed out that it depended on the subject being dealt with. 'In the present complex script it would be impossible because the sex-element is a part of the matter.' 'Emotional and sexual satisfaction' were emphasized as a general requirement to enable 'intellectual desire'.
80. ibid., 377ff.
81. To Pond, 15 Oct. 1919, SIUC.
82. JBY to Rosa Butt, 23 June 1920, Bodleian, letter 201, and to AG, n.d., Berg.
83. To AG, 27 Jan. 1920, Berg.
84. For JBY's sympathy, see his letter to Rosa Butt, above. For the rich New Yorkers, Anne Freemantle, *Three Cornered Heart* (London, 1971), 267.
85. WBY to AG, 8 Feb. 1920, Berg.
86. WBY arrived at New York on 22 Jan. and spent the first fortnight based there. On 2 Feb. he was in Toronto, 3 Feb. Montreal, 13 Feb. Northampton, Mass., 17 Feb. New York, 18 Feb. Yale, 19 Feb. Washington, DC, 20 Feb. New York, 24 Feb. Pittsburg, 29 Feb.

and several days thereafter, Chicago. On 14 Mar. he was in Salt Lake City, and on 21 Mar. Portland, Oregon, which he left on 22 Mar. for a two-day journey by train to San Francisco, arriving on 24 Mar. From 28 until (at least) 30 Mar. he was in Pasadena, and on 8 Apr. in Santa Barbara; he then went to New Orleans, and by 13 Apr. was travelling from there to San Antonio for a lecture on 14 Apr., whence he went to Austin and Waco. On 17 Apr. he was in Dallas, on 18 Apr. in Sherman, Texas, and by 23 Apr. in Kirksville, Missouri. By 29 Apr. he was on a train from Cleveland to New York, arriving at the Algonquin on 30 Apr. New York remained his base until he sailed from Montreal on 29 May. This itinerary has been reconstructed from letters, newspaper reports and the invaluable Ph.D. thesis by Karin Strand, 'W. B. Yeats's American Lecture Tours', Northwestern University, 1978.

87. To Rosa Butt, 23 June 1920, Bodleian, letter 201.

88. *Statesman* [Austin], 16 Apr. 1920, quoted in Strand, 'W. B. Yeats's American Lecture Tours', 190. At Waco shortly afterwards, he was deemed 'above the heads of his audience'.

89. To William Phelps, 12 Feb. 1920, Yale.

90. JBY to JY, 7 May 1920, Boston College; he boasted that his own weight never rose above eleven stone.

91. To AG, 28 Feb. 1920, Berg.

92. To AG, 30 Mar. 1920, Berg.

93. See WBY to Pond, 18 and 26 Apr., SIUC, and to AG, 2 Jan. 1921, Berg.

94. WBY to AG, 14 June [1920], Berg.

95. *New York Times*, 25 Jan. 1920, quoted in Strand, 'W. B. Yeats's American Lecture Tours', 173–4.

96. This statement was provided for the Palestine Restoration Fund Campaign committee, and reported in the *San Francisco Call and Post*, 26 Mar. 1920, quoted in Strand, 'W. B. Yeats's American Lecture Tours', 187–8.

97. *Toronto Evening Telegraph*, 3 Feb. 1920, quoted in Strand, 'W. B. Yeats's American Lecture Tours', 177–8.

98. See Strand, 'W. B. Yeats's American Lecture Tours', 200–2.

99. ibid., 196.

100. *Oberlin Review*, quoted in Strand, 'W. B. Yeats's American Lecture Tours', 205.

101. 14 Mar. [1920], *L*, 661.

102. *Waco Daily Times-Herald*, 17 Apr. 1920: my thanks to Declan Kiely. Also see papers in Armstrong Browning Library, Baylor University, which reveal that William Howard Taft spoke there the same day, getting $600 to WBY's $150.

103. *Chicago Daily Tribune*, 1 Mar. 1920, quoted in Strand, 'W. B. Yeats's American Lecture Tours', 183.

104. Robert J. Carey in *Chicago Daily Tribune*, 2 July 1955.

105. WBY to Dulac, 22 Mar. 1920, HRHRC. Junzo Sato, 'A Sketch of My Life' in Shotaro Oshima (ed.), *W. B. Yeats and Japan* (Tokyo, 1965), 132–3.

106. To Pond, 18 and 26 Apr. 1920, SIUC. A telegram to Quinn on 30 Apr. stresses his anxiety to have Pond book some May lectures (NYPL).

107. To AG, 14 June [1920], Berg.

108. *I & R*, i, 126–31.

109. 18 May 1920, Berg.

110. Quinn to JBY, 13 Jan. 1919, NLI MS 31,114: a very threatening letter, listing the expense of his upkeep, including illnesses and costs of departure, estimated at $1,000. 'I have told W.B.Y. that the longer you stay here the longer you will be in debt. If he can stand that burden, and if the idea of your returning home has no appeal to you, and if you are willing and your family is willing to run the risk of another attack of pneumonia here

then I have done all that I can do, all that any friend can do. I have not the strength to keep on indefinitely in the role of Cassandra.' Also Quinn to WBY, 16 Jan. 1919, accusing JBY of 'deliberately taking advantage of my good nature . . . If he dies all the unpleasant things will be up to me.' This was indeed the case. It should be added that Quinn, who was a legendary hypochondriac, was also convinced (it is not known on what evidence) that the old man had tuberculosis, and feared for his own health whenever he was near him.

111. 28 Feb. 1920, Berg.
112. *MYV*, ii, 394.

Chapter 5 : 'Weight and Measure in a Time of Dearth' 1920–1921

1. Ronan Fanning, Michael Kennedy, Dermot Keogh and Eunan O'Halpin (eds.), *Documents on Irish Foreign Policy. Volume 1: 1919–1922* (Dublin, 1998), no. 3, 5.
2. See WBY to Robinson, 23 July 1920, SIUC.
3. *Journals*, i, 187 (entry for 27 Sept.).
4. See WBY to AG, 18 May 1920, Berg, and to Robinson, 24 Feb. 1920, SIUC.
5. To JBY, 10 Nov. 1919, transcription by William M. Murphy. For the attempts at a match, also see IG to WBY, 17 Nov. 1919 (copy), in Ellmann Papers, Y.2, Tulsa, giving her version of the dinner with SMY and adding: 'Robinson is a nice young man but . . . A man. How could you seriously think that I could marry him? And *do* you seriously think it?' For Dublin's assumption about Robinson's sexual orientation, see Frank O'Connor in *I & R*, ii, 340–1, where he indicated that WBY shared this belief.
6. See IG to WBY, 'Monday' [early Dec. 1919], Jeffares, White and Bridgwater. On 17 Nov. she had written describing her new 'great friend' Stuart and praising his poems. 'He has an adoration which amounts to a religion for you, but he is very shy and I cannot get him to send you any of his work.'
7. IG's friend Margaret Barrington had insisted that she go and tell Purser that she had given her name as a reference for a lease on a flat. My thanks to Margaret Barrington's daughter Pegeen O'Flaherty for this reminiscence.
8. See a note of MG's, '14 May', at Kansas, probably to P. S. O'Hegarty. 'A Cara, thank you so much for letting me know of the activities of Mr Stuart. It is very kind of you – I had given those books as real treasures to my cousin herself who loves her library – I do not think she can know of this.' The 'cousin' is evidently IG.
9. WBY to GY, 4 Aug. 1920, MBY.
10. 14 Jan. 1920, Jeffares, White and Bridgwater. She put Stuart in either Phase Fourteen or Seventeen of the 'System', reinforcing the bond with WBY.
11. ibid.
12. 24 Feb. 1920, SIUC.
13. 'Thursday', from Glenmalure, Jeffares, White and Bridgwater: apparently written before WBY was summoned by MG.
14. WBY to GY, 1 Aug. 1920, MBY.
15. WBY to AG, 1 Aug. 1920, Berg.
16. To Quinn, 2 Sept. 1920, transcription by William M. Murphy.
17. AG to WBY, 5 Aug. 1920 and 'Friday' [6 Aug.], NLI MSS 18,673 and 18,675.
18. WBY to GY, 'Sat.' [31 July 1920], and GY to WBY, '[3] Aug. 1920', MBY.
19. 7 Aug. 1920, transcription by William M. Murphy. Though Mead had once been described by WBY as possessing 'the intellect of a good-sized whelk' (see *AM*, 102), he turned up about twice a month at Woburn Buildings (Virginia Moore, *The Unicorn*,

New York, 1954, 455), and his ideas actually considerably influenced *AV*: see *YA* 13 (1998), 47ff. He had founded the Quest Society in 1909.

20. WBY to GY, 4 Aug. 1920. Previous quotations come from GY to WBY, 4 and 6 Aug., and WBY to GY, 7 Aug.: all in MBY.

21. GY to WBY, 4 Aug. 1920, MBY: this could possibly refer to her own pregnancy and miscarriage, but in context, and from WBY's reply, seems to relate more easily to Iseult's.

22. This letter, written 4–6 Aug., is at Emory: probably a draft sent to AG for approbation.

23. 'Monday' [probably 9 Aug. 1920], MBY.

24. IG to WBY from 67 Fitzwilliam Square, n.d., NLI MS 18,673.

25. To Solomons, 4–6 Aug. 1920, Emory, and to AG, 3 Aug. 1920, Berg.

26. WBY to AG, 3 Aug. 1920, Berg, and to GY, 1 Aug. 1920, MBY.

27. WBY to Iseult, 10 Apr. [1921], Kansas.

28. 9 Aug. 1921, Berg. Iseult wrote him a heartbroken letter from Lough Dan describing the child's illness and death.

29. See peremptory letters of 28 Sept., 27 Oct., 9 Nov. 1920 to JBY, as well as several to Quinn in Nov.

30. See WBY to Pound, 7 Oct. 1920, Yale. 'I have just finished a long poem of 100 lines & I think it good, as [*recte* at] least as good as "The [*sic*] Prayer for my Daughter" & much the same sort of thing. It describes Horton & Mrs Emery & Macgregor.'

31. The section covering MG's arrival in his life is much the most extensively reworked part of the draft: NLI MS 30,016.

32. SMY to Quinn, 14 Oct. 1920, NYPL. SMY had been determined to keep these treasures out of AG's clutches.

33. See WBY to Pound, 8 Dec. 1920, Indiana, telling him he had written 8,000 to 9,000 words. On 12 Dec. he told AG 14,000 (Berg).

34. *Au, CW*, iii, 111.

35. ibid., 132.

36. ibid., 166.

37. 14 Mar. 1921, *L*, 665.

38. The handwritten MS in NLI 30,472 contains statements such as 'I had again to realise that intellectual freedom and social equity are incompatible . . .'

39. This is as it appeared in *Au*. But in the MS at NLI 30,536 this last famous passage is much crossed out and rewritten, in an otherwise fluent manuscript.

40. This is the last passage in *Au*, but both in the 1921 version and in NLI MS 30,536 this appeal does not end the book. Instead it is followed by a Section XXIII which would later supply the opening to 'Ireland after Parnell', but much altered. The original manuscript version of *Four Years* thus ends with an attack on Rolleston, later deleted from all published versions. 'He was my first public disappointment & because of it I have tried to choose my moralists from the unwholesome side of the Mareotic Sea where a man whips his own shadow.'

41. *Au*, 192, and WBY to AG, 1 Aug. 1921, Berg.

42. To Boyd, 11 Nov. 1920, Healy.

43. SMY to JBY, 7 June 1920, 9 Dec. 1920; William M. Murphy's transcription.

44. Diary, 10 Oct. 1920, Plunkett Foundation, Oxford; my thanks to Gary Peatling for this reference. Also see Bernard G. Krimm, *W. B. Yeats and the Emergence of the Irish Free State 1918–1939 – Living in the Explosion* (NY, 1981), 51, for a meeting between WBY and Asquith later in Oct.

45. He went to Dublin on 9 Oct.; SMY told Quinn on 11 Oct. (NYPL) that he and GY had been in town for two days and that he had been at Plunkett's the night before. He was

to go into the Elpis nursing-home 'tonight' for the operation, which took place on the 13th. He also fitted in a visit to MG at Glenmalure; this was probably the occasion when he wrote 'On a Picture of a Black Centaur by Edmund Dulac', as described by Cecil Salkeld (also staying there): TS, 'Memories of W. B. Yeats', HRHRC. See also letters to Robinson, 7 Oct., SIUC; AG, 16 Oct., Berg; JBY, 27 Oct., Boston College.

46. See *Nation*, 16 Oct. 1920, 63–4, 'A Week in Ireland'; 23 Oct. 1920, 123–4, 'Another Week in Ireland'; 4 Dec. 1920, 333, 'A Third Week in Ireland'; 18 Dec. 1920, 413–14, 'A Fourth Week in Ireland'; 1 Jan. 1921, 472–3, 'A Fifth Week in Ireland'. She may also have written 'Murder by the Throat' in ibid., 13 Nov. 1920, 215–16.

47. *Journals*, i, 197.

48. 21 Mar. 1921, Berg, discussing a joint letter to the *TLS*.

49. To Robinson, 26 Sept. [1920], SIUC. By 14 Nov., however, with the hunger strike in Cork Gaol over, he thought it might not be worth putting on the play. His own *King's Threshold*, when played in Dublin, struck the young Thomas MacGreevy as 'one of the great occasions of my youth'. Notes for a speech at Reading, MacGreevy Papers, TCD.

50. 29 Oct. 1920, SIUC.

51. *Journals*, i, 207–8. She was particularly sensitive about Shaw's repeating that Robert claimed he had never been happier than during his year as an airman. There is an odd echo of Shaw's own *O'Flaherty VC*, where the hero prefers the battle-front to the difficulties of Ireland, mother, and sweetheart.

52. 3 Dec. 1920, Berg.

53. ibid. 'Did I tell you that Lord Henry Cavendish spoke of you here as "that remarkable woman" & that he attributed to you, mistakenly I imagine, some article in "the Nation"'. His letter of 12 Dec., quoted below, shows that he swiftly tried to make amends.

54. WBY to AG, 27 Dec. 1920, Berg, *Journals*, i, 216.

55. WBY to AG, 12 Dec. 1920, Berg.

56. 12 Dec. 1920, Berg; he repeated the message three days later.

57. To J. C. Squire, 13 Dec. 1920, HRHRC.

58. See an important letter of 23 Dec. 1920, BL Add. MSS 55003.

59. To Quinn, 3 Mar. 1921, NYPL.

60. WBY to AG, 30 Dec. 1920, Berg, and to SMY, 21 June 1921, Boston College.

61. WBY to AG, 8 Feb. 1921, Berg.

62. See WBY to Harold Monro, 10 June 1921, marked 'Private', HRHRC. 'Macmillan & I go on disputing on the question [of his books' availability]. He signed an agreement to re-issue all my work in a certain form & now that printing has got so much more expensive, wants some other arrangement. He keeps evading the point. I want to get out a uniform edition of all my poems & prose. If that should be impossible I have a com-promise in my head which involves however some negociation with Unwin.'

63. 6 Jan. 1921, Berg.

64. WBY to AG, 15 Jan. 1921, Berg.

65. AE to ECY, 7 Jan. 1921, Healy; also see ECY to John J. Gallagher, 12 Aug. 1937.

66. n.d. [but late Jan. 1921], NLI MS 18,673.

67. WBY to AG, 18 Jan. 1921, SIUC; 17 Jan., Berg, for the 'fountain of news'; 22 Mar. 1921, Berg, for his reasons for living in Oxford.

68. See AG to Robinson, 23 Dec. 1921, SIUC. For her worries about WBY and the army benefit, AG to WBY, 13, 17 and 19 Jan. 1921, NLI MS 18,673. His letter denying that he ever intended to attend 'Warriors' Day' is NLI MS 30,890. 'Though I might try to think of men who served in France or Italy with a good conscience, & who now perhaps need help, I would think instead of certain ex-servicemen called "auxiliary police" who in my own country rob and murder without hindrance.' NLI MS 30,080 is a draft letter to *The Times* complaining about British soldiers' behaviour around Labane. AG

approved: 'I am glad you wrote that protest – it will be good to have it to quote if your name as a supporter is again used.'

69. 31 Jan. 1921, SIUC.

70. James O'Reilly, 'Memories of W. B. Yeats and Undergraduate Oxford', HRHRC.

71. 'Yeats sat enthroned at the head of our table looking very distinguished and exceedingly bored with tortoiseshell spectacles . . . Yeats and Plunkett chatted to each other, which they found difficult as they were deaf in the wrong ears. Yeats was far too distinguished unfortunately to give a speech of more than four or five sentences though I believe he is exceedingly good if roused.' Butler would later see him 'roused' at the celebrated Union debate: see below. Butler to his mother, 1 Dec. 1920, family papers; my thanks to Rob Tobin.

72. WBY to AG, 18 Dec. 1920, Berg. He said the same thing to Robinson, 18 Dec., SIUC.

73. *Oxford Magazine*, 39, 14 (25 Feb. 1921), 225.

74. O'Reilly, 'W. B. Yeats and Undergraduate Oxford'.

75. According to the *Oxford Chronicle*, 18 Feb. 1921.

76. *Westminster Gazette*, 18 Feb. 1920, is the most detailed report, though it does not target the phrases which O'Reilly recorded, and which anticipate 'Nineteen Hundred and Nineteen'. J. S. Collis, Balliol, moved 'that this House would welcome complete self-government in Ireland, and condemns reprisals'. H. C. McKisack, Queen's, opposed. Speeches were also reported from J. G. Morgan, St John's, for, and Major the Hon. H. Lygon, against.

Mr William Butler Yeats was loudly cheered on rising. He said that not law, only English law, has broken down in Ireland. Sinn Fein brought real justice into his part of Ireland for the first time in centuries. The only complaint was that they protected property perhaps a little too vigorously. He spoke of the murder of a young man and of a girl in his district. The men of the neighbourhood pathetically thought the troops – all officers – would at least spare a woman. Everything done by Germany in Belgium is being done by England in Ireland. Have an Inquiry! (Tremendous cheering.) The Irish farmers are, foolishly, adopting the world-old policy of guerrilla warfare. Did we call it 'murder' in our allies of the Peninsular War? As Burke says, you cannot indict a nation. Mr Yeats said he did not know which lay more heavily on his heart – Ireland or England. Ireland will come but strengthened by suffering but England – ? We all speak of liberty and law; but there is truth in the gibe that the war 'made the world safe for hypocrisy'. It is untrue that the Black and Tans were hardly tried men whose nerves gave way. This might be said of the soldiers, who have for the most part behaved well. Who sent the Black and Tans? If England were the England of Victoria she would find out *who sent them* and indict them.

The division was 219 for, 129 against.

77. 24 Feb. 1921, Berg.

78. To Quinn, 3 Mar. 1921, NYPL.

79. *I & R*, i, 148.

80. WBY to OS, 9 Apr. 1921, HRHRC, and *L*, 667–8.

81. WBY to Robinson, 21 May 1921, SIUC. It was an extremely good deal: copyright reverted to WBY after three years, and he kept serial rights.

82. 9 Apr. 1921, HRHRC, and *L*, 668.

83. 10 Apr. [1921], Berg.

84. For this memory, and some of the thought behind the poem, see NLI MS 30,273, a MS fragment probably intended for *Wheels and Butterflies*:

Someone has informed me that we stand at the verge of our Hellenistic age . . . Forty years ago I heard Churton Collins say 'York Powell's Rome is Oxford. By 1900 war will have come to an end and by 1920 there will be no more poverty.' A fortnight before the Great War broke out a Labour member of Parliament at a review in Hyde Park said 'It s a fine sight, it is nothing but a fine sight and there will never be another war' & yet for some ten or fifteen years the change had been upon us in increasing violence of life & art, & an increasing despondence or sullenness, & we had begun to desire whatever life seemed most undisturbed by our understanding, our hard outlines or purposes . . .

85. This is as it appeared in the *Dial*, Sept. 1921 – except that in the first line, 'ingenious' appeared as 'ingenuous'. Since 'ingenious' appears in all the MS drafts (see Curtis Bradford, *Yeats at Work*, Carbondale, Ill., 1965, for an illuminating survey) it seems to have been a printer's error.

86. See George Watson, 'Yeats's View of History: The Contemplation of Ruin', *Maynooth Review* 2, 12 (1978), 35.

87. Loie Fuller's dancers were in fact Japanese; they toured Europe in the early 1900s. Her own speciality was the 'moth dance', using sticks and a huge floating skirt. Fuller was a pioneer in the use of electric-light projection, especially from below; her performers danced on transparent panels. WBY may have seen her in a private performance; compare *Au*, 126, where he remembers 'a dance I once saw in a great house, where beautifully dressed children wound a long ribbon in and out as they danced'. Fuller's 'Dancing Girls' had recently returned to the Coliseum, in Apr. 1919, and she produced a 'ballet of light' there in Aug.

88. See WBY to GY, 8 Apr. 1921.

89. WBY to GY, 9 May 1921. For a report of WBY's performance, see *The Times*, 6 May 1921. He told amusing stories about controversies associated with the early plays, and emphasized the theatre's non-political stance. Nonetheless, WBY declined to give another under Mrs Fowler's auspices when she refused to advertise it as 'for the benefit to the Abbey Theatre', on the grounds that 'Ireland was so unpopular': the lectures made over £500 for the Abbey. WBY to AG, 10 June [1921], Berg; partly in *L*, 669–70.

90. 21 June 1921, SIUC; also see WBY to AG, 22 May 1921, Berg. For interference with mail, WBY to Quinn, 30 May [1921], NYPL, and to ECY, 6 July 1921, Boston College.

91. WBY to AG, 1 July 1921, Berg, and to Dulac, 17 July [1921], HRHRC.

92. 13 July 1921, Boston College. Throughout 1921 Quinn sent angry letters about JBY, telling Pound 'the financing of [WBY's] father staying on here is up to me, flatly dumped on my doorstep' (12 Dec. 1920, copy, NYPL) – which is not really accurate, given the above. As to JBY's hurt feelings, WBY was less tough in a letter to AG, 13 July 1921: 'It is about my treatment of my father that I am anxious. My hope is that it is something else that without knowing it he really minds: my whole point of view about the people we have known differs from his. He always thinks I lack "humanity".' (Berg).

93. 3 July 1921, NLI MS 18,678.

94. 1 Aug. 1921, Berg.

95. NLI MS 9968 (no. 777); partly in *Some Passages from the Letters of A. E. to W. B. Yeats* (Cuala, 1936), 55.

96. *Au*, 178.

97. ibid., 247.

98. To AG, 9 Sept. 1921, Berg. 'It was brave of her [GY] as she thought the child could not live till morning & all the time I was bringing up to her letters & telegrams of congratulation.' SMY's version to JBY is more vivid: 'George wouldn't let the doctor and nurse tell Willie a word about the danger. He wrote away in his study oblivious to it all, while Delia, the pretty Galway maid went to and fro with telegrams, tears covering her face. And George only wrote to me when he was a fortnight old and quite out of danger.' (16 Sept. 1921, Boston College).

99. See SMY to JBY, 23 Aug. 1921, and WBY to ECY, 22 Dec. 1921, Boston College.

100. 19 Oct. 1921, Berg.
101. To Quinn, 7 Nov. 1921, NYPL. He was WBY's maternal grandmother's brother's son.
102. He pointed this out in letters to AG, and one new passage is particularly telling:

> He needs no help that joy has lifted up
> Like some miraculous beast out of Ezekiel.
> The man that dies has the chief part in the story,
> And I will mock and mock and mock that image yonder,
> That evil picture in the sky – no, no!
> I have all my strength again, I will outface it.

This was typed out, probably by GY, and attached with a letter of 27 Oct. 1921 to AG's copy of vol. 3. of *Plays for an Irish Theatre*, now in Berg.
103. 22 Dec. 1921, *L*, 675.
104. ECY to James Drake, 1 Feb. 1922, HRHRC.
105. Including the singing of the National Anthem in the middle. When his Aberdeen engagement had to be cancelled, WBY told GY, 'I have felt here, under the very friendly surface, a current of political hostility, though no hostility to myself' (10 Nov. 1921, MBY).
106. 22 Dec. [1921], *L*, 675.
107. 7 Sept. 1921, NLI MS 16,678. She would add her voice too. See WBY to Quinn, 2 Sept. 1921: 'Lady Gregory writes to me that she is at her Memoirs, so the work of this generation in Ireland will not lack its chronicle.' (NYPL).

Chapter 6 : LIVING IN THE EXPLOSION
1922–1924

1. James Stephens, 'Arthur Griffith, President of Dáil Éireann', *Review of Reviews*, 65, 317 (Mar. 1922).
2. Mary Fitzgerald, 'Ezra Pound and Irish Politics: An Unpublished Correspondence', *Paideuma*, 12, 2 (1983), 393.
3. See Tom Garvin, *1922: The Birth of Irish Democracy* (Dublin, 1996), 30; also ibid., 176–7, for the pseudo-legalistic arguments querying the reality of the new state.
4. 12 Jan. 1922, Indiana. AE wrote to WBY (16 Jan.):

> Griffith is proving himself a competent chief I think. His speech winding up Dail debate was astonishing from him. He is generally cold and ineffective. There his voice was resonant, his thinking clear, his sentences incisive, and that dear, woolly-minded de Valera appeared a sheep beside an exceedingly clever and yet not too wicked goat. Ireland is intensely interesting, more so than I have found it since I was a boy. The young men are full of possibilities, and I watch them and study their minds, and I am full of hope not indeed of an ever peaceful country but for a country with a great many fine personalities.

NLI MS 9968 (no. 381) and partly in *Some Passages from the Letters of A. E. to W. B. Yeats* (Cuala, 1936).
5. For full quotation and context, see M. Hopkinson, *Green Against Green: The Irish Civil War* (Dublin, 1988), 52.
6. This cosy concept was advanced by the South African Irish paper, the *Republic*: see Gerard Keown, 'The Irish Race Congress, 1922, Reconsidered', *Irish Historical Studies*, 32, 127 (May 2001), 365–76. Also see Ronan Fanning, Michael Kennedy, Dermot Keogh and Eunan O'Halpin (eds.), *Documents on Irish Foreign Policy. Volume 1: 1919–1922* (Dublin, 1998), no. 3, 5.

7. Another reason for stressing 'cultural' connections was the uncomfortable fact that the creation of an Irish state 'at home' raised difficult questions regarding the extent to which the Irish abroad could claim citizenship of the new Free State – as many of the sundered Gaels vehemently (but mistakenly) expected to.

8. 29 Jan. 1922, NLI MS 18,678. Pound's judgement is in a letter to Quinn, 21 Feb. 1922, NYPL. 'Affable but no impact. Still, the Abbey, and putting Synge across [to] the public, is about all the propaganda one can ask of a man, especially if he is a damn great lyric poet.'

9. 15 Jan. 1922, Berg.

10. See Donald T. Torchiana, *Yeats and Georgian Ireland* (Washington, 2nd ed., 1992), 114.

11. n.d. [but early 1922], NLI MS 18,677.

12. WBY to AG, 27 Jan. 1922, Berg. His comments about the 'impossibilists' are in a letter of 12 Jan. For the fears of ill-informed English friends, see G. Bottomley to T. S. Moore, 15 Apr. 1922, Sturge Moore Papers, University of London, MS 978/17/148. AG wrote enthusiastically about WBY as minister for Arts, 31 Jan. (NLI MS 18,678).

13. WBY to AG, 23 Feb. 1922, Berg.

14. 12 Jan. 1922, Berg.

15. WBY to Gogarty 1 Feb. 1922 (in GY's hand), Bucknell, and to May Morris, 2 Apr. 1927, Bodleian MS Top. Oxon. c. 369, and *L*, 724–5.

16. See *AM*, 412.

17. 1 Feb. 1922, SIUC.

18. WBY to AG, 23 Feb., 1 Mar., 9 Mar. 1922, Berg.

19. To Rosa Butt, n.d. [but 1902]; also 17 July 1908: 'one reason why I get irritated with Merrion Square is that it is full of class people'. (Bodleian).

20. 26 Feb. 1922, MBY. The $14 is recorded (without comment) by Quinn to WBY, 4 Apr. 1922, MBY.

21. 3 Feb. 1922, Boston College. He wrote in similar terms the same day to ECY.

22. WBY to Jeanne Foster, Foster–Murphy Collection, NYPL. Foster told GY that all his clothes had been burned and the room fumigated for fear of TB (12 Feb. 1922, NLI MS 31,115) but this may have been an obsession of Quinn's.

23. *Dial*, Feb. 1922.

24. *BG*, 3–5. Tattwa symbolism uses a yellow square for earth, a blue disc for air, a black egg for spirit, a red triangle for fire, and a silver crescent for water, a symbolism familiar to both Yeatses. My thanks to Deirdre Toomey for guidance on this point.

25. To Quinn, 5 June 1922, NYPL.

26. For this distinction, see Garvin, *Irish Democracy*, 143.

27. AG, *Journals*, i, 358.

28. Postcard to GY, 21 Mar. 1922, MBY; the phrase is repeated in a letter to AG. (He arrived at Coole on 27 Mar.)

29. *Journals*, i, 366. De Valera's attack on 'cowardly reason' is quoted in Garvin, *Irish Democracy*, 49.

30. To J. C. Squire, 16 July [1922], HRHRC.

31. HRHRC. Also see *Journals*, i, 383, entries for 2 and 6 Aug.; WBY to Sturge Moore, 15 Aug., HRHRC; and to T. Spicer-Sampson, 8 Aug. 1922, Princeton. At the time of purchase the bridge was exhaustively discussed: see Sir Henry Doran to WBY, 1 Mar. 1917, and J. O'Brien to WBY, 26 Mar. 1917, MBY. For GY's negotiations, see Brigit Patmore in the *Massachusetts Review*, 8, 4 (Winter, 1968), 152–9. The Irregulars asked her to 'never breathe it again'.

32. Lucille O'Malley McLoughlin, recorded by James Charles Roy, 7 Nov. 1997. AG's account of the visit is in *Journals*, i, 370: she does not mention Lucille's presence.

O'Malley wrote three articles in the *Boston Post* describing his experiences (19, 26 and 27 July 1922). His expressed scepticism about the Irish people's faith in what he called a 'shadowy republic' may owe something to his conversation with WBY and AG at Coole.

33. To Quinn, 5 June 1922, Foster–Murphy Collection, NYPL.

34. So GY told Joseph Hone, in a letter of 14 Dec. 1940, HRHRC.

35. *Journals*, i, 368. But she missed the point in believing that he was representing the landlord class as abdicating through 'virtue rather than necessity'.

36. A parallelism usefully discussed in Daniel Harris, *Yeats: Coole Park and Ballylee* (London, 1974), Chapter 6. The version of 'My House' printed here is that first published in the *Dial*; the third stanza was later excised. In the *Dial* 'founded' in the last stanza appeared as 'found it', which seems to have been an error.

37. See Elizabeth Butler Cullingford, 'How Jacques Molay Got Up the Tower: Yeats's "Meditations in Time of Civil War"', *ELH* (formerly *Journal of English Literary History*), 50 (1983), 763–89. 'Vengeance on the murderers of Jacques Molay' was a Masonic code; the eighteenth-century Freemasons saw themselves as heirs of the Templars, as WBY pointed out in a note. Cullingford shows that in 1921 WBY (and GY) were plagued by Christina Stoddart, a fellow member of the Stella Matutina who was obsessed by the fear that the Order was being infiltrated by Illuminati determined to overthrow civilization: it was all the fault of the Jews. The Russian Revolution featured largely in these diatribes, and may lie behind WBY's 'Phantoms of Hatred', which also owe something to George Sand's novels *Consuelo* and *The Countess of Rudolstadt*, dealing with the theme of the Illuminati, which AG was reading aloud to WBY at this time. See *L*, 687–8: 'They fill one with reverie – secret societies of the eighteenth century, all turmoil of imagined wisdom from which came the barricades'.

38. AG to Lennox Robinson, 23 Aug. 1922, SIUC.

39. WBY to Louis Purser, 3 Sept. 1922, Purser Papers.

40. 4 Oct. 1922, Yale.

41. Or so Pritchett claimed in his autobiography. But in his *Christian Science Monitor* articles, written at the time (23 June and 8 July 1923), he gives a less colourful version, where WBY simply removes a stone from his shoe. *I & R*, ii, 347. For other descriptions, see ibid., i, 158–63, 160–71, 191.

42. See AG to WBY, 31 Dec. 1922 NLI MS 18,679.

43. As itemized in Willard Conneely, 'Recollections of A. E. and Yeats', TS in HRHRC.

44. 10 Aug. 1922, NYPL.

45. *The Masterpiece and the Man: Yeats as I Knew Him* (London, 1959), and *Black List Section H* (London, 1975).

46. NLI MS 13,376 has a relevant entry dated '1922' under 'Style as a form of good breeding'.

47. WBY to AG, 30 Sept. [1922], Berg, for his remark about the unpolitical society. See Elizabeth Butler Cullingford, *Yeats, Ireland and Fascism* (London, 1981), 172 ff.; NLI MS 30,887, for WBY's correspondence with Blythe about the Gonne motor-car.

48. WBY to Ricketts, 5 Nov. 1922, *L*, 691–2.

49. 19 Oct. 1922, NYPL.

50. 9 Oct. 1922, *L*, 690.

51. See WBY to OS, '7 Dec.' [but actually 7 Nov. 1922], MBY. 'Elsewhere I find constant stories and phrases that seem now the logical result of the mathematical system of which I knew nothing at the time.'

52. 18 July 1922, NYPL.

53. 24 Nov. 1922, MBY. This letter also includes a marvellously vivid description of a bullet-ridden night in Dublin.

54. GY to WBY, 28 Nov. 1922.

55. Garvin, *Irish Democracy*, 60.
56. See WBY to GY, n.d. [but 2 Dec. 1922], MBY. At the Savile Club, Gosse had said, in WBY's hearing,

'Have you seen that disgraceful book Ulysses? The author is a Sinn Feiner and a spy.' I waited a moment or two & then got up & strayed over to Gosse's side & said 'Mr James Joyce is very grateful to Mr Gosse, who got him quite a large sum from the Royal Bounty Fund.' Gosse then said 'The Portrait of the Artist was a very different book from Ulysses' & I said 'It is hardly less obscene in places' after a word or two more of quite a mild nature I strayed to the far end of the room. I heard Gosse (who evidently thought I had left the room) say 'was Yeats embarrassed' and another voice reply 'Yes but I think he got rather well out of it.' I did not like to over hear any more & went down stairs.

The previous Jan. Gosse had mounted in the *Sunday Times* what Bottomley called a 'dastardly, odious, unpardonable and fundamentally unintelligent attack upon Yeats': to Sturge Moore, 15 Jan. 1922, Sturge Moore Papers, University of London, MS 978/17/143. Gosse would later write a mocking review of *The Bounty of Sweden* in Aug. 1925: see *UP*, ii, 453–4.

57. 29 Nov. 1922, MBY.
58. As he recalled when unveiling a plaque to Thomas Lyster, the librarian of the day, on 27 Mar. 1926: see NLI MS 30,868.
59. HRHRC: misdated 1 Dec. [1922], from Merrion Square. WBY was not back in Dublin before 10 Dec., and when he wrote this letter had already attended several sessions. It may be 1 Jan. 1923.
60. *I & R*, i, 392.
61. To Quinn, 29 Jan. 1924, NYPL. Jameson also had a Sligo connection: his maternal grandfather was James Cochrane of Glen Lodge, Strandhill, a friend of the Pollexfens (see *PF*, 325). Jameson was chairman of John Jameson & Son from 1905 to 1941, and a friend and patron of JBY; he commissioned portraits from him, contributed largely to the fund intended to send JBY to Italy in 1907 (but which took him to New York instead), and visited him at Petitpas's in 1911. The Jamesons lived in plutocratic splendour at Sutton House, Howth, looking south over Dublin Bay. For WBY's connection with this group in the Senate, see Torchiana, *Yeats and Georgian Ireland*, 172–3.
62. Pearce, 38–9.
63. Hopkinson, *Green Against Green*, 140.
64. WBY to Cyril Fagan, 21 Dec. 1922, NLI MS 5918. For Gogarty's reference, see letter to 'Harry' [probably Stuart or Clifton], 17 Oct. 1938, copy in HRHRC; the same phrase recurs in an incomplete letter to Shane Leslie. Anti-Semitic comments disfigure most of Gogarty's letters, notably those to Mab Moltke in Bucknell, a feature which remarkably goes unmentioned by his biographer Ulick O'Connor.
65. 26 Dec. 1922, Berg.
66. See WBY's letter to *IT*, 8 Feb. 1926. The episode is dealt with by Torchiana, *Yeats and Georgian Ireland*, 207ff., and in Bernard G. Krimm, *W. B. Yeats and the Emergence of the Irish Free State 1918–1939 – Living in the Explosion* (NY, 1981), 66–9 – with some far-fetched extrapolation to WBY's late poem 'The Black Tower'. Letters between Southborough and Granard (5 and 6 Apr. 1923) in MBY suggest intermediaries.
67. To GY, 21 Jan. [1923], MBY. His disillusionment refers to a long talk with one such lady 'on the most profound subjects' who suddenly asked him what he meant by the word 'aphorism'.
68. Curtis memorandum, 'Yeats on the General Position, Secret', 27 Jan. 1923, PRO CO 739/19 (reproduced on pp. 668–9). A letter from WBY to GY shows that he met Curtis on 20 Jan. For his part, Curtis made the strange suggestion that WBY and his friends set up voluntary armed vigilante forces to police the streets.

69. WBY to GY, 21 Jan. [1923]. Buckmaster, an Asquithean, had been lord chancellor in the coalition government of 1915.

70. 31 Jan. 1923, Emory. He mentions his wish to meet GY somewhere in Wales '& to think out . . . if we cannot find some means of putting the children in safety from Dublin noise of shot & bomb. It is very bad for Anne who has nerves. I have only had telegrams & it is possible George has already sent Anne to a nursing home.'

71. Hopkinson, *Green Against Green*, 222–3.

72. ibid., 257.

73. *Journals*, i, 445; WBY to Quinn, n.d., NYPL; WBY to Pound, 18 May 1924, Indiana. 'No. Maud and Iseult are both out of jail, Iseult through pressure brought by me, and Seaghan escaped some months ago.'

74. Hopkinson, *Green Against Green*, 264.

75. See a letter to General MacGrath, 18 Oct. 1923, in FitzGerald Papers, UCDA, which details the arrangements.

76. 26 Dec. 1922, Berg.

77. To Dulac, '1' Dec. 1922 [but misdated], HRHRC.

78. Pearce, 30; 18 Dec. 1922, *L*, 694.

79. WBY to AG, 19 Dec. 1921, Emory.

80. ibid., a very long letter, written while Robinson was staying with him at Oxford, and AG to WBY, 21 Dec. [1921], NLI MS 18,678. A draft letter was produced, to this effect.

81. To WBY, 7 Jan. 1922, NLI MS 18,678.

82. To AG, 19 Dec. 1921, Emory.

83. WBY to AG, 2 Jan. 1922, Berg.

84. *Journals*, i, 319, 329.

85. See Appendix 1, below.

86. Memo accompanying a letter from Robinson to FitzGerald, 21 Oct. 1922, FitzGerald Papers, UCDA.

87. See GY to FitzGerald, 11 Dec. 1922, and 17 Jan. '1922' [*recte* 1923], FitzGerald papers, UCDA.

88. *Journals*, i, 435, 446–7. A letter from her to WBY of 20 Oct. [1922], NLI MS 18,679, makes clear that she thought the statement 'a little too much of an S.O.S. signal' and would have preferred to hold on longer and then hand it over completely. 'I am not obstructing your proposal, only taking care the financial items are right.' It was, therefore, very much his initiative.

89. NLI MS 18,677; Robinson to AG, 2 July 1923, and to Ernest Blythe, 1 Nov. 1924, Berg.

90. 'The Abbey Subsidy', speech at the Abbey, 8 Aug. 1925, TS, MBY. For the actual arrangements, see FitzGerald to Robinson, 5 Feb. 1925, FitzGerald Papers, UCDA.

91. To Ernest Boyd, 14 June 1923, Healy.

92. Recorded in NLI MS 30,864.

93. Torchiana, *Yeats and Georgian Ireland*, 176–7.

94. Andrew Boyle, *Poor Dear Brendan: The Quest for Brendan Bracken* (London, 1974), 126; Charles Lysaght, *Brendan Bracken* (London, 1979), 62.

95. See *Journals*, i, 432, 434. WBY's Senate speech is reported in *FJ*, 10 May 1923; also see Pearce, 460–9. There is a useful clippings collection in NLI MS 30,250, showing that WBY collected reports of cases where a codicil had been disputed and upheld; it also contains some notes for his Senate speech.

96. AE to WBY, 21 Mar. 1922, *LTWBY*, ii, 407–8. There had been a long report in the *IT* of 28 Feb. 1922, showing that planning meetings had been taking place over a number of months. The eleven members of the Drafting Committee were nearly all academics from the National University (Trinity was unrepresented). The secretary was Father Timothy Corcoran, scourge of liberalism in general and Protestantism in particular.

97. See AE to WBY, 30 Mar. 1922, *LTWBY*, ii, 408–9, and to Ernest Boyd, 19 June 1922, Healy; also WBY to AG, 23 Mar. [1922], and to Pound, 27 July 1922, Buffalo.

98. Pearce, 57–8; see also *I & R*, i, 162, for an evasive answer about compulsory Irish, in 1924. V. S. Pritchett noted, 'I suspect he dislikes the teaching of Irish': *Christian Science Monitor*, 8 Dec. 1923.

99. Quoted in Garvin, *Irish Democracy*, 118.

100. *Journals*, i, 463, 527.

101. ibid., 485.

102. *AM*, 194.

103. WBY to AG, 19 July 1923, Berg.

104. See ECY to Quinn, 10 July 1917, 18 July 1922, 16 Jan. 1923, 31 July 1923, NYPL. The limited company option was eventually embraced; see SMY to R L-P, 26 Sept. 1933. 'The accounts [in bank] are Lolly for the press, George for the embroidery & Lolly & I are partners & Cuala ceases to be a society, which is what we wanted for these ages, as we had all the responsibility & risk.'

105. To AG, 17 July 1923, Berg.

106. 'How I would enjoy life if I wrote like that.' WBY to AG, 4 Sept. 1923, Berg.

107. ECY to Clement Shorter, 2 Jan. 1924, Berg.

108. A fairly random collection of bills (Boston College) add up to £418. 4s. 9d. and there must have been more. 'Roseneath' cost eight guineas a week without medicine, and she was there for eight months.

109. WBY to Robert Simpson, 3 Apr. 1924 (copy), Boston College. For the matron's letter, ECY to GY 'Friday evening' [1924], Boston College; also see Robert Simpson to WBY, 20 Mar. 1924. SMY to GY, 12 Mar. 1924, Boston College, describes ECY's advent. 'She came to see me four times & made me wish I was dead. She spoke of coming over again "to see me". I do hope she will not.' Also SMY to WBY, 30 Mar. 1924, Boston College: 'I wish you could use some magic, white or black, & cure Lolly of her temper & insane jealously. It has stood between me & everything for 15 years or more & even now I cannot escape. Her visit over here was one of venomous mischief.'

110. WBY to AG, 30 Oct. 1923, Berg. 'Bracken has come and gone. Curzon said to him "I did not want to give up those pictures but I find that I must." Curzon then told him that the Commission would decide he thought that they were to be given back on permanent loan as the difficulties of bringing in a bill were too great. I brought him over to the President & got him to repeat his story. The President said that he would consult the law officers, or rather I asked him to do so & he agreed.' Also *Journals*, i, 543, for T. M. Healy contradicting Bracken's assertions, and WBY to AG, 16 Oct. and 2 Nov. 1923, Berg.

111. See his correspondence with the infuriated Thomas Bodkin in June–July 1923, who felt WBY had blocked his candidacy for the National Gallery: Bodkin Papers, TCD.

112. WBY to AG, 16 Oct. 1923, Berg.

113. Plunkett to AG, 10 Feb. 1923, Berg.

114. 4 July 1923, Berg.

115. See *AV (1925)*, p. xxiii, and WBY to AG, 30 Oct. 1923, Berg.

116. 1 Aug. [1923], NLS.

117. *Journals*, i, 477.

118. Giorgio Melchiori, *The Whole Mystery of Art: Pattern into Poetry in the Work of W. B. Yeats* (London, 1960), discusses probable inspirations: such as an illustration in Andrew Lang's edition of *The Strife of Love in a Dream*, transcribed by WBY for Nutt in his youth (*AM*, 556, n. 64). Michelangelo's painting was originally considered the most direct source, though Melchiori made a good case for Moreau (153 ff.). However, Charles Madge in the *TLS* of 20 July 1962 suggested a bas-relief in the Etruscan Room

of the British Museum, and since this is reproduced in Élie Faure's *History of Art*, which was owned by WBY, it may indeed have been the image he showed AG when she visited him. In the *TLS* of 16 Nov. 1962 Madge argued convincingly against Charles Gullam's suggestion (*TLS*, 9 Nov. 1962) of Sturge Moore's woodcut. For the best summary, see Ian Fletcher, '"Leda and the Swan" as Iconic Poem' *YA* 1 (1982), 82–113.

119. *AV (1925)*, 181.

120. *I & R*, ii, 324.

121. SMY to Quinn, 22 Nov. 1923, NYPL; Thomas MacGreevy, 'Uileacháin Dubh Ó', *Capuchin Annual* (1952), 224.

122. To Sir John O'Connell, 25 Nov. 1923, Yale (in a copy of *Poems*, 1895).

123. For the coat, see *AM*, 315, 316, 327. It was lined in Dublin, relined in London en route at double the cost, and never worn in Sweden, where the weather was mild and balmy: SMY to R L-P, 26 Dec. 1923. After WBY's death in 1939 it was offered to several Dublin furriers, but nobody wanted it.

124. See an article in *New Church Life* (Apr. 1926), quoting the *Nya Kyrkans Tidning* of Dec. 1923.

125. Robert McAlmon retreated under a barrage of high-flown clichés about the artist's search for beauty: see *Being Geniuses Together 1920–1930* (rev. ed., London, 1984), 227.

126. SMY to R L-P, 26 Dec. [1923]. Hill, who was only thirty-six when he won the Nobel, went on to a long and distinguished career; he died in 1977.

127. To Stead, 20 Nov. 1923, Yale; to Quinn, 3 Nov. 1923 and 29 Jan. 1924, NYPL.

128. 13 Jan. 1924, Berg, and *L*, 701–2. For the commitment to Cuala, see GY to R L-P, 17 June 1925: my thanks to William M. Murphy.

129. The stockbrokers were Perry & Cairnes, 31 College Green. Between 7 and 15 Jan. 1924 WBY purchased £2,000 Great Southern & Western Railway 4% Debenture Stock at 68 and 69 (£1396. 8s. 0d.), £500 G. S. and W. 4% Railway Debenture Stock at 69 and a half (£347. 10s. 0d.), £1,150 Great Northern Railway 4% Debenture Stock at 70 (£805. 0s. 0d.), a further £600 of the same (£420), £250 ditto at 71 and a half (£178. 15s. 0d.) and £500 ditto at 72 (£360. 0s. 0d.). (NLI MS 30,646 gives slightly higher figures, which include the brokers' commission.) The G. S. and W. stock declined steadily until 1933, when WBY's investment of £1,743. 18s. 0d. was worth only £925. It recovered over the rest of the decade, reaching a record high in 1936, when WBY's holding would have been worth £2,125, but by the time of his death it was down again (his shares, if he still had them, would have been worth £1,412. 10s. 0d.). His Great Northern stock followed much the same pattern; his holding, worth £1,763. 15s. 0d. in 1924, had declined to £1,56. 5s. 0d. in 1934, recovering to a high of £2,075 in 1937, but falling again to £1,122. 10s. 0d. at the time of his death. His railway investments therefore brought neither a large income nor capital growth. Information from *IT* stock listings in early Jan. 1924–39. According to W. R. Rodgers, 'Notes for the Radio', HRHRC, Lennox Robinson was responsible for the advice to invest in railways.

130. To AG, 13 Jan. 1924, Berg.

131. As suggested in A. Hartfeldt to WBY, n.d., from the Swedish Academy, MBY.

132. NLI MS 30,813. He changed it to 'delighted in history and tradition'.

133. Nonetheless, Frank Fay sent a friendly congratulation, and WBY replied that he had 'spoken of you and your brother, & of all those who helped in those old days'; the applause had been for them as well (NLI MS 2652). Mrs W. G. Fay was not so generously minded: see below, p. 460.

134. This reaction was true of other areas of activity too. See for instance A. P. Graves to Mrs Todhunter (Reading), reacting to the *Mercury* extracts from *The Trembling of the Veil*. 'I wonder Squire printed them: it is a record of self-glorification as regards the Irish

Literary Society for which Willie Rolleston & I worked hardest tho' no doubt he [WBY] did a good deal though I should imagine very injudiciously for the National Literary Society of Dublin.'

Chapter 7 : BAD WRITERS AND BISHOPS
1924–1925

1. 29 Jan. 1924, NYPL.
2. 25 Feb. 1924, HRHRC.
3. *CB*, 13, 12 (Dec. 1923), 817–18.
4. ibid., 19, 1 (Jan. 1924), 6. Gogarty had said in the Senate:

    For more than twenty-five years Senator Yeats has set his face against any false enthusiasm, or false idealism, or any attempt to make poetry into patriotism; he has invited and sustained a good deal of unpopularity, but on no occasion has he written tawdry poetry to make his purse heavier. The civilisation of countries, ancient and modern, has been assessed by outstanding names in literature, and Ireland's civilisation will be assessed by the name of Senator Yeats.

5. ibid., 14, 2 (Feb. 1924), 91.
6. To AG, 26 Jan. 1924, Berg.
7. *Journals*, i, 525.
8. 23 Mar. 1924.
9. WBY to GY, n.d. Her illness was probably pleurisy, but she also suffered from recurrent arthritis; she had had scarlet fever and subsequently jaundice in 1923.
10. O'Connell's letter and memorandum is in NLI MS 30,680. The letter makes clear that Jameson and WBY were the unnamed senators in the document, and were to remain unknown. It is an important statement, clarifying the rival existences of the IRB (with Mulcahy 'at the very head and centre') and the Irish Republican Army Organization (IRAO) in the army and the threatened breakdown of efficiency and discipline. According to O'Connell, the Cork, Kerry, and Waterford commands were all in chaos, the generals believed that the army had kept the government in power and could put it out, and the general officer commanding the Limerick division asserted 'the only difference between the Irregulars and ourselves was that we had won'. The IRAO was ready to revolt, and the IRB was a 'virus' destroying army discipline from within. Plans for seizing camps at the Curragh and elsewhere had been made, assassination plots against senior officers were in existence, and the guard at Baldonnell had to be swiftly changed. A brother officer (almost certainly MacManus) had approached him 'and said to me privately that he knew a particular Senator of outstanding integrity, judgement and patriotism, and asked if I would put the case before him, and abide by his decision as to whether or not the state of things justified approaching a member of the executive'. Later WBY told OS that MacManus was 'one of the two men who came to me when we were threatened with a mutiny' (*L*, 812–13). For O'Connell, see Donald T. Torchiana, *Yeats and Georgian Ireland* (Washington, 2nd ed., 1992), 222, n. 1. Also see GY's diary, NLI MS 30,065, for the dinner with O'Higgins. For the mutiny, see Maryanna Valuilis, *Almost a Revolution: the Irish Army Mutiny of 1924* (Cork, 1985); John Regan, *The Irish Counter-Revolution 1921–1936* (Dublin, 1999), Chapter 8. WBY's attitude is dealt with by David Fitzpatrick in 'W. B. Yeats in Seanad Éireann' in R. O'Driscoll and Lorna Reynolds, *Yeats and the Theatre* (1975), 162; Hone, 382; Francis MacManus (ed.), *The Yeats we Knew* (Cork, 1965); and Bernard G. Krimm, *W. B. Yeats and the Emergence of the Irish Free State 1918–1939 – Living in the Explosion* (NY, 1981); but none of these authorities seem to have followed through the implications of the O'Connell memorandum.

11. Regan, *Irish Counter-Revolution*, 180.
12. *Dublin Magazine*, I, 9 (Apr. 1924).
13. See *Journals*, i, 445, and for the first night, Robert Hogan and Michael J. O'Neill (eds.), *Joseph Holloway's Abbey Theatre: A Selection from His Unpublished Journal 'Impressions of a Dublin Playgoer'* (London, 1967), 215–16, 226–7.
14. *Journals*, i, 514–15.
15. ibid., 512. Also see WBY to Pound, 18 May 1924, Indiana. 'I don't think his "Juno and the Paycock" reads particularly well, but played by our people who know the slum people it is extraordinarily moving and amusing. It is a tragic farce about the assassinations and counter-assassinations that have gone on here, and is the greatest success the Abbey has had for years. We turned away hundreds of people one night.'
16. *Journals*, i, 541.
17. Articles on the subject appeared in the *Irish Ecclesiastical Record, Studies, The Catholic Mind*, and elsewhere: see Senia Paseta, '"A Time of Particular Danger and Particular Hope": Literary Censorship and Its Opponents in the Irish Free State 1922–1932', *Past and Present*, forthcoming.
18. 27 July 1922, Buffalo. The point that Joyce never altogether abandoned a certain *fin de siècle* shimmer in his descriptive style is astute.
19. To GY, 3 Dec. [1922]. 'I am charmed with Eliot & find that I have a reasonable liking for his "Sacred Wood". He told me a strange story. Joyce is related through his mother to the Macsweeneys family [*recte* MacSwiney], the hunger strikers family, & was stirred by the death of the Mayor of Cork to his first political interest or emotion.'
20. See Richard Ellmann (ed.), *Letters of James Joyce. Volume 3* (London, 1966), 77; WBY wrote on 26 June 1923.
21. *IT*, 9 Nov. 1923.
22. 20 May [1924]. 'At least I am told so, for I never see the Catholic popular press.'
23. 17 June 1924, Indiana. Pound's effusion was dated 14 June 1924. WBY's original temporizing letter was written on 18 May 1924, Indiana. It continued: 'Do you happen to know whether the seizures were made in connection with the League of Nations, that body has a clause in its constitution about stopping the transit from one country to another of what its officials consider indecent literature. You should get people in the press to watch the use made of that clause.'
24. WBY to Pound, 26 June 1924, Indiana.
25. 17 June 1924, Indiana.
26. Pound to FitzGerald, 16 and 24 Oct. 1928, quoted in Mary Fitzgerald, 'Ezra Pound and Irish Politics: An Unpublished Correspondence', *Paideuma*, 12, 2 (1983).
27. Regan, *Irish Counter-Revolution*, 91.
28. MBY. 'Aonach Tailteann' had been first dreamt up in 1922, but postponed because of the civil war. Its origins lay in a legendary sports festival organized by King Lugha in honour of Queen Taillte, at Telltown on the plains of Meath.
29. 28 May 1924; MacGreevy Papers, TCD.
30. See Gogarty to Ernest Boyd, 14 Feb. 1924 (copy), HRHRC. Also on the invitations committee were Sir Henry McLaughlin, Sir Simon Maddock, and the Marquis MacSwiney. WBY told Joyce (1 June 1924, Cornell), 'At first the Committee only intended to invite people of other nationalities but at the last moment they decided, for more or less political reasons, to invite Lavery and Shaw. Then the question arose of asking other Irishmen.'
31. See Pound to WBY, 19 June 1924, Indiana: an exceptionally deluded letter, for this period in Pound's life, which begins 'To the President of the Howly Synod: William by the grace of God; Butler by descent uterine; on the male side Yeats.' He repeated his condition of a passport to Quinn, 10 July 1924, NYPL.

32. WBY to Joyce, 1 June 1924, Cornell. As to the formal invitation, he warned Joyce, 'I do not, however, expect to succeed. I can imagine the horror with which the suggestion will be received by, for instance, the Marquis MacSwiney, Chamberlain to the pope.'

33. This continued: when the next Aonach Tailteann tried to confer a 'National Award for Imaginative Literature' on GBS, they got a characteristic missile from Cap d'Antibes: 'If Aonach Tailteann can do no better with a gold medal than to give it to a man of 72 to whom it is not of the slightest use . . . then the sooner A. T. is dropped into the dustbin the better.' He finally accepted only on condition that he was not 'made a party to the transaction' (Shaw to Lennox Robinson, 26 July 1928 and 3 Aug. 1928, SIUC).

34. See *Journals*, i, 574–5, which give GY's irreverent version of diplomatic difficulties.

35. *IT*, 4 Aug. 1924.

36. This is from the version printed in the *Irish Independent*, 4 Aug. 1924; there is an earlier draft in NLI MS 30,097 which runs less easily.

37. See *AM*, 499–501.

38. This is taken from NLI MS 30,097, not the *Independent* report.

39. The Persian poet proved a disappointment to devotees of Omar Khayyám but gave WBY material for a good story told to Maurice Bowra:

    'I asked the poet [through an interpreter] what poetry he wrote, and the Persian replied that he used to write love-poetry, which was so beautiful that it became a model of decorum and was studied in all the girls' schools of Persia, but that was a long time ago. So I asked him what he wrote now, and the Persian replied that he wrote useful poetry.' (At that point Yeats' voice became indignant.) 'So I asked what that might be. And the Persian replied that he went as the representative of Persia on the League of Nations, and sent all his reports in rhyme.'
    (*I & R*, ii, 397).

40. See WBY to AG, 30 Apr. [1924], Berg, suggesting that he see the Provost of Trinity about 'a plan I have for the R.I.A. in connection with the Taltian [*sic*] Games'.

41. For the background to this prize, see WBY to Dunsany, 27 July 1924, Berg, looking for a subscription. WBY's citation is reported in the *IT*, 11 Aug. 1924. He continued:

    'Will his expression clarify, his music grow strong and confident, or will his promise remain unfulfilled? That will probably depend upon his critical capacity, upon his intellect, and of these we have no means of judging. His genius, if genius it be, is the opposite of Dr Gogarty's, for he desires all that is faint, cold and shadowy.'

    (Here, as elsewhere, he seems to be casting Stuart for the part of a youthful WBY: another attempt to appropriate Iseult by proxy.) Stuart's account is to be found in his fictionalized autobiography, *Black List Section H* (1995 ed., Dublin), 118–121. According to him, WBY said two of the poems 'so disturbed my imagination that they kept me from my sleep'.

42. *Black List Section H*, 120.

43. WBY to Pound, 12 Aug. 1924, Indiana. Also see *Irish Statesman*, 28 Aug. 1924.

44. *CB*, 14, 4 (Apr. 1924), 265–6.

45. ibid., 14, 9 (Sept. 1924), 746–7.

46. ibid., 14, 10 (Oct. 1924), 836–7.

47. Eoin Ua Mathghamhna, 'Obscenity in Modern Literature', *Irish Monthly* (Nov. 1924).

48. Quoted *CB*, 14, 10 (Oct. 1924), 837.

49. 21 June [1924], partly in *L*, 705–6.

50. 28 June 1924, Berg.

51. See WBY to Pound, 5 July 1924, Indiana: 'Lennox Robinson & I have given them contributions.'

52. NLI MS 30,278.
53. 25 July 1924, HRHRC. In the same letter he recounted his pleasure at AG's response to the Ampthill peerage case, which hung on the assertion by the claimant's mother that she had become pregnant while remaining *virgo intacta* through using a sponge containing her husband's semen.

    [AG] hates all clergy though she never misses church & is a great reader of her bible & as she believes very orthodox – furthermore she is a great prude so far as what others say to her is concerned. She suddenly astounded me by saying – a propos of nothing – a couple of weeks ago – & with an air of gratified malice – 'that Russell [Ampthill] case sheds a new light on immaculate conception' – she evidently felt that a doctrine which belonged in an especial sense to the clergy had been hit . . . If I had said such a thing as this I would have been in disgrace for the afternoon.

54. 28 July 1924, SIUC, and Richard Taylor (ed.), *Frank Pearce Sturm: His Life, Letters and Collected Work* (Urbana, Ill., 1969), 82–3. Compare WBY to L. A. G. Strong, same date, HRHRC: 'I know nothing of the paper's contents except the leading article which is most inflammatory & a poem which I have sent them.' He wrote the same to Harriet Monroe the same day (Chicago).
55. For more details see Ulick O'Connor, *Oliver St John Gogarty* (London, 1964 ed.), 194–8, 219–21.
56. *CB*, 14, 11 (Nov. 1924), 930.
57. To Ernest Boyd, 19 Nov. 1924, Healy.
58. 5 July, 12 July 1924.
59. See *Journals*, i, 563, and WBY to AG, 30 Oct. 1923 and 26 Jan. 1924, Berg, for Robinson's wish to become director rather than manager, and subsequent plan to withdraw to London. 'He has taken St John Ervine's place on the Observer & should grow to be a man of influence. Bracken got him the job. He does the more general articles while a man in London goes the round of the Theatres. Lennox gets £500 year – & so with his other incomes is worth the attention of ambitious mothers.' As with much else in Robinson's life, this did not work out as planned.
60. *Journals*, i, 563.
61. ibid., 558.
62. ibid., 593.
63. His letter of resignation is in the MacGreevy Papers, TCD, sent by Robinson.
64. *Journals*, i, 593, 595.
65. WBY to Robinson, 23 Oct. 1924, SIUC.
66. *Journals*, i, 596.
67. Minute of Carnegie Library Committee meeting, 22 Oct. 1924, MacGreevy Papers, TCD.
68. On 31 Mar. 1925 WBY wrote to Desmond FitzGerald that, following recent conversations, he could not possibly ask Robinson to resign his position as director. Even though the Abbey's life would be very short without government support, Robinson 'has been for many years the very life of the institution and I would not under any circumstances subject him to what might seem a slight, and what might seem in the future a very bad precedent.' FitzGerald replied soothingly the next day, assuring him it was 'very unlikely that the question of resignation will arise': he had simply raised it as a possible hitch. (UCDA, FitzGerald Papers). It is significant that WBY was, apparently, prepared to risk the subsidy if it meant giving in to government pressure over Robinson; AG would not have been thus inclined.
69. *Journals*, i, 599. Also Iseult to WBY, 'Wednesday' [late 1924, probably Oct.], Jeffares, White and Bridgwater.

70. *Journals*, i, 605. For the *To-Morrow* affair and its possible influence on the campaign for literary censorship, see F. C. Molloy, 'Francis Stuart, W. B. Yeats and *To-Morrow*', *YA* 8 (1991), 214–24.

71. *AV (1925)*, p. xi.

72. To GY, 13 July 1924.

73. To GY, 26 Aug. 1924.

74. To GY [early Sept. 1924].

75. 11 Oct. Sturm pointed out that Costa Ibn Luca, 'whom you call Kusta ben Luka', was 'still hard at work with his pen' fifty-seven years after the death of the Caliph Harun El Rashid, so 'could not have been an old man when the Caliph made him a present of the sleep-walking girl, unless he lived to a very great age indeed. I know you hate pedantry [*sic*], & so do I, but if "A Vision" is to be founded on supposedly existing MS, the dates will have to be right.' Taylor, *Frank Pearce Sturm*, 83.

76. WBY to GY, early Sept. 1924; GY to WBY, n.d. [but late 1924].

77. n.d. [but Aug. 1924]; 28 Aug. 1924; n.d. [but early Sept. 1924], MBY.

78. WBY to Finberg, 18 May and 23 Sept. 1924, Boston College.

79. To Pound, 15 June 1921 [copy], NYPL.

80. 10 Aug. 1924, Foster–Murphy Collection, NYPL.

81. ibid.

82. Iseult to WBY, '29th' [probably Sept. 1924], Jeffares, White and Bridgwater; also see WBY to GY, n.d. [but probably Sept. 1924], MBY.

83. *Journals*, i, 532.

84. See Pearce, 68–77, for this interesting debate.

85. *UP*, ii, 439–49.

86. Pearce, 87. The assertion that he 'knew nothing about the border' came, perhaps significantly, in a letter to Lady Londonderry, wife of an Ulster Unionist grandee (12 Nov. 1924, PRONI). His speech was weakened by a rather contrived reference to Burke, and the British government sending scalping knives to American Indians: according to AG, airing this snippet was the *raison d'être* of the speech in the first place. If so, it transcended its origins.

87. See several leaders in *IT* during Oct. 1924; and *CB*, 14, 11 (Nov. 1924), 937–8.

88. Thomas Gillman Moorhead, Regius Professor of Physic at TCD and a leading Dublin consultant. Less than a year later he was blinded by retinal detachment, but continued a successful career: see J. B. Lyons, *Oliver St John Gogarty: The Man of Many Talents* (Dublin, 1980), 166–7.

89. 21 Oct. 1924, HRHRC. Gogarty to Ernest Boyd, 2 Mar. 1925 (Healy) adds some details. 'Pain in the region of the heart, when excited with oratory in the Senate – blood pressure 220!! ...... Moorhead sent him off [to Sicily], *not* I this time.'

90. Apparently dated 3 Oct., when he was not in fact at Coole. It must actually be 3 Nov. He continued: 'I wish you could write to me but I know you are always busy.'

91. See *Journals*, i, 604, 585–6.

92. ibid., 602–3. WBY left Coole on 15 or 16 Nov.

93. ibid. The 'absurd' reference is in a letter to GY, 13 Nov. [1924].

94. WBY to Lady Londonderry, 12 Nov. 1924, PRONI.

95. A letter apparently dated 15 Nov. 1924. But WBY was still at Coole then; he went to London on 26 Nov., according to the letter to Lady Londonderry.

96. 29 Nov. 1924.

97. See Virginia Moore, *The Unicorn* (New York, 1954), 300, for Ezra's memory. The interest began with his visit to Ravenna in 1907.

98. See WBY to Dulac, 23 Apr. 1925, HRHRC.

99. Hone, 367.

100. See below, Chapter 8, n. 16.

101. *AV (1925)*, p. xiii.

102. *The Masterpiece and the Man: Yeats as I Knew Him* (London, 1959), 82. Monk Gibbon recorded visiting Merrion Square and being shown the TS, finished that day – though he dates it wrongly as 1926.

103. 23 Apr. 1924, HRHRC. For the Great Wheel diagram, see material in Pierpoint Morgan Library, which indicates that WBY's initial ideas were much more complex than Dulac's final version.

104. Ursula Bridge (ed.), *W. B. Yeats and T. S. Moore: Their Correspondence 1901–1937* (London, 1953), p. xvi.

105. To WBY, 14 Feb. 1926, quoted in John Harwood, 'Olivia Shakespear: Letters to W. B. Yeats', *YA* 6 (1988), 60.

106. See Gogarty to L. A. G. Strong, 26 Jan. 1926 (copy), HRHRC, and *Journals*, i, 465 (an entry for 15 June 1923, at Merrion Square). 'Yeats went up to write but came down excited by finding that Einstein's theory brings in the spirals that are the foundations of his own philosophy. Einstein has done away with materialism, he says, and that his theory is banned from the Soviet schools in Russia because it could upset the proleteriat. I can only follow very dimly all this.'

107. *AV (1925)*, p. xi.

108. See *AM*, Chapter 7.

109. Eugene Jolas's recollection: see Richard Ellmann, *James Joyce* (London, 1982), 596n. Parodies of *AV* would recur in *Finnegans Wake*.

110. NLI MS 30,865, 'Notes Rejected from "Wheels and Butterflies"'.

111. A useful discussion in T. R. Whitaker, *Swan and Shadow: Yeats's Dialogue with History* (Chapel Hill, NC, 1964), 32, takes these themes back to the 1890s.

112. See *AV (1925)*, pp. xxxvi–xlvii.

113. Iseult to WBY, [probably 28 Jan. 1926], Jeffares, White and Bridgwater.

114. The idea that truth can be revealed but not discovered recurs in a famous letter at the very end of his life; see below, pp. 649–50.

115. Harper paraphrases it about as clearly as anyone can. '*Will*, the essential definition of personality, is pure choice and defines the self; what it chooses as ideal personality its *Mask*. *Creative Mind*, something of a misnomer, is less related to Romantic imagination than to philosophical reason, bound by the *Body of Fate* or set of environmental truths which it perceives.' (*AV (1925)*, 10). Compare Ellmann, *IY*, 160: 'Yeats divided the self into two sets of symbolic opposites, Will and Mask, Creative Mind and Body of Fate. These may be roughly translated as Imagination and the Image of what we wish to become, and Intellect and Environment.'

116. Whitaker, *Swan and Shadow*, 32, is perceptive on these connections.

117. Michael B. Yeats, *Cast a Cold Eye: Memories of a Poet's Son and Politician* (Dublin, n.d., but 1998), 28.

118. *AV (1925)*, 24–5.

119. Ellmann, *IY*, 161–2.

120. *AV (1925)*, 28–9.

121. ibid., 126–7.

122. ibid., 131–2.

123. In the concluding section of Book II, WBY points out the parallels to Plotinus's philosophy – but with 'a fundamental difference, though perhaps only of expression . . . In Plotinus the One is the Good, whereas in the System God and Evil are eliminated before the soul can be united to Reality, being that stream of phenomena that drowns us.'

124. *AV (1925)*, 180.
125. ibid., 183.
126. ibid., 190–1.
127. And in Ravenna: Thomas MacGreevy was struck by the exactness of WBY's memory of these (see below, p. 303). *AV (1925)*, 53, lists the major authorities studied by WBY for this section: W. G. Holmes, O. M. Dalton, Mrs Arthur Strong, Gibbon, the *Encyclopedia Britannica*, and the *Cambridge Medieval History*.
128. *AV (1925)*, 195. For the omissions, see ibid., 53, n. 190.
129. ibid., 202.
130. ibid., 206–7. James Joyce may lie behind a subsequent reflection: '... the modern novel is created, but even before the gyre is drawn to its end, the happy ending, the admired hero, the preoccupation with desirable things, all that is undisguisedly *Antithetical* disappears.'
131. ibid., 209.
132. ibid., 211–12.
133. Or, yet again, 'mathematical Babylonian starlight'.
134. ibid., 213–14.
135. ibid., 215.
136. See also his remarks on Dickens's 'democratic qualities' in lecture reported in *IT*, 9 Nov. 1923: quoted in *AV (1925)*, 62.
137. 22 Sept. 1923, Yale.
138. *AV (1925)*, 66, n. 217, quoting a note by WBY which Curtis Bradford dates 'about 1929'.
139. See, for instance, 'The Separation of the Four Principles' as glossed by Harper in ibid., 69, n. 232. Experiments with GY's 'Sleeps' are also transposed, as accounts by Robartes of a Judwali seer's findings.

Chapter 8 : VANITY AND PRIDE
1925–1927

1. *CB*, 14, 9 (Sept. 1924): the same issue contained a leading editorial denouncing the Tailteann literary awards inspired by WBY.
2. *IT*, 30 July 1924; *CB*, 14, 11 (Nov. 1924).
3. *UP*, ii, 450. There is a MS and corrected TS in the Robinson Papers at SIUC, implying that Robinson was closely consulted.
4. ibid., 451.
5. ibid., 452.
6. ibid., 463–4.
7. *Journals*, ii, 11 (15 May 1925).
8. WBY to AG, 26 Mar. 1925, Berg. The *CB*'s reaction to AE's caution is worth quoting; it appeared under the title 'Purging the Pride of Pollexfen' in 16, 9 (Sept. 1926).

The Irish Statesman HAS ACTUALLY COLD-SHOULDERED SENATOR YEATS! These 'notes' were sent once again, as usual. But they were sent back, unbasted and ungarnished!! No admittance!!! 'Cold-storage' was the treatment now editorially administered!!!! No editorial butter was now melted for the choice service of the Visionary Viands!!! That editorial commodity had to be taken away! ... Driven from Home! Thrust from the Haughty Portals of Plunkett House, with his Occasional Literary Offspring in his arms!! Why did not a score of sabres leap from their scabbards, to counter this cold-shoulder, cleave it to the chine, and vindicate the vanishing Visionary?

This was in response to the eventual British appearance of the piece in the *New Criterion* of Apr. 1926, retitled 'Our Need for Religious Sincerity'.

9. NLI MS 30,080.

10. Pearce, 94. On the day, WBY referred to Archbishop [Edward] Byrne as the 'Most Rev. Dr O'Donnell', and was sharply corrected by Joseph Byrne, CSSP, provincial of the Fathers of the Holy Ghost, in a public letter: see *CB*, 16, 6 (June, 1926), 685, and *Irish Independent*, 13 June 1925. Dr Byrne had quoted Archbishop O'Donnell, and WBY conflated the two men.

11. AG had tried to make him spare the bishop of Meath, but WBY showed her a report of his speech to the Mothers' Union in which he stated that 'the immoral person should not be treated as at present just as a sinner, but as a criminal, and should receive the punishment meted to other criminals such as robbers or forgers or murderers'. 'After that,' she admitted, 'what could I say? Our church dignitaries instead of standing against R. C. pressure are supporting it.' (*Journals*, ii, 14).

12. Pearce, 97.

13. See TS dated 10 June 1925, NLI MS 30,080.

14. He gleefully borrowed this observation from Francis Hackett: see Lis Pihl, 'Francis Hackett's "Monuments": A Yeats Letter in the Royal Library, Copenhagen', *YA* 11 (1995), 106–204.

15. Burke and Swift, interestingly, were added to the TS at a late stage: see NLI MS 30,080.

16. See *Journals*, ii, 27, 29. Joseph Hone acted as 'secretary' for this group; he had written a piece in the *Irish Statesman* suggesting some guiding policies, including – in AG's words – 'a dual monarchy', the suppression of the *IT*, 'No Freemasons', and – at WBY's suggestion – bringing back Grattan's body from Westminster to St Patrick's, an edifice which might itself be offered to the Catholic Church. Not all of these ideas may have been ironic, but none of them was carried very far. To judge by a letter from him to WBY (22 May [1925], MBY), they had discussed a new 'National Unionist Party' when on holiday in Italy which would advocate a status like that before 1800, making the British monarch king of Ireland and using the imperial connection to advantage. 'INTERNAL policy anti-democratic, but in a progressive, modern sense.' A 'hierarchic form of society' was called for, along with protection of wealth and intellectual liberty. The Italian example was specifically invoked.

17. *CB*, 15, 7 (July 1925). The full report of WBY's speech from the *Official Records* was reproduced in the same issue. The *Irish Independent* of 12 June 1925 carried a long and appalled report, with many subheadings. *Sinn Féin*, however, approved (AG to WBY, 15 June 1925, NLI MS 18,681).

18. To R L-P, n.d. [but *c.* 11 June 1925]. Also see *Journals* ii, 16.

19. To L. A. G. Strong, 25 June 1925, *L*, 708–9.

20. *Journals*, ii, 15. As reported by AG, the original letter added: 'Tommy Bodkin went up to Father Peter Finley at the Governor-General's garden party – Gogarty says – & said "Are you not ashamed to appear in public after the castigation Dr Yeats gave you in the Senate." Father Finley is said to have hurried away making no answer.'

21. ibid., 17.

22. 12 Nov. 1925, *Journals*, ii, 51.

23. See his exchange with FitzGerald, 31 Mar. and 1 Apr. 1925, UCDA. FitzGerald hastily recanted the suggestion and assured him that it was very unlikely that any question of resignation would arise.

24. See above, pp. 233–6.

25. See WBY to Blythe, 11 and 12 July 1925, NLI MS 20,704. For the arrangements worked out, see FitzGerald to Robinson, 5 Feb. 1925, and reply, 6 Feb. 1925, UCDA. At the dinner Michael Dolan and Gabriel Fallon were also present, with their wives.

26. MBY. On 28 June 1925 Robinson had written to MacGreevy describing WBY's excitement about the 'intensity' of Anglo-Ireland: MacGreevy Papers, TCD.

27. He had changed 'Irishmen' to 'a section of the Irish people', and deleted a slighting reference to the lower standard of debate in the Oireachtas.

28. For dislike of MacNamara, see WBY to AG, 16 Apr. 1926, Berg; for his view of Richards, Robinson to AG, 28 Nov. 1925, Berg.

29. Interview with Molly Howe [Mary Manning], Boston, 7 June 1992: she described GY as 'a deeply genuine person out of her depth' in Dublin. After more than sixty years Manning still felt sharply resentful of the way WBY's and AG's plays were repeatedly forced on the company.

30. WBY to AG, 15 Dec. 1925, MBY.

31. SMY to R L-P, 31 Dec. 1925. The event took place on 22 Dec.

32. At AE's behest: see his letter to AG, 18 May 1926, Berg.

33. See *IT*, 9 Aug. 1925, for a summing-up article which he found too defeatist and for which he blamed Bodkin.

34. *Journals*, ii, 16.

35. See a letter to AG, 24 Mar. [1926], Berg. 'When may I speak of the King's intention to open the Tate gallery's new wing? I want to consult the chair, about a vote of protest in the Senate: I shall speak to it as befits our placid house, but will be followed as befits their kind by the Labour & Republican press. Yours in old age & the friend of bankers but still an incendiary, W. B. Yeats.' This probably lies behind his long-suppressed poem, 'Cracked Mary's Vision': see below, p. 386.

36. To AG, 15 June 1928, Emory.

37. *UP*, ii, 453–4. For publication of *The Bounty of Sweden*, see ECY to Drake, 14 July 1925, HRHRC.

38. 1 Oct. 1925.

39. SMY to R L-P, 5 June 1928 ('one-act plays'), 14 June 1927 ('hysterical egoism'), 14 June 1927 ('insane jealousy'), 18 Sept. 1925 ('distasteful duty'); for WBY and Cuala, ECY to Symons, 22 Mar. 1926, HRHRC.

40. MacGreevy's notes for a speech opening the Yeats exhibition in Reading, 1961, TCD.

41. *Voice of Labour*, quoted in Robert G. Lowery (ed.), *A Whirlwind in Dublin: 'The Plough and the Stars' Riots* (Westport, Conn., 1984), 51–2. The anonymous reviewer continued: 'I waited till the close of the act for some justification of the use of sentences that were and are still part of our spiritual and national life. I did not find it.'

42. Nicholas Grene, *The Politics of Irish Drama: Plays in Context from Boucicault to Friel* (Cambridge, 1999), 142.

43. 10 Sept. 1925: quoted in Lowery, *A Whirlwind in Dublin*, 13.

44. See ibid., 21ff.

45. *I & R*, i, 183.

46. Lowery, *A Whirlwind in Dublin*, 31.

47. Horace Reynolds's notes of WBY's speech at Wellesley, 8 Dec. 1932, Harvard, b Ms Am 1787[662]. Kathleen O'Brennan also told Holloway that WBY went round to the *IT*: Lowery, 36. GY told the same story to Ellmann: Interview Book, Ellmann Papers, Y.9, Tulsa.

48. *I & R*, i, 185. On 18 Feb. 1926 WBY wrote to Lady Londonderry: 'It will be some years before the Southern Irishman looks upon the police as his own.' PRONI.

49. Lowery, *A Whirlwind in Dublin*, 35, 37.

50. 15 Feb. 1926.

51. *Journals*, ii, 65.

52. Lowery, *A Whirlwind in Dublin*, 62.

53. 26 Feb.; there is a corrected version in David Krause (ed.), *The Letters of Sean O'Casey. Volume 1: 1910–1941* (London, 1975), 168–71. The full exchanges with Sheehy-Skeffington can be found in Lowery, *A Whirlwind in Dublin*, 77–82. Her later attacks did, unwisely, shift to the 'morality' question.

54. Lowery, *A Whirlwind in Dublin*, 66.

55. 'Several writers of the new Irish school believe that Mr O'Casey's work is a crude exploitation of our poorer people in an Anglo-Irish tradition that is now moribund . . . May one hope that your paper [the *Irish Statesman*], ignoring the recent revival of Anglo-Irish coterie criticism, which is doing so much harm to our art, will open its columns to the discussion of the artistic values in question?' (Lowery, *A Whirlwind in Dublin*, 71). However, for Clarke's appreciative review of *The Tower*, see below, p. 364.

56. Lowery, *A Whirlwind in Dublin*, 73.

57. See *CB*, 16, 4 (Apr. 1926).

58. *IT*, 25 Feb. 1926, quoted in Donald T. Torchiana, *Yeats and Georgian Ireland* (Washington, 2nd ed., 1992), 130–1. The 'Cromwellian' reference was provoked by a meeting at the Dublin Literary Society, where George Reddin had claimed 'the spirit of the Abbey Theatre was Cromwellian . . . this Kiltartan jargon, and the venerable authors of it, were the creation of the same foreign biased mind as evolved, for the same political motives, that mirth-provoking buffoon, stage-Irish Pat. The Cromwellian tradition and the native tradition would never blend.' There are notes for WBY's reply in NLI MS 30,097. Hyde was mischievously enlisted as a Cromwellian too.

59. '28th' [Jan. 1926], Jeffares, White and Bridgwater.

60. To MacGreevy, n.d., MacGreevy Papers, TCD.

61. See letters to F. P. Sturm, 1 Mar. 1926, SIUC, and to OS, 4 Mar. 1926, *L*, 711–12.

62. *CB*, 16, 3 (Mar. 1926). 'Loony slovenliness' is in 18, 8 (Aug. 1927). AE's review was in the *Irish Statesman* of 13 Feb. 1926 and is reprinted in *CH*, 269–73.

63. Reminiscence in W. R. Rodgers MSS, HRHRC. One of the post-prandial guests was Sean O'Faolain, on his first visit.

64. 19 Jan. 1926, Richard Taylor (ed.), *Frank Pearce Sturm: His Life, Letters and Collected Work* (Urbana, Ill., 1969), 87.

65. 20 Jan. 1926, ibid., 90.

66. 'Speculum Angelorum et Homenorum' rather than 'Hominum'. WBY wondered if he could get away with it as 'dog Latin', but Sturm condemned it under any form – though he did suggest changing it to 'homunculorum', thus introducing 'manikin' – 'the artificial men that the alchemists of [Giraldus's] day were forever trying to concoct in their stew-pans. Of course the proper title: *Speculum Angelorum et Hominum* is the more dignified.' [3?] Feb. 1926, Taylor, *Frank Pearce Sturm*, 94. For Mead's review, see the *Quest*, 18, 1 (Oct. 1926), 96–8. My thanks to Warwick Gould.

67. 13 May 1925, HRHRC.

68. To W. F. Stead, 30 July [1926], Yale. Also see WBY to TSM, 26 June, in Ursula Bridge (ed.), *W. B. Yeats and T. S. Moore: Their Correspondence 1901–1937* (London, 1953), 104–5.

69. Bridge, *W. B. Yeats and T. S. Moore*, 148, 150.

Your world despises Spengler because it writes for or reads *The New Statesman* and *The Nation* which have their roots in mere whistling air if he is right, but Wyndham Lewis dislikes him because he suspects him – rightly – of taking over from Bergson certain convictions, a belief in the 'datum' in fact, which commits him to the eternal flux.

I too quarrel with this element in Spengler, which your *New Statesman* friends would like could they read him at all, but I think him profound and salutary for all that. There are no doubt errors of historical detail but his vast enlargement of Henry Adams's *History as Phase*, for that is what it is, is, if it were nothing more, magnificent as a work of imagination. (9 Apr. 1929).

70. To Ignatius MacHugh, 28 May [1926], Huntington.
71. 31 July 1925, TCD.
72. 10 Jan. 1926, *Journals*, ii, 59.
73. Bridge, *W. B. Yeats and T. S. Moore*, 113.
74. 23 May 1926, Bucknell. She mentions 'Among School Children' in *Journals*, ii, 101.
75. WBY's note that he wrote the poem in 'spring 1928' is amply contradicted by the drafts, which establish its composition in autumn 1927. See W. B. Yeats, *The Winding Stair (1929): Manuscript Materials*, edited by David R. Clark (London, 1995), p. xxv.
76. ECY to Symons, 18 Apr. 1926, HRHRC.
77. 5 July 1926, PRONI.
78. For an exemplary treatment of this, see Deirdre Toomey, 'Labyrinths: Yeats and Maud Gonne', *YA* 9 (1992), 60–94.
79. 3 Jan. 1926; see John Harwood, 'Olivia Shakespear: Letters to W. B. Yeats', *YA* 6 (1988), 65.
80. See WBY to OS, 15 Apr. 1926, *L*, 712–13, and SMY to R L-P, 6 Apr., 1926.
81. James Olney, 'W. B. Yeats's Daimonic Memory', *Sewanee Review*, 85 (1977), 595.
82. For a full and intelligent treatment, see Patrick J. Keane, *Yeats's Interactions with Tradition* (Columbia, Miss., 1987), 113.
83. There is some disagreement on the question. Ellmann assigns some of the poems in the sequence to 1927, Jeffares and Hone to 1926. See Jon Stallworthy, *Between the Lines: Yeats's Poetry in the Making* (Oxford, 1963), 139, for a discussion – and for the demonstration that 'Chosen' and 'Parting' were originally one poem. Sturm's reference to Macrobius, acknowledged in WBY's notes, suggests that he was working on it in Feb. 1926, and he sent some of the poems to OS on 2 July 1926 (*L*, 716).
84. Keane, *Yeats's Interactions with Tradition*, 127–8. Donne's voice is also echoed in 'Parting': see Stallworthy, *Between the Lines*, 143. On 'Consolation' see ibid., 206–9, where it is pointed out that the poem becomes less and less subjective in successive drafts.
85. *L*, 716. Keane convincingly relates this comment to 'A Last Confession' and not 'The Friends of Youth' as previously supposed.
86. On 27 Oct. [1926] MBY. WBY wrote to OS of 'my own mood between spiritual excitement & the sexual torture & the knowledge that they are somehow inseparable', relating this to Dante's pursuit of Beatrice.
87. *CB*, 16, 5 (May 1926), responding to a Senate speech on 24 Mar. (reproduced in Pearce, 106–14). The *Bulletin* further remarked:

He had, of course, a good word for 'Catholic Austria', which he reviled last Autumn in the choice atmosphere of Trinity College, Dublin; he had a good word for one school in Dublin, and for one school – managed, he tells us, by the Sisters of Mercy – in the South of Ireland. To our amazement, there was nothing about the Danish high school, no inspiration from Stockholm. But by way of compensation there is an effort to push the latest craze of the Plunkett House Coteries, the educational theories of Gentile. That very distinctly non-Catholic theorist was for a few months Minister of Education in Italy, until the Italian Strong Man sent him into retirement. A belated Vision of the Gentile Ideals was vouchsafed a few months ago to the Great Ego, and was forthwith enunciated in the Subsidised Weekly. For an idealist creation, the Gentile Scheme is a paltry plan, indeed a mere patchwork of platitudes: and this is virtually confessed by the pompous Pensionary himself. It is, he informs us, 'a system of education in philosophy', which turns out '*men and women who can manage, in the fields, to do all the work of the nation*'. Yet this portentous philosophy is, according to Loquacity-at-Large, so curious an article that 'its teachers do not need special training to carry it out'. No wonder that it attracts the Orator at large, a genus of which the Combined Coteries can exhibit numerous examples.

For WBY's pronouncements on education at this time, see *UP*, ii, 454–5, and Pearce, 168ff.

88. 14 Dec. 1925.

89. As the *CB* pointed out; above, n. 87. See, e.g., 'Education Policy in the Free State', 17 Apr. 1926, 'Education and Civil Strife', 24 July 1926, 'Education Policy in the Free State', 7 May 1926, 'Irish Education', 21 Apr. 1928, 'Some Problems of National Education', 11 Aug. 1928. These articles often invoked Gentile's ideas and argued for a Council of Education, modern methods, and an integrated approach to learning, geared towards an education shaped for the needs of the new Irish citizenry, rather than relying on Irish-by-rote and the emigration route.

90. On 15 June 1926 he spoke pointedly about the necessity to have teachers eligible as Dáil deputies and senators, against a motion which implied their exclusion – an idea which WBY suggested came from clerical pressure on behalf of Catholic school managers. Pearce, 116–18.

91. 23 Mar. 1926, Berg.

92. 26 Mar. 1926, MacGreevy Papers, TCD.

93. 'The Paddler's Heritage: Yeats's Visit to St Otteran's School, 1926' in *YA* 7 (1990), 287–8. Also see Donald T. Torchiana's valuable and detailed article '"Among School Children" and the Education of the Irish spirit' in A. Norman Jeffares and K. G. W. Cross (eds.), *In Excited Reverie* (London, 1965), 123–50.

94. Quoted in Torchiana, '"Among School Children"', 129–30. The TS of this speech is in NLI MS 30,162.

95. ibid., 131–2.

96. ibid., 140.

97. See F. P. Sturm to WBY, 20 Feb. 1921, Taylor, *Frank Pearce Sturm*, 79, for reflections on dancing, and a verse which includes the line 'Understand, by dancing, what I do'. Symons's many dance-poems must be a subconscious influence too, notably 'Nora on the Pavement' (see Karl Beckson, *Arthur Symons: A Life*, Oxford, 1987, 109). The dancer-figure in the Tarot, it should be remembered, 'merges self-consciousness with subconsciousness': see Gwladys V. Downes, 'W. B. Yeats and the Tarot' in Robin Skelton and Ann Saddlemyer (eds.), *The World of W. B. Yeats* (Seattle, 1965), 53. But the key passage comes from Shelley:

Poetry is indeed something divine. It is at once the centre and circumference of *knowledge*; it is that which comprehends all science, and that to which all science must be referred. It is at the same time the *root* and *blossom* of all other systems of thought; it is that from which all spring and that which adorns all; and that which, if blighted, denies the *fruit* and the *seed*, and witholds from the barren world the nourishment and the succession of the scions of the *tree* of life. It is the perfect and consummate surface and *bloom* of things . . . I appeal to the greatest poets of the present day, whether it be not an error to assert that the finest passages of poetry are produced by *labour* and *study*.

98. *L*, 721. For the portrait, see *AM*, facing 161.

99. Cullingford, *Gender and History in Yeats's Love Poems* (Cambridge, 1993), 174–5.

100. W. G. Holmes's *The Age of Justinian and Theodora: A History of the Sixth Century AD* (London, 1912) was a key text for WBY: for the later 'Byzantium' it is joined by Mrs Arthur [Eugenie] Strong, *Apotheosis and After-life: Three Lectures on Certain Phases of Art and Religion in the Roman Empire* (London, 1915). A. Norman Jeffares, 'The Byzantine Poems of W. B. Yeats', *Review of English Studies*, 22 (Jan. 1946) pioneered study of the influences in these poems; it is usefully collected with other commentaries in Richard J. Finneran (ed.), *W. B. Yeats: The Byzantium Poems* (Columbus, Ohio, 1970). This also includes Frederick L. Gwynn's 'Yeats's Byzantium and Its Sources', which traces many images back to Holmes. F. A. C. Wilson, in *Yeats's Iconography*

(London, 1960), stresses the importance of Gibbon's *Decline and Fall*; but it is joined by sources as diverse as the *Cambridge Modern History* and Hans Christian Andersen's 'Emperor's Nightingale'. Melchiori has also pointed out that WBY's idea of Byzantium may have been, bizarrely, inspired by his experience of Stockholm: quoted in Finneran, 87.

101. To Katharine Tynan Hinkson, 23 Aug. 1926, SIUC. He signed the Muckross visitor's book on 1 Sept., which was probably the day he left: my thanks to Mr William Bourne Vincent for showing it to me, and for his recollections of the visit. There is a sketch of WBY by a Miss Eley, one of the other guests.

102. WBY to GY, 22 Aug. 1926, MBY.

103. 21 Aug. 1926, PRONI.

104. T. R. Henn, *The Lonely Tower* (London, 1950), 222.

105. Notes to accompany a broadcast on 8 Sept. 1931, quoted in Stallworthy, *Between the Lines*, 96–7.

106. 14 Dec. 1926, BL Add. MSS 55003.

107. *AV (1925)*, 190: see above, p. 288. For the Morris connection, see T. McAlindon, 'The Idea of Byzantium in William Morris and W. B. Yeats', *Modern Philology* (May 1967), 307–19.

108. George Bornstein, *Yeats and Shelley* (Chicago, 1970), 185 ff., makes interesting connections to 'Hellas'; and for 'The Revolt of Islam' see Harold Bloom, *Yeats* (Oxford, 1970), 345–9. Also illuminating are T. R. Whitaker, *Swan and Shadow* (Chapel Hill, NC, 1964), 121 ff., and Daniel Albright, *Quantum Poetics: Yeats, Pound, Eliot and the Science of Modernism* (Cambridge, 1997), 44–5.

109. 'Memorable birds that sing by machinery' had, in fact, been part of his imaginative armoury since 1899 at least: see his letter to the *Daily Chronicle* about dramatic stagings, 27 Jan. 1899, *CL*, ii, 349.

110. Jeremy Silver (ed.), 'George Barnes's "W. B. Yeats and Broadcasting" 1940', *YA* 5 (1987), 191.

111. Stallworthy, *Between the Lines*, 97, traces these connections from conversations with GY as well as the drafts themselves.

112. *Journals*, ii, 95–6.

113. Pearce, 119–20. NLI MS 30,287 and 30,104 contain drafts and copies of letters from the 1926 campaign.

114. 5 July [1926], PRONI.

115. To AG, 11 Oct. 1926, Kentucky, and 20 Oct. 1926, private collection. The latter recounts a long exchange with D'Abernon, who hinted at a 'loan in parcels' arrangement. WBY rejoined, 'You must not ask a man of letters to accept a compromise – it is the ruin of good literature.' Beaverbrook tried to lure him down to Cherkley several times, which WBY courteously tried to avoid.

116. *Journals*, ii, 124. For WBY's speech and the debate, see Pearce, 125–32.

117. See exchange of letters, 4 and 7 Mar. 1926, NA P.4/14/0.194 35.

118. Pearce, 126.

119. To MacGreevy, 31 Dec. 1925, TCD.

120. 29 Apr. 1927, House of Lords Library.

121. To Blythe, 22 June 1925, UCDA.

122. On 3 Mar. 1926, WBY made a pointed speech thanking the Ministry of Finance for promising to appoint a committee: Pearce, 105. The relevant government file is NA D, Taoiseach S 6244A. Useful documents are reprinted in *W. B. Yeats and the Designing of Ireland's Coinage: Texts by W. B. Yeats and Others*, edited with an Introduction by Brian Cleeve, New Yeats Papers 3 (Dublin, 1972).

123. To Lady Londonderry, 19 June 1926, PRONI.

124. n.d., HRHRC.

125. Same to same, 1 Aug. [1926], HRHRC.
126. This is referred to in correspondence in the Bodkin Papers in TCD, and in a letter from Bodkin to WBY, 28 Nov. 1927, MBY; correspondence with J. McElligott shows that they had threatened resignation, though the report of the committee (NLI MS 30,866) gives no indication.
127. WBY wrote to 'Harrison' on 13 Dec. assuring him that he did not hold him responsible for 'paragraphs which accuse Dermod O'Brien, the Director of the National Gallery, Thomas Bodkin and myself of deliberately cheating our artist competitors'. MG's letter was to *An Phoblacht*, Dec. 1928, and was preserved by WBY: see NLI MS 30,911. For other reactions, see Cleeve, *W. B. Yeats and Ireland's Coinage*, 56.
128. 18, 8 (Aug. 1927).
129. 22 Dec. 1926, Yale.
130. SMY to R L-P, 24 Nov. 1926. For WBY's continuing interest in Swedish architecture, see Torchiana, *Yeats and Georgian Ireland*, 103.
131. AE to Katharine Tynan Hinkson, 2 Aug. 1927, SIUC.
132. *Journals*, ii, 164.
133. WBY to his sisters, 29 Oct. 1925, Boston College, itemized his payments on their behalf as £2,020. 11s. 1d., and an overdraft guarantee of £100 for each of their departments, which he could not exceed. He also outlined their average losses (£135 p.a.) over the past twenty years. It is a notably businesslike letter. In that same year the erratic Pollexfen shares paid nothing, and he made up SMY's income by £40, making it clear that he could not afford to repeat the gesture. In fact he did so when the dividend dried up again in 1930, to SMY's discomfiture: 'I know he has no margin.' See SMY to R L-P, 19 July 1927, 26 Dec. 1930. Things remained hand-to-mouth at Cuala; ECY had to sell off her own run of their books for £120 in 1928.
134. 1 Nov. 1925, Berg. For the income from *Au*, see GY to Pound, 8 Oct. 1927, Yale.
135. NLI MS 30,694 for accounts; also Robinson to MacGreevy, 25 July [1927], MacGreevy Papers, TCD.
136. See a revealing letter from WBY (in Dublin) to GY (in London), 3 Nov. 1925, MBY, about a 'thunderbolt' in the form of a bill from Heal's

that may be a shock to you. I think that my large ballance at the bank may have been left there to meet it, but as things stand I cannot do so. Can you meet it, & charge to me either the whole ultimately or the part that went to pay for the things in my room. Or would you prefer that I sold out something? I am most anxious that you sell out nothing more – you must keep a rampart round the children.

For GY's legacy, see a letter to MacGreevy, 31 Dec. 1925, TCD, celebrating the death of 'my great-aunt-in-law devil', which released a third of her father's capital and would bring in £250 p.a.
137. MacNamara was violently offended by WBY's 'insulting' and 'contemptuous' reaction to a play of his in Jan. 1926, and wrote telling him so – HRHRC, n.d. Also see a long letter from WBY to Lennox Robinson, 23 Sept. 1926, SIUC.
138. To MacGreevy, 31 Dec. 1925, MacGreevy Papers, TCD.
139. 27 July 1926, MBY.
140. See *CB*, 16, 6 (June 1926). The sculptor, ironically, was Albert Power, who had sculpted WBY himself, to the subject's approval: see above, p. 90.
141. n.d., SIUC.
142. See David R. Clark and James B. McGuire, 'The Writing of *Sophocles' King Oedipus*: Manuscripts of W. B. Years', *YAACTS* 2 (1984), and *AM*, 455–6, 612–13.
143. To OS, 6 and 7 Dec. [1926], *L*, 719–20.
144. See J. T. Hayes in *New York Times*, 26 Dec. 1926 ('it is not only great, it is magnificent'),

and *IT*, 8 Dec. 1926. The best treatment of the play's genesis is David R. Clark and James B. McGuire, 'W. B. Yeats: The Writing of *Sophocles' King Oedipus*', 30–74. Also see R. Tracy, 'Intelligible on the Blasket Islands: Yeats's *King Oedipus*, 1926', *Éire-Ireland*, 28, 2 (Summer, 1993), 116–28.

145. To OS, 6 Dec. [1926], *L*, 719–20.
146. 20 Feb. [1927], Yale.
147. *Irish Statesman*, 4 Dec. 1926.
148. To GY, n.d., MBY.
149. *Journals*, ii, 194–5.
150. Now in Harvard, b Ms Am 1787[5803].
151. *Journals*, ii, 203.
152. See John Regan, *The Irish Counter-Revolution: 1921–1936* (Dublin, 1999), 86–7.
153. n.d., *L*, 726–7.
154. Horace Reynolds's diary, 12 July 1927, Harvard.

Chapter 9 : Striking a Match
1927–1930

1. Unionists refused the 'Kingdom of Ireland' idea at once. See John Regan, *The Irish Counter-Revolution 1921–1936* (Dublin, 1999), 266–71, and Sinead McCool, *Hazel: A Life of Lady Lavery* (Dublin, 1996), 118–35.
2. Regan, *The Irish Counter-Revolution*, 271.
3. For the visit to Cosgrave, see WBY to OS, 2 Oct. [1927], MBY, and *G–Y L*, 431–6. Cosgrave told him that 'three classes of people ought not to be in public life, because their preoccupation with the sick & infirm unfits them for it – women, doctors and priests'. Seán MacBride was eventually released, Major Bryan Cooper having testified that he was – as claimed – travelling to the Continent at the time of the murder. WBY had had his suspicions. 'He was & probably is a friendly simple lad but has been subject to a stream of terrible suggestion & may not have been able to resist. Any one ordinary would think him devoted to making peace but there are others who have a different story & it is impossible to sift out the truth.' To OS, 7 Sept. [1927], MBY. The killers were in fact Archie Doyle, Tim Murphy, and Bill Gannon: see Afterword to Terence de Vere White, *Kevin O'Higgins* (Dublin, 2nd ed., 1986), 256.
4. 28 Sept. [1927]; *G–Y L*, 433.
5. 29 Sept. [1927]; ibid., 434.
6. 3 Oct. [1927]; ibid., 437.
7. Exchange of 3–4 Oct., ibid., 436–7. Anti-Semitism was common currency in the Gonne household: Gonne's friend Kathleen Lynn was shocked by Iseult's anti-Semitism in the late 1930s. My thanks to Margaret Ó hÓgartaigh for this observation, based on Lynn's diaries.
8. Appended to a letter of 7 Oct., *G–Y L*, 439. For his earlier analysis, see *CL*, ii, 355.
9. For a suggestive commentary, see Donald T. Torchiana, *W. B. Yeats and Georgian Ireland* (Washington, 2nd ed., 1992), 197, n. 95.
10. He was struck by the Swift quote when he read it in Edward Young's *Conjectures on Original Composition*: see Daniel Harris, *Yeats: Coole Park and Ballylee* (London, 1974), 215.
11. *Journals*, ii, 199.
12. See *AM*, 129, 443.
13. W. B. Yeats, *'The Winding Stair' (1929): Manuscript Materials*, edited by David R. Clark (London, 1995), 7.

14. 7 Sept. [1927], MBY. For Markievicz and the Treaty debates, see my *Paddy and Mr Punch*, 304.

15. *Journals*, ii, 204.

16. 13 Nov. [1927], Berg. He refers to this arrangement, set up by James Wells, in several letters from mid Sept. See Colin Smythe, 'Crosby Gaige and W. B. Yeats's *The Winding Stair* (1929)', *YA* 13 (1998), 317–28. The Fountain Press, partly owned by Wells, took over the project from Gaige.

17. 20 Aug. 1927, HRHRC.

18. 29 Nov. [1927], TCD.

19. See GY to Robinson, 29 Nov. 1927 ('the most perfect oyster') and 'Maundy Thursday' [1926?] for 'hand-holding', Huntington. Her letters to Robinson allow insight into WBY's artistic inspiration as well as more mundane aspects of family life; see a postscript to the latter letter. 'A conversation on a windy day on March. *George Yeats*: "Why do you like Norman? He is a vile little boy." *Anne Yeats*: "But he has lovely hair & eyes as cold as any March wind." Or we might call it "Any woman's reply on being asked why she loves a scoundrel."' (MacGreevy Papers, TCD). WBY, of course, was equally struck, and noted it in a MS book (dated Mar. 1926). 'I should put this into verse, for it is the cry of every woman who loves a blackguard.' My thanks to Warwick Gould. It became the first poem in 'A Woman Young and Old'.

20. To MacGreevy, 1 July 1928. See also a letter of 9 Nov. 1926, for an account of Robinson's intense and quarrelsome relationship with Alan Duncan.

21. 9 Mar. 1926, MacGreevy Papers, TCD.

22. See Robinson to MacGreevy, 4 May [1927], and 'Monday', TCD, telling him his hopes of the job were unrealistic. Bodkin was backed by Hugh Kennedy and T. M. Healy. For his career at the gallery see Anne Kelly's article in *Irish Arts Review* (1991–2), 171–7.

23. To MacGreevy, 10 July [1925?], TCD.

24. 9 Nov. [1926], TCD. For their introduction, see Robinson to MacGreevy, 28 Oct. 1926, TCD.

25. 15 June 1927, TCD; for the cinema plan, see Robinson to MacGreevy, 4 May 1927, TCD.

26. WBY to OS, 2 Oct. 1927, MBY.

27. See WBY to OS, 9 July 1928, *L*, 744.

28. 27 Dec. 1930, TCD.

29. To R L-P, 24 Oct. 1927. For GY's bulletin, see *Journals*, ii, 207.

30. Same to same, 31 Oct. 1927; for earlier plans, see GY to Pound, 8 Sept. 1927, Yale.

31. 19 Nov. [1927], TCD.

32. To Robinson, 27 Nov. 1927, Huntington.

33. 12 Dec. 1927, Bucknell.

34. To OS, 29 Nov. 1927, *L*, 732–3.

35. 29 Nov. 1927, *L*, 733.

36. See Robinson to Dolly Travers Smith, n.d., and 11 Dec. 1927, Robinson Papers, TCD.

37. GY to MacGreevy, 19 Feb. 1928, MacGreevy Papers, TCD.

38. To Robinson, 17 Jan. 1928, Huntington.

39. 15 Mar. 1928, MacGreevy Papers, TCD.

40. The automatic writing from 1917 shows an interest in Lewis, reciprocated by the medium. See Peter L. Carraciolo and Paul Edwards, 'In Fundamental Agreement: Yeats and Wyndham Lewis', *YA* 13 (1998), 110–57, much the fullest account of their intellectual relationship. W. K. Rose (ed.), *The Letters of Wyndham Lewis* (London, 1965), 75, indicates that in 1916 Lewis thought WBY was suspicious of his claims to a Royal Literary Fund pension, had not yet met him and knew only of his work as a painter.

41. Carraciolo and Edwards, 'Yeats and Wyndham Lewis', 125.
42. 13 Jan. 1928, Berg. Also see Robinson to MacGreevy, 21 Jan. 1928, MacGreevy Papers, TCD.
43. 20 Jan. 1928, printed in *YA* 7 (1990), 11–12.
44. To SMY, 19 Mar. 1928, Boston College.
45. GY to Robinson, n.d., Huntington. Sassoon was in Rapallo with Stephen Tennant in Nov. 1929, but he had also made an earlier visit.
46. See, e.g., Pound to John Drummond, 18 Feb. 1928, in D. D. Paige (ed.), *Selected Letters of Ezra Pound* (London, 1971), 240.
47. See Donald T. Torchiana, 'Yeats and Croce', *YA* 4 (1986), 3–12.
48. *L*, 739. For a valuable article setting Pound's hatred of Palgrave in perspective, see Warwick Gould's 'The Unknown Masterpiece: Yeats and the Design of the *Cantos*' in Andrew Gibson (ed.), *Pound in Multiple Perspective* (London, 1993), 40–92.
49. 29 Nov. 1927, Huntington.
50. To Robinson, 27 Feb. 1928, SIUC.
51. 23 Feb. 1928, *L*, 736–7.
52. To AG, postmarked 24 Feb. 1928, *L*, 738.
53. See Robinson to Dolly Travers Smith, 1 Apr. 1928, Robinson Papers, TCD, and MacGreevy to GY, 11 June 1928, MBY.
54. See SMY to R L-P, 17 Apr. 1928, and WBY to Hone, 6 May 1928, Gilvarry Collection. 'Fire of Straw' is a constant metaphor: see above, pp. 126, 243, 693, n. 100.
55. These accounts are in letters from WBY to GY, 'Wednesday' and 28 Aug. [1928], MBY.
56. SMY to R L-P, 29 June 1928. She added that WBY was a governor of the Rotunda Hospital, and Solomons did not charge GY for medical attention.
57. 28 May 1928. Also see AG to WBY, 1 Aug. 1928, NLI MS 18,682. 'Sad to think of 82 – I shall feel lonely when I pass it. I had so many comfortable visits there – such a help in the troublesome times that turned up in late years – but I hope are now over –' She had spent three weeks with the Yeatses in May, when GY was organizing the sale and looking for a new home.
58. 12 Mar. [1928], Berg.
59. 18 Mar. 1928, NLI MS 18,682. She noted the same look in a photograph of Michael.
60. 10 Apr. 1928.
61. Ronald Bush, 'Yeats, Spooks, Nursery Rhymes' in *YAACTS* 3 (1985), 23.
62. To OS, 23 Apr. 1928, and to AG, 24 Feb. 1928, *L*, 738.
63. To AG, postmarked 1 Apr. 1928, Berg, and *L*, 740.
64. *TLS*, 1 Mar. 1928, reprinted in *CH*, 282 ff.
65. *CH*, 288.
66. London, 1931, 42.
67. See Robinson to AG, 22 Oct. 1925, Berg, for the background.
68. See, e.g., Robinson to AG, 28 Nov. 1925, Berg: 'All the effects "off" have me heart-broken; in some ways I think it's the worst written of his plays, "Juno" was child's play compared to it. It will go all right because of good character[s] and good acting but he hasn't made it easy for players & producer.'
69. See *Journals*, ii, 213–14, 229, and Robinson to AG, 9 Nov. 1927, Berg. WBY wanted to put it on and face the row, but he gave way.
70. O'Casey to Robinson, 5 Apr. 1928, SIUC.
71. 30 Mar. 1928, Berg.
72. 2 Mar. 1928, Berg.
73. 20 Apr. 1928, *L*, 740–2.

74. HRHRC.

75. Annotating WBY's second letter to her strangely: 'This just arrived this morning. I couldn't bear to put it in for you to see.' It seems likely that she meant to write 'not to put it in'.

76. 4 May 1928, Berg. SMY's account is in SMY to R L-P, 5 June 1928. AG to WBY, 29 Apr. 1928, NLI MS 18,682 tells him his 'very fine' letter to O'Casey has just come, and she is sending it on with his letter to her, and Robinson's also. She thought O'Casey would 'value [WBY's letter] later tho' it will be a blow now'.

77. Her own letter to O'Casey certainly emphasizes WBY's initiative in the rejection. 'It must hurt you – or at least disappoint you (as his criticisms did me of my first draft of Sancha). But it is right you should know at once what he – what we all – feel & think.' (29 Apr. 1928, Berg). O'Casey's daughter Shivaun believes 'Lennox was never his friend and I don't think Yeats was really a friend although Sean admired the man and his work until his dying day. The main regret Sean ever had about the rejection was Lady Gregory, who was his friend and remained his friend.' (To RFF, 30 Nov. 2000).

78. 2 May 1928, David Krause (ed.), *The Letters of Sean O'Casey. Volume 1: 1910–1941* (London, 1975), 240.

79. For St John Ervine's part, see Robert Bell to Robinson, 5 June 1928, SIUC. On the same day AG wrote to WBY:

We all lost our heads at the last when the play was about to be returned or we wd no doubt have had Starkie there & a formal letter. It is very distressing & I think Garvin [editor of the *Observer*] deserves more blame than Casey about the publication of the letters. He has lived in a different world & must have known it was not an honourable proceeding. We had not remonstrated with Casey when he said he wd publish them in the book & he may have taken that for permission.

(NLI MS 18,682). NLI MS 30,897 is WBY's correspondence with legal advisers about claiming damages after O'Casey published the correspondence.

80. Quoted in Garry O'Connor, *Sean O'Casey: A Life* (London, 1988), 256.

81. See Nicholas Grene, 'The Class of the Clitheroes: O'Casey's Revisions to *The Plough and the Stars* Prompt-book', *Bullán*, 4, 2 (Winter, 1999/Spring, 2000), 57–66.

82. 22 May 1928, MBY; excised from the version in *L*, 743–4.

83. WBY to AG, 4 June 1928, Delaware. For her reply, see n. 77 above.

84. O'Connor, *Sean O'Casey*, 257.

85. *Journals*, ii, 462–3. Significantly, she wrote: 'We should have held out against L.R. that last evening of the season when the order to return it was given – it was rejected.'

86. O'Connor, *Sean O'Casey*, 257.

87. Dan H. Laurence and Nicholas Grene (eds.), *Shaw, Lady Gregory and the Abbey: A Correspondence and a Record* (Gerrards Cross, 1993), 184–6 (letters of 19 and 26 June 1928 to AG).

88. O'Connor, *Sean O'Casey*, 275.

89. *CB*, 16, 3 (Mar. 1926).

90. *Irish Statesman*, 8 Jan., 12 Feb. 1927.

91. See *CB*, 17, 3 (Mar. 1927), replying to the *Irish Statesman*, 12 Feb. 1927 – a diatribe notable for its attack on J. M. Turner, who 'executed many hundreds of drawings which were most vilely obscene and indecent', now under lock and key at 'John Bull's British Museum'.

92. *Irish Statesman*, 13 Oct. 1928.

93. See WBY to AG, *L*, 744.

94. 26 Aug. 1928, Rachewiltz Collection, University of Toledo.

95. *CB*, 17, 10 (Oct. 1928).

96. See *UP*, ii, 477–85. Drafts of censorship articles exist in NLI MSS 30,807, 30,116 and 30,105, as well as in his Rapallo Notebook A, NLI MS 13,578, enormously scored out and rewritten: he put a great deal of care into the campaign. The final draft of 'The Irish Censorship' is dated 22 Sept.

97. See *Journals*, ii, 277–8.

98. 13 Nov. 1928, Yale. In 1930 Pound was still in touch with FitzGerald, sharing ideas about pamphlets and suggesting liaison with Page, Raven Thompson, and other British Fascists. For an overview of the relationship, see Mary Fitzgerald, 'Ezra Pound and Irish Politics: An Unpublished Correspondence', *Paideuma*, 12, 2 (1983), 378–417.

99. NLI MS 30,105.

100. This has been glossed in *UP* as referring to AE, but WBY to Pound, 23 Sept. 1928, Rachewiltz Collection, University of Toledo, records 'Maud and I are at one over it, the only thing we have agreed about for years.'

101. *UP*, ii, 481–2.

102. The draft in the Rapallo Notebook A, NLI MS 13,578, has more detail about the Abbey's proud history of controversy; he may have felt it was too confrontational, given the government subsidy.

103. According to Torchiana, who probably asked GY, the 'revolutionary soldier' is Jephson Byrne O'Connell; but it could conceivably be Dermott MacManus.

104. Rapallo Notebook A, NLI MS 13,578.

105. See *CB*, 18, 12 (Dec. 1928). The *IT* found it 'disquieting' that no one declared an intention to vote against the second reading, even though the Protestant minority had 'a representation which is not unfair in proportion to its number'.

106. 13 Aug. 1929, NLI MS 30,877 has an (unattributed) newspaper cutting listing the seventy amendments proposed.

107. *Journals*, ii, 306.

108. The operation came at a time when the Yeatses were in Rapallo. See AG to WBY from a Dublin nursing-home, 3 Feb. 1929, NLI MS 18,681. 'You may imagine how much I have missed you & George & all you did for me.' For Margaret's marriage, see SMY to R L-P, 3 Oct. 1928. '"Aunt Augusta" they say is fifteen years younger since she gave away her daughter-in-law. Captain Gough is rich and what is known as "a very decent fellow", which I think means dull but knows how to behave.'

109. *Journals*, ii, 317. But see below, p. 379, for a visit to Monte Carlo. There is an undated fragment from Gogarty in NLI MS 30,584. 'Mrs Phillimore has returned and proceeded by a series of arguments to Kilmacurragh which she speaks of buying and presenting "to the Nation" as if it didn't burn down houses like that when it could get the chance. After her book on [St] Paul she is to write a sex novel. (In this case it is better for a press to burn.)' During his burst of verse-writing in Feb. 1929, WBY produced a quatrain based on an argument with her:

> 'I learned to think in a man's way
> And women's toys forget.'
> 'None learned like you that think today
> Like the first man you met.'

She was a regular on the Riviera in the early 1930s, on one occasion offending her hosts so much by her views on the Virgin Birth that they refused to speak to her for a week: Gogarty to WBY, 26 June 1936, NLI MS 30,584.

110. *Journals*, ii, 327. GY's letter, dated 16 Oct. 1928, is in Berg.

111. *Irish Independent*, 22 Oct. 1928, quoted in Torchiana, *Yeats and Georgian Ireland*, 143.

112. Judge Richard Campbell to AE, 1 Dec. 1928, Healy; WBY to OS, 12 Aug. 1928, *L*, 745–6.

113. See WBY to OS, 23 Nov. 1928, *L*, 748, and to SMY, 27 Nov. 1928, Boston College.

114. To R L-P, 19 Mar. 1929.

115. Bright Patmore, notebook in HRHRC: a draft of the reminiscence published in *Texas Quarterly*, 8, 3–4 (1965), 152–9, and reprinted in *I & R*, ii, 355–63. Following references are to the *I & R* printing, since the version in Brigit Patmore, *Reminiscences: My Friends when Young* (London, 1968) is truncated.

116. George Antheil, *Bad Boy of Music* (London, 1947), 180. Virgil Thomson later remarked that literary people liked Antheil 'because, with his violence and infantile boyish charm, he was a literary man's idea of a musical genius.' Thomas Dilworth, 'Virgil Thomson on George Antheil and Ezra Pound: A Conversation', *Paideuma*, 12, 2 (1983), 349–56.

117. For a detailed description of a Hauptmann dinner, see GY to Robinson, n.d. [but Mar. 1929], TCD.

118. 21 Jan. 1929, Berg.

119. Basil Bunting, 'Yeats Recollected', *Agenda*, 12, 2 (Summer, 1974), 36–47.

120. GY to Brigit Patmore, n.d., UCLA; WBY to OS, 2 Mar. 1929, *L*, 758–9.

121. To AG, 24 Mar. 1929, Berg.

122. For Montale, Piccolo, and WBY, see Fiorenzo Fantaccini, 'Montale, Lucio Piccolo e le opere di William Butler Yeats', in F. Marroni, M. Costantini, R. D'Agnillo, *Percorsi di poesia irlandese da W. B. Yeats a Desmond Egan* (Pescara, 1998), 63–94. Lampedusa's essay was 'W. B. Yeats e il risorgimento irlandese', first published in *Le opere e i giorni*, ii (1926), 36–46: see Jeffrey Meyers, 'Lampedusa on Yeats: A Newly Discovered Essay' in *YAACTS* 6 (1988), 72–5.

123. Patmore, 358: the 'gunman', who apparently did not arrive, may have been Seán MacBride, Frank O'Connor, or possibly Peadar O'Donnell.

124. Patmore, 361–2.

125. 22 Aug. 1920, Yale. See also Gould, 'The Unknown Masterpiece', for the Pound–Yeats relationship.

126. 26 Aug. 1928, Rachewiltz Collection, Toledo.

127. 23 Sept. 1928, Rachewiltz Collection, Toledo. Shortly after WBY's death, GY wrote to Pound: 'WBY wrote to me from London that you had said some of his recent poems were "quite good. This is very high praise from Ezra" – Glad you said it – he referred to the remark with evident pleasure several times while we were in France.' ([early 1939], Yale).

128. This is copied from WBY's own copy of *A Packet*, in Emory, used to set the corresponding part of *A Vision*; but it was deleted from the published version.

129. NLI MSS 13,579, 13,582.

130. *Packet*, 3.

131. ibid., 8.

132. ibid., 5.

133. See Carraciolo and Edwards, 'Yeats and Wyndham Lewis', 110.

134. NLI MS 13,579.

135. *Packet*, 33.

136. See *BG*, 405–6.

137. To AG, 9 Mar. 1929, Berg.

138. There are five of these in NLI. MSS 13,578–9 contain drafts of 'The Great Year', the censorship articles, his 1930 diary, and much of *A Packet*. His diary notebook (MS 13,580) has early drafts of a striking number of poems, dated Jan.–Mar. 1929; GY listed the poems written in Rapallo in NLI MS 30,891.

139. 23 Nov. 1928, Faber and Faber. Rapallo Notebook A was finished on 9 Oct. 1928, according to WBY's note on the cover.

140. 29 Jan. 1929, *LTWBY*, ii, 492.

141. 11 Feb. 1929, TCD.

142. To AG, 9 Mar. 1929, Berg.

143. NLI MS 30,891. The dates are, respectively: 4 Feb., 9 Feb., 12 Feb., 14–24 Feb., 24 Feb., 2 Mar., 6 Mar., 8 Mar., 29 Mar., 27 Mar., n.d. [but Mar.], and 29 Mar. (or possibly later).

144. Introduction to *Letters to the New Island*.

145. *L*, 786, postmarked 23 Nov. 1931.

146. AG transcribed it, dating it 5 Aug. 1929; another copy in Ellmann Papers, Y.2, Tulsa, is dated 'Rapallo Feb. 24 1929'. The *Amherst Literary Magazine* printed it in 1964, believing it previously unpublished, from a version memorized by Gogarty, who had in fact printed a version in *It isn't that Time of Year at All!* (London, 1954), 255. For WBY's wish to publish it, see his letter to AG, 20 June 1929, Berg. See *Journals*, ii, 451–2, for WBY's feelings about the king, and for his protests in the Senate at the time, Pearce, 118–24. At the Irish Academy of Letters banquet in Aug. 1937, WBY remarked that in 1926 George V

> had an impulse of generosity; he sent us word through a member of his household that he would not open those rooms while they contained the thirty-nine pictures. We let our agitation quiet down. Then the king gave way, patriotic Irish men and women offered to march up and down in front of the Gallery with sandwich boards. I greatly regret that, owing to some new promise from somebody or other, we refused. (*IT*, 18 Aug. 1937).

147. WBY's letter to Sir Frederick Macmillan, 30 Sept. 1928, BL Add. MSS 55003, introducing Joseph Hone, is illuminating.

> He wishes to edit Berkeley's *Commonplace Book* and translate for it the only adequate commentary. The commentary has been published in Bologna by Mario Rossi . . . I have given some time to trying to understand the *Commonplace Book* and know therefore the great need for explanatory notes and introductions. The *Commonplace Book* is of great philosophic importance. Giovanni Gentile begins his chief work with an account of it, finds in it the prophecy of modern idealism; but thinks what Berkeley published during his life-time but a compromise and a falling away. It remained in MSS until Frazer published it in 1875.

148. On 4 May; see WBY to OS, same date, *L*, 763.

149. 5 May 1929, Bucknell. He told Ottoline Morrell (5 June) that she, the Dulacs, and OS were the only people he would see in London in the future. The Ghost Club occasion is retailed in Henry Yorke to Ottoline Morrell, 5 May 1929: Yorke's brother Gerald, the club's president, thought the occasion 'magnificent'. My thanks to Jeremy Treglown for this reference. WBY told GY: '"The Ghosts" received my account of the philosophy & its origin with enthusiasm.' (5 May [1929], MBY). The mediums and the steamboats are also mentioned in an undated letter to GY. At one seance JBY came through and told him: 'You have a son who is slow to learn but he is slow and sure. When older he will be brilliant.'

150. To AG, 19 May 1929, repeated in her *Journals*, ii, 444.

151. WBY to AG, 20 June 1929, Berg.

152. SMY to R L-P, 29 July 1926.

153. WBY to AG, 2 July 1929, Berg; Robinson to Dolly Travers Smith, 6 July 1929, Robinson Papers, TCD.

154. ECY to Sean O'Faolain, 10 July 1929, Ellmann Papers, Y.8, Tulsa.

155. Holloway's diary, quoted in Sylvia C. Ellis, *The Plays of W. B. Yeats. Yeats and the Dancer* (London, 1995), 328–9.

156. Ursula Bridge (ed.), *W. B. Yeats and T. S. Moore: Their Correspondence 1901–1937* (London, 1953), 146.

157. 24 Aug. 1929, *L*, 768.
158. To Dolly Travers Smith, 16 July 1929, Robinson Papers, TCD.
159. SMY to R L-P, 20 Sept. 1929.
160. Quoted by Torchiana, *Yeats and Georgian Ireland*, 175. Reminiscence of Peter Cooper to RFF, Feb. 2001.
161. NLI MS 13,581. The holograph in the Berg Collection says 7 Sept., but he seems to have been still working on it in early Oct.: *Journals*, ii, 460.
162. NLI MS 13,581. For further variations, see Jon Stallworthy, *Between the Lines: Yeats's Poetry in the Making* (Oxford, 1963), 186, 193–4.
163. To Katharine Tynan Hinkson, 27 Sept. 1929, SIUC.
164. Robinson to Dolly Travers Smith, 29 June 1928, Robinson Papers, TCD. For Japan, see WBY to OS, '31 Aug' [but probably 31 July 1929], *L*, 765–6.
165. There is a list of projected engagements in NLI 13,581; he planned to see Stephen Gwynn, Hazel Lavery, Ottoline Morrell, and Bessie [Radcliffe] Gorell.
166. SMY to R L-P, 5 Nov. 1929, reports a letter from GY in London. 'It is nothing at all to worry about – he has again had haemorrhage from the left lung. He had it about a year and a half ago, and then the doctors said it was not serious. The London doctor this time sent him to see Dr [R.A.] Young, who saw me . . . He looked very well when here, and G. says he is now in very good spirits but just has to stay quiet for a short time.' See also WBY to GY, 30 Oct. [1929]. She had followed him to London, where they stayed until mid November.
167. 'Thursday' [28 Nov. 1929], MacGreevy Papers, TCD; for WBY's remarks, a letter to Robinson of 25 Nov. 1929, SIUC.
168. NLI MS 30,201.
169. SMY to R L-P, 4 Feb. 1930; also letters from GY to Gogarty, Healy, which give medical details (with impressive exactness).
170. 'Estrangement', LIV; first published in the *Dial*, Nov. 1926, 383.

Chapter 10 : ONE LAST BURIAL
1930–1932

1. *Journals*, ii, 494–5.
2. 13 Feb. 1930 Huntington. NLI 30,759 is her detailed notes on the progress of the illness. Also see GY to Gogarty, 9 Feb. 1930, giving temperature charts, references from the *British Medical Journal*, the name of the bacillus, state of excreta, etc. Nicola Pende was the local doctor. On 28 Feb. WBY went out for the first time.
3. SMY to R L-P, 18 July 1933, where 'prescription' appears as 'subscription'.
4. 26 Mar. 1930, NLI MS 18,683. Also see AG to WBY, 29 Apr. 1930, quoting 'Topics for Comment' in *IT*, and WBY to AG, 19 Mar. 1930, Reading.
5. 9 Apr. 1930, NLI MS 30,584.
6. See Donald T. Torchiana, *Yeats and Georgian Ireland* (Washington, 2nd ed., 1992), 124, and WBY to Gogarty, 20 Mar. 1930, Sligo.
7. Published as *Pages from a Diary Written in 1930*. The proofs are in NLI MS 30,823. For variants see M. Gibson, *Yeats, Coleridge and the Romantic Sage* (London, 2000).
8. To AG, 7 Apr. 1930, Berg, and *L*, 773–4; the same day he began his diary as eventually published.
9. To L. A. G. Strong, 18 Apr. [1930], HRHRC.
10. *Ex*, 292–3.
11. ibid., 312.
12. ibid., 314–15, entry for 9 Aug.

13. See AG to WBY, 13 Nov. [1930]. 'I remember when you originally rejected Johnston's play you had, as you walked up & down, thrown out some suggestions.' (NLI MS 18,683). A detailed consideration is given in Bernard Adams, *Denis Johnston: A Life* (Dublin, 2002), 86–9, 97–9. By 1932 Johnston was a director of the Gate, which ruled him out.

14. WBY to Robinson, 28 Feb. 1930, SIUC.

15. To AG, 15 Apr. 1930, and 1 May 1930, Berg.

16. On 1 May 1930 he wrote to AG (Berg) wondering what O'Casey would do after the 'failure' of the *Tassie*: 'he has no constructive power, nothing but curiosity about life, and that is the last thing a London manager values'.

17. 12 July 1930, Robinson Papers, TCD.

18. Donal O'Sullivan had described an academic study of folk music as slovenly and incompetent, precipitating an endless and expensive hearing; the jury disagreed but the costs broke the bank. AE sent a hilarious description to John Finlay, 1 Feb. 1929, Healy, and to many other correspondents. Campbell's TS memoir of AE says that an American syndicate contributed 'over $100,000' to the *Statesman* over 8 years. Horace Plunkett to Gogarty, 14 Jan. 1929, and AE to Campbell, 11 Dec. 1928 (both at Stanford) stress WBY's concern and his readiness to drum up money. Also see Henry Summerfield, *That Myriad-minded Man: A Biography of George William Russell 'A.E.' 1867–1935* (Gerrards Cross, 1975), 250–1. There was much controversy over the mismanagement of the subsidies received, but the paper was probably doomed anyway.

19. 13 Apr. [1930], Indiana; AE's reply is in Alan Denson (ed.), *Letters from A.E.* (London, 1961), 60–1.

20. 7 May 1930; printed in *Massachusetts Review*, 11, 1 (1970), 159–62.

21. WBY to AG, 25 May, Emory, 21 June 1930, Berg.

22. *Ex*, 300.

23. ibid., 307–8. Gogarty's letter was written on 28 May and is in NLI MS 30,584.

24. See dedication to *The Winding Stair*, quoted in *VP*, 831.

25. 16 Apr. 1930, Ursula Bridge (ed.), *W. B. Yeats and T. S. Moore: Their Correspondence 1901–1937*, 162.

26. *Ex*, 290, note dated 30 Apr. 1930; and see Jon Stallworthy, *Between the Lines: Yeats's Poetry in the Making* (Oxford, 1963), 115ff.

27. For a brilliant exploration of the drafts (which are in NLI MS 13,581) see Stallworthy, *Between the Lines*.

28. WBY to AG, 1 May 1930, Berg.

29. *I & R*, ii, 400.

30. 25 May 1930, Emory. AG had floated the idea in a letter of 29 Apr. 1930. Masefield told SMY that WBY's claims were pre-eminent and that he 'considered himself W.'s pupil and disciple': SMY to R L-P, 2 and 27 May 1930. SMY, Pollexfen-like, promptly sold Masefield's letter for £10.

31. To AG, 25 May 1930, Emory. The long-banished juvenilia reprinted by O'Faolain were 'Wisdom and Dreams' and 'Remembrance' (*VP*, 704, 743): he was reviewing WBY's 1929 *Selected Poems* in the *Criterion*, 9, 36 (Apr. 1930), 23–8. For Gogarty's financial crisis, see his letter to Richard Campbell, 14 Jan. 1932, Healy. He was practically dealing in Augustus Johns at this time. Also see Gogarty to Shane Leslie, 20 Mar. 1930 (copy), HRHRC. The price asked was £1,000. For Cork and the portrait, also see a cancelled section of WBY's 'Pages from a Diary' (quoted in Torchiana, *Yeats and Georgian Ireland*, 153) where he remarks that this was a portrait he had never seen – clearly a study for the famous portrait in the Tate.

32. 'Very well and gay, her clothes pitched on her,' reported SMY to R L-P, 29 July 1930.

33. *Ex*, 310.

34. Christine Longford's TS autobiography, 84–5: my thanks to Selina Hastings and Thomas Pakenham.

35. AG to WBY, fragment, probably Mar. 1930, Berg.

36. Quoted in Michael Holroyd, *Augustus John* (Harmondsworth, 1976), 636.

37. WBY to GY [Aug. 1930]. For details of this Renvyle visit, see Christine Longford's TS autobiography, 84, Holroyd, 636, and WBY's letters to GY. The hangers-on included Lady Alington, her sister Lady Ashley-Cooper, and Kit Dunn; they were joined by an American, Hope Scott.

38. n.d. [25 July 1930], MBY.

39. Gogarty, who wildly overpraised the portrait (see the Montreal *Gazette*, 24 Apr. 1943), sold it to the Glasgow Art Gallery for, he claimed, the equivalent of $10,000. The rug may be the 'coonskin' travelling-rug immortalized by Pound in the *Pisan Cantos*.

40. *YA 7* (1990), 16.

41. To R L-P, 30 Sept. 1930; also 8 Sept. 1930.

42. *Journals*, ii, 550; WBY to AG, 23 Aug. 1930, Berg.

43. *Journals*, ii, 553.

44. See above, pp. 279, 719, n. 16.

45. To Hone, 20 Nov. 1930, Buffalo.

46. 9 Sept. 1930, *Ex*, 318.

47. See Rapallo Notebook E, NLI MS 13,582.

48. 23 Apr. 1932, TCD.

49. The TS draft is in NLI MS 30,325. It appeared in the *Dublin Magazine*, Oct.–Dec. 1931 and Jan.–Mar. 1932: see below for the circumstances of its composition. For 'intellectual nationalism', see WBY to OS, 2 Dec. 1930, *L*, 779–80.

50. *Ex*, 347–8. It should be read against Daniel Corkery, *Synge and Anglo-Irish Literature*, (Cork, 1931), 38–9.

51. 23 Oct. 1930, *L*, 777.

52. To L. A. G. Strong, 14 Dec. [1930], HRHRC.

53. Recorded in a pamphlet, *Words Spoken at the Music Room Boar's Hill in the Afternoon of November 5, 1930, at a Festival Designed in the Honour of William Butler Yeats, Poet* (there is a copy in the Pierpont Morgan Library). The performing girls were Betty Bartholomew, Dulcie Bowie, Rose Bruford, Sybil Hertz-Smith and Judith Masefield; the plays were Highet's 'The Apple' and Coghill's 'The Tudor Town'.

54. To GY, 8 Nov. [1930], MBY.

55. Anne Olivier Bell and Andrew McNeillie (eds.), *The Diary of Virginia Woolf. Volume 3: 1925–1930* (London, 1980), 330; also see Nigel Nicolson and Joanne Trautmann (eds.), *The Letters of Virginia Woolf. Volume 3: A Reflection* (London, 1978), 250, 253; and Hermione Lee, *Virginia Woolf: A Biography* (London, 1996), 575. For de la Mare's impression, see Russell Brain, *Tea with Walter de la Mare* (London, 1957), 110.

56. Introduction to *Fighting the Waves*, 1934.

57. Sent to GY in a letter of 8 Nov. [1930], MBY.

58. 21 Nov. 1930, HRHRC.

59. NLI MS 30,231.

60. See Robinson to MacGreevy, 31 Jan. 1931, MacGreevy Papers, TCD, and to WBY, 31 Jan. 1931, Berg – this last in reply to a letter of WBY's. 'It doesn't seem to me to make us "responsible" for his poverty, we are in the same category as the other names that will be associated with it. I don't think that anybody is ignorant enough to believe that the theatre treated him badly, everyone knows that he left of his own accord.'

61. See Gogarty to WBY, 17 June 1930, *LTWBY*, ii, 512. The objective was to cure his 'dark

weeping' and give him leisure and confidence. GBS and Charlotte Shaw gave £25 each, as did Horace Plunkett, Sarah and Louis Purser £100 each.

62. To R L-P, 26 Dec. 1930.

63. 24 Sept. 1931. She wrote in similar terms on 22 Nov. 1932 and 1 May 1933. GY provided a telephone for the Dundrum house and various payments such as 'cash to take drives with'. On 21 July 1931 SMY had told Ruth, 'My Cuala embroidery dept is in a rocky state'; in Sept. GY and WBY had encouraged her to let it 'fade out slowly' by Christmas, and to sell her steamer shares to Arthur Jackson, along with some Pollexfen shares, and accept the weekly allowance from the Yeatses.

64. 6 Aug. 1931.

65. Michael went to Baymount and then St Columba's; Anne to Hillcourt the following year.

66. 27 Dec. 1930, L, 780–1. For other references, see WBY to Seumas O'Sullivan, 14 Dec. 1930, Indiana.

67. 20 May [1931], Berg.

68. n.d. [but late October], MBY.

69. See WBY to Albert Bender, 10 Mar. 1931, Mills College. For WBY's relations with Macmillan, see Warwick Gould, 'W. B. Yeats on the Road to St Martin's Street 1900–1917' in Elizabeth James (ed.), Macmillan: A Publishing Tradition (London, 2002), 182–217.

70. Draft, 17 June 1931, MBY.

71. For a summary see Warwick Gould's Appendix to A. Norman Jeffares (ed.), Yeats's Poems (London, 1989) and his 'W. B. Yeats and the Resurrection of the Author', the Library, 16, 2 (June 1994), 101–34.

72. 5 Jan. 1931. The penultimate line originally read 'Since Time and Change are Streams of Light'.

73. To Pound, 5 Feb. [1931], Rachewiltz Collection, University of Toledo. He was at Coole from 22 Jan. to 9 Feb.

74. To OS, postmarked 9 Feb. 1931, MBY, and L, 781.

75. 19 Mar. 1931, University of Vermont. For the description of South Hill, WBY to AG, 19 Feb. 1931, Berg.

76. The case of the Geohegan infants, whose mother had surrendered custody and now faced the prospect of the children being sent to an institution following her estranged husband's illness, was reported in the Independent, 21 Apr. 1931: WBY had noticed an altercation between the solicitors, Messrs Roger Greene & Sons, and the Protestant archbishop of Dublin, Dr Gregg, who had reportedly denounced the 'squalid scene enacted in the Courts of Law a few months ago, when the children of a Protestant mother were torn from her in the name of religion, or law'. Since an appeal was pending, the solicitors objected to the archbishop raising the issue. WBY was following this incident rather than the original reportage of the case in the Law Reports section of the Independent on 30 Mar. 1931.

77. To AG, 8 Apr. 1931, Berg.

78. To GY, n.d. [but May 1931], MBY.

79. Bowra's description is reprinted in I & R, ii, 399–400. Bowra dates it as 'early June' but the actual date seems to have been 26 May. The reference to being asked 'what had deepened my poetry' is in WBY to GY [May 1931], MBY.

80. A letter to GY dated 1 June (a Sunday) indicates that he will see Macmillan the next day.

81. It appeared in a volume called Writers at Work later that year. The (corrected) TS is in HRHRC: following quotations are from I & R, ii, 199–203.

82. SMY to R L-P, 18 May 1932. 'No hat has cured this.'

83. Torchiana, Yeats and Georgian Ireland, 114, quoting GY.

84. WBY, reporting to GY, 12 Sept. [1931]. The marriage took place on 5 Sept., in London.
85. WBY to OS, 4 Jan. 1932, MBY.
86. To Dolly Travers Smith, 22 Aug. 1931, Robinson Papers, TCD.
87. n.d. [Aug. 1931], MBY.
88. 30 Aug. [1931], MBY; excised from *L*, 783.
89. 29 Aug. 1931, MBY.
90. Letters of 1 and 25 Nov. 1931, MBY.
91. 25 Nov. 1931, MBY.
92. 22 Oct. [1931], MBY.
93. 25 Oct. 1931, HRHRC, and Bridge, *W. B. Yeats and T. S. Moore*, 169–70. The Berkeley Introduction is reprinted in *E & I*. It is striking how many phrases and ideas had been tried out on Louise Morgan six weeks before.
94. NLI MS 30,103.
95. WBY to GY, 31 Aug. [1931], MBY.
96. 29 Sept. 1931, Yale.
97. Corkery, *Synge and Anglo-Irish Literature*, 38–9. For WBY's use of the clay image in *Per Amica*, see *Myth*, 366.
98. ibid., 3.
99. ibid., 4, 212.
100. ibid., 41.
101. ibid., 17, 56–7.
102. *E & I*, 411. Since Corkery also used the image of 'topsy-turvy', this may be a coded response.
103. He also takes up Corkery's reference to O'Grady's attack upon the Ascendancy: see *Ex*, 350, compare Corkery, 53.
104. *Ex*, 344–5. There is a TS draft of the *Dublin Magazine* version in NLI MSS 30,325 and 30,874; page proofs are in NLI MS 30,771. The TS shows that he dropped some passages of personal recollection, those dealing with Mrs Wriedt's seances among other things.
105. *Ex*, 354.
106. Notebook begun 23 Nov. 1930, quoted in Torchiana, *Yeats and Georgian Ireland*, 140.
107. To Judge Campbell, 12 Feb. 1934, Healy. This outburst was occasioned by WBY attending, as a layman, the Church of Ireland Synod, where Archbishop Gregg 'shut him up'. According to SMY in 1931, WBY and GY were worried at the prospect of 'mixed marriages' for their children (to R L-P, 27 Oct. 1931).
108. NLI MS 30,159 is a typed statement by WBY. 'The misunderstanding about Sunday's meeting is all my fault. I went to the office on Wednesday, found Mr Peadar O'Donnell there, and began talking about his novels. I had read "Storm" and "The Knife" and was in the middle of "Adrigoole" and had long wanted to meet him. I came away with a vague memory that he had said something about having just hired the Abbey for a meeting or convention. However, my mind was on "Adrigoole" and I thought nothing more of the matter until next day when a fellow Director came round with the advertisement of a revolutionary meeting at the Abbey on Sunday.' NLI MS 30,675 is a superb broadside from O'Donnell dated 28 Sept. 1931, calling the Abbey directors 'the crust of a dying order' for having given in to government censorship.
109. 'Friday' [Aug. 1931]. For a commentary, see Jeremy Silver (ed.), 'George Barnes's "W. B. Yeats and Broadcasting" 1940', *YA* 5 (1987).
110. See Karin Dorn's edition of this broadcast in *YA* 5. The original is in NLI MS 30,109.
111. In an interview in the *Northern Whig and Belfast Post*, 9 Sept. 1931, he denied he had experienced any stage fright, and said he had listened to music over the wireless but never a human voice.

112. 25 Oct. 1931, Bridge, *W. B. Yeats and T. S. Moore*, 169–70.
113. To GY, 8 Feb. 1932. He wrote enthusiastically to Sturge Moore the same day.
114. 3 Feb. 1932. The reference to Wilde is based directly on a passage in 'The Decay of Lying', where Wilde asserts 'the nineteenth century, as we know it, is largely an invention of Balzac'. See Richard Ellmann, *The Artist as Critic: Critical Essays of Oscar Wilde* (London, 1970), 309.
115. *Journals*, ii, 627.
116. To Verschoyle, 17 Jan. 1932, private collection; my thanks to John Kelly.
117. There had been an *IT* leader about this on 18 Apr. 1931, followed by correspondence on 16 and 18 Apr.
118. *UP*, ii, 490; the article is reprinted on 486–90.
119. 'The Rise and Fall of Anglo-Ireland: A Race Has Passed Away – Why?', *Irish Press*, 3 Mar. 1932.
120. To Hone, 9 Feb. 1932, Kenyon. De Blácam's correspondence is in HRHRC (WBY Misc.), politely reiterating that the Anglo-Irish got their just deserts.
121. See my article '"When the Newspapers Have Forgotten Me: Yeats and His Obituarists' in *The Irish Story* (London, 2001), 89–90.
122. To AG, 22 Feb. [1932], Colin Smythe.
123. To Richard Campbell, *c*. 17 Jan. 1932, Healy. For his comments on the new government, same to same, 21 June 1932, Healy.
124. To Monk Gibbon, 12 Mar. 1932, printed in *Yeats: The Masterpiece and the Man: Yeats as I Knew Him* (London, 1959), 7.
125. This moment is also described in 'Anima Mundi' (*Myth*, 364–5). The reference to his age suggests after June 1915. GY would later tell Ellmann how important this epiphany was to WBY, 'the only such experience he had': Interview Book, Ellmann Papers, Y.9, Tulsa.
126. The letter to OS is in *L*, 789–90. The evolution of 'Vacillation' is illuminatingly discussed in Curtis Bradford, *Yeats at Work* (Carbondale, Ill., 1965), 128–34, and Ellmann, *IY*, 268–74.
127. To Sturge Moore, 8 Feb. 1932, BL Add. MSS 45732.
128. 6 Mar. 1932, *LTWBY*, ii, 531.
129. To GY, 16 Mar. 1932.
130. 12 Mar. 1932, Gibbon, *Yeats: The Masterpiece and the Man*, 137–8.
131. AG to WBY, 25 Feb. 1930, Berg.
132. For an incisive commentary, D. McMahon, *Republicans and Imperialists: Anglo-Irish Relations in the 1930s* (London, 1984), 44ff.
133. WBY to GY, n.d. [early Apr. 1932].
134. ibid.
135. John Harwood, *After Long Silence* (London, 1989), 174–5.
136. The Sturge Moores' marital correspondence for Apr. 1932 in the University of London has many references to this. However, WBY spent 12 Apr. working on the autobiography with Sturge Moore, having lunched with Mrs Foden on 7 Apr.; he visited her again on the 17th. (Engagement diary, NLI MS 31,061). He may have been at a meeting on 31 Mar. set up to arrange a settlement between the Swami and Sturge Moore: Patrick French, *Younghusband: The Last Great Imperial Adventurer* (London, 1995 ed.), 351–2.
137. NLI MS 30,107.
138. To GY, 18 Apr. 1932.
139. To OS, 9 May 1932, MBY.
140. Quoted in WBY to GY, 28 Apr. 1932.
141. SMY to R L-P, 24 May 1932.

142. To GY, 10 May [1932].
143. Berg.
144. This account is in NLI MS 30,257; printed as an Appendix to *Journals*, ii, 633–8.
145. ibid., 634.
146. 31 May [1932], *L*, 796.
147. 23 May 1932; Denson, *Letters from AE*, 197.
148. 6 June 1932, Delaware.
149. To Sydney Cockerell, 9 June 1932; Sydney Cockerell, *Friends of a Lifetime*, edited by Viola Meynell (London, 1940), 273.
150. 16 Aug. 1932.
151. 3 Feb. [1932].
152. This stanza was later removed and printed as a separate poem: perhaps because in this context it reflected rather badly on the quality of AG's 'work' compared to her 'life'.

Chapter 11 : STRUGGLES TOWARDS REALITY
1932–1933

1. *VP*, 855.
2. To Richard Campbell, 24 Aug. 1932, Healy.
3. To T. G. Keller, 1 Oct. 1932, Major Gregory Collection.
4. ibid. He added: 'I am not quoting her words, the difficulty of the situation was rather understood between us than spoken.'
5. T. J. Kiernan to Keller, 21 June 1933, quoted in Colin Smythe, Afterword in *Journals*, ii, 652 – a very detailed and valuable account of the publishing history of AG's diaries.
6. Smythe, Afterword, *Journals*, ii, 635–6.
7. WBY to Kiernan, 17 Mar. 1933 [wrongly annotated 1935], Berg. In the same letter he suggested Robinson as biographer. Other names considered were Una Pope Hennessy, Ethel Colburn Mayne, and L. A. G. Strong. WBY crisply dismissed Austin Clarke on the grounds that 'unbalanced people waste endless time and vitality' (to Sturge Moore, 5 July 1932, HRHRC).
8. 'Modern Ireland: An Address to American Audiences 1932–1933', edited by Curtis Bradford, *Massachusetts Review*, 5 (1964), 256. WBY claimed that the immediate inspiration was L. P. Jacks's article 'Over-production of Ideas' in the *Observer*, 31 July 1932. Karin Strand has pointed out differences between this version and reports of the lecture as delivered in the USA, and convincingly surmises that it is an early draft. The lecture was refined through repeated performances, and finally transplanted (in part) into the 'Commentary' on 'A Parnellite at Parnell's Funeral'. It was aired in Dublin under the title 'Modern Irish Literature' (at the R.D.S.) and spliced into his 'Irish Dramatic Movement' lecture: see *Irish Independent*, 18 Feb. 1933. This was the lecture that infuriated Bridget Fay: see below, n. 57.
9. Bradford, 'An Address to American Audiences', 266.
10. To GY, n.d. For SMY's embroidery and his reading, WBY to OS, 30 June and 5 July [1932], *L*, 797–9.
11. 25 July [1932], MBY, and *L*, 799–800.
12. 6 Sept. [1933], Kansas.
13. See his correspondence with GY. All the same, a story told by SMY to R L-P (2 May 1929) is revealing: he lectured Anne at Rapallo on the importance of working hard, like all his family, and Michael jealously demanded a lecture too. 'They felt so important, because father had never lectured them before. It was an event.' For details of Anne's

739

education, see same to same, 5 Oct. 1932; for WBY at St Columba's, personal reminiscence of Cedric Sowby in 1993.

14. 14 Aug. 1932, Kansas, and WBY to Thomas Bodkin, 20 Aug. 1932, TCD. For the walk to Churchtown, WBY to SMY, 4 Sept. 1932, Boston College.

15. To OS, 5 and 25 July [1932]. The lease cost £700, according to NLI MS 30,650, and they anticipated future difficulties with building plans in the area.

16. NLI MS 31,006 has letters from WBY to the secretary of the Royal Irish Academy, 27 July 1926 and 27 Nov. 1927, suggesting 'an autonomous committee of men of letters who would give [the RIA] the character of the French institute'. Names suggested were GBS, James Stephens, AE, Robinson, WBY, Stephen MacKenna, Sean O'Casey, and 'let us say' St John Ervine or Forrest Reid from Northern Ireland. It would have 'no difficulty in finding out duties for itself' as the new state took shape. There was a chilly response, so WBY resigned from the main body. On 29 May 1928 AE had prepared the way with Blythe for a meeting with himself, WBY, and Starkie: 'It is not the censorship we are wishing to discuss, so do not be alarmed – but a project of importance to the future of literature in Ireland'. (NLI MS 20,707).

17. To Sturge Moore, 6 Sept. 1932, HRHRC.

18. 2 Sept. 1932, L, 800–1.

19. MacGreevy to GY, 17 Apr. 1928 (NLI MS 30,859) records Joyce 'speaking very kindly of W. B., recalled that he met him once at Euston at 9 a.m. to bring him to his rooms and talk'. It was actually 6 a.m. – on 2 Dec. 1901. See AM, 277. WBY gave his version of Joyce's reasons for declining Academy membership in a New York Times interview, 28 Oct. 1932.

20. According to WBY it represented an intellectualizing of the Irish novel, as Synge had intellectualized Irish drama. O'Flaherty had also managed to transcend political testimony. 'This book will come secretly into Ireland, go from man to man as if it belonged to some hidden religion, and if I am right in my belief that it is a great book, it will so travel for generations to come.' (Manchester Guardian, 24 Feb. 1932).

21. AE to Richard Campbell, 14 Aug. 1932, Healy.

22. To Shane Leslie, 24 Sept. 1932, HRHRC.

23. WBY to Hazel Lavery, 4 Oct. [1932], private collection: my thanks to John Kelly. For a copy of the Rules, NLI MS 30,725.

24. 17 Dec. 1932, LTWBY, ii, 547.

25. 10 Mar. [1932?], NLI MS 27,884. My thanks to Rob Tobin.

26. See WBY to F. R. Higgins, n.d. [but probably autumn 1932], HRHRC.

27. 17 Dec. 1932, LTWBY, ii, 547.

28. Interview in Time and Tide (who had accepted an O'Casey story), 14, 21 (27 May 1933). For further details, see Ronald Ayling, 'Theatre Business, Management of Men: Six Letters by W. B. Yeats', Threshold, 19 (Autumn, 1965), 48–52. For WBY and Dunsany, New York Times, 28 Oct. 1932; for Gogarty's views, a letter to James Healy, 31 May 1944, Healy; for Milligan's and Hyde's reactions, see their letters to AE, 3 Apr. [1933] and 14 Oct. 1932, NLI MS 10,864.

29. Quoted in Charlotte Shaw to T. E. Lawrence, 22 Sept. 1932; A. W. Lawrence (ed.), Letters to T. E. Lawrence (London, 1962), p. 214.

30. New York Times, 28 Oct. 1932.

31. To Patrick McCartan, 12 July 1933, Boston University. AE to Richard Campbell, 4 Apr. 1933, Healy, shows they were trying to raise enough capital to fund £100 p.a.

32. 4 Jan. 1934, Berg.

33. Quoted in the Nation, 14 Dec. 1932.

34. The visit to Ruttledge may be ben trovato, but WBY certainly pursued him: see his account to GBS of an encounter during the interval at an Abbey play, 30 July 1933 [draft], NLI MS 31,020.

35. *IT*, 20 Oct. 1937 in NLI MS 30,877. The bibulous Ruttledge was a particular target. The week after he was bearded by the Academy over the *Black Girl* issue, WBY watched him guided to a seat in the Abbey 'as the lame and blind are guided, & slurring his consonants' (to Shaw, 30 Aug. 1933, NLI MS 30,020).

36. WBY's engagement diary (NLI MS 31,060) shows he was in Manchester on 6–7 Oct., visited the Laverys in London on 10 Oct., Gogarty on 11 Oct., Putnam and Macmillan on 19 Oct., saw Ottoline Morrell on 20 Oct., and sailed on the 21st. The same source shows he had visited the Swami and Mrs Foden on 13 and 17 Apr. 1932.

37. Sturge Moore Papers [late 1932], University of London, MS 978/37/8.

38. He arrived on 26 Oct. and gave interviews at once. There was a dinner in his honour in the Authors' Club on the 27th, and the tour proper began on the 31st. On 1 Nov. he was in Bangor, Maine, and on 4 Nov. in Waterville, where he spoke at Colby College. (He also lectured at Bowdoin at this time.) He then returned to New York for some engagements. On 10 Nov. he lectured in Ann Arbor, on the 11th he was in Detroit giving interviews and touring the Ford factories, and on the 14th he was in Cleveland. On 15 Nov. he lectured at Kent State. On 17 Nov. he was in Minneapolis, 18 Nov. Cincinnati, 23–25 Nov. Toronto, and thence to Montreal on the 26th. He gave two lectures there, on the 27th and 28th. On 29 Nov. he travelled to Dartmouth, Colgate, and Groton for lectures, arriving in Boston on 3 Dec. Though he returned to New York in the interim and spoke on 7 Dec. at Bryn Mawr, he was back in Boston to lecture at Wellesley on 8 Dec., and attended a seance at Mrs Crandon's on the 11th. On 15 Dec. he gave his last large public lecture, at Brooklyn. From then until his departure on 22 Jan. he concentrated on 'drawing-room lectures' to raise money for the Academy, arranged by Richard Campbell and Patrick McCartan. He also attended lunch parties in his honour, visited museums, and spoke at the opening of an exhibition of JY's paintings at the Museum of Irish Art on 29 Dec. On 4–8 Jan. he returned to Boston for seances with the Crandons and then visited South Bend, Indiana, to lecture at Notre Dame on 9 Jan. The last fortnight was spent in New York, following a busy social schedule, speaking at a special performance of *King Oedipus* on 15 Jan., and attending a dinner to honour Gogarty, John McCormack, Hamilton Harty and himself on the 16th. Details of his social life and financial arrangements are taken from SMY to R L-P, 16 Nov. 1932, and Alan Duncan to GY, 16 Dec. 1932, HRHRC.

39. Uncharitably recalled by Gogarty. 'Mrs Duncan was the foundress of the United Arts Club. She got people to join a "Club" in which she dwelt and so escaped much of the cost of living. She is the wife of an ex-civil servant who was in the old Dublin Castle in the Ministry of Education. He took his pension and though over 70 lives in Paris up a narrow stair with a woman.' To Horace Reynolds, 21 Feb. 1936, Harvard, b Ms Am 1787[140].

40. Flyer from M. C. Turner Southwestern Music Bureau, Dallas, in the Armstrong Browning Library, Baylor University, Waco.

41. In Cleveland on 14 Nov.; see Karin Strand, 'W. B. Yeats's American Lecture Tours', Ph.D. thesis, Northwestern University, 1978, 217.

42. *Boston Evening Transcript*, 9 Dec. 1932; quoted in Strand, 'W. B. Yeats's American Lecture Tours', 222–3.

43. 28 Oct. See Brooks Atkinson in *New York Times*, 29 Oct. John Mason Brown also reported the occasion in the *New York Evening Post*, but hated the play.

44. *America*, 10 Dec. 1932.

45. *Nation*, 135, 3,519 (14 Dec. 1932).

46. Francis Russell, 'The Arch-poet', *Horizons* (Nov. 1960), 66–9: my thanks to James Earl Roy for this reference.

47. See letters to GY, 12 Dec., 18 Nov., and (for Lawrence) 4 Nov. 1932. He went on to *The Rainbow* and *Sons and Lovers*; though he decided the writing was clumsy, he continued to admire Lawrence's passion.

48. 11 Dec. 1932.
49. *Brave Spirit* (London, n.d.), 79–80. For her impressions of him in 1914, see *AM*, 515.
50. Strand, 'W. B. Yeats's American Lecture Tours', 212.
51. 'Eliot told me give WBY his love which I did and WBY said ₀ down there like that' (to GY, 28 Nov. 1926, NLI MS 30,859). Eliot gave great prominence to WBY's work in his 'Contemporary English Literature' lectures at Harvard: see Stuart Daley, 'Eliot's English 26, Harvard University, Spring Term 1933' in *T. S. Eliot Review* (Fall, 1975). The story about the Wellesley dinner is in Ellmann's *Eminent Domain: Yeats among Wilde, Joyce, Pound, Eliot, and Auden* (Oxford, 1967), 89, and the anecdote from Bowdoin is in Francis Russell, 'The Arch-poet'.
52. The lecture was on 8 Dec. Reynolds preserved his notes and they are in his papers at the Harvard, b Ms Am 1787[662].
53. *New York Times*, 23 Jan. 1933.
54. 10 July 1936, Harvard, b Ms Am 1787[140].
55. Harvard; reprinted in George Bornstein and Hugh Witemeyer (eds.), *Letters to the New Island: A New Edition* (London, 1989), p. xviii.
56. To GY, 16 Dec. 1932, HRHRC.
57. 27 Feb. 1933, NLI MS 2652. The lecture was reported in the *IT* and *Irish Independent* on 18 Feb.; it is very similar to the one recorded by Reynolds at Wellesley. Bridget Fay also wrote to the *Irish Independent* on 3 Mar. WBY replied on 13 Mar., in a fairly mollifying way, denying that he had been contemptuous, though a friend to whom he had shown the article had agreed that 'perhaps the word "stage-struck" might have seemed so'. Also see above, n. 8.
58. NLI MS 30,658. Expenses had been very closely monitored, down to 3 cents for a paper, 10 cents for oranges, etc. In 1934 he was still calculating his income very tightly: jottings in the back of his engagement diary (NLI MS 31,661) show him carefully listing his income from serial publications.
59. These figures are put together from NLI MS 30,659.
60. See letter from Macmillan, 15 Apr. 1932, NLI MS 30,248.
61. See letters of 29–30 Mar. 1933, NLI MS 30,248.
62. WBY to R.N.D. Wilson, n.d., private collection.
63. 24 Oct. 1933, Delaware.
64. *E & I*, 436.
65. 16 Feb. 1934, Delaware.
66. Hone, 382.
67. See J. McElligott to Lennox Robinson, 27 Feb. 1933, NLI MS 30,575. For a typical Magennis performance, see *IT*, 9 Nov. 1923, where he clashed with WBY over 'the modern novel' (in effect, Joyce).
68. See NLI MS 26,198 (Joseph Brennan Papers).
69. *Irish Monthly*, 61 (Apr. 1928), 658.
70. Letter to editor of *Sunday Times*, printed 7 Oct. 1934. For de Valera's response in the Dáil, see Paul Scott Stanfield, *Yeats and Politics in the 1930s* (London, 1988), 33; it was discussed in *The Times*, 9 Apr. 1934. There was also a clearly 'inspired' paragraph in the *Irish Independent*, 7 Apr. 1934, giving WBY's side of things, and criticizing de Valera for never setting foot in the Abbey; and a long and gossipy piece on 13 Apr. ('Leaves from a Woman's Diary') reviewing the theatre's relationship with the government, but criticizing it for resting on its laurels. The *Manchester Guardian*, 13 Apr. 1934, carried a long piece giving the Abbey's side: repr. in *I & R*, ii, 240–5. De Valera's letter to Robinson of 17 Apr. 1934 is in SIUC.

Chapter 12 : A New Fanaticism
1933–1934

1. To R L-P, 8 Aug. 1932.
2. WBY's friend Andrew Jameson headed a committee of former southern Unionists to raise money for Cumann an nGaedheal in 1931: see John Regan, *The Irish Counter-Revolution 1921–1936* (Dublin, 1999), 313.
3. To Richard Campbell, n.d. [but Oct. 1932], Healy.
4. Regan, *The Irish Counter-Revolution*, 287–304.
5. The report of the state of the army in 1924 (NLI MS 30,878) states that MacManus had been marked down for demobilization, but the high command urgently requested his retention, as he had been a crucially effective deputy governor of Mountjoy Prison and camp commander at Portobello. He stood for 'stern military discipline' and had broken IRA prisoners' spirits as well as clearing up 'an almost incredible mess of indiscipline and maladministration' at Portobello.
6. See *I & R*, ii, 409.
7. See WBY to Mrs Arndt, 27 Mar. 1934, Penn State. The correspondence in the Frankfurt State Archives between WBY and the ober-burgomeister shows clearly that WBY connected the award strictly to Goethe himself (whose head adorned the medal), rather than the political party in power there. The *Irish Press* of 17 Feb. 1934 reported that the award was now very rarely given to persons distinguished for cultural achievement, unlike under the 'old regime'. SMY to R L-P, 29 Aug. 1929, mentions WBY's following in Germany. The whole issue is examined in K. P. S. Jochum, 'Yeats and the Goethe-Plakette: An Unpublished Letter and Its Context', *YA* 15 (2002), 281–7.
8. JY to Hone, 8 May 1948, HRHRC; MG to Ethel Mannin, 24 July 1946, and an undated letter of the late 1940s, NLI MS 17,875. For the comment to Rothenstein, see *Since Fifty: Men and Memories 1922–1938* (London, 1939), 283; though it should be pointed out that when WBY encountered a similar idea in Toynbee's *Study of History* he rather took exception to it (See 'General Introduction to my Work') and that he supported the foundation of a Jewish homeland (see above, p. 165).
9. 2 Mar. 1933, Yale.
10. Scrap in NLI MS 30,011, dated 30 May 1933.
11. To Blythe, July 1931: quoted by Regan, *The Irish Counter-Revolution*, 283.
12. 19 Dec. 1932, UCDA, P80/1212 (1). A letter from Coole about Berdyaev, 4 Dec. [1931], is in ibid., 1211 (1).
13. *New York Times* magazine, 13 Nov. 1932.
14. 'Modern Ireland: An Address to American Audiences', edited by Curtis Bradford, *Massachusetts Review*, 5 (1964), 256.
15. To OS, 9 Mar. 1933; *L*, 806.
16. To Hildegarde Coghill, 6 Mar. 1933; my thanks to Gifford Lewis for this reference.
17. Journal, 19 Dec. 1933; my thanks to Adrian Goodman for this reference.
18. NLI MS 30,546; probably late July 1933.
19. See Michael Cronin, *The Blueshirts and Irish Politics* (Dublin, 1997).
20. WBY had consulted Brown on senatorial and Academy matters (see WBY to Blythe, 11 July 1925, NLI MS 20,704, and 4 Oct. 1928, UCDA) and been visited by him in Italy.
21. *L*, 808.
22. 30 Mar. 1933, UCDA.
23. *L*, 811–12.

24. 28 Oct. 1947, Interview Book, Ellmann Papers, Y.9, Tulsa.

25. NLI MS 30,280; also see the version sent to FitzGerald on 30 Mar. 1933 in UCDA.

26. 'Notes for the Radio', W. R. Rogers Collection, HRHRC.

27. *L*, 813 (postmarked 25 July).

28. Journal, 19 Dec. 1933; my thanks to Adrian Goodman.

29. Annotated 'August', HRHRC.

30. Starkie became a member of *Le Centre International d' Études sur la Fascisme* and edited its journal; Mike Cronin, *The Blueshirts and Irish Politics* (Dublin, 1997), 93–7.

31. UCDA. (This though Blythe would declare later that he possessed no correspondence with WBY.) WBY's accompanying, undated letter tells Blythe that 'the Spectator is printing them at once' and also identifies Larchet, director of music at the Abbey, as his adviser on whether they were 'singable'. A following letter is postmarked '30 Nov. 1933'. In the event, of course, the *Spectator* did not publish them until Feb. 1934. In a letter dated 'Nov 22' [1934], UCDA, WBY told Con Curran that he had been 'absorbed in an attempt to put tolerable words to the tune of O'Donnell abu. Having completed three versions my mind is at peace again.'

32. The 'National Song' debate took place on 22 Nov., introduced by an argument as to whether the state possessed copyright in the 'Soldiers' Song'. Frank MacDermot called for a committee to select 'an old Gaelic air worthy of the country' and in fact suggested 'O'Donnell Abu'. Nearly a month before (26 Oct. 1933) the Blueshirt newspaper had published 'O'Duffy Abu' by 'Volunteer A. Lacey'. This sequence of events has been incisively traced in an unpublished paper by the late Síle ní Shúilleabháin, to which I am much indebted.

33. HRHRC. The concert of poems, to be sung by F. R. Higgins, was advertised for 19 Feb. and following nights: *Irish Press*, 19 Feb. 1934.

34. GY's opinions are reported in the Ellmann Interview Book, as above.

35. *United Ireland*, 10 Feb. 1934. An even worse version appeared on 3 Feb. 1934.

36. HRHRC.

37. 7 Mar. [1934]; Richard Taylor (ed.), *Frank Pearce Sturm: His Life, Letters and Collected Work* (Urbana, Ill., 1969), 103.

38. 3 Oct. 1933, MBY.

39. 2 Apr. 1934. The Swami's advances remained obdurately unearned; only twenty-seven copies were sold in the USA (letter of 22 Oct. 1933, MBY).

40. See GY to WBY, 5 Jan. 1934, for Edwards; for O'Faolain, his letter to WBY of 14 Jan. 1930, MBY.

41. 27 Feb. [1934], *L*, 820.

42. 9 Mar. 1934, BL Add. MSS 55003.

43. To OS, 24 Jan. 1934, MBY. This follows straight on from a remark that his Gregory letters had been returned to him. The recurring apparition is recorded in a notebook (NLI MS 30,546). It began as a coat on a coat-hanger, subsequently became an actual body, and approached his bed to offer him a drink. A version of this was famously relayed to Virginia Woolf, and also finds its way into the refrain of 'The Apparitions'.

44. The following comparisons come from the draft MS in Houghton.

45. WBY tells an anecdote about 'a beautiful woman whose love affairs were notorious' [Daisy Fingall], and who feared a lecture from the bishop of Tuam less than one from AG. He originally added: 'Lady Gregory would have been as wise as the Bishop, & perhaps because her philosophy was like her brothers . . .' but stopped there and deleted the observation, perhaps feeling he was getting into deep water.

46. Diary, 12 July 1927, Harvard, b Ms Am 1787[5803].

47. This is in the Harvard draft; it is put more lengthily in the published version. The affectation that he had 'forgotten' what marriage coarsened the Moore blood is a subtle

riposte to Moore's claim in *Ave* that he had 'forgotten' what WBY told him about his sexual relations with MG: see *AM*, 507.

48. Notebook, 2 July 1927, Harvard.
49. Deleted from final version.
50. The generous encomium on Fay which appears at the end of Section XX in the published version is not in the Houghton draft.
51. *Saturday Review* (New York), 16 May 1936.
52. WBY to Margaret Gough, 24 Nov. 1934, private collection – a letter which shows that he at one stage intended to add 'another hundred pages'. Quinn's judgement is in a letter to Jeanne Foster, 21 June 1922, Foster–Murphy Collection, NYPL. He, of course, had a special knowledge of AG's life denied to many.
53. The annotations survive in Reynolds's papers in Harvard; WBY suggests among other things that Reynolds underestimated Joyce's productivity.
54. *CH*, 318.
55. ibid., 322ff.
56. ibid., 341. This is a poet's insight: compare Tom Paulin's thoughtful analysis of 'In Memory of Eva Gore-Booth and Con Markiewicz', *LRB*, 20, 2 (22 Jan. 1998).
57. There is a text in NLI MS 30,722, and a version in the *Listener*, 4 Apr. 1934, reprinted in *UP*, ii, 495–9.
58. George Buchanan in *CH*, 329.

Chapter 13 : PASSIONATE METAPHYSICS
1934–1935

1. NLI MS 30,061.
2. For Steinach, see Harry Benjamin in *Scientific Monthly* (New York) (1945), 427–44.
3. See Ivan Crozier, 'Becoming a Sexologist: Norman Haire, the 1929 London World League of Sexual Reform Congress, and Organizing Medical Knowledge about Sex in Inter-war England', *History of Science*, forthcoming. I am indebted to Diana Wyndham for further information.
4. By the 1940s he was back in Australia, where he survived accusations of spying for Germany to become a much reviled but widely read contraception advocate and sex guru for a popular magazine. At his death in 1959 he left a considerable fortune, to found a chair of sexology at the University of Sydney (he told Anthony O'Connor this was to annoy 'the wowsers': Anthony O'Connor, unpublished TS). It still endows annual fellowships in his name.
5. Crozier, 'Becoming a Sexologist'.
6. This was the book recommended by WBY to Sturge Moore, who had a Steinach operation performed by Geoffrey Keynes two years after WBY (Ellmann interview with Haire, 13 Dec. 1946, Interview Book, Ellmann Papers, EJ-12, Tulsa). WBY wrote to Sturge Moore on 10 July 1934, telling him Haire was expensive and suggesting that Dulac might advise somebody more reasonable: University of London, MS 978/2/76.
7. H. Montgomery Hyde, 'Yeats and Gogarty', *YA* 5 (1987), 156.
8. Woolf to Stephen Spender, 29 Oct. 1934, Nigel Nicolson and Joanne Trautmann (eds.), *The Letters of Virginia Woolf. Volume 5: The Sickle Side of the Moon 1932–1935* (London, 1979), 342; also Harold Nicolson, *Diaries and Letters 1930–1939*, edited by Nigel Nicolson (London, 1966), 88 (entry for 9 Nov. 1936). The coat-hanger apparition is recorded in a notebook: NLI MS 30,546.
9. See, e.g., WBY to Brigit Patmore, 4 Nov. [1934], UCLA.

10. WBY to Macmillan, 15 May 1934, BL Add. MSS 55003. For vasectomy and libido, see *The Times*, 6 June 1995.

11. WBY to OS, 1 June [1934], MBY.

12. To Horace Reynolds, 11 Oct. 1934, Harvard.

13. 28 June 1947, Interview Book, Ellmann Papers, Y.8, Tulsa. L. A. G. Strong recorded that WBY said AE should have the operation, since he was 'physically enfeebled': though, he added, 'with a flash from his strong lenses, "he would die sooner"'. Undated newspaper cutting (reviewing Hone), NLI MS 5919.

14. WBY to OS, 9 May 1934, MBY, censored in *L*, 822. The letter goes on to discuss the love-life of 'the daughter of a Bishop' whose promiscuous and eccentric lifestyle has no shock-value in the modern world. 'The shepherds of Theocritus return & you & I are old.'

15. WBY to OS, 17 Sept. 1934, MBY; partly in *L*, 829–30.

16. The best commentary on this process is Tim Armstrong, 'Giving Birth to Oneself: Yeats's Late Sexuality', *YA* 8 (1991), 39–58.

17. *CH*, 358.

18. Mary Fitzgerald, 'Ezra Pound and Irish Politics: An Unpublished Correspondence', *Paideuma*, 12, 2 (1983), 392.

19. *The King of the Great Clock Tower, Commentaries and Poems* (London, 1935), pp. vi–vii.

20. 25 Aug. 1936; my thanks to John Kelly.

21. At this very time, he wrote to Dolmetsch introducing the young American musician Harry Partch, 21 Nov. 1934, Dolmetsch Papers, Haslemere.

22. *CH*, 362.

23. 24 July 1934, *L*, 824.

24. In a letter to OS, 25 Aug. [1934], censored in *L*, 827–9.

25. 24 July 1934, *L*, 824–5.

26. Margot was born on 25 Sept. 1907, according to WBY to Dulac, 6 Nov. 1934, HRHRC.

27. *ASD*, 19–20.

28. 5 Oct. 1934, *ASD*, 21.

29. 11 Oct., from Rome; *ASD*, 23. 'The old version of the play is bad because abstract and incoherent. This version is poignant and simple – lyrical dialogue all simple. It takes years to get my plays right.'

30. Interview with GY, 24 Sept. 1947, Interview Book, Ellmann Papers, Y.9, Tulsa.

31. An interpretation he would later build into 'The Municipal Gallery Revisited'. See NLI MS 30,113 and 30,336 for versions of the Rome speech. The first version was printed by the Reale Accademia as a pamphlet, 'The Irish National Theatre', the following year.

32. n.d. [but from context late Oct. 1934]. Other letters of 27 Oct. and 'Tuesday' [probably 30 Oct. 1934] give more details of the project. The best discussion is Michael Sidnell, *Dances of Death: The Group Theatre of London in the Thirties* (London, 1984), 266–9.

33. To GY, n.d., and 23 Oct. [1934]. For Allen's recollection, see Sidnell, *Dances of Death*, 20.

34. It had been scheduled for Oct. but actually appeared in mid Dec.; WBY to R. A. Scott-James, n.d., HRHRC.

35. *ASD*, 24–6.

36. Or so WBY told Gogarty: see Gogarty to Norah Hoult, apparently dated 2 Jan. 1935 [but probably Feb.], Bucknell.

37. SMY to R L-P, 20 Sept. 1930.

38. 'How the devil am I to "write a novel" if people ask how it progresses and I get involved therefore with biographical matter? I am doing it to amuse myself, and if I attempt to publish it shall do so under a pseudonym. Probably it will be burnt, but it is meant as an

interest to myself, is not Irish or English, has no autobiographical or biographical associations. So leave me to stew in my solitary juice.' 29 Dec. [1935], MBY.

39. Interview with RFF, 26 Nov. 1987. For WBY at *Sweeney*, Sidnell, *Dances of Death*, 103. WBY's revived interest in *Diarmuid and Grania* is corroborated by GY to H. O. White, 29 Apr. 1949, TCD, which describes WBY looking through the play in 1935 to see if it could be reshaped for the Abbey, 'but [he] rejected it with groans'.

40. WBY to Dulac, 'Monday' [10 Dec. 1934], HRHRC. The visits to Morrell and Dulac were 20 and 11 Dec. respectively.

41. 18 Dec. 1934, HRHRC.

42. The account in Mannin's TS diary in Boston University differs very little from that published in *Privileged Spectator* (London, 1939).

43. This poem is penetratingly discussed by Warwick Gould in *YA* 6 (1988). There is a MS version in NLI MS 30,189. Ellmann, *IY*, believed it to be part of the poem-sequence 'Margot'; Gould separated out two strains of composition, and their redrafting into three numbered stanzas on a different sheet, together with the date, suggests that the verses quoted are intended for Mannin.

44. Mannin's proud boast in *Young in the Twenties* (London, 1971), 85.

45. Anthony O'Connor, unpublished TS.

46. Interview on 11 Dec. 1946, Interview Book, Ellmann Papers, Y.9, Tulsa.

47. Information from Diana Wyndham.

48. Interview, 7 Jan. 1947, as above.

49. 30 Dec. 1934, Sligo. Gogarty's version is in a letter to Horace Reynolds, 9 Mar. 1955, Harvard, b Ms Am 1787[140], and the 'swan song' reference is in a letter from Mannin to Ellmann, 11 Feb. 1946, Tulsa.

50. 5 Feb. 1935, *L*, 821.

51. Private collection. SMY to R L-P, 4 Feb. 1935.

52. Gogarty to James A. Healy (to whom he was trying to sell the letter), 25 June 1950, Healy.

53. 'Tuesday Jan. 21 [or 22?]'. The context is 1935. In fact WBY was probably looking for letters from Mannin, but it is uncertain whether GY yet knew about her, and she was not a friend of Dulac.

54. 1 Jan. 1935.

55. To R L-P, 4 Feb. 1935.

56. To Norah Hoult, '2 Jan.' [but it must have been Feb.] 1935, Bucknell.

57. n.d. [but Feb. 1935], Sligo.

58. *Privileged Spectator*, 117.

59. 4 Mar. 1935, *L*, 831–2.

60. 2 Apr. [1935] – a letter which mentions Mannin bringing Toller to see WBY on a previous occasion, but does not clarify whether this was the occasion described in *Privileged Spectator*, and dealt with below, pp. 518–19.

61. Sidnell, *Dances of Death*, 115.

62. Robert Medley, *Drawn from the Life: A Memoir* (London, 1983), 154.

63. Probably 7 Apr., to judge by a letter to GY of 8 Apr., MBY. The text of the *Dog* was not published until 25 May. It is possible that the play they discussed was the new production of *The Dance of Death*, which the Group Theatre put on the following Oct. At least twice in later life Auden remarked that he had 'known' three great poets (Brecht, Frost, and Yeats) and that they were all 'shits', which suggests that there was indeed a meeting. See Joseph Brodsky, *Less than One: Selected Essays* (New York, 1980), 34. Brodsky also expressed this in a poem ('Each/One a prize son of a bitch'): see 'In England' in Ann Kjellberg (ed.), *Collected Poems in English* (New York, 2000), 137. My thanks to

Nicholas Jenkins. WBY had earlier mentioned to GY his wish to meet Auden: n.d. [but late Oct. 1934].

64. Humphrey Carpenter, *W. H. Auden: A Biography* (London, 1981), 135.
65. Doone to Dulac, 18 Mar. 1935, HRHRC, shows as much. Also see *ASD*, 37 n.
66. Dulac to WBY, n.d., and 16 Mar. 1935, HRHRC.
67. To GY, 'Monday' [22 Apr. 1935]; SMY to R L-P, 15 Apr. 1935.
68. Quoted in *I & R*, ii, 213, where it is misdated to Jan. 1933; but evidence of letters, and the Lancaster Gate Terrace setting, firmly fix it in Apr.–May 1935. O'Casey may have conflated more than one occasion. The 'black oxen' refers to the conclusion of *The Countess Kathleen* – an image WBY originally lifted from Walter Scott.
69. Rothenstein, *Since Fifty: Men and Memories 1922–1938* (London, 1939), 241–2.
70. *Privileged Spectator*, 84. Also see my edition of Hubert Butler, *The Sub-Prefect Should Have Held His Tongue and Other Essays* (London, 1985), 237–40, for more details of Ossietzky – who did win the Nobel in 1935, but died in Nazi custody.
71. 23 May 1936; my thanks to John Kelly.
72. See *Dublin Magazine*, i, 12 (Jan. 1924); my thanks to Nicholas Allen.
73. She often quoted this, but possibly its first appearance is in her letter to Rothenstein immediately after WBY's death, 6 Feb. 1939, HRHRC. Rothenstein took the credit for introducing her to WBY (*Since Fifty*, 249–50), but Ottoline Morrell had at least as strong a claim.
74. WBY to Mannin, 1 Feb. 1934 [*recte* 1935], Sligo, and to OS, 5 Feb. 1935, *L*, 831.
75. 1 June 1935, HRHRC.
76. Copy in Marie Belloc Lowndes Papers, HRHRC.
77. n.d., HRHRC. 'Off-handed' is presumably a slip for 'open-handed'.
78. To Rothenstein, 11 July 1935, Harvard, b Ms Eng 1148[1650].
79. To R L-P, 17 June 1935.
80. As WBY proudly emphasized to Gwyneth Foden, n.d. [but July 1935], HRHRC.
81. 13 June 1935.
82. NLI MS 30,590, TS of RÉ interview with Deirdre MacDonough.
83. NLI 30,817.
84. It arrived on 4 July (WBY to Dulac, 6 July 1935, HRHRC). He wrote delightedly to Wellesley the same day. For the poem it inspired a year later, see below, pp. 550–2. Harry Clifton was born in 1907, the son of John Talbot Clifton and Violet Mary (née Beauclerk) who had a house near Gogarty in Connemara as well as a castle in Islay and a country house at Lytham St Anne's. The money came from vast Lancashire estates, including 'half of Blackpool' (Seymour Leslie, *The Jerome Connection*, London, 1964, 114). He wrote *Dielma and Other Poems* (1932), *Flight* (1934) and *Gleams Britain's Day* (1942) – the last dedicated to JY and to the memory of AE. All were published by Duckworth, probably with some financial inducement. Clifton died in the London Ritz in 1978, having become markedly eccentric.
85. SMY to R L-P, 17 June 1935.
86. To R L-P, 30 June 1935.
87. Several letters in the Healy Collection at Stanford chronicle this sad progress; including one from AE to James Stephens, asking him not to respond to begging-letters from his son. See also SMY to R L-P, 3 July 1933, who (after discussing the Russell family) adds: 'Willy says he never asks any of his friends about their sons, as they have all turned out badly.'
88. *LTWBY*, ii, 574.
89. 10 June 1935, Berkeley.
90. 23 July 1935.

91. To DW, 26 July [1935], Meisei.
92. SMY to R L-P, 30 July 1935; for his 'remorse' at not going to Bournemouth, WBY to James Stephens, 2 July 1935, Harvard; for surprise at WBY not giving the funeral oration, Richard Campbell to Gogarty, 16 Aug. 1935, Healy.
93. 26 Aug. 1935, *LDW*, 13.
94. See O'Casey to WBY, 19 May 1935, MBY, and WBY to Richard Hayes, 1 Feb. 1935, SIUC.
95. *IT*, 26 Feb. 1935 (the interview took place on 23 Feb.).
96. To Eric Gorman, 4 May 1935 (headed Riversdale, but written in London), NLI MS 31,002.
97. See below p. 532. The directors' rejoinder is reported in the *IT*, 3 Sept. 1935; they said that MacNamara had never spoken against *The Silver Tassie* at Abbey Board meetings, and attacked it only when the press campaign began. Sean McCann (ed.), *The Story of the Abbey Theatre* (London, 1967), 152–3, gives a useful account of the 1935 controversy, and the campaign against the play by Catholic Action and the Gaelic League.
98. See President James Conant to WBY, 25 May 1935, and draft reply in GY's hand, NLI 31,003. The contract involved six lectures, to be published by Harvard University Press, with a payment of $4,500 and $500 travelling expenses.
99. 24 July [1935], Sligo, and *L*, 835–6.
100. *Dublin Magazine*, 10, 1 (Jan.–Mar. 1935).
101. Interview Book, Ellmann Papers, Y.9, Tulsa.
102. 14 June 1935, *LDW*, 4.
103. E. T. Williams and Helen M. Palmer (eds.), *Dictionary of National Biography 1951–1960* (Oxford, 1971), 1,041–2.
104. Victoria Glendinning, *Vita: The Life of Vita Sackville-West* (London, 1983), 124.
105. ibid., 214.
106. 21 June 1935, *LDW*, 7.
107. *DNB*, 1,041.
108. 15 Nov. [1935], *LDW*, 41. 'Cumulative' may be a misreading of 'combative'.
109. *LDW*, 73.
110. WBY to Macmillan, 18 Nov. 1935, BL Add. MSS 55003. The book was published with WBY's Introduction and the drawing of Wellesley by Rothenstein: see above, p. 527.
111. 21 Dec. 1935. He rephrased it the next day. 'With you it is not a question of the speech of the common people – as with Synge and Lady Gregory – but the common speech of the people.'
112. To Gogarty, 14 Sept. 1940, Healy.
113. For WBY's admiration, see Richard Shone, *Bloomsbury Portrait: Vanessa Bell, Duncan Grant and Their Circle* (London, 1993), 229. The paintings are now in the University of Southampton. My thanks to Lady Elizabeth Clyde for her reminiscences.
114. Lady Elizabeth Clyde, who was sixteen at the time, admits to thinking her mother's guest 'pompous, arrogant and patronizing'.
115. 17 July 1935, Meisei, and *LDW*, 5 (with excisions).
116. 21 July 1935, Meisei, and *LDW*, 7.
117. *ASD*, 42.
118. SMY to R L-P, 19 July 1935, and WBY to DW, 1 Sept. 1935, *LDW*, 23.
119. 11 Aug. 1935, *LDW*, 21.
120. 'Sunday' [1 Sept. 1935], MBY.
121. 3 Sept. 1935, Meisei.
122. 2 Oct. 1935, Price Collection, Princeton.
123. This is the version he sent to Price, now at Princeton.

124. WBY to GY, 31 Oct. [1935], MBY. For the tiny audience, see Rothenstein, *Since Fifty*, 245–6.

125. Glendinning, *Vita*, 279.

126. To GY, n.d., MBY.

127. To Harold Macmillan, 18 Nov. 1935, BL Add. MSS 55003.

128. For the story of the Scribner edition, see Edward Callan (ed.), *Yeats on Yeats: The Last Introductions and the 'Dublin' Edition* (Dublin, 1981), and Warwick Gould, Appendix 6: 'The Definitive Edition' in A. Norman Jeffares (ed.), *Yeats's Poems* (London, 1989), 706–49. The Scribner & Sons Archives at Princeton (Author Files I, Box 170) record the initial moves. On 7 Nov. 1935, Charles Scribner wrote to Charles Brett at Macmillan (New York) suggesting a subscription set of seven or eight volumes, priced at $10 per volume, 600 to 700 sets in all, the first volume to be signed by WBY. Royalties would be at 10 per cent, two thirds to the author; this would mean '$6000 divided between you and Yeats'. Brett wrote to WBY the next day, suggesting a 'definitive' edition with new material: this would, in the end, amount to little more than the General Introduction, which was the major plum offered (though new Introductions to each volume had originally been mentioned). Scribner cooled a little in 1936, but by Oct. of that year it was reported that WBY 'now seems a lot keener . . . and has volunteered to make more of an effort' (7 Oct. 1936). The appearance of a surprising amount of new work by WBY after this date complicated matters. Moreover, Macmillan (and Watt) seem to have kept quiet about the British edition de luxe – as is clear from a discomfited letter from Charles Kingsley to Wheelock, 4 Apr. 1939. WBY wrote to Harold Macmillan on 18 Nov. 1935: 'I would naturally like to accept this offer but I don't want to do anything unfair. You have an English expensive edition of my work on hand and partly printed. I have therefore sent Brett's letter to Watt and asked him to consider the matter with you.' He wrote in similar terms to Watt the same day, doubting that the two editions would clash, and expressing impatience at Macmillan (London) for delaying the edition de luxe. It seems clear that his priority was to maximize income.

129. To Gwyneth Foden, 12 Nov. [1935], HRHRC.

130. Same to same, 6 July 1935, HRHRC

131. Interview of 21 Sept. 1947, Interview Book, Ellmann Papers, Y.9, Tulsa.

132. 9 Dec. 1935.

Chapter 14 : FIRE AND EATING
1936–1937

1. Anne Olivier Bell and Andrew McNeillie (eds.), *The Diary of Virginia Woolf. Volume 4: 1931–1935* (London, 1982), 271.

2. For a particularly direct transposition, see Denis E. Smith and F. A. C. Wilson, 'The Source of Yeats's "What Magic Drum"', *Papers on Language and Literature*, 9 (1975), 197–201.

3. Naresh Guha, *W. B. Yeats: An Indian Approach* (Calcutta, 1968), 114ff., makes the connection between these poems and the 'Katha' *Upanishad*, a dialogue with death.

4. 6 Jan. 1932, MBY.

5. 29 Sept. 1935, *Calcutta Municipal Gazette*, 22 Feb. 1936.

6. n.d., Pierpoint Morgan Library.

7. See Shankhar Mokashi-Punekar, 'Shri Purohit Swami and W. B. Yeats' in M. K. Nair, S. K. Desai, S. T. Kallapur (eds.), *The Image of India in Western Creative Writing* (Khamatak University, Dharwar, 1970); A. Davenport, 'W. B. Yeats and the *Upanishads*', *Review of English Studies*, 3, 9 (Jan. 1952), 55–62; Shri S. Viswantha, 'Yeats

and the Swami: The Poetic Use of an Indian Tradition', *The Anuyan Path* (Bombay), 34, 8 (Aug. 1968); Guha, *An Indian Approach*, Chapter 5; Sankaran Ravindran, *W. B. Yeats and Indian Tradition* (Delhi, 1990), Chapter 4.

8. As established by Guha, *An Indian Approach*, 144.

9. See Guha, 108ff., and Elizabeth Butler Cullingford, *Gender and History in Yeats's Love Poems* (Cambridge, 1993), 252–3, 256–7.

10. J. Masson, 'Yeats's *The Ten Principal Upanishads*', *Jadvapur Journal of Comparative Literature*, 19 (1973), points out the inadequacy and omissions of most of the material offered, blaming the Swami for giving only a sketchy approximation of the texts.

11. 16 June 1935, MBY.

12. See WBY to Foden, 6 and 28 July, and 12 Nov. 1935: 'Get rooms and bed at £2 a week, I will pay £3 a week and that will bring your share of total expenses to £3. If we go to a hotel and pay £3 then you will have the monstrous sum of £6 to pay for I cannot pay more than £3.' He intended to use the £60 left over from his birthday gift to finance the venture. His margins were distinctly narrow. (HRHRC).

13. John Harwood, *After Long Silence* (London, 1989), 175.

14. Alan Hugh Hillgarth R. N. (1899–1978) became consul at Palma in 1937, before moving as naval attaché to Madrid in 1939. He pursued a distinguished career in naval intelligence during the war, subsequently retiring to Ballinderry, County Tipperary.

15. WBY to DW, 19 and 20 Jan. 1936, Meisei.

16. See WBY to EM, 19 Dec. 1935, *L*, 845, and to DW, 21 Dec. 1935, *LDW*, 47–8. For a full discussion, see below, Chapter 15.

17. *Privileged Spectator* (London, 1939), 55.

18. See WBY to Riding, 26 Apr. [1936], HRHRC. The story about Graves is retailed in a letter from Edith Sitwell to Hone, 22 Mar. 1941, NLI MS 5919.

19. GY to WBY, 20 Jan. 1936.

20. The sequence of attacks is difficult to date exactly. GY received a letter on 21 Jan. saying he had been 'laid up with food poisoning but was better'; post took five days, so this was probably written on 16 Jan. On 26 Jan. WBY told DW that he had been ill 'for about twelve days'. The date of GY's presentiment seems very close to the first attack. On 20 Mar. ECY told Margaret Sutcliff (Columbia University) that he had been in bed '8 weeks', which went back to 22 Jan.

21. WBY to TSM, 1 July 1936, MBY.

22. WBY to DW, 24 Apr. 1936, Meisei; interview with GY, 17 Jan. 1947, Interview Book, Ellmann Papers, Y.9, Tulsa.

23. Now in HRHRC. For other references, see GY's correspondence with the Sturge Moores, 1936–7, University of London, MS 978/31/188–199. A letter from Sean O'Faolain to Foden, now in Harvard, shows she was offering material to him in the late 1930s (see above, p. xxi). On 17 Nov. 1936 the Swami wrote indignantly to WBY: 'Let Ethel Mannin speak or write as much as she likes, it is all water on a duck's back. She is herself struggling. She has no peace, how can she give peace to others? She wants peace as she told me when you introduced her; and she will have to come to India for that.' (Delaware).

24. 10 Apr. [1936], *L*, 852.

25. SMY to R L-P, 24 Mar. 1936.

26. Donald Pearce, 'Hours with the Domestic Sibyl: Remembering George Yeats', *Southern Review*, 28, 3 (July 1992), 490–1.

27. *L*, 850–1.

28. *LDW*, 61.

29. *ASD*, 81; n.d. [but her reply was dated 9 Apr.].

30. *ASD*, 68–9, 82.

31. Meisei (omitted from *LDW*).

32. Nonetheless, the draft in NLI MS 30,321 (dated Dec. 1936) has some deletions of material suggesting lunacy rather than ecstasy.

33. 20 July 1936, Harvard, b Ms Am 1787[140].

34. 23 Aug. 1937, Meisei (not in *LDW*). For the previous negotiations, see a draft of WBY to the Swami, NLI MS 31,019, and a letter of 23 Apr. 1937, Delaware. Letters from the Swami to WBY of 13 Jan. and 8 Apr. 1938 show that Margot was eventually repaid, but not WBY.

35. 14 June 1936, Sligo.

36. 1 Feb. 1936, not in *LDW*.

37. 14 Feb. 1936, not in *LDW*.

38. *LDW*, 69–70.

39. NLI MS 30,508. The poem is in *YAACTS* 9 (1991) and in fact derived from one of Gogarty's bawdy lyrics. See A. Norman Jeffares, 'Know Your Gogarty', *YA* 14 (2001), 298–305.

40. This is the version in *LDW*, before later adaptations. Cullingford (*Gender and History*, 271–2) makes an interesting connection between WBY's presentation of the Furies, his reading of Woolf (at DW's instigation), and Jane Harrison's interpretation of the *Orestia*, which points out that the Furies can bring blessing as well as vengeance.

41. To Horace Reynolds, 15 Aug. 1936, Harvard, b Ms Am 1787[140]: having heard that WBY's ankles were still swollen due to kidney trouble which, with a strained heart, boded ill for the future.

42. 19 Sept. 1936, MBY.

43. 23 July 1936, MBY. The meeting had taken place before 20 July; Harrison had sent WBY R. C. K. Ensor's endorsement in his *Oxford History of England* volume.

44. Meisei. Misdated 2 July in *LDW*, where the passage from 'I was furious . . .' to 'Rest of night . . .' was deleted.

45. 13 Aug. 1936, Meisei, not in *LDW*.

46. 8 Sept. 1936, Meisei, not in *LDW*.

47. 1 Aug. [1936], Sligo.

48. *E & I*, 522–3.

49. *LDW*, 8–9. For enlightening commentaries on the poem, see Ellmann, *IY*, 185–7; Jeffares's essay in Jon Stallworthy (ed.), *Yeats's 'Last Poems': A Casebook* (London, 1968), 16–65; Edward Engelberg, *The Vast Design: Patterns in W. B. Yeats's Aesthetic* (Toronto, 1974), 170–5.

50. *Vast Design*, 171.

51. To Harriet Monroe, Jan. 1916, *Poetry* Archive, University of Chicago.

52. To GY, 23 Oct. 1934, MBY.

53. 6 July 1935, *LDW*, 8.

54. WBY to OS, 25 Feb. 1935, MBY; to DW, n.d. [but July 1936], *LDW*, 81.

55. See WBY to Masefield, 19 Sept. [1935], HRHRC.

56. Kenneth Siswam to Humphrey Milford, 13 Nov. 1934, Clarendon Press Archives. Quoted in Clare Hutton, '"Caprice and Partiality": A Study of *The Oxford Book of Modern Verse*, Edited by W. B. Yeats' (M.Phil., Trinity College, Dublin, 1993). My thanks to Dr Hutton for giving me access to her work and providing enlightening commentary.

57. 24 Oct. 1935, quoted in Stallworthy, 'Yeats as Anthologist' in A. Norman Jeffares and K. G. W. Cross (eds.), *In Excited Reverie. A Centenary Tribute to W. B. Yeats* (London, 1965), 181.

58. n.d. [but Oct. 1935], HRHRC.

59. [probably May 1935], Sligo.

60. Sitwell to Hone, 22 Mar. 1941, NLI MS 5919.

61. See F. P. Sturm to W. Force Stead, 4 June 1936 (Yale), where he remarks that the poems in *Eternal Helen* (1921) 'were chosen by Yeats during a few days I spent with him in Oxford'.

62. Stallworthy, 'Yeats as Anthologist', 179.

63. Recollected by E. R. Dodds, *Missing Persons: An Autobiography* (Oxford, 1968), 88.

64. WBY had a budget of £500 for permissions, and over-spent it by £50. He told Pound he could only have twenty pounds' worth and to give him what he could for that sum. 'I know you have no dislike for anthologies as you have published a couple yourself' (12 Dec. 1935, Yale). A certain brusqueness in the correspondence suggests that the epithet 'putrid' still rankled.

65. 'He has been charmed with an American poetess who wrote about an eagle ['The Eagle and the Mole'],' wrote Gogarty to Reynolds, 11 Oct. 1934, Harvard, b Ms Am 1787[140]. 'I'll get her name when he forgets to forget it.'

66. A series of letters to 'Mr Wilson', in GY's hand, profile his book orders; also see his letter to Charles Williams, quoted in Stallworthy, 'Yeats as Anthologist', 178. He had read Rosenberg as early as 1932, to judge by a note in his MS diary (NLI MS 31,061).

67. [late Apr. 1936], HRHRC.

68. This rationalization did not do justice to the casualness with which he adapted Wilde. A letter to OUP on 4 Sept. (Clarendon Press Archives) shows that by 'an unfortunate error' he had dropped the last two stanzas from Housman's 'Soldier from the Wars Returning' and, to make room, WBY blithely ordered the excision of yet another verse of *Reading Gaol*. 'Leaving it out will do no injury to Wilde's Ballad; it is just the kind of thing I have left out elsewhere in the poem.'

69. 26 Oct. 1936, HRHRC.

70. Introduction to *The Year's at the Spring: An Anthology of Recent Poetry*, compiled by L. D'O. Walters (London, 1920).

71. See *AM*, 36.

72. Quoted in Stallworthy, 'Yeats as Anthologist', 174–5.

73. ibid., 185.

74. 30 Aug. 1936.

75. 19 Sept. 1936, *LDW*, 107.

76. 5 Aug. 1936, censored in *LDW*.

77. To Horace Reynolds, 25 Apr. 1946, Harvard, b Ms Am 1787[140]. This was in the summer of 1938.

78. See WBY's subsequent letter to Mannin, 4 May 1936, Sligo. He had dined with Ruddock the night before.

79. n.d., Price Collection, Princeton; the context fixes it as autumn 1936.

80. See WBY to EM, 27 Sept. [1936], Sligo – apologizing for not writing because he was too unwell to leave the house and 'I thought it unwise to leave on the hall table letters which might become a theme of domestic meditation'.

81. See Jeremy Silver, 'George Barnes's "W. B. Yeats and Broadcasting" 1940', *YA* 5 (1987), 189–90.

82. To Ottoline Morrell, 26 Oct. 1936, HRHRC.

83. Rachel Cecil to Lady Salisbury, 16 Oct. [1936]; my thanks to Hugh Cecil.

84. 29 Oct. 1936, Meisei, partly in *LDW*, 109, where 'alas' is misread as 'also'. This was written from the Savile Club, en route back to Ireland.

85. 8 Nov. 1936, *LDW*, 110.

86. 28 Nov. 1936, *LDW*, 118. Economical as ever, he sent a version to Mannin as well on 30 Nov. (Sligo).

87. ibid., 125.

88. See Dodds, *Missing Persons*, 132.

89. 21 Feb. 1936, Harvard, b Ms Am 1787[140].

90. 27 Nov. 1936.

91. 20 Nov. 1936, reprinted in *CH*, 378–81.

92. 21 Nov. 1936, reprinted in *CH*, 381–5 and discussed in Stallworthy, 'Yeats as Anthologist', 188.

93. Mar. 1937, reprinted in *CH*, 385–7.

94. *Daily Worker*, 16 Dec. 1936; *LDW*, 126.

95. 19 Dec. 1936.

96. Jan. 1937.

97. *LDW*, 124.

98. To the *Spectator*, 4 Dec. 1936, taking the responsibility on to his own shoulders for deciding to limit the input of expensive writers like Pound and Kipling.

99. *LDW*, 127.

100. See a letter from Andrew Dillon to the *IT*, 30 Nov. 2001.

101. 14 Nov. 1936, Harvard, b Ms Am 1787[140]. He repeated much of this in another letter of 23 Nov., and in a letter to Shane Leslie, 12 Nov. 1936, HRHRC.

102. *English* (1937), 339–40.

103. 4 Feb. 1937, quoted in Stallworthy, 'Yeats as Anthologist', 192.

104. See ibid., 189–91.

105. Humphrey Carpenter, *W. H. Auden: A Biography* (London, 1981), 223. WBY's comment is in a letter to Moya Llewellyn Davies, 19 Mar. [1937], HRHRC, and *L*, 885–6. How and where he had read Auden's unpublished work remains mysterious, and he may well have been bluffing.

106. Miranda Seymour, *Ottoline Morrell: Life on the Grand Scale* (London, 1992), 473ff.

107. There are drafts of Morrell's letters of 7 and 10 Mar. 1937 in HRHRC with WBY's letters of 8, 10, 11 and 14 Mar. He defended Turner's work and described him as 'almost the only writer in England with whose general philosophical position I am in sympathy' (10 Mar.); also see Seymour, 541. Morrell had had early warning; her diary for Nov. 1935 records tea with Ethel Smyth, Eliot, de la Mare, Hope Mirrlees, Dilys Powell, and WBY, who astonished her by praising Turner, though he knew about the rift between them.

108. Rapallo Notebook, NLI MS 13,581.

109. See a letter of 24 Mar. 1937 to DW, *LDW*, 146, where he boasts that his having decided 'to scold [Ottoline] instead' had mended things – a complete misreading of the situation.

110. Richard Taylor (ed.), *Frank Pearce Sturm: His Life, Letters and Collected Work* (Urbana, Ill., 1969), 55. Sturm suspected GY had a lot to do with the choice of poems, but she robustly denied it to Taylor.

111. *The Masterpiece and the Man: Yeats as I Knew Him* (London, 1959), 183.

112. His accounts show that between Apr. 1937 and Mar. 1938 the *OBMV* earned him £227. 1s. 10d.

113. Forensic and scholarly opinion generally accepts that the diaries were genuine. For the complicated story of Maloney's book, see W. J. McCormack, *Haunting the Free State: Roger Casement in the 1930s* (Dublin, 2002).

114. 15 Nov. 1936, Sligo.

115. 2 Dec. 1936, Meisei (wrongly printed as 4 Dec. in *LDW*, 119, where this passage is suppressed).

116. In Maloney's book, Gilbert Murray is mentioned on p. 61 as the author of 'Shall Sir Roger Casement Hang?' in the *Providence Journal*, 20 June 1916. Murray indeed worked for the propaganda wing of the Foreign Office, but this article had nothing to do with the diaries. Murray in fact sent Quinn a message supporting his plea for clemency. Gilbert Parker played a much more interventionist role, as detailed in Maloney, 103–4 – pages that also mention Noyes and Spring-Rice, whose names occur in close proximity to Murray's in the first drafts of WBY's ballad (though an early draft has Gilbert Murray as 'Arthur') (NLI MS 13,592).

117. *LDW*, 121.

118. To Reynolds, 14 Nov. 1936, Harvard, b Ms Am 1787[140]. Retelling this anecdote later, Gogarty gave the 'Lord of Upper Egypt' story as a *bon mot* of WBY's own: see same to same, 16 Dec. 1951 (Harvard), and several published reminiscences.

Chapter 15 : FOLLY AND ELEGANCE
1937–1938

1. Jeremy Silver, 'George Barnes's "W. B. Yeats and Broadcasting" 1940', *YA* 5 (1987), 194.

2. 13 Dec. 1936, HRHRC, asking her for 'The King of China's Daughter' for the series.

3. WBY to M. J. MacManus, 29 Jan. 1937, NLI MS 5460. The previous flirtation with the *IT* is mentioned in a letter to Mannin, 30 Nov. 1936, Sligo.

4. 18 Feb. 1937, *LDW*, 141. On 2 Dec. 1936, when he still thought Gilbert Murray had been involved in the publicity campaign, he had written to Wellesley a passage suppressed in *LDW*.

   But suppose the evidence had been true, suppose Casement had been a homosexual & left a diary recording it all, what would you think of a Government who used that diary to prevent a movement for the reprieve of a prisoner condemned to death? Charles Ricketts & Lawrence of Arabia were reputed homosexuals – suppose they had been condemned on a capital charge some where, what would you think of a proffession who insured their execution by telling the middle classes that they were homosexual. (Meisei).

5. In 1916 Noyes (who then worked for the Ministry of Information) had been teaching at Princeton, from whence he had written to the *Philadelphia Public Ledger* stating that Casement's 'confessions about himself . . . were filthy beyond transcription . . . I have seen and read them and they touch the lowest depth of human degradation ever reached. Page after page of his diary would be an insult to a pig's trough to let the foul record touch it.' For Gogarty's hopes of a libel case, see John Unterecker, 'Yeats and Patrick McCartan: A Fenian friendship' in Liam Miller (ed.), *The Dolmen Press Yeats Centenary Papers 1965* (Dublin, 1968), 387 – an essay which brings together much of the relevant material. Also see W. J. McCormack, *Haunting the Free State: Roger Casement in the 1930s* (Dublin, 2002).

6. 30 Nov., 11 Dec. 1936, *L*, 869, 873.

7. According to Pablo Neruda: see Elizabeth Butler Cullingford, *Yeats, Ireland and Fascism* (London, 1981), 223. For the previous quotation, WBY to Mannin, 1 Mar. 1937, *L*, 885. For his support of Unamuno against Primo de Rivera's government in 1924, see above, p. 519.

8. Ellmann, *IY*, dates it to this month, as is also implied by WBY to Moya Llewellyn Davies, 18 Dec. 1936, HRHRC, and the poem is annotated '1936' in some draft lists. On 11 Feb. he told Mannin, 'I shall return to the matter in a new ballad,' but this must have been a projected third salvo.

9. *LDW*, 131, 135.

10. 20 Feb. 1937, to McCartan, Unterecker, 'Yeats and McCartan', 397.

11. As reflected in the first epigraph to this chapter, which was written at this time.

12. 30 Jan. 1937, NLI MS 30,581; also *YA* 5 (1987), as above.

13. A process recorded at length in his correspondence with Rothenstein since 1930 (Harvard). WBY complained of the fruit and vegetable carts rumbling past the windows of the Savile in the small hours, on their way to Covent Garden; though, he gloomily told Rothenstein, they made up so much of his diet that he tried to 'cultivate towards them an interested affection': 14 Sept. 1936, Harvard, b Ms Eng 1148[1650].

14. He wrote to her on 8, 10, 11 and 14 Mar. HRHRC, sending copies to GY; the addresses varied from 'My dear Ottoline . . . Yours always' to 'Dear Lady Ottoline . . . Yours sincerely'.

15. 24 Mar. [1937], Sligo.

16. See WBY's correspondence with Doone, 13 and 18 Mar. 1937, Berg. He wrote that the *Dog* 'would certainly not play at the Abbey, where the audience has popular & Irish traditions'.

17. See *YA* 5 (1987), as above, 191, 195; WBY to Moya Llewellyn Davies, 13 Mar. [1937], HRHRC; and TS text in NLI MS 30,580.

18. 8 Feb. [1937], *LDW*, 139. The corpse-factory image reveals the influence of Maloney's Casement book, which attacked the government for circulating rumours during the First World War that the Germans were recycling corpses to produce glycerine.

19. 3 Apr. [1937].

20. To Moya Llewellyn Davies, 9 Apr. [1937], HRHRC.

21. WBY had replied to him in Nov. 1936, pleased that Berryman liked poems which he himself favoured. As Berryman remembered it, these were 'The Second Coming', the poems in *Words for Music Perhaps*, 'Sailing to Byzantium', 'The Fisherman', 'Among School Children', and 'In Memory of Major Robert Gregory'. See Richard Kelly (ed.), *We Dream of Honour: John Berryman's Letters to His Mother* (London, 1988), 69–73, 99–100.

22. *YA* 5 (1987), as above, 190. Wellesley's criticism is in a letter of 23 Apr. 1937, Meisei.

23. 18 Dec. 1936, HRHRC. WBY to Higgins, 1 Feb. 1937, HRHRC, mentions her literary productions.

24. 28 Apr. 1937, HRHRC.

25. Delaware. A letter to Colquhoun of 3 May 1937, Tate Gallery, thanks her for 'making understanding easy that afternoon' and suggests further meetings; her autobiography refers to his 'powerful magnetism . . . even in old age'. My thanks to Deirdre Toomey for these references.

26. She was born on 27 Mar. 1899, and died in Sept. 1975, by which time she was living in a flat in Mecklenburgh Square, which she never allowed to be cleaned and which was crammed with books on mysticism (and, presumably, letters from WBY, now lost). She had retained her left-wing opinions and thoroughly approved of the Cultural Revolution in China. Her husband, Captain Charles Murray Beazley, had died ten years before. I am most grateful to the earl of Chichester and Dione, Lady Gibson, for their memories of her.

27. *LTWBY*, 588–9.

28. Delaware.

29. 15 May [1937], Delaware.

30. 27 May [1937], HRHRC.

31. In a radio programme, *Yeats in Sussex*, broadcast 15 Aug. 1966, ESH said they met briefly in 1910; WBY was indeed lecturing in the north of England in this year. (My thanks to Jon Stallworthy and Heather Clark for providing a transcript of this broadcast.) In 1929 she wrote an article describing WBY's 'graceful manner and melodious conversation',

but these could have been observed at a distance. When Mair died in 1926, ESH was one of the very few people at his funeral; my thanks to W. J. McCormack for this detail.

32. Letters to Dulac, 15 May, 1 June, HRHRC, and to ESH, 18 and 29 May 1937, Harvard, b Ms Eng 338.12.

33. 13 May 1937. For WBY's defence of the Pillar, see Manning Robertson to Sarah Purser, 30 Mar. 1926, NLI MS 10,201.

34. Described in detail to Dulac, 4 May 1937, HRHRC.

35. *BG*, 523.

36. The fullest description of this visit is Bose's own account in R. K. Dasgupta (ed.), *Rabindranath Tagore and William Butler Yeats: The Story of a Literary Friendship* (Delhi, 1965), 18–24. Trench's account, written for Hone, is in NLI MS 5919.

37. Bose in *Tagore and Yeats*, 20–1.

38. 'He is a prophet. It is as a sort of St John the Baptist that he calls on my people to repent and change their outlook. There was none of the idealism of St John the Baptist yet it is clear that he lives in the wilderness and feasts on honey and locusts.' Trench's account written for Hone, NLI MS 5919.

39. He wrote to Rothenstein on 9 Sept. 1933 that Indians should 'start a boycott of the English language': Harvard, b Ms Eng 1148[1650].

40. See n. 7, above. Cullingford's authority is a recollection of Pablo Neruda's, and I can find no other corroboration.

41. 29 May 1937, Harvard, b Ms Eng 338.12.

42. SMY to R L-P, 28 May 1937 and 2 Aug. 1947.

43. See WBY to GY, 16 June 1937 (the 'two elderly women' crossed out in the copy sent to Hone), and to McCartan, 24 June 1937, Unterecker, 'Yeats and McCartan', 404.

44. In fact, it was a different pier – the old Chain Pier, by then demolished. Edith's memories are from the *Yeats in Sussex* broadcast.

45. Kingsley to Wheelock, 24 June 1937, Scribner Archive, Princeton.

46. 19 June 1937, Harvard, b Ms Eng 338.12.

47. See WBY to Dulac, 27 May [1937], HRHRC.

48. He and Wellesley would argue this in a 'Broadside' Preface later that year. For WBY and music, see also the comments by Arthur Duff in transcripts of W. R. Rodgers's 'W. B. Yeats: A Dublin Portrait', HRHRC.

49. Now in HRHRC.

50. GY to WBY, 7 July 1937; Margot Lovell [Ruddock] to Dulac, 25 June 1937, HRHRC.

51. See Dulac to WBY, 7 July 1937, and associated correspondence, HRHRC.

52. 14 July 1937, HRHRC.

53. WBY to Dulac, 15 July 1937, HRHRC; another letter of 17 July elaborated on these points, which also occur in letters to Wellesley that summer. Dulac's 'thesis', titled 'Music and Poetry', is in HRHRC. This exchange has been the subject of intensive commentary by Wayne McKenna in *YA* 8 (1991), 225–34.

54. Turner to WBY, 9 July 1937, MBY. He had written about the broadcast in the *New Statesman* the same day. In the letter, he was severe about the programme as a whole.

55. 29 Nov. 1937, Yale.

56. The 'General Introduction' is to be found in *E & I*, but the best text and most interesting apparatus is in Edward Callan, *Yeats on Yeats: The Last Introductions and the 'Dublin' Edition* (New Yeats Papers 20, Dublin, 1985). Callan, 17, suggests convincingly that the 'First Principle' is a reference to Blake's conversation with the Prophet Ezekiel in *The Marriage of Heaven and Hell*: 'We of Israel taught that Poetic Genius (as you call it) was the first principle and all others merely derivative.'

57. Excised unintentionally from the version in *E & I*.

58. On 16 Nov. 1936 Watt had told WBY that Harold Macmillan wanted 'to hold over our edition for the time being' and preferred not to let Scribner use their sheets or corrected proofs: 'the more divergence there would be between our edition and Scribners', according to Macmillan, 'the better it would be in the interests of the former'.

59. NLI MSS 30,659, 30,696.

60. NLI MS 30,778.

61. Starting at about £50: see NLI MS 30,662.

62. In 1932 he sold out a quantity of war loan stock for £500: NLI MS 30,602.

63. See Gogarty to Reynolds, 4 Jan., 26 Feb., 23 Apr. 1936, Harvard, b Ms Am 1787[140].

64. SMY to R L-P, 15 Jan. 1937, 21 Aug. 1937.

65. As GY reported to WBY, 19 Oct. [1936]. For their earlier exchange, see above, pp. 230–1.

66. The negotiations are traced in Unterecker, 'Yeats and McCartan', 396ff.

67. To R L-P, 2 Aug. 1937.

68. ECY to John J. Gallagher, 6 Dec. 1937, and to James Healy, 12 May 1938, Healy.

69. Postmarked 2 Aug. 1937, Harvard, b Ms Eng 338.12. For the marriage 'ode', see *LDW*, 156–7.

70. Eugene Kinkead, treasurer; James Farrell, chairman; George MacDonald, vice-chairman; W. P. Maloney, secretary. (This last was a cousin of the author of *The Forged Casement Diaries*.) Also Joseph S. Cullinan, Cornelius P. Kelly, Thomas J. O'Neill, Edward F. Tilton, James A. Healy, Patrick McCartan, and James Reeve. The committee is profiled at length in Healy to WBY (copy), 1 Oct. 1937, Healy. There is material about this endeavour in Unterecker, 'Yeats and McCartan'; the McCartan Papers, Boston University; Healy; Berkeley; and NLI MS 30,667.

71. See James Farrell to Garret McInerney, 27 May 1937, Berkeley.

72. To Kinkead, 12 May 1937, Healy.

73. 12 May 1937, Healy.

74. Kinkead to Farrell, 6 Oct. 1937, Healy. The Healy Papers show how company vice-presidents from General Motors to the General Tire & Rubber Company, Akron, were targeted. Irish Hollywood remained a disappointment.

75. He owed Healy $2,000 by 1944.

76. *Irish Independent*, 18 Aug. 1937.

77. This is taken from *A Speech and Two Poems*, printed in Dublin, 1937, in an edition of seventy. WBY first visited the new Gallery with SMY in Aug. 1933, to see their father's pictures: see SMY to WBY, 31 Aug. 1933. In his speech as reported in the *IT* and *Irish Independent*, 18 Aug. 1937, he also attacked the king for opening the Tate wing and regretted that he had not encouraged a public demonstration; see above, p. 742, n. 146.

78. The 'Dedication' started life as a projected first stanza of 'The Municipal Gallery Revisited', followed by the even more banal reflection that thanks to the Testimonial he no longer needed to go to the Gallery by bus, but could use 'more expensive wheels'. NLI MS 13,593. See *'New Poems': Manuscript Materials*, edited by J. C. C. Mays and Stephen Parrish (London, 2000), 316–17.

79. NLI MS 13,593.

80. 5 Sept., *LDW*, 119.

81. See ESH in the *Yeats in Sussex* broadcast. But she also said that Elizabeth Pelham had no memory of having started that train of thought, and the first surviving draft was apparently written at Riversdale. For the Theosophical imagery, see T. R. Henn, 'The Ascent of Yeats's *Last Poems*', reprinted in Jon Stallworthy (ed.), *Yeats's 'Last Poems': A Casebook* (London, 1968), 125–6.

82. See WBY to de Valera, 15 Jan. 1937, NLI MS 30,161. Regarding the Abbey, complex negotiations with the government throughout the summer of 1937 envisaged extending the original site towards the river and incorporating three auditoriums – a new National

Theatre seating up to 1,000, a theatre similar in size to the existing Abbey, and a studio theatre accommodating 250 for Gaelic and experimental work. (NLI MS 30,727).

83. 12 Sept. [1937], Harvard, b Ms Eng 338.12.

84. 10 and 12 Dec. 1937, Harvard, b Ms Eng 338.12.

85. NLI MS 13,593. For drafts, see *'New Poems': Manuscript Materials*, edited by Mays and Parish, 290.

86. NLI MS 30,320.

87. *YA* 5 (1987), 194.

88. Pound, many years later, remarked of *AV*: 'I tried for God's sake to prevent him from printing anything. I told him it was rubbish. All he did was print it with a preface saying *I* said it was rubbish.' But he had confused it with *The King of the Great Clock Tower*. George Plimpton (ed.), *Writers at Work: The 'Paris Review' Interviews*, second series (New York, 1963), 43.

89. *L*, 627.

90. 4 May 1937, *LDW*, 149; WBY to OS, 12 Oct. 1937, MBY.

91. See a note on p. 81, linking the idea of a fully realized life to Fascism. 'Individual and classes complete their personality and then sink back to enrich the mass.' The story of surrogate sex was based on the experience of Alan Porter, who later married Wyndham Lewis's lover Iris Barry.

92. 'Unity of being' was now more directly associated with sexual union, while references to the 'ego' were dropped.

93. Such as a long section on 'The Daimon, the Sexes, Unity of Being, Natural and Supernatural Unity' (*AV* (1937), 26ff.), which had contained a strong autobiographical insinuation in commenting on the way a man chooses a woman.

94. With some corrections: the odd image of a woman writing on the snow with the point of a parasol is changed to a more seasonal umbrella (127).

95. p. 200.

96. pp. 205–6. 'Schneider' is Hermann Schneider, *The History of World Civilization*, translated by Margaret M. Green (London, 1931).

97. See *AV (1925)*, p. xi.

98. My thanks to Jeremy Clyde for showing me this book.

99. pp. 248–9.

100. p. 255.

101. See especially pp. 256–7.

102. See Helen Vendler, *Yeats's 'Vision' and the Later Plays* (Oxford, 1963), 9–11.

103. 'This Extraordinary Book', *YA* 1 (1981), 204.

104. Vendler, *'Vision'*, 30. See, for instance, her illuminating explication of the significance of the Jupiter–Saturn conjuction (207).

105. See Colin McDowell's discussion of Hazard Adams's *The Book of Yeats's 'Vision': Romantic Modernism and Antithetical Tradition* in *YA* 13 (1998), 357–66.

106. *London Mercury*, 37, 217 (Nov. 1937), 69–70.

107. To ESH, 10 Dec. 1937, *L*, 901.

108. WBY to DW, 11 and 20 Nov. 1937, *LDW*, 163–4, and to ESH, 28 Nov. 1937, *L*, 901.

109. *LDW*, 159.

110. 17 Dec. [1937], *L*, 903. He made the same point about profitability to DW on 11 Nov., *LDW*, 163.

111. SMY to R L-P, 12 July and 1 Nov. 1937. Actually GY visited her mother at Sidmouth about once a year.

112. Same to same, 27 Nov. 1934, 20 Aug. 1933. Also see same to same, 10 May 1934. 'Willy & George asked Lolly to tea at the Shelbourne to discuss the agreement. George thought

the place & the tea would create a good atmosphere & Willy said it would also keep him from "shouting at Lolly".' WBY's celebrated remark that he and ECY 'quarreled at the edge of the cradle & are keeping it up at the grave's edge' is excised from a letter printed in *LDW*, 151, but is to be found in the original at Meisei.

113. Same to same, 26 Dec. 1933. In June 1937 he was providing her with designs from Rothenstein and Diana Murphy; SMY described the resulting embroideries in letters to R L-P on 18 Nov. 1937 and 28 Feb. 1938. WBY brought 'The Land of Youth' to London in late Sept. 1937, but these works did not find buyers easily.

114. SMY to R L-P, 18 Nov. and 14 Dec. 1937.

115. 21 Oct. [1937], Boston College. The crisis at Cuala is dealt with in *FS*, 250ff.

116. Letters of 14 and 18 Dec. 1937, NLI MS 30,904.

117. 21 Dec. 1937, Boston College.

118. 2 Jan. 1938. Scroope to ECY, 23 June 1938, Boston College, shows that by then the No. 2 account, to which she was restricted, was overdrawn by £54, and that she informed WBY of the balance every week.

119. 10 Dec. [1937], Harvard, b Ms Eng 338.12. This may lie behind a claim in Sean O'Faolain's autobiography that GY 'once advised [WBY] when they were discussing the logistics of one of his romantic excursions not to ignore his mistress on the railway platform and occupy a distant carriage until the train moved out, as he was proposing to do, but rather to go forward to her and greet her joyfully before the world'. *Vive Moi!* (London, 1964), 308.

120. Gogarty to Healy, 1 Dec. 1937, Healy, and to Reynolds, 16 Mar. 1938, Harvard, b Ms Am 1787[140].

Chapter 16 : DYING LIKE AN EMPIRE
1938–1939

1. 25 Jan. 1938, Yale.

2. To GY, 26 Jan. 1938.

3. To Sturm, 21 Jan. 1938, Richard Taylor (ed.), *Frank Pearce Sturm: His Life, Letters and Collected Work* (Urbana, Ill., 1969), 109; to OS, 10 Feb. 1938, Indiana. For 'Mr and Mrs Shackleton', ECY to James Healy, 10 Feb. 1938, Healy.

4. 20 Feb. [1938], to Blacker. Blacker's reply admitted the difficulties and sent an extract from Lewis Terman's *The Measurement of Intelligence*. See NLI MS 30,583.

5. 17 Feb. 1938, Sligo.

6. 10 Feb. 1938, Indiana. The play was conceived and (mostly) written when WBY was absorbed by Shri Purohit Swami, the *Upanishads* and Shri Hamsa's autobiography. See Sankaran Ravindran, *W. B. Yeats and Indian Tradition* (Delhi, 1990), 101–10, which is enlightening about the Tantric concept of the Cosmic Egg containing seven elements, and other Indian inspirations for the character of Attracta the ascetic. The Karmic origins of the reincarnation motif at the end of the play are also suggestive. Naresh Guha, *W. B. Yeats: An Indian Approach* (Calcutta, 1968), 131–40, connects the play more closely to Tagore's *The King of the Dark Chamber*.

7. 24 May [1938], Harvard, b Ms Eng 338.12.

8. NLI MS 30,280.

9. 15 Mar. 1938, Harvard, b Ms Eng 338.12.

10. To GY, 31 Mar. 1938; for their journey back, SMY to R L-P, 28 Mar. 1938.

11. GY to ESH, 12 May 1938, WBY to ESH, 2 and 15 Mar., Harvard, b Ms Eng 338.12.

12. 6 Apr. [1938]. It was apparently completed on 4 Apr. (compare Ellmann, *IY*, 294, where it is assigned to Nov. 1937).

13. *AV B*, 293–4; see Giorgio Melchiori, *The Whole Mystery of Art: Pattern into Poetry in the Work of W. B. Yeats* (London, 1960), 237ff. The final Michelangelo reference may owe something to a poem by James Guthie which WBY had printed in the first 'Broadsides' series (vol. 3, Aug. 1909): 'To a Painter on a Scaffold'.

14. This is illuminatingly discussed in Jefferson Holdridge, *Those Mingled Seas: W. B. Yeats, The Beautiful and the Sublime* (Dublin, 2000), 214–18. There are also interesting parallels with a psychological questionnaire on creativity which WBY answered for a project based in Cambridge. '"Do you feel that you have voluntary control over ideas so that you can force them to come?" "Usually. The actual ideas comes [*sic*] in a moment of unconsciousness & forgetfullness but the effort must be kept up until the stream produce what may be only a momentary passivity." "Do you find that actual execution starts with a series of apparently futile attempts to work?" "Always."' NLI MS 30,098, probably from the 1930s.

15. For the status of the final TS, see W. B. Yeats, *'Last Poems': Manuscript Materials*, edited by James Pethica (London, 1997), pp. xlvii–xlviii; also Jon Stallworthy, *Vision and Revision in Yeats's 'Last Poems'* (Oxford, 1969), 123ff.

16. F. A. C. Wilson, *Yeats's Iconography* (London, 1960), 290–303, is a closely argued and enlightening reading with a useful paraphrase of this stanza: 'the modern India worshipper, who has been caught up in the materialist "tide" and has become almost wholly objective, so that his true gods are the witch's cat and the dragon-monster of eastern art, even today at the hour of prayer is ironically compelled to pay homage to subjective religion'. At the end, however, Wilson's judgement that this is a poem of 'inner reconciliation' which reintegrates beauty and the self seems to miss an important dimension.

17. The first draft (Pethica, *'Last Poems'*, 205) put it more baldly:

> Where are you now. Is it true you shed the
> Sun-burn & became pale white; did you appear
> In the Post Office in 1916 is it True that
> Pearse called on you by name of Cuchullin
> [Certainly?] we have need of you. The vague flood is upon us
> Not from one quarter alone, from all four quarters is [coming?]
> Come back with all your Pythagorean numbers.

18. 'Race', he had written in 1933, 'which has for its flower the family and the individual, is wiser than Government and . . . is the source of all initiative.' ('A Race Philosophy': for a commentary, see Marjorie Howes, *Yeats's Nations: Gender, Class and Irishness*, Cambridge, 1996, 162). But 'kindred' in this passage seems to imply aristocracy and authoritarianism rather than racial purity – given his belief in the composite nature of the Irish nation.

19. 15 Mar. [1938], Harvard, b Ms Eng 338.12.

20. See W. Evans Wentz, *The Fairy Faith in Celtic Countries* (Oxford, 1911), 363–4, 384. Hyde and Henri d'Arbois de Jubainville also discussed Purgatory theories in Irish tradition. For reports on progress, WBY to GY, 6 Apr. 1938.

21. *LDW*, 195.

22. 'Perhaps when the Spirits speak to us they give us thoughts that we would not have had the courage to express ourselves.' (*Journals*, ii, 40) and ibid., i, 362, for the may-blossom tradition.

23. For a fuller treatment of this connection, see my 'Protestant Magic' in *Paddy and Mr Punch*, 218.

24. Marjorie Howes follows W. J. McCormack (*Ascendancy and Tradition in Anglo-Irish Literary History*, Oxford, 1985, Chapter 10) in suggesting that the Old Man's lament is intended to be a foolish and nostalgic idealization, but this seems unconvincing, if only because WBY is evoking the Gregorys and Coole.

25. As explored by Melchiori, 253ff., and Wilson, 159–60, who relates it to *King Lear*.

26. *Poetry and Drama* (London, 1951), 23.

27. 16 June 1938, Jeremy Silver (ed.), 'George Barnes's "W. B. Yeats and Broadcasting", 1940', *YA* 5 (1987), 196.

28. To GY, 26 Apr., 27 Apr., 3 May 1938.

29. *I & R*, ii, 402–3.

30. For his previous queries to Blacker, see NLI 30,583 and David Bradshaw, 'The Eugenics Movement in the 1930s and the Emergence of *On the Boiler*' in *YA* 9 (1992), 189–215. For the Oxford evening I am grateful to Sir Stuart Hampshire, for a conversation in Oct. 2001. He also wrote to me (21 Oct. 2001): 'I suffered a shock when I met Yeats for a very long evening in All Souls with Edith Shackleton and John Sparrow at the height of his ultra fascist phase writing "On the Boiler". As we talked in a very small room I suddenly saw (as I think) that Yeats had that strange Irish coldness which often lies beneath the magnificence of language and of gesture and which permits great cruelty.'

31. Sold at Christie's in 1978; quoted by Ellmann in *W. B. Yeats's Second Puberty: A Lecture delivered at the Library of Congress on April 2, 1982* (Washington, 1985), 26. It is written in Edith's hand, dated 'Oxford May 8 1938', and signed by WBY.

32. To SMY, 19 Apr. [1938], Boston College.

33. On 13 and 19 Dec. 1938 the *IT* published letters from Stuart which Kathleen Lynn correctly described as 'v. anti-Semitic', provoking some angry replies. See also Brendan Barrington's Introduction to his edition of *The Wartime Broadcasts of Francis Stuart* (Dublin, 2000). My thanks to Margaret Ó hÓgartaigh for references from Lynn's diary; on 16 Nov. 1938 she was also shocked by Iseult's 'v. anti-semitic' response to news of persecion of Jews in Germany and Central Europe.

34. WBY wrote (following MacLeish) 'meanings' in the original; it was later changed to 'meaning'.

35. To DW, 24 May 1938, *L*, 908–9. The essay, 'Westron Wind', was in the *Yale Review*, Mar. 1938. It also, as Richard Finneran has pointed out, supplied WBY's closing image, since MacLeish quoted the anonymous 'Christ, that my love were in my arms/And I in my bed again.'

36. Her name was Cora Hughes; my thanks to Richard English for this reminiscence of George Gilmore's. However, WBY told DW 'it is not a real incident, but a moment of meditation'.

37. Michael B. Yeats, *Cast a Cold Eye: Memories of a Poet's Son and Politician* (Dublin, n.d., but 1998), 28.

38. *L*, 903.

39. To GY, 25 and 26 Apr. [1938]. ECY printed 450 copies of *New Poems*, and WBY wanted her to destroy 100.

40. See ECY to Quinn, 3 Aug. 1915, NYPL, for the co-operative status as 'a great farce'.

41. To ESH, 13 June [1938], Harvard, b Ms Eng 338.12. Also see WBY to Blythe, 23 June 1938, suggesting that Higgins manage the Abbey on a daily basis, leaving plays to Robinson; and ECY to James Healy, 31 May 1938 and 2 Dec. 1938, Healy.

42. To R L-P, 29 June 1938.

43. Though not very successfully. For a summary account, see NA, COMP I, Dissolved Companies Files. The business was established on 6 Oct. 1938 [Ivy Day] with £2,000 share capital, and WBY, ECY, GY, and Higgins as directors. The certificate of Incorporation is dated 12 Oct. WBY chaired two directors' meetings, on 12 and 19 Oct., before leaving for Sussex and France. The £2,000 was, however, completely notional, representing the money WBY had put in – a subterfuge that worried him, according to ECY to Healy, 3 Dec. 1938 (Healy). Shareholders in 1939 were GY, ECY, Higgins, Eileen Colum, Esther Ryan, Molly Gill, and Katharine Banfield. ECY died in 1940, and Higgins in 1941. He was replaced by Michael O'Donovan (the writer Frank O'Connor). The company was threatened with being struck off the registered list in

early 1955 and ceased trading as a limited company the same year, though it continued its activities in a reduced form.

44. Digges to Healy, 16 June 1938, and Kinkead to WBY, 27 June 1938 (copy), Healy.

45. 4 July 1938 (copy), Healy. This letter was widely quoted. A useful letter from Kinkead to John Francis Neylan, 22 June 1939, Berkeley, transcribes it and gives the final financial account. $6,000 had been contributed, by means of 17 contributions of $200 (paid in two instalments, 1937 and 1938) and 26 donations of $100. £600 (*c.* $3,000) was given to WBY in Aug. 1937, £400 (*c.* $2,000) in June 1938, and £200 (*c.* $1,000) to GY after WBY's death, holding back $105.20 for miscellaneous expenses.

46. To R L-P, 7 June 1938.

47. Unpublished reminiscence of George White, Mar. 1985, RFF.

48. 28 June 1938, Harvard, b Ms Eng 338.12.

49. It stands to this day, an elegant Greek temple with Latin inscriptions (provided by John Sparrow) and a tablet 'to the poets who loved Penns' – WBY, de la Mare, Turner, Ruth Pitter, Vita Sackville-West and DW. Quotations from Thomas Nashe as well as Shelley's *Julian and Maddalo* ('They learn in suffering what they teach in song') suggest WBY's influence. His own epitaph from 'Under Ben Bulben' is also engraved, matched by a plaque recording a poem of DW's own. Strangely, a tribute to Hilda Matheson, 'amica amicarum', was later excised on DW's orders, though it is still just visible.

50. Stallworthy, *Vision and Revision*, 73.

51. WBY to Higgins, 9 Aug. 1938, HRHRC, and to GY, 4 Aug. 1938, MBY.

52. To WBY, 25 July 1938.

53. To Hone, 26 Feb. 1940, HRHRC.

54. 29 June 1938, Frank O'Connor Papers, Boston University; for report of the first night, *IT*, 10 Aug. 1938.

55. 15 Aug. 1938, Harvard, b Ms Eng 338.12.

56. Another version of this thought occurs in a prose draft of 'Under Ben Bulben'; see Stallworthy, *Vision and Revision*, 157–8.

57. 19 June 1938, Harvard, b Ms Eng 338.12. A coat of arms might be added, on a border of poet's laurel: 'no shamrocks of course'.

58. Though Dan Stone has pointed out that 'the broad political appeal of eugenics at this time, however, does not invalidate the claim that it was essentially reactionary, predicated on the fear of degeneration. Although many schemes for both "positive" and "negative" eugenics are indistinguishable from public health measures – in fact, the presence of an established public health bureaucracy was key in restraining the growth of the eugenics movement as a single-issue movement – they all rested on an analysis of society which saw it as somehow in decline, and hence in need of rescue.' *Breeding Superman: Nietzsche, Race and Eugenics in Edwardian and Inter-war Britain* (Liverpool, 2002), 6.

59. *Women and the Revolution* (New York, 1938), 248.

60. Stone, *Breeding Superman*, 76–7, 119–20.

61. 'Is National Intelligence Declining?', *Eugenics Review*, 28, 3 (Oct. 1938), esp. 99; WBY possessed a copy.

62. See ibid., 50–5, 84.

63. See Bradshaw, 'The Eugenics Movement', 207–8, for the evolution of this through various drafts.

64. ibid., 208.

65. Harvard, b Ms Eng 338.12; censored in *L*, 915.

66. 9 Oct. 1938, Sligo. See Stallworthy, *Vision and Revision*, 148ff. Also see William Rose's account of his exchanges with WBY about Rilke in *German Life and Letters*, 15, 1 (Oct. 1961), 68–70. WBY (who knew Rose through Dulac) wrote to him on 17 Aug. that he

read the book – *Rainer Maria Rilke: Aspects of His Mind and Poetry*, edited by G. C. Houston and Rose (London, 1938) – in early Aug.

At first I was repelled by the brooding on death & the importance given to it, a theme foreign to Irish literature, & wrote upon the margin

> Draw rein; draw breath
> Cast a cold eye
> On life, on death.
> Horseman pass by.

Then I saw that I did not understand & could not because all your quotations are in german . . .

67. In one version a line follows: 'The Soul's perfection is from peace.' For a summary of the tangled textual problems raised by the poem, see Pethica, '*Last Poems*', pp. xxxvi–xl; for the two versions, ibid., 41–5. I have followed the second.

68. 7 Sept. [1938], Meisei.

69. 7 Sept. [1938], Meisei.

70. ibid.

71. Pethica, '*Last Poems*', p. xl, n. 53, suggests various reasons.

72. To DW, 2 Oct. 1938, HRHRC.

73. To R L-P, 21 Jan. 1938.

74. 21 Sept. 1938, Harvard, b Ms Am 1787[140].

75. 26 Sept. 1938, Meisei. On 12 Sept. de Valera had been elected president of the Assembly of the League of Nations.

76. To Horace Reynolds, 26 Mar. 1940, Harvard, b Ms Am 1787[140].

77. The drafts are in NLI MS 13,593, discussed by Pethica in '*Last Poems*', pp. xxx–xxxvi.

78. Pethica, '*Last Poems*', p. xxxv, suggests that the development of the poem replicates WBY's intended arrangement of the volume of verse he was planning: from bitter and rhetorical declamation about the modern world to a meditative recognition of the sources of private inspiration.

79. 2 Oct. [1938], HRHRC.

80. 7 Oct. 1938, Delaware.

81. WBY to Shastri, 21 Dec. 1938. See Hari Prasad Shastri, 'Reminiscences of W. B. Yeats' in *Self-Knowledge: A Quarterly Journal Devoted to Spiritual Thought and Practice*, 5, 4 (Autumn, 1954), 117. My thanks to John Kelly for this reference.

82. 8 Oct. 1938, *L*, 916.

83. Isaiah Berlin to Cressida Bonham-Carter, n.d. [but Aug. 1938]. It seems clear that 'a young woman and what appears to be her brother' were Mannin and Reynolds, who did look rather alike, and were entertained to dinner by WBY in the Shelbourne on Sunday 28 Aug. – when Berlin was in Dublin en route to Bowen's Court. My thanks to Lady Berlin and Henry Hardy for this reference.

84. 16 June 1938, *G–YL*, 451.

85. Stephen Gwynn (ed.), *Scattering Branches: Tributes to the Memory of W. B. Yeats* (London, 1940), 34; also in *I & R*, ii, 280–1. The original version, written out for Hone, is in HRHRC.

86. 1 Nov. [1938], Emory.

87. 27 Oct. 1938, MBY.

88. For the significance of McTaggart's ideas in his *Human Immortality and Pre-Existence*, see the brilliant exposition by Deirdre Toomey in 'Labyrinths: Yeats and Maud Gonne', *YA* 9 (1992), 119–20.

89. WBY to GY, 17 Nov. [1938], MBY.

90. 18 Nov. 1938, HRHRC.
91. To GY, 18 Nov. 1938.
92. W. Conneely, 'A Talk with W. B. Yeats', HRHRC.
93. See DW to Higgins, 14 Nov. 1938, NLI MS 10,864.
94. NLI MS 30,485.
95. WBY's rebuke, at least in its first version, is replete with snobbery (Wingfield's husband was the future Viscount Powerscourt). 'That you who have not the excuse of ignorance or poverty [like Katharine Tynan] should do this vulgar thing fills me with all the more regret, because I have liked your work & found some pleasure in our brief acquaintance.' (Draft, MBY). Wingfield's husband replied on her behalf, and she got her own back with a dismissive and insinuating description in her autobiography of WBY in a state of near-dotage on a railway journey: *Sun Too Fast* (London, 1974), 125–6.
96. 20 Oct. [1938], Sligo; some small differences in *L*, 917–18.
97. Jeremy Silver, 'George Barnes's "W. B. Yeats and Broadcasting", 1940', *YA* 5 (1987), 194. Also see WBY to V. Clinton-Baddeley, 13 Dec. 1938, NLI MS 5918, ECY to Healy, 19 Oct. 1938, Healy.
98. 23 Dec. 1938, Sligo.
99. SMY to R L-P, 2 July 1938.
100. GY told Ellmann they were 'bitter enemies': interview of 28 Oct. 1947, Interview Book, Ellmann Papers, Y.9, Tulsa.
101. *Since Fifty: Men and Memories 1922–1938* (London, 1939), 305–6.
102. *Wheels and Butterflies* (London, 1934), 71. For the 'Instructors', see above, p. 107.
103. To ESH, n.d. [but early Jan. 1939], Harvard, b Ms Eng 338.12.
104. In an unpublished note: see Patrick J. Keane, *Yeats's Interactions with Tradition* (Columbia, Miss., 1987), 153.
105. She is named in an early draft: see W. B. Yeats, *'The Death of Cuchulain': Manuscript Materials*, edited by Phillip L. Marcus (London, 1982), 7–8.
106. See ibid., 13–16, for a subtle analysis of the connection, which is much more unambiguously 'patriotic' in the first draft.
107. In a cancelled passage Aoife says she 'hated men/But loved the sword'. ibid., 12.
108. The original is NLI MS 30,196; it at one stage belonged to DW, who printed it in *LDW*, 212 ff., but was eventually returned to GY. The close resemblance to Dante's imagery, and the date of the letter to Heald, suggest that WBY's 'dream' (on the night of 7 Jan.) was by no means its single inspiration.
109. *AV (1925)*, 229–31; Helen Vendler, *Yeats's 'Vision' and the Later Plays* (Oxford, 1963), 249.
110. *Finn and His Companions* was published in 1892 and chosen by WBY as one of his '30 Best Books' in 1895; for connections to 'The Black Tower', see Patrick Diskin, 'A Source for Yeats's "The Black Tower"', *Notes and Queries*, 206 (Mar. 1961) and 210 (July 1965). But Síle ní Shúilleabháin suggested in an unpublished article that the *Masque* was closer still, and WBY had had a much more recent acquaintance with it.
111. See *AM*, 399; he called it 'The Coming of Finn'.
112. Jon Stallworthy, *Between the Lines: Yeats's Poetry in the Making* (Oxford, 1963), 232.
113. To *The Times*, 9 Feb. 1939.
114. NLI MS 30,280: on Idéal Séjour notepaper, dated 23 Dec. 1938.
115. 4 Jan. 1939, *L*, 922. In a copy which GY sent to Patrick McCartan she wrote 'Man can embody truth but he cannot find it' but this seems to have been a mistranscription from Pelham's copy. The original has never surfaced.
116. *The Symbolist Movement in Literature*, 162–3 ('Maeterlinck as Mystic'). There is also an echo of *AV (1925)*, 114. See Marcus, 7–8, for assonances between this letter and the Prologue to *The Death of Cuchulain*.

117. To Louise Morgan in 1930, *I & R*, ii, 203.
118. *FS*, 376.
119. DW to Rothenstein, 6 Feb. 1939, HRHRC, printed by Rothenstein in *Since Fifty*, 306–7. She sent a similar letter to Ethel Smyth, 7 Feb. 1939, HRHRC.
120. Dermod O'Brien to Sarah Purser, 30 Jan. 1939, NLI MS 10,201.
121. To Rothenstein, 6 Feb. 1939, as above. She claimed she called for a few minutes the next day, Friday, but GY told Ellmann that DW was last there two days before WBY's death: interview of 28 Oct. 1947, Interview Book, Ellmann Papers, Y.9, Tulsa. The fullest contemporary account of the last days is Mabel O'Brien to SMY, 29 Jan. 1939, NLI MS 30,732; also see ECY to 'Olga', 24 Mar. 1939, HRHRC.
122. The contents list is in Pethica, '*Last Poems*', 466. Also see Warwick Gould, 'W. B. Yeats and the Resurrection of the Author', the *Library*, 16, 2 (June, 1994), 101–34.
123. The death certificate recorded two thirty; evidence from letters usually says two o'clock.
124. To GY, 2 Feb. 1939, quoted by GY to Healy, 20 Feb. 1939, Healy.
125. For the MS's subsequent history, see Marcus, 'The Death of Cuchulain', 4; for the gifts to ESH, *Yeats in Sussex*, BBC broadcast.
126. 6 Mar. 1939, TCD. For further consideration of this question, see my '"When the Newspapers Have Forgotten Me": Yeats, Obituarists and Irishness' in *The Irish Story* (London, 2001), 80–1.
127. SMY to R L-P, 4 Feb. 1939.
128. Same to same, 4 Feb. 1939.

Epilogue: Genius and History

1. Kansas; also quoted by Hone in 'Yeats as Political Philosopher', *London Mercury*, 39, 233 (Mar. 1939), 496.
2. '*Last Poems': Manuscript Materials*, edited by James Pethica (London, 1997), 35.
3. SMY to R L-P, 4 Feb. 1939.
4. GY to R. A. Scott-James, 18 Feb. 1939, HRHRC.
5. ECY to P. S. O'Hegarty, 11 Feb. 1939, Kansas.
6. To R L-P, 27 Feb. 1939. For a description, see my *The Irish Story*, 251, n. 7. Hilda Matheson thought it an 'unworthy and ill-prepared affair': to GY, 3 July 1939, MBY.
7. NLI MS 30,765 gives details of the estate, as does *The Times*, 23 Oct. 1939.
8. To R L-P, 17 Apr. 1939, 27 June 1939.
9. 26 Apr. 1939, NLI MS 30,248.
10. To James Healy, 13 Mar. 1939, Healy.
11. See *The Irish Story*, 82–94, for a fuller consideration.
12. See Jon Stallworthy (ed.), *Yeats's 'Last Poems': A Casebook* (London, 1968), 44.
13. *New York Times Book Review*: see *Irish Story*, 81.
14. Several appeared after his death in the *London Mercury*. Cuala published *Last Poems and Two Plays* in July 1939, following a sequence left by WBY. Macmillan's *Last Poems and Plays* (1940) brought together *New Poems* and the final Cuala volume, and added three more from *On the Boiler*. As Curtis Bradford first pointed out, this diluted the impact and the bleakness of the work composed in the last year of his life, as well as its coherence. However, see Phillip L. Marcus, 'Yeats's *Last Poems: A Reconsideration*', *YA* 5 (1987), 3–14.
15. Stallworthy, '*Last Poems': A Casebook*, 32.
16. SMY to R L-P, 10 Apr. 1939.
17. Same to same, 8 Mar. 1943.

18. Same to same, 10 Oct. 1946.

19. Same to same, 11 Nov. 1941.

20. See Diana Souhami, *Gluck 1895–1978: Her Biography* (London, 1988), and *BG*, 604ff. My own account relies on papers in the possession of Roy Gluckstein, to whom I owe thanks, in MBY, and in the archives of the Bibliothèque Princesse Grace, Monaco – including correspondence about the Dulac plaque, in which the local authorities refer to 'Butler, Wm. Yeats . . . dont les restes se trouvent dans l'ossuaire' (12 Nov. 1947). Edith (and, oddly, the French native Dulac) thought the 'fosse commune' meant a pauper's grave, but it actually designated the part of the cemetery owned by the municipality, not individuals. There seems to be a disagreement as to whether a lease there could run for more than five years. For the Hollis family view, see Louise Foxcroft, 'Diary', *London Review of Books*, 7 Sept. 2000.

21. See Patrick Mahony, *Unsought Visitors* (privately printed, New York, 1953), 35: the seance was allegedly in a cottage near Lissadell immediately after the re-interment, with Robinson trying to get through to WBY for advice about staging *Cathleen ni Houlihan* ('Oh, I've talked to him on more important things than this, I can tell you . . .'). But rumours were well established by then. The *News Chronicle*, 22 June 1948, had a comment about the grave being moved, Louis MacNeice mentioned the confusion publicly at the re-interment (Jon Stallworthy, *Louis MacNeice*, London, 1995, 372), and the *Picture Post* reporter had followed up the story from its origins in Roquebrune.

22. Derrick Hill to RFF, 27 Jan. 1992.

23. The fullest accounts were in the *Sligo Independent and West of Ireland Telegraph*, 25 Sept. 1948, and *Irish Independent*, 18 Sept. 1948. The novelist Kate O'Brien, who was there, wrote an atmospheric piece in the *Spectator*, 24 Sept. 1948. John Ormond Thomas wrote a long account in *Picture Post*, 9 Oct. 1948, with striking photographs – he not only publicized the doubts about identifying WBY's remains, but revealed some evasions and inconsistencies in the Roquebrune authorities' handling of the issue.

24. It seems likely that these included the two volumes of Visions Notebooks, which MacBride's daughter remembers being sent to her father at the Ministry of External Affairs by GY. Thus GY was in effect returning them to MG – a gesture both graceful and generous. My thanks to Deirdre Toomey.

25. Robert Speaight in *Commonweal*, 31 Mar. 1939.

26. *The Egoist* 4, 16 (July 1917), 90: reviewing Pound's Cuala edition of JBY's letters. He continued: 'Ordinary writers of verse either deal in "imagination" or in "ideas"; they escape from one to the other, but neither one nor the other nor both together is truth in the sense of poetic truth. Only old ideas, "part and parcel of the personality", are of use to the poet. (This is worth repeating to our American contemporaries who study Freud.)' In *Au*, 273, WBY himself instanced Dante and Shakespeare as artists who created out of their own experience something so unified that it amounted to 'the re-creation of the man through the art, the birth of a new species of man'.

27. TCD: notes for a speech opening an exhibition at Reading, 1961. He also wrote it up into a lengthier and more florid version for the *Capuchin Annual* (1952), 237–8.

28. Gwynn in *Observer*, 5 Feb. 1939.

29. 'John Eglinton', *United Irishman*, 9 Nov. 1901, reprinted in *UP*, ii, 260.

30. Quoted in Karin Strand, 'W. B. Yeats's American Lecture Tours', Ph.D. thesis, Northwestern University, 1978, 203.

31. 'Yeats as I Knew Him', a talk to the Irish Literary Society, Nov. 1948, TS in HRHRC. Compare 'A Prayer for Old Age': 'O what am I that I should not seem / For the song's sake a fool?'

32. 'Anima Hominis' in *Per Amica Silentia Lunae, Myth*, 332–3.

INDEX

THE abbreviations used are as in the notes. Writings by WBY (including *Samhain*, which was largely his own work) are gathered in his composite entry. The journals and newspapers listed are those which recur in the text, or which were particularly important to WBY. The notes are also indexed when they contain substantial additional information rather than a short or passing reference. Pseudonyms are indexed, but not fictional personages (such as Michael Hearn or Michael Robartes).

INDEX

Russell, George William ('AE') (cont.):
praises Easter Rising martyrs 52; on WBY's
Per Amica 79; and 'Convention of Irishmen'
82, 88, 687 (n. 116); visits WBY in Dublin 90;
on George's role with WBY 122; opposes
conscription in Ireland 123; and MG's flight
from London to Ireland 124; and Seán
MacBride 127; on WBY's view of Ireland 138;
and WBY's criticism of Russian communism
147; on WBY's book on philosophy of
mysticism 155–6; and WBY's view on Irish
unity of culture 178; in Irish troubles 180;
place in Irish history 180; WBY quarrels with
Lolly over 186; resumes correspondence with
WBY 200; in WBY's 'Ireland after Parnell'
200; and WBY's view of Anglo-Irish Treaty
206; Magee praises 209; memoirs 217; on
WBY in Dublin 224; believes WBY neglecting
writing 237; and proposed National Academy
238; edits *Irish Statesman* 242–3; on WBY's
'Leda and the Swan' 243; and 'New
Ascendancy' 256; accused of attacking
Catholicism 261; and Tailteann Games 266;
on *To-Morrow* 271–2; WBY's relations with
276; refuses to print WBY's 'On the Need for
Audacity of Thought' 295; portrait 302;
reaction to WBY's *A Vision* 310–12; *Catholic
Bulletin* mocks 311; entertains WBY 335–6;
supports founding of literary academy 337;
reviews WBY's *Autobiographies* 339; and row
over O'Casey's *The Silver Tassie* 369–70;
censors WBY's 'Crazy Jane on the King' 386;
and closing of *Irish Statesman* 399; public
subscription for 414; visits Coole 422; lacks
common Irish nature 424; on dangers of de
Valera government 433; and Irish Academy of
Letters 436, 448, 450; on AG's death 438;
congratulates WBY on seventieth birthday 523;
decline, death and funeral 523–5; and status of
Cuala Press 623; on Anglo-Irish 629; *New
Songs* (anthology) 136; 'Thoughts for a
Convention' 88, 687 (n. 116)
Ruttledge, Patrick Joseph 452, 615
Ryan, W. P. 66

Sackville-West, Vita 522, 527–9, 533, 600, 652;
The Edwardians 541–2
St George family 618
St George, Lady Harriet 618
Salkeld, Cecil 155
Sand, George 222
Santayana, George 401
Saor Éire (movement) 426, 466
Sassoon, Siegfried 357, 522, 555
Satie, Erik 38
Sato, Junzo 167, 522, 586
Savile Club, London 85, 101, 228, 393, 401, 452,
578
Scatcherd, Felicia 678 (n. 49)

Schepeler, Alick 27, 29–30, 39, 87, 98, 127
Schmidt, Peter 497; *The Conquest of Old Age* 498
Schnabel, Artur 644
Schneider, Hermann 604
Scott, William 86, 88, 121, 131, 213
Scott-James, R. A. 539, 544, 583
Scribner, Charles & Sons (US publishers) 534,
587, 592, 617, 654, 750 (n. 128)
Scroope, S. F. 609, 623
Scrutiny (magazine) 565
Senate (Irish): WBY's membership of and
activities in 228–9, 231, 233, 236, 238–9, 242,
254, 276–7, 329; members terrorized 230; WBY
leaves 378
Seymour, St John: *Irish Witchcraft and
Demonology* 23, 197
Shackleton, Edith *see* Heald, Edith Shackleton
Shakespear, Dorothy *see* Pound, Dorothy
Shakespear, Henry Hope 688 (n. 131)
Shakespear, Olivia: relations with WBY 3, 67, 111,
143, 153, 317, 319, 421, 483, 498–9, 509, 638–9;
manner 55; psychic practices 72, 106; and
Nelly Tucker and George 92, 94–5, 101, 104;
letter from WBY in Utah 166; and WBY's
poetic images 191; and WBY's idea of
recurrence 193; and WBY's memoirs 203; and
WBY's pessimism over Irish politics 203; and
WBY's relations with JBY 211; chooses shoes
as WBY's gift for George 223; and WBY's
conservatism 226; and WBY's Senatorial
activities 233; and WBY's defence of *Ulysses*
261; and WBY's idealization of Mussolini 265;
and WBY's anti-clerical campaign 268–9; WBY
sends *To-Morrow* circulars to 270; WS meets
in London 274; on WBY's 'System' in *A Vision*
280; in WBY's *A Vision* 281; circle of friends
294; WBY complains of Abbey plays to 301;
and WBY's love poetry 319; photograph 324;
and WBY's reaction to O'Higgins murder 341;
WBY describes Irish hatred to 349; WBY sends
poems to 350; letters from WBY 353–4, 359,
370, 387, 498–9, 503–4, 510; and WBY's decision
to leave Senate 378; WBY describes 'Cracked
Mary' ('Crazy Jane') to 386, 430; WBY visits in
London 388; WBY tells of ballet version of
Fighting the Waves 389; cares for Omar Pound
400; and WBY's *The Words upon the Window
Pane* 411; and WBY's not dictating to George
412; and proposed de luxe edition of WBY's
collected works 415; and WBY's revised
A Vision 417; and WBY's relations with Margaret
Gough 421; WBY writes of 'Vacillation' to
431; and Shri Purohit Swami 435, 452; WBY
recommends Stuart's *The Coloured Dome* to
446; and WBY's 1930s political views 473;
WBY writes of proposed memoir on AG 483;
scepticism over Gwyneth Foden 538; and
WBY's stay in Majorca 545; and WBY's *Oxford
Book of Modern Verse* 553; WBY neglects 599;

786

SOURCES OF ILLUSTRATIONS

Front endpaper Colin Smythe

797

25 (*bottom*) BBC Photo Library
26 The Huntington Library, San Marino, California, 278 (15)
27 (*top*) ibid, 278 (26)
    (*bottom*) ibid, 278 (12)
28 (*top*) By permission of the Houghton Library, Harvard University
    (*bottom*) By courtesy and permission of Louise Foxcroft
29 Julian D'Arcy
30 Hulton Archive/Getty Images
31 Sligo County Libraries Local Studies Collection
32 Bord Fáilte

TEXT ILLUSTRATIONS

p. 40 British Library
  86 Courtesy of the Department of Special Collections, Stanford University Libraries
 159 Robert H. Taylor Collection, Department of Rare Books and Special Collections, Princeton University Library
 215 University of London Library, MS 978/2/78
 334 Central Bank of Ireland
 363 The Estate of Thomas Sturge Moore
 493 Sterling Library, University of London Library
 527 © The Duke of Wellington/The Syndics of Cambridge University Library (Dorothy Wellesley, *Selections from the Poems of Dorothy Wellesley*, 1936)
 573 *Irish Press*
 595 *Irish Times*

Back endpaper Collection Trinity College Dublin

In a few instances we have been unable to trace the copyright holder prior to publication. If notified, the publisher will be pleased to amend the acknowledgements in any future edition.